FACING ARMAGEDDON:
The First World War Experienced

FACING ARMAGEDDON

The First World War Experienced

LEO COOPER
LONDON

First published in Great Britain in 1996
by
LEO COOPER
190 Shaftesbury Avenue, London WC2H 8JL
an imprint of
Pen & Sword Books Ltd,
47 Church Street,
Barnsley, South Yorkshire S70 2AS

A CIP record for this book is available from the British Library

ISBN
0 85052 506 3 Hardback edition
0 85052 525 X Paperback edition

Typeset by Phoenix Typesetting, Ilkley, West Yorkshire.

Printed in Great Britain by Redwood Books Ltd,
Trowbridge, Wilts

This book is dedicated to the memory of all the known and unknown warriors, the willing and unwilling participants in the First World War.

Contents

Part III   THE NAVAL AND AIR WAR

Part IV   SOLDIERS: NATIONAL AND UNIT IDENTITY – GENERAL

Part V   SOLDIERS: NATIONAL AND UNIT IDENTITY – BRITISH

Part VI   SOLDIER MORALE

Part VII   MEDICINE AND EXPERIENCE

Part VIII   PEOPLES AT WAR

Part IX   RESISTERS: REBELS AND DISSENTERS

Part X   THE WAR EXPERIENCE PROJECTED: PROPAGANDISTS
AND THEIR AUDIENCES

List of Illustrations

16. J.T.B. McCudden, V.C., D.S.O, & Bar, M.C. & Bar, R.F.C. (E.D.G. Galley: Liddle Collection).
17. The first take-off by an operational military aeroplane from the deck of a naval carrier at sea. November 1915. (Via J.M. Bruce).
18. Lieutenant Oscar Bechtle, Moorsele, Belgium. (Via Oscar Bechtle).
19. Trench drainage: A problem for the French Sappers (Charles Thierry: Liddle Collection).
20. Turkish soldiers with something to celebrate, Gallipoli. (Liddle Collection).
21. Private Maurice Moser (American Expeditionary Force). (James Cooke).
22. Easter 1916: Prisoners under escort, Trinity College, Dublin. (Peggy Goodwin: Liddle Collection).
23. Ludendorff, the Kaiser and Hindenburg. (Liddle Collection).
24. Ernst Jünger, 1920.
25. French cavalry, 5 September 1914. (R.C. Money: Liddle Collection).

Between pages 648 and 649.
26. Officers, 10th Battalion, Essex Regiment at Lamotte, France, December 1916. (R.A. Chell: Liddle Collection).
27. The Band of the 6th Battalion Highland Light Infantry leading the battalion near Gaza, May 1917. (T.M. MacQuaker: Liddle Collection).
28. A member of 186 Company RE, Special Brigade, France 22.5.16 with a gas cylinder and barrow (G.I. Higson: Liddle Collection).
29. 'The Smilers' – comradeship within the Q.M.A.A.C. (Nora Steer: Liddle Collection).
30. German soldiers in an underground bunker: (Charles G. Adams (A.E.F.): Liddle Collection).
31. Austro–Hungarian wounded on the Izonzo Front, 1916. (Österreichisches Kriegsarchiv, Vienna).
32. Russian prisoners under guard. (H. Meyer: Liddle Collection).
33. Italian troops, Autumn 1917, not long before defeat at Caporetto. (L. Struthers: Liddle Collection).
34. Caporetto casualties. (L. Struthers: Liddle Collection).
35. A Medical Officer and stretcher case. (Dr R.S. Goodman: Liddle Collection).
36. Corporal A.E. Clay RAMC at work in an improvised Advanced Field Laboratory, 27.4.18, Mesopotamia. (A.E. Clay: Liddle Collection).
37. Sir Harold Gillies. (British Association of Plastic Surgeons).
38. Private Bell, facial surgery. (St. Mary's Hospital N.H. Trust Archives, Sidcup).

Illustrations within the Text

* The spelling of this regiment with a "c" dates officially from 1920 though unofficially the "c" was in widespread use before this date.

Acknowledgements

This book has widened its scope far beyond its original concept as the publication of papers offered at the Leeds International 1914–18 Commemoration Conference in September 1994 but we must begin with a grateful acknowledgement to our main sponsor, the Argyll Group and to our Travel Sponsor, Woodcock Travel facilitating the presence in Leeds of historians from all over the world.

For the larger concept of the First World War Commemoration with its international exhibitions and city based events, all with a link to the conference, we benefitted from the support of many local and national and some international agencies. Of our many personal supporters we gratefully make special mention of the Duke of Devonshire, the Viscount Cranborne, Kenneth Rose, Arnold Ziff, Mrs Audrey Burton, Mrs Audrey Faber and Bernard Atha. To Graham Stow we owe particular thanks for his sustained concern to be of help in answering each and every need; also to Adam Smith and Matthew Richardson who shouldered Liddle Collection responsibilities in the University Library and exhibition responsibilities in the city so that the conference and commemoration work could be more easily managed.

The support of Friends of the Liddle Collection has especially to be recognised. In several ways this book has been aided by Albert Smith, Braham Myers, Terry Mumford, Jacqueline Wynne Jones, Alasdair Cheyne, Keith and Brenda Clifton and in a specific way by Carolyn Mumford who has transcribed tapes recorded more than twenty years ago making them far more accessible as material for those of us concerned with the recall of the experience of war. Alyson Jackson brought professional experience to bear on the presentation of the photographs copied by David Bailey in the photography division of Leeds University Media Services. Relatedly Philip Thody and Paul Brooke prepared the translations of papers sent to us in French, a gift of their scholarship and time without which we would have been seriously disadvantaged. John Morison and Richard Davies helped us with our Russian scholars and their work. In preparing the book for publication, we commend the co-operation of Alan Twiddle and Barbara Bramall of Pen and Sword for their zeal, efficiency and friendliness – our fellow proof readers, Steve Brumwell and Peter Edwards have been meticulous in their support too.

For sponsorship of this volume we are deeply indebted to the Viscount Ridley and the Trustees of the Sir James Knott Trust set up in memory of two sons of Sir James Knott, Captain H.B. Knott and Major J.L. Knott, killed in action on the Western Front in the First World War. The generosity of the Trustees ensured publication of the book with the scope and structure we considered essential.

Claire Harder, Secretary in the Liddle Collection, has in effect been secretary to the production of this book, always keen and interested in its development. Readily we thank her. As Editors we can write with pleasure that we have been blessed in bringing together the most co-operative of contributors and the same may be said of the staff and trustees of those agencies from which the photographs for the book were selected. Every effort has been made by contributors to locate current holders of copyright in text and illustrations but we apologise for any omissions and would welcome information so that amendments can be made in future editions. It would be appropriate here to add a word of appreciation of those whose presence at the Conference contributed significantly to the debate which is continued in this volume, Max Egremont, Brian Holden Reid, Phil Taylor, Al Thomson, Claire Tylee and Caroline Zilboorg. Angela Gaffney and Chris McCarthy too made helpful contributions.

Editing a volume of this nature has been a greater task than either of us has undertaken in our own published work. It would have been impossible had we not had such a generous response from our colleagues within and outside of the University of Leeds. We thank all those who accepted our initial invitation more than two years ago and then those who in the last year have joined the team to make the study more comprehensive.

All authors and editors with family commitments need supportive understanding at home. Our wives, Mirabel Cecil and Louise Liddle, have given us this. We thank them and everyone who has assisted us towards the production of a work which we hope will help those who now and in the future look for an insight into the experience of the First World War.

Hugh Cecil and Peter Liddle – The University of Leeds
April 1996

Introduction

Hugh Cecil, Peter Liddle

It is over eighty years since the beginning of the great global conflict which in 1914 ushered in a new era of armed struggle and shaped this century. Among historians, the interpretation of this event remains as lively a battle-field as at any time. Their chief efforts have concentrated on the burning questions of why the 1914–18 war happened, what its effects were, how it was run, and according to what strategies. However, in this long and serious debate on the major issues, there would seem to be room for a more comprehensive scholarly treament of one area, namely, the subject of this book: the experience of men and women in a world war, leaders and led alike.

In every land where a war is within living memory, former participants will meet to remember it. They seek above all to recollect the companion-ship in days of youth and great danger and the memory of lost comrades to whom they feel forever bound; to recall times when they had been ready to put first, and before self, a cause in which they believed. Experience of total war is at the heart of the culture and societies of twentieth century Europe and America – as indeed it is for some parts of Asia and Africa. Quite as much as the First World War's causes and impact on world politics, this field therefore merits academic investigation. What did people of most ages, in every class, in combatant and non-combatant roles, in command or under orders, really pass through? How did the war affect them?

This volume shows that there is ample research material available for examining these questions in the ever-accumulating personal archives and in the mass of imperfectly-explored official documents, such as censorship and intelligence reports. In tackling this subject, however, scholars find themselves frequently up against well-established popular myths, such as that of an universally disillusioned soldiery reluctantly engaged in futile destruction throughout Europe – myths which persist in the face of strong contrary evidence and dominate contemporary fiction and above all, television programmes, the greatest influence in moulding opinion today.[1]

Historians cannot ignore popular misconceptions; their duty is to enlighten the public as well as one another. For the very reason that the subject of war experience is so emotionally charged, it needs cooler, more balanced examination. This book demonstrates that the truth is far from simple.

It is now possible and desirable to look at 'the myriad faces of war' from a broad perspective, on an international level, recognising that the experience of war for one country's citizens is not necessarily true for those of all the other participating nations, as some British and American commentators have assumed. This is what H.G. Wells meant when he wrote in 1927 of his hope that in the future a publisher would put together what he called 'a living, many-sided view of the immense multiplex occurrence.'[2] Only with such a sense of proportion can one realise, for example, that any despondency among British troops on the Western Front was a long way from the breakdown of morale in the Russian army in 1917 – a distinction a recent BBC film on the history of the twentieth century completely failed to make.[3]

Thanks to the efforts here of over sixty scholars from as far afield as Russia, Australia and the U.S.A., some from disciplines other than history, the varied nature of responses to the First World War becomes clear. This book sets out, first, to analyse the kind of war it was. Its technology, as explained by John Terraine, was the context in which soldiers, sailors and airmen fought; while Imanuel Geiss reminds us that women and children, non-combatants, old and young, had scant protection in war zones, throughout the European continent.

It was a war of machines against machines, as well as machines against men. In such an impersonal storm of destruction, the schoolboy's dream of heroic single combat became impossible – save occasionally for airmen. But the human courage required was as great as ever before. It was a war of industries – the industries that produced the supplies to maintain the troops in the trenches and the shells to kill their enemies; the industries that on the battlefield created a more blighted scenery than any polluted factory landscape and a noise more ear-splitting than the loudest steam-hammers.

We should remind ourselves however, that the war did not take place only on the Western Front, the location for which it is best remembered and which was in truth, the decisive area of the fighting. It covered two-thirds of the globe, affecting populations from Tahiti to the Orkneys. It meant, as this volume tells us, vagabondage for countless Russian children, acute hunger in Germany and Austria, riots in Italy, hangings in Mesopotamia, ancient university buildings blazing in Belgium, merchant seamen drowning in the Atlantic and forced labour in East Africa.

It was a war which brought countless new opportunities of employment, particularly for women; a war in which political reputations were triumphantly won or disastrously lost, a war bringing stress, happiness and grief to love and marriage, a war in which unwanted 'war babies' were born and children orphaned.

Much of this volume is devoted to those who fought, looking first (Part ii) at their leaders – Ludendorff, Churchill, Foch, Pétain, Mangin, Pershing, Beatty, Lloyd George and Haig. Amid the critical attention devoted to these decision-makers, little is normally paid to the physical and psychological cost of their work. This section focuses on the burden of executive office and its impact on the office holder. At any given moment, the fate of literally a million men might be in one man's hands – a responsibility which took a heavy toll on nerves and vitality.

Part iii of the book looks at naval activity, German, Italian and British, in the North Sea and English Channel, in amphibious operations off the Gallipoli peninsula, in the Adriatic and in the Atlantic convoys. While giving a view of overall strategy, it concentrates, too, on the pressures faced by ordinary seafarers, civilians and servicemen alike. In the last two chapters the experience of British and German airmen, pioneers of the most modern arm of warfare, is examined. While high strategy and technology affected these branches of the services, many of the wartime ordeals at sea could have occurred in earlier days. Tony Lane shows how merchant seamen reacted dutifully to their First World War trials much as they reacted to disaster at any time. Strikingly we can see how sailors were often called on to fight on land as well as sea or to take part in amphibious operations, and also how airmen, a great many of whom had started as soldiers (and rather fewer, as sailors) worked closely with ground forces, with whom they retained an affinity.

The most eloquent symbol of the conflict was of course the soldier – particularly the infantryman of the trenches – whether patriotic, disaffected, cheerful, enraged, glum, or stoical. Parts iv, v and vi analyse the morale and loyalties among soldiers of Germany, France, Austria–Hungary, Russia, Italy, America, Turkey and Great Britain. Despite great differences in the levels of equipment and organisation, much of the fighting had an universal character. What emerges, perhaps unsurprisingly, is the importance of collective loyalty and purpose – both national and regimental. Where these were strong and where the officers and command were respected, the will to fight endured, even when there were serious shortages of equipment. For much of the time this was as true of the badly-fed, under-equipped but sometimes victorious Turkish army as it was of the efficient, well-armed land forces of Britain (where the new women's army corps shared in the unit pride and individual honours for courage) and of Germany. The importance also of small group loyalty emerges in John Bourne's examination of a working-class citizen army predisposed towards such solidarity by the nature of their pre-war existence and in Tom Nevin's chapter on German Storm Troopers as chronicled by Ernst Jünger. The *ésprit* of strongly cohesive German, British and French units contrasted with that of many in the Russian and Austro-Hungarian armies. The Russian soldiers, despite a strong sense of national identity, felt that they had been betrayed by their leaders. Austro–Hungarians were riven by ethnic divisions intensified by a poor performance in the field. The Italian army, after two years of low morale, became more effective when a detested leadership was replaced, finding also a national purpose in the urgent drive to avert total defeat.

The efficiency of armies and their endurance in the field was directly related to the health of their men and the swift, effective treatment of casualties. Some of the grimmest but also inspiring chapters of the war's history deal with medical care of the wounded. The next section of the book (Part vii) describes lessons learned by the medical profession in treating wounds and disease, particularly shell-shock and facial injury; and they tell much of the conduct of the army doctors at the front, who despite harsh things sometimes said of them in personal reminiscences, emerge on the whole with great credit.

Part viii, on *peoples* at war, elaborates the theme, emphasized in Professor Geiss's introductory essay, that the war was not just a war of military organisations but of whole nations, whether their citizens took part as temporary service personnel, as non-combatant war workers, or simply as passive sufferers – and even beneficiaries. Two chapters highlight the differences between a unified Britain and Russia, where social fissures ran deep. The chapters on Germany and Italy present dissimilar societies under pressure of shortages, and the failures of their leaders to keep public opinion fully behind them on the home front. These failures, the social fractures exacerbated by shortages and the hardship on many who were children at the time, were among the causes of the rise of fascism in these two countries. This section concludes with an examination of an important and hitherto largely neglected area of study – the experience of the peoples of the undeveloped, chiefly colonial, countries.

There were many for whom war involved a struggle on home territory, either with an occupying power, or against an imperial power which they no longer recognised as legitimate. Some there were, too, who fell foul of a state machine forcing them into a war they regarded as immoral. Part ix describes the French and Belgian resistance to German occupation, the opportunist dissidence of Arab and Jugoslav nationalists against their Turkish and Austrian overlords and the conscientious objectors in France and Britain – whose path in some senses was the loneliest.

In Part x, we are reminded that war was not only something which happened, but which was being continually re-written for the benefit of those at home. Two chapters show how British and American propagandists idealised – and sometimes distorted – the nature of war service in industry and at the front. Moreover the people involved in dispensing propaganda, as, for instance, German schoolteachers or British war correspondents, had their own particular experience of war, marked by great dedication and sacrifice and, more than occasionally, mixed feelings about what they were doing. To be on the receiving end of all this, as were schoolchildren and cinema audiences, was to experience the war in yet another way. These contemporary efforts to influence public opinion have played a large part in the later misrepresentation of the First World War, either because they have perpetuated a misleading picture of how things were or because they have driven people into the opposite error of disbelieving what was in some cases, although propaganda, substantially true.

Finally, in Part xi, this book looks at ways in which the First World War has been perceived, sometimes after an interval, by some of the most imaginative and articulate individuals who experienced it – painters, novelists, poets and one eminent soldier of a reflective and literary outlook – Sir Ian Hamilton. To what extent is it ever possible to describe war? Can poetry, a formalised medium of expression, evoke the raw reality, however shortly after a battle it is written? Can a novel, finished after long pondering, tell a greater truth than contemporary letters and diaries, or is its message inevitably distorted by later events and by literary conventions? However honestly conceived, some of this creative effort may have failed because the artists' perceptions had been altered by disappointments after the war or new hopes of better times leading them to reinterpret their experience. Much war art, produced by both soldiers and civilians, however, was not of course intended to be a literal interpretation but allegorical, the 'vocabulary of mourning' as J.M.Winter puts it, helping people in an age of mass bereavement to cope with the enormous catastrophe of war.

Inevitably, even in so large a volume, there are gaps of which the editors are all too aware – for example to do with day-to-day wartime political and diplomatic life, with espionage, with soldier priests, or with the Armenian massacres only touched on in Imanuel Geiss's chapter. In another volume or edition of this book one may hope that this will be rectified.To address at least some of the lacunae, Ian Beckett's concluding chapter, a bibliographical essay which looks back over the last ten years of historical writing on the experience of the Great War, directs readers towards such subjects as British Empire experience and feminist studies of the conflict.

In this bibliographical chapter, Dr. Beckett also makes a brief reference to the international historical conference in September 1994 held during the week organised by the University and City of Leeds to commemorate the eightieth anniversary of the First World War. Over those eight days, from morning until night, there took place a series of events on the Great War theme: lectures, exhibitions, staged commemoration of former war poets, popular musical culture and film of the day and re-enactments of the wartime life of the city. At the end, on Sunday, 11 September, there was a service near Leeds City Art Gallery, beside Henry Charles Fehr's powerful war memorial, attended by representatives from foreign embassies. It was a moment for contemplation of those days of struggle – and for acceptance and symbolic reconciliation, after eighty years. To some it seemed appropriate that the Winged Victory which had formerly topped the monument, had been replaced in 1992, after being shaken in high winds, by a new sculpture symbolising peace.

In a sense there was a finality about the whole week, for it was surely one of the last major commemorations of the Great War at which veterans could be present. Ten years before at another commemorative occasion at Sunderland, survivors from the Great War had taken an active part in conference debates and had sung their old songs with gusto in the evenings. In 1995, sadly, only one solitary frail figure, ninety-six year old Walter Hare, former Somme veteran, was able to represent, at any of the ceremonies, the millions of soldiers who had marched away to serve their countries between 1914 and 1918.

Yet this volume, which drew its inspiration from that week of commemoration, is not intended as a finishing post – rather, a fresh starting line in the historical scholarship about four years which changed the course of history. This book is guided by the desire to cross the ever-widening divide between that tragic conflict and the present, to deepen our understanding of what it was like to go through it and to prevent the actuality of the Great War from being swamped by the distortions of popular mythology.

Notes

1 See for example, Ben Elton & Richard Curtis's 'Blackadder Goes Forth' (1992), Alan Bleasdale's 'The Monocled Mutineer' (1986) and 'The People's Century' (1995).

2 H.G.Wells: preface to A.D. Gristwood, *The Somme, also including the Coward*, London, Cape, 1927.

3 The People's Century (1995).

Part I

A World at War

Chapter 1

The Substance of the War

John Terraine

During an academic lifetime of study and writing about the First World War, it was not until my tenth book on this subject, *White Heat: The New Warfare 1914–18*, 1982, that I ventured to say in the Introduction, that it dealt with 'the very nature of the war'; that is to say, a factor shared in varying degrees by all the combatants, and with those variations of degree playing decisive parts in the conduct and outcome of the event. This, I wrote, 'is a book about the sinews of the greatest *First* Industrial Revolution War.' It had taken me about forty years to reach that perception.

To avoid confusion, I think I must now explain what I mean by '*First* Industrial Revolution'. I mean the enormous change brought about in human life and transactions by the introduction of steam-power – i.e. the transition from horses to horse-power, and the virtually simultaneous introduction of steel as a prime material. Steam was produced by heat from coal, steel was evolved from iron: the possession of these commodities in large supply was an economic and political asset of fundamental importance, both in peace and war. A second Industrial Revolution added the internal combustion engine, based on petroleum, as a further power source, along with electricity and light metals. A third Revolution contributed nuclear energy, plastics and electronics. A process of emergence, dominance, decline and fall is apparent. There are no fixed dates; elements of all three Revolutions operate today, and so do such pre-Industrial power-sources as oxen, horses and mules, and pre-Industrial materials like bronze and wood. But the 'natural laws' that govern us are the laws of Industrial society. They certainly govern war. They supply the sinews.

I wrote in *White Heat* that the transformation of war by industrialism had two aspects, which I called 'qualitative' and 'quantitative': 'The qualitative aspect embraces that continuing stream – or flood – of inventions

3

and developments of techniques which characterises the entire period. The quantitative aspect goes far beyond the matter of productive capacities, though these are impressive and important: it has a profound social significance also.'[2]

I was referring to the unprecedented increases in population which (with one conspicuous and curious exception) accompanied the rising levels of industrialisation of the great world powers. But a few examples may be illuminating: Between 1880–1911, America's population rose from 53 million to 94 million; an increase of 41 million. Between 1880–1913, Britain's population rose by 12 million. In the same period Germany's population rose by 22 million. The exception to the rule was France, where a population of just over 30 million in 1821 only reached 39 million in 1921 – a century later. I added: 'These large population increases are central to the great wars of the First Industrial Revolution; the mass populations supplied the mass armies which are the particular feature of those wars.'[3]

There was never any doubt that the mass populations would turn into mass armies. Germany's 67 million people entered the war with just under 4½ million trained and partially trained soldiers; France's 39 million had 3½ million under arms on mobilization; Russia's estimated 167 million mobilized just over 4 million in the army. Britain alone ignored the portents, resolutely refused to adopt conscription and clung to what Lord Esher called 'the Principle of Unequal Sacrifice' and what others had more cruelly called 'conscription by hunger'. In August 1914 her army numbered 733,514,\ including Territorials and Reserves. But she was never able to escape the hard realities: Lord Kitchener's implementation of the much-admired Voluntary System produced 1,186,357 recruits by the end of 1914, a number which most public figures would have regarded as impossible, indeed ludicrous, five months earlier, but which was multiplied by nearly five before the War was over – a total of about one seventh of the population. It seemed a very high figure to us, but comparatively it was not; the German enlistment total was 11 million – about a sixth of the population; the French was 8 million – one in five. I would not like to even guess at the Russian figures – their proportion would almost certainly be considerably smaller, their total distressingly high. It was a war of unwieldy hordes.

They all had to be clothed in the distinctive fashions of their calling, equipped with all its accoutrements, accommodated, moved over land and sea, medicated, fed – and buried. The Industrial Revolution took care of all these matters in a manner never before possible. The picture is awesome – the production figures of the war; the astronomical mileage of telephone wire and barbed wire; the quantities of sandbags; of pit-props; the diversity and numbers of trench warfare supplies; acreage of cloth for uniforms; horseshoes; tonnages of lint for bandages; the unimaginable totals

4

of weapons: rifles, machine guns, small arms ammunition, artillery of all calibres, shells . . . shells . . . shells. Winston Churchill became Minister of Munitions in July 1917 – it is arguable that it was, next to becoming Prime Minister in 1940, his most successful post, the man and his task fitting like a hand in a tailored glove; as he described it, 'We were in the presence of requirements at once imperative and apparently insatiable.'[4] But thanks to the unending progress of industrial technology, by 1918 the insatiable greed of battle was propitiated almost effortlessly. As Churchill said, 'The whole island was an arsenal.'[5]

By 1918, he tells us, describing this great Ministry over which he presided, 'Nearly all the mines and workshops of Britain were in our hands. We controlled and were actually managing all the greatest industries. We regulated the supply of all their raw materials. We organized the whole distribution of their finished products. Nearly five million persons were directly under our orders, and we were interwoven on every side with every other sphere of the national economic life.'[6]

If that is not a description of a revolution, I don't know what is. And referring to the sundry satrapies within his empire, he continues:

> There was very little in the productive sphere they could not at this time actually do. A requisition, for instance, for half a million houses would not have seemed more difficult to comply with than those we were already in process of executing for a hundred thousand aeroplanes, or twenty thousand guns, or the medium artillery of the American army, or two million tons of projectiles.[7]

He is, of course, describing total war: war affecting the totality of the population, absorbing all its economic resources; the only limitation was its ultimate capacity. That was the substance of the war; in total war, the sinews are the sinews of the nation – everything, material and human.

The mass armies drawn from the world's mass populations could only be equipped and maintained by mass production and mass logistics. Those who had practised these matters had the advantages of experience and apparatus – and this is a key word. The apparatus of the war made it an astonishingly different experience from all its forerunners. Contrary to much ill-informed supposition to the effect that it was a single, mindless repetition of sterile acts, it was in fact a novelty from the first, a novelty breeding novelties to the very end. It became a pendulum performance of invention, antidote, counter-invention, and new antidote.

The Royal Navy encountered undersea-warfare for the first time on the third day of the war, when the light cruiser *Amphion* struck two German mines and sank with the loss of 150 officers and men. Three days later HMS *Birmingham* rammed and sank *U-15*; the new warfare was under way and its most significant form appeared on 20 October when the British steamer *Glitra* was sunk by *U-17* – the first merchant ship to be sunk by a submarine – so beginning the U-boat blockade. The Royal Navy now had to invent and master what was virtually a new profession – Anti-Submarine Warfare. This would ascend almost into the realm of magic during World War II, but it had to begin somewhere, and this was the time. From 1914 to 1944 it revolved around an unremitting process of experiment, trial and completion of weapons and systems; at the centre of them all was the problem of locating a submerged submarine, and a prime system for doing that was what was then called ASDIC and is now called SONAR. This was invented in 1917, and just as the war was ending it was possible to install it in naval vessels, with what were described as promising results. It had taken that long.

The conventional (surface) element of the Royal Navy also quickly found itself in the presence of alarming novelties: on 22 September three old cruisers were sunk in quick succession off the Dutch coast by a single U-boat, *U-9*. Just over a month later a modern battleship, *Audacious* (she was launched in 1912), was lost off the north coast of Ireland; the reason why she was there was that the Grand Fleet's base at Scapa Flow was considered insecure, and Admiral Jellicoe adopted the expedient of taking the fleet round to the west of the British Isles to avoid attack by U-boats – only for *Audacious* to fall victim to the other underwater weapon, the mine. As the Naval Official History remarks of these events. 'Nothing that had yet occurred had so emphatically proclaimed the change that had come over naval warfare.'[8]

Yet the most remarkable, unforeseen novelty of naval warfare resided from the first, and continued to do so, on the other side of the North Sea. Nothing had done more to promote Anglo–German hostility than the building of the German High Seas Fleet, a powerful instrument pointed directly at British sea supremacy, the very foundation of the British Empire. When war broke out a decisive trial of strength, a modern Trafalgar, was confidently expected and awaited. For nearly two years nothing of the kind occurred; when it did (at Jutland in 1916) it was a messy, inconclusive-looking affair – but decisive all the same, because it never happened again. And within the messiness lay one of the new wonders of technology: thanks to Wireless Telegraphy and ability to intercept it, Jellicoe's Grand Fleet was already at sea on its way to meet the Germans before they had left port.

Major-General J.F.C. Fuller, a perceptive and sympathetic observer of techniques, even if he was rather more dubiously gifted in the fields of strategy and politics, identified two of the 20th Century's novelties as the most fateful: the internal combustion engine and wireless telegraphy – W/T. The former, says Fuller, by solving the problem of flight, lifted warfare into a third dimension; he continues: 'The latter virtually raised it into the fourth dimension; for all intents and purposes the wireless transmission of energy annihilated time as well as space. Thus *two new battlefields* were created – the *sky* and the *ether*.'[9]

Thanks to W/T, the Royal Navy, between 1914–18, enjoyed an enviable advantage: by the end of 1914 all three of the German Navy's operational codes were in the hands of the Admiralty. This was a defeat from which, says Patrick Beesly, 'The Imperial German Navy was never to recover.'[10]

It has been said that the German Navy, in that war, could not move a picket-boat in its harbours without the Admiralty in London immediately knowing about it. Not only that, but the art of Direction-Finding by plotting wireless signals advanced so rapidly that by May 1915 a U-boat's movement could be followed across the North Sea. By 1917 the practice was commonplace – and by 1941 D/F was tracking them right across the Atlantic; later it would be a prime instrument of their swift destruction. The implication of this great stride forward in communication and naval Intelligence procedures was that the Admiralty itself now became a commander-in-chief, a rôle admirably performed in 1982.

On land also, for a time, W/T offered the promise of valuable Intelligence gathering – it was probably General Joffre's most important source during the calamitous early days and the retreat to the Marne. But this potential was so obvious that wireless soon ceased to be a main means of communication (though it never ceased to be used). After all, in the Western theatre there was no lack of land lines; the telephone was the prime instrument of command. But it was in conjunction with the internal combustion engine, in the form of air power, that W/T achieved its highest significance.

All aviation was in its early infancy; the Wright brothers made their breakthrough towards the moon and the stars in December 1903; military aviation could be said to have had its beginning in 1908, when the French Army showed a marked interest in the exhibits at the Le Mans meeting. Aircraft featured strongly in the French Army manoeuvres of 1911, especially in the matter of co-operation with artillery.

In Britain an Air Committee was set up to advise on the creation of an Aeronautical Service, and Colonel J.E.B. Seely (later Secretary of State for War) was chairman of its technical sub-committee. He told members: 'At the present time in this country we have, as far as I know, of actual flying men in the Army about eleven, and of actual flying men in the Navy about eight, and France has about two hundred and sixty-three, so we are what you might call behind.'[11]

The Committee got the message; three months later the Royal Flying Corps was formed, with a Military and a Naval Wing. It made its practical début at the Annual Army manoeuvres of 1912, in which the two sides were commanded by the two rising stars, Lieutenant-Generals Sir Douglas Haig and Sir James Grierson, both to be Corps Commanders in the BEF in August 1914. Each had a small squadron of aeroplanes and an airship; Haig's airship broke down almost at once, but Grierson's performed such service that he emerged from the manoeuvres as the clear winner; he said in his report: 'The airship, as long as she remained afloat, was of more use to me for strategical reconnaissance than the aeroplanes as, being fitted with wireless telegraphy, I received her messages *in a continuous stream and immediately after the observation had been made.*'[12]

It was what you might call a perfect laboratory result, and Grierson was deeply impressed by his air component; he added, 'The impression left on my mind is that their use had revolutionized the art of war.'[13] In 1913 he went further: 'Warfare will be impossible unless we have the mastery of the air.'[14]

It is one of the wonders of history that the French Air Force in 1914, with some 136 operational aircraft, completely missed the mass of about a million men forming the right wing of the German Army, advancing through Belgium in accordance with the Schlieffen Plan. The German Air Force equally failed to spot the landing of the BEF and its advance to Mons where its presence came as a great surprise, and they also overlooked the formation of a whole new French Army, threatening their advancing right wing. The Royal Flying Corps missed very little; it reported the German outflanking movement against the BEF and monitored their advance, and together with belatedly awakened French airmen it reported the fatal swing to the south-east which wrecked the Schlieffen Plan and made possible the Battle of the Marne.

Reconnaissance in this style has always been a classic function in war; it has been well named 'the eye in the sky', and from time immemorial has emphasized the value of high points – hills, tall buildings, and it now looks down on the whole earth from circling satellites. In 1914 the eye was lodged in very frail vehicles, but effective none the less. When the war of movement stopped on the Western Front there were few opportunities of observing manoeuvre, but the war lost no time in signalling what was to be its predominant characteristic: it was going to be an 'artillery war'.

In 1914, no sooner was the Battle of the Marne decided by the wide retreat of the German right flank to the River Aisne and the heights over-looking it than the quite unexpected phenomenon of *trench warfare* made its appearance, and this was to be the mode – indeed, the substance – of the war for the next three years. It spelt tactical deadlock: the deadlock of two unbroken lines of trenches, fronted by aprons of barbed wire and defended by the whole apparatus of fire power, rifles, machine guns and artillery. And artillery, as well as being part of the deadlock was also the only means of overcoming it. Artillery – and the ammunition which gives it life – was of the very essence of trench warfare which, from 1915 to November 1917 *was* the war.

Until the second half of 1916 this fact was entirely to the German advantage. The French entered the war with some 4,000 pieces of artillery, but virtually all of them were 75mm field guns, the famous *soixante-quinze* Quick-Firing gun which was sometimes referred to at the *Ecole de Guerre* as 'God the Father, God the Son, and God the Holy Ghost'. It was pretty certainly the best field gun of that war, with excellent qualities, but it did not have divine powers; above all, it was not very effective against entrenchments or fortifications of any kind. The French had no field howitzer and only about 100 howitzers of any description with their armies. Their prime task became the rapid expansion of their heavy gun and howitzer production – and ammunition production too – and pulling heavy ordnance out of their fortresses. These tasks were tackled with such vigour that for the great autumn battles in Artois and Champagne in 1915 they were able to back their 3,000 field pieces with 2,000 heavies.

Their allies were in even worse plights. The Russian fortress systems swallowed up huge numbers of heavy guns and mountains of ammunition. From beginning to end a marked characteristic of the Eastern Front would be the thin provision of Russian battlefield artillery – in marked contrast with World War II.

Britain's Expeditionary Force took to France precisely 410 pieces of artillery in August 1914 – a ridiculous number for the warfare of the continental masses. But there were encouraging features: schooled by the Boers in South Africa, the British took a very good heavy gun into the field – the 60-pdr, but there were only 4 guns (one battery) per division, which means just 16 for the original BEF. More satisfactory was the allocation of the 4.5-inch field howitzer, authoritatively called 'the best field howitzer in the world'; each division had 3 batteries of these, which gave the BEF 72. The fact remains that the British were painfully weak in artillery as well as in numbers generally, and that this weakness was perilously compounded by that of the munitions industry, which had to be built up virtually from scratch.

The Germans had no more anticipated trench warfare than anyone else, but they had expected to besiege fortresses, and went to war with large siege warfare supplies, including great numbers of heavy guns, and they were able to put substantial numbers of 210mm (8-inch) and 280mm (11-inch) howitzers in the field. The German 150mm (5.9-inch), often referred to as the 'best gun of the war', was always plentiful.

For a long time artillery preparations of attacks on enemy trenches took the form of what I have called 'blazing away at a landscape', drenching it with hot metal, the chief effect of which was to create cratered swamps which became virtually impassable in bad weather. The long bombardments made surprise impossible; movement was deadly slow in the fire zone; casualties mounted appallingly; progress seemed negligible. But help was on its way, in technology's good time.

As early as September 1914, on the Aisne, the special value of the 'eye in the sky' became apparent. Thanks to two ex-Royal Engineer subalterns, Lieutenants James and Lewis, the Royal Artillery very soon made long strides towards effective Air co-operation by W/T. By 1915 it was clear that in modern battle a bad day for flying was a bad day for the guns, and a bad day for the guns was a very bad day indeed for the infantry. But it also became clear that air co-operation went far beyond marking targets and fall of shot.

It was in that year that the Royal Flying Corps undertook, by aerial photography with infinite labour and much peril, in conjunction with the new Royal Engineer Field Survey Companies, the making of a new map of the Western Front to replace the existing very inaccurate French maps (which the Germans continued to use). This co-operation bore fruit in November 1917 at Cambrai, when the onset of some 350 fighting tanks was simultaneously accompanied by the crash of 1003 guns, firing unregistered by this map by what was called predicted shooting. This was the saviour; by this means,

Surprise was restored to battle; there were no warning shots;
Precision was conferred by calibration of guns, an art well understood by the Royal Garrison Artillery, but unfamiliar to Field Gunners until now;
Protection was given to the infantry by the lavish use of smoke-shell.

The war of movement had returned, after three years' absence.

After Cambrai the continuous trench-lines faded away. They became, for most of the time, places where the armies waited in varying degrees of danger and discomfort for battle to begin. When it did, the bombardment would be short, violent and highly destructive and the attack would follow immediately upon it. Linear defences were considered shell-traps; the defence would be conducted by mutually supportive posts, with the attackers attempting to infiltrate between them. Dramatic results were achieved in this way by the Germans in March 1918, and decisively repeated by the Allies in the Final Offensive from July to November. Movement became virtually continuous; when it was held up in front it spread to the flanks, and when they halted it returned to the original thrust-line. It was never very fast movement, because the internal combustion engine was not yet able to produce sufficient horse-power for speed. The Medium Mark 'A' tank (generally known as the 'Whippet'), which made its battle début at Amiens on 8 August 1918, had a road speed of 8.3 m.p.h., but across-country it was lucky to exceed 2 m.p.h. As I have said before, this makes any resemblance to dogs of the greyhound breed very tenuous.

So the great advance was a slow business. The motor transport of the period performed prodigies, particularly when the weather broke, but the factor which kept the battle moving was always the guns, and they were also a prime factor in slowing it down. The BEF reached its highest level of shell expenditure between noon on 28 September and noon 29 September 1918: 943,847 rounds; just under a million shells in 24 hours, for the breaking of the 'Hindenburg Line'. The logistical implications are appalling. Nevertheless, this was victory; as Lloyd George himself expressed it, 'the conclusion is inescapable that Germany and her allies were in fact defeated in the field.'[15]

There can be no escaping the argument that the possession, or lack, of the sinews of war was, for all who had to wage it in the Industrial Age, its very substance. I don't think one can begin to make sense of the war, or make many sensible observations about it, without grasping the effect of shortages of war matériel. Think of the Russian soldiers entering battle without rifles, having to wait to take them from fallen comrades; think of facing poisonous gas without masks; think of standing beside cold guns in the heat of battle, with no shells to fire; think of the French gunners trying to engage long-range heavy artillery with field guns; think of infantry trying to defend a trench against attack by showers of hand-grenades, having nothing similar to reply with; of flying an outclassed aircraft in the face of a skilful enemy, and so on, and much else besides. Think of trying to command such a battle. And then think of the relief, the anticipation, the great expectations when, at last, the necessities appear. This is what I mean by the war's 'inner nature'.

At first the penury pressed hardest on the Allies, who then became over-excited when their needs began to be satisfied and riches smiled upon them. Over-confidence set in – the French were always very prone to this; from their first blind faith in the all-out offensive to the seeming wisdom of the 1916 dictum, 'It is artillery that captures places and infantry only helps it to do so.'[16]

In 1917 General Nivelle promised that he had a key to victory which would perform it in 48 hours. 1,185,000 dead Frenchmen bore witness to the error of these beliefs. Yet in the last two years it was the Central Powers who came to understand penury, facing what they called the 'Materialschlacht' (the war of matériel) – the absolute Allied supremacy in munitions of all descriptions. It reached the point where, in the words of Robin Prior and Trevor Wilson, the British Armies '. . . were now employing such massive quantities of artillery in so co-ordinated and skilful a manner that it is not certain that any defensive positions could have withstood them';[17] or, as Prior and Wilson also write: 'the enemy was fundamentally outmatched by the British weapons system.'[18]

What a transformation! I began to appreciate the extent of it in 1962, when an ex-officer of the Royal Artillery wrote to me, referring to the Second Battle of Ypres in early 1915, 'I remember the period when it was almost "reasons in writing" for firing away a shell.'[19] That definitely helped me to understand what General Haig meant when he wrote in his diary, 'It is impossible to fight battles on a scale of ammunition like that.'[20] He meant *successful* battles, of course. How right he was.

The impression of those evil times, when the BEF lacked everything it needed except amazing courage, was hard to efface. I can see a direct line from 'impossible to fight battles' in the first part of the year, to the quite inadequate 153 heavy guns and 788 field guns which were all the BEF had for its biggest battle in 1915, Loos, in September; then to November, the war being 15 months old, and General Robertson (soon to be CIGS) only then being able to say, 'For the first time since the commencement of the War the supply of munitions on an adequate scale is assured.'[21]

And so we arrive at 1 July, 1916, when General Rawlinson found himself the proud possessor of 1,437 guns for his attack on the Somme, no fewer than 427 of them being heavies. This seemed to be a very great number, and now there were mountains of ammunition beyond the dreams of earlier years, allowing the firing of 150,000 rounds a day and 50,000 per night. The infantry was assured that 'nothing could exist at the conclusion of the bombardment in the area covered by it.'[22]

It was a delusion; at least twice as many guns and twice as much ammunition were required to produce such a result, as the battles of 1917 showed. But in 1916 the delusion led to horrible disaster. In 1917 the infantry did indeed make a virtually unopposed capture of the enemy position – at Messines; in 1918 the Germans had the same gratifying experience, for the same reason at the Chemin des Dames on 27 May, when they made the deepest one-day advance of the War – about 12 miles.

I stress these dates. It has long been my belief that chronology is the spinal column of history, and that every step away from chronological sequence is highly dangerous. This seems to me to be unmistakably the case with the First World War. As I have stated, the industrial process turned the war into a 'pendulum performance', a concept devoid of meaning without a chronological base. Each phase of the war, each year, each novelty requires to be separately examined; the air war – outstandingly – is only intelligible in the context of incessant change. Much of this is closely linked to the name of Anthony Fokker, which came to the fore in 1915. Air reconnaissance and artillery co-operation called for countermeasures, and these led directly to air combat to achieve that 'mastery of the air' that General Grierson had prophesied in 1912. In 1915 Fokker produced his *Eindecker* – the monoplane with a machine gun firing forward through the propellor by means of synchronization. This was the first pure fighter aircraft; its coming produced the 'Air Aces'. New Allied aircraft countered the *Eindecker*; the 'Aces' were countered by formation flying. It was a sequence of developments; *the War* was a sequence of developments.

It was also certain other things; it was from first to last a Coalition war – a highly significant matter for the Allies, but also applying to the Central Powers. Not for nothing did German staff officers speak of the Austrian alliance as being 'fettered to a corpse'. It became fashionable in influential quarters in Britain to refer to Germany's allies as her 'props'; this was a complete and very serious misreading of the strategic fundamentals.

The same influential people – conspicuously Winston Churchill (First Lord of the Admiralty until late May 1915), Lloyd George (Prime Minister from December 1916) and the ubiquitous, indefatigable Colonel Hankey (Secretary of the War Cabinet), dangerously misjudged Britain's own alliance situation. It irked Lloyd George from the start. He could not rid himself of the belief that Britain still possessed freedom of action, as she had done in past wars. During the great strategic debate in early 1915 he asked his friend Churchill, 'Are we really bound to hand over the ordering of our troops to France as if we were her vassal?'[23] Churchill's reply – if any – is not recorded; both he and Lloyd George were actively promoting alternative strategies to the Western Front, both were finding the French alliance an insuperable and detestable obstacle.

To the French, the strategic problem was simple and so was its solution. General Joffre, the French C-in-C, expresses both quite clearly: The best and largest portion of the German army was on our soil, with its line of battle jutting out a mere five days' march from the heart of France. This situation made it clear to every Frenchman that our task consisted in defeating this enemy, and driving him out of our country.[24]

I am bound to say that I find this proposition entirely reasonable, and so did a substantial number of people at the time. In the BEF there were few who doubted it; General Haig summed up a majority view succinctly in March 1915: 'We cannot hope to win until we have defeated the German Army.'[25]

And General Robertson retrospectively dotted the 'i's and 't's of defeating the Germany Army: where was this to be done? He had little doubt: 'In the Great War the decisive front was fixed for us by the deployment of the enemy's main masses in France and Belgium.'[26]

In much British writing about the war there are two conspicuous absentees: the enemy and the Allies. During the war itself, the enemy and our Allies spoke with one voice: France and a tiny portion of Belgium were to them, and remained, the main front of the War. The Russians fought a hard war on a big front, and when it collapsed in 1917 it was sorely missed; but unlike 1941–45 it was *not* the main front. Nor did the German General Staff ever consider it being allowed to become that.

The underlying strategic reality of the War, which makes so much feverish discussion quite sterile, is that although the Schlieffen Plan failed in its main purpose in 1914, it bequeathed to Germany a strategic initiative which continued until July 1918. The effect of this bitterly simple fact, as I have often said, was that for virtually four years, 'the French had to dance to the German tune and the British danced at their coat-tails – an activity neither dignified nor rewarding.'[27]

I have also remarked that for this reason, 'One may even say that the First World War was structured by the Schlieffen Plan.'[28]

When I say that obedience to the discipline of the Coalition was not rewarding, I am, of course, thinking of the British war cemeteries. Once seen, never forgotten. I preside over an Association dedicated to 'Remembering'. But there is so much to remember. The Western Front averaged about 450 miles in length. The British portion of it never rose above 123 miles. We need to remember that. We need to remember, when we recall the terrible cost of the Western Front to all who fought there, that French casualties by the end of 1914 – just 5 months of war – were 955,000 and Britain's were just over 90,000; that by the end of 1915 the French had lost about 2 million, and the British about half a million. The war's French total of 1,385,000 dead represented 3.5% of their whole population; Britain's three-quarters of a million represented 1.5%. Again, 17.7% of French enlistments were killed, 11.8% of British. We need to remember that for two years France bore by far the heavier burden of the war, waiting for Britain to make up for lost time.

To those who became aware of its effect, this disproportion was heavy with meaning: how long could France stay in the war? In August 1915 Lord Kitchener told Haig, 'We must act with all our energy, and do our utmost to help the French, even though, by so doing, we suffered very heavy losses indeed.'[29] And that is precisely what took place – at Loos. But Kitchener's words (and his own observations) remained in Haig's mind; on New Year's Day 1916, just a fortnight after being appointed C-in-C, Haig sent for the Head of the French Mission at GHQ, and showed him his orders from the Government: 'I pointed out that I am *not under* General Joffre's orders, but that would make no difference, as my intention was to do my utmost to carry out General Joffre's wishes on strategical matters as if they were orders.'[30]

This became Haig's guiding principle, under Joffre and his successors, and if he had done nothing else (foolish thought!) in a Coalition war this perception earned his pay. But it was Kitchener who put the whole terrible reality into words: 'We cannot make war as we ought, we can only make it as we can.'[31] That was the heart of the matter; you could call it the epitaph of the war.

Notes

1   John Terraine: *White Heat: The New Warfare* 1914–18 p. 6
2   Ibid p. 7
3   Ibid
4   Churchill: *The World Crisis* ii (Odhams edition) p. 1171
5   Ibid
6   Churchill: *The World Crisis: The Aftermath* p. 32
7   Ibid p. 33
8   Corbett: *Naval Operations* i p. 177
9   Fuller: *The Decisive Battles of the Western World* iii p. 184
10 Beesly: *Room 40* p. 70
11 Walter Raleigh *The War in the Air* i p. 202
12 Ibid p. 227

13 Ibid p. 226
14 Lieut.-Gen. Sir J. Grierson, lecture at the Royal Artillery Institution, Nov. 6 1913
15 Lloyd George *War Memoirs* ii (Odhams edition) p. 1946
16 Official History (*Military Operations France and Belgium 1916* ii f.n. 1)
17 Prior & Wilson *Command on the Western Front* p. 350
18 Ibid p. 339
19 Correspondence with Lieutenant-Colonel Neate RA, Oct. 1962
20 Haig Diary Nov. 15 1914
21 Field-Marshal Sir William Robertson: *Soldiers and Statesmen i* p. 199
22 Official History (op. cit. i p. 288)
23 Martin Gilbert *Winston S. Churchill iii* Companion Volume i p. 472
24 *The Memoirs of Marshall Joffre ii* p. 327
25 Haig Diary March 28 1915
26 Robertson op. cit. p. 75
27 Royal United Services Institute Journal Sept. 1981 p. 4
28 *Army Quarterly & Defence Journal* July 1985 p. 279
29 Haig Diary Aug. 19 1915
30 Haig Diary Jan. 1 1916
31 Churchill: *The World Crisis: The Eastern Front* p. 271

Chapter 2

The Civilian Dimension of the War

Imanuel Geiss

The eruption of the American Civil War as the first really modern industrial mass war, in particular its end with Sherman's devastating march
through the South, foreshadowed a future where war would distinguish
less and less the soldier from the civilian. However America was far away
from Europe, and the implications of the U.S. Civil War were soon
forgotten or simply ignored. The American message for the future was
overshadowed by the shock caused by the Prusso–German artillery
bombardment of besieged Paris in early 1871, when the Second German
Empire was founded amidst the thunder of German Krupp cannons, as it
was phrased in naïve, but unwittingly revealing terms, in German history
textbooks. More far-reaching was the franc-tireur war – men, without military uniform, sniping at regular troops of the invading enemy.

The Great Oriental Crisis of 1875–78, culminating in the 8th
Russo–Turkish War, settled by the Congress of Berlin in 1878, was accompanied by mutual massacres of Christian and Muslim Balkan peoples. Here
Europe, in particular Liberal England, only saw the 'Bulgarian atrocities'
committed by the 'unspeakable Turk' of Gladstone's rhetoric, not the
corresponding crimes committed against Muslims. They took place
beyond the periphery of civilised Europe. Europe's own efforts in institu-
tionalising civilised warfare led to the founding of the Red Cross in 1864
and several Geneva Conventions, sanctified by International Law through
the Hague conventions for land warfare in 1907. On paper, it completed
the separation of regular armies and civilian populations. Occupation
forces had to spare civilian populations and even political structures in
war-time, while irregular forces had to wear at least visible badges and had
to have responsible command structures. Everything else was considered a
war crime.

Against that background the war of the future was optimistically considered. Self-destructive complacency prevailed, with trust in the strength of

civilisation and international law to shield non-combatants from the rigours of war. In fact, the collective weight of industrial weapons and of sheer masses in uniformed national armies was so terrific as simply to sweep aside many formal international obligations on 'scraps of paper', as if they were spiders' webs. For this became the general message of the First World War. The concept that the military and civilian spheres were separate was smashed by demands of the first total industrial war, both on military fronts, by land and on seas, and on home fronts. A few realistic pessimists from opposite ends of the political spectrum, like the Conservative Swiss–German historian Jacob Burckhardt and the affluent revolutionary Friedrich Engels in his comfortable English exile, warned in vain about the destructive character of modern industrial warfare.

War atrocities committed by Serbs and Montenegrins against Muslim Albanians in Kosovo and in Northern Albania during the Second Balkan War in 1912/13,[1] were seen by Germany as a first precedent for 'ethnic cleansing' or 'völkische Flurbereinigung', later to be picked up by the Pan-Germans as precedents for the ethnic cleansing they proposed for their 'Greater Germany'. All such considerations were at best *'cura posterior'* for many Europeans when the world war broke out in early August 1914.

In their blissful ignorance of what the warlike future had in store for them, capitals and provincial towns – as well as many individuals – were seized with enthusiasm. Even if jubilant masses were not the majority, their patriotic noises had the greatest impact, politically and historically. They gave the solid basis of jingo chauvinism of all national shades and to clamours for expansive war aims as a punishment for aggressors.

War had suddenly become immensely popular in Europe. The famous or notorious 'Augusterlebnis' in Germany, the 'Union Sacrée' in France, are expressions of quasi-religious sentiments that bordered on blasphemy. God, of course, was invoked from all sides and the nation-state was raised to the heights of a secular religion. This side of the coin with its high emotions deserves attention, if only in contrast to the suffering which civilian populations would endure.

The grim warnings of those who could imagine what the Great War might mean, were hushed by the hurrahs on all sides, but their reaction may best be summed up by one short word which the commander of Napoleon's Old Guard uttered when ordered to surrender to the British at Waterloo. In legend his reply was: 'The Old Guard will die, but will not surrender'. In reality he is reported to have said: *'Merde'*. Just as prophetically but in a more gentlemanly fashion, the British Foreign Secretary, Sir Edward Grey, on 4 August 1914 expressed his verdict. 'The lights have gone out over Europe. They will not be lit again in our time.' The realism of such pessimists had political effect only towards the end of the war – on the losers' side, in a desperate attempt to end the war by Revolution, and on the winning side in pleading for moderation in a war *à l'outrance*.

The first to bear the shock of real warfare were civilian populations of countries invaded by foreign armies. Even here, we have to distinguish between harsh realities and national legends. The shock must have been rudest for the Belgians, apparently safe in their neutrality, guaranteed by International Law, but breached by Germany for strategic reasons. The German invading armies fell immediately below the level of the civilised warfare of the previous two centuries by exacting war contributions from occupied Belgian and French cities. Anxious memories of the franc-tireur warfare in 1870–71 made German soldiers trigger-happy, in particular at night. Real or imagined incidents of civilian sniping, often enough turning out to be German soldiers shooting each other, in the belief that they had been attacked by snipers, led to the terrible burning of Louvain with its famous University Library by German troops, as a reprisal for alleged sniping.[2] The burning was repeated in May 1940, in the Second World War.

The East suffered comparably, but this is less well-known. The Polish counterpart, all but ignored because of Louvain, was Kalisch, a Polish provincial town next to the Silesian border. After the withdrawal of Russian troops, German units moved in on 6 August. After real or alleged sniping over eight days, they pulled out and shelled Kalisch systematically from surrounding hills.[3] Later, Germans wondered why Poles did not greet German armies as liberators. On their first retreat in Poland from Warsaw in late autumn 1914, German troops systematically destroyed bridges, railways and roads in order to slow up the advance of Russian troops, including the flooding of coal mines[4] – something which German troops did on their retreat from the Western Front in the final months of the war. In contrast, alleged atrocities of Russian troops in East Prussia in August 1914 did not take place. They were German propaganda myths. One Prussian Landrat who stayed behind the Russian lines with his civilian population, made some sobering remarks in his official report after the return of the German Army: Russian troops behaved with exemplary discipline. The few incidents of unjustified harshness were immediately and severely punished by Russian officers. Houses were only destroyed when German troops were firing from them. There were no rapes, and no plundering, and the few thefts were the work of Germans staying after the Russian invasion. The honest Landrat ends on a bitter note on the morality of the German civilian population. His report[5] is the more remarkable, as the behaviour of Russian troops in August 1914 contrasts favourably with German practices in both World Wars and with Soviet troops entering Germany in the Second World War.

No wonder, then, that a new phenomenon for Europe was that of masses of refugees, right from the beginning of the war. Refugees in little Belgium could hardly know where to move, but refugees in France, fleeing before the Germany Army were also very numerous. In the East – East Prussia,

Poland and Lithuania – too, millions were on the move, adding stresses on civilian life, largely unknown before. To refugees, who fled on their own, must be added those deported from border areas for being politically unreliable or 'fifth columns' as they would have been called following the Spanish Civil War. More tragically still, such deportations could also perpetuate past policies of discrimination and oppression.

The most dramatic example was that of the Armenians, who, indeed, sympathised with the Russians, because they appeared to them as liberators from the Turkish yoke of enforced assimilation and pogroms. The Armenian tragedy is full of historical ironies. They were marched, shot and hacked to death in 1915–16 in massacres that bordered on intended genocide, to the embarrassment of the German Government which hushed up scandalised reports by German consuls on the spot. This Turkish version of 'ethnic cleansing' against Christian Armenians was executed by Muslim Kurds who today are suffering a similar fate in secularised Turkey. One of the German vice-consuls was Scheubner-Richter, Hitler's early close associate, who was killed at the Munich putsch of 1923. Through him, Hitler must have learned about the Armenian massacres, but he used this knowledge in a perversely twisted way to dismiss world reaction to intended mass murder almost thirty years later when he remarked during World War II in one of his table talks: 'Who remembers the Armenian Massacres? Thus, it will be the same with the Jews'.

A parallel incident, less known and less bloody, was the deportation of Jews from the Western provinces of Russia, who were wooed by German leaflets in Yiddish, promising liberation from Tsarist pogroms. Hardship for Jewish deportees in Russia was a harbinger of worse to come – from irregular pogroms during the Russian Civil War on both sides, 'White' and 'Red', to the regular and systematically organised Holocaust, one World War later, on industrial lines. The grim historical irony is too obvious to be made explicit: one generation later, those very Jews became the victims of the German Holocaust in the next World War.

In the First World War, German policy-makers were split over what to do with Jews in Poland living in areas adjacent to the German borders in the East and secretly earmarked for annexation and Germanisation after a German victory: Pan-Germans and their allies in military and government circles followed their anti-semitic instincts and wanted to expel them, along with Poles, from the countryside,[6] while more liberal Germans considered Jews a Germanising element, because of their Yiddish language and their admiration for German culture.

Further deportees were those Belgians sent to Germany as forced labour. This had one memorable side-effect – an outstanding piece of modern historiography: one Belgian patriot who protested against German policies to split Belgium into Walloon and Flemish districts, was the great Medieval historian, Henri Pirenne. Sent to Germany, he landed up in an officers' camp at Holzminden, Northern Germany. There he was asked by well-educated Russian officers to give them lectures in his field. Pirenne agreed, and out of his lectures – without books or source material to hand – emerged his 'History of Europe in the Middle Ages from the Invasion of the Barbarians to the Reformation', one of his many fine books.

After the German conquest of Lithuania and southern Latvia in summer 1915, the Germans installed a military government *Oberost* under General Ludendorff which again pointed the way to practices in the next World War: economic exploitation and the treatment of the civilian population was so harsh that, as a recent doctoral dissertation of a Lithuanian has shown, Lithuanians felt a nostalgic desire for the return of Russian rule and even fought the Germans in a hitherto largely ignored partisan war.[7] Latvians, who had burned down the manors of German–Baltic barons in the First Russian Revolution of 1905, formed élite regiments in the Russian Army to fight the Germans.[8] Later they became Lenin's watch-dogs of the Bolshevik Revolution, as depicted in George Orwell's 'Animal Farm', furtively paid with German gold marks which had been supplied by the Kaiser's Government to Russia. Austrian troops re-occupying Eastern Galicia in 1915, hanged from trees Ruthenian (i.e. Ukrainian) peasants by the thousands for having collaborated with the Russians.

As to the sufferings of civilian populations of the Balkans in the war, it is easy to imagine what happened, given the tradition of 'Balkan massacre'[9] and experiences in the region since the Macedonian Uprising in 1903. Muslim Bosnian regiments commanded by German Austrian officers, fought well against Orthodox Serbs and Russians, when attacking with their favourite weapon – knives between their teeth.

The further away from the actual battlefields, the more indirect were the effects of war: the normal anguish of wives and fiancées for their men in the war, the shortages of food and other necessities of daily life. They were most severe in belligerent countries, more or less blockaded from the rest of the World – Russia and the Central Powers – in particular predominantly industrialised Germany.

Since most had cherished the illusion of the short war, no preparations had been made in advance. The British blockade, aiming at and hitting mostly the civilian population, gradually pushed Germany and Austro–Hungary into widespread and chronic hunger. There were great differences: industrial areas were harder hit than agrarian ones; as a rule of thumb, the closer to the level of subsistence, the less devastating were the effects of the blockade, although agrarian production suffered badly from the lack of fertilizers, draft animals and male labour. The wealthier people in urban and rural areas were, the better-off they were, with political consequences. Hatred against war-profiteers of all sorts could become explosive. Anti-Semitism in Germany made its first creeping breakthrough in the terrible home front crisis of the central years of the Great War.

By the winter of 1916–17, the less favoured segments of German and Austrian society were restricted to hunger diets by official rationing. A small detail may suffice here, as reported in the memoirs of the leading Social Democrat Philip Scheidemann. After he had spoken about the suffering of the urban population, in particular the working class, in the steering committee (*Hauptausschuss*) of the Reichstag, he received a bag of potatoes from one of the arch-reactionary members of Parliament, Oldenburg-Januschau.[10] By and large, polarisation between the better-off and undernourished sectors of societies marked the breaking-line in the hour of defeat.

The working-classes were the weak spots in the home front of industrialised societies in war. Here, national enthusiasm at the beginning of the war first turned into hatred towards its end, leading to social revolution, in 1917 in Russia, in 1918/19 in Germany, Austria and Hungary, each in their different way. In Russia, the few pockets of industrialisation became centres of Bolshevik agitation, whilst their working-class mates serving on the then technically most sophisticated branch of the Armed Forces, as sailors of the battle-fleets, became pioneers of social revolution to end the war for the losers.

France was geographically split into her eastern and north-eastern fringes, occupied by the German Army, ravaged by industrialised total war, and the area behind the French front. In the latter, life for the civilian population went on almost as normal, except for rigours imposed by the national war effort. Britain, in her splendid isolation, was even more sheltered from direct warfare. She, however, had to depend on her vital sea-links for the supply of foodstuffs and raw materials after Germany opened her submarine campaign in order to break the British blockade.

As for women, since women had often to do a man's job, their new burdens and responsibilities tended to strengthen the movement for emancipating women from the patriarchal grip of men. This was a peculiarity of Europe and Northern America dating from the Age of Enlightenment and the French Revolution. With 'the Rights of Man' spreading to the whole of democratic national societies in the West, women were belatedly making their demands. Equal rights for women were to break the unspoken assumption that 'rights of man' were reserved for males only.

Although the First World War was largely a European Great War – all Great European Powers against each other at the same time – our Euro-centred perspective should not prevent us from considering the civilian dimension of war outside Europe, in particular in Black Africa. With the German U-boat warfare, sailors took additional risks on commercial ships. Blacks from the British Empire, often the West Indians, more traditionally Lascars from the East Indies, constituted a fair proportion of the crews of

British merchant vessels. After the War, those who had survived tended to stay in Britain, forming the nuclei of black ghettoes in British seaports. During the Second World War the same happened again, now quantitatively on an even bigger scale. This became an important mechanism to bring blacks into Britain *en masse* in two world wars.[11]

The French equivalent was a straightforward military parallel. In her peril, France increased the numbers of her colonial troops, recruited mostly in French West Africa, and not just from Senegal, as the usual name for them suggests. Many of those who had fought in and for France stayed or returned after the war. They also concentrated around seaports, Marseilles and Bordeaux in particular.

In Africa, the impact of war was twofold: British and French colonies took part in the war efforts of their Mother Countries, the British more indirectly in the economic sphere, the French more directly in the military. Actual fighting on African soil was short-lived except in East Africa. In all cases, colonial powers mobilised Africans almost as conscript labour, usually for porterage in the service of their colonial armies (Many of them, admittedly, were already slaves of African masters). By the same token, three-quarters of recruited soldiers in French West Africa were said to have been slaves.[12] In one case, the stresses of colonial rule and the First World War escalated into open revolt, that of John Chilembwe in Nyasaland (Malawi) in 1915, with its not so unusual mixture of Western (Euro–American) Christian fundamentalism and indigenous elements.[13] Although, or because, Chilembwe's movement was swiftly and harshly suppressed by the British, he became the great martyr for the Nyasaland national independence movement after World War II. The parallel to the Irish Easter Rising of 1916 is obvious, where the English converted what was a military defeat for the Irish Republicans into a political victory by turning the leaders of the Irish Rebellion into martyrs.

In the Belgian Congo, although not directly hit by colonial war, the equivalent agitation took the form of religion in the rise of Joseph Kimbangu immediately after the War. In South Africa it crystallised in the African National Congress (A.N.C.) originally modelled on the Indian National Congress in South Africa, launched by the later Mahatma Gandhi, and also in the first African Trade Unions. In general, colonial societies tended to press, after World War I, through their new intelligentsias as their mouth-pieces, for autonomy, roughly in proportion to their participation in the metropolitan war effort, though it was only after World War II that they agitated for sovereignty and full independence.

The sufferings of civilians in war, whether in uniform on the military fronts, on the home front, or as refugees or deportees, were too great to make them the wiser for a better future. From the victors came the cries: 'Squeeze them till the pips squeak!' and 'Hang the Kaiser!' From the losers came 'No more War!' ('*Nie wieder Krieg!*') right after the war, followed by the drive for revenge, which in itself sufficed to land Germany and the world into a Second World War. On top of this came the flight of the mightiest of the losers into ideologically opposing totalitarian camps, which, between them, secretly collaborated against parliamentary democracy and gave the kiss of death to world peace for a second time. Yet the Second World War, the most spectacular offshoot of World War I, proved destructive to totalitarian régimes, first directly, through Nazism's defeat and later indirectly, through Soviet Communism's eventual collapse in the long 'peace' of the Cold War following apparent victory, with its dialectical after-effects, in the 'hot' Second World War. The legacies of these regimes were more chaos and confusion everywhere.

We may draw little but cold comfort from the end of the Cold War and its implied threat of global World War III between the Super-Powers, because post-colonial and post-Communist successor states are plunging the world into a maze of hot local civil and international wars. However, it may be that a rational analysis of the First World War could help to avoid greater catastrophes, as long as people are prepared to draw peaceful lessons from Great Wars.

Notes

1 *The Other Balkan Wars.* A 1913 Carnegie Endowment Inquiry in Retrospect with a New Introduction and Reflections on the Present Conflict by George F. Kennan, a Carnegie Endowment Book, New York 1993.

2 Peter Schöller: *Der Fall Löwen und das Weißbuch*, Böhlau, Köln/Graz 1958; Lothar Wieland; *Belgien 1914*, Peter Lang, Frankfurt/Main u.a. 1984; Wolfgang Schivelbusch: *Eine Ruine im Krieg der Geister. Die Bibliothek von Löwen August 1914 bis Mai 1940*, Fischer Taschenbuch Geschichte 10367, Frankfurt/Main 1993, p. 10.

3 First mentioned by Werner Conze: *Polnische Nation und Deutsche Politik im Ersten Weltkrieg*, Böhlau, Köln, Graz 1958, p. 58, in a longish footnote; also Imanuel Geiss: Der polnische Grenzstreifen 1914–1918. Ein Beitrag zur deutschen Kriegszielpolitik im Ersten Weltkrieg, *Historische Studen 378*, Matthiesen Verlag, Lübeck, Hamburg, 1960, p. 33. Material on the (negative) reactions of the Polish legions in the (former) Deutsches Zentralarchiv, now Bundesarchiv, Merseburg, Rep. 77, Tit. 863 A, Nr. 7, 'Die polnischen Legionen'. A detailed study would be worth while.

4 I. Geiss: *Der polnische Grenzstreifen*, p. 33.

5 Material in: Staatliches Archivlager Göttingen, Re. 2 Oberpräsident Ostpreußen.

6 I. Geiss: *Der polnische Grenzstreifen*, p. 105, 133f., 158, 161, 169.

7 A. Strazhas: *Deutsche Ostpolitik im Ersten Weltkrieg. Der Fall Ober Ost 1915 bis 1917*, Veröffentlichungen des Osteuropa-Instituts München (Reihe: Geschichte, Bd. 61), Harrassowitz, Wiesbaden 1993, pp 13–27.

8 Peter Krupnikov: *Letten und Lettland im Spiegel der deutschen und deutschbaltischen Publizistik 1895–1950*, Hirschleydt, Hannover-Döhren 1988, p. 188–192.

9   The term used in I. Geiss: *Der Jugoslawienkrieg*, Diesterweg. Frankfurt/Main 1993, pp. 27–29.
10 Philipp Scheidemann: *Memoiren eines Sozialdemokratien*, Reissner, Dresden 1928, p. . . . .
11 Kenneth Little: *Negroes in Britain. A study of Racial Relations in English Society*, London 1947.
12 John Iliffe: *The African Poor. A History*, Cambridge University Press. Cambridge 1987, p. 144.
13 George Shepperson/Thomas Price: Independent African: *John Chilembwe and the Origins, Setting and Significance of the Nyasaland Native Rising of 1915*, Edinburgh University Press, Edinburgh 1958.

Part II

Command: Responsibility and Stress

Chapter 3

Winston Churchill and the Strain of Office, 1914 – 1915

Martin Gilbert

For the first ten months of the First World War, Winston Churchill was First Lord of the Admiralty, and, from the moment of its inception, a member of the War Council*. He was not yet forty years old when war broke out, but had been First Lord for almost three years.

Churchill was a compulsively hard worker. Contrary to legend, he neither drank nor smoked more than his fellow-politicians. He certainly drank less than Asquith. In terms of the mass of technical material with which he was confronted as First Lord, he could absorb substantial submissions and memoranda: it is a fiction that he had no time for a submission longer than a single page. His marginal and textual notes on long documents show how thoroughly he could study them. His office was his home: he lived and slept at Admiralty House, at the north-east corner of Horse Guards Parade, the building next to the Admiralty Building, where the rooms most essential to his daily work were located. He was supported at his work by a devoted Private Office, headed by Eddie Marsh, who had been seconded to him at the Colonial Office at the end of 1905 and had never left his employ (he was still his Private Secretary in 1929). His Admiralty Secretary, James Masterton Smith (later his Permanent Under-Secretary of State at the Colonial Office), was equally devoted and hard-working. One evening, as Asquith was finishing his work in the Cabinet Room, he wrote to his friend Venetia Stanley: 'Through the opposite window across the Parade I see the Admiralty flag flying and the lights 'beginning to twinkle' from the rooms where Winston and his two familiars (Eddie and Masterton) are beating out their plans.'

Churchill was always on the move. Between 10 September 1914 and 5 May 1915 he made eight visits across the Channel to France and Belgium to examine Admiralty, Naval Air Service and Royal Naval Division units, and to discuss naval policy with his French and Belgian opposite numbers.

His comparative youth gave him an edge among his Cabinet colleagues not only in terms of his travels across the Channel, but in the hours that he spent at work, and the energies he expended not only at his desk, but in his continual visits to Admiralty installations and ships around the United Kingdom. He was twenty-six years younger than Kitchener, twenty-four years younger than Asquith, and twelve years younger even than his fellow 'young Turk', Lloyd George. Each of them envied his capacity for sustained hard work, and could be jolted by his ability to raise in Cabinet some issue with which they assumed he was unfamiliar, but which he had somehow, amid his other responsibilities, found the will and time to master.

The impact of the First World War on Winston Churchill's life and career was to prove decisive on many aspects of his future career, although, with his removal from the Admiralty in May 1915, it was assumed by many observers of the political scene that his career was over. His departure for the trenches of the Western Front in November 1915, after he gave up the essentially sinecure post of Chancellor of the Duchy of Lancaster, confirmed this. The mocking rebuttal of his speech in the House of Commons in March 1916, when he returned from the trenches to demand the re-appointment of Admiral Lord Fisher as First Lord, seemed further evidence that he had no political future; that, as far as his political behaviour was concerned, the balance of his mind was disturbed.

When Churchill was dismissed by Asquith in May 1915 he was convinced that an injustice had been done to him, and in one sense he was right. The Conservative leaders, who regarded Churchill as a renegade and an adventurer, irrevocably and dangerously hostile to their party's interests since he had left their ranks a decade earlier, had insisted on his removal from the Admiralty as a condition of their joining Asquith's all-Party government. Churchill's sense of grievance was deep, and was supported by his wife Clementine, who, despite her own deep Liberal sentiments, felt that Asquith had failed to support her husband's abilities at the moment when they were most needed by the nation. In what Asquith described privately as 'the letter of a maniac', Clementine Churchill wrote to him at the height of the May 1915 political crisis: 'If you throw Winston overboard you will be committing an act of weakness and your Coalition Government will not be as formidable a War machine as the present Government. Winston may in your eyes and in those with whom he has to work have faults but he has the supreme quality which I venture to say very few of your present or future Cabinet possess, the power, the imagination, the deadliness to fight Germany. If you send him to another place he will no longer be fighting. If you waste this valuable war material you will be doing an injury to this country.'

From the moment of his removal from the Admiralty, perhaps even from the moment that war had been declared, Churchill believed that had he been called upon to direct the nation's affairs, he would certainly have made an effective war leader. He was convinced, he wrote to his wife from the trenches in January 1916, that he could use power 'better than any other living Englishman to determine the war policy of Britain'. He was confident that he had the ability to drive forward the machinery of government with vigour and cohesion, and that his ideas for national organisation and naval, military and aerial strategy could have averted the disasters and broken the stalemates of 1915 and 1916. When he was nearly killed by a German shell in March 1916 he expressed his thoughts on death in national as well as in personal terms, writing to his wife (in words that would have had a chilling resonance for all those who were alive in 1940, had they known of them) about 'a final gift, unvalued, to an ungrateful country – an impoverishment of the war-making power of Britain which no one would ever know or measure or mourn'.

Churchill's confidence in his abilities was absolute, and had been since his experiences as a soldier twenty years before the outbreak of the First World War. This confidence was not shaken by the political setbacks of May and November 1915. As a Cabinet Minister since 1908 he had shown this confidence to his colleagues, and it had always been a striking feature of his public speeches. It was a strong and vaunted confidence, applauded at first both by his colleagues and by the public, who appreciated in August 1914, and were inspired by, his combination of faith in the outcome of the war and recognition of the difficulties still to come. But to be accepted fully, to be trusted and rewarded, such confidence needed to be set against successful results.

The series of failures at the Dardanelles and Gallipoli, however much they can be explained by errors other than Churchill's own, or, as he came to explain them, by his lack of overall authority to drive the enterprise to success, set up a barrier between the confidence which he felt in himself, and the public assessment of him. Nor was it the Dardanelles alone that kept this barrier in place, depriving him of the power which he believed he could use effectively, and relegating him first to political impotence and then, under Lloyd George, to a position (Minister of Munitions) outside the inner Cabinet. Irrespective of particular successes or failures between August 1914 and May 1915, and in spite of such explanations and documentation which he was able to give in subsequent newspaper articles and books, Churchill was unable to convince many of his contemporaries that he had a claim on their respect and trust. He was believed by many to be wanting in certain essential qualities of statesmanship; and was judged more deficient in these qualities by the winter of 1916 than he had been in the autumn of 1914.

Churchill's wartime work at the Admiralty, for which he believed himself entitled to the praise and support of his fellow-countrymen, was interpreted in such a way as to confirm in many minds the doubts that had already been formed during the previous decade, and to create doubts where none had earlier existed. He believed that his war policies and war-making zeal had been both unique and beneficial, making him indispensable to any successful wartime administration, and qualifying him for the highest public office. But the very enthusiasm with which he entered into war policy created suspicion and even fear, destroying his chances after May 1915 of directing the war from 10 Downing Street, the Admiralty or the War Office. Any other place he regarded as insufficient challenge to his abilities, and as a waste of his energies.

Churchill did not understand why it was that he created mistrust where he expected to secure approval. He believed that his abilities and achievements were such that only a malicious critic would deny them. Clementine Churchill realised why he did not inspire trust. She saw how far his strident confidence frightened those with whom he worked and to whom he had to look for support. She alone of those closest to him told him of his faults. Others, like Asquith and Lloyd George, added to his self-deception by frequent praise and encouragement when they were with him, but by severe censure on him in their private talk and correspondence. Clementine Churchill cautioned her husband directly. In her letters to him she stressed the danger to his career of the impatience and scorn which he often showed towards those who disagreed with him. She rebuked his tendency to take provocative or unexpected measures without regard to the likely reaction of others. She stressed how much he harmed himself by acting upon ideas which he had not given others time to accept, or which he had failed adequately to explain. She warned him that these weaknesses of character were accentuated by his often brusque and dictatorial manner, and by his overriding impatience. She saw clearly that the ideas which he produced with such extraordinary energy and conviction were seen by others as lacking in judgement; and that the more fiercely he pressed forward with a course of action, the more lacking in perspective he appeared to those colleagues without whose support he could not act.

These criticisms were all justified; Clementine Churchill understood her husband's failure to convince others. But there was a deeper failure. Churchill had always to be at the centre; he wanted to be responsible for the principal decisions of the war, and to be known to be. He believed that risks had to be taken, and he failed to understand why others were repelled by his evident relish for warmaking. At the Admiralty he proposed several swift and bold actions. Those who hesitated to accept those proposals sensed his disapproval. Those who wanted to wait longer upon events found his scorn direct, outspoken and even galling. Those who could not make up their minds, or who did so with reservations, felt his disapproval.

As 1915 progressed, his arguments at the War Council became increasingly ineffective. Because of his forceful and assertive manner he often appeared to his colleagues over-simple and over-dramatic. His counsel was weighty and sober, but at times it was perceived as hasty and immature.

Churchill was often unable to make his diverse moods, his growing obsessions, or his seemingly dictatorial approach to dissent, understood for what they were, a determination to 'neglect no means' (his favourite Latin tag) to achieve victory over Germany. His contemporaries found themselves making frequent and caustic reference to his ambition, which they interpreted as overriding his undoubted grasp of naval and military strategy, his perceptiveness and farsightedness.

Asquith and Lloyd George, whose respective patronage had been essential to Churchill for him to remain in Government or return to it, both felt that their imaginative, constructive, hard-working colleague of pre-war years was being eaten up by personal ambition, and that his judgement had been impaired. An example of how Churchill was spoken about, behind his back, can be seen in Lloyd George's remarks to Margot Asquith, at the time of Churchill's relegation in May 1915, about his mood at the time of the outbreak of war. Margot Asquith recorded them in her diary. 'Winston dashed into the room,' she recorded Lloyd George as recalling, 'radiant, his face bright, his manner keen, one word pouring out on another how he was going to send telegrams to the Mediterranean, the North Sea, and God knows where. You could see he was a really happy man.'

The doubts felt by Asquith and Lloyd George about Churchill's reliability kept him from office for nearly two years, two years when he felt he had so much to contribute to victory. His political position was isolated, so that whatever good ideas he might have about the conduct of the war, and in due course about the nature of peacemaking (where he urged magnanimity) could not find a political base. No influential section of the Liberal Party considered him their leader. No significant political groups regarded him as their spokesman. The hostilities which he had aroused by the end of 1915 cut him off from all but a small group of isolated allies of no political strength, a few of those seen as mavericks like himself.

Churchill craved the allegiance of large numbers, both in Parliament and outside it. He was convinced that his foresight and his abilities, if understood by his fellow-countrymen, would win that allegiance for him. But faith in his powers of leadership was held by few; by a small family circle, and by friends who had been captivated by his driving force. They alone regarded his consuming self-confidence, his impatience and his brooding as a necessary counterpart to his positive qualities, and felt that without them his powers of judgement, and his remarkable energy, could indeed not flourish.

Churchill could not dispel the doubts and distrust which he had created. All the faults to which people pointed seemed to spring from an egoism which would be dangerous if allowed to control, or even influence, a War Cabinet. Only an overriding concern with self seemed adequate to explain the different phases of his wartime career: his excitement at the preparations for war, his exhilaration when it came, his personal involve-

31

ment in the siege of Antwerp, his desire at the time of Antwerp to give up the Admiralty for a military command, his brooding concern for vindication over each of the several disasters of his wartime months as First Lord, his growing obsession with making known the precise evolution of policy and planning at the Dardanelles, his gnawing impatience at his reduced powers at the Duchy of Lancaster, and, most fatal of all for public perceptions, his appeal in March 1916 for the return of Lord Fisher to the Admiralty. As it was Fisher's desertion of his post in May 1915 that had enabled the Conservative leaders to demand a coalition, and with it Churchill's head, it seemed ill-judged, to say the least, that Churchill should, within a year, argue publicly and forcefully that the proper prosecution of the war depended on Fisher being given high office and substantial powers. The selfishness and irresponsibility which these concerns seemed to indicate could be set against substantial achievements in naval policy, and considerable wisdom and foresight in counsel. But the mistrust which Churchill aroused prevented these comparisons being made, and his substantial achievements failed to restore public confidence.

During 1916 Churchill realised he could do nothing to curb the continuous criticisms of his past actions, or to allay suspicions about his motives. He came increasingly to fear that his contemporaries would never recognise what he believed were the extent of his achievements, and of his capabilities. He felt that these had come to be blotted out of the public mind by malice, partisanship and prejudice. His bitterness against Asquith for not publishing the documents about the Dardanelles was acute. His dislike of the Press for condemning him without the evidence was severe. He became convinced that only when the archives of the Admiralty and the War Council were made public would his true worth be known. He believed that although contemporaries belittled his achievements, historical research would show his actions to have been prudent, wise and remarkable. He fell back upon the belief that, despite the harsh judgement of his contemporaries, the judgement of history would support him.

Cut off from power, denigrated and condemned, Churchill saw history as the final refuge of his reputation. But his immediate career, and his influence on the course of the war, depended entirely, not upon the historical but upon the contemporary verdict. In December 1916 that verdict was outspokenly hostile and seemingly irreversible. As Churchill himself had written to Asquith in September 1915, urging publication of the Dardanelles documentation: 'I am repeatedly made the object of very serious charges in all these matters, which have never been contradicted, and seem in some way to be confirmed by my leaving the Admiralty. Sometimes the charges appear in print . . . but much more they are kept alive by conversation, or by constant references in newspaper articles; and there is no doubt whatever that the belief is widespread that I personally acted in these events wrongfully and foolishly. You know the facts. I have made them known to some of my colleagues. But that does not help me outside, and I still remain under the shadow of utterly false aspersions which are a serious injury to me.'

As a result of his sense of historical truth, Churchill began, even while he was Chancellor of the Duchy of Lancaster, to collect the documents bearing on his conduct of naval affairs. When neither Asquith nor, after December 1916, Lloyd George, would agree to publish them, he decided to write the history himself. His first essay had been in a series of newspaper articles. But his greatest energies were to be put into presenting his case in book form. When, in July 1915, he had expected to go to the Dardanelles to see the situation at first hand (a project which the Conservative members of the Cabinet stopped at the last moment, after Asquith had approved it), he wrote to his wife that, in the event of his being killed on his mission, 'I am anxious you should get hold of all my papers, especially those which refer to my Admiralty administration . . . There is no hurry; but some day I should like the truth to be known.'

The truth which Churchill wanted told related to all the decisions he had made between August 1914 and May 1915, and to the pressures surrounding those decisions at the time. In the days leading up to war it had been his initiative, supported by Asquith, that had kept the Fleet at its war stations. Had this become known to the Cabinet, it might have led to a reversal of the decision by those, including at that moment Lloyd George, for whom it might have seemed a provocative rather than a precautionary measure. The strain of the decision, compounded with its secrecy, was something Churchill alone knew. In May 1915, when he was packing up his office at the Admiralty, Churchill was momentarily cheered when Lord Kitchener came to see him to discuss the crisis and, as he was about to leave, turned to Churchill with the words: 'Well, there is one thing at any rate they cannot take from you. The Fleet was ready.'

On the eve of war, Churchill's attempt to prevent the two German warships, *Goeben* and *Breslau*, from reaching Turkish waters after they had bombarded two French naval installations in North Africa, was likewise a time of great anxiety. The measures he had put in train to intercept the ships were negated by a Cabinet decision not to allow a German act of war on France to be responded to until after the British ultimatum against Germany had expired. The few hours involved made the difference between success and failure: yet it was the failure that most influenced the public, and even colleagues who knew the full story.

A further strain at the outbreak of war was the convoying across the Channel of the British Expeditionary Force. Had this force been attacked in any way, by warship, submarine or from the air, the blame for having taken too great a risk, or for not having taken adequate precautions, would have been put at Churchill's door. Yet the transfer, in ten days, of 120,000 men, without the loss of a single life, was due in considerable measure to his careful planning. So too was the movement of 50,000 Indian troops from Bombay and Karachi to Marseilles, and 25,000 Canadian volunteers across the Atlantic. These were considerable numbers of men. At the time, praise was given to Churchill for this, the Manchester Guardian commenting: 'We remember nothing like this feat in the whole of naval history'. But for Churchill, it had been a time of anxiety, and it was this very word which he used in an unpublished note, written just after the war, to describe it: 'This was a period of great anxiety to us. All the most fateful possibilities were open. We were bound to expect a military descent upon our coasts with the intention of arresting or recalling our Army, or a naval raid into the Channel to cut down the transports, or a concentrated sub-marine attack upon these vessels crammed with men. The great naval battle might begin at any moment independently or in connection with any of these operations. It was a period of extreme psychological tension.'

There were also personal anxieties which affected the man who knew that the German navy was a powerful striking force. His wife and children were on holiday at Cromer, on the North Sea. 'It makes me a little anxious that you should be on the coast,' he wrote to her five days after the British declaration of war on Germany. 'It is 100 to 1 against a raid – but still there is a chance, and Cromer has a good landing place near. I wish you would get the motor repaired and keep it so that you can whisk away at the first sign of trouble.'

The pressures of the early weeks and months of war were considerable. It was the danger of a rapid German advance to the Channel Ports, cutting off the Expeditionary Force from its line of withdrawal to the coast, that made Churchill decide to make a personal journey to Antwerp in October 1914, and to seek to remain there, helping stiffen the resolve of the defenders as the German siege lines tightened. 'Antwerp' was to be one of the strongest nails in his political coffin, a constant jibe by Conservative and Liberal critics alike, and part of the charge of irresponsibility against him for many years to come. At the time, it had seemed possible that Churchill might just be able to strengthen the Belgian resolve by his personal presence. As Asquith informed his friend Venetia Stanley after Churchill had left: 'The intrepid Winston set off at midnight and ought to have reached Antwerp by about nine this morning. He will go straightway and beard the King and his Ministers, and try to infuse into their backbones the necessary quantity of starch.'

Churchill's mission to Antwerp was effective; he did manage to persuade the Belgians, with the help of British reinforcements, to hold on for an extra few crucial days. But the Conservative opposition used the mission, the background and evolution of which was unknown to them (it is described on pages 96 to 120 of volume three of the Churchill biography), to criticise his judgement publicly and ferociously. As speculative accounts of Churchill's mission circulated in Whitehall, a senior civil servant, Sir

Francis Hopwood, wrote to the King's Private Secretary Lord Stamfordham, 'I don't think Winston can come away now with credit,' to which Stamfordham replied: 'Our friend must be quite off his head!' This became the accepted view, and from his anguished reading of the newspapers, Churchill knew it. He did not know that Asquith had written to the Cabinet Secretary: 'That week at Antwerp was well spent, and had a real effect on the general campaign.'

The question of pressure and policy is seldom seen more clearly than in the evolution of the Dardanelles campaign. Churchill had wanted the Gallipoli Peninsula attacked as soon as Turkey entered the war in October 1914, if possible in conjunction with the Greek Army. Within two months, as the trench lines were established on the Western Front, he became convinced that the Eastern Mediterranean was not the right area for British military effort. When, at the beginning of January 1915, his recently-appointed First Sea Lord, Admiral Fisher, pressed for a series of attacks on Turkey, including at the Dardanelles and Gallipoli, using Greek and Bulgarian as well as 75,000 British troops, Churchill wrote to him: 'I would not grudge 100,000 men because of the great political effects in the Balkan peninsula: but Germany is the foe, and it is bad war to seek cheaper victories and easier antagonists.'

It was at that very moment that an appeal was sent to London from the Grand Duke Nicholas, the Russian Commander-in-Chief, whose troops were being hard pressed by the Turks in eastern Anatolia, asking for emergency action by Britain. As soon as the appeal reached the War Office, Kitchener wrote to Churchill: 'The only place that a demonstration might have some effect in stopping reinforcements going East would be the Dardanelles – particularly if, as the Grand Duke says, reports could be spread at the same time that Constantinople was threatened.' Kitchener's letter was the first link in the chain that led, not only to a purely naval 'demonstration' at the Dardanelles, but to a naval attempt to break through the Narrows into the Sea of Marmara. Churchill became the principal and most determined advocate of this, and of effective, properly supported military landings on the Gallipoli peninsula. But the preparations for the landings were the responsibility of Kitchener, and Churchill spent many unsuccessful interventions in the War Council failing to convince Kitchener to act with a greater sense of the military obstacles that might lie ahead.

In Volume Three of the Churchill biography I have described, and in the companion volumes of Churchill documents that accompany the biography I have elaborated on Churchill's frustrations when, at each stage, and almost on each day of the preparations for naval action at the Dardanelles something went wrong, some new factor was thrown into the discussion, some existing plan countermanded, or some change of plan authorised. It was a time not only of anxiety and worry, but also of anger

35

and sometimes almost despair for him. He was obliged to stand by and watch the ill-effects (about many of which he had warned) of the volatile nature of the decision-making process. Sometimes Kitchener as Secretary of State for War, sometimes Asquith as Prime Minister, and even Grey as Secretary of State for Foreign Affairs, would introduce some new factor. These involved, by turns, alterations to technical and logistic plans, to wider strategies, and to the whole concept for which the men in action were being asked to risk, and to lose, their lives. In the Second World War Churchill was determined to avoid such a situation, hence his creation of the Chiefs of Staff system.

With regard to the period August 1914 to May 1915, and in particular the Dardanelles, Churchill had no illusions about the role of history and the historians (himself included). Two months after being removed from the Admiralty he wrote to a soldier friend: 'I am hopeful that the truth may be published. But failure and tragedy are all that are left to divide.' It was a cry of anguish, based upon a traumatic period of hopes raised and expectations dashed.

* Editorial note: See in particular Martin Gilbert, *Churchill*, Vol III, 1914–16, London, Heinemann, 1971, and companion volumes.

Chapter 4

Kitchener at the War Office

George Cassar

Even if Kitchener had not drowned when the *Hampshire* sank off the Orkneys in June 1916, it is unlikely that he would have written his memoirs in retirement. Secure in himself, at no time did he feel the need to justify his actions, content to leave that judgment to history. During his long career as a soldier and administrator he rarely committed his views to paper, still less sharing them with acquaintances and associates. He shunned publicity, was unsociable and only a few friends were privy to his innermost thoughts. To his contemporaries he was an enigma and even today there are aspects of his life which remain unclear or unknown to us. This paper focuses on his role as Secretary of State for War and in particular on how his struggle to preserve his carefully formulated military strategy in the face of serious obstacles, plus his increasingly troubled relationship with cabinet colleagues, heightened the pressure of managing Britain's effort in the Great War.

Kitchener had the initial benefit of great popular and political support when he accepted the seals of the War Office on 5 August 1914, one day after the nation found itself at war. He was the quintessential Victorian imperial hero with military achievements which included annihilating the dervishes in the epic battle of Omdurman and crushing Boer guerilla resistance in South Africa. The public believed he could do no wrong, and greeted his appointment as Secretary of State for War with relief and ecstatic approval, while the cabinet, in awe of his reputation and dazed by the outbreak of war, left him free to do as he saw fit.

Kitchener's was a one-man show; he rarely availed himself of the General Staff which could have relieved him of a mountain of trivial decisions.[1] Directing the whole military machine, he assumed responsibility for strategic planning, mobilizing the nation's industries for war, protecting the empire and recruiting and supplying the army in the field.[2] It was a burden that no man could sustain for long.

Kitchener knew that Britain was poorly prepared for the kind of war that he envisaged. He scoffed at the notion that it could fight a European war along principles of limited liability.[3] He alone predicted that the conflict would be a long one and would be won after many bloody battles fought on the continent.[4] His shrewd assessment of the relative strengths of the opposing continental armies had convinced him that Russia and France lacked the means to defeat so formidable and determined an adversary as Germany. It was unrealistic to think that Britain's meagre army of six divisions would be able to redress the military imbalance. If Britain was to do its fair share of the fighting it would need to expand its army many times over – ultimately he set the number of divisions at seventy. He wanted the 'new armies' to reach maximum strength in 1917 by which time he calculated that the continental powers would have fought each other to a standstill.[5] The British army, with its resources practically untapped, would be in a position to administer the final blow against Germany and dictate peace terms to friend and foe alike.

Kitchener's strategy was based on a sophisticated understanding of the nature of a two-front war. He considered inseparable the conduct of the war on the Eastern and Western fronts. He never thought of Russia as a dominant military nation but valued its effective fighting presence as pivotal for the success of his war aims. Although he expected that war would be won on the Western front he was fully aware that Britain and France were years away from gaining that objective. While the new armies were being prepared it was imperative that the Russians should hold down a sizeable segment of the German army. If Russia were knocked out of the war early and Germany able to concentrate all its forces in the west, he was not at all confident that the French and the British could hold the line.[6]

Kitchener would have been sensible to disclose his plans to the Cabinet. But he viewed his colleagues warily, with the soldier's usual mixture of contempt and trepidation. He was accustomed to keeping his views to himself and he distrusted his colleagues' discretion, suspecting that they revealed everything to their wives or girl friends. He stayed at cabinet meetings only as long as was necessary to disclose the essentials. The Prime Minister, H.H. Asquith, did not press him for details or encourage others to do so. He had no wish to add to Kitchener's immense labours. Although the cabinet contained many contentious and brilliant personalities, all were relieved to place the responsibility for managing the war in his hands.[7] On the whole their trust in his judgment was not misplaced.

Wearing the blue field dress of a field-marshal, Kitchener arrived at the War Office at 9 a.m. and, except for lunch and an occasional tea break, worked at his desk until dusk. He maintained this arduous schedule from Monday to Friday and occasionally came in to work on Saturdays. Those who saw much of the Secretary for War could not fail to wonder how he was able to keep going at such a pace. His ability to do so was a testament to his physical fitness. For a man of sixty-four he was remarkably energetic and spry. He had never been self indulgent. He ate light meals and for exercise took long daily walks. He was never more than a moderate drinker, consuming a little wine at dinner and a scotch and soda later in the evening.[8] His chief indulgence was smoking cigars, which he puffed while deep in thought or throwing out orders to his staff.

Kitchener assumed the burdens of office with confidence and composure. He shook up War Office personnel by introducing methods of work it had never known and by discarding long established procedures.[9] Terrified messengers, their coat-tails streaming behind, raced down the corridors when summoned to his office. Seated behind a large desk, usually littered with papers, he dealt personally with each major problem as it arose; but because he scrupulously weighed and analyzed all factors he was slow in arriving at a decision.

Kitchener was quite imperturbable, neither depressed by defeat nor unduly elated by success. He was used to working under pressure, for when serving on the fringes of the Empire he had faced almost insuperable difficulties, sometimes for days on end. He was accustomed to making decisions on which rested the fate of thousands. Since much had to be improvised in the opening months of the war, Kitchener, a proven master of expedients, was in his element.

He felt that he was defrauding his country if he were not doing his full duty, but it would have been better in the long run if he had taken off more time so that he could maintain his stamina and focus. As it was he took no leave and had few outlets to relieve the tensions in his mind. He avoided social gatherings and had no interest in such popular pastimes as fishing and golf. He never married and, outside his immediate entourage, had only a few friends with whom he could relax.

Ironically, while Kitchener disliked social gatherings he disliked solitude even more. After leaving the War Office, normally around 8 p.m., he would sometimes cross over Trafalgar Square to the Beefsteak club, of which he had been a member since 1899, and after dinner, where diners were served, as they still are, at a long communal table, he would sit back and listen, without saying much, to the conversation around him.[10] As a rule, however, he would dine at home with a close friend or his private secretaries, George Arthur and Lieutenant-Colonel O.A.G. Fitzgerald. Among Kitchener's intimates it was understood that conversation at the table would not be connected with the war.

Occasionally Kitchener would pay a brief visit to Broome Park, his country house near Canterbury, motoring down on Saturday mornings and returning the following evening. He had purchased the estate in 1911 from the bankrupt Oxenden family and for the remaining five years of his life lavished attention and money on reconstructing the interior of the building and beautifying the grounds. At Broome he stayed at his agent's house and took great delight in poring over plans, or digging and hoeing in the garden. Here he could forget War Office business, if only for a few hours.

The first real test of Kitchener's leadership came within a month of the outbreak of the war. He was shaken to receive a telegram at 2 a.m. on 24 August, from Sir John French, commander-in-chief of the B.E.F., who had decided to retire behind the Seine, the consequence of which would be to desert the French.[11] Kitchener saw that such a course of action would not only fracture the Entente, but also assure the piecemeal destruction of the British and French armies. At 7 a.m. the next morning, he went over to Admiralty House to break the news to Churchill who was sitting in bed working on papers. Churchill was disturbed by the Field-Marshal's appearance. His eyes were rolling and his face appeared distorted and discoloured.[12] Nevertheless Kitchener's manner was calm and he knew what needed to be done. With the consent of the cabinet he set off for Paris and in a stormy interview with Sir John French at the British Embassy ordered him to remain in the battle line.[13] Kitchener's action may well have saved the Entente from defeat.[14]

Although Kitchener could never shake the nagging feeling that he could do more,[15] even he must have been happy with the progress that had been made by the close of 1914. The new armies were rapidly taking shape and war equipment was being turned out faster than anyone had hitherto expected. Not only was the Empire secure but military operations had been initiated against German colonies in Africa and the Pacific. In the main theatres there were grounds for optimism. Kitchener's timely intervention in overruling Sir John French had permitted the French to counter-attack successfully at the Marne, thwarting Germany's plan to gain a quick victory in the west. The Russians, although badly shaken in the opening weeks of the conflict, still possessed a formidable army.

Unfortunately, in 1915 events did not follow Kitchener's script, forcing him to deviate from his strategy. The onset of trench warfare at the close of 1914 created many unprecedented problems which were not easily resolved. Another complication was the Cabinet which now emerged from its shell to play a more active role in the direction of the war. In these circumstances mistakes were inevitable, often resulting when Kitchener, against his better judgment, was hurried or coerced into a course of action.

From November 1914, Kitchener had to resist demands from the French government for an immediate commitment of additional British troops to France. Trained manpower in Britain was in short supply. It had been necessary to replace the heavy losses suffered by the British regular army during the initial battles. Kitchener refused to send the new armies anywhere until they were trained or equipped. Besides he did not want a premature outlay of manpower which would inhibit accumulating reserves and prevent Britain from taking the chief role in winning the war. He understood that in 1915 Britain lacked the military capability to make decisive military interventions. His colleagues never did.

He had no greater insight than any of the French or British generals on how to overcome the stalemate on the Western Front.[16] But he knew that their policy of concentrating resources in France and hammering at impregnable positions was not the answer. Instead he wanted the Anglo–French armies to adopt a passive defence in the west, undertaking limited attacks only out of military necessity such as straightening out an awkward salient or easing the pressure on the Russians. He meant to use the first of the new armies to strike in another theatre, such as in the eastern Mediterranean, where Germany was more vulnerable, thus eroding its moral and material strength.[17]

Things began to unravel for Kitchener early in 1915 when several members of the cabinet, disillusioned by the carnage on the Western Front, suggested strategies for achieving decisive results at less cost. One, advocated by Lloyd George, involved an expeditionary force to the Balkans and, in co-operation with the states in the area, to strike at Germany by the back door.[18] Kitchener disliked the proposal. The communications inland were inadequate and he considered it improvident to rely on the dubious allegiance of neutral states. On the other hand he was attracted to Churchill's idea of a purely naval attack on the Dardanelles.[19] Requiring few troops, this enterprise would advance British interests in the Middle East, satisfy those in the cabinet who chafed at a passive stance, provide an excuse to delay sending reserves to France and give the appearance of assisting the Russians who were already complaining of British inactivity.[20]

The newly established War Council[21] sanctioned the operation but it was not long before Churchill, at the Admiralty, became embroiled in a dispute with Kitchener over the fate of the last regular division in Britain. At a War Council meeting on 19 February Kitchener announced that the threat to France caused by recent Russian setbacks had compelled him to delay the departure of the 29th division for the Dardanelles – a prudent measure in view of the potential dangers to the Western Front. But Churchill wanted the 29th on hand to exploit gains made by the fleet.

In this and the next meeting, Churchill was supported by several ministers, including Asquith, and faced with this onslaught Kitchener was at pains to fight a rearguard action. In the past he had dealt directly with politicians on a one-to-one basis or behind the scenes and had rarely experienced outside interference. Now he was plunged into collective decision-making. He lacked gifts of verbal expression and was ill at ease with the practice of free discussion to which his colleagues were accustomed. Churchill presented his case lucidly and with the skill expected of him, but Kitchener exasperated his colleagues by his lengthy silences and inability to argue briefly and coherently. Although War Council sentiment sided with Churchill, no one at this stage suggested overruling Kitchener.[22]

Still it was clear that the Cabinet no longer considered Kitchener's pronouncements as having gospel authority and this was an unhappy harbinger of things to come.

As predicted by naval experts, the fleet, by itself, was unable to get through the Straits. The last thing that Kitchener wanted was a long term commitment to a secondary theatre. However, he was convinced that to discontinue the operation would deal a damaging blow to British prestige in the Muslim world. Without reference to the General Staff, which almost certainly would have pointed out the pitfalls, Kitchener, normally prudent, acted precipitously and agreed to send in the army. With his low opinion of Turkish capabilities, he counted on doing the job with a modest force. His assessment might have proved accurate if the Turks had not been alerted by the naval attack.

British troops under General Ian Hamilton landed on the Gallipoli peninsula in April 1915 but despite heroic efforts they found it impossible to storm the higher ground overlooking their small beachheads. Kitchener's disappointment was acute, all the more so because he had been virtually certain of victory. Kitchener received another jolt at the War Council meeting on 14 May when Churchill announced that, in view of the increasing U-boat danger in the Mediterranean, he was recalling the *Queen Elizabeth*[23] to home water. Kitchener's habitual composure in trying circumstances left him and he turned on Churchill, virtually accusing him of treachery.[24]

That same day an article, 'The Need for Shells', in the *Times*, had not improved Kitchener's disposition. On 9 May Sir John French, after assuring the War Office that he had sufficient ammunition on hand, had launched an attack on Aubers Ridge which was repulsed after a promising start. To distract attention from his muddled leadership, French told the *Times* correspondent, Colonel Repington, that his attack had failed as a result of a shortage of shells.[25]

The article caused a sensation in Britain because in the previous month Asquith had denied in a speech at Newcastle that operations on the Western Front had been hampered by want of munitions. Asquith did not take kindly to press criticism which accused him of dereliction and of lying to the nation and he blamed Kitchener, from whom he had obtained his information. In fact he was so angry that he briefly considered leaving Kitchener out of the coalition government which he was compelled to form in the latter part of May. Kitchener, however, was immovable because of his unshakable grip over the nation. Still Asquith relieved him of all responsibility for the supply of munitions by creating a separate Ministry of Munitions.[26]

Kitchener was himself attacked by the Northcliffe press to which he did not bother to reply. He felt he had nothing to reproach himself for; he had done everything humanly possible to meet the army's munition needs.

Existing supplies were indeed inadequate but it was hardly his fault that the country had been unprepared to wage a modern war.

No less a concern to Kitchener was the widening gap between himself and his cabinet colleagues. Impatient because victory was nowhere in sight, they were less willing to tolerate his methods. As they shared collective responsibility for every executive action he took, they resented being kept in the dark. More and more they pressed him for information which they required before making up their minds. One minister in particular, Lloyd George, developed an undisguised hatred for Kitchener and resorted to every kind of political chicanery, not excluding prevarication, to drive him out of the War Office.

By the late spring of 1915 the strain of confrontations with the politicians was beginning to tell on Kitchener's nerves. He had never complained about the long hours spent at the War Office wrestling with problems which exceeded all previous experience. But he found it wearisome during or after a hard day's work to engage in verbal jousting for which he was ill-equipped. All he wanted was to be left in peace to do his job by the methods to which he was habituated. He resented the Cabinet's lack of appreciation for what he had accomplished and also the intrigues of certain members against him. At one point during the reconstruction of the government in May he thought of leaving the War Office and returning to Egypt. His close supporters, however, dissuaded him.[27]

His problems mounted as the year wore on: the war continued to go badly. Moreover, the Tories in the Cabinet distrusted the Liberals and themselves took a more active role in overseeing the war effort, which resulted in Kitchener coming under much greater scrutiny than he had in the previous administration.

The most pressing task facing him after the formation of the coalition government was to advocate a course of action in the Dardanelles. Kitchener saw no way in which General Sir Ian Hamilton could succeed, in view of the current estimates of Turkish strength on the peninsula, but he could not bring himself to order an evacuation. In a memorandum dated 28 May, Kitchener suggested making good Hamilton's losses and leaving him to make such progress as he could.[28] Meeting for the first time on 8 June the restructured War Council, now known as the Dardanelles Committee, rejected Kitchener's advice and agreed to send Hamilton three divisions, in addition to one already sent, to enable him to mount a second major landing. A fifth division was subsequently added.

The second assault in August was no more successful than the first, ending in a stalemate. Hamilton's new demand for reinforcements could not be met. Kitchener, it turned out, had committed the British army to support a major French offensive in the fall.

All along, Kitchener had favoured an essentially defensive posture in the west and continued to reject pleas from France for more troops. He knew that any forces sent to France would be squandered in senseless attacks. He preferred to let the Germans attack in France and to suffer the heavy losses that he felt would surely follow. In July he relented somewhat and agreed to send over some new divisions on condition that they be used primarily to take over additional lengths of the line.[29] But Kitchener had to contend with Britain's allies and he was not always able to do what he wanted.

In mid-August he crossed over to France and during a conference with General Joffre, the French commander, gave his approval for a large British attack at Loos in September. The agreement was inconsistent with his previous strategic thinking and signalled the beginning of Britain's heavy commitment to the continental land war. However, it was governed by two crucial considerations: one was to avoid a split with the French and the other to assist the Russians who, it was feared, were on the verge of a complete military collapse.[30]

Kitchener's proposed change in Britain's military policy was assailed in the Dardanelles Committee, particularly by Churchill, and it was only because he had Asquith's support that he was able to win over his reluctant colleagues.[31] As it happened, the British attack at Loos was checked with heavy losses and, although it had been badly mismanaged in the field, Kitchener could not escape criticism for having sanctioned it. It became increasingly difficult for him thereafter to maintain his grip over the conduct of the war.

The manpower losses at Loos renewed demands in political circles for the introduction of conscription. It was a contentious issue and fought more or less along party lines. The Liberals opposed conscription, on the grounds that it was contrary to democratic principles. The Conservatives saw it as the only way effectively and fairly to determine the needs of the army and the economy. Given Kitchener's immense popularity with the public, the government would have been compelled to adopt universal military service if he had thrown his weight behind it. The Conservatives looked to Kitchener to give the lead and force the issue. Had Kitchener done so, life for him in the cabinet would have been easier, as his principal antagonists also happened to be ardent conscriptionists; but he refused to be drawn into the controversy. He stood loyally by the Prime Minister who convinced him that compulsion was premature and would divide the nation. In so doing Kitchener brought down on his head the full wrath of the Conservatives.[32]

Nothing, however, caused Kitchener more harm than the Central Powers' invasion of Serbia in October 1915. A month previously, on 6 September, Bulgaria, lured by promises of territorial gains, signed a military convention with Germany and Austria and pledged to join them in an attack on Serbia. The collapse of Serbia would give the Central Powers a direct route to Constantinople. With Turkey resupplied and in possession of heavy artillery, British forces clinging to their narrow beachheads might be driven into the sea.

A fortnight later the Entente received a warning of what was coming when Bulgaria began to mobilize its army. Serbia was a landlocked state and the only route by which aid might be sent was through the Greek port of Salonika. Greece announced it would stand by its treaty commitments with Serbia and place 150,000 men in the field if the Entente contributed an equal number. The French grasped eagerly at the offer and put intense pressure on the British to supply their quota of 75,000 men. With Lloyd George and his Conservative allies, Edward Carson and Andrew Bonar Law, forcefully arguing the case for succouring gallant little Serbia, the Dardanelles Committee acceded to the French request. But as soon as Allied troops began disembarking at Salonika on 5 October the Greek Government withdrew its offer and reaffirmed its intention to remain neutral. The last glimmer of hope for Serbia was gone regardless of what the French and the British might do. The Central Powers attacked a few days later, severing the link between the Serbian army and Salonika.[33]

The only sensible course, it seemed, was for the Allied forces in Greece to re-embark and return home even though it meant leaving Serbia in the lurch. But the pro-Salonika faction in the Cabinet asserted that ties with the Serbs could be re-established and threatened to bring down the government unless the Allies remained in Greece.[34] In the heated debates that followed, Lloyd George, in particular, sought to use Kitchener as a scapegoat for the Serbian tragedy. He resented what he considered was Kitchener's indifference to Serbia and the Balkans. Why, he asked, had the War Office not made the slightest preparation to deal with the German invasion? What galled him most was that Kitchener had neglected to double the carrying capacity of the single-track railway from Greece to Serbia as directed by the War Council last February. He remarked superciliously that some months ago he had warned against this very disaster and held that it was Kitchener's irresolution and want of foresight that had prevented timely action in the Balkans.[35] His cause was argued with messianic assurance and had a considerable impact on his colleagues who were even less well informed than he was.

The scenario which Lloyd George depicted bore no relationship to reality. He ignored the jealousies and hatreds – created in the aftermath of the Balkan wars – which posed an insuperable barrier to uniting the Balkan states against the Central Powers. He ignored the fact that the requisite engineers and building materials to increase and improve the transport facilities of the Salonika–Nish rail-line could only be obtained from the Western Front where they were already at a premium. He even disregarded the distance between Salonika and Nish (about 250 miles), the topography of the area (mostly mountainous)[36], and the work involved. To conduct surveys, double the line where possible, construct sidings and increase the rolling stock would have required years, not months; not to mention that the project would have been vulnerable to damage or destruction by enemy raids unless protected by a fairly large force. Finally Lloyd George shrugged off the illegality of occupying a neutral country.

Kitchener was exceedingly sensitive to the dangers of creating a new front at a time when his resources were stretched to breaking point. Understandably he did not want to be dragged into another pointlessly wasteful sideshow. All along he had known that Britain would be unable, alone, to stop a determined German bid to break through to Constantinople. He had not evolved an independent Balkan strategy because he lacked the troops to carry it out. Rather he hoped that any major military effort to counteract enemy designs in the Balkans would be undertaken by Bulgaria or Rumania. When Foreign Office initiatives failed to entice either state, Kitchener realized that with such Allied troops as could be mustered, an expedition to relieve Serbia was doomed before it began. He had serious doubts about the belated Greek offer. A General Staff paper on 24 September had warned that there was little chance of rescuing Serbia even with Greek assistance.[37] Kitchener had no hesitation in writing off Serbia the moment Greece turned its back on the Entente. A number of his colleagues, particularly Lloyd George and to a lesser extent Carson, were vehement in opposing him.

Kitchener, as on other issues, lacked the ability to articulate convincingly either the flaws that he recognised in Lloyd George's thinking, or his own reasons for pursuing his Balkan policy, whereas Lloyd George and Carson were such masters of rhetoric that they could make a ludicrous position seem plausible. Their outmanoeuvring of Kitchener in debate made him, at times, look foolish, especially when a proposition came up for the first time and caught him by surprise. On such occasions he retreated into sullen silence or rambled incoherently. He thus made it easy for his enemies to claim that he was no longer fit to manage the war.

Kitchener's isolation from his colleagues became complete during the final months of 1915. His secretiveness, lack of candour and obduracy had often driven them to distraction. No doubt they would have shown more forbearance if his efforts had produced a clear success. But the war was not going well for the Entente. An influential section of the Cabinet came to see his methods as the principal cause of the setbacks and, consequently, he rapidly began to lose his remaining prestige.

Kitchener was as exasperated with his Cabinet colleagues as they were with him. He often felt he was waging a war on two fronts, one against the Germans and the other against the politicians. He complained that he spent more time at meetings and preparing for them than in fighting the Germans. He despaired at the backbiting and confusion reigning in the upper councils of war. He could not understand how his colleagues could be so adamant on issues about which they obviously knew little. Their decisions were invariably shortsighted and they never seemed to take into consideration the larger aspects of the war. Interaction with politicians, never a priority, now became an ordeal. The harassments, cross-examinations and demands for lengthy explanations in the Cabinet and the Dardanelles Committee robbed him of his vigour and inhibited his capacity for bold and imaginative action which had characterized his early conduct of the war. He became indecisive, frequently changed his mind and lost touch with his own aims.

By the end of October, opinion in the cabinet was virtually unanimous that Kitchener ought to leave the War Office. To evade an almost certainly violent reaction from the public, Asquith took the ingenious course of sending him on a fact finding mission to the eastern Mediterranean and assuming personal control of the War Office in his absence. Asquith hoped that ultimately Kitchener might be persuaded to go to Egypt as a sort of *generalissimo* of the British forces in the Near East. Kitchener, however, turned down the suggestion. Although he had had his fill of politicians, he did not wish to leave the War Office with his great task unfinished. When Kitchener returned to London on 30 November he discovered that Asquith had assigned Sir William Robertson to become effective controller of military strategy. Kitchener, seeing his duties reduced to recruiting and administration, immediately tendered his resignation. Asquith refused it – Kitchener was regarded by the public as indispensable. He wanted him as a figurehead with his actual authority transferred elsewhere.[38]

Before any change could be implemented, Kitchener resumed his place in a cabinet still divided over Gallipoli and Salonika. Kitchener always viewed Salonika with distaste and, although he had strongly supported Gallipoli in the past, his own personal inspection during his recent trip to the eastern Mediterranean had convinced him that it was impractical to stay on the Gallipoli peninsula.

Early in December the Cabinet was assailed by an impending disaster. In Mesopotamia, the British Cabinet, against Kitchener's advice, had sanctioned a bold and foolish march in the desert towards Baghdad. The British force was checked and forced to fall back to Kut where it was surrounded. In a move designed to counter the ill-effects of this defeat, Kitchener changed his mind about the Dardanelles and proposed to launch another offensive as soon as Salonika was evacuated. The idea was abandoned when it became apparent that the survival of the French government depended on the Allies remaining at Salonika.[39] Since the British did not have the resources to sustain two sideshows it was decided to evacuate Gallipoli.

A terrible despair swept over Kitchener in the days immediately before the evacuation. Quite apart from the admission of failure, which he believed would damage Britain's aura of invincibility in the East, he anticipated heavy losses during the course of withdrawal. 'I pace my room at night' he confided to Asquith 'and see the boats fired at and capsizing, and the drowning men.'[40] Happily the British withdrawal from Gallipoli was accomplished without the loss of a single life.

There could be little doubt that 1915 was the most difficult year of Kitchener's career. Gradually but steadily the pressure had built up to an almost explosive level. Apart from the staggering work load, each personal and professional setback took its toll. He had to endure successive military defeats, the ruin of his strategy and the repudiation of his leadership in the Cabinet. On top of this he was distressed by the lengthening casualty list, including, particularly, the names of close friends and former subordinates. The cumulative effect eroded his health and spirits. His intimates and co-workers were struck by how much he had aged in recent months. He had lost weight, the lines in his face had deepened and his hair was turning white. At the start of the week he was able to keep up with his work but by Thursday and Friday he would lose some of his alertness in the late after-noon and evening. There were even signs that he was on the verge of a nervous breakdown.[41]

Although in a state of extreme exhaustion, Kitchener rallied magnifi-cently as he entered the sunset of his career. The appointment of Sir William Robertson as Chief of Imperial General Staff at least lifted a heavy burden of responsibility from his shoulders and enabled him to spend his weekends at Broome and enjoy more leisure. Within a few months he had regained his health and buoyancy.

Kitchener's pride was hurt when he was compelled to surrender control of the war but he came to appreciate Robertson's ability and integrity and, to the chagrin of the Cabinet, the two soldiers got on well together.[42] Kitchener did not always agree with Robertson on military matters but supported him wholeheartedly in the cabinet. The politicians soon discov-ered that Robertson, committed to a policy of concentrating all British troops in France, was as dogmatic and impatient of interference as Kitchener. In the absence of a rift between the two soldiers, they could scarcely reject the advice of their own appointee. The intrigues against Kitchener resumed in an effort to remove him from office. But the old soldier determined to stay on until the end of the war when he hoped to be a member of the peace delegation.[43] If fate had not cut short his life, he also would have been rewarded with the knowledge that he had been right on nearly all the major issues and that the measures he had introduced at the outset of his tenure had proved indispensable in winning the war.

Notes

1   Brian Bond, *The Victorian Army and the Staff College*, London, 1972, pp. 302–3.
2   Philip Magnus, *Kitchener: Portrait of an Imperialist*, New York, 1959, p. 283.
3   Before 1914 the government's rejection of the option to create a continental size army had compelled Britain's defence planners to revert to the traditional

policy of fighting a European war by naval and economic means. France and Russia were to bear the burden of the land war and, if necessary, suffer very heavy casualties, while Britain contributed a token military force to the continent and devoted itself mainly to clearing the seas of enemy ships, blockading Germany, and providing its allies with money and munitions. See David French, *British Economic and Strategic Planning, 1905–1915*, London, 1982, passim.

4 Winston S. Churchill, *The World Crisis*, New York, 1951, vol. 1, p. 253.

5 Sir George Arthur, *Life of Lord Kitchener*, London, 1920, vol. 3, p. 9.

6 The best discussion of Kitchener's strategy can be found in Keith Neilson's 'Kitchener: A Reputation Refurbished', *Canadian Journal of History*, vol. 15 (2), pp. 207–227.

7 *First Report of the Dardanelles Commission*, London, 1917, pp. 4–5; David Lloyd George, *War Memoirs*, London, 1938, vol. 1, pp. 51.

8 In 1915 the King, to set an example for workers, pledged his abstinence from drinking for the duration of the war and, at his request, Kitchener did the same. It was an unwise privation which led him to eat more and thus resulted in unnecessary weight gain.

9 On Kitchener's early months at the War Office see Major-General Sir C.E. Callwell, *Experiences of a Dug-Out, 1914–1918*, London, 1920, ch. 3.

10 Magnus, *Kitchener*, p. 282.

11 French to Kitchener, 24 August 1914, Kitchener papers, PRO 30/57/49.

12 Churchill, *The World Crisis*, vol. 1, pp. 289–90.

13 John Terraine, *Mons*, New York, 1960, pp. 186–91.

14 George H. Cassar, *The Tragedy of Sir John French*, Cranbury, NJ, 1985, p. 138.

15 Earl of Denby, 'K' in Sir Hedley Lebas, ed., *The Lord Kitchener Memorial Book*, London n.d., p. 1.

16 Sir Edward Grey, *Twenty Five Years*, New York, 1925, vol. 2, pp. 71–72.

17 George H. Cassar, *Kitchener: Architect of Victory*, London, 1977, pp. 268–70.

18 Lloyd George, 'The War – Suggestions as to the Military Situation', 1 January 1915, CAB 42/1/8.

19 Minutes of the War Council, 14 January 1915, CAB 42/1/16.

20 Neilson, 'Kitchener: A Reputation Refurbished', p. 213.

21 The Cabinet, assisted by the Committee of Imperial Defence, had dealt with strategic planning during peacetime and for the first three months of the war. It was a slow and cumbersome arrangement and in November Asquith delegated that responsibility to a small committee, the War Council, consisting mainly of service department heads as well as army and naval experts. Nevertheless the Cabinet retained executive authority with the right to review and debate War Council decisions.

22 Michael and Eleanor Brock, ed., *H.H. Asquith: Letters to Venetia Stanley*, Oxford, 1982, pp. 445–46, 449: Minutes of the War Council, 19 and 24 February 1915, CAB 42/1/36, 42.

23 The newest and most powerful dreadnought, the *Queen Elizabeth*, had been sent to test its 15-inch guns against the Turkish forts.

24 Minutes of the War Council, 14 May 1915, CAB 42/2/19.

25 David French, 'The Military Background to the "Shells Crisis" of May 1915',

Journal of Strategic Studies, vol. 2, 1979, pp. 200–3; Cassar, *Sir John French*, pp. 210–14.

26 George H. Cassar, *Asquith as War Leader*, London, 1994, pp. 87–88, 102–3.

27 Cassar, *Kitchener*, pp. 367–68.

28 Lord Kitchener, 'The Dardanelles', 28 May 1915, CAB 37/128/27.

29 Cassar, *Kitchener*, p. 381.

30 Neilson, 'Kitchener: A Military Reputation Refurbished', p. 222; Cassar, *Kitchener*, p. 388; David French, *British Strategy and War Aims, 1914–1916*, London, 1986, p. 110–111.

31 Meeting of the Dardanelles Committee, 20 August 1915, CAB 42/3/16.

32 Magnus, *Kitchener*, pp. 351–53.

33 Paul Guinn, *British Strategy and Politics, 1914–1918*, Oxford, 1965, pp. 97–103; French, *British Strategy*, pp. 140–42.

34 Memorandum by Bonar Law, 12 October 1915, CAB 137/135/23; Memorandum by Lloyd George, 1 October 1915, CAB 37/136/9; Minutes of the Dardanelles Committee, 11 October 1915, CAB 42/4/6.

35 Memorandum by Lloyd George, 14 October 1915, CAB 37/136/9; Minutes of the Dardanelles Committee, 11 and 14 October, CAB 42/4/6,9; Lloyd George, *War Memoirs*, vol. 1, pp. 295–97.

36 It is very mountainous between Salonika and Uskub (a distance of 145 miles) and only slightly less between Uskub and Nish.

37 'Appreciation of the situation in the Balkans by the General Staff', 24 September 1915, CAB 42/3/19.

38 Cassar, *Asquith*, pp. 133–37.

39 Lord Hankey, *The Supreme Command*, London, 1961, vol. 2, p. 462.

40 Arthur, *Life of Lord Kitchener*, vol. 3, p. 185.

41 Murray to Ian Hamilton, 10 May 1921, 79/48/3, Murray papers; Callwell to Robertson, 1 December 1915, 1/8/379, Robertson papers; Esher to Brinsley Fitzgerald, 11 December 1915, 3/29, Esher papers; Hankey diary, 30 September and 1 October 1915, Hankey papers; Major General Sir C.E. Callwell, *Stray Recollections*, London, 1923, vol. 2, p. 278.

42 Victor Bonham-Carter, *Soldier True*, London, 1963, pp 137–39.

43 Randolph S. Churchill, *Lord Derby 'King of Lancashire'*, London, 1959, pp. 209–10.

Chapter 5

Ludendorff and Germany's Defeat

Martin Kitchen

The German Spring offensive which began on 21 March 1918, was the last desperate *va banque* play of the war. The Schlieffen Plan had failed, the Verdun offensive had ended in a bloody slogging match, unrestricted submarine warfare proved to be a disastrous mistake. It was clear that the outcome of the war depended on this offensive and it was planned down to the last detail. In the two months before it was due to begin Ludendorff worked himself into a state of near complete physical and mental exhaustion. In the past three-and-a-half years he had only taken four days leave. His exophthalmic goitre heightened his irritability and nervous tension. The task before him was immense, the strain intolerable. Almost 40 divisions, totalling 600,000 men, were moved from the Eastern, Italian and Serbian fronts to the West.[1] Industrial output had to be increased, massive reserves of munitions had to be assembled, in spite of the strike by munitions workers in January 1918. Troops had to be brought forward and concentrated without being noticed by the enemy. Logistical support by rail for nearly 4 million men demanded minute planning.[2] Elaborate deception plans successfully fooled the Entente into believing that the attack would be mounted against the French in the Champagne and not against the British.[3]

Of the 240 German divisions on the Western Front, 52 were specially equipped for attack with a machine-gun section, air support, a signals section, a horse-drawn howitzer battalion and logistical support.[4] The troops were well supplied with arms and munitions, thanks in large part to the success of the 'Hindenburg Programme' to increase industrial output, a programme in which Ludendorff played a key role.[5] The major problem was the shortage of draft horses which meant that the amount of artillery and heavy machine guns and mortars in the 'mobile' (Mob.) divisions had to be reduced. Shortages of raw materials meant that only 80 per cent of the heavy artillery which Ludendorff required for the offensive was available, but he hoped to make up for this deficiency by bringing additional mortars up to the front.[6] The Germans had air superiority at the front and adequate supplies of ammunition. Their major problem was a lack of motor vehicles and of tanks. They had a mere 36,000 motor vehicles in March 1918, the Entente more than 300,000. The British had 432 tanks, the French 383 heavy tanks and 150 light tanks. The Germans had no tanks that could be used at the front.[7]

The Mob. Divisions were given two months intensive training according to principles laid down by Ludendorff in his 'Attack in Trench Warfare' (*Der Angriff im Stellungskrieg*). Having examined a number of offensives in detail Ludendorff concluded that surprise was the key to success. He argued that attacks should be made by mixed formations which were designed for specific tasks, and which ignored the artifical categories of battalion or division. This was the origin of the battle groups (*Kampfgruppen*) and combined operations used extensively in World War II.

The battle groups were completely independent. Their task was to penetrate as far as possible behind the enemy lines and to cause the maximum amount of confusion. They were followed by heavy battle groups which were to wipe out pockets of resistance which the first wave had by-passed. The forward groups were then to press on, following the line of least resistance. Ludendorff ordered that the light battle groups should reach the enemy's artillery positions by the first day. What happened later would depend on the situation on the ground according to the German doctrine of *Auftragstaktik*, first adumbrated by the older Moltke and perfected by Ludendorff. The German army was trained in modern tactics to the point that, in the view of many experts, the infantry was better trained in modern warfare in 1918 than in 1939. The artillery had adopted new methods developed by Captain Pulkowski, the High Command's (OHL) brilliant artillery specialist, which were enthusiastically endorsed by Ludendorff, and which made it possible to lay down accurate fire immediately on any spot which could be identified on the map. The troops believed that everything possible had been done to secure the success of the operation and were full of confidence.[8]

The deployment of this huge force, for which Ludendorff was chiefly responsible, was a brilliant operation carried out almost without a hitch, but the offensive still remained a desperate gamble. The Germans had a 2:1 advantage on the 'Michael' front around St. Quentin, where the main thrust was concentrated, but this advantage would soon be lost once reserves were brought in by the defence. The British had had a 4:1 advantage in Flanders in 1917, but had still failed. A number of senior officers were understandably concerned that they did not have sufficient forces for a successful offensive.[9]

Considerable confusion was caused on the eve of the offensive when

Ludendorff suddenly changed its strategic goals. Initially 17 Army to the north, and 2 Army in the centre, both from Army Group Crown Prince Rupprecht, were to form the *Schwerpunkt* of the offensive against the British, while 18 Army of Army Group German Crown Prince supported the left flank against the French. Now Ludendorff ordered each army to conduct separate offensives.[10]

Although 17 Army met with determined opposition, 2 and 18 Armies made excellent progress in the first day of the offensive. The OHL then made the surprising decision to strengthen 18 Army and allow it to push forward. This had the effect of switching the operational *Schwerpunkt* from the right flank to the left, a decision that resulted from the optimistic assessment of the situation by von der Schulenburg, the Crown Prince's chief of staff, which he relayed to his friend Lieutenant Colonel Wetzell at the OHL. He in turn convinced Ludendorff to place tactical above strategic considerations. Ludendorff thus abandoned a clear strategic objective and was hoping that luck would be on his side. He was losing overall control over the offensive and began to interfere persistently at the tactical level, thus causing great resentment among subordinate commanders. It was a highly stressful situation which further aggravated his precarious nervous condition.

By the afternoon of 23 March, 2 and 18 Armies had advanced more than 22 kilometres and were now able to deploy freely. 2 Army began to push North-West in accordance with the original plan. The British army was in disarray, the Germans had driven a wedge 15 kilometres wide between 5 and 3 armies, and Pétain was unable to give Haig any immediate assistance. Ludendorff was fully aware that the battle had reached a critical point. He called von der Schulenburg and the chief of staff of 2 Army, von Kuhl, to a conference in Avesnes. Once again Ludendorff changed the operational goals of the offensive. Whereas the original plan was to divide the British and French armies to the North of the Somme and drive the British back to the Channel coast, Ludendorff now ordered a push South as well as North of the river. This meant that 17 Army had to move North-West, West and South-West. 2 Army, the spearhead of the offensive, had now to advance on both sides of the Somme, and was to push South-West rather than North-West.[11]

Ludendorff thus completely changed the plans for the 'Michael' offensive as laid down in the original orders of 10 March. The *Schwerpunkt* was changed from the right to the left flank and a mere 27 divisions in 17 Army were now pitched against the 50 British divisions North of the Somme. The German offensive was now hopelessly diffused, and far too many of the fresh reserves were allocated to 18 Army – 14 divisions of a total of 28.

The Germans continued to advance rapidly in spite of this strategic confusion, then once again Ludendorff modified the plan. At 1630 hours on 24 March he ordered 17 Army to move West towards Doullens rather than North-West towards St. Pol, thus virtually abandoning the attempt to drive the British to the sea, an operation that had every chance of success had he concentrated all his forces towards the North-West.[12] The British were in a desperate situation and Haig and Wilson believed that the end was near. Crown Prince Rupprecht's staff realised that the British were at the end of their tether and argued that 17 Army and the right flank of 2 Army should be strengthened to deliver the *coup de grâce*. Ludendorff disagreed. He was convinced that a major victory could be won South of the Somme. On the evening of 26 March he ordered the South-Western thrust to be strengthened and 2 Army was to concentrate their efforts against the French.[13] The goals of the offensive were now Boulogne to the North and Compiègne to the South. 175 kilometres separated the two positions, and each of the German armies were given widely separated goals. Small wonder that Crown Prince Rupprecht became seriously worried that the front was far too broad.[14]

On 28 March Ludendorff heard that the 'Mars' offensive at Arras had run into difficulties. He therefore ordered 2 Army to continue its offensive against the French but also to advance in a North-Westerly direction towards Doullens to put pressure on the British. Once again Ludendorff had changed the direction of the offensive. For five days it had been towards the South-West, now it was being partially redirected towards its original objectives, but with inadequate forces. Ludendorff made matters worse by moving the bulk of 17 Army's artillery to the left flank and by virtually bringing the 'Michael' offensive to an end by ordering limited attacks against the British positions to tie them down.

By now it was clear that Ludendorff was without a clear strategic concept. He was unable to decide whether the main thrust should be by 17, 2 or 18 Army and changed his mind whenever one ran into temporary difficulties. He was beginning to panic and was frantically improvising in an attempt to impose his will on the battle. Having abandoned strategy he was bound to be further frustrated. As a result he missed the opportunity to deliver the British a crippling blow. By 28 March the 'Mars' offensive had clearly failed. On 29 March the offensive on the left flank against Noyon ground to a halt. A final desperate push on 30 March was poorly planned and executed and was unsuccessful.

Ludendorff refused to accept the fact that he had failed on the Somme just as von Moltke had failed on the Marne. He now argued that the 'Michael' offensive, far from being designed to bring a decisive victory, was simply the first action of what he now called 'The Great Battle in France'. In fact it was now simply a matter of time before the German army was totally exhausted.

Ludendorff had prepared 'Michael' brilliantly and the new tactics paid handsome dividends in the early stages of the campaign. But he made many glaring errors. It was a mistake to have two Army Groups rather than a unified command. Constant meddling by the OHL in the minutest details of the operation was bitterly resented and only caused confusion. Although he had correctly elected to concentrate the attack against the British to the North of the Somme he made the serious mistake of changing the *Schwerpunkt* to the left flank where 18 Army, which had been given an essentially defensive role, had advanced rapidly. As on the Marne in August 1914 the Germans had attacked where they had intended to defend, thus making nonsense of the original strategic concept. By advancing beyond the Crozat canal 18 Army exposed its left flank to counter-attacks by the French and thus lost momentum. Ludendorff broke the golden rule of German strategy that all efforts should be concentrated on the decisive point – in this case the right flank – and thus frittered away his limited resources by pushing in three directions simultaneously.[15]

By the evening of 30 March the OHL realised that the 'Michael' offensive had failed. The strategic goal had been sacrificed to tactical successes. These successes were considerable. The German army had advanced an unprecedented 60 kilometres, the Entente had lost 320,000 men killed, wounded and taken prisoner, and lost 1300 pieces of artillery. But the Germans had lost 230,000 men, and these men were irreplaceable. They were now forced to defend a deep salient. No attempt had been made to exploit the early successes politically by opening peace negotiations. The only possible course of action for the Germans was to withdraw to the Siegfried Line and to begin peace talks. But Ludendorff thought otherwise. He ordered another offensive, 'Georgette', around Armentières, and thus sought to hide the fact that 'Michael' had failed. The offensive began on 9 April. The Germans advanced 20 kilometres and were then halted by 20 April. The Germans had created another deep salient which needed large numbers of men to defend.

Although he had gained no strategic advantage whatsoever from 'Georgette', Ludendorff ordered another 'hammer blow' at Chemin les Dames. Forty-one under-manned German divisions attacked on 27 May and once again the superbly trained troops had startling initial successes, advancing 45 kilometres and crossing the Marne. During this operation Ludendorff had once again placed tactics above strategy. Initially the offensive was designed as a feint to attract British reserves, but blinded by success he allowed the troops to push forward, thus creating another highly vulnerable salient.

On 18 July the French counter-attacked from Villers-Cotterêts. The Germans were never to regain the strategic initiative. The 20 top quality French divisions, 4 double-sized American divisions and 750 tanks advanced against 11 under-strength and inferior divisions. The Entente advanced 4 miles and threatened the entire German position on the Marne. Ludendorff was by now suffering from a severe psychological crisis which made it impossible for him to perform his duties satisfactorily. An increasing number of officers at the OHL were convinced that he had to go, and the politicians who were anxious to reassert the primacy of the political over the military were determined to exploit his misfortunes to their advantage.[16]

Ludendorff shabbily blamed the failure on the Marne on Colonel Wetzell, the chief of the operations division at the OHL and advocate of a 'hammer blow' strategy. General von Lossberg, an outstanding tactician with a particular expertise in the mobile approach to defence, reported back from the Marne front and insisted that the army should be withdrawn immediately to the Siegfried Line. Ludendorff agreed that this was militarily correct but that it would have a disastrous effect on morale and give undue encouragement to the Entente. On 30 July Ludendorff gave an absurdly optimistic account of the situation to the recently appointed secretary of state for foreign affairs, Admiral von Hintze. A number of officers felt that he had taken leave of his senses and was living in a world of vain illusions.[17]

On 20 July Major Neimann had circulated a memorandum in the OHL arguing that peace negotiations should begin at once after a drastic reconsideration of war aims, for if there was any delay Germany would be in a hopelessly weak situation.[18] Even the extremist Colonel Bauer, Ludendorff's closest political associate, agreed, but insisted that Germany would have to keep Alsace and Lorraine and annexe Longwy and Briey.[19] Even this unrealistic position caused Bauer to be denounced by the Ludendorff camp as a pessimist.[20]

At first Ludendorff was prepared to give Bauer a hearing, but when the Entente was unable to exploit its initial successes at Villers-Cotterêts he began to think of yet another 'hammer blow', and he refused to consider any further withdrawals. He was in such an optimistic mood that Hintze was reluctantly forced to agree with those officers who felt that he was no longer able to make a realistic assessment of the overall situation. Then the shattering news arrived that the Entente had made a major breakthrough on the Somme and that crack units of the German army had lost their nerve and fled in panic. This day, 8 August 1918, is remembered as the *dies ater* of the German army.

Two major setbacks in three weeks were too much for Ludendorff's frayed nerves and he suffered a severe nervous collapse. He had been seriously depressed since Viller-Cotterêts and was now no longer able to issue coherent orders and was in a permanent state of extreme agitation.[21] He blamed the situation on the 2 Army where a Württemberg division was denounced by a guards division as 'strike breakers' and 'prolongers of the war' when they launched a counter-attack. The large number of Germans taken prisoner was further evidence of demoralization.[22] The Kaiser defended the troops against this attack, saying that they had reached the limits of their defensive ability and that the war would have to be ended.

He therefore ordered a Crown Council to be convened on 14 August which was to be attended by Hindenburg, Ludendorff, the chancellor, Count von Hertling, Hintze and the Crown Prince.[23]

Ludendorff now at least realised that any further offensives were out of the question, but clung to the illusion that it would be possible to adopt a defensive stance which would wear down the enemy to the point that they would have to sue for peace.[24] He put this view forward forcefully at the Crown Council and Hintze, who argued that time was on the side of the Entente with their overwhelming superiority of men and material, and that Germany's allies Austria, Bulgaria and Turkey were on the verge of collapse, found himself isolated. Faced with the new found optimism of the OHL, Hintze felt obliged to give way.[25]

Ludendorff and his supporters at the OHL were now living in a world of fantasy. They imagined that the war could be won by a defensive strategy on the Western Front and that extensive war aims could still be achieved. The Secretary of State for Foreign Affairs knew that this was nonsense, but lacked the courage to confront the generals whose reputations were as high as ever.

In spite of his expressed optimism and confidence, Ludendorff's nervous depression did not improve. Colonel Bauer brought in a brilliant young officer, Colonel Heye, to relieve his chief of some of the immense burden of work. Ludendorff's critics at the OHL were not impressed. They felt that Heye was too young and too much under Ludendorff's influence to provide an independent voice. They were soon proved wrong. Heye was sharply critical of Ludendorff's assessment of the situation at the front and became the principal spokesman of the 'pessimists'. He was soon to replace Colonel Wetzell, the leading 'optimist', as head of the operations division and thus became one of the most influential officers in the OHL. Ludendorff had serious misgivings about Heye's appointment, and only agreed because the other candidates were even more objectionable to him.[26]

Wetzell, smarting under Ludendorff's accusation that he was responsible for the failure on the Marne, complained that he was no longer able to make rational decisions and was constantly prevaricating.[27] He was horrified when he learnt that Ludendorff admitted that he had given Hintze a deliberately false impression of the situation at the front for fear that the government might panic. He felt that the only hope was to try to stiffen Hindenburg, distance him from Ludendorff, and ensure that the Kaiser was put fully in the picture. Unfortunately he was posted from the OHL before he could do anything.[28]

Wetzell was part of a group of officers who managed to persuade Ludendorff to seek medical help. Unexpectedly the general agreed. Dr Hochheimer, the staff psychologist at the Imperial Headquarters in Spa, examined Ludendorff and diagnosed that he was suffering from overwork.

He ordered his patient to take it easy, take more exercise and ensure that he got a good night's sleep. Ludendorff meekly agreed, to the surprise and delight of his staff.[29] Some of the good doctor's prescriptions were somewhat less than orthodox. He instructed Ludendorff to sing German folk songs on waking in the morning and to take special pleasure in the roses in the garden of his villa.[30] History does not record whether he complied.

Ludendorff was now virtually isolated at the OHL. Even those officers who believed that Germany should not open armistice negotiations, because of the disastrous effect on morale, wavered in their support of Ludendorff. Most were convinced that his powers had to be radically reduced and some even argued that he would have to go. They felt that there should be closer co-operation with the majority parties in the Reichstag and that armistice negotiations should begin before the army was completely defeated. Colonel Bauer was horrified at such suggestions and still believed that satisfactory peace terms could be achieved by a determined defensive strategy. He had now lost all confidence in Ludendorff whom he saw as a broken man, weak-kneed, prevaricating and lacking the 'fortuna' which Frederick the Great had always insisted was the essential ingredient of military success. Bauer, and his friend General Bartenwerffer, now felt that Ludendorff had to be replaced by a stronger man, possibly Schulenburg. He blamed the critical situation on the politicians, particularly on the ex-Chancellor Bethmann Hollweg, for undermining morale on the home front and for failing to discipline the workers.[31]

Bauer and Bartenwerffer's influence at the OHL depended on their close association with Ludendorff. They were thus sawing off the branch on which they were sitting. As his star waned so did their influence, enabling the younger officers who were calling for an armistice to gain the initiative. Bauer had also undermined his own position by pressing for the appointment of Heye and Stülpnagel, both of whom played a key role in setting the armistice negotiations in motion. Ludendorff's position now depended entirely on Hindenburg. When he withdrew his support his fate was sealed.

By the end of September the 'pessimists' were convinced that the war could not only not be won, it had been lost. What had seemed to some to be at best a stalemate was now defeat, and it was feared that the army might fall apart and there would be revolution at home. Ludendorff refused to accept this gloomy assessment of the situation. On 24 September he gave Groener an encouraging account of developments on the Western Front and Groener discounted Heye's vigorous objections on the grounds that he was a well-known 'pessimist'.[32] On the following day Ludendorff issued an order to all army groups saying that there would be no retreat and that the decisive battle would be fought from existing positions. Heye simply refused to forward the order and told Ludendorff that he should go immediately to Berlin and tell the Kaiser and Hintze that the situation was critical and that armistice negotiations should begin at once. Stülpnagel also pleaded with Ludendorff to make the fateful journey to Berlin.[33]

Ludendorff was elated when he heard that Spanish 'flu had broken out in the French army, and told the army surgeon general, Dr Schjerning, that this was Germany's 'last chance'. The doctor was appalled by Ludendorff's attitude and immediately reported the conversation to Heye who called a meeting the following morning, 26 September, to discuss the latest developments.[34] The atmosphere at the meeting was tense. The Entente was hammering at the German positions at Cambrai and Ypres, in the Champagne and on the Meuse. News had arrived during the night that the Bulgarians were about to capitulate. Heye and Stülpnagel were frustrated that they had not been able to convince Ludendorff to travel to Berlin and now proposed to tell Hintze that the military situation was hopeless and that he should come immediately to the OHL's headquarters at Spa. It was decided to invite Hintze without first informing Ludendorff.[35]

At midday Heye screwed up his courage and told Ludendorff that Hintze had been invited to Spa. To his great relief Ludendorff did not object. He had now come to the reluctant conclusion that an armistice was inevitable, but it was not until the evening of 28 September that he first raised the question with Hindenburg. The Field Marshal solemnly announced that he had already come to the same conclusion. But both men still harboured dangerous illusions. They imagined that the armistice would merely provide a breathing space to allow Germany to recuperate and resume the struggle. They also assumed that the Entente's fear of Bolshevism was such that they would not object to Germany maintaining its positions in the east and turn a blind eye to extensive annexations.[36]

Hintze, who no longer took Ludendorff's opinion seriously since he had announced in the middle of July that Germany would defeat the Entente 'finally and decisively', relied increasingly on information relayed directly from the front from which he concluded that the situation was hopeless. After discussions with his colleagues in the foreign office he decided, in the traditional Prussian manner, to orchestrate a 'revolution from above' in order to prevent a 'revolution from below'. When he arrived in Spa on 29 September he was thus well briefed and had a carefully prepared plan of action.[37]

Hintze argued that the chancellor, Hertling, would have to resign and that a new broadly based government would have to be formed. Armistice negotiations would begin on the basis of President Wilson's fourteen points. The chancellor was informed at the last moment that the OHL agreed that he would have to go. Angered that these intrigues had been conducted behind his back he left immediately for Spa.[38]

Hindenburg, Ludendorff, Heye and Hintze met in the Hotel Britannique in Spa at 10 a.m. on 29 September. Hintze was shocked when Ludendorff told him that armistice talks would have to begin immediately, for he imagined that he had plenty of time to prepare the ground politically. Ludendorff endorsed the state secretary's plans for a 'revolution from above' remarking that responsibility for Germany's defeat would have to be spread as widely as possible. When Hindenburg remarked that Longwy and Briey had to be annexed Ludendorff snapped that there could no longer be any question of annexations in the west.[39]

Once the OHL had endorsed Hintze's plan they went to see the Kaiser who agreed that a new government which included members of the Social Democratic Party (SDP) would have to be formed. Poor old Hertling arrived in Spa after these decisions had been taken. He was appalled at the suggestion that Germany should become a parliamentary democracy and pleaded with the Kaiser to wait at least two weeks to see if there was any improvement in the military situation. Hindenburg and Ludendorff insisted that the situation at the front was so grave that armistice negotiations would have to begin at once. Hertling offered his resignation which was promptly accepted.[40]

Although all the officers at the OHL knew that Hindenburg and Ludendorff had decided that an armistice had to be signed as soon as possible, it was not until 1 October that Ludendorff addressed the section chiefs of the OHL to make a formal announcement to this effect.[41] He appeared pale and in a state of great agitation, but one officer was so carried away by the drama of the moment to write in his diary that he was 'a truly beautiful German hero. I had to think of Siegfried with the mortal wound in his back from Hagen's spear'.[42] Hagen was symbolic of the Socialists, particularly the radical Spartacus group, who, according to Ludendorff, had undermined morale and sabotaged industrial production. He said of the SPD: 'I have asked His Majesty to bring those people into the government who are largely responsible that things have turned out as they have. We shall therefore see these gentlemen enter the ministries, and they must now make the peace which has to be made. They must now eat the soup which they dished out to us!' This was the origin of the 'stab in the back' legend which proved such a powerful weapon against democratic forces of the Weimar Republic.

In a frantic attempt to find scapegoats Ludendorff blamed the defeat of Bulgaria on the Foreign Office for failing to secure the removal of the American chargé d'affaires from Sofia, and the collapse of the western front on the War Ministry for not enforcing the auxiliary labour law with sufficient vigour and thus failing to provide enough additional manpower for the army.[43] Ludendorff was now beginning to panic and insisted that a peace offer should be made immediately, even before Prince Max of Baden had formed a new government. Then he reluctantly agreed to wait for another twenty-four hours.[44]

Prince Max arrived in Berlin early on the morning of 1 October. He was adamant that he should be given at least a fortnight in which to prepare the ground politically, both at home and abroad, before the armistice talks began. At 4.30 a.m. the OHL's envoy, Haeften, told him that the army needed an immediate armistice. Later in the day Hintze said that the decision had already been made at the meeting on 29 September that armistice talks should begin at once. Haeften relayed Prince Max's concerns to Ludendorff who said that the army needed an immediate respite which would give it the chance to recover its strength and continue the struggle.

Hindenburg travelled to Berlin on 2 October to meet Prince Max. He said that the OHL was expecting a fresh enemy offensive which could very well lead to a catastrophe. There could thus be no question of delaying the armistice talks. The two met again the following day and Prince Max made a further fruitless attempt to secure a delay. He then asked Hindenburg to state in writing that the situation was so serious that the army could not possibly wait.[45]

Hindenburg discussed the wording of this note with Ludendorff over the telephone. The result was a curious document which argued that an armistice was needed to save lives. There was no mention of imminent collapse.[46] Haeften concluded that Hindenburg was less insistent on an immediate armistice than was Ludendorff, and Prince Max felt that a delay might be possible.[47]

When it was pointed out that an immediate armistice would mean that Germany would lose Alsace and Lorraine as well as the Polish speaking districts of the Reich, the OHL told Prince Max that the army could probably hold on until the spring and that there could be no question of ceding any territory other than a few French speaking parts of Alsace-Lorraine.[48] Ludendorff flatly rejected the suggestion that a peace offer should be made rather than a request for an armistice, repeating that the army needed pause to catch breath.[49]

A note was sent to President Wilson calling for an immediate armistice. A reply reached Berlin on 9 October and Ludendorff continued to argue that an immediate armistice was essential and much to Prince Max's relief he rejected Walther Rathenau's preposterous suggestion for a *levée en masse*. He told the chancellor that the army could withdraw from France and Belgium, with the exception of Metz, which would have to be held 'for reasons of military honour'.[50]

Right-wing politicians were appalled when they heard that he was prepared to abandon the territorial gains in the west and there were loud calls for his resignation. Colonel Bauer now set about undermining Ludendorff's civilian support by arguing that his nervous breakdown in August meant that he was no longer able to function properly.[51]

Hindenburg and Ludendorff knew of these intrigues, but were not aware of the key role played by Colonel Bauer. Hindenburg announced that he would resign if Ludendorff were dismissed. Prince Max supported Ludendorff against his critics even though Ludendorff was beginning to take a firmer stance in response to their attacks.[52] Wilson's second note, which was far firmer in tone than the first, arrived in Berlin on 16 October and prompted Ludendorff to propose that troops should be sent from the east to the western front for a 'fight to the bitter end'.[53]

The following day Ludendorff travelled to Berlin and told Prince Max that there was now no question of the front collapsing. He said that the Entente was incapable of making a decisive breakthrough and that he saw no cause for alarm if negotiations with the American President were broken off.[54]

Wilson's third note on 23 October insisted that the armistice would have to make any resumption of hostilities impossible. Hindenburg and Ludendorff agreed that this was unacceptable, and Ludendorff issued an order to all army commanders that the war would have to be continued with the utmost determination.[55] They then set off for Berlin.

Prince Max decided that Ludendorff would have to be dismissed and that armistice negotiations should continue.[56] Hindenburg and Ludendorff arrived in Berlin determined to offer their resignations if the armistice negotiations were not broken off at once. They assumed that the mere threat of their resignations would be enough to get their way, as it had been on numerous occasions in the past. They first met the vice-chancellor, Friedrich von Payer, as Prince Max was in bed with influenza. There was an ugly exchange between a furious Ludendorff and a horrified Payer. Ludendorff argued that if the armistice talks continued 'within a few weeks you will have Bolshevism in the army and at home, and then you can think of me!' To lend force to his arguments Ludendorff announced that he would offer his resignation to the Kaiser.[57]

Ludendorff went off for an audience with the Kaiser on 26 October in a state of extreme agitation. The Kaiser complained that he had first demanded an armistice, and then a month later had asked for negotiations to be broken off and the war to be continued. Ludendorff shouted at the Kaiser who had to remind him that he was addressing his King and Emperor. Ludendorff offered his resignation which the Kaiser angrily accepted. Hindenburg muttered that he too would resign. The Kaiser ordered him to remain in office, the Field Marshal bowed in acquiescence, wherepon Ludendorff stormed out of the room in a towering rage. He waited outside in the corridor for Hindenburg to appear, fully expecting that he also had resigned. When he heard that the Field Marshal had failed to support him he refused to travel in the same car back to the offices of the general staff and returned to Spa in an ordinary express train.

Thus ended Ludendorff's military career. He fled to Sweden at the war's end, took part in the Kapp putsch of 1920 and the Hitler putsch of 1923, but broke with Hitler for what he considered to be his too tolerant attitude towards the Catholic Church. He devoted most of his energies to the Tannenburg Association which mounted vicious attacks on Jews, Masons and Jesuits and furthered the bizarre aims of his second wife's 'German Religion' (*Deutsche Gotterkenntnis*). He died in 1937 and was given a state funeral by the Nazis, even though he had never reconciled with the man he insisted on calling 'Herr Hitler'.

He was a brilliant organizer who mastered all the details of arming and training his troops, and his ingenious defensive strategy in 1917 has earned him the right to be considered the finest general of World War I. His withdrawal to the 'Alberich' positions in 1917 was probably the outstanding operation of both World Wars. His preparations for the 'Michael' offensive, apart from his failure to grasp the importance of tanks, were masterly. Then everything began to fall apart. By placing temporary tactical success above strategic aims he allowed an offensive, which might have been as successful as Hitler and von Manstein's similar 'sickle strategy' of 1940, to dissipate and to degenerate into what Foch was to call a 'buffalo strategy'. As Crown Prince Rupprecht of Bavaria commented in his diary Ludendorff was a 'brilliant organizer, but not a great strategist'. He had no clear idea of the relationship between political and military goals, indeed he despised Clausewitz and insisted that war was a matter for soldiers alone. Politicians were only useful as 'lightning conductors' when things went wrong. Had the 'Michael' offensive succeeded Ludendorff would have secured a place in the pantheon of the truly great commanders. As he realised his failure and as work overwhelmed him, his nerves cracked. His private life was in ruins. His wife was a morphine addict, two of his stepsons to whom he was devoted died in action at the beginning of the 'Michael' offensive. He sought solace in countless affairs which resulted in blackmail attempts and many compromising situations. He was never to recover his balance and lived on in the twilight world of extremist politics and pseudo-religious fanaticism. Such was the 'Ludendorff tragedy'.[58] Helmuth von Moltke went further than Frederick the Great by saying that a general needed 'four Gs – *Geld, Geduld, Genie und Glück*' '(money, patience, genius and luck). It cannot be denied that Ludendorff had a touch of genius, but he certainly lacked the other three 'G's.

Notes

1   *Der Weltkrieg 1914–1918*, edited by the Reichsarchiv, Reichskriegs-ministerium und Oberkommando des Heeres, 14 vols, Berlin 1925–1944, vol. XIV pp. 29 and 38.
2   Erich Ludendorff, *Meine Kriegserinnerungen*, Berlin 1919, p. 473.
3   Reichsarchiv XIV p. 98.
4   Reichsarchiv XIV p. 41.
5   On the Hindenburg programme see: G.D. Feldman, *Army, Industry and Labor*

in Germany, 1914–1918, Princeton 1966; Martin Kitchen, The Silent Dictatorship: The Politics of the German High Command under Hindenburg and Ludendorff, 1916–1918, London 1976; Wihelm Deist, Militär und Innenpolitik, 2 vols, Düsseldorf, 1970.

6 Rupprecht von Bayern, Kronprinz, Mein Kriegstagebuch, ed. Eugen Frauenholz, 3 vols, Berlin 1921, vol. 2, p. 328.

7 Reichsarchiv XIV, p. 94.

8 William Balck, Ordnung im Chaos, Osnabrück 1981, p. 221. Ernst Jünger, Im Stahlgewittern, Berlin 1925, p. 214.

9 Among them Prinz Rupprecht of Bavaria and General von Kuhl. Rupprecht, 2, p. 326.

10 Rupprecht, 2, p. 243.

11 Reichsarchiv XIV, p. 167; von Kuhl, Entstehung, Durchführung und Zusammenbruch der Offensive von 1918, Berlin 1927, p. 134.

12 Reichsarchiv XIV, p. 180.

13 Reichsarchiv XIV, p. 215.

14 Rupprecht, 2, p. 260.

15 See the critique by Wilhelm Groener, Lebenserinnerungen. Jugend, Generalstab, Weltkrieg, ed. Friedrich Freiherr von Gaertringen, Göttingen 1957, p. 565ff.

16 By far the best account of the atmosphere in the OHL at this time can be found in Fritz von Lossberg, Meine Tätigkeit im Weltkrieg 1914–1918, Berlin 1939.

17 Bundesarchiv Militärarchiv Freiburg, Nachlass Groener N46/63, Tagebuch Generals von Mertz 31-7-1918.

18 Das Werk des Untersuchungsausschusses der Verfassungsgebenden Deutschen Nationalversammlung und des Deutschen Reichstages. IV Reihe: Die Ursachen des Deutschen Zusammenbruches. 12 vols., Berlin 1919–1929, vol. 2, p. 214. Joachim Petzold, 'Die Entstehung vom 29 September 1918', Zeitschrift für Militärgeschichte, 5, 1965.

19 Bundesarchiv Koblenz, Nachlass Bauer, vol 2.

20 Max Bauer, Der Grosse Krieg in Feld und Heimat. Erinnerungen und Betrachtungen, Tübingen, 1921, p. 225.

21 Bayerisches Hauptstaatsarchiv, Abteilung IV, Kriegsarchiv M.Kr. 1832, Bevollmächt. im Gr. HQ 1918, 8-8-1918. Attempts by Ludendorff, supported by Mertz, Thaer and others to show that he did not suffer a nervous collapse in 1918 do not convince since they rest on hair-splitting arguments about the precise medical definition of a nervous breakdown. See also: Ludendorff, Urkunden der OHL, p. 526.

22 Bundesarchiv Militärarchiv Freiburg, Nachlass Haeften N35/5, Erinnerungen.

23 A Neimann, Kaiser und Revolution. Die entscheidenden Ereignisse im Grossen Hauptquartier im Herbst 1918, Berlin 1922, p. 44. A more extensive version in Der Tag, 185, May 1922.

24 Amtliche Urkunden zur Vorgeschichte des Waffenstillstandes 1918, 2nd ed., Berlin 1924, p. 7.

25 Ibid., p. 3.

26 Albrecht von Thaer, Generalstabsdienst an der Front und in der OHL. Aus Briefen und Tagebuchaufzeichnungen 1915–1919, ed. Siegfried A. Kaehler (Abhandlungen der Akademie der Wissenschaften in Göttingen. Phil. Hist. Klasse 3, Folge Nr. 40) Göttingen 1958.

27 Bundesarchiv Militärarchiv Freiburg, Nachlass Groener N46/63, Tagebuch Generals von Mertz 4–8–18.

28 *Ibid.* Tagebuch Mertz 1–9–1918.

29 Siegfried A. Kaehler, *Zur Beurteilung Ludendorffs im Sommer 1918*, Studien zur deutschen Geschichte des 19. und 20. Jahrhunderts, Göttingen 1961, p. 21.

30 Bundesarchiv Militärarchiv Freiburg, Nachlass Heye, N18/5, Lebenserinnerungen, p. 72.

31 BA Koblenz, Nachlass Bauer, vol. 21. Many of those who were calling for an armistice in the summer of 1918 were related to officers involved, in a similar situation, in the 20 July plot on Hitler's life in 1944, among them Mertz, Haeften, Harbou and Stülpnagel.

32 Bundesarchiv Militärarchiv Freiburg, Nachlass Haeften N35/4, diary entry 24–9–1918.

33 Wolfgang Foerster, *Der Feldherr Ludendorff im Unglück*, Wiesbaden 1952, p. 85. Bundesarchiv Militärarchiv Freiburg, Nachlass Stülpnagel N5/27.

34 Bundesarchiv Militärarchiv Freiburg, Nachlass Haeften N35/4, diary entry 25–9–1918.

35 *Ibid.*, 26–9–1918.

36 *Ibid.*, 28–9–1918.

37 PA Bonn AA Weltkrieg 23 Geheim, vol. 32. *Amtliche Urkunden*, p. 47.

38 Siegfried A. Kaehler, *Vier quellenkritische Untersuchungen zum Kriegsende 1918*, Nachrichten der Akademie der Wissenschaften Göttingen, 1960, Nr. 8, p. 433. Bundesarchiv Koblenz, Nachlass Bauer, vol 23.

39 *Untersuchungsausschuss IV Reihe*, vol. 2, pp. 260, 386.

40 Prince Max von Baden, *Memoirs*, vol. 2, London 1928, p. 21.

41 PA Bonn AA Weltkrieg 23 Geheim vol. 32. Amtliche Urkunden, p. 61 fn 36.

42 Thaer, *Generalstabsdienst*, 1 October 1918.

43 Bayerisches Hauptstaatsarchiv Abteilung IV Kriegsarchiv M.Kr. 1832, Bevollmächt. im Gr. HQ 1918, 7–10–1918.

44 *Amtliche Urkunden* pp. 60 and 62. Ludendorff, *Urkunden der OHL*, p. 529. Prince Max von Baden, *Memoirs*, vol. 2, p. 4.

45 Prince Max von Baden, *Memoirs*, vol. 2, p. 14.

46 *Amtliche Urkunden*, p. 73.

47 Bundesarchiv Militärarchiv Freiburg, Nachlass Heften, N35/3.

48 Ludendorff, *Urkunden der OHL*, p. 540.

49 Prince Max, *Memoirs*, vol. 2, p. 21.

50 *Ibid.*, p. 66.

51 *Ibid.*, p. 71. For Rumours of Ludendorff's impending resignation see press conference 4–10–18 in Wilhelm Deist, *Militär und Innenpolitik*, vol. 2, Düsseldorf 1970, p. 1300.

52 Bundesarchiv Militärarchiv Freiburg, Nachlass Heften N35/4, diary entry 12–10–1918. PA Bonn AA Weltkrieg 23 Geheim, vol 22, Berckheim to foreign office 12–10–1918.

53 Ludendorff, *Urkunden der OHL*, pp. 109 and 123.

54 DZA Potsdam, Reichskanzlei, Beschlüsse des Kriegsrats 2462/1. Prince Max von Baden, *Memoirs*, vol. 2, p. 102.

55 Bundesarchiv Militärarchiv Freiburg, Nachlass Heye N18/4 25–10–1918.

According to Thaer, *Generalstabsdienst*, the order to the army commanders was sent by Ludendorff without Hindenburg's knowledge.

56 Prince Max von Baden, *Memoirs*, vol 2, p. 195.
57 Bundesarchiv Militärarchiv Freiburg Nachlass Heye N18/5, p. 115.
58 The title of W. Breucke, *Die Tragik Ludendorffs*, Oldenburg 1953.

Chapter 6

Haig and Pershing

Frank Vandiver

By the end of 1914 men burrowed in a labyrinth of ditches stretching from Switzerland to the Channel. A new and different war was spawned in the trenches, a war against movement, against surprise, a siege that short-circuited many received principles of war.

Trenches were far from new and had of course affected the Russo–Japanese war as well as the ending of the American Civil War. But those of 1914 that lingered until 1918 brought differences beyond expectation and stresses beyond imagination. The thousands of books devoted to this war attest to stresses, to twisted psyches and minds blasted by a maelstrom that created new realities. Many of the more recent volumes speak of common soldier's suffering or of baffling battles beyond gallantry that eddy on to history in an awful churning of the world.

In those books on High Command, some of the figures centrally important are damned by blunders to the dustbins of history. Politicians probably receive the meanest treatment in the smallness of their goals but military leaders in particular are excoriated for a butchery made worse by their supposed ignorance of modern times. All commanders of the war are stained by the same brush of damnation. Douglas Haig, Commander-in-Chief of the British Armies in France, and General John Pershing, Commander of the American Expeditionary Forces, are no exceptions – save in the sense that they get some of the worst brushing. Haig suffers history's barbs though he succeeded albeit at a fearsome cost; Pershing, because his apparent inexperience and that of his men represented the intrusion of a wealthy upstart into Europe on the brink of bankruptcy.

These two men played vital roles in war and in the final Allied victory. How did they bear the buffets of high command, or, to borrow the question from Lord Moran's *Anatomy of Courage*, how did they 'wear' in war?[1] A difficult question, because both Haig and Pershing were wrapped in the veil of command on a lonely peak of their own. They were alike, these two, in more ways than were obvious but were chasms apart in surface personalities.

Both had ambition – all great captains have it – and they developed considerable skill in advancing themselves by finding influential friends in and out of the army. Both married advantageously – Haig close to Windsor and Pershing close to Congress and the White House – and each chose careful paths of experience. Both were professionals though they came to a military life differently. Pershing perhaps excelled Haig in brainpower since he was graduated First Captain of his West Point class, but Haig had the determination almost to memorize his way to Oxford and to Sandhurst. Pershing lacked Haig's speed in promotion and if he missed the kind of opportunities enjoyed by Haig in the River War under Kitchener, then in the Second Boer War and in India, he had his own sound colonial apprenticeship against Plains Indians, against the Spanish at Kettle Hill, against warrior Moros in the southern Philippines and led an expedition into Mexico against Pancho Villa's *bandidos*. Pershing caught up in rank – President Theodore Roosevelt promoted him from captain to brigadier-general in one jump.

Both in a way were waiting for their moment in the years just before the war. Haig held the prestigious Aldershot command in 1914 and took the field at the head of the British I Corps. Through the first year of a war to beggar precedents he learned more about manoeuvre and defence than ever before; he learned, too that a good many absurdities had gone into preparing for campaigns in Belgium and France.

In 1915 Pershing sustained a psychic shock that nearly unhinged him. In August, his wife and three daughters perished in a fire at the San Francisco Presidio while he was at Fort Bliss, Texas. Only son Warren survived. His wife had been his confidante, guide and confessor – without her he seemed, for a time, adrift and groping for direction. His father-in-law tried to comfort him, one of his sisters came to Fort Bliss to help with Warren, but Pershing found his own way, finally, to reintegration of his personality by doing, in the words of a psychiatrist, 'what many strong minded and moderately perfectionist personalities do; reassert their self-worth by plunging into hard work.'[2]

Pershing suffered more trauma when he arrived in Europe. The war exceeded all estimates in complexity and though he had guessed the need for an army of a million men, he had underguessed the intricacies of trench fighting.

Haig and Pershing reacted differently to their first large command experiences and the differences stemmed partly from their respective positions. Pershing served under no field superior; he ran his own show, but missed his former moments of being in the field and in the action, of seeing things for himself. Haig served under a former cavalry officer well known to him but one whose capacity for large operations he had come to doubt. When he led I Corps into the fighting at Mons and during the subsequent days, Haig had been troubled by cooperating with Sir Horace Smith-Dorrien's II Corps, often irked by Commander-in-Chief Sir John French's orders and intentions, had yielded to some confusion of his own and finally on August 25, 1915 – and for the only recorded time in France – became 'violently sick'.[3]

For Haig, the war's first sixteen months were a harsh school in strategy, tactics, human relations and patience. About all that he found useful from past experience were staff lessons and logistics – both of which he understood well. At first, when the war moved rapidly, old things worked, but as stasis set in and grids of rail lines and complex road systems sustained the trenches and engineering overwhelmed everything, a new world emerged. Slowly Haig built his own confidence by going forward 'to get the feel of the battle,'[4] and on 17 December, 1915, he took formal command of all the British Armies in France. He handled supreme command with customary stoicism – but he did feel elation. Brigadier-General John Charteris, in Field Marshal Earl Haig, mentions admiringly that 'if ambition had been Haig's aim he had now achieved it in full measure; but, although ambition played a large part in Haig's earlier life, in the face of the tremendous issues at stake his keen sense of relative values had long since made personal ambition tawdry in his eyes.'[5] That assessment insults Haig's humanity – he was proud and glad of the command and knew he would handle it well.[6]

Pershing had a different path to the top. Called to Washington in April 1917 from departmental command in Texas, he learned he would lead the first Americans into the Great War. And on 12 May, Secretary of War Newton D. Baker told him he would be commander-in-chief of America's forces in France. Baker watched him carefully, saw him take his own measure. Like Haig, Pershing had 'no doubt in my mind then, or at any other time, of my ability to do my part . . .'[7]

On the the Western Front Haig and Pershing shared some similar pressures, especially pressures from the French over manpower. Early on with Haig, French demands to take over more line were followed later by demands for many of Pershing's men to fill thinned poilu ranks. French efforts often spilled over to embroil politicians in London and Washington, efforts which involved Haig and Pershing in testy conferences with disgruntled allies. Logistics bothered both as rail communications were inadequate and locomotives in short supply. All these problems added stress to the daily business of running huge armies. To these enormous worries must be added the individual pressures endured by each man before a full appreciation of their full burdens can be reached.

Haig had his own impatience against him. Battles of 1916 and 1917 gradually eroded his confidence in the French, forcing him increasingly to cover for their failures. His diary and his nearly daily letters show rising resentment, yet with the crisis of March 1918, he recognised the compelling arguments for the establishment of a supreme Allied commander-in-chief who would have to be French.

On 6 April 1918, in the midst of the great German drive launched on 21 March, Haig, certain of enemy intent to destroy the British positions in France, asked the new Commander-in-Chief, Ferdinand Foch, for help. Next day Haig told Foch he believed firmly that 'the main enemy attack would fall on the British front . . . an attack by some 35 to 40 Divisions.' Foch demurred at length and Haig assessed their meeting caustically: 'Personally, I do not believe that Foch or Pétain have any intention of putting French Divisions into the battle!' Certainty came a day later. Foch's intransigence on 8 April sparked this remark in Haig's diary: 'How difficult these "Latins" are to deal with! They mean to bleed the British to the utmost.' On the dull and foggy ninth of April 1918 Foch came to Haig at a moment of crisis as the British line sagged between Armentières and the La Bassée Canal. The meeting had some strain. '*Foch declined to take over any part of the British line*,' Haig fumed in his diary. During their talk Foch announced his determination to put four French divisions in reserve 'immediately West of Amiens.' Since this would disrupt Haig's whole logistical skein behind his Fourth Army, he protested to no avail. 'I found Foch most selfish and obstinate,' Haig noted, adding 'I wonder if he is afraid to trust French Divisions in the battle front?'

As the Germans pressed on, Haig kept close to the front, shifted British units from place to place and waited for the French. In the morning of 10 April he tried Foch again. 'I requested him to arrange to take over *some portion* of the British line in order to set free Reserves and enable me to continue the battle and hold our positions.'[9] Foch came to see Haig about 10 o'clock that night. Agreeing on the enemy objective at last, Foch promised 'a large force of French troops ready to take part in the battle.' After Foch left him about 11:30, Haig vented his feelings in his diary: 'I am glad that the French at last are beginning to realize the object of the Germans. The French losses in this battle are about 20 to 25,000. Ours are 160,000 and will be more. This shows their share of the fight so far! But personally I have come to the conclusion that Foch is afraid to put any French Division into the battle, and that he won't do so until force of circumstances, as a last resort, compel him.[10]

Haig, remaining outwardly calm, became increasingly nervous as German attacks pressed on. Edgy, as Passchendaele was conceded, the Ypres Salient contracted and inundations round Dunkirk were considered, Haig saw Foch again at Abbeville on 14 April. He urged swift help since heavy losses were eroding his divisions and all his troops were weary. 'Foch spoke a lot of nonsense, that as we were in the battle, there must be no Divisions withdrawn for rest . . .' Haig stressed the urgency of the situation around Hazebrouck – a prime enemy objective – but Foch refused giving immediate aid. Haig watched him in mounting disgust and saw a man 'unmethodical' with a 'short view' of the situation. 'He does not,' Haig thought, 'look ahead and make a forecast of what may be required in a week in a certain area, and arrange accordingly. He only provides from day to day sufficient troops to keep the railway accommodation filled up!'[11]

During the whole time of Germany's win-the-war offensive in 1918, Haig endured stresses beyond the battlefield that created a special sense of insecurity. Prime Minister Lloyd George, never an admirer of Haig's, nor of British professional officers, had sniped at the 'Western Front' advocates since becoming War Minister in mid-1916 and Prime Minister that December. Openly seeking alternatives to both the Western Front and to Haig, Lloyd George connived with the French to put Haig and his armies under General Robert Nivelle's command in the spring of 1917 and in the midst of the German 1918 attacks, he ordered the removal of General Sir Hubert Gough, whose V Army had nearly collapsed. Haig carried out the order with distaste and noted that 'L[loyd] G[eorge] seems a "cur" and when I am with him I cannot resist a feeling of distrust of him, and of his intentions.'[12] Haig's instincts were sound – during the heaviest fighting in April, the Prime Minister made a public address distorting the British effort in France.[13]

Not a day passed without the threat of 'the Little Welshman' looming beyond the Channel, lurking, waiting to find another commander. In early April, in fact, the War Cabinet had an angry discussion about a new commander in France. The New Chief of the Imperial General Staff, Sir Henry Wilson, probably saved Haig by suggesting the danger of removing a commander in the middle of a battle.[14] None of this missed Haig's tuned ears; none of it sat well with him, especially as danger piled high around his armies that month. Faced with dissolution of his front as the German drives continued, Haig rose above his worries in one of his greatest personal acts of command during the war.

By 10 April he realized that Messines Ridge and the vital rail junction at Hazebrouck were in jeopardy, and the next morning he went into his field office, sat down, took out paper and pen and began writing. His chaplain thought he might have had a restless night,[15] but no one could tell that day – he seemed calm as ever, immaculate, hair carefully brushed. And yet he had that morning worries beyond his own tongue-tied voice to tell. He could always write, though, the things of the heart and he began a Special Order of the Day

TO ALL RANKS OF THE BRITISH ARMY IN FRANCE AND
FLANDERS
Three weeks ago today the enemy began his terrific attacks against us
on a fifty-mile front. His objects are to separate us from the French, to
take the Channel Ports and destroy the British Army.

71

In spite of throwing already 106 Divisions into the battle and enduring the most reckless sacrifice of human life, he has as yet made little progress towards his goals.

We owe this to the determined fighting and self-sacrifice of our troops. Words fail me to express the admiration which I feel for the splendid resistance offered by all ranks of our Army under the most trying circumstances.

Many amongst us now are tired. To those I would say that Victory will belong to the side which holds out the longest. The French Army is moving rapidly and in great force to our support.

There is no other course open to us but to fight it out. Every position must be held to the last man: there must be no retirement. With our backs to the wall and believing in the justice of our cause each one of use must fight on to the end. The safety of our homes and the Freedom of mankind alike depend upon the conduct of each one of us at this critical moment.

D. Haig, F.M.
Thursday 11 April 1918

This was no hysteric's message, but it resolutely gave the alarm. How had he worn through the year so far? Outwardly the same, of course, unruffled; when Colonel Marshall Cornwall rushed to France as the German drive began in late March he found far less commotion at British Headquarters than anywhere else. Everyone there, including Haig, exuded confidence. It had not always been so. On earlier occasions soldiers had seen a worried commander-in-chief.[16] And in March and April Haig's tension could be glimpsed in frequent tugs on his moustache, by comments punctuated by a jabbing arm, frequent asthmatic breathing bouts and some digestive trouble. At the height of the worst, though, Haig settled in and wore better than usual. He paid attention to his health at all times, rode almost every day near various parts of the front, did not smoke, drank little and ate carefully. Frustrations and complaints of most days he shared in letters to his wife – showing his impatience at unjust accusations of remoteness from the front (a charge refuted often during and after the war),[17] with obstructive generals and politicos and with a government's animosity, as well as his not always flattering characterisations of colleagues and allies[18].

Probably the charge most hurtful to him was of glacial unconcern for casualties. He never rebutted it in any confessional way, but he often rebutted it unconsciously in remarks deflecting credit from himself to the troops. Consider a remark made to Sir William Orpen, who came to paint Haig's portrait: 'Why waste your time painting me? Go and paint the men. They're the fellows who are saving the world, and they're getting killed every day.'[19] After the war his devotion to the veterans became legendary.

It was bitter also to be accused by contemporaries, such as Winston Churchill, of pursuing the worst of strategies – attrition on the Western Front. Haig read Churchill's book in proof and asked no change; he commented, though, that 'no one knows as well as I do how far short of the ideal my own conduct both of the 1st Corps and the First Army was, as well as of the B.E.F. when C.-in-C.'[20]

Churchill perhaps tells Haig's pressures better than anyone: 'No anodyne of danger, no relief in violent action; nothing but anxiety, suspense, perplexing and contradictory information; weighing the imponderable, assigning proportions to what cannot be measured, intricate staff duties, difficult personal negotiations, and the muttering of far-distant guns. But he endured it all.'[21]

How? Was it because of that quality Lord Moran called 'phlegm'? Or did Haig turn to the covenanting faith of his mother for sustenance? His personal chaplain for most of the war, Reverend G. S. Duncan feels that Haig had a firm and growing, but somewhat eclectic faith, a personal one to fit his needs. Whatever the label, it gave him strength and he relied upon it. Duncan records Haig saying that his job was hard and 'I am frequently asked how I managed to do it?' But having things put 'into proper perspective on Sundays,' Haig recalled, and especially by lines Duncan read from Second Chronicles: 'Be not afraid nor dismayed by reason of this great multitude; for the battle is not yours, but God's.' More than that, the feeling of higher guidance built a growing assurance of destiny in him as he sought to 'do my best and trust in God.'[22] The sentiments could be Ireton's or Stonewall Jackson's. Religion surely gave him strength. But, like John Pershing, he turned, too, in times of turmoil to duty – the thing that he did best.

Pershing's duty in France was made clear – and easy – by almost model orders from President Wilson and Secretary Baker. Empowered with 'all necessary authority to carry on the war vigorously . . . towards a victorious conclusion,' Pershing worked under specific instruction to co-operate with the Allies 'but in so doing the underlying idea must be kept in view that the forces of the United States are a separate and distinct component of the combined forces, the identity of which must be preserved.'[23] Amalgamation of Americans with Allied armies would be restricted and would be one of Pershing's most constant pressures. Arguments for temporary amalgamation were logical. Veteran French and British units already blooded in trench warfare could teach tactics quickly and the intricate staff work needed to co-ordinate logistics, artillery support, air liaison, intelligence. But Pershing's native Missouri stubbornness helped him resist all kinds of suasion for amalgamation and he pushed hard to make the American Expeditionary Forces into an American Army.

The issue bubbled continually and Allies intrigued with each other against him. While he worried and was embroiled with myriad organizational details he found himself sniped at from behind and forced to wage an unexpected two-front war. British and French diplomats bustled in Washington seeking Baker's or Wilson's agreement to amalgamation – all over Pershing's head.[24] They were steadily referred back to the AEF's commander! But they kept trying and Pershing worried lest repetition have effect.

Right he was to worry. Baker visited France in March 1918, almost coincidentally with Germany's big offensive. Pershing had been wanting Baker to come – needed his presence in support[25] – but there was a downside to his coming. Called often to social gatherings with high Allied leaders and lost for a time in England, Baker fell victim to constant badgering. On 25 March, as the 'Michael' drive gathered momentum, Baker sent a jolting cable from London. American divisions, he suggested, ought to replace French divisions in quiet areas, all US engineers might well be stripped from the lines of communication and put to work on secondary British defences, and he thought that only infantry should be shipped from America for the present. Obviously Lloyd George had not abandoned old hopes of amalgamation. The Supreme Allied War Council, on 28 March, also agreed to sending only infantry and machine-gunners from America.

Pershing reacted quickly. On the 28th he met with Baker and America's representative on the Supreme Allied War Council, General Tasker Bliss, to untangle the messy matter of precedents. The suggested arrangement, Pershing said, would put the coming American troops entirely at the disposal of the War Council and likely would 'destroy all possibility of . . . forming an American Army.' Baker swiftly backed Pershing and a compromise came in the form of allowing temporary precedence to special troops but with their final disposition up to the AEF's commander.[26] Confirmed authority did not stop Allied grasps for American troops, so the worry continued.

There were other worries. Shifting demands for manpower confused the War Department in Washington – where a new Chief of Staff, General Peyton March, sought to bring order out of chaos. He imposed rigid control on logistics and apparently worked to rearrange Pershing's Services of Supply. Stray indications of War Department concern about AEF supplies caught Pershing's attention, but he missed the seriousness of the problem. In July 1918, he found out.

As he read a 6 July letter from the Secretary of War, Pershing nearly panicked: 'The President and I have had several conferences about your situation in France, both of us desiring in every possible way to relieve you of unnecessary burdens, but of course to leave you with all the authority necessary to secure the best results from your forces and to supply all the support and assistance we possibly can.' After that softening up, Baker suggested that Pershing be relieved of worries about supplies by having General George Goethals take over the logistical situation in France, with him 'rather in a co-ordinate than a subordinate relationship to you . . . and you could then forget about docks, railroads, storage houses, and all the other vast industrial undertakings to which . . . you have given a good deal of your time . . .'[27] Anguished, Pershing noted a loophole – think it over, Baker said, 'and tell me quite frankly just what you think of the subject.'

Swiftly Pershing pulled General James Harbord, commanding the 2nd Division, out of the fighting line and put him in charge of the Services of Supply. To Baker, Pershing cabled honestly that 'any division of responsibility or co-ordinate control in any sense would be fatal.' Baker, slightly amused by Pershing's hasty but effective flank-guarding, did not send Goethals.[28] Still, the whole episode was a harsh reminder – commanders' jobs often hung by threads of intrigue.

When, at last, the American First Army took the field, Pershing hoped for an end to intrigue – but knew better. On 30 August, 1918, at the height of planning for the American attack on the St. Mihiel Salient, Marshal Foch visited Pershing's Headquarters. Limit the attack, he urged, prepare to switch north to the Argonne and join the French II Army, put another American Army between the French II and IV Armies in the Aire River sector – this would set the stage for a great Franco–American drive toward Mézières and a link with Haig's attack on Cambrai. Pershing argued that these moves would foil formation of an American Army. Foch sadly agreed. What did Pershing propose? A shift of American troops to the whole sector of the Meuse-Argonne after the St. Mihiel attack. Foch doubted the shift possible, but finally agreed – and left Pershing worried about how long his American Army would exist.

Everything went well. The St. Mihiel Salient evaporated under Pershing's attack and the switch to the Meuse-Argonne went better than anyone expected. When Pershing launched his main offensive in late September, initial successes were impressive and Clemenceau came to visit. He praised what had been done but traffic conditions behind the US front appalled him. Soon he would demand Pershing's removal. Meantime, there were other worries. After the initial drive stalled, Pershing reorganized his army, sacked numbers of slothful generals and made ready to attack again.

Personal costs, though, were high. Those who knew him saw the effects of strain on Pershing – he grew thinner, his old Mexican tan faded to an almost ashen gray, his eyes sank into dark holes, and – most significantly – he sometimes slumped at his desk. That, more than anything, concerned Colonel George C. Marshall, the wizard who planned the move to the Argonne. Pershing had told him once that a commander, no matter how weary, should never slump at his desk!

Beyond the outward signs of strain Pershing suffered bouts of gloom as the battle dragged and Foch kept threatening to replace him. 'I feel like I am carrying the whole world on my shoulders,' he said, and once, motoring toward the front, he put his face in his hands and called to his dead wife, 'Frankie . . . Frankie . . . My God, sometimes I don't know how I can go on.' Foch noted how bad he looked and wondered who could take over. But his will held. To one of his divisional commanders he confessed that 'things are going badly . . . But by God! . . . I was never so much in earnest in my life and we are going to get through.' Marshall noted with increasing admiration that his chief kept up the pressure on his commanders and his men, and later told him how much that had meant: 'With . . . heavy casualties, disorganized and only partially trained troops, supply troubles . . . due to the devastated zone so hurriedly crossed, inclement and cold weather, flu, stubborn resistance . . . on one of the strongest positions on the Western Front, pessimism on all sides and the pleadings to halt the battle made by many of the influential members of the army, you persisted in your determination to force the fighting over all difficulties and objections . . . Nothing else in your leadership throughout the war was comparable to this.'[29]

With victory looming in October, Pershing caught the 'flu – one of the rare times he took to his bed. Victory came in November as Douglas Haig's long drive – starting in August – broke the Hindenburg Line. In the last one hundred days, Haig had 'fitted events as a hand fitted a glove.'[30] Like Pershing, Haig's determination made the difference. Alone and against Cabinet opinion he made the essential decision to launch an attack on 8 August, and Ludendorff remembered that as 'the black day of the German Army . . .'[31] Haig pushed the attack as Pershing pushed his – never had he been so active, alive and everywhere.

Both Haig and Pershing rose above pressures of high command with dogged determination. They survived all the furies of the World War and were great contributors to its outcome. The steel forged in them over years of soldiering did not break – though it bent often in a ceaseless cauldron of stresses.

End Notes

1   Lord Moran, *The Anatomy of Courage* (London: Constable, 1945), p. ix.
2   Bevan Steadman, M.D., 'Psychiatric Assessment of John J. Pershing,' College Station, Texas, August 12, 1995, p. 11. Manuscript in author's possession. The author wishes to express special gratitude to Dr. Steadman (who has made a study of stress in war) for advice and counsel throughout the preparation of this article.
3   E.K.G. Sixsmith, *Douglas Haig* (London: Weidenfeld and Nicolson, 1976), p. 73.
4   *Ibid*, p. 81.
5   (New York, Charles Scribner's Sons, 1929), p. 185.
6   *Ibid*.
7   John J. Pershing, *My Experiences in the First World War* (paperback edition, two volumes in one, New York: Da Capo Press, Inc., 1995), I, p. 18.
8   Entries in the Diary of Field Marshal Earl Haig, National Library of Scotland, Edinburgh (microfilm copy in author's possession).
9   Haig Diary.
10 *Ibid*.
11 *Ibid*.

12 *Ibid.*, April 3, 4, 1918.

13 *Ibid*, April 12, 1918.

14 Sixsmith, *Haig*, p. 157.

15 G.S. Duncan, *Douglas Haig As I Knew Him* (London: George Allen and Unwin, Ltd., 1966), p. 82.

16 See text in Sixsmith, *Haig*, p. 197.

17 See Diary of 2nd Lt S.C. Dumbreck (Royal Dragoons), September 21, 1915, noting that Haig 'said goodbye and good luck with some emotion which made me wonder what was up'; Letter, 2nd Lt Harry Oldham (9th Bn West Yorks), October 11, 1916, saying 'we've been reviewed today by Sir Douglas Haig. He looked frightfully pale and worried. I suppose it must be an awful strain'; Letter, Capt N.M. McLeod (RFA), February 6, 1918, noting that Haig 'looks done up and I thought he looked very dejected and old.' (All of these sources are in the Liddle Collection, Brotherton Library, University of Leeds, England.)

18 See Haig's correspondence with his wife in the Haig Papers, National Library of Scotland.

19 See, for example, letter from Christopher C. McDowell, Hampden Park, March 18, 1971, in Bemersyde Archives (Black Box), writing as an 'other rank' who often saw Haig near the trenches and knew he sympathized with the troops and 'felt with him – as I *knew* he felt for us.' In a conversation with the author in 1972 Charles Carrington recounted the story cited in Philip Warner, *Field Marshal Earl Haig* (London: The Bodley Head, 1991), p. 4,: that Haig made a personal reconnaissance of Carrington's section of the front (as I recall near Gommecourt) and decided to cancel a scheduled attack. There are many accounts of Haig's perhaps surprising popularity with the troops. John Buchan, who served with him, 'loved him' and thought 'he diffused a gentle compelling radiance.' (*Memory Hold-the-Door* [London: Hodder and Stoughton Ltd., 1950], pp. 185, 187) and General Marshall-Cornwall stated in 1974 that 'I think he was a very fine and inspiring leader of men ...' (Taped interview with Peter Liddle in May 1974 (tapes 225 and 226, Liddle Collection, Leeds University). Churchill wrote (*Great Contemporaries*, pp. 199–200) that Haig's 'qualities of mind and spirit ... came to be known by occult channels throughout the vast armies of which he was the Chief,' and that nothing dimmed 'the confidence of the soldiers in their Commander.'

20 Duff Cooper, *Haig* (Garden City, N.Y.: Doubleday, Doran & Co., 1936), p. 370.

21 Winston Churchill, *Great Contemporaries* (Freeport, N.Y.: Books for Libraries Press [Essay Reprint Series], first published 1937, reprinted 1971), pp. 195, 199.

22 Duncan, *Douglas Haig*, pp. 119–120, 124, 127. Duncan quotes a revealing letter from Haig written during the April 1918 crisis: 'I *know* I am sustained in my efforts by that Great Unseen Power, otherwise I could not be standing the strain as I am doing.' (*Ibid.*, p. 122).

23 Pershing, *My Experiences*, I, pp. 38–39.

24 See, for example, accounts of various meetings, especially of one between Georges Clemenceau and Pershing on January 9, 1918, in which Pershing threshed out the matter of going over his head. Pershing put the issue to Clemenceau in a pre-conference note: 'May I not suggest to you ... the inex-

pediency of communicating such matters to Washington by cable? These questions must all be settled here . . . on their merits . . . and cables of this sort are very likely, I fear, to convey the impression of serious disagreement between us when such is not the case.' Vandiver, *Black Jack: The Life and Times of John J. Pershing* (2 vols., College Station, Texas: Texas A&M University Press, 1977, II, pp. 845–846.

25 Pershing's position put him in a 'support vacuum,' which increased the stresses on him. He used wide discretionary powers without benefit of a superior's validation – a situation which increased the loneliness of command. See Steadman, 'Psychiatric Assessment.'

26 Vandiver, *Black Jack*, II, pp. 874–875.

27 *Ibid.*, p. 903.

28 For the Goethals embroglio, see Edward M. Coffman, *The Hilt of the Sword: The Career of Peyton C. March* (Madison, Wisc.: University of Wisconsin Press, 1966), pp. 104–109; Coffman, *The War to End All Wars: The American Military Experience in World War I* (New York: Oxford University Press, 1968), pp. 175–176; James Harbord, *The American Army in France, 1917–1919* (Boston: Little, Brown, 1936), pp. 345–355; Peyton C. March, *The Nation at War* (Garden City, N.Y.: Doubleday, Doran & Co., 1932), pp. 193–196; Pershing *My Experiences*, II, pp. 135–137; Vandiver, *Black Jack*, II, pp. 902–904.

29 Donald Smythe, *Pershing: General of the Armies* (Bloomington: Indiana University Press, 1986), pp. 208–209.

30 J.F.C. Fuller, quoted in Sixsmith, *Haig*, p. 191.

31 Quoted in Warner, *Haig*, p. 261.

Chapter 7

The French High Command and the Mutinies of Spring 1917

Len Smith

For all the attention devoted to the *decisions* of generals in the military history of World War I, our understanding of their *experience* is probably inferior to that of common soldiers. If asked to describe the experience of senior commanders, most historians would probably refer to a huge phys-ical and especially psychological distance between generals and the front lines, and of a frequently intentional detachment from the suffering their commands had to evoke. But this experience would also probably be described as logical and predictable. In *On War*, Clausewitz maintained that war differs from any form of state administration only in its use of violence.[1] If we were to accept his view we would expect to see generals experience the war as senior administrators, making decisions, justifying them, and seeing to their enforcement.

But the French army mutinies of May and June 1917, in which constituent parts of nearly half of the divisions in the French army refused at one point or another to move into the front lines, must have disrupted the assumptions underpinning the experience of rational, logical adminis-tration. For the mutinies were a huge if limited affront to military authority as conventionally conceived. Soldiers' demonstrations put generals in a limbo, in which they were neither obeyed nor directly assaulted. To be sure, many mutineers expressed dismay with the quality of their leadership. But perhaps surprisingly, they directed their anger more often at 'the war' than at the generals per se.[2]

My purpose here is to explore how French generals confronted the mutinies of 1917 as a cognitive experience. The generals struggled to understand a situation that St. Cyr and the Ecole Polytechnique had not trained them to anticipate, and that they were not fundamentally control-ling. With their actual power temporarily in abeyance, they imposed an understanding of unimpeded military authority on a situation in which that authority did not actually exist. I will conclude that although soldiers did not understand the mutinies the way the generals did, historians of the mutinies have largely accepted the assumptions about French soldiers built into the generals' interpretation.

Exploring the mutinies as a challenge to the normal cognitive processes of senior military administration suggests a 'high politics' approach quite distinct from my earlier work on the mutinies.[3] My main focus here will be on generals who led armies and army groups, right up to General Philippe Pétain.[4] However, I will have occasion to refer to army corps and division commanders, insofar as they contributed to the picture formed by those who exercised the highest levels of command.

GENERALS ON THE MARGINS: BEHAVIOUR AND RESPONSIBILITY

To the extent that policy is made by administrators rather than simply applied by them, it is striking to observe how little operational or strategic policy there was even to make during the mutinies. The key operational decision involved scaling down the objective of the Chemin des Dames offensive from a rupture of the German lines to the all-too-familiar 'attrition' of the enemy. This decision was taken by General Robert Nivelle a good three weeks before Pétain assumed supreme command on 15 May, and well before the most acute phase of the mutinies.[5] Indeed, there was little in the short run that Pétain could do differently from his predecessor. The irregular gains of the offensive had rendered the front highly unstable. The French position had to be either consolidated or abandoned. Pétain surmised that abandoning the gains would constitute a shattering confession to discontented soldiers and civilians alike that the whole Chemin des Dames effort had been a colossal waste of blood and resources. He chose the alternative policy of simply holding the line, and consolidating gains whenever possible.

The mutinies involved collective and categorical refusals by particular units to take up positions in the front lines. Upon choosing open disobedience, soldiers would hold demonstrations in which they would air a wide array of grievances. I have argued that the mutinies ended without the widespread application of force because of the ways French citizen-soldiers prioritized their demands and because of the critical mediation of non-commissioned and junior officers.[6] But micro-dramas of persuading discontented soldiers to re-accept formal military authority were not matters for generals. For reasons explored further below, senior commanders seem to have kept their distance from troubled units until after something resembling calm returned. In the interim, and paradoxically, this meant that senior commanders found themselves to a surprising degree on the margins.

Indeed, it is no easy task to find out just *how* senior commanders spent their time during the mutinies. Sometimes generals were concerned about putting things down on paper. After most of the disturbances were over, a memo from Pétain's headquarters to his senior subordinates warning of a possible return of antiwar activities concluded: 'it is essential to refrain from all written communication on this subject. The troops always find out about such communications.'[7] Perhaps in part because of an erratic uncertainty about documents falling into the wrong hands, generals spent a considerable amount of time in personal meetings, most often with superiors and immediate subordinates. Army Group North Commander Louis Franchet d'Espérey was a prolific memo writer to Pétain, yet his journal records almost daily meetings (usually over meals) during the worst part of the crisis.[8]

In their struggle for normalcy in a highly abnormal situation, generals seem to have spent a good deal of their time gathering and processing information. And like senior administrators in more typical circumstances, generals were sometimes displeased with the quality of the information they received. In May 1917, reports of a rash of desertions and 'a deep moral depression', in the 152nd Regiment reached Tenth Army Commander General Denis Duchêne not through the regimental commander, but through the postal censors.[9] It was up to Duchêne to order an investigation.[10] Likewise, Second Army commander General Marie Louis Guillaumat expressed dissatisfaction with the flow of information at all levels:

> Too often, it happens that commanders *hide* acts committed by their subordinates, the information suppressed by them out of a harmful sense of fear of being held responsible, or even out of a hope of being able to take care of things all by themselves. When they alert their superiors, it is too late, the damage has been done.[11]

If the extent of the paper trail were any judge, generals spent a considerable amount of time generating the information about the mutinies as well as gathering it. The bulk of the documentary record comprises memos and reports which interpret the events and propose solutions.[12] These documents could be highly repetitious, and given their sensitivity, promiscuously distributed.[13] Many generals were also avid letter writers, whether to their wives or to friendly politicians. Second Army commander Guillaumat described to his wife his own response to the mutinies in considerable detail.[14] General Joseph Micheler, commander of the Army Group of Reserves and later the Fifth Army, maintained a brisk correspondence with his friend and president of the Senate, Antonin Dubost.[15]

Certainly, the upper reaches of military command structures tend to be famous for political intrigue, worthy of Namier-style investigation.[16] Generals also ostensibly disdained colleagues who sought support from civilian politicians, even as they carefully nurtured their own patrons in the cabinet and the Chamber of Deputies.[17] And like many ambitious and accomplished people, generals sometimes had harsh words to say about their peers. Guillaumat wrote to his wife upon General Ferdinand Foch's elevation to chief of the General Staff that the army had promoted 'a crazy and sick man.'[18] After a meeting on May 22 with Guillaumat, his corps commanders, and Army Group Centre commander (and future Marshal of France) General Marie Emile Fayolle, Guillaumat wrote of 'the emptiness, the drivel, the waste coming out of a tap you can't turn off.'[19]

But only Nivelle openly turned on his subordinates, in an unsuccessful effort to stave off his own deposition, which occurred on 15 May . As early as 1 May, according to War Minister Paul Painlévé, Nivelle requested that Fifth Army commander, General Mazel, be removed because of 'his ignorance of questions of the artillery and the defective organization of provisioning.'[20] On 3 May, Nivelle wrote to Painlévé that Sixth Army commander, General Charles Mangin, 'having given himself over to the ardour of a military temperament, otherwise remarkable, did not bring to the calculation and preparation for the attacks the method and the precision indispensable to the command of an army.'[21] On 6 May, according to Michelle, Nivelle was preparing to sack his own chief of staff and the director of his Third Bureau (operations).[22]

But as a group, senior French commanders presented a common front in explaining the mutinies. Guy Pedroncini has shown that none of the senior French generals sought to blame the mutinies directly on Nivelle.[23] Pétain resolutely refused to criticize Nivelle at the time, and even in a 1926 report made only a glancing reference to a 'fantastic strategic overconfidence' on the part of the high command.[24] To some extent, this involved a simple herd instinct of self-preservation. Generals hesitated to make Nivelle the scapegoat for the mutinies because they understood how deeply they were all implicated in the offensive strategy that culminated in the Chemin des Dames. Nivelle certainly had not strengthened his own position by proclaiming the incompetence of men he had raised so high.

But the whole question of responsibility proved one around which generals had to tread lightly. In the short run, assigning blame for the mutinies was not easily separable from the immediate problem of resolving them. Theoretically, responsibility for ending the mutinies was a simple issue. At all levels, the gaze of the commander was supposed to be everywhere. His duties comprised predicting and preventing any movement that threatened to disrupt the untrammelled exercise of authority. Personal engagement, combined with perfect intelligence, ostensibly provided the key to regaining control.

In an 11 June memo to army and army group commanders, Pétain outlined this ideal situation, as it transpired in an unidentified army corps.[25] The corps commander, warned that a mutiny was going to erupt in a battalion ordered into the front lines, realized that he had to 'intervene personally and went immediately to the point at which the recalcitrant soldiers were assembled.' He encircled the would-be mutineers with cavalry and gendarmes, and barred access to all motor vehicles. In the presence of the assembled officers and NCOs, he gave the soldiers a certain amount of time to rejoin their unit, and ordered the company commanders to take out five men from each company, 'chosen among the proven leaders, or failing that, among the bad soldiers.' No one protested, and all the others rejoined the battalion within the prescribed time. The general announced to the battalion that if these measures did not suffice, 'they could await many others, of much more pitiless rigour.' Pétain concluded:

> Here is how a leader, worthy of the name, who knows how to join firm words with energetic action, can bring back together a group of men led astray and terrorized by a few leaders. [26]

But Pétain had good reason to know that this approach could hardly be applied to the army as a whole. At no point did the command structure have enough force at its disposition to suppress the mutinies. Only the cavalry were deemed certain to fire on demonstrators if ordered, and their numbers were certainly insufficient if soldiers decided to resist.[27] And at lower-level commands, untimely personal intervention on the part of a general could show the discrepancy between theoretical and real power all too clearly. In the Forty-first Infantry Division, the brigade commander tried to speak to demonstrating soldiers from his two regiments, only to have stones thrown at him and his stars pulled off. The (apparently unmolested) division commander standing at his side kept the assault from going farther only by promising that he would not make the two regiments go into the front lines for the time being, and that he would take up their complaints with the Fifth Army commander.[28]

It seems that senior commanders only appeared before particular units once the demonstrations had ended. For example, the Fifth Division proved by Pedroncini's reckoning the most mutinous in the whole French army. Yet Army Group North commander Franchet d'Esperey handled the delicate matter of removing two of its regiments in the early morning hours of 30 May over the telephone.[29] The last incident occurred on 6 June, a demonstration that was technically mutinous, but so fleeting that all the soldiers had returned to their billets by the time the regimental commander penned the last paragraph of his report.[30] Yet Franchet d'Esperey visited the Fifth Division only on 13 June, after it had taken up positions along the Chemin des Dames.

Much of the paper coming from senior commanders about responsibility, then, involved generals trying to get more junior officers to take more of it. A memo from Pétain dated 8 June maintained that 'certain officers have hidden from their superiors the poor spirit that has been reigning in their regiments' and warned that 'inertia equals complicity.'[31] Third Army commander General Georges Humbert echoed similar views on 17 June, when he alleged that officers charged with maintaining order at train stations 'have given the impression that they are afraid of their men; quite far from intervening, they claim to have seen nothing and not to have been aware of the facts to which they have been witnesses.'[32] Yet even these appeals to junior command's sense of responsibility had their limits. As Pedroncini has shown, there is no archival evidence that the high command sought summary executions, and he found only one execution outside the military justice system.[33]

COMMANDING THE NARRATIVE: SUBVERSION, 'LEADERS,' AND THE IMPRESSIONABLE MASSES

At stake in the mutinies was nothing less than an understanding of the nature of military power itself. In *Between Mutiny and Obedience* I have argued that the marginalization of the senior command structure created a situation in which the discontented soldiers became for a time essentially free political actors, able to debate among themselves the rights and responsibilities of citizen-soldiers. When the time came to choose between accepting the return of military authority in some form and losing the war, soldiers chose obedience when no external force existed to compel them to do otherwise. In agreeing to return to the trenches, they re-entered a complex symbolic economy of concessions coupled with highly selective repression. Underpinning this symbolic system was Pétain's tacit promise not to embark on any more quixotic offensives until tanks and American reinforcements gave France a decisive advantage.[34]

But such an understanding of the mutinies was fundamentally unacceptable to the French senior command, because it meant accepting an essentially two-way notion of military authority. Generals understood power in a military organization as operating in one direction only, from superior to subordinate. Various forms of what Clausewitz called 'friction' (including non-obedience) might slow a given military machine down and in some situations even break it. [35] But friction does not alter the way the machine itself is understood.

Clausewitz's ideal of a frictionless military machine depended on a strict separation of the practice of war and 'politics'. This notion sat poorly with the idea of thinking, partly empowered citizen-soldiers. Some glimmers of understanding appeared of the basic impossibility of a frictionless army of citizen-soldiers. An intelligence report of 21 July given to army group, army, army corps, and division commanders counselled that 'haughtiness provokes real sentiments of hostility. "We are not soldiers, we are citizens," is a fairly constant theme. The men do not wish to be treated like children.'[36] In a memo dated 16 July , the ever-thoughtful General Guillaumat fretted that soldiers might understand the mutinies all too well:

Rightly or wrongly, the good as well as the bad soldier is not far from thinking that the regrettable mutinies were not without usefulness and that because of them, soldiers have received certain concessions, or at least certain promises.[37]

The conception of one-directional military authority uncomfortably re-imposed the question of responsibility for the mutinies. For if soldiers serve as cogs in a military machine, as simple reflections of the will of their commanders, the latter are also implicated if soldiers fail to obey. Consequently, unable fully to command the situation during the mutinies, generals sought to regain command of the narrative explaining them. According to this narrative, generals could not be held responsible for the mutinies because the civilian politics of pacifist and defeatist subversion had 'infected' the military sphere. 'Leaders' in the army itself had carried the germs of this infection to the fundamentally loyal but highly impressionable mass of French soldiers.

Guy Pedroncini has shown in compelling detail how tightly the senior French command grasped subversive civilian politics as the principal cause of the mutinies, with the implicit scolding of the civilian authorities for not keeping their own house in order.[38] Army Group East commander de Castelnau telegraphed Pétain that 'the origin of these movements seem more and more clearly to come from secret organizations from the interior, whose decisions are transmitted by soldiers returning from leave.' Tenth Army commander Duchêne wrote of 'a secret and more or less entrenched movement coming primarily from Paris, which seeks through these special circumstances (the events in Russia, the strikes in Paris, etc.) to win over the troops and to demoralize them.'[39] Army Group North commander Franchet d'Espérey recommended that all of France be declared under a state of siege, with the expulsion of foreigners from neutral countries, the repatriation of civilians even from Allied Countries, and the imprisonment of residents from enemy countries, specifically Turks and Armenians.[40] My own work suggests that at lower command levels, officers shifted their explanations of the mutinies virtually day by day away from varieties of war-weariness toward civilian subversion.[41]

But Pedroncini has overstated the degree to which Pétain differed from his colleagues in explaining the mutinies. Pétain, after all, had helped see to it that French socialists were denied passports to attend a meeting in Stockholm to discuss peace. As early as 29 May, he wrote to Painlévé that 'the movement has deep roots in the interior,' and suggested a variety of repressive measures directed at civilians and particularly soldiers on leave. And the first explanatory cause of the mutinies cited in Pétain's 1926 report was 'the launching and exploitation of a pacifist propaganda campaign.'[42]

The infection of civilian subversion and defeatism was transmitted to the French army through 'leaders' of the mutinies. As Sixth Army commander Joseph Maistre observed:

There have been leaders. No better proof of the kept secret than the uniform attitude of the men toward the remonstrations of their officers, the slightly affected respect toward them the officers speak of, the nearly complete absence of over-excitement and of drunkenness – I note that the soldiers were obliged by their comrades to empty their canteens – in a word, obedience to instructions, which give the revolt a character marked by organization.'[43]

Presuming 'leaders' solved several difficulties for the senior command. Far too many men were involved in the mutinies for them all to have been tried.[44] 'Leaders' could thus be selected to pay the price for the collectivity. These could be construed as bad parts in the military machine, potentially lethal to the machine if left in place but harmless enough once removed.

Yet the category of 'leader' proved much more self-evident to the generals than to the junior officers actually dealing with the discontented soldiers. To judge by events in the Fifth Division, the very concept goes essentially against the facts.. Junior officers were struck by the spontaneous and very collective nature of the demonstrations, and identified 'leaders' only when commanded to do so.[45]

The court martial became an instrument not just for repressing the mutinies, but for identifying the 'leaders'. In the Fifth Division, some soldiers were selected for trial simply because of their judicial antecedents, and some because of even more dubious criteria.[46] In one company of the Seventy-fourth Regiment, four soldiers were identified simply because of their 'poor spirit and their usual manner of service.' Another soldier was marked as a leader because he was 'intelligent and well-instructed.' At the trials themselves, the defendants admitted taking part in the demonstrations, but denied leading them. When asked why they took part, virtually to a man they responded, *'J'ai suivi les camarades* [I followed the comrades.]'

The third component of the senior-command narrative of the mutinies comprised the impressionable mass of soldiers, who would be swayed either by subversion or by efficiently exercised command authority. Generals understood that they were dealing with a highly socialized and highly literate population. 'Every Frenchman talks well,' General Guillaumat observed, 'and as a result, talks a lot.'[47] Eighteenth Army Corps commander General Hirschauer noted that: 'The soldier reads a great deal. He awaits with impatience the arrival of newspapers from Paris; he receives newspapers from the provinces.'[48] Moreover, Hirschauer understood that reading and socializing were plainly parallel processes:

'And not only are the newspapers read, but they are also commented upon. And everything in the articles touching on current events–the action of the Russians, the action of the Americans, the duration of the war, peace efforts, etc.–give rise to long conversations in the shelters and in the bivouacs.'

Generals also understood that soldiers had complex and constant links to civilian society. Soldiers were, after all, fighting in their own country, many less than a day's train ride from the front. Franchet d'Espérey cautioned that 'we must not forget that in effect, nearly a fifth of the army is always in the interior, on leave or convalescing. There is thus a floating and idle mass; available to all suggestions and bringing with each incessant and inevitable exchange ideas between the country and the army.'[49] The civilian and military spheres continued to intersect further up the army hierarchy. Pétain became sufficiently irked by unauthorized contact between officers and civilian authorities to complain of 'a grave lack of discipline . . . [and] an absence of professional courage that verges on cowardice.'[50]

Precisely *because* soldiers were known to be socialized and literate, it became a matter of the utmost significance to command the information they received. The efforts to do so constituted the administrative counter- part of using the court martial to identify and punish the 'leaders' of the mutinies.

Commanding the information received by the ostensibly impressionable mass of soldiers involved finding a narrow path between the hated *bourrade de crâne* (fancifully optimistic propaganda) and renderings of military experience deemed defeatist. Eighteenth Army Corps commander General Hirschauer observed that: 'Accounts should be true. But truth doesn't mean realism.'[51] The commander of the Thirty-second Army Corps provided some additional hints concerning this delicate task: the press should

'cultivate and develop heroism, whether by stories or news items in which the imagination gives itself free reign, or by "Eyewitness Accounts of War". But these last should maintain a truthful character, banning hollow phrases and the bombastic style that angers rather than inspires soldiers who have lived through such experiences.'[52]

But anything questioning the idea that military authority operated in only one direction was deemed harmful. As Thirty-third Army Corps commander General Tantot put it, 'relations between officers and soldiers are defined by our regulations; they must be commented upon and super- vised only by the chain of command. Intervention from newspapers on this question only complicates the task of the responsible commanders, without benefit to the troops.'[53] At the same time, several generals noted the need to play up the heroism of the high command. As Pétain put it, a bit defen- sively, newspapers needed to stress that 'the shelters are not designed to protect the generals, but to permit the command to exercise regular, constant action, indispensable to the good conduct of combat.'[54]

Opinions differed as to how the crises of 1917 in other countries should be handled in the French press. Concerning events in Russia, Ninth Army Corps commander General Mangin believed that the press should explore in depth 'the disastrous consequences of the theories of the ideologues, the reign of indiscipline and insubordination, in contrast to German organization and discipline.'[55] Yet General Tantot in the Thirty-third Corps believed that any mention of resistance to authority in Russia was to be avoided: such accounts 'will awaken ideas of turbulence, leading to evil ferments.' Colonel Steinmetz, provisional commander of the 126th Division, believed that reports even of the mutinies in the German navy should be played down.[56]

Of course, just where truth should leave off and political realism should begin proved no easy matter to negotiate. The more truthfully one wrote about World War I combat, the more difficult it became to represent it in an inspiring manner – particularly in the second half of 1917. Accounts of soldiers' experience in the civilian press could influence soldiers' impressions of civilian society, but were unlikely fundamentally to shape the way soldiers understood their own ordeals. Generals also assumed a 'read no evil, do no evil' approach to military authority. The French army had just been through a major mutiny; they hardly needed the newspapers to alert them to the possibility of resistance to formal command. Likewise, praising the hard work of the generals was not going to make anyone forget the Artois in 1915, Verdun in 1916, and the Chemin des Dames in 1917.

CONCLUSION: GENERALS AND THE HISTORIANS
Over time, historians appear to have discarded much of the generals' narrative of the mutinies, even before most of the archival record became accessible. French-language historiography has tended to seek a story line that divided Frenchmen least. Jean Ratinaud and R.G. Nobécourt played down the role of internal subversion, and emphasized command overconfidence and material hardship.[57] Anglophone historians such as John Williams and Richard Watt – always on the lookout for early symptoms of the moral collapse of France in 1940 – have been more attracted to the idea of a military sphere infected by the viruses of pacifism and defeatism.[58] But military historians have long been fixated on the assignation of blame, preferably personalized. Consequently, they have pointed the finger of responsibility far more directly toward Nivelle than did generals at the time.

Pedroncini's Les Mutineries de 1917 was the first study to make extensive use of the archival record. Unsurpassed as a comprehensive study of the mutinies twenty-eight years after its publication in 1967, his work definitively laid to rest an unreconstructed version of the generals' narrative. Pedroncini argued that the mutinies were 'military' rather than political. They involved a sophisticated and limited protest against years of tried-and-failed offensive tactics that culminated in Nivelle's Chemin des Dames offensive. Pétain understood what his predecessors had not; that war had become fully industrialized, first and foremost a matter of *matériel*. The mutinies thus became a matter of what John Keegan called the 'survivability' of the French army.[59] Pacifist subversion had meaning only against this brute physical reality.

But like his predecessors, Pedroncini kept the historiographical focus on the generals. Pedroncini himself has been keenly, perhaps primarily, interested in the rehabilitation of Pétain. I would argue this is a very incomplete way to understand the mutinies. Pedroncini oversold the distinctions between Pétain and his colleagues, which were certainly of degree rather than of kind. He does not question the existence of 'leaders,' but rather concentrates on the (no doubt correct) point that Pétain had many fewer of them shot than would have most of his colleagues. Nor does he question the fundamental impressionability of the mass of French soldiers.

In short, the historiography of the mutinies has accepted the most basic assumption shared by generals at the time, whether a particular historian supported a particular general's conduct or not. Specifically, historians have accepted the generals' time-honoured Clausewitzian ideal of mechanistic military authority in which power flows untrammelled from superior to subordinate . The mutinies thus become a matter of the French military machine breaking down, whether through dubious generalship or through the intrusion of the the the civilian politics of pacifism or defeatism. It is this assumption of mechanistic one-directional military authority that needs to be rethought. The French army mutinies of 1917 were *both* 'military' and 'political' in that they involved a multi-layered confrontation between French citizen-soldiers and the formal authority over them – an authority which drew its very legitimacy from those citizen-soldiers and their compatriots. Clausewitz would probably have found this confrontation as confusing as the French generals of 1917. How military authority *actually* functioned in this situation is a far more complex matter than how it 'should' have functioned, or how generals and military historians believed it functioned.

Notes

1   See the famous passage on war as the continuation of politics by other means in Carl von Clausewitz, *On War*, Michael Howard and Peter Paret, trans., Princeton: Princeton University Press, 1976, Book 1, Chapter 1, Section 24, p.87.

2   See Guy Pedroncini, editor, 1917: *Les Mutineries de l'Armée Française*, Paris: Julliard, 1968, Chapter II. This is primarily a collection of primary documents distinct from Pedroncini's classic monograph, *Les Mutineries de 1917*, Paris: Presses Universitaires de France, 1967.

3   See Leonard V. Smith, *Between Mutiny and Obedience: The Case of the French Fifth Infantry Division during World War I*, Princeton: Princeton University Press, 1994, pp.175–214.

4   Pétain was the most senior general at the time of the mutinies, though he was not general-in-chief of all the French armies, as General Joseph Joffre had been at the beginning of the war. Like General Robert Nivelle, Pétain's formal title was commander of the Groupe des Armées du Nord et du Nord-est.

5   See the chronology in Pedroncini, *Les Mutineries de 1917*, Chapter 4.

6   See Smith, *Between Mutiny and Obedience*, pp.187–206.

7   'Le Général en chef des Armées du Nord et du Nord-Est aux Généraux Cdt. les Groupes d'Armées [et] aux Généraux Cdt. les Armées,' No. 5. S.R.A./2, [undated, probably late June or early July 1917], Groupe d'Armées de l'Est, 1ᵉ Bureau, 18 N 298, Service Historique de l'Armée de Terre, Château de Vincennes, Vincennes, France. All archival references come from this source. All translations are my own unless otherwise noted.

8   Sometime after 1937, Franchet d'Espérey had his journal typed out and added various recollections. The entire memoir comprises twelve carnets. The relevant one here is Carnet IX, "Commandement du Général Nivelle," Papiers Franchet d'Esperey, 1 K Mi 44.

9   Commission du Contrôle Postal, Gare Régulatrice de Noisy-le-Sec, 'Unité controlé: 152e RI, sp.206: Rapport,' 25 May 1917, Xᵉ Armée, 3ᵉ Bureau, 19 N 1667.

10 'Le Général Duchêne, Commandant la Xe Armée à Monsieur le Général Commandant le 18e C.A.,' (2ᵉ Bureau, S.R., No. 12.263), in ibid.

11 'Note pour les commandants de C.A.,' No. 196 bis/C (undated, June 1917), IIe Armée, 2ᵉ Bureau, 19 N 305.

12 A good cross-section of the documentary record had been published in Pedroncini, ed., *1917: Les Mutineries de l'Armée française*.

13 It is not uncommon to see in the archives multiple copies in multiple cartons of reports marked *'Secret'* or *'Confidentiel.'*

14 See the transcriptions in Papiers Guillaumat, 1 K Mi 52.

15 See the untitled, undated memoir by Micheler in Fonds Micheler, 1 K 113.

16 That is to say, analysis based in personality rather than ideology, and heavily steeped in the minutiae of primary sources. See, for example, Louis Namier, *The Structure of Politics at the Accession of George III* (London: Macmillan, 1929).

17 See the well-preserved study based entirely on published sources, Jere Clemens King, *Generals and Politicians: Conflict between France's High Command, Parliament, and Government, 1914–1918*, Berkeley and Los Angeles, University of California Press, 1951.

18 Papiers Guillaumat, 17 May 1917.

19 Ibid., 23 May 1917.

20 'Le Ministre de la Guerre à Monsieur le Général Commandant en Chef les Armées du Nord et Nord-Est,' (undated, around 18 May 1917) in G.Q.G. 1ᵉ Bureau, 16 N 495.

21 Letter from Nivelle to Painlévé, 1 May 1917, quoted in 'Le Ministre de la Guerre au Général Commandant en Chef les Armées du Nord-Est,' 3 May 1917, in ibid.

22 Fonds Micheler.

23 Pedroncini, *Les Mutineries de 1917*, pp.281–88.
24 See ibid., p.288n; 'A Crisis in the French Nation at War,' Rivers Scott, trans., in Major General Sir Edward Spears, *Two Men who Saved France: Pétain and De Gaulle*, London: Eyre & Spottiswoode, 1966, p.82. Nivelle did not return Pétain's favour, and blamed the mutinies on the decision to close down the offensive and his own removal from supreme command. Pedroncini, *Les Mutineries de 1917*, p.287.
25 'Note aux Groupes d'Armées et Armées,' No. 10.221, 11 June 1917, G.Q.G., 1ᵉ Bureau, 16 N 298.
26 Pétain maintained a striking silence on the conduct of the division, regimental, and battalion commanders in these events.
27 See Pedroncini, *Les Mutineries de 1917*, pp.183–85.
28 Ibid, pp.135–36.
29 Papiers Franchet d'Esperey, 29 May 1917. On the mutinies in the Fifth Division, see Smith, *Between Mutiny and Obedience*, Chapter VIII.
30 Smith, *Between Mutiny and Obedience*, pp.186–87.
31 'Télégramme chiffré,' No.2.433 et 2.434, quoted in ibid., p.207.
32 'Note pour M.M. les Généraux Commandant les C.A., le 1ᵉʳ C.C., la 70ᵉ D.I.. et les Brigades Territoriales,' No. PS/195, 17 June 1917, IIIe Armée, 1ᵉ Bureau, 19 N 528.
33 See Pedroncini, *Les Mutineries de 1917*, p.187. On May 29 (during the most difficult phase of the mutinies), a second lieutenant from the Ninth Infantry Regiment was actually tried (but acquitted) for shooting dead on April 9 one of his soldiers who refused to advance to the front lines. General Guillaumat wrote that 'I cannot explain to myself how they put this officer before a court martial, when he deserves to be greatly congratulated for having done his duty and nothing but his duty.' But he did not encourage other officers to behave likewise. Hand-written addendum by Guillaumat in 'Le Général Eon, Commandant la 33e Division d'Infanterie, à M. le Général Commandant la IIᵉ Armée,' No. 8.111, 8 June 1917, in IIᵉ Armée, 1ᵉ Bureau, 19 N 277.
34 See Smith, *Between Mutiny and Obedience*, Ch. VIII-IX, pp.206–30.
35 See Clausewitz, *On War*, Book I, Chapter 7, pp.119–21.
36 'Bulletin confidentiel No. 3, Résumant la situation morale aux Armées dans la semaine du 15 au 21 juillet 1917,' in Groupe des Armées de l'Est, 1ᵉʳ Bureau, 18 N 298.
37 'Réponse à la Note du G.A.C. en date du 30 juin 1917,' 16 July 1917, in IIᵉ Armée, 1ᵉʳ Bureau, 19 N 277.
38 Pedroncini, *Les Mutineries de 1917*, passim, especially pp.281–88.
39 Both quotes may be found in ibid., pp.282 and 283.
40 'Le Général de Division Franchet d'Espérey, Commandant le Groupe d'Armées du Nord, au Général en chef,' No. 8231, 31 May 1917, in Groupe d'Armées du Nord, 1ᵉʳ Bureau, 18 N 37.
41 Smith, *Between Mutiny and Obedience*, pp.203–206.
42 Pétain, 'A Crisis of Morale,' p.72.
43 Untitled response to report from Third Army Corps commander General Lebrun, 30 May 1917, VI Armée, 3e Bureau, 19 N 1093.
44 Pedroncini's estimate is 25,000–30,000. *Les Mutineries de 1917*, p.307.
45 See Smith, *Between Mutiny and Obedience*, pp.206–14.
46 Ibid., pp.210–12.

47 'Note pour les commandants de C.A.,' No. 196 bis/C, undated, June 1917, in IIe Armée, 2ᵉ Bureau, 19 N 305.

48 'Rapport sur l'orientation à donner à la presse,'(18e C.A., 2e Bureau, 28 July 1917), in Groupe des Armées de l'Est, 2ᵉ Bureau, 18 N 312.

49 'Le Général de Division Franchet d'Espérey, Commandant le Groupe d'Armées du Nord au Général Commandant en Chef (Cabinet),' No. 9.154, 10 June 1917, in Groupe d'Armées du Nord, 1ᵉ Bureau, 18 N 37.

50 'Secret: Notes aux Armées,' No. 18749, 18 July 1917, in G.Q.G., 1ᵉ Bureau, 16 N 298.

51 Hirschauer, 'Rapport sur l'orientation.' He probably made here a thinly veiled reference to the anti-war 'realism' of Henri Barbusse's Le Feu, published in November 1916.

52 Untitled, unsigned response, 27 October 1917, No. 4.320/2, from 32e C.A., 2ᵉ Bureau, in ibid.

53 'Le Général Tantot, Commandant provisoirement le 33ᵉ Corps d'Armée au Général Commandant la VIIᵉ Armée: Influence des journaux sur le morale des troupes,' 33ᵉ C.A., 1ᵉ Bureau, No. 2448/1 (undated), in ibid.

54 'Le Général Commandant en Chef à Monsieur le Ministre de la guerre (Cabinet) à Paris,' No. 26.204, 23 August 1917, in 6ᵉ Armée, 2ᵉ Bureau, 19 N 1037.

55 'Le Général Mangin, Commandant le 9ᵉ Corps d'Armée, à M. le Général Cdt la VIIIe Armée, 2ᵉ Bureau,' 9ᵉ C.A., 2ᵉ Bureau, No. L.3128, 27 December 1917, in ibid.

56 'Compte-Rendu sur les directives à donner à la presse,' 126ᵉ D.I., 2ᵉ Bureau, No. 816/R, 8 November 1917, in ibid.

57 Jean Ratinaud, 1917 ou La Révolte des poilus, Paris: Fayard, 1960; R.G. Nobécourt, Les Fantassins du Chemin des Dames, Paris: Robert Laffont, 1965.

58 John Williams, Mutiny 1917, London: William Heinemann Ltd., 1962; Richard M. Watt, Dare Call it Treason, New York: Simon and Schuster, 1963. Watt accepts the generals' interpretation much more uncritically than Williams.

59 In a sometimes cranky but not actually unfavourable review of Between Mutiny and Obedience, Keegan took me to task for conceptualizing the mutinies beyond this. See 'An Army downs tools, mutiny in the First World War: theory and the poor bloody infantry,' Times Literary Supplement, 13 May 1994, pp.3-4.

Chapter 8

British Decision-making 1917: Lloyd George, The Generals and Passchendaele

Trevor Wilson and Robin Prior

I

It is part of the mythology of the First World War that Britain's military strategy was determined, not by its responsible political leaders, but by the military command. In this view, there were always far-sighted civilians, in and out of government, proposing a more fruitful and imaginative way of conducting the war than that adopted. Their insights availed nothing. The nation's military chiefs always secured the last word.

This view is neatly summed up in an eminent biography of H H Asquith, Britain's Prime Minister during the first two years of the war.[1] Roy Jenkins writes of Asquith: 'he never thought it his duty to impose strategic decisions upon the service chiefs. They were the experts . . . he would no more have thought it right to issue a directive which ran counter to their united voices than to tell the Lord Chief Justice what judgements he should deliver.'

The consequences, it is generally concluded, were regrettable. According to Roy Jenkins: 'the Government permitted the generals to engage in frontal attacks on heavily fortified positions, with the frightful losses which were inevitably involved . . .'. That is, Western Front operations such as Loos in 1915 and the Somme in 1916 and Third Ypres in 1917 were in good measure the product of military misjudgement exercised in circumstances where civilian authority had gone into abeyance.

There is no warrant for this view. At every stage, the fundamental decisions about Britain's involvement in this war, and the manner of its participation, were reached in accord with orthodox constitutional practice. That is, they were made by the nation's civilian rulers, after consultation (where appropriate) with their service chiefs.

We need only observe the major decisions taken in the opening years of the war to recognise that civilian control continued to function. In the diplomatic crisis of July–August 1914, no one asked the military to decide whether Britain should participate in a European war; any more than, in the ensuing days and months, the High Command was asked whether Britain should abandon its small-army, 'business-as-usual' orientation, in favour of a mass army and a war economy. Equally, it was as a result of a protracted political tussle, not a military *diktat*, that Britain ultimately abandoned voluntary recruitment and imposed military conscription on adult males.

So in the area of grand strategy, it was the Prime Minister and his political colleagues who decided that the overwhelming proportion of Britain's fighting forces would be engaged first in the essential task of holding the line in the West and then in the attempt to drive the invader from the soil of France and Belgium. That decision remained in place to the end of Asquith's Premiership in December 1916. Certainly, during 1915 a sub-committee of the Cabinet with special responsibility for strategic matters made decisions concerning operations elsewhere: an intended naval offensive at the Dardanelles which came to develop military implications; and an undertaking at Salonica which only the inclinations of the French and the demands of coalition warfare persuaded the British to persist in. These sideshows, nevertheless, were never seen by Britain's rulers as alternatives to, or substitutes for, the prime task, of driving the forces of Germany out of Western Europe.

There were, admittedly, thoughtful men in Britain's governing circles who jibbed at their nation's resort to offensives in the West. Lloyd George, for one, argued from early 1915 that some other front be sought for Britain's endeavours. That he failed to carry the day, however, did not signal a victory for military stupidity over civilian common sense. Neither Lloyd George nor any other well-placed civilian managed to propose an actual area of operations which seemed to offer a better prospect than the Western Front. Indeed by the end of 1915 the abortive undertakings at Gallipoli and Salonica had left such views utterly at a discount.

The consequence was the great Anglo–French offensive on the Somme in the second half of 1916. Its outcome would prove profoundly unsatisfactory, in its human cost and failure to yield significant gains. Yet that does not mean that the Somme campaign was only embarked on, and persisted in, because of the determination of the British high command. In British governing circles generally, there were great hopes for the outcome of what would be Britain's first major land campaign of the war. And even among those less-than-confident, none could suggest a more hopeful way of proceeding, or argue that – given France's mounting peril – British forces could sit back and do nothing.

These events set the scene for Britain's part in the war on land in 1917. That year was noteworthy for many things. But as far as the British army was concerned it is memorable for the great offensive which British forces waged in Flanders from late July to mid November – what is officially the Third Battle of Ypres, but popularly known as the Battle of Passchendaele. This campaign is often judged the most futile and purposeless of World War One's many offensives.

What is to be said of this? One thing cannot be said: that in 1917 Britain was burdened with a Prime Minister prepared, against his better judgement, to bow to the dictates of the military command. In December 1916 Asquith had been ousted from office by his erstwhile lieutenant, Lloyd George. One particular consideration that had inspired Lloyd George to seize power was his despair at the military plans being hatched in November 1916 by the high commands of France and Britain. Their schemes for 1917, in Lloyd George's view, looked like nothing but a repetition of 1916's futile endeavours on the Somme. Secure in the Premiership by January 1917, he made it plain that he would not be a party to further such proceedings. He told his private secretary:

> Haig does not care how many men he loses. He just squanders the lives of these boys. I mean to save some of them in the future . . I am their trustee.[2]

Lloyd George would still be Prime Minister six months later, when British troops went over the top on the first day of Third Ypres, and 3½ months after that, when the campaign came to its miserable conclusion on Passchendaele Ridge. It is unlikely that the boys whose trustee Lloyd George had declared himself to be were profoundly conscious of any attempts made by him to preserve their lives – where, that is, they remained conscious at all.

How had it happened that the elevation to power of a British Prime Minister already thoroughly disenchanted with the country's military leaders, and utterly disbelieving in a Western Front strategy, had allowed this particular Western Front offensive to go its appalling way? The conventional answer is that Lloyd George was powerless to stop it. Though supreme in many areas of government, he was helpless in this. As a new Prime Minister who had broken with his own party and was dependent for office on the support of the Conservatives, he could not sack a Commander-in-Chief who was a favourite of the King and had many friends in high places. Lloyd George was expendable, Haig was not.

This line of argument is specious on every ground. First, far from being dispensable, as long as he lived Lloyd George was the one indispensable man in Britain in 1917. He alone could plausibly offer the nation the national government without which it could not function at this time: a government predominantly Conservative in composition and orientation, but including a section of Liberals and the endorsement of the fledgling but important Labour party. What sort of government, one would like to know, would the Labour party be prepared to enter in the aftermath of Lloyd George's being kicked out by the King in order to placate Sir Douglas Haig?

Secondly, the notion that in order to forestall or terminate the Third Ypres campaign it would have been necessary for Lloyd George to sack Haig is unwarranted. Indeed it constitutes a fraudulent requirement invented to explain the seemingly inexplicable. All that the situation required was for the nation's civilian rulers, with whom responsibility for control of grand strategy indubitably rested, to inform the Commander-in-Chief on the Western Front that, after due consideration, they could not authorise his proposed Flanders campaign. They could explain that they lacked the weapons and manpower, or that they possessed them but intended to employ them in another theatre upon a different campaign, or that they chose – on account of perilous events on the French and Russian fronts and the hopeful prospect of eventual American military intervention – to refrain from large offensive action anywhere until circumstances were more propitious.

That Lloyd George knew that he possessed ultimate control of strategy, had no inhibitions about telling Haig his business, and indeed was prepared to downgrade Haig even from control of British operations in the Western sector, was blindingly clear. It had become so within weeks of Lloyd George's seizure of the Premiership. Following the overthrow of Joffre by the rulers of France, Haig had proposed as his main endeavour for 1917 a British campaign in Flanders. Lloyd George let it be known that he had quite other plans. His strong inclination was towards a great campaign in Italy which would draw Germans as well as Austrians to that front. However the Italians proved quite unwilling to launch an offensive on their front in the absence of a campaign on the Western Front to occupy the Germans. Lloyd George then turned to the French. He embraced the proposal of their new Commander-in-Chief, General Nivelle, to launch a great French offensive in the Champagne region, with British forces mounting subsidiary operations under his overall direction. That is, far from Lloyd George's dancing to Haig's tune, Haig would do the dancing. Lloyd George had placed him under French direction.

The arrangement proved short-lived. But that was not because Haig induced the King and maverick Conservatives to unseat Lloyd George. It was because Nivelle, in the view of Lloyd George's secretary, let Lloyd George down: that is, conducted so disastrous an offensive that the French army mutinied and the French government sacked him. This debacle was a setback to Lloyd George, but it did not mean that he was now obliged to agree to Haig's renewed proposal in June and July for a campaign in Flanders. He could still opt for a campaign in Turkey, or decline to resume any sort of large-scale offensive until the French had recovered and the Americans had begun to put in an appearance. Haig might have argued otherwise, but no one feared that he would consider resigning if he did not get his way.

<h1 style="text-align:center">III</h1>

So, seemingly, the question remains. Why, in mid-1917, did the civilian rulers of Britain abdicate their clear control over British strategy and allow Haig to launch the 3½ month campaign which terminated in the mud and blood of Passchendaele? The answer is that they never did: never, that is, authorised an extended campaign employing vast resources without regard to timespan or lack of achievement. In June and July Lloyd George created a new body, the War Policy Committee, just to adjudicate on this matter of strategy. (It looked very much like the established War Cabinet, minus the Labour representative.)[3] Haig presented to it his grand strategic design: a breakout from the Ypres salient by Sir Hubert Gough's Fifth Army supported by Plumer's Second Army, supplemented at an appropriate stage by a strike up the coast and a landing from the sea behind enemy lines directed by Sir Henry Rawlinson and Admiral Bacon. The War Policy Committee argued the pros and cons, with Lloyd George always indicating a preference for his mythical campaign in Italy.

In the outcome the Committee did not decide for Italy, if only because it had no power to initiate an operation there. But neither did it agree to an extended undertaking in Flanders whose extent and duration would be decreed by Haig. What they finally opted for was just the first phase of a Flanders campaign. When that had taken place the situation would be reviewed. If Haig's grand vision seemed to be developing, then operations would continue. If it did not, and all that was emerging was a Somme-type slogging match, then that would end the matter. Attention would turn to Italy or elsewhere, and the word Passchendaele would never enter the demonology of the First World War.

All this made a sort of sense. But it did so only in the context that the War Policy Committee would go on meeting and monitoring Haig's progress and deciding if anything of note was being achieved at less than excessive cost. The record reveals a quite different scenario. The War Policy Committee, far from meeting and scrutinising and assessing and deciding for or against continuation on the basis of results, never met from the day the campaign started (31 July) to a date, late in September, almost two months later. And when it was hastily reconvened, it was not in response to what had been happening in Flanders. (There a first month of campaigning in drenching rain had achieved so little that, at least temporarily, Gough had been sidelined and a new type of operation instituted under Plumer). The War Policy Committee was reactivated in consequence of events on the Italian front.

In the course of September Lloyd George, along with General Foch, had exercised considerable pressure on Haig to divert 100 batteries of guns to the Italian front to aid General Cadorna in his continuing operations against the Austrians. No sooner had Haig handed over the guns than Cadorna had informed the British government that he would be launching no more offensives that year. Adding insult to injury, he had reminded them that whether he did or did not do so was entirely a matter for the Italian government to decide.

In response to this *démarche* the War Policy Committee was hastily reassembled, to beat its breast about Italian backsliding, to take back control of its guns, and to proclaim that weapons and strategic initiative would now proceed east. A campaign against Turkey would replace operations by the Italians. Germany, Lloyd George proclaimed, could not be defeated until it was isolated. In a reversion to this 'knocking away the props' mentality of 1915 – but with Turkey rather than Austria the prop now in his sights – he argued for a campaign in Palestine. This might give Turkey a good knock, and at the same time the Turks should be offered generous peace terms ('peace at any price'). This combination of stick and carrot might persuade the Turks to leave the war during the European winter, and the campaign in Flanders would be resumed in the spring of 1918 in more hopeful circumstances. Two aspects of this extraordinary farrago require comment. First, there was no attempt to argue the case that Germany could only be beaten following its deprivation of its allies – quite apart from the fact that just the loss of Turkey would hardly leave Germany isolated. And secondly, and of far more importance, nothing was being said here about the actual progress of the campaign in Flanders, where rain and thwarted large objectives under Gough in August had, in September, given way to fine weather and decidedly modest goals under Plumer.

It is often said that the government was the victim of misinformation: that the military command, while attaining next to nothing, was proclaiming one victory after another.[4] In truth there was no possibility of this. Haig in order to sell his project in the first place had needed to be disarmingly specific about his objectives. Lloyd George to his dying day would remember Haig's hand sweeping across the map of Belgium and ending up across the German frontier. No one could pretend that Haig was accomplishing anything of the sort.

Anyway, it was simply not the case that the military authorities were trying to put it across their political masters. As we have seen, the War Policy Committee did not meet in August and most of September, so the military could not report to it and suffer cross-examination. But the War Cabinet, its parent body, was meeting, although it seemed inclined to spend more time on less-than-momentous subjects such as air raids on London than on Britain's major military campaign. Nevertheless, 'Wullie' Robertson, the CIGS, did offer them regular accounts of what was happening in Flanders. His reports were sometimes wildly optimistic concerning what might soon be accomplished, but as to what had so far been achieved they were strictly accurate; and it was not hard to detect how expectations overall were diminishing from Haig's earlier promises.

Yet what is noteworthy about these transactions is not what Robertson had to say but how the War Cabinet responded. If the minutes of meetings are any guide, he spoke in silence, evoked no questions, and was subjected to no expressions of dismay that this operation was proving no better than a re-run of the Somme. Members of the War Cabinet might, in response to his reports, take off into speculations about alternative strategies directed against Austria or Turkey. They never, during August and the opening weeks of September, demanded to know whether the Third Ypres campaign was nearing its objectives and how great was the price being paid.

Indeed it was Robertson who, far from trying to fob them off, endeavoured to force the members of the War Cabinet to do their duty. On 28 August, after Lloyd George had first pressed for the sending of some guns to Italy (without at all suggesting that this meant halting operations in Flanders), Robertson demanded that the War Cabinet review the whole issue of strategy. The cabinet, he reminded them, had all along decided this matter. The first decision for a Flanders operation had been made by the Asquith cabinet in its concluding days. Then the Lloyd George cabinet in February 1917 had opted for a switch to Nivelle. And in July the same body had made the decision to revert to the campaign at Ypres. Now it must decide again: either to continue the Flanders operation, or to opt for Italy. The War Cabinet ducked this challenge. It said that it was impressed by what was being achieved in Italy, but would not override the military if they concluded that events in Italy did not warrant the abandonment of Third Ypres. That is, in face of Robertson's clear challenge, the War Cabinet steadfastly refused to engage the question, what was actually being accomplished in Flanders and at what cost.

Yet it steadily becomes clear that, whatever the reason for this abdication of decision-making, it was not that the Prime Minister and his colleagues were under any illusion about the progress of events on the Western Front. Their eagerness to send guns to Cadorna while he was willing to act, like their subsequent thrashing about for an operation against the Turks at Alexandretta or in Palestine, constitutes evidence enough of their dissatisfaction with events in the main sector. So Lloyd George spoke in the War Cabinet immediately after the Third Ypres campaign had yielded its first entirely successful action – Plumer's limited attack on the Menin Road on 20 September. The Prime Minister argued devotedly for a large reinforcement to the army in Palestine 'to make sure of one army being successful'. Regarding Plumer's attack, he said that for a war-weary country 'the effect of an advance such as the recent one in Flanders did not last long'. In his most bizarre contribution, Lloyd George proclaimed as the one truly successful Western Front operation of 1917 the Nivelle offensive in April, far more rewarding than the operation proceeding in Flanders. Regarding the latter, he made clear his negative judgement. The French, he said, had repeatedly reneged on their promises to aid the Third Ypres campaign by launching complementary attacks elsewhere on the Western Front, and they would do so again. The War Cabinet had been misled by Haig's optimistic predictions concerning the offensive: 'no one would have voted for the offensive if they had not been considerably influenced by his optimism'. There was no prospect, Lloyd George concluded, even in the judgement of the military authorities of getting even as far as the Klerken Ridge this year.

At a meeting of the War Cabinet on 11 October, following Plumer's third successful small-scale attack and in the absence of Robertson, the Flanders operation was subjected to general condemnation. Lord Curzon announced that he was 'ready to assume that Field Marshal Haig and General Robertson were wrong in their views about the Western Front'. And General Smuts held that the Western Front 'had always presented an insoluble problem' which, should Russia drop out of the war, 'would become a hopeless problem'. (What Smuts perceived as the difference between an insoluble and a hopeless problem, no one seems to have inquired). As for Lloyd George, after delivering another panegyric to the Nivelle offensive – 'the most successful operation undertaken by the Allies this year' – and proclaiming a Palestine campaign 'the only operation to undertake', the Prime Minster went on to make this prediction:

> we would not capture the Klerken Ridge and he would call the War Cabinet's attention to this in three weeks' time. In fact, he believed that he himself had taken too sanguine a view of Sir Douglas Haig's prospects in the Flanders offensive. Unless something of the kind now contemplated were done in Turkey[,] in a year's time we should find ourselves in exactly the same position as we were in now.

If this, early in October, was the government's view of the Flanders campaign, two events gave it the opportunity to halt Third Ypres there and then. One resulted from action by the War Cabinet, the other action by the French government. For the first time, the War Cabinet demanded to know the human cost of the Flanders offensive. Indeed it complained that casualty figures had never been supplied, overlooking the fact that it had never requested them, and hitherto had evinced little interest in the cost and progress of the campaign. The figures provided to the Cabinet at its meeting on 17 October made grim reading: that is, the War Office made no attempt to mislead it concerning the extent of British losses, however over-optimistic its conjectures regarding German losses. From 31 July to 5 October, the British army in Flanders had sustained casualties of 150,000, with, according to the War Minister Lord Derby, a further 40,000 casualties since the start of October. That is, the War Cabinet learned that after 2½ months of campaigning, with Haig's army not in sight of the Belgian coast and not even expected to reach the Klerken Ridge, with the projected invasion from the sea plainly vanished from sight, and with rain now falling unrelentingly, Haig had sustained casualties approaching 200,000 men.

At the same time, the War Cabinet was coming under pressure from the French to take over more line on the Western Front, so as to facilitate French operations elsewhere and enable them to employ troops in bringing in the harvest. Haig and Robertson made it clear that this course was incompatible with continuation of the Flanders offensive.

Here then were two powerful reasons for forthwith abandoning the offensive: its appalling toll in casualties, and the needs of Britain's major ally. The War Cabinet declined to seize either opportunity. On 24 October it concluded that it could not agree with the French to extend the British sector of the Western Front while the present offensive was proceeding and while the matter of whether or not to resume it in the spring remained unresolved. Yet more bizarre was the War Cabinet's response to casualty figures. Far from being dismayed by the huge losses so far sustained, what led to expressions of concern were the exaggerated reports circulating in the country regarding the extent of casualties. The opinion was expressed that the only way to scotch these false accounts was to publish the true figures.

In short, therefore, the civilian rulers of Britain, having expressed themselves utterly disenchanted with the campaign Haig was conducting, turned their backs on straightforward opportunities to bring it to a halt. What is painfully evident, at every stage from 31 July onwards, is the Prime Minister and War Cabinet's refusal to accept responsibility for military operations occurring only with their authority. First they appeared reluctant to notice what was going on in the major area of Britain's military endeavours, while devoting much attention to areas of but trivial importance. Then they began noticing what was going on, drawing the most negative conclusions and rejecting opportunities to act on these conclusions.

These are the actions of onlookers, of commentators, of Cassandras, of a body feeling no responsibility for the course of events. They are not the responses of men who, having hesitatingly authorised the campaign, intend to act on their assertion that they will stop it the moment it becomes evident that it is not producing the promised results. That was not because Lloyd George and his colleagues were unaware that, under the British constitution, strategy was their business. They understood it perfectly well when Nivelle's offensive was on offer, or when operations against Turkey were under discussion. There, they would take the decision, and the military authorities would act accordingly. But for no evident reason, the campaign in Flanders was different. The War Cabinet foresaw failure, and refused to call a halt. Indeed there was a large positive consequence of Lloyd George's chillingly negative announcement on 11 October that 'we would not capture the Klerken Ridge and he would call the War Cabinet's attention to this in three weeks' time'. This forewarning of failure and futility constituted his authorisation that, for another terrible month of rain and mud, the Passchendaele campaign would continue.

Notes

1   Roy Jenkins, *Asquith: Portrait of a Man and an Era*, Collins, London, 1964, pages 350–1, 371.
2   A.J.P. Taylor (ed.), *Lloyd George: a diary by Frances Stevenson*, London, Hutchinson, 1971, p.139.
3   Quotations from the War Cabinet and War Policy Committee in the following pages are drawn from their minutes contained in CAB 23 and CAB 27.
4   See, for example, Arthur Bryant, *English Saga (1840–1940)*, The Reprint Society, London, 1942, pages 293–294.

Chapter 9

War Experience and Armistice Conditions: Generals and Politicians

Bullitt Lowry

The German request in October 1918 that Woodrow Wilson should arrange an armistice caught the Allied generals and admirals, like the Allied politicians, by surprise. Only six months before, the generals had been planning what to do should their front lines collapse, but in mid-summer, the situation had turned dramatically in favour of the Allies.[1] Since 8 August, the advance of the Allied armies had been continuous. Yet German resistance remained strong, and even in September, none of the generals suspected that the Germans were nearing the end of their will to fight. Indeed, with the Allied and American forces extending their supply lines to inefficient lengths and the winter's adverse conditions approaching, the Allied and American generals were preparing for a great offensive in 1919, not an armistice in 1918.[2]

Then in September, Bulgaria sued for, and got, an armistice. The Bulgarian surrender materially worsened the already declining fortunes of the Germans, cutting their south-eastern supply lines. With Bulgaria out of the war and with Austria-Hungary not far behind, the Germans sooner or later would have to face an Allied assault on their undefended southern frontier. When realisation of that fact was added to their defeat on the Western Front and the long-term effects of the blockade, Ludendorff, perhaps hoping for a respite as much as for an end to the war, pushed Germany's political leaders to seek an armistice.[3] The German request went to President Wilson on 3 October, 1918.

The Allied prime ministers (the United States was not an Ally, but an 'Associated Power') were meeting to discuss the strategic situation stemming from the surrender of Bulgaria when they got word of the German request.[4] To put the discussion that followed in context, it is necessary to remember that the German note of 3 October was not the first time the warring nations had mentioned peace talks. In early October 1918, the Allied leaders had no more reason to suspect that this overture would lead directly to peace than any earlier proposals had. They saw the First German Note as a splendid omen, but it offered no assurance of a quick German surrender.

Another important point is that prior to World War I, an armistice – historically, a temporary suspension of hostilities – usually was arranged so that diplomats could discuss a peace treaty. For that reason, an armistice usually provided simply that hostilities cease. Thus, it might have been expected that an armistice in the fall of 1918 would specify only a pause in the fighting, with the opposing armies remaining in place while the diplomats negotiated peace terms. Instead, the armistice with Germany became a peace treaty in miniature, and in that metamorphosis, the Allied and American generals and admirals played a crucial role.

The command structure that had emerged from four years of war reflected different attempts to get efficient direction over the Allied and American armies. Until late 1917, no instrument of overall control, political or military, existed. Then, following the terrible Italian defeat at Caporetto, the Allied political leaders gathered at Rapallo and created the Supreme War Council, composed of the prime minister and a 'member of the government' of each of the Allied nations, with the United States, finally a belligerent, usually represented by diplomatic liaison officers.[5] At Rapallo, the politicians also established a military committee, the Military Representatives to the Supreme War Council, to give them military advice, while at the same time keeping the generals at arm's length from decision-making. At first, the generals nominated as Military Representatives were powerful ones, but after the crisis over unified command in the spring of 1918, when Ferdinand Foch of France became Commander-in-Chief of the Allied and American armies on the Western Front, power moved to him from the Military Representatives, who thereafter limited their actions to technical advice at the call of the Supreme War Council.

The Allied prime ministers, responding to the German note of 3 October, drew up a brief guide of eight points as an outline of what they wanted an armistice to contain. The central requirements of that eight-point guide were that the Germans should evacuate French, Belgian, and Luxembourger territory immediately, and that the German army should retire behind the Rhine – which would mean a German evacuation of Alsace, Lorraine, and the Rhineland. Without spending a great deal of thought on the matter, the political leaders referred their sketchy eight-point draft to the Military Representatives to the Supreme War Council. At the same time, on the orders of French premier Georges Clemenceau, Marshal Foch drew up his own set of terms.

The Military Representatives, along with some admirals, fattened out the politicians' eight-point guide, but their draft never became a basis for further discussion.[6] Marshal Foch's draft did, and in fact, it became the core of the final armistice document signed on November 11.[7] That draft reflected not only Foch's military analysis, but also what he had learned from four years of war and seven months of supreme command.

Ferdinand Foch was a devout Catholic and devoted patriot. His moral courage was great, and he persevered with determination when he was faced with any reverse, but of course, only generals who exhibited that level of perseverance survived the test of the Great War. It is possible that the deaths in action early in the war of Foch's only surviving son and of one of his two sons-in-law further committed him never to seek any sort of compromise with Germany, so that at the end of the war, whatever moderation he showed demonstrated an intellectual evolution of sorts.

His mind was incisive and penetrating, but not subtle; his thought moved in straight lines. Before the war, his theoretical approach to war was a bit sterile, even metaphysical.[8] Although he had never, perhaps, adopted the extremist offensive doctrines of Colonel Grandmaison, he still had little use for the defensive, and he favoured too much what was almost a spiritual approach to combat. To him, moral factors were pre-eminent: will and courage would triumph. Before the war, he did not see that they do indeed triumph when they are supported by superior fire power and superior tactics and strategy, but by themselves they are only a reckless recipe for frightful casualties. The blackboards and library of the *Ecole Supérieure de Guerre* simply had not provided him with the reality of modern war, but four years of immersion in the Great War modified his thinking. Tempered in the fearsome battles of the war, his audacity became less pronounced, and he matured dramatically, both as a strategist and as a tactician.

In his draft of armistice terms, Foch required the evacuation of Belgian, French, and Luxembourger territory and the provinces of Alsace and Lorraine, which the Allies would occupy immediately. Foch required the Germans to carry out the evacuation of all this land within two weeks, which would require an extremely rapid German withdrawal, and he stated that the blockade would remain in force.

Another clause was inauspicious for Germany. Foch demanded 'possession of securities (*gages*)' for reparations. The Allies would get those securities in the form of an occupation of all German territory on the left bank of the Rhine. Foch did not necessarily foreshadow the annexation of the Rhineland here, but he was hinting at large reparations and probable later territorial acquisitions. In that way, Foch believed, the war would have meaning for France, and the sacrifice of so much blood and treasure would not have been without result. The absolutist in Foch was always near the surface. He had fought too long and too hard to let victory slip away.

Foch also required bridgeheads *across* the upper Rhine at Rastadt, Strasbourg, and Neuf-Brisach, the bridgeheads to consist of thirty-kilometre semi-circles on the right bank. With this provision, Foch was demanding territory on the eastern bank of the Rhine. His insistence on control of the great defensive barrier of the Rhine suggests that the war had taught him a more balanced view of the power of modern defence than he had once supported.

Foch's military proposals, given on 8 October, formed the core of the armistice Germany signed on 11 November. The only major additions were a demand for the surrender of specified military and railroad *matériel*, financial clauses, clauses concerning the Eastern Front, and naval terms. In summary, where the prime ministers had created a brief document that retained, but did not greatly increase, the military supremacy of the Allies and the United States, Foch's clauses would magnify that supremacy immensely. Furthermore, Foch's demand for what was, in effect, the immediate retrocession of Alsace and Lorraine, the occupation of the entire left bank of the Rhine, and bridgeheads across the upper Rhine also had major political implications not included in the prime ministers' draft.

With the prime ministers having several drafts for an armistice before them, they nonetheless avoided making decisions and adjourned when they were satisfied that President Wilson was on the right course in his negotiations with the Germans. For the next week, the Allied High Commands did very little concerning an armistice. Then, on 19 October, the British cabinet began a series of meetings to define what they wanted from an armistice and what terms they wanted an armistice to contain. The cabinet brought Field Marshal Sir Douglas Haig, the British Commander-in-Chief in France, back from the Continent and heard him and Sir Henry Wilson, the Chief of the Imperial General Staff, as well as their admirals, describe what terms an armistice should include.

Field Marshal Haig was far more than a dour Scot of limited imagination, the picture derived from the character assassination of World War I generals that took hold of the public mind between the wars. To begin with, he was poised and courteous, a man who seldom raised his voice or lost his composure. His heritage and training, as well as his ingrained shyness, had taught him not to let his emotions show to others, although his strong feelings and sorrow at the terrible slaughter of World War I emerge clearly from the pages of his manuscript diary.

He was tenacious, and although there is a fine line between tenacity and obstinacy, no one less tough-minded could have exercised the command he held successfully. After he took command of the British Expeditionary Force, he was subjected to the soul-searing pressures of ultimate responsibility, and he rose to the challenge. His refusal to accept honours and awards until Parliament arranged pensions for survivors and widows is well-known, but his finest hour came at Doullens in March 1918, when he subordinated himself to Foch for the common good.

Some generals go through the fire of war and become inhuman, partly because of knowing that they were responsible for the deaths of countless thousands. Others emerge stronger and more deeply impressed with the true value of human life. Haig was one of the latter. In contrast, the Chief of the Imperial General Staff, Sir Henry Wilson, never really saw soldiers, or his subordinates, or his colleagues, as people. They were marionettes jerking to scripts based on his own intrigues. He manipulated people, but he never developed any true sympathy for them.

Haig had seen Foch's terms and feared them, for he believed that they would lengthen the war to no real purpose.[9] He had even told Clemenceau that all the Allies needed to do was order the Germans to hand over Metz and Strasbourg as a sign of good faith, and then the Allies could draft peace terms.[10] Unlike Haig's compassionate moderation, Sir Henry Wilson, driven by fear of Bolshevism, loathing for Woodrow Wilson's Fourteen Points, and a vain hope that somehow he could impose conscription on restive Ireland, had little use for an armistice. If there were to be one, however, it must afford the Allies a complete and indisputable victory. Insofar as Sir Henry's thinking went, he wanted an armistice that would totally disarm the Germans and provide for the occupation of all German territory up to the Rhine, but not across it.

Neither Sir Henry nor Haig thought that Germany was about to collapse. Haig believed that it was enough for the Allies to propose moderate terms the Germans would accept. To be sure, the terms must give the Allies victory, but it was unnecessary to crush the Germans to the dust. Sir Henry, for his part, would accept nothing short of a Carthaginian victory; if he could not get that sort of victory now, he preferred nothing at all.

In front of the cabinet, each maintained his position.[11] Haig, usually taciturn, waxed voluble as he expounded his belief that the only effective army in the fall of 1918 was the British one. Expanding on this point in his diary, Haig commented that 'the British alone might bring the enemy to his knees. But why expend more British lives – and for what?' Haig was prepared to end the war quickly, if it could be done sensibly and in a way that protected British interests.

In the meantime, the British naval leaders had been developing their proposals for an armistice. Admiral Sir Rosslyn Wemyss, the First Sea Lord, had been in contact with the dashing commander of the Grand Fleet at Scapa Flow, Sir David Beatty.[12] Beatty was a man of great personal bravery, with his most conspicuous characteristic being his impetuosity. Supporting those two pieces of his personality was sheer, continuing, good luck in his professional life. If Haig, earlier in his career, had borne the nickname of 'Lucky', Beatty had more of the reality of it. Owing to his luck and his bravery, Beatty had distinguished himself as a junior officer in operations up the Nile against the Mahdi. This had set him on the road which saw him a rear-admiral before he was forty, an age that was the average for making captain. All his life had been one easy lope to success, and he never seemed to believe that others could fail to share his inclinations and intentions. Their failure to do so was, to him, only a wilful denial of facts. And most important, in the matter of the armistice, like other matters, he abhorred compromise, and his experiences in the war had taught him nothing to the contrary.

Beatty rose to highest command because of dash, bravery, and luck. Wemyss, the First Sea Lord at the end of the war, was a bureaucratic seaman, well-connected to the monarchy, and widely regarded within the Senior Service as only a 'Court' sailor. Although he had succeeded Admiral Sir John Jellicoe at the Admiralty in a murky power struggle late in the war, he never really gained the moral authority of his predecessors, even though he was an able and thoughtful administrator. He got on poorly with Beatty, who spent a great deal of his time after 1919 trying to ensure that Wemyss shared in none of the rewards given the most senior leaders of the army and navy. Yet despite their personal strains at the end of the war and later, they worked together well enough on armistice terms.

Between them, they wanted the surrender of all German submarines, dreadnoughts, and battle cruisers, as well as six light cruisers and fifty destroyers. When Wemyss presented these terms to the cabinet, the politicians appeared stricken. 'This amounted to abject surrender,' Prime Minister David Lloyd George exclaimed. The cabinet adjourned without making a decision.

On the 21st, they reassembled, and Admiral Wemyss stood firmly behind the navy's extreme terms.[13] Wemyss explained that his thinking was based on the assumption that the nation would not renew hostilities once the armistice was signed. As a consequence, 'the terms of the armistice should approximate to what it was desired to obtain in the peace.' If the British reduced their claims, the naval victory would not be equal to the victory 'on shore' and 'we should not reap the fruits of victory at sea.'

Admiral Beatty had left the Grand fleet at Scapa Flow and hurried to London so that he might present the harsh terms he thought were indispensable. A major British war aim, he said, was to destroy German naval militarism. The naval terms must reduce Germany to a 'second-rate Naval Power.' The standard by which Beatty judged how many ships Germany must surrender was the result of a hypothetical battle between the two great war fleets. In such a battle, Germany would lose most of its ships, he claimed. Judging from the results of Jutland in 1916, that was an optimistic claim, but optimism was, after all, Beatty's stock-in-trade. His conclusion was that the Allies must force Germany to surrender all the ships listed earlier. Once again, the cabinet made no final decision on the issue.

Facing the admirals' continued insistence on those extreme terms several days later, Lloyd George said he feared that demanding the surrender of all those German ships would be so 'humiliating' that the Germans would

TERMS OF ARMISTICE WITH GERMANY.

(The French text is the official one; the English and German texts are translations).

CONDITIONS DE L'ARMISTICE AVEC L'ALLEMAGNE.

Entre le MARÉCHAL FOCH, Commandant en Chef des Armées Alliées, stipulant au nom des Puissances Alliées et Associées, assisté de l'AMIRAL WEMYSS, First Sea Lord, d'une part ; et

M. le Secrétaire d'État ERZBERGER, Président de la Délégation Allemande,

M. l'Envoyé Extraordinaire et Ministre Plénipotentiaire COMTE VON OBERNDORFF,

M. le GÉNÉRAL-MAJOR VON WINTERFELDT,

M. le CAPITAINE DE VAISSEAU VANSELOW,

munis de pouvoirs réguliers et agissant avec l'agrément du Chancelier Allemand, d'autre part,

il a été conclu un Armistice aux conditions suivantes.

CONDITIONS DE L'ARMISTICE CONCLU AVEC L'ALLEMAGNE.

A.—SUR LE FRONT D'OCCIDENT.

I.—Cessation des hostilités, sur terre et dans les airs, 6 heures après la signature de l'Armistice.

II.—Évacuation immédiate des pays envahis : Belgique, France, Luxembourg—ainsi que de l'Alsace-Lorraine—réglée de manière à être réalisée dans un délai de 15 jours à dater de la signature de l'Armistice.

Les troupes allemandes, qui n'auront pas évacué les territoires prévus dans les délais fixés, seront faites prisonnières de guerre.

L'occupation par l'ensemble des troupes alliées et des États-Unis suivra, dans ces pays, la marche de l'évacuation.

Tous les mouvements d'évacuation ou d'occupation sont réglés par la Note Annexe No. 1, arrêtée au moment de la signature de l'Armistice.

TERMS OF ARMISTICE WITH GERMANY.

Between MARSHAL FOCH, Commander-in-Chief of the Allied Armies, acting in the name of the Allied and Associated Powers, with ADMIRAL WEMYSS, First Sea Lord, on the one hand, and

HERR ERZBERGER, Secretary of State, President of the German Delegation,

COUNT VON OBERNDORFF, Envoy Extraordinary and Minister Plenipotentiary,

MAJOR-GENERAL VON WINTERFELDT,

CAPTAIN VANSELOW (German Navy),

duly empowered and acting with the concurrence of the German Chancellor on the other hand.

An Armistice has been concluded on the following conditions :—

CONDITIONS OF THE ARMISTICE CONCLUDED WITH GERMANY.

A.—CLAUSES RELATING TO THE WESTERN FRONT.

I.—Cessation of hostilities by land and in the air six hours after the signing of the Armistice.

II.—Immediate evacuation of the invaded countries — Belgium, France, Luxemburg, as well as Alsace-Lorraine—so ordered as to be completed within 15 days from the signature of the Armistice.

German troops which have not left the above-mentioned territories within the period fixed shall be made prisoners of war.

Occupation by the Allied and United States Forces jointly shall keep pace with the evacuation in these areas.

All movements of evacuation and occupation shall be regulated in accordance with a Note (Annexe 1) determined at the time of the signing of the Armistice.

BEDINGUNGEN DES WAFFENSTILLSTANDES MIT DEUTSCHLAND.

Zwischen MARSCHALL FOCH, Oberbefehlshaber der Alliierten Armeen, bevollmächtigt durch die Alliierten und Assoziierten Mächte, zugleich mit ADMIRAL WEMYSS, dem Ersten "Sea Lord," einerseits, und dem Staatssekretär ERZBERGER, Präsident der deutschen Gesandtschaft, ausserordentlicher Gesandter und Bevollmächtigter Minister GRAF VON OBERNDORFF, Generalmajor VON WINTERFELDT, Kapitän zur See VANSELOW, beauftragt mit regelmässigen Vollmachten und bevollmächtigt durch die Autorität des deutschen Kanzlers andererseits.

Ein Waffenstillstand ist unter den folgenden Bedingungen geschlossen worden :—

BEDINGUNGEN DES MIT DEUTSCHLAND GESCHLOSSENEN WAFFENSTILLSTANDES.

A.—AN DER WESTFRONT.

I.—Ende der Feindseligkeiten auf dem Lande und in der Luft sechs Stunden nach der Unterzeichnung des Waffenstillstandes.

II.—Sofortige Räumung der überfallenen Länder : Belgien, Frankreich, Luxemburg, wie auch Elsass-Lothringen, die auf eine solche Weise zu folgen hat, dass sie 15 Tage nach der Unterzeichnung des Waffenstillstandes vollzogen worden ist.

Deutsche Truppen, welche die obenerwähnten Länder nicht in den festgesetzten Fristen verlassen haben, werden zu Kriegsgefangenen gemacht.

Besetzung dieser Gebiete durch die Truppen der Alliierten und der Vereinigten Staaten zusammen, wird mit der Räumung jener Hand in Hand gehen.

Alle Bewegungen der Räumung und der Besetzung sollen, gemäss einer Anmerkung (Anhang 1), die zur Zeit der Unterzeichnung des Waffenstillstandes festgesetzt wird, geregelt werden.

(i)   The terms as finally agreed: Part of the first page of an eleven-page document.
[S.G.R. Baker: Liddle Collection]

refuse to sign an armistice.[14] Here the cabinet produced a hazy formula and adopted it as policy:

> The naval conditions of the armistice should represent the admission of German defeat by sea in the same degree as the military conditions recognise the corresponding admission of German defeat by land.

The critical British cabinet meetings dealing with military and naval armistice terms made no binding decisions concerning terms to offer Germany. In his diary, Sir Henry Wilson summarized the whole sprawling debate: Haig 'weak in his terms of armistice. David Beatty excellent. Most of Cabinet including L[loyd] G[eorge] and S[ecretary of State for War] Milner rather weak.'[15] In any case, Lloyd George could go off to negotiate with the Allies and Americans with his hands free.

In France during this same period, there were no great arguments over armistice terms. There was real animosity between Clemenceau and Foch, but it sprang from personality conflicts, not differences over what the armistice with Germany should contain. Clemenceau distrusted Foch's clerical and conservative politics and disliked him personally, but he was entirely happy with Foch's terms and never made any real effort to amend the marshal's draft. Both the Premier and the marshal wanted terms that would mean an incontestable victory over Germany. Foch's terms met those wishes.

The two men did quarrel over other matters during these weeks in October. First, Foch wanted an active role in the negotiations among the Allies and the United States over the armistice, and Clemenceau, jealous of his own power, refused to cede an iota of it to Foch.[16] Except for that issue, the most important matter over which Foch and Clemenceau fought in October 1918 was Clemenceau's belief that Foch was not getting full value from the American soldiers. Clemenceau felt that the Commander-in-Chief of the American Expeditionary Forces, General John J. Pershing, was incompetent. He wanted Foch either to replace Pershing or to force him to act effectively.

Ever since the United States declared war on Germany in April 1917, the Europeans had wanted to shift the burden of fighting to American shoulders. During the weeks of the rapid Allied advance after August 1918, the American forces were not doing as well as the French and British were. That situation disappointed the Europeans, who had counted on using American soldiers to protect their own men. More battle experience would teach the American Expeditionary Forces what they needed to be effective, but as the days passed and more Allied soldiers died while the Americans were learning the necessary lessons of modern war, the European leaders became increasingly testy about the price being paid.

Foch understood all the elements of this situation, and he refused to do what Clemenceau wanted.[17] He did speak to Pershing about pressing forward more effectively than Pershing was doing, and more important, he moved the American Expeditionary Forces organisationally from under the French Army to give it a status equal to that of the British.[18] That move may have helped American pride, but the only thing that the United States' forces really needed to become more effective was experience, which they were gaining daily.

Early on the morning of 25 October, Marshal Foch sent messages to the Allied commanders asking them to meet at his headquarters in Senlis that afternoon to discuss terms of armistice for Germany.[19] The day before, Foch, Clemenceau, and the Commander-in-Chief of the French Armies, Henri-Philippe Pétain, had met to go over Foch's draft of armistice conditions.[20] Pétain, in contrast to Foch, was an exponent of the defence, not the offence, but he was thoroughly overshadowed by Foch and played no truly independent role here or elsewhere in the armistice negotiations. The prime minister and the two military leaders made no major changes in Foch's original draft; the only substantive change was to substitute bridgeheads on the middle Rhine – Köln, Mainz, and Koblenz – for the upper Rhine bridgeheads specified in Foch's original draft.

Now, on the 25th, Foch met with the national commanders and their chiefs of staff. At this meeting, Pétain presented Foch's draft, which he and Clemenceau had examined the day before. Haig predictably argued that the German army was not so beaten that the Germans would accept Foch's harsh provisions. Pershing presented his own set of terms, which duplicated Foch's in nearly every particular. At Senlis, there was no free discussion, and Foch adjourned the meeting without a vote. Nevertheless, it was clear that Pershing supported Foch's terms, and Haig thought them too difficult. In fact, Haig left the meeting thinking that severe terms would only encourage Bolshevism in Germany, and he continued to believe that French insistence on occupying the left bank of the Rhine was simply an underhanded way to get control over the Rhineland.[21]

When Foch got back to Paris, he amended his original draft slightly and gave it to Clemenceau.[22] First, Foch required the Germans to evacuate Allied territory and Alsace-Lorraine within fourteen days, and to surrender 2,500 heavy cannon, 2,500 light cannon, 3,000 trench mortars, and 30,000 machine guns, numbers that Foch explained would constitute about one-third of Germany's artillery and one-half of its machine guns. The Germans must evacuate the left bank of the Rhine, with the Allies establishing bridgeheads having a thirty-kilometre radius at Köln, Mainz, and Koblenz; the Germans must evacuate a neutral zone along the right bank from the Netherlands to Switzerland. The Germans also had to surrender 5,000 locomotives and 150,000 railroad cars, and the blockade would remain in effect. Foch's post-Senlis draft differed from his 8 October draft only in a few details and in the selection of bridgeheads.

On 29 October, when the political leaders of the Allies and the United

States met in Paris and began their deliberations over granting Germany an armistice, the issues that Foch's terms raised and other political issues were by no means settled. Foch assumed occupation of the left bank of the Rhine, to which Clemenceau gained grudging British and American agreement. Foch also assumed large reparation payments, to which the Allied and American leaders agreed in seeming defiance of President Wilson's principles, although in return the American representative got superficial agreement to Wilson's Fourteen Points. Thus, the Allied and American leaders assured some of their main war aims by inserting them in the armistice document.

The British naval leaders got the Allied Naval Council to support almost without exception the naval terms the British admirals wanted in the armistice, the terms given to the cabinet ten days before.[23] The terms of armistice, the British First Sea Lord continued to argue, must duplicate what they wanted in the peace.[24] As Admiral Wemyss summed up the naval terms, 'The naval terms are stiff – but not more so than they should be nor more than we deserve and is good for Europe.'[25]

There were a number of attempts to modify the British admirals' draft of naval terms, some by the French, who were not entirely convinced of the contribution that sea power had made to victory, others by the British Prime Minister, who may have wanted to make the armistice document seem more palatable to the Germans.[26] Foch was outspoken against the need for the armistice to do any more regarding the German navy than take the German submarines.[27]

After discussing internment of some ships, as opposed to surrender (surrender being what the British admirals wanted), the Allied and American leaders agreed on requiring the surrender of only Germany's submarines and the internment, not the surrender, of Germany's listed surface ships – the Dreadnoughts, battle cruisers, light cruisers, and destroyers. Those surface vessels would go to neutral ports 'or failing them (neutral ports) Allied ports.'[28] That was a farce. No real attempt was ever made to locate a neutral nation willing to supervise the internment of those warships, and the major German vessels ended up at Britain's great wartime harbour of Scapa Flow, for all practical purposes, surrendered.

One event startled the Allied leaders. The commander of the American Expeditionary Forces delivered a letter to the Allied leaders on 30 October in which he seemed to oppose granting an armistice at all.[29] His motives are obscure. Pershing was not a subtle man, being self-contained, a bit plodding in his mental processes, and not given to introspection.[30] Sufficient evidence of the barrenness of his imagination can be seen in his *Final Report* of 1919, which, in the words of one of his biographers, 'lacked life, warmth, color, and names.'[31]

Nevertheless, Pershing could be personally charming, he was certainly capable of tact and graciousness in social situations, and in his personal habits (other than women) he was abstemious. Capable of prodigious effort, he could sustain it over long periods of time. He needed that ability because he was loathe to delegate responsibility to his subordinates and thus did far more of the detailed work of the headquarters than he should have. For his slowness of mental processes he compensated with an attention to detail and an energetic doggedness, which went a long way to repair any deficiencies he may have had.

He tended to see the war as a way for the United States to make its mark on world affairs, and perhaps as a way that he, himself, might make a mark on world affairs. After all, someone had to win the Republican nomination for President of the United States in 1920, and successful generals had won presidential nomination and election handily enough in the past. In fact, every major American war to that time had propelled a general into the presidency.

Two schools of thought exist on Pershing's motives for sending his letter to the Supreme War Council opposing the granting of any armistice. One is that he mistrusted President Wilson and Wilson's Fourteen Points. Therefore, he wanted to undermine his commander-in-chief and force a very harsh armistice on Germany. Thus, there would never be any question of Germany's seeking refuge behind the Fourteen Points and possibly evading retribution.[32] The other explanation is more repellent: Pershing had not yet had a great battlefield victory, and he wanted to have one to his credit before ending the war.[33] Neither interpretation does Pershing much honour, and whatever the truth, his letter had no effect on the drafting of the armistice.[34]

The critical piece of the politicians' thinking about granting an armistice came with the question asked of Foch on 31 October.[35] Was it better to make an armistice or to continue the war? Foch had answered bluntly:

> I do not make war for the purpose of making war but for the purpose of getting results. If the Germans sign an armistice with the conditions recognized as necessary to guarantee to us the results, I am satisfied. No one has the right to prolong the bloodshed longer.

With the terms that Foch had proposed for the land forces and the terms that the British admirals had proposed for the German navy (however modified they may have been by the requirement for internment, not surrender, of the surface fleet), the Allies and the United States would have their 'guarantee' of results. When to those terms were added terms requiring the Germans to evacuate the Eastern Front when the Allies demanded it and other provisions securing all the loose assets of Germany, there was no way that Germany could resume the war if peace negotiations broke down after the armistice went into effect. The Germans would have to accept whatever peace provisions the Allies and the United States chose to impose on them.

None of the Allied leaders, political or military, expected the Germans to accept these armistice terms immediately. The belief was that Germany would reject them initially, but ultimately accept them after another Allied offensive, probably in the spring of 1919. The sudden deterioration of the German domestic situation in the first days of November caught everyone, Germans as well as Allies, by surprise. By 8 November, when Marshal Foch and Admiral Wemyss presented the armistice terms to the German delegates in the railroad car at Rethondes, the Germans had little choice other than to accept them.

Some obvious points emerge from this brief examination of the various High Commanders and the armistice with Germany. What terms the Allies would give the Germans was ultimately a political decision, of course; and for one reason or another, none of the military or naval leaders trusted their political superiors. Therefore, the generals and the admirals exerted their full strengths to support their visions of what an armistice must contain. In many cases they came perilously close to insubordination, the most obvious instances being Pershing's letter of 30 October and the British admirals' fight against leniency in the naval terms.

To be sure, the generals and admirals ought to have been the ones to determine the technical conditions for ending the fighting, because they were the experts. In 1918, however, Foch and the British admirals ventured far beyond technical armistice terms and moved into what were really peace provisions, and they became one of the forces that caused the armistice to metamorphose into a preliminary peace treaty.

It is also clear that the generals did not speak with one voice; nor did they function even as a loosely co-ordinated group. The agency that had been established expressly to give military advice to the political leaders, the Military Representatives, played no role in ending the war. The national commanders met as a group only once, on 25 October at Senlis, and then they did not act jointly. It was Marshal Foch who dominated the content of the military terms, and the British admirals who dominated the content of the naval provisions.

The five-week period considered in this survey of the high command and the armistice does allow insight into what the experience of the war had done to those leaders of millions of fighting men. Some leaders had grown; some had not. Neither John J. Pershing nor David Beatty changed dramatically as a result of the high commands they held. Pershing was insulated from events, perhaps by the comparatively short time he served on the Western Front as much as by any deficiencies of mind or spirit. His ambition for post-war political office may also have served as a countervailing force to growth.

So far as Beatty was concerned, it is hard to escape observing that he did not fight in the same kind of war as his colleagues on land did. Indeed, he is the only one of the High Command who consciously and openly gloated over the discomfiture of the Germans during surrender ceremonies, which strikes a somewhat sour note.[36] He had led his forces into battle only a handful of times, and the nature of naval warfare was such that he was a participant in those actions, exposed to death or disability as much as the youngest seaman. His personal bravery was beyond reproach, and he certainly carried as much of a burden of the responsibility for ultimate success as any general could have shouldered – as, in a different world, he would have carried the onus of failure. But the circumstances of land and naval war differed from each other. Naval warfare in World War I between giant battleships and battle cruisers may have held a few moments of sheer terror, but those moments were not like the spirit-numbing ferocity of trench warfare. On the sea was none of the constant attrition of the trenches; it was a question of being on watch, but usually not at arms. Thus, Beatty did not have to develop the same mental qualities that the generals had to develop: the ability and the moral strength which enabled them to order men into battle, day after day.

In that crucible of war on land, Haig grew. From the sometime commander of the 17th Lancers, he grew through the chaos, and failures, and deaths of 1916 and 1917 to emerge in 1918 as one of the great men of the twentieth century. His strengths in generalship were enormous, his compassion was clear, but in the final analysis, he does not measure up as one of the great captains of history. In fact, for whatever reason, none of these men in highest command from 1914 to 1918 did, except Foch.

Although Foch's theoretical shortcomings, noted above, handicapped him at the start of the war, he grew past them. His audacity lessened, which is seen most vividly in his postponement of the proposed Lorraine Offensive, a great Franco–American attack that would have involved more than 30 divisions and 600 tanks.[37] Responding to a spirit of parsimony concerning the lives of soldiers now that an armistice was possible, Foch postponed that attack several times, and it was never launched. The theoretical Foch of the *Ecole Supérieure de Guerre* would not have postponed it.

The theoretical Foch of prewar years would not have stopped before the visible destruction of the enemy, either. A wiser Foch, tempered in the Great War, did. It was essential to realize, Foch argued in his memoirs a decade later, that in November 1918, the Allies did not have the power to bring about the immediate destruction of the German army in the field.[38] The Allies and the United States could have continued forcing the German soldiers to retreat, taking prisoners and capturing guns, but they could not have prevented the Germans from crossing the Rhine and fortifying themselves behind it. The Allies and the United States could have spent many lives to get, later, perhaps no more than they got in November, and what they got in November, Foch believed, was entirely sufficient.

'Because war is a means,' Foch said just before his death in an echo of

Clausewitz. 'it is not an end.'[39] A nation makes war 'solely to make the adversary submit to his will, *all his will.*' The Germans, when they signed the armistice, were submitting to all the will of their foes. 'What would it gain to ask more?'

Notes

1 PRO War Office Archives; W.O. 33/878, Organisation of Lines of Communication in Event of Operations in United Kingdom, May 1918. PRO Foreign Office Archives: F.O. 371/3214, No. 111908, Derby to Foreign Office, 20 June 1918.

2 One telling point is that they had made no preparations for an armistice. The British War Cabinet had ordered the army and navy leaders to prepare material on armistice terms for Germany, but nothing had come of it yet, PRO Cabinet Office Archives: CAB 23/8, War Cabinet 480, 1 October 1918. Edmonds states that the General Staff had studied armistice terms before October 1918, but no fruits of that effort had reached high-level discussion, J.E. Edmonds and R. Maxwell-Hyslop, *Military Operations, France and Belgium, 1918*, vol. 5, London, H.M. Stationery Office, 1947, p. 183; Charles, Lord Hardinge, *Old Diplomacy*, London, Murray, 1947, p. 229. David Stevenson, *French War Aims Against Germany, 1914–1919*, Oxford, Clarendon Press, 1982, p. 110.

3 Because many of the relevant German General Staff documents were destroyed at the end of 1945, it may never be possible to piece all the German events together, but see Lernser to Foreign Office, General Headquarters, 1 October 1918, Germany, Reichskanzlei, *Preliminary History of the Armistice*, trans. Carnegie Endowment for International Peace, New York, Oxford University Press, 1924, p. 40.

4 PRO Cabinet Office Archives: CAB 28/5, I.C. –76, Procès-verbal of a Conference, 5 October 1918.

5 Rapallo Agreement of November 1917, Minutes of a Conference, Rapallo, 7 November 1917, Annex I, United States Department of the Army, *The United States Army in the World War, 1917–1919*, vol. 2, Washington, Government Printing Office, 1948, p. 72; this work cited hereafter as *U.S. Army*.

6 Bliss to Adjutant-General for Baker and March, 8 October 1918, *U.S Army*, vol. 10, pp. 6–7. To the usual Military Representatives, Generals Sackville-West, Belin, and di Robilant, were added the British CIGS and several admirals. The United States' Military Representative, Tasker Bliss, chose not to attend, fearing unnecessarily some deep Allied plot, and he sent several staff officers in his place.

7 PRO Cabinet Office Archives; CAB 28/5, Appendix I to I.C.–80, Conference of Prime Ministers, 8 October 1918. Ferdinand Foch, *Mémoires pour servir à L'histoire de la guerre de 1914–1918*, vol. 2, Paris, Plon, 1931, pp. 270–272.

8 Stefan D Posany and Etienne Mantoux, 'Du Picq and Foch: The French School,' *Makers of Modern Strategy*, ed. Edward Mead Earle, Princeton, Princeton University Press, 1952, p. 220.

9 National Library of Scotland, Papers of Field Marshal the Earl Haig of Bemersyde; H 132, Haig diary, 10 October 1918.

10 Ibid., 13 October 1918.

11 PRO Cabinet Office Archives; CAB 23/17, War Cabinet X–29, 19 October 1918. The diaries of Haig and Wilson (Wilson's is in the Imperial War Museum) agree with each other and the minutes. See also David Lloyd George, *War Memoirs*, vol. 6, London, Ivor Nicholson and Watson, 1936, pp. 3299–3304. Admiral Wemyss attended, but no representative of the newly independent air force was present, the Chief of the Air Staff giving his recommendations only on 22 October, PRO Cabinet Office Archives; CAB 24/67, Cabinet Paper G.T.–6076, Main Requirements of the Royal Air Force.

12 [British] National Maritime Museum, Papers of Admiral of the Fleet Earl Beatty; BTY/13/40/6, Wemyss to Beatty, 16 October 1918, BTY/13/40/7, Beatty to Wemyss, 17 October 1918, and BTY/13/40/9, Wemyss to Beatty, 18 October 1918.

13 PRO Cabinet Office Archives; CAB 23/14, War Cabinet 489A, 21 October 1918 (the minutes of this meeting were rearranged later).

14 PRO Cabinet Office Archives, CAB 23/14, War Cabinet 491B, 26 October 1918.

15 Imperial War Museum, Manuscripts, Papers of Field Marshal Sir Henry Hughes Wilson; HHW 1/32, Wilson diary, 21 October 1918. See also PRO War Office Archives; W.O. 158/25, 24 October 1918.

16 Foch to Clemenceau, 16 October 1918, Réné M.M. L'Hôpital, *Foch, L'armistice et la paix*, Paris, Plon, 1938, pp. 27–30. Clemenceau to Foch, 23 October 1918, ibid., pp. 33–34; Foch, *Mémoires*, vol. 2, pp. 276–279.

17 Henri Mordacq, *Le ministère Clemenceau: journal d'un témoin*,, vol. 2, Paris, Plon, 1931, pp. 244, 249. Library of Congress, Manuscripts Division, John J. Pershing Papers; box 4–5, Pershing diary, 3 and 8 October 1918.

18 Weygand, *Idéal vécu*, p. 628. Mordacq, *Le ministère Clemenceau*, vol. 2, pp. 277–278. Foch to Pétain, 16 October 1918, France, Ministère de la guerre, État-major de l'armée, Service historique, *Les armées françaises dans la Grande Guerre*, Tome 7, *Le campagne offensive de 1918 et la marche au Rhin (18 juillet 1918–28 juin 1919)*, Paris, Imprimerie Nationale, 1938, Annexes, p. 422; this work cited hereafter as *AFGG*. Foch, *Mémoires*, vol. 2, pp. 245–246.

19 Proceedings of a Military Conference at Senlis (Contemporary Translation), Notes on Conference Held at Senlis, 25 October 1918, *U.S. Army*, vol. 10, pp. 19–22. For additional material, see U.S. National Archives, Records of the American Expeditionary Forces; RG 120, box 1572, Proceedings, 25 October 1918. See also Henri Mordacq, *L'Armistice du 11 novembre: récit d'un témoin*, Paris, Plon, 1937, p. 156, and André Tardieu, *The Truth About the Treaty*, Indianapolis, Bobbs-Merrill, 1921, p. 60.

20 Maxime Weygand, *Idéal vécu*, Paris, Flammarion, 1953, pp. 634–635.

21 National Library of Scotland, Papers of Field Marshal the Earl Haig of Bemersyde; H 132, Haig diary, 25 October 1918.

22 Foch to Clemenceau, [26 October 1918], L'Hôpital, *Foch*, pp. 60–65.

23 [British] National Maritime Museum, Papers of Admiral of the Fleet Earl Beatty; BTY/7/11/9, Allied Naval Council, Report of the Six Meetings Held. . . October 28th to November 4th, 1918.

24 Churchill College, Cambridge University, Papers of Admiral of the Fleet Lord Wester-Wemyss; WMYS 7/11/4, Wemyss, Notes, 27 October–3 November 1918.

25 Ibid.
26 PRO Cabinet Office Archives; CAB 23/8, War Cabinet 497, Imperial War Cabinet 36, 5 November 1918.
27 PRO Cabinet Office Archives; CAB 28/5, I.C. −93, Procès-verbal of a Conference of Heads of Governments, 4 November 1918.
28 Service Historique des Armées de Terre, Archives, 6 N 42, text filed under date of 5 November 1918. The number of ships to be surrendered was marginally reduced from the admirals' first list of 18 October.
29 Pershing to Allied Supreme War Council, 30 October 1918, *U.S Army*, vol. 10, pp. 28–30.
30 Donald Smythe, *Pershing: General of the Armies*, Bloomington, Indiana University Press, 1986, pp. 238–244.
31 Ibid., p. 264.
32. See my 'Pershing and the Armistice,' *Journal of American History*, 1968, vol. 55, pp. 281–291.
33 That theory is supported by Daniel Beaver in an unpublished paper read to the annual meeting of the Society for Military History, Royal Military College, Kingston, Ontario, 1993. Pierre Renouvin comes to no conclusion between the two theories, giving them equal weight, *L'Armistice de Rethondes*, Paris, Gallimard, 1968, pp. 260–261.
34 Yale University, Edward M. House Collection; House diary, 30 October 1918. Library of Congress, Manuscripts Division, Woodrow Wilson Papers; Series II, House to Lansing for Wilson, 14, 31 October 1918. No discussion of the subject is recorded in the procès-verbal.
35 No secretary was present at that 31 October meeting. Weygand, *Idéal vécu*, p. 635, and Foch, *Mémoires*, vol. 2, p. 285, give substantially the same text. Some sources suggest that Foch said this first on 1 November, but it makes no difference. See also the variation in Paul Mantoux to House, 6 July 1920, Charles Seymour, *The Intimate Papers of Colonel House*, vol. 4, Boston and New York, Houghton Mifflin, 1928, p. 91.
36 Stephen Roskill, *Earl Beatty: The Last Naval Hero*, New York, Atheneum, 1981, p. 277.
37 Foch, *Mémoires*, vol.2, pp. 263–264. A French army group would attack on a 30-kilometre front from Metz to the Vosges while the Americans attacked along the French flank. De Castlenau to Foch, 23 October 1918, *AFGG*, tome 7, Annexes, pp. 553ff; Foch to Castlenau, 3 November 1918, ibid., p. 739; Foch to Pershing, 27 October 1918. ibid., p. 637; Foch to Pershing, 3 November 1918, ibid., p. 741.
38 Foch, *Mémoires*, vol. 2, pp. 269, 322: cf. Weygand, *Idéal vécu*, p. 633.
39 Raymond Recouly, *Le mémorial de Foch: mes entretiens avec le maréchal*, Paris, Editions de France, 1929, p. 30. Original in italics.

Part III

The Naval and Air War

Chapter 10

The German Naval War 1914–18: Strategy and Experience

Werner Rahn

Owing to the German Reich's position in Central Europe, with potential enemies in both East and West, the build-up of its navy was for a long time overshadowed by the Army. Until 1897, its strategic horizons were limited to forward coastal defence. It was not until the time of Alfred Tirpitz[1] that the systematic and determined building of a battle fleet got under way. Tirpitz regarded Great Britain as the most dangerous opponent at sea against whom Germany must have a certain degree of naval strength as an instrument of political power. Cruiser warfare was out of the question because of a lack of bases. The German Fleet would therefore have to deploy its greatest war effort between Heligoland and the Thames.

At the beginning of the twentieth century, the build-up of the German High Seas Fleet came at a time of enormous technical change in which weaponry quickly became obsolete.[2] In his strategic concept for the building of the Fleet, Tirpitz assumed that the Royal Navy would always act offensively in a war against Germany, establishing a blockade close in to the German coast. Such a blockade by major elements of the British Fleet would then create favourable conditions for Germany to enter into a decisive battle. On Germany's part, both strategic planning and practical fleet training were aimed at such an engagement. There was however, a great deal of confusion regarding the true purpose of a battle.[3] Notwithstanding the fact that the German Naval Command had willingly adopted Mahan's theory of sea power, they had paid only lip-service to a central element of that theory, namely the importance of geographical position and the resultant strategic options. This led to a wrong assessment of British strategy. Despite the tradition of offensive action in the Royal Navy, Britain never had a definite war plan which included a close blockade of Germany. It was considered that the development of such modern means of naval warfare as mining and the submarine made such an operation too risky.[4]

In August 1914 the German Imperial Navy was under the spell of the great superiority of the enemy in terms of material. In the North Sea alone the Royal Navy had twenty-six modern capital ships (battleships and battle cruisers) compared to only eighteen equally modern units of the German Navy. The British superiority in older ships of the line as well as cruisers and torpedo boats was even more striking.[5]

In view of this situation, the German Naval Command placed all its hopes on a reduction of enemy forces to be achieved through offensive submarine and mine-laying operations. Then, the fleet was to be employed in a battle 'under favourable conditions', still assuming that the opponent would seek battle as well.[6] It was not until the hoped-for balance of forces failed to materialise that long discussions took place on the remaining operational possibilities of the fleet. Plans for farther-reaching sorties involving greater danger were opposed by the Kaiser who formally was the Commander-in-Chief. He considered that the function of the High Seas Fleet was more and more a factor of political power that was to be kept intact and combat-ready until peace had been achieved. These thoughts were undoubtedly based on the hope that the question of winner or loser would be resolved by the land forces before long. The spiritual constraint under which High Seas Fleet personnel were thus held captives nicely contrasted with the liberty given to the then independent German raiders. In his book *Emden*, Prince Franz Joseph of Hohenzollern nicely captures the sense of freedom felt when the signal came '*Emden* detached. Good luck'. In the whole ship there was great rejoicing and excitement. 'At last we were to be on our own and could act independently, as we, or our Captain pleased. No sailor could ask more.'[7] This freedom was to bring further bounty in the variety of food supplies captured from the *Emden*'s victims though fate was to bring swift retribution to the German warship.

To return to the question of the employment of the High Seas Fleet, all considerations were eclipsed by the controversy about the political and military problems brought about by the submarine merchant war. Basically, the submarine warfare against the British sea lines of communication was a completely new strategic concept which could have had appropriate consequences for the employment of the High Seas Fleet. Instead, the Naval Command operated by a 'system of half measures'[8] and without clear focusing: on the one hand, there was submarine warfare against the British sea lines of communication; on the other, fleet activities in the North Sea under the motto: 'Something must be done with the fleet, but nothing must happen to it'.

After it had bombarded the British east coast twice in November and December 1914, the British had to expect further offensive operations threatening their coasts and North Sea lines of communication. But being in possession of the German radio code they were able to intercept the German battle cruisers with superior forces at Dogger Bank on 24 January 1915, involving them in a battle in which the armoured cruiser *Blücher* was lost. Accounts survive of the dreadful experience to be endured when in a ship receiving such concentration of enemy fire:

All loose or insecure fittings are transformed into moving objects of destruction. Open doors bang to and fro. Closed doors bend outward like two tin plates and through it all, the bodies of men are whirled about like dead leaves in a winter blast to be battered to death against the iron walls – men were swept from the deck like flies from a tablecloth. Everywhere blood trickled and flowed.[9]

After Dogger Bank the Kaiser relieved the commander-in-chief of the fleet, Admiral von Ingenohl, for inadequate preparation of the sortie.[10] His successor, Admiral von Pohl, made a total of seven shorter sorties in 1915 which neither had any strategic impact nor even led to any kind of enemy contact.

When Vice-Admiral Scheer took over command of the High Seas Fleet in January 1916, he developed no new concept for employment of the fleet, either, since he wanted at all costs to avoid a battle with the entire British fleet. The only difference from the former doctrine was that Scheer planned to make sorties further towards the British coast to achieve partial success if possible. However, sporadic bombardments of coasts were nothing but pinpricks that could irritate the opponent but not seriously threaten him. This also applied to the interruption of the sea routes linking Scandinavia and Scotland which had no vital importance for Great Britain. In the end, only the English Channel in its function as supply line for the Allied Powers was a strategic objective worth attacking; but that would have required common strategic planning and close co-operation with the Army on the basis of an overall strategy.

However, operational thinking still focused on battle between big ships. This was the reason why the basic strategic questions of naval warfare against Great Britain never found a convincing solution.

After two sorties of the High Seas Fleet in spring 1916, 31 May saw the Battle of Jutland, and, for the German sailors involved, the thrill of a first major encounter with the fleet of their British enemy. As Torpedo-Oberbootsmannsmaat Milewczyk recalled:

The Vth torpedo boat flotilla secured the High Seas Fleet to its starboard side. Amongst us prevailed an extraordinary excitement like a child feverishly waiting on Christmas Eve before seeing the glittering Christmas tree for the first time. We knew nothing for sure. But something was in the air that gripped us all. Everything took too long. We were burning with impatience. One thing was clear – two giants would measure up today, and the outcome of the struggle would largely depend on how well we were fulfilling our duties.[11]

The élan with which the crews joined battle can be judged from Obermaschinist Karl Kieffer's account of the battle-cruiser *Seydlitz* in the heat of action:

The feeling in the engine-rooms and coal bunkers was unique. No lack of steam! 24 knots and more were kept up steadily for hours, and but for the forward electric station, the engines worked in perfect order, despite receiving the heaviest impact from enemy shells. We were hit hard many times and there were some casualties. But the 'black bay' supplied coal and steam untiringly. In the hellish noise which even at times drowned the thunder of the guns, news which reached us from above was welcome. When our Captain passed on the memorable order for the battle-cruisers ''*Ran an den Feind!* (go for the enemy!)' and crowned it with: '*Drauf Seydlitz!* (Forward – *Seydlitz!*)' the enthusiasm knew no more bounds. The engine-room crew yelled like hell and were beating their shovels against the bunkers so that the captain surely must have heard it![12]

With the result of that battle, however, neither Great Britain nor Germany could be satisfied. The British had not achieved the final victory like the Trafalgar they had hoped for. Germany had to realize that the battle had not even brought about the change in the balance of forces hoped for as a partial success, for the strength ratio between the two fleets had remained unchanged. In his realistic assessment of the situation on 4 July 1916, Scheer came to realize

that even the most successful outcome of a Fleet action in this war will not force England to make peace. The disadvantages of our military-geographical position in relation to that of the British Isles, and the enemy's great material superiority, cannot be compensated by our Fleet to the extent where we shall be able to overcome the blockade or the British Isles themselves . . . A victorious end to the war within a reasonable time can only be achieved through the defeat of British economic life – that is, by using the U-boats against British trade.[13]

Thereafter, the entire High Seas Fleet made only two more North Sea sorties (towards the British East coast in August 1916 and off Bergen in April 1918), without direct enemy contact. The fact was, the Fleet primarily performed the function of a 'Fleet in Being': protecting the German coast, blocking Baltic approaches and keeping submarine exit routes clear. A realistic cost-benefit analysis shows, however, that, in the end, the fleet did not achieve what it expected to do.

German cruisers overseas, such as *Emden* and *Königsberg* in the Indian

Ocean, scored early successes, sinking merchantmen and tying up Allied naval forces, but were soon neutralised by the Royal Navy.[14 & 15] In the Atlantic, the 28 knot light cruiser *Karlsruhe* evaded opponents but sank following an explosion in the fo'castle. After Japan entered the war against Germany, von Spee, the commander of the East Asiatic Cruiser Squadron, with its two armoured cruisers *Scharnhorst* and *Gneisenau*, attempted to break out home from the South Pacific, destroying, en route, two outmatched British armoured cruisers off Coronel, Chile. In view of lost prestige and the threat to lines of communication, the British Admiralty sent two Grand Fleet battle cruisers which sought out and sank almost all the German Squadron off the Falklands in the South Atlantic.[16] This example serves as evidence to show that the Imperial Navy neither recognised nor utilised the strategic interplay between naval operations overseas and in home waters.[17]

However, one small, but powerful German Task Group was to influence the balance of forces and the overall course of the First World War. It was the Mediterranean Division comprising the Battle Cruiser *Goeben* and the Light Cruiser *Breslau*. The breakthrough of the two vessels to Constantinople and their formal handover to Turkey in August 1914 so enhanced German influence on that country that it joined the war on the side of the Central Powers at the end of October 1914. Thus the Turkish Straits – Dardanelles and Bosphorus – became impassable to the Allies. The second most important sea route to Russia after the Baltic remained closed and this contributed to that country being lost as an ally to the Entente in 1917.[18]

The fast German auxiliary cruisers often had difficulties on account of their high coal consumption. Two ships were destroyed by British naval forces in August 1914. Three others entered American ports at the end of their long time of operation in spring 1915 and were interned there. Because of coal supply problems, the German Navy later used slower freighters with a speed of approximately fourteen knots as auxiliary cruisers and minelayers. They could stay at sea for a long time because of their large coal supplies and low consumption rates. The main operational problem was how to break through the British blockade in the northern North Sea. Two ships were lost during this operation. One unusual camouflage proved to be the use of a square rigger with auxiliary engine (*Seeadler*) in 1917 that sank fourteen vessels, but was stranded on a coral reef in the Pacific. The auxiliary cruiser *Wolf* even had a seaplane and stayed at sea from December 1916 to February 1918 – 452 days in all.

During the first months of the war the submarine had proved a surprisingly efficient naval weapon, although its early successes also gave both military and political leadership in the Reich an exaggerated idea of its capabilities. In the face of the British threat to 'strangle the economy with the help of the blockade' as Churchill had put it in a speech on 9 November,

Tirpitz said in an interview two weeks later that Germany could 'play the same game' by torpedoing all British ships.[19] In Germany, this interview triggered passionate public debates that in turn had their repercussions on the naval command. As a result, the naval command succeeded in persuading the Government to agree to the employment of submarines against British trade routes, although initially only fourteen boats were available to operate west of the British Isles.

By employing submarines against merchant vessels Germany entered new ground in military terms and in terms of international law, for it was evident that submarines would have problems in acting according to the prize regulations, especially after the British began to arm their merchant ships and to deploy Q-ships. On the other hand it is a fact that submarine commanding officers, with some caution and experience, did manage to comply with these regulations, achieving remarkable results by using their gun armament. It is true that the submarines, for lack of space, were not able to take aboard any individuals, but in some cases lifeboats were towed to within close reach of the coast.

The German government proclaimed a war zone, in which all merchant ships would be sunk 'without it always being possible to avoid danger to the crews and passengers'[20] In addition, the declaration included the warning that neutral shipping was also endangered as a result of the British abuse of flags. Without giving the submarine commanding officers any clear instructions, the naval command obviously proceeded on the assumption that most ships would be torpedoed without warning, thus deterring neutral shipping. Lieutenant Commander Freiherr von Spiegel has described vividly in a 1916 publication the tension within a submarine while herself being stalked and then the elation of a successful sinking of the U-boat's quarry: 'a real wave of enthusiasm, arising from hearts freed from suspense, a wave which rushed through the whole boat and whose joyous echoes reached one in the conning tower.'[21]

This new form of naval warfare soon brought about a serious crisis in relations with the United States: one need only think of the *Lusitania* catastrophe of 7 May 1915. The problem of how to use the submarine in the most effective military way against Great Britain, whilst still being able to justify attacks on merchant shipping politically to the neutral powers, led to repeated arguments between the political and military leadership which lasted until the end of 1916.

During this period, a remarkable submarine operation was undertaken. On 7 October 1916, U-53 entered the harbour at Newport, Rhode Island for a few hours as a quasi-warning demonstration for the U.S. Navy of the capabilities of German submarines. Following its departure from Newport, U-53 sank 3 merchant ships outside American territorial waters off the Nantucket Lightship, while still complying with the Prize Regulations.[22]

Notwithstanding the successes achieved against merchant shipping whilst following the Prize Regulations in summer and fall 1916, the German Naval Command called again and again for 'unrestricted submarine warfare' – in other words the sinking of all merchant ships in the War Zone without warning, even if it did mean that the United States would break off relations as a direct result. The atmosphere and attitudes at that time among naval officers are described by Lieutenant Ernst von Weiszäcker in his diary:

> The naval officers sit around, eat, drink, politicize, intrigue, and even believe that they are being patriotic in trying by sordid means to bring about the adoption of unrestricted submarine warfare. Submarine warfare is supposed to cover up the stupidities (committed) in the fleet construction and in the wartime deployment of the fleet. The bad conscience emerges in this forbidden propaganda for it.[23]

The propaganda Weizsäcker mentioned was, however, effective. At the end of 1916, the new military leadership of the Reich, Field Marshal von Hindenburg and General Ludendorff, realized that victory in ground war was becoming more and more unlikely. Therefore, they saw unrestricted submarine warfare as a last means to gain victory.

With the start of an unrestricted campaign on 1 February 1917, came the expected break with the United States, though that country for the time being limited its reaction to 'armed neutrality'. On their part, the Entente were trying to bring the U.S.A. into the war, so as to take full advantage of the America's entire economic resources. This goal was soon reached, thanks to Germany's extremely maladroit diplomacy. She aimed at keeping the Americans militarily engaged on their continent and in the Pacific ocean. To this end, an alliance, which she also invited Japan to join, had been offered by cable to Mexico as early as 16 January 1917. In the meantime, however, the British Naval Intelligence was able to decipher all secret German diplomatic cables transmitted between Berlin, Washington, and Mexico.

To speed up the United States' decision – making process in view of its entry into the war, the British government handed over the deciphered German cables to Washington where President Wilson had them placed in the hands of the press on 28 February. The revelation of the German alliance offer to Mexico finally turned American public opinion against Germany; a dislike aggravated by the sinking of American ships that had occurred in the meantime. Early in April the U.S. entered into the war on the side of the Allies. There is no doubt that this step was not triggered by unrestricted submarine warfare alone, but the German position toward that issue possibly contributed to that decision in a substantial way.

On 1 February 1917, Germany had 105 operational submarines available for 'unrestricted submarine warfare'. By June 1917 their number was increased to 129. However their intensive use between February and July, 1917, meant in the end longer refitting periods in the shipyards and in consequence, fewer and fewer were available for operations.

In April 1917, the great success of the submarines in sinking ships led to a severe crisis among the Allies, so that they temporarily feared losing the war if it continued.[24] However, the strategic objective – effective disruption of the British sea lines of communication – was not achieved, and, subsequently, the introduction of the convoy system and an enhanced anti-submarine defence, from the summer of 1917, led to the submarine successes becoming fewer and fewer. The Naval Command had calculated the enemy's available merchant shipping tonnage too vaguely, and now the submarines almost everywhere had to operate submerged when launching a torpedo attack. Many convoys were not detected at all, owing to inadequate reconnaissance. It became apparent that there had never actually been enough operational submarines for convoy action west of the British Isles. The Royal Navy's intensive mining of the U-Boat sailing channels in 1917–1918 caused heavy losses that could not be replaced. After July 1917, it was no longer possible to increase the number of operational submarines – indeed their number gradually decreased. With that, the submarine war was practically in ruins. Ironically, through its part in provoking the entry of the U.S.A. into the war it proved to be a decisive factor in the German defeat.

The dull and monotonous defence patrols of the High Seas Fleet just offshore and the shift of naval warfare to the light forces, especially submarines, shook the self-confidence of the naval officers. They were now confronted with the new and difficult task of organizing the fleet's training and stand-by duty to maintain the fighting efficiency of the Fleet. Here, the human factor, the sympathetic treatment and care of the crews, played a decisive role. It seems that admirals and senior officers underrated the far-reaching effects of these psychological leadership problems. They failed to make the uneventful stand-by duty sufficiently interesting to keep the discipline and reliability of the crews at a high level. Furthermore, there was a frequent exchange of personnel due to the requirements of the submarine warfare, which deprived the capital ships of many of its medium-rank officers. In any case, it was especially in these units that the officers were in a privileged position. For example, they received different, usually better rations than the ratings. This intensified the differences within the military hierarchy and contributed towards the loss of a trustful relationship, the basis of military discipline. On Whit-Monday of 1915, a seaman wrote in his diary:

> There is now a greater gulf between the officers and the men than at any other period in my naval career. The fact that the officers have made no sacrifices at all so far, contributes significantly to this painful situation. While we have to content ourselves with living on half-rations of bread,

in the officers' mess they hold feasts and drinking bouts at which six or even seven courses are served. No one objected to this in peacetime. But is this proper at the present critical juncture?[25]

Characteristically the decline in morale did not extend to the crews of submarines, torpedo boats, and minesweepers, which were kept very active, received uniform rations, and lived cheek by jowl with their officers.

In summer 1917, ration shortages and minor duty problems resulted in hunger strikes and open insubordination on several capital ships and cruisers. In June, a hunger strike developed from action taken in *Prinzregent Luitpold* because of a regular diet of turnips, dehydrated vegetables and '*Drahtverhau*'. The stokers declared that they 'would gladly eat whatever food was given them if the officers would do the same'.[26] To re-establish discipline on these ships the naval command took drastic action – for example, carrying out two death sentences. This created indignation and bitterness among the sailors that lasted until 1918.[27]

At the end of September 1918, after a long internal struggle, the German Army High Command admitted military defeat and demanded an immediate armistice. The termination of the unrestricted submarine warfare seemed to be a precondition for establishing first contact with the United States via Switzerland. Suddenly, senior naval officers realized that the navy had to end the war without having had any important influence on its course. To them, the future *raison d'être* of a fleet seemed to be questionable. Out of these considerations arose the idea of a final fleet action which was designed to be the last spectacular encounter with the Grand Fleet. Admiral Scheer, now Chief of Naval War Staff, stated on 16 October 1918 what he wanted to accomplish through an attack by the fleet:

> It is impossible for the Fleet to remain inactive in any final battle that may sooner or later precede an armistice. The Fleet must be committed. Even if it is not to be expected that this would decisively influence the course of events, it is still, from the moral point of view, a question of the honour and existence of the Navy to have done its utmost in the last battle.[28]

A sortie of the fleet towards the English channel and the mouth of the River Thames was to provoke British defensive action and thus lead to a battle. The chances of success of such an operation are a matter of mere speculation. on the other hand, there can be no doubt that the basic idea did not result from a sober military estimate of the situation taking into account the entire political and military situation of the Reich. In a strange manner senior naval officers regarded the fate of their service as totally isolated from the overall political picture.

Furthermore, the fleet command entirely misjudged the mood of the crews. It ignored the warning signs from the unrest in the High Seas Fleet in the summer of 1917 and did not doubt the sailors' reliability at all. As usual, the planning of the fleet sortie was kept strictly secret. The crews were not even generally informed on the situation and possible fleet operations, an omission that would soon have far-reaching consequences, since certain preparations could not remain secret: as they were not informed by their superiors, the rumour of an impending risky mission of the fleet quickly spread among the ratings.

The behavior and statements of individual officers reinforced the impression of a planned 'final battle' or a 'death ride'. An officer told his fellow officers: 'We shall fire our last two thousand rounds at the English and then go down with honour. Better an honourable death than a life of shame.'[29] Informed by the press of the exchange of notes between the government of the Reich and President Wilson as well as of the German desire for an armistice, the ratings considered the fleet sortie an arbitrary action undertaken by the officers that was no longer compatible with the new parliamentary government's desire for peace and their own hopes for peace.

On some cruisers and capital ships, therefore, part of the crews refused to obey orders and put up passive resistance as early as 27 October 1918, in order to prevent the departure of the fleet. Insubordination reached its first climax on the evening of 29 October when one squadron had to stop its sailing preparations. When other commanders also doubted the reliability of their forces, the Chief of the High Seas Fleet, Admiral Hipper, dropped the original plan on 30 October and ordered a submarine sortie supported by seven capital ships. Again the crews prevented the capital ships from leaving port and Hipper was forced to withdraw the second sailing order, too. During these days a seaman noted in his diary:

Long years of accumulated injustice have been transformed into a dangerously explosive force which now erupts with great power all around. My God – why did we have to have such criminal, conscienceless officers? It was they who deprived us of all our love for our Fatherland, our joy in our German existence, and our pride in our incomparable institutions. Even now my blood boils with anger whenever I think of the many injustices I suffered in the navy.[30]

In order to prevent the rebellious crew members from contacting each other and to restore order and discipline in his forces, Hipper decided to deploy the squadrons to other ports. The disciplinary and intimidating measures, however, resulted in a further spreading of unrest and more cases of insubordination among the crews. In the end, any remaining authority held by superior officers was completely lost.

In view of the critical situation, the senior officers of the Kiel station area discussed possible countermeasures. They decided to bind the sailors to their units and commands by means of a general alert for the whole city. At the same time, a first report was sent to the Naval Office in Berlin with the request to send an 'excellent social democratic member of parliament' to Kiel who could talk to the sailors 'in order to avoid a revolution and rebellion'.[31] The city alert, however, that was sounded in the afternoon had no pacifying effect. Rather, it whipped up emotions. This resulted in a large protest rally with demonstrating sailors, stokers, and workers marching through the inner city. After several patrols and officers had been disarmed, there was a bloody incident when a military patrol fired into the crowd: eight persons were killed and twenty-nine injured. After this incident, the ratings took the bull by the horns. On the following day (4 Nov), they armed themselves, formed sailors' councils and seized the initiative in the city and aboard the ships. At the same time, the shipyard workers started a strike in sympathy with them. Lacking support from the population or reliable troops at his disposal, the senior naval officer in Kiel, Admiral Souchon, was forced to negotiate with representatives of the sailors' council to avoid a further escalation of the violent clashes.

Next day all ships flew the red flag as a symbol of the victory of the sailors' councils. The only bloodshed which occurred was aboard the battleship *König* when the captain and his officers defended the Naval Ensign. Two officers were fatally wounded and the captain, who was also seriously injured, shot a sailor who had tried to lower the flag.

Astonishingly, the officer corps made no serious attempt during this severe crisis of military discipline to suppress the sailors' revolt by force or at least limit it to a few ships, although this might have been successful, given energetic leadership and the support of picked, reliable ratings who were still available. Although the course of the Russian revolution, the cases of insubordination in the summer of 1917 and similar events in the Austrian fleet in January 1918 had given clear warning, the German naval command failed to study the problems of mutiny in detail and take preventative countermeasures.

In consequence, most officers 'were in no way prepared for such a development'.[32]

The collapse of military discipline took them so much by surprise that they lost all their initiative and leadership qualities, as if paralysed. In view of their helplessness and the arrests carried out by the rebellious sailors, many officers saw no alternative but to leave their posts and garrison towns. Within a few days, the revolt of sailors and stokers led to the collapse and end of the Imperial Navy and accelerated the general uprising in the Reich.

The outbreak and the course of the First World War had shown that the German Naval Command's political and strategic concepts did not work. During the July crisis of 1914 the High Seas Fleet was no deterrent. The

German Naval Command overestimated the possibilites of taking on Great Britain in a naval war because of the geographical conditions, the British were capable of achieving their strategic aims with regard to Germany without entering into a decisive battle. Despite tremendous individual successes up to the autumn of 1918, the German Navy was faced with a bitter result at the end of World War I. Its strategic designs for the employment of the High Seas Fleet as well as for the merchant war with submarines had failed. Furthermore, it was the starting point of a revolt triggering the political overthrow of the Reich. Under these circumstances the question was bound to arise in everyone's minds as to whether and how the further existence of a navy could be justified. The answer was provided by the victorious Allied powers, who laid down important military stipulations in the Versailles Peace treaty of 1919.

Notes

1   Cf Volker Berghahn, *Der Tirpitz-Plan. Genesis und Verfall einer innenpolitischen Krisenstrategie unter Wilhelm II*, Düsseldorf 1971; and Ivo N. Lambi, *The Navy and Power Politics, 1862–1914, Boston 1984;* and Jonathan, Steinberg, *Yesterday's Deterrent: Tirpitz and the Birth of the German Battle Fleet*, London, Macdonald, 1965, pp. 208–210.

2   With its first capital ship, H.M.S. *Dreadnought*, the Royal Navy achieved in 1905–6 an enormous leap forward in battleship combat capability. Tirpitz had to take the same step if the Imperial Navy were to remain equal to the potential enemy ship for ship. Cf. in this context: Jon Sumida, *In Defence of Naval Supremacy, Finance, Technology and British Naval Policy, 1889–1914*, London, New York, Routledge, 1989.

3   Cf. Paul M. Kennedy, 'Maritime Strategieprobleme der deutsch-englischen Flottenrivalität', in H. Schottelius, and W. Deist, eds., *Marine und Marinepolitik im kaiserlichen Deutschsland 1871–1914*, 2nd edn., Düsseldorf, Droste, 1981, pp. 178–210; see also Edward Wegener, 'Die Tirpitzsche Seestrategie', ibid. pp. 236–262.

4   Kennedy, op.cit. pp. 197–198.

5   Numbers according to: Otto Groos, *Der Krieg in der Nordsee*, vol. 1, 2nd edn. Berlin,E.S. Mittler 1922, p. 45.

6   Operations order for North Sea theatre, 30 July 1914, quoted in Groos, op.cit., p. 54; cf. also Paul G. Halpern, *A Naval History of World War I*, Annapolis Md, 1994, p. 23.

7   Prince Franz Joseph of Hohenzollern, *Emden*, London, Herbert Jenkins, n.d. p. 33.

8   Formulated by Captain Michaelis, Chief of Staff, High Seas Fleet in a letter to his friend Captain Zenker, Chief of Staff, Naval Staff, Berlin, 15 July 1914, quote in Groos, op.cit., vol.4, Berlin 1924, p. 241.

9   Liddle Collection, Brotherton Library, University of Leeds: translation of 1915 report captured in German Consul's office, Kamerun.

10 For details see Groos, op.cit. vol.3, Berlin 1923, pp. 50–121; cf. also Halpern, op.cit., pp. 44–46, and Arthur J. Marder, *From the Dreadnought to Scapa*

Flow: the Royal Navy in the Fisher Era. 1904–1919, vol. II: The War Years: To the Eve of Jutland, London, O.U.P., 1965, pp. 156–175.

11 Fritz Otto Busch: Das Volksbuch vom Skagerrak. Augenzeugenberichte deutscher und englischer Mitkämpfer, Berlin, Wilhelm Limpert, 1938, p. 106.

12 ibid., p. 197.

13 Marder. op.cit., vol III, Jutland and After (May–December 1916), London 1966, p. 206.

14 After her sinking, Emden's landing corps, which had failed to get on board before the action, succeeded in getting to Constantinople by adventurous routes via Arabia during the following months.

15 After she was sunk in the Rufiji Delta, the ten guns of Königsberg were recovered and used to defend the German colony until 1917.

16 Marder op.cit., vol II, pp. 117–120.

17 See Erich Raeder, Der Kreuzerkrieg in den ausländischen Gewässern, vol. 1, Das Kreuzergeschwader, 2nd edn., Berlin, E.S. Mittler, 1927, pp. 253 & 265.

18 Richard Hough, The Great War at Sea. 1914–1918, Oxford U.P., 1983, pp. 81–82,: and Ulrich Trumpener, Germany and the Ottoman Empire 1914–1918, Princeton 1968, pp. 25–27.

19 See Arnold Spindler, Der Handelskrieg mit U-Booten, vol. I, Berlin, E. S. Mittler, 1932, pp. 24–25, 34–35 & 243–245.

20 Marder, op.cit., Vol. II, p.344.

21 Lieut. Cmdr. Freiherr, von Spiegel, U-Boat 202: the War Diary of a German Submarine. (Eng. tr.) London, Mews pb. edn., 1976, p. 32.

22 Halpern op.cit., p. 336.

23 Ernst von Weiszäcker, diary 27 Sept. 1916, quoted in Die Weiszäcker-Papiere 1900–1932, ed Hill, Leonidas E., Berlin, Frankfurt, Wien, 1982, p. 215. Cf. also Holger H. Herwig, The German Naval Officer Corps: a Social and Political History. 1890–1918, Oxford 1973, p. 188. [Herwig wrongly identified the note as a letter from Weiszäcker to his father.]

24 Marder, op.cit., Vol. IV, 1917, Year of Crisis, 1969, pp. 113–114 & 144–152.

25 Daniel Horn, ed. & tr., War, Mutiny and Revolution in the German Navy. The World War I Diary of Seaman Richard Stumpf, Rutgers U.P. New Brunswick N.J., 1967. p.97.

26 ibid. p, 98. 'Drahtverhau' was a vile concoction of vegetable & sausage in vinegar and water.

27 Daniel Horn, The German Naval Mutinies of World War I, New Brunswick N.J., Rutgers U.P., 1969, passim.

28. Quoted in Marder, op.cit., Vol. V, Victory and Aftermath, London 1970, p. 173.

29 Horn, op.cit., p. 221.

30 ibid., pp. 418–419.

31 Message of Admiral Souchon to Naval Office, Berlin, 3 Nov. 1918, quoted in Rahn, Werner, 'Führungsprobleme und Zusammenbruch der kaiserlichen Marine 1917/18'. 'Die deutsche Marine. Historisches Selbstverständnis und Standortbestimmung, ed. by Deutsches Marine Institut, Herford and Bonn, 1983, p. 183.

32 ibid. p. 186 [Vice Admiral (ret.) Friedrich Ruge, quoted by Werner Rahn].

Chapter 11

The British Experience of Enforcing Blockade: The Armed Merchant Cruisers in 1915

Chris Page

Accounts of the war at sea tend to focus on the major engagements: Jutland, Zeebrugge, the heroics of the submariners, and the U-Boat campaign. Little has been written on the experiences of naval combatants, and the way that sailors coped with the daily problems of war at sea. Their personal experiences I have chosen for this chapter are those of fairly junior officers in one of the vital but more routine areas of naval activity, the blockade of the Central Powers. I have selected two men serving in ships enforcing the blockade during 1915. My principal characters are uncelebrated men who found themselves confronted by the challenge of war, and the particular problems of patrolling to enforce an embargo.

Their ships were no mighty gun platforms, or greyhounds of the oceans, but Armed Merchant Cruisers, commissioned from merchant ship operators, with minimal conversion of accommodation and storage spaces, fitted with a few six inch guns and the necessary magazine, and a small, but vital extra amount of communications equipment. They engaged in no glorious action against the enemy, (although some AMCs did), but month after month pounded their patrol areas searching for merchant vessels to stop and search. In writing this chapter I was fortunate enough to have access to the unpublished journal of Surgeon James Shaw RNVR of HMS *Changuinola*, and the diary of Lieutenant Commander F.J. Stenson, RNR, of HMS *Marmora*; these documents are now in the Liddle Collection at Leeds; both have an authentic ring of truth about the wartime experiences of their authors.

To some, the performance of the Royal Navy in the First World War was disappointing: the hoped-for and expected Trafalgar-like encounter with the German High Seas Fleet did not occur, and the results of the only major Fleet action, off Jutland in May 1916 seem to support the feeling of disappointment. Too little tends to be made of the major successes. These include the maintenance of sea communications with Britain's friends and allies, enabling us to feed their people and import the necessary materials vital for the continued prosecution of the War. This involved a titanic struggle to defeat the U-boats in the Northern Atlantic and Western Approaches. John Terraine has pointed out that a further critical role of the Royal Navy was to ensure the transport of many millions of our troops and those of their allies to the appropriate theatre of operations with tiny losses.[1] But perhaps the Navy's prime achievement in the Great War was the enforcement of the naval blockade. Opinion is divided on the extent of the contribution of the embargo of the Central Powers to their eventual defeat,[2] but there is little doubt that it was a vital factor.

Blockade was not a new phenomenon in British naval strategy during the First World War. It has formed the core of the way Britain has employed her maritime forces in times of conflict for hundreds of years.[3] The Germans were, of course, aware of how the Royal Navy was likely to fight the war at sea, and had taken steps to negate the British plans. First, they declined to offer their inferior battle fleet, (the High Seas Fleet), in a major action against the Grand Fleet, and kept their ships as a 'fleet in being', large enough to require almost all of the British capital ships to be retained in the waters of the North Sea. Second, they adopted the traditional strategy of the weaker naval power, that of 'Guerre de Course', attacking British sea communications with submarines and a variety of raiders, from the squadrons of powerful cruisers, like that commanded by Von Spee, to individual merchant cruisers. They also attempted to use neutral shipping to break the blockade. Later, they adopted the unrestricted submarine campaign against British sea communications.

The Royal Navy countered in the time-honoured way by hunting down all the surface raiders as early as possible, and using their own armed merchant cruisers to enforce the maritime blockade. During the course of the War the measures adopted by the Royal Navy to close any loopholes in the maritime embargo became progressively more stringent, so much so that a certain amount of ill-feeling was generated among those neutral countries endeavouring to continue their maritime commerce. The main nation so affected was, unsurprisingly, the United States, and care was taken not to antagonize the Americans so much that their support for, and eventual participation in, the War was prejudiced.

Surgeon James Shaw was a young Scot from Coatbridge, who joined up at the outbreak of the War, and served for a while in HMS *Druid*, a small destroyer of 750 tons, built by Denny, and part of the 1910/11 programme. He saw action in her at the Battle of the Dogger Bank in January 1915. In March 1915 he was appointed to HMS *Changuinola*, a modern (1912) steam turbine powered refrigerated cargo ship of 6000 tons, taken up from

(ii)   Maintaining the blockade: A painting by Surgeon James Shaw of H.M.S. *Changuinola*, North of Iceland. [Dr J. Shaw: Liddle Collection]

Elder and Fyffes. She had originally been owned by the Hamburg-Amerika line, but under her British owners, had been employed on the banana trade. *Changuinola* was commissioned as part of the 10th Cruiser Squadron, whose beat initially was the northern British waters, and the Iceland/Faeroes gap. Later in the War the squadron ranged further afield, to the seas north and west of Iceland, and nearer the Norwegian coast.

Lieutenant Commander F.J. Stenson, an officer in the Royal Naval Reserve, was appointed to the Armed Merchant Cruiser HMS *Marmora* in August 1914 as the Third Hand and Boarding Officer. He survived the War, and eventually became Commodore Captain of the Clan Line. *Marmora* was a unit of the 9th Cruiser Squadron, which patrolled the warmer North Atlantic waters from Sierra Leone, to the Cape Verde Islands, the Canaries, and even as far as the Caribbean. *Changuinola* appears to have been a happy ship, with generally high morale, while *Marmora* had repeated instances of quarrelling between officers, disciplinary problems with sailors, and fairly low morale. Some of the reasons for the differences between the two ships will become apparent.

Very soon after the outbreak of the war, the Admiralty realised that the enforcement of a full trade embargo of Germany would involve many more ships than were currently serving under the White Ensign, and they hastily requisitioned merchant vessels, with minimal conversion to fit them for the task, and formed them into 'Cruiser Squadrons'. The Tenth, the one which was to bear the brunt of enforcing the blockade, under Admiral de Chair, was originally intended to consist of about twenty-four vessels large enough to provide the sea-keeping qualities necessary for operations in some of the roughest seas in the world, and economical enough to stay on patrol for long periods.

In 1915, the Squadron intercepted 3,098 ships, mostly Scandinavian neutrals, of which 743 were 'sent in', i.e. suspected of carrying contraband, and despatched, either under escort, but much more commonly, with small prize crews, to British ports for closer examination. Only eight vessels whose interception was considered important evaded the patrol.[4] During the course of the war, the ships of the 10th Cruiser Squadron intercepted and boarded nearly 13,000 ships at sea, while 2,039 more decided it was not worth trying to slip through and voluntarily reported at British examination ports. It is estimated that only 642 vessels managed to escape interception and beat the Northern blockade.[5] Each of these vessels had to be boarded by a naval party sent from the cruiser in a small open boat powered by oars sometimes in atrocious weather conditions. By the middle of 1917, with the entry into the war of the USA, and the disinclination of neutrals to risk running the gauntlet, the blockade was no longer required to be maintained at the same intensity, and the 10th Cruiser Squadron began to be redeployed to convoy escort duties.

The ships were vulnerable, and in 1915 alone, five were lost – two torpedoed by German submarines, one mined, two more lost with all hands in appalling weather, and two seriously damaged, one in a collision, and the other by a mine. Their fragility mirrors that of the countless number of merchant vessels involved in the U-Boat campaigns of both World Wars: one torpedo, a mine, or even relatively light shellfire could spell the sudden end of the ship and her crew. The strain on the officers and men was considerable. The year's total casualties for the squadron were 63 officers and 800 men out of an approximate total complement of 9,000.[6] The flagship, *Alsatian*, was at sea for 262 days, and steamed 71,500 miles and burned nearly 41,000 tons of coal.[7]

In the same way that the perspective of the War of the typical infantryman in the trenches was dominated by the matters closest to his immediate world, so the existence of the men of the blockade-enforcers was similarly governed. The comparison with their army counterparts went further, for the bulk of the men in the Squadrons were civilian: typically, only three or four of the officers were likely to be Royal Navy – the Captain, invariably, and two Warrant officers, the Gunner and the Boatswain. The navigator was often the previous ship's master. There were some regular Chief and Petty Officers, both seamen and engineers, a Royal Navy Master-at-Arms, in charge of discipline, and a Royal Marine detachment, consisting of a sergeant and between twenty and forty depending on the ship's size. The rest were merchant seamen and firemen who had signed on for hostilities only. Finally, each ship had a few seamen from the Newfoundland section of the RNR, mostly ex-fishermen, who were invaluable for working the small boats in heavy seas.

In *Changuinola*, the total complement was twenty seven officers and 190 men. The ship was based at Glasgow. All ships of the squadron worked similar routines: the men were in three watches, i.e. four on and eight off, while the officers operated a one in four system. When off watch in the day time the men would carry out normal maintenance and cleaning duties, and trimming coal.

Changuinola was not taken up for Naval service until March 1915, and her first patrol lasted from 10 April to 1 May. After only four days out they had already stopped two vessels. Apart from the interception and boarding of merchant vessels, the main interest and excitement came from periodic alarms occasioned by possible sightings of submarine periscopes. They, and mines, were the most credible and fearsome threats to the thin-skinned armed merchant cruisers. The next patrol was from 13 May to 1 June, followed by a few days to coal. For the rest of the year her routine alternated between patrols and short coaling stops, either at their home port, Glasgow, or in the Shetlands at Swarback Minns. From Shaw's diary it would seem that *Changuinola*'s endurance was about twenty-two days. Some of the larger ships in the squadron carried huge amounts of extra coal in their former holds; while increasing their time at sea, this meant that a heavy extra burden was imposed on the crew to ship the stocks to the coal bunkers.

Coaling was the continual bugbear of all such ships of the time, none more so than those of the 10th C.S., who, apart from time in harbour for boiler cleaning and defect rectification, were continuously at sea and thus burning coal. Coaling for *Changuinola* took about sixteen working hours, involving the whole ship's company, including the officers; only the officer of the watch and the medical staff were exempt. The evolution was followed by a similar period to clean the ship, and remove at least most of the black dust and grime. Apart from the relatively few days when the ship was in her home port, shore leave was restricted to walks in the Shetlands, although Shaw managed an hour and a half in Iceland when the ship put in there for a brief visit: he noted that the houses were all wooden, and fitted with electric light, but that the most noteworthy feature of the town, Siglisford, was the 'overpowering smell of fish'.[8] Life in the Shetlands offered very little more during coaling stops; Shaw confined himself to walks and the occasional visit to church. Other than the beautiful scenery and a 'keenness in the atmosphere which gave one an appetite',[9] the main point of interest in this visit was the fact that Shaw noticed that there were 'almost as many black sheep as white'![10] On the other three times that *Changuinola* was in port in 1915, she was alongside in Glasgow. Here Shaw was fortunate that he could go home occasionally to Coatbridge. He also had relatives and friends in Glasgow itself and enjoyed taking them to the Alhambra Theatre. Shaw's diary reveals that life was not particularly scintillating for him ashore, but at least he saw his family on a fairly regular basis, if only for a very few days at a time.

This is in sharpest contrast with the life of Lieutenant-Commander Stenson of *Marmora*, one of the units of the 9th Cruiser Squadron: her beat, in the tropics, was ostensibly the more attractive. The time spent at sea was similar in both squadrons, but the shore time of the 9th C.S. was passed alongside in Gibraltar, St Vincent (in the Cape Verde Islands), Tenerife, Bahia and Rio in Brazil, and Madeira. Even these exotic locations did not move Stenson. His only favourable comments on his land surroundings were that the Sugar Loaf at Rio was a 'splendid landmark'[11], and that Bahia was 'a very pretty place'.[12] Unlike Shaw, and the crew of *Changuinola*, Stenson – a married man – did not get home during 1915, which rankled with him.[13] Stenson, who had been at sea in the Merchant Service since 1893, had had his fill of foreign parts, and did not enjoy his surroundings and time ashore as Shaw did: he was older, and, arguably, wiser.

At sea, there is no doubt that the motivation of the ships of the 10th C.S. was high: they realized that they were the cutting edge of the blockade, and their patrols produced a continual stream of vessels to stop, many more than the less frequent interceptions of the 9th C.S. *Changuinola* was fortunate in her Captain, Commander H.C.R. Brocklebank, who ran a happy ship. He took pride in the speed and efficiency of his boat's crews, effectively the ship's main armament on these duties, and Shaw noted with pride that they were the 'crack ship' in this regard.[14] The ship had sporting facilities in the form of a rudimentary gymnasium, and competitions on deck when the weather permitted. In the ship's sports meeting, the officers and senior ratings participated, and ten of the twenty seven took part in the obstacle race in the form of an assault course. All the officers managed to finish this arduous race, 'unlike some of the men'.[15]

The Captain presented the prizes: the men received small cash awards, while winning officers were given iron crosses, much to the amusement of the sailors. A.B. Karr, who had entered many events and won none, was presented with a special large brass cross with 'Nil Desperandum' inscribed on it.[16] On completion the men gave three cheers for the Captain and officers. Shaw records that 'It is pleasant to have such good feeling between the officers and men'.[17] The situation was not so good in other vessels of the squadron: officers returning from temporary duty away from *Changuinola*, reported that some ships had no recreation at all; their attitude seemed to be 'We are at war and therefore we must make ourselves miserable'.[18]

One of the most serious problems for those in the blockade ships was that of monotony: even the 10th C.S., which was far busier in terms of interceptions than the 9th, life inevitably became tedious at times. Both diary accounts emphasised the boredom, and the feeling of dullness and apathy engendered. For Shaw, optimistic by nature, this seemed to coincide with periods of rough weather, when the chances of detection of any blockade runners were less, and it was not possible to use the upper deck for recreation. 'It is the awful monotony and confinement enough at times almost to drive me crazy', he wrote on 23 September; but Shaw was not one to stay depressed for long, and a spell ashore soon revived his spirits.

For the more distant 9th C.S., the lack of regular mail exaggerated the boredom. As early as January 1915 Stenson voiced his deep resentment at being in 'steamy, unhealthy heat – barest scraps of news – deadly dull monontony . . . and a half insubordinate engine room crew'.[19] By August, boredom gave way to apathy: 'Nothing seems to matter . . . a bit lonely. The juniors won't ask me to go ashore with them, . . . and so I exist in a solitary state'.[20] Towards the end of the year, disillusion, bitterness, and rancour peppered his diary. He commented that he had dreamed all his life of the part that he would play in wartime, but never imagined himself 'wandering, practically in exile, all over the Atlantic'.[21]

The ships were not bad to serve in compared with some of the other vessels used by the Royal Navy in the War. They were reasonably large, and quite good sea-boats. Shaw noted that the food on board was much better than on his previous small ship, there was plenty of good coffee, and always the prospect of a decent night's rest. He particularly appreciated the fact that he has 'never been wet to the skin which I frequently was on the destroyer'.[22] After some nasty experiences early, a largely self-help programme was instituted in the plushly-furnished ex-merchant ships to remove a large number of the more dangerous fittings: the wooden panelling had to be taken down, while those suspended light fittings, decorative glass panels and mirrors which had survived the first test firings of the guns, were all stripped out; in *Marmora* even the charcoal sheeting used as insulation for the decks was cut out and burnt.[23] Later, even more bitter experience of the need to increase the buoyancy of the ships to withstand action damage led to the stowage of large quantities of wood and empty metal drums low down. Stenson observed waspishly that having got rid of a tremendous amount of valuable woodwork to reduce the fire risk, the magazine was now surrounded by empty packing cases![24]

Thus it can be seen that life aboard the AMCs, some of them formerly luxury liners, was not without its trials and tribulations; and, despite their size, especially in the patrol areas of the 10th C.S., heavy weather could make things very unpleasant for the crews: in *Changuinola*, the doctors regularly saw men injured as a result of violent ship's motion.[25]

For example, in HMS *Edgar*, another ship of the 10th Cruiser Squadron, Midshipman Michell recounted the effects of a particularly bad storm in terms which will be all too familiar to those who have spent their lives at sea:

> I was woken by a tremendous crash which sounded like a very large explosion and then the seas broke right over us and we shivered from stem to stern. I thought for a moment that we had struck a mine . . . The main deck was soon flooded and the Lower Deck as well . . . All went well until about 6.0 am when we dived into a head sea and before we had time to recover another sea struck just abaft the bridge on the Port side and completely submerged the upper deck . . . In the Engine Room . . . the water rose in the bilges to just above the main bearings. The main deck was a sight – a mixture of tins, cups, broken plates, sugar, tea, potatoes, and everything you can think of floating about in 2 feet of sea water! All the cabins were washed out and the Wardroom was a mass of upturned tables, chairs, piano and book cases on the deck . . . Charging wildly about in several inches of water.[26]

Rough weather brought other miseries: the ventilators and doors were all closed, so the atmosphere rapidly became vile and unhealthy. Not surprisingly therefore, the sick lists were long, and the doctors carried by all ships were kept busy.[27] Sometimes the doctors were unable to make the correct diagnoses; Stenson himself records that his treatment for peritonitis was to have his side 'rubbed with camphor',[28] while his violent toothache could only be alleviated by a 'wad of carbolic' until *Marmora* arrived in Madeira two weeks later.[29]

Discipline on board was the responsibility of the Master-at-Arms, in the last resort backed by the Royal Marine detachment. Some ships sensibly practised the rapid calling out of their Marines to deal with serious breaches of discipline, but few had to implement such a procedure in earnest. An exception was in *Alsatian*, the flagship of Admiral Tupper's 10th Cruiser Squadron. Admiral Tupper dealt with a strike by his firemen, as the ship was in the process of leaving harbour. Tupper was from the old school, and in the other ships he had commanded, it had always been his custom 'to periodically assemble the Marines detachment by the Marines' regimental call on the bugle'.[30] The Marines were assembled within three minutes, and sent to the mutinous mess, where, after interrogation of each man and giving him the choice to resume duty or be shot, the firemen returned to work.

Changuinola seems to have been a remarkably well-disciplined unit: even seen through the eyes of a naïve young officer, there appear to have been none of the myriad of offences, some petty, some very serious, which occurred in *Marmora*. Morale and discipline in a ship are inextricably linked, and this is most clearly demonstrated by Stenson's experience: *Marmora*'s first Captain, Farie, seems to have been a reasonable man. Stenson notes him as being a 'nice chap and so very tactful';[31] his job was made more difficult by the bickering of his officers. A continual source of friction was that the engineers, being ex-Merchant Navy men, messed with the other officers as part of their terms of engagement. It often rankled with the more RN-minded officers of the RNR, that most of these engineers should not be officers at all, but senior ratings. In most ships this did not lead to severe friction, but in *Marmora*, it seems that this was a contributory factor at least to the poisonous atmosphere in the Wardroom. Stenson, the Third Hand, rowed with the Chief Engineer, 'a pig-headed Scotchman a regular merchant seaman full of their idiosyncracies'.[32]

Stenson reports other sources of tension in the Wardroom: some are not on speaking terms with others: the First Lieutenant, Lieutenant-Commander Mayne, (RN not RNR) is 'irresponsible, thick skinned and petty'.[33] Mayne becomes almost an obsession with Stenson, and comes in for the rasp of his tongue on many occasions: 'Mayne has been running down his brother officers . . . Some day he'll be told the truth about himself. More out and out despicable caddishness I've never met'.[34] Even Mayne's use of the Captain's boat to go ashore irritates Stenson.[35] At the end of the year, Mayne left *Marmora*, and Stenson relieved him as the First Lieutenant.

On 6 November 1915, *Marmora* captured only her fourth ship in fifteen months, a fact which illustrates the fundamental difference between the 9th and 10th Cruiser Squadrons. In the latter, stopping and searching was an almost daily occurrence, and the officers and men had no difficulty believing in the vital nature of their task. *Marmora*'s crew had far less pressing urgency and sense of purpose, and yet still endured the fear of an attack without warning by a German submarine in waters where sea traffic was not so dense that early rescue of survivors was likely. It is small wonder, therefore, that in *Marmora*, monotonous patrols, squabbling officers, and the generally unhealthy conditions, led to disciplinary problems among the men.

In the course of only one year, Stenson reports at least four serious cases of drunkenness; on a couple of occasions the trimmers refused to trim coal, and there was one case of sodomy on board, 'A Catholic I'm sorry to say', notes Stenson, the senior Roman Catholic on board.[36] Stenson himself survived a Court Martial in July for 'pushing the Chief Engineer', the charge was 'not proven'.[37] Other offences included a trimmer striking an officer,[38] and disobedience.[39] On one day, thirty-two men were seen by the Captain for minor offences,[40] and there were two attempts at suicide during the course of the year: in May, a fireman jumped overboard, but was rescued,[41] and in August the Marine butcher tried to cut his throat, and was packed off to hospital.[42]

Stenson, who was so critical of the other officers, struggled to improve things in *Marmora* when he became First Lieutenant, but the ship had reached such a low ebb that discipline and morale were still far from satisfactory in 1916. Nevertheless, he left the ship on promotion in October 1917; after the War, he had the unusual experience for an RNR officer of commanding the Detention Quarters at Chatham, before returning to the Clan line on demobilization in 1919.[43]

It is easy to be sympathetic to the attractive character of Surgeon Shaw, rather than the continual, rather bitter, complaining of Lieutenant-Commander Stenson, but both their diaries have the ring of truth about them: neither recoils from self-criticism, although the younger man, Shaw, is much less introspective. There appears to be no attempt to conceal some of the more unsavoury aspects of life in the ships of the Cruiser Squadrons. It is clear from their journals that life in ships enforcing the blockade during the early part of the First World War was arduous, and for the most part, more or less unpleasant. It is difficult to gauge whether life at sea was worse or better than that of those in the trenches. Undoubtedly, the Royal Navy in the First World War was, statistically, much safer than service in the infantry on the Western Front. However, quite literally, men at sea are all in the same boat, and there are many recorded instances of ships being lost with all hands, i.e. a casualty rate of 100 per cent.

As with all fighting organizations, there was a huge spectrum of abilities to be found among the thousands of vessels in Royal Navy service during the First World War. As on land, these tended to range from a very few elite groups, to an equally small number of units with almost no battle value, with a largest portion of reasonably combat-worthy units in between. The examples of the officers whose experience forms the basis of this short chapter illustrate some of the possible reasons for those differences. In times of general mobilization, it is impossible to fit all square pegs into square holes, and therefore most units, ashore and afloat, had to make the best of the men they were given. In the end, this proved sufficient to bring victory, at sea and on land, against one of the most dangerous and implacable enemies Britain has ever been called on to face.

Notes

1   John Terraine, *Business in Great Waters*, London, Leo Cooper 1989. p 150.
2   There is no doubt that the blockade resulted in very serious privations for the German people: see John Williams, *The Other Battle Ground, – Britain, France and Germany 1914–1918*, Regnery 1972; C.R.M.F. Cruttwell, *A History of the Great War 1914–1918* Oxford, OUP 2nd ed. 1936; Cyril Falls, *The First World War*, London, Longman's Green 1960; Basil Liddell Hart, *History of the First World War*, 1973 edn, (by arrangement with Cassel); For a German opinion see R.H. Lutz, *The Causes of the German Collapse in 1918*

partic.ch.V 'Report by General von Kuhl on the "Stab in the Back Question".' For a different view, see J.N. Tracy, *Attack on Maritime Trade*, (Chapter 2), London, Macmillan/UTP, 1991, who does not doubt the effectiveness of the blockade in depriving the German populace of essential goods, but contends that the overall effect on the performance of the German Army in the field has been exaggerated. Both sides have had reasons for stressing the importance of the blockade on the outcome of the War: Britain, for reasons of maritime tradition, the need to show that the Royal Navy played a key role in the victory, and to justify to a certain extent the suffering inflicted on the German people; and the Germans, to explain that their Army was not defeated in battle, but undermined by Communists and defeatists at home.

3   For a good resumé of the theory and practice of blockade in history, see J.N. Tracy, *Attack on Maritime Trade*, quoted above. Also S.W. Roskill, *The Strategy of Sea Power, Its Development and Application*, London, Collins 1962 and P.M. Kennedy, *The Rise and Fall of British Naval Mastery*, London, Allen Lane 1976, give an excellent background.

4   Statistics quoted in this section are from CB 917E, *Naval Staff Monographs, (Historical) Fleet Issue, Volume VII*, Sept. 1922.

5   Admiral Sir Reginald Tupper, *Reminiscences*, London, Jarrolds, 1929, p. 267.

6   *Naval Staff Monograms (Historical) Fleet Issue Volume VII*, Monograph 19 Sept. 1922.

7   ibid.

8   Diary of Surgeon James Shaw, entry for 30 Sept. 1915, Liddle Collection, henceforth referred to as 'Shaw's Diary'.

9   ibid. Entry for 17 Sept. 1915.

10 ibid.

11 From The Journal of Lieutenant-Commander F.J. Stenson RNR, held by the Liddle Collection, entry for 29 Oct. 1915. Hereafter referred to as 'Stenson's Journal'.

12 Stenson's Journal, 20 Nov. 1915.

13 In fact, *Marmora* did not return to her home port, Liverpool, until the end of June 1916, by which time Stenson had been away from home for two years.

14 Shaw's Diary, 17 June 1915.

15 ibid, 21 June 1915.

16 ibid, 22 June 1915.

17 ibid.

18 ibid, 11 September 1915.

19 Stenson's Journal, 28 January 1915.

20 Stenson's Journal, entry for 26 August 1915.

21 ibid, 21 October 1915.

22 Shaw's Diary, entry for 23 April 1915.

23 Stenson's Journal, 28 October 1915.

24 ibid, 19 April 1915.

25 Shaw's Journal, entry for 29 December 1915 is an example.

26 From the Diary of Midshipman R.A.C. Michell, of HMS *Edgar*, of the 10th Cruiser Squadron, entry for 11 November 1914. Liddle Collection.

27 Examples are to be found in Stenson's Diary, entries for 6, 11, 14 February, 8 March, 20 April, 14 August 1915, among others.

28 Stenson's Diary, entry for 7 February 1915.

29 ibid, entries for 15, 22, 27 May 1915.
30 *Reminiscences*, by Admiral Sir Reginald Tupper. p. 266.
31 Stenson's Diary, entry for 12 December 1914.
32 ibid, 14 January 1915.
33 Stenson's Diary, entry for 12 December 1914.
34 ibid, 22 June 1915.
35 ibid, 20 June 1915.
36 ibid, 28 April 1915.
37 ibid, 22 July 1915.
38 ibid, 3 August 1915.
39 ibid, 6 May 1915.
40 ibid, 7 May 1915.
41 ibid, 7 May 1915.
42 ibid, 26 August 1915
43 From an article in the Journal of Commerce and Shipping Telegraph, 7 June
    1930.

Chapter 12

The British Merchant Seaman at War

Tony Lane

War came to merchant seafarers as it did to no other civilians. The advent of mass submarine warfare literally brought the crews of passenger and cargo ships into the front-line: 14, 287 seafarers on British ships lost their lives in the war at sea, nearly ninety per cent of them aboard ships sunk by submarines.[1] And yet despite the hazards and the lionizing rhetoric heaped upon them, seafarers persisted in cleaving to the culture of their occupation. In their attitudes and in their behaviour they stuck to what they knew. If like everyone else they were capable of indulging in passing patriotic enthusiasms, the rhythms and routines of everyday life kept them immune from the fantasies of the professional super-patriots. When circumstances presented, seafarers might do brave things. But the bravery was bred of the needs of the moment and the mores and habits of seafaring rather than of the call of colours and country.

Britishness, indeed, was not the most obvious feature of the crews of British ships. Ships' crews were *normally* cosmopolitan in composition and war made little difference to this. When the *Cabotia* was sunk 120 miles west of Ireland in October 1916 her seventy-four man crew, besides British, included Greeks, Italians, Portuguese, Americans, Danes and Norwegians.[2] 'British', furthermore, denoted a legal and imperial status rather than a simple national one. Some twenty per cent of British seafarers were from the Indian sub-continent and another ten per cent from Crown Colonies and Protectorates in the Caribbean, Arabia, Africa north, south, east and west and South East Asia including Hong Kong. Seafarers from these regions, whether Punjabi or Yemeni firemen, Cayman Islands able seamen or Kru cooks and stewards could all legitimately declare themselves British.[3] This pattern of crewing simultaneously reflected Britain's imperial status, its extraordinary dominance of the world shipping industry where British ships carried half the whole world's external seaborne trade, and ships' regular need to replenish crews in ports abroad due to death, illness and desertion.

Indian seamen, invariably referred to at this time as 'Lascars', had been employed on British ships since the seventeenth century and by the outbreak of war in 1914 formed the entire non-officer crew of almost all ships engaged in the very substantial Indian trade. Chinese crews were at this time being regularly employed in the Far Eastern trade and Kru and Nigerians to West Africa.[4] Additionally, West Indians, Europeans of all nationalities and Northern, Southern and Central Americans together formed a transient seafaring population temporarily lodged in the 'sailor-towns' of the larger ports of the world.

Given the size of the British merchant fleet, transient seafarers were more likely to find British employment than any other. And when shipmasters went looking for whole new crews to sign-on in Europe at the commencement of voyages or for replacements in ones, twos and handfuls when abroad, they cared more about making up numbers than about nationality. In 1901, thirteen per cent of able seamen sailing from Liverpool in steamships and forty-five per cent leaving in sailing ships were foreign. Ships arriving in Liverpool in 1901 had even higher proportions of foreigners – fifteen per cent of able seamen in steam and sixty-two per cent in sail. The greater number of foreign seamen on arriving ships reflected the need to replace British seamen who had deserted or been left ashore ill in overseas ports.[5] Ad hoc crewing practices, combined with the systematic employment of sons of empire, meant that up to forty per cent of seamen killed on British ships were not natively British.

The view of merchant seafarers available to the public consisted largely of newspaper accounts of the experiences of particular ships and their crews or collections of similar reports published in books. Books' prefaces were apt to offer resounding celebrations of stoicism, such as the following by L.Cope Cornford:

> He must navigate unlighted channels amid unlighted ships. He must steer new courses and learn the art of war. He never failed nor flinched. And you shall mark in these chronicles the merchant seaman . . . stumbling over mines, attacked by raiding cruisers, torpedoed or shot to pieces by submarines, sent adrift to go mad or drown in open boats, still sturdily going undaunted about his business, and gradually becoming a wary and valorous fighting man. He is the same merchant seaman who, but three years since, was the drudge of commerce, and who now in his own right is entered of the chivalry of the sea.[6]

The stories introduced in this manner related the experiences of stoical British seaman, in which readers were invited to see themselves as they ought to be. When the story's cast contained other 'friendly' Europeans they were predictably characterized as equals of the British in courage and

Germans and Austrians were by no means seen uniformly as barbarians.[7] Different vocabularies, codes and conventions, however, were used to highlight the subordination of non-Europeans. Cornford gently cut Chinese seamen down to size when he said of the crew of the *Goldmouth* that it consisted of twelve British and forty-seven 'Chinamen' and that: 'All behaved well, especially the British.'[8] More crudely, Harold Wheeler wrote of the *Delmira*'s attempts to run from an attacking submarine by cracking on steam:

> Unfortunately the black squad below [the firemen] were not British. They were Chinamen, and inhabitants of the Yellow Kingdom do not possess a reputation for bravery at sea. Somehow they got to know of the presence of the enemy . . . and swarmed on deck and went on strike. There were only eight white men, including officers, all told. In ordinary circumstances the minority would have quelled the rabble, and sent them back to their work in double quick time.[9]

The German naval tactics as used against merchant ships were not initially controversial. In the first three months of the war forty merchantmen were lost to German surface ships and only one to submarines. This was conventional warfare. Merchant ships were stopped and their crews given time to assemble a few belongings and get into boats before their ships were sunk. The evacuated crews were then normally taken prisoner aboard the intercepting ship and often landed subsequently in neutral ports. It was the commencement of mass submarine warfare by Germany from January 1915 that led to allegations of German brutality and atrocity against merchant seamen.

By convention merchant seamen were civilian non-combatants who could expect to be rescued if their ships were sunk. Submarines, however, were generally too small to make rescue practicable if they were operating on the surface and needed to make their escape if under water. The 'brutalities' allegedly committed by submariners were, therefore, acts of *omission*. It was not a case of acts perpetrated but of rescues not undertaken. In the event, the record of German submariners in respect of merchant seamen was overwhelmingly honourable given the limitations of their operational circumstances. Indeed the populist British literature, intending to illustrate the perfidiousness of German submarine crews, actually provides many examples of correct behaviour and even substantial assistance. In the instance of the *Delmira* cited above, wine was offered to the survivors who declined, 'but the offer of a tow was accepted. For an hour and a half the submarine acted as a tug; then the commander of the U-boat sighted a large ship, cast off, and descended to the nether regions. Why he did not attempt to destroy the vessel on the horizon is known only to himself.'[10] And when the *Hanna Larsen* was sunk in the North Sea: 'The master told the commanding officer of the submarine that one of his crew was badly wounded in the head, whereupon the German officer ordered one of his people to fetch lint and dress the wound.'[11]

British official statistics of merchant shipping lost to submarines have two principal categories. Ships are described as having been sunk without warning by torpedoes from submerged submarines or captured by submarines operating on the surface. In the latter case crews were allowed to leave before their ships were subsequently sunk by gunfire, torpedo or planted explosive. August 1915, the worst month in the war for merchant seamen until February 1917, saw forty two ships sunk by submarine – five 'without warning' (12 per cent) and thirty seven 'captured' (88 per cent). The very worst month in the war at sea was April 1917 when submarines sank 155 ships – 101 'without warning' (65 per cent) and forty four 'captured' (24 per cent). This change in submarine tactics was principally a response to the British introduction of convoys.

If convoying undoubtedly offered ships more protection, the submarines response of sinking without warning also increased the risks to merchant seamen. The practice of convoying also sent submarines further out into the Atlantic in search of prey. This in turn meant that survivors of sunken ships had to launch and sometimes make voyages in their boats in conditions far more hostile than when ships were sunk in coastal waters. None of the ships sunk in August 1915 were more than 100 miles from a point of land but in April 1917, sixty five of the ships (42 per cent) were sunk more than 100 miles from land.[12]

Nothing was so threatening as the possibility of being sunk although one might not know this from the prosaic accounts in the seamen's diaries. Harold Taylor was a sixteen-year old apprentice aboard the *Jersey City* on 24 May 1917. In a subsequent recollection he wrote that he was dressed 'sketchily in thin singlet and greasy very worn dungarees on the fore end of the lower bridge polishing the captain's ports with brickdust and oil'. Taylor recorded the ship sinking slowly since she was full of grain and this gave everyone a chance to get off the ship. In another brief and entirely unsensational paragraph he wrote that since the boat could not sail to windward she was unable to make for the Flannan Islands, about thirty miles to the west of Stornoway in the Hebridean Isle of Lewis. Obliged to sail eastward across the top of Scotland, the survivors were rescued three days later by a Naval patrol boat when they were off Scapa Flow in the Orkneys.[13] B.A. Hardinge, 2nd officer of the *Clan Davidson* and on his way up Channel after an uneventful voyage from Fremantle, was far more economical. He recorded without supporting detail of 24 June 1917, 'torpedoed and sunk by German submarine'. Of 25 June, Hardinge entered, 'landed Plymouth by British Destroyer.'[14] Only slightly less matter of fact was E.T.N. Lawry who avoided evoking any light, shade or emotion in respect of the three ships sunk under him when he was in his later 'teens. The first two ships were sunk in the Channel and rescue was immediate.

In the case of the third, the *Port Hardy* was 200 miles west of Gibraltar and Lawrey, by then a 19-year old 3rd officer, was in a boat with nine others when rescued a day later. He was apparently impressed by nothing so much as the fact that the Danish schooner which picked them up was fifty days out from Iceland on a voyage to Cadiz![15]

C. Mather, a 19-year old radio officer on the *Sturton* which was sunk off the Cote d'Azure in February 1918, was unusually literary in his later reconstruction of events. Wondering how his ship had been spotted at night by the U-boat which sunk it, he asked 'did the steward (a tall lout, Danish, taken on in Baltimore to replace a British steward who absconded with the ship's linen and stores) show a light in his porthole [?] This steward was a laudanum addict and was frequently causing trouble.' After the rescue the *Sturton*'s crew were put in the charge of the UK Consul in Nice who having given 'the impression that he was much more accustomed to officiating at diplomatic afternoon teas than dealing with a nondescript crew of ship-wrecked mariners', mishandled the hotel arrangements for the survivors by inverting the customary hierarchy. The ratings got put in a good class hotel and the officers in something rather inferior with the result that 'some of the Arab firemen, no doubt stunned by the luxury of white table linen, elegant cutlery and too much wine, had a riot and smashed the glassware in their dining room.'[16]

A harsher story but as sparely written as a logbook was recounted by the master of the *Coquet*, sunk after 'capture' by an Austrian submarine in January 1916 when 200 miles east of Malta. The 31-man crew got away in two boats. Fifteen of them in the chief officer's boat were never seen again. From the master's boat there were only two survivors although the seventeen men in it all made it safely to land NW of Tobruk in Libya, after a six-day voyage. The next day the master and two other crew members set off in search of help and after several hours met with an Arab who went back with them to the survivors camp on the beach. The master then sent two Greek firemen off with the Arab to find help – one fireman spoke Arabic and the other Italian. The following day, but before help arrived, the remaining fifteen survivors were attacked by 'Beduin'. Ten men were taken off as prisoners and the other five, including the master, were left dead or wounded. In his report to the Admiralty the master said: 'the carpenter was horribly mutilated but still alive. He asked me to drag him away from the sea; I tried to but he was a big man and my wound very painful. A little way out in the water the steward was floating face downward [and] the little Italian messroom boy was lying dead.' Help arrived the same day in the form of a small Italian steamer with an Italian army officer and a squad of Arab soldiers. The 'Beduin' and the prisoners were not found, leaving the master and a badly wounded able seaman the only apparent survivors.[17]

Epic voyages of fourteen and more days made by merchant seamen survivors in ships' boats were a regular feature of the Second World War but almost unknown in the Great War.[18] One who did make such a voyage was Cecil Foster, who when serving as a first officer was sunk 320 miles WSW of the Scillies and then sailed for nine and a half days to the coast of N Spain. This was to prove a training and initiation for a far longer ordeal after the war: in June 1923 Foster was master of the *Trevassa* when she sank in a storm 1600 miles from Fremantle. After 22 days and 1700 miles Foster's boat arrived safely in the Mauritius group of islands.[19] This was an extraordinary achievement but as in the case of other diaries and logs cited here, Foster's book managed nevertheless to render the narrative detail of an exceptional episode as mundane.

There are two things to say about this almost universal tendency to exclude 'atmosphere'. Keepers of logs, were trained to write with economy. In logs things happen in sequence and have an immediate cause. Anything else is idle speculation which might later give encouragement to average adjusters, insurers and Admiralty Courts.

Secondly, the formal as well as the customary routines of shipboard life were finely drawn and deeply etched. Ships at the time of the Great War were relatively small and densely populated. If crews were to function effectively in their collective social life and in the formal division of labour, the whole web of routines needed minimal disturbance. War conditions which threatened to disrupt the always fragile social order of the merchant ship, needed to have their significance reduced so that the familiar and well-worn patterns of everyday life could remain sovereign. Merchant seamen succeeded splendidly in marginalizing war. They may have been conscious of the critical importance of their labours in keeping the home front and the armed services supplied but the nature of their work meant that they still continued to lead a life apart. The customs and practices which together formed the occupational culture of seafaring were hardly affected by war.

Of thirty-six ships sunk by U-boats in December 1916 only four were sunk on Atlantic routes and perhaps this added to the confidence of the catering crew members of a Port Line ship berthed in New York over Christmas. Seeing no reason to cook and wait upon the officers on Christmas Day, they gave themselves the day off and went ashore. [20] It would be surprising if at least some of them did not decide to cut their losses and desert. Labour was scarce in New York and wages, including those for seamen on US ships were far higher than in the UK. Desertion by seamen from British ships in North American and Australasian ports had been a major problem for shipowners pre-war. In 1908, 23,311 crew members had deserted in ports abroad, 11,000 in the USA and Canada. Philadelphia was a convenient port for desertion: in the spring thaw men left to go north and west to work on Great Lakes' traders.[21] British seamen had been deserting their ships in North America since the early nineteenth century[22] and were still doing so during the Great War. In 1917 it seems that Britons accounted for more than half the membership of the American Seamen's Union and seventy-five per cent of the union's members in the Atlantic trade.[23]

Once ashore in foreign ports seamen did mainly what seamen of all nationalities had always done unless they were closely guarded apprentices – like Harry Forrest – with little money. Young Forrest spent most of the war on voyages to the Mediterranean and having on one occasion been given a half-holiday, was taken by the chief officer to see a bull-fight. Momentarily lapsing from logbook codes he wrote to his mother: 'I don't wish to see another one, it's the most sickly affair I have ever seen.' A more uplifting experience was provided for young Harry while his ship was in a Tunisian port. A resident Englishwoman wrote to his mother that she had taken him to Carthage to see 'where the early martyrs sealed their faith with their blood.'[24]

Drinking excessively rather than sampling cultures was what a very large proportion of seamen of all ranks did when they went ashore. Drink accounted for a much higher proportion of seamen's expenditure than prostitutes. The fact of war was if anything only likely to increase the level of drinking because the payment of wartime bonuses and wage increases had almost doubled seamen's pay. Stories of 'epic' drinking exploits were a staple item of sailor-talk and it would be hard to exaggerate the centrality of 'booze' to the seafarer's sense of what it meant to be a 'proper seaman'.[25] The ability to 'hold drink' was regarded as one of the more important measures of 'manliness', a quality taken seriously in an all-male occupation where hazard and risk-taking was built into the job even without the additional dangers of war.[26] If severe alcoholism were not as widespread as might be expected, when it did occur it was more likely to afflict officers who unlike the rest of the crew, had access to drink at sea.

The 16-year old apprentice E.T.N. Lawrey was rather shocked at the behaviour of the chief officer of the Braunton, one Paddy Kane from Island Magee in northern Ireland. When the ship was in Baltimore shortly after war began Kane 'went on the booze' and later when discharging American grain in St. Nazaire, he fell out with the chief engineer and threatened him with violence: 'In consequence of these threats the old Chief left his room at nights and used to sleep on top of the boilers. So Paddy was arrested and kept locked up until the ship left [port]'. On the ballast passage to Barry, Kane was locked in his room having had his razor and knife taken from him. The replacement chief officer was another alcoholic. On Lawrey's next voyage and while the ship was in St Lucia in the West Indies 'the Mate took to drinking Bay Rum and finally got the DT's . . . On passage to Cuba the Mate was lashed into a hammock until he recovered.' Lawrey seemed surprised to be able to record of the new Mate that he was 'rather a gentlemanly type for a Tramp Ship' which presumably meant that he did not drink excessively.[27] It need hardly be said that if drinking exploits were often recounted as heroic, the opposite was more likely to be true. When a young engineer officer aboard the tanker San Gregorio, R.D.F. Powell said the chief engineer was permanently drunk while the ship was under repair at Hebburn: 'He used to knock his wife about at night, and the Donkeyman [engine room petty officer] heard him and went and thrashed him'. And as if to balance the account as between deck and engineroom officers, Powell observed that in matters of drink the master was no better than the chief.[28]

Tramp ship life elsewhere seemed to run to form. R.D. Hoskins aboard the Carlisle Castle in Philadelphia noted of 15 October 1917: 'Chief Engineer fell into dock. Pulled out by Chief Officer.' And of 17 October: 'Pantryman attempted suicide by drowning. Rescued. Taken ashore and detained as a lunatic.'[29] Lawrey, meanwhile, was now at the end of his apprenticeship and equipped with his 2nd Mate's Certificate, and had escaped into a cargo liner company where officers thought themselves gentlemen. Describing runs ashore with shipmates in Argentina in June 1918, he noted: 'Life was very gay at the River Plate. We attended Race Meetings at La Plata.'[30]

The extent to which war intruded on everyday life during voyages varied according to rank, route and place in the division of labour. A bored Leslie Davies, an 18-year old radio officer, was keeping four-on-four-off watches in convoys between Milford Haven and Gibraltar. All that was required of him was that he received SOS and ALLO messages, the latter reporting sightings and positions of submarines. He took to reading and with 'some advantage, because I had decided that after the war I would like to do medicine [and] would have a university entrance examination to face – so, after the first voyage, I provided myself with some school text-books and I got down to Latin and French.'[31]

In Atlantic convoys weather might often interrupt the unremitting tedium of the crossing. R.D. Hoskins entered in his diary for the three days between 17 and 20 November 1917:

> All ships in convoy hove to. Driving rain and spray obliterate surrounding ships. 10/00 Gale increases. Give up attempting to keep station. Every ship for itself . . . Huge confused sea running. Shipping very heavy water. Bosun's store and lamp room stove in. 7/00 p.m. this night shipped bad sea over port lower bridge. Smashed wing house and tore asunder iron rails on fore and after part of same . . . Nov. 20th rejoined Escort. Starboard lifeboat stove in and port lifeboat badly damaged. Carpenter and hands in repairs. Captain in his cabin in nervous breakdown.[32]

Sailing in company with other ships was wholly unfamiliar to merchant seamen. Where ships of the Royal Navy typically sailed in formation and crews were accordingly accustomed to the skills of station-keeping, merchant ships on leaving port invariably went their own way and saw other ships as offering risks of collision. Merchant ships, furthermore, were cumbersome, slow to respond to the helm at low speeds and with low power to weight ratios. Where the average destroyer could make twenty five knots comfortably, most merchant ships which were three or four times larger would struggle to make ten. Convoys which had to proceed at the speed of the slowest ship were often, therefore, regarded by navigating and engineer officers alike as a new form of occupational examination where even average competence was hard to achieve. The constant problem was maintaining a safe distance from the ship in front. Ships' telegraphs linking bridge and engine room were not calibrated for adjustments in propeller revolutions and telephones were a novelty even aboard the newest and best equipped passenger ships. The voice pipe was the only way and as I.P. Ellis, a young third officer said: 'All the navigating officers had a lovely case of swollen lips by the end of the passage from continual contact with the brass pipe.'[33] In the early days of convoying, excitability was another hazard, Ellis saying of a convoy formed off the Eddystone Light:

> We had hardly been going a few hours when one ship fired its gun and went off at an angle wailing with fear on her syren. We were awfully excited, and everyone saw periscopes all over the place till the sea bristled with them, but the cease-fire went and the submarine degenerated into a box someone had thrown overboard against regulations.[34]

Real encounters with German submarines and surface ships where merchantmen fought back were not uncommon once ships had been equipped with guns and crews trained to use them. In March 1917 when 350 miles east of the Azores, the *Otaki* was approached by the famous German armed merchant cruiser, *Moewe* and told to stop. The *Otaki*, whose master was a Lieutenant in the Royal Naval Reserve, refused and replied with gunfire when attacked, killing five of the *Moewe*'s crew and wounding ten others. The *Otaki*, however, was outgunned having one against the *Moewe*'s seven. Being set on fire the *Otaki*'s crew abandoned ship having lost six men in the encounter, including the master, and with nine wounded. The *Otaki*'s Captain Bisset Smith, was posthumously awarded the Victoria Cross, the chief officer the DSO, two gunners the DSM, the carpenter was Mentioned in Dispatches and so also but posthumously, were two young apprentices.[35] The crew of the *Ramsay* had better luck, having been missed by two torpedoes; the submarine was then sunk by the *Ramsay*'s gun. Remarkable success was not met with scenes of triumph. This was war, not a football match. Radio officer Mather recalled:

The psychological atmosphere on board was very strange. Everybody was quiet and subdued. There was no jubilation or bravado, no argument or discussions. Gooderidge, the gunner [and a son of a Methodist minister] was uncommunicative – he was not elated but rather sad at his responsibility.

The *Ramsay*'s master, another RNR officer, and who later received a DSO was less reticent. Greatly to Mather's disapproval, the master understandably bragged of the exploit to consular officials when the ship arrived in Buenos Aires. The encouragement he received only added to his general tendency to belligerence. When the ship was sailing homeward from the Plate, he shouted through his megaphone at two German merchant ships at anchor in the estuary and blockaded by the Royal Navy: 'Get away to sea, you bloody cowards.'[36] On other occasions such encounters with German seamen produced a playful form of warfare. Captain Atkinson, a young apprentice in 1915, said that when his ship sailed out of the Plate past an anchored German ship the firemen 'started pelting clinkers [stokehold wastes] over on to the deck of a German ship because they were all standing nice and clean watching [us] go out and a fight started between the two of them with ashes and clinkers'[37]

The crews of passenger ships converted to trooping and acting as hospital ships for the Dardanelles campaign in the Mediterranean saw regular evidence of the war at sea *and* on land. H. Hiscock, crew member of the *Goorkha*, wrote:

a derelict raft, probably from a French transport, was sighted and passed. We also steamed towards a drifting lifeboat on September 20th but no human beings were seen . . . Each incident happened a few miles from Malta a favourite hunting ground for submarines. Among the patients carried were usually a few mental cases one of whom jumped overboard on September 19th notwithstanding the fact that a protection net was always thrown across the ship's side. He evidently came to his senses upon striking water for when we sighted him ten minutes later he was swimming in good style towards us.[38]

At least in the early days of the war there was no doubting the patriotism of the merchant seamen crews of the transports taking troops to the Dardanelles. H. Atkinson aboard the *Aragon* wrote on 20 April 1915, near the beginning of his 85-page diary covering the first six months of the Dardanelles campaign:

A notice was issued this morning asking for volunteers to assist in the loading of troops and ammunition on the Peninsula. Almost everyone volunteered but only 25 from each department were taken, as the

Admiral's request was for 75 from each ship. What this entails I don't know. But everybody else is taking a chance. So'm I.[39]

Five days later, on 25 April, his diary entry was given a title in large letters, *A Day in History*, and the opening paragraph ran: 'It is now 12 p.m. and events have taken place today that will never be forgotten by those who saw them as long as ever they live.'[40] The terror of war had been instantly revealed:

Then came the order to land our troops, and they fell in to load the boats. But before we landed a single man, there were three boats alongside full of dead, dying and wounded. A horrible spectacle. They were the remains of some of the first landing parties. One sailor in the bows of one boat had half his head shot away, and had just fallen back where he had been stood. Several more in that boat were quite dead, while others with terrible wounds in all parts of their bodies lay across the thwarts and in the bottoms of the boats which were saturated with blood. In one of the boats was a dog which when the troops were landing, was being taken ashore as a mascot. But the occupants of these boats, and also many more had never had the chance being riddled with machine guns as soon as ever they were within range, and this dog's master had been shot quite dead, and the dog stood beside him whining and shaking. It was brought aboard here and we tried to comfort it. But all the coaxing was of no avail.[41]

At nine in the evening of 27 April, Atkinson wrote:

Taken aboard about 200 more wounded off the *Soudan* and are now moving up to the fleet again to await orders. The sooner we get away from here with this crowd, the better. The ship reeks of mutilated flesh and stale blood. It is sickening. But everyone is doing their best. We have only one doctor (Military) on board here and one Chaplain. No nurses or R.A.M.C. And this doctor has been hard at it all the time amputating, and dressing, and as others have died, we have been removing them to the poop ready for burial. I hope we can get some sleep tonight. This will be the first time since Friday night. I am tired.[42]

The *Aragon*'s crew were rewarded. The ship sailed two days later with a cargo of 1500 dead, dying and wounded. Some of the dying and all of the wounded were landed in Alexandria and then Malta. On Sunday afternoon of 9 May Atkinson and friend got ashore in Valletta and watched a Maltese team beat the Army 1–0 in a local cup final, hired bikes for a ride into the countryside in the afternoon, went to the pictures in the evening. Coming out at 11 p.m. and 'rather too late to go anywhere else we dropped into an Italian Cafe for half an hour, and then made our way back to the ship . . . being both of the same emphatic opinion, that we had had a ripping good time.'[43]

When Atkinson's ship returned to the Dardanelles she became a floating command and administrative centre, with the 'heads' as Atkinson referred to the generals and admirals, regularly arriving aboard the *Aragon* for meetings, lunches and dinners. For six months from the end of April, Atkinson and shipmates became spectators to the daily traffic of the military elite and privileged listeners to staff officers' casual talk about the progress of the war locally and this formed the substance of Atkinson's diary. And then suddenly events aboard the *Aragon* took a dramatic turn, unconnectedly marked by the arrival of Lord Kitchener for lunch on 11 November, 1915.

Although plainly awed by Kitchener ('his dignity of bearing, and general appearance proclaim him to be what he truly is "A man with an iron will".') Atkinson was nevertheless willing to join a dissentient meeting of the crew which voted unanimously to remind the captain that their agreement expired in 14 days and that 'a relief crew was necessary to take our places as we had decided to discontinue on [25 November].' The crews discontents were a blend of frustration (' every privilege has been denied us, and we are tied here like a lot of prisoners')[45] an awareness that there were 'heads' who shared their sense of futility and a conviction 'that this campaign is a great and unnecessary expense to the Empire.'[46]

Another meeting of the crew a week later ominously 'conveyed to the Captain that we intended to cease work midnight 25 November.'[47] On the morning of the 25th the crew's dissidence was strengthened after a threatening speech from Rear Admiral Weymss – only to be weakened when promised payment of their balance of wages if they would sign clear of the *Aragon* and work another ship homeward. But this successful tactic of dividing the ranks of the strikers-to-be was then undone by a touch of senior officer arrogance and stupidity:

> At 5.30 p.m. a party of [thirty] armed Marines came on board the *Aragon*, and a little later the Captain and Chief Officer walked through the ship telling the men in by no means a polite manner to pack their boxes and get off the ship in an hour. A great many men had already decided to stay, but upon the word being passed all the men handy just packed their gear and went with the crowd. We were straight away hustled off the *Aragon* and on to a government tug . . . There were 107 of us all told.[47]

After a cold and hungry night while the tug was at anchor they were taken ashore the next morning and 'handed over to a Military Guard, who had been led to believe that we were really a desperate crowd. Of course they soon learned different. However for the time being we were subject to military discipline.'[48]

At this point the diary stops abruptly and what seems to be a remarkable event disappears into nothingness. But perhaps what happened subsequently to Atkinson and his shipmates is of no great consequence for there was in fact nothing exceptional in the actions of this crew nor in the punitive action that was certain to follow. Crews or parts of them had habitually being doing this *sort* of thing for many decades before the Great War and continued to do so afterwards, including during the Second World War. Known for their robust readiness to seize well-timed moments to stand up for themselves because they had learned over many generations that this was usually the best way to get grievances remedied, merchant seamen in the *Aragon* as elsewhere continued to do what was customary. Merchant seamen also continued to sail the ships which provisioned the nation and the armed forces. But this was what merchant seamen always did and it did not make them heroes. Neither did it make them villains when they rebelled. Like anyone else they were people of their time and of their circumstances.

Notes

1 Not quite true. Chinese and Africans drafted into the European battlegrounds as labourers.

2 L. Cope Cornford, *The Merchant Seamen In War*, London, 1918, p 138.

3 See, Tony Lane, 'The Political Imperatives of Bureaucracy and Empire: The Case of the Coloured Alien Seaman Order, 1925', *Immigrants and Minorities*, 13 (1994), 2 & 3, 104–129; Laura Tabili, *We Ask For British Justice*, Ithaca & London, 1994.

4 Between 1911 and 1913 the number of Chinese employed on British ships increased by 73 per cent – from 5366 to 9286 men. *The Times*, 10 July 1914.

5 *BPP* Report of the Committee Appointed by the Board of Trade to Inquire into Certain Questions Affecting the Mercantile Marine, Cmnd.1608, Minutes of Evidence, Appendix B, No.3.

6 L. Cope Cornford, op.cit., p. xvi.

7 Alfred Noyes' *Open Boats*, Edinburgh & London, 1917, is a good example of a thoroughly ambivalent text which on its high notes is shrill but elsewhere and often albeit in lower key, acknowledges considerate conduct by German submariners.

8 L. Cope Cornford, op.cit., p. 121.

9 Harold F.B. Wheeler, *Daring Deeds of Merchant Seamen in the Great War*, London, 1918, pps. 51–2.

10 ibid., p. 52.

11 ibid., p. 215.

12 HMSO British Vessels Lost at Sea, 1914–18 and 1939–45, Wellingborough, 1988.

13 Liddle Collection, Captain H.N. Taylor.

14 Liddle Collection, Captain B.A. Hardinge.

15 Liddle Collection, E.T.N. Lawrey.

16 Liddle Collection, C. Mather.

17 *The Times*, 30 March 1916.

18 See, Tony Lane, *The Merchant Seamen's War*, Liverpool, 1993, chap.9.

19 Cecil Foster, *1700 Miles in Open Boats*, London, 1924.

20 E.T.N. Lawrey, op.cit.

21 *BPP* Return Respecting the Number of Desertions from British Ships, CMND. 4803, 1909, pps. 10–19.

22 It was said of the 4,136 deserters in US ports in 1847 that most had gone to fight in Mexico: "An offer was made of seventy dollars for volunteers to supply troops for Mexico . . . whole crews entered for soldiers. At New Orleans and Charleston, and Mobile and the Southern ports of the United States they deserted in shoals." *BPP* House of Lords Select Committee on the Navigation Acts, 1847, Minutes of Evidence, Q.7620.

23 A.H. Jenks, 'Continuity of Employment in the Merchant Navy', Unpublished M.A. thesis, University of Liverpool, 1953, p.26.

24 Liddle Collection, Harry Forrest.

25 At the time of the Great War chanties were well-known to seamen even if their innovative moment had passed. Among the more popular themes in chanties were those dealing with the peronal costs and consequences of drink. See, Stan Hugill, *Shanties from the Seven Seas*, London, 1961 and A.L. Lloyd, *Folk Song in England*, London, 1975.

26 In the period 1901–10 the death rate in sailing ships was 1 in 76 and 1 in 163 in steam – see F.J. Lindop, 'A History of Seamen's Trade Unionism to 1929', Unpublished M.Phil. thesis, University of London, 1971, p.30. Seafaring in sail was roughly four times more dangerous than coalmining.

27 Lawrey, op.cit.

28 Liddle Collection, R.D.F. Powell.

29 Liddle Collection, R.D. Hoskins.

30 Lawrey op.cit.

31 Liddle Collection, Professor L.J. Davies.

32 R.D. Hoskins, op. cit.

33 Liddle Collection, I.P. Ellis.

34 ibid., p.155.

35 S.D.Waters, *From Clipper Ship to Motor Liner*, London, 1939, pps. 74–6.

36 C.Mather, op.cit.

37 Liddle Collection, Captain Atkinson.

38 Liddle Collection, H. Hiscock.

39 Imperial War Museum, 289, H. Atkinson ms, pps. 10–11.

40 ibid., p.12.

41 ibid., p.14.

42 ibid., p.24.

43 ibid., p.37.

44 ibid., p.75.

45 ibid., p.76.

46 ibid., pps.77–9.

47 ibid., p.84.

48 ibid., p.85.

Chapter 13

Brothers in Arms: The British Army and Navy at The Dardanelles

Geoffrey Till

Historically, amphibious operations have been central to the conduct of the 'British Way in Warfare' which maximised Britain's maritime advantages, avoided pitched battle on the continent of Europe but called instead for the imaginative use of an expeditionary army against the exposed vulnerabilities of a land-bound adversary. It was a demanding form of war since it required the closest cooperation of the Army and the Navy. Indeed, as a commentator writing in the mid-eighteenth century once shrewdly observed: 'the Fleet and Army acting in conjunction seem to be the natural bulwark of this kingdom.'[1]

This paper explores the relationship between the two services at all three levels of the Dardanelles campaign, namely the strategic, the operational and the tactical. How well did they co-operate? What strengths and weaknesses did they bring to bear? What did they think of each other? How did their experiences of war compare? The thesis presented here is a simple one: the higher the level of war, the worse the degree of co-operation between the services, the lower, the better. But without good co-operation, the British way in warfare was likely to prove a chimaera.[2]

ARMY-NAVY RELATIONS AT THE STRATEGIC LEVEL: THE INCEPTION OF THE CAMPAIGN

Despite the extent to which amphibious operations had been a feature of British strategic practice for several centuries, it was a rather neglected area of defence at the beginning of the century. The result was inevitable. As Roger Keyes told the Dardanelles Commission, the division of responsibility at Gallipoli was decided, impromptu, on the basis of 'some army book' and the King's Regulations. Much of the detail had to be re-learned in combat.[3]

This lack of inter-service agreement also reflected the fact that the two services were quite unable to agree a vision of the future role of amphibious operations in modern warfare. The Admiralty as a whole tended to be wary of diverting too much of the fleet away from its true purpose into the support of amphibious operations, unless, that is, these operations could themselves be seen as a way of improving the prospects for winning command. Before the war, army reactions could be more sceptical still, especially of the idea of opposed landings in modern conditions, but Army thinkers like Charles Callwell, the Director of Military Operations, were surprisingly keen on subsidiary operations against the Turks, outside Europe.

Despite such hesitations, and despite the immediate preoccupations of the war on the Western Front and/or the North Sea, there was soon in Sir Julian Corbett's words 'a stirring of the old instinct' for combined operations, once it became clear that there was no prospect of a quick decision on the Western Front, and provided not too many resources were committed. But when it was realised that the required investment of resources was going to be heavier than was at first thought, elements of both the Army and the Navy began to back-track.

The consequence of all this indecision was an incremental campaign in which the objectives changed as it went along, in which fundamental questions and issues were not addressed and in which both naval and land forces were fed into the theatre too late and in dribs and drabs. Naval and Army commanders regularly complained that the campaign would have been won had the forces in theatre at the end of the campaign been present at the beginning. Thus Lord Moyne, on 8 November 1915:

> We heard this morning that Lord Kitchener is on his way out. It is difficult to see how we can withdraw from here without great losses. Never can a campaign have been worse managed. Although 17 Divisions have been sent out here, it has always been by driblets which have not even sufficed to replace the wastage. If all the men who have been out here could have been available simultaneously, something might have been done.[4]

Some of the reasons for this have little to do with the fact that this operation required the co-operation of the two services from the highest level downwards. For instance, it is certainly true that the strategic environment against which the planners conceived and conducted the campaign was not static, but, on the contrary, constantly shifted in a way which undermined the strategic assumptions upon which the campaign had been built. Perceptions of Russian vulnerability for example did much to inspire early action, but worries about French resilience limited the number of troops thought to be available. Later it became clear that neither worry was so justified. Strategic uncertainty and change was a fact of life but separate from the problems of inter-service co-operation.

It was nonetheless true that each service had its own agenda and that their priorities were hard to reconcile. Kitchener was in favour of Eastern operations so long as that whatever was done would not suck so many forces away from the Western Front that the Allied position in France would be jeopardised. He was prepared to support a campaign lead and mainly fought by the Navy. Fisher's view was similar, although played out in a different dimension. He would support an operation in the Dardanelles just so long as it did not threaten the naval balance in the North Sea. He could spare a squadron of old surplus warships to blast their way through the straits; if more effort were required, he would support a joint operation in which the Army predominated. But the third of the three Titans, Churchill, also representing the maritime dimension of British defence, took a different line from either. He thought the Turkish Empire a ripe fruit ready to fall if the branches were shaken a little. In the Dardanelles British sea power could have a disproportionate effect on the outcome of the whole war, much more cost-effectively than feeding yet more men into the slaughter of the Western Front. Churchill remained confident that the Navy could get through on its own, with perhaps a little help from the Army on the way in and for garrisoning purposes afterwards.

The apparent inability of both services clearly to articulate their perspectives on the matter made successful co-ordination of these two dimensions of what should have been a joint national strategy prohibitively difficult. Two reasons can be adduced for this. Firstly, both services suffered from internal bureaucratic deficiencies which prevented them from developing both a real understanding of the requirements of joint operations and of the strengths and weaknesses of the enemy. The Admiralty's war staff was embryonic at best and failed even to identify the crucial differences in approach between Churchill and Fisher. Kitchener had a much more developed staff, but largely ignored it. Key figures in the War Office who might have restrained him, had already gone to France leaving him, in the admiring Hamilton's words, 'like a powerful engine from which we have removed all controls, regulators and safety valves'.[5]

Secondly, the machinery for high-level co-ordination *between* the services was also grievously defective and this was recognised even at the time. Hankey noted in his diary on 19 March;

> Wrote a memo to Prime Minister imploring him to appoint naval and military technical committee to plan out military attack on Dardanelles in great detail, so as to avoid repetition of naval fiasco, which is largely due to inadequate staff preparation.[6]

But, sadly too little was done. Inter-service co-operation at the strategic level remained largely a matter of the interaction of key personalities, rather than of the workings of an established machinery.

At this exalted level, the experience of war was a matter of high strategy, far removed from the clamour, discomforts and dangers of battle. It was a question of deciding the overall approach to the Dardanelles campaign, of weighing strategic options and of making choices. Those conducting the war at this level found the burden of exercising their responsibilities in the 'miasma' (as Fisher called it) created by continual change and continual uncertainty hard to bear. However energetic they might otherwise be, the strain was considerable for men like Fisher at 74, Kitchener at 65, Asquith at 63. Only the youthful Churchill, at 41, seemed to revel in the pulse of day-to-day events. But, in the end, both he and Fisher fell victim to their circumstances. Even the prestigious and magisterial Lord Kitchener, found himself thwarted (such as over Fisher's insistence on bringing home the *Queen Elizabeth*), his opinions disputed by his own War Office and, towards the end of the campaign, lost his personal sense of certainty, eventually going out to the Dardanelles, not as supreme arbiter, but more as an umpire between the 'evacuators' (led by General Monro), and those who wanted to carry on, led by Commodore Keyes. 'I could not help feeling sorry for him,' Keyes noted afterwards. 'He looked so terribly weary and harassed'.[7] In their own way, Britain's strategic leaders were also victims of the Dardanelles campaign.

It was the same, moreover, for all the participants, whether they represented the Army or the Navy. Indeed the issues and the loyalties cut right across service lines. Some of the most strident arguments, for example, were inside the Admiralty, between Fisher and Churchill. Both were masterful, peremptory, decidedly not 'organisation men'. They had a warm regard for each other, compounded by long association. Even after the debacle of May 1915, Fisher could write of Churchill: 'I backed him up till I resigned. I would do the same again! He had courage and imagination! He was a War Man!'[8] Despite this, Fisher eventually cracked for a variety of reasons, amongst them a growing sense that the Dardanelles campaign was putting too many ships and men at risk, sucking too many resources away from the war against the High Seas Fleet and growing sense of frustration at the way in which Churchill increasingly interfered in the Admirals' business. Their argument percolated downwards too. Keyes, ardently for the campaign, was dismissed by Fisher as 'very shallow . . . (and) a special pet of the First Lord'. Their dislike and the distrust were plainly mutual.[9] For his part Churchill was frustrated by the reluctance of his subordinates, first Carden and later De Robeck, to initiate and then to resume the scheme to force the straits. Curiously, in some of these intra-naval quarrels, the Army could sometimes act as mediator, as happened, most famously, at the War Council of 28 January when only Kitchener's intervention prevented Fisher from resigning and storming out of the meeting, there and then.

Later, when Keyes fought his last ditch campaign to prevent the evacuation and came to argue his case over the head of his local naval commander, he found Kitchener, not the new Admiralty Board, to be most sympathetic to his point of view. But it all came to nothing, and as he later remarked, 'Thus the Admiral [de Robeck] and the General [Monro] who were really entirely responsible for the lamentable policy of evacuation left the execution of this unpleasant task to an Admiral [Wemyss] and a General [Birdwood] who were strongly opposed to it'.[10]

This is not to say that the two services did not sometimes find themselves at odds, at the strategic level. There were quarrels between the khaki and the dark blue, most obviously over the recall of the *Queen Elizabeth*. And the fact that they were two different services was a factor in the debate. Quite clearly, for example, Hamilton did not feel he could appeal directly to Churchill for support against Fisher's reluctance to despatch proper landing craft, because this might have lacerated Kitchener's sensitivities. '[A]lthough the sailors [in the theatre] want me to pull this particular chestnut out of the fire, it is just as well they should know I am not going to speak to their Boss even under the most tempting circumstances'.[11] Nonetheless, at the Grand Strategic level, decisions were based less on service loyalties, than on differing, and changing, perceptions of the strategic issues and on the crucial interaction of personalities under acute strain. Not surprisingly perhaps, and given the absence of an effective inter-service machinery to manage this necessary process effectively, the result was an incremental, unsure, approach to the campaign which left those conducting it in theatre with the dismaying, indeed demoralising, impression that their leaders were making up their strategy as they went along.

ARMY/NAVY CO-OPERATION AT THE OPERATIONAL LEVEL

The experience of war of commanders at the operational level was fundamentally different from that of the strategic planners at home, for they were so much nearer to the action. All the operational commanders found it hard to bear, for what Hamilton called 'the strain of waiting' was not 'softened by distance. Here we see the flashes, we hear the shots; we stand in our main battery and are yet cut off from sharing the efforts of our comrades. Too near for reflection, too far for intervention: on tenterhooks, in fact, a sort of mental crucifixion.'[12] The Commanders were debilitated by a variety of stomach disorders, physical ailments and nervous strain, and several had to be invalided home (including Admiral Carden and General Hunter-Weston). They did not of course share the daily privations and dangers of the troops ashore, but occasionally came uncomfortably close to it. Compton Mackenzie, then working in the Intelligence section on the *Arcadian*, went ashore regularly. On one visit he recalled:

> Looking down I saw squelching up from the ground on either side of my boot like a rotten mangold the deliquescent green and black flesh of a Turk's head.[13]

Despite this, theirs was generally the experience of command, rather than of fighting. At this level of war, moreover, there did not seem to be much difference in the experience of the Commanders in both services, a fact which reinforced their support for each other.

In the theatre of operations, inter-service co-operation was better than it was in London since decisions were consciously and deliberately made, and many of them look sensible even in retrospect. For instance, after the failure of the Navy on 18 March, a joint conference was held on *Queen Elizabeth* in Mudros harbour of all the Admirals and Generals in which it was agreed that combined action was now necessary but 'must be postponed until plans had been developed and perfected.' Arrangements for the next few weeks were agreed.

> And so the meeting came to an end with perfect accord between the Navy and the Army, and we each went our way to our several tasks.[14]

Nonetheless the machinery for joint action was plainly far from perfect. Corbett was rather proud of the fact that there was no joint force commander since he preferred a 'combination of equals'. The Army and the Navy went about their complementary business largely in isolation. Consultations were largely a matter of telling each other what was going to be done. Hamilton was absolutely clear that he had no right to interfere in the naval side of the campaign. '. . .Obviously I cannot go out of my element to urge the Fleet to actions, the perils of which I am professionally incompetent to judge.' Even when de Robeck was plainly hoping for a steer from Hamilton, it was not forthcoming. De Robeck for his part was equally scrupulous in not interfering in the General's affairs. Interestingly, Hamilton clearly thought there should have been a theatre commander on the *medical* side of the campaign, but did not apparently extend this logic to the operational area.[15]

There was also only rudimentary machinery for co-ordination between the two services. Hamilton was usually on one ship, the *Arcadian* at Alexandria or Lemnos, but was later at Imbros.[16] De Robeck was usually somewhere at sea. During the landings on 25 April Hamilton joined De Robeck on *Queen Elizabeth* but this meant 'his staff being incarcerated in gun turrets and other clanging recesses where they were quite useless'.[17] Putting the staffs of both Rear-Admiral Wemyss and General Hunter-Weston both on the *Euryalus* off W beach was certainly a mistake. The latter's Chief of Staff operated in a chart room 20 yards from A turret. 'The 9.2" gun was firing about every five minutes and whenever it went off, it made chaos of the divisional signals and reports which had been laid out in neat rows on the chart table'.[18] At Suvla, Hamilton once again had his own ship, but this was immobilised with boiler trouble for six frustrating hours while, as he suspected, Stopford frittered away the possibilities of victory ashore. Such physical separation encouraged both services to take decisions independently. On 9 May the Navy held a big conference aboard *Queen Elizabeth* to consider the prospects for a renewed naval assault on the narrows, without the presence of a single soldier, even though the Army might well have been virtually marooned on the peninsula if the attack had gone badly wrong.[19]

These faults were, however, sometimes ascribable to the deficiencies of the services themselves rather than to problems deriving from the fact of their having to co-operate. Hamilton's initial dismay at his own ramshackle staff was clear:

> My staff still bear the bewildered look of men who have hurriedly been snatched from desks to do some extraordinary turn in some unheard-of theatre. One or two of them put on uniform for the first time in their lives an hour ago. Leggings awry, spurs upside down, belts over shoulder straps! I haven't a notion of who they all are.[20]

They settled down, but Hamilton himself was obsessed with the supposed benefits of a small Headquarters staff and separated it from his administrative staff, clearly regarding the latter as a tedious encumbrance.[21] He quite consciously took a non-interventionist view of his command function, often contrasting the Army style of command, with the more centralised and proactive Navy style. But in the circumstances of the Dardanelles when the fleet was untypically disaggregated down a long coastline, instead of concentrated into battle order on the high seas, even the Navy had to delegate more than it was used to.[22]

Nonetheless, Keyes in particular was sometimes incensed at what he regarded as the administrative inefficiency of the Army, viewing them as suffering from 'overstaffing and the water-tight compartments and miles of red tape which tightly bound them up and add enormously to *our* difficulties'. Supplying the troops ashore, he thought, was made unnecessarily difficult 'if his [Hamilton's] people are so absolutely careless and callous.'[23]

Many of these potential inter-service hazards were, however, compensated for by the fact that the Naval and Army leaders got on so well together. This was partly a function of deliberate policy by all concerned. Keyes was quite insistent that 'this was going to be an expedition in which there should be no quarrels and the Admiral would send home anyone responsible for friction [with the Army] at once without the slightest hesitation'.[24] Keyes was already a friend of Hamilton's Chief of Staff,

General Braithwaite, and Hamilton too was a family friend. Everyone liked and admired De Robeck, and all these close personal relationships do much to explain why the two services were not at loggerheads despite such difficult circumstances. To a large extent, the fact that they did get on so well, and the fact that they did come to complementary conclusions, if by independent routes, rather concealed the huge deficiencies in the mechanics of their co-operation.

Curiously enough, it was much the same story when things began to go badly wrong and the end of the campaign came into sight. As we have seen, service affiliation played little part in determining positions for or against evacuation. Keyes was as angry with De Robeck as he was with Monro for their decision to withdraw, but in neither case did this disagreement become personal.

It was, finally, also true that what Corbett called the 'relative primacy of the land and sea element'[25] shifted backwards and forwards according to the changing nature of the campaign, in a way which much complicated the co-ordination process, making it difficult to see who really should have been in charge. This also contributed to key decisions often later considered to have been mistakes. These include:

- Independent naval operations at the beginning of the campaign conducted without the presence of immediate available land forces should their use be proved necessary.

- Initial landings at the tip of the peninsula in order directly to facilitate the naval passage, instead of at easier sites further to the north, perhaps Suvla.

- Dispersing forces between seven beaches, rather than one or two in a manner which made it difficult for success to be reinforced.[26]

However, with the wisdom of hindsight such criticisms are easy. It is important to remember that amphibious operations were recognised to be inherently difficult in that they did require the closest operational co-ordination between participating services. As Hankey warned,

It must be remembered that combined operations require more careful preparation than any other class of military enterprise.[27]

Moreover, even as amphibious operations went, this was an ambitious exercise in that it was opposed from the start, and conducted in a distant area in the most demanding of climatic and topographical conditions.

It is indeed important not to be seduced by the advantages of hindsight into failing to recognise the scale of the administrative achievement involved into improvising at such short notice so large and difficult an amphibious undertaking.[28] The tendency to focus on the problems of the campaign should not blind observers to the fact of its successes. Getting the Army ashore in such numbers and keeping them there for so long remains an impressive achievement. The Suvla landing and even more the final evacuation showed how much had been learned during the course of the campaigns by both services, separately and jointly. As so often, Corbett put the point particularly well:

> In that marvellous evacuation we see the national genius for amphibious warfare raised to its highest manifestation. In hard experience and successive disappointments the weapon had been brought to a perfect temper, and when the hour of fruition came to show of what great things it was capable, it was used only to effect a retreat.[29]

ARMY/NAVY CO-OPERATION AT THE TACTICAL LEVEL

The successful conduct of the Dardanelles campaign required the closest tactical co-operation between the two services in the performance of a variety of functions. Firstly, the troops and their material had to be transported safely into the battle area, in some cases from thousands of miles away. This was an uncomfortable process for all concerned. Diaries and letters home are full of complaints that the men were not allowed ashore enough along the way in places like Malta or Alexandria. The cynical observed that the officers were much better treated in this respect. Even so, these were merely inconveniences. Before the April landings, there were very few losses in transit, thanks largely to the extent the Royal Navy commanded the sea.

Inefficiencies were perhaps more noticeable in the theatre, than outside it. Admiral Wemyss, trying to make sense of the problem back at Mudros, was incensed at the monumental incompetence of the loading authorities in England and at Alexandria. Nearly all the supplies had to be cross-decked and restowed and, given the inadequate facilities at Mudros, this was often a major problem. Waste and the delayed despatch of huge quantities of war material were the inevitable consequences.[30] Experience grew, but it was a painful process. Later the prospect of local U-boat and torpedo boat attack provided extra complications.

Once in the theatre, the troops had to be conveyed to the landing area. This was not easy. In order to produce a speedy landing on 25 April and later at Suvla, they were mainly packed onto operational warships, often in situations of acute discomfort. The experience of the men of XIth Division was not untypical. The day before they sailed, on 5 August, they had been inoculated against cholera, a process which in 1915 had a sledge-hammer effect on the strongest constitution. At dawn on the 6th, they went aboard a variety of destroyers and little steamers like the SS *Partridge*. The men stood, crushed together with very little elbow room.

1. French heavy artillery: 240mm gun in action, Cape Helles, Gallipoli, 1915 (J. Bareille: Liddle Collection). See Chapter 2: The Substance of War.

2. Imperial Germany exerts its authority in East Africa. (R. Bennett: Liddle Collection). 'If the British public only knew the full tale of death and suffering bravely endured by Africans' (the Bishop of Zanzibar, 1920). See Chapter 3: The Civilian Dimension of War.

3. Winston Churchill with H.M. King George V leaves Blandford Railway Station, Dorset, February 1915 on his way to reviewing the Royal Naval Division before its departure for Gallipoli. (W.E. Bland: Liddle Collection)
See Chapter 4: Churchill and the Strain of Office.

4. A less familiar photograph of Lord Kitchener captures a fleeting smile. (Liddle Collection).
See Chapter 5: Kitchener at the War Office

5. Field-Marshal Sir Douglas Haig
   (Earl Haig of Bemersyde).
   See Chapter 7: Haig and
   Pershing

6. General Pershing arrives in
   France, Boulogne, May 1917.
   (Liddle Collection).
   See Chapter 7: Haig &
   Pershing.

7. Bleak outlook.(C.Thierry: Liddle Collection) 'from our ranks rose the lament "It'll never end - never!"' (a French soldier describing the Chemin des Dames offensive, April 1917). See Chapter 8: The French High Command and the Mutinies of Spring 1917.

8. Photographically in step, the war won and their own armistice expressed in a smile: Prime Minister Lloyd George and Field-Marshal Haig in Paris. (Associated Newspapers). See Chapter 9: British Decision Making 1917.

9. A sailor of S.M.S. Deutschland gets a hug from the ship's mascot.
(Militärgeschichtliches Forschungsamt, Potsdam)
See Chapter 11: The German Naval War 1914-18.

10. Lt Cdr F.J. Stenson of H.M.S.
    Marmora (F.J. Stenson: Liddle
    Collection)
    See Chapter 12: The British
    Experience of Enforcing Blockade

11. Merchant seamen of the "Clan
    Macrae". From left to right, the
    2nd Refrigerating Engineer, the
    Ship's Carpenter and the 4th Mate.
    In 1915, the year of this
    photograph, the Clan Macrae had
    evaded attack by a U-boat in
    Liverpool Bay. (A.B. Cumming:
    Liddle Collection)
    See Chapter 13: The British
    Merchant Seaman at War.

12. (In the foreground, left to right) General Sir Ian Hamilton, Rear Admiral C.F. Thursby and Lieutenant-General W.R. Birdwood on a newly erected pier a few days after the 25 April 1915 landing at Anzac Cove. (L.S. Ormsby Johnson, Liddle Collection). See Chapter 14: Brothers in Arms.

13. MAS boat ready for action. (Italian Naval Archives, Rome) See Chapter 15: Italy and the War in the Adriatic.

One by one we began to nod and doze, like old tired cart horse standing asleep in their stalls. And one by one we began to lean heavily against each other, to lurch and sag and give at the knees, until at last we sank slowly down into a sprawling overlapping heap. We had been on our feet since dawn. Most of us had 'gyppy tummy' and many were suffering from sand-fly fever, a mild form of dysentery.

By the time they landed many of these men had been on their feet for 17 hours. That these relatively inexperienced men of Kitchener's new divisions did not seem to display particular energy at Suvla Bay hardly seems surprising.[31]

If and when the enemy resisted the landings it became a question of suppressing his defence and somehow protecting the landing troops against his fire. On 25 April the only means available for this were cutters towed towards the beach by steam pinnaces, and then rowed ashore by sailors. The gallantry of the young midshipmen conducting this activity, of the defenceless sailors rowing backwards and forwards and of the 30 to 40 enduring soldiers wedged tightly into each cutter is well known. Although at several crucial places the Turks fortunately withheld fire, the carnage on landing confirmed Callwell's worst fears, especially at V and W beaches. The converted steamer *River Clyde* (a rudimentary landing craft complete with platforms, pontoons and bow-mounted machine guns) was an imaginative response to the problem, but its arrival did not go according to plan, and the fact that there was only one of them meant that its un-fortunate passengers attracted a fatal concentration of Turkish fire. At Suvla steel-plated motor driven 'beetles' carried the soldiers safely ashore, showing how well the awful lessons of 25 April had been absorbed.

The Navy had also to provide gunfire support against the defences the Turks and the Germans had been assiduously building ever since the arrival of the Allies in this theatre. Its moral effect on the Allied soldiers was quite clear from countless contemporary sources:

> The soldiers in my boat were simply enthralled with the sight of the cliff face being literally blown away by the ship's guns and the spectacle of the ship steaming in firing was magnificent. . . .The change in their atti-tude towards what lay ahead during that short run in alongside the ship was quite phenomenal.[32]

On occasions, reality conformed to appearance, and naval gunfire support proved decisive. Naval shrapnel fire against counter-attacking Turkish troops advancing in the open could be particularly devastating. On 28 April, a single shrapnel shell from *Queen Elizabeth* destroyed an entire company of Turkish troops advancing on the hard-pressed defenders at Y Beach. At Suvla, Kemal's six battalions counter-attacking the Allied position on Chunuk crest were hit heavily by naval gunfire. 'Thank God we've got a Navy!' said private Fred Boler, 'We'd all be dead as mutton now, or else.'[33]

But it is equally true that very often the moral and physical effect that such gunfire had on the Turks was much less than appearances suggested. Thus Lieutenant Clayton of the Lancashire Fusiliers:

> We thought nothing could survive the ship's guns, but they bombarded too far inland and the trenches overlooking the landing beaches were not touched, so the rifle and machine-gun fire poured into us as we got out of the boats and made for the sandy shore. There was tremendously strong wire where my boat landed. I got my wire cutters out but could not make the slightest impression. The front of the wire was now a thick mess of men, the majority of whom never moved again. The noise was ghastly and the sights horrible.[34]

So what went wrong? Why did the naval gunfire support so often fail? There were many reasons for it. In the first place, the scale of the requirement had been underestimated. Captain Dent in *Arcadian* recorded that he was 'chilled to the bone' by how sanguine the headquarters were over the landing prospects. Eighteen battleships and twelve cruisers were provided in support of the landing operation, which sounds generous enough but they were mostly old ships not needed for more important duty in the North Sea and had poor fire-control systems. The ships' holdings in shells might have been appropriate for a sea battle, but were not ideal for the support of landing operations. They had too few fused shrapnel shells and their delayed action HE shells were inappropriate to their targets. The fire distribution was debatable too, with a paradoxical concentration of effort at S and Y beaches where little resistance was expected. The ships at Y were supposed to keep the heavy Turkish batteries further inland on Achi Baba quiet, while the ships at S did the same to the Turkish guns on the Asiatic shore. The result was rather thin coverage at V and W beaches where it was, as things turned out, most needed.

This partly explains the widespread view that the navy fired too far inland, on the crests of the hills overlooking the beaches or even behind them, leaving the defences on the beaches themselves often largely untouched. A fire co-ordination meeting on 21 April on *Euryalus* had concluded ambiguously. Some attendees apparently received the impression that they had after all been expressly forbidden to come in close for fear of grounding or to engage targets on the beach lest they hit the landing troops. It is easy to see possible reasons for this last decision. The poor fire-control systems of most of the ships meant they would fire on a flat trajectory, initially perhaps 60 feet above the departing soldiers' heads. As the troops approached the shore, they would obviously become vulnerable to naval fire themselves, unless it were lifted. The concentrations of fire needed therefore, to cut a path through thick wire were never achieved. In many cases also, the Turkish defences were practically invisible. The confusion ashore made it difficult for the ships to distinguish friend from foe, even if there were observation parties to hand.

According to Captain Lockyer, present at the *Euryalus* meeting, some of these deficiencies would have been improved had the ships come in closer. He left the meeting believing that he had discretion to do so, and four days later steamed in the *Implacable* at X Beach blasting everything in sight at a few hundred yards range, where most of his colleagues elsewhere kept a mile or two back from their beaches. After the war, Lockyer claimed that his close support had been instrumental in getting his soldiers ashore on X Beach with very few casualties, and argued that had others followed his example, the 29th Division would have got ashore much more easily, consolidated a much bigger bridgehead before the Turkish counterattacks began, probably altering the nature of the whole campaign.[35] The same sense of opportunities lost informed the view of the then Lieutenant-Commander Cunningham in command of the destroyer *Scorpion*:

> . . . we destroyers lay off the beaches (on 25 April) . . . though for some incomprehensible reason we had the strictest orders not to open fire in support of the Army. I have never discovered who was responsible for this stupid edict, for many opportunities were missed of directly helping the landings by destroyers – so close inshore they could even see the Turks bobbing up and down in their trenches. The *Scorpion* itself lay stopped for a considerable time off V Beach, 500 yards off a trench full of the enemy firing on our troops, and unable to do anything. We could see our infantry lying flat on their faces on the beach under withering fire, and every now and then one or two men dashing out to cut the wire . . . only to be quickly shot down. It was a tragedy and a mortifying situation for a well-gunned destroyer; but a few days later . . . an order that never should have been given was rescinded.[36]

Although we should be careful about accepting such testimony at face value, since at X Beach, there were in any case only some twelve Turkish defenders and post-attack analysis showed that their minimal defences had not in fact been much affected by *Implacable*'s fire,[37] it does seem fair to conclude that naval gunfire support could have been better than it was.

But because the landed forces were unable to win themselves enough elbow room, the amphibious phase of the operation had to last much longer than originally anticipated. The Navy needed to stay in close attendance for months, rather than for hours, days or even weeks. For the oceanic British used to the pursuit of decisive and dramatic encounters on the high seas, these littoral operations were an unfamiliar business.

The support of the landed force involved transportation, ferrying troops in and out. It required a logistic operation, huge by contemporary standards that depended on maintaining local command of the sea, and when the U-boats arrived in the Mediterranean, this had to be fought for.[38] It also required a considerable effort in simple transportation at every stage of the process from the despatch of supplies from Britain to their delivery to the soldiers from supply dumps organised on the beaches themselves. A huge forward base was established at Mudros, and streams of little boats shuttled backwards and forwards every day conveying supplies to the jetties, small harbours and supply dumps provided by naval logistics parties ashore. It was a gigantic and largely unfamiliar business, but in the end the logistics system impressed observers like the newspaper man Ashmead Bartlett[39] and seems to have worked reasonably well.

The supply of medical services followed the same pattern. Initially the scale of the casualties was underestimated and the evacuation of the wounded was at first little short of scandalous. Contemporary accounts are full of almost unbelievably grisly descriptions of the sufferings and neglect of the wounded. Poor organisation exacerbated shortages in all types of medical supplies and hospital ships especially at the beginnings of the campaign, and the heat, continuing problems with water and flies made everything worse, but, once again, hard experience taught many lessons, and things improved.

Naval gunfire support had a continuingly vital role to play, not least because the Army's own artillery was woefully deficient through most of the campaign. Hamilton was forever lamenting the shortage of shells and of the plunging fire of howitzers needed against the well protected Turkish trenches. According to Lord Moyne, moreover, 'our artillery arrangements (are) astoundingly primitive.'[40] The army's guns were frequently sited down on the beaches, from where it was as difficult for them to deliver the pin-point accuracy up on the hill tops that the close proximity of friend and foe demanded, as it was for the naval gunners out to sea. In Callwell's view, Hamilton's artillery deficiencies were 'undoubtedly . . . one of the contributory causes to bringing about the failure of the Dardanelles venture.'[41] Clearly the Navy was still needed to help rectify the situation.

But the artillery problems encountered in the landing phase carried on afterwards. The fleet, like the army, was short of shells of the right sort. As the soldiers moved inland in very difficult terrain, they moved out of sight, and this often made it difficult to provide close gunfire support safely. On 7th August British troops at last fought their way over the crest of Chunuk Bair above Suvla and gazed down in triumph for the first time on the Dardanelles. They were then shelled by their own side and forced to abandon their hard-won position, never subsequently regaining it. There is still some doubt about whether it was naval or army shells that did the damage (although majority opinion inclined at the time and has remained that the Navy was to blame) the tragic mistake on Chunuk Bair, was simply the inevitable consequence of a spotting/communication system that was too primitive for such complicated warfare.[42]

The Navy's tasks were more difficult in other ways too. Now the ships themselves were subjected to regular artillery attack from Turkish batteries ashore. Worse still, Turkish torpedo boats and German submarines inflicted significant casualties. The battleship *Goliath* was sunk by a torpedo boat on the night of 12/13 May in Morto bay; the U-21 sank the battleship *Triumph* in broad daylight and in full view of the troops at Anzac cove on the 25th. The Navy moved to increase the defences of its other big ships on site, but to no avail. Three days later, the battleship *Majestic* was sunk, and all the big ships were pulled back. Only later was the inshore submarine and torpedo boat menace mastered and normal service resumed.

There was, finally, always the notion that if things went badly, the navy would be needed for a final evacuation. Many expected appalling losses. Lord Curzon painted an apocalyptic scene:

> A moment must come when a final *sauve qui peut* takes place, and when a disorganised crowd will press in despairing tumult on to the shore and into the boats. Shells will be falling and bullets ploughing their way into this mass of retreating humanity ... Conceive the crowding into the boats of thousands of half crazy men, the swamping of craft, the nocturnal panic, the agony of the wounded, the hecatombs of the slain.[43]

But in fact it was not like this at all. Retreats are never victories, but this one came close to being one. It was meticulously organised in two separated stages first from Anzac and Suvla and then from Helles. The Turks were fooled into missing their opportunity to inflict huge casualties by careful deception and inspired organisation at every level of the operation. Amazingly there were virtually no casualties; everyone got away and much of the supplies that would have been of use to the Turks was skilfully destroyed. The withdrawal was a graphic demonstration of how much had been learned in this campaign, by both services.

Overall, at the tactical level this was a campaign in which the two services were closely enmeshed to unique degree, and for much longer than anyone anticipated. One young naval officer on the *Prince of Wales* was perceptive about the implications of such complex operations:

> An exaggerated but quite plausible case: e.g. a battery concealed by bushes opens fire on our troops, a captive balloon approximately locates them. The battleship opens fire on the battery directed by the balloon which has a telephone; an aeroplane attacks the balloon, the battleship's anti-aircraft guns open fire on the aeroplane, a submarine attacks the battleship and she sinks. In the meanwhile, after the first shells, our soldiers have discreetly returned to their dugouts and are watching the show through the front door![44]

So, given the close proximity of the Army and the Navy fighting their own separate but interconnecting wars, how did their experiences compare, and what did their people think of each other? For several reasons, historians might have expected a degree of resentment from the soldiery towards the Navy. After all, if the Navy had done its job in the first place and fought its way through the narrows, these terrible landings would not have been necessary in the first place. Admiral Keyes, watching the unfolding horror on V Beach, was acutely aware of this fact; it was, he told a companion, '. . . the most humiliating day of my life'.[45] There were also many instances where things went awry: the troops landed at the wrong place, the naval bombardments that missed their targets, the water that did not arrive, the inadequate medical services and so on.

It was also undeniably true that even for the ratings, and certainly for the officers, conditions afloat were so much better than they were ashore. Visitors aboard immediately noted the absence of flies and smells, the presence of clean linen, the simple pleasures of taking a hot bath, or a whisky and soda. On *Euryalus*, Major John Gillam of the Army Service Corps, recorded his impression:

> Never, surely, was Army and Navy so closely allied. I go below to get breakfast . . . I feel shamed to be there . . . The Steward calmly hands the menu around, just as he might on a peaceful voyage. What a contrast! Two boiled eggs, coffee, toast and marmalade. Here we are sitting down to a good meal and men are fighting on the cliffs a few hundred yards away.[46]

The naval officers sometimes had the curious feeling that they were more witnesses to the action than participants. Here is one officer writing home:

> This afternoon, I've been lying on your chair on the upper deck listening to the *Queen*'s band playing waltzes 500 yards on my starboard side, while a mile on my port side, projectiles are flopping into the sea from some Turkish Battleship in the Narrows – when they get closer, we get under way and steam about. Right ahead of me is incessant rifle fire and on the beach is shrapnel bursting from a gun three miles away which we cannot locate.[47]

Naval accounts are full of a kind of appalled admiration for the suffering and stoicism of their mates ashore. Thus Boy Telegraphist Blamey, on 29 April:

> It's a sight to watch the army shore of a night time; to look at it, one would imagine it impossible for anything human to live in it . . . Big shells bursting in mid-air and all over the land white searchlights are playing

on both parties. If a shell bursts on the earth, a huge sheet of flame and sparks shoot up – To see it makes one wonder if there is such.a thing as civilisation. And to think while our mates ashore are going through it, some shirking . . . devils who could be here are asleep comfortably in their beds in England.[48]

More surprising perhaps is the fact that the diaries and letters of the soldiers reveal little resentment against their more fortunate naval colleagues afloat.

A good deal of this no doubt was due to a recognition of how much their futures depended on the Navy, for all the reasons described earlier. This was nowhere more apparent, than when it suddenly seemed as though the Navy might be forced to abandon them. The gloom with which the soldiers watched the enforced departures of the big ships on 28 May is evidence of the extent of the psychological as well as practical support they had hitherto provided. Compton Mackenzie described the scene graphically:

I saw them in full flight, transports and battleships, the *Agamemnon* seeming to lead the van. The air was heavy that evening and, what wind there was being in the south, the smoke of every ship was driven down astern, which gave the effect of a number of dogs running away with their tails between their legs. The sense of abandonment was acute. There was a sudden lull in the noise of the beach, as if every man had paused to stare at the unfamiliar emptiness of the water and then turned to his neighbour with a question in his eyes about their future here. It is certain that the Royal Navy has never executed a more demoralising manoeuvre in the whole of its history.[49]

Fortunately, in due course, the big ships returned in time to ensure that this sense of abandonment was only temporary.

But the soldiers' acceptance of their naval colleagues' somewhat better lot was also reinforced by their awareness of the fact that they were in constant peril too. For the men afloat, there were also periods of boredom and mere discomfort and occasions of high drama, desperate fear and supreme courage. At sea, the experience of war could be as searing as anything ashore. Here for instance is the account of an ordinary rating of a minesweeping attempt in the Narrows in early March:

I left the ship at 6 pm this night [11 March] with officers in charge, to enter the enemy's mine field, with 7 trawlers. We lost one trawler sunk by gunfire but the crew were saved. It was a very dirty night. Never shall I forget that night so long as I live. We were close to the shore and I think that they fired everything at us from 11" gun to a pistol and the screaming of the shells was enough to drive you off your head, but our Officer was very cool. He gave orders for mine sweepers to retire. We destroyed several lines of mines, after being in the minefield for about 4 hours. We returned to the ship at 8 am the following morning after being in the boat for 14 hours without anything to eat or drink, cold and wet through. I was very bad after it as it had shaken my senses very much. We were all recommended to the Admiralty and they acknowledged it, but have heard nothing more about it since. We were lucky to get away with our lives. *Another escape.*[50]

The soldiers knew that their comrades afloat had gone through many other such experiences. Their accounts show that the attempt to force the straits on 18 March was another example – and so was the often remarked courage of the young Midshipman and sailors rowing their cutters backwards and forwards to the landing beaches under gunfire on 25 April.

There were of course distinctive differences between this kind of experience and those ashore. At sea it was more a matter of striking contrasts. At one moment a ship could be safely proceeding in relative comfort and apparent security, at the next a torpedo or mine hit could overwhelm it in a sudden catastrophe for all on board. The accounts frequently remark on the distinctive characteristic of naval warfare. Its implications for readiness were realised too. It meant that a ship's company had to be instantly ready for action at all times; preparation for action was a matter of minutes, not hours or days.

Nonetheless there were also many similarities between the sailors and the soldiers, in experience and requirement. Here a junior officer on the *Prince of Wales* ruminates on the lessons he has learned about the nature of leadership and courage, in terms that could apply to any fighting situation:

That the fighting efficiency of the ship depends largely on the nerves of the officers. When shells come your way, one is conscious that [the] men look to see the effect on you, and if giving an order or speaking at all one must on no account break the sentence or show any perturbation whatever. That one very soon becomes used to the 'ping' of bullets and the noise of shells and unless they are *very* close take no action whatever. That one becomes quickly immune to the sight of wounded and dead, that you acquire a totally different view of life and death, that England and all its associations become vague and unreal, and that the crash of guns and shell are the natural accompaniment to one's thoughts which are entirely taken up with the strain and excitement of the fight. That the man who in quiet moments has something cheery to think about is lucky.[51]

For all these reasons, personal relations between soldiers and sailors of all ranks remained excellent. A few days before Suvla, Lieutenant-Colonel Foster was hospitably entertained afloat, enjoying a 'wondrous' whisky and soda.

I learned that sailor men call soldiers 'leather-necks' and get called 'bilge-rats' in return. So you see relations between the services are of the most cordial nature.[52]

Ten years after the event, the correspondent of *The Times* indeed remarked:

It is an uncommon thing for all classes of His Majesty's ships to fight almost in first line with His Majesty's troops, and the mutual respect felt by the Services for one another at the close of the action was not among the least of the benefits derived from this co-operation. Gone, we hope for ever, are the stories of the old wars which so often told of dissensions between seamen and soldiers.[53]

By the end of the campaign, the Army and the Navy really had become brothers in arms, and nowhere more so than at the tactical and operational levels. But, sadly, when peace returned, the two services went back to their old ways and their individual preoccupations. As a result, many of the same lessons had to be re-learned in the experiences of the Norway and Dakar operations of 1940, and the 'British Way in Warfare' turned out at first to be more an aspiration than a reality.

Notes

1   Thomas More Molyneux, *Conjunct Expeditions, or Expeditions that have been carried on by the Fleet and Army*. London, 1759.
2   I am grateful to Sub Lt Andy Yeomans, Royal Navy, for his research efforts at the Imperial War Museum and for Nigel Steel at the same institution for his help to both of us.
3   Dardanelles Commission, Evidence p 1453. Public Record Office, Cab 19/33. For this and for much that follows in the next two paragraphs I am grateful to David Massam of the University of Oxford.
4   Entry for 5th Nov 1915, in B. Bond and S. Robbins [Eds], *Staff Officer : The Diaries of Lord Moyne*, London, Leo Cooper, 1987, p. 49.
5   General Sir Ian Hamilton, *Gallipoli Diary*, Vol I. London; Edward Arnold, 1920.
6   Sir Maurice Hankey, *The Supreme Command 1914–1918*, London, Allen and Unwin, 1961, Vol 1. p. 293.
7   Alan Moorehead, *Gallipoli*, London, Andre Deutsch, 1983 pp 269–271. Keyes, Diary Entries for 17–24 November 1915. *The Keyes Papers*, London: Naval Records Society, 1972, pp. 243–255.
8   Admiral of the Fleet Lord Fisher, *Memories*, London, Hodder & Stoughton, 1919, p. 57.
9   For Fisher's views on Keyes see his letter to Beatty of 3 February and to Jellicoe 4 April 1915, in A.J. Marder [Ed] *Fear God and Dread Nought*, Vol III London, Jonathan Cape, 1959, see *Keyes Papers*, op. cit., p. 229.
10 Quoted Moorehead, op. cit., p. 271.
11 Hamilton, Vol I. Entry for 22 March 1915, p. 45.

12. Hamilton, Vol I, pp. 192–3.

13 Compton Mackenzie, *Gallipoli Memories,* London, Cassell, 1929, p. 83.

14 Adm. of the Fleet Lord Wester Wemyss,*The Navy in the Dardanelles Campaign*, London, Hodder and Stoughton, 1924, pp. 40–2.

15 Hamilton, Vol II, p. 32. Also see their discussion of 20th August, Hamilton, Vol II, pp. 124–5. For his medical point see Vol I, p. 367.

16 ibid, pp. 104–5.

17 General Sir Hugh Beach, 'The Murderous Responsibility' *Gallipoli Memorial Lecture Series*, 1985, p. 16.

18 *The Naval Memoirs of Admiral J.H. Godfrey* Unpublished, 1964. Vol II, p. 4.

19 ibid.

20 Hamilton, I, Vol I, p. 16.

21 Beach, op. cit. p. 16.

22 Hamilton, I, pp. 132–3, 127.

23 *Keyes papers*, op. cit, pp. 165, 167.

24 Vol II, Letter to his wife, 2 July 1915, p. 157.

25 Sir Julian Corbett, *Naval Operations*, London, Longmans, Green, 1921, Vol II, pp. 177–8.

26 Callwell for example believed strongly that all the troops should have been landed on the littoral north of Gaba Tepe in the area subsequently known as Anzac Cove. Major-General Sir Charles Callwell, *The Dardanelles*, London, Constable, 119, pp. 128–9.

27 Quoted in J. Laffin, *Damn the Dardanelles : The Story of Gallipoli*, London, Osprey, 1980, pp. 40–1.

28 Peter Liddle, *Men of Gallipoli*, London, Allen Lane, 1976, p. 98.

29 Corbett, op. cit., p. 245.

30 Wemyss, op. cit., pp. 186–7, p. 37.

31 J. Hargrave, *The Suvla Bay Landing*, London, Macdonald, 1964, p. 78.

32 Letters from the then Midshipman Stanley Norfolk to Captain Hughes Lockyer R.N. of 2 Sep 1936, cited in Nigel Steel and Peter Hart, *Defeat at Gallipoli*, London, Macmillan, 1994, p. 84.

33 Cited in Hargrave, op. cit., p. 197.

34 Cited in Field Marshal Sir Nigel Bagnall, 'The Human Story' *Gallipoli Memorial Lecture Series*, 1992, p. 4.

35 For this claim, and related correspondence see Capt. H. Lockyer, RN 'The Tragedy of the Battle of the Beaches' [privately published pamphlet of 1936] in Lockyer MSS at Imperial War Museum 75/56/1.

36 Adm. of the Fleet Viscount Cunningham, A *Sailor's Odyssey*, London, Hutchinson, 1951, p. 72.

37 Callwell, op. cit. p. 67.

38 Wemyss, op. cit. p. 54 and pp. 104–5.

39 Ellis Ashmead-Bartlett, *Despatch from the Dardanelles*, London, George Newnes, 1915, pp. 106–7.

40 Entry for 14 Oct 1915, Moyne diaries, op.cit. p. 38.

41 Callwell, op. cit. pp. 188–9.

42 See Laffin, op. cit. p. 122 and letter of Lt Col C.E. Foster, 11 Aug in Foster MSS at Imperial War Museum. Also Robert O'Neill, 'For Want of Critics . . . The Tragedy of Gallipoli' *Gallipoli Memorial Lecture Series*, 1990.

43 Cited Steel, op. cit. p. 378.

44 Undated memoir of Lt Bampton, HMS *Prince of Wales* in Bampton MSS at IWM 77/45/1.
45 Cited in Brig.Gen. C.F. Aspinall-Oglander, *Roger Keyes*, London, Hogarth Press, 1951, p. 163.
46 Cited in Laffin, op. cit. p. 50.
47 Lt Cdr R.W. Wilkinson Letter of 11 May 1915, Wilkinson MSS, IWM Boy Telegraphist W.J.H. Blamey.
48 Diary Entry for 29 April, Blamey MSS 86/53/1.
49 Compton Mackenzie, op. cit. pp. 75-6.
50 Able Seaman P. Rooke, HMS *Canopus*, Diary entry for 11 March 1915, Rooke MSS IWM.
51 Lt Bampton HMS *Prince of Wales*, Undated memoir, Bampton MSS, IWM 77/45/1.
52 Lt Col C.E. Foster, Letter of 3 August, Foster MSS, IWM 85/15/1.
53 Lt Col C. Repington 'Ten Years Ago: The Gallipoli Landing' *Daily Telegraph*, 25 April 1925.

Chapter 14

Italy and the War in the Adriatic

Renato Sicurezza

The First World War can be seen as the final chapter of Italy's struggle for independence. When she entered the war in 1915, she had existed as a nation for little more than fifty years and was not fully unified. Her enemy at the time, Austria, was also the same enemy against whom the Italian people had fought many bloody battles to achieve liberty in the previous century. The very names of Austrian ships, *Tegetthof*, *Radetzky*, *Custozza*, *Novara* and *Lissa*, evoked memories of Austrian victories. Lissa, the naval defeat of 1866, still weighed heavily on the mind of every Italian sailor. Tradition has it that the black scarf which forms part of the Italian naval uniform is a symbol of mourning for those killed in that battle.

Compared with what remains from World War Two, personal accounts or memoirs of the First World War in the Italian Naval Archives in Rome are scarce. They yield little direct evidence of the experience of the 'ordinary seaman' of the 1915–18 period whose individual experiences merge with those of his fellow crewmen. Only 'Leaders' or 'Heroes' stand out. Even so, the archival records do yield a distinctive picture of the Italian sailor's war in the Adriatic.[*]

Even before Italy went to war, the Entente Powers dominated the Mediterranean. The Austro-Hungarian fleet, clearly inferior to that of its opponents, sought to counter the blocking of the Straits of Otranto by making use of the few light surface and submarine forces at its disposal, but when Italy joined the Entente powers in 1915, it became possible to oppose these Austrian efforts in the Adriatic.

Italy faced difficulties, however. Her Adriatic coastline was largely exposed, whereas her adversary's shores, which were protected by the

---

[*] Except where otherwise stated all the documents quoted are from the Italian Naval Archives in Rome.

natural defences of the Dalmatian Archipelago. Moreover, Italy's bases were far apart – at Venice, Brindisi and Taranto. The Austrians, by contrast, had bases at Pola, the Island of Lussin and at the port of Trieste in the north, at Sebenico in the central Adriatic and Cattaro in the south. Additionally, Austrian naval movements, especially of light vessels and cable-laying craft, could be undertaken within the security of the Dalmatian Channel, which also offered freedom of internal communications. Finally, the seabed, frequently less than 100 metres deep, especially in the Central and Northern Adriatic, lent itself to mine warfare, while not presenting an insurmountable obstacle for submarines.

The fleets of both sides were intended to undertake a 'classical' type of sea war – battles between capital ships to win strategic advantage with torpedo craft in support, whilst torpedo boats and submarines attacked enemy ports and ships – rather than to protect merchant shipping. Both sides also had squadrons of seaplanes and airships, designated for reconnaissance and bombing operations. The Italian fleet had more battleships, whether pre-dreadnought or dreadnought, than her opponent. Austria-Hungary had superiority in heavy cruisers and in various categories of light cruisers, and in submarines, many of which could be used in the open sea, but was behind in the development of reconnaissance craft and modern destroyers.

The Austrians maintained their defensive-offensive strategy with forces 'in being', based at Pola and Cattaro, whilst making use of light naval units and submarines for surveillance purposes, surprise attacks on enemy ships and attacks on the Italian coastline. Their decision to hold all large naval units in port and the absence of any merchant shipping to protect, allowed them to use a large proportion of their light naval units offensively.

Italy initially pursued an offensive naval strategy in co-ordination with the Italian army plans aimed at capturing Vienna. The Italian fleet was to operate in the Upper Adriatic, blockading Trieste and Pola and preventing the Austrian navy from supporting their land forces. If Austrian units tried to break out, the Italians would immediately engage with them. In case of extended naval operations, Italy's allies were asked to help with light naval vessels, submarines, aircraft and battleships.

The picture soon altered. First, the Italian Army's offensive possibilities changed drastically as it failed to achieve a breakthrough on the southern flank of the front. Secondly, because of the position of their bases, Italian naval forces were unable to intervene effectively against continual surprise attacks on the coastline. The Chief of their Naval Staff, Admiral Paolo Thaon de Revel, quickly revamped all operational plans, giving orders for mines and submarine patrols along the enemy coastline, regular reconnaissance missions by light naval and air forces, while concentrating the main battle fleet at Taranto and Brindisi, with a battleship force at Venice to support land operations and counter the Austrian forces at Pola and Trieste.

To protect their coast, and to reciprocate Austrian attacks, the Italian Navy, in the absence of adequate bases, ordered permanent patrols by substantial naval forces. However, a new naval weapon, the submarine, was claiming numerous victims, chiefly in merchant navies. Italy was to lose forty-nine per cent of its total merchant tonnage. In the Adriatic, April 1915 saw the Austrian submarine U5 sink the French cruiser *Leon Gambetta*. In the absence of an appropriate doctrine and adequate counter-measures, life became difficult for the surface fleets. Despite Italy's apparent control of the Adriatic she sustained two major losses in July 1915. The heavy cruiser *Amalfi* was sunk by the German submarine U14 and the heavy cruiser *Garibaldi* by the Austrian U4.

The Italians therefore resorted to the concept of the 'fleet in being', while they worked on new methods and techniques to counter this threat, including motor- and patrol-boats for coastal reconnaissance and anti-submarine warfare, armoured trains for coastal defence (twelve were eventually deployed in the area between Cervia and Brindisi) and the strengthening of coastal batteries and air units. The task of patrolling the Adriatic and of conducting naval operations against Austrian light naval units fell to the Italian and Allied surface fleets, to their submarines and to their seaplanes.

In the absence of a decisive encounter, the war at sea, by nature mobile and fluid, changed into a 'war of fixed positions' like the land war, almost as if the Adriatic were a maritime trench across which the two opposing fleets faced each other, barricaded into their respective fronts, whilst rapid reconnaissance in force was undertaken by minor forces. Some of the 'major' confrontations between the light naval forces of the two sides developed from these reconnaissances towards the Italian coast of the Straits of Otranto, notably on 5 June and 29 December 1915. Allied naval units appeared badly organised in the face of sudden enemy actions when the Austrians broke out into the open sea from the Dalmatian Channel. In the second attack, however, two Austrian destroyers were sunk.

The major naval action of the war in the Adriatic took place in the southern region of the sea on 15 May 1917. The Austrians had planned an attack by light naval forces on Italian communications in the Lower Adriatic and on the Otranto barrier. A force comprising five destroyers and air units attacked an Italian convoy passing through the Straits of Otranto at night, sinking a steam ship and an escorting destroyer and attacking the barrier. The naval command at Brindisi intervened with an Allied force of two British light cruisers, four Italian destroyers, three French destroyers and two submarines. This time there was better co-ordination between the various forces. The encounter developed into a fragmented battle in which the coastal defences of the two sides also took part, along with Austrian reinforcements from Cattaro comprising one battleship and three torpedo boats. The outcome was two Austrian destroyers damaged, one Italian and two British destroyers hit, and one French destroyer sunk by a mine. One witness recalled the exciting moment when the battle began:

> We were at last confronting the enemy we had previously searched for in vain. Our fire was very good as we could see from the closeness of the fountains of water thrown up by the impact of our shells. Unfortunately we were not able to maintain our action for long; at 9.35 a.m. a thick white smoke rose from the Austrian file-leader, the 'Novara' . . . The cruisers had released a thick screen of artificial fog to escape our fire, and hauling to port in a few minutes, they hid entirely from us.[1]

Meanwhile, the vulnerability of the low-lying, easily accessible Italian coastline called for a powerful and extensive system of fixed and mobile coastal defences (coastal batteries, minefields, armoured pontoons and armoured trains), to counter bombing raids or beach landings directed against military and industrial targets. A large and powerful battery, The Amalfi, had been installed to defend the northern maritime sector around the naval base at Venice, of great importance from the start of hostilities. The purpose of the naval defences at Venice was to complement the army's three batteries of 305/50 mm guns, and thus jointly protect a 22 kilometre stretch of water around Venice and the Italian Naval Arsenal. The navy's weapons consisted of four pairs of 1914-model 381/40 mm Vickers-Terni guns originally destined for the battleship *Francesco Caracciolo*, whose construction had been suspended because of financial constraints.

Work on the defences took seventeen months, from the end of September 1916. The unusual decision to install guns destined for ship-borne use necessitated many time-consuming changes in order to adapt them to their new setting. The guns' range – 19,800 metres with an angle of elevation of twenty degrees – along with a 360 degree arc of fire, permitted their use in land operations; and the monitor *Capellini*, equipped with a turret mounting a 381 mm gun, was added to the fixed defences of the Venice lagoon.

Owing to Austro-Hungarian air raids on these emplacements, with incendiary and explosive bombs, the need arose for adequate anti-aircraft and anti-torpedo defences, and four 102/25 mm weapons were eventually installed in the area east of the main guns some 1,500 metres apart. Once completed, the entire battery came temporarily under the command of the Italian Third Army. When the unfavourable outcome of Caporetto brought Italy's enemies perilously close to Venice, the Amalfi battery was given the opportunity of firing against the land enemy, thus totally altering the reason for their existence, namely as a maritime weapon. The problems of defending Venice were formidable, as gunners have testified:

The conditions for fighting weren't good in the Lower Isonzo river; but at least the Grado Lagoon had plenty of islands dotted about it with good solid ground on them. It had some groups of forest trees . . . Here (in the Venice Lagoon) we have to defend a flat and bare area, it is desperately slimy; there's not a single r'ace above sea level.[2]

In this contest, armoured trains, an economical and rapid means of concentrating a volume of fire wherever required, were also deployed. The Italian Navy first introduced them in 1915 to counter surprise Austrian attacks on Italy's Adriatic coast,which was poorly protected by fixed artillery positions. From the very first day of the war, in direct violation of international law, Austrian ships, aiming more at civilian morale than strategic targets, had bombarded heavily-populated urban centres along the coast, destroying civilian industries and causing many civilian casualties. In the opening hours of the conflict, the city of Ancona, including its hospital, suffered an intense bombardment by units of the Austrian navy comprising the battleships *Viribus Unitis* and *Tegetthof*. There were sixty-eight casualties. It was repugnant to Italy to retaliate by bombarding the opposite shore, which was largely inhabited by people of Italian origin, desiring unity with their homeland. Instead, armoured trains, equipped with medium and light calibre weapons and able to repel Austrian attacks to good effect, were deployed along tracks running the whole length of the coastline.

All the trains were capable of travelling at sixty to seventy-five km/h and each operated along about sixty km. of track, so that by staying at a centre point, it would never have to travel more than half an hour to reach any point where coast was being threatened. The trains were kept at the ready, with their teams on board and boiler pressure up, awaiting the alarm at any minute – usually at first light, the enemy fleet having crept up to the coast under cover of darkness. To prevent the recoil of the guns deforming the rails, there was a breathless minute when the crew, after it reached the battle area, jacked up the train, removed its wheels, and anchored it securely to the bed of the track.

Outstanding instances can be given of their vital role: on 3 February 1916 Armoured Train Number VI, with intense and accurate fire, drove off the enemy (the Austrian cruiser *Saint George*, three destroyers and two motor torpedo boats) who was bombarding Ortona and San Vito Lanciano. On 23 June, two destroyers shelling Grottamare were forced to disengage; on 5 November, Armoured Train Number III, firing for some ten minutes, damaged two out of three Austrian *Tatra* class destroyers attacking the town of S. Elpidio a Mare (Ascoli Piceno) and killed several crewmen; and on 28 November 1917, after bombarding Porto Corsini, an Austrian *Novara* class cruiser and three *Tatra* destroyers were deflected from Rimini by Armoured Train Number I, which opened fire from a distance of 6,800 metres with its 152 mm guns (having found the range with its second salvo), scoring a direct hit on the base of the cruiser's funnel and killing twenty men.

From the spring of 1916, the conflict in the Upper Adriatic became increasingly a war of attrition. Given the limited initiatives of the Austrian naval forces, part of the Italian battleship fleet was moved away from its base at Venice, whilst coastal and port defence measures were increased by adding armoured pontoons and monitors (one of which was British) so that they could now also support army units. As a result of the effectiveness of the armoured trains and a more efficient system of raising the alarm, Austrian coastal attacks diminished. The enemy seemed increasingly reluctant to commit himself, preferring the safety of his bases at Pola, Fiume and Trieste.

As was now the case in the land campaigns, it therefore became necessary to go in search of the enemy in a sort of 'assault with fixed bayonets', without precedent in naval conflict, the methods for this type of operation being developed effectively from scratch. MAS – motorboats armed with torpedoes, each having a small displacement, carrying very little equipment on board, and fitted with oil-powered engines capable of high speeds – were evolved from the obsolete steam-powered torpedo boats after various experiments. These small vessels, displacing no more than thirteen tons, inflicted substantial losses on Italy's opponents. During the war some 300 were built and used with increasing frequency.

The number of MAS deployed for strategic use amounted to twenty in 1916, sixty-five in 1917 and a remarkable ninety-nine in the last ten months of the war in 1918. Their overall performance was excellent, and losses were minimal – in all just twenty boats: nine following petrol explosions, seven following accidents or collisions and four due to heavy seas. No MAS was lost through either maritime or land-based enemy action.

During this era the Italian navy also developed highly specialised weapons of war. One was a type of vessel equipped with tracks and able to surmount obstacles blocking port entrances. Towards the end of the war a naval officer, Major Rossetti, designed and built the *mignatta*, effectively a torpedo able to carry a crew of two and an explosive payload – the forerunners of the midget submarines (*maiali*) used with such success against Gibraltar and Alexandria during the Second World War. One of these weapons sank the battleship *Viribus Unitis* in the port of Pola on 3 November 1918. However, most such operations in the North Adriatic were undertaken by the newborn MAS boats which successfully harassed Austrian capital ships and other major naval units, in the open sea or in enemy ports. They were manned by determined individuals with strong personalities, eager for success. These included Goiran and Cavagnari (subsequently Chief of Naval Staff under Mussolini), not to mention Commander Costanzo Ciano, father of Italy's future Foreign Minister. On 16 November 1917, Ciano, commanding a force of two MAS, thwarted a coastal bombardment by two Austrian battleships, *Wien* and *Budapest*, near Cortellazzo.

But it was Luigi Rizzo who achieved the most successes in the MAS. Between 1915 and 1918 he won two Gold Medals, four Silver Medals, two War Crosses and promotion in the field. On the night of 19 December 1917, he cut through defensive steel cables sixty mm thick to enter the port of Trieste with two MAS. After a brief reconnaissance of the harbour, he noticed the distinctive silhouettes of *Wien* and *Budapest*, the very same ships which had bombarded Cortellazzo. He moved, undetected, to within fifty metres of the ships to check whether anti-torpedo nets were in place, which they were not. Then his two vessels fired two torpedoes at 250 metres distance, one sinking the battleship *Wien* . Unchallenged, the two MAS rapidly left the harbour and returned to Venice. This brilliant action, crowned by such a significant success, won Rizzo his first Gold Medal for Military Valour.

The Austrian navy also understood the need to carry the offensive to the enemy's ports, in their case, through sabotage, for which they established a cell in Italy. In September 1915, this launched a mission against the port of Brindisi, planting explosives which quickly sank the pre-dreadnought *Benedetto Brin*, with the loss of 456 lives. In August 1916 the new dreadnought *Leonardo da Vinci* exploded at Taranto, leaving 248 dead, victims of the same methods. One witness recalled his experience of seeing the stricken hulk of the *Leonardo da Vinci*:

> On one occasion I saw a terrible sight in a quiet bay – the keel of the *Leonardo da Vinci* rising to the surface from the cerulean blue of the sea, close to the shore. It seemed all the more monstrous because of the pleasant calm of its surroundings. It was greenish, spotted, like the dappled flank of a vast whale.[3]

The Austrians also set up an excellent espionage network. It was only in February 1917 that the Italian Naval Intelligence Service delivered its own coup – the agent was actually a naval officer – by forcing the safe of the Austrian consulate in Zurich and thus obtaining a list of all Austrian saboteurs operating in Italian territory.

A major land defeat called for extra efforts by the Italian navy. When, on 24 October 1917, Italy's enemies broke through the front held by II Army at Caporetto, the army began to retreat. The Chief of the Italian Naval Staff, Admiral Thaon de Revel, gave orders on 26 October that monitors and pontoons should abandon their existing positions to provide added firepower to III Army, which was retreating beyond the Isonzo. On the 28th Monfalcone was cleared, followed by Grado next day. The largest monitors moved along the coast while lighter ones used the inland waterway, 150 km long, linking Venice with Grado.

Resistance on the Tagliamento was impossible and a line was chosen at

Lemene, fifteen kilometers further back. A company of 230 sailors from Venice, supported by Rizzo's MAS boats, was sent there. The sailors were attacked on the night of 7 November and, despite the support of the MAS which had covered the area from Lemene to Portoruaro, were compelled to retreat first to Caorle and then to Venice. The line at Lemene also fell.

The area between the Piave and Sile rivers was flooded, creating an obstacle stretching from S. Dona to Porto di Cortelazzo. Here Thaon de Revel proposed to establish the final line of defence. Fully aware of the strategic importance of Venice – should the port fall, the navy would need to relocate to Brindisi – Admiral Thaon de Revel had, by 1 November, expressed the view that Venice should be defended 'to the ultimate limits possible'.

The company of sailors initially deployed was increased to battalion strength (twenty-two officers, 900 men and twelve machine guns) and given the name 'Monfalcone'. On 8 November, the battalion was placed under the orders of III Army and saw action for the first time at Cortelazzo next day. On the thirteenth, the battalion repelled two enemy attempts to cross the river and land at Cortelazzo. A second battalion, the 'Grado', entered the line in mid-November. The 'Monfalcone' battalion was composed of naval ratings already assigned to the defence of Monfalcone and Grado, but subsequent detachments were also despatched to the coastal defences at La Spezia, Naples and Messina. A third battalion – 'Caorle' – was established during the course of 1917, whilst a fourth battalion – named 'Navi' – made up of 400 men taken from various naval vessels and destined to defend Ancona was also sent into the line under the name of 'Galometto'. These battalions formed the Naval Infantry Regiment.

On 14 November the Naval Artillery Group was formed and subdivided into eight smaller groups which could be assigned to various sectors; from the 28th the Group was placed under the command of XXIII Army Corps, whilst it s larger 190 mm guns remained under the control of III Army. The Artillery Group was gradually strengthened until it consisted of 106 guns. The Naval Infantry Regiment and the Artillery Group together formed the Naval Brigade, its headquarters being situated in Venice.

The Naval Brigade, which totalled some 13,000 men, was deployed often and distinguished itself on various occasions. During the battle of the Piave (June–July 1918), the Naval Regiment suffered 142 dead and 467 wounded, but took over 500 prisoners. Detachments of the regiment were at Trieste on 3 November 1918 when that city once again became part of Italy. In all the Naval Regiment suffered 384 dead and 772 wounded; no member of the Regiment was ever taken prisoner.

The continued Italian attacks on their ports, and the inactivity of the bulk of the main fleet, created a profound sense of discontent among the Austro–Hungarian crews, culminating in open revolt at Cattaro in

February 1918. Basically the crews wanted to taste action. The government was not insensitive to these demands. In March 1918 Captain Nicola Horthy di Nagy-Banya Miklos, a Hungarian nobleman, was promoted to the rank of rear-admiral and made commander-in-chief of the fleet. The new commander-in-chief immediately planned a naval operation against the Otranto barrier and the naval bases of Brindisi and Valona.

The new situation had in fact already been correctly assessed by the Italian Naval Staff. As early as 6 March 1918, the Chief of Naval Staff, Admiral Thaon de Revel, wrote to the fleet commander:

> It would appear that some changes have been made within the High Command of the Austrian Navy and that the Commander-in-Chief of the Fleet has recently been replaced by a younger admiral.
>
> It is not unlikely that this new Commander-in-Chief will seek to assert himself by following a more active policy which may result in a certain imprudence from which we should be ready to take advantage.
>
> I therefore ask Your Excellency to pay heed to the above in the hope that we might take advantage of every enemy movement by attacking immediately . . . with submarines . . . destroyers, torpedo boats and MAS.

The barrage defences at Otranto had been attacked some nineteen times during the course of the war, and Admiral Horthy had participated in four of these attacks while in command of the *Novara*, suffering minor injuries on 15 May 1917, when the ship was badly damaged. Between Horthy and the sea defences there existed, therefore, an unsettled account that seemed almost a personal one.

The planned Austrian operation was due to take place between 5 and 11 June 1918, and was to coincide with a land offensive. Specifically, the plan envisaged the deployment of four battleships divided into two groups, each with torpedo boats acting as an escort. The first, comprising the *Viribus Unitis*, the *Prinz Eugen* and the torpedo boat escorts, left Pola on the evening of 8 June, steaming southwards by night to avoid detection. The second group, *Svent Istvan*, *Tegetthof*, six torpedo boats and a destroyer escort, also set sail from Pola the following evening. Their meticulously staged operation was destined to fail.

The Italians, for their part, had prepared an ambush by MAS units for both evenings. On the evening of the 8th a section of MAS were in position off the port of Pola in order to await the exit of the two Austrian battleships, but the latter had already sailed undisturbed past that point earlier that evening. On the night of 9/10 June things went differently. This time the MAS force comprised MAS 15, aboard which was Captain Rizzo, and MAS 21, under Midshipman Guiseppe Aonzo. The units lay in ambush at 11.30 p.m. They had prepared a general ambush against possible enemy targets exiting from the port, as the Italian navy had no detailed information about the enemy's plans.

Meanwhile the two battleships had sailed from Pola about half an hour later than scheduled owing to difficulty in opening the port defences. Once outside port they set their course, but at a slightly slower speed than planned because of engine problems aboard the *Svent Istvan*. They gradually fell an hour behind schedule, so that they passed close to the two MAS boats which, after a vain wait in ambush, were returning to base.

At 3.15 a.m. Rizzo spotted a 'huge cloud of smoke', and believing that it must signal enemy forces, he decided to take advantage of the light, which was still poor, to move closer and assess the situation more clearly. he quickly realised that a unique opportunity now presented itself; 'here were two large warships escorted by between eight and ten destroyers protecting them at the bow, the stern and alongside'. We now know that it was a considerably smaller escort – six torpedo boats and one destroyer to be exact – but it was still a sizeable force. As Rizzo reported:

> Having decided to fire my torpedoes from the shortest distance possible, I therefore manoeuvred in such a way as to pass between the destroyers which flanked the first vessel. In order to slip past the destroyer on my left I moved at a speed of between 9 and 12 knots, and having succeeded in reaching a point 100 metres beyond the range of the two vessels unnoticed, I fired two torpedoes at the first battleship at a distance of no more than 300 metres. Both torpedoes hit their target and exploded, the one on the right hitting the area between the first and second funnel, and the one on the left the area between the rearmost funnel and the stern, raising two great clouds of water and black smoke as they did so. The torpedoes had been prepared for attacking torpedo boats, and were set for a depth of 1.50 metres. The battleship took no evasive measures.

While all this was taking place MAS 21 also launched its attack, firing its own torpedoes from a distance of about 500 metres but unfortunately missing its target, the second Austrian battleship *Tegetthof*. At this point, as dawn began to light up the skies, both MAS decided to retreat. An enemy torpedo boat sighted MAS 15 and gave chase whilst firing with its forward gun. Luckily the shots fell harmlessly in front of the Italian vessel, probably because the light did not yet permit the range to be easily estimated. To prevent the Austrian torpedo boat from finding his range, Rizzo chose not to reply with machine-gun fire but threw off his pursuer by firing two depth charges. After they had exploded the Austrian boat broke off the chase.

The *Svent Istvan* had been seriously damaged in its vitals: the sea had penetrated the boiler room and extinguished all the fires. The great ship thus suddenly found itself without either power or electricity. There was little the crew could do to save her, although they did their best. It was not possible to repair the damage, or to pump out the flooded sections. The ship began to tilt ever more to starboard, and an attempt at towing by the *Tegetthof* was eventually abandoned because she was listing too badly. After some two-and-a-half slow and agonising hours the *Svent Istvan* capsized and sank. The disaster claimed the lives of eighty-nine men; 1,005 were saved. An Austrian officer described the final moments of the battleship in these words:

> I looked up to the bridge and saw that the captain was still there, clinging to the ship's bell as the ship began to capsize. A great cry of 'hurrah' erupted from everyone. This was at 06.05 hours.

On 11 June 1918, the day after these events, the fourth session of the Inter-Allied Naval Council met in London to discuss the progress of the war at sea. The news of Rizzo's victory was received with enthusiasm by all the representatives of the Allied navies. The Commander-in-Chief of the British Grand Fleet sent a telegram congratulating the Italian Fleet 'on the magnificent achievement carried out with such valour and daring against the Austrian enemy'. The operation planned by Horthy, which was to have restored the morale of both the Austro-Hungarian Navy and Army before a major offensive on the Piave thus failed miserably and was terminated by 6.30 a.m. on 10 June due to the brilliant efforts of a tiny MAS and the heroism of Luigi Rizzo. David had beaten Goliath. Lissa had been avenged.

The First World War at sea has a distinctive, perhaps unique, character, combining the last of ' traditional' warfare with the new. Among its more 'traditional' aspects seem the short distances at which attacks were launched by such as Paolucci and Rossetti, with their *'mignatta'* (human torpedo), sinking the *Viribus Unitis*, and Rizzo, at Trieste, and against the *Svent Istvan*. Today, when ballistic missiles target cities thousands of miles away, these minimal distances seem nearer to the age of the medieval tournament, though there is also a parallel with the close proximity of both sides in 1914–18 trench warfare.

Again, the saving of the retreating Serbian army by the French and Italian navies, reminds us of earlier ages. The Italian navy alone succeeded in carrying to safety not only 260,895 men but *10,153 horses*. One gets the same sense of continuity with the past from the barrier of the straits of Otranto, which recalls the chain across the surface at Corno d'Oro barring the entrance to ships in the 17th century. The system at Otranto was effective despite its relative simplicity, as the report on the loss of the German submarine U 53 demonstrates:

> UB 53 left Pola 2100 German time on 1 August (1918) proceeded at 12 knots on the surface until 1600 on August 2nd, when she did a practice

dive for a short time. She dived again at 0400 August 3rd and proceeded submerged at about 3 knots ('slow') all that day. At 1830, when at a depth of 50 metres, she ran into the net of the Otranto fixed barrage. Most of the crew were asleep at the time. (They state that they had orders to sleep when the boat dived in order to economise on air. The helmsman at once called the Captain who ordered 'half speed'. Shortly afterwards the mines of the net exploded abreast the stern compartment and all the lights went out. The Captain gave orders to blow all tanks and the boat came to the surface at a big angle with her bows in the air. Orders were given to abandon ship. All the crew got out on deck, put on life belts (where those were available) and jumped into the water. UB 53 remained on the surface for 4 to 5 minutes and then sank stern first.

On the other hand, the First World War also witnessed some particularly significant 'innovations', such as wide use of the submarine, aeroplanes for naval reconnaissance and offensive operations, 'human torpedoes' and light torpedo boats.

Unchanged, however, was the vital importance of sea power: 'the sea', reflected one commentator, ' has always offered us the means of reversing a defeat, of remedying a disaster, or rebuilding an army (such as the Serbian army) and in this way, of resolving any conflict successfully. Indeed, everything came to us by sea: steel, grain, coal; meanwhile the enemy was denied everything, so that when this enemy found his own resources exhausted . . . he was compelled to give in'.

Lastly the men who fought this naval war must be considered. During the four years of war, the Italian Navy doubled its number of officers and tripled that of its non-commissioned officers and ratings. In all, 3065 were killed, that is: 167 officers, approximately 6.64 per cent of the total, and 2,898 NCOs and men, approximately 2.13 per cent – a lower casualty rate than the very high rates suffered by the army, as one would expect, given the very different circumstances.

Personal records of the war in that period are hard to find, not least because some 38% of the Italian population was illiterate. Valuable evidence, however comes from the military censorship reports, such as those by the head of the Military Censor's office at the naval base of Taranto for the period 1 June 1916, to 30 May 1917. The jurisdiction of the base then extended over both city and outlying areas, and it was also a 'site for the concentration of troops going to and from the eastern front'. In just one year of operations, this office handled some 6,000,000 letters and 200,000 telegrams destined for both civilian and military personnel. On only twenty-one occasions was it deemed necessary to refer cases to a military tribunal, and only two of these cases involved sailors. One dealt with information about the torpedoing of a merchant vessel, and the other was a case of insubordination towards a superior officer. Both cases resulted in disciplinary action. Thirty-eight cases of absence without leave were similarly punished, only five of which were due to 'impatience with, and criticism of, military life'.

Overall, very few serious cases emerge from the various reports of the Censor's Office. In actual fact, the fortnightly reports on morale among the troops, the reports from the Commander-in-Chief of the naval base at Venice (derived from an examination of all personal correspondence) and the reports of the Military Censor's office during the period 1917–18 all display extremely positive feelings of love of country, belief in an overall victory and the will to fight. Though there were isolated, if serious, cases of sabotage, the behaviour of all personnel, generally speaking,was excellent and morale was high, even in the sadder moments of the war. This was especially true of the crews of the MAS boats. Many sailors and non-commissioned officers also distinguished themselves individually as pilots or gunners of planes and airships.

The behaviour of naval personnel deployed ashore was also of the highest order. The 682 survivors of the cruiser *Amalfi*, torpedoed in July 1915, were formed into two companies which manned the floating batteries of the Grado sector, supporting III Army. When these duties ended in January 1916, the commander of that army, Lieutenant-General Emanuele Filiberto di Savoia, thanked them wholeheartedly for their courage, calm orderliness, and 'the great military spirit which constantly inspired them.'

In practice, after Caporetto, the Italian Navy, with its shore-based personnel, assumed and sustained the defence of Venice; and for the 13,000 men involved there was further praise from the commander of III Army. But perhaps the ultimate compliment came from Hungarian prisoners-of-war: 'If all Italian soldiers fight like the sailors did at Cortellazzo, any hope of breaking through on the Piave has gone.' In May 1918, the city of Venice repaid its debt by giving the San Marco Regiment its battle flag.

Many courageous acts, both great and small, were performed by shipboard personnel. Three Gold Medals, the highest of all military honours, went to non-commissioned officers and sailors, as well as 292 Silver Medals. In the final analysis, Italian sailors fought with both conviction and dash during the Great War. Like Italy's soldiers and people, they never wanted for resolution or bravery. Men of a young nation, they endured a difficult trial by determination, a will to succeed and a spirit of sacrifice.

Notes

1   Slaghek Fabbri, Luigi, *Con Gli Inglesi in Adriatico*, Roma, Ardita, 1934, p. 190.
2   Maffii, Maffio, *Dal Piave a Premuda*, p. 65
3   Maffii, Maffio, *Guerra di Mare*, Milano, Alfieri & Lacroix, 1917. p. 126.

Chapter 15

The War in the Air: The Men and Their Machines

Jack Bruce

On 7 September 1914, in his first dispatch from France, Field Marshal Sir John French, commander of the British Expeditionary Force, recorded this tribute to the Military Wing of the Royal Flying Corps:

> I wish particularly to bring to your Lordships' notice the admirable work done by the Royal Flying Corps under Sir David Henderson. Their skill, energy and perseverance have been beyond all praise. They have furnished me with the most complex and accurate information, which has been of incalculable value in the conduct of operations. Fired at constantly both by friend and foe, and not hesitating to fly in every kind of weather, they have remained undaunted throughout. Further, by actually fighting in the air, they have succeeded in destroying five of the enemy's machines.[1]

The Naval Wing, which had unilaterally named itself the Royal Naval Air Service, had gone to wage war on the Continent with a motley collection of aeroplanes, and was making its presence felt elsewhere. On 6 September Commander C. R. Samson, RN, styling himself (for the benefit of the enemy) 'Officer in Command of an English Force at Dunkirk', had formally occupied Lille, an action accomplished by armed motor cars rather than aircraft. The cars were subsequently armoured, and Samson used them to considerable effect and to the discomfiture of the enemy.

The Military Wing might not have done so well if it had been equipped with the type of aeroplane that had been declared the winner of the Military Aeroplane Competition held at Larkhill in August 1912 – the alarmingly unsuitable Cody biplane. That it won was the fault of the specification that entrant aircraft were supposed to meet. This contained no requirement that any weaponry, camera, or any form of signalling equipment should be carried; but fortunately the men of the Military Wing had their own and more realistic ideas about that sort of thing, and had experimented for themselves, sometimes at their own expense, with various forms of armament, cameras, and with signalling.

The competition specification did nothing more than define a flying observation platform for reconnaissance purposes; one, moreover, that did not expect to have to defend itself against enemy aircraft. Despite all the enterprising experiments undertaken by the flying officers of the R.F.C., and by the staff of the Royal Aircraft Factory at Farnborough, Sir Walter Raleigh (author of Volume I of the official history *The War in the Air)* was still to write:

> The single use in war for which the machines of the Military Wing of the R.F.C. were designed and the men trained was (let it be repeated) recon-
> naissance.[2]

Of the officers in the group photograph shown here taken about August 1912, Captain Dawes was the earliest certificated military pilot. His Royal Aero Club aviator's certificate was No. 17, taken privately on a Humber monoplane at Wolverhampton on 26 July 1910. In this he was the immediate predecessor of that great pioneer, A.V. Roe, whose certificate was No. 18.

Samson has already been mentioned. He was one of the most remarkable of the earliest officers of the Naval Wing, and he left a characteristic account of many of his wartime experiences in his book *Fights and Flights* (London, Ernest Benn Ltd, 1930). One of the first four Naval officers to learn to fly (R.Ae.C. aviator's certificate No. 71. dated 25 April 1911), he commanded the Eastchurch Squadron, R.N.A.S., at Ostend and Dunkerque, 1914–15. His was a warlike nature that believed that war should be carried to the enemy at all times, with all possible vigour, and in whatever way was effective. He had a hand in making armoured cars, and in fighting in them, as well as flying. In the Gallipoli campaign he operated in the Aegean area; on 14 May 1916 he took over command of the East Indies and Egypt Seaplane Squadron, and of the seaplane carrier HMS *Ben-my-Chree* until she was sunk on 8 January 1917. His experience of war was gained on land, at sea, and in the air.

Sykes was the first Commanding Officer of the Military Wing, but for the wartime R.F.C. the most important officer in the group was Brooke-Popham, a man who had long recognised the great military potential of aircraft, and foresaw aerial combat as early as 1910. He had joined the Air Battalion of the Royal Engineers, the precursor of the R.F.C., in March 1912, took over command of its Aeroplane Company in late April, and on 13 May 1912, that unit became No. 3 Squadron of the Military Wing, R.F.C. Brooke-Popham was an outstandingly dedicated squadron commander, and showed great energy, inventiveness and resourcefulness in the operation of his squadron, especially in the experiments that it conducted.

When the R.F.C. went to war in August 1914, Brooke-Popham was on the Headquarters staff. As the R.F.C. expanded and Wings were formed he, as a Lieutenant-Colonel, formed the Third Wing, which comprised Squadrons No.1 and 4, based at St-Omer, soon supplemented by Nos 7 and 8. On 26 May 1915 Brooke-Popham became G.S.O.1 at R.F.C. Headquarters. He saw clearly the importance of establishing air superiority, writing in August 1915 a memorandum in which he pointed out that whereas the British Expeditionary Force had expanded from its original four divisions to thirty the number of aeroplane squadrons had risen only from four to eleven, despite the addition of new duties to their original task of reconnaissance. He wrote:

> If the enemy brings troops over from the Eastern Front and resumes his offensive, he will doubtless make a determined effort to prevent our discovering his movements. Then will commence the real struggle for air supremacy where numbers will be one of the essentials for success.[3]

Timely words, not least because it was just then that R.F.C. aircrew began to encounter the Fokker monoplanes. With the growth of the R.F.C. the Headquarters establishment was increased commensurately, and the new post of Deputy-Adjutant and Quartermaster General was filled by Brooke-Popham, promoted to Brigadier-General. From then until the end he oversaw, with extraordinary zeal and efficiency, virtually everything the Military Wing did and flew. It is doubtful whether any other British officer knew more about the aerial war than he did. What cannot be comprehensively or accurately assessed is the extent to which his individual influence and competence affected the R.F.C.'s and R.A.F.'s conduct of the war, but it must have been very substantial. It seems that he never received any very public recognition of his outstanding work.

These men in our 1912 photograph, their successors and counterparts in the ranks of our Allies and enemies, were to experience – indeed, to a very large extent, invent – a new form of warfare. This implied and demanded unforeseen and largely unforeseeable experimentation and development, not only in the specific field of aeronautics but in various inseparably associated technologies. Aviation had barely reached a level of practicability when war broke out, yet by 1918 there were fighting, bombing, reconnaissance and training aircraft, in both landplane and seaplane forms, and in great variety of size, configuration and performance. Aerial photography and its interpretation were universally practised and developed; armament had progressed from hand-held pistols, carbines and rifles to batteries of machine-guns, some with various synchronizing mechanisms and speeding-up devices, and from rifle grenades to bombs of 1,650 and 3,300 lb; radio telephony was in limited but growing use; heated clothing and rudimentary oxygen equipment had begun to bring a measure of comfort to occupants of open cockpits. The practitioners of military aviation had to adapt to these and other developments, their experience of war being forcibly modified in the process.

Aircraft performance, in all its various aspects, was of paramount importance. That, in turn, depended fundamentally on aero-engines. The British flying services never had enough of them, especially the really good designs such as the Rolls-Royce Eagle and Falcon. Some catastrophically bad choices were made, for example the appalling A.B.C. Radials and the Sunbeam Arab: the large amount of manufacturing capacity taken up by their production could have been better utilized. Initially our military aircraft were dependent on French aero-engines: all of the aircraft that first went to France and Belgium to join the B.E.F. in the Field had Gnome or Renault engines. More extraordinarily, virtually all our magnetos were of German manufacture; not until the autumn of 1916 did deliveries of British-made magnetos begin, and then only in small numbers. This made a bad situation worse.

Cold statistics provide a rough measure of magnitude, but their anonymity conceals the extent of human endeavour, endurance and sheer effort that underlay so much of the progress of the war. In August 1914, the Military Wing of the R.F.C. had 146 officers and 1,097 other ranks, the Naval Wing (R.N.A.S.) 130 officers and 700 lower-deck men: in all, 276 officers and 1,797 men in the British flying services. In November 1918 the Royal Air Force's strength comprised 27,333 officers, 16,681 cadets and NCOs under training, and 247,161 NCOs and men, a total of 291,175.

The four Military Wing squadrons that joined the B.E.F. in France in August 1914 had between them a total of 41 aircraft of five different types. According to C.F. Snowden Gamble in his classic book *The Story of a North Sea Air Station,* (London, Oxford University Press, 1928)[4] the R.N.A.S. had, at the outbreak of war, a total of 40 aeroplanes of 20 different types, 31 seaplanes of 12 types, and 7 airships, all of different types. By November 1918, on the Western Front alone there were 99 squadrons with 1,799 aircraft, of which 747 were single-seat fighters, 138 fighter-reconnaissance two-seaters, 526 bombers, and 370 corps aeroplanes. To these must be added squadrons and other units in the Middle East, Italy, the Aegean and Macedonia, on Home Defence, and training units. On 31 October 1918, the Royal Air Force had on charge 22,171 aircraft, with production continuing into 1919.

Fortunately for the infant Military Wing, the War Office had the good sense not to order the competition-winning Cody biplane in quantities, but chose more practical types. One of these was an early product of Geoffrey de Havilland's talent, the B.E.2a, which was built in modest numbers by several contractors. When the Military Wing went to France on 13 August 1914, No. 2 Squadron took twelve B.E.2as, No. 4 Squadron eleven.

There also went to France the R.F.C.'s Aircraft Park, forerunner of the later extensive organization of Aircraft Depots, Aeroplane Supply Depots and other support units. Its personnel arrived at Boulogne on 18 August 1914, to the evident perplexity of the doubtless harassed British Landing Officer there. He sent a telegram to British General Headquarters: 'An unnumbered unit without aeroplanes which calls itself an Aircraft Park has arrived. What are we to do with it?'[5]

From the B.E.2a and the very similar B.E.2b came the B.E.2c, developed by Edward Teshmaker Busk as an automatically stable aeroplane, in pursuit of the pre-war theoretical ideal of a military aircraft that was to be merely an aerial observation post. The B.E.2c was a good aeroplane *qua* aeroplane, and it did reasonably well, even up to mid-1916 and despite the advent of the Fokker monoplane a year earlier. It and its derivatives, the B.E.2d and 2e, were kept in production and operational use far beyond their effective life, and well past the time when they should have been withdrawn from operational use.

The B.E2c shared with contemporary tractor aircraft the difficulty of providing defensive armament that could be effectively used by the observer. For want of a device enabling a machine-gun to fire through the plane of rotation of a tractor airscrew, gun-carrying aircraft had to be constructed with the engine and propeller at the rear. One such was the Vickers F.B5, specifically designed as a gun-carrier. The front-seat observer of an aircraft of this configuration could have a wide and unobstructed field of fire, and could, within the limitations of whatever form of gun-mounting was provided, use this gun with fair freedom. Unfortunately, the F.B5's performance was so poor that it was soon outclassed in combat. A vivid impression of operational flying in the F.B.5 was given by A. J. Insall, sometime of No. 11 Squadron, in his book *Observer* (London, William Kimber, 1970). A. J. Insall's brother Gilbert was awarded the Victoria Cross for his action of 7 November 1915, involving a Vickers F.B.5.

Air combat, aeroplane against aeroplane, had been foreseen by Brooke-Popham in 1910 and, with great clarity, by Captain Bertram Dickson in 1911; and when it came it brought to its combatants an experience of warfare that no earlier fighting men had known. Soon their greatest concerns became the ease and accuracy with which they could use their weapons, and their field of view from the cockpit. Equally vital were their aircraft's performance and manœuvrability.

No pusher aircraft could match the performance of a comparably-powered tractor, and the way ahead for fighter aircraft was pointed by that great French pilot, Roland Garros, who adopted Robert Saulnier's idea of fitting armoured wedges to the propeller of a tractor aircraft, in line with the barrel of a fixed machine-gun. He applied this operationally to a

Morane-Saulnier Type L parasol monoplane, here photographed at Dunkerque, and shot down several German aircraft before he himself was obliged, on 18 April 1915, to land in enemy territory by a lucky rifle shot. This capture of his armed aeroplane led to a fanciful but spurious account by Tony Fokker that is deservedly discredited, claiming the creation, almost overnight, of a mechanical synchronizing device to enable a machine-gun to shoot between the blades of a rotating propeller on a tractor aeroplane.

For want of a gun-synchronizing gear, the alternative to some form of bullet deflector was to put the gun in a single-seat pusher aircraft, retrograde though that was. Geoffrey de Havilland designed the D.H.2 in this form, and it equipped R.F.C. Squadrons Nos 24, 29 and 32, a few examples also going to Nos 5, 11 and 18; others served in Macedonia and Palestine.

In February 1915 the French Spad company patented the basic design of an extraordinary aircraft, in which the object was to combine the clear field of fire of a pusher with the performance of a tractor. A small nacelle for an observer/gunner was perilously positioned immediately in front of the tractor airscrew of a Le Rhône rotary engine. The American pilot, Bert Hall, who flew with the French, saw some of these Spads Type A at Avord and left this note in his book *One Man's War* (London, John Hamilton Ltd, 1929):

> 'The first one they tried turned over taking off and mashed the observer as flat as a flapjack. Everybody on the field tried to argue them out of trying the second one, but nothing would do but a test flight . . . The machine took off all right but when Stromeyer [the pilot] tried to pull it out of a gradual glide, the front nacelle came off, the wings buckled up, and that was the end of the first model Spad.'[6]

These fatalities notwithstanding, various Spads Type A saw some operational service in French and Russian squadrons.

The Royal Aircraft Factory, either by imitative intent or by coincidence, employed the same hair-raising configuration in its B.E.9, which emerged in mid-August 1915. It was a modified B.E.2c. When it was tested at Central Flying School, the Commandant himself, the redoubtable Captain Godfrey Paine, RN, reported the B.E.9 to be excellent, its crew's view and range of action for the Lewis gun better than on any type previously seen at C.F.S. So inevitably it went to France. There, on 13 September 1915, Brooke-Popham flew in the forward cockpit and, somewhat surprisingly, generously approved of the aircraft.

Later, R. R. Money was to write in his book *Flying and Soldiering* (London, Ivor Nicholson & Watson, 1936) that: 'Brooke-Popham . . . lives in my memory because he went up in a horrible contraption called the Pulpit B.E.2c and refused to condemn it.'

The B.E.9 was briefly flown by three squadrons (one of its pilots was Lieutenant W. Sholto Douglas, then of No. 8 Squadron but later Marshal of the Royal Air Force Lord Douglas of Kirtleside) but no-one had a good word to say for it, and it returned to Farnborough on 9 January 1916, never to be heard of again.

By then, fortunately, a new Sopwith prototype was about to be tested. This was the quaintly-named 1½ Strutter, initially ordered for the R.N.A.S but quickly adopted by the R.F.C. This British aircraft had the unusual distinction of being built in much greater numbers by French constructors than at home in Britain. When fully equipped with a fixed and synchronised Vickers gun for the pilot and a Lewis gun on a Scarff ring-mounting for the observer, the 1½ Strutter was at first quite successful, but was soon out-performed on the Western Front. French production was so slow to deliver Sopwiths to French units that the type was obsolete by the time it went into action in numbers. In British service it was another type flown operationally by Sholto Douglas, and by Norman Macmillan, both of whom recorded their experiences in their respective books, *Years of Combat* (London, Collins, 1963) and *Into the Blue* (London, Duckworth, 1929).

Early in February 1916 Sopwith brought out the little single-seat fighter that quickly – but unofficially – became known as the Pup. It was extremely popular with contemporary pilots, and was widely used, most notably on experimental work that it alone could undertake because it was so outstandingly docile and controllable.

The Pup was closely followed, in May 1916, by the Sopwith Triplane, a revolutionary design and the world's first fighting triplane. Its performance and combat successes so impressed (and probably alarmed) the Germans that they asked their aircraft manufacturers to design triplane fighters. A profusion of German prototypes followed, but only the Fokker design, the V.4, was produced in significant numbers and almost a year later than the Sopwith triplane. The Fokker, too, proved to be a formidable weapon in its time, but the prototype did not fly until late June 1917, and production Fokker Dr.Is did not begin to reach the *Jagdstaffeln* until late August 1917. The Sopwith Triplane was used operationally only by R.N.A.S. fighter squadrons, and was almost as well liked as the Pup.

Much brave and invaluable work was done behind the scenes by designers and test pilots. One of the truly great pilots of his time was Frank Widenham Goodden, a test pilot at the Royal Aircraft Factory, Farnborough. He played a leading part in establishing the method of recovering from a spin. On 23 August 1916 he deliberately put an F.E.8 into a spin, recovered safely and positively, and set down his actions in Reports & Memoranda No. 168. At that time, this was a great and gallant achievement, but Goodden received no honour, decoration or any public recognition for it. He was to lose his life on 28 January 1917, when the second prototype S.E.5 broke up in the air over Farnborough. His death was seized upon by C. G. Grey, then editor of the weekly magazine *The Aeroplane*, as an excuse for one of the cruellest and most cowardly of his vitriolic outpourings: to Grey, the Royal Aircraft Factory and anyone who worked there deserved nothing but contempt and abuse, even in death; and it was in that odious vein that he, a man who had never flown anything, vilified poor Goodden, whose skill and courage were exceptional. Goodden was 27 when he was killed.

The S.E.5 survived its initial difficulties and became one of the standard British fighters of the latter half of the war in its S.E.5a form. One of its most successful exponents was James McCudden. From being a humble but highly competent mechanic, he rose through the ranks, flew as an observer, trained as a pilot, and became one of the R.F.C.'s most successful fighter pilots, having flown operationally on F.E.2ds, D.H.2s, Sopwith Pups and S.E.5as. His book, *Five Years in the Royal Flying Corps* (London, Aeroplane & General Publishing Co., Ltd, 1918), reveals clearly that he was the complete professional, scrupulously attentive to detail, constantly thinking about his job as a fighter pilot and how he might improve his success rate, all with a kind of clinical detachment – no great drama is written into his narrative. No German pilot could claim to have defeated him in combat: he met his death on 9 July 1918 at Auxi-le-Château in a take-off accident while he was flying out to take command of No. 60 Squadron, R.A.F. He had received his Victoria Cross while still alive, and was only 23 when he was killed.

A great contemporary of the S.E.5a in the fighter squadrons was the Sopwith F.1 Camel, the first British fighter to have twin synchronized Vickers guns. Widely used by both R.F.C and R.N.A.S. squadrons, the Camel was built in very large numbers and saw extensive service in France and elsewhere. To the inadequately trained young men who had to fly the Camel in combat it was a difficult aeroplane to master, but those who lived long enough to learn its capabilities regarded it as a flexible and highly responsive fighter.

One of the Camel's greatest exponents was William George Barker, who had many combat successes on B6313 on the Italian Front. He was awarded the V.C. for his great single-handed combat on the Camel's successor, a Sopwith Snipe, on 27 October 1918, against at least 15 enemy fighters, of which he shot down four despite being wounded in both legs and an arm.

Much successful air fighting was done by a two-seater of outstanding quality, the Bristol F.2B. It proved, after an uncertain start in its F.2a form, to be formidable as a fighting aircraft: indeed, at one time crews of No. 11 Squadron found that enemy pilots would not attack or join combat if more than three Bristols were flying together. And it lived on in the post-war R.A.F until 1932.

14. Some officers of the Royal Flying Corps, August 1912. From left to right, front row:
2/Lt Geoffrey de Havilland , Captain R.R. Gordon, (Royal Marines), Major H.R.M.
Brooke Popham, Major F.H. Sykes, Commander C.R. Samson, RN, Lieutenant B.H.
Barrington-Kennett. Rear row: Captain G.W.P. Dawes, Lieutenant A.E.B. Ashton,
Lieutenant C.J. L'Estrange-Malone, R.N., Lieutenant Spenser D.A. Grey, RN,
Lieutenant A.G. Fox. (RAE 0.790 Crown Copyright)
See Chapter 16: The War in the Air.

15. The Morane-Saulnier Type L monoplane flown by Lieutenant Roland Garros, at
Dunkerque. It was armed with a fixed Hotchkiss machine-gun firing through the
plane of rotation of the airscrew, the blades of which were fitted with protecting steel
wedges to deflect any bullets that did not pass freely through. (Via J.M. Bruce).
See Chapter 16: The War in the Air.

16. James Thomas Byford McCudden V.C.,D.S.O. & Bar, M.C. & Bar, one of Britain's greatest fighting pilots of the war, and a brilliant exponent of the S.E. 5a. A mechanic in the RFC in 1913, he went to France with No. 3 Squadron in August 1914, flying occasionally as an Observer for which work he was awarded the Military Medal and Croix de Guerre. In January 1916 in the U.K. he learned to fly and was posted back to France achieving successes attributed to his scientific approach. He was to reach a total of 57 victories over enemy aircraft, the majority from the single seater S.E. 5a when he was with 56 Squadron. He was killed in a stall after take-off in July 1918 as he was leaving Britain after a period as an Instructor and on being posted to take over Command of 60 Squadron (E.D.G. Galley: Liddle Collection) See Chapter 16: The War in the Air.

17. The Royal Naval Air Service evolved and pioneered virtually every significant technique and development in deck flying. This photograph records an historic event: the first take-off made by an operational military aeroplane from the deck of a naval carrier whilst under way at sea. Flight Commander Bernard Fowler, flying Bristol Scout No. 1255, here departs from the flying deck of H.M.S Vindex on 3 November 1915. The relative wind over the ship's deck was at 27 kt; the measured take-off run was 46 ft in length. (Via J.M. Bruce).
See Chapter 16: The War in the Air.

18. Lieutenant Oscar Bechtle stands in the doorway of Fl. Abt. 33 Officers' Mess, (73 Wittemolenstraat), Moorsele, Belgium. Of the other officers of this squadron pictured here, one can be indentified, Hans Bertsch, on Bechtle's immediate right framed by the backs of the two men in the foreground (Via Oscar Bechtle).
See Chapter 17. A German Airman and his War: Oscar Bechtle.

19. Trench drainage: A problem for the French Sappers. (Charles Thierry: Liddle
Collection). See Chapter 18: The French Soldier in the Trenches.

20. Turkish soldiers with something to celebrate: the British evacuation of the Gallipoli Peninsula. (Liddle Collection). See Chapter 19: Little Mehmet in the Desert.

21. Private Maurice Moser (first on the left, second row, with men of the 89th Division). (James Cooke). See Chapter 20: The American Soldier in France 1917-19.

22. Easter 1916, Prisoners under escort inside Trinity College, Dublin. (Peggy Goodwin: Liddle Collection). See Chapter 21: The Reaction of the Irish Officers in the British Army to the Easter Rising of 1916.

23. From right to left, Ludendorff, the Kaiser and Hindenburg at General Headquarters, January 1917, before the onset of pressures still more intense. (Liddle collection). See Chapter 6: Ludendorff and Germany's defeat.

24. Ernst Jünger photographed at the time of the publication of *Storm of Steel*, 1920. He wears the Pour le Mérite medal.
See Chapter 22: Ernst Jünger: German Stormtrooper Chronicler.

25. French cavalry, 5 September 1914, passing Cameronians. (R.C. Money: Liddle Collection). See Chapter 23: The Last Hurrah.

Another great two-seater was the D.H.4, Geoffrey de Havilland's finest wartime design. Particularly when fitted with the excellent Rolls-Royce Eagle VIII engine the D.H.4 had an outstanding performance, and saw operational service with both the R.F.C. and the R.N.A.S. as a bomber and as a reconnaissance aircraft. The type was built, with the Liberty 12 engine, in great numbers in the United States.

Night bombing in World War I was a hazardous undertaking, for navigation equipment was crude, sketchy and inaccurate; and such aids to night flying as existed were primitive and scanty. It did have the advantage that low speed in the bombing aircraft was no great handicap. Nothing makes that clearer than the extensive use, by the R.F.C., R.A.F. and the Independent Force, of the versatile and durable F.E.2b. Originally designed in 1914 as a fighter-reconnaissance two-seater, it was still in production at the time of the Armistice as night bomber.

The first true heavy bomber for the British flying services was the Handley Page 0/400. This was a development of the 0/100, which had been first built for the R.N.A.S. in 1915. The operational 0/400s only came into service in the spring of 1918; by the end of hostilities the type was equipping three R.A.F squadrons and five of the Independent Force.

The R.A.F.'s first four-engine bomber was the Handley Page V/1500 of 1918, its engines installed in two tandem pairs: four Rolls-Royce Eagles VIII or four Galloway Atlantics. It was hoped to bomb Berlin from bases in England, but the Armistice came before any such raid could be made. As on the earlier 0/100 and 0/400, the wings could be folded to conserve hangar space.

From the outbreak of war, the Royal Navy had a great dread of Germany's rigid airships, perceiving them primarily as a very great threat to its ships. The R.N.A.S. therefore devoted a great deal of effort and experimentation to devising means of attacking and destroying airships. The means of doing so were meagre, and even some of the outlandish ideas that were conceived got as far as being translated into prototype hardware. One such was a brainchild of Noel Pemberton Billing M.P., an ardent advocate of retaliatory bombing of civilian targets in Germany. He proposed the idea of a heavily armed aeroplane designed to have a very long flight endurance and the ability to loiter at low airspeeds in the misguided expectation that, by hanging about in this way, it could shoot down any Zeppelin that obligingly came by at just the right altitude and within range. From an early but short-lived prototype twin-engined quadruplane was developed the Supermarine P.B.31, also a quadruplane which, as an aircraft, embodied several very advanced ideas and equipment, but it had no performance to speak of. Equipment included a nose-mounted searchlight, an on-board auxiliary power unit, rest space for one crew member (a maximum flight endurance of 18 hours was claimed), and a Davis non-recoil shell-firing gun. Many of the drawings for this aircraft survive, and the signature on them is that of one R.J. Mitchell – a mere 20 years before his immortal design, the Spitfire, made its first flight. The two aircraft were worlds apart.

A far greater man than Pemberton Billing was John Cyril Porte, a true pioneer pilot in the pre-war period, and later a great designer of flying boats. He had been invalided out of the Navy, and was to have been co-pilot of the Curtiss H-1 flying boat that had been designed and built to attempt the transAtlantic flight in 1914. When the outbreak of war frustrated the project (though the aircraft would never have made it) he returned to Britain, persuaded the Air Department of the Admiralty to order a batch of Curtiss H-4 flying-boats, and then went on to design far more workmanlike and durable flying-boat hulls. This led to the great family of Felixstowe flying-boats, but first he designed a large three-engine flying-boat, known as the Porte Baby. It was not an unqualified success, but the first Baby was used in combination with a Bristol Scout single-seater to form the world's first composite aircraft. The objective was to provide a rapid reaction to enemy airships with a fighter aircraft already airborne on its carrier: the Scout was to fly off the Baby when an airship was sighted. A faultless in-flight separation was made on 6 April 1916, but was never repeated. On that occasion the Baby was flown by John Porte himself, the Scout by Flight Lieutenant M. J. Day.

In the official history, *The War in the Air*, Vol. I Sir Walter Raleigh acknowledged John Porte's extraordinary achievements: 'The shortest possible list of those who saved the country in its hour of need would have to include his name.'[8] Sadly, John Porte died in 1919.

His most significant development was to take the Curtiss H–8, No. 8650 in the R.N.A.S., and replace its boat-built hull by a simpler and sturdier structure, his Porte II design. In its modified form, 8650 was named Felixstowe F.2, and it served as the prototype for the production type F.2A, which was widely used. In an instance of the wheel turning full circle, the Felixstowe F.2A was built in the U.S.A. by Curtiss as the H–16. Later British developments, also produced in quantity, were the F.3 and F.5: the latter, too, was built in the U.S.A. as the F–5L, the suffix L denoting Liberty engines in place of the Rolls-Royce Eagles of the British-built aircraft.

The R.N.A.S. displayed great inventiveness and resourcefulness in developing naval aviation. The possibility of launching torpedoes from aircraft had been first discussed by several British naval officers in 1911. In Italy, a dummy torpedo was dropped from a special monoplane seaplane on 26 February 1914. The first serious attempt to create a British torpedo aircraft was the big Sopwith Special Seaplane No. 170, which arrived at Calshot on 1 June 1914, but never succeeded in flying with a torpedo. The first successful drop was made from a Short Folder seaplane, No. 121, flown by Squadron Commander Arthur Longmore, on 28 July 1914.

Experiments in dropping torpedoes continued during the war, but a persistent limiting factor was the lack of suitably powerful engines for the seaplanes – combined with the basic fact that the R.N.A.S. for long persisted in using for this task only seaplanes, handicapped by their heavy and drag-creating float undercarriages. Eventually, progress was made with flying from the decks of carrier vessels, which made it feasible to entrust torpedo-dropping to aircraft with wheel undercarriages. The first British torpedo-dropper with wheels instead of floats was the Sopwith T.1, later named Cuckoo. Production Cuckoos were just too late to see operational use before the Armistice. Preparatory training began in 1918, and a Torpedo Aeroplane School was set up at East Fortune, the aircraft operating from the sands at Belhaven.

It had been in the anti-airship field of activity that the technique of flying-off small fighter landplanes from abbreviated decks on available seaplane carriers had earlier been practised. The first take-off made by an operational fighting aeroplane from a carrier vessel under way at sea was made on 3 November 1915; the aircraft was the Bristol Scout C No. 1255, its pilot Flight Commander B. F. Fowler; the ship HMS *Vindex*.

Such signal achievements led to the protracted and assiduous experimentation conducted at the Isle of Grain with the object of developing deck flying to the point of operational practicality. Taking off was relatively easier than landing-on, not least because the day of the through-deck carrier had not yet dawned. HMS *Furious* had a good flying-off deck for'ard, but retained her funnel and conventional superstructure amidships. Despite these obstructions, Squadron Commander E. H. Dunning succeeded in landing a Sopwith Pup on that for'ard deck by flying alongside and crabbing in over the deck, whereupon his aircraft was hauled down manually, its relative speed over the deck being virtually nil. That was done on 2 August 1917. He made a second successful landing on 7 August, but was killed in attempting a third.

The feasibility of flying suitable fighter aeroplanes from tiny platforms on cruisers was proved by Squadron Commander F. J. Rutland. He said he could take off in a Sopwith Pup from a run of only 15 feet, and did so, from HMS *Yarmouth* on 28 June 1917: his run was in fact 14ft 9in. This could only have been done by a Pup. Rutland was a man of brilliant skill, great determination and courage, matched with imagination and ingenuity. He had been the pilot of the Short 184 seaplane that was the only aircraft of any type to fly during the Battle of Jutland in 1916, and went on to become one of the outstanding pioneers in the development of deck flying in the Royal Navy. Such a man deserved a far better end than he had. Because he had worked in Japan in the inter-war period, he was imprisoned without charge or trial during World War II. He was released without apology or explanation in the autumn of 1943, but finally took his own life on 28 January 1949.

A pivotal figure in the history of wartime aviation – indeed, of world-wide aviation – was Robert Smith-Barry. To him the entire aviation world is indebted for his creation, in the autumn of 1917, of the School of Special Flying at Gosport, with its all-important system of flying instruction. Up to that time, flying instruction had been a somewhat hit-and-miss affair, largely given by instructors who often had little more flying experience than their hapless pupils: inevitably this proved to be disastrously inadequate. Smith-Barry's chosen instrument at Gosport was at first the Avro 504J, and subsequently his station played a part in the evolution of the later 504K, which remained in service with the Royal Air Force well into the post-war period, and was further developed into the 504N, which had an Armstrong-Siddeley Lynx radial engine and an improved undercarriage. Smith-Barry himself had seen operational flying from the earliest days of the war: he had gone to France with the R.F.C. in August 1914, but had been injured in the crash of a B.E.8. He later flew Morane-Saulnier Bullets in No. 60 Squadron as a fighter pilot, and commanded that Squadron from July until December 1916.

Of the men of Britain's flying services, the late Sir Walter Raleigh, the author of Volume I of the official history, *The War in the Air* (Oxford, The Clarendon Press, 1922), wrote:

> The recruits of the air were young, some of them not more than boys. Their training lasted only a few months. They put their home life behind them, or kept it only as a fortifying memory and threw themselves with fervour and abandon into the work to be done. Pride in their squadron became a part of their religion. The demands made upon them, which, it might reasonably have been believed, were greater than human nature can endure, were taken by them as a matter of course; they fulfilled them, and went beyond. They were not a melancholy company; they had something of the lightness of the element in which they moved. Indeed, it would be difficult to find, in the world's history, any body of fighters who, for sheer gaiety and zest could hold a candle to them. They have opened up a new vista for their country and mankind. Their story, if it could ever be fully and truly written, is the Epic of Youth.[9]

Sir Walter Raleigh died in 1922 and did not see the completion of the official history. Nor did he see the events of 1940, a time when a succeeding generation of young flying men was to uphold with honour the tradition but recently established by the Royal Flying Corps and the Royal Naval Air Service. Sir Walter would, I believe, have written of them in similar terms.

Notes

1   Quoted in *The War in the Air*, Vol. I, p. 329 (Oxford University Press, 1922).
2   *The War in the Air*, Vol. I, p. 260.

3   *The War in the Air*, Vol. II, p. 144.
4   *The Story of a North Sea Air Station*, C. F. Snowden Gamble, Oxford University Press, 1928; pp. 81–82.
5   *The War in the Air*, Vol. I, p. 284.
6   *One Man's War*, Bert Hall; John Hamilton Ltd, 1929; p. 122.
7   *Flying and Soldiering*, R. R. Money; Ivor Nicolson & Watson, 1939, p. 40.
8   *The War in the Air*, Vol. I, p. 466.
9   *The War in the Air*, Vol. I, p. 408.

Chapter 16

A German Airman and his War: Oscar Bechtle

Peter Kilduff

At mobilization on 1 August 1914, the German Army's *Fliegertruppe* [Flying Service] had 254 trained pilots and 271 qualified observers serving with 48 Prussian and seven Bavarian units.[1] Despite the unity of purpose and nominal responsibility accorded to the *Inspekteur der Fliegertruppen* [Inspector General of the Flying Service], Germany's first air arm had a weak command structure. The flaws were corrected some two years later, when the *Fliegertruppe* was reorganized as the *Luftstreitkräfte* [Air Force], under its own commanding general.[2]

A good example of the development and deployment of German airmen during this transitional period can be seen in the career of Oscar Bechtle, who had joined the German Army in 1913 to become a career infantry officer. Commissioned a *Leutnant* [Second Lieutenant] in *Grenadier-Regiment König Karl (5. Württembergisches) Nr. 123*, Bechtle remained with that unit until, as he noted, he became frustrated by the lack of progress in the ground war:

> In the spring and summer of 1916, the early morning hours were very peaceful along our sector of the Flanders Front, where the 26. and 27. *Infanterie-Divisions* [on the German 4 *Armee* Front] were positioned to attack Ypres. Occasionally, a shot would ring out, aimed at one of the pheasants among the tree stumps. Otherwise, it was quiet and we . . . could enjoy the sweet idleness, while viewing from our position atop Hill 59 the white teeth-like towers of the city of Ypres, which, surrounded by green hedges, made a tranquil scene.[3]

Seeking more action, Bechtle applied for transfer to the *Luftstreitkräfte* and, on 12 November 1916, he was assigned to the aviation training facility *Versuchs-und Übungspark Ost* in Warsaw. At the time, officers were trained as observers and as pilots, while aviation enlisted men served only as pilots (in the sense of 'aerial drivers'), gunners and ground personnel. By the spring of 1917, the 23-year-old Bechtle was back on the 4. *Armee* Front, now assigned to *Flieger-Abteilung 33*, an aerial reconnaissance unit. There, he was reunited with three former regimental comrades: *Ltns* Gustav Eichler (33 years old), Alfons Reichle (18) and Willy Semmler (20).

'THE GOOD LIFE'

Bechtle confirmed that, relatively speaking, service in the *Luftstreitkräfte* was 'the good life'. Living in a comfortable expropriated château in Moorsele, Belgium, the aircrews of *Fl.-Abt 33* soon forgot the indignities of eating and sleeping within musty, vermin-infested earthen battlements; now, they could fight for their country, while enjoying fresh air, good food and drink, and clean beds, within a relatively well-protected area behind the lines.

'What a difference from life in the trenches,' Bechtle wrote. 'In less than ten minutes, with no waiting for the artillery shelling to end, we were able to go straight to and over the Front. We had to keep our eyes open, however, to avoid suffering the mishap that befell our regimental comrade *Ltn* Albrecht Jäger [of nearby *Fl.-Abt 30*], who, while returning . . . [from] one of his first flights over the lines,[4] was attacked above his own airfield by a British "*Gitterschwanz*" [lattice-tail, rear-engined] aircraft that gave him a good working over and severely wounded him in the arm.'[5]

Bechtle also observed the battleground's new perspective, as seen from his seat in the rear of a reconnaissance biplane:

The focal point . . . was the white ruins of the shattered city of Ypres. To the north, protected by the overflow of the Yser River, was a broad reddish band of emplacements, bounded on either side by green parcels of land. In and around Hill 60, Bastion and St. Eloi, yawned the big craters that had swallowed up so many human lives.

'North and south of Poperinghe, site of an important rail junction, could be seen the smoke of the locomotives of British transport trains and then the British camp at the foot of Mount Kemmel, near Dickebusch Lake. The all-seeing eye of the aerial camera revealed the location and extent of these activities.[6]

Flying in a DFW C.V reconnaissance aircraft, Bechtle and his pilot, *Vizefeldwebel* (Sergeant Major) Erich Bahr,[7] climbed to 5,000 metres altitude. Bechtle paid particular attention to the movement of heavy artillery pieces, which German batteries would try to silence before their own front-line units were battered.

Bechtle's value as a ground-war veteran was recognized on 16 March, when he and the commanding officer of *Fl.-Abt 33*, *Hauptmann* [Captain]

Plaeschke, were ordered to 4. *Armee* Headquarters to brief the staff on British activities.[8]

Their host was *Hptm* Otto Bufe, *Kommandeur der Flieger der 4. Armee* [Officer in Charge of Aviation for the 4th Army]. 'Other higher ranking Staff officers observed silently, as Bufe put a series of questions to us,' Bechtle said. 'After his brief interrogation, we were sent on our way. The Staff did not waste time on amenities.'

COMBAT IN THE AIR

'Operation Alberich,'[9] the orderly, gradual withdrawal of German forces to the much-better fortified Siegfried Position, from 16 March through 6 April 1917, encouraged a general British advance from Arras to Roye which began on 17 March.[10] Bechtle recalled *Fl.-Abt 33*'s increased activity that day:

> As part of these efforts, a special mission was undertaken by *Ltn* Alfons Reichle, the well-liked former commander of the *3. Kompagnie* [3rd Company] of the *123. Grenadier-Regiment*. [That day], he started out three times to photograph enemy artillery batteries. The first time he had to return because his engine was damaged during an air fight. The second time, an engine defect forced him to return home. Only on the third attempt was Reichle able to take the required photographs – and then only after a fight. . .[11]

A 4. *Armee* report described the encounter:

> *Leutnant* Reichle and *Unteroffizier* [Corporal] Weiss, *Flieger-Abteilung 33*, during a photo-reconnaissance flight[12] at 2:50 p.m., got into a fight with an enemy aeroplane [B.E.2], which, after a few shots, disappeared in a steep turn, leaving a trail of smoke, and was observed to crash within enemy lines north of Bastion. Confirmation [of the aerial victory] seems assured.[13]

The crew's mission was reconnaissance, but, successful defence in aerial combat was regarded by commanders and comrades alike as a great achievement. Indeed, there were tangible rewards for shooting down any enemy aircraft. On confirmation of the first aerial victory, each German airman received a silver *Ehrenbecher für den Sieg im Luftkampfe* [Cup of Honour for the Victor in Aerial Combat] to mark the occasion. Often, the crew received decorations, an *Orden* [order] for the officer, a lower-ranking *Medaille* [medal] for the enlisted man.

'Such a triumph was cause for a good party,' Oscar Bechtle told this author. '*Hptm* Plaeschke let it be known that an LVG C.V had been used during the air fight. It had been rumoured that the aircraft companies were generous and, the next day, a lorry arrived at our officers' mess with several cases of good wine – courtesy of the aeroplane manufacturer *Luft-Verkehrs-Gesellschaft*. Flyers from nearby units also brought treats such as a good sausage or a nice wheel of cheese, and stayed to help us consume them.'

The joy of victory was short-lived. Exactly a week later, Bechtle remembered: 'We waited in vain for Reichle to return from his regularly scheduled mission. Subsequently, we discovered his shattered aeroplane [near Hollebeke[14]], only a few metres from a trench position he had used during his infantry days. We recovered Reichle's body; his perpetual happy smile was still on his lips. He now rests in his native [Württemberg].'[15]

BLOODY APRIL

That month, German air superiority inflicted such heavy losses on the Royal Flying Corps – one-third of its frontline airmen, 912 pilots and observers in 50 squadrons – that the period has come to be known in military aviation history as 'Bloody April'.[16] From Oscar Bechtle's viewpoint, it was a time of trouble for Germans, too:

> There was no rest for us and, as we flew along the edge of Ypres, to observe in the evening darkness the muzzle flashes of the enemy artillery positions from Ypres to Kemmel, often we thought of our comrades on the ground. We could visualize them cowering in their sand-bagged positions, wishing the night would end, while we in the air shouted with joy whenever a long suspected [hostile] battery fired a salvo and thereby betrayed its position.[17]

British gains on the ground out-weighed losses in the air. Those same British gains helped to forge a closer relationship between Bechtle and his former comrades on the ground:

> The battle for Wytschaete raged. Our aeroplanes flew day and night. During brief lulls in the fighting, it was a particular pleasure to travel by car to our beloved regiment, then stationed at Roulers. On our homeward flights we would announce our intentions by dropping a note on the company's machine-gun billets. And how happy we were when the visit was returned at our airfield in Moorsele.[18]

During the battle for Bullecourt, on 11 April 1917, Bechtle had an especially close connection with his old regiment. When British tanks and infantry penetrated a spot in the German defences, he and Bahr were sent out to evaluate the situation. 'As I flew over the trenches, I recognized the territory and my old regiment's positions. Within moments, I understood the situation – the British had broken through, but were stalled – and I directed Bahr to fly to *Hptm* Bufe's advance field post,' Bechtle told the author:

On our arrival, it was so quiet I feared the post had been overrun, but then an orderly emerged from a small house. 'Where is the officer in charge?' I asked. 'He is having breakfast with the staff,' he said. 'Would you mind waiting?' 'Yes,' I replied sharply. 'There is a battle going on and I have important information to report.' The orderly disappeared and moments later, an *Oberleutnant* [First Lieutenant] came out, apologized for the delay and took down my information. He said he would inform the staff – probably as they finished their breakfast. Bahr and I left in disgust and made a full report when we returned to Moorsele.

IN THE AIR OVER CAMBRAI

Ultimately, Oscar Bechtle and his comrades aided the 4. *Armee* in a generally successful effort to hold the Hindenburg Line. Next, they took part in plans to help stop the British offensive at Cambrai, on the neighbouring German 2. *Armee* Front, beginning on 19 November 1917.[19] The following day, additional fighter aircraft were sent to reinforce the object of the concentrated attack, as reported in an optimistic *Luftstreitkräfte* weekly summary of events:

A great battle [is taking place] in the 2. *Armee* [area]; The aviation units of [that] *Armee*, supported by fighter aeroplanes of the 7. *Armee*, made numerous low-level flights to keep its leaders continually apprised of the battle situation. Low-hanging clouds have made flights at only 50 metres [altitude] necessary. [There have been] numerous artillery adjustment and low-level machine-gun attacks, [as well as] successful battles against tanks. Along the rest of the Front, activity is slight.[20]

Despite prevailing bad weather, the bold advance at Cambrai affected German units in the adjacent areas for weeks to come. When the weather cleared[21] on 28 November 1917,[22] *Fl.-Abt 33* and other units were diverted to support German defences at Cambrai. But even during those grim struggles, Bechtle and his comrades found at least an element of rude humour in the introduction of British tanks:

To be sure, [he recalled] these [tanks] were not yet fully developed and frequently they lay stuck in the mud. At the time we called them 'masculine' and 'feminine' tanks; the former armed with cannons, the latter only with machine-guns.[23]

REWARDS FOR VALOUR

Ltn Oscar Bechtle's audacity and bravery were recognized by various components of the German Empire. He had received Prussia's Iron Cross 2nd Class on 4 October 1914 and the Iron Cross 1st Class on 16 August

1916. Only thirteen days later, Bechtle became one of only 164 aviation recipients of his native Kingdom of Württemberg's Knight's Cross of the Military Merit Order with Swords.[24] Receipt of Prussia's second-highest bravery award[25] – the Knights Cross of the Royal Order of the House of Hohenzollern with Swords – on 24 November 1917,[26] confirmed his value to the *Luftstreitkräfte*.

Not to be outdone by *Kaiser* Wilhelm II, a smaller royal house with troops in the area decorated Bechtle, who recalled:

> The minor *Fürsten* [Princes] paid scrupulous attention to their own sovereignty. Their seats of court were mostly made prominent by being honoured to be small garrisons. The local unit commander was usually the Prince, who [otherwise] had no command authority. . .This Prince *did* have troops at the Front within our area,[27] and so [on 19 December 1917], I received the Principality of Schwarzburg-Sondershausen's War Cross of Honour 3rd Class for provisioning and relieving enemy pressure on these troops from the air.[28]

AIR VIEW OF THE MARCH 1918 OFFENSIVE

In recognition of his outstanding service and leadership, on 18 March 1918, Bechtle was appointed commanding officer of *Schlachtstaffel 2*, one of 38 'battle flights' created for intense close air support during the coming offensive. These *Schlastas* succeeded the former *Schutzstaffeln* [protection flights][29] assigned to escort reconnaissance and infantry-support aircraft; the main difference was the more aggressive role taken by the newly reconstituted units, as Bechtle recalled:

> The *Schlastas* were . . . [primarily] equipped with two-seat Halberstadt [CL.II] and also less-esteemed Hannover [CL.IIIa] aircraft. We had about twenty 1-kg small bombs aboard, two fixed, forward-firing machine-guns and the *Fliegerschütze* [rear-seat aerial gunners] had a swivel-mounted machine-gun. In my experience as the leader of *Schlasta* 2, such a unit was successful only when our opponents were unnerved or in retreat.
>
> There were some successes recorded, [but] as soon as the opposition counter-attacked in April 1918, we suffered high casualties. By the time I was shot down from 100 metres altitude by ground-fire at the end of April, there were only two serviceable aeroplanes out of the original eighteen [assigned to *Schlasta* 2].[30]

All this, Bechtle recorded, despite arduous training and availability of considerable resources:

> Behind the Front [prior to the offensive], I had drilled my black-tailed, fast-turning two-seat Halberstadt CL.II aircraft daily. Every pilot, every

aerial gunner was secure in the feeling: no one can single me out when I am in the *Staffel* and stay close to the leading aircraft. In addition to our own dependable aircraft, we also had three reserve aeroplanes, well hidden in two old barns, and they could be made ready for action within a few hours.

Our *Staffel* also had three of the best heavy duty lorries, which could be quickly mobilized as an 'aviation supply column' and loaded with tools and spare parts, fuel and ammunition – ready to set out immediately when we changed airfields . . .

We just wanted to get on with it! The endless rain and fog during most of the month got on our nerves. At last, on 20 March, a car came to the farm where we were billeted and brought orders for us to take part in the opening attack the next day. Now there was feverish activity to get everything ready. Even the reserve machines were assembled for use.[31]

The German spring offensive began under the cover of a heavy mist at 0445 hours on Thursday, 21 March 1918. Extensive heavy artillery fire was followed at about 0800 hours by waves of assault troops, escorted by low-flying *Schlasta* aircraft.[32]

Schlasta 2's aircraft – based near St. Martin Rivère,[33] a few kilometres east of Busigny – had been readied before daybreak and the aircrews were eager to get underway, as Bechtle remembered:

In every Halberstadt there were two to three 12.5-kg bombs, in addition hand grenades and machine-gun ammunition. Many a pilot did not make a happy face when his aerial gunner . . . [tried] to smuggle aboard a few more kilos of hand grenades and the 'crate' would hardly be able to get off the ground[34]

During a break in the weather at about 0800 hours, *Schlasta* 2 set out almost due south for Grougis Lesquielles, to rendezvous with *Schlastas* 6 and 32[35] and thence to operate broadly along the *18. Armee* Front against elements of the British Fifth Army.[36] Bechtle later wrote:

One aeroplane after the other went headlong into the veil of fog that hung over us at scarcely 50 metres altitude, circled the airfield until each could see the white band around the fuselage of [my] aircraft, which flew just below them and then headed south. Following one another like Indians on the warpath, they flew at the lowest altitude along the tree-lined country road, anxiously staying with every bend in the road; they knew that anyone who lost his direction in the fog would become so completely lost that he would never be able to find his way home in one piece.[37]

Steady control of movement was a key part of deploying the small, agile two-seaters in support of German ground troops. Amidst the fog, signal fires were set to direct *Schlachtstaffeln* to airfields. As luck would have it, all six *Schlasta 2* pilots were deceived by an ambulance column's blazing campfire and landed nearby, only to find their Halberstadts in soft mud up to their axles. The undamaged aircraft were extricated by teams of horses, but Bechtle's plan to arrive at the Front in strength of numbers had to be delayed. Thus, his unit was not called into action until 1500 hours. He recalled:

> Less than ten minutes later we were in the air, anxious about the situation, as no news about conditions at the Front had reached us. Only the location of the attacks had been given and we were left to determine what progress had been made. Therefore, I especially impressed upon my crews not to fire a shot until I shot a flare as a signal to begin the attack. Above all, they were to avoid giving our infantry a false signal to attack. On the contrary, the [infantry] were to make their advance with us.[38]

Upon arriving over St. Quentin, *Schlasta 2* was briefly exposed to gunfire near the city's cathedral. Unable to recognize the battle line, Bechtle led his crews northward, whereupon he reported:

> Everywhere beneath us columns were moving westward. At our 200-metre altitude, we felt and heard the short bark of guns here and there, as . . . our artillery was still firing over a wide area. Therefore, the attack could not make much headway; it behoved us to be doubly cautious. We flew up and down our old positions . . .
>
> Then came signal flashes from the secondary enemy positions; a German battalion commander displayed the square cloth panel [to mark his degree of advancement]. Now we understood. Here and there small groups [of German infantry] moved forward in leaps and bounds; now the attack could be risked. . .
>
> A flare appeared above the foremost line. On that signal we loosened our machine-gun belts and went into a shallow dive at about 180 kilometres per hour toward the enemy. Tack, tack, tack . . . my pilots tested their guns. At the beginning of the attack, they opened up with their forward-firing machine-guns, pouring tracer and regular bullets through their propeller arcs and into the enemy positions . . . We passed over the British defences quicker than we thought we would and their troops were waiting for us behind hillocks and in shell holes. Down went our hand grenades, followed by black smoke rising from the ammunition stockpiles that we had ignited.
>
> After a sharp turn to the right, the swivel-mounted machine-guns were put to good use by the aerial gunners . . . We noticed only a little return fire. Now it was back to our infantry and repeating the show two or three times more . . . For a long time on our return flight we saw bright-red shell flashes illuminated by the stores of artillery ammunition we had hit.[39]

Oscar Bechtle was promoted to *Oberleutnant* the following day and, a short time later, was honoured by the Kingdom of Saxony for his work with Saxon ground units. He was awarded the Knight's Cross 2nd Class of the Order of Albert with Swords.[40]

The *18. Armee* pushed ahead and *Schlasta 2* was in the forefront, helping to sweep aside opponents above and below. During one flight along the old Roman road from Vermand to Amiens, Bechtle recalled:

> Cheerfully, we flew along . . . bathed in the late afternoon sunshine at an altitude of 400 metres. Aside from bright flames and thick dirty clouds of smoke, there was nothing to be seen for some distance . . . Suddenly my wingman wagged his tail three times to get my attention. I looked over and saw, below us and to the right, three aeroplanes bearing tri-colour cockades. Blithely flying into German-held territory [were] big two-engined Caudrons, uprooted hastily from some other area, and apparently totally new . . . [to this] area.
>
> 'Immediately, all five of us turned and went after the three cumber-some Frenchmen, and attacked them from above and below. Two dived for the ground and made emergency landings. The third tried to steal away, but two of us got below and behind him and, firing with our swivel-mounted machine-guns over our top wings, silenced his engine and knocked out everything else, so that he went down leaving a steep trail of smoke and hit a swampy bank of the Somme.[41]
>
> 'Flying over the Somme, the presence of heavy artillery fire required us to reconnoitre very cautiously. The enemy was well hidden in the hills on the other side and supported below by considerable infantry, whose presence was made known to flyers when rifle bullets struck their aero-planes. We were not easily diverted from our mission, however; to the north, at Villers Carbonnel, we caught up with an [enemy] infantry column and got them to move. Farther south, [enemy] artillery was firing on an open field and soon the whole bank was alive, as our artillery joined the action.[41]

For the *Schlastas*, April 1918 became nearly a reversal of a year earlier. *Schlasta 2* proceeded south and east, where Bechtle observed that 'resist-ance met in the air and on the ground became stronger. Every day at the Front we were involved with three divisions engaged in heavy fighting, or escorting reconnaissance aircraft on flights that lasted for hours. Enemy defensive positions were continually being readied by troops whose blue uniforms we recognized as being French.'[43]

Ultimately, the failure of the last German offensive took its toll on Oscar Bechtle. He and his pilot were attacking French troops from 100 metres altitude over the forest near Grivesnes when a great crash rocked their aeroplane. In a moment, the pilot was slumped over the controls, unconscious. Bechtle later wrote:

I had to shake him several times to awaken him. When I asked if he had been wounded, he held up his bleeding right arm and shouted in my ear: 'Yes, I believe so.' On the return to our airfield . . . hardly had the machine come to a halt, when out jumped my brave pilot, who proudly began to count the bullet holes in his 'crate.' But then he fell to the ground unconscious.[44]

The pilot had been hit by a bullet that passed from his left hip through the right shoulder. His life was saved by a speedy journey to a field hospital.

Bechtle's own flying career ended only days later, when his patched-up aircraft was brought down by infantry gunfire. After crashing inside German forward lines, the wrecked Halberstadt was shelled by nearby British batteries. Both crewmen survived uninjured, but that mission turned out to be Oscar Bechtle's last combat flight.

His wealth of extensive combat experiences made Bechtle a valuable instructor for the new, ever younger aircrews entering the training cycle. Despite his protests to remain at the Front, on 24 July 1918, Bechtle was assigned to the Aviation Replacement Section in Böblingen, not far from his home town of Esslingen, and served there until the war's end.

Bechtle never forgot his comrades at the Front[45] and noted that, after his departure, 'Schlasta 2 went on to perform new deeds of valour during very successful attacks between the Aisne and Marne Rivers. In the successful completion of their missions, the Schlachtflieger [Battle Flyers] were like the cavalry of earlier days, ever charging into the fray.'[46]

Notes

1   C. Neumann ed., *Die deutschen Luftstreitkräfte im Weltkriege*, Berlin, 1920, p. 62.
2   H. Nowarra, *Eisernes Kreuz und Balkenkreuz*, Mainz 1968, p. 37.
3   O. Bechtle, 'Württembergische Flieger-Erinnerungen aus Flandern' in O. von Moser, ed., *Die Württemberger im Weltkrieg*, Stuttgart 1938, p. 635.
4   *Kommandeur der Flieger der 4. Armee* weekly report, No. 14370/19, 18 March 1917, p. 1 reports that on the morning of 17 March 'a flight of three "pusher" biplane and two fighter aeroplanes went as far [over German lines] as Menin and a second [flight] of three units went as far as Roulers.'
5   Bechtle in von Moser, op.cit.; at the time, Jäger was 22 years old.
6   ibid.
7   Bechtle Letter to the author, 14 November 1978, which also notes; 'after his promotion to *Leutnant der Reserve*, Bahr was transferred in November 1917 to *Jagdstaffel 11* [commanded by *Ltn* Lothar *Freiherr* [Baron] von Richthofen, brother of Germany's highest-scoring fighter ace of World War I, *Rittmeister* Manfred *Freiherr* von Richthofen]. Bahr was killed in action [on 3 March 1918] just before the Spring 1918 Offensive.'
8   Confirmed in *Flieger-Abteilung 33 Tätigkeitsbericht Nr 194/17*, 18 March 1917, p. 1.
9   Named after a character in the Teutonic legend *The Ring of the Niebelungs*; the dwarf king Alberich was the keeper of the treasure of the Niebelungs.

Accordingly, the fallback line was called the Siegfried Position, which was named the Hindenburg Line by *Entente* forces.

10 H. Jones, *The War in the Air*, vol III, Oxford, 1931, p. 307.

11 Bechtle in von Moser, op.cit., pp. 635–636.

12 Made on behalf of *Infanterie-Regiment Nr 413* [Ref: *Flieger-Abt 33* weekly report No. 194/17, 18 March 1917. p. 1.

13 *Kofl 4. Armee* weekly report, op.cit., p. 5. Despite this favourable report, official credit for shooting down an aircraft near the British-held fortified position opposite the German 27. *Infanterie-Division* was not confirmed in the German Air Force's weekly summary of events; presumably, Reichle's and Weiss's claim was disallowed [Ref: *Nachrichtenblatt der Luftstreitkräfte*, Vol I, No. 7, 12 April 1917, p. 14]. Worthy of note, however, is that No. 4 Squadron, RFC, reported that B.E.2c #2755 was 'brought down by [the] enemy' in the area at 1:45 p.m. (British Time, an hour ahead of German Time), indicating that this aircraft might have been shot down by Reichle and Weiss [Ref: *RFC Western Front Casualty List in the Field*, 17 March 1917].

14 *Ehrentafel der Flieger und Luftschifferformationen der Königlichen Württembergischen Armee*, Stuttgart, 1934, p. 51. Hollebeke was then within German lines, but available German records do no indicate what caused Reichle's aircraft to crash, nor the fate and disposition – or even identification – of the pilot.

15 Bechtle in von Moser, op.cit.

16 A. Morris, *Bloody April*, London 1967, p. 15.

17 Bechtle in von Moser, op.cit., p. 636.

18 ibid.

19 B. Liddell Hart, *The Real War 1914–1918*, New York 1964 ed., p. 344.

20 Kogenluft, *Nachrichtenblatt der Luftstreitkräfte*, Berlin 1917, vol. 1, No. 39, 22 November, 1917, p. 400.

21 Ref: *Nachrichtenblatt*, No. 41, 6 December 1917, p. 431.

22 The date is confirmed in the *Personal-Bogen* [personnel records] of Oscar Bechtle and other members of *Fl.-Abt 33*.

23 Bechtle letter to the author dated 4 June 1979.

24 N. O'Connor, *Aviation Awards of Imperial Germany in World War I and the Men Who Earned Them*, vol. IV, *The Aviation Awards of the Kingdom of Württemberg*, Princeton 1995, pp. 40–41.

25 N. O'Connor, vol. II, *The Aviation Awards of the Kingdom of Prussia*, (1990), p. 132. The same reference also notes that this honour 'came to be the intermediate award for officers between the Iron Cross 1st Class and the *Orden Pour le Mérite*,' Prussia's highest bravery award, commonly known as 'the Blue Max.'

26 Bechtle *Personal-Bogen*, op.cit.

27 *Fürst* [Prince] Günther of Schwarzburg-Rudolstadt and Sondershausen commanded *III. Bataillon des 7. Thüringeschen Infanterie-Regiments Nr. 96 (Rudolstadt)* [ref: *Thüringen im Weltkrieg*, Vol I, Leipzig 1921, pp. 300–301.

28 Bechtle letter to the author dated 17 April 1987.

29 *Kriegsministerium, Teil 10 Abschnitt B, Flieger-Formationen* [organization manual], Berlin 1918, pp. 222–223, 246–253.

30 Bechtle letter to the author dated 16 March 1977.

31 Bechtle, *Mit der Schlachtstaffel von St. Quentin nach Amiens* in Neumann (ed), *In der Luft Unbesiegt* (1923), p. 167.

32 Jones, *The War in the Air*, vol IV, (1934), pp. 292–293.

33 ibid., Map 10, p. 364; geographically located just within the southern boundary of the *2. Armee, Schlasta* 2 operated on the German *18. Armee* Front.

34 Bechtle in Neumann, op.cit.

35 Jones, Map, op.cit.

36 ibid.

37 Bechtle in Neumann, op.cit.

38 ibid., p. 168.

39 ibid., p. 169.

40 O'Connor, vol III, *The Aviation Awards of the Kingdom of Saxony*, (1993), p. 170, notes that there were 790 non-Saxon recipients of this award.

41 Kogenluft, *Nachrichtenblatt der Luftstreitkräfte*, Vol II, Berlin 1918 No. 17, 20 June 1918 lists no confirmed victories for any *Schlasta* 2 aircrews from 21 through 31 March 1918.

42 Bechtle in Neumann, op.cit., p. 171.

43 ibid., p. 173.

44 ibid., p. 174.

45 Having survived the rigours of two World Wars, Oscar Bechtle died peacefully at his home in 1990 at the age of 94.

46 op.cit., p. 175.

Part IV

Soldiers: National and Unit Identity – General

Chapter 17

The French Soldier in the Trenches*

Stephane Audoin-Rouzeau

Of all the great powers involved in the war, no other country mobilised on such a vast scale as France or suffered such a high rate of casualties. The direct sacrifices asked of the French people were greater than elsewhere and French soldiers were in a much less advantageous position than the Germans when it came to fighting since, until the middle of 1918, the theatre of war was largely unfavourable to French interests. How and why was it that the majority of these eight million French soldiers were able to hold out in the trenches for more than four years?

In fact, we cannot understand the amazing staying power of the French soldier without knowing something of his frame of mind; knowledge of this is to be sought in (unpublished) accounts of personal experience written at the time and not in accounts written long after the events they describe, for memory has distorted history to a considerable extent in the accounts written by ex-servicemen who have often set themselves up as the only historians qualified to speak of their experience of the war.[1] Progress in research now makes it easier to have an overview of the French army in its diversity, as interest shifts towards the most numerous category of combatant, paradoxically the least well known, namely the *soldats-paysans*, soldiers recruited from the agrarian classes. What did the men in the trenches say about what they were living through as they were experiencing it?

The stereotypical '1914–1918 *poilu*' is obviously a myth. Given that the front was being renewed constantly it was not always the same men who held the line. In view of the frightful losses of 1914 and 1915, only part of the soldiers who were in at the start of the war were able to see it out.

* This is an edited translation of an article which appeared in '*14–18: Mourir Pour La Patrie*, L'Histoire Spécial no 107 p. 31 ff., Paris, Seuil 1992.

Infantry accounted for 80 per cent of the army in 1914 but only 50 per cent in 1918; war had taken on a different aspect with the development of modern weaponry. Furthermore, the trenches did not wipe out sociological diversity: soldiers from rural areas, who were in the majority, cannot be assimilated to ones from the towns, any more than soldiers from the middle classes can be to those from the working classes. They were not all equally well off, they had different preoccupations and their attitudes remained distinct right up to the end of the war.

Geographical origin was another form of difference. A soldier from the Midi knew his family was safe; but a soldier from the *départements* which had been invaded remained virtually without news of his relations for the duration of the war. With *patois* sometimes representing a real obstacle, soldiers from different regions did not always find it easy to make contact. A last but essential difference lay in the fact that they were not all equal in the face of death. Infantrymen of the line were very exposed, artillery and territorial divisions a little less so.

Nevertheless, life in the trenches created a certain community of life and feelings, even if the army was never totally homogeneous, even if the comradeship engendered among those who had been in the front line (which was to be exalted later by veterans) was largely a myth. The sufferings of everyday life and the shared experience of a long confrontation with death created a peculiar 'war culture' which affected the soldiers, whatever their origins.

Death . . . We must start there because the combatants lived under the threat of it during the whole of their stay at the front. It was in their trench newspapers that certain soldiers were able to communicate the deep anguish it caused in them: 'How quickly the rest period passed', wrote *L'Argonaute* in 1917. 'On leaving a peaceful village more than one man wondered 'Will I be back here next time?'. He thinks no more about it but behind his thought lies a vague image of bodies lying in the plain and roughly-made crosses standing askew. The lottery is starting up again. Happy indeed are those who draw a lucky number. 'Death lies ceaselessly in wait especially before an attack', wrote the same journal in 1917: 'Just a few moments ago in the front trench people's eyes met and were quickly turned away but it was long enough to read the secret anguish of the "any minute now". And I felt my thoughts inclining this way. I was going to feel fear in the face of the unknown, be afraid to go up, to fight. However, the attack freed you from the terrible anguish of waiting, which disappears as soon as the action starts.'

'There's nothing like this during bombardments, an even more terrible ordeal; nothing else to be done but wait for death for hours, sometimes days.' 'There's nothing more horrible in war than being shelled', wrote another trench newspaper, *La Saucisse*, in April 1917. 'It's a form of torture that the soldier can't see the end of. Suddenly he's afraid of being buried alive . . . He conjures up the atrocious agony . . . And there's a vision of loved ones, his wife, mother, child . . . And the man stays put in his hole, helplessly waiting for, hoping for a miracle'. Unlike the letters, such texts are not destined for soldiers' families but for the fighting men themselves: the better-educated ones write them for their close comrades. Is it a means by which the group can tame death, keep it at bay, exorcise it? The risk of death creates a deep rift between the soldiers and the rest of the population and, in their view, cuts them off from the society from which they come and which it is their mission to defend. From what they say, the fact that death is ever present makes the front an 'island', it creates a world apart.

Shells and bullets, the former rather than the latter, killed 1,300,000 French soldiers.[2] Only Serbia, Turkey, Roumania and Bulgaria recorded higher rates of casualties than France. But, with 16.5 per cent of those called up becoming casualties, France tragically outstrips Germany – 15.4 per cent, Great Britain – 12.5 per cent, the Austro-Hungarian Empire – 12.2 per cent, Russia – 11.5 per cent and Italy – 10.3 per cent. For the actual combatants the casualty rate reached 18 per cent compared with 3 per cent for the service regiments. The saddest record is held by the officers, usually of middle class origin, who suffered most in the war: the agrarian class came second ahead of the working class. Losses among officers reached 19 per cent of their number and even 22 per cent for those commanding troops in the front line. This calamitous superiority of the French over the principal powers involved in the conflict is reflected in the overall casualty rate: France lost 3.4 per cent of its total population, a figure exceeded only by Serbia and Turkey. Somewhere in the region of three million French soldiers were probably wounded, either slightly or more seriously and once or several times, which comes to 40 per cent of the total forces mobilised.

This makes it easier to understand a certain indifference to the death of others among those whose first reaction was happiness at feeling themselves alive after each ordeal. 'While we were at the barbed wire and during rest periods', wrote a sergeant to his wife in December 1914, 'stretcher bearers from the Ambulance Service took away a dead man and passed a few feet from us and whilst some asked about the dead man, others went on playing cards as if nothing were amiss. One comes to accept death, suffering and horror as everyday occurrences.'

The rigours of everyday life are set against this tragic backdrop. Conditions in the trenches were lamentable, especially on the French side. In its anxiety not to get bogged down permanently in a war of position and not to appear resigned to this form of combat, the High Command for a long time neglected the soldiers' welfare. On both the German and the British sides, however, the High Command endeavoured to ensure a certain minimum comfort for their men. Thus the conditions of life were harder for the French soldier than for the combatants of the principal Western powers all the more so as, when they were relieved, combatants found poor facilities for resting up behind the lines: action taken by Pétain on food and billeting did not take effect until the second half of 1917.

In the limited world of the trenches, where discomfort was extreme and lack of privacy intolerable, everything was suddenly aggravated when bad weather set in.

Le Crapouillot, the only trench paper whose title still exists, described the hardship caused by the cold thus: (to appreciate it) 'you need to have remained for six days and six nights of this winter sitting tight, your belly frozen, your arms hanging loosely, your hands and feet numb, you need to have felt despair, convinced that nothing could ever thaw you out again.' Rain was even worse than the cold. According to *L'Horizon* this simple word encapsulates all the horror experienced by a soldier during a campaign. To sum up, the only thing which made me really feel wretched during the war was the rain. Rain led inevitably to the formation of the infamous mud in the trenches which became cess pits where stagnant water mingled with earth from the parapets which kept giving way on all sides. This liquid mass sometimes came up to knee-level. 'Sticky, liquid mud', 'oily tide', 'an enormous octopus with vile slaver dripping from its mouth': these are the terms used by the fighting men in their newspapers to conjure up the scourge of the mud. 'Hell is not fire' affirms *La Mitraille*, 'it would not be the worst form of suffering. The real hell is the mud.'

In these frightful conditions, tremendous physical exertion is often demanded of the combatants. When he is exhausted from lack of rest, fatigue duty and guard duty at night the foot soldier also fears the interminable marches towards the advanced positions or a new sector: 'We end up marching when half asleep, unaware of our surroundings, with no semblance of order, without seeing or thinking, just like animals', *Le Crapouillot* admitted.

'Like animals' – the word is important, for physical suffering is also a moral ordeal, so humiliating is it. For example the filthy state of their bodies, which they modestly refrain from mentioning but sometimes admit: 'We're sad because we smell bad' noted *Le Crapouillot* after a trying relief operation. Another form of suffering which is rarely referred to is the lack of a female presence which gives even the briefest meeting a precious quality. 'These girls from the mining villages were nice to look at', *L'Echo des tranchées* wrote. We left for the trenches and we thought of them at night in the dugouts, when the shells were falling'. Another trench newspaper *Tacatacteufteuf* put it rather more crudely: 'especially in the morning, soldiers experience persistent urges'. *L'Echo des tranchées-ville* speaks of the men as feeling sad and isolated. Such admissions about emotional and sexual misery are rare and to be found exclusively in newspapers destined for soldiers' eyes; letters and later accounts are even more discreet about such forms of suffering.

When added to the boredom and the risk of death these tribulations increase the soldiers' depression, an often endemic sickness which was part of their everyday lot. 'Every *poilu* has known depression', wrote *L'Echo des tranchées-ville* in 1916. 'It hits you suddenly, you don't know why and you start looking for all the reasons for being sad. It's a form of moral lassitude which comes over you. Everything is black. You're even tired of living. Things outside you lose all interest.'

Another reaction is revolt, which becomes inevitable after a certain period of time and a certain level of suffering. In 1917 exasperation reached a peak and led to mutinies. But the spirit of revolt had manifested itself much earlier. For instance, soldiers were indignant about patriotic propaganda. In May 1917 a Territorial who was not very well-educated but nobody's fool, however, wrote: 'I prefer a letter to a newspaper because newspapers bore us stiff when they go on talking about the final thrust'. Soldiers considered nationalistic indoctrination an insult to their experience of the war, to their human dignity and their courage, all of which had been discounted by people who conveniently stayed out of danger.

The attitude of the home front was another source of indignation. The soldiers thought civilians were indifferent to the sufferings of those doing the fighting and concerned only about their own well-being. Some soldiers' newspapers almost accused them of treason: 'Their stupid negligence runs the risk of destroying the benefits gained by our three years' of resistance and sacrifice. Let's tell them straight that what they're doing is shooting us in the back' wrote *Tacatacteufteuf* in June 1917. Sometimes the combatants' exasperation was so great that they resolved to lay down the law to all these people as soon as the war was over: dreams of vengeance colour their hopes for victory and demobilisation. HQs which show little concern about the amount of bloodshed among the fighting men are judged even more harshly. Even in October 1914 sub-lieutenant Abel Ferry, a former Secretary of State, who would be killed in 1918, was writing to his wife in these terms: 'Men have been sent to their deaths senselessly . . . All day long they lie there, being decimated, getting themselves killed, next to the bodies of those killed earlier, and yet they don't move or retreat. The battalion has lost three hundred men. Now, I'm just back from Verdun where the general of the Third Army declared that the Governor of Verdun had made us attack points of no strategic significance and had not understood his orders . . . We are wasting men and saving on ammunition and material'. Refusal to be sent over the top in such deplorable circumstances lies at the root of the crisis of 1917.

One can understand the soldiers feeling exiled on this immense 'island' that the front seemed to them to be. Cut off from the rest of the world they might be, but they were less completely so than they said. The home front was a source of exasperation but they were passionately interested in whatever was going on there. All their thoughts were directed towards the family and community they had left behind. Leave, letters and parcels kept the links going; the soldiers were moreover almost obsessively attached to these fragile bridges between the home front and the front line. Thanks to letters received and written – on average one a day in periods of inactivity – they were able to have some share in family life from afar. They gave a wife or relatives advice on how to run the farm, they kept an eye on prices and sales if they were shopkeepers. They concerned themselves with the education of children, enquired about the slightest incidents that had taken place in the village and informed their families whenever they had news of fellow-soldiers from villages near their own.

Even after several years in the trenches, the soldiers remained civilians in uniform: they still belonged to the civilian society they had left and hoped to rejoin. Hence the front was not an island but a peninsula with solid links to the rest of the community. The soldiers remained attached to it through every fibre in their bodies, whatever feelings of resentment they might harbour, and such feelings were in any case much less in evidence among those recruited from the countryside than those from the towns. In addition, the combatants worried about the fate of the national community. Admittedly, even the most highly-educated ones sometimes claimed to be uninterested in news about the war: immediate concerns took priority in their everyday lives. Nevertheless, the postal censorship service for 1916 proves that the main news items concerning the war were known in the trenches and that morale varied in direct proportion to whether the information received was judged to be favourable or ominous.

Could the soldiers' national sentiment be the key to understanding why they held out so long? Recent research reveals a strong feeling of national identity; this feeling is stronger than is generally thought and stronger than what the combatants had to say about it after the war, in a very different context.

French people today find it hard to acknowledge the depth of the hostility felt by the soldiers towards their adversaries. Ex-servicemen have obstinately denied it for reason of pacifism or because of their concern to give a more elevated sense to the nightmare they went through. But the notion that the soldiers held the line without feeling hostility towards the enemy is without foundation, a myth; at the time, things were felt in a very different way by the great mass of the troops. Admittedly, they did not feel blind hatred for the troops in the trenches opposite; occasionally they might come to a tacit or explicit agreement with them so as to make life a little less difficult. They respected their adversary and had good reason to appreciate his courage and tenacity; nothing irritated them more than suggestions in the home press concerning the mediocrity of the enemy forces. It made little difference: the Germans were above all 'the Boches' and hostility towards them was unfailing from start to finish of the war. At best, a feeling of difference prevailed in the accounts such as this one in *Le Crapouillot* as a column of German prisoners went by: 'Not a murmur, not a shout. A frosty silence. The men looking on have the definite impression that they are not of the same race as the men filing past. No trace of arrogant hatred for the vanquished . . . but something of scorn for the never-ending line of these soldiers who have surrendered and allow themselves to be led like so many sheep by a few hussars with drawn swords'.

Hostility is more apparent in this miner from the Nord, fighting close to the region he came from: 'You must never show mercy to a "*Boche*" because they are really savage brutes. As for me, I never show mercy to a "*Boche*" because anyone who does, it's because he's afraid, because the first one I come across can be sure he'll be killed.' Virulent hatred, too, in this agricultural worker from the Puy-de-Dôme who, in February 1915, wrote to his parents: 'I get a terrible rage against this barbaric people I'd be pleased to see a whole lot of them come along I guarantee there wouldn't be any left alive for very long . . . I'm proud when I see them fall on the field of battle.'

This amazing discourse proves that many of the troops had adopted the terminology of nationalistic propaganda statements, while yet rejecting the doctoring of information and the propaganda itself. But hostility towards the enemy was not the only basis for national sentiment among the troops. As surprising as it may seem, confidence in ultimate victory seems to have wavered little from the beginning to the end of the war and the fact that, until July 1918, war was being waged on French territory did not sow doubt in the soldiers' minds. Put off from month to month, victory seemed slow in coming, but it *would* come, no one had any doubt about it. In 1915 an NCO wrote: 'In spite of everything I think we shall succeed'. Belief in victory was an act of faith, for reasons which were essentially moral ones. France had right on its side and couldn't lose the war. This simple reasoning was sufficient for the majority of the fighting men.

Other reasons for fighting and for holding out can be added to this incredible feeling of confidence. But the chief patriotic themes, which were inculcated by the schools, – France a beacon of civilisation, the lost provinces etc. – played only a modest role. Was Antoine Prost right in suggesting that these themes were too abstract in face of the reality of the front line?

On the other hand the concept of duty was very much in evidence; you did your duty, that's all there was to it. A wine-grower wrote to his cousin in 1916: 'In a few days' time, we'll be launching a major attack – what can I do, I'll just do my duty.' You showed little enthusiasm when consenting to do your duty and accepted it with resignation; this was well put by Jean Galtier-Boissière:[3] 'the poor devil, alone in a shell-hole, with the elements doing their worst, has a clear sense of "what must be done" and "what must not be done"?' When it's freed from all grandiloquent phraseology, the idea of duty comes down to a feeling about self-esteem, whether personal or collective, on the part of soldiers taking a professional pride in their fighting. This idea of 'a job well done', which was characteristic of this army of *paysans*, led to their defending every inch of the ground. 'If only we can hold our positions', writes one of them before an enemy attack in December 1914. Defending ground in which the soldiers are holed up for days on end strikes a chord with these farmers turned infantrymen. It becomes even more necessary to defend this precious earth since comrades have died on it, have even been buried in it, sometimes under the survivors' feet. To defend the soil of France is to defend those who died for it.

Such is the specific nature of the French soldier's defensive patriotism. In May 1918 *le Crapouillot* described in colourful language the exodus of the civil population which preceded the advance of the German forces: 'These people were not weeping but you felt they were in the grip of immense distress and they were fleeing like wretched creatures driven from their lairs, without really knowing where they would stop . . . So, 'we were unable to prevent this; I feel a kind of shame about it'. The map of the areas affected by the war, by isolating, partially or wholly, about ten *départements*, which had to be left in enemy hands, gave a special sense to the French fighting men's ability to hold out. By forcing them to fight on and for their own soil, by obliging them to hold on in order to defend their own people, it reinforced in a more palpable way than was the case for German or British soldiers, the feeling that they were fighting to defend their own native land.

And yet an objection comes to mind; were not the 1917 mutinies the most serious crisis experienced by the European armies, if we except Austria-Hungary and Russia? In fact the army in its totality was not affected, even if the feeling of latent discontent was very widespread. And it seems that the mutinies did not stem from a crisis in the feeling of national unity. At all events, even if the soldiers' feeling for their country gradually became dulled as an interminable war brought continuing tribulations, the will to resist was never broken. Patriotism was moral armour for the majority of the combatants; in the last analysis, they drew their ability to hold out from the strength of their links with the nation.

Notes

1 Personal Accounts.

   Personal accounts, written by 1914–1918 soldiers in the heat of battle, are not subject to the distortions of memory. First of all come the letters written by combatants; these were very numerous, on average one per day for each soldier in periods of inactivity. Unfortunately, the majority of these exchanges of correspondence are lost to the historian, or are hoarded by families as a mark of respect, which comes to the same thing. Nevertheless, in addition to personal collections which we can always make, interesting but unclassified series of letters exist at the Invalides (Bibliothéque de Documentation Internationale Contemporaine, BDIC), and also in the Archives Nationales (series AP) and in certain departmental collections of archives (series J). The majority of the letters quoted in this article come from these archive collections.

In recent years some exchanges of correspondence as well as personal diaries have been edited; some examples are to be found at the BDIC and at the SHAT (Service historique de l'armée de terre). But, as regards correspondence, the postal censorship service is the only means of obtaining an overview. Having been set up in late 1915, the postal censorship service kept on refining its methods. It allows us to take a reliable, representative sample of letters written by soldiers each month. But, obviously, it cannot give us an overall view of the correspondence of any one individual over several months or years.

Moreover, the censors form as it were a screen between the raw documents and what they tell us about them; in addition, the censorship they exercise is feared by the soldiers, who fear their letters will not get through if they express themselves too freely.

Trench news sheets constitute another, very different, source of information, out of a probable total of approximately 400 for the Army, 170 are held at the BDIC, at the SHAT and at the Bibliothèque Nationale. These news sheets, which had a very limited run and were often duplicated in a very primitive way, were aimed at the soldiers themselves, at squad, section, company or regimental level. If they refer sometimes crudely to certain realities which were omitted from their letters home (so as not to cause panic in their families), they have the disadvantage of reflecting chiefly the views of the 'educated', often commissioned men. Furthermore, censorship and self-imposed censorship temper excessive sincerity. (On this point see: S. Audouin-Rouzeau, '14 – 18. Les combattants des tranchées' Paris, A. Colin, 1986. p. 223.)

To sum up, none of these personal sources of information is without its faults or free from risk, even though they may have been written as the events were happening.

Crosschecking the information they provide enables us and will continue to enable us to deepen our knowledge of the soldiers of the Great War.

2   See the article by J.J. Becker, 'Mourir à Verdun', in *14–18, Mourir pour la patrie*, Paris, Seuil, 1992, pp. 152–169. The calculation of the number of deaths is subject to considerable variation according to the method of calculation and the period chosen. The figure quoted here is a low estimate.

3   Attaining the rank of corporal during the war, he was the editor-in-chief of *Le Crapouillot*, and a journalist and writer after the war. After 1918, *Le Crapouillot* became an avant-garde artistic and literary journal.

Chapter 18

Little Mehmet in the Desert: The Ottoman Soldier's Experience

Erik Zürcher

THE LIMITS OF THE SOURCES

For some twenty-five years now a certain approach to the history of the war has been popular, an approach which is epitomized by Martin Middlebrook's famous *The First Day on the Somme* (1971). This is the attempt to write the war's social history, to concentrate on the war *experience*, viewing the experience of the First World War from below, through the eyes of the men who served in the trenches, the people who drove the ambulances, the women who filled the shells in the factories. In Europe, there is ample material available for this way of writing history: letters and diaries, stories, poems and paintings, autobiographies and oral history. Where Turkey, or rather – until 1923 – the Ottoman Empire, is concerned, the situation could not be more different and the reason is a simple one: the common soldier of the Ottoman army was – almost without exception – illiterate. Even as late as 1927, four years after the establishment of the Turkish republic, only slightly over ten percent of the population was able to read and write.[1] This means that the Ottoman soldier has not left much in the way of written monuments: no letters home, no diaries. Sometimes subalterns functioned as the official scribes for a company, writing letters which were dictated to them; but it was more usual for someone from a village to travel to the front and bring the news orally – and take the messages of the soldiers from a particular area back the same way.[2] Naturalist painting was not a Middle Eastern tradition (being frowned upon by Islam), so we have no sketches. Oral history has come into fashion in Turkey, but only recently – in the last three or four years – twenty years too late to be of much use for the study of the First World War.

We do have a number of sources which tell us something about the conditions in which the Ottoman soldier tried to survive, but with one exception they are typical 'top-down' documents, which view the war from the standpoint of high-ranking officers. There are a number of memoirs and autobiographies both of Ottoman officers (Ali İhsan Pasha Sâbis, Cemal Pasha, Ahmet Izzet Pasha (Furgaç), Selâhettin Adil Pasha, Halil Pasha (Kut), Mustafa Kemal Pasha (Atatürk), Kâzim Pasha Karabekir and others) and of German ones (Liman von Sanders, Kress von Kressensteim, Kannengiesser, von Gleich, von Seeckt and others. The main source for the recollections of the members of the German military mission serving in the Ottoman Empire is the journal *Mitteilungen des Bundes der Asienkämpfer* (Bulletin of the Society of Veterans of Asia) and its yearbooks, entitled *Zwischen Kaukasus and Sinai* (Between Caucasus and Sinai).[3] The German archives contain reports and evaluations by leading members of the mission (Liman von Sanders, von Seeckt), some of which have also been published. The complexities of the German-Ottoman alliance have been studied exhaustively, but these studies are essentially diplomatic, not so much military in nature.[4] As far as histories of the Ottoman war effort go, there is the large-scale official history, published by the War History and Strategic Studies Directorate of the General Staff in Ankara,[5] but very little in the way of regimental histories or histories of specific battles or fronts, as far as the First World War is concerned. Most efforts in this field in Turkey seem to be concentrated on the independence war which followed between 1919 and 1922. In European languages the only detailed history of the Ottoman war is Maurice Larcher's *La guerre turque dans la guerre mondiale* (Paris, 1926). For the economic and social history of the war, Ahmet Emin Yalman's *Turkey in the World War* (Yale, 1930) is indispensable.

The Turkish General Staff archives are almost completely closed to foreigners (and to most Turkish scholars as well). Among the foreign archives the German military archives in Freiburg are obviously the pre-eminent source, which has been used by a number of scholars. I have consulted the political reports from the Constantinople embassy in the Dutch state archives. The Netherlands being neutral, these continue throughout the First World War.

What all these sources have in common is that they share a 'top-down' vision which keeps us distanced from the realities of the war experience; which see casualties as a manpower problem rather than as something involving pain and death. The only exception is formed by the records of the interrogations of captured Ottoman soldiers on the part of the British troops in Palestine and Mesopotamia.[6]

THE OTTOMAN WAR EFFORT

The most amazing thing about the Ottoman army in the First World War is that an army which had been beaten comprehensively by four small Balkan states a year earlier, managed to fight for as long as it did and as well as it did. During the war, the general opinion among the British and French was that this was wholly due to the efforts of the German officers and troops serving in the empire, but it was also the result of the reforms pushed through in the year following the Balkan War by Enver Pasha, the Young Turk leader and Ottoman War Minister and his German advisers and which entailed the retirement of a large number of older officers, many of whom had risen from the ranks, and their replacement with modern educated younger officers. The level of staff work in particular was greatly improved.

From the start, the army was burdened with two almost insurmountable problems: lack of manpower and lack of communications. Lack of manpower had been a problem for the Ottomans all through the nineteenth century, that is to say, once they came up against large conscripted European armies. The Ottoman population, even though it had been growing quite fast over the last thirty years, was still comparatively small: about 19,000,000 people in the core provinces and if the outlying areas (where no reliable census existed) are included and the undercount of the Ottoman census system is taken into account, perhaps between 23 and 25 millions.[7] Not all of the adult males in this population were available for military service, however. Generally, the non-Muslims (Christians and Jews, about 20 per cent of the population in 1914) paid an exemption tax. Many Muslims also made use of this possibility, but for them the exemption tax was considerably higher so it was mostly the more affluent city and town-dwellers who managed to raise enough money. From 1909, the Young Turk government had started to enforce conscription for non-Muslims as well, but in practice the majority of eligible Christians still managed to avoid military service, paying the higher rate Muslims paid. In the war the units composed of the poorer Greeks and Armenians who could not pay the exemption fee were employed in unarmed labour battalions. Sheer lack of manpower meant that, increasingly during the war, the Ottoman government had to use Arabs from Syria and Iraq in fighting units, but these were considered inferior to the Turkish troops. This showed for instance when prisoners of war were exchanged. The Ottomans used to insist that they be given 'real Turkish troops, not Arabs' in exchange for Englishmen, only accepting Arabs in exchange for Indian troops.[8] In Liman von Sanders's opinion the Arab troops were not necessarily bad, but needed 'just but strict command'.[9] Some of the nomad tribes of the empire, notably the Kurds, did contribute to the war effort, but largely as irregular cavalry units which were only loosely attached to the regular army. So the burden of military service in the regular units fell overwhelmingly on the Turkish peasant population of Anatolia, which constituted about 40 per cent of the total population, or nine to ten millions.

After deduction of those who could pay the exemption tax instead, about

100,000 men were called up for military service each year and of these only about three quarters actually turned out. This meant that the peacetime strength of the army was about 150,000 (two classes). When fully mobilised, this was raised to slightly under 800,000.[10] Mobilisation, however, was extremely slow and took at least six months to be fully effective. This meant that even after full mobilisation, only about 4 per cent of the population was under arms and on active duty (compared with, for instance, 10 per cent in France, which also had a population nearly twice as big).[11]

Neither the Ottoman nor the German military leadership took the manpower problem into account when deciding on the strategy to be followed. Even though lack of manpower in the face of the British and, especially, the Russian army was a major headache, the offensive strategy adopted by the Ottoman government from the outset wasted human life on a grand scale. The greatest disaster was the ill-conceived winter offensive Enver Pasha unleashed towards Kars in December 1914. The troops were forced to cross mountain ridges deep in snow and as a result of the combined effects of cold, starvation and typhoid, of the 90,000 troops of the Third Army, only 12,000 survived into Spring. The attack on the Suez canal in August 1916 and the attempt to round the British flank in Mesopotamia through an adventurous offensive in Persia, although much less costly, were also irresponsible adventures which brought no tangible results. The decision to hold on to Yemen and the Hejaz (with the holy cities of Mecca and Medina) was a purely political one, which left the army stretched out along a thousand mile railway and extremely vulnerable.

The high point of the Ottoman war effort of course was the Gallipoli campaign. After the repulse of the Franco-British attempt to force the straits by naval force alone had ended in a totally unexpected Ottoman victory, the Ottoman army just managed to block the Allied attempt at a breakthrough overland on the Gallipoli peninsula. There can hardly be any doubt that this was a great strategic victory which gave the empire a new lease of life (or prolonged its misery, whichever way you choose to look at it). The victory over first the British fleet and then the Allied armies was a tremendous morale booster for the Ottomans, but in the long run it broke the back of the army. The Dardanelles campaign cost the Ottomans nearly 90,000 dead and 165,000 wounded and sick (by their own official figures which are certainly an underestimation),[12] almost all of them from the best-equipped and most experienced divisions in the army. In spite of the carnage at the Dardanelles, the Ottoman army reached its peak numeric strength at the beginning of 1916, the year Townshend had to surrender to them at Kut-al-Amara, but in terms of quality the damage caused by Gallipoli could not be repaired. After 1916, quality went down and numbers started to dwindle: When the unfortunate Third Army in Eastern Anatolia was again thrown into the attack against much superior Russian forces over terrain where neither its supply trains nor its medical service could follow in the summer of 1916, the offensive failed and in its wake a large part of the Third Army simply melted away.

The Second Army lost about two thirds of its strength (over 60,000 men) on the same front in the Winter of 1916–1917.[13] As a result the total number of combatants went down to 400,000 in March 1917 and 200,000 in March 1918. When the armistice was signed, less than 100,000 troops remained in the field.[14]

This dwindling of the numeric strength of the army was due mainly to two causes: disease and desertion. Malaria, typhoid, syphilis and dysenteria were rampant.[15] Seven times as many men died of illness as died of wounds during the war.[16]

Desertion became a problem of unmanageable proportions. As early as May 1916 we find a report by the Dutch embassy that the army has replaced prison sentences with corporal punishment in the field in order not to deplete the strength of the army further.[17] By December 1917 over 300,000 men had deserted.[18] By the end of the war the number stood at nearly half a million. These deserters as a rule did not go over to the enemy. They fled while en route to the front, or from the army on the march. They roamed the countryside, living off the land and turning into robber bands. Further troops had to be detached in ever greater numbers to deal with the insecurity these bands created behind the front lines.[19]

The reason for the mass desertions were clear and are identified in the German reports: the troops were ill-paid or not paid at all, worn out marching, undernourished and badly clothed. Footwear seems to have been an especially serious problem, which is mentioned time and again in the reports. It was not unusual for Turkish troops to fight – and march – barefoot.[20] As a matter of fact, the war is still known as 'the barefoot war' in Syria today.[21] These problems were closely linked to the lack of adequate communications, but also to financial mismanagement and corruption.

There was no overall shortage of food, in spite of the fact that the production of foodstuffs dropped by forty per cent during the war. In fact, it has been computed that the Arab provinces produced enough grain to support the local population and the armies on the Palestinian and Mesopotamian fronts. Anatolia had a wheat surplus and so had Syria except after the disastrous locust plague of 1915.[22] Nevertheless, the troops on the Eastern and Southern fronts received only between one half and one third of their nominal rations, the troops in Palestine surviving on 350 grams of bread a day. The problem was transport. The empire had been dependent on sea transport for bulk goods before the war and the British blockade now made shipping impossible anywhere but in the Black Sea and the Sea of Marmara. Even in the Black Sea the shipping, for instance of coal from the Ereğli coalfield, was often interrupted by the Russian fleet. The railways were totally overburdened. There were only 5700 kilometres of railway (one kilometre per 304 square kilometres of territory – the figure for France was one in ten and for India one in sixty).[23] They were single track everywhere and the key connections between Anatolia and the Arab provinces through the Taurus and Amanos mountain ranges had not been completed yet (the crucial tunnels were only finished by September 1918). There were no railways at all between Ankara and the Russian front. There was a lack of locomotives (Turkey had only 280 of them) and of carrying capacity (troops were transported sixty men to a freight car)[24] and freight cars were allocated on the basis of corruption and political influence. The roads were so primitive that the lorries which the Germans sent constantly broke down. According to Yalman, even ten years after the war their remains could still be encountered everywhere along the roads in 1930.[25] There was a lack of transport animals (primarily camels), because the Bedouins who were able to supply them had to be paid in gold and anyway from 1916 onwards many of the Arab tribes revolted. As a result of the lack of transport facilities, prices of foodstuffs differed widely (in 1916 wheat was over six times as expensive in Istanbul as it was in the central Anatolian grain growing area of Konya), so fortunes could be made by those who managed to get hold of freight cars – and a government permit to use them.[26]

Corruption was widespread and encouraged by the fact that army commanders received the money for their army as a lump sum, with complete discretionary powers as to how to spend it – as one German observer put it: 'on food for his troops, or on building a cinema'.[27]

As a result of the combined effect of disease and desertion, the actual strength of most of the units by 1917 was at or below 50 per cent of their nominal strength, battalions numbering 300 to 400 rifles, regiments 800 to 1500 and divisions between 2500 and 4000.[28]

THE VOICE OF THE SOLDIER

The numbers do indeed tell a tale, a tale of extreme hardship which again makes one wonder at the ability of this army to keep on fighting so well for so long, but the voice of the Turkish 'Tommy Atkins' or *Mehmetçik* ('Little Mehmet') as is the Turkish pet-name for the soldier, remains largely unheard. The one authentic expression on the part of the soldiers we do have, is contained in songs. Many of these were older than the war itself. Sometimes the melodies were older and new lyrics were added, reflecting experiences of '14-'18. This is the case with, for instance, the *Çanakkale Türküsü* ('Dardanelles Song'), one of the best known of them all:

> 'At Chanakkale I was hit;
> Alive they dumped me in a grave;
> Goodbye, sweet youth, goodbye.'

Even when the songs were new, they reflected the experience of the past hundred years rather than of the war itself. The great wars against the Russians of the nineteenth century (1828–1829, the Crimean War, the disaster of 1876–1878) and the attrition caused by continuous small-scale warfare against rebel bands and tribes in places as far apart as Albania and Arabia, meant that those who were unfortunate enough to be conscripted into the Ottoman Army and who did not have the means to buy off conscription, had very little chance of returning alive.

The prevailing sentiment in the lyrics of the songs is therefore nearly always that those who went on campaign had no chance of returning and that they would die in some far off desert: *The* symbol for this feeling and for the idea that young lives were being wasted to keep some unknown faraway area within the empire, is the *Yemen*.

YEMEN AND THE 'YEMEN SONGS'

The Yemen had been conquered by the Ottomans as part of their victory over the Mamluks in 1517, but the territory had never been held firmly and in 1636 the Ottomans were expelled from the Yemen by the Imam (ruler and religious leader) Muhammad. In 1849 the Ottoman government, which had been reasserting its authority over the provinces since the 1820s, decided to re-occupy Yemen. They managed to occupy the coastal strip, but only after the opening of the Suez canal improved communications in 1869 could they muster enough force to move inland. The capital, Sana'a, was occupied in 1872. Over the following decades, the country remained unruly, with major insurrections in 1882, 1898 and 1904. The cost of the constant harassment by Arab bands to the Ottoman army varied from a few hundred to a few thousand casualties a year all through this period, while the major rebellions really caused large-scale slaughter: the 1904–5 rebellion caused the death of 30,000 out of 55,000 Ottoman troops. 1910–1911 saw another rebellion, with the mortality rate again going up to between 30 and 50 a day. It is clear, therefore, that the Yemen had earned its bloody reputation.[29]

'Yemen songs' form a category in themselves and one which became very popular, especially with the troops serving in Syria, Palestine and Mesopotamia. There are at least a dozen with names like 'Does grass grow in Yemen?', 'The Band is Playing', 'The Mobilisation Song', 'The Exercise Song', 'No Water Flows in Yemen', 'No Cloud in the Sky', 'On the Road to Yemen', 'In the Desert of Yemen' and, of course 'The Yemen Song'.[30] Just to give an idea of the type of song we are dealing with, there follows here a translation of a few stanzas from some of them:

'The band was playing – did you think it was a wedding?
A banner, red and green – did you think it was a bride?
Those who left for Yemen – did you think they would return?'

'No cloud in the heaven, so whence this hazy sky?
No one died in this village – so what is that cry?
Mother, why this dirge? – Your son did not die.

Behind the barracks three fig trees stand;
A chain around my neck, handcuffs on my hand;
My God, how cruelly they hurt, these bands.'

'Here in Yemen the waters never flow;
No surgeon comes to look after the sick;
Who falls ill there will without question die.
In Yemen I stay behind and cry.'

and, finally:

'Merciless rulers let their soldiers stand
For ten years in the Hejaz's sand;
Those who go will stay there till the end.'

As we can see, the feelings expressed are not startlingly original, but they are telling: There is no heroism here, and no patriotism. Nor do the songs express the kind of dogged determination of contemporary Western front hits such as 'Pack up your troubles' or 'Keep right on to the end of the road'. More than anything they express a feeling of hopelessness and doom, of being sacrificed. In the eyes of the people who sang these songs, being called to the colours was a death sentence. In many cases, of course, they were right. The Ottoman army suffered 725,000 certified casualties during the war, with the percentage of dead being as high as 45 per cent. To these should be added over a million and a half sick and missing (these latter including the deserters). Proportionally, these are very high numbers, but the true horror of the situation in Turkey only comes out when we look at the changes in the population of Anatolia between 1913 and 1923.

If we are to understand the Ottoman war experience, we must realise that for the Ottomans the war did not stand on its own. It was the second phase in a period of almost continuous warfare lasting from 1912 until 1922.

In October 1912, the allied Balkan states of Montenegro, Serbia, Bulgaria and Greece had declared war on the Ottoman Empire. This Balkan War ended in a crushing defeat for the Ottoman arms, even though they managed to recover a small portion of the territorial losses when the Balkan states started warring amongst themselves. The Empire lost nearly all its European territories, over 60,000 square miles with nearly four million inhabitants. These areas formed the richest and most developed provinces of the empire and had formed the Ottoman heartland for over five hundred years. Nearly half a million Muslims from the Balkans fled the new Balkan states and had to be resettled in the Asiatic provinces, where they played an important part in the growing tensions between Muslims and non-Muslims in the Empire.

The Balkan War officially ended in September 1913. Thirteen months later the Ottoman Empire entered the First World War. The four war years not only saw fighting on four different fronts, but also, from 1915 onwards, inter-ethnic violence between Muslims and Armenians, and the deportation – and virtual extermination – of up to 800,000 Armenians from Anatolia.

After the war, a nationalist resistance movement developed in Anatolia, which aimed at the preservation of the independence of those areas which had a Muslim majority. In two wars, first (1920–1921) against Armenia in the East, then (1921–1922) against the Greek invasion army in the West, the resistance movement fought off attempts to partition Anatolia.

What this means is that for the Ottoman population the war experience was fundamentally different from that of the European peoples. It was part of a decade of war and the end of a process of disintegration and communal violence which had been going on for a century. After ten years of almost continuous warfare what remained of the country was depopulated, impoverished and in ruins to a degree almost unparalleled in modern history.

Some 2,500,000 Anatolian Muslims lost their lives, as well as up to 800,000 Armenians and 300,000 Greeks. All in all, the population of Anatolia declined by 17.7 per cent through mortality. Compare this to the case of France, where those killed totalled 3.5 per cent of the population. If we use the more useful definition of 'population loss' – the difference between the actual population and what would have been the population total had normal growth continued during the war years – the difference is even more striking: 26 per cent loss in Turkey compared to 1 per cent in France. Even this number is deceptive, however. In the war zones the loss was higher: in some Eastern provinces half of the population was dead and another quarter had become refugees. There were twelve provinces, most of them in the West, where the percentage of widows among the female population exceeded 30 per cent (more than double the normal rate)![31]

Next to mortality, migration was the major demographic phenomenon. During and after the World War several hundred thousand Armenians emigrated from Anatolia, mainly to the Soviet Union, France and the U.S.A. Their example was followed by large numbers of Greeks from Western Anatolia. Finally, under the provisions of the treaty of Lausanne, the remainder of the Greek orthodox population of Anatolia (but not that of Istanbul), about 900,000 people, were exchanged against the Muslims from Greece (except the community in Western Thrace) who numbered about 400,000.

The population changes meant that, culturally also, Anatolia in 1923 was a completely different place from what it had been in 1913. The larger Christian communities were practically gone (the Armenian community had shrunk to about 65,000 and the Greek community was down from around 2,000,000 to 120,000) and Anatolia, which had been 80 per cent Muslim before the wars, was now approximately 98 per cent Muslim.

Again the numbers tell a story. A story of ten years of suffering which makes the war experience of the Ottoman peoples rather different from the experiences of the peoples of Western and Central Europe – horrendous as those were. Therefore, one legacy would be an unshakeable determination among the leadership of the Turkish Republic to avoid being drawn into the Second World War at all cost.

Notes

1   Cavit Orhan Tütengil, 1927 yılinda Türkiye [Turkey in the year 1927], in: *Atatürk'un büyük soylevi'nin 50. yılı semineri. Bildiriler ve tartışmalar*, Ankara: Türk Tarih Kurumu, 1980, p. 56.

The overall average of 10.6 per cent literacy hid vast differences. While of the men in the towns of over 10,000 inhabitants 41.5 per cent were able to read and write, at the other end of the scale only 1.4 per cent of the women in the villages could do so. However, of the total population between eighty and eighty-five per cent lived in the villages . Therefore, the most relevant statistic is that of the 11.4 per cent of male villagers who were literate. Because the numbers quoted refer to 1927, the villagers concerned are almost exclusively muslim, the Armenians and Greeks, who had a much higher rate of literacy, having left or having been killed.

2   Hans Kannengiesser, *The Campaign in Gallipoli*, London: Hutchinson, 1927, p. 157.

3   A complete collection of the journal is to be found in the library of the Oriental Institute of the University of Bonn, while the university library of Tübingen has a collection of the yearbooks.

4   Apart from Jehuda L. Wallach's *Anatomie einer Militärhilfe. Die Preussisch-deutschen Militärmissionen in der Türkei 1835–1919*, Düsseldorf: Droste, 1976, which does concentrate on military matters, the other leading studies are: Ulrich Trumpener, *Germany and the Ottoman Empire 1914–1918*, Princeton, 1966, and F.G. Weber, *Eagles on the Crescent. Germany, Austria and the Diplomacy of the Turkish Alliance, 1914–1918*, Ithaca, 1970. the pre-war German-Ottoman rapprochement is studied in: C. Sullivan, *Stamboul Crossings. German Diplomacy in Turkey 1908–1914*, Ph. D. Vanderbilt University, Nashville, 1977.

5   Fahri Belen, *Birinci cihan harbinde Türk harbi* [The Turkish war in the First World War], Ankara: Genelkurmay harp Tarihi ve Stratejik Etüt Başkanligi, 1963–1967, 5 vols.

6   The existence of this source was kindly pointed out to me by Dr Yigal Sheffy of the Dayan Center, Tel-Aviv. As yet I have not been able to study this material, but it can be found in the monthly intelligence summaries, ref. PRO/WO 157/687ff (Egyptian front) and PRO/WO 157/776ff (Mesopotamian front).

7   Yalman, *Turkey in the World War*, p. 79.

8   Halil Kut, *Bitmeyen savaş. Kütulamare kahramanı Halil Paşa'nın anıları* [War

239

without end. The memoirs of Halil Pasha the hero of Kut] (ed. by M. Taylan Sorgun), Istanbul: Yedigün, 1972, p. 191. This is confirmed on the British side by Aubrey Herbert in *Mons, Anzac and Kut*, London: Hutchinson, 1919, p. 253.

9   Liman von Sanders, *Fünf Jahre Türkei*, [Five years in Turkey], Berlin: Scherl, 1920, p. 242.

10   Maurice Larcher, *La guerre turque dans la guerre mondiale* [The Turkish war in the world war], appendices 44 and 50. Larcher bases himself on the official statistics released by the Ottoman War Ministry in 1919. The number of 800,000 refers to the number of armed and trained regulars. A much higher number (around 2,000,000) is also mentioned, but this seems to include the – often unarmed – territorials and reservists of all types. Larcher considers the higher number 'questionable' and it does indeed seem unrealistically high. This is also true for the total number of men called up, which is put at 2.85 million. All numbers are in fact rough estimates.

11   Larcher, appendix 45, 48.

12   Figures given in Robert Rhodes James, *Gallipoli*, London: Pan, 1974, p. 348. Rhodes James estimates the actual number of casualties at about 300,000. Liman gives the even more optimistic estimates of 66,000 dead and 152,000 wounded (Liman, p. 135).

13   Liman, p. 240.

14   Larcher, appendix 50.

15   Cf. Yalman, *Turkey in the World War*, p. 81.

16   Larcher, appendix 51, p. 602.

17   Erik Jan Zürcher, Weligelichte kringen? De politieke berichtgeving van de Nederlandse ambassade in Istanbul in de eerste wereldoorlog [Well-informed sources? The political reports of the Dutch legation in Istanbul during World War I], *Shargiyyat* 1/1 (1988), p. 78.

18   Liman, p. 241.

19   Liman, p. 241.

20   Cf. Ali İhsan Sâbis, *Hatıralarım. Birinci dünya harbi* [My memoirs. The First World War], İstanbul: Nehir, 1991, Vol. 3, p. 331.

21   I am indebted to my colleague Dr Dick Douwes for this observation.

22   Cf. The report by General von Seeckt in Jehuda L. Wallach, *Anatomie einer Militärhilfe. Die Preussisch-deutschen Militärmissionen in der Türkei 1835–1919* [Anatomy of a military support operation. The Prussian-German military missions in Turkey 1835–1919], Düsseldorf: Droste, 1976, p. 263.

23   Yalman, p. 85.

24   Yalman, p. 86.

25   Yalman, p. 88.

26   The problems with the food supply and the attendant corruption are discussed in an (as yet unpublished) paper by Selim İlkin and İlhan Tekeli, *Osmanlı İmparatorluğu'nun I. dünya savaşındaki ekonomik düzenlemeleri içinde ve Kara Kemal Bey'in yeri* [The place of supply minister Kara Kemal in the economic organisation of the Ottoman Empire during World War I], which was graciously sent to me by the authors.

27   von Seeckt, in Wallach, p. 263.

28   Sâbis, p. 332.

29 These data are taken from: John Baldry, 'Al-Yaman and the Turkish Occupation 1849–1914', *Arabica* XXIII (1976), p. 156–196.

30 'Yemen songs' are published in a number of collections of folksongs, for instance in: Mehmet Özbek, *Folklor ve türkülerimiz* [Our folklore and songs], İstanbul: Ötüken, 1975.

31 These data are taken from: Justin McCarthy, *Muslims and Minorities. The Population of Ottoman Anatolia and the End of the Empire*, New York: New York University Press, 1983, p. 117–144.

Chapter 19

The American Soldier in France, 1917–1919

James Cooke

Early in the morning of 9 May 1919, a line of French '40 and 8' freight cars (to hold 40 men or 8 horses) moved slowly through the old St. Mihiel battlefield. On one of the cars was Corporal Maurice L. Moser, 355th Infantry Regiment, 89th Infantry Division. Moser, from Little Rock, Arkansas, was just twenty years old and had been in Europe a little over a year. As he looked out over the field upon which he fought, he wrote in his diary, 'Pass through the St. Mihiel sector again. Looks different than when I was here before. Pass an American graveyard where the crosses seem literally to cover the ground. I wonder how many I know are resting there'.[1] In just over 365 days Moser had seen France, Belgium, Luxembourg and Germany, had fought in the St. Mihiel and Meuse-Argonne, and had fallen in and out of love with a German girl. He was now on his way to a port of embarkation for the trip home.

On 15 May Moser sat on the deck of the SS *Huron* writing in his diary, 'I want to once more look on the fields where friends were lost, I want to see again those odd little villages along the Mosel. I wonder if I ever shall. And then my thoughts turn homeward. I can't help but wonder what is waiting for me there. I know no young people'.[2] Before he was twenty-one, before he could vote, Moser felt that he knew no young people. They were a part of a different world that had not been seared by shot, shell, gas and blood. Like so many of his fellow Doughboys, Moser felt an ambivalence about home.

By 11 November 1918, there were over two million Americans in the American Expeditionary Forces, with a combat strength of a million men on the line. Of that million, 646,000 served in the infantry and machine-gun units at the front. The 1st Infantry Division had an authorized strength of 28,000 officers and men. By the Armistice, 30,206 replacements had

242

passed through the division. The 28th Division, from the Pennsylvania National Guard, with same authorized strength, had 21,717 replacements before war's end.[3]

The war had begun for the United States on 6 April 1917. It came as a shock to many who, just the year before, firmly believed that President Woodrow Wilson had been right not to involve America in this European squabble. In 1916 one of the best-selling songs in sheet music and records had been 'I Didn't Raise My Boy to be a Soldier'. Another catchy Tin Pan Alley tune proudly proclaimed, 'We take our hats off to you Mr. Wilson', in tribute to American isolationism. In a few short months 'Over There' would outsell any anti-war song produced the year before.

At the University of Alabama a venerable professor was in the midst of his lecture when he was handed a telegram. With solemnity he opened the envelope, read, and then stated to his charges, 'Ladies and Gentlemen: Congress voted a declaration of war against Imperial Germany at ten o'clock. The gravity of this hour is so impelling that I will omit the remainder of today's lecture. Meanwhile may we regain composure and carry on next meeting.'[4] In a few days, thirteen men in his class joined the United States Army. At Columbia University eleven students immediately left school to form a balloon company.[5]

In April, 1917, the United States had no really modern army to send to Europe to fight, and there were questions about the European's desire for American troops unless they could train and lead them into battle. The cadre of professionals was small, scattered over forts and garrisons in the United States and stationed in far-flung colonial posts such as the ones in the Philippine Islands. The last war the United States waged, the one against Spain in 1898, was a fiasco of poor planning, unworkable logistics and movement, and suspect leadership. Fighting Germans rather than Spaniards and Philippine Moros would be a very different matter.

The embarrassment of 1898 began a period of reform in the American military structure, but parsimonious Congresses and public indifference kept great changes from occurring. Divisions existed only on paper. Wilbur and Orville Wright had pioneered air flight at Kitty Hawk, North Carolina, in 1903, but the US Army had but one squadron of antiquated, totally unserviceable airplanes in 1917. The Americans had been known for the quality and craftsmanship of their weapons, but, in 1917, most of the eager soldiers would train with wooden mock-ups of rifles, machine guns, and mortars, and some would go to France without even the most rudimentary instruction in rifle assembly, care and cleaning, or marksmanship.[6]

The United States had a vast reservoir of motivated, but untrained and untested, manpower. When war came, America had a Regular Army of 138,000, of which 5,800 were officers. Many of the officers were of low rank but of older age, due to an agonizingly slow promotion system. Precious few had seen real experience above the battalion level, and all were ignorant of command and staff functions at the divisional level. The National Guard, the province of the then 48 states, had 70,200 men, 3,200 being of officer rank. The vast majority of these citizen-soldiers had seen little or no realistic training.[7] What made the National Guard so important to the military structure of the United States was the simple fact that they represented the cities, towns, and villages where the units were raised.

The Regular Army wanted the forces going to France to be totally professional. The Regulars could train, and, most importantly, command the mass of draftees. But Pershing and others failed to see the reality. The reality of the situation was not lost on Woodrow Wilson who, although an idealist, was also a politician. The vote in Congress to declare war had not been unanimous, and those politicians who occupied positions of power in Columbus (Ohio), New York City, Montgomery (Alabama), Sacramento (California), and elsewhere, had to be kept happy. One way to aggravate those men who got out the vote was to deny to the local citizen-soldier their place in this great crusade in Europe. The National Guard would be called, and they would fight and die. Who would command those men would be another matter again. War was too serious to be left to officers who owed their commissions to a civilian governor, and the regulars reasoned that, once in France, steps could be taken to replace those citizen-officers with eager regulars.

There was a major fallacy in Pershing's thinking about the force that would eventually represent the United States on the battlefields of the Western Front. The Regular Army was indeed the professional force, but how really professional was it? Only on a very theoretical plain were the regulars knowledgeable about command above the regimental level. The concept of a division which would manoeuvre on the battlefield had been created in 1912. Divisions had been deployed to the Mexican border in 1916, but they did not function as such. There were few experienced staff officers, and, worse yet, the American army was bereft of officers with the necessary rank to run divisions and corps, let alone armies.

On 5 June 1917, over nine million American men registered for the draft, instituted by a new war-time law which was hotly debated by the United States Congress. There was very little resistance to either registration or to being called for service. The vast majority of those conscripts would fill the ranks of the divisions of the new National Army, and a number of those units saw good service such as the 77th, 78th, 82nd, and 89th Divisions. Some of the draftees would serve as replacements for the regular and National Guard Army divisions. The collar disks worn by the troops of the AEF bore the US for regulars, state initials or USNG for guardsmen, and USNA for the National Army men. By the late summer of 1918 the War Department sought to do away with these distinctions between the three components of the army by prescribing the US insignia only. Many of the guardsmen or National Army men simply ignored the new regulations and kept their distinctive disks. But, there was no difference in the high state of morale in the components. As the AEF formed corps (3 to 4 divisions) all components fought side by side watching the corps. However, by the end of the war the competition between components was still strong as each assured the other that they had fought as well or harder than the other,

By the end of the war, fully four-fifths of the Regular Army rank and file would be green recruits, sturdy volunteers with no prior military training. To say in April, 1917, that the American Expeditionary Forces would be comprised of regulars and a regular-led National Army of conscripts was to ignore the basic fact that no one segment of the American military establishment was ready for the Western Front. When soon-to-be Major General Robert Lee Bullard, as hard a fighter as the AEF had, visited Washington's War Department in the summer of 1917, he was aghast. Bullard recalled that, 'I found the War Department not very busy, certainly not as busy and hard worked as at the out-break of the Spanish-American War. This has surprised me. Nobody seems very busy or very worried. I wonder if we are really awake.'[8]

The War Department in Washington never did adjust to the necessities of war in France. Many times the AEF was a beggar army relying on the Allies for everything from uniforms, helmets, artillery, machine guns to airplanes. There did not even exist on 6 April 1917, a plan to put together such a large force as the one now needed. Indeed, Woodrow Wilson, the pacific President who was 'too proud to fight', had even forbidden such warlike planning.[9]

There was activity, however, across the vast country. National Guard units prepared to leave for camps after being called to the colours by Wilson. Young men rushed to enlist and were enrolled by the thousands. But there were no camps to train them, sergeants to instruct them, officers to command them, or equipment to give them. Some with military training found themselves in charge of groups of men who were just a little more ignorant of drill and the military life than they were.

Every measure had to be employed to create large numbers of leaders, hoping that thousands were not killed in the process. Despite popular concepts of the United States the majority of the eager soldiers had never handled a rifle or a hand gun of any kind. Care had to be taken to make sure in the first weeks of training that recruits did not shoot themselves or any other man standing in the ranks. Most of the trainers had only the vaguest knowledge of weaponry and few had ever thrown a grenade or fired a machine gun. This was true in the regular, National Guard, and National Army units, and once in France the army welcomed battle-wise teachers from both the French and British Army, the lion's share coming from the French army. Prior to US entry into World War One, Congress had created the Officer Reserve Corps, and the Army opened a training camp at Plattsburg, New York. Normally associated with a college or university, the Officer Reserve Corps was an attempt to attract young men with a potential for leadership. It was possible for an older man with proven skills and abilities to be commissioned to a rank as high as major, but even they had to attend the camp. The army, however, believed that the vast majority of men who would go through the Plattsburg program would be from the colleges, and would be commissioned as second lieutenants.

The Plattsburg course of study was a basic training course, a hodge-podge of various military subjects. Drill was conducted throughout the year, and an encampment of several weeks was held in the summer for the student to hone his skills.

In the manual, which seemed to be fully ignorant of harsh realities of war, prospective Plattsburg officers were advised to, 'Bring a pair of sneakers or slippers. They will add greatly to your comfort after a long march or hard day's work. A complete bathing suit often comes in handy.'[10] Even though hundreds graduated from the Plattsburg camp, the army found itself seriously short of officers in 1917. Officers combed the ranks of incoming soldiers for those with potential, and they were sent off to a three-month program which was much more severe and intense than the Plattsburg program.

There were those mentally and physically fit to become officers who refused. This was especially true of the National Guard, where being with one's buddies was more important than the gold bar of the second lieu-tenant. The well-known poet Joyce Kilmer, of the 165th Infantry Regiment, consistently refused any chance of becoming an officer because, 'I would be sent as an officer, not back to the 69th (now known as the 165th United States Infantry), but to some other outfit. I want very much to stay with the regiment; I have many good friends here, and I would feel lost in any other military organisation.'[11] Sergeant-poet Joyce Kilmer would be killed in battle on the Ourcq River in late July, 1918.

Private Walter Hill of the 311th Field Artillery Regiment, 79th Division, had been in the army only a few weeks when he wrote to his mother, 'Well I hope you people feel satisfied that we are pretty well cared for although it is not like home, but we will do our best. I expect to begin to go to non-commissioned officers school which they have for one hour Monday, Tuesday, Thursday and Friday evenings'.[12] So critical was the need that Hill, who did not yet have a complete uniform, was learning the skills of an NCO four hours a week!

Pershing knew that his troops were poorly trained and unready to face the rigours of combat. From Camp Coetquidan on the Brittany Peninsula to Le Valdahon near the Swiss Border to Tours on the Loire River, American soldiers began to train for war. For the Allies it was an agonis-ingly slow process, especially when men were so badly needed to stem the German offensives of 1918. Within the ranks, however, there was high morale and a sense of wonder at being so far from home. The vast majority of the Doughboys were from small towns scattered throughout the United States, and many had never been out of their counties, let alone outside the continental United States, before. Private Everett Scott of the 168th Infantry, made up the National Guardsmen from the farm state of Iowa, wrote to his mother, 'All of the houses both in Ingland (sic) and here are made of stone or bricks. There are very few wooden buildings, and all of the people wear wooden shoes.'[13]

The vast majority of the infantry trained in France, and their association with the French became the subject of many letters home. They bought French-English phrase books by the hundreds of thousands, trying to learn enough French to get a meal or haltingly converse with French girls.

Since all soldiers everywhere are in a perpetual state of hunger, buying food, when the situation allowed, became of prime importance. Elmer Sherwood of Indiana, serving in the 150th Field Artillery Regiment of the 42nd Division, recalled, 'Along the road passed (Camp) Coetquidan many peddlers and tradesmen established shops so that soon the route began to resemble a county fair, where we could buy everything from wine to souvenirs . . . For four to five francs we could buy a meal consisting first of soup . . . The next course was meat, steak, or perhaps a fish . . . Next came French fried potatoes. A bottle of wine was, of course, always served at four or five francs additional cost. About all the French use water for is to wash clothes in. If one asked for it the waitress might have to make a special visit to the town pump.'[14] The sense of being in a strange, but likeable, land never wore off.

Douglas Walker of the 5th Machine Gun Battalion, 2nd Infantry Division, wrote to his parents in Oxford, Mississippi, 'This is a pretty place. I can't understand anything these people say.'[15] The language was not the only thing that was new to the Doughboys of the AEF. Private Joseph Gray of the 1st Balloon Company could only gawk as he moved through France to begin training at the Balloon Training Center at Camp Souge, near Bordeaux. 'The French girls wore short skirts and silk stockings. In our country the girls had their skirts to their shoe tops',[16] Gray recalled. The beauty and coquetry of the French girls had reached mythical proportions by the time the American soldiers reached France. While they fantasized about the 'Mademoiselle from Armentières', as the popular soldier song went, they were drawn like magnets to Paris.

'They'll never want to see a rake or plow, and who the deuce can parleyvous a cow?' So went the very popular song which ended with 'How you gonna keep 'em down on the farm after they've seen Paree?'[17] Only a minority of enlisted American soldiers ever had the opportunity to see Paris, but the thought of it ran through the letters which they sent home. Second Lieutenant Hamilton Coolidge a former student at Harvard University, had the chance to take leave from the 94th Aero Squadron,

Pursuit, to visit the city. All he could write to his mother was that, 'Paris is wonderful'.[18] He would be killed in aerial combat over the Western Front during the Meuse-Argonne Offensive in October, 1918.

There was a great gulf between what the folks back home believed about the war and what the soldiers actually experienced in combat. The differences were to become greater as the war went on. General Pershing, at the start of the war, insisted on a very strict censorship of all mail between the AEF and the United States. Within each company an officer was assigned to read letters and literally cut out such material as might indicate where the troops were, or the extent of American casualties. Very quickly the soldiers learned that 'Somewhere in France' was the only heading they could use. In letters the war became sanitized for the home front. Newspaper correspondents knew that the AEF leadership would not tolerate stories of failures, shortages of supplies, casualties, troop movements and the like.

What most of the Doughboys saw during the war were the towns near the camps or trenches where they trained. The first divisions which came into France were to spend weeks training with the French behind the lines, and then they would move into trenches which were in so-called 'quiet' areas. There they would become accustomed to the miseries and the perils of trench warfare. American airmen were sent to training fields like Issoudun, Tours, and elsewhere to learn the ins and outs of flying deadly combat missions over trenches. Near those areas thousands of small bars, restaurants, souvenir shops, and houses of prostitution sprang up to cater to the Americans.

Private Albert Ettinger of the 165th Infantry, a motorcycle dispatch rider, had been given a sheaf of business cards from a Madam who ran a bordello near the town of Baccarat. If he handed out the cards to his mates the Madam would not charge him when he visited the place.[19] Private Craig S. Herbert of the 2nd Balloon Company marvelled at the ability of the French to find souvenirs to sell to the Doughboys, recalling that:

> The Frog merchants peddled all sorts of cheap silk articles to those who had partaken of cognac or wines a bit too liberally. The articles included handkerchiefs, panties, bras and other unmentionables to send home. The colors that predominated were pink and lavender. I imagine there were young ladies back in the states going around dressed in some of these bits of wearing apparel, with the crossed flags of the U.S. and France displayed in the most unusual locations.[20]

The Americans were souvenir buyers *par excellence*, and they sent back to the United States everything from German helmets to the above-mentioned items of clothing. When they were out of the line they became tourists, obsessed with buying something from *La Belle France* for the folks back home.

There developed a love-hate relationship between the Doughboys and France (and the French). The wonder of being in France never diminished, but as combat continued and bad weather set in during the fall of 1918, Doughboys began to complain, as all soldiers have since armies began. The most obvious focus of their anger was the country they were in. AEF Sergeant Alexander Woollcott summed up some of the problems in 1918 when he pointed out that Doughboys had the aggravating tendency to loudly proclaim that they had saved France. In a country where almost every woman wore black and every family had been touched by death or had a loved one maimed, such bravado fell on very deaf ears. Except for the larger towns and cities, Frenchmen lived in small villages dominated by interlocking family systems. Outsiders were not really welcomed, and the loud, youthful Americans were only tolerated. Almost every Doughboy account of France talked of the open prostitution and high-priced bars which catered to the American soldiers. But, Woollcott wrote, at the bottom of it all was a great cultural difference. 'The young American,' the AEF veteran wrote, 'dislikes the Frenchman because he is not clean.'[21]

Americans had developed a mania for bathing, and the cultural climate of France was such that nightly full baths were not a high-priority item. It also appeared that the filth of the battlefield, intestinal disorders caused by the poor quality of food, and the ever-present, merciless cooties (lice), bred a condition with which many Americans – certainly not all – were unfamiliar. When the combat divisions of the Army of Occupation arrived in Germany in late 1918 they found the Germans' standards of cleanliness to be higher, and their towns cleaner and neater. Of course, the German towns on the West bank of the Rhine had not been fought or marched over for four years, either. It is little wonder that the French came to resent the Americans' attitudes toward their hated enemy. Sergeant Andrew Sullivan summed up what many have claimed as the prevailing sentiment in the AEF when he recalled, 'Somehow I never really hated the Germans; I doubt that soldiers around me did either,'[22]

When they were in the trenches, however, their lives, like those of the British and French, were miserable. In combat they died in vast numbers. Since the Doughboys received little real training in the United States, they were exposed to realistic conditions in the training areas or in quiet sectors very close to the enemy. Even so-called quiet areas would see shelling, small arms fire and poison gas. The majority of the AEF infantry divisions trained under the supervision of the French and British, who felt that too much time was taken to prepare for combat. French reports usually reflected a higher opinion of the Doughboy's potential than did inspectors from the General Headquarters of the AEF.

Those early divisions which so impressed the French were prepared for both trench and manoeuvre combat, and they were among the best that the AEF had to offer. However, as more units poured into France, the training time was cut drastically, and by the fall campaigns of 1918 many units had little or no time to prepare. Consequently, there would be radical differences in the way the 1st or 42nd Division looked at combat experiences compared with the 35th or 79th Divisions. Those divisions which arrived in France in late 1917 up to the early spring of 1918 had time to prepare for combat under the direction of the French and British. The new units had little of the luxury. The later units recalled being rushed to the front or having just enough training to begin battle.

Private Walter Hill is typical of the men of the late-arriving 79th Division. On 19 September 1918, Hill told his mother, 'It sure was a tiresome trip [across the Atlantic]. We are kept very busy at present receiving different instructions which is very interesting. Our whole battery is going on the target range tomorrow . . . The guns we are using over here are [French 75s] guns. They are very powerful and I think they will be the means of helping to defeat the Huns to a great extent. At present we have the guns which we will use in actual service at the front whenever that will be I do not know.'[23] Hill's 79th Division had no days of training in line prior to commitment to combat on the first day of the Meuse-Argonne offensive. [24]

The miseries of the trenches for the early units were very striking, and the memory runs through their narratives of the war. Lieutenant Hugh Thompson of the 42nd Division's 168th Infantry Regiment recalled his first exposure to life in the trenches when he wrote that, 'The sight that greeted us brought an immediate and positive reaction. "Desolate" was the only name for it. A mass of rusty barbed wire was strung on crisscrosses of posts that seemed to grow from the ground. Ghostlike trees to the right were splintered with shell scars. Some had fallen into the mass of twisted wire and upturned earth.'[25]

One can see similarities in the letters written by the Doughboys of the AEF and those written by British and French soldiers. What marks a difference in 1918 is the innocence of the American soldier who had not experienced battle. The Americans who arrived in France came with a self-righteousness and a bravado which soon wore off. Most of them had been raised on stories of the American Civil War, decades after the fact, where there were heroic deeds of daring-do, and where blood and maiming were obscured by the lessons they were to teach. The reality came quickly.

No amount of training, however realistic, can prepare a soldier for the shock of battle, of death, of the maiming of comrades. Andrew Sullivan, who had left the University of Alabama a year before, heard that the 167th Infantry Regiment of the 42nd Division was close by. He had two brothers serving with that unit, and he went to find them. He was told that one brother had been killed fighting for a village named Fére-en-Tardenois on the Ourcq River in late July, 1918. The second brother was so overcome that he fell into depression, and during the fight became a shell-shock casualty. In fact, his condition was so bad that he had to be evacuated to the United States, a situation rare in the Great War. The Sullivan family of Alabama had lost two of three sons, and Andrew fought through St. Mihiel and the Meuse-Argonne.[26]

The shock of casualties was greater on those new divisions which had not had the period of training in the trenches to experience losses in raids, bombardments, and gas attacks. The situation in the Meuse-Argonne led to a vast amount of 'straggling'; men just fell out of the ranks and wandered about.[27] Many of the frontline combat troops were not being fed. The American logistics system had simply broken down under the strain, and the road network servicing the AEF in the Meuse-Argonne was a quagmire of mud due to shelling and constant rains. The poor diet, when it could be gotten to the Americans, began to take its toll on strength and on morale. Captain Raymond Cheseldine of the veteran 166th Infantry Regiment recalled that, 'Canned meat, dehydrated potatoes and onions, and hard bread were staple articles for two weeks.'[28] Regardless of what General John J. Pershing wrote in his memoirs later, the American Expeditionary Force was reaching the end of its tether during the last week of October, 1918.

There were no differences among the various AEF divisions and units over the end of the war. A sense of relief spread over all of the troops. In the United States, where the majority of the manpower was, there was a definite feeling that they had been left out of the great adventure. The AEF's insistence that stateside units wore no overseas cap, no Sam Browne Belt, no distinctive unit shoulder patches, widened the gulf between those who went to France and those who did not. There were no overseas stripes for those who did not cross the Atlantic. This severe gulf was uniquely an American problem, one which would have great consequences later.

Pershing began, as soon as the fighting was over, to move Doughboys back to the United States as quickly as possible. By the Christmas season of 1918 there was a flood of returning troops. The divisions which served in Belgium, Luxembourg, and on the West bank of the Rhine river were the experienced combat units. The old veterans deeply resented the fact that those who went home first were those who had arrived most recently in England and France and had seen the least action, but the Army of Occupation was configured to begin combat operations if the tense situation warranted it. By spring and the signing of the Versailles Treaty, however, the AEF began sending many of those occupying divisions back to the United States. By that time the public euphoria over returning masses of troops had subsided.

When Brigadier General Douglas MacArthur and his veteran Rainbow (42nd) Division brigade arrived in New York on 25 April, 1919, there was no one to greet them, no bands, no throngs of grateful countrymen. A newspaper boy asked what unit this was, and when MacArthur told him, the lad shrugged his shoulders and asked if they had ever been in France.[29] Of course, there were local celebrations when regiments returned to their homes, but by and large the American public had seen enough of soldiers. Many Doughboys were so quickly mustered out of the service that no one took the time to present them their Victory Medals. Leslie Langille of the Illinois 148th Field Artillery Regiment recalled that each man in the regiment was given sixty dollars and transportation home. There were no speeches, no final pass-in-review.[30]

The combat soldiers worried about jobs and conditions back home. Those who remained on occupation duties saw their prospects dim as months went by. Sergeant Eustace Fielder of Sales Commissary Unit No. 24 in Antwerp, Belgium, wrote to his mother on 25 July, 1919, 'Well I am finally on the sailing list. We'll leave about the 30th of August . . . Say, mother dear when Dad is feeling good tell him to take a walk down to [Mr. Bonelli's store], and see if I have still got a job waiting me and let me know in your answer to this. If there is nothing doing I will try to get me something to do when I reach the states . . .'[31] It was a bitter joke among those who did the hardest fighting that the best jobs would be taken by those who had never gone in the army or by those who had done none of the heavy fighting.

When they finally reached home they found a wall that separated them from their family and friends. The experience of combat in the Great War had left none unscathed. On the night of 11 November, 1918, First Lieutenant Percival Gray Hart of the 135th Aero Observation Squadron and his friends, went to Nancy, bought out the Café Liègeois, and drank the night away. There was a sense that they had been through something which could not be shared. Hart wrote that there they, 'celebrated the end of an era in our lives, an era of adventure and romance such as in our younger days we had never dreamed could come to pass – filled with memories and friendships which only death itself can take from us.'[32]

Most of them already knew that America had changed while they were gone. Fourteen years later, Private Leslie Langille wrote, 'Then, too, did we not come back to a world that had become foreign to them, and with sixty dollars donated by a grateful government – barely enough to buy civilian attire – again become law-abiding citizens.'[33]

Unlike the civilian populations of Britain, France, and the other major belligerents, the civilians in the United States did not come face to face with the horrible realities of war. The magnitude of the human loss was an abstract for Americans. When the Doughboys returned home they found that no one really had any idea of what they went through. Letters had been censored, news reports were geared 'to support the troops,' and military dispatches talked only about victories. How could the soldier relate what he had seen in the Meuse-Argonne when there was no common ground to start with? For the home front the war had been hectic work schedules, bond selling tours, work for the YMCA, Red Cross, Knights of Columbus, the Jewish Welfare Board and the like. Their impression of the Doughboy experience in France generally featured the mademoiselles of Paris. How, then, could they relate their experiences? In the 1920s and 1930s the great generals, including Pershing himself, wrote their experiences, but by and large, as useful as they were (or were not), they were cold, stark, not really relating the horrors of battle on the level where mortal combat took place.

A glance at the music on the piano told the Doughboy very quickly what the home folks sang. His songs were sometimes risqué barracks ditties, or favorites like 'Over There,' 'A Long Way From Tipperary,' and so forth. The home folks played such absurd tunes as 'Your Lips Are No-Mans' Land But Mine,' 'You'll Find Old Dixieland in France,' 'You'll Have to Put Him to Sleep With the Marseillaise and Wake Him Up with Oo-La-La,' or 'When the Sun Goes Down in France.' None of them described the ever-present rancid corned beef the soldiers universally called Corned Willie. None reflected the horrors of mustard gas or the gut-wrenching fear before an attack against German machine guns in the Kriemhilde Stellung in October, 1918. There was a wall of non-understanding that the returning soldier seemed content to rest behind.

Then there were those who wore the uniform but never made the trip across the Atlantic Ocean, and had no great desire to hear the AEF veterans recount their efforts in France. This is, of course, a universal trait, but what made the American experience so different was that the majority of those who answered the call to arms voluntarily, and those who were conscripted into the ranks, never left the shores of America. The AEF had the jaunty overseas cap, the Sam Browne Belt, the overseas and wound stripes, and the left shoulder insignia. These had been denied to the soldiers who remained and had not experienced the vagaries of war. Those gaunt men who had been in the Argonne, be it in supply, the combat divisions, the aero squadrons, had no reason to discuss 'the war' with those who were not there.

Then there was the failure of the United States to ratify the Versailles Treaty, to join the League of Nations, and by 1923 conditions in Europe were troublesome again. But that was Europe, and Americans poured into Europe to enjoy the great cities, like Paris, where there was no prohibition. Writers would define the 'Lost Generation,' but it appears that the Doughboys who served in Europe preferred not to think of themselves in those terms. Veterans' organizations flourished, and reunions were held all over the United States. They were closed organizations, however, and they developed their own iconography. As each old veteran 'Went West' (the Doughboy's terminology for death) his grave was marked with divisional insignia, sometimes after mourners left the graveside. That was too personal a moment to share, too private, too protected.

'I saw Gold Star mothers, sisters, and brothers, what a sacrifice they made,' so went a line in a 1925 song 'My Dreams of the Big Parade.' A movie entitled *The Big Parade*, which appeared the same year, purported to show the Western Front and the AEF. Most veterans did not comment on the widely attended film except to say it was close, but not close enough. By the end of the war most veterans had had their fill of war, were disgusted with the course of politics and wrangling over the Versailles Treaty and the like. Private Walter Hill summed up the prevailing feeling when he told his mother, 'I am only too glad to be among the living, a person surely must be healthy to endure all exposures over here,'[34] Their memories were ones which could not be shared. As the 1925 song went on, 'valleys of ruins, mountains of mud, beautiful rivers and rivers of blood . . . pieces of shrapnel, pieces of shell, many a cross where somebody fell.' They drew in on themselves because they could not bridge the gap which chasmed between themselves and family. Those who did not make the crossing to France were not part of the fraternity. A silent bitterness crept into the memories of the Doughboys. The song ended: 'I saw one-legged pals coming home to their gals, in my dream of the Big Parade.'

Notes

1   Diary Entry, Moser Diaries, Author's Personal Collection.
2   ibid.
3   Laurence Stallings, *The Doughboys: The Story of the AEF, 1917–1918* (New York: Harper & Row, 1963), pp. 377, 380–81.
4   Andrew Sullivan, *Yesterdays* (Brooklyn, NY: Theo Gaus Sons, Inc., 1974, p. 73.
5   First Lieutenant Fred Squier Dunn, 24th Balloon Company, World War One Questionnaire, US Army Military History Institute Archives, Carlisle Barracks, Pa.
6   Paul F. Braim, *The Test of Battle: The American Expeditionary Forces in the Meuse-Argonne Campaign* (Newark: The University of Delaware Press, 1987), p. 101.
7   James W. Rainey 'The Questionable Training of the AEF in World War I,' *Parameters* XII, 4 (Winter, 1992–93), p. 89.
8   Robert Lee Bullard, *Personalities and Reminiscences of the War* (Garden City: Doubleday, 1925), p. 24.
9   Rainey, 'Questionable Training,' p. 90.
10 Captain O.O. Ellis and Captain E.B. Garey, *The Plattsburg Manual: A Handbook for Military Training* (New York: The Century Co., 1917), p. 11.
11 Kenton Kilmer, *Memories of My Father Joyce Kilmer* (New Brunswick: The Joyce Kilmer Foundation, 1993).
12 Letter from Hill to his Mother, Camp Meade, 5 December, 1917. The Walter Hill Letters, Author's Personal Collection.
13 Letter from Scott to his mother, France, 29 December, 1917, in the Everett Scott Letters, Author's Personal Collection.
14 Elmer Sherwood, *Rainbow Hoosier* (Indianapolis: Printing Arts Co., c. 1925), pp. 36–38.

15 Letter from Walker to his Parents, France, 27 October, 1918, The Douglas Walker Letters, Author's Personal Collection.

16 Private Joseph Gray, 1st Balloon Company, World War One Questionnaires, US Army Military History Institute Archives, Carlisle Barracks, Pa.

17 'How Ya Gonna Keep 'em Down on the Farm . . .' by Joe Young and Sam M. Lewis (New York: Watterson, Berlin and Snyder, Co., 1919).

18 Letter from Coolidge to His Mother, Paris, 15 August, 1918, in *Letters of an American Airman* (Boston: Private Printing, 1919), p. 4.

19 A. Churchill Ettinger (ed.), *A Doughboy With the Fighting 69th* (Shippensburg, Pa: White Mane, 1992), p. 91.

20 Craig S. Herbert, *Eyes of the Army* (Private Printing, 1986), p. 60.

21 Alexander Woollcott, 'Them Damned Frogs,' *The North American Review*, September 1919, p. 497.

22 Sullivan, *Yesterdays*, p. 101.

23 Letter from Hill to his mother, France, 19 September 1918, Hill Letters.

24 Stallings, *The Doughboys*, p. 377.

25 Hugh S. Thompson, 'Following the Rainbow,' *The Chattanooga* (TN) *Times*, 27 January 1934.

26 Sullivan, *Yesterdays*, p. 92.

27 Braim, *Test of Battle*, p. 135.

28 R.M. Chesledine, *Ohio in the Rainbow: Official Story of the 166th Infantry, 42nd Division in the World War* (Columbus: F.J. Heer, 1924), pp. 256–57.

29 Douglas MacArthur, *Reminiscences* (New York: McGraw-Hill, 1964), p. 72.

30 Leslie Langille, *Men of the Rainbow* (Chicago: The O'Sullivan Publishing House, 1933), pp. 192–93.

31 Letter from Fielder to his Mother, Antwerp, 25 July, 1919, in the Fielder Letters, Used by permission of Mrs Gail Fielder Andrews, Huntsville, Al.

32 Percival Gray Hart, *History of the 135th Aero Squadron* (Chicago: Chicago Law Printing Co., 1939), p. 154.

33 Langille, *Men of the Rainbow*, p. 192.

34 Letter from Hill to his Mother, Boncourt, 29 March, 1919, Hill Letters.

Chapter 20

The Reaction of Irish Officers in the British Army to the Easter Rising of 1916

Jane Leonard

'These men will go down to history as heroes and martyrs and I will go down – if I go down at all – as a bloody British officer'. The comment was attributed to Captain Tom Kettle before he was killed in action with the 9th Royal Dublin Fusiliers during the 16th (Irish) Division's attack on Ginchy in September 1916. Kettle was a prominent nationalist, poet and university lecturer. From 1906 to 1910 he had been MP for East Tyrone.[1]

The men Kettle referred to had been executed for their part in the events in Dublin during Easter that year. Easter 1916 occupies a key place in the semantic war underpinning Anglo-Irish relations. In contemporary correspondence and newspaper reports, the week's happenings were commonly described as a riot, a disturbance and 'local troubles'. Irish and British sensitivities ever since as to whether the week should be defined as a rising or a revolt have been discussed by Charles Townshend in a recent stimulating article. He also noted that similar perspectives have dictated the choice of verb used to describe the British response. These range from crush, suppress, quell and put down to neutralize, counter and pacify.[2]

This article will explore the impact of the rising on Irishmen holding commissions in the British forces. Irish involvement in the war had been a sensitive political issue right from the start. Implementation of the Home Rule Act for Ireland, given assent in September 1914, was suspended for the duration of the war. Two paramilitary bodies had been founded in Ireland in the previous year. Ulster unionists established the Ulster Volunteer Force (UVF) in January 1913 to oppose the introduction of Home Rule while in November 1913, Irish nationalists set up their own force, the Irish Volunteers, precisely to safeguard the measure. The UVF provided the bulk of early recruits for the 36th (Ulster) Division.

In recognition of the implementation of Home Rule, the Irish parliamentary nationalist party led by John Redmond backed the war effort and pledged that the Irish Volunteers would enlist in the British forces. A minority within the Irish Volunteers (some 11,000 out of 190,000) dissented and left the movement. This splinter group retained the original name of Irish Volunteers while the majority pro-war membership became known as the Irish National Volunteers (INV). A considerable proportion of recruits for the two new southern Irish divisions in the army – the 10th and the 16th – were former INV members.

The 10th (Irish) Division suffered heavy losses in the Suvla Bay landings at Gallipoli in August 1915. Casualties were especially heavy among battalions of the Royal Dublin Fusiliers recruited from the inner quarters of the capital. The 36th (Ulster) Division and 16th (Irish) Division only arrived on the Western Front in late 1915 and neither had yet experienced a major campaign. The timing of the Rising was therefore significant. Its impact on morale in the Irish divisions would presumably have been more severe had it followed their losses on the Somme and further harsh winters in the trenches. An additional factor affecting morale at home was that conscription, introduced into the rest of the United Kingdom in early April 1916, did not extend to Ireland. Had it done, nationalist alienation from the war effort might have translated into solidarity with the rebellion. This was to be the case in 1918 when all sections of the nationalist population united with Sinn Fein to stop conscription being applied to Ireland. As it was, the inner Dublin community was still traumatised from its losses at Gallipoli and on other fronts and the only alienation it initially felt was with the rebels.[3]

The Easter Rising was staged by the Irish Volunteers, supported by even smaller groups including the Irish Citizen Army, a labour militia led by James Connolly. In total, less than 2500 men were involved in the revolt. British intelligence had monitored telegrams passing between Ireland, Germany and America. The Royal Navy intercepted a German submarine carrying Roger Casement and weapons off the Kerry coast on Good Friday. As a result, the Irish Volunteers cancelled an Easter Sunday parade in central Dublin which had been planned to mask the rebellion. The order not to parade was rescinded by a more militant section led by Patrick Pearse and a much smaller revolt began in central Dublin on Easter Monday when parading volunteers seized public buildings around the city centre. The Irish civil administration and military command were taken by surprise – many army officers were at the traditional Easter race meeting at Fairyhouse outside Dublin and were unaware of events until that evening.

The Rising lasted for six days. Most infantry battalions stationed or drafted into Dublin were Irish and their ranks were augmented by soldiers on leave and colonial troops spending Easter in Ireland. The Dublin University Officer Training Corps (the only such unit in the British Isles to see active service during the war) was helped in its defence of the college by Australian, New Zealand and Canadian soldiers. Cadets at the Curragh in Kildare and Fermoy in Cork were posted to flying columns sent to counter smaller outbreaks in the south-east. Additional infantry, artillery batteries and a gun-boat, were sent to Dublin. There was heavy shelling of rebel-held buildings. By Saturday there were 16,000 British troops in Dublin and the rebels surrendered.

At this stage public sympathies were totally against them. Some 258 non-combatant civilians had been killed in addition to 132 soldiers and policemen. Casualties were heavy among locally recruited regiments. The city centre was devastated and jobs had been lost (though the pickings for looters had been good during the week). Many newspaper offices had been destroyed in the bombardment. When newspapers re-appeared, they were subject to strict censorship. Most were heavily critical of the rebels.

A gradual shift in public opinion came over the next weeks and months with the executions over a protracted period of the principal leaders and with the arrest of a massive 3,500. Almost half had taken no part in the rising and were subsequently released. The remaining 1,800 were sent to internment camps in England and Wales. Popular condemnation of the rising was gradually converted into retrospective solidarity with the rebels over the next five years.

Of eight by-elections contested by both parties in 1917 and 1918, Sinn Fein won five to the Home Rule party's three. Sinn Fein consolidated its position by dominating the united nationalist opposition to the proposed introduction of conscription in the spring of 1918. In the general election of December 1918, it won a massive victory over the Home Rule party. January 1919 saw the establishment of the party's abstentionist assembly in Dublin, Dail Eireann and the inauguration of the IRA's military campaign which ultimately led to the Anglo-Irish Treaty of December 1921. By the time of the sixth anniversary of the Easter Rising in 1922, British garrisons had left or were preparing to depart from the Irish Free State and the six British infantry regiments recruited from within this part of Ireland were preparing for disbandment.[4]

How did Irish officers serving with the British forces react to the Rising? Did the reactions of unionists markedly differ from those of nationalists? How did officers stationed or on leave *in Ireland* during or soon after the Rising react? How did those serving *outside Ireland* respond to news of the Rising?

It should be emphasised that, at the time of the Rising, most Irish officers in the British forces were not nationalists. The majority of officers in Irish regiments in early 1916 held regular commissions and were either not Irish or else came from Irish unionist backgrounds. Nationalists who received temporary commissions generally served in southern Irish battalions of the 10th and 16th (Irish) Divisions or with other corps such as the artillery and the Royal Army Medical Corps.[5]

It is important to stress that nationalist and unionist officers had similar initial reactions. Like any serving officer faced with a domestic rebellion, they expressed shock and dismay at the physical damage to Dublin, sorrow at military and civilian casualties and anger at the disruption to the war effort.

The stock phrase uttered by Irish Great War veterans about the Easter Rising was that it was 'a stab in the back'. The phrase was used equally in contemporary accounts and in later interviews and memoirs. The term was used by both nationalist and unionist officers.[6]

Where their reactions diverged it was over what caused the most damage – the 'stab in the back' or the methods used to neutralise the assailants. Nationalists felt that the Rising damaged the prospects for Home Rule but that the suppression of the Rising did even greater harm to the prospect of a lasting settlement in Ireland. For unionists, the Rising disrupted the war effort but was a useful reminder of nationalist treachery. A blunt editorial in a County Down newspaper commented that 'if Ulster were sufficiently unpatriotic to place her private interests before that of the Empire, we might even congratulate ourselves in relation to what has occurred. It certainly has not helped the cause of Home Rule.'[7]

After the war, unionist politicians and propagandists regularly contrasted the disloyalty of southern Ireland in April 1916 with the heavy Ulster Division losses at the Somme the following July. Political expediency ruled the 16th (Irish) Division's own Somme losses in September 1916 out of this equation. When Prime Minister of Northern Ireland in the late 1960s, Lord Brookeborough cited his memories of the Easter Rising as a major influence on his political thinking. Then a regular officer, he was home on special leave as his wife was having a baby in Dublin. He felt ashamed 'for his country, for his regiment and for those who had died in the war'. He and his wife were 'impressed at the manner in which the rebels paralysed the city. This made them determined to withstand any such rising in the North.'[8]

Raw young officers were more likely to appreciate the opportunity of combat experience than to grasp its political significance. One later described his first days on the Western Front: 'I've never spent a week in the army that I enjoyed half as much as this last one here, with the possible exception of the rebellion in Dublin last year.'[9] For two subalterns of the Connaught Rangers, the 'spinoffs from the row in Dublin' included a comic raid on a suspect's house where a wake was in progress and the chance to lead a flying column by motor-bike.[10] Convalescent officers also enjoyed the return to action. Lord Dunalley, a Rifle Brigade officer recuperating in Tipperary, instructed his mother 'to shoot any of the maidservants who showed symptoms of treachery' before he set off to join GHQ staff in Dublin.[11]

The Rising was a maturing experience for John Carrothers, home on leave from the Inns of Court Officer Training Corps at Berkhamsted and attached to a Royal Irish Rifles battalion in Portobello Barracks. By the end of the week, he had seen 'enough of the horrors of war without going to France to see any more.'[12]

Few expressed qualms about firing on friends and former comrades, although one officer in the Leinster Regiment declined to command the firing party at the execution of Joseph Plunkett. He cited their childhood friendship and was excused this duty. Captain Stephen Gwynn of the Connaught Rangers, a nationalist MP for Galway, noted that the 10th battalion Royal Dublin Fusiliers included men who 'had been active leaders in the Howth gunrunning. It was not merely a case of Irishmen firing on their fellow countrymen: it was one section of the original Volunteers firing on another.'[13]

At the same time, however, nationalist officers were keen to emphasise the sensitivity with which Irish regiments handled the early days of the revolt and contrasted this with the heavy-handed methods used by non-Irish units subsequently. Captain Eugene Sheehy, son of a former Home Rule MP and brother-in-law of Tom Kettle, stressed the restraint with which his battalion, the 4th Royal Dublin Fusiliers, had conducted itself.[14]

Those who had direct contact with the rebels were impressed by their bravery and courtesy. While a prisoner in the General Post Office, Captain George Mahony, an Indian Army doctor, became friendly with the wounded James Connolly. Fifty years later, his widow objected to a BBC programme on the rising which mistook Mahony's nationality. Her letter illustrated the ambivalent position of Irish officers serving under the crown. Her husband, she wrote, 'was born and bred in Cork . . . and was very proud of being an Irishman and would have been most distressed to hear himself being called an English doctor.'[15]

Some officers felt sorry for their opponents. Carrothers found it 'pitiable to see some of the Sinns [sic] that have been captured by women in the back streets. They are all scratched and stabbed with hat pins.'[16] Lieutenant John Wilson-Lynch sent a vivid account of escort duty to his family in Galway:

> It was a sad sight. In the pouring rain, these poor unfortunate dupes were marched along the quays. Not a cheer the whole way – women crying, and the prisoners miserable, dirty, unshaven and wet through. They must have begun to realise what fools they had been. They hardly looked up the whole way.[17]

Two officers jointly protested at an action by British forces during the week. Captain Sir Francis Vane and Second Lieutenant Monk Gibbon, stationed at Portobello Barracks, notified the War Office of the circumstances of the murder there of Francis Sheehy Skeffington, a prominent pacifist and nationalist. Vane and Gibbon based their joint protest on the fact that the mentally unstable officer who killed Sheehy-Skeffington was allowed to remain on duty. They enlisted the help of nationalist politicians and eventually the officer was court-martialled and committed to a mental hospital.[18]

After the war, one Irish officer expressed his reservations about British handling of the rising to the senior officer responsible. At a lunch in Northern Command, York in 1919, Brigadier William English-Murphy, a pre-war teacher in Belfast, quizzed General Sir John Maxwell (GOC Ireland in 1916) about the decision to execute the leaders. The general did not respond positively to such criticism but English-Murphy was due for demobilisation and escaped a reprimand.[19]

Those who privately expressed some solidarity with the rebels included Robert Barton and David Robinson. A Wicklow landowner and a pre-war Irish Volunteer, Robert Barton was gazetted from the Inns of Court OTC to the Royal Dublin Fusiliers just as the rebellion began. He spent the week in Richmond Barracks, Dublin and was in charge of gathering prisoners' effects after the surrender. Those involved in relief work for the next of kin of interned prisoners found Barton sympathetic and helpful. He is popularly supposed to have resigned his commission immediately after the rising in protest although he did not actually leave the army for another year (sanctioned in order to increase tillage on his Wicklow estate). But disenchantment had set in. By June 1916 he felt that 'everyone is a Sinn Feiner now . . . Ireland will never again be as friendly disposed to England as she was at the outbreak of war'. In December 1918 Barton was elected Sinn Fein MP for West Wicklow. He was one of the Irish signatories to the Anglo-Irish Treaty in December 1921.

His friend, Captain David Robinson, Royal Marine Light Infantry, was in France when he heard of the Rising. An understanding commanding officer, aware of his politics, allowed him to go home on leave. On arrival in Dublin, he joined Barton in Richmond Barracks. Among those awaiting deportation were familiar faces from the Irish Volunteers and the Gaelic League. Robinson returned to France and later transferred to the Tank Corps. He was invalided out of the army after Cambrai and had joined the IRA by late 1918.[20]

There is one further incident of strong solidarity with the rebels. On Easter Monday, Charles Duff was returning to the Inns of Court OTC from Easter leave in Fermanagh. He published two accounts of what followed. A general history of the rising published in 1966 briefly referred to his 'few adventures' before being hurried with other Irish and colonial soldiers on to the mailboat for Holyhead. Duff was relieved not to have served during the Rising as he 'had joined the British Army as a volunteer in Dublin – to fight Germans.'

In Duff's autobiography, there is a more detailed account of what happened when troops waiting at Kingstown for the mailboat were told to report to various barracks for duty. He and about twenty others decided to protest on the grounds of their Irish nationality. Senior officers quizzed them about this decision and then locked them up for the night. Next morning, Easter Tuesday, they and about 250 other Irish and colonial troops (who had presumably made similar protests or else would have been posted for duty in Dublin) sailed for Holyhead. No recriminations followed. Years later Duff met the Irish major who had interviewed the protestors. He explained to Duff that he had persuaded the army that 'it would not be common sense to turn against Irish rebels Irishmen who did not want to fight their own countrymen and who might even sympathize with them'. The Irish major had himself arranged to be sent back to France. One of the interesting aspects to this protest was the commonsense military response it produced. The decision to allow this particular conscientious objection was an antidote to the standard image of the British army's crude handling of the Rising.[21]

How did officers serving *outside* Ireland react? Initial reports were confused and sketchy and it was several weeks before soldiers fully grasped that the home front had become a war front, or 'Ypres on the Liffey', as one Dublin magazine described it. On 29 April, Lt Patrick Hemphill, serving in Salonika, referred to the 'Dublin riots' in a letter, but it took another month's news before he realised 'that it was anything more than a glorified strike.'[22]

In some Irish battalions, news of the Rising had little impact. The majority of Irish officers interviewed long after the war had little or no recollection of exactly when they heard about the Rising. Delayed post and interrupted circulation of Irish newspapers may have contributed to this uncertainty. Frank Law, himself the son of a Home Rule MP, was puzzled by the lack of comment among Irish Guardsmen. Law recalled 'no talk about the Rising or its implications. Perhaps the problems, all day and every day, of staying alive, made news from home unreal and very irrelevant'.[23]

When newspapers did resume publication, they reported that Irish troops felt betrayed and angered by the Rising. The Germans and Roger Casement were seen as the villains – the names of Pearse and Connolly and the other leaders were strikingly absent from soldiers' criticisms of the revolt. There were calls for heavy penalties. On 29 April, Lieutenant Patrick Hemphill speculated:

I suppose they'll hang all the ringleaders. It's what the traitors deserve. It appears to have been got up by Roger Casement. A jolly good thing they caught him all right. He's another for the noose. The beauty of the thing is that they will all be tried by court martial which has no lenient tendency.[24]

Similar satisfaction was expressed by a future Unionist MP for North Down. From Russia, where he was serving with a Royal Naval Armoured Train, Lt Walter Smiles reported in late May that Irishmen in his unit were pleased that the rebellion was over. They hoped that Carson would be appointed Chief Secretary for Ireland.[25]

Press reports emphasised that nationalists in the trenches felt let down. Particular bitterness was felt by the 16th (Irish) Division who had survived a heavy gas bombardment at Hulluch while the Easter Rising was taking place. Lt Edward Gallagher, a nationalist from Strabane serving with the 7th Inniskilling Fusiliers, was relieved to have come through this attack. Then news came of 'this terrible Rebel rising in Dublin. Poor old Ireland. Betrayed again'. An unnamed officer who survived Hulluch wished:

> to God the War Office would send the 16th Div over to Dublin to settle things. After going through the 27th [April] we are game for anything, and we would soon settle the German puppets. I am getting along as well as can be expected but it takes time to get the gas out of one's system.[26]

Following these gas attacks, the 16th Division was incensed when German troops raised placards opposite them urging them to desert and join the uprising in Dublin. The ensuing raids on German trenches and capture of the offending placards received heavy coverage in Irish newspapers. The official war diarist of the 9th Royal Munster Fusiliers recorded a revenge taunt on 21 May when his battalion hung up an effigy of Roger Casement in full view of the German trenches. Thus although the Rising dismayed and embittered men in the trenches, it nonetheless buoyed up rather than weakened morale.

Both the 36th (Ulster) Division and the 16th (Irish) Division acquitted themselves in their first real blooding in July and September 1916 on the Somme. Separate studies by Terence Denman and Lyn Lemisko of the 16th (Irish) Division have both concluded that the Rising had no serious effect on it. As Denman has pointed out 'it is clear that whatever disquiet the events in Ireland produced they did not damage its fighting performance'.[27]

While the rising did not directly damage front-line morale in Irish units, it had a long-term alienating effect on the pysche of nationalists, especially on those with brothers, cousins and friends among the rebels. William Kent, the brother of Eamonn Ceannt, an executed leader, was killed in action with the Royal Dublin Fusiliers in 1917. Eamon de Valera, reprieved from execution on account of his American birth, had been taught by Father Bernard Carey, who served during the war as a chaplain with the British West India Regiment. News of the role of his former pupil reached Carey in East Africa. The only Irishman in his mess, he

> had a good deal to suffer from insulting remarks on the occasion of the Irish rebellion. My ears often tingled as I heard from a captain at a table

near where I sat such expressions as 'These bloody Irish, they want another Cromwell to blow the whole bloody crew out of existence.'[28]

The poet and teacher Thomas MacDonagh was one of the sixteen executed leaders. For his former pupil, Arthur Dickens, then an Indian Army cadet, 1916 'was a blot on the family escutcheon, for it was my father who was in command of the Artillery during the Easter Rising and it was to him Thomas MacDonagh surrendered.'[29]

Home Rule MPs serving in the trenches were in despair. They initially wanted to return home and then decided that the best example they could set would be to remain with the Irish soldiers under their command. Stephen Gwynn and William Redmond realised their war service would compromise them should the Irish electorate change its views in the wake of the Rising. Redmond prophesied that he would be seen 'as a traitor to his country and a leader of traitors.' Redmond was killed on the Messines Ridge in 1917. Like Tom Kettle the previous year, Redmond was popularly supposed to have lost his will to live after news came of the Rising.[30]

While nationalist politicians serving in the army expressed genuine sympathy for the internees and sorrow at the executions, they were angry that the cause of Irish constitutional nationalism and the service of its supporters in the war was now eclipsed. This resentment was directed equally at Sinn Fein and the British Government. Capt Stephen Gwynn's subsequent speeches to the House of Commons and his letters to the press were bitter about the damage done to Home Rule. In a letter to the Observer in March 1918 he complained that England had 'so managed the affair that Pearse and his handful of half-armed men have effected more against the Allies than all the Irish troops together in all their fighting have effected against Germany'.[31]

Similar unease was expressed by those stationed in post-Rising Ireland. In 1917, Owen Tweedy was transferred from a reserve battalion of the Connaught Rangers in Cork to a staff posting in the Middle East. Keen to leave Ireland, Tweedy felt that 'after the Easter Rising things were never really comfortable again. There was everywhere the distressing feeling that we were now locked in a bitter struggle with others who were as Irish as we were'.

There was no significant transfer of allegiance from nationalist ex-officers returning to Ireland after the war. I have traced only about twenty former supporters of John Redmond who served as officers in the Great War and then became prominent in Sinn Fein or the IRA after the Armistice. The most famous was Lieutenant-Commander Erskine Childers, a decorated naval aviator. Childers (a cousin of Robert Barton) had been a civil servant in London, a Boer War hero and an acclaimed novelist. In 1914, he had smuggled guns into Ireland for the Irish Volunteers. Dismayed by the rebellion, he remained a constitutional nationalist for the rest of the war and did not join Sinn Fein until after his demobilisation.[32]

Instead of converting to militant nationalism, many Redmondite officers either remained in the British army or found civilian careers outside Ireland after the war. Among them were some sons and grandsons of former Home Rule MPs who became barristers in England, colonial civil servants in Africa and officers in the Indian Army. Many ex-officers who had supported Home Rule never lived in Ireland after the war although some did return at the start of the civil war in 1922 and joined the Free State army. This they saw as a logical resumption of the defence of constitutional nationalism which had led them to join up during the Great War. Lt Walter Joyce, ex-South Irish Horse and Irish Guards, had served in a cavalry unit of John Redmond's National Volunteers in 1914. He recalled coming back in 1922:

By the time I got my degree (a 3rd in history!) and came down from Cambridge, Ireland was in a state of civil war. The Irish representatives had rejected an agreement, which amounted to Dominion Status. Ireland to be called the Free State of Ireland. De Valera rejected the agreement and was followed by a large body of Irish. I thought we should have stood by the agreement and joined up on the pro-Treaty side . . . I left immediately the fighting was over and through Cambridge University Appointments Board got a job in B.P. (British Petroleum) as a district manager in Ireland.[33]

In conclusion, what long-term effect did the Rising have on nationalist officers? We know that it did not have a major adverse effect on morale in Irish units although the drop in Irish enlistments following the Rising directly affected the long-term viability of the two southern Irish divisions. While nationalist officers certainly experienced some degree of alienation from the British Army in the aftermath of the Rising, they simultaneously felt out of place in the new political culture of Sinn Fein. Their support for the now unpopular concept of Home Rule and the fact that they had served in the same army as General Sir John Maxwell rather than with Patrick Pearse militated against their integration into the newly republican society of Ireland.[34]

Nationalist officers who left Ireland retained conflicting emotions about this physical, mental and cultural displacement caused by their service in the British Army. Capt Daniel D. Sheehan was an independent nationalist MP for North Cork who had served with the Royal Munster Fusiliers during the war. His four sons also served in the war. Two were killed and two became regular officers after the Armistice. After the war, Sinn Fein boycotted his legal practice and the IRA expelled him from Cork. By 1921, bankrupt in London, he could still praise the action of the 1916 rebels who arguably had initiated much of his bad luck. Sheehan argued that 'not the least of their performances [was] that they gave back to the people of Ireland the right of thinking and acting for themselves.'[35]

Residual guilt about his service with the Royal Dublin Fusiliers during the rising marked the correspondence of one old survivor. Writing from Rhodesia to a fellow ex-officer in the early 1970s, William Mount constantly recalled the search parties, sniping and shelling that marked the week. Although from a unionist background, Mount had been a friend of Sean Heuston, one of the executed leaders of the Rising. A letter of April 1970 linked British policy in the worsening northern Irish situation to that of 54 years earlier:

It is a relief to know that President Dev[alera] and Mr Lynch have not followed the mean, cowardly lead given by [Harold] Wilson. You know, Denis, my opinion of the English sagged greatly following that affair in April 1916. When they started putting those chaps including my friend Huston [sic] up against a wall there were times when I wondered if we were on the right side. That was a cowardly, unforgiveable thing to do.[36]

The overwhelming impression is that the Rising unsettled the identity of nationalist officers while it reinforced the confidence of unionists. For nationalists, the essential uncertainty was how the new Ireland would regard their wartime service. Those who did return to Ireland in 1919 went back, in Captain Stephen Gwynn's phrase, 'with doubtful eyes'. Another, Eugene Sheehy, though he became a Free State army officer and then a District Justice, remained uncomfortable about Easter 1916. Thirty five years later, he still maintained that it was

a source of heartbreak to me and to the many tens of thousands of Irish nationalists who had joined the British Army . . . As the tide of Irish public opinion gradually changed and hostility to England grew we did not quite know where we stood, or where our duty lay.[37]

Notes

1   J.B. Lyons, *The Enigma of Tom Kettle*, Dublin, Glendale, 1983, p.293.
2   see for example *The Irish Builder and Engineer*, 13 May 1916; C. Townshend, 'The Suppression of the Easter Rising', *Bullan*, 1994, vol. 1 no. 1, p.29.
3   A comprehensive account of the raising of the Irish divisions is given in chapters 1–3 of T. Denman, *Ireland's Unknown Soldiers, The 16th (Irish) Division In World War I*, Dublin, Irish Academic, 1992; see also P. Orr, *The Road To The Somme, Men Of The Ulster Division Tell Their Story*, Belfast, Blackstaff, 1987, pp.3–47; K. Myers, 'The day the sea turned red at Gallipoli', *Irish Times*, 25 April 1985.
4   G. Hayes McCoy, 'A military history of the Easter Rising', in K.B. Nowlan (ed), *The Making of 1916*, Dublin, 1969, pp. 255–304; the social and economic impact of the week are vividly assessed in J.B. O'Brien, *Dear Dirty Dublin: A City In Distress, 1899–1916*, Berkeley, University of California Press, 1983, pp.258–274; a fascinating recent analysis of the interaction of

political cultures in pre- and post-Rising Ireland is given in P. Bew, *Ideology And The Irish Question: Ulster Unionism And Irish Nationalism, 1912–1916*, Oxford, OUP, 1994.

5   The backgrounds of officers in Irish infantry regiments are analysed in chapter five of M. Staunton, *The Royal Munster Fusiliers In The Great War*, MA Thesis, University College, Dublin, 1986.

6   See May 1916 issues of the *Freemans' Journal, Irish News* and *Cork Examiner*. Comments made in author's interviews with Frederick Dixon, Edward Gahan, Terence Poulter, William Ruttle, William Hurley, Ralph Cusack, Fitz Brabazon and Walter Joyce.

7   *County Down Spectator*, 28 April 1916.

8   T.P. Coogan, *The IRA*, London, Fontana, 1970, p.58.

9   *The Whitest Band* (7th Officer Cadet Battalion Journal, Fermoy) vol 11 no 6, October 1917.

10   Seymour Jourdain interview, Imperial War Museum, Department of Sound Records 11214/12; C.A. Brett, *Recollections*, n.d., p18 (unpublished memoirs deposited in Linenhall Library, Belfast).

11   Lord Dunalley, *Rifle And Khaki Green*, London, 1944, p.200.

12   J.C. Carrothers, *War Memoirs Of A Young Lieutenant*, Enniskillen, nd, privately printed, 29 April 1916, p.21; despite the title, this consists of letters.

13   M. Gibbon, *Inglorious Soldier*, London, Hutchinson, 1968, p. 71; S. Gwynn, *John Redmond's Last Years*, London, Edward Arnold, 1919, p.227.

14   E. Sheehy, *May It Please The Court*, Dublin, Fallon, 1951, p.90.

15   Mrs G. Malone to Mr McCarthy, 5 May, 1966, National Library of Ireland Manuscripts Department, Ms 15 017.

16   Carrothers, ibid, 30 April, p. 22.

17   John Wilson-Lynch to his aunt, Wilson Lynch Ls 1 Breise 118.5, University College Galway, Hardiman Library.

18   Gibbon, ibid, pp.28 passim; F. Vane, *Agin The Governments*, London, Sampson Low, 1929, pp. 261–282; Gibbon was later invalided out of the army following a nervous breakdown, Vane was dismissed from the army and moved to Italy; the officer who murdered Sheehy-Skeffington was subsequently released from Broadmoor and became a bank manger in Canada.

19   Unpublished memoir quoted by his grandson, K. Murphy, in *William Richard English-Murphy: His Early Life And Career In The British Army Till 1919*, Maynooth College BA thesis, 1993. Murphy became a Free State Army general during the Irish Civil War, 1922–23 and was subsequently Commissioner of the Dublin Metropolitan Police and Deputy Commissioner of the Gardai. He dropped the first part of his surname in 1923.

20   Service record in Robert Barton papers, National Archives of Ireland, 1093/9; P. O'Farrell, *Who's Who In The Irish War Of Independence*, Cork, Mercier, 1980, p.14; Robert Barton to Molly Childers, 30 June 1916, Childers papers Ms 7833/14, Trinity College, Dublin Dept of Manuscripts; ms, autobiographical account by David Robinson, n.d., Childers papers Ms 7847–51/1077, Trinity College, Dublin, Dept of Manuscripts.

21   C Duff, *Six Days To Shake An Empire*, London, Dent, 1966, p.105; C. Duff, *No Angel's Wing*, London, 1947, pp. 44–46;Duff became a Foreign Office diplomat after the war. His appears to be the sole account of this protest.

22 *The Lady Of The House*, 15 May 1916; Hemphill correspondence, Liddle Collection, Leeds University, 29 April 1916 and 22 May 1916.

23 F. Law, *A Man At Arms*, London, Collins, 1983, p.69.

24 Hemphill letters, ibid, 29 April 1916.

25 Lt Walter Smiles to his parents, 27 May 1916 D3437/B/1–5 Public Record Office of Northern Ireland.

26 *Belfast Evening Telegraph*, 6 May 1916; *Cork Constitution*, 10 May 1916.

27 L.S. Lemisko, *Politics, Performance And Morale: 16 (Irish) Division, 1914–18*, University of Calgary MA, 1992, pp.68–71; Denman, ibid, p.144.

28 Staunton, ibid, 173; B. Carey, *Leaves From The Diary of a Catholic Chaplain In The Great War*, Pittsburgh, n.d., pp.44–45.

29 A. Dickens, 'Return to Rockwell' in *Rockwell College Annual* 1970, p.37.

30 See Monsignor Arthur Ryan's foreword in *Major Willie Redmond: In Memoriam*, London, privately printed, 1917, pp15–16; Redmond's depression after the Rising is analysed in Terence Denman's biography, *A Lonely Grave. The Life and Death of William Redmond*, Dublin, Irish Academic Press, 1995.

31 See also his comments in the *Ulster Guardian* 8 July 1916 and Hansard, LXXXV, cols 2569–2577, 22 August 1916.

32 T. Crowe (ed), *Gathering Moss. A Memoir Of Owen Tweedy*, London, Sidgwick & Jackson, 1967, P.52; B Wilkinson, *The Zeal Of The Convert. The Life of Erskine Childers,* New York, Second Chance Press, 1985, pp.149–157.

33 These findings on the post-war political outlook and career patterns of nationalist ex-officers are taken from the London University thesis I am completing on '*Ex-servicemen and political change in Ireland, 1919–1939*'; Walter Joyce to the author, 13 March 1989.

34 Intimidation of ex-servicemen was a feature of the IRA's campaign after 1918; some preliminary findings on murders of ex-soldiers are in my article 'Getting them at last': the IRA and ex-servicemen' in D. Fitzpatrick (ed.) *Revolution? Ireland 1917–23*, Dublin, Trinity History Workshop, 1990, pp.118–129.

35 Interviews with Sheehan's son and grandson, Dublin, 1990; D.D. Sheehan, *Ireland Since Parnell*, London, Daniel O'Connor, 1921, p.298.

36 I must thank Kevin Myers for access to William Mount's correspondence with Denis O'Brien.

37 S. Gwynn, 'Irish regiments' in F. Lavery (comp.) *Great Irishmen In War And Politics*, London, Melrose, 1920, p.186; Sheehy, ibid, p. 91.

Chapter 21

Ernst Jünger: German Stormtrooper Chronicler

Thomas Nevin

Storm troops were first employed in the Argonne forest, some fifteen miles west of Verdun, in December, 1914. German rifle divisions had met resistance there in late September, and the fighting quickly developed into a positional contest of trenches and what the Germans called a fortress war *(Festungskrieg)* of trench mortars and revolving artillery. At 8 a.m. on December 20, 'storm divisions' were sent out with hand-grenades, axes and wire shears. They gained 800 metres, 200 prisoners, four machine guns, a cannon and eight mortars.[1]

After the Argonne, the German High Command tested the usefulness of an initial line of attack by troops fortified with metal shields who were thus capable of hitting the enemy from rear and flank positions. The initial force came from two companies of pioneers and one division armed with a 3.7 cm. cannon. It was successfully engaged in its *coup d'essai* at the battle of Loretto Heights northwest of Arras (March 1915), but its conspicuous and clumsy protective shielding drew artillery fire so effectively that half of the personnel were lost.

The survivors were re-assigned and a new troop formation was left to Capt. Willy M. E. Rohr of the Guards Defence Battalion. He dispensed with the awkward protective cover, preferring to co-ordinate troop movement with machine guns and artillery. To insure co-ordination he schooled his troops behind the lines and used live ammunition to encourage their learning.

This training paid off in Alsace, 22–23 December, 1915. At Hartmannsweiler, 3 miles north of Cernay, Rohr's troops aided the 82nd Militia Brigade in the recapture of the town's summit. According to the field reports,[2] the Germans captured 23 French officers and 1,530 of their men. The logistics here were far different from those at the Argonne, but

Rohr's success satisfied the High Command, and his troops, known there-after as *das Sturmbataillon Rohr*, were incorporated into the Fifth Army under Crown Prince Wilhelm. This minor victory also gave the impetus for the creation of new stormtroop battalions, eight of which were formed from the regular infantry.

The equipment of the stormtroopers singled them out from the regular infantrymen. Instead of a rifle, each carried a sling carbine; cartridges were carried in pockets rather than in belts. Two small sacks of egg-size grenades were buckled crosswise over both shoulders. A large pioneer's spade with a half-length shaft projected from the shoulder. A pack holding a coat and blanket wound round the chest and back.

Intensive training became *de rigeur* through the last three years of the war, but as the tactical need of well-disciplined troops proved more urgent, it grew more difficult to meet. Too many men had been wasted in the initial campaigns, so that recruits were finally too raw to fight effectively. According to Lt. Gen. Wilhelm Balck,

> The infantry was essentially different from the one we had in the war's initial offensive. Battalions and companies were led by young, in part very young officers, who though experienced in the war, lacked that which made the strength of our officers during the peacetime [who were] schooled for all situations, untiring in solicitude for subordinates, a model of exertion and self-denial in danger and endurance . . . there was still a sound spirit among the men; they followed their leaders confi-dently. Of course the training was no longer as before: you couldn't get the same results in six months as in two years of peacetime service, that was especially the case in the use of rifles and projectiles . . . The young reserves, grown up without the influence of their fathers and other older relatives in the field, weren't even morally on the same high level of old.[3]

Balck's generalities are pertinent to the best known chronicler of the storm troops' course in the war. I refer to one of their lieutenants, Ernst Jünger of the 73rd Hanoverian Fusiliers. He was very young – nineteen when he enlisted – yet war-seasoned; he served in all but the first two months of the war. He had no experience whatever of the peacetime career corps of officers; his real training was in the exigencies of the field. By the war's final year, he was burdened with youngsters, only a few years his juniors, whom he had to lead chiefly by the example of his own endurance, performance (2 Iron Crosses by March, 1918) and – no small matter – luck.

Jünger survived to write three memoirs of his service: *In Stahlgewittern* (1920), known to English readers in Basil Creighton's translation, *The Storm of Steel* (1929); *Das Wäldchen 125* (1924) or *Copse 125*, another translation by Creighton; and *Feuer und Blut* (1925), which remains untranslated. The first of these spans all four years of Jünger's service; the second, four weeks in the summer of 1918; the third, one day of combat:

21 March, 1918, the beginning of the Michael Offensive. Complementing the memoirs is a long, rather expressionistic essay, *Der Kampf als Inneres Erlebnis* (1922), a work often quoted but still untranslated.

In Stahlgewittern was one of the first published accounts of the war. It came amid a wave of apologetic literature from the officer class, much of which was dedicated to explaining away the military catastrophe.[4] Jünger, a junior officer, dispassionately recounts the war not in strategic or tactical terms but at the ground level of immediate perceptions. His prose vividly compacts daily hazard with an at times lyrical distancing from that hazard. He is at once soldier and spectator. His accounts survive because they are for the greater part free of the hysterics of war rhetoric and its anamorphic vision.

Consider for a moment the following idealized caricature of the stormtrooper which the soldier-poet Franz Schauwecker, later Jünger's colleague in journalism, provided in his wartime dispatches to a homefront press:

> ... he moves from shellhole to shellhole in raging fire, by leap and bound, by creep and crawl like a seal, close to earth like an animal, never discouraged, never irresolute, never forfeiting intent, always full of recourse, schemes and self-reliance, ripe for every situation, answering every blow with counterblow ... a new kind of man, a man in the highest exaltation of all manly qualities so harmonized and from a single caste that one sees a man in the word 'fighter'.[5]

'Never . . . never . . . always . . . every,' and of course 'highest'. It is a pity that this hyperbole fails to convince, for a more earthbound diction would suffice, and it is because Jünger provides it that he, and not Schauwecker, deserves our reading still. Besides, Schauwecker poses a strange incongruity: the almost comic bulk the stormtroopers had to carry comports oddly with his heady choreography for a primitive yet nimble and vicious creature, the 'new man'. But this is precisely the sort of warrior Jünger himself depicts in 'Battle as Inner Experience'. A Homeric motif sounds in two particulars: distinctively armed (carbine and grenades), the stormtrooper carries like Achilles a peculiar menace with which, being in the forefront, he can garner the lion's share of the honorifics of violence. He is a man become force. But he is also a master of animal cunning, enduring like Odysseus as much through wiles as through brute vitality. Such were the initiatives required by defence-in-depth tactics from 1916 on: they begot the anomaly of soldiers without command.

Here is one of Jünger's lively descriptions of these men in action:

> Cracks of thunder showed us our way. Behind rifles and machine-guns hundreds of eyes lay in wait upon the goal. We were already far in front of our own lines. From all sides shots whistled round our steel helmets

or shattered with a harsh clap on the trench's rim. Every time one of the egg-shaped clumps of iron appeared on the horizon, the eye fastened upon it with that final sharpness of which only a man facing a decision of life and death is capable. Then we hurled ourselves forward. Scarcely had a look glanced over the crumpled body of a foe who had played out his hand than a new duel began. The hand-grenade exchange reminds you of foil fencing; you have to spring as in a ballet. It's the deadliest of contests for two, and it's ended only when one of the opponents goes flying into the air.[6]

We find not only brisk writing here (only obliquely suggested in translation) but also substantial warrant for Jünger's ascription of 'prince' to the stormtrooper in the trench. The complement to death, so capriciously egalitarian, is the ennoblement of all those, whatever their station in former peace, who confront it as individuals, matching terror with their own ruthlessness. That was the promise of King Harry to his death-dealing commoners at Agincourt.[7]

500 years later in the battle at Cambrai just described, however, there was no royalty present to elevate the commoner. Stormtroopers became αριστοι by fiat or forfeit, roaming, crawling, springing over shell pits and trench channels with an Homeric one-to-one imminent at every step. Options were stark: annihilation (a misstep in the pas-de-deux); the ignominy of capture; survival, as likely as not with wounds. One marvels at the irony in Ludendorff's post-war remark on the stormtroopers (his memoirs give them one paragraph), that 'They were examples to be imitated by the other men'.[8]

That Jünger himself was exemplary amongst his subordinates is simply attested by evidence within *Stahlgewitter* yet external to his narrative. In the summer campaign of 1918, after Ludendorff had expended his last offensives, and there remained no possible hope of German victory – demoralized troops in retreat mocked as 'scabs' those units advancing from the rear – Major General von Busse, commander of the 111th Infantry Division, commended the 73rd Hanoverians for sustaining their reputation for bravery 'in defence and counter-attack' against the overwhelming enemy (25 July at Copse 125), 'for I well know,' says his report of 12 August, 'what high demands of endurance and trust in duty had to be placed on the division's troops in its lengthy operation on a difficult front. In particular, Lt. Jünger, already wounded six times and this time as always a shining model for officers and men deserves recognition'.[9]

No less important was the testimony of his fellows. One morning during the campaign around Cambrai (December 1917), Jünger and some other officers were taking breakfast in a blockhouse only 100 metres from the English. A brief exchange of grenades and machine-gun fire prompted a deputy officer from a neighbouring regiment to call out volunteers for a raid. 'It represents one of those remarkable interludes,' writes Jünger, 'in which the war's history is so rich on both the large and the small scale . . . Courage, the mad-keen (tollkühn) operation of the individual always works inspiringly. We, too, were gripped with *Draufgängertum* and rushed on, gathering up some handgrenades, to participate in the improvised attack.'[10]

In this impromptu clash Germans and British exchanged grenades like snowballs. In the midst of it, Jünger's helmet was shot through and his head grazed. Shortly after, blood flowed down his face. He had been lacerated by the splinters of a wounded comrade's helmet. Weakened, he managed to get back via the village of Moeuvres to the command post and later received a silver bowl from the battalion's three other company commanders. It was inscribed 'To the Victor of Moeuvres'.

Jünger proudly nominated three of his subordinates for the Iron Cross, First Class. Eighty men had gone over; they had taken 200 prisoners and a good deal of weaponry. But the losses, noted almost parenthetically, were massive: fifty per cent.[11] Here precisely lay the absurdity of the stormtrooper as Ludendorff's example for the regular infantry's imitation: the human cost was too great and too grievous the waste. If the Cambrai assault is at all representative of losses among these highly trained personnel, it would indicate that the margin of disaster had not been reduced in the nearly three years since the initial stormtroop effort in the Argonne Forest. Of courage there was an ample store. The men, especially when fortified by drink (neither consolation nor mere relaxation, schnaps and beer were generously allowed in the army's regulations) were intrepid. They were only too few.

Their hazard points to the essential weakness of the defence-in-depth tactic, that it could not be converted effectively into an offensive. Not that the Germans did not try. They learned the lessons of trench warfare all too thoroughly. Willy Rohr's essential insight, that squads had to replace conventional skirmish lines, placed maximal weight upon the decisiveness and alacrity of youthful company commanders, most of whom were second lieutenants. The Germans had quickly realized that assault troops needed substantial and carefully timed support from artillery in order to break through the enemy's trench system. Ideally, barrages would immediately precede by as little as a few yards the first wave attack. The enemy would be stunned (it is commonly maintained that artillery did not of itself achieve high casualties – the weightiest lesson of 1 July, 1916), and the troops storming the trench lines would have a vital interval in which to 'roll them up' with hand grenades. Success in this brief time was imperative: unless the trench system was cleared, the second wave of troops could not enter its lines securely, and then the first wave it had come to support would risk being cut off by counter-attack. The stormtroops, their store of grenades likely spent, were in constant peril of disorientation, as Jünger had learned firsthand in Alsace, and distraction, especially when the enemy left foodstores and liquor visible. (Stormtroops were fed better than regulars but as the war continued, even the élite's diet became impalatable.) Besides, there was no guarantee that enemy troops, no matter how tremendously pounded by artillery, would be even momentarily incapacitated.

The German command went to elaborate lengths to prepare troops for these assaults. Whenever possible, a replica of the enemy trenches would be reproduced to scale behind the lines, sometimes in Germany itself, according to aerial reconnaissance. The attack would be planned and in rehearsal live ammunition would be employed. Grenades were at half strength. Whatever the waste of powder and even of lives, this kind of instruction was psychologically far more effective than any manual or classroom alone could have been, for by this preparation, the troops would have been through the battle before it began, they would have honed the precious arts of timing and gait, and gained confidence in their own endurance and caution within demonstrated limits. Knowing the particular trench system in advance, including its concatenated pillboxes, machine-gun nests and blockhouses, was indispensable. The stormtroops were commonly delivered from the rear by vans (a convenience bordering on luxury in that war) and under night's cover; their first view of the terrain they were to master would come in the effort itself, early in the morning.

In his well-known book on the Germans during the war[12] Hans Fried contends that stormtroopers were contemptuous of regular infantry, and infantry hostile to them. The élite troops were indeed given special consideration merited by their training and the risks they inevitably ran (extended leave and rest billets), and they did not have to endure regularly the trench's tedium, confinement and precipitous terror. Besides, in their exuberance they had developed an ésprit de corps that included familiar address of their officers, an unheard-of break with military protocol. Finally, the surviving stormtroops would be withdrawn from combat once they had achieved their mission. They did not have to face retaliatory missiles. But the assumption of commonplace antagonism between them and the regulars is probably overdrawn. For all their daily miseries and the occasional shelling, the regulars knew that the stormtroops faced intense and exceptional dangers, that they were capable of daring and stress such as most others, certainly the family men, could not have shown or endured with comparable élan.

The stormtroops, moreover, were breaking up the cosmic monotony – most men in the war were most of the time idle – striking effectively, though at high cost, at the unseen foe, and probing the line forward.

Psychology apart, logistics in fact brought the stormtroops and the regulars closer together as the war went on. Less than two months after Ludendorff took command of the German forces in the West (29 August, 1916), he had each army form an assault battalion from its ranks. By then some regiments without assault units formally assigned had been creating them ad hoc. Even before Ludendorff's authorization, Captain Rohr had written an instruction manual detailing the stormtroops' rôle: with light trench mortars, machine guns and flame-throwers, they would clear the way and so lead an attack by regular infantry companies. Following in small and irregular columns, the infantry was thus initiated into the assault.

As production of machine guns and light mortars increased, the number of common riflemen declined. By 1918, the infantry platoon was composed of a machine gun squad, a rifle squad and an assault unit. That parity allowed platoon commanders a high degree of tactical potential since the rifle squad could now be manoeuvred with the assault unit while both were sustained by the machine-gunners. 'The idea that the battlefield was a place where infantry regiments and battalions fought for general fire superiority and then clashed with each other as complete units was gone forever. In its place grew the conception that the attack of a regiment or battalion was really a series of much smaller combats, where each platoon and squad attempted to obtain a very local fire superiority and then exploit that with very local movement.' [13]

The predicate 'very local' is all important. It suggests that in adaptation to a positional war, Ludendorff unwittingly sacrificed strategy to tactics, the end to the means. Breaking through the enemy trench system became so important that its desired effect, operational freedom and its potential for destroying the enemy, virtually fell away from view.

The March 1918 campaign, initially devastating in its thrust westward, stalled because the forward lines could not be relieved sufficiently quickly from the rear. The German High Command's official directive, issued 1 January 1918, actually prescribed that the reinforcement of leading units, because it might cost time, should be secondary to their maintenance of initiative and advance. It is all the more peculiar, then, that Ludendorff seems to have betrayed this tactic in the March offensive when the Allies marshalled a strong resistance around Arras. Rather than circumventing it, he became stubbornly resolute about taking Arras, thus confounding both the substantial gains of his southern (left) flank movement and the strategy of a northward rollback of the Allies into Belgium. The stormtroops, it could be said, were obliged not only to advance the line of combat but to become it, and in the brutal *mise en scène* of a large scale offensive, their particular advantages – their smallish autonomy, their light-arms mobility – could only play calamitously against them. In all three spring offensives – 21 March, 9 April (between Ypres and Béthune) and 27 May (from north of Soissons-Reims south to Chateau Thierry) – the success of the German advances amazed the High Command as well as the Allies. But then the infantry turned a tactical triumph into a strategic disaster, exposing itself in bulges around which its foe was able to gather reinforcements. Breakthroughs evolved into entrapments, ironically the very snare which the High Command's defence-in-depth tactic had prepared for the enemy.

So much for the lure of space. And time? The high expectations placed upon timing, upon surprise, had to be dashed. The forward line could overwhelm only for so long, and then the most elementary of facts played into Germany's catastrophe: the stormtroops could go just so far on their own – three days set the approximate limit of effectiveness – before their own material and human resources were spent.

Besides, it is of the very nature of surprise to be brief. It is also double-dealing: the Germans were themselves surprised, not least by the latest Allied reinforcements, those greenest of troops from far-distant lands named Missouri and Georgia who had an undaunted and therefore daunting vim that no tactician either side of Belleau Wood could have accounted for.[14]

In 1918 Germany was undone politically and militarily by its successes in the East. Russia's concessions of land in the treaty of Brest-Litovsk convinced the Western powers that Germany was resolved upon the conquest of territory, and so they became as obdurate as the German High Command itself towards any peace initiatives. Ludendorff's Western offensives pushed against terrain that was studded with villages, woods and canals, a landscape cumbrous and defensible compared to the steppes over which Germany had scored its greatest victories in the war.

In a sense, the stormtroops themselves helped Germany to lose the war. They were well trained and then squandered. In an horrendous irony of loss, they made the tactical advances that shortchanged strategic goals.

For his part, Ernst Jünger emerged triumphant, a victor among the defeated. Having received in the war's last weeks the highest German military award, *Pour le Mérite*, he went on to write the chronicle that to this day has given the stormtroops of the Great War the image of a tenacious valour.[15]

Notes

1   These figures come from Wilhelm Kranzler, *Für Vaterland und Ehre*, Hamburg, Hansa, 1916, II:187, a consistently biassed chronicle of the first two years of the war, but indispensable because it affords the Germans' militant view of the war as it proceeded. It includes a summary index of day-to-day events on all fronts as well as lengthy citations of officers' battle reports. Despite the purport of his subtitle, *Wahrheitsgetreue Geschichte des grossen Krieges*, Kranzler does not always report German losses. It is not clear why the introduction of stormtroop divisions was not decisive. Instead, we find the rationalization which became standard after 1918, that against Allied quantitive superiority in *matériel* and manpower, the Germans brought the qualitative heroism of 'toughness, steadfastness and a lust for the attack' (II, p. 185).

2   Reported in Kranzler, III, p. 215.

3   Lt. Gen. Wilhelm Balck, 'Organisation und Taktik im deutschen Heere,' in

Max Schwarte, ed., *Die militärischen Lehren des grossen Krieges*, Berlin: Mittler, 1923, p. 56.

4 See, for example, *Im Felde unbesiegt*, Gustav von Dickhuth-Harrach, ed., Munich: Lehmann, 1921; *Auf See unbesiegt*, G. von Mantey, ed., Munich: Lehmann, 1921.

5 Franz Schauwecker, *Im Todesrachen*, Halle: Dickmann, 1919, pp. 282–283.

6 Jünger passes over some crucial facts about the egg grenades. The German *Eierhandgranate* had a distinctive advantage over its British counter: weighing only 11 ounces it could be thrown as far as fifty yards. The British (Mills) grenade weighed over twice as much, 23 ounces. The German egg needed no detonator. So efficient was it that the British copied it, reducing their own grenade weight to 12 ounces.

7 *King Henry the Fifth*: 'For he today that sheds his blood with me shall be my brother; be he ne'er so vile, this day shall gentle his condition.'

8 Erich Ludendorff, *My War Memories 1914–1918*, London: Hutchinson and Company, n.d., I, p. 273. German edn. was 1919.

9 *Stahlgewitter*, 1st ed., p. 172. For some reason, Jünger omitted von Busse's commendation from the 1934 edition.

10 *ibid.*, p. 131–132. *Draufgängertum* might be defined as an over-the-top or "up-an'-at-'em" spirit among the troops.

11 This episode is recounted by Desmond Young, *Rommel: The Desert Fox*, New York: Berkeley, 1961, pp. 25–26. Young, who had served near Cambrai at the time, read Jünger's account and takes it as evidence of how 'The German professional soldier has always taken war with a seriousness with which only sport is treated by the British.' He depicts the *Draufgängertum* as a break from a Sunday afternoon brandy: '"Why not let's go over and raid the English?" someone suggested.' But Jünger makes clear that the initiative came from an officer's boldness, intoxicated by drink to rage. The ensuing action had had some grenades' provocation. Young almost trivializes the result: ' . . . because the early afternoon was not the recognized time for raids' (bad sports, these German chaps) 'it was successful and the company officers returned ten minutes later in triumph, bringing with them two or three prisoners and leaving behind them two or three dead.' In fact some 200 prisoners, some 40 German dead.

12 Hans Ernst Fried, *The Guilt of the German Army*, New York, Macmillan, 1942, pp. 167–168.

13 Bruce Gudmundsson, *Stormtroop Tactics: Innovations in the German Army, 1914–1918,* New York, Praeger, 1989, pp. 101–102. As Gudmundsson notes, p. 152, n.2, the December 1916 training manual, though recognizing the need for training officers (including the non-commissioned) in stormtroop tactics, assumed 'that infantry tactics would revert, more or less, to those which had been taught in peacetime once the war of movement resumed.' The January 1918 revision of the manual, however, required that every infantryman be trained for storm trooping.

14 For that kind of fighting see the definitive account, *Fix Bayonets!* by U.S. Marine Corps Captain John W. Thomason, Jr., New York: C. Scribner's Sons, 1926.

15 The English translation of *In Stahlgewittern, The Storm of Steel*, has recently been reprinted by Constable Publishers, London.

Chapter 22

The Last Hurrah: Cavalry on the Western Front, August–September 1914

Richard Holmes

The First World War was not one war but many. The differences start with
terrain and climate: British soldiers fought everywhere from midwinter
Flanders (and even colder north Russia), through searing Mesopotamian
summers and steamy East African autumns to a drenching Gallipoli winter.
We tend to associate Gallipoli with the midsummer misery of flies, but it
is worth remembering that this little dog-leg peninsula itself had radical
swings of climate: on 26–7 November 1915 1st Lancashire Fusiliers lost
20 men drowned, 19 frozen to death and another 536 evacuated sick.[1]

Even the Western Front contained contrasts so stark as to suggest that
it was the theatre of several campaigns for which, to my mind, Haig's
description of 'one great and continuous engagement' is singularly inapt.[2]
Try it now. A day's hard driving will take you from alluvial Flanders,
across the dreary post-industrial Douai plain, and over Vimy Ridge to
Artois limestone and Picardy chalk. Then comes the great sweep of dry
Champagne, bubbling into the bottleneck of the Argonne and out onto the
bleak uplands around Verdun. The sticky Woevre plateau, between Meuse
and Moselle, strikes a chord with Flanders, and little more than an hour's
drive south, under the blue line of the Vosges, stand rocks where
Gebirgsjäger and *Chasseurs Alpins* came into their own.

There were different opponents against whom one played by different
rules. Germans, Turks, Austro-Hungarians and Bulgarians all behaved
differently, in the line and out of it. And 'German' is itself too large a
package to contain martial Brandenburgers, who never let up; more
indolent Saxons, who were often prepared to come to a quiet understanding; and almost *méridional* Bavarians who might, in the same week,
give you a trench raid (they were fond of using the sharpened shovel in
such brawls) and a moonlight serenade. A British soldier captured by the

Germans might expect hard but correct treatment. If he fell into Turkish hands he would be more likely to die than to survive. The Australians, in contrast, at first suspected the Turks of atrocities and were inclined to take few prisoners, but soon their respect for the Turks grew. 'Little Mehmet' was known almost affectionately, as 'Abdul', 'Johnny Turk' or 'Jacko'. When the 3rd Light Horse Brigade was evacuated from Gallipoli its commander left a message announcing: 'we Australians desire to express appreciation of the fine soldierly qualities of our TURKISH opponents and of the sportsmanlike manner in which they have participated in a very interesting contest, honourable, we trust, to both sides.'[3] But the Australians tended to regard the fighting on the Western Front as something of a needle match. 'I was filled with delight to see so many Huns killed,' wrote one, 'and could not help laughing.'[4]

Command in any war is situational, and we should not be surprised that in a compendium of so many wars a general might fail in one and succeed in another. Allenby was scarcely a success as an army commander on the Western Front: the waspish Sir James Edmonds called his career there 'one of gross stupidity from first to last.'[5] The Battle of Arras in April 1917 cost 150,000 British and Dominion casualties, with a daily loss-rate exceeded only during the German March offensive of 1918.[6] Canadian seizure of Vimy Ridge – no less momentous in terms of enduring national symbolism than the Australian capture of Pozières eight months before – was the only splash of colour on a gloomy canvas. It was the Bull at his most bullish. As Aylmer Haldane ruefully observed, it took enormous moral courage to question an operation foredoomed to failure, since the result would be a wrecked career. In the freezing weather Allenby's order that troops would not wear or carry greatcoats was not widely appreciated. His insistence that 'all troops must understand that the Third Army is now pursuing a defeated enemy and that risks must be freely taken' was regarded with incredulity, but his cavalry loyally trotted off to calamity in the crater fields around Monchy-le-Preux: some sang the Eton Boating Song as they disappeared into the blizzard.[7] And yet the same Allenby was successful in Palestine. Not necessarily because he had learnt much – but because his style of command, which produced only the worst sort of shoving-match on the Western Front, worked better when there were flanks to be found.

Robin Prior and Trevor Wilson point to a similar situational ingredient in Rawlinson's leadership. He did not learn in a smooth curve, going from divisional commander at Ypres in 1914, through corps commander at Neuve Chapelle in 1915 to army commander on the Somme in 1916 and at Amiens in 1918, amassing useful knowledge as he went. He showed no consistent advance in wisdom, and displayed an infirmity of purpose often laced paradoxically into a doggedness which even Allenby might have envied. Perhaps the single most important reason for his army's stunning successes in 1918 was that his permissive style of command, which had not worked well when his subordinates lacked experience and the enemy front was rock-solid, was more fruitful when he presided over a galaxy of talented subordinates facing an enemy on the back foot. Arms, not the man, had changed.[8]

So we have a war which Trevor Wilson was entirely correct to see as having a myriad faces.[9] And some of these faces were more ancient than modern, which brings us to the summer of 1914. In many respects the war's first campaign, which took the contending armies from their homes and barracks to stalemate on the Aisne, had more in common with the Franco-Prussian War thirty-four years before (and within the military memory of Kitchener, Joffre and Moltke, each of whom bore its marks in different ways) than it did with First Ypres only six weeks later.

Let us ask ourselves what was really new about the armies of 1914. Certainly not the way they looked. Captain Walter Bloem expressed the continental soldier's surprise at the unmartial dress of the British when he saw his first British soldier at Terte, near Mons on 23 August 1914, clad in what he took to be a golfing-suit.[10] At least British officers still carried swords: Lieutenant Alan Hanbury-Sparrow of the Royal Berkshires ran his man through with one at First Ypres, and even at Neuve Chapelle five months later some British officers went over the top, like their grandfathers assaulting the Redan before Sebastopol, with sword and pistol.[11] German regular and reserve formations marched away in field-grey tunics, generously garnished with piping, frogging, collar patches, and lace in a dozen colours, topped with pikelhaube, shako, schapka, busby or dragoon helmet. Uniform is scarcely the word for the embellishments to Austrian regulation pike-grey, and Patrick Leigh-Fermor's friend Istvan wistfully remembered that even in 1917: 'You should have seen us moving off for Galicia and Bukovina. The Uhlans in the square czapkas and red trousers, dragoons in long Waffenrocks, and hussars like us in pale blue.'[12]

The French had retained uniforms of traditional colour and cut. A prewar Minister of War had assured the Chamber of Deputies that the red trousers of French infantry were sacrosanct, because *Le pantalon rouge, c'est la France*. French cavalry struck their British counterparts as particularly old-fashioned. Corporal Percy Snelling of the 12th Lancers complained that 'they do not fight much dismounted and their carbines are very unreliable.'[13] A sapper officer, Second-Lieutenant Kenneth Godsell, found French cuirassiers 'easy to see at long distances, as the sun flashed in all directions from their shining breastplates. As the latter were not bullet-proof, it was difficult to understand their exact function.'[14]

Weapons and tactics were as much ancient as modern. The weapon carried by the most numerous of the men of 1914, the infantry whose long dusty columns filled the roads that aching and interminable summer, was the bolt action magazine rifle, product of Nineteenth-Century technology. It would not have seemed bizarre to the men who had plied needle-gun or

Chassepot at Rezonville. The French Lebel had come into service in 1886, the German Mauser thirteen years later, and the British Short Magazine Lee-Enfield as recently as 1902.

And what of the use to which these rifles were put? The Franco-Prussian War had shown what happened to infantry who attempted to assault others in a position which favoured defence: the fate of the Prussian Guard at St Privat on 18 August 1870, was as militarily instructive as it was socially calamitous. In its aftermath a new air of realism blew through infantry drill-books. The French 1875 Regulations forebade close-order formations within effective range of the enemy's fire, and decreed that the skirmish line – which had traditionally preceded the main body of attacking infantry – was actually to be 'fed' so as to constitute the attack itself. But there was a speedy reaction. In part this was founded on the misplaced conviction that to attack was manly, to shirk from it cowardly. In part, too, it reflected Ardant Du Picq's warning that on the fire-swept battlefield 'cohesion is no longer ensured by mutual observation.'[15] What would happen when these new, loose formations, composed, for the most part, of conscripts, collided with enemy fire? They would go to ground and, as history so abundantly demonstrated, many of them would stay there. From the 1880s till the outbreak of war infantry theorists grappled with this problem. Many concluded that the answer was to weld men together just as tightly as in the past, throwing them into battle shoulder to shoulder to the sound of drum and bugle. This would result in appalling losses in the short term – but it would at least produce a decision, not sterile butchery. And it would avoid what one caustic French officer described as 'acute Transvaalitis' – paralysis by fire.[16]

Even the British army, which had, after all, studied the epidemiology of Transvaalitis at some collective cost, concluded, in *Infantry Training* 1914 that 'The object of infantry in the attack is . . . to get to close quarters as quickly as possible.' Once there, the commander on the spot was to judge when superiority of fire had been achieved and then order the assault. And now, believe it or not, I quote.

> The commander who decides to order the assault will order the charge to be sounded, the call will at once be taken up by all buglers, and all neighbouring units will join in the charge as quickly as possible. During the assault the men will cheer, bugles be sounded, and pipes played.[17]

This looks to me no different in principle to the infantry tactics in vogue when the line was red rather than khaki. Establish what passes for superiority of fire, and when you believe you have done so, take the bayonet to the other fellow: the chances are that he will not wait for its arrival. My old colleague Paddy Griffith has written about this to good effect in *Forward Into Battle*, showing that despite the apparent improvements in infantry weapons over the period of the firepower revolution of the second half of the Nineteenth Century, the range at which infantry combats took place did not significantly increase.

Although *Field Service Regulations Part 1 (Operations)* declared that the effective fighting range of infantry was 600 to 1400 yards and anything under 600 was close range, the majority of British infantry combat in the summer of 1914 was much, much closer.[18] I would not pretend that the easy availability of anecdote can compensate for the absence of reliable statistics. But let me just pick two descriptions, almost at random. Lieutenant George Roupell's battalion of the East Surreys stood in II Corps' line west of Mons on 23 August. 'We got into a position on the embankment,' he wrote,

> and as the enemy came through the wood about 200 yards in front they presented a magnificent target . . . Despite the short range a number of them were firing high but I found it difficult to control the fire as there was so much noise. Eventually I drew my sword and walked along the line beating men on the backside, and, as I got their attention, telling them to fire low. So much for all our beautiful fire orders taught in peacetime.[19]

On the afternoon of 25 August the German 48th Infantry Regiment and B Squadron 15th Hussars, divisional cavalry of 2nd Division, clashed on the Sambre bridge at Maroilles, home of a delightfully pungent cheese. The hussars carried the Short Magazine Lee Enfield and were skilled in its use. Private Ted Fowler remembered that:

> We sent our horses back. We could see Germans creeping across the bridge and we fired away at them but they kept coming. Close enough for me to see a man with big Kaiser moustaches. He came running forward and I was sort of sorry when I shot him down. Then the Berkshires came up and we went back.

And what happened when the Berkshires arrived? There was no distant fusillade, making the most of the SMLE's long-range sight, but what Private Alfred Green called 'a rare old hand-to-hand fight, bayonet and butt, and, as our other companies came up, the Germans fell back to the bridge.'[20]

Nor, at this stage in the war, did machine-guns change the old-fashioned nature of infantry combat. There were really very few of them. The British had two per battalion and there were six in a three-battalion German regiment's machine-gun company, with another 17 independent machine-gun detachments with six guns apiece. The entire German army, better-provided with these weapons than allies or enemies, had only 2,400 machine-guns with its field armies and fortress troops in August 1914 at a time when there were a staggering 3,840,000 Germans under arms, over two million of them with the field armies. All these weapons were water-cooled and belt fed, and while they could be carried or dragged short distances they relied for mobility on horse-drawn wagons and limbers. Finally, although they were unquestionably effective, they were best suited to positional defence, when the flanking fire of one detachment could sweep the front of another.

But was it not a gunners' war? That it became one is not in doubt, and for the war as a whole guns and mortars were the main producers of battle casualties, hitting (and statistics invariably vary between armies and fronts) around 70% of those killed or wounded. But in 1914 artillery was generally smaller in calibre and thinner on the ground than it was even a year later. In the British army there was a single four-gun battery of 60-pounder heavies in each division: the remaining 72 pieces were 18-pounders or 4.5 howitzers. The 77mm gun was the workhorse of German field artillery, and it is not until we reach the foot artillery regiment at corps level, with its 15cm howitzers (5.9s to the British), that we encounter real muscle. In August 1914 many of these 15cms were the elderly 1900 pattern with a maximum range of only 6,616 yards: the much better 1913 pattern, which reached out another 3,000 yards, was being brought into service as war broke out. At the other extreme, trench mortars were a rarity. The British had none; the Germans only 160: by the war's end no less than 18,000 had been used in the German army.[21]

If weapons were generally light, the shells they fired were unsophisticated. British field guns – 13-pounders for the Royal Horse Artillery and 18-pounders for the Royal Field Artillery – fired only shrapnel and had no high explosive until First Ypres. German gunners were better-equipped and had both HE and shrapnel, giving an important advantage in actions like Le Cateau and Néry when gun sometimes took on gun with direct fire.

Gunners on both sides could use indirect fire, engaging targets invisible from the gun-line, their fire controlled by observation officers forward with the infantry, or up trees, towers or even collapsible ladders. But there were several reasons why direct fire was more popular in August 1914, and communications were the most important. Forward observation officers could pass messages to the guns by telephone or semaphore, neither method ideal in a mobile war. More often than not guns were wheeled into line, detachments hunched up behind the gunshields, taking on a target they could see. In the flank-guard action at Elouges on 24 August (more costly to the British than the battle of Mons the day before) both British batteries engaged – L Battery RHA and 119th Battery RFA – used direct fire, L Battery against a mass of German infantry debouching down the valley of the Honnelle, and 119th Battery against nine German batteries on the Mons-Valenciennes road.

At Le Cateau two days later the Commanders Royal Artillery of the British 3rd and 5th Divisions decided that the infantry might not stand without the intimate support of their gunner brothers, and batteries were pushed well forward. Some guns were dug right into the infantry firing line with orders not to fire till the final assault. Second-Lieutenant Clarrie Hodgson of 122nd Battery, part of XXVIII Brigade RFA, remembered his division's Staff Captain Royal Artillery riding over and telling the officers and men in his battery that the situation was 'very, very serious and he was depending on us. He left us in no doubt as to what we were expected to do when we went into action. He said it was up to us, that we'd done well and he knew we'd do well again and wouldn't let him down.' By the time it was told to withdraw the brigade had lost CO, adjutant and two of its three battery commanders.[22] The Royal West Kents, just behind the gun line (in itself a telling point), rose to their feet to cheer the drivers and their teams as they hurtled up in an effort to haul their pieces to safety, but the story ended sadly, as it did for so many 18-pounder batteries that day. Lieutenant Lionel Lutyens glanced back as he galloped off the position to see: 'an extraordinary sight, a wild scene of galloping and falling horses, then everyone gone, dead horses and dead men everywhere, four guns left solitary on the position, a few wagon limbers lying about, and one standing on the skyline with its pole straight up in the air. *Voilà Tout.*[23]

If I had said that this quote came from Sedan or Königgrätz, or even Waterloo, you would probably have believed me, for it tells the old story of gunners at war from the Sixteenth Century onwards: at their business amongst the ranks of the infantry, standing the fire of infantry and artillery alike, taking on targets they could see, kept brave by the knowledge that their infantry expected much of them, and set a gallant example by their officers. Lieutenant Tom Butt, whose King's Own Yorkshire Light Infantry battalion was fighting to a finish on the Roman Road at Le Cateau, saw the last gun in one of XXVIII Brigade's batteries, just behind him, served by the battery commander and his sergeant-major.[24]

And as to command, not much of the methodology of August 1914 would have shocked the elder Moltke. Most generals lived in the saddle. The fact that Douglas Haig of I Corps was so unwell that he had to use his staff car not his charger on 25 August was remarkable enough for Captain John Charteris of his staff to note it in his diary, and at Le Cateau when Horace Smith-Dorrien of II Corps wondered what was happening on his left flank, he galloped over to it, going like a good 'un across the stubble out under the shrapnel-bursts.[25] Of course the telephone was available, but despite the efforts of the Royal Engineers Signal Service it was little use at brigade level or below, and even communications between corps and GHQ were patchy. In a broader sense it was not primarily the growth of killing-power that gave the Western Front its distinctive character: it was the fact that communications consistently lagged behind weaponry. It was always easier for a defender, driven back on his own communications, to reinforce his failure than it was for an attacker, his communications stretched across the abrasive edge of the battlefield, to reinforce his success. The question is intimately bound up with that of styles of command – *auftragstaktik* as opposed to *befehlstaktik* – and I am sure that it is in these areas that some of the most fruitful research on the war will soon be carried out.

The picture I have painted so far is one of an essentially Nineteenth Century campaign, and had the war ended in September 1914 – by no means impossible had Moltke been more, or Joffre less, resolute – it would have seemed a logical continuation of the pattern of 1866 and 1870–71. It is in this context that we ought to consider cavalry. There are few subjects where prejudice has a clearer run than with the mounted arm in the First World War. John Terraine took a good cut at the myth with 'Cavalry Generals and the "Gee" in Gap', but it canters on into the sunset, as brainless as the stereotyped cavalry officers it likes to depict.[26]

It is not my aim to fight my way over the same ground already crossed by Mr Terraine, who is chiefly concerned with debunking the myth that 'all generals were cavalrymen.' He maintains, not unreasonably, that 'the overwhelming majority of the generals actually handling troops in battle came, as one might expect, from the arm which produced the over-whelming majority of those troops: the infantry.' He might usefully have added that, of the many cavalry generals who commanded infantry forma-tions, several earned the respect of their adoptive arm. Both Tom Bridges and David Campbell, extreme specimens of what we might term *homo caballus*, made robust infantry divisional commanders.[27] And far from all cavalry officers being neck-or-nothing merchants, he quite rightly accuses Lieutenant-General Kavanagh of the Cavalry Corps of having too little dash at Cambrai in 1917, rather than the more commonly-diagnosed cavalry disease of too much.

I shall address instead the question of cavalry in the opening weeks of the war. Here I contend that there was indeed a place for it, for it could carry out functions which could not be performed by any other arm. My arguments apply to the Western Front in particular, but can be writ far larger for the Eastern. There troop and weapon density, those two important ingredients of trenchlock, were always thinner than on the Western Front. Both geography and the natural aptitudes of many of the combatants helped ensure that cavalry remained important in the east not merely throughout the First World War, but on into the Russo-Polish War and even into the Second.

Cavalry was unquestionably but not unreasonably numerous. At the outbreak of war Germany fielded 110 regiments with a strength of a little over 700 officers and men apiece, or 77,000 cavalrymen in a field army over two million strong. The BEF of August 1914 had nearly 10,000 cavalry for its 66,000 infantry, a higher proportion of sabres to rifles than at any other time in the war.[28] Although details varied with national and personal preferences, there was broad agreement between cavalry theorists that these mounted men existed to carry out three functions. First came what was then called 'deep strategic reconnaissance and exploitation,' the job of independent cavalry corps tasked directly by the commander-in-chief. We would now shrink from the description strategic, and place this activity firmly at the operational level of war, for these horsemen were intended to provide the theatre commanders and their senior subordinates with crucial information. Next was the protection of the moving army and its lines of communication, entrusted to what the British termed 'protective cavalry', and finally came close reconnaissance and communications within the division, the task of divisional cavalry.[29]

We might pause and ask ourselves just who else might have done these jobs in 1914. Deep reconnaissance was already becoming a task of the air arm. But in 1914 there were few aircraft available, and those that existed were technically too limited to carry out this role with much success. The RFC's first wartime mission was, as a recent history admits, 'not a very convincing performance', while thick morning mists played havoc with von Kluck's air reconnaissance, helping ensure that he bumped the BEF at Mons with no idea of what he was stumbling into.[30] The British had better information. Some of it came from air reconnaissance, however rudimentary; some from Lieutenant Colonel George Barrow's unofficial expedient of phoning post offices to see how far the Germans had got, and much from the cavalry.[31] When Tom Bridges' squadron of the 4th Dragoon Guards met a German patrol at Casteau, north-east of Mons, on 22 August, it brought back information of a quality then unmatched by anything the air could do. The Germans were the 4th Cuirassiers of 9th Cavalry Division, part of von der Marwitz's II Cavalry Corps. GHQ's intelligence branch suspected that this pointed to a wide outflanking move, for an independent cavalry corps was exactly the sort of formation one would expect to find on the outer edge of a broad right hook. The fact that the British cavalry division and a substantial amount of the BEF's artillery was shifted to cover the left flank on the night of 22/23 August was due to this, and information like it. Had GHQ shown more preparedness to credit the cavalry's reports rather than to believe the sort of moonshine which still beamed from GQG, the BEF would have been even better placed to fight its first battle.

If deep reconnaissance faced a technological gulf which air power was only beginning to fill, exploitation was in an even deeper abyss, which only the development of light armour, nearly four years on, was to bridge. As to the other functions of cavalry, the answer is clear: the mounted arm could exercise functions that no other could. True, some of the more mundane and road-bound tasks of divisional cavalry could be carried out by cyclists, but the British expedient of collocating the divisional cavalry squadron with the divisional cyclist company enabled the staff to get the best out of both arms.

The debate over the way in which cavalry would carry out these functions has been capably summarised elsewhere: Edward Spiers' 1979 article on 'The British Cavalry in 1914' has still not been bettered for a general study, and I do no more than sketch out the discussion here. There was wide recognition that cavalry would operate by a mixture of mounted shock and dismounted fire. By 1914 many theorists, citing examples from the American Civil and Franco-Prussian wars, agreed that there would be few opportunities for shock action. The prolific and experienced Prince Kraft zu Hohenlohe-Ingelfingen reckoned that the unique value of cavalry lay in its rapid movement rather than its ability to charge home, while his countryman Lieutenant-General Friedrich von Bernhardi argued that most of the problems which would present themselves to cavalry could only be solved by fire action.[32]

However, it was not only traditionalists who remained convinced that there would be times when shock action was necessary. There would be moments when elements of a large conscript army would become demoralised and vulnerable to cavalry attack. And in any event, the first act of a future war would be a battle between the opposing cavalries, and only troopers who had the necessary mounted skills and confidence in their ability to charge home could hope to win it. Even Douglas Haig, well out on the traditionalist flank as far as the British army was concerned, freely admitted that fire action was nine-tenths more likely than shock action. But without the confidence to take shock action, cavalry would be emasculated – perhaps that metaphor is precisely the right one – for the dash upon which it depended as an arm would be gone for ever.

Support for shock action was, then, not merely about the utility of a particular form of tactics. It was about faith, and in this context the charge was at least as much a ritual as a battle-drill. There is also more than a little read-across into infantry tactics, for theorists, mounted or foot, were uncomfortably aware that one result of firepower might be paralysis: the Aisne was to prove just how right they were. Sir John French, no tactical genius in 1914, but a cavalry officer of wide experience, was quite clear that the trick lay in combining the mental attitude which would encourage horsemen to take advantage of fleeting opportunities with the recognition that fire kills. His 1906 preface to von Bernhardi's *Cavalry in Future Wars* emphasised that he was 'absolutely convinced that the Cavalry Spirit is and may be encouraged to the utmost without in the least degree prejudicing either training in dismounted duties or the acquirement of such tactical knowledge on the part of leaders as will enable them to discern when and where to resort to dismounted methods.'[33]

As far as the British army is concerned we should not make too much of the endless wrangling over the phraseology of the cavalry drill book. Such niceties had a much-blunted impact by the time they filtered down to regimental level, where so many officers and men had heard:

The flying bullet down the pass
That whistles clear: 'All flesh is grass.'

The adoption of the Short Magazine Lee Enfield rifle (the same weapon carried by infantry and cavalry alike) in 1902, linked to the experience of the Boer War inspired a revival in cavalry shooting. The following year Private Bertie Seed of the 4th Hussars won the Indian musketry prize at 600 yards, and in 1908 the 14th Hussars had 354 marksmen, 212 first class shots, 35 second class shots and a mere four 3rd class shots.[34] In 1910 Lieutenant-Colonel Edwards, an Indian Army officer who had won a DSO in South Africa, summed up what most cavalry officers regarded as a decent compromise. 'The desire to use sword or lance should be predominant,' he wrote, 'but it should be held in check by a thorough knowledge of the power of the firearm.'[35]

That the British cavalry was ahead of its allies and opponents is beyond question. Lieutenant-General von Poseck, inspector-general of German cavalry, admitted that his own army had got the balance wrong:

> the greatest emphasis was placed by us on the skilful grouping of forces in the mounted combat since, at the beginning of the campaign, we calculated more particularly on this kind of fighting . . . Despite the improvements made in fighting dismounted, there was nevertheless a lack of schooling in firing practices in the larger units.

The French were in a worse state because cavalry tactics had, not unnaturally, trotted in step with the doctrine of the offensive battle, and the French alone retained armoured cuirassiers for use in shock action in the opening cavalry engagement which was so confidently expected.[36]

In the summer of 1993 I rode the route of the Retreat from Mons. I was accompanied by a genial Grenadier, Brigadier Evelyn Webb-Carter and, I am ashamed to say, by a small support crew, prominent amongst whom was John O'Flaherty, late Corporal of Horse in the Household Cavalry Mounted Regiment. It was the right time of year; I followed the right route, village by village, and at the end of a fortnight the realities of the campaign were etched deep into mind – and backside. I had read letters and diaries extensively before departing, and by way of conclusion will consider a few historical points underlined by hoof-prints and sweat.[37]

There can be no escaping the cavalryman's symbiotic relationship with what that doughty Napoleonic *beau sabreur* F. de Brack called 'part of himself' – his horse.[38] It was a horsey summer, as Walter Bloem, mobilising with the Brandenburg Grenadiers, saw.

> Then there were the horses – snorting, rearing, stamping everywhere. Sturdy cart-horses, powerful runners, light hacks from gentlemen's stables, prancing thoroughbreds, steeple-chasers, browns, blacks, chest-

nuts, bays, all sorts and colours, excited by the change from their daily routine, the railway journey, the great gathering of their kind, by the cracking of many whips, and the shouting – all sweat and commotion.[39]

A good horse meant everything – Brack was right to declare that 'the strength of the horse is the fortune of its rider' – and scarcely a day went by when I did not have cause to thank my horse's gentleness and courage. Private Garrod of the 20th Hussars (privates in line cavalry regiments did not officially gain the title 'trooper' till after the war) was not as lucky, and mobilised with a horse nicknamed 'Syphilis' because nobody wanted to catch it. When it was being winched aboard the transport at Southampton it kicked out and broke the farrier sergeant-major's arm: in the ensuing confusion the winch crew lost its presence of mind and 'Old Syph' disappeared into the water, never to be seen again. Garrod went to war on the sergeant-major's horse, and all was well.[40] Lieutenant Henry Owens, a hunting doctor hastily commissioned into the RAMC, knew what he was about, and drew 'a nice horse, a long tailed bay, well bred, nice mouth and manners and nice paces . . . a topping ride.'[41]

There was inevitably a sad side to all this. Private Nobby Clarke of the Bays was shocked by his first sight of multiple death in battle at Néry on 1 September. But what hurt him as much was the fact that:

I never saw my horse again. She was called Daisy. She was a lovely, docile, intelligent girl. I had a quick look for her but I suppose she's been either blown to bits or stampeded and ended up as someone else's mount in another regiment.[42]

Frank Pusey of 31st Howitzer Battery RFA recalled that 14 September was his first bad day, when:

the Battery was shaken at the loss of so many old friends. One gun team of black horses – the pride of No 1 Section – which were used for funerals at Woolwich, were all killed while standing with the gun limber on the flank of the battery.[43]

Nobby Clarke was not alone in finding the plight of blameless horses harder to bear than that of men. 'We were often hungry,' he remembered,

and so were the mules and horses and how those poor creatures suffered. I think they must have been more tired and out of condition then we were. Innocent victims of man-made madness. They broke your heart, especially when you passed the injured ones, left to die, in agony and screaming with pain and terror.[44]

British accounts are highly critical of the horsemastership of the French cavalrymen, who rarely dismounted on the line of march. Second Lieutenant Kenneth Godsell wrote that:

> The French cavalrymen was rarely seen off his horse. He had a rooted objection to dismounting. His animals were looking very thin and tired as a result of long and trying marches in this hot weather.[45]

On our march we dismounted regularly and took the girths down a hole or two to make the horses more comfortable. This caused as much local surprise in 1993 as it had seventy-nine years before.

We were off roads most of the time and, once we knew the form we grew quite cavalier about riding anywhere that was not under crops. This gave me a feel for the ground that had eluded me on my many visits to the same battlefields and emphasises the importance of 'microterrain' which is so often massaged out of the heavier end of military history. Riding the retreat showed just how the British cavalry managed to combine mounted and dismounted action so successfully, and how there was simply no other arm that could have done the job.

The little action at Cerizy was fought on 28 August between 5th Cavalry Brigade, part of a flank-guard screening I Corp's left in the valley of the Oise, and the Guard Cavalry Division, point of the German 2nd Army. The leading German regiment, 2nd Guard Dragoons, bumped the British rear-guard, C Squadron of the Royal Scots Greys, fighting dismounted. J Battery RHA joined in and helped pin the Germans, who had themselves dismounted, to a forward slope in front of Puisieux Farm. The 12th Lancers, resting in the nearby village of Moy, got a squadron and the machine-gun section into action on the German left flank, followed by the remaining two squadrons, who worked their way forward dismounted. The lancers' adjutant then discovered that one of the re-entrants nudging up into the slope would enable the leading squadron to get within charging distance without being seen. I suspect that the lancers moved faster than middle-aged historians on sturdy hunters – having the lances of the second rank a foot or two from your spine would certainly encourage you to kick on – but it took us well under thirty seconds for us to emerge from the re-entrant and gallop over the German position. The Germans got off one volley – which wounded the lancers' CO and killed the squadron leader – but were wiped out by sword, lance and pistol. 2nd Guard Dragoons were badly mauled, and, fortuitously, as J Battery lifted its fire when the charge went in its shells burst amongst the Guard Rifle Battalion, which was just coming up to help the dragoons. The Guard Cavalry Division had the edge taken off its ardour for the rest of the day, and that very vulnerable gap between the British corps was protected. Could any other arm have got there in time but withdrawn rapidly enough? And could mounted infantry, so beloved of the pre-war reformers, have used shock to present for payment the cheque made out by fire? Emphatically not.

The action points up another of the eternal truths of war. Whatever the law may say, it is difficult to persuade men who have just passed through the zone of the enemy's fire and seen their comrades killed to cease aggression on the instant. The lancers' adjutant recorded cheerfully that he was not carrying the new pattern thrusting sword but 'the old cutting sword which went in and out of the German like a pat of butter.'[46] He killed five dragoons, and another officer got three with his sword and one with his revolver. I am not altogether persuaded that all were offering resistance. Paul Maze, interpreter with the Greys, arrived on the position as the Greys charged to support the lancers, and observed:

As a few Germans were hiding in the corn stooks lances and swords were thrust through the hay and I heard fearful yells. The horses were very excited, as were the men, who were showing to one another the blood dripping off their sword-blades. Others were picking up souvenirs.[47]

As we swung back across the stubble we passed the village cemetery in Moy, and there, behind a Second World War bomber crew, all Australians, we found Captain Michel of the 12th Lancers who fell, as the inscription on his headstone proudly proclaims, 'gallantly leading his squadron.' His squadron quartermaster-sergeant lies beside him, and in the same little row is Major Swetenham of the Greys, killed while directing the fire of his regiment's dismounted squadron.

These graves of men who died as their great grandfathers might have done at Waterloo, sword in hand and horse beneath them, again emphasise the old-fashioned character of those first few weeks. Perhaps Major Swetenham and Captain Michel were lucky in their way, for the open warfare for which they had trained would outlive them for only a month or so. And once firepower began to freeze mobility into deadlock on the Aisne so the character of the war changed. Captain Arthur Osburn, the increasingly disillusioned medical officer of 4th Dragoon Guards, heard modern smash squarely into ancient as two heavy shells slammed into one of those fortress-walled farms on the dry limestone overlooking the Aisne.

Fragments of stone, manure, pieces of clothing and hair came falling about me as I ran through the archway and beheld one of the most heartrending sights I have ever seen, even in war. The detachment of 9th Lancers had almost completely disappeared. In the centre of the yard where I had seen them but a moment before, there was now a mound four or five feet high of dead men and horses . . . Around this central heap of dead men the wounded lay on all sides. Some had been blown to the back of the yard, their backs broken. One sat up dazed and whimpering, his back against a wall, holding part of his intestines in his hand.[48]

Small wonder that when Richard Chant of the 5th Dragoon Guards was reminiscing about his own days under arms, he focused not on the white heat of the new war but on the rough familiarity of the old, and paid whimsical tribute to his mates who had died as a trooper ought.

So good luck to all the Pals I know
That's had the life-long run
Especially those who took the jump
On the back of his long-faced Chum[49]

Notes

1   George Ashurst, *My Bit: A Lancashire Fusilier at War 1914–18* (Ed Richard Holmes), Ramsbury, Crowood Press, 1987, pp.69–70.

2   Field-Marshal Sir Douglas Haig, 'Final Despatch' 21 March 1919, Lieutenant-Colonel J.H. Boraston, *Sir Douglas Haig's Despatches*, London, J.M. Dent, 1920, p.319.

3   Supplementary material, War Diary 3rd Light Horse Brigade, quoted in Bill Gammage, *The Broken Years: Australian Soldiers in the Great War*, Canberra, Australian National University, 1974, p.113. For a penetrating analysis of the Anzac legend see Alistair Thomson, *Anzac Memories*, Melbourne, Oxford University Press, 1994.

4   Corporal W.D.Gallwey, letter 2 August 1917, quoted in Gammage *Broken Years*, p.225.

5   Quoted in Lawrence James, *Imperial Warrior: The Life and Times of Field-Marshal Viscount Allenby*, London, Weidenfeld and Nicolson, 1993, p.107.

6   John Terraine, *The Smoke and the Fire: Myths and Anti-Myths of War 1861–1945*, London, Leo Cooper, 1992, pp.46, 98–9.

7   James, *Imperial Warrior* p.101.

8   Robin Prior and Trevor Wilson, *Command on the Western Front: The Military Career of Sir Henry Rawlinson 1914–1918*, Oxford, Blackwell, 1992.

9   Trevor Wilson, *The Myriad Faces of War*, Cambridge, Polity Press, 1986.

10   Walter Bloem, *The Advance from Mons*, London, Peter Davies, 1938, p.57.

11   Alan Hanbury-Sparrow, *The Land-Locked Lake*, London, Arthur Barker, 1932, p.127. For Neuve Chapelle see John Baynes, *Morale: A Story of Men and Courage: The Second Scottish Rifles at Neuve Chapelle 1915*, London, Cassell, 1967.

12   Patrick Leigh-Fermor, *Between the Woods and the Water*, London, Penguin, 1986, p.127.

13   Diary of Captain Percy Snelling, 12th Lancers, 22 August 1914, Department of Documents, Imperial War Museum.

14   Diary of Lieutenant-Colonel K.B. Godsell RE, 25 August 1914, Liddle Collection, University of Leeds.

15   Charles Ardant de Picq, *Etudes sur le combat: Combat antique et moderne*, Paris, Berger-Levrault, 1942, p.110.

16   General Langlois, founder of the *Revue militaire générale*, quoted in Joseph C. Arnold 'French Tactical Doctrine 1870–1914', *Military Affairs* vol 42 no.2 (April 1978).

17   *Infantry Training (4-Company Organization) 1914*, Calcutta, Government Printing House, 1917, p.146.

18 *Field Service Regulations Part I (Operations) 1909*, London, HMSO, 1914, p.17.

19 Quoted in David Ascoli, *The Mons Star: The British Expeditionary Force 5th August – 22nd November 1914*, London, Harrap, 1981, p.69.

20 Quoted Ascoli, *Mons Star* pp. 92–3.

21 For British establishments in August 1914 see J.E. Edmonds, *History of the Great War . . . France and Belgium 1914*, Vol 1, London, Macmillan, 1922, pp.427–9. Details of German establishments and weapons are from D.B. Nash, *Imperial German Army Handbook 1914–18*, Ian Allen, 1980.

22 Quoted in Lyn Macdonald, *1914*, London, Michael Joseph, 1987, p.170.

23 Account in the papers of Major E.G. Lutyens MC RFA, Department of Documents, Imperial War Museum. This was available to the official historian, who used it almost verbatim: Edmonds *France and Belgium 1914* Vol 1 p.163.

24 Account in the papers of Lieutenant-Colonel T.B. Butt KOYLI, Department of Documents, Imperial War Museum.

25 Brigadier-General John Charteris, *At GHQ*, London, Cassell, 1931, p.17, Edmonds *France and Belgium 1914*, Vol 1 pp.174–5.

26 John Terraine, 'Cavalry Generals and the "Gee" in Gap' in *The Smoke and the Fire* pp.161–6.

27 Lieutenant-General Sir Tom Bridges (4th Dragoon Guards) lost a leg as a divisional commander at Passchendaele, characteristically walking in the open when it was 'raining old iron'. General Sir David 'Soarer' Campbell (9th Lancers) commanded the 21st Division from May 1916 until the end of the war.

28 See 'Cavalry in European Armies: Regiments by Type' in Terraine *The Smoke and the Fire* p.169.

29 This definition is from Major-General Douglas Haig, *Cavalry Studies*, London, Hugh Rees, 1907, p.4. For British cavalry on the eve of war see Edward M. Spiers 'The British Cavalry, 1902–1914', *Journal of the Society for Army Historical Research*, Summer 1979, B.J. Bond 'Doctrine and training in the British cavalry 1870–1914' in Michael Howard (ed), *The Theory and Practice of War*, London, Cassell, 1965, and vol 4 of The Marquess of Anglesey, *A History of British Cavalry 1816–1919*, London, 1986.

30 Ralph Barker, *The Royal Flying Corps in France*, London, Constable, 1994, p.34.

31 Barrow, an Indian Army officer on leave in England when war broke out, was attached to Cavalry Division headquarters. See General Sir George Barrow *The Fire of Life*, London, Hutchinson, 1941.

32 See Prince Kraft zu Hohenlohe-Ingelfingen *Letters on Cavalry*, London, Edward Stanford, 1889, and Lieutenant-General Friedrich von Bernhardi *Cavalry in Future Wars*, London, John Murray, 1906.

33 Bernhardi, *Cavalry*, p.xxii.

34 Anglesey, *British Cavalry*, p.424–5.

35 Lieutenant-Colonel F.M. Edwards, *Notes on the Training, Equipment and Organisation of Cavalry for War*, London, William Clowes, 1910, p.67.

36 Lieutenant-General M. von Poseck, *The German Cavalry in 1914 in Belgium and France*, Berlin, E.S. Mittler, 1923, p.232.

37 For an account of the ride see Richard Holmes, *Riding the Retreat: Mons to the Marne 1914 Revisited*, London, Jonathan Cape, 1995.

38 F. de Brack, *Light Cavalry Out-Posts*, London, W. Mitchell, 1876, p.xix.

39 Bloem, *Advance from Mons* p.15.

40 Papers of R.G. Garrod, 20th Hussars, Department of Documents, Imperial War Museum.

41 Diary of Captain H.B. Owens MC RAMC, 11 August 1914, Department of Documents, Imperial War Museum.

42 Account of Private William Clarke, 2nd Dragoon Guards (Queen's Bays), Liddle Collection, University of Leeds.

43 Quoted in Ascoli, *Mons Star* p.30.

44 Clarke Papers, Liddle Collection.

45 Diary of Lieutenant-Colonel K.B. Godsell RE, 25 August 1914, Liddle Collection.

46 Regimental War Diary, 12th Lancers, 28 August 1914, Public Record Office WO 95.

47 Paul Maze, *A Frenchman in Khaki*, London, Heinemann, 1934, p.47.

48 Arthur Osburn, *Unwilling Passenger*, London, Faber and Faber, 1932, pp.132–4.

49 Poem in the papers of Richard Chant, 5th Dragoon Guards, Liddle Collection.

Part V

Soldiers: National and Unit Identity – British

Chapter 23

The War Experience of a Typical Kitchener Division: The 18th Division, 1914–1918

Peter Simkins

It is now recognised by a growing number of historians that, far from being 'the bluntest of swords' – as Denis Winter has described it[1] – the British Expeditionary Force under Haig not only steadily improved its tactics and organisation between the Somme and the Armistice but also played a key role in the final Allied offensive.[2] Scholars are, in addition, beginning to emphasise the increasing tactical decentralisation that occurred in the BEF from 1916 to 1918.[3] Tim Travers contends that, during the 'Hundred Days' in 1918, Haig and GHQ became largely irrelevant from a tactical standpoint. In the transition from positional to mobile warfare, when the BEF had to cope with a mixture of set-piece assaults and periods of movement, the methods employed, Travers writes, 'had nothing to do with the pre-war principles preached by the top brass at GHQ, but resulted from developments at army, corps and divisional level.'[4] Dr Paddy Griffith too pays special attention to the fighting methods used within the corps, division, brigade or battalion. Such formations, he argues, frequently 'invented their own characteristic tactics and operating procedures . . . The whims of commanders, in fact, were always a very major determinant of how every battle would be fought.'[5] In view of these trends in First World War studies, the need for a more systematic examination of divisional organisation, composition and performance in the BEF has assumed a new importance.

As a barometer of divisional performance and war experience, the 18th (Eastern) Division is a particularly rewarding unit to study since, in many respects – such as the manner of its raising, its social composition and its subsequent battle honours – it was a typical enough New Army division; in other respects – for instance, its commanders and its fighting performance, especially on the Somme in 1916 and in the 'Hundred Days' – it was outstanding. It can certainly be viewed as a symbol of the evolution of the BEF from 1915 to 1918 in that it offers a splendid example of what could be achieved, after a chaotic and unpromising start, by an 'ordinary' New Army division, raised in the Home Counties, without the élitist selection processes of some Territorial units, without the distinct social cohesion of the northern Pals formations, and without the sectarian and political binding of the 36th (Ulster) Division.

The 18th Division was part of the Second New Army – the second series of new infantry divisions created in 1914 following Lord Kitchener's decision to expand the Army. Its 53rd Infantry Brigade included the 6th Royal Berkshire Regiment, the 10th Essex, the 8th Norfolks and the 8th Suffolks; the 54th Brigade comprised the 6th Northamptonshires, the 11th Royal Fusiliers, the 12th Middlesex and the 7th Bedfordshires; and the 55th Brigade contained the 7th Queen's, 7th Buffs, 7th Royal West Kents and the 8th East Surreys. The 8th Royal Sussex Regiment became the divisional Pioneer battalion. The 55th Brigade's first camp was at Purfleet, while the 53rd and 54th Brigades, the 8th Royal Sussex and the four brigades of divisional artillery – the 82nd, 83rd, 84th and 85th Brigades, Royal Field Artillery – began their real training at Colchester, though some battalions, such as the 8th Norfolks and 10th Essex, had assembled initially at places like Shorncliffe. All of these infantry battalions remained with the division until the reorganisation of the BEF early in 1918, along with the Pioneer battalion and the 82nd and 83rd Brigades RFA.[6] There was, then, a strong thread of continuity in the divisional organisation throughout the war. When one considers the organisational changes experienced by many British divisions on the Western front during the conflict, the 18th was relatively fortunate to retain seven of its original infantry battalions to the end – a factor which undoubtedly contributed to its consistently high standards of battlefield performance.[7]

The rapid expansion of the Army in 1914 caused acute shortages of almost everything needed to make it function: officers, NCOs, accommodation, uniforms, weapons, equipment and, initially, even food. A.P.B. Irwin, the original adjutant of the 8th East Surreys (and eventually the commanding officer) was the only Regular officer of the battalion when the bulk of the recruits who were to form it reached Purfleet on 10 September 1914. 'They arrived, a thousand strong, with no officers, no non-commissioned officers – rather like a football excursion crowd . . . They knew no words of command'.[8] An officer of the 8th Norfolks recalled that 'it was impossible to prevent new recruits coming. A company would start a route march 300 strong and return with 310, and no one knew or could find out who were the new men'.[9] With improvisation the order of the day, the shortages were felt perhaps more painfully by the gunners than by the infantry. Months passed before the batteries had their own guns. Detachments had to be trained with one wooden gun per battery, and once a week were allowed to drill with a real 18-pounder. There were no dial sights and they practised gunlaying over wooden sights upon which the degrees were roughly marked. As late as November 1914, relates the divisional historian, 'no battery had more than two dozen horses to its two hundred men, and any battery going out in drill order had first to scout round and borrow animals from other batteries'.[10]

Few New Army units in the autumn of 1914 contained enough competent re-enlisted soldiers to fill all their non-commissioned ranks, and hard-pressed officers had to make up the required numbers simply by choosing promising recruits. According to Irwin of the 8th East Surreys: 'We were given a dozen old Reservists, who were promptly made lance-corporals, much to their horror and indignation. Then the whole battalion was paraded and an appeal was made for anyone who had ever been in charge of anyone else, or who wanted to be. About forty men stepped forward; we tied white tape around their arms and made them lance-corporals too. A rough and ready system, but it worked out well, and nearly all of them made good . . .'[11] In the 12th Middlesex, a man was selected as a corporal simply because he kept himself clean and also because, being a fish seller from near Billingsgate, he had a powerful voice.[12] There was inevitably much 'grousing' but the mutual goodwill and enthusiasm of the recruits and of the newly-commissioned officers sufficed to surmount most obstacles. In the words of one officer of the 8th Norfolks:

> men lived, ate, slept and worked in their sections and platoons in which they were to fight in France. Some sections never actually changed between the day of their first formation and the day on which they first suffered casualties in France. The officers not only knew their men by sight and by name, and by their military proficiency, but knew many of the details of their private life . . . Thus was the morale and ésprit de corps of the battalion fostered.[13]

The division was exceedingly fortunate in that its first commanding officer was Major-General Ivor Maxse, one of the truly outstanding tacticians and trainers of his generation and a general who, as much as any senior British officer in the Great War, demonstrated that not all of his kind were 'butchers and bunglers'. Originally commissioned into the Royal Fusiliers, he transferred to the Coldstream Guards in 1891 and commanded the 1st Guards Brigade from 1910, taking it to France in August 1914 at the age of fifty-one and leading it on the Marne and Aisne before being brought home to command the infant 18th Division.[14] Blessed with a quick and independent mind, Maxse had, prior to the war, written on tactics and battalion organisation. In 1912, for example, he urged the reorganisation of the infantry battalion from eight smaller companies into four larger ones – a measure subsequently adopted for Regular units in January 1914.[15] He was never one to cultivate easy popularity and has been described by historians as 'hard swearing' and 'intolerant' or 'bumptious and outspoken'.[16] Basil Liddell Hart, who knew him well after the war, portrayed him as a 'Tartar' in dealing with 'lazy or inefficient seniors and subordinates' but added that Maxse's fierce manner 'concealed a very warm heart, and he particularly liked people who showed that they were not afraid of him'.[17] Paddy Griffith maintains that Maxse was as keen as anyone on saluting and close-order drill and that he emphasised the importance of regularity in route marches and of intensive digging. Nevertheless, as Dr Griffith observes, 'one should not scorn his extension of the same drill principle into such combat functions as platoon organisation, deployment into tactical formations, or the advance to contact'.[18] Maxse himself stressed that 'all details such as "forming up" lines, formations, objective, etc., must be prepared beforehand and rehearsed beforehand. It won't be "all right on the night"'.[19] He thought that tactics should be 'so ingrained on the training ground as to become second nature in battle'.[20] Maxse's belief in regularity and system, Paddy Griffith argues, was combined with a desire for lively training methods, based upon proper evaluation of the lessons of battle and upon the need to encourage individual initiative. All was designed to make sense to the average soldier and guide him through the shock of real action.[21]

Maxse's methods were undeniably appreciated by the majority of his junior officers. Harold Hemming, an officer in the 84th Brigade RFA in 1915, wrote: 'Attending his fortnightly conference, listening hard and taking notes, was like a university course on how to make a fine fighting division out of 20,000 semi-trained albeit enthusiastic soldiers'.[22] An officer of the 10th Essex remarked: '. . . one remembers with marvelling the feat he used to perform when he would pass the Battalion, Brigade and later the Division on the line of march, and greet by name every subaltern that passed. It went right home, for you felt you were working for a chief who knew you, and not merely for an abstraction in a brass hat'.[23] Maxse's performance as a trainer of troops later drew a glowing tribute from Hubert Gough, under whom the 18th Division fought on the Somme in the autumn of 1916:

> no division in the Army was more efficiently trained . . . Maxse had an immense capacity for grasping the important points in training . . . Quick and energetic, . . . he never failed to encourage initiative among his subordinates; he drove them hard, but one and all, long before they had finished their experiences of fighting the Germans under his command, realised the soundness and value of his training, and thanked him for it.[24]

The division crossed to France at the end of July 1915 and, for the best part of a year, served its trench warfare apprenticeship on the Somme, mainly in the Tambour sector at Fricourt and at Carnoy and La Boisselle. Even in late 1915 these were scarcely 'cushy' sectors and the division suffered 1,247 casualties by the end of that year, but this prolonged period of trench warfare helped it to 'shake down' into an effective fighting formation.[25] It was arguably the most consistently successful British division in the 1916 Somme offensive, taking part in the capture of Montauban on 1 July as well as securing Trones Wood on 14 July – despite initial difficulties – and then seizing Thiepval, one of the strongest German positions on the Western Front, on 26 and 27 September. The division subsequently played a major role in the struggle for the formidable Schwaben Redoubt at Thiepval and in the capture of important sections of Regina Trench and Desire Trench. By my calculations, the 18th Division carried out more big attacks (seven) than any other British or Dominion division on the Somme and, by the end of 1916, was certainly part of what Paddy Griffith has identified as an emerging 'assault élite' in the BEF.[26]

Maxse's contribution to these successes was considerable. His tactics on 1 July, when he deployed his assaulting troops in No Man's Land before zero hour, so that they won the 'race to the parapet' on their first objective, proved invaluable in the capture of the Pommiers Redoubt and Montauban Ridge – as did his use of a form of creeping barrage (then by no means a standard ingredient of assaults) to take the infantry through to their next objective,[27] although the key role of Alan Brooke, then the division's Brigade Major Royal Artillery (BMRA) in preparing this creeping barrage must be acknowledged. At Thiepval his emphasis on thorough battle drill and previous preparation were key factors in the set-piece phase of the attack. As Maxse himself wrote in his report: 'With sufficient time to prepare an assault on a definite and limited objective, I believe a well trained division can capture almost any "impregnable" stronghold, and this doctrine has been taught to the 18th Division'. Before the attack, Maxse covered almost every conceivable detail in a conference with twenty-two main agenda headings. The Chief of Staff of II Corps addressed all brigade and battalion commanders at Maxse's request and several told Maxse that 'it made them put life and intelligence into their work of preparation. They felt they were being trusted . . .'[28] This thoroughness meant that the effect of inevitable casualties among junior leaders was reduced because every soldier, with frequent rehearsals, knew his task. Thus, at Thiepval, when the set-piece phase was over and the operation became a bitter, close-quarters, soldier's battle in the labyrinth of trenches and strongpoints around the village, it was, in the official historian's view, 'the prowess of the individual soldier' that 'largely decided the issue. For the most part, the enemy fought to the death; he was only to be overcome by desperate courage, skill-at-arms, and the enterprise of small groups of men, often led by privates after officers and NCO's had been killed or wounded'. The official historian adds that the deeds of Privates F.J. Edwards and R. Ryder – two men of the 12th Middlesex who both won the VC at Thiepval – 'were not isolated acts'.[29]

Maxse left the division in January 1917 to command XVIII Corps, but his spirit remained. One Maxse-trained officer was Lieutenant T.R. Price, the adjutant of the 6th Northamptonshires, who, after his commanding officer was killed, extricated the battalion from a dangerous position in the teeth of a German counter-attack at Boom Ravine, near Miraumont, in February 1917. When congratulated on his handling of the situation, Price replied that he had based his actions upon what his former divisional commander had taught him ought to be done.[30] Maxse's successor was Major General Richard Lee, a sapper who had previously served as CRE of the 7th Division and as Chief Engineer of Gough's Fifth Army. The divisional historian states that Lee 'displayed infinite knowledge, quick grip and decision ... He had a great gift for map-reading, and consequently never failed to make full use of ground'. Lee also apparently had a 'distaste for frontal attacks: the large hauls of prisoners and correspondingly small casualties in the successful actions in the closing stages of the war can be traced to his determination to manoeuvre'.[31]

Lee's first sixteen months in command coincided with the division's most difficult period of the war, though its problems often stemmed from factors outside his personal control. The start of this period was, in fact, reasonably encouraging. The largely forgotten battle which led to its capture of Boom Ravine and cost it nearly 1,200 casualties on 17 February 1917, helped to break the back of German resistance on the Ancre and seems to have precipitated the planned German withdrawal to the Hindenburg Line.[32] This was followed by a brilliant surprise assault by the 53rd Brigade leading to the capture of Irles on 10 March.[33] However, at Chérisy on 3 May, during the Battle of Arras, the division received its first 'definite and substantial check'. The setback can be ascribed to various causes, including the fact that the attacking brigades had less than three days to become acquainted with the ground. A side-step of 500 yards to the left had to be made immediately before the action; the artillery failed to cut the wire opposite the 54th Brigade; an assault in darkness at 0345 had an adverse 'knock on' effect on operations throughout the day; and parties of the 7th Buffs and 8th East Surreys, which had reached the final objective, retired in the face of a strong German counter-attack.[34]

On 31 July, the first day of the Third Battle of Ypres, the 53rd Brigade, at heavy cost, again displayed the stubborn fighting qualities of the division's infantry, gaining 1,000 yards of ground against fierce opposition, but the troops were stopped short of their objective at Glencorse Wood, partly due to the earlier failure of the 30th Division in front. On 10 August, once more at heavy cost – the 11th Royal Fusiliers (54th Brigade), for example, lost 17 officers and 335 other ranks – the division attacked towards Inverness Copse and Glencorse Wood for a second time and managed to hold on to the north-west corner of Glencorse Wood, though forced back elsewhere.[35] All the same, Third Ypres ended on a brighter note for the 18th Division, with the formation again serving under Maxse, as part of XVIII Corps. During rehearsals for subsequent operations at Poelcappelle, Maxse, typically, told officers: 'I have arranged a very nice battle for you gentlemen, with lots of Huns to kill'. In the event, the 'battle' began badly in thick mud on 12 October, but on 22 October the 53rd Brigade won an impressive victory, taking Poelcappelle Brewery, Meunier House and Tracas Farm in a model operation in which Brigadier General H.W. Higginson bluffed the Germans with a dummy attack south of the village and outmanoeuvred them with a thrust to the north.[36]

Not surprisingly, memories of the division's experience in the great German offensive of March 1918 are contradictory, reflecting the confusion of the fighting. For some, like Private G.A. Fleet of the 7th Queen's, the opening day of the offensive, 21 March, was one of chaos, bewilderment and fear.[37] But it is all too often overlooked that not every British unit in Picardy simply retired in disorder, and that many, often ad hoc, small groups of men conducted a fighting withdrawal, inflicting severe casualties on the German infantry. The 18th Division, for instance, held most of its main Battle Zone intact throughout 21 March and even retained some strongholds in the Forward Zone.[38] As late as 25 March, its 54th Brigade still had the capacity to mount a determined, delaying counter-attack at Baboeuf, retaking the village for a while and capturing ten German machine-guns.[39] The following month, particularly on 4 and 24 April, the division fought hard alongside the Australians at Villers-Bretonneux in the defence of Amiens.

It was during the 'Hundred Days', however, that the 18th truly reinforced its reputation as an outstanding division. Even here it suffered setbacks. Two days before the opening of the British offensive at Amiens, the division was the victim of a sudden German attack, which disrupted its own preparations, forcing it to spend most of the final forty-eight hours regaining ground that had been lost. The 54th Brigade was temporarily replaced by a brigade from the 12th Division and, in these circumstances, the 18th Division did not perform as effectively on 8 August as it might otherwise have done.[40] Yet, later in the month, it played a leading part in the Battle of Albert, fighting again over the 1916 battlefield and retaking Trones Wood, over two years after its first success there. The Trones Wood attack on 27 August 1918 offers a particularly good example of the improved all-arms, small unit tactics of the BEF by that period, as the successful companies of the Berkshires and 10th Essex received direct support not only from the 53rd Trench Mortar Battery but also from two 18-pounders which fired 200 rounds in ten minutes at close range.[41] Despite a further 'sticky patch' in the struggle for the Hindenburg Line outposts (18–24 September), the division gained some or all of its objectives in over 70 per cent of its attacks during the 'Hundred Days', making it one of ten British divisions with a success rate of 70 per cent or better in ten or more opposed attacks between 8 August and 11 November 1918.[42] General Lee surely deserves some credit for the victories of the final weeks, conceiving and overseeing a masterly turning movement at Frégicourt, near Morval, on 1 September, where 700 prisoners were taken at trifling cost and, according to the divisional historian, 'there was most workmanlike co-operation between artillery and infantry in bringing off a bold and unusual coup'.[43] Lee appears at last to have come into his own in the mixture of positional and semi-open warfare of the 'Hundred Days'.

One can, of course, find exceptions to any rule, but it is probably fair to say that the quality of leadership in the division, from brigade comman-ders to NCOs, was generally high – an assessment which the division's battle record seems to support. To the instances of good planning and personal leadership already mentioned, one might add the achievement of Lieutenant-Colonel Frank Maxwell VC, the CO of the 12th Middlesex, when he revived a flagging attack at Trones Wood on 14 July 1916, and personally led men of the 54th Brigade through the wood to the final objec-tive, participating in an assault on a German strongpoint on the way. He is reported to have said earlier to a padre: 'I am going this night to instil the spirit of savagery into my battalion'. In the same operation a VC was won by Sergeant William Boulter of the 6th Northamptonshires. Boulter was an almost archetypical Great War citizen-soldier – a kind of First World War 'Kipps' – as, before enlisting, he worked in the haberdashery department of the Co-operative store in Kettering.[44] One might also cite the case of the night relief at Thiepval on 26–27 September 1916, which was organised by Brigadier-General T.H. Shoubridge of the 54th Brigade and Lieutenant-Colonel G.D. Price of the 7th Bedfords – an operation described by Maxse as 'the finest example of efficiency and battle disci-pline' seen to date in the division; of the five NCOs of the 11th Royal Fusiliers who won DCMs at Glencorse Wood and Inverness Copse in August 1917 for taking charge of officerless companies and inspiring waverers to repel repeated counter-attacks; of the initiative demonstrated by Second Lieutenant W. Tysoe of the 7th Bedfords in organising and conducting the defence of the sector between the Bois l'Abbé and Hangard Wood, from 24 to 26 April 1918, during the fight for Villers-Bretonneux; of the coolness of Brigadier-General E.A. Wood of the 55th Brigade in the thick of the battle for Ronssoy in the Hindenburg Line outposts in September 1918, when, unarmed and single-handed, he captured over twenty Germans by pelting them with chalk and old boots; or, alterna-tively, of the consistent bravery and capable leadership shown over a long period by officers such as Irwin of the East Surreys or A.E. Percival of the Bedfords.[45] These examples hardly tally with Bruce Gudmundsson's judge-ment that British small unit leadership was largely in the hands of 'tactically incompetent schoolboys'.[46] On the contrary, I would argue that any detailed analysis of the division's operational record will indicate that the standards of junior leadership in the BEF from 1916 to 1918 were higher than has previously been supposed by the majority of historians.

In this connection one can also conclude that the officer–man relations in the division were, on the whole, good – and certainly sufficiently sound to sustain it through all the horrors of the Western Front and to help maintain its fighting reputation. Captain 'Billie' Nevill of the 8th East Surreys – who gave his men footballs to kick into No Man's Land on 1 July 1916 – told his family of his feelings soon after taking over 'B' Company in March that year: '. . . 220 odd men all to myself. Their meals, clothes, pay, and lives too all to my responsibility. They are a topping lot . . .' In April he claimed that the responsibility 'doesn't worry me a bit or awe me; though the thought of it in England used to frighten me a bit, but I know I've got real good officers to back me up and I feel absolutely confident in the men themselves and that's why I can feel confident in myself'.[47] Other officers like Tom Adlam of the 7th Bedfords – who, as a subaltern, won the VC at Thiepval – took special care to keep the men happy, partly by being open-minded and willing to recognise their own limitations. Adlam himself had served both as a private and as a sergeant in a Hampshire Territorial battalion before the war. He later recalled: 'Some officers would think they had to do better than their own men. But if I found a man who could do something better than me I'd say "Well, you do that". And I think they liked it . . . A man likes to be recognised as being a responsible person.'[48]

The commanding officer of the 12th Middlesex on the Somme in 1916 was Lieutenant-Colonel Frank Maxwell – a VC winner in South Africa and former ADC to Kitchener, who nicknamed him 'The Brat'. Maxwell believed in speaking directly to his men when the occasion demanded. Early in June 1916 he addressed the entire battalion, instructing the men to gather close round him and to sit down, smoke and listen, adding that 'when we can be a family, we'll be one and talk to each other as one'.[49] However, he revealed less enlightened attitudes in a letter of 26 July 1916:

'Shell shock' is a complaint which, to my mind, is too prevalent everywhere; and I have told my people that my name for it is fright, or something worse, and I am not going to have it. Of course, the average nerve system of this class is much lower than ours, and sights and sounds affect them much more. It means . . . that they haven't got our power of self-control, that's all.'[50]

Courage in battle on the part of an officer inevitably won respect. Describing the attack on Thiepval, Private C. Cooksey of the 10th Essex wrote: '. . . here I and the chaps in my section witnessed one of the bravest incidents of the day . . . in my mind, I met the bravest man I had seen in my life. Lieut. Goddard of our company walking up and down our line . . . with his map and compass in his left hand and the revolver in his right one, stopping now and again to glance at his map or to shout an order as to direction to our section leaders, cool as a cucumber taking no notice of the machine-gun bullets . . .'[51] Sergeant Barrett, of the same company, remarked that Goddard was 'strolling along as if in the Strand!' and called his officer's conduct 'thrilling'.[52] 'Billie' Nevill was also clearly held in esteem and affection by men of his company of the 8th East Surreys. Even allowing for the platitudes of condolence, this is evident in letters sent to his family after he was killed on 1 July 1916. Sergeant Humphrey Cunnington wrote: 'It is seldom, even in the Army, that a man gains the love of his fellow men, but our feelings towards Capt. Nevill were deeper than mere admiration, and there wasn't a man in the Battn. who would not have followed him anywhere'.[53]

Not all officers earned such glowing tributes. Robert Cude, originally a battalion runner with the 7th Buffs and later a runner for the 55th Brigade, described one officer in August 1917 as 'a self-opinionated idiot' and, on another occasion, in mid-1918, called an officer an 'imbecile'.[54] Maxse himself did not escape Cude's biting criticisms. When Brigadier General T.D. Jackson was removed from command of the 55th Brigade, after the operations at Thiepval and the Schwaben Redoubt, allegedly for refusing to commit battalions to an action he considered impracticable, Cude was full of sympathy for him but expressed little admiration for the divisional commander: 'He [Jackson] will carry with him the well wishes of the whole Bde. and we can never forget the man who would wreck his career rather than be a party – however unwilling – to the annihilation of troops under his command. What would the Bde. like to do with Gen. Maxse, the man with a breast full of decorations – not one earned'.[55] Jackson's successor, G.D. Price, never won Cude's approval. In October 1916 Cude commented scathingly, '. . . whatever price was asked for it would have been dear'. When Price, in turn, was succeeded by Brigadier General E.A. Wood in November 1917, Cude noted: '. . . at a first glance he suits, for he looks a thorough soldier. The other old woman [Price] has gone back to England to act as house-keeper to a Suffragette, at least, that is all he is fit for . . .'[56] Wood indeed lived up to Cude's expectations and, during the critical days of March 1918, Cude found time to describe him as a 'Grand Old Man' and an 'English Gentleman'. So long as Wood remained with the brigade, wrote Cude, 'I shall not mind going through Hell itself'.[57] Cude, moreover, was ready to admit when he had misjudged an officer. Thus, in the case of Lieutenant-Colonel A.L. Ransome, the CO of the 7th Buffs, who led his battalion with distinction in March 1918, Cude conceded that he had been 'transfigured from the best hated man in the Bde. to a man who will now be strictly respected by us all'. Ransome, he declared, 'has infused such a spirit into his battn. that the men on one occasion made 3 counter-attacks to get him out of Jerry's hands, where he had got simply through sheer bravery'.[58] Officer–man relations in the 18th Division may not have been ideal, but as in most other British units, they were good enough to sustain the formation through the tribulations of 1916, 1917 and 1918 and enable it to keep pressing forward in the final weeks of the war.

Discipline in the division appears to have been strict, although possibly no harsher than that exercised in the rest of the BEF. In June 1916, shortly after taking command of the 12th Middlesex, Frank Maxwell informed his wife that he had decided to end the hated Field Punishment No. 1 in his battalion: 'A most vile form of punishment, to my brand of mind, as it is shameful and lowers a man's self-respect'. But Maxwell – like others of his day – was prepared to recommend, or at least acquiesce in, the impo-sition of the death penalty. On 7 July 1916, he wrote of two men who had gone missing when the unit moved up to the front and had made their way to Boulogne: 'Poor devils, I suppose it was cold feet, and they are going to lose their lives dishonourably now, instead of taking the chance of doing so honourably a week ago'.[59] So far as I can trace from the evidence recently presented by Putkowski and Sykes, the men to whom Maxwell referred were not executed. In total, five privates of the 18th Division were executed, for desertion, during the war – about the average number for New Army divisions on the Western Front. All five executions took place between September 1917 and August 1918, four of them in the last quarter of 1917. The first to be shot was a soldier of the 8th Norfolks from the 53rd Brigade, the others all being from the 55th Brigade – two privates from the 7th Buffs and one each from the 7th Queen's and 8th East Surreys.[60] As with the men described by Maxwell, the evidence available indicates that the executions represented only the tip of the iceberg and that there were numerous cases of desertion and cowardice where the soldiers concerned had their death sentences commuted or suspended. Indeed, around 90 per cent of the 3,080 death sentences passed under the Army Act between 1914 and 1920 were commuted. It is also worth noting that the five men executed in the 18th Division had each committed at least one previous, and equally serious, offence.[61]

Few officers and men were immune to the terrors of the Western Front but most of those who went through one or more of the big battles were able to carry on without cracking, provided that they were allowed some time to recover from the experience. Second Lieutenant Eric Miall-Smith, of the 8th Norfolks, reassured his parents after the attack of 1 July 1916: 'I am glad it is over, and I am quite sound. I am not shaken and my nerves are all right so long as we are given a rest'.[62] Confused and frightened as he had been during the early days of the German March offensive in 1918, Private Fleet of the 7th Queen's recalled: '. . . with rest, food and drink we became normal human beings again'.[63] The constant regeneration of units with new drafts to replace casualties meant that new section, platoon or battery loyalties were continually being created and, with each 'rebirth', morale was, in the main, quickly restored. Robert Cude may again be taken as a good yardstick of 18th Division morale for, besides being an incorrigible 'grouser', he was with the division throughout its time in France and finished the war with the MM and Bar, so he was clearly made of the 'right stuff'. Like many others, Cude had bouts of disillusionment and war weariness, particularly during and after the Somme and Third Ypres. In January 1917 he confessed that peace was 'the heartfelt wish of all the troops operating on [the] "Somme". Let the politicians fight the war now I have had enough'. And, in August 1917, he wrote: '. . . everyone out here (in line of course) is heartily sick of it all, and wish it was over. Personally, I do not think that anyone troubles as to which side will ulti-mately win . . .' However, Cude could also take great pride in the division's exploits, such as the counter-attack at Baboeuf in March 1918. 'This is the stuff to give the troops . . .', he stated: '. . . I have never seen such a glorious attack'. He was in little doubt, by mid-August, that victory was in sight. A phrase written by Cude in October 1916 – 'we are on "Active Service", so must grumble but carry on' – could be taken as a perfect summary of the attitude of the vast majority of British soldiers during the war.[64]

Continuity of personnel cannot really be claimed as a key factor contributing to the 18th Division's success in battle. The 10th Essex alone, for example, lost 1,103 killed out of 5,500 officers and men who passed through the battalion, and the division as a whole lost approximately 550 officers and 13,000 other ranks killed and died of wounds from 1915 to 1918.[65] In effect, therefore, the division – like all the others – was constantly changing its personnel. The coming of conscription and the reorganisation of the reserve and drafting system in 1916 further diluted the original, highly-localised character of many units. A random glance through the relevant pages of Soldiers Died in the Great War will show that the 7th Queen's, by 1917–1918, contained soldiers from Northumberland, Middlesborough, Hull, Poole, Eccles, Leicester and County Sligo, while the 7th Buffs, at the same time, included NCOs and men from Berkshire, Norfolk, Liverpool, Yorkshire, Devon, Worcestershire, North Wales, Sunderland and Derby.[66] Given that the division had only two commanding officers during its entire time on the Western Front, it is tempting to believe that continuity of command was an important ingredient in its success. But, by the same token, one should note that the 9th (Scottish) Division, which possessed a fighting record equal to that of the 18th, experienced nine changes of command and seven different commanders after crossing to France.[67] What was perhaps more important was a division's ability to rebuild and reorganise itself periodically around a nucleus of combat veterans, and to maintain its divisional ethos – a way of doing things which could be passed on to others, however frequent the changes of personnel.

What, then, were the factors that shaped the battlefield success of the 18th, and other divisions, especially in the last three months of the war? First, the BEF was obviously a much better-balanced force by 1918 than it had been two years earlier. As Trevor Wilson has written, by the 'Hundred Days' infantry, artillery, machine guns, tanks, aircraft and wireless 'all functioned as parts of a single unit. As a result of meticulous planning, each component of the offensive was integrated with, and provided maximum support for, every other component . . . It was not that the British had developed a war-winning weapon. What they had was a weapons system: the melding of the various elements in the military arm into a mutually supporting whole'.[68] Within this 'weapons system', the generally high level of performance of the gunners, whose techniques and skills had improved out of all recognition since 1915, exerted a decisive influence. Secondly, a parallel improvement in small unit infantry tactics and changes in platoon organisation – processes in which Maxse and the 18th Division played no small part – also helped to ensure victory in 1918. Thirdly, ultimate success must, of course, be ascribed to the troops themselves. During the 'Hundred Days', after a moderate start at Amiens, the 18th Division pushed across the old 1916 battlefield between 22 August and 5 September 1918, recapturing Albert, Montauban, Trones Wood, Leuze Wood and Combles as well as seizing Frégicourt, St Pierre Vaast Wood and Vaux Wood. In this period, at a cost of 2,852 casualties, it advanced seventeen miles. The division then had a fortnight's rest before several days of bitter fighting, between 18 and 24 September, for the Hindenburg Line outposts. By this time, the division, now containing a large proportion of young conscripts, was tired and depleted, the average company strength being down to seventy men. Nevertheless, the division fought on doggedly until 5 November, winning further honours at Corbeau, Richemont Mill, Epinette, Bousies, Robersart and Renuart Farm.[69] In the long run, it was possibly the British soldier's bloody minded persistence and his powers of endurance – two of his outstanding qualities – that mattered most in the BEF's vital contribution to the defeat of Germany.

Notes

1 Denis Winter, *Haig's Command: A Reassessment* London, Viking, 1991, p.150.

2 See, in particular, Paddy Griffith, *Battle Tactics of the Western Front: The British Army's Art of Attack, 1916–18*, New Haven and London, Yale University Press, 1994; Bill Rawling, *Surviving Trench Warfare: Technology and the Canadian Corps, 1914–1918*, University of Toronto Press, 1992; Robin Prior and Trevor Wilson, *Command on the Western Front: The Military Career of Sir Henry Rawlinson, 1914–18*, Oxford, Blackwell, 1992; and 'What Manner of Victory?: Reflections on the Termination of the First World War', in *Revue Internationale d'Histoire Militaire*, No. 72, 1990, pp.80–96.

3 Prior and Wilson, *Command on the Western Front*, pp.300, 305, 339.

4 Tim Travers, *How the War was Won: Command and Technology in the British Army on the Western Front, 1917–1918*, London, Routledge, 1992, p.145; see also pp.109, 146–51.

5 Griffith, *Battle Tactics of the Western Front*, p.27; see also pp.22–3.

6   Major A.F. Becke, *History of the Great War: Order of Battle of Divisions, Part 3A, New Army Divisions (9–26)*, London, HMSO, 1938, pp.79–85; Captain G.H.F. Nichols, *The 18th Division in the Great War*, Edinburgh and London, Blackwood, 1922, particularly p.3.

7   For a summary of these organisational changes see Peter Simkins, 'The Four Armies, 1914–1918', in David Chandler and Ian Beckett (eds.), *The Oxford Illustrated History of the British Army*, Oxford University Press, 1994, pp.241–62.

8   Lieutenant-Colonel A.P.B. Irwin, quoted in Nichols, *The 18th Division in the Great War*, p.2.

9   Account by Major H.P. Berney-Ficklin, the former adjutant of the 8th Norfolks, quoted in F. Loraine Petre, *The History of the Norfolk Regiment, 1685–1918: Volume II, 4 August 1914, to 31 December 1918*, Norwich, Jarrold, 1924, p.209.

10   Nichols, op.cit., pp.8–10.

11   Lieutenant-Colonel A.P.B. Irwin, quoted in Martin Middlebrook, *The First Day on the Somme: 1 July 1916*, London, Allen Lane, 1971, p.19.

12   Account by Major L.A. Newnham, quoted in 'E.R.' (ed.), *The 54th Infantry Brigade, 1914–1918: Some Records of Battle and Laughter in France*, Aldershot, Gale and Polden, 1919, p.5.

13   Major C.F. Ashdown, unpublished typescript account, Imperial War Museum (IWM), Department of Documents, 75/30/1. It should be noted that, in places, there are marked similarities between Ashdown's reminiscences and the account by Major H.P. Berney-Ficklin quoted in Volume II of *The History of the Norfolk Regiment* (see, in particular, p.211).

14   See the entry on Maxse by Correlli Barnett in E.T. Williams and Helen T. Palmer (eds.) *The Dictionary of National Biography, 1951–1960*, Oxford University Press, 1971, pp.727–8.

15   Shelford Bidwell and Dominick Graham, *Fire-Power: British Army Weapons and Theories of War, 1904–1945*, London, Allen and Unwin, 1982, pp.35–7; see also Brigadier General F.I. Maxse, 'Battalion Organisation', in *Journal of the Royal United Services Institute*, Vol.56, 1912, p.53.

16   Middlebrook, *The First Day on the Somme*, p.279; Griffith, op.cit., p.184.

17   B.H. Liddell Hart, *The Memoirs of Captain Liddell Hart*, Volume I, London, Cassell, 1965, p.43.

18   Griffith, op.cit., p.99.

19   Lieutenant-General Sir Ivor Maxse, *Hints on Training issued by XVIII Corps*, London, HMSO, 1918, p.10; see also pp.5, 20.

20   ibid, p.6.

21   Griffith, op.cit., pp.99–100.

22   Lieutenant-Colonel H.H. Hemming, unpublished account, IWM, Department of Documents, PP/MCR/155.

23   Lieutenant-Colonel T.M. Banks and Captain R.A. Chell, *With the 10th Essex in France*, London, Gay and Hancock, 1921, pp.21–2.

24   General Sir Hubert Gough, *The Fifth Army*, London, Hodder and Stoughton, 1931, pp.147–8.

25   Nichols, op.cit., p.16.

26   Griffith, op.cit., pp.79–83; Nichols, op.cit., pp.35–136; 18th Division, General Staff, War Diary, July 1915-December 1916, PRO, WO 95/2015.

27 Nichols, op.cit., pp.35–50; 18th Division, General Staff, War Diary, July 1915-December 1916, PRO, WO 95/2015; 18th Division, Commander Royal Artillery, War Diary, July 1915-November 1916, PRO, WO 95/2019; Middlebrook, op.cit., p.279; Prior and Wilson, *Command on the Western Front*, pp.161, 173, 177, 184; Maxse, 'The Battle of the Somme', unpublished manuscript, Maxse papers, IWM, Department of Documents, 69/53/6; Bidwell and Graham, *Fire-Power*, pp.84–5. For Alan Brooke's contribution, see David Fraser, *Alanbrooke*, London, Collins, 1982, pp.68–73.

28 Major General F.I. Maxse, *The 18th Division in the Battle of the Ancre*, printed report, December 1916, pp.3–4. A copy of the report is held by the Imperial War Museum's Department of Printed Books.

29 Captain Wilfrid Miles, *Military Operations: France and Belgium, 1916*, Vol.II, London, Macmillan, 1938, p.407.

30 Nichols, op.cit., pp.149–50.

31 ibid, p.138.

32 ibid, pp.139–53; see also 18th Division, General Staff, War Diary, January-December 1917, PRO, WO 95/2016; Captain Cyril Falls, *Military Operations: France and Belgium, 1917, Vol.I*, London, Macmillan, 1940, pp.75–82, 115; Field Marshal Crown Prince Rupprecht of Bavaria, *Mein Kriegstagebuch*, Vol.II, edited by E. von Frauenholz, Munich, Deutscher National Verlag, 1929, p.100.

33 Nichols, op.cit., pp.155–63; 18th Division, General Staff, War Diary, January-December 1917, PRO, WO 95/2016; Falls, *Military Operations: 1917, Vol.I*, pp.105–7.

34 Nichols, op.cit., pp.164–88; Falls, op.cit., pp.436–8; 18th Division, General Staff, War Diary, January-December 1917, PRO, WO 95/2016; 55th Infantry Brigade, Headquarters, War Diary, January-December 1917, PRO, WO 95/2047; *A Short History of the 55th Infantry Brigade in the War of 1914–18* (printed for private circulation, London, circa 1919), p.15. J.R. Ackerley, an officer of the 8th East Surreys (and subsequently Literary Editor of the *Listener*), who was wounded and taken prisoner at Chérisy, writes that men of his company 'deserted me and bolted' when counter-attacked: see his *My Father and Myself*, London, Bodley Head, 1968, p.73.

35 Nichols, op.cit., pp.194–231; 18th Division, General Staff, War Diary, January-December 1917, PRO, WO 95/2016; 11th Royal Fusiliers, War Diary, July 1915-April 1919, PRO, WO 95/2045; Brigadier General Sir James Edmonds, *Military Operations: France and Belgium, 1917, Vol. II*, London, HMSO, 1948, pp.153–5, 186–8.

36 Nichols, op.cit., pp.232–46; 18th Division, General Staff, War Diary, January-December 1917, PRO, WO 95/2016; 53rd Infantry Brigade, Headquarters, War Diary, January-December 1917, PRO, WO 95/2035; Edmonds, *Military Operations: 1917, Vol.II*, pp.343–4.

37 Private G.A. Fleet, quoted in Peter H. Liddle, *The Soldier's War*, London, Blandford, 1988, pp.221–2. Fleet's manuscript recollections are in the Liddle Collection, The Library, University of Leeds.

38 Nichols, op. cit., pp.253–74; 18th Division, General Staff, War Diary, January 1918-March 1919, PRO, WO 95/2017; Edmonds, *Military Operations: France and Belgium, 1918, Vol.I*, London, Macmillan, 1935, pp.170, 172, 183–5, 194–8, 210.

39 Edmonds, *Military Operations: 1918, Vol. I*, p.456; Nichols, op.cit., pp.293–301; 18th Division, General Staff, War Diary, January 1918-March 1919, PRO, WO 95/2017; 54th Infantry Brigade, Headquarters, War Diary, June 1917-April 1919, PRO, WO 95/2042; 'E.R.', *The 54th Infantry Brigade*, pp.138–40.

40 Nichols, op.cit., pp.335–56; 18th Division, General Staff, War Diary, January 1918-March 1919, PRO, WO 95/2017; Edmonds, *Military Operations: 1918, Vol.IV*, London, HMSO, 1947, PP.75–7, 79–81, 82–3; 'E.R.', op.cit., pp.164–70.

41 Edmonds, *Military Operations: 1918, Vol.IV*, pp.321–3; Nichols, op.cit., pp.377–83; 18th Division, General Staff, War Diary, January 1918-March 1919, PRO, WO 95/2017; 53rd Infantry Brigade, Headquarters, War Diary, January 1918-March 1919, PRO WO 95/2036.

42 These statistics were compiled from the appropriate volumes of the British official history, as well as divisional war diaries, for my recent essay 'Co-Stars or Supporting Cast? : British Divisions in the "Hundred Days", 1918', due to be published by Frank Cass in a volume, edited by Paddy Griffith, entitled *British Fighting Methods in the Great War*.

43 Nichols, op.cit., p.384, see also pp.385–93; 18th Division, General Staff, War Diary, January 1918-March 1919, PRO, WO 95/2017; Edmonds, *Military Operations: 1918, Vol.IV*, pp.376–7.

44 Nichols, op.cit., pp.51–69; 'E.R.', op.cit., pp.43–50; Miles, *Military Operations: 1916, Vol.II*, pp.47–9, 75–8. Maxwell's own account of the action, given in letters to his wife, is contained in Charlotte Maxwell (ed.), *Frank Maxwell, Brigadier-General, VC, CSI, DSO: A Memoir and Some Letters*, London, John Murray, 1921, pp.152–61.

45 Major-General F.I. Maxse, *The 18th Division in the Battle of the Ancre*, p.11; Miles, op.cit., p.416; 'E.R.', op.cit., pp.103–116; Nichols, op.cit., pp.325–9, 399; Edmonds, *Military Operations: France and Belgium, 1918*, Vol.II, London, Macmillan, 1937, pp.356–8, 391–4, 397; Major W. Tysoe, typescript recollections, Liddle Collection, Leeds; see also Liddle, *The Soldier's War*, pp.244–5. Percival subsequently rose to the rank of Lieutenant-General. He was the officer who, as GOC Malaya, surrendered Singapore to the Japanese in February 1942.

46 Bruce I. Gudmundsson, *Stormtroop Tactics: Innovation in the German Army, 1914–1918*, New York, Praeger, 1989, p.175.

47 Captain W.P. Nevill, letters to his family, 16 March and 5 April 1916, IWM, Department of Documents, CON/WPN; see also Ruth Elwyn Harris, *'Billie': The Nevill Letters, 1914–1916*, London, Julia MacRae Books, 1991, pp.165, 168–9.

48 Interview with Lieutenant-Colonel T.E. Adlam VC, 1973, IWM, Department of Sound Records, 35/5.

49 Maxwell to his wife, 2 June 1916, quoted in Charlotte Maxwell (ed.), *Frank Maxwell, VC*, pp.138–40.

50 ibid, pp.164–5.

51 Private C. Cooksey, pencilled note, 6 January 1917, in Colonel R.A. Chell papers, Liddle Collection, Leeds.

52 Sergeant Barrett, pencilled note, n.d., probably late 1916 or early 1917, in Chell papers, Liddle Collection, Leeds.

53 Sergeant Humphrey Cunnington, letter to mother of Captain W.P. Nevill, 18 July 1916, IWM, Department of Documents, CON/WPN. J.R. Ackerley, on the other hand, described Nevill as 'the battalion buffoon', see *My Father and Myself*, p.57.

54 Robert Cude, unpublished typed transcript of diary, entries for 8 August 1917, and 12 June 1918, IWM, Department of Documents, CON/RC.

55 Cude diary, entry for 8 October 1916, IWM, CON/RC.

56 ibid, entries for 15 October 1916, and 13 November 1917, IWM, CON/RC.

57 ibid, entries for 24–26 March 1918, IWM, CON/RC.

58 ibid, entry for 4 April 1918, IWM, CON/RC.

59 Maxwell, letters to his wife, 3 June and 7 July 1916, see Charlotte Maxwell, op.cit., pp.140–1, 150.

60 See Julian Putkowski and Julian Sykes, *Shot at Dawn*, Barnsley, Wharncliffe, 1989, pp.217, 231–2, 248–9, 251–2, 290–3, 325.

61 *Statistics of the Military Effort of the British Empire during the Great War, 1914–1920*, London, HMSO, 1922, pp.648–9; Putkowski and Sykes, *Shot at Dawn*, p.8.

62 Second Lieutenant G.E. Miall-Smith, letter of 4 July 1916, quoted in *Two Brothers*, printed for private circulation, 1918, p.37. A copy is to be found in the Liddle Collection, Leeds.

63 Private G.A. Fleet, quoted in Liddle, *The Soldier's War*, p.222.

64 Cude diary, entries for 6 October 1916, 17 January 1917, 25 March 1918, and 22–23 August 1918, IWM, CON/RC.

65 Nichols, op.cit., pp.472, 476.

66 *Soldiers Died in the Great War, 1914–19*, London, War Office, 1921, *Part 7: The Queen's (Royal West Surrey Regiment)*, pp.46–61; and *Part 8: The Buffs (East Kent Regiment)*, pp.48–62.

67 Becke, *Order of Battle of Divisions, Part 3A*, p.3; see also John Ewing, *The History of the 9th (Scottish) Division, 1914–1919*, London, John Murray, 1921.

68 Trevor Wilson, *The Myriad Faces of War: Britain and The Great War, 1914–1918*, Cambridge, Polity Press, 1986, p.586.

69 Nichols, op.cit., pp.302–476; 18th Division, General Staff, War Diary, January 1918-March 1919, PRO, WO 95/2017.

Chapter 24

The Scottish Soldier at War

Edward Spiers

During the First World War 557,618 Scots enlisted in the Army, that is, 41.4 per cent of males aged between 15 and 49 and some 147,000 of these men sacrificed their lives.[1] They served in every theatre of the war and in every branch of the Army not only in the well-known Scottish regiments (and the six Scottish infantry divisions formed during the conflict),[2] but also in locally-formed batteries of gunners and field companies of engineers[3] and in English formations (the 15th and 16th Royal Scots served in the English 34th Division). The broader Scottish diaspora included numerous dominion forces, notably the Canadian battalions either affiliated or associated with Scottish regiments, the South African Scottish and the battalions of London, Liverpool and Tyneside Scottish (although some of these units were far from exclusively Scots in composition).[4] In reviewing the Scottish wartime experience, some 150 personal diaries, collections of correspondence and memoirs have been consulted. The sample includes recollections from every Scottish regiment, from regulars, Territorials and New Army soldiers, and from soldiers serving in all major theatres of the war. Although officers are disproportionately prominent, NCOs and other ranks bequeathed illuminating testimony, too, underlining the enduring relevance of Alexander Somerville's quip, uttered over half a century before, that 'It was the writing quite as much as the fighting of the Scottish regiments that distinguished them'.[5]

In the late Victorian and Edwardian Armies, Scots had been slightly under-represented as a proportion of the UK population. This reflected recruiting difficulties not only in under-populated Highland districts but also in urban areas (for example, the two regular battalions of the Highland Light Infantry had to recruit from all over Scotland and not simply from their Glaswegian district. Hence the irony of the HLI's first two Victoria Crosses in the Great War being won by Edinburgh men,

Lieutenant Brodie and Private Wilson, a fact quickly noticed by *The Scotsman*, Edinburgh's local newspaper).[6] The Scots, though, responded enthusiastically to the outbreak of war: throughout the months of voluntary enlistment (August 1914 – December 1915) Scotland produced 320,589 recruits, the highest proportion of enlistments in the UK. At a time when, as Lord Reith recalled, the Territorials were cheered and not jeered on the streets of Glasgow,[7] Scots enlisted from every class and region of the country. Like the rest of the Army, they may not have constituted an exact cross section of the country (and Scottish recruitment rates fell as key industries were protected during conscription),[8] but the Scots formed companies from the universities and the stock exchange, or, like the 7th Battalion The Black Watch, drew disproportionately from a particular industry in one region (in its case the coalfield of Fife), or constituted predominantly 'working class' or 'slum' battalions in others.[9] 'My favourite Battalion,' wrote Major-General G.G. Egerton, while serving in Gallipoli, 'is the 8th Scottish Rifles, – what is left of them; recruited from the lowest slums of Glasgow, many of them awful little ruffians, just "Glasgow Keelies", but cheery game fellows'.[10]

Scots enlisted individually and in groups; they responded to local recruiting drives and the exhortations of local élites. They formed pals battalions, notably the 15th HLI (raised in 16 hours from the tramways depots of Glasgow, largely in response to the appeal of James Dalrymple, the manager of the Tramways Department), the 16th HLI (officered and manned to a considerable extent by current and former members of the Glasgow Battalion of the Boys' Brigade) and the 17th HLI (raised by the Glasgow Chamber of Commerce).[11] They also joined bantam battalions in Edinburgh and Glasgow.

Scottish recruiting, like recruiting throughout the UK, reflected a mixture of patriotic and personal motives which cannot be quantified with any precision. The letters, diaries and memoirs reflect desires to serve King and Country, to fight the 'Hun', to see the war before it was over at Christmas, to escape from mundane employment or from hardship and unemployment.[12] Some, like C.N. Barclay, would have been ashamed had they not enlisted, and anyway wanted to join friends in the London Scottish;[13] David Smith desperately tried to follow his father and brother into the Army despite his height of 5ft 1½ins (and eventually entered the Seaforth Highlanders via the Royal Scots bantams);[14] Second Lieutenant Kenneth Kershaw, 2nd Battalion Gordon Highlanders, was simply delighted to be off to the Western Front: 'Thursday will be the happiest day of my life without exception. I am chosen at last to fight for my country, my whole and only one ambition in life'.[15]

Martial enthusiasm, none the less, only gripped just over one in four Scottish males aged between 15 and 49 (some 26.9 per cent) in the period up to December 1915. Just as recruiting throughout the UK began to dwindle after the initial surge in 1914, for all the reasons adduced by Dewey and Simkins,[16] Scottish numbers plummeted. Nor were all Scottish Territorials eager to serve overseas; while 'practically the whole' of the 5th Battalion, The Black Watch and over 90% of the 8th Battalion, Scottish Rifles (Cameronians) volunteered, the 51st (Highland) Division showed nothing like the same enthusiasm,[17] and only intense pressure, as Lionel Ferguson recalled, enabled the Liverpool Scottish to increase its response rate from 'about 15%' to 50 per cent and then to 79 per cent after nine days.[18] By June 1915 Private N.J. Fowler regarded his recruiting task in Edinburgh as 'a rotten job . . . They are coming in slowly. We generally manage to get one a day. There are about 15 of us out looking for them but my pal and I spend most of our time in the Gardens'.[19] The consequences were only too predictable. Contrary to popular mythology, the local and territorial connections of some Scottish units were eroded and, in some instances, their national composition diluted, too. As early as April 1915, the 51st (Highland) Division accepted a Lancashire brigade, and, in the following month, the under-strength 11th Battalion The Black Watch had to send recruiting parties off to Edinburgh, Glasgow and Manchester. When the 16th HLI was based at Nieuport in 1917, it received a draft from the Notts, Derby and Yorkshire depots.[20] Nevertheless, in ethos and cultural mores these units remained distinctively Scottish, and few Englishmen, serving in these units, would be left under any illusion on that point.

In many respects the Scottish military experience largely mirrored that of their English counterparts. Scottish special reservists, like the other special reservists, felt the marching across northern France in the hot autumnal conditions of August/September 1914. Captain E. Campion wrote of the 2nd Battalion Seaforth Highlanders that 'their marching could have been better but their coolness under fire is admirable and at night they are not excitable . . .'.[21] Scottish Territorials and those in Kitchener's first 100,000 endured, as others did, the cramped accommodation, the lack of proper uniforms and the obsolete equipment. Many of those who trained south of the border experienced a culture shock. The residents of Basingstoke and Bedford were somewhat alarmed at the prospect of having kilted highlanders billeted amongst them (the 6th Cameron Highlanders and the Territorials of the 51st Division respectively). Although the sewage and drainage system of Bedford was strained by men who knew little about modern sanitation, the residents treated them kindly. Alexander Runcie even recalled a girl who asked him if he 'didn't feel the cold at night on the hills with only my plaid to cover me while sleeping'.[22] Nevertheless, the experiences of training camps helped to forge *ésprit de corps*, even if they hardly prepared men for the peculiar demands of the Western Front, Gallipoli, Mesopotamia et al.

Once in the trenches, the experiences of the Scots were not exceptional.

Like other soldiers, they wrote of trench labour,[23] rations,[24] snipers,[25] rats,[26] lice,[27] and mud (Major-General Sir Aylmer Haldane reported two Cameron Highlanders who drowned in the mud and another Royal Scot who was trapped for four days in a communication trench before dying within an hour of his release).[28] They also wrote despairingly of the flies which harried soldiers in every theatre, not least in Egypt.[29]

Yet the Highland battalions, the 9th battalions of the HLI and the Royal Scots and some diaspora Scottish units had a distinctive trench experience by virtue of wearing the kilt. The merits and demerits of the kilt as a form of battledress have been keenly debated ever since. Worn under a wrap-around khaki cotton-kilt apron, with a pocket at the front to replace the sporran, the kilt kept men warm where they had to be warm and prevented them from having to stand in wet trousers. Private Jack Mackenzie, 5th Cameron Highlanders, wrote of his first night in the trenches, working knee-deep in rain-water and mud with his kilt tied around his waist.[30] If it became soaked or caked with mud, the kilt would become extremely heavy while the rim would cut the backs of knees. When soldiers replaced their boots and puttees with gumboots, the latter would chafe the bare thighs of kilted soldiers.[31] The kilt was more expensive than other uniform, consumed more space in ordnance wagons, and proved an encumbrance whenever soldiers had to swim across canals or, more frequently, when they had to move through uncut barbed wire.[32] It also attracted lice and insects, forcing highlanders to improvise delousing techniques, running heated forks down the pleats or experimenting with sheep dip, which produced horrendous burns on the Gordon Highlanders concerned (who were doubly unfortunate as they were refused hospital treatment for self-inflicted wounds), or more systematic disinfecting, which in the opinion of Captain A.R. Boyle, 1st Battalion Argyll and Sutherland Highlanders, merely 'served to arouse the vermin and spoilt the kilt'.[33]

The kilt, though, had three major disadvantages in the Great War: for soldiers drafted into kilted battalions from Lowland or English units, the change of garb could be quite a shock (in the severe winter of 1916, the Glasgow Highlanders had the highest incidence of frostbite and trench feet in the 100th Brigade, mainly among Scottish Yeomen drafted into their ranks).[34] Secondly, even some units devoted to the kilt, like the Gordon Highlanders, had to admit defeat in the Somme and abandon their mud-encrusted garments, albeit temporarily. Finally, mustard gas with its propensity to burn the sweatier parts of the anatomy, signalled the death knell of the kilt: 'in these circumstances', wrote A.M. McGilchrist, 'the kilt is not an ideal garment'.[35] Even before the threat of mustard gas, the 51st (Highland) Division had sought to dispense with the kilt. Only a few hundred of the Territorials, as Colonel Nicholson averred, had worn the kilt before the war; men readily wore trousers on road control or when detached from duty, and, on a famous occasion when the Division was left

317

guarding the XVIIth Corps sector (as other units were withdrawn to prepare for the Somme), the troops in the line donned khaki trousers lest they revealed that the sector was manned by highlanders alone.[36] The authorities, however, insisted upon the wearing of the kilt: quite apart from tradition, recruiting appeal and regimental distinctiveness, the kilt had rapidly become part of the battlefield imagery (with the Germans dubbing kilted soldiers as the 'women from hell', thereby adding to their legendary reputations).[37]

Apart from the vexed issue of the kilt, Scottish memoirs make several more general points about their trench existence. While many officers and other ranks allude to the sordid battlefield conditions, with grim descriptions of burial details, the smell of corpses and the desolate scenery encountered,[38] they also recognise that some trenches were much more comfortable, as well as better designed and drained than others. As early as June 1915 Lieutenant Hugh Munro, 1/8th Argyll and Sutherland Highlanders, wrote that

> Our own trench is a magnificent piece of work, exceedingly strong and comfortable. The parapet is well bullet-proof with cunning snipers' lairs and loopholes. Dugouts are numerous, and those of the officers luxurious. Captain Henderson has a suite of rooms! He has a sitting-room . . . , a dressing room with chest of drawers and full-length mirror, a bedroom with a spring bed and mattress. A pull bell connects the bedroom with the sitting room and orderlies; the bedroom has a stained glass window with muslin curtains and a flower box outside, with pansies! Men's dug-outs are simpler but equally safe and comfortable.[39]

There are several less graphic, but equally reassuring, accounts of improved conditions in other parts of the front.[40] Indeed some non-commissioned officers and other ranks positively preferred the trenches to the periods of so-called 'rest' in the billets behind the front lines. Lance Corporal Ramage, 1st Battalion Gordon Highlanders, noted that 'were it not for the scarcity of food, water and sleep in the trenches, we have a much harder time when we return for rest at billets, a rest crammed full of parades from early morning till eve'.[41] Private Mackenzie was equally emphatic: 'I would much rather be in the trenches than out here, as it is nothing else but parades and inspections'.[42]

How then did Scots respond to battlefield conditions in the Great War? In many respects just like any other group of British soldiers. In their letters they testify to feelings of comradeship and fellow-feeling in the mess or front-line, not just with their own comrades (although there are plenty of these, including one from a prisoner of war from the King's Own Scottish Borderers (KOSB), yearning to be back with his battalion and resume 'the good times we had in France',[43] but also with Lancashire Tommies, described by Captain Eric Townsend, 1/5th Battalion HLI, as 'really a treat they were so cheerful' in Gallipoli,[44] Gurkhas, Sikhs and many others with whom they were sharing the dangers and duties at the front.[45] Scots, though, were hardly oblivious of the shortcomings of others. In his Gallipoli diary, Captain Alexander M. Shaw, 1st Battalion KOSB, records that 'We have Terriers – Lincolns – next to us on the left. They are very casual. Sanitation shocking and the men are allowed too much freedom so they expose themselves and get shot'.[46] In France, Second Lieutenant R.W.F. Johnston, 9th Battalion Royal Scots, was even more critical of a neighbouring company of Cameron Highlanders, who marked 'Stand To' each morning and evening by firing fifteen rounds rapid at the enemy, inevitably provoking a counter barrage of artillery fire. While the Camerons claimed that this tactic accustomed their men to firing in the half-light, to be unafraid of looking over the top of their trenches and 'to intimidate the Boche', the Royal Scots groused that the retaliatory fire all too frequently fell on them.[47]

If comradeship was critically important to the functioning of the unit, so was the quality of officer leadership. As in non-Scottish units, this was variable. Lance Corporal Ramage had scant respect for most of his officers, describing one as a fat, conceited, unsoldierly liar – a 'braggard' and 'therefore untrustworthy'; another, he wrote, had threatened to shoot any man who hesitated in the charge. Nor did he warm to an officer promoted from the ranks; while he respected the courage and technical knowledge of Lieutenant Thom, MC, Ramage complained that he

> pestered the men with unnecessary parades – knew his work better than the other officers and very keen but not a gentleman – thought him trying to curry favour with our Capt. Hume Gore.[48]

Runcie also recalled that one of his officers put his own comforts before those of his men, while Haldane encountered a company commander of the Royal Scots who had been on duty for twenty-four hours without ever visiting his men.[49]

These examples hardly detract from the high standards of conscientious endeavour, self-sacrifice, and heroic leadership set by many other officers. 'We saw our Company Commander often', wrote Robert W.F. Johnston, 9th Battalion Royal Scots, 'He visited us twice each day and once by night speaking to every soldier. He was a member of the Scottish Bar and a delightful man in his thirties'.[50] Contrary to the oft-mooted claim that Scottish battalions differed from their English counterparts because of the relative absence of caste differences between officers and men, these diaries and correspondence seem to indicate that what officers did and how they did it mattered much more than who they were. Officers of gentry stock, such as Second Lieutenant George Buchanan Smith, 2nd Battalion Gordon Highlanders, shared the labouring duties in the trenches. He wrote to his mother, describing how he dug through the night clad only in his kilt, stockings and boots.[51] Scottish soldiers appreciated these efforts: 'We are all so proud of our officers', noted Private Mackenzie, 'it is fine to be under men like them . . . Our two just went at it with the rest . . . , digging and filling sand bag [SIC] . . . and passing jokes the whole time'.[52]

In the task of motivating men, keeping them keen and alert, Commanding Officers such as Winston Churchill, when CO of the 6th Battalion Royal Scots Fusiliers, proved critically important. Unlike Colonel A.E. Holland, who always took an interpreter whenever he inspected Scottish units, Churchill made a determined effort to master the local dialect. Full of vigour and vitality, Churchill had, in Holland's view, transformed 'his battalion from a moderate one into a d—- good one'.[53] Lieutenant-Colonel F.J. Duncan, 2nd Battalion Royal Scots, also impressed, not least because, in spite of his Roman Catholicism, he regularly attended the Presbyterian services of his unit, which was overwhelmingly Protestant.[54] When Major Jack assumed command of the 1st Battalion, The Cameronians, in 1918, he was immediately recognised as a 'pukka soldier' of the old school with firm ideas on discipline. Lieutenant Joseph MacLean described him as 'a fine looking chap, tall and thin, with a fine string of medals on his chest, and a regular live wire'.[55]

Jack recognised that officers had to lead from the front, albeit not as numerously and rashly as they had done at the battle of Neuve Chapelle (14/15 March 1915).[56] Officers who possessed nerve and courage were certainly respected by their men. Second Lieutenant Gillespie never doubted that he had to lead his men into battle, dying when he did so at the battle of Loos. In the same battle Lieutenant-Colonel A.F. Douglas-Hamilton rallied the 6th Cameron Highlanders to mount four separate charges, before incurring a fatal wound and earning the Victoria Cross.[57] Moreover, in battle, many officers displayed not only personal heroism but also a genuine concern for the well-being of their men. Writing from an advanced dressing station in Gallipoli, Lieutenant-Colonel James Young, Field Ambulance 52nd Division, recalled that an officer of the Argyll and Sutherland Highlanders, brought in with a shattered thigh, was only concerned with the water supplies for his men, who were fighting in extremely hot conditions.[58]

Officers, though, had few illusions about the men under their command. If the regulars of the British Expeditionary Force, including the 1st Battalion The Black Watch, moved through England and France in an impressively disciplined manner, disdaining the wine and cider proffered en route,[59] such self-restraint was not so prevalent among all later units. Officers complained of drunkenness among Black Watch soldiers on their arrival in Southampton (November 1914), among drafts of Gordon Highlanders leaving Invergordon for France (March 1915), and among several Royal Scots with 'a large number' falling out on the line of march in France.[60] Captain John A. Liddell reported 'awful trouble' in trying to keep the 3rd Battalion Argyll and Sutherland Highlanders in order *en route* to France, while Lieutenant A.A. Macfarlane Grieve described the 4th Battalion HLI, while in camp near Plymouth, as a 'rabble of half-clothed ruffians with a marvellous talent for getting drunk'.[61]

Drunkenness was relatively less of a problem in France where, as Captain Jack observed, 'the penalties are severe and estaminets are carefully watched by our military police',[62] but looting and other forms of unruly behaviour occurred in French billets. In admitting indiscretions by the 2nd Battalion Argyll and Sutherland Highlanders, Gillespie argued that 'The finest officers and training couldn't make saints of men straight from Falkirk High Street and the south side of Glasgow'.[63] Many Scots supposed, and apparently were told, that they had a special appeal in France. If the kilts and/or pipes attracted crowds of women and children, the Scots' readiness to fraternise quickly forged closer relations. Within days of landing in France, Second Lieutenant Alexander Williamson, 2nd Battalion Seaforth Highlanders, wrote that 'The Jocks have been making friends already and are trying on their french [sic]'.[64] Ramage, a former schoolteacher, described subsequent scenes in which young French girls waved the soldiers off, while shouting English sexual obscenities and causing immense hilarity in the ranks, as an 'annoying linguistic memento of our help which the British patriot will not relish'.[65]

As in other units, there were more serious derelictions of duty and infractions of discipline. On 25 January 1915, Haldane recorded that the 'RSF [Royal Scots Fusiliers] are behaving badly and one man is under sentence of death for cowardice', and, twelve months later, noted that 'The Liverpool Scottish had done and were doing little . . . The British soldier is, as regards work, a close second to the lazy type of British workman'.[66] Such aspersions were offset by the effusive compliments paid towards the other ranks. Once he had instructed English soldiers and found them very 'slow in the uptake', Lieutenant John D. MacLeod, 2nd Battalion Cameron Highlanders, appreciated the value of a Scottish education – a point endorsed within the 51st Division, where the 'leap frog' infantry tactics of Major-General G.M. Harper were absorbed by sustained training and put into effect in a series of battles.[67] Haldane also lauded the 'gallantry and staunchness' of the 4th Battalion Gordon Highlanders, 2nd Battalion Royal Scots and 1st Battalion Royal Scots Fusiliers at Loos, while Captain Claud Low of the London Scottish was filled with admiration for the way in which The Black Watch and the Camerons launched their assault on Aubers Ridge (9 May 1915): 'throughout the whole day and night I saw no cowardly act, no sign of flinching, scarcity or sign of fear . . .'.[68]

These were only a few of the many tributes paid to Scottish soldiery whether in France, Gallipoli, Salonika or Palestine, and they raise the question of how Scottish formations were welded into much vaunted fighting formations. In his splendid study of the 2nd Scottish Rifles at Neuve

Chapelle, Lieutenant-Colonel John Baynes has identified many of the critical aspects of morale within the context of the Great War. He envisaged morale built upon several layers, beginning with administrative support in good food, adequate rest, mail, proper medical care and good welfare services for families at home. While there were occasions, as Baynes admits, when Scottish forces fought courageously without many of these prerequisites, soldiers frequently testified to the general importance of rum, rations, the receipt of mail and medical care.[69]

Building on this foundation, Baynes adumbrates the importance of battalions being smart, disciplined, and attentive to sanitary detail. Haldane was particularly keen on trench discipline and reckoned that 'The discipline in Scottish, or at any rate in Highland, units, is . . . stricter than in English ones'.[70] Some Highlanders certainly agreed. 'The 2/5th Seaforths', recalled Private David Smith, 'was one of the most best behaved Battalions I ever had the pleasure to serve under', while another Seaforth, Second Lieutenant William Paterson, maintained that there was nothing worse for a man than 'to have time on his hands', therefore 'elementary training, such as saluting, drill, squad drill and so on' was vital to sustain the requisite standards of efficiency and discipline.[71]

Complementing smartness and discipline as aspects of morale were cheerfulness and high spirits within the ranks. Whereas Baynes and several Great War soldiers acknowledged these factors,[72] many of the latter emphasised that among the customary motivating factors (sports, leave, inter-regimental competitions etc.), the bagpipes had a particular impact upon Scottish morale. Although at first dispensed with in the war, pipe bands were soon restored as conspicuous components of the Scottish military presence.[73] They were employed in recruiting, in parades, on the line of march, in billets, in battle (where debates about their audibility recurred) and in funerals. Gillespie maintained, as many others did, that the pipes inspired men while tired, enlivened their spirits, and reminded them of home.[74] Bagpipes reinforced the bond between officers and men since they were played by Scottish gentlemen, and so, if pipers were injured in battle, officers like Second Lieutenant John G. Scott, 1st Battalion The Black Watch, could assist in piping men back to their trenches.[75] Some pipers distinguished themselves in battle; at Loos, Piper Munro piped the 2nd Gordons through a gas cloud, while Piper Laidlaw kept playing the pipes when wounded and earned the first Victoria Cross awarded to a Scottish Borderer in the Great War. Piper Archie Angus, 2nd Battalion London Scottish, was even willing to risk and lose his life to retrieve bagpipes left in No Man's Land.[76] So important had the pipes become that divisional commanders authorised the pipes and drums of their three infantry brigades to play at ceremonial and other occasions. As Colonel Nicholson remarked, 'a Retreat played by a hundred or more pipers . . . once heard and seen . . . was not soon forgotten'.[77] Arguably there were few symbols of Scottish identity and cultural distinctiveness more evocative than the bagpipes. The Americans, wrote Lieutenant R.L. Mackay, 8th Battalion Argyll and Sutherland Highlanders,

> were fascinated by our bag-pipes. Lord! How we held our heads up high and stepped out when THEY were watching, just to show them that we – WE – were winning the war – and then the Americans would fall behind . . .'[78]

Baynes identified two further factors in maintaining the morale of the 2nd Cameronians – a sense of sheer 'bloody-mindedness' and a nobility of spirit. By the former he meant a determination to persevere irrespective of the conditions and circumstances in battle and by the latter, love of a cause, love of one's country, loyalty, *ésprit de corps*, and unselfishness.[79] Corroborating these points are the many tributes paid to the steadfastness and resolve of Scottish soldiers in actions such as, the storming of Beaumont Hamel (13 November 1916) and the defence of the Frankfurt Trench (a second line German trench held for eight days from 8 November 1916 by 100 officers and men of the 16th HLI and the 11th Borders against the repeated assaults of an entire German brigade).[80]

This resilience and dogged determination probably derived from more fundamental feelings. Pride in their country may have motivated some; it had certainly helped in recruiting, and, if not terribly prominent in diaries and letters home (which may only reflect a reluctance to comment on a patriotism taken for granted), it was apparent in some correspondence.[81] Several soldiers emphasised a clear sense of Scottish identity and fighting tradition, and the former could embarrass members of the so-called Scottish diaspora. The Liverpool Scot, Stainton, recalled that he 'felt a rank imposter' when he first met a Gordon Highlander and found that neither of them could understand each other. As an Englishman, Stainton had invented a Scots grandfather to join

> a kilted regiment partly because of friends who had already done so, partly because of a great love for the sweet, stirring and mournful music of the pipes, and partly because I knew of the Battalion's deservedly good reputation.

After meeting a Gordon Highlander, though, he doubted whether he had any 'moral right' to wear the Forbes tartan.[82]

If some Scots regarded themselves as distinctive or as heirs to a distinctive military tradition, the British regimental system cut across these loyalties. Many had chosen to join specific regiments or, once they had joined, became aware of their regiment's reputation and, accordingly, developed a high sense of exclusive self-esteem. 'The B[lack] W[atch] have got a great name out here', wrote Private J.P. Fowler, 'especially the 4th'.[83]

Soldiers often revelled in their regiment's fighting reputation, even if they did not always share the enthusiasm with which senior officers, like Haldane, dwelt upon their history and traditions. Ramage recalled that in one parade when the 1st Battalion was reminded by an officer of the Gordons' history and the Scottish martial traditions, old soldiers were heard to murmur in the ranks: 'Same old bloody muck'.[84] Nevertheless, the exclusiveness of Scottish regiments and their ancient rivalries readily came to the fore. Just as Captain James B. Lorimer found it 'sickening' to be transferred from the Cameron Highlanders to the 7th Battalion Rifle Brigade, Second Lieutenant C.N. Barclay was 'naturally' disappointed to be transferred from the Cameronians to the Royal Scots.[85]

The reception accorded to incoming officers was none too warm either as Lieutenant Lionel Sotheby found on joining the 2nd Black Watch from the Argylls. As the first incoming officer, he had an 'uphill fight' to get accepted: 'You can have no idea', he wrote, 'how a regiment such as this views the appearance of comparative strangers'.[86] Indeed, officers resented any dilution of their regimental identity. The Hon. William Fraser regretted that his 6th Battalion Gordon Highlanders had to receive a draft of 60 Argylls: 'it does not make for *ésprit de Corps*', he observed.[87] Lieutenant MacLeod was even more alarmed when he heard that the Cameron machine-gun sections might be transferred into a separate corps in Salonika: 'Some of my men', he wrote,

> have been 10 and 11 years in the Regiment, and they will feel it fright-
> fully if they lose the kilt, to join a parvenu and unaristocratic corps,
> particularly after seeing the specimens of the M[achine] G[un] Corps
> who maggoted about in France.[88]

There were, too, ancient rivalries to be overcome in the brigading of some Scots units together (and later in amalgamating battalions of the same regiment). In 1916 the 6th Cameronians reputedly lodged a formal protest against being brigaded with Highland units since their forefathers had fought against Highlanders.[89] Haldane never doubted that such animosities could be overcome by service at the front and so brigaded the Royal Scots and the Royal Scots Fusiliers together.[90] Indeed regimental differences could be overcome from a most unexpected quarter. When the Germans, in 1917, reportedly rated the 51st Highland Division as Britain's fiercest fighting division, this provided a powerful boost to divisional *ésprit de corps*.[91]

Like other battalions, the Scots took pride in their standards of discipline and in their aggressive patrolling (with the 9th Cameronians claiming to have pioneered the tactic of daytime raids upon enemy trenches).[92] In Salonika, moreover, where men could be trained for some five months continuously, officers claimed extremely high standards of discipline and efficiency, as well as derisory sick lists.[93] Any localised successes bolstered regimental pride still further: after the 8th Cameronians had assisted in the forcing of the Auja river in Palestine (20–21 December 1917), Colonel J.M. Findlay noted how the battalion had been transformed since its baptism of fire in Gallipoli, not merely in the degree of trust between officers and men but also in 'the sense of self-reliance and knowledge of how to deal with situations . . .'.[94] When such successes did occur, Scots relished one particular accolade, namely the assertion that they were upholding the standards of the pre-war British Army. At the Marne in September 1914, Major John Crabbe, Royal Scots Greys, recalled seeing a Lowland Scottish battalion, advancing 'as on a parade ground and we were all very impressed'.[95] In describing a notable defensive action in which only one German reached the British ramparts, Sotheby claimed that 'the Seaforths behaved just as on peace parades in Scotland and their discipline was excellent'.[96] Finally, in Salonika, when Lieutenant James C. Cunningham, 2nd Battalion Argyll and Sutherland Highlanders, described the routing of the Bulgars by the Argylls, Camerons, Royal Scots and the 2nd Glosters, he dubbed this body, 'the flower of the British Army. Regular troops that had not fought since Ypres'.[97]

Underpinning any sense of collective motivation derived from national, regimental and professional feelings were more personal sentiments. While religion undoubtedly influenced some Scots, Baynes is fairly sceptical about its prevalence. Based upon the results of his questionnaire, he reckons that it had more influence among officers, especially regulars, than men, and only a vague, intermittent, or no influence upon the vast majority of soldiers.[98] Whether his statistics apply to all Scottish regiments, Highland as well as Lowland, is impossible to prove, but several memoirs testify to the comfort gained (and the sense of duty buttressed) by reading scripture or by attending voluntary church parades.[99] Admittedly some battalions served for lengthy periods without attached padres (for eight months in the case of the 10th Battalion Argyll and Sutherland Highlanders in 1916),[100] and criticism of wartime chaplains was often virulent. 'Most chaplains out here', wrote Lieutenant MacLean, 'are only a nuisance, occupying good billets and drinking our drinks and doing nothing notice-able toward the spiritual welfare of the troops. As a class they are cordially disliked with very few exceptions'.[101] While this may corroborate a sense of spiritual loss or erosion during the war, it may also indicate that many officers believed that religious feelings should have been cultivated more assiduously among the rank-and-file.

Arguably, the depth of the lingering hostility towards the Germans was more important. In *Death's Men* Dennis Winter argues that the Scots, like the Canadians and Australians, had 'no close season' in their enmity towards the Germans. In this respect, he asserts, they differed from the New Zealanders and the men from southern England, and that these differ-ences derived from their distinctive cultural backgrounds (the male-oriented family circle in Scotland, with an emphasis on toughness in personal relations and a concentration on past military glories).[102] If a study of Scottish sources cannot confirm or refute such comparative claims, it can certainly confirm the depth of animosities felt by some Scotsmen, even if these feelings have to be placed in context. However hostile towards the enemy, Scots readily acknowledged the fighting qualities and the military preparations, especially the trench construction, of the Germans. They also participated in the Christmas truce of 1914, and, in some cases, fraternized subsequently with Saxon soldiers. Private Runcie, nonetheless, recalled that a Gordon Highlander, on returning from the Christmas truce, showed him a concealed dagger, saying 'I don't trust these Bastards . . .'.[103]

Of more significance, though, was the real sense of enmity towards the Germans. Many Scots were incensed by the atrocity allegations, abuse of the White Flag, the torpedoing of ships, and the recourse to weapons such as the flame thrower and, above all, poison gas.[104] If the first use of gas had put men on their mettle in the trenches, making them 'ten times keener' in Gillespie's opinion (based upon reading their letters as the battalion censor),[105] it was still regarded by several officers and men as an underhand 'trick' and an 'unforgivable sin'. Private Young, 9th Royal Scots, described it as the 'devil's work . . . an utterly wrong thing. The enemy had burned their boats, and now it was war to the end, bitter and implacable'.[106] Lest it be thought that such sentiments were merely a passing sense of outrage at the first use of gas, many Scots, if not Gillespie, favoured retaliation-in-kind. The irrepressible Ramage argued that 'All war is foul. Why object to gas and not to bullets . . . we object to the Germans using chlorine scientifically. Why the hell dont [sic] we use it? Humbug, hypocrisy and want of clear intelligence I expect'.[107] In spite of the disappointment occasioned by the first British use of gas at Loos, where clouds of chlorine blew back over many Scottish soldiers, concern about German gas persisted, especially with the introduction of mustard gas in July 1917.[108]

The enmity of some Scots was striking in its intensity. Major (later Lieutenant-Colonel) John Stewart, 9th Battalion The Black Watch, was especially bitter. Appalled by tales of female voices being heard in German trenches and of a Frenchwoman being shot while trying to escape from the German lines, he described 'Fritz as a fat brute with the manners of a monkey and the morals of a maggot'.[109] In letters to his wife, he emphasised that 'THE B.W. TOOK *VERY* FEW PRISONERS' at Loos, exulted in the shelling and gassing of German trenches, yearned to get 'close' to 'the HUN' with a bayonet, deplored any distractions from the central war effort, such as the 'Irish riot' by 'a few irresponsible persons', and urged that 'the main thing is to kill plenty of HUNS with as little loss to oneself as possible: its a great game and our allies are playing it top hole'.[110]

Combat experience accentuated such feelings. After Neuve Chapelle when Lieutenant Lionel Sotheby found himself in charge of a company of 25 Black Watch instead of 200, he vowed that 'Next time the Germans *will* get it. Giving [sic] a chance with wire down and at close quarters, they will be slaughtered and I feel quite mad at it, and long for a decent smack at them'.[111] Even when the Allies assumed the offensive and moved through formerly occupied country, the resentment persisted. In his diary of 22 October 1918, Lieutenant Mackay described 'Pitiable scenes outside H.Q. with refugees. Appalling beyond all description. I feel bitter against the Hun, as never before'.[112]

In their desire to close with the enemy, many Scots chafed at the war on the Western Front. Captain Sir Edward Hulse, 2nd Battalion Scots Guards, bemoaned the loss of fire and movement, and, in February 1915, wrote that 'There is damned little mobility or latitude now'.[113] Several wished to engage in 'square fighting' and hence relished the prospect of service in the Near East, where they regarded the Turks as 'clean' fighters by comparison with the Germans and where they hoped to resolve matters at the point of a bayonet. 'It will be a pucher [sic] war', wrote Lieutenant Thorburn *en route* to Mesopotamia, 'and as one imagines what War is . . .'.[114] It took only one disastrous frontal attack across dead flat ground without any cover at Shaikh Sa'ad (7 January 1916) to dispell these illusions. After the 2nd Battalion The Black Watch had suffered horrendous casualties, Captain R.H. Dundas noted that 'In almost every way [except gun fire] this is universally voted far worse than France, and more slaughterous'.[115] The Scots, nonetheless, would eventually realise their preference for open warfare, both in Mesopotamia and Palestine, thereby bolstering their battalions' sense of achievement. Writing from Palestine in November 1917, Major R. Brown asserted that the 5th Argyll and Sutherland Highlanders have 'done awfully well, and we are all rather bucked about it . . .'. As he added a few days later, 'Could you believe the Battalion has walked 69 miles in the last ten days or so . . . and fought four battles?'[116]

All these aggressive attitudes and values, though, have to be placed in a broader perspective. Like other British soldiers, the Scots endured often lengthy periods of stultifying routine between bouts of combat and, in the main, were besotted neither with thoughts of battle nor with hatred of the enemy. They had the capacity to turn the abnormality and awfulness of warfare into the normal and the ordinary, laced with a degree of fatalism. When Private (later Captain) A. Thomson, 4th Battalion The Black Watch, first arrived in the trenches, he was amazed to meet two regulars of the 2nd Battalion, who were utterly nonchalant about the enemy's rifle fire while they were looking for a 'sigharee' (a sort of brazier) to cook their ham on.[117] John Hay Beith, an Argyll and Sutherland Highlander, who wrote under the pseudonym 'Ian Hay', claimed that the British Tommy was 'chiefly concerned, as in peacetime, with his holidays and creature comforts', and so regarded battle as 'a mere incident between one set of billets and another'.[118]

Overall the wartime experience of the Scots had many similarities with the experience of other British soldiers, but it had distinctive aspects, too. Undoubtedly good morale, underpinned by a highly positive self-image, fortified Scots in coping with the conditions and in confronting the enemy. Like others, they met with failure as well as success and received not only plaudits but also mockery on occasions (as when the Camerons and Glosters ended up charging each other in a night attack in 1916).[119] After serving with the 10th Cameronians, Captain L. Gameson, Royal Army Medical Corps, remarked of the Scots that 'With some notable exceptions, whom I keep in my thoughts, they are as a race so ready to admire themselves that an outsider's opinion passes them unheeded'.[120] Seeing themselves as others see them is not a bad point on which to conclude a study of Scotsmen at war, and, if the latter sometimes earned ridicule for embellishing or exaggerating their wartime exploits, this should not detract from a contribution which was often distinctive and never less than considerable.

Notes

I should like to thank the Trustees of the Imperial War Museum for access to their manuscript collections and those holders of copyright material who allowed me to quote from their papers: Mrs J.J.H. Swallow (Ferguson Mss.), Mr Felix Gameson (Gameson Mss.), Mr Edward Hulse (Hulse Mss.), Mrs E.G.M. Clayton (Liddle Mss.), Mr J.M. Morgan (Low Mss.), Mrs J.S. Brown (MacKenzie Mss.), Mrs I. Lock (H.H. Stainton Mss.), Colonel A. Thorburn (Thorburn Mss.) and Mrs M. Sinclair (Townsend Mss.). Also Peter Liddle, the Liddle Collection, Leeds University.

1   War Office, *Statistics of the Military Effort of the British Empire during the Great War*, London, HMSO, 1922, part v; J.M. Winter, 'Britain's lost generation of the First World War', *Population Studies*, 1977, vol.31, p.451; S. Wood, *The Scottish Soldier*, Manchester, Archive Publications, 1987, p. 88.

2   The 9th, 15th, 51st (Highland), 52nd (Lowland), 64th (2nd Highland) and 65th (2nd Lowland) Divisions.

3   'Locally Raised Units', War Office, August 1916, P[ublic] R[ecord] O[ffice], Kitchener Mss., PRO 30/57/73, pp.I-II; see also J. Johnston, *A Souvenir of the Great War*, Aberdeen, Aberdeen Daily Journal Office, 1915, p.47; *War Record of the 2nd City of Edinburgh Battery*, Glasgow, R. Maclehose, 1923, pp.1, 9–10.

4   P[riva]te E. Herd, diary, 9 December 1914, Herd Mss., I[mperial] W[ar] M[useum], DS/MISC/48; Pte H. Stainton, 'A Personal Narrative of the War', p.10, Stainton Mss., IWM, 78/11/1; C. Hughes, 'The New Armies' in I.F.W. Beckett and K. Simpson (eds.), *A Nation in Arms*, Manchester, Manchester University Press, 1985, p.106.

5   A. Somerville, *The Autobiography of a Working Man* (1848), ed. by J. Carswell, London, Turnstile Press, 1951, p.116.

6   L[ieutenan]t-Col[onel] L.B. Oatts, *Proud Heritage: The Story of the Highland Light Infantry*, 4 vols, Glasgow, House of Grant, 1961, vol.3, p.165.

7   J. Reith, *Wearing Spurs*, London, Hutchinson, 1966, p.25.

8   See note 1 and P.E. Dewey, 'Military Recruiting and the British Labour Force during the First World War', *The Historical Journal*, 1984, vol.27, pp.199–223; Lt-Col R.R. Thompson, *The Fifty-Second (Lowland) Division 1914–1918*, Glasgow, MacLehose, 1923. p.10.

9   *Historical Records of the Queen's Own Cameron Highlanders*, Edinburgh, Blackwood, 1931 vol. IV, p.46; E. and A. Linklater, *The Black Watch: The History of the Royal Highland Regiment*, London, Barrie & Jenkins, 1977, p.143; Lance Corporal (L/Cpl) G. Ramage, diary, 17 April 1915, Ramage Mss., N[ational] L[ibrary of] S[cotland], Ms 944; Col W.N. Nicholson, *Behind the Lines*, London, Jonathan Cape, 1939, p.38: Maj[or]-Gen[eral] G.G. Egerton, diary, 1 July 1915, PRO, CAB 45, p.28.

10 *ibid.*, 12 September 1915, pp.116–17.

11 T. Chalmers, *An Epic of Glasgow: History of the 15th Battalion The Highland Light Infantry (City of Glasgow Regiment)*, Glasgow, John McCallum, 1934, p.x; T. Chalmers (ed.), *A Saga of Scotland: History of the 16th Battalion The Highland Light Infantry (City of Glasgow Regiment)*, Glasgow, John McCallum, 1930, pp.2–3; J.W. Arthur and I.S. Munro (eds.), *The Seventeenth Highland Light Infantry (Glasgow Chamber of Commerce Battalion) Record of War Service 1914–1918*, Glasgow, D.J. Clark, 1920.

12 Second Lieutenant (2nd Lt) A.D. Gillespie, *Letters from Flanders*, London, Smith Elder, 1916, pp.2, 12; W.L. Andrews, *Haunting Years: The Commentaries of a War Territorial*, London, Hutchinson, 1930, pp.12–13; Brigadier C.N. Barclay, 'Recollections', p.2, Barclay Mss., L[iddle] C[ollection].

13 *ibid.*

14 Pte D. Smith, diary, p.1, Smith Mss., S[cottish] U[nited] S[ervices] M[useum], 72/78.915.1.

15 2nd Lt K. Kershaw, letter, 30 June 1915, Kershaw Mss., LC.

16 P. Simkins, *Kitchener's Army: The Raising of the New Armies, 1914–16*, Manchester, Manchester University Press, 1988, pp.104–119; Dewey, *op.cit.*, pp.206–21.

17 Nicholson, *op.cit.*, p.19; Maj.-Gen. A. G. Wauchope, *A History of The Black Watch [Royal Highlanders] in the Great War 1914–1918*, 3 vols. London, Medici Society, 1926, vol.2, p.40; Col J.M. Findlay, *With The 8th Scottish Rifles 1914–1919*, London, Blackie, 1926, p.5.

18 Lionel Ferguson, 'War Diary 1914–1919', Ferguson Mss., IWM, 77/166/1.

19 Pte N.J. Fowler to his niece, n.d., Fowler Mss., IWM 82/3/1.

20 Wauchope, *op.cit.*, vol.3, p272; Maj. F.W. Bewsher, *The History of the 51st (Highland) Division 1914–1918*, Edinburgh, Blackwood, 1921, p.8; Chalmers, *A Saga of Scotland*, p.45. Compare with G.Y. Cheyne, *The Last Great Battle of the Somme: Beaumont Hamel 1916*, Edinburgh, John Donald, 1988, pp.27, 144.

21 Capt[ain] E. Campion to Maj.-Gen. G. Egerton, 17 September 1914, Egerton Mss., SUS; Sir J.A.L. Haldane, diary, 12, 31 August 1914, Haldane Mss., NLS, Ms 20248, ff. 28, 51.

22 A. Runcie, 'Territorial Mob', p.7, Runcie Mss., IWM, P.185; see also Lt-Col

J. Stewart and J. Buchan, *The Fifteenth Scottish Division 1914–1919*, Edinburgh, Blackwood, 1926, pp.4–11; Nicholson, *op.cit.*, pp.38, 60; Bewsher, *op.cit.*, p.2; *Historical Records of the Queen's Own Cameron Highlanders*, vol.IV, p.139.

23 Pte J.B. Mackenzie to his wife, 6 July 1915, Mackenzie Mss., IWM, 87/62/1; 2nd Lt G. Buchanan Smith to his mother, 14 September 1915, Buchanan Smith Mss., NLS, Acc 9446, no 198.

24 Ramage, diary, 23 April 1915, Ramage Mss., NLS, Ms 944.

25 *ibid.*, 23 and 26 April 1915, Ramage Mss., NLS, Ms 944; Lt H. Munro to his father, 23 May 1915, Munro Mss., NLS, Ms 26930, f.44; Pte J. Laing, diary, 29 December 1914, 4 and 9 January 1915, Laing Mss., B[lack] W[atch] A[rchive, Balhousie Castle, Perth, item] 0768.

26 Ramage, diary, 24 April 1915, Ramage Mss., NLS, Ms. 944.; Capt G. Stewart to his mother, 30 August 1916, Stewart Mss., LC, f.51; Pte P. Macgregor to his wife, 6 August 1916, Macgregor Mss., IWM, 76/153/2; Pte A.H. Hubbard to his family, 9 June 1916, Hubbard Mss., IWM, Con Shelf.

27 Pte A. Clark, diary, 15 August 1916, Clark Mss., IWM, 84/1/1; Ramage, diary, 24 April 1915, Ramage Mss., NLS, Ms 944; Capt J.B. Lorimer to his mother, 15 and 20 September 1916, Lorimer Mss., NLS, Acc. 6592, ff.107, 108.

28 Haldane, diary, 15 January 1915, Haldane Mss., NLS, Ms 20248, f.143; Lt A. Knight to his mother, 15 December 1915, IWM, P303; Capt J. Hay-Young to his father, 15 January 1915, Hay-Young Mss., LC, f.5; L/Cpl J. Dalziel, diary, 18 and 21 February 1915, Dalziel Mss., A[rgyll] and S[utherland] H[ighlanders] Museum, [Stirling Castle], N-El DAL; Lt J. MacPhie, diary, 7 May 1918, A&SH Museum, N-E6 MAC 15286.

29 Munro to Winifred, 20 June 1915, Munro Mss., NLS, Ms. 26930, f.97; 2nd Lt J.D. Milne, diary, 27 May 1916, Milne Mss., LC; L/Cpl R. Loudon, memoirs, IWM, 87/17/1, ff.13, 54; Capt E.T. Townsend, letters to his mother, 19 July 1915, 30 April and 6 May 1916, Townsend Mss., IWM, 86/66/1.

30 Mackenzie to his wife, 18 June 1915, Mackenzie Mss., IWM, 87/62/1; see also Lt-Col H.G. Hyslop, diary, 26 November 1915, vol.2, Hyslop Mss., A&SH Museum, N-E2 HYS, p.40; Wood, *op.cit.*, p.89.

31 Stainton, 'A Personal Narrative of the War', p.20, IWM, 78/11/1; L/Cpl H.S. Taylor, 'Reminiscences of the Great War 1914/1918', IWM 80/19/1; Col A.K. Reid, *Shoulder to Shoulder: The Glasgow Highlanders 9th Battalion Highland Light Infantry 1914–1918*, Glasgow, A. Aiken, 1988, p.169; C. Falls, *The Gordon Highlanders in the First World War 1914–1919*, Aberdeen, The University Press, 1958, p.118; T.M. Lyon, *More Adventures in Kilt and Khaki*, Kilmarnock, Standard Press, 1917, p.70.

32 *ibid.*, pp.12–13; Smith, diary, p.36, Smith Mss., SUS, 72/78.915.1.

33 Lt-Col G.S. Hutchinson, *Footslogger: An Autobiography*, London, Hutchinson, 1931, pp.132, 149–50; Ramage, diary, 30 May 1915, Ramage Mss., NLS, Ms 946; Captain A.R. Boyle, diary, 1 October 1915, p.66, Boyle Mss., LC.

34 Reid, *op.cit.*, p.169.

35 A.M. McGilchrist, *The Liverpool Scottish 1900–1919*, Liverpool, Henry Young, 1930, p.117; see also Falls, *op.cit.*, pp.118–19 and Wood, *op.cit.*, p.89.

36 Nicholson, *op.cit.*, pp.145–6; Bewsher, *op.cit.*, p.65; see also L/Cpl T. Dalziel, diary, 12 February 1915, Dalziel Mss., IWM 86/51/1.

37 Maj. C.J. Low to Noanie, 18 May 1915, Low Mss., IWM, 79/54/1, p.107; see also A. Drummond, 'A Journey to India', p.8, BWA, 0770/1.

38 Findlay, *op.cit.*, p.26; Ramage, diary, 20 May 1915, Ramage Mss., NLS, Ms. 945; Mackenzie to his wife, 6 July 1915, Mackenzie Mss., IWM 87/62/1; Munro to his mother, 21 May 1915, Munro Mss., NLS, Ms. 26930, ff.41–2.

39 Munro to his father, 27 June 1915, Munro Mss., NLS, Ms 26930, f.106.

40 W.S. Churchill to Clementine Churchill, 20 January 1916, in M. Gilbert, *Winston S. Churchill*, Vol.III, London, Heinemann, 1971, p.643; J. Terraine (ed.), *General Jack's Diary 1914–1918*, London, Eyre & Spottiswoode, 1964, p.134; 2nd Lt J.A. Fraser to G. Fraser, 5 October 1917, Fraser Mss., LC, f.29.

41 Ramage, diary, 8 June 1915, Ramage Mss., NLS, Ms 946.

42 Mackenzie to his wife, 6 July 1915, Mackenzie Mss., IWM, 87/62/1.

43 Capt H.W. Samson, letter from Freiburg, 3 November 1917, Samson Mss., K[ing's] O[wn] S[cottish] B[orderers Regimental] Museum, [Berwick Castle] T1/14; see also Capt A.M. Shaw, letter to his family, 20 May 1916, Shaw Mss., KOSB Museum, T1/13; Gillespie, *op.cit.*, p.255; Pte H.W. Mann to Jess Mann, 13 May 1917, Mann Mss., NLS, Acc 10007.

44 Townsend to his mother, 5 July 1915, Townsend Mss., IWM, 86/66/1.

45 Runcie, 'Territorial Mob', p.29, Runcie Mss., IWM, P.185; Andrews, *op.cit.*, pp.64–5.

46 Capt A.M. Shaw, 'A Diary of Gallipoli', 9 September 1915, Shaw Mss., KOSB Museum, T1/13.

47 2nd Lt R.W.F. Johnston, 'Experiences of War', p.33, Johnston Mss., LC.

48 Ramage, diary, 20 April 1915, NLS, Ms. 944.

49 Runcie, 'Territorial Mob', p.33, IWM P.185; Haldane, diary, 11 February 1915, Haldane Mss., NLS, Ms20248, f.149.

50 Johnston, 'Experiences of War', p.11, Johnston Mss., LC.

51 Buchanan Smith to his mother, 14 September 1915, Buchanan Smith Mss., NLS, Acc 9446, no. 198; see also 2nd Lt A.D.M. Jameson to his mother, 25 February 1917, Jameson Mss., NLS, Ms 10305, f.265. Compare with Cheyne, *op.cit.*, pp.144–5 and C. Harvie, *No Gods and Precious Few Heroes: Scotland 1914–1980*, London, Edward Arnold, 1981, p.11.

52 Mackenzie to his wife, 6 July 1915, Mackenzie Mss., IWM, 87/62/1.

53 Col A.E. Holland to C. Churchill, 18 February 1916, in M. Gilbert, *Winston S. Churchill*, Vol.III Companion Part 2 (London; Heinemann, 1972), p.1431.

54 Barclay, 'Recollections', p.13, Barclay Mss., LC.

55 Lt J.B. MacLean to A. MacLean, 25 July 1918, Maclean Mss., LC, f.68.

56 Capt J. Jack, diary, 19 February 1916 in Terraine (ed.), *op.cit.*, p.127.

57 Ramage, diary, 20 April 1915, Ramage Mss., NLS, Ms 944; L/Cpl A. McLachlan, diary, 9 November 1914, McLachlan Mss., A&SH Museum, N-E2 McLA 16152; Gillespie, *op.cit.*, p.312; Stewart and Buchan, *op.cit.*, p.44; *Historical Records of the Queen's Own Cameron Highlanders*, vol.IV, pp.149–50.

58 Lt-Col J. Young, 'A Doctor's Letters from Gallipoli', p.27, SUS, RAMC.v.915.1.

59 Maj A.D.C. Krook, diary 1914, BWA, 0170.

60 D. Fraser (ed.), *In Good Company: The First World War Letters and Diaries*

of The Hon. William Fraser Gordon Highlanders, Wilton, Michael Russell, 1990, pp.36–7; Capt C. Low to Noanie, 25 November 1914, Low Mss., IWM, 79/54/1; 2nd Lt D.J. McDougall, diary, 4 October 1914, McDougall Mss., IWM, 79/51/1.

61 Capt J.A. Liddell, diary, 5 September 1914, Liddell Mss., IWM, PP/MCR/281; Lt A.A. Macfarlane Grieve, letter, 29 September 1914, Sir J. Fraser Mss., LC.

62 Jack, diary, 10 October 1914, in Terraine (ed.), *op.cit.*, p.60.

63 Gillespie, *op.cit.*, pp.57, 233; see also 2nd Lt M.S. Goodbahn, diary, 3 July 1915, Goodbahn Mss., IWM, P371; Capt R.H.W. Rose, diary, 3 and 11 September 1914, Rose Mss., LC, pp.15, 19–20; Lorimer to his mother, 13 November 1916, Lorimer Mss., NLS, Acc 6592, f.134.

64 2nd Lt A.J.N. Williamson, diary, 23 August 1914, Williamson Mss., IWM, 89/2/1; see also Lyon, *op.cit.*, p.178; 2nd Lt W. Surrey Dane, diary, 30 September 1915, Surrey Dane Mss., LC, p.20; Capt J.B. Muir, notebook, 25 July 1915, Muir Mss., BWA, 0748; S. Wood, *The Auld Alliance: Scotland and France: The Military Connection*, Edinburgh, Mainstream Publishing, 1989, p.144.

65 Ramage, diary, 30 April 1915, Ramage Mss., NLS, Ms 944.

66 Haldane, diary, 25 January and 10 December 1915, Haldane Mss., NLS, Ms 20248, ff.145, 373; see also Capt A.T. Wyllie, diary, 9 November 1916, Wyllie Mss., IWM, 75/102/1.

67 Lt J.D. MacLeod to his mother, 27 March 1917, MacLeod Mss., LC, f.264; Lt J.A. Fraser to Rev. C. Fraser, 2 August 1917, Fraser Mss., LC, f.13; Bewsher, *op.cit.*, p.47.

68 Haldane, diary, 26 September 1915, Haldane Mss., NLS, Ms 20248, f.341; Low to Nono, 11 May 1915, Low Mss., IWM, 79/54/1; see also Lt J.B. MacLean to A. MacLean, November 1917, Maclean Mss., LC, f.31; Shaw, 'A Diary of Gallipoli', Shaw Mss., KOSB Museum, T1/13, f.11; Capt J. Hay-Young to Mag, 4 March 1917 and to his father, 11 December 1917, Hay-Young Mss., LC, ff.101, 152.

69 J. Baynes, *Morale: A Study of Men and Courage: The Second Scottish Rifles at the Battle of Neuve Chapelle 1915*, London, Leo Cooper, 1967, p.101; Lt A. Knight to his mother, 15 December 1915, Knight Mss., IWM, P.303; Anonymous [Rev. W.P. Young], *9th Royal Scots (T.F.) B Company on Active Service From a Private's Diary February – May 1915* (1915), p.27; Pte J. Campbell to his parents, 25 November n.d., Campbell Mss., A&SH Museum, N-E8 CAM; Wyllie, diary, 8 August 1915, Wyllie Mss., IWM, 75/102/1.

70 Baynes, *op.cit.*, pp.95–6; Haldane, diary, 9 September 1916, Haldane Mss., NLS, Ms 20249, f.187.

71 Smith, diary, p.14, Smith Mss., SUS, 72/78.915.1; 2nd Lt W. Paterson, diary, pp.144–45, Paterson Mss., SUS, M 1993.420.1; see also Capt. Sir E. Hulse to his uncle, 2 February 1915, Hulse Mss., IWM, 86/30/1.

72 Baynes, *op. cit.*, p. 94; Kershaw to his family, 19 July 1915, Kershaw Mss., LC, f.9; MacLean to A. MacLean, November 1917, MacLean Mss., LC, f.31.

73 Hutchison, *op.cit.*, p.146; Jack, diary, 10 November 1915 in Terraine (ed.), *op.cit.*, p.118.

74 Gillespie, *op.cit.*, pp.22–3, 232, 256; Buchanan Smith to his mother, 12 September 1915, Buchanan Smith Mss., NLS, Acc 9446, no. 198; see also

Wood, *The Scottish Soldier*, p.96; E. and A. Linklater, *op.cit.*, p.142; *Historical Records of the Queen's Own Cameron Highlanders*, vol.III, p.151.

75 2nd Lt J.G. Scott to his father, 31 January 1915, Scott Mss., LC; see also D.M. Henderson, *Highland Soldier: A Social Study of the Highland Regiments, 1820–1920*, Edinburgh, John Donald, 1989, pp.234–62.

76 Falls, *op.cit.*, p.60; Capt. S. Gillon, *The K.O.S.B. in the Great War*, London, Thomas Nelson, 1930, p.390; Pte C. Brown, letter, 26 November 1915, Angus Mss., NLS, Acc 7658.

77 Nicholson, *op.cit.*, p.143; see also Maj. The Hon. W. Fraser, diary 22 May 1917 in D. Fraser (ed.), *op.cit.*, p.110 and Milne, diary, 13 June 1916, Milne Mss., LC.

78 Lt R.L. Mackay, diary, 21 July 1918, Mackay Mss., A&SH Museum, N-E11 MAC, p.68.

79 Baynes, *op.cit.*, pp.97–8.

80 Andrews, *op.cit.*, p.249; Bewsher, *op.cit.*, p.85; Chalmers (ed.), *A Saga of Scotland*, pp.56–67.

81 Lt Stewart to his father, 15 February 1916 and 7 July 1916 in *Letters of Lieutenant J.W.H. Stewart, 16th and 9th Royal Scots, 1914–1919*, Edinburgh, private, 1936, pp.218, 240; MacLeod to his mother, 27 March 1917, MacLeod Mss., LC, f.264.

82 Stainton, 'A Personal Narrative of the War', p.10, IWM, 78/11/1.

83 Fowler to his niece, 18 March 1916, Fowler Mss., IWM, 82/3/1; see also Ramage, diary, 16 April 1915, Ramage Mss., NLS, Ms 944; Smith, diary, p.14, Smith Mss., SUS, 72/78.915.1; Hutchinson, *op.cit.*, p.130; Andrews, *op.cit.*, p.249.

84 Ramage, diary, 12 May 1915, Ramage Mss., NLS, Ms 945; Haldane, diary, 23 February 1916, Haldane Mss., NLS, Ms 20249, ff.27–8.

85 Lorimer to his mother, 2 January 1917, Lorimer Mss., NLS, Acc 6592, f.168; Barclay, 'Recollections', Barclay Mss., LC, pp.12–13.

86 Lt L. Sotheby, diary, 3 January 1915, Sotheby Mss., LC, p.19.

87 Fraser, diary, 24 June 1917 in D. Fraser (ed.), *op.cit.*, p.122.

88 MacLeod to his mother, 16 March 1916, MacLeod Mss., LC, p.165.

89 Terraine (ed.), *op.cit.*, p.246; on amalgamation difficulties see Mackay, diary, 12 and 14 June 1918, Mackay Mss., A&SH Museum, N-E11 MAC, p.63.

90 Haldane, diary, 19 April 1916, Haldane Mss., NLS, Ms 20249, f.84.

91 2nd Lt J.A. Fraser to G. Fraser, 5 August 1917, Fraser Mss., LC, f.14; see also Nicholson, *op.cit.*, p.48; Bewsher, *op.cit.*, p.410.

92 Col. H.H. Story, *History of The Cameronians (Scottish Rifles) 1910–1933*, Aylesbury and Slough, Hazell Watson Viney, 1961, pp.142–3; see also Buchanan Smith to his mother, 10 September 1915, Buchanan Smith Mss., NLS, Acc. 9446, no.198; Jack, diary, 30 January 1915 in Terraine (ed.), *op.cit.*, p.98.

93 Johnston, 'Experiences of War', Johnston Mss., LC, p.49; MacLeod to his mother, 2 April 1916, MacLeod Mss., LA, f.167.

94 Findlay, *op.cit.*, p.142.

95 Sir J. Crabbe, memoir, Crabbe Mss., LC.

96 Sotheby, diary no. 3, 15 March 1915, Sotheby Mss., LC, f.5; see also Pte A. Thomson, diary, 10 March 1915, Thomson Mss., BWA, 0783, f.52.

97 Lt J.C. Cunningham to his mother, 6 October 1916, Cunningham Mss., LC.

98 Baynes, *op.cit.*, pp.202–5.

99 Shaw, 'A Diary of Gallipoli', 22 August 1915, Shaw Mss., KOSB Museum, T1/13; J. Lush, *Letters and Memories*, Oxford, Blackwell, 1916, p.108; Paterson, diary, pp.137–8, Paterson Mss., SUS, M 1993.420.1; Maj. J. Stewart to his wife, 26 April 1916, Stewart Mss., BWA, 0264; The Officers, *The Fifth Battalion Highland Light Infantry in the War 1914–1918*, Glasgow, MacLehose, 1921, p.43.

100 Pte H. Wren, diary, 6 August 1916, Wren Mss., A&SH Museum, N-E10 WREN; Hyslop, diary, 27 September 1914, vol. 1, Hyslop Mss., A&SH Museum, N-E2 HYS, p.58.

101 MacLean to A. MacLean, 12 December 1917, MacLean Mss., LC, f.33; see also 2nd Lt J.A. Fraser to his father, 11 August 1917, Fraser Mss., LC. f.17; Haldane, diary, 26 November 1916, Haldane Mss., NLS, Ms 20249, f.209; Fraser, diary, 24 June 1917 in D. Fraser (ed.), *op.cit.*, p.122.

102 D. Winter, *Death's Men: Soldiers of the Great War*, Harmondsworth, Penguin, 1979, p.209.

103 Runcie, 'Territorial Mob', p.31, Runcie Mss., IWM, P.185; Capt. A.G. Ritchie, diary, 25 October 1914, Ritchie Mss., LC; Jack, diary, 8 August 1915 in Terraine (ed.), *op.cit.*, p.107; Herd, diary, 23, 25, 27, 28 November 1915, Herd Mss., IWM, DS/MISC/48; Lt-Col C.W.E. Gordon, diary, 6 July 1916, vol.3, p.84, Gordon Mss., BWA, 0164; Lt-Col H.G. Hyslop, diary, 6 November 1916, vol.III, Hyslop Mss., A&SH Museum, N-E2 HYS, p.42.

104 Gillespie, *op.cit.*, pp.2, 113–116, 257; C. Simpson, diary, 22 October 1914, Simpson Mss., IWM, 89/7/1; Lt-Col D.H. MacDonell to his mother, 5 March 1916, MacDonnell Mss., IWM, 88/39/1.

105 Gillespie, *op.cit.*, p.146.

106 Anonymous, *op.cit.*, pp.66–7; Andrews, *op.cit.*, p.220; Gillespie, *op.cit.*, p.146; MacLeod to his mother, 5 May 1915, MacLeod Mss., LC, f.88.

107 Ramage, diary, 15 May 1915, Ramage Mss., NLS, Ms 945; see also Gillespie, *op.cit.*, pp.147, 149; Capt. W. Fraser to his father, 3 May 1915 in Fraser (ed.), *op.cit.*, p.52; 2nd Lt W. Surrey Dane, diary, 24 September 1915, Surrey Dane Mss., LC, f.17.

108 Mackay, diary, 12 October 1916, Mackay Mss., A&SH Museum, N-E11 MAC, p.4; MacLean to A. MacLean, 15 August 1917, MacLean Mss., LC, f.17; on the gas failure at Loos see 2nd Lt W. Surrey Dane, diary, 26 September 1915, Surrey Dane Mss., LC, f.19; Maj. C.W.E. Gordon, diary, 26 September 1915, vol.2, pp.8–9, Gordon Mss., BWA, 0164.

109 Maj. J. Stewart, diary, 9 August 1915, Stewart Mss., BWA, 0171 and Stewart to his wife, 5 May 1916, Stewart Mss., BWA, 0264.

110 Stewart to his wife, 7 August 1915, 1 September and 1 October 1915, 9 March, 3 and 28 April, 3 and 15 May 1916, Stewart Mss., BWA, 0264.

111 Sotheby, letter, 11 May 1915, Sotheby Mss., LC, f.23.

112 Mackay, diary, 22 October 1918, Mackay Mss., A&SH Museum, N-E11 MAC, p.78.

113 Capt. Sir E. Hulse to his uncle, 2 February 1915, Hulse Mss., IWM, 86/30/1.

114 Lt M. Thorburn to his parents, 1 November 1915, Thorburn Mss., IWM, 88/56/1 (P); see also Lt Col D.H. MacDonnell to his mother, 5 March 1916, MacDonnell Mss., 88/39/1.

115 Capt. R.H. Dundas, diary, 14 January 1916, Dundas Mss., BWA 0640/3.

116 Maj. R. Brown, letters, 12 and 16 November 1917, Brown Mss., A&SH Museum, N-E5 BRO.

117 Pte A. Thomson, diary, 6 March 1915, Thomson Mss., BWA, 0783, ff.39–40.

118 I. Hay, *Carrying On – After The First Hundred Thousand*, Edinburgh, Blackwood, 1917, p.243; see also J. Buchan, *The History of The Royal Scots Fusiliers (1678–1918)*, London, Thomas Nelson, 1925, p.459.

119 Lt E. Chadband, memoirs, 22/23 July 1916, Chadband Mss., IWM, PP/MCR/32, p.39.

120 Capt. L. Gameson, diary, 11 November 1918, Gameson Mss., IWM, Con Shelf, p.382.

Chapter 25

The British Working Man in Arms[1]

John Bourne

The social history of the Great War has generally avoided the battlefield.[2] Its principal concern has been to analyze the relationship between war and social change. Questions of class, gender, social welfare, and – increasingly – remembrance have been at its heart.[3] This is understandable. More then five-and-a-half million men served in the British Army during the war,[4] 22.11 per cent of the male population of the United Kingdom and 10.73 per cent of the population as a whole.[5] It took the efforts of many more, male and female, to keep the troops armed, equipped and supplied. Such a degree of mobilization ensured that the war was socially as well as militarily important.

This paper is equally concerned with the war as a social experience. It is also a modest attempt to relate the social history of the war to the military history. It is not concerned with the impact of the war on society, however, but with the impact of society on the war.

The First World War is often approached for the first time through the medium of literature rather than of history. This has had the unfortunate effect of embalming the war in the image of the public school subalterns who wrote many of its most famous memoirs and poems. Such men should neither be devalued nor disparaged. Many displayed outstanding leadership and devotion to duty. They suffered disproportionately high levels of casualties.[6] But it should be stressed that mass recruitment from a society which, in 1914, was overwhelmingly working-class and overwhelmingly urban, produced, by 1916, an overwhelmingly working-class, urban army.[7] The British soldier of the Great War was essentially the British working man in uniform.[8] This had important consequences for the way in which the war was experienced and endured.

The British look back on the Great War with dismay. A.J.P. Taylor delivered the judgement of posterity: 'brave, helpless soldiers; blundering, obstinate generals; nothing achieved'.[9] The war was the calvary of the common man. At the heart of this perception lie the casualties. Nothing in Britain's military experience before 1914 prepared the nation for the scale of loss. Britain's subsequent wars have happily failed to repeat it. The familiar images of trench warfare on the Western Front haunt the national memory. The fascination with the suffering of ordinary soldiers and junior officers remains. A question constantly recurs: 'how did they manage to stick it?'

One answer was supplied by a famous recruiting poster. In it a vast column of men, four abreast, curves into the distance. In the foreground civilians from a variety of occupations and social classes, a bewigged barrister, a navvy with his pick, a bowler-hatted clerk, rub shoulders with one another. But as the column swings away it is transformed into one of soldiers, uniformed, united, indistinguishable, inculcated and armed with military values.

Regtl. No.	RANK AND NAME	Married or Single	Date of Enrollment or re-commencement of Service	Age on Enlistment	Term of Service	Religion	G. C. Badges	Class Service or Proficiency Pay	Musketry Classification	No. of Rifle	No. of Rifle Bolt	No. of Equipment
5168	Rfm. MARKS	S	25.3.16	22	Heb.							
4951	" DUFTON	S	29.11.15	19	CE			2				
8053	" LYNCH	S	23.3.16	37	RC							
5172	" HIGGINS	S	25.3.16	33	CE							
4950	" WHITHAM	S	29.11.15	39	CE							
3888	" HAIGH	M	16.6.14	33	CE							

(iii)   Working class occupations: soldiers of 2/7 West Yorks (Leeds Rifles) have their background formally noted in their officer's Platoon Roll Book. [G.E. Raven: Liddle Collection]

The British Army which the wartime volunteers and conscripts entered was a peculiar institution. Its system and social values were the product of its historical experience as a colonial police force. They owed little to the values of British society, which the army's social composition poorly reflected.[10] The army's need was for a small, highly trained workforce capable of operating effectively in remote parts of the world, often in the face of local political hostility and public indifference at home. This put a high premium on morale. The army understood this and knew how to achieve it.

The army's method with recruits was to divest them of their civilian values and recreate them in the army's image. They were able to do this relatively easily. In 1907 the army's annual intake of recruits was fixed at

337

no more than 37,000 men a year. Recruits often came from among the least well educated sections of British society, the urban and rural poor. They were mostly young and impressionable. Once in the army, they would find themselves a minority among a majority already socialized into the army's way of doing things. They would also spend long periods abroad remote from their parent culture. The focus of their lives would be the battalion. The battalion would house them, feed them, clothe them, entertain them and sometimes punish them. It was the only institution on which they could fully depend for their security and welfare and even, on occasions, their survival. Their training and indoctrination could be thorough and systematic.

The pre-war Regular Army's attempt to turn civilian recruits into the kind of soldiers it wanted was based on the inculcation of military values. Central to this process were regimental pride, leadership and discipline. All recruits were expected to know their regimental history and to take inspiration from the heroism of the past. Historic rivalries and friendships with other regiments were skilfully fostered and maintained. The private soldier was expected to be hardy and uncomplaining, to know his job and to obey orders at all times. He was kept to this by the example of his officers. Relations between officers and men were generally cordial but not close. Officers were not expected to be 'pally' with their men. They were expected to set an example of physical courage and devotion to duty. They were also expected to uphold a disciplinary code of uncompromising severity. Military 'crime', petty theft, drunkenness, insubordination, was soon visited with retribution. This system worked well. It created a secure, ordered and, in many ways, comfortable world which provided soldiers with both a sense of belonging and a sense of obligation. It proved itself in the exacting conditions of combat during the battles of 1914 and 1915.

However, the massive intrusion into this ordered world of Kitchener's volunteers confronted the army with an unprecedented challenge to its historic practices. By Christmas 1914 the Regular Army was faced with the task of inculcating military values into a 'New Army' four times its own size. It had to do this while fighting a war on the Western Front in which it suffered heavy casualties, and while also carrying out its traditional colonial garrison duties. It was an impossible task.

The shortage of officers and NCOs was severe. Only the battalions of twelve New Army divisions had any Regular officers at all. The remaining eighteen divisions averaged only one former officer, 'dug out' of retirement, in each battalion.[11] The traditional situation was reversed. Instead of a minority of civilians entering a world of experienced professionals, a handful of experienced professionals was swamped by a mass of civilian amateurs. Many of the latter were much better educated than the normal army recruit. Many of them were also much older and far less impressionable. Some would serve in units where the regimental tradition still meant something, but an increasing number would belong to units – the Royal Flying Corps, the Machine-Gun Corps, the Tank Corps – which had no regimental history to draw on.

Men who fought on the Western Front were never entirely severed from civilian society. British newspapers were available in the trenches, sometimes on the same day of issue. The great engineering firm, Stewarts and Lloyds, even sent a monthly periodical, *Stories and Letters from Broad Street Chambers,* to Birmingham members of its staff on active service. The extraordinarily efficient army postal service kept up a constant flow of letters and parcels to the front. The consequences of this were very great.

One explanation for the tribulations of the British Army during the First World War and for its eventual triumph is that the painstaking struggle by a small number of senior commanders, in the most difficult of circumstances, eventually succeeded in turning civilians into soldiers in the Regular Army's image. 'We may have cursed the Germans, the mud, our loads, but NOT our senior commanders,' recalled James Jack, 'who, experienced officers, did their level best, often with amateur staffs.'[12] This is the theme which underpins the official history of the war and other writing by military 'insiders'.[13]

Not everyone has been so charitable. Denis Winter has condemned the Regular Army for failing to understand or make appropriate use of the magnificent human material which the First World War placed in its hands and for mindlessly hammering the wartime volunteers and conscripts into a Regular Army shape which destroyed their enthusiasm and initiative. He contrasts this unfavourably with the more democratic spirit of the Dominion forces, which he considers to have been more innovative and militarily effective.[14]

These two views, however different, share a common belief that the Regular Army's values did eventually prevail. This may be doubted.

'The pride of arms was . . . an abiding source of strength in the Regular Army during the early part of the last war,' recalled Lord Moran, who served as medical officer with a battalion of London working-class Royal Fusiliers. 'But it never took root in the citizen force upon which the brunt of the struggle later [fell].'[15] On the contrary, the 'citizen force' took a perverse pride in being unmilitary. Their self-image was self-deprecating. Soldiers' songs and slang provide a constant reminder of the army's civilian ethos.[16] 'Thank Gawd, we've got a Navy!' ordinary soldiers exclaimed. This did not mean that the citizen army lacked determination or fighting spirit. It did not. They may have been 'Fred Karno's Army', but when they got to Berlin even the Kaiser would have to admit that they were 'a bloody fine lot'. They would do their bit as best they could, but they were soldiers only for 'the duration'. When the 'lousy war' was over they would put the army and the war swiftly behind them; there would be 'no more soldiering' for them. The courage and devotion to duty of the Regulars could produce admiration and respect, but rarely comprehension.[17] The bulk of Britain's urban working-class army did not find the courage to stick it out by accepting and internalizing the values of the pre-war Regular Army. Their values and their inspiration remained obstinately civilian.

This has sometimes been questioned. Much has been made of the 'preparation' of the British people for war by the efforts of quasi-military organizations such as the Boy Scouts, The Boys' Brigade, and the Lads' Drill Association.[18] It has been calculated that as many as forty-one per cent of male adolescents belonged to some form of youth organization by 1914.[19] This has been offered as an explanation for the success of Kitchener's call-to-arms and for the later steadfastness of the British army in the field.

It is difficult to believe, however, that these organizations, even if they were as 'militarist' as some commentators have claimed, did anything more than scratch the surface of working-class life. Working-class values were shaped by the much more potent experience of family, work and community. Working-class attitudes to the army did not noticeably change during the Edwardian period. The army was still viewed with considerable hostility and suspicion. Respectable working-class families remained appalled by the idea of having a son who had 'gone for a soldier'. The Territorials certainly failed to benefit from the 'militarization' of the working class. They represented fewer than one per cent of males on the eve of war.[20] 'Saturday-night soldiers' were regarded with mild contempt. The Territorial Force entered the war seriously undermanned and with no real claim on public affection and esteem. Seven-eighths of those who served in the British Army during the war were wartime volunteers and conscripts, a higher proportion than any other major belligerent.[21] The vast majority had no pre-war military experience or training and no thought of ever getting any.

The Regular Army itself quickly realized that it was dealing with a different and more problematic kind of recruit, not one who had already been 'militarized', but its response was rather piecemeal until February 1918. The spectre of the French army mutinies and the Bolshevik revolution finally convinced the high command that something different would have to be done. Haig himself ordered a comprehensive scheme of education to be established in order to give the men a clearer understanding of the cause for which they were being asked to fight. The honour of the regiment and the memory of Albuhera were no longer enough. The army became committed not only to producing 'good soldiers' but also 'good citizens'. This was a significant moment in the history of the British Army.[22]

The debate about the pre-war 'militarization' of the working class has been important, however, in directing attention to the relationship between civilian social values and the war. This has been an antidote to the tendency in writing on the First World War to regard it as an experience without parallel, one for which previous existence provided little preparation, a sundering. The argument of this paper rests on the belief that the British working-class was well adapted to the challenge of war. Working-class culture provided the army with a bedrock of social cohesion and community on which its capacity for endurance rested. The existential realities from which this culture evolved were remarkably similar to those of military life, both in the army and on the battlefield.[23]

There was no 'average' experience during the First World War. The nature of the war itself changed dramatically over time. The British Army in 1914 was a small, highly trained force of craftsmen. Its soldiers dressed like gamekeepers. They wore soft caps and were armed with little more than rifles and bayonets. The battles they fought had more in common with Napoleonic warfare than they did with the 'modern' war which eventually evolved.

During the next two years the army underwent a rapid expansion, but at the price of widespread 'de-skilling' at all levels. By 1918 the army had evolved again into a vast force of specialists and technicians closer in spirit to the world of mass production. There was a significant decline in the proportion of infantrymen and an increase in the number of support units. The proportion of infantrymen who were simple rifle-carriers also declined in favour of increased numbers of machine-gunners and trench mortar men. The small scale of these units, typically half-a-dozen men, their hierarchical structure, typically a skilled gunner and several ammunition carriers, and their functional cohesion presented a scene familiar to most industrial workers, the majority of whom worked in small units. At the turn of the century the average British workshop employed only 29.26 male employees. Only four heavy industrial firms – Armstrong Whitworth, Vickers, John Brown, and Stewarts and Lloyd – employed more than 10,000 people.[24] Even in large-scale enterprises the primary unit of production was often quite small. Men worked in gangs, often under the immediate control of a skilled worker or foreman, rather than a 'boss', a trend reinforced by increasing industrial specialization. In a sense the soldier of 1918 even dressed like a factory worker. He wore a steel helmet and carried a respirator to protect himself against gas. He was as likely to be armed with an automatic weapon as with a rifle. His entry into battle might be by truck. He would be supported by an artillery barrage of crushing density, by tanks and by ground attack aircraft.

The nature of the war also varied from place to place. Some fronts saw more combat than others as did different parts of the same front. Experience of the war in an élite assault division was different from that in a run-of-the-mill trench holding one. There were considerable differences in attitude and perception in Regular Army, New Army and Territorial units, though these tended to even out over time. By 1918 the army had more of the flavour of a 'National Service' force. Other

341

differences, however, became more prominent, particularly those between specialists and 'ordinary' infantry. Combat was often the exceptional experience. Boredom, drudgery and physical discomfort were much more common.

Whatever the nature of the experience, however, it presented three basic challenges to the citizen soldier: learning to cope with a new and alien authority system; learning to do a new job of work; and learning to create a new form of community. The context may have been different from civilian life, but the challenges were familiar and recognizable. Working-class culture was shaped by the struggle with alien authority, and by the experience of work and community.

The fundamental reality of working-class life was inequality of power. This took many forms. Economic inequality was pronounced. Nearly ninety per cent of Britain's wealth was owned by ten per cent of the population. Fewer than a million people paid income tax by 1900. The division between the 'classes' and the 'masses' was everywhere apparent: not only in wealth but also in dress, speech, leisure pursuits, manners, education. Some working-class males, especially skilled workers in unionized industries, enjoyed substantial and rising incomes, but this could never be entirely relied upon. Unemployment, ill health and old age could have devastating effects on individual and family fortunes.

Political inequality was also apparent. Perhaps as much as forty per cent of the adult male working class was effectively disfranchised by the complexities of voter registration and property qualification.[25] Female disfranchisement also discriminated against the working class as this was the class to which most women belonged.

Economic and political inequality conspired to produce inequality of opportunity, not least in education and training. The final inequality was, perhaps, inequality of ambition. Outside observers were often appalled by what appeared to them the acquiescent and defeatist attitudes of working-class people.[26]

Working-class values were conditioned by the response to these inequalities. This response was marked by a pragmatic and contingent attitude to authority, by a distinctive work ethic and by an extraordinary degree of mutuality.

The urban working-class volunteers and conscripts of the First World War did not enter the alien authority system of the Regular Army naked and without tried and tested survival strategies. The most important source of these was the workplace. This was the battlefield of working-class life. Here, the inequality of power was felt most keenly and the need to respond most urgent.

The most significant working-class response – and certainly the most successful – was the trade union. The scale of trade union membership should not be overestimated. By 1914 some seventy-five per cent of working-class males, and an even greater proportion of working-class females, were un-unionized. Trade union membership had increased before the war, but this tended to be in areas like textiles and engineering where membership was already strong.[27]

These reservations, however, should not diminish the importance which trade unions have for deciphering working-class attitudes. Trade unions grew out of the working class. They owed little or nothing to middle- and upper-class patronage or ideas. They addressed the fundamental realities of working-class life, especially its industrial experience. This has not always endeared them either to free market liberals or to the middle-class left.

At the heart of trade unionism were the interests of the myriad of skilled workers. Spinners, weavers, boilermakers, fitters, turners, carpenters, tool-makers, engine drivers, miners were the aristocrats of labour. It was men like these who had established the first really successful unions in the aftermath of the collapse of Chartism. The unions they formed were often small, sometimes tiny. They used their strategic position at the heart of the industrial process, heavily reliant on handicraft skills, to exact privileges from their employers. They were also instrumental in setting up the Trades Union Congress in 1868 and dominated its proceedings. Larger-scale unions of general labourers followed in their wake from the 1880s, but enjoyed far less authority and success until the post-war foundation of the Transport and General Workers Union by Ernest Bevin and others.

Skilled unions undoubtedly helped to articulate a wider sense of workers' rights, but in practice their interests were sectarian. The activities of skilled unions were often directed as much against the interests and pretensions of other workers, skilled and unskilled, as they were against employers.

This sectarianism re-inforced the other principal characteristic of late-Victorian trade unionism, its defensive orientation. Trade unions did not seek fundamental changes in society. They wished to restrain the inequalities of power, not to remove them. They sought accommodation, a recognition of their rights, a fairer share of the cake. Within these limits the unions (especially the skilled unions) enjoyed considerable success. Unions possessed a formidable capacity for disruption. Their principal weapon was withdrawal of labour, the strike. It was a weapon against which, in practice – despite the law's hostility to trade unions – individual employers were poorly equipped to protect themselves. Workers struck because strikes were effective. Small employers, the majority, had limited resources with which to survive a prolonged withdrawal of labour. And there was always another small employer down the road only too pleased to take over their business. The prudent employer avoided alienating his workers, creating an atmosphere of compromise rather than conflict. Despite the image of industrial chaos engendered by the strike-prone years of 1912–13, British industrial relations before the war were characterized by a 'live and let live system' in which both sides recognized the limits of their power and the dangers of exceeding it.

Nowhere is the working-class attitude to authority more clearly expressed than in the trade union movement. British society during the Edwardian period was, perhaps, remarkably cohesive, but it also exhibited a very low level of social integration. The working-class was imbued with a strong sense of 'them and us'. 'Them' were clearly important. As landlords, employers, legislators, policemen, they exercised much influence on working-class life. 'Them' had power which it was often prudent to obey. But the acquiescence was not simply deferential. It was contingent on a generalized sense of 'fair play'. Both sides recognized limits. If these were crossed, the working-class was quite prepared to use its resources to challenge, to soften and – not least – to ignore the authority of 'them'.

Resort to the strike was not easily available during the war. But other forms of trade union practice were. The issue which concerned the manufacturing unions most was not wage rates or wage differentials (though these were important) or health and safety (on which the record of the unions was as bad as that of the employers) but productivity. Controlling the pace of production was central to union strategy.[28] This sometimes provoked an acute response in the form of a strike. But it more usually resulted in chronic shopfloor guerrilla warfare: demarcation disputes between different groups of workers, 'go slows', re-assertion of the prerogatives of skilled men, defence of the apprenticeship system, opposition to employers' attempts – such as piece rates or bonus schemes – to set worker against worker in an individual competition for better pay. This produced an attitude known as 'dead levelism'. It was the dominant ideology of the unionized working-class and one which employers found it almost impossible to overcome.

From the outside, armies appear to be uncomplicated authority structures. Those at the top decide and those at the bottom obey. If those at the bottom do not obey they can be punished with a range of sanctions, including, during the First World War, the death penalty. The reality is often less clear cut. Even in armies 'orders' at all levels are often 'negotiated'. The poet Ivor Gurney was lying in No Man's Land when an officer in 'the politest voice', a 'finicking accent', said 'Do you think you might crawl through there Gurney: there's a hole'? Gurney smiled and politely replied, 'I'm afraid not, Sir'.[29] It is difficult to imagine this incident happening in 1914. The pre-war Regular Army's uncompromising code was not always evenly applied. Territorial units were frequently criticised for the laxity of their discipline and for their 'family' atmosphere. There is some empirical evidence that the death penalty was disproportionately applied to those serving in Regular units.[30]

The apparent clarity and rigidity of the army's formal command structure which prescribed behaviour through rules and regulations could be subverted, modified and softened in practice. The new citizen army was never completely docile in the face of military authority even on first acquaintance. 'I expect in pre-war times such a barrage of words was meant to terrify half-witted recruits,' Private E.W. Prosser recalled of his first meeting with a bullying, foul-mouthed Regular Army NCO. 'They left us unmoved. We even had a good laugh out of it.'[31] Incidents of indiscipline were frequently widespread in the army.[32] These varied from the quite trivial to the clearly criminal, but they did not threaten the army's ability to function. Such strikes as there were took place in rear areas and base depots. They were not strikes against the war itself, but against the worst excesses of Regular Army practice. In this they were very similar to pre-war industrial unrest.

Soldiering was, after all, a form of work. A Canadian volunteer, Brian Brooke Claxton, explained the realities. It meant having 'the know-how to behave on all occasions like a tried and experienced man. It meant knowing who and how to salute, laying out your kit, getting your rations, having enough coal, getting leaves, escaping extra-duty, digging a trench, getting "your rights" – all by fair means or foul, but with a minimum of effort.'[33] This was very little different from the getting of knowledge by industrial and other workers. An important aspect of learning about work was learning how to avoid it, to make it easier, to dodge the foreman, to sneak off for a smoke without getting caught.

The British working man was shaped by the workplace, which he had probably entered between the ages of twelve and fourteen. British workers to an overwhelming extent (eighty-five per cent) were employed by someone else. Most of these (perhaps eighty per cent) were manual workers.[34] Much of the work undertaken was dirty, dangerous and boringly repetitive. Much was also physically arduous and required considerable strength. Employers, such as the Cadbury brothers, who took an interest in the physical and spiritual well-being of their workers, were few and far between. The workplace commonly offered only the most basic facilities for washing, changing and eating, if it offered any at all. Hours, too, were often long, not least for shop and office workers.

Tedium, regimentation, subordination and physical hardship were the common lot of the British working man. Industrial accidents were commonplace. Those in mining could produce casualty figures almost on a military scale. During the war the British worker merely substituted one set of hardships for another. Recruits from poorer working-class families actually enjoyed a higher standard of living and comfort in the army. When exposed to fresh air, physical training and plentiful quantities of army food they put on weight and height and discovered a new self-respect.[35]

The British worker at war also exchanged one set of compensations for another. Chief among these was comradeship. Comradeship made the war bearable. For some it even made it worthwhile. Membership of a 'primary group' of 'buddies' or 'pals' is now seen as essential to the maintenance of military morale. The army's commanders showed only a limited understanding of this. Such groups developed in spite of rather than because of official sponsorship. Even a superficial contemplation of British working-class life shows why this was likely to be the case.

Membership of trade unions was only one important example of the wider working-class characteristic of association. Mass membership of a wide-range of self-governing bodies was one of the fundamental features of working-class life.

The most important of these associations were probably the Friendly Societies. They were much larger than the trade union movement both in membership and resources, not least perhaps because they met with none of the legal hostility which trade unions faced. On the contrary parliament smiled benevolently on this manifestation of working-class thrift. The Friendly Societies provided, for a few pence a week, an affordable bulwark against the ultimate working-class nightmare, a pauper's funeral. They are indicative of working-class aspirations to respectability, one of the great social forces of the nineteenth century.

The third characteristically working-class organization after the trade unions and the Friendly Societies, was the Co-operative Movement, with its chain of retail stores which paid a regular dividend to members ('co-operators') depending on the amount of goods purchased.

The vocabulary of these quintessential working-class organizations – 'friendly', 'co-operative', 'union', 'dividend', 'mutual' – testifies to the sense of community and the idea of sharing. It was reflected in a network of more informal, more local organizations, often devoted to leisure activities: choral singing, brass banding; gardening; sport, 'the fancy'; the pub.[36] Here the vocabulary was of 'mates', 'chums', 'pals', words which were to find a poignant place in the history of the Great War.

The existence of this rich diversity of working-class 'civil society' is indicative of a much wider community solidarity. It would be easy to sentimentalize this. Working-class people did not choose community solidarity because of their innate moral superiority to the thrusting, individualistic, selfish bourgeoisie. They were forced into it by the demands of their situation. Community solidarity was the product of shared adversity. This produced a quite extraordinary degree of mutuality.

Sharing was at the heart of working-class culture. Its importance was learned at home. Although working-class demography conformed to the general decline in fertility and reduction in family size experienced nationally and internationally after 1870, working-class families remained large. Working-class homes remained small. Sharing began with space. Working-class people experienced a degree of physical closeness which is now unusual. There was little privacy, few places to be alone, nowhere to go and sulk. Selfish and irresponsible behaviour had immediate repercussions for everyone else in the house. Mutual toleration and clear lines of demarcation were essential.

Possessions were also shared. It was a world of hand-me-down clothing, of patch and mend. Working-class husbands gave their wives what they thought appropriate for housekeeping, but all other members of the household were expected to make a financial contribution as soon as they could. This was particularly so in the case of children, otherwise a major drain on family resources. The household was much more of an economic unit than it is now. This re-inforced the idea of belonging to a group rather than confronting the world as an isolated individual.

The group solidarity and mutuality forged at home was reinforced in the overlapping network of communities which made up working-class life. In areas of older working-class housing, there was the community of the yard or close, with its shared washing and toilet facilities. Everywhere there was the community of the street. Working-class life was street life. Children played in the street. Women gossiped in it. Men gathered in it and separated in it. There was also the community of the surrounding network of streets, the neighbourhood or urban village, its boundaries defined perhaps by a park, a main road, a canal, a railway line, or a factory, beyond whose familiar and secure features it could be dangerous to wander. And, finally, to those residential communities must be added the communities of association, in the workplace, the pub, the club and the team.

Most of these communities were intensely local. At this level most people knew one another. Many were inter-related. Many worked together at the same factory or mine located close to their homes. They drank together, played together, sometimes even prayed together. All faced the same difficulties and problems. All enjoyed good times and bad. The sense of mutual obligation was very strong.

This powerful sense of community can clearly be seen in working-class use of language. People did not speak of 'my house' but of 'our mom's', of 'my brother' but of 'our Billy', of 'my street' but of 'our street'.

There were advantages to this way of life. Working-class values did not encourage morbid introspection. Working-class life was psychologically comforting, at least for those who conformed to social norms. Working-class people were protected from the extremes of personal anguish found in more individualist, competitive and atomised cultures. Fate had singled no one out. Everyone was in the same boat. Your lot was the lot of everyone else you knew, or at least of everyone you knew well. There was no point bemoaning this. It was much more sensible to get on with life and make the best of things. This meant making the most of opportunities for celebration, excitement and distraction. Middle-class moralists regularly expressed their dismay at hedonistic working-class expenditure on drink and gambling, on vulgar music hall entertainments and the 'unnecessary' knick-knacks with which they loved to furnish their homes.

There was, however, a price to pay for this. Working-class life was deeply conformist. Psychological comfort was not extended to those who did not conform. It was easy for a sense of community to degenerate into intrusive prying. It was difficult to keep things private. In such a world gossip was a formidable instrument of social control. And so was ridicule. This is what would be handed out to those who 'got above themselves', who 'thought they were better than everyone else', who were 'posh' or 'toffee-nosed'. (In the Nottinghamshire mining village of Eastwood, D.H. Lawrence's father, portrayed as a vulgar brute by his son, is remembered as a 'good bloke who liked a drink and a joke'; Mrs Lawrence is remembered as a 'stuck up snob who put ideas above his station into her son's head'.) Working-class culture offered few incentives for those who wanted to 'get on'. Rather, it restrained them. Working-class aspirations remained limited and essentially inward-looking.

These limits were not only mental but also physical. The intense parochialism of working-class life expressed itself in hostility towards outsiders, even towards seemingly identical people from neighbouring communities. These tensions often surfaced at the beginning of the war when unfortunate 'foreigners' found themselves dropped like some extra-terrestrial being into locally-recruited Kitchener battalions.[37]

The cohesiveness of working-class communities was the product not only of conformity but also of hierarchy. Working-class society was not egalitarian. It offered many opportunities for the exercise of power and social condescension. Petty snobberies and petty tyrannies abounded. Skilled workers who could afford to keep their wives at home thought themselves a cut above mere labourers. They would discourage their daughters from marrying 'down'. Streets themselves had hierarchies. Some had bow-fronted houses with small gardens and net curtains or, even posher, leaded windows, the sign of the well-paid artisan. Others were less plush but equally neat and tidy. Women soap-stoned their steps and fought a constant battle against the encompassing grime. Other streets were regarded as dens of iniquity, the homes of drunkards who neglected their children, and who frequently came to the attention of the police. Even these could be categorised. One elderly Birmingham man was able to distinguish between streets in his childhood which were 'roughish, rough and dog-rough'.[38]

The working-class volunteers and conscripts who made up the over-whelming majority of the British Army during the Great War were, therefore, not unpromising military material. They were used to subordi-nation and tedium, two of the principal features of military life. They were inured to a certain degree of physical discomfort and material deprivation. They had quite low levels of expectation. They could put up with a lot provided there was an occasional festive intermission. The provision by the army of a huge network of welfare facilities, including YMCA canteens, concert parties and organized sport was a vital element in the maintenance of morale.[39] 'Given the chance we were always ready to live gaily,' recalled Private W.H. Groom of the London Rifle Brigade. 'And this particularly applied to our concert party evenings . . . Concert party night was one of the highlights of our rest periods. The troupe did a wonderful job, their work was of immeasurable value in raising morale.'[40] The pattern of working-class life in the army was allowed to replicate the pattern of its civilian life: conformity, community, celebration.

Working-class people were used to doing what they could to make life bearable. They could rely on a dense network of community loyalties for comfort and support. Their culture was riven with petty distinctions and sectarian divisions. They were comfortable with the idea of hierarchy and knew their place within it. They were not hostile to authority, though within certain limits, which they were prepared to defend. They were conservative and conformist. They harboured a reservoir of affection and respect for the monarchy and parliament. In short, they were biddable.

The war presented far more severe existential realities than those of civilian life, but they were recognizable realities, even to some extent familiar ones. Dying and killing and maiming were horrors for which little preparation was possible and many men's minds were destroyed by them. But there was nothing new about material poverty, physical hardship, disruptive and unpredictable outside authority with an alien agenda. Nor was there anything new about the strategies which were adopted to cope with them. These were the familiar strategies of working-class life.

Chief among them was loyalty to community and comrades, particularly those in the primary group of immediate 'mates', sometimes defined by function, at other times by choice. The army, like civilian life, provided an overlapping network of communities beyond the primary group: the section, the platoon, the company, the battalion, the brigade, the division. Some or all of them provided a focus for allegiance, a source of support, a duty or obligation. So did a man's trade: infantryman, gunner, sapper; or his particular skill, Vickers or Lewis gunner, bomber, trench mortar man. This helped to ensure that the soldier was more than an anonymous figure, a terrified statistic lost in a vast, impersonal bureaucracy of killing and dying. He belonged. And because he belonged he did not face the terrors alone.

Working-class values produced an army which was comfortable with hierarchy, formal and informal, and one which understood authority and its limits. In war, as in peace, men learned to make the best of things, to make do and mend, to grasp any opportunity to improve living conditions, to stick by their pals, to establish and maintain social norms, to draw lines of demarcation and acceptable behaviour, to find distraction in sport, entertainment, gambling and drink. It was an army with a remarkable degree of social cohesion, imbued with a resilient optimism, built to resist and to endure.

Notes

1   I should like to thank Dr R.W. Bushaway, Dr C.S.A. Chinn and Dr R.M. Robbins for their helpful comments on this paper.
2   Tony Ashworth's *Trench Warfare 1914–1918*, London, Macmillan, 1980, is a notable exception.
3   Arthur Marwick's *The Deluge. British Society and the First World War*, 1965, 2nd edn. 1991, is the key text. J.M. Winter, *The Great War and the British People*, London, Macmillan, 1986, and Bernard Waites, *A Class Society at War. England 1914–1918*, Leamington Spa, Berg, 1987, are also important. See also, Bob Bushaway, 'Name upon name: the Great War and remembrance', in Roy Porter, ed., *Myths of the English*, Cambridge, Polity Press, 1992, pp. 136–67; David Cannadine, 'War and Death, Grief and Mourning in Modern Britain', in J. Whaley, ed., *Mirrors of Mortality. Studies in the Social History of Death*, London, Europa, 1981, pp.187–252; and Adrian Gregory, *The Silence of Memory. Armistice Day 1919–1946*, Oxford, Berg, 1994.
4   The actual figure was 5,704,416, see *Statistics of the Military Effort of the British Empire during the Great War*, London, HMSO, 1922, p. 364.
5   Ian Beckett, 'The Nation in Arms' in Ian F.W. Beckett and Keith Simpson, eds., *A Nation in Arms. A Social Study of the British Army in the First World War*, London, Tom Donovan, 1990, p. 13.
6   Peter Parker, *The Old Lie: The Great War and the Public School Ethos*, London, Constable, 1987, pp. 16–17, gives the astonishing casualty figures suffered by many public schools. The casualty rates of officers were consistently higher than those of their men, see Winter, *Great War and the British People*, p. 111.
7   Jose Harris, *Private Lives, Public Spirit. A Social History of Britain 1870–1914*, Oxford, Oxford University Press, 1993, p. 45, pp. 147–48.
8   The importance of this concept was brought home to me by Dr Bob Bushaway, when he pointed out Sir William Orpen's description of the soldiers in the wartime paintings of C.R. Nevinson as 'the British workman in disguise'. See Sir William Orpen, *The Outline of Art*, London, George Newnes, nd, p. 374. The French journalist Michel Corday similarly described the French soldier as 'merely a peasant in a steel helmet': *The Paris Front: An Unpublished Diary 1914–1918*, London, 1933, pp. 154–55. Britain's new citizen army, however, did not represent a simple cross-section of the British work force, see P.E. Dewey, 'Military recruiting and the British labour force during the Great War', *Historical Journal*, 1984, vol. 27, pp. 199–223.
9   A.J.P. Taylor, *An Illustrated History of the First World War*, Harmondsworth, Penguin, 1965, p. 105.
10 For the pre-war army, see Edward Spiers, *Army and Society, 1815–1914*, London, Longman, 1980.
11 Martin Samuels, *Doctrine and Dogma. German and British Infantry Tactics in the First World War*, London, Greenwood Press, 1992, p. 177.

12 John Terraine, ed., *General Jack's Diary 1914–1918. The Trench Diary of Brigadier-General J.L. Jack, D.S.O.*, London, Eyre and Spottiswoode, 1964, p. 309.

13 See, for example, G.A.B. Dewar and Lieutenant-Colonel J.H. Boraston, *Sir Douglas Haig's Command, 1915–1918*, 2 vols., London, 1922, I, p. 151.

14 Denis Winter, *Death's Men. Soldiers of the Great War*, London, Allen Lane, 1978.

15 Lord Moran, *The Anatomy of Courage*, London, Constable, 1945, p. 184.

16 See John Brophy and Eric Partridge, *The Long Trail. Soldiers' Songs and Slang 1914–1918*, London, Sphere, 1969.

17 Both admiration and incomprehension can be glimpsed in Sidney Rogerson's 'Foreword' to Jack's diary.

18 J.O. Springhall, 'The Boy Scouts, class and militarism in relation to British youth movements, 1908–1930', *International Review of Social History*, 1971, vol. 16, pp. 125–58, and 'Lord Meath, youth and empire', *Journal of Contemporary History*, 1970, vol. 5, pp. 97–111; P. Wilkinson, 'English youth movements, 1908–1930', *Journal of Contemporary History*, 1969, vol. 4, pp. 3–24; Ann Summers, 'Militarism in Britain before the Great War', *History Workshop*, 1976, vol. 2, pp. 104–23; and M.D. Blanch, 'Imperialism, nationalism and organised youth', in J. Clarke, *et al* eds., *Working Class Culture*, London, Hutchinson, 1979, pp. 103–20.

19 Beckett, 'Nation in Arms', p. 5.

20 Ian Beckett, 'The Territorial Force', in Beckett and Simpson, eds., *A Nation in Arms*, p. 129.

21 Samuels, *Doctrine and Dogma*, p. 149.

22 For this, see S.P. Mackenzie, *Politics and Military Morale. Current Affairs and Citizenship Education in the British Army 1914–1950*, Oxford, Oxford University Press, 1992, pp. 3–39.

23 Clearly, a similar argument could be made for other classes. Roger Cooper and John McCarthy have, in recent times, reminded us of the utility of a public school education in learning to cope with material deprivation and psychological stress.

24 Ross McKibbin, *The Ideologies of Class. Social Relations in Britain 1880–1950*, Oxford, Oxford University Press, 1990, pp. 6–7.

25 Neal Blewett, 'The franchise in the United Kingdom', *Past and Present*, 1965, vol. 32, pp. 27–56.

26 McKibbin, *Ideologies of Class*, p. 165.

27 McKibbin, *Ideologies of Class*, p. 2.

28 Robert Currie, *Industrial Politics*, London, Oxford University Press, 1979, puts this aspect at the centre of his brilliant analysis of trade union strategy.

29 P.J. Kavanagh, *The Collected Poems of Ivor Gurney*, Oxford, Oxford University Press, 1984, p. 102.

30 Ian Beckett, 'Review of *Shot at Dawn*', *Journal of the Society for Army Historical Research*, 1990, vol. 68, p. 132.

31 Peter Simkins, *Kitchener's Army*, Manchester, Manchester University Press, 1988, p. 200.

32 See J. Brent Wilson, 'The Morale and Discipline of the British Expeditionary Force, 1914–1918' (Unpublished MA thesis, University of New Brunswick, 1978).

351

33 Sandra Gwyn, *Tapestry of War*, London, Harper-Collins, 1992, p. 465.
34 Harris, *Private Lives, Public Spirit*, pp. 147–48.
35 Jay Winter, 'The Army and Society', in Beckett and Simpson, eds., *A Nation in Arms*, p. 196.
36 Ross McKibbin's essay 'Why was there no Marxism in Great Britain?' in *Ideologies of Class*, pp. 1–41, is suggestive of the importance and significance of these affiliations.
37 Peter Simkins, *Kitchener's Army. Raising and Training the New Armies 1914–1916*, Manchester, Manchester University Press, 1988, p. 208.
38 In an interview with Dr C.S.A. Chinn.
39 This is one of the major themes of J.G. Fuller's *Troop Morale and Popular Culture in the British and Dominion Armies 1914–1918*, Oxford, Clarendon Press, 1990.
40 W.H.A. Groom, *Poor Bloody Infantry. A Memoir of the First World War*, London, William Kimber, 1976, p. 63.

Chapter 26

The Experience of the British Special Brigade in Gas Warfare

Donald Richter

Poison gas[1] retains to this day connotations of horror, revulsion, and panic, conjuring up visions of a thick greenish cloud gliding relentlessly across the trenches of the Great War's Western Front like the Bible's Last Plague of Egypt, sinister, deadly, and implacable.

How does this popular perception tally with actual experience? Was gas relentless, sinister, deadly, implacable? Was it even effective? How did it work? Was it inhumane? What were the attitudes of those soldiers most associated with British offensive use of gas?

The facts of the case are well known.[2] Although each side experimented freely with a wide array of gases from relatively innocuous smoke and tear gas combinations to the most deadly poisons available at the time, three chemical agents predominated; chlorine, phosgene and Yperite. At Langemarck on the outskirts of Ypres on the afternoon of 22 April 1915 German soldiers, after waiting many hours for a favourable wind, released chlorine into the atmosphere and watched it drift silently toward Allied lines.[3] The panic which ensued in the French colonial units directly in its path gave warning of possibly a new era in modern warfare. Chlorine was deadly enough, as initial casualties demonstrated, but even more lethal gases followed. The introduction of phosgene, carbonyl chloride ($COCl_2$), in December 1915 raised the lethal capacity considerably. It did not signal its presence by the telltale detectable odor that chlorine had, nor did it give immediate warning of its ingestion by inducing severe coughing as did chlorine, and phosgene was many times as toxic as chlorine. Both these gases, however, disperse rather quickly, which was not the case with the third major gas, one which raised blisters, dichlorodiethyl sulphide, more commonly known as mustard gas, introduced in 1917, also at Ypres, and therefore called Yperite as well. Many early mustard gas injuries resulted when soldiers slept following a barrage of artillery shells containing the gas, waking to the slow realization that the moisture of morning dew and/or their own bodies had triggered release of the deadly gas into the atmosphere, blistering eyes, lungs, and other moist places.[4]

For those exposed to lethal concentrations death came slowly and unmercifully in excruciating agonies of suffocation. Most of us have no doubt known or met survivors, or relatives of survivors, who received less than lethal doses, and who tell of lingering lung problems and life-long incapacities. Walter Hare, a distinguished veteran of West Yorkshire, told me at the 1994 conference where this paper was delivered, of his encounter with a cloud of chlorine at Vimy, and although he was at the time only out of the line several weeks, he had suffered from lung congestion to this day and had constantly to resort to an inhaler during our conversation. Such acquaintance lends substance to the view that there is something sinister, a lurking unfairness about a weapon that wreaks such internal agony or reaches out over the years to continue to punish a veteran long after the war is over. On the other hand, we are aware that artillery was undoubtedly the single most deadly weapon of the war and have seen countless horror pictures of its physically mangled victims, many incapacitated likewise for life. Yet we have never branded artillery as inhumane or unfair, seemingly a moral paradox of the first order.

In actuality, while injuries attending the initial surprise gas attacks were gruesome enough, anti-gas defence evolved almost as fast as new gases were brought into play.[5] Even the early admonition to 'Piss on your handkerchiefs and tie them over your faces,' was surprisingly effective in neutralizing chlorine.[6] An increasingly more practical series of smoke helmets, though uncomfortable, and even suffocating, soon superseded this makeshift improvisation and proved efficient when properly used.[7] Gas was soon sinister only to the untrained, unwary or careless soldier. The Great War gas mask, when properly and promptly worn, soon afforded better protection to the ordinary soldier from gases than he had from any other Great War weapon.[8] The vast majority of gas injuries resulted from improper wearing of the defence equipment, its premature removal, or not wearing it at all. Typical of those injured in this way were Walter Hare and his comrades, whose commanding officer had not alerted the platoon to the gas component of the cloud they marched through and who therefore had not donned the helmets they carried with them. Against the constant danger from artillery shells, there was no equivalent protection so readily available.

Virtually all British soldiers of the Great War who fought for any extended period along the Western Front during 1915 and after confronted the gas menace at some point and their stories are legion. The unique experience which is the special subject of this chapter, however, is that of the men responsible for British gas 'retaliation,' the men of the unit called the

Special Brigade. This was a special unit hastily recruited and trained in the weeks following 2nd Ypres, a unit composed at first largely of chemists, grouped in only two Special Companies, expanded to four for the Battle of Loos, and gradually increased to a strength of just under 6,000 and ultimately designated the Special Brigade.[9] Its leader was Major Charles Howard Foulkes, an energetic and independent-minded young officer in the Engineers who confessed at the time of his appointment that he knew nothing whatsoever about chemical warfare. He and his band of chemists learned quickly: the Special Companies were able to carry out the first British cloud gas attack at Loos in September, 1915, then went on to attempt capability in flame-throwers, smoke screens, gas projectors. In the last months of the war, they staged massed train-car discharges in vain attempts to catch up with a retreating target. Although the Artillery increasingly added gas to shrapnel and explosive shells, the Special Brigade was the only British unit whose primary and sole mission was gas.

The earliest form of British retaliation fairly replicated the German procedure in which chlorine was discharged into the air from ordinary acetylene cylinders. The British initially chose chlorine simply because that was the only poison gas available in the required quantities, but early on Foulkes urged the use of 'the deadliest gases procurable,'[10] and it was only for lack of time and availability that British use of phosgene followed rather than preceded its German use. By 1916 a mixture of phosgene and chlorine replaced pure chlorine. If phosgene, a light gas, were to be discharged in cloud form, as Foulkes intended, as opposed to direct delivery by shell, it performed better mixed with a heavier gas to keep the cloud from rising harmlessly into the atmosphere too soon. The natural choice for the heavier gas was chlorine, thereby solving the weight problem and combining the lethal effects of both gases. In late January, 1916, following lengthy experiments with various proportions, Foulkes decided on a fifty percent mixture of both gases, which came to be called White Star. Though continuing to experiment with a wide assortment of chemical poisons, the Special Brigade adopted the White Star mixture as the staple cylinder filling for most of the remainder of the war.[11] Foulkes and his unit never employed mustard gas, for reasons which will later be made clear. After 1916, however, the Artillery used combinations of all three in its gas shells.

The initial experience of the British gas soldiers in Foulkes's unit was certainly not as they had imagined. Most of the early recruits expected to serve in laboratories, to pour and calibrate, to collect and analyze German gases, and in general to put their chemical expertise at the service of their country in a professional capacity. They were to be severely disappointed, for there developed little need for these specialized services, though the earliest did serve for a time as emergency advisors in gas defence. The primary mission of Foulkes's unit was for gas offensive, and it quickly became clear that the successful carrying out of this undertaking required more brawn then chemical expertise. The chemist recruits found themselves digging emplacement pits in wet trenches, portering heavy equipment, connecting pipes and cylinders, in general performing the jobs of ordinary navvies and labourers. The work was arduous and difficult, the equipment bulky and unmanageable, the procedures unfamiliar. In short it was exasperating in the extreme and no one could be certain it would all work as intended.

The actual installation of the cylinders likewise required sheer muscle rather than much technical skill. Upon arrival in the front trenches, the gas personnel prepared the cylinder emplacements by first digging away part of the fire-step and then excavating a pit about two feet deeper than the level of the trench bottom, using timber to shore up the sides to the level of the trench floor. The cylinders then had to be hauled through the communication trenches, securely buried in the deep emplacement pits, and sand-bagged for safe storage until needed. Under battle conditions the gas troops had to attach a maze of connecting pipes, throw one end over the trench parapet into No Man's Land, and synchronize the gas discharge by simultaneously turning on the valves. Upon contact with air, the liquid chlorine vaporized instantaneously and the rest depended entirely on a favourable wind.

The five-and-a-half foot long cylinders which Foulkes selected weighed (empty) about seventy, and full, up to one hundred and thirty pounds.[12] The gasmen nicknamed them 'Rogers' as Foulkes had decreed that the words gas and cylinder never be used. An amusing incident in which an infantry commander ordered double the number of men for carrying out the empty cylinders on the false notion that they were no longer buoyant illustrates how little the ordinary soldier knew of gas. Gas fatigues were unpopular with infantry units detached for such carrying and portering. Even after discounting the amount of grousing that was mandatory in the interests of morale and camaraderie, the intensity of the complaints was revealing. 'I thought I should have died,' wrote one nineteen-year-old recruit after his first cylinder fatigue.[13] Robert Graves and his company of Welch Fusiliers were later to perform this duty and found it extremely onerous. 'This was worse than carrying the dead; the cylinders were cast iron, heavy and hateful. The men cursed and sulked . . . I felt like screaming.' This painful experience may account somewhat for the contemptuous sentiments about the whole concept of gas warfare which Graves expressed in Good-bye to all That.[14]

If the cylinders were heavy and cumbersome, the maze of connecting pipes were no less difficult to handle and transport. Manoeuvring the awkward and unwieldy bundles of pipes, some reaching ten feet in length, through the twists and turns of communication trenches and traverses proved both extremely fatiguing and frustrating.

Despite critical shortages of material and manpower, four of the Special Companies were able to organize the first retaliatory gas attack in concert with the Loos Offensive of 1915. On that occasion Foulkes hoped that, provided the wind proved favourable, the gas would constitute a protective shield behind which the infantry would advance without danger. Perhaps unwarrantedly impressed with a gas demonstration arranged by Foulkes in August, Haig too embraced the gas component as the only way to overcome shortages of other weapons. Though warned by General Gough that 'Gas might be a boomerang ally – a tremendous but treacherous friend,'[15] Haig felt increasingly that all hopes for a decisive breakthrough rested on the success of the gas mission.[16] Thus on the morning of 25 September Haig gave the go-ahead to the gas officers in spite of disappointingly uncertain winds. Not only did the equipment perform imperfectly, but drifting wind did indeed turn treacherous in several places along the line and large amounts of gas leaked or blew back into British trenches with deadly effect. In one section (26) exploding shells filled the trench with dense smoke, and Luther Mitchell, a gas corporal, returning from another traverse where he had rushed to apply an emergency field dressing, found his mate 'half suffocating with our own gas. We all had gas helmets on, but they got so stuffy that the temptation is to remove them for a breath of air, which proves to be a breath of chlorine.'[17] Another remembers getting 'a big mouthful with the first cylinder,' and later wrote 'God, what a game! The rotten apparatus they had given us was leaking all over the place and we were working in a cloud of gas.'[18] It remains questionable whether this first British gas attack helped or hindered the offensive, but it clearly had not lived up to expectations.

Although the first big test of gas proved keenly disappointing the mission continued and problems compounded. Undischarged cylinders left in the front lines had to be guarded twenty-four hours a day until discharged, a particularly unwelcome duty. The party typically consisted of one corporal and two pioneers who were responsible for dealing with any leaks that occurred, either burying or carrying off any faulty cylinders. Men of the Special Companies had daily to rotate to the front lines for this purpose, while additional fatigue parties retrieved empty cylinders, manhandled them back to railheads, repaired damaged emplacement pits, and prepared more new pipe kits.

Repeated cancellations, called 'wash-outs,' added to the sense of frustration. Not only did companies in charge of front line cylinders have to mount round-the-clock surveillance, but, anxious as they naturally were to get the gas off, several sections had to go up the line each evening on the chance of the favourable wind. Night after night sections of gas companies trudged 'up the line,' heaved away the sandbags, connected up the pipes, and, more often than not, just before Zero Hour, received word that contrary winds had washed out the stunt, thus requiring them to repeat the whole operation in reverse. Luther Mitchell remembered a particularly cold December night spent waiting a favourable wind in an abandoned dugout near the front line. 'I slept for an hour or two and woke up shivering. During the rest of the night I stood outside the dugout stamping my feet in the endeavour to keep them warm.'[19] The next day concentrated German shelling devastated much of his trench ramparts, killing two Specials and wounding many others. C Company once 'stood to' twenty successive nights in the summer of 1917 (21 June to 9 July) nursing over a thousand cylinders in the front lines, during which time enemy firepower buried over 100 of them.[20] Such repeated disappointments must surely have exacerbated an already tedious and dangerous operation, but such was the experience of the gas soldier.

Perhaps most disturbingly, the problem of leaking gas remained unsolved. No unit was more vulnerable than the men of the Special Brigade for they were in almost constant proximity if not contact with gas apparatus. In 1916 the greater toxicity of the added phosgene component of the White Star, more insidious because of its delayed effects, meant more serious injuries among the complacent. Even the Specials themselves underestimated the new gas, having worked so long with the relatively milder Red Star (chlorine). A sergeant with K Company, deployed around Ypres, received a slight dose of White Star in disconnecting a gas pipe. According to a War Diary at the Public Record Office: 'He paid no attention to it, did not even report it and carried on with his work. He returned to billet, slept well, collapsed while taking breakfast the following morning and was dead within 24 hours.' On the same occasion a shell bursting on a trench parapet sent billows of gas into one of the bays. Though a gas corporal and two pioneers stationed there reported only slight irritation, their section commander sent them to a dressing station at once. The corporal, protesting that he felt 'quite well', returned to the line, but was again ordered back. All three men were dead in the morning.[21] Gas certainly proved sinister in these cases, but the imprudence of the victims unwittingly contributed to their unfortunate deaths.

Despite improvements in the cylinder and piping apparatus, gas equipment still performed imperfectly throughout the rest of the war. Gas leaked as previously from piping joints. Contrary wind eddies blew gas back into British trenches. Enemy shells and shell fragments ruptured gas pipes. Human error or human carelessness generated additional difficulties. Problems inherent in cloud gas attacks seemed insurmountable and both the French and the Germans gave up on the technique by mid-1916. Except for the Special Brigade, the gas war from then on was fought with gas artillery shell.

An alternative delivery system devised by the more ingenious among the gas personnel, but not favoured by Foulkes, was a gas mortar gun, called a projector, a three-foot long steel tube resembling an ordinary mortar and positioned for firing on a heavy base-plate. The projectile was filled with thirty pounds of pure phosgene. A wire threaded through the apparatus allowed remote firing. The crew fired projectors from above ground positions situated behind the front lines, typically between the support lines and reserve lines. Range and direction were not very accurate, but since large numbers could be fired in quick succession, as long as they fell somewhere in enemy lines it was thought worth the effort.

The projector, however, entailed dangers and disadvantages as well. The heavy guns tended to become more easily buried both from natural sinking and from repeated recoil. They had constantly to be dug out of soft earth with picks and shovels and ropes. Deeply buried projectors had frequently to be abandoned. Installed on open ground behind the front lines, the unloaded projector itself, while not chemically dangerous if hit by shell fire, clearly posed a more visible and vulnerable target for enemy shelling than the cylinders sandbagged deep in the firestep. Moreover the projector operators had to work above ground rather than in the relative safety of the trenches. When, in mid-May 1918, C Company was to carry out its first projector stunt, Sidney Fox, gas corporal, wrote of feeling 'naked' working out on top for the first time: 'A deep protecting trench seemed Heaven compared to this.'[22]

Though the use of projectors involved less heavy carrying than the cylinders, the base-plates, detonators, cables and projectors were clumsy and heavy enough. Each base-plate weighed about 40 pounds and the projector tubes weighed about one hundred pounds each. Where trench duckboards were either unsteady or damaged by enemy shelling, it was almost impossible to transport such heavy equipment. In an effort to reduce the carrying involved in projector shoots, Z Company tried firing the projectors without the base plates. In soft ground, however, projectors without base-plates were too easily buried, sometimes to a depth of nine feet. Another way to reduce the recoil was to reduce the charge, but this also decreased the range.

Heavy rains periodically turned the trenches and dugouts into rivers of mud and muck.[23 & 24] In thigh-length gum boots, leather jerkins and thick leather gloves, the gas soldiers used ash poles to measure mud depth as they waded through stretches of opaque knee-deep water. One diarist, Richard Gale, recalled a trench dubbed 'Pudding Lane'.

The coming of winters added lengthened periods of darkness and cold to the dampness, with nights 'black as Hades.'[25] The winter of 1916–17 was the coldest since 1880, with icy ground hard as iron, particularly exacerbating the trench work of the Gas Specials whether working with cylinders or projectors.[26,27 & 28] Drenching rains during the first months of the winter of 1915–16 had buried hundreds of trench-stored cylinders. Gale reconnoitred the front line trenches in mid-November, 1915. 'We found everything in an awful state; floods of mud and water everywhere, trenches collapsing, and cylinders disappearing into the mud . . . In the front line the slush was knee deep . . . and the reserve trenches about waist deep.'[29] The thick mud tended to suck the gas cylinders downward in a vice-like grip, the hollow base acting as a vacuum. On occasion water rose so high in some communication trenches that gas soldiers found they could actually float the empty cylinders out. Tending the near-frozen and slippery cylinders and pipes became doubly onerous. 'I had to lie on my stomach in the mud in order to connect the pipes to the nozzles of the cylinders. We lit candles to see what we were doing.'[30] Gale's section tried unsuccessfully to drain a trench almost submerged in mud and water by running a pipe along a mine gallery under the embankment and out into a shell crater on the canal bank. Some emplacements were accessible only by 'crawling out across a sea of mud.'[31]

Soldiers who spent any considerable time in the forward areas commonly remembered a shared experience of danger and mutilation associated with randomly falling artillery shells. This was what defined experience in the front lines, and the chemists were as frequently in the front lines operating in and near No Man's land as any common soldier. The men of the Special Brigade were never asked to go over the top infantry fashion, but they lived and worked in locations and circumstances which rendered them no less vulnerable to enemy artillery, rifle, and sniper fire than any Tommy.

In one particularly tragic incident in the Arras sector in 1917, Z Company had assembled 250 projectors, gas projectiles, propellants and detonators near Bullecourt. The carrying parties were grouped thickly round the off-loading point when a chance shell landed in their midst. Z Company lost fourteen killed and seven wounded; P Company, which came to be known as the 'Suicide Company,' twenty-one killed and fourteen men wounded; G Company, eight men and one officer killed, seventeen men wounded. The dead were buried where they lay. The total number of casualties in this, the brigade's most costly single accident of the war was eighty-eight.[32] Total wartime casualties in the brigade were severe, 5,384, close to 100 per cent of its highest strength.

When the Germans had first introduced gas warfare the Allies had branded it an atrocity, the act of a barbarous nation. 'An atrocious method of warfare,' a 'diabolical contrivance,' this 'enormity' wrote The Times.[33] No other weapon of war supposedly carried such a despicable reputation, not even the dreaded submarine which ran a distant second. So the question naturally occurs – what did our chemical soldier think of wielding such a weapon?

To find the answer to this question the researcher must forsake the characteristically prosaic official war diaries at the Public Record Office and probe the more revealing personal diaries, memoirs, and letters of the individual members of the Special Brigade held in various archives. Most of us I dare say still regard poison gas an unacceptable means of warfare – witness the Geneva Protocol of 1925 – but examination of the men's own testimony indicates they seem not to have been so anguished. While the available evidence is largely anecdotal, even anecdotal evidence becomes compelling when a particular sentiment is found in overwhelming instances. After all, the Germans 'had done it first.' It was merely 'Paying the Hun back in his own coin.'[34] 'It is a vile method of warfare,' wrote one soldier, 'but the Bosches have brought it on themselves.'[35] Foulkes claimed that he was on hand to greet every arriving contingent and gave every man the option of returning to his original unit if he objected to gas warfare. Few did so. An entry in the diary of Charles Ashley reflects the general sentiment in the unit: 'subsequent experience did not lead me to suppose that gas was more objectionable on moral or any other grounds than high explosives.'[36] A gas captain, Norman Campbell, whose diary reveals a deeply religious and conscientious temperament, wrote to his wife that 'in case you have any doubts . . . as to whether my particular job is an honourable one or not, I should just like to say this, that except for a few days at the very beginning out here, I have never had any doubts about it being right.'[37] Any lingering ethical considerations quickly dissipated in the heat and pressure of preparing for the front lines.

Although repeated disappointments must have clawed grievously at morale, the personal diaries of the men of the Special Brigade reveal no demoralization or loss of determination to try again. Their improvised songs and marching ditties, like those of any other combat unit, resound to the good-natured sentiments of self-deprecation and humorous good will. A favourite stanza of the ever-fruitful Fred Karno's song ran as follows, sung irreverently to the tune of 'The Church's One Foundation:'

> We are Fred Karno's Army,
> The Roger Corps R.E.
> We cannot march, we cannot fight,
> What bloody good are we?
>
> We go up to the trenches,
> And let off ruddy gas:
> We make such awful stenches,
> And wither all the grass.[38]

Other enthusiastic improvisations carry the same message. The chemical soldiers felt that they were doing their bit and were proud of their contribution.

As for the conscientious Foulkes, his experience leading the Special Brigade must have been frustrating in the extreme. Forced to hurry his initial experimental operation, he extemporized as best he could only to watch helplessly as contrary winds turned his Herculean efforts to failure. Support for the gas mission never fully recovered from this first disappointment. Putting the best face on things, he carried on, never acknowledging failure, ever enthusiastic in the face of increasing resistance and even obstruction on the part of infantry commanders, many of whom considered gas more of a hindrance than a help. Haig, an early enthusiast, quickly lost confidence after the disappointing results at Loos. General Headquarters concluded early on that gas was, if not a waste of time and effort, far too labour-intensive to assign it more than an ancillary role. Both the French and the Germans had given up on cloud gas as a decisive weapon and had relegated its use to a supportive role. The last German cloud gas attack took place on 8 August 1916. Foulkes alone remained convinced to the end that under the right conditions gas could clear a path for the infantry and break the deadlock on the Western Front: he believed that a cloud of gas timed for release just before the infantry went over the top was the only method that would serve this purpose, which was why he never introduced mustard gas, which could only be delivered by shell. Emphasis on such a release system would also assure a leading role for the Special Brigade rather than the Artillery, which was using gas in shells from 1916 onwards.

Forced to a marginal operation, he never gave up the dream of a more central, decisive one in which his unit led the way to victory. Others might well have done it differently, but no one could have done it more conscientiously or with more optimism and enthusiasm.

At every level, then, the experience of gas warfare was not what its initial recruits thought they were getting into. For the most part it proved to be laborious and tedious work, long waiting, punctuated by periods of extreme danger. Nonetheless the chemical soldiers performed this work with a professionalism and *ésprit de corps* that was quite exemplary. The unfortunate aspect of their contribution was that on the whole results were disappointing. Gas was never decisive. The Loos trial was the first and last serious attempt to synchronize a gas attack with a major offensive. All who have studied the gas effort first hand, that is, from original documents, have concluded that at the end of the day it was not worth it. The labour, the danger, the time, the manpower required made it not a cost-effective weapon. This was especially true of the cloud gas attacks which Foulkes favoured. Even the gas component of the artillery war was merely ancillary, troublesome, and, as the author of the Official History put it, it made war uncomfortable to no decisive effect.

As with so many popular notions of the war, much of the popular perception of gas warfare thus turns out to be myth; and as always, the actual experience, harrowing enough, is gleaned not from post-war poets and ideologues, but from the soldiers themselves.

Notes

1   Most of the 'gases' used during World War I were actually pressurized liquids. Vaporization took place only at the instant of discharge when the poison hissed forth as a gas, for the most part clinging to the ground, and carried on the wind. Dichlorodiethyl sulphide, commonly called mustard gas, likewise remained a liquid till reaction with atmospheric or body moisture.

2   The best summary of twentieth century gas warfare in general is Guy Hartcup, *The War of Invention*, London, 1988. The definitive study of Great War gas warfare remains L.F. Haber, *The Poisonous Cloud*, Oxford, 1986. Critical to any scholarly study of the subject on the German side is the Hartley Report, PRO/WO/33/1072, Harold Hartley, 'Report on German Chemical Warfare Organization and Policy, 1919.'

3   See James L. McWilliams and R. Steele, *Gas! The Battle for Ypres, 1915*, St Catharines, Ontario, Vanwell Publishing, 1985.

4   The experience of these myriad victims has been told, eloquently and well, by others, included among them Edward Spiers, *Chemical Warfare*, Urbana and Chicago, 1986.

5   See Simon Jones, 'Gas Warfare: The British Defensive Measures. Part I: The Second Battle of Ypres,' *Stand To!*, September, 1985, pp.15–23, and 'Under a Green Sea: The Defensive British Responses to Gas Warfare,' *The Great War, 1914–1918*, August, 1989, pp. 126–132, and November, 1989, pp. 14–21.

6   McWilliams and Steele, *op.cit.*, p. 86.

7   Like many others, Grossmith felt so stifled when wearing the mask properly that he threw it away during the battle of Loos. George W. Grossmith, letter 27 September 1915, Liddle Collection, University of Leeds.

8   The clear exception to this was mustard gas which assailed other moist parts of the body.

9   See my own *Chemical Soldiers: British Gas Warfare in World War I*, University Press of Kansas, 1992, re-published by Leo Cooper, London, 1994.

10   PRO/WO32/5171, Memo by Col. Lucius Jackson, 'Gas in Trench Warfare – Summary of What has been done to Date, June 30 1915.' See also Charles H. Foulkes, *Gas! The Story of the Special Brigade*, Edinburgh and London, 1934, p. 40.

12   Haber, *op.cit.*, p. 52. See also Foulkes, *op.cit.*, p. 56. Throughout the war cylinders of a variety of sizes saw service as it proved impossible to supply the necessary number of uniform cylinders. This accounts for infantry carrying parties' widely divergent estimates of the weight of cylinders.

13   T. Eden Papers, Liddle Collection, University of Leeds.

14   Robert Graves, *Good-bye to All That*, London, 1929, p. 143 and p. 129.

15   Sir Hubert Gough, *The Fifth Army*, London, 1931, p. 101.

16   PRO/CAB45/121, R.D. Whigham to J.E. Edmonds, 1925. See also Robert Blake, ed., *Private Papers of Douglas Haig 1914–1919*, London, 1952, entries for 16 and 20 September, 1915.

17   L.G. Mitchell Diary, 25 September, 1915., Imperial War Museum.

18   G.O. Mitchell Diary, 25 September 1915, Imperial War Museum.

19   Luther Gordon Mitchell Diary, 20–23 December, 1915, Imperial War Museum.

20   PRO/WO95/549, War Diary, C Company, 9 July, 1917.

21 PRO/WO95/121, War Diary, 3rd Battalion, Special Brigade, 30 June, 1916. The sergeant was W. Harrower.

22 Sidney Fox, *Corporals All*, typescript, 1965, pp. 103–104.

23 *ibid*, p. 32.

24 Richard Gale Diary, 13 December, 1915, Imperial War Museum.

25 Fox, *op.cit.*, p. 31.

26 Fox, *op.cit.*, p. 64.

27 Memoirs of H.J.C. Marshall, Vol. III, p.4, Imperial War Museum, WM, 84/11/2.

28 T. Eden Papers, Liddle Collection.

29 Gale Diary, *op.cit.*, 13 November 1915.

30 John Thomas Diary, 21 December, 1915, Royal Engineers Museum.

31 Gale Diary, *op.cit.*, 13 December, 1915.

32 PRO/WO95/486, War Diary, Z Company, Report No. Z/632 by Lieutenant Bansall, 20 May, 1917.

33 *The Times of London*, 29 April, 1915. Of personal diaries etc., the Royal Engineers Museum holds a small collection, as does the entirely separate Royal Engineers Library, both located at Chatham. Others may be found at Churchill College, Cambridge; at the National Army Museum in Chelsea; and at the Liddell Hart Centre for Military Archives at King's College London. By far the best collections of gas diaries and memorabilia may be found in the manuscript division of the Imperial War Museum at Lambeth and in the Liddle Collection at the University of Leeds. Many reminiscences as well appear in the pages of the brigade's own post-war Special Brigade Newsletter, which continued for over fifty years.

34 Henry Williamson, *A Fox Under My Cloak*, (1955), p. 272.

35 Diary of Adrian Hodgkin, 30 January, 1916, Imperial War Museum.

36 R.H. Atkinson, 'Recollections of the Gas C'oys,' *Special Brigade Newsletter* #40 (February, 1977), p. 1; Charles Ashley Diary, 19 July, 1915, Imperial War Museum.

37 Mrs Norman P. Campbell, *N.P. Campbell: Scientist, Missionary, Soldier*, Cambridge, 1921, pp. 35–36.

38 File 8102–03, Royal Engineers Museum.

Chapter 27

The Forgotten Army of Women: The Overseas Service of Queen Mary's Army Auxiliary Corps with the British Forces, 1917–1921

Diana Shaw

For centuries before the Great War, women camp followers, *vivandières* and *cantinières*, were the traditional purveyors of food to the warring armies – the real pioneers of women's army service. In the Peninsular campaign, for example, official provisioning did not stretch beyond essentials and it was the wives of soldiers who cooked, washed, nursed and arranged accommodation.[1] The establishment of Britain's Women's Army Auxiliary Corps formally recognised as a necessity what in the past had been accepted by custom and in his final dispatch, the Commander-in-Chief, Field Marshal Sir Douglas Haig, readily acknowledged that through the aid it gave Britain's declining manpower, it 'contributed materially to the success of our arms.'[2]

By the war's end, the Corps had employed a total of 40,850 women. Of these, 17,000 had served overseas, though never more than 8,777 at any time.[3] Despite these large numbers, researchers on British women at war have tended to concentrate more on such aspects as nursing and munitions. This paper examines the overseas experience of the Corps and its significance for the women's movement.

Late in 1916, facing a manpower crisis, the military authorities found 12,000 servicemen fit for active service tied up in non-combatant duties and recommended seeking alternative labour sources.[4] The case for using women volunteers was convincingly canvassed by Mary 'Mona' Chalmers-Watson, a distinguished Scottish doctor with all the dynamism and patriotism of her brothers, Sir Auckland Geddes, the Director of Recruiting, and Sir Eric Geddes, in charge of Western Front railways.[5] In

February 1917, she was gazetted Chief Controller, in overall charge of a newly-formed Women's Corps, while Mrs. (later Dame) Helen Gwynne-Vaughan, a botanist before the war, administered it in France. It was run by the Army Council, aided by a staff liaison officer, the first of whom, Colonel Leigh-Wood, found difficulty in accepting Chalmers-Watson's authority and was replaced by a more amenable colleague.[6]

Six base camps for a women's corps were set up at Etaples, Calais, Abbeville, Le Havre, Boulogne and Rouen,[7] and, later, St. Omer and Dieppe. These, with smaller camps along the lines of communication, eventually housed around 8000 women, releasing at least 6000 men for the fighting. [8] From the first the organisation was on military lines. There were four main branches of the Corps – 'motor transport', 'clerical', 'household' and 'mechanical and miscellaneous' – denoted by differently coloured shoulder straps. In 1918, a further branch incorporated the Corps' police. The Corps was not allowed military titles but its structure was closely akin, the 'officials' being the officers, the 'forewomen' the non-commissioned officers, and the 'workers' the rank-and-file. These last-named had a brief training before being sent to Folkestone for inoculations and embarkation. Officials trained for three weeks, followed by a fourteen-day probationary period.[9] The very first draft, however, which left for France only days after the official creation of the Corps, had no such preparation – indicating how urgently it was needed. For those on overseas service – where discipline came under the Army Act (section 184), as opposed to civil law for those at home – the minimum age was twenty, as opposed to eighteen for home service, and there were direct benefits such as cheaper postage, free travel to and from home when on leave and free medical and dental treatment.[10] However, no member of the Corps was entitled, as men were, to army pensions, dependence allowances, retention bonuses or gratuities. Instead they were covered by the National Insurance Act and the War Compensation Act of 1914. [11]

The response to the original request for women was enormous. By April 1917, 35,000 had registered,[12] proving that the campaign, begun in 1914, for women's right to serve, reflected a strong nation-wide desire to help their country. Nevertheless, not all those who joined supported the system without thought for themselves. The first recruits signed a civil contract, but after May 1917 all enrolments came under regulation 42c of the Defence of the Realm Act, which meant that existing members had to re-enlist. Domestics, to whom it made no material difference, did this as a matter of course, but those clerks already working long hours in France, refused to do so (since it involved a reduction in wages and an end to over-time pay) until October 1917, when the War Office decided that only those members who re-enrolled would be eligible for promotion.[13] Significantly for women's history, the Corps was also the setting for one of the first successful battles for equal pay in the twentieth century: Dr. Laura Sandeman refused to accept her position in France until she and her doctors were paid at the higher civilian rates. As there was no other way of obtaining a medical service for the WAAC in France, the government was forced to agree, despite objections from the War Minister, Lord Derby, who believed it was 'outrageous that no medical woman will accept an appointment under £700 a year.'[14]

Given prevailing prejudices it is not surprising that the military, including Haig, had been initially sceptical about women's ability to acquire 'military knowledge' quickly.[15] It was not a change in conventional attitudes but the terrible cost of the war in lives,which had brought the Corps into existence – as popular opinion recognised: 'things', one woman was heard to say, were coming to something when they had to send women![16] The effect of women's involvement was that more men were released to go 'up the line' and this may explain why the use of women in army camps was sometimes resented. In 1915, cooks in the Women's Legion found that the ovens at Sommerdown Convalescent Camp, Eastbourne had been sabotaged.[17] Although the personal documents studied for this paper make no mention of such extreme behaviour, they show that the idea of women undergoing military discipline was, for many, if not anathema, a source of amusement: there is much comment on the humorous gibes to which women were subjected, especially while drilling. Ada Potter has described first arriving in France as a WAAC, 'to be confronted by rows of curious soldiers on the other platform. Their comments on our drill were derisive of course. It was hard to keep a stoney (sic) face. A rather beautiful girl was blushing from many propositions.'[18]

If some women were made to feel like 'usurpers', they won the respect and friendliness of the troops once it was understood that they had come to work, rather than to 'find husbands'.[19] Indeed, the disappearance of waitresses from officers' messes aroused the same degree of complaint in 1919 as their arrival had in 1917.[20] The Corps may not have been created as a result of a change in attitudes but its existence had changed attitudes.

Although the Corps was one of the first women's voluntary organisations to admit members of the working classes, social distinctions endured, as to be expected in that period. At mealtimes during training, for example, upper-class women went straight to the head of the queue.[21] The division of branches according to occupation further reinforced class distinctions: 'motor transport' claimed the upper and middle classes; 'clerical', 'mechanical and miscellaneous', the middle classes; 'household', the working classes. Although, as time passed, promotion through the ranks was encouraged,[22] the administration was dominated by the upper and middle classes, for at first it was assumed that only these women had the 'well-educated' and 'good' background required for officials..

The women worked long hours. Allowed one day off and a half-day off, on alternate weeks, they usually spent these in town, treating themselves to such luxuries as a visit to the hairdresser.[23] Many of their diverse jobs had formerly been a male preserve. Most commonly, they served as domestics, clerks and drivers, but also as gardeners, shoemakers, machinists, printers, photographers, painters, turners and tracers. They worked as their own car mechanics and as sandblasters, acetylene welders, electricians, coppersmiths, vulcanisers and tin smiths[24] – not without danger: Dorothy Loveday, for example, was burned on face and hands when the engine of the car she was driving exploded.[25]

The hostels where some of them lodged ranged from small guesthouses to chateaux. Others, in the camps, lived either in Nissen huts, housing eight women, or Adrian huts, accommodating nineteen. Administrators were allowed a bedroom and office each, sharing the latrine reserved for them. Every camp had a general store, a vegetable and grocery store, a dining room and cookhouse connected by a scullery, a duty room for at least forty women and later, usually, a Young Women's Christian Association hut for relaxation. Bath and ablution huts had to be near a water heater and provided with a surface channel for water, while latrines, consisting of a wooden bucket and seat, had to be kept away from the living area but within easy walking distance. Each camp had to provide enough lavatories for eight per cent of their strength, enough baths for five per cent, enough wash basins for fifteen per cent and a sick bay which could accommodate eight per cent.[26]

Such guidelines ignored the difficulties of running these camps in wartime. Inspectors in 1918 found conditions excellent in some, but very bad in others, usually the smaller ones. Often their locations were unpleasant. One had horse carcasses rotting outside the entrance.[27] In the worst camp, at Guinnes,[28] the women lived in sodden tents, and slept in canvas sleeping bags. Apart from the usual problems with rats and lice, the water supply was frequently unreliable. One Christmas, the French authorities cut it off altogether from a camp, claiming the women used too much.[29] Another camp had no means of heating water,[30] while in Dorothy Loveday's, as she complained in a letter to her former headmistress, Miss Robertson: 'The water supply comes up in carts and is put in a large tank, from there it is carried in army buckets or petrol tins by Chinese, *generally from the VD compound* [author's italics], and filled into open dirty tanks in our own two camps.'[31]

Not that women, in this respect, were worse-treated than male soldiers; and, as everywhere, there was sometimes a minority who were less than stoical: in a short story published in 1931, Charis Grundy re-enacted fellow-WAACs' grousing, despite her own camp having *four* bathrooms – 'the four most precious possessions of the unit':

" . . . don't forget to turn on my tub. It'll be as cold as heaven on a morning like this [Daniel was grumbling]. Why the blazes they can't provide the troops with hot water I can't understand. Two nights a week indeed! Thank you for nothing, Haig, old thing!"

"You're jolly lucky to get baths at all, Danny, announced Morgan, sententiously. "You forget there's a war on."[32]

In rainy weather, pools of mud frequently made it difficult to get to and from work. Water froze in the cold and with only one bucket of coke provided per week, scrounging fuel became a major preoccupation:[33] 'we knocked out all the wood from the old-fashioned dressers in the kitchen drawers,' recalled Edith Willison, 'and just left the front panels as a blind and as long as the wood lasted we had a fire.'[34] Another problem was that of the latrines. Attacks of dysentery led to their overflowing and as the military authorities deemed it inappropriate for Corps members to carry out the heavy fatigue of spreading lime, waiting for outside (male) labour often slowed the process of sanitation.[35]

The Corps ate standard army food – plentiful but monotonous and nutritionally inadequate, as frequent cases of anaemia and debility showed.[36] Edith Willison disdained the stale biscuits 'saved from the Boer War', but found that by cutting out their centres they made excellent frames for the snaps on her office desk.[37] On the whole, however, the women's health benefited. For most it was the first time they had regular medical check-ups and free medical and dental treatment. The authorities' practical attitude about proper hygiene during the menstrual period put paid to superstitions which had caused unnecessary gynaecological problems in the past – a revolution in many women's lives.[38]

Also revolutionary for British women of that era was being, like nurses, under fire on a large scale for the first time. Until Spring 1918, apart from air raids, the only physical dangers usually facing members of the Corps were from mines and submarines on the channel crossing which claimed the lives of two women.[39] After 21 March, however, when the German offensive forced the Allies back and brought the fighting zone nearer, WAACs suffered shelling and aerial bombardment. Sheltering in trenches or breastworks during air raids, they were not issued with steel helmets; but throughout this period they carried on working [40] So crucial had their role become that only one attempt was made by General Headquarters to remove some of them – women signallers at Saint Omer – out of danger, to England, at the beginning of the German offensive; even this order was rescinded.[41] In some cases the women's bravery was recognized and Military Medals were awarded.

The event which, above all, won the Corps admiration was its first experience of an enemy air raid at Abbeville, with nine fatalities. As one article put it : 'This incident, they feel, has confirmed their right to khaki and makes them one in sympathy and sacrifice with the fighting forces'.[42] It was a turning point. The women were buried with full military honours, nine artillery wagons carrying the coffins, draped in Union Jacks, to the cemetery. The respect of the troops was evident: pilots from the Royal Flying Corps circled the cemetery during the service and soldiers lined the route, standing at attention and saluting the coffins as they passed.[43]

Only a few years before, such terrifying bombing attacks had been inconceivable for male troops, let alone women. Ada Potter recalled the distressing effects of an air raid on her best friend, revealing incidentally how her own warm nature triumphed over fear on this occasion: 'M. crouched next to me. Suddenly her usual high colour drained out her face to ashen white. She was trembling all over. I could do nothing but hold her hand and say "Soon be over now" like talking to a child in a thunderstorm.'[44] Despite the women's courage, the ordeal caused some major, and many minor, nervous reactions.[45]

Women's history had been made by the deaths in the Corps, for these were the first British female military personnel to die on active service. The tragedies silenced politicians who had argued against female suffrage on the grounds that women were taking no part in the defence of their country and, if given votes, would try to stop the war, fearing for their sons' and husbands' safety.[46] WAACs were now no longer kept away from the battle zone because of their sex – something which had frustrated many of them till then: 'O how hopelessly casual and futile everything seems,' Dorothy Loveday had told a friend, ' when one thinks of what is going on . . . I passionately want to go within sound at least of the guns.'[47] Significantly too, when, without the approval or assistance of the military, a women's rest camp was set up at Mesnil Val for their eighty-odd cases of neurasthenia, these females showed themselves tough enough to carry out all the fatigues by themselves.[48]

At the same time as the Women's Army was earning points for courage, its moral reputation was under attack. As Antonia Fraser, in her study of women war leaders, *The Warrior Queens*, has observed: 'because her sex is first and foremost what makes the [woman] Warrior remarkable, her sexuality must always be called into question.'[49] From the start, misleading accounts reached home both of immorality and of the officious measures designed to prevent it. One of the first drafts was informed by its administrator, a Mrs. Pratton Beaton, that the military commandant could enter their rooms at any time. There were outraged complaints from parents at the lack of trust – and privacy – this implied and the administrator was replaced; but the damage had been done.[50]

The section of the Army Act dealing with the Corps' discipline referred to the women as 'camp followers' and was, therefore, open to misinterpretation. Sir Neville Macready, the Adjutant General, had been only half-joking when he told Mona Chalmers-Watson in December 1916, that the army ran the risk of being held up as organisers of vice if they set up the Women's Corps![51] At least one politician took at face value the jest that women of the Army Corps were being employed in *maisons de tolerance*,[52] while a leading cleric publicly declared that some WAACs were being paid to produce children.[53] Another cleric was told by mischievous servicemen that a group of pregnant Frenchwomen were off-duty members of the Corps.[54] 'I expect you have heard the rumours about these war babies among the WACKS' Dorothy Loveday wrote to Miss Robertson: 'There is a tale the government is encouraging likely circumstances as a method of increasing the population. 150 are supposed to have been sent back from France and a maternity home started in Aldershot.'[55] Further scandalous stories, supposedly spread by owners of *estaminets*, who felt they had lost custom when the Corps arrived in France, as well as derogatory impressions arising from some soldiers' letters home, and the actions of French prostitutes, dressing in the Corps' uniform to attract custom, are claimed to have added credence to such beliefs.[56] These rumours were reinforced by comic postcards, such as one which asked 'Would you rather have a slap in the eye or a WAAC on the knee?'[57]

In fact, the founders of the Corps had created a rigorous code of behaviour to ward off allegations of immorality and indiscipline. This was maintained by a system of graded punishments consisting of admonitions, small fines, the forfeiture of pay and downgrading of rank. In extreme circumstances the women were liable to stand trial before a summary court of justice and could face up to six months' imprisonment and or a fine of up to £100. [58] However, in contrast with the men's army, the strictness with which administrators adhered to the code of discipline varied widely. Dorothy Loveday was shocked by the slackness in her camp where women came to dinner with their hair down and the roll call was not strictly observed.[59] There were indeed widespread problems with untidiness, unpunctuality and irregularity of dress, as, for example, the wearing by the workers of light collars – a privilege reserved for forewomen.[60]

Towards the war's end, although a majority was sustained by an *ésprit de corps*, patriotism and the wish to share their menfolk's hardship, some instances of insubordination were recorded, a small number of women being sent home. Inevitably war strain told, especially on those who had done other work at the front before joining the WAACs. One of these, in a somewhat over-dramatic account, described how in her camp, ' a sort of mutiny broke out' in August 1918, starting with an Irish girl who threatened to strike a superior officer, and followed by groups of women refusing to obey orders and quarrelling violently with each other. Authority, however quickly re-asserted itself :

Four girls were called to orderly room and addressed in person by a High Authority . . . They had gone in with heads up, jaws set, fire in their eyes, splendidly defiant. They were not going to be dictated to, ordered to do this and that, 'bullied like lodging-house slaveys,' as one of them prettily put it.

They remained behind those closed doors for over half an hour. I happened to be passing as they came out. Their eyes no longer flamed . . . Two were in tears . . . from then onward there were no further signs of 'rebellion'.[61]

Among other regulations, smoking was prohibited on duty and in public places. Alcohol was forbidden – except when prescribed 'for medicinal purposes' – and no member of the Corps was allowed even to enter an establishment which sold it.[62] All letters were read by administrators,[63] while a stringent system of chaperoning existed – theoretically at least. The barbed wire fences around the camps served to keep the women in, as well as the men out.[64] Married women were not allowed to serve in the same theatre of war as their husbands. Men were forbidden inside the camps without authorisation and members of the Corps even required permission to speak to officers.[65] No social contact was allowed with the French or Belgians.[66] The fact that roll call in France was at ten to nine and lights out at ten-thirty, together with the long hours that these dedicated women worked, left little time or energy for sexual escapades.[67] Indeed, as WAAC Marjorie Holme claimed, many arrived innocent and left innocent.[68]

This was, of course, not true of all. Dorothy Loveday confided to her friend Miss Robertson: 'Why does uniform have such an odd effect? The girls at once try and pick up with someone . . . Perhaps they feel they don't show up so much individually, lost in a crowd and can throw off all restraint. Of course it isn't all, perhaps not even half, but they are giving all the dogs a bad name.'[69] She blamed the lack of supervision for the unde-sirable behaviour of the younger WAACs when at close quarters with male soldiers: 'I went up one day,' she wrote, 'and found the Sergeant with a girl on either knee and we all had tea and another Sergeant came in and a girl sat on his knee. No superior of any kind, and no girl made responsible. Isn't it asking for trouble?'[70] Bearing in mind the battle-stress that many young women of normal sexual feelings were undergoing close to the line, it is not surprising that some, like their male equivalents, felt an urgent need for emotional and physical release.[71] Such a situation forced on 'respectable' women a fuller understanding of their sexuality than had been possible in their often sheltered backgrounds.

Although the scandalous rumours surrounding the Corps were mostly misinterpretations of the facts, they were so widely believed that by 1918, when Florence Burleigh Leach replaced Mona Chalmers-Watson, she had to swear an affidavit stating that to her knowledge no member of the Corps was being used for immoral purposes.[72] Shortly after this, a Commission of Enquiry spent eight days in France investigating the allegations, inter-viewing eighty women, and visiting three hospitals, eighteen hostels and twenty-nine camps. Helen Gwynne-Vaughan had sensibly recorded the reason for all dismissals and transfers and this evidence made it easy to refute accusations. Out of the 8,000 or so women who had served in France between 1 July 1917 and 11 March 1918, only *eighty -eight* had been disciplined. Of the 119 sent home since the formation of the Corps, only nineteen had been on disciplinary grounds, twenty for inefficiency, twenty one on compassionate grounds and fifty-nine for medical reasons, including twelve cases of venereal disease. There had been only twenty-one pregnancies, most of which had begun before the women arrived in France. The Commission agreed that the accusations were largely unfounded and recommended the formation of a Corps Police and greater vigilance in lonely camps and those nearer the front line, where there were more men about.[73] Taking the whole period of the Corps' overseas service, the final figures show that there were only a few more pregnancies and, out of the 17,000 WAACs who served in France, a mere *twenty seven* – including several long-term sufferers – were treated for V.D.[74]

With the war's end, the circumstances which had led to the creation of the Corps no longer obtained. There were soon calls in the once supportive press for its speedy demobilisation, largely in the interest of Britain's male population. The editor of *John Bull,* Horatio Bottomley M.P., asserted that the women's place was in the home, looking after the family, not taking men's jobs [75] In a less strident vein, *The Times* claimed that while the experiment had been a success, the continuing existence of the Corps would cause too many social and emotional problems in the army, not to mention the costly care and supervision required.[76]

It was actually three years before the Corps was completely disbanded. Contrary to press opinion, it proved itself vital to the post-war military machine, in such areas as the apprehension of female smugglers with the Army of Occupation, where body searches had to be carried out. The Corps also shouldered an important share of the huge clerical and administrative burden of demobilisation.[77] There was even talk of a permanent peacetime Corps, consisting of 150 officials and 10,000 other ranks, but this idea was widely opposed and never fully explored.[78]

Demobilisation had begun immediately the war ended. Priority was given to married women, widows with children, and those who had served more than one year. Personal reasons were also considered. If a woman had served less than one year and did not fall into one of the above categories she had to prove that she had a job to return to in England.[79] Mass demobilisation did not occur until those members of the Corps serving with the American Expeditionary Force were disbanded in June 1919.[80] After this the rate of demobilisation changed from between 500 and 600 a week to 2000 a week.[81] When the women were demobilised, they were allowed to keep their uniform and received a chit which they could exchange for a ration book.[82] 'Workers' were given twenty-eight days paid furlough and 'officials' two months pay, plus benefits.[83]

The signing of the Peace Treaty in 1919 ended the jurisdiction of the Defence of The Realm Act and, accordingly, on 1 January 1920, the Corps ceased to exist as a corporate body.[84] By February 1920, there were only 284 staff at the Corps' headquarters in London and sixty women involved in grave registration in France.[85] On 30 April 1920, all members, apart from those serving at St Pol military cemetery, were demobilized.[86] The women at St Pol continued to work there, re-enlisting every three months until their demobilisation in September 1921. By this time the number of women serving in France had dwindled to thirty-four.[87]

There was much positive writing about the new type of woman emerging from war service: 'The more I have seen of the WAACs, the firmer my belief that a new virile feminine element will come marching back,' commented one enthusiastic journalist, H.M. Love.[88] Service had broadened women's horizons, especially those of WAACs from conventionally-minded backgrounds:

> it made them – with some exceptions – singularly tolerant. Many even of those County women who before the war I had rather despised because they seemed so banal and provincial and self-centred, I grew to admire and respect . . . Pulled up by the roots from their native soil, and replanted in the middle of the war area, they gradually developed an entirely changed mental attitude. They saw what others did and set to work to do the same. The feeling of contempt they had entertained for those slightly beneath them socially, also for what are called the lower classes, vanished completely.[89]

The exceptions the same witness found to this rule were among those who were in areas far removed from the shells and bombs: 'I was forcibly struck by the difference that existed between the women – and the men too – who had seen something of the actual war, and those who had all the time remained in safety.'[90]

As a padre on the Western Front, the Reverend Robert Keable, later a best-selling author and advocate of greater sexual freedom, was struck in 1918 by the WAACs' emancipated approach to the opposite sex:

> When . . . one does get a chance talk with a Waac, the noticeable thing is that the girl is so enormously more independent. One feels that wooing has gone out of fashion, or at least wooing on the old lines . . . I take out my cigarette case and as a matter of course offer it to her. As a matter of course she takes it. She crosses her legs, and the short skirts just suffice to cover her knees, and we chat of England and the world. She shall certainly go to the colonies after the war, she says, blowing out the smoke. Yes, very likely motor-driving . . . I suggest that we have a walk

374

one afternoon. Certainly, she agrees, unperturbed; we can meet out of town.[91]

Though many returned to their homes and domesticity, some to their previous jobs, the women who returned from France tended to have greater expectations. Some used skills acquired in the Corps, such as driving.[92] Administrators became bursars, superintendents and matrons in educational establishments, while Corps doctors continued their professional work into civilian life. There were those, however, who readjusted with difficulty to old ways and subjection to their parents. Though some settled for traditional women's training, such as cooking lessons, there were those who resented not having their male counterparts' opportunities for study.[93] Those entering domestic service wanted fixed hours and their uniforms provided, and to be called 'domestics' rather than 'servants.'[94] They were often disappointed: there was a proliferation of job advertisements which stated: 'No WAAC Need Apply'.

Others, like many male ex-soldiers, felt England had little to offer them. Two women are recorded as moving to the Channel Islands to set up a farm,[95] others as carrying out relief work in Warsaw, Vienna and Serbia.[96] Most of these female emigrants chose South Africa, New Zealand, Australia and Canada, encouraged by the government, which was prepared to pay their fares.[97] The Old Comrades' Association's Gazettes were full of letters from women who had already emigrated or were about to do so, emphasising their new-found freedom.[98] This was before the days of symbolically burning brassières, but Jolie Buck, a former army driver, who in 1922 settled on Tahiti with the man she loved, rejoiced to be in a society where she did not have to wear stays.[99]

As with male ex-servicemen, the war had left such a deep mark on so many servicewomen that there was a widespread wish for some form of association: 'We've had such ripping times for more than two years, barring the poor dears who were killed of course, and we can't bear to let everything just fade away, and we want to keep it on.'[100] The Old Comrades' Association was formed at the end of 1919[101] and held its first reunion dinner on 25 June 1920.[102] By July it was publishing its own magazine. It met every Thursday between 7.30and 10.30 p.m. at 91 Belgrave Road, London.[103] Eventually it was to have its own social club, a clothes store to provide help for members who had fallen on bad times, a holiday home at St. Leonard's and a camp on the River Thames.[104] Through the association the spirit of the Corps was maintained, ready to be made flesh once more in 1938 with the creation of the Auxiliary Territorial Service.

The demise of the Corps should not be seen as a sign of failure, for it had received recognition for its services. All the members received the General Service Medal and the Victory Medal.[105] They were represented by three members and an administrator at the Peace March of 1919.[106] A select few visited Buckingham Palace for a garden party and were presented in uniform.[107] At York Minster, the 'Five Sisters Window' was installed and dedicated to the memory of all the members of the women's organizations who died whilst serving their country.[108] The Corps had proved that women could organize themselves, carry out essential work and be self-reliant. When a second world war loomed, the authorities did not wait, but instigated a women's army corps *a full year* before the outbreak. With Helen Gwynne-Vaughan in charge, continuity – loosely maintained for seventeen years by the Old Comrades' Association – was finally restored. Because the organization and training of the Auxiliary Territorial Service was based on the WAACs' Great War experience,[109] the Women's Army Auxiliary Corps was not a mere isolated episode in military and social history. Individual women, moreover, regarded having done their duty to their country with the pride that the majority of men did. Their service in the Corps had been a unique, intense period of hardship, excitement and camaraderie: as Dorothy Mary Bruce, who returned after the war to a conventional woman's existence, wrote in 1992: 'I always looked back on it as my one adventure.'[110]

Notes

Thanks should here be given to Claire Harder, Liddle Collection, Leeds, for research assistance in the later stages of writing, to the staff of the Liddle Collection, to Mrs A. Dale and Mrs. M. Walkington for typing and to the staff of the WRAC Museum at Guildford where the official files of the WRAC used here were consulted. They have since been transferred to the Imperial War Museum.

1   B. Ewing, *Women in Uniform throughout the Centuries*, 1975, p.31.

2   R.H. Boraston, *Haig's Despatches*, 1919, p.343.

3   R. Miles, *A Women's History of the World*, 1989, p.16.

4   Imperial War Museum, Women's Collection, Army 3/2, Lt. Gen. Lawson's Report, 8 Dec., 1916.

5   'Geddes' (The Rt.Hon. Auckland Campbell, Baron Geddes, G.C.M.G., K.C.B.,(Mil.), M.D., *The Forging of a Family: a family story studied in its genetical, cultural and spiritual aspects and a testament of personal belief founded thereon*, London, Faber & Faber, 1952, ch.xvii (Mona's Record) pp. 251–260.

6   IWM Women, Army 3, 12/6, interview with M. Chalmers Watson, 9 June 1918.

7   IWM Women., Army 3, 10/10, H.Gwynne Vaughan Diary, March 1917.

8   ibid., Army 3, 4/2, letter from Director Gen. Transport, to Adj. Gen., 4 Feb. 1917. He believed 161 women could replace 143 men, a 4:3 ratio.

9   *Times*, 13 Feb. 1918.

10   See *Times* 22 Aug. 1917; L[iddle] C[ollection], Brotherton Library, Leeds, Women's File, D. Fillis, Waac regulations; *Hansard* 5 Series, 1917,xcv,1481; ibid., 1918,cvi,563; ibid., 1918,cvi, 60; ibid.,1920,cxxv, 1516 & 1714.

11   ibid., 1917, xcviii, 1195.

12   ibid.,1917,xcii,1319.

13 See *Times*, 13 August 1917; and J.M.Cowper, *A Short History of the Queen Mary's Auxiliary Army Corps*, p.30.

14 IWM, Women, Army 3, 12/6, interview with M. Chalmers Watson, 9 June 1918.

15 ibid., Army 3, 5/3, Haig's Alternative Report.

16 WRAC Museum, Guildford, K. Bottomley (née White) written reminiscence.

17 Cowper op. cit., p.11.

18 L.C. Women, Miss A. Potter, WAAC telegraphist, typed reminiscences, 1916–19, p.3.

19 L.C. Women, tape 687, D.Fillis, R.White.

20 WRAC Museum, official WAAC scrapbook, *Daily Mail*, 6 March, 1919.

21 L.C. Women, Dorothy Loveday to Miss Robertson, Dec. 1917.

22 *Times*, 13 Feb. 1918.

23 L.C., Women, N.Steer, diary.

24 ibid, D. Fillis.

25 ibid., D. Loveday to Miss Robertson, 11 Dec., 1918.

26 IWM, Women, Army 3, 27/12.

27 L.C. Women, Tape 687.

28 ibid., Army 3, 13/114 Inspection Report 1918.

29 ibid. L.C. tape 687.

30 L.C., D. Loveday, letter to Miss Robertson (N.D.).

31 ibid.

32 C.W. Grundy, in Conal o'Riordan ed., *A Martial Medley*, London, Scolartis Press, 1930.

33 L.C., Women, Ada Potter.

34 L.C. Mrs. Edith Willison, typed reminiscences, p.15.

35 L.C. D. Loveday to Miss Robertson (n.d.).

36 See R. Terry, *Women in Khaki*, pp.53, 55; IWM Women, Army 3, 27/10, précis of medical services to QMAAC in France; ibid., Army 3, 27/13, medical returns of diseases 1918; WRAC Museum, *Daily Telegraph* 16 March 1981, loose cutting; IWM, Women, Army 3, 27/0; L.C., Dorothy Bruce, WAAC telegraphist, typewritten reminiscences, p.5.

37 L.C. Mrs. Edith Willison, typed reminiscences, pp.13–14.

38 IWM, Army 3, 15/8 Personal Hygiene Recommendations; S. Holdsworth, *Out of the Doll's House*, 1988, p.88; L.C., Women, A. Potter.

39 *Hansard* 5 1918, cx,775.

40 WRAC Museum, I.A.Turner, written reminiscences; ibid., O.B. Graham written reminiscences; L.C. Women, tape 447, Mrs. Sarsfield-Hall; ibid., A Potter; IWM, Women, Army 3, 29/5, H.Gwynne Vaughan notes on résumé of QMAAC; WRAC Museum, O.B. Graham; ibid., G.E. Watkins; Terry, op.cit., p. 61.

41 Cowper, op.cit., p. 48.

42 *Times*, 7 June 1918.

43 WRAC Museum, letter, Chief Controller Overseas to Controller-in-Chief, May 1918, official correspondence.

44 L.C. Women, Ada Potter p.13.

45 IWM Women, Army 3, 27/13; L.C. Women, Tape 447.

46 Miles, op.cit., pp.187–188.

47 L.C., D. Loveday to Miss Robertson, 24 March 1918.

48 IWM, Women, Army 3, 27/13.
49 Antonia Fraser, *The Warrior Queens*, 1989, p.12.
50 IWM, Women, Army 3, 12/6.
51 Geddes op.cit., p.258.
52 WRAC Museum, E.Lawrie's scrapbook, article, no date or source given.
53 *Times*, 16 April 1918.
54 Terry, op.cit., p.69.
55 L.C., Women, D. Loveday to Miss Robertson, 14 Jan. 1918.
56 WRAC Museum, report by Commision of Enquiry, official correspondence.
57 Terry op.cit., p.73.
58   L.C. Women, D.Fillis.
59 ibid., D.Loveday to Miss Robertson, 6 March 1918.
60 See M. Izzard, *A Heroine in Her Time*, 1969, pp.164–5; C.W.Grundy op.cit.;
    L.C., Women, N. Steer, diary, 17 Sept. 1918; WRAC Museum, M.L. Emsley;
    letter to father 18 Sept. 1918.
61 Anon., *WAAC, The Woman's Story of the War*, [memoir], London, T. Werner
    Laurie, 1930. p.211.
62 IWM Women, Army 3, 2/15, 3rd draft for organisation of Women's Army
    Corps.
63 L.C., Women, D. Loveday to Miss Robertson, 7 March 1918.
64 WRAC Museum, official WAAC scrapbook, article by Lady Baden Powell, in
    The Gentlewoman (n.d.).
65 IWM, Women, Army 3, 8/3, draft of WAAC regulations.
66 L.C. Women, D. Loveday to Miss Robertson, 7 March 1918.
67 WRAC Museum, minutes of QMAAC Conference 29 March 1918, official
    correspondence.
68 WRAC Museum, M. Holme, written reminiscences.
69 L.C., Women, D. Loveday to Miss Robertson, 6 Feb. 1918.
70 L.C., Women, D. Loveday to Miss Robertson, 14 Jan. 1918.
71 Anon., WAAC [memoir] pp. 128–130.
72 Terry op.cit. p. 73.
73 WRAC Museum, report by Commission of Enquiry.
74 IWM Women, Army 3, 27/10.
75 WRAC Museum, official WAAC scrapbook, article by H. Bottomley M.P. in
    Sunday Pictorial, n.d.
76 *Times*, 28 Aug. 1919; see also for a sympathetic comment, R.M. Bradley,
    'Women After the War', in *The Nineteenth Century and After*, lxxxvi, 1919,
    p.836.
77 Hansard 5, cxviii, 1919, 1162.
78 *Times*, 29 March 1919.
79 IWM, Women, Army 3, 31/2, report by War Resettlement Committee.
80 WRAC Museum, Col. D. Stone, A.E.F., to F. Burleigh Leach, 29 June 1919,
    official correspondence.
81 *Times*, 25 Sept. 1919.
82 WRAC Museum, M. Emsley, discharge documents.
83 IWM, Women, Army 3, 31/2.
84 *Times*, 31 Dec. 1919.
85 ibid., 18 Feb. 1920.
86 ibid., 4 March 1920.

87 WRAC Museum, official WAAC scrapbook, *Daily Sketch*, 27 Sept. 1921.

88 WRAC Museum, E. Lawrie's scrapbook, H.M. Love, 'The WAAC Nut' (n.d., no source given).

89 Anon., *WAAC*, [memoir] pp. 200–201.

90 ibid., p. 178.

91 R. Keable, *Standing By*, London, Nisbet, 1919, p.243.

92 See Oliver Onions, *Cut Flowers*, London, Chapman & Hall, 1927, p.34.

93 L.C. Women, A.Potter.

94 WRAC Museum, official WAAC scrapbook, F. Burleigh Leach, 'Why WAACS Dislike Domestic Work' (n.d., no source given).

95 ibid., *Daily News* cutting, 26 Jan. 1920.

96 *Times*, 29 Sept. 1920.

97 ibid., 2 Dec. 1920.

98 IWM, Women, Army 3, 26/26–34, Old Comrades Assocn. Gazettes.

99 Jolie (Buck) Keable to Mrs. Elliott, 23 March, 1923 (see Hugh Cecil, *The Flower of Battle, British Fiction Writers of the First World War*, London, Secker & Warburg 1995, p.175.)

100 Oliver Onions, op.cit. p. 65.

101 *Times,* 25 June 1920.

102 ibid., 28 June 1920.

103 ibid., 15 July 1920.

104 ibid., 20 June 1921.

105 E.C. Joslin et al. (eds.) *British Battles and Medals,* 1988, pp.228, 230.

106 IWM, Women, Army 3, 17/5, instructions for Peace March.

107 WRAC Museum, M. Holme.

108 WRAC Museum, official WAAC scrapbook, 21 June 1925 (no title nor source given).

109 Terry, op.cit., pp.92–5.

110 L.C., Dorothy Mary Bruce, WAAC telegraphist, to P. Liddle, 1992.

Part VI

Soldier Morale

Chapter 28

The Morale of the German Army, 1917–18[1]

Hew Strachan

In his study of German armaments policy published in 1984 Michael Geyer posited two basic forms to early twentieth-century warfare. The first was manpower driven. The second – the 'true' conception of modern war – was shaped by technology. He argued that in 1916 the new German supreme command of Hindenburg and Ludendorff, 3 O.H.L., embraced this latter approach, causing machines to substitute for men, and ousting tradition and hierarchy in favour of 'the functional organization of violence'.[2] The consequences which preoccupied Geyer in his original study were those felt in the management of the war economy. But the impact was also tactical: 'discipline and military socialization were rebuilt around weapons skills and performance'.[3]

Tim Travers, writing the conclusion to *The Killing Ground,* published in 1987, was impressed by Geyer's argument. 'Ludendorff's technical rule led to the full rationalization of machine war.'[4] For him the contrast between the German army's response to the battles of 1916 and that of the British army was complete. The former shaped tactics around the characteristics of the new weapons systems thrown up by technological innovation: the latter remained bound to an approach which grafted the new weapons onto existing and unchanging concepts. Haig's solutions to the problems of the western front remained mired in calculations about manpower and did not, as the Germans did, begin with machinery.

Both Geyer and Travers have produced works of considerable scholarship, packed with stimulating insights and fertile debates. But the generalizations, however crude, to be distilled from their analyses – that modern war is machine war, and that the Germans embraced it in 1916–18 but the British did not – present as many difficulties as they resolve.

The first objection is simplistic but still powerful. They do not tell us why Germany lost and Britain won. Or at least they imply that explanations for the outcome of the war must be found removed from the battlefield.

The second set of objections is specifically German. The reworking of German tactics associated by G.C. Wynne and Timothy Lupfer[5] with Hindenburg's and Ludendorff's arrival at O.H.L. was initiated not in late 1916 but began in 1915. Short artillery bombardments were the practice from Gorlice-Tarnow in May 1915 and infiltration tactics were employed at Verdun in February 1916. This was a 'bottom-up' response to circumstances on the ground, and Falkenhayn as much as Ludendorff must get the credit for listening to what junior commanders were saying. Indeed Ludendorff himself did not look very modern in 1915: he was still pursuing operational solutions on the eastern front that were Schlieffenesque and even Napoleonic in their grandeur, and which paid scant attention to logistics or to artillery firepower. Thus the change in high command in 1916 looks less dramatic. This is true not only when put in the context of 1915 but also when projected forward to that of 1917–18. Geyer's argument assumes that 3 O.H.L. had a total conception for a total war – covering the span from domestic output to tactical deployment. But there is little evidence that the weapons production targets achieved later in the war were the fruit of the Hindenburg programme rather than of the steady accretion of orders placed by the Prussian war ministry since 1914.[6] Indeed the consequences of the Hindenburg programme confirm how ill-thought out were its implications – as well as its execution: it generated inflation, and it exacerbated the shortages of men, coal and transport which were all to prove crucial to Germany's final collapse. Finally, it seems bizarre to see Germany as the home of machine warfare when the most obvious technical innovation in land fighting during the war, the tank, was embraced with enthusiasm by Britain and France but not by Germany.

The third set of objections to the Geyer/Travers thesis is therefore comparative. Germany was not alone in concluding that machines must substitute for men in 1917–18. If the German adoption of machine warfare is seen as the product not of virtue but of necessity – a series of responses to a desperate and worsening manpower position, its similarity to the behaviour of the other belligerents is more striking than its peculiarity. Moreover, it was the British application of war industry on the Somme that so stunned Hindenburg and Ludendorff, and led the Germans to coin the word *Materialschlacht*.[7] For all the belligerents, production bottlenecks ultimately proved easier to overcome than manpower problems – particularly for the Entente, which had access to American industry before it had the use of the U.S. Army. One obvious illustration of this point – if we put aside (and there is no reason why we should) the tank as well as the crushing artillery superiority of the Allies in 1918 – is the reorganisation of the division. The cutting of the British division from 12 infantry battalions to 9 resulted in a proportional increase in artillery and machine guns in relation to manpower. Even more striking is the French example. Pétain's reorganisation of the heavy artillery to give it flexibility and strategic mobility complemented, at the other extreme, the French use of infiltration tactics and their widespread distribution of automatic weapons.[8]

Pétain's views were not of course the product of any great sea change in 1916 or 1917; he had argued that firepower should substitute for men in 1914 and 1915. But for Pétain machinery was not enough: on 27 December 1917 he told Pershing that 'morale has become one of the essential factors of the struggle'.[9] For a commander-in-chief whose first task had been the suppression of mutinies affecting half his army that may seem no more than a rather crass statement of the obvious. But for the present discussion it has particular pertinence. The positing of manpower and machinery as alternatives has had the effect of excluding morale from the picture. Furthermore, when morale is recognised it is associated with the 1914 'spirit of the offensive', and so ranged on the side of traditionalism rather than modernity. But morale is clearly central to any discussion of operational effectiveness in 1917 and 1918. In the former year both the Russian and Italian armies, as well as the French, suffered internal collapse. The fact that both the British and the German armies apparently came through unscathed has not gone unremarked. Arguments have been put which suggest that both had their come-uppance, albeit in differing degrees, in 1918. The unusually high proportion of captured among the British 5th Army's casualties on 21 March 1918 may point to a failure of morale. But in that case recovery followed soon after.[10] Much less contentious is the argument that, although the German army did not stop fighting until 11 November 1918, its effectiveness was being sapped by desertions, stragglers and mass surrenders for several months before the armistice. Wilhelm Deist, reflecting the language of Guy Pedroncini when discussing the French mutinies of 1917, has referred to a 'veiled military strike'.[11]

Ludendorff was as aware as Pétain of the centrality of morale. The famous document of 1 January 1918, 'The attack in position warfare', emphasises the requirement for surprise, the need to press on regardless of losses, and the centrality of independent decision-making. Mental attitudes are pivotal: its focus is as much on the 'reckless drive and initiative on the part of every individual man' as on machinery. Furthermore, its language and expression are more traditional than Geyer's portrayal of radicalism and technocracy would lead one to expect. 'The great military principles which formed the backbone of our military training in peacetime and to which we owe all great successes of the war are still the old ones. Where they may have been forgotten they must be resurrected.'[12]

The critical features of the two key tactical texts of 3 O.H.L., 'The defence in position war' of December 1916, and 'The attack in position war', were that they represented the experience and views of those at the front and that these were then disseminated through training and instruction. In this instance, therefore, the views of the high command were not at odds with those who were required to execute their directives: the fact that this was not the case in the French army in April 1917 has been given as the cause for 'the military strike' that assailed that army after the failure of the Nivelle offensive. By arming the infantry with automatic weapons, the Germans re-empowered the individual foot-soldier despite the advent of industrialised warfare and its domination by artillery timetables. Training gave him confidence in his ability to complete his task even in a *Materialschlacht*. Thus O.H.L.'s tactical instructions were designed to recover morale and had the effect of averting, at least for the time being, a 'military strike'.[13]

Ludendorff's reaction to the tank was somewhat different. Germany's own failure to respond in kind was, admittedly, more the product of material shortages than of doctrine. But the division in the latter caused by the need to take steps for anti-tank defence showed that when it suited O.H.L. it did not respond to pressures from the front but reacted out of its own conviction as to the primacy of morale. While reports from the front urged defence in depth, the distribution of artillery at lower levels of command, and the construction of broad anti-tank ditches, the German supreme command said that effective resistance to armoured fighting vehicles was simply a matter of nerves. Ludendorff talked disdainfully of 'tank-panic'.[14]

Like much else in Ludendorff's military thought, his preoccupation with morale was not innovatory but traditional. He, after all, had been the prime advocate of a manpower-intensive solution to Germany's strategic problems when chief of operations on the general staff in 1912 and 1913. The fact that Germany nonetheless had to anticipate fighting a European war from a position of numerical inferiority meant that less quantifiable factors – like doctrine and, of course, morale – had to be adduced as factors that would make the difference between victory and defeat. The dazzling advance in the first six weeks of the war, combined with Tannenberg, and then the overrunning of Poland and Serbia in 1915, confirmed the belief that German soldiers, man for man, were individually superior to those of other armies. This conviction was never far away in the calculations of their commanders.

Equally insensitive to the real feelings of the front-line soldier was O.H.L.'s response to declining morale in July 1917. On the 29th of that month Ludendorff issued guidance on 'patriotic instruction' for the army: each division was to make arrangements for lectures on French and Russian responsibility for the war, and on Germany's successes and invincibility.[15] Most recent discussion of 'patriotic instruction' puts it in the context of civil-military relations, of the army's effort to propagate its own political objectives, and cites it as evidence of O.H.L.'s right-wing credentials and its advocacy of annexations. Ludendorff was undoubtedly worried by trends at home: the Reichstag had adopted the peace resolution ten days previously, and mutiny was to break out in the High Seas Fleet the following month. The idea of 'the stab in the back', used by the army after the armistice to protect its own reputation and shift the blame for defeat to the home front, was not retrospective but was already emerging as clearly articulated both in the programme of patriotic instruction and even earlier, in 1916.

But Ludendorff's anxiety to insulate the army from the effects of socialism and pacifism in the rear must not simply be subsumed in the war aims debate. It was also a reflection of his worries about the mood at the front. The head of the field medical service warned O.H.L. that prolonged absence from home and lack of leave were taking their toll. He pointed out that the depressing effects of news and views worked in both directions, home and front interacting with each other in a downward spiral.[16] The writer Rudolf Binding, who was serving on the Western Front, concluded his diary's review of the events in Berlin in July, with the words: 'One shuts one's eyes because there is nothing but pettiness to look at. Perhaps it is just as well that one can shut them because it becomes intolerable to look on. Perhaps there lies hope in the very fact that the situation seems hopeless.'[17]

The programme of 'patriotic instruction' was a dismal failure, and not just because it was attacked by the centre/left majority in the Reichstag. From its title to its schoolmasterly organisation, it totally miscalculated the true mood of the soldier.[18] But the scheme is evidence both of the primacy of morale in Ludendorff's calculations and of his perception that that of the German army was already in decline in 1917.

It seems reasonable to conclude that the German army's internal strains began not in 1918, in the aftermath of the spring and summer offensives, but in 1917. Like the French, and unlike the British, the Germans had been continuously engaged at full strength since 1914. Like the French, the Germans had been through the mincing machine of Verdun; unlike the French, they had failed to achieve their objectives, and they had then been put on the rack at the Somme. Inter-war German writers emphasised how close the army was to collapse in August 1916 – albeit to heighten the effectiveness of Hindenburg's and Ludendorff's arrival.[19] Concrete evidence for what followed is remarkably hard to come by, and it is mostly French. P. Camena d'Almeida, writing in 1919, and who from internal evidence served in French military intelligence, reported large-scale German desertions in August 1917. Pierre Miquel goes one stage further and describes what happened as mutiny. He catalogues a string of mutinies between May and August 1917, principally in units from Wurttemberg and Saxony, but also embracing Hessians, Silesians and even Prussians. Furthermore, the crisis spanned the length of the front: mutiny broke out in the 26th Württemberg Division at Poelcapelle in May, and in the 80th Pomeranian Division at Verdun in August.[20] In November 1917 Wilhelm

Groener was ousted from his job as head of the *Kriegsamt* and took over the 33rd Infantry Division in a quiet sector of the Western Front. He found no evidence of direct fear in his new command, but he could not fail to notice that the men did their duty without enthusiasm and with a relief born from the knowledge that their positions were secure and their rations adequate. The division's problems were in its rear areas and its base camps.[21] Friedrich Altrichter, a patriotic but not uncritical observer, writing in 1933, denied that there were mutinies in 1917, but then – in referring to the transport services – promptly contradicted himself.[22]

Therefore the difficulty in assessing the scale of the crisis is not only the success with which it was masked by O.H.L., but also the imprecision of the terms which are used to describe it. At what stage do massive desertions by Poles become mutiny in the German army? The former suggests an act of individual desperation; the latter a collective and considered conspiracy to achieve a specific objective. Part of Altrichter's confusion is his uncertainty as to the distinction. Part of O.H.L.'s skill in obfuscation is its emphasis on the former – on the unreliability of non-German minorities within the army – in order to protect the collective reputation of the latter.

Whatever the precise nature of the crisis, the German army surmounted it with sufficient *élan* to weather the third battle of Ypres and then to launch the spring offensives of 1918. Assuming that this resilience cannot be attributed to the scheme of 'patriotic instruction', to what – Ludendorff's tactical instructions apart – can it be attributed?

Some of the answers may be found in the internal organisation of the army itself. Most recent work on morale focuses on the importance of the primary group, the section of seven to ten men; it stresses that men fight not for a higher cause but for their 'mates' and 'buddies', bound by war in a relationship which, however utilitarian, can achieve great intensity.[23] The German army made the section or *Gruppe* not only its basic social unit but also its key tactical formation. Thus the drift of the main fighting instructions worked with the grain of good morale, not against it.[24]

Junior leadership was vital to the success of the small group. Here Germany profited from its own heritage, which emphasised the delegation of command forward and the exercise of individual responsibility (*Auftragstaktik*), and which created a special class of NCOs, socially distinct from the private soldiers and imbued with its own ethos. Both these elements took a battering during the war. Ludendorff had to reinculcate the principles of *Auftragstaktik* precisely because they were lost in the centralizing tendencies of divisional command so easily generated in the circumstances of position warfare. By 1917 only *Kompaniefeldwebeln* were still pre-war regulars, and the influx of new NCOs, without the training and long service of their predecessors, eroded the distinction between them and the rank and file.[25] But the decline was relative to

388

Germany's past rather than to the standards of other armies. In the British pre-war army there was never a social distinction between the NCO and the private, both of them coming from the lower reaches of society; the comparative lack of initiative to be found in the former was reflected in the higher number of commissioned officers per battalion than was the case in Germany. By simultaneously embracing both conscription and the notion of an aristocratic officer corps, Germany drew in men of middle-class backgrounds but then cut off many of their paths to commissions: such arrangements meant that men of professional and educated back-grounds – schoolmasters, lawyers, managers – still occupied non-commissioned rank in the German army.

Nor had the status and attributes of the officers themselves been as eroded by the expansion of the officer corps as the pre-war defenders of the aristocratic principle seemed to expect. Germany commissioned 226,130 reserve officers during the war: most of them came from middle-class backgrounds, and numerically they swamped the 50,960 active officers. But the decision was taken not to lower educational standards, and, as was also evident in some British regiments, the newcomers embraced the prevailing standards of the officer corps rather than subverted them. Casualties among the active officer corps (24.8 per cent were killed) were higher than those of the reserve (15.7 per cent). But if more than 75 per cent of the active officers survived this was clearly a proportion sufficient to ensure the perpetuation of traditional values. The continuation of promotion by seniority, despite pressure for change in 1917, confirmed this. Of Prussian officers in service in 1914, about 40 per cent were killed in the war. This is a high death rate, but in this context it is more noteworthy that 60 per cent survived.[26]

Ultimately the problems that would assail the German officer corps were not those of too little continuity but of too much. The maintenance of educational standards excluded the senior NCOs from commissions: the best that they could hope for was promotion to *Feldwebelleutnant* as a 'substitute officer', a rank below that of the most junior lieutenant, and this after twelve years' service. The situation was not rectified until October 1918. It was too late. As in the German navy, the grievances of this group would push them to the forefront of the soldiers' councils in November 1918.[27] Furthermore, within the officer corps proper, the decision to stick with the principle of seniority blocked the promotions of the able and ambitious, who therefore moved sideways to the stimulus and excitement of responsible positions on the staff and in the war ministry. The effect was to leave only a rump, either ageing and lacking ability, or young and inex-perienced, serving with the regiments in the field.[28] Thus the German army bought stability in 1917 at the expense of instability in late 1918.

The third internal factor – after small group loyalty and junior leader-ship – which could help explain the resilience of German morale is the perpetuation of local links. The trend during the war was to form divisions of distinct regional groupings: a wounded man who returned to service on recovery would not necessarily return to his original unit, but he would go to a formation from the same geographical area.[29] Germany therefore avoided the evils of the excessively tight community links characterised by the British 'Pals' battalions: heavy casualties in a single battalion would not devastate a street or suburb. But they nonetheless exploited the identities of Germany's constituent states. Again this would rebound by November 1918: anti-Prussianism would grip Bavaria, and the north/south division was exploited by British propaganda. In the interim, however, local links served to sustain morale rather than to subvert it.

The explanations so far adduced for the maintenance of the German army's cohesion are internal and conform to most of the traditional explanations for good morale in other armies and in other epochs. A further reason for the army's resilience is more contentious. It has become remarkably unfashionable to explain high morale in terms of broader political goals and even of military victory. The notion that men fought for the nation could not, we are constantly reminded, survive the ordeal of the trenches.

The rise in British morale in late 1918, already referred to, confirms the unwisdom of this approach. Germany's experience of the First World War was, for much of the time, strikingly successful. However dour the struggle on the western front, the initial advance in 1914 ensured it was waged on enemy soil. More importantly, the eastern front in 1915 and again in 1917 brought substantial gains. By July 1918 the German empire stood on frontiers which would only be exceeded by Hitler. Furthermore, those victories not only redounded to the credit of the army, they also – more self-interestedly – pointed the soldier on the way home. Dogged defence, however successfully conducted over however long a period, did no more than ensure the war's continuation. Decisive victory promised a quick peace. The enthusiasm and determination manifested in the 1918 offensives were, in this sense, no more than the positive expression of war weariness.[30]

The failure of those offensives to achieve a strategic decision therefore rekindled the disintegrating effects barely held in check in 1917. The consequences of Germany's gains meant that Germany's subsequent defeat can be explained in material terms alone. Between 21 March and 25 June 1918 the length of front held by the German army increased from 390 kilometres to 510, while at the same time about a million men had been lost. Furthermore, many of these casualties were borne by exactly the groups which had sustained the army's morale thus far. Company officers suffered particularly heavily. The policy of distinguishing between 'mobile divisions' and 'position divisions', giving the former better equipment, rebounded when they also bore the brunt of German losses. The physical consequences could not but have psychological effects.[31]

The indications of declining German morale were evident to all on both sides of the line in the summer of 1918. Gerhard Ritter, who himself served as a front-line officer in the 18th Army in March 1918, wrote of the 'crushing disappointment' caused by the failure of the April offensive.[32] Mass surrenders, precipitate flight, recurrent desertions – all are elements in explaining the rapidity of the Allied advance. But it nonetheless remains true that enough units retained sufficient military commitment to sustain a continued defence. On 19 October Haig reported that, 'The German Army is capable of retiring to its own frontiers and holding that line.'[33] Not all the factors contributing to the collapse of the German army are to be found at the front. As in the French army in 1917, problems arose more often when troops were out of the line than when they were in it: the immediacy of fighting seems often to have sustained unit cohesion rather than undermined it.

One of the principal grouses of the German soldier was food. This is of course a standard complaint among all soldiers. But in the German case it had two specific twists.

First, there was the conspicuous difference between officers and men; the former when out of the line fed in style and the latter fed – as in the line – from field kitchens. This distinction gave substance to the front-line soldier's animosity towards the staff. But it also subverted the solidarity created in action between the junior officer and his men: once in reserve soldiers became aware that comradeship only went so far. Reserve officers in particular, it has been suggested,[34] were not as attentive to the gastronomic needs of their men as regular officers. In the army, as in the navy,[35] food divided officers from men.

The services were therefore similar to civilian society: the maladministration of the food supply deepened rather than alleviated the effects of the blockade. The latter meant that hunger was not only a relative problem, but also an absolute one. Soldiers' supplies were a top priority in Germany's rationing system and mobile divisions were a priority within the army. But pauses to plunder, and to eat and drink, still dissipated the advance of March 1918. Deist reports that corned beef was particularly popular. On 1 June, one Guards division tried to minimise the disordering effects of looting by creating special booty commands within each battalion.

The army's preoccupation with food, and its relationship to the blockade, serves to remind us that the division between front and rear can be overdrawn. Post-war memoirs emphasise the soldier's sense of solidarity, the common bond that bridged both sides of no man's land, and stress the veteran's alienation from civil society. But, as Stéphane Audoin-Rouzeau has so successfully argued,[36] the underlying rationale for the war has to be the defence of home in the most literal sense. French soldiers' postcards, however maudlin, testify to the longing for wife and hearth – a point confirmed in one of the more bizarre episodes in Barbusse's bizarre book, *Le Feu*, when a French soldier gets behind German lines to have a glimpse of his family in a German-occupied town.

The problem was that the home the soldier went off to defend in 1914 had changed irreversibly by 1918. Georg Pabst's film, *Westfront 1918* (1930), contains a remarkable evocation of this mood. A German soldier returns from leave to find his wife in bed with another man; he goes to see his mother but she is not at home; eventually he finds her, frail and exhausted, queuing for bread.

The most important indications that the war was not being fought for its primary objectives – that even military victory would not prevent the collapse of a way of life – were social. The Reichstag peace resolution and the 1917 naval mutinies made the doubts of those in the rear palpable. But there were also political and constitutional challenges to the legitimacy of what the army was doing. These went to the heart of its existence, to its very *raison d'être*.

Before the war the army was a symbol of the nation but not its representative. It was the custodian of the principle of kingship – both in the sense that historically, in 1813 and 1848, it had protected the monarchy from itself, and in the sense that it was a bulwark against socialism. Conscription had not been achieved at the expense of these values. The ethos of the army was regular and professional. Its officer corps, for all that the general staff was becoming increasingly bourgeois and bureaucratic, took its tone from the aristocracy. It drafted only 56 per cent of the available manpower, and so was able to take those from agricultural backgrounds, spurning urban workers who might have been prey to socialist influences. In 1914 the army faced inwards as well as outwards in its defensive mission.[37]

The effect of the war was to create a true nation in arms within Germany. Pre-war opponents of expansion had argued that a bigger army would inevitably involve the incorporation of larger numbers of middle-class officers and more socialist-minded soldiers. The battles of 1916 made these conservative fears reality. Descriptions of the army as no more than a militia were current by the winter of 1916–17 and increased in 1917–18. In his emphasis on training and on patriotic instruction Ludendorff was doing no more than respond to the existing expectation that such a change in the army's social composition would create an internal crisis.

Simultaneously there arose the question of whose service this national army was called upon to fulfil. The war witnessed the completion of the decline in the Kaiser's power: the notion that the soldiers owed personal fealty to their king became increasingly absurd as Wilhelm was marginalised, and was finally crushed by the army's role in his abdication. But no new authority replaced that of the Kaiser. Significant here was the failure to introduce constitutional reform. Rousseau's rationalisation of conscription, that civic obligations were the corollary of civil rights, did not find fulfilment. The idea of Germany itself was insufficient substitute as the fissiparous tendencies of the component parts of the empire took hold in response to adversity.

One focus of the constitutional debate, and at times a substitute for it, was the issue of war aims. Public disagreement as to what Germany was fighting for divided its citizens during the war just as surely as the shape of the constitution threatened to do so after hostilities were over. Ludendorff's programme of patriotic instruction was an acknowledgement that these debates could rupture the fabric of the army just as easily as they could define parties in the Reichstag.

Of course, front-line soldiers were preoccupied with far more immediate and pressing issues than these. Food, warmth, survival – all were more important than constitutionalism or war aims. But the failure of the state to tackle the pressing matters, especially the first, or its efforts to do so with effects that were unequal, helped rob the state of its legitimacy. Social issues and political issues were linked. In November 1918 the army's behaviour testified to its support for at least some of the more abstract political objectives.

The links between the front and the rear were never severed. 'Men on leave', Philipp Scheidemann told the Reichstag on 17 October 1918, 'come from the army with ugly stories; returning from home they carry bad news back to the Army'.[38] The corollary of the creation of a nation in arms was that the army's ills were the nation's, and the nation's the army's. Ludendorff may have wished to create a *cordon sanitaire* around the army, but he could not. Soldiers went home on leave; soldiers criss-crossed Europe moving from front to front, and in so doing passed through Germany; soldiers wrote letters home. Significant in this latter context is the fact that censorship of the field post was not established until as late as 1917. However, much the most significant force for integration rather than separation was the army's need for men.

Reinforcements for the western front in 1917–18 were culled from three main sources, all of them, in O.H.L.'s eyes, tainted in varying degrees.

First were the troops brought from the eastern front to the west in 1917. Fraternisation with the Russians had taken hold between the two revolutions, and many Germans had begun to reckon on an early return home. Many of the wagons which they boarded for the journey westward bore the slogan, '*Schlachtvieh für Flandern*'.[39] The German railway system itself was over-extended by the growth of the empire and under-maintained for lack of labour. As in France, railway stations became the focus for agitation. Many who set out on the journey failed to reach their destinations. Societies to aid deserters were established in Berlin, Hamburg, Cologne, Stuttgart and Munich. They were provided with food cards, forged papers and money, and then pointed towards the Dutch frontier.[40] Richard Bessel reckons that up to 10 per cent of those moved from east to west deserted: it would be interesting to know more about how many got to Holland and Switzerland, and the routes they used.[41]

The second source of men were the prisoners of war released by the Russians. Many of these had become socialists, and some opted to stay in Russia rather than be repatriated. Again, the expectation that for them at least the war was over ill-prepared them for the war in the west. The army recognised this and created special camps to retrain and reinvigorate them. By the summer of 1918 the manpower position was so desperate that O.H.L. had to employ them, but many regimental commanders refused, seeing them as a hindrance, not a help, and preferring a battalion that was under-strength but reliable.[42]

Finally, there was Germany itself. Over a million men had been released from the army by January 1918 to meet the needs of the Hindenburg programme: over two million within Germany were eligible for military service but were retained at home on other work. O.H.L. set about reversing the flow, albeit with limited overall success. But, if the effect on aggregate numbers was limited, its impact on the army's political attitudes may have been much more significant. The Berlin strike of January 1918, whose aims included peace and constitutional reform, was organised by the shop stewards. Many of the most militant, including Richard Müller, were promptly conscripted into the army.[43] As a strike-breaking device it was crude; as a military measure it was ill-conceived. Two interpretations are possible. One draws a line between the conscripted shop stewards and the soldiers' councils of November 1918. The other points to the tensions between those exempted from military service and battle-hardened veterans: these were vented in recruit training of particular severity.[44]

The most palpable evidence of declining morale was to be found not at the front, for all its sponginess in the summer of 1918, but on the lines of communication. The rear of the front line, not the home front, was the physical focus for all these elements. The arrival of replacements, transport and supply difficulties, tensions over food, training and retraining – all could simmer and seethe here without the direct pressure of the enemy to suppress them. Men in the rear were less frequently members of formed units; their officers were temporary and their authority did not rely on familiarity and shared experience. Here too the rearward flow of men from the front was most evident, further clogging the railways and straining the food supplies. Men did not all flee the front as deserters. Some claimed to have lost their units; others were lightly wounded or slightly sick. About a million men came into this last category between March and July 1918: about 40 per cent of them were capable of marching. The cynic might reasonably enquire whether they could have marched forwards as well as backwards. He might also, looking at the very high sickness rate in June and July 1918, wonder for how many the influenza epidemic was a convenience rather than an encumbrance. Erich Otto Volkmann reckoned that in the latter stages of the war there were up to a million shirkers lurking in the rear and making their way back to Germany.[45]

The decline in the legitimacy of the army is evident in O.H.L.'s failure to take control of this situation. British commentators tend to observe with favour the infrequency of capital punishment in the German army. After the war, the Germans themselves observed how the British and the French both hardened their application of military law in response to the social transformation of their armies, whereas they had softened it. In April 1917, the German army, overly sensitive to its evolution as a 'militia', issued a new legal code which, while retaining the existing maximum punishments, moderated the minor ones: the minimum sentence of ten years' imprisonment for disobedience in the face of the enemy was put to one side, and the definition of what constituted 'the face of the enemy' was adapted to the circumstances of trench warfare and incorporated the reserve areas. The worst punishment for desertion was penal servitude or transfer to a punishment company: both could seem preferable to a return to the trenches.

The army's efforts to restore order in 1918 were little and late. Special trains moved behind the front collecting stragglers. But many of the latter then had their desires met, as they were sent back to Germany for creation into fresh units. Some were drafted into the nearest available battalions. But this could have the effect of weakening good units, and put officers in command of men they did not know. Ludendorff's directive of July 1918, which allowed officers *in extremis* to use their weapons on their own soldiers, completed this rupture in internal cohesion.[46]

The significance of the chaos in the German army's rear, of the disturbances at railway stations and of the flow of deserters, shirkers and stragglers along the lines of communication, is that this was the interface between the army and civil society, between front and home. What it suggests is that the currents followed by demoralisation flowed in both directions. Ludendorff and others were not wrong to fear the implications of divisions and dissent within Germany for the solidity of the army. But equally correct were those who realised that soldiers could undermine the morale of those at home. Many who went back took their weapons with them; as early as June and July 1917 the deputy commanding generals reckoned that soldiers on leave were participating in riots and disturbances.[47] This interaction was the inevitable consequence of the creation of a nation in arms.

The argument about the *Dolchstosslegende* is therefore a sterile one. Both camps were right in that there was revolution at home *and* the army suffered internal collapse. It is significant that two of the inter-war authorities on which this essay has drawn, Erich Otto Volkmann and Friedrich Altrichter – both friends to the army, and the latter a venerator of

Hindenburg and Ludendorff, embraced criticisms that could not permit them to espouse the stab-in-the-back argument *tout court*. They recognised the interactive effects between front and rear. But they still tended to see Germany as formed of two entities – the army on the one hand and the nation on the other. The essence of the sterility lies in the fact that Germany had become one: its army was made up of citizen soldiers, and its civilian society was, through the Auxiliary Service Law, conscripted for the prosecution of the war. Thus the divisions within Germany ran not along its frontiers, between those tending the hearth and those in the field, but flowed throughout the fabric of its society, the army included.

Notes

1 What follows is more an agenda for research than its consequence. It is informed in part by comparative considerations arising out of our knowledge of the morale of the other belligerents in 1917–18. The low-level experience of the First World War, so extensively covered in the British literature and increasingly in the French, has not received comparable attention in Germany. Hence Wolfram Wette (ed.), *Der Krieg des kleinen Mannes: eine Militärgeschichte von unten* (Munich, 1992), has been greeted as a pathbreaking study. Relevant to the present theme is Wilhelm Deist's piece in that collection, 'Verdeckter Militärstreik im Kriegsjahr 1918?'.
See also Deist, 'Der militärische Zusammenbruch des Kaiserreichs: zur Realität der "Dolchstosslegende"', in Ursula Büttner (ed.), *Das Unrechtsregime: internationale Forschung über den Nationalsozialismus. Bd. 1. Ideologie – Herrschaftssystem-Wirkung in Europa* (Hamburg, 1986): this important article was reprinted in Deist, *Militär, Staat und Gesellschaft: Studien zur preussischen–deutschen Militärgeschichte* (Munich, 1991), and will appear in an English translation in *War in History*, III, 1996.

2 Michael Geyer, 'German Strategy in the Age of Machine Warfare, 1914–1945', in Peter Paret (ed.), *Makers of Modern Strategy from Machiavelli to the Nuclear Age,* (Oxford, 1986), p. 541. See also Geyer, *Deutsche Rüstungspolitik 1860–1980* (Frankfurt, 1984), esp. pp. 13, 91–2, 99–103.

3 ibid, p. 541.

4 Tim Travers, *The Killing Ground: The British Army, the Western Front and the Emergence of Modern Warfare, 1900–1918* (London, 1987), p.261.

5 G.C. Wynne, *If Germany Attacks: the battle in depth in the west* (London, 1940); Timothy Lupfer, *The Dynamics of Doctrine: the changes in German tactical doctrine in the First World War* (Fort Leavenworth, Kansas, 1981). My own *European Armies and the Conduct of War* (London, 1983) needs revising on this point.

6 Ernst von Wrisberg, *Wehr und Waffen* (Leipzig, 1922), pp. 17–18, 96–8.

7 ibid, p. 90.

8 Guy Pedroncini, *Pétain: Général en Chef 1917–1918* (Paris, 1974).

9 Guy Pedroncini, 'L'Armée Française et la Grande Guerre', in *Histoire Militaire de la France, 3. de 1871 à 1940,* (Paris, 1992), p. 162.

10 G.D. Sheffield letter to the editor, *Times Literary Supplement*, 8th July 1994.

11 Deist, 'Militärische Zusammenbruch', p. 122; see also the title of Deist's contribution to Wette, *Der Krieg des kleinen Mannes*.

12 R.H. Lutz (ed.), *Documents of the German Revolution: fall of the German empire 1914–1918* (Stanford, 1932), I, p. 647. For the full text and subsequent revisions, see Erich Ludendorff (ed.), *Urkunden der Obersten Heeresleitung über ihre Tätigkeit 1916–18* (Berlin, 1920).

13 This is not a new interpretation; it is implicit in the only synoptic treatment of the German army's morale in the war, Friedrich Altrichter, *Die seelischen Kräfte des Deutschen Heeres im Frieden und im Weltkriege* (Berlin, 1933), pp. 95–6, 126.

14 Heinz-Ludger Borgert, 'Grundzüge der Landkriegführung von Schlieffen bis Guderian', in Militärgeschichtliches Forschungsamt, *Handbuch zur deutschen Militärgeschichte*, IX, pp. 527–8; see also Lutz (ed.), *Fall of the German Empire*, II, p. 490; Lutz (ed.), *Causes of the German Collapse* (Stanford, 1934), pp. 68–71.

15 For the text, see Herbert Michaelis and Ernst Schraepler (eds), *Ursachen und Folgen vom Deutschen Zusammenbruch 1918 und 1945 bis zur staatlichen Neuordnung Deutschlands in der Gegenwart* (6 vols, Berlin, 1958), I, pp. 220–3.

16 Oberkommando des Heeres, *Der Weltkrieg*, XIII (Berlin, 1942), p. 23.

17 Rudolf Binding, *A Fatalist at War*, translated by F.D. Morrow (London, 1929), p. 174.

18 Altrichter, *Seelischen Kräfte*, pp. 226–7.

19 ibid, pp. 91–2; Erich Otto Volkmann, *Der Marxismus und das deutsche Heer im Weltkriege* (Berlin, 1925), p. 161.

20 Pierre Miquel, *La Grande Guerre* (Paris, 1983), p. 407; see also P. Camena d'Almeida, *L'Armée Allemande avant et pendant la guerre de 1914–1918* (Nancy, 1919), p. 283.

21 Wilhelm Groener, *Lebenserinnerungen* (Göttingen, 1957), pp. 375–7.

22 Altrichter, *Seelischen Kräfte*, p. 120.

23 S.L.A. Marshall, *Men against Fire* (New York, 1947); J. Glen Gray, *The Warriors: reflections on men in battle* (New York, 1970). See also John Lynn, *The Bayonets of the Republic: motivation and tactics in the army of Revolutionary France 1791–94* (Urbana, 1984), pp. 30–5, 163, 168, 182.

24 Friedrich Seesselberg, *Der Stellungskrieg 1914–1918* (Berlin, 1926), p. 62.

25 Altrichter, *Seelischen Kräfte*, pp. 233, 236.

26 ibid, pp. 232–3.

27 ibid, pp. 216–17; compare Holger H. Herwig, *The German Naval Officer Corps: a social and political history 1890–1918* (Oxford, 1973).

28 Volkmann, *Marxismus und das deutsche Heer*, pp. 153–56.

29 P. Camena d'Almeida, *L'Armée Allemande*, pp. 269–72.

30 Altrichter, *Seelischen Kräfte*, p. 127.

31 Wilhelm Deist, 'Militärische Zusammenbruch', has fully explored these points and it is not proposed to cover the same ground here.

32 Gerhard Ritter, *The Sword and the Sceptre: the Problem of Militarism in Germany* (4 vols, London, 1970–3), IV, p. 232.

33 Robert Blake (ed), *The Private Papers of Douglas Haig 1914–1919* (London, 1952), p. 333.

34 Volkmann, *Marxismus und das deutsche Heer*, p. 159.

35 Daniel Horn, *The German Naval Mutinies of World War I* (London, 1969).

36 Stéphane Audoin-Rouzeau, *Men at War 1914–1918: national sentiment and*

trench journalism in France during the First World War (Providence, 1992), pp. 128–54.

37 See Martin Kitchen, *The German Officer Corps 1890–1914* (Oxford, 1968); Bernd Schulte, *Die deutsche Armee 1900–1914: zwischen Beharren und Verändern* (Dusseldorf, 1977).

38 R.H. Lutz (ed.), *Fall of the German Empire* (2 vols, Stanford, 1932), II, p. 481.

39 Altrichter, *Seelische Kräfte*, p. 122.

40 R.H. Lutz (ed.), *Causes of the German Collapse in 1918* (Stanford, 1934), pp. 140–1; A.C. Bell, *A History of the Blockade of Germany* (London, 1937), pp. 689–90.

41 Richard Bessel, 'The Great War in German Memory: the soldiers of the First World War, demobilization and Weimar political culture', *German History*, VI, 1988, p. 24.

42 Volkmann, *Marxismus und das deutsche Heer*, pp. 164–5.

43 Stephen Bailey, 'The Berlin strike of January 1918', *Central European History*, XIII, 1980, pp. 166–7.

44 Altrichter, *Seelische Kräfte*, p. 160.

45 Deist, 'Verdeckter Militärstreik', pp. 155, 157.

46 Altrichter, *Seelische Kräfte*, pp. 157–8, 220–5; Volkmann, *Marxismus und das deutsche Heer*, pp. 157–8, 195, 313–14.

47 Volkmann, *Marxismus und das deutsche Heer*, pp. 166, 193.

Chapter 29

Morale in the Austro-Hungarian Army: The Evidence of Habsburg Army Campaign Reports and Allied Intelligence Officers

Geoffrey Wawro

The theory that World War I was as much the product of internal political as of external tensions is perhaps nowhere more applicable than in the case of Austria-Hungary. Here was a Great Power that by 1914 was severely undermined by national divisions. In the parliament, schools and streets of Austria, Czechs and Slovenes regularly did battle with Germans, and in Hungary, Croatia periodically rebelled against Magyar rule and the sorely oppressed Rumanians of Transylvania eagerly awaited their rescue by Bucharest in a future war.

Even the Habsburg army, traditional bastion of multinational loyalty in Austria-Hungary, was not proof against these nationalistic tendencies. In 1908, well before the Great War, Czech regiments convened to celebrate the sixtieth anniversary of Emperor Franz Joseph Habsburg's reign refused to join in the singing of the Imperial Anthem at the Emperor's Jubilee Review.[1] Four years later, there were many cases of insubordination and outright mutiny during the Habsburg army's partial mobilization of 1912, when Franz Joseph tried unsuccessfully to frighten Serbia into renouncing its gains in the First Balkan War.[2]

Franz Joseph's embarrassment at this display of imperial weakness was such that he restructured his army in 1912, increasing the complement of German officers, NCOs and recruits in Austria's non-German regiments in the hope that 'Germanization' would stiffen them. In 1916, an Austro-Hungarian officer captured by the Italians recalled that, in reality, the new German 'core troops' had only exacerbated ethnic tensions in the Austro-Hungarian regiments. 'It was rare,' he wrote, 'to encounter [an Austro-German] who had *any* affection for his Slavic, Italian or

Rumanian comrades. Germans, from the lowliest corporal all the way up to the battalion commandant, attributed every error or oversight [on the part of the non-German] to "ill will" or, worse, "treachery." When they were not administering beatings with their swagger canes, their favourite epithets were: *"dalmatinische Bagage," "italienische Schweine," "croatische Schufte," "Hunde,"* and *"feige Kerle."* ' ³ This captured Austro-Hungarian officer made the no less illuminating observation that Habsburg officers frequently summoned Serbian and Croatian recruits not by name or rank, but with a racial slur one still hears in Vienna today: '*cus.*' This hissing sound, originally employed by Balkan shepherds to drive their flocks, had by 1914 been adopted by some Habsburg officers and non-commissioned ranks as a disparaging form of address akin to 'nigger' or 'wog.' Even allowing for an element of hyperbole on the part of a captured soldier anxious to placate his captors, such French evidence is important in illustrating a widespread grievance within the Austro-Hungarian army – such reports having also an inevitable impact on Allied perceptions.

The army which went to war in 1914 was approximately 44 percent Slav, 28 percent German, 18 percent Hungarian, 8 percent Rumanian and 2 percent Italian.⁴ It had been split, after the Austro-Hungarian Military Compromise of 1868, into four distinct bodies employing nine different 'regimental languages' for everyday business and three 'languages of command' in battle: German in both the Austro-Hungarian Common Army and the Austrian *Landwehr*, Magyar in Hungary's *Honvéd,* and Croatian in Croatia's *Domobran.* Although these units could be mingled in times of war, in peacetime they were a source of intense, demoralizing bickering, as the Hungarians in particular sought to increase their share of military resources at the expense of the Common Army and its supranational mission.⁵

The First World War, it is argued here, revealed as never before, Austria-Hungary's social, political and military weaknesses . I take issue not only with historians who suggest that the monarchy's survival through four years of total war was evidence of its essential durability and legitimacy, but also with those more temperate ones who assert that the army 'mixed' great successes and failures.⁶ Besides Austria's defensive victories on the Isonzo Front, which consisted of some almost unassailable positions, the Habsburg army's record in the war was one of chronic failure. After examining a broad range of evidence collected in Vienna, Paris, and London – chiefly Habsburg army battle reports and Entente interviews with captured Austro-Hungarian officers and enlisted men – it seems clear that confronted as it was in 1918 by a formidable and well-equipped enemy and worn down by four years of blockade, the army had also been continually and severely undermined by the indifference or hostility felt by so many of its own men towards the Habsburg cause. It should be here stressed however that there were variations in the degree of disloyalty or apathy even within separate ethnic groups. Some Croat regiments, for example, were for a time considered, according to army sources, to be fairly reliable, while some Magyar units continued to hold together until the end. Nonetheless in the eyes of the military authorities – and with good reason – disaffection was feared from the start and from such as the Bosnian Serbs and Czechs in particular. Clearly care had to be taken in selecting the war theatres to which soldiers of different origins could safely be sent. Finally we should remember that many German-Austrian soldiers surrendered on the battlefield as readily as the rest. However, though so complicated a picture may make historians chary of sweeping judgments, some overall conclusions can be attempted.

Two wartime episodes and two types of evidence would seem to illustrate clearly the failure of the Austrian army's record and how this was linked with ethnic divisions. First, I will look at the Austro-Hungarian invasion of Serbia in 1914 through the eyes of Austro-Hungarian officers at the front. Second, I will assess the morale and performance of the Habsburg army in 1918 from the perspective of Austro-Hungarian enlisted men of various nationalities captured in Italy and France. I find that a comparison of these two war years and these two quite different archival sources – the *Kriegsarchiv* in Vienna and the *Archive de l'Armée de Terre* in Vincennes – suggests that the Habsburg army in one way or another showed indications of being as slack, refractory and demoralized in 1914 as it was four years and four million casualties later in 1918. An earlier collapse was not averted because of dogged loyalty to the Habsburg cause, but simply because the Reich Germans intervened massively after 1914 to prop up the Austro-Hungarian army and because it was physically difficult for Austro-Hungarian soldiers to desert the front in the absence of major, disorganizing Entente offensives, which were intermittent until the last months of the war. In the interludes between enemy pushes, Austro-Hungarian regiments were literally imprisoned by their own wire and field gendarmes who made sure that their less ardent comrades did not try to escape across no-man's-land.

For the Austro-Hungarian army the war began in 1914 with humiliating defeats in Galicia and Serbia. Although Emperor Franz Joseph could plausibly blame the rout of his 'North Army' in Russia on Germany's failure to complete its Schlieffen Plan in time to transport reinforcements to the east, the defeat in Serbia was not so easily rationalized. Since Austria-Hungary was a European Great Power and the Serbs and Austrians deployed equal numbers of troops on the Balkan Front, the repulse of the Austrian invasion and the desperate, bedraggled flight of General Oskar Potiorek's 'South Army' out of Serbia in December 1914 was humiliating.[7] Even neutral correspondents well disposed toward the Habsburg Monarchy did not trouble to conceal the disdain they felt for the

Austro-Hungarian army after witnessing its panic-stricken rout from positions around Belgrade and the atrocities it meted out to Serbian civilians in the course of its retreat.[8]

In 1915, the Austrians recovered briefly. They were bolstered by German divisions sent east from France and Belgium by General Erich von Falkenhayn, who devoted the year 1915 to beating the Russians. It was in 1915 that the Austrians, aided by the Germans, rolled back the Russian gains of 1914 and, in league with General August von Mackensen's German South Army, finally beat the Serbs. It is important to note, however, first, that the Austro-German eastern offensive of 1915 was German-planned, German-led and used German tactics imported from the Western Front; secondly, that it did not go without a hitch. Three Austro-Hungarian regiments deserted to the Russians *en masse* and one had to be formally dissolved by the Habsburg emperor at a time when he required more recruits than ever due to Italy's declaration of war on Austria-Hungary in May 1915.[9]

In 1916, Falkenhayn decided to return many of the units he had sent east in 1915 to the Western Front to launch the battle of Verdun and, later, to blunt the British Somme offensive. This brought him into heated arguments with Austria-Hungary's staff chief, General Franz Conrad von Hötzendorf, who insisted on a continuation of Germany's eastern push to secure Austria's war aims.[10] Falkenhayn's refusal even to consider Conrad's point of view foretold the future: by 1916, Austria-Hungary seemed increasingly to be little more than a German recruiting station.

In 1916, stripped temporarily of their German supports, the Austrians staggered again, this time under the weight of the Russian general Brusilov's highly effective offensive, which cut through Austria's eastern trench lines, taking 327,000 prisoners. In a few days of fighting, more than a third of the entire Austro-Hungarian army on the *Ostfront* surrendered to the Russians. Magyar regiments joined with Slav ones in the undignified rush to surrender.[11] All at once, the Austro-German gains of 1915 were erased. Karl Pflanzer-Baltin, an Austro-Hungarian general operating in Bukovina, spoke of his *'ruinierte Armee.'* Seeking to exploit this ruin, the Rumanians declared war on the Central Powers in August and invaded Hungary. At its wits' end, Vienna turned again to Berlin for aid, and received another German army, under Mackensen, which halted the Rumanians in Transylvania.

On the Italian Front, an Austro-Hungarian offensive in Tyrol was shattered; on the Isonzo the Austrians were forced to yield the key positions of Gorizia and Doberdo.[12] The twin failures of the German push at Verdun and the Austrian defence of the Ukraine put the Central Powers in a very difficult position. They were encircled by the Entente, but lacked the troops and material to break out, not least because, as Norman Stone put it, 'the Austrian army was useful only in so far as it could be joined with German troops.'[13]

After 1916, the Austrians fundamentally changed their order-of-battle. Like some other armies, they introduced 'storm troops,' but in Austria-Hungary *ethnic* considerations figured prominently in the selection of the new assault formations. Acknowledging that most of the nations of Austria-Hungary were unwilling to sacrifice themselves for the Habsburg cause, the Austro-Hungarian commandant in Italy – General Svetozar Boroevic – divided his million-man Isonzo Army into two, quite separate parts, characterized by the French General Staff as '*une masse de choc*' and '*une masse de résistance*.' The 'shock mass' was relatively small, was largely German and Hungarian, and was reserved for attacks and counter-attacks. To ensure that the troops reserved for this kind of fighting were kept at the peak of fitness and could be quickly switched to any part of the line, 'shock troops' were given extra rations and were withdrawn to the rear immediately after battle. They were not called upon to defend trenches or endure enemy bombardments in the long intervals between offensives.

The much more numerous, largely Slavic and Rumanian 'resistance mass' formed the bulk of the Habsburg army. These men were charged with the task of defending Austria-Hungary's extensive trench lines against enemy bombardments and raids.[14] Due in part to this pragmatic reorganization, 1917 proved to be an *annus mirabilis* for the Habsburg army. In defiance of all expectations, it aided in the final destruction of Russia and joined the German-led Caporetto breakthrough on the Isonzo. But a closer look reveals that these successes were owed chiefly to the Germans. It was General Felix von Bothmer's manoeuvre north of the Dniester that broke the back of the Kerensky Offensive, and it was General Otto von Below, who surged through Tolmein to exploit the breakthrough at Caporetto and drive the Italians back to the Piave. In fact, each time the Austrians fought *alone* in 1917 they were beaten with huge losses in men and material: in May on the Carso, in July in Galicia, and in August on the Plateau of Bainsizza. Taking stock of this reality, the French General Staff noted in January 1918 that the apparent success of Habsburg arms in 1917 was 'an illusion, for, stripped of German aid, the Austro-Hungarian army is incapable even of defending itself.'[15]

This French observation proved accurate in 1918. When the Germans withdrew much of their strength from Italy to reinforce the Ludendorff offensive in France, the Austrians hazarded a push of their own across the Piave in June. This attempt to administer a post-Caporetto *coup de grâce* to the tottering Kingdom of Italy backfired. Austria's two best generals – Conrad and Boroevic – were stopped in their tracks and Emperor Karl's carefully planned operation, which was intended as a display of Austro-Hungarian might and independence, had to be called off after just six days. In October, the Italians began a long-awaited offensive and the Austro-Hungarian army quickly collapsed.[16] Thus the Habsburg army's Great War ended as it had begun four years earlier in Galicia and Serbia, with rout and defeat.

How can we explain this unsatisfactory record? Austrian leadership was, in general, not much worse than that exercised by other First War Armies. Austrian tactics, though unevenly applied, did approximate those employed by the Germans and the Entente. Given the problems of supply and with ethnic minorities at home, the *crucial* weakness of the Austro-Hungarian army lay in the frequently dubious loyalty of its rank and file. Throughout the war, Austro-Hungarian units tended to desert, straggle and surrender in large numbers and Habsburg efforts to overcome this defeatism with patriotic propaganda were in vain. In all, 1.7 million Austrian prisoners-of-war were taken, a total that was second only to the Russians in absolute terms and first in relative terms. By comparison, 180,000 British were taken prisoners-of-war, 500,000 French, and less than 600,000 Italians.[17]

To illustrate the points I am making, I turn first to the Austro-Hungarian invasion of Serbia in 1914. Here was a campaign where the Austro-Hungarian will to conquer ought to have been at its height. At this stage one would not have expected signs of war-weariness. The army was deployed against 'Dog Serbia' – the alleged assassin of Austria-Hungary's crown prince – and it was still manned by its best-trained, most deeply-committed officers, NCOs, and conscripts.

What in fact happened in Serbia was shocking. General Oskar Potiorek's Austro-Hungarian South Army entered Serbia from southern Hungary and Bosnia, wasted itself in crude, frontal assaults on Serbia's mountain bastions, then broke and disbanded deep inside the enemy kingdom. At the outset, the Austrians were confident of victory. General Oskar Potiorek, at that time well-enough regarded, planned to invade the north-western corner of Serbia in a pincer movement. One of his three armies would cross the Sava River and descend on a southerly course from Sabac; the two others would cross the Drina River and push eastward. Potiorek assumed that the Serbs would advance their entire army to oppose these river crossings, and be trapped between them. In a brief, Moltke-style 'Strafexpedition,' Potiorek's three armies would envelop Serbia's ten divisions and destroy them. Potiorek did not bother to contain his optimism in an order-of-the-day published on 13 August 1914. 'Soldiers!' he announced. 'In hot combats we will force the [Serbs] to recognize Austria-Hungary's mastery. My army, which combines all the nations of the [Habsburg] Monarchy, will demonstrate that, as formerly in the days of Prince Eugen and Radetzky, all the peoples will do their utmost for Kaiser, King and Fatherland.'[18] Potiorek would shortly be disabused of his high hopes.

The Serbs easily repulsed the Austro-Hungarian Second Army –

Potiorek's leading pincer – when it crossed the Sava in August. Under fire for the first time, whole Austro-Hungarian units dissolved amid terrible confusion.[19] The Austro-Hungarian 44th Regiment received three-quarters of its casualties from its own errant artillery before disbanding in panic. An officer of this largely Hungarian unit described it – after just one day of battle – as 'morally shattered.'[20]

While Potiorek retracted this blunted pincer from Sabac, the Serbs turned their attention to the Drina sector, where the Austrian Fifth and Sixth Armies had successfully crossed the river. In a few days of bitter fighting, the Serbs forced the Austrians back to the Bosnian bank. Austria's 21st Landwehr Division panicked and disbanded completely on 16 August, forcing Potiorek to place the entire division under arrest for insubordination and mutiny.[21] Similiar problems afflicted regular army units as well. On 22 August, the commandant of Potiorek's Fifth Army complained that, at rest, the men of his mixed Czech and German 9th Infantry Division refused to salute their superiors and, in battle, contrived to 'lose' their rifles during marches to the front, where they vied with one another for the right to escort field kitchens and wounded comrades to the rear.[22]

Potiorek regrouped and invaded Serbia a second time in September. This campaign, which immediately bogged down in trenches, went no better than the first.[23] Once more, the field correspondence of the Habsburg army revealed only apathy and hostility on the part of Austro-Hungarian troops for the Emperor's *Strafexpedition*. In the September 1914 campaign reports of the largely Croatian 36th Division, for example, there is this hastily pencilled note from a Fifth Army staff captain entitled: 'My Observations of our Troops.' After touring the 36th Division's sector of the Drina Front, this captain wrote that disorder reigned everywhere he went. Whenever Austrian trenches were pushed forward, the disused ones were left littered with discarded ammunition, rifles, backpacks and clothing. New trenches were not deepened and masked by fatigue parties, but simply left 'in the most primitive condition.' Captured Serbian trenches were not reversed and adapted to Austrian tactical needs, but simply occupied and left as they were 'before the storm.'

In the trenches of the Croatian 53rd Regiment, the captain found the men lunching on their iron rations in flagrant defiance of orders to conserve them for a pending offensive. Trench walls and battery positions caved in by enemy artillery were invariably left unrepaired. In the trenches of the Croatian 96th Regiment, infantry companies sprawled in ditches without fire steps or parapets. 'It was impossible to shoot *out* of them,' Fifth Army's staff observer complained. When he questioned sentries on duty about this, 'they showed neither understanding nor interest in the problem.'[24] Although it strongly suggests the probability of severe disaffection, the evidence cited above does not on its own prove this, only that there was poor discipline among wild and sometimes very hungry young men, as was also to be found in the Russian army at the time; but in any case such slackness, when coupled with pre-war ethnic tensions and the urgency of organising a co-ordinated force in a modern war, clearly gave rise to mutual resentments between army commanders and troops from the ethnic minorities.

In October 1914, as the Austro-Hungarians battled into Serbia from the Drina, a 9th Division brigadier had to remind his men that 'the purpose of a skirmish line is to *shoot* at the enemy, not carry wounded comrades to the rear, which, in any case, is usually just a comfortable pretext for a man to withdraw himself safely from battle. In future,' the brigadier warned his men, 'officers will make stinging examples of these kinds of shirkers (*Drückeberger*).'[25]

Austro-Hungarian infantrymen who did advance in battle revealed a disappointing tendency simply to flatten themselves against the earth to crawl safely home at the first opportunity. This explained the increasingly strident orders in the Habsburg campaign papers that attacks be carried forward 'at any price,' and that retreats be forbidden under all but the most hopeless conditions. On 15 September, General Joseph Panesch – Austria's VIII Corps commandant – protested that since so many of his men were breaking off promising attacks, he would henceforth apply strictly 'Article 60 of the Tactical Manual.' To wit, no officer below the rank of brigadier general could order a retreat! If, in the smoky moil of no-man's-land, brigadier generals were nowhere to be found, troops were to fulfil Point 623 of the Tactical Manual to the letter: 'Defend all captured ground to the last man.' Lest anyone try to evade these orders under pressure from an enemy barrage or counter-attack, Panesch stipulated that, even in the heat of battle, 'all retreat orders must be formally witnessed and set down on paper.' He concluded with a rodomontade truly worthy of Hašek's *Good Soldier Švejk*: 'Remember our old army saying: "Only troops who have resolved never to yield will remain unvanquished to the end." '[26]

Such examples are legion. Unsurprisingly, Austria-Hungary's campaign reports began to fill with examples of disobedience, mutiny and malingering as the summer turned to autumn and autumn to winter in the Serbian mountains. Ultimately, the Austro-Hungarian invasion came undone in December, when Potiorek's regiments broke apart and retreated – raping, burning, and plundering the whole way – across the Danube and the Sava amid scenes of crazy abandon that seemed to be the true and unaffected measure of the Austro-Hungarian army.[27]

Many of the same pernicious faults afflicting the army during the first year persisted into the last campaigns of the war, as is underlined by hitherto unexplored French intelligence sources. Austria-Hungary's military situation had stabilized somewhat after 1914 thanks in large part to German aid. But in 1918, with the Russians beaten and most German troops and material reserved for Ludendorff's 'Victory Offensive' in France and Belgium, the Austro-Hungarian army was forced to stand alone. The timing was propitious, for whereas in June 1917 the Habsburg army had been thinly stretched between the Italian and Russian Fronts, with one million men on each, by 1918, with the final collapse of the Russian Empire, the Austro-Hungarians were able to concentrate much of their strength in Italy[28] (apart from those troops engaged in a massive bread-gathering operation in Poland and the Ukraine). This explained Conrad von Hötzendorf's willingness to risk an all-out offensive over the Piave in June 1918.

Conrad's Piave Offensive was intended not only to knock Italy out of the war, but also to restore faith in Austro-Hungarian arms. There had been mutiny in the Habsburg navy in February 1918, and, well before June, the Austro-Hungarian army too had begun to melt away. The situation is well illustrated in the testimony of the numerous deserters from it. In February 1918, to give but one example, two Slovakian deserters from the 1st Hungarian Honvéd Regiment crossed over to Italian lines. When questioned as to their motives for deserting, they cited 'cruel treatment, bad food and the hostility they felt for their German and Hungarian' comrades.[29] Typical also was a Rumanian prisoner from the Austro-Hungarian 64th Regiment who described the same morale problems in his unit, where, he claimed, 'Rumanians received bad treatment from their Hungarian officers, even blows.'[30] Here he echoed what the Slovaks before him had said: 'The Austro-Hungarian soldier receives more blows than bread.'

Widespread and unhappy sentiments such as these must have contributed to a severe erosion of morale at the time of Conrad's Piave offensive, though bad weather, miscalculation, and poor feeding and equipment were central to its failure. Far from consolidating the gains of Caporetto, Conrad and Boroevic were actually hurled back as their thrusts broke against Italian resistance and provided 12,000 more Austro-Hungarians with the opportunity to cross over to the enemy lines.[31] In July, the Italians and their Entente allies began probing the Austro-Hungarian defences on the Piave in preparation for a great autumn offensive. What they received were indications that the Habsburg regiments, far from grimly 'holding out,' were in fact fairly yearning for a big Italian push so that they would have the opportunity to surrender. This sentiment was universally expressed by Austro-Hungarian prisoners taken by the Entente on the Piave Front. Two Czech uhlans taken by the Italians in July 1918, for instance, claimed that their comrades were united in a 'hatred of the Germans' and were 'hoping for an Allied offensive so that they might find an opportunity to surrender.'[32] Even allowing for the natural instinct of surrendered men to justify their perfidy by implicating their comrades, it is plain that these feelings were widely held. The same attitude is well summed up by the words of a Polish gunner who successfully deserted to the Italians in August and informed his captors that 'many other [Austrian] Poles wished to desert, but were put off by the prospect of having to swim across the Piave' to reach Italian lines. Thus, most of them were deserting northward, into Austria-Hungary itself, where brigandage and mass arrests of young and middle-aged men suspected of desertion became commonplace in 1918.[33]

Further light is thrown on the collapse of the Austrian offensive on the Piave by subsequent intelligence reports at the front in France, where the Austrians sent four divisions to aid the Germans in 1918. There is, for example, the evidence of two Hungarian deserters who in August explained to French staff officers that once their division had been beaten in the Piave offensive, the men had mutinied and refused to renew the attack. Instead of resting and restoring the unit, the Austro-Hungarian command had disarmed it, and transported it to France to dig trenches for the Germans. The Germans, however, in need of men to occupy their most vulnerable forward positions, promptly rearmed the Hungarians and sent them to defend a particularly hazardous sector of the Western Front near Verdun, whereupon the Hungarians as promptly deserted, losing one of their comrades to French fire as they sprinted across no-man's-land.[34] This incident, which was by no means exceptional, and which was concealed from the Hungarian parliament by the removal of all regimental insignia from the intended *Kanonenfutter*, suggested the real nature of Austro-German 'co-operation' in the last stages of World War I.[35]

Back in Italy, Austrian army records tended to play down the fact of desertions, but Italian reports described, for instance, how a batch of some 105 Czechs and Hungarians deserted to them *en masse* in September 1918, and told their Italian captors that the demoralization in their units was so extensive that another Austro-Hungarian offensive was quite out of the question. All of their comrades, they claimed, were only waiting for a successful Italian push to give them the opportunity to surrender.[36] While evaluating this evidence, the Italians captured the operations journal of the Austro-Hungarian 96th Regiment, a Croatian unit. In it were orders from Vienna commanding police surveillance of the regiment's battalions and weekly 'patriotic rallies,' which were to 'exalt love for the Fatherland' by, among other things, loud renditions of Haydn's imperial anthem. 'Officers,' the journal importuned, 'are required to attend *and* sing.'[37]

One German soldier from Vienna, who deserted his regiment in September, suggested that the only reason many of Austria-Hungary's generally reliable German troops were not deserting was that they were frightened by rumours of famine at home. By 1918, many of the principal cities of the Empire, such as Vienna, were literally starving, and recruits from Vienna discovered that even the *Ersatz* bread, the 100 grammes of horsemeat, and the thin broth that they received daily were a feast by civilian standards.[38] This realization certainly helped keep Austria-Hungary's surging desertion rate within limits.

Even so, in October 1918, desertion from the Austro-Hungarian trenches on the Italian Front quickened as the Italians intensified their bombardment of Conrad's lines prior to General Armando Diaz's final offensive. Heavily outgunned in this phase of the war, many Austro-Hungarian soldiers realized that it was safer to brave the perils of no-man's-land than to await death passively in their trenches, where companies sometimes lost half their strength to Italian bombardments lavishly supplied with high explosive.[39] On a single day in the first week of October, the largely Hungarian 65th Regiment reported 1,451 deserters.[40] Army command tried to plug the leak by increasing surveillance, but also by promising the men that warm winter quarters far from the trenches were being prepared for the winter of 1918–19. Deserters from the largely Rumanian 31st Regiment told their Italian captors that their officers had promised them that they would not have to endure another winter in trenches, but would instead be withdrawn to a cosy 'Winterstellung' behind the lines.[41]

The last part of October 1918 was a 'black week' for the Austro-Hungarian army, as grim as any in 1916. On 24 October, Italy's final offensive began, when Diaz brought his rebuilt army out of its post-Caporetto recuperation and blasted through the sixty Austro-Hungarian divisions deployed on the Grappa and the Piave. The Italians took an astounding 500,000 Austro-Hungarian prisoners in the week between 26 October and 3 November. Considering that Austro-Hungarian battle casualties numbered only 30,000 in this period, it was clear that the mass desertion Austro-Hungarian prisoners had been predicting since the New Year had come at last.[42] Whole Austro-Hungarian divisions threw away their weapons and fled over to the enemy. This was not a proud army that had doggedly resisted to the end for Kaiser and Fatherland, but rather a pitiful one that had been *willing* an Italian offensive since the previous winter to deliver it from an unpopular régime. Now that the Italians were finally on the march, the Austro-Hungarians voted with their feet, defying orders, shooting their officers, and tumbling into the arms of the advancing Italian columns.[43]

In short, the evidence both of Habsburg Army campaign reports *and* of Allied intellence officers strongly suggests that the Austro-Hungarian army was indeed a 'prison of the nations'. Each major Habsburg army campaign of the Great War revealed major nationality problems, which called into question the Monarchy's very reason for being. Did the Habsburg Monarchy in fact unite and protect the small nations of East Central Europe against foreign domination, or was the Monarchy itself a foreign oppressor and, in the end, a mere front for Reich German domination? Austria-Hungary's record in the Great War, from its early defeats to its final acceptance of Ludendorff's supreme command, suggests that the latter case cannot be lightly ignored. The fact that there was some variation in the degree of disloyalty or indifference within the various non-German ethnic groups, and that many German-Austrian soldiers shared in the general decline in morale does not alter the fact that the ethnic divisions within this army, exacerbated by irredentist agitation on the home front, were a fundamental cause of its ineffectiveness under the strain of a modern war.[44]

Notes

1 Norman Stone, 'Army and Society in the Habsburg Monarchy, 1900–1914,' *Past & Present* 33 (1966), p. 101.

2 Vienna, Kriegsarchiv (KA), B/1503:5, Vienna, 18 December 1912, GdI Conrad. *Neue Freie Presse,* 12, 13 and 17 December 1912. István Deák, *Beyond Nationalism* (New York, Oxford: Oxford Univ. Press, 1990), p. 197.

3 Vincennes, Archive de l'Armée de Terre (AAT), Etat-Major de l'Armée (EMA), 7N846, Rome, 13 April 1916, Col. François to Minister of War, 'Observations of "Lt. X," a captured Austro-Hungarian officer.'

4 Vincennes, AAT, EMA, 7N852, M.I. 3B, War Office, June, 1918, 'Handbook of the Austro-Hungarian Army in War, June 1918.'

5 Norman Stone, 'Constitutional Crisis in Hungary, 1903–1906,' *The Slavonic & East European Review* 40 (1967).

6 Deák, *Beyond Nationalism,* pp. 190–91. Jay Luvaas, 'A Unique Army: The Common Experience,' in *The Habsburg Empire in World War I,* ed. Robert A. Kann (New York: East European Quarterly, 1977), pp. 88–89, 100. Gunther E. Rothenberg, 'The Habsburg Army in the First World War, 1914–1918,' in *East Central European Society in World War I,* ed. Béla Király (New York: Atlantic Research, 1985), p. 293. István Deák, 'The Habsburg Army in the First and Last Days of World War I: A Comparative Analysis,' in *East Central European Society in World War I,* p. 311.

7 Rudolf Jerabek, *Potiorek* (Graz, Vienna: Verlag Styria, 1991). Gunther E. Rothenberg, 'The Austro-Hungarian Campaign Against Serbia in 1914,' *The Journal of Military History* 4 (1989), p. 144.

8 Vienna, Haus-Hof-und Staatsarchiv (HHSA), Politisches Archiv (PA) I, 819, 2a, FPA 305, 12 Feb. 1915, FML Krauss to FZM. Potiorek. A discussion of William Shepheard's exposé – 'Austria's Retreat from Serbia' – which was published in two instalments in December 1914 by New York's *Evening Sun.*

9 Manfried Rauchensteiner, *Der Tod des Doppeladlers* (Graz, Vienna: Verlag Styria, 1993), pp. 205–206.

10 Rudolf Jerabek, 'Die Brussilowoffensive 1916: Ein Wendepunkt der Koalitionskriegführung der Mittelmächte,' 2 vols. (University of Vienna, phil. Diss., 1982), vol. 1, pp. 67–75, 114–115.

11 Norman Stone, *The Eastern Front, 1914–1917* (London: Hodder & Stoughton, 1975), p. 254.

12 Márton Farkas, 'Doberdo: The Habsburg Army on the Italian. Front, 1915–16,' in *East Central European Society in World War I,* pp. 330–31. Jerabek, 'Brussilowoffensive,' vol. 1, pp. 308–9.

13 Stone, *Eastern Front,* p. 254.

14 Vincennes, AAT, EMA, 7N845, Paris, 13 October 1917, 'Renseignements sur les "troupes d'assaut" de l'Armée Austro-Hongroise d'après enquête faite au camp de prisonniers de Bagnaria-Arsa.'

15 Vincennes, AAT, EMA, 7N852, Paris, 10 January 1918, 'Note sur la Situation de l'Autriche-Hongrie au début de 1918.'

16 Vincennes, AAT, EMA, 7N852, M.I. 3B, November 1918, 'Dispositions of the Austro-Hungarian Army on the Italian Front during its Last Battle from 24 October to 4 November 1918.'

17 Gaston Bodart, 'Die Menschen-Verluste Österreich-Ungarns im Weltkriege 1914–18.' Manuscript in Vincennes, AAT, EMA, 7N848. Bear in mind the Good Soldier Švejk's interview with Baloun before an Austrian offensive in Galicia. When Baloun considered doing his duty, Švejk patiently reminded him that this would be 'a crime against the glorious spirit of our glorious army,' which compelled desertion and surrender rather than heroic resistance. Jaroslav Hašek, *The Good Soldier Švejk and his Fortunes in the World War,* trans. Cecil Parrott (orig, 1921; New York: Penguin, 1974), p. 594.

18 KA, B/1503:6, Sarajevo, 13 August 1914, Armee-Kommando-Befehl Nr. 1.

19 KA, Neue Feld-Akten (NFA), 1846, 32. ITD, Tagebuch, 19 August 1914.

20 KA, Gefechts-Berichte (GB), 21, 15 August 1914, Maj. Jeskowski, 'Bericht über meine Eindrücke in Sabac am 15. August.'

21 KA, NFA, 475, Bijelina, 27 August 1914, FML Przyborski.

22 KA, NFA, 170, Brcko, 22 August 1914, GdI Frank. NFA, 529, Etappenkdo. 170, 21 August 1914, GdI Frank. Noting the spread of defeatist sentiments among Austro-Hungarian units after the Serbian victories at Sabac and on the Drina, Frank, the Fifth Army commandant, implored his men 'to recount examples of glorious Austrian heroism rather than [Serbian] horror stories *(Schaudermären).'*

23 Jerabek, *Potiorek,* p. 142.

24 KA, NFA, 2115, Megjasi, 12 September 1914, Capt. Bubin, 'Wahrnehmungen bei eigenen Truppen.'

25 KA, NFA, 528, 20 October 1914, GM Daniel.

26 KA, NFA, 529, Grk, 15 September 1914, GdK Giesl.

27 HHSA, PA I, 819, 2a, Vienna, 1 March 1915, FML Krauss to k.u.k. Kriegsüberwachungsamt.

28 Vincennes, AAT, EMA, 7N846, Italie, 28 June 1918, 'Effectifs globaux.'

29 Vincennes, AAT, EMA, 7N847, 2eme Bureau, 26 Feb. 1918, 'Interrogatoire de Prisonniers.'

30 Vincennes, AAT, EMA, 7N847, 2eme Bureau, 21 Sept. 1918, 'Interrogatoire de Prisonniers.'

31 Vincennes, AAT, EMA, 7N846, 2eme Bureau, 28 July 1918, 'Les Pertes Autrichiennes dans l'Offensive sur la Piave et la Brenta de Juin 1918.'

32 Vincennes, AAT, EMA, 7N847, 2eme Bureau, 29 July 1918, 'Interrogatoire de Prisonniers.'

33 Vincennes, AAT, EMA, 7N845, 2eme Bureau, July 1918, 'Etat Moral, Punitions, Rébellions' and 14 August 1918, 'Le Moral de l'Armée Austro-Hongroise.'

34 Vincennes, AAT, EMA, 7N847, 2eme Bureau, 29 August 1918, 'Interrogatoire de Prisonniers.'

35 Vincennes, AAT, EMA, 7N847, 2eme Bureau, 16 Sept. 1918, 'Interrogatoire

de Prisonniers.' An officer from the 5th Honvéd Regiment captured in France divulged that he had been ordered upon arrival in France to remove all his insignia and burn his papers to conceal the presence of Hungarians on the Western Front. He added that his entire regiment was seeking the opportunity to desert to the French or Americans.

36 Vincennes, AAT, EMA, 7N847, 2eme Bureau, 27 Sept. 1918, 'Interrogatoire de Prisonniers.'

37 Vincennes, AAT, EMA, 7N847, 2eme Bureau, 5 Sept. 1918, 'Interrogatoire de Prisonniers.'

38 Vincennes, AAT, EMA, 7N847, 2eme Bureau, 26 Sept. 1918, 'Interrogatoire de Prisonniers.'

39 Vincennes, AAT, EMA, 7N847, 2eme Bureau, 1918, 'Renseignements fournis par l'interrogatoire d'officiers autrichiens capturés.' Describes two Bosnian companies that lost 50 and 70 percent of their strength respectively to an Italian bombardment at Monte Tomba.

40 Vincennes, AAT, EMA, 7N846, Paris, 13 October 1918, 'Recrutement.'

41 Vincennes, AAT, EMA, 7N847, 2eme Bureau, 7 Oct. 1918, 'Interrogatoire de Prisonniers.'

42 London, Public Record Office (PRO), War Office (WO) 106/593, 'The State of the Austro-Hungarian Army in May 1918.'

43 Vincennes, AAT, EMA, 7N847, 2eme Bureau, 29 Oct. 1918, 'Interrogatoire de Prisonniers.' A German deserter from Tyrol testified that the Slovenian 17th Regiment massacred its officers in October 1918, and that Austro-Hungarian 'morale had sunk so low that refusal to go to the front had become a daily event' in the last weeks of the war. 7N852, M.I. 3B, Nov. 1918, 'Dispositions of the Austro-Hungarian Army on the Italian Front during its Last Battle.'

44 For a close analysis of ethnic divisions, 'the influence of the hinterland' and the counter-propaganda in the army, the reader is referred to Mark Cornwall's article, 'Morale and Patriotism in the Austro-Hungarian Army, 1914–18', in John Horne ed., *State, Society and Mobilisation in Europe during the First World War*, C.U.P. (publication forthcoming).

Chapter 30

Officer–Man Relations, Discipline and Morale in the British Army of the Great War[1]

Gary Sheffield

In 1935 a British wartime Temporary officer wrote that 'An army, like any other human society, is an organism, whose well-being depends on the interplay of human relationships'.[2] This paper examines the relationship of leader and led in the British army of 1914–18 and the impact of this relationship upon morale. My remarks are confined largely to infantry and artillery units on the Western Front, and to regimental officers of the rank of lieutenant-colonel or below.

It is necessary to examine some of the pre-war foundations of wartime officer–man relations. Modern scholarship has confirmed the essential accuracy of JFC Fuller's view that the pre-war Regular army was 'Recruited from the bottom of Society' but 'led from the top'.[3] An education at a public school, especially a Clarendon school, was an almost essential *rite de passage* for the aspirant officer while, in sharp contrast, working-class men filled the ranks. Thus in 1913 unskilled and skilled labourers accounted for over 68 per cent of recruits, while clerks accounted for only 3 percent.[4] A whole series of influences, including those of the landed interest and the reformed public schools, ensured that by 1914 virtually all Regular officers were thoroughly paternalistic. The core of the officer's creed was *noblesse oblige*, the belief that privilege entailed responsibility for the well-being of their men. A pair of paintings displayed side by side in the Officers' Mess at Sandhurst gives a graphic illustration of this paternal and pragmatic concern. The first depicts a squire and groom standing beside a horse. The squire is saying 'Well, Jim, has he fed all right?' The second shows a group of soldiers sitting round a campfire. An officer is asking 'Dinners all right, men?'. Both paintings share a single caption: *Noblesse oblige.*[5] Somewhat paradoxically, the army combined exemplary paternalism with a rigidly hierarchical approach to discipline and distant, although generally mutually respectful, relations between officers and men.[6]

Things were rather different in the pre-war part-time Territorial Force. A whole series of factors, not least the social composition of the ranks and the officer corps, and the practical difficulties involved in enforcing strict discipline on a part-time amateur army, produced a style of officer–man relations and discipline very different from the Regular varieties.[7] An officer of 7/Manchesters wrote of the 'comradeship' which produced an 'easy relationship between officers and men . . . [that] was the despair of the more crusted Regular martinet'. A Regular brigadier-general described the discipline of another northern Territorial battalion, 6/West Yorkshires, as being that of 'good will'. In this unit, it was claimed, orders were at first obeyed 'because of a mutual confidence and respect' between the ranks, 'similar to that in a workshop or any small society'. Neither battalion set much store by formal discipline. On one occasion in January 1914, the 6/West Yorkshires marched off parade 45 minutes late, only eighty strong, and 'Even this was considered a good attendance!'[8]

Thus there were not one but two distinct strands of officer–man relations and discipline co-existing in the pre–1914 British army, a 'Regular' and an 'Auxiliary' variety. The paternalism of the Regular officer was passed on to his Temporary wartime successor, and many units raised during the war adopted a 'Regular' style of discipline. However, wartime inter-rank relations tended more towards the 'Territorial' than the 'Regular' end of the spectrum. Most wartime units took elements from both traditions, in varying proportions depending on the battalion, to create a style of officer–man relations and discipline that showed traits inherited from both parents.

It can be misleading to generalize about an organisation as large as the British army of 1914–18. It consisted of three, initially distinct, types of units – Regular, Territorial and New (or 'Kitchener's') Army, and officer–man relations could differ from unit to unit and even from platoon to platoon. Moreover, soldiers had greater opportunities to forge informal relations with their officers on active service than while training at home.[9] Nonetheless, it is possible to make a broad assessment of the subject.

A theme that runs through many wartime officers' letters, diaries and memoirs is that of devotion, even love, for their men. The circumstances of the Western Front were particularly well suited for officers to become fond of their men. While the officer's lot was in many ways better than that of the other ranks,[10] all men who served in the trenches suffered from poor living conditions, and the fear of sudden death or mutilation. Many officers came to see their men as partners in adversity. In November 1916 Sergt H.H. Munro (the author 'Saki') was killed. Despite his advanced age and privileged social background Munro had refused a commission, preferring to stay in the ranks of 22/Royal Fusiliers. One of his officers, Maj Christopher Stone, commented that Munro was

> 'one of the men that I really and honestly admire and revere in this war ... He did very finely for us all.'

Two years later Stone expressed similar sentiments about the death of a working-class NCO, describing him as one of 'my friends'. Having served as a private in the 16/Middlesex, albeit in training in England, Stone had no illusions about the hardships of life in the ranks, and indeed experienced some guilt about the '1,000 comforts' available to him as an officer.[11]

(iv) "Never a better lad or soildier [sic] ever stepped on a field". Wounded Private Sam Woodhead enquires after his officer, Lt J.W.B. Russell (9th Battalion Duke of Wellington's Regiment). The officer had in fact been killed in the same attack in July 1916 on the Somme. [J.W.B. Russell: Liddle Collection]

What might be called the 'bureaucracy of paternalism' ensured that their men were never very far from the thoughts of junior officers. The Regular officers who dominated the wartime army seem to have been concerned that Temporary officers, many of whom lacked the social and educational background of pre-war Regulars, might have neglected their duties towards their men. This concern lay at the root of the much-derided obsession of the staff with apparent trivialities, which were, in fact, manifestations of institutionalised paternalism. Wyn Griffith, a temporary officer of 15/Royal Welch Fusiliers, described the bureaucracy of paternalism in these words:

every man above the rank of private is his brother's keeper . . . this concern . . . can be harassing, and it often is, but it is omnipresent throughout the hierarchy of the command and staff.[12]

Even on the beaches of Gallipoli, one subaltern recorded in 1915, 'endless returns have to be made about one's men – health, clothes, equipment . . . etc.'.[13]

Most Temporary officers confounded official fears by displaying an extremely high level of paternal care for their men, which in practice meant ensuring that soldiers were well fed, well clothed, and given at least the minimum of comfort. Officers' training emphasised that the well-being of their men should always come before their own comfort. Thus at the end of a march, an officer would routinely ensure that the men were comfortably billeted before even thinking of retiring to his own billet.[15] Many officers provided extra comforts out of their own pockets. Officers' letters home are littered with requests that chocolate, cigarettes and the like be sent out for their men, although the request of one Coldstream Guards officer in December 1915 for 200 large mince pies was perhaps at the upper end of the scale of generosity.[14]

Officers attended to more than just the creature comforts of their men. After breaking down at the graveside of his brother, a private of 1/Coldstream Guards was sent to a convalescent camp by a sympathetic officer.[16] In a revealing casual aside in his memoirs, a Temporary subaltern of 1/North Staffordshires wrote of his disappointment at not being able to keep a 'swanky German' pipe, which would have made his men laugh. Clearly this officer believed that keeping his men amused was an essential part of his duties.[17] What is more important, many officers believed that they had a duty to protect 'their' men against what many perceived as an impersonal and arbitrary coercive military machine. Some officers, such as the CO of 1/Duke of Cornwall's Light Infantry in September 1916, risked their careers by refusing to attack in unfavourable circumstances.[18] Most officers did not take such a personally risky stand. Regimental officers, like the men they commanded, were trapped by the military system, and could only modify that system at an extremely local level.[19]

There were many ways in which officers could make life more bearable for their soldiers. Officers quietly woke exhausted men discovered sleeping on sentry duty and saved them from the full rigour of the disciplinary code.[20] If men were 'crimed', an officer could award minor punishments at company or battalion level to prevent disciplinary cases from going forward to the lottery of a court martial.[21] More simply, the paternal officer could turn a blind eye to illegal but harmless activities that made the ranker's life worth living. In his great prose/poem, *In Parenthesis*, David Jones (15/Royal Welch Fusiliers) wrote memorably of surreptitious smoking 'under the turnip stack'. Although the 'kind' platoon officer affected not to notice, a look-out watched for signs of authority in the form of 'the Adjutant, or that shit Major Lillywhite'.[22]

By 1917–18, approximately 40 per cent of British officers were of working-class or at least lower-middle-class origin.[23] The experiences of such officers varied from individual to individual. Henry Williamson, in his semi-autobiographical novel *A Fox Under My Cloak*, wrote of the problems experienced in 1915 by a lower-middle class former ranker in adjusting to commissioned status. In one scene the central character, 'Phillip (sic) Maddison', a rather gauche and desperately insecure young man, is subjected to the ordeal of a subaltern's court martial for infractions of the unwritten social code. By contrast, John Lucy, a former Regular ranker, was treated with kindness when he joined his old battalion as an officer, and had few problems in adapting to his new status.[24] On the whole, it seems that rather more prejudice was experienced by Temporary officers in the earlier years of the war than the latter, and that most were accepted with the same degree of pragmatism that lay behind their commissioning.

There was, however, considerable contemporary criticism of 'Temporary Gentleman'. This nickname reflects not just social snobbery but also a genuine concern that, lacking a traditional social and educational background, such officers would not be paternalistic. This concern was misplaced. The system of officer training introduced during the war was a pragmatic and highly successful attempt to give potential officers a crash-course in, among other things, paternalistic behaviour.[25] Moreover, the bulk of officers commissioned in the later stages of the war had served in the ranks and knew very well the importance of an officer's care for his men. T.A.H. Nash, for instance, served as a junior NCO in 1/4 Gloucestershires, and the experience served him in good stead when he was commissioned into 16/Manchesters, his divisional commander later paying tribute to Nash's understanding of, and sympathy with, his men.[26] It is true that it is much rarer to find references to officers buying food for their men in 1917–18 than it is for the earlier period, but this can be explained by purely practical factors, such as food shortages at home and the fact that many officers did not have enough spare cash to buy gifts in bulk for their men.

The language used by officers when writing about their men indicates that their attitudes were not determined solely by pragmatism or a sense of duty. The bond between the subaltern and his platoon was often described in terms of marriage and parenthood. Both neatly capture the idea of a tender, loving relationship. Sharing, to a greater or lesser degree, the hardships of war, it is perhaps not surprising that boys of similar ages made friends across the rank and class divide, or that older officers had a thoroughly paternal concern for their men, or sympathized with men of their own age enduring life in the ranks. Many officers came to admire the fortitude of their men. 'A private's life out here is a very rotten one' wrote an officer of 9/Duke of Wellington's Regiment in 1916, 'the more one thinks about it, the more one admires the men – they're absolutely wonderful to stick what they do stick'.[27]

The picture was not entirely rosy. Many officers felt that their men seemed incapable of doing anything without their help; the creation of a dependency culture was an almost inevitable consequence of the bureaucracy of paternalism. In 1916 a *Times* journalist commented that the extent to which even intelligent soldiers relied upon their officers was on occasion 'so absolute as to be embarrassing'. This writer believed that this state of affairs was the consequence of the surrender of individual liberty by men when they joined the army.[28] Officers also had to square the circle of demonstrating friendship for their men while retaining their authority as hierarchical leaders by avoiding undue familiarity. Curiously, few officers articulated this dilemma, although it lay at the heart of the question of officer–man relations. One who did succinctly summarized what seems to have been the credo of most officers: 'The men are all topping fellows. But one has to let them know who is master. First an officer has to be an officer, and then he may become a man.'[29] Once this had been established, both officers and men generally observed the principle of 'on parade, on parade; off parade, off parade'; that is, the recognition by both officers and men that 'what was permissible on certain occasions might be a military crime on others'.[30]

What did other ranks think of their officers? They tended to judge them by a simple set of criteria. Officers, wrote a private of 2/5 Lancashire Fusiliers,

> fell in into two categories. If they passed dirty rifles, handled a spade, or carried a bag of cement they were 'aw reet'. If not, they were 'no bloody *bon*'.

A middle-class private of 2/5 Gloucestershires recorded the views of his working-class comrades in similar terms:

> A bad officer, that is, a bully, is a —! A good officer, that is, a considerate (sic), is 'a toff'. 'I'd follow him anywhere. The men's friend'; or simply, but in significant tones 'gentleman'![31]

As these quotations show, other ranks tended to judge officers largely in terms of deference, which can be defined as 'respect for, and obedience to, "leaders" of society'. Deference was one of the principal bonds of Edwardian society. It was both a pragmatic response of working-class men to economic realities, and a 'natural' way of life, inculcated through religion and education. Deference was not, however, the same as subservience. Men in the ranks saw deference as 'the natural exchange' for paternalism. Officers who did not look after their men, who did not show leadership qualities in battle, or who did not behave in a gentlemanly fashion had, in the eyes of the ordinary soldier, forfeited all rights to commissioned status, and the privileges that went with it, including the right to expect rankers to follow them.[32] This point is graphically illustrated by the reaction of some sergeants of 4/5 Black Watch to the unedifying spectacle of a drunken and sexually-aroused Temporary officer chasing the hostess around an estaminet. The sergeants, working-class slum dwellers by origin, were 'incensed by such behaviour in an officer of our regiment'.[33]

It is rare indeed to find a blanket condemnation of officers in the writings of other ranks. A furious denunciation of one officer is likely to be followed by a complimentary reference to another; thus Pte Abraham of 8/Queens attacked the character of one officer, yet went on to say that other officers were natural leaders, who enjoyed the trust and esteem of their soldiers. It is uncommon to discover an officer who was actively hated by his men, as opposed to one who was criticized for neglecting his men or for thoughtlessness. A private described a Northants Yeomanry officer as 'the most detested and hated officer I ever met.' The interesting point is that this officer suffered by comparison with the popular officer he had replaced. Precisely because most officers were paternal and lived up to their side of the unspoken bargain, rankers regarded with especial distaste officers who did not conform to the general pattern of officer–man relations. Pte S.B. Abbot (86th Machine Gun Company) was scathing about one officer, who simultaneously risked his men's lives unnecessarily and seemed over-concerned with his own safety. More typical of Abbot's officers was a paternalistic subaltern who was killed at Arras in April 1917, much to Abbot's grief.[34]

The writings of men in the ranks frequently contain favourable references to officers, although not as often as complimentary remarks about soldiers appear in officers' memoirs, letters and writings. In part this is a reflection of differing perceptions of the relationship, but also of the 'unspoken assumption' that officer–man relations were good unless stated otherwise. Only if an officer was exceptionally good, or exceptionally bad, or if he suddenly came to mind through being killed or wounded, was he likely to be mentioned. The first specific death mentioned in the diary of Pte Joe Griffiths of 1/King's Royal Rifle Corps was that of 2nd Lt Bentall. His sense of loss prompted Griffiths to record his appreciation of this officer which otherwise would have gone unknown.[35]

Middle-class rankers were more inclined to complain about the officer–man relationship than their working-class counterparts. The former were perhaps less sympathetic to the concept of deference as a return for paternalism, and tended to resent officers' privileges, particularly if they had been passed over for a commission.[36] For the most part men in the

419

ranks accepted the superior lifestyle of the officer as part of the natural order of things – provided, of course that the officer did not behave in an 'unofficer-like' way. This obviously placed ranker-officers, that is, officers without a public school education who had previously served in the ranks, in a potentially very difficult situation when faced by a middle-class soldier like John Tucker of 1/13 Londons who criticised a subaltern for speaking with 'a slight cockney accent', or indeed working-class soldiers who preferred officers to be distinctive in their speech and behaviour.[37] However, if lower-class officers had been widely mistrusted by the men they commanded, the British army's cohesion would have been placed under severe strain in 1917–18. In reality, most lower-class ranker officers did meet other ranks' expectations of officer-like behaviour, and inter-rank relations remained cordial throughout the war. An officer's leadership skills, competence, paternalism, and courage determined his relations with his men, not his social class.

Some soldiers emerged from the khaki mass and formed close relationships with officers. Informal night-time chats between a duty officer and a lonely sentry; the peculiar relationship between officer and soldier servant; the shared experience of battle – all of these circumstances offered opportunities for the barriers of rank to lower, albeit briefly. NCOs, who deserve a major study to themselves, co-operated closely with officers to ensure the smooth running of a unit, although the problems of balancing friendship and discipline could be acute. The officer and NCO had to strike a delicate balance between being part of the platoon or company 'team' and being slightly aloof from it. The successful partnership between the officer and NCO, which was in many ways the lynchpin of the entire disciplinary structure of the army, had to be founded upon mutual goodwill and recognition of the difficulties inherent in the relationship.[38]

In 1915 Donald Hankey, a gentleman-ranker of 7/Rifle Brigade, published 'The Beloved Captain', a short story about an officer who was Christ-like in his concern for his men. 'Beloved Captains' are often to be found in the writings of ordinary soldiers. Some younger soldiers engaged in hero-worship, while other more mature men expressed more measured, but very positive, opinions of some officers. Ernest Shepherd, a prewar Regular NCO of 1/Dorsets, described Captain Algeo as 'Absolutely fearless . . . [his] first and last thought [was] for his men'[39] A balanced view of the officer corps as a whole appeared in an article published in 1938 in a popular magazine aimed at the ex-servicemen's market. In assessing his officers the author, an anonymous former ranker, certainly did not shrink from pointing out their defects. Nonetheless, like Hankey, he expressed his admiration of brave and paternal officers, and recognised their role in making life bearable for the ordinary soldier: 'We can have nothing but admiration . . . tinged with affection . . . for almost all of them'.[40]

The generally excellent state of officer–man relations had important consequences for the morale of the army of 1914–18. As Correlli Barnett has written, British soldiers on the Western Front 'had the moral and material support of an immense organization' devoted to their welfare.[41] Regimental officers had an important role in this organization; not merely as providers of 'buckshee' cigarettes but as buffers between the soldier and the army, for as a conscript private noted, while recalling a friendly officer, 'It makes all the difference when one is treated with kindness and consideration by one in authority'.[42] In June 1917 a 'Soldier's and Worker's Council' – a body that would not, one would have thought, have been a natural defender of the officer class – passed resolutions demanding 'more generous treatment' of junior officers and that 'The general treatment of soldiers be brought into line with the spirit of officers and men in daily contact' which alone 'make life endurable.'[43]

British other ranks were perfectly capable of conveying their opinions to their superiors by a variety of methods.[44] The most dramatic way was to carry out an act of large-scale mutiny. The only such British mutiny to take place on the Western Front during hostilities occurred at Etaples base camp in September 1917. Here, the army's disciplinary system ran riot and seasoned troops were, much to their disgust, treated as raw recruits. Moreover at Etaples officers were kept well away from the men. The creative tension that existed at unit level between discipline and protective paternalism of regimental officers was thus absent. Significantly, military police and instructor NCOs, not regimental officers, were the main targets of the mutineers' fury.[45] Without the paternal role of the regimental officers, there might well have been many more such mutinies on the Western Front.

It is important to note the limitations of the paternalistic/deferential relationship. It could not prevent cases of 'rough justice'.[46] It could not prevent the imposition of tough 'Regular' discipline on citizen volunteers and conscripts, although it could help to modify its effects. It helped to sustain a 'dependency culture' in which men relied too heavily on their officers. However, drawing up the balance sheet, the advantages of the inter-rank relationship far outweighed the disadvantages. The excellence of relations between other ranks and regimental officers was a factor of absolutely crucial importance in maintaining the morale of the B.E.F. throughout four gruelling years of attrition on the Western Front.[47]

Notes

Crown Copyright material in the Public Record Office is reproduced by permission of the Controller of Her Majesty's Stationery Office and material in the Liddle Collection by kind permission of the University of Leeds. It has proved impossible to trace the holders of copyright in the GS Chaplin papers held in the Imperial War Museum.

1   This paper is based upon G.D. Sheffield, 'Officer–Man Relations, Morale and

Discipline in the British Army, 1902–22', PhD., University of London, 1994. This thesis is currently being prepared for publication by Macmillan.

A.D. Thorburn, *Amateur Gunners*, Liverpool, W. Potter, 1933, p.5.

3 J.F.C. Fuller, *The Army in My Time*, London, Rich and Cowan, 1935, p.6. For a modern study of the social composition of the Victorian and Edwardian army, see E.M. Spiers, *The Army and Society*, London, Longman, 1980.

4 'Trades of men offering for enlistment, year ending September 30th 1913', pp. 1921, XX, CMD 1193.

5 The paintings appeared as plates in E.A.H. Alderson, *Pink and Scarlet, or Hunting as a School for Soldiering*, London, Hodder and Stoughton, 1913, pp. 198–9.

6 See Sheffield, 'Officer-Man Relations' pp.15–22; unpublished account, p.2, W.J. Nicholson papers, Imperial War Museum [IWM]; J. Lucy, *There's a Devil in the Drum*, London, Faber and Faber, 1938, p.94.

7 Sheffield, 'Officer-Man Relations', pp.24–50.

8 G.B. Hurst, *With the Manchesters in the East*, Manchester, Manchester University Press, 1917, p.2 (see also Hurst's comments in S.J. Wilson, *The Seventh Manchesters*, Manchester, Manchester University Press, 1920, p.xiii); E.V. Tempest, *History of 6th Battalion the West Yorkshire Regiment*, Bradford, Percy Lund, Humphries, 1921, pp.1–3, 6, 12. For (generally disapproving) views of Regular officers on the discipline of auxiliary units, see the series of 'Reports . . . on the progress made by the Territorial Force . . .', War Office Library.

9 Unpublished account, p.4, J. Woollin papers, PP/MCR/110, IWM; Notebook I, B.D. Parkin papers, 86/57/1, IWM.

10 I.F.W. Beckett, 'The British Army, 1914–18: The Illusion of Change' in J. Turner (ed.) *Britain and the First World War*, London, Unwin-Hyman, 1988, p.107.

11 G.D. Sheffield and G.I.S. Inglis, eds., *From Vimy Ridge to the Rhine: The Great War Letters of Christopher Stone DSO MC*, Marlborough, Crowood, 1989, pp. 20, 135 (letters of 12 February, 16 November, 1916, 9 September 1918). For another example, see Lt R.E. Wilson, letter, 9 July 1916, K.R. Simpson Questionnaires [KRS Q]. All quotations from these questionnaires appear by the permission of Mr Keith Simpson, to whom I am grateful for giving access to this unique archive.

12 W. Griffith, *Up to Mametz*, Norwich, Gliddon, 1988, pp.202–3 (first published in 1931). For an example see memo. from AA&QMG, 66th Division, 28 Feb. 1918, in P. Ingleson papers, Liddle Collection, University of Leeds. [LC]

13 P.M. Campbell, *Letters from Gallipoli*, Edinburgh, privately printed, 1916, p.26.

14 See Examination paper 1, Dec. 1916, in 'Officers: Officer Cadets' files, LC.

15 Sir W. Baynes Bart, letter, 24 Dec. 1915, LC.

16 H. Venables, diary, 3 June 1915, LC.

17 B. Martin, *Poor Bloody Infantry*, London, John Murray, 1987, p.115.

18 E.W. Flanagan to J.E. Edmonds, 17 Nov. 1935, CAB 45/133, Public Record Office [PRO].

19 R. Graves, *Goodbye to All That*, Harmondsworth, Penguin, 1960, p.192 (first

published 1929); letter, 7 Oct. 1916, G.S. Taylor papers, Liddell Hart Centre for Military Archives.

20 [A.M. Burrage] 'Ex-Pte.-X', *War is War*, London, Victor Gollancz, 1930, p.74; G.H. Cole, KRS Q.

21 P.W. Turner and R.H. Haigh, *Not For Glory*, London, Robert Maxwell, 1969, pp.86–7; C.E. Carrington, *Soldier From the Wars Returning*, London, Hutchinson, 1965, pp.169–70.

22 D. Jones, *In Parenthesis*, London, Faber and Faber, 1963, p.15 (first published 1937).

23 Figures are calculated from *Statistics of the Military Effort of the British Empire during the Great War*, London, HMSO, 1922, p.707; see also J.M. Winter, *The Great War and the British People*, London, Macmillan, 1987, pp.83–99.

24 H. Williamson, *A Fox Under My Cloak*, London, Macdonald, 1985 (first published 1955) pp.218–23; Lucy, *op cit*, pp.352–9.

25 R.T. Rees, *A Schoolmaster at War*, London, Haycock Press, nd, p.79; Sheffield, 'Officer-Man Relations', pp.138–50; R. Graves, p.203.

26 T.A.M. Nash (ed.) *The Diary of an Unprofessional Soldier*, Chippenham, Picton, 1991, pp.ix, 27.

27 P. Beaver, (ed.) *The Wipers Times*, London, Macmillan, 1988, p.79 (first published 1916); G. Macleod Ross, KRS Q; J.W.B. Russell, diary, 15 May 1916, LC.

28 'A Citizen Army from Within', part III, *The Times*, 5 Dec; see also E. Taylor, Letters, 12, 13 Dec. 1914, LC. The lack of initiative of the British soldier can be overstressed. For a corrective, see an excellent, and very positive, recent analysis of British tactics: P. Griffith, *Battle Tactics of the Western Front*, New Haven and London, Yale University Press, 1994.

29 R.W. McConnell to father in L. Housman, *War Letters of Fallen Englishmen*, London, Victor Gollancz, 1930, p.186. An excellent description of this dilemma can be found in R. Coldicott, *London Men in Palestine*, London, Edward Arnold, 1919, pp.66–70.

30 J. Brophy and E. Partridge, *The Long Trail*, Andre Deutsch, 1965, p.225.

31 V.W. Tilsey, *Other Ranks*, London, Cobden-Sanderson, 1931, p.126–27; I. Gurney, (R.K.R. Thornton, ed.) *War Letters*, London, Hogarth Press, 1984, p.217.

32 For the concept of deference, see H. Newby, 'The Deferential Dialectic', *Comparative Studies in Society and History*, 17, 2, (1975); P. Joyce, *Work, Society and Politics*, London, Meuthen, 1980, pp.91–5.

33 E. Linklater, *Fanfare for a Tin Hat*, London, Macmillan, 1970, p.61.

34 Unpublished account, pp.8a, 54, 84, A.J. Abraham papers, IWM; unpublished account, (unpaginated), G.S. Chaplin papers, IWM; unpublished account, S.B. Abbot papers, 78/36/1, IWM.

35 J. Griffiths, diary, 3 Oct. 1915, IWM.

36 See for instance A. Moffat, diary, 16 Feb. 1916, LC; H. Innes, letter, 5 Sept. 1918, LC; Burrage, *op cit* pp.9, 13, 70–1.

37 J.F. Tucker, *Johnny Get Your Gun*, London, W. Kimber, 1978, p.41; G.W. Grossmith, KRS Q.

38 W. Griffith, *op cit* pp. 135–6; R.L. Mackay, diary, 2 Aug. 1917, p.374, IWM; S.F. Hatton, *The Yarn of a Yeoman*, London, Hutchinson, nd, pp.87–8.

39 D. Hankey, *A Student in Arms,* London, Andrew Melrose, 1916, pp.59–70; G. Coppard, *With a Machine Gun to Cambrai,* London, Macmillan, 1986, p.5; W.M. Jenner, letter, 24 June 1969, P. Blagrove papers, Liddell Hart Centre for Military Archives; E. Shepherd, (B. Rossor, ed.) *A Sergeant-Major's War,* Marlborough, Crowood, 1987, op cit, pp.82, 97.

40 Anon, 'Memories V', In Sir E. Swinton (ed.) *Twenty Years After,* supplementary vol., London, George Newnes, nd, pp.369–72.

41 C. Barnett, *The Collapse of British Power,* Gloucester, Alan Sutton, 1984, p.432 (first published in 1972).

42 C. Haworth, *March to Armistice 1918,* London, William Kimber, 1968, p.28.

43 WO 32/5455, PRO.

44 For a study of 'power relationships' in the French army, which makes some points of relevance to this present study, see L.V. Smith, *Between Mutiny and Obedience: The Case of the French Fifth Infantry Division during World War I,* Princeton, NJ, Princeton University Press, 1994.

45 J.H. Dible, diary, 11 Sept. 1917, IWM; War Diary of Commandant, Etaples Base camp, 9–10 Sept. 1917, WO 95/4027, PRO; G.D. Sheffield, *The Redcaps,* London, Brassey's, 1994, p.80.

46 This is the title of a novel which centres around a military miscarriage of justice that results in an execution. C.E. Montague, *Rough Justice,* London, Chatto and Windus, 1926.

47 The comments on officer-man relations and discipline in J.G. Fuller's otherwise excellent study of an aspect of the B.E.F.'s morale merit some adjustment in view of the research presented in this paper; J.G. Fuller, *Troop Morale and Popular Culture in the British and Dominion Armies 1914–1918,* Oxford, Clarendon Press, 1991, pp.47–57.

Chapter 31

The Russian Soldier's Morale from the Evidence of Tsarist Military Censorship

Irina Davidian

To a greater degree than most other wars, the First World War can be called the 'war that shook foundations' – foundations, not only material, but also (and principally) of the human spirit . The latter is especially true for the people who directly participated in the war and experienced all the physical and mental suffering it entailed: that is, the ordinary soldiers. What they thought about, what they believed in, what they dreamed of – in a word, what was 'the soldier's truth' and how it changed during the war, is the theme of my paper. To examine 'the soldier's truth' I took a very interesting and rarely used source – summaries and reports of Russian military censorship which were compiled after the censoring of soldier's letters.

The war divided fighting Russia (as other fighting countries) into two worlds: the front and the rear. The only cord connecting them were letters – small scraps of paper bearing the thoughts and feelings of soldiers, their attitudes to the war and peace, to the Tsar and God, to a company commander or the government of Russia – and many other topics. The significance of this channel of communication was also clear to the Tsarist Government, which introduced military censorship of soldiers' correspondence from the first days of the war. The purpose of this innovation was not only to watch out for breaches of military secrecy, but also, more and more openly, to check up on the morale of troops.

Though the censorship itself is not a subject of my research it is worth saying something about the organization and functioning of this institution. The job of military censor appeared in Russia for the first time in 1812, during the war against Napoleon, but it was only during the First World War that military censorship became an established institution, in line, most likely, with the new global character of the war and the extreme bureaucratization of the Tsarist regime. The functions of Russian military censorship were determined by two principal documents: 'The temporary regulations on military censorship' adopted on July 20, 1914, and 'The list of information, prohibited for publication', adopted on July 26, 1914.[1] According to these documents, 'perlustration' (i.e., going through the letters) was one of three main activities of military censorship. The military censorship at the front was comprehensive – every letter or telegram, (except those fixed in the regulations) was subjected to it; in the rest of Russia, only international correspondence and some interior correspondence were censored – at the discretion of a military district commander. In the battle zone there were departments of military censorship attached to staffs of fronts, armies and other military units, and in the rear there were commissions of military censorship subordinated to the Chief Commission. As with any new undertaking, military censorship developed throughout the war. The main tendency of this development was the further strengthening and bureaucratization of the apparatus. Thus, the initial sphere of the censor's activity was exclusively military. But in late 1915 they were ordered to pay attention to political questions as well. A connection between military censorship and the Gendarme Department developed. The post of 'senior censor' was introduced and personal stamps of censors with their names were replaced by impersonal stamps with numbers . By the end of the war military censorship had turned into such a perfectly organized machine that it went on working even when the Russian military regime was in complete disarray. Moreover, military censorship continued its functions after the overthrow of Romanovs in February 1917 and even after the Bolshevik revolution in October 1917. It was abolished only in 1918 (but was revived half a year later in the Red Army).

The work of the military censors as in any bureaucratic institution was subject to detailed regulation. According to the 1914 regulations, the Censor was to open a letter and look through it. If he found nothing wrong, he was to stamp the letter with the words 'opened by military censorship' and with his personal stamp and send it on to its destination. If some part of it contained any undesirable information or view, this part was to be deleted. If the whole letter failed to pass the requirements of military censorship, it could be confiscated and sent to the appropriate authority.

Going through correspondence was not the only duty of censors. Every ten days, they were also obliged to compile summaries of quotations from the letters which were most typical and widespread in their message, retaining the original style and language of their author. These were sorted into the following categories: patriotic letters; letters expressing wishes for peace; letters complaining about food, treatment and so on; letters containing forbidden information; critical letters and so-called 'ignorant' letters (i.e., not mentioning the war). The data of these summaries were used by a chief military censor in his regular reports to the chief of staff.

After analysing the censorial summaries and forming a general judgement, he made his resumé about the troops' morale and fighting power. Since reports, unlike summaries, were concerned, not with the letters themselves but with the percentage of 'contented' 'depressed' and 'ignorant' letters, quotations in them are rare. Summaries are therefore, of course, a more attractive source for the study of the soldiers' moods. They are, however, somewhat subjective. Censors were only human and could not be absolutely dispassionate. This was first of all because of the great volume of the censor's work, as some figures will show: one field post-office daily received eighteen to twenty thousand letters. One rear post-office daily received from 5 to 50 thousand letters (in Petrograd up to 200 thousand). One censor, however, could look through only 200–250 letters a day.[2] There was one case of a censor who looked through about fourteen thousand letters for two weeks (i.e. a thousand a day), but that was a record.[3] Certainly, it was very difficult for censors to be careful and objective in such conditions.

Secondly, censorship was overtime work for civilian officers in the postal service. They got no salary for it and hence were not interested in the result. And the third factor was personal. One censor might want to attract the chief's favourable notice, and so might deliberately cite only 'contented' and 'patriotic' letters. Another censor, on the contrary, might pay attention only to 'depressed' and 'critical' letters. A third might be only interested in compiling a formal summary, putting both sides for the record, so he distributed quotations evenly and not necessarily in proportion to their incidence. There was, however, one thing a censor could not do – he could not fabricate letters.

All in all, the by-products of military censorship constitute a vivid historical source, and though not very objective – sometimes decidedly the opposite – they brought together and preserved people's real thoughts and feelings, united by one time and one great event – the First World War.

The documents used and cited here are kept in the Russian State Military Historical Archive in Moscow. These are the files of the Supreme Commander-in-Chief's Headquarters (f. 2003) and the files of Front Commanders-in-Chiefs' Headquarters (ff. 2019,2031, 2048, 2067). Besides that, the documents of local military censorship commissions are kept in some provincial archives (at Kazan, for example). As I mentioned earlier, these documents have not often been used. I can cite only two or three publications which have drawn evidence from them.[4] The Soviet researchers into this subject examined the censorship materials exclusively in connection with the 'development of a revolutionary movement in the Tsarist Army during the World War I.' But to my mind, these documents can yield much more information.

The letters cited by censors are rich in material that gives an idea of the changes in the thoughts and spirit of the Russian soldier during the first World War. These changes were brought about by a number of circumstances. The most important of these were the situations at the front and at home.

When the war began in the summer of 1914, there were few people in Russia who could foresee what it really would entail and how it would finish. Society was gripped with so-called 'hurrah-patriotism' and with eagerness to 'help our Serbian brothers' and to destroy the Germans before the onset of winter. All this found ample expression in the first letters from the front:

I'm eager, as is every warrior, for the soonest possible victory over the enemy of our motherland, and we'll return only when we have won.[5]
We must show the German, what the Russian four-edged bayonet means!
Russia, of course, will smash the snotty nose of the damned German.

But already first defeats at the front brought disappointment and raised doubts about Russian superiority.

Soldiers have no more confidence in victory, everybody is in low spirits now. Failure is everywhere. And now there is the bad weather as well. Poor Russia has no luck at all.

Shortages of food, boots and overcoats became evident at once. Soldiers wrote with bitterness:

It is very bad now. We haven't received bread for two weeks, only rusks; that's what we are expected to fight on. There is a shortage of rusks too and no snuff at all.
I am at my post all the time – frozen, soaked and, on top of that, hungry as a dog. Some days I have nothing to eat but bread. What a waste of energy and health!
They feed us very badly. We walk barefoot or in rope-soled shoes. It's incredible that soldiers of the Russian army are in rope-soled shoes!

But the shortage of bread and boots was nothing compared with the shortage of arms:

Everybody is in bad spirits . . . The main thing is lack of arms. Here we have 1000 men who have been waiting four days for a weapon – in vain.

When the situation about shells changed soldiers wrote:

Things are good now. Our artillery pull the guns to the positions . . . Soldiers seeing big guns, kiss them with joy.

The 'trench warfare', into which the fighting settled in 1915, was unexpected not only for the Russian High Command, but also for the soldiers. In the new conditions when technical equipment, especially heavy artillery, was decisive, infantrymen (being the majority of the army) began to feel their uselessness and impotence.

The Germans are right who say about us: 'Russians fight with God, and we fight with heavy guns.'

Moreover, the most far-sighted men began to understand that soldiers in this war were consigned to a role as cannon-fodder:

> Our position is bad, we are still retreating and the main reason is the lack of shells. This is what we've fought for! And it is the war ministers who did it. And now we have to use up men instead of shells.

Indeed, by August 1915, up to thirty per cent of the Russians at the front were without arms. This is largely the reason for the exceptionally huge losses by the Russian Army during the war (about five million killed, crippled and captive – that is, a third of all those mobilized during the war) – given the appearance of new weapons of mass extermination (gas, for example). 'The war becomes more tricky', wrote soldiers in their letters.

A series of defeats, mass losses, shortages of ammunition and supplies – all these forced soldiers to think about the reason for Russia's failures:

> All our divisions were defeated by the Germans . . . It is annoying to think, all the same: who's to blame for our lack of success? Who made thousands people unhappy and their children orphans? It certainly is not the soldiers themselves who are guilty of all that.
>
> 'We are not guilty, we're betrayed.
>
> This war is worse then the Japanese one. That was spent drinking, in this we were betrayed.
>
> Perhaps, we'll have soon to admit that our war campaign is lost and, above all, that it has been betrayed'

In the opinion of the soldiers, betrayal was universal: from a company's cook who stole the soldier's bread, to the Tsar and his generals who left the army to the mercy of fate. There was nothing left of the former unity believed to exist between the Tsar and the army and, within the army, between the soldiers and their commanders. The number of letters with complaints against the way their commanders treated them increased very much in 1915 when flogging in the army was legalized:

> Our company commander is a very bad man, he beats us very hard.
>
> War is everywhere: at the front we're beaten by the German and in the reserve – by our own commanders.

The phrase 'war is everywhere' expressed the soldier's understanding of the world, universal war. If war was everywhere and everywhere was evil, so war itself was the main evil:

> The war has dragged on and one cannot see the end. Battles and battles again go on every day. Human blood is shed, but there is no result.
>
> This damned war will soon have been lingering on for two years, the war which deprived all of us of freedom and cut us off from our families and friends. And in addition there is no end to this war in sight. So oppressive is this war and so hateful, that the whole world has become loathsome!

This deep hatred felt by ordinary soldiers towards the war was to be prevalent in the letters of 1916–1917. It had nothing to do with anti-patriotism or sedition on their part – simply that they did not understand the sense or purpose of this mass slaughter.

Soldier's letters show that not only were they looking for someone to blame but also for a means of escape. Some soldiers, though they felt deeply the wrong and injustice of the war preferred, even so, to endure to the end; but others sought to end their unhappiness by getting to the front-line as soon as possible and fall in battle; and a third element sought to avoid suffering through voluntary surrender or desertion – an attitude which became widespread by the end of 1915. A censor of the Moscow military district wrote in his report on 12 November 1915:

> One encounters frequent evidence of voluntary surrender by large groups.

Interestingly, the letters which mentioned such occurrences almost never condemn them; indeed the soldiers who wrote them seemed to support mutineers and be ready to follow them:

> There is no order and the troops bore the brunt of everything, but now they don't want to urge each other to attack . . . They say: 'Stop murdering people!' Our soldiers in some regiments drove their bayonets into the ground and we, perhaps, shall do the same.

The soldier's anti-war solidarity was shown more clearly in mass refusals to attack the enemy and in fraternization. The first information on such actions appeared in letters of late 1915, and in 1916 it became widespread. The most interesting phenomenon, of course, was fraternization. Though in the Russian army it appeared later than in the armies of France, Germany or Britain, it signified a great change in the mind of the Russian soldier. Now he saw neither any purpose in the war, nor any enemy. The enemy had turned from the newspaper caricature into the same kind of ordinary man as himself who believed in Jesus Christ in the same way and celebrated Christian holidays on the same days (the mass fraternization at the Russian front was most common during Easter week of 1916):

> On the first day [of Easter] we and Austrians came together, shook hands and I must confess that they are very kind people. Don't believe what our books write of them.
> There was no battle at Easter. On the first day of Easter the Germans put white flags out of their trenches and we did the same. We made peace for two days and then Germans treated our people to their cigars and drinks. So we've lived a little for two days.

Fraternization was not only a demonstration of the universal soldier's thirst for peace, but also an attempt, albeit expressed in religious form, at peace-making over the head of governments. In this sense, fraternization can be considered as a prototype of a future 'people's diplomacy'.

The world war phenomenon manifested itself not only in fraternization with other armies, but in a 'globalization' of mind too. Contrasting themselves with foreign soldiers and comparing such experiences with their own, Russian soldiers began to realize the universal scale of the current catastrophe. They understood that such a catastrophe must inevitably entail deep changes in the world:

> After the war there will be great troubles in our country and abroad.
> Perhaps, war will ruin all of us and not only us, but the whole world is suffering and will be suffering because of war. War can bring us nothing good. We're tired of war.

The letters of 1916 were full of the soldier's thirst for peace and hopes of 'finishing the war this year.' The words 'we're tired of war' sounded as a refrain in almost every letter. Soldiers were interested in the situation not only on their own front but also on the other fronts of the world war. Every event, however insignificant, they interpreted in terms of how it would bring a speedy end of the war. Perhaps this very peace enthusiasm can explain the success of the last Russian decisive offensive in the summer of 1916 (the so-called 'Brusilov break-through'). However, this final drive of the Russian army to change the situation at the front failed. The total retreat of Russians from Galicia which followed caused a deep despondency in the army. 'There was never before such depression in the correspondence from the front', wrote military censors at the end of 1916. Cheerful expectations of peace were replaced by apathy or open hate. The percentage of 'indifferent' letters (the letters which did not mention war), increased significantly. Now soldiers were most interested in the events at home which began developing at high speed in the winter of 1916/17.

Information about the situation in the rear was the other factor influencing the soldier's mood. About eighty per cent of the Russian army were peasants who suffered very much because of their separation from home and land, and it is small wonder that the number of 'indifferent' letters increased, from the censor's evidence, in spring and autumn, when work in the fields was at its most intensive. A steady interest in home events had arisen only by the end of 1915. Just at that time the front defeats and letters from home about the bad situation in the rear had come together in the soldier's mind in a vague guess that the fate of the war would be decided in Russia:

> Everybody here is interested, not in the war theatre, but in Petrograd. The fate of war is decided there, that is, whether we shall be successful or not.

Now, what kind of information from the rear could disturb the army? First of all, there were complaints from relatives about the poor harvest, hunger, high prices and the bad conditions of soldiers' families:

'Most of all the army is interested. as usual, in high prices in Russia', was written in a summary of censors' reports of 12 June 1916.

'At the front soldiers fight and struggle, and in the rear instead of help they steal and rob,' wrote soldiers indignantly. At first they tried to encourage their families, advising them to trust the Government and Duma. However, as time went by, these hopes passed; then disappointment was replaced by irritation: 'We all placed our hopes on the Duma: maybe, it would do something good for us. But the hope seems to be weak.'

Then, inevitably, the development of political events in Russia influenced the soldier's mood:

> One cannot but notice [wrote the chief of the Petrograd military censorship commission in November 1916], that in letters from the army as well as, mainly, in letters to the army, discontent arising from internal political situation of the country is beginning to grow ... Rumours about disorders and strikes at factories, about disturbances in reserve units are reaching the army and these rumours, often exaggerated and embroidered, cause depression in the soldiers' morale and much worry about the fate of relatives left at home.

The information from home (letters and newspapers) convinced soldiers that they had nobody and nothing to fight for:

> I don't know what to do and why I should serve and I don't want to go under ... What is there to fight for?

Comrades in the village have saved up big money and we must suffer.
For what? When will it end?

That is why the news about the overthrow of autocracy in February
1917 was taken by the soldiers as an opportunity to free themselves from
the hated war:

Now we all have come to life.

However, the change of power in Russia did not bring soldiers their
desired peace, and other problems now came to the fore:

Our soldiers are divided into two parties now: one is the Bolsheviks who
are keen to finish the war as soon as possible and the other is the
Mensheviks who support the bourgeoisie and want to continue with the
war up to the victory. It's a dangerous time in Russia now. A civil war
can break out, because one party is opposing the other.

At this point, the soldier's truth about the world war was to be replaced
by the soldier's truth about the coming civil war in Russia.

Notes

1 See: Sobranie uzakonenii i rasporyazhenii pravitelstva, izdavaemoe pri
   Pravitel- stvuyushchem Senate, 1914, Otdel I, nos. 192, 203.
2 Russian State Military Historical Archive (RGVIA). Collection 2003, description 1, folder 1482, folio 121.
3 Revolyutsionnoe dvizhenie v armii i na flote (1914-fevral 1917): Sbornik
   dokumentov, Moscow, 1966, p.292.
4 See: Tsarskaya armiya v period mirovoi voiny i Fevralskoi revolyutsii, Kazan,
   1932; 'Soldatskie pisma v gody mirovoi voiny (1915–1917)' in Krasnyi
   Arkhiv, no. 405, 1934; Revolyutsionnoe dvizhenie v armii i na flote (1914-
   fevral 1917): Sbornik dokumentov, Moscow, 1966.
5 This and all following quotations are cited from: RGVIA, Collection 2048,
   description 1, folder 901, 904, 905; Collection 2031, description 1, folder
   1180, 1181, 1182, 1183; Collection 2067, description 1, folder 2930, 2933,
   2934, 2935, 2936, 2937, 2938, 2941.

Morale and Discipline in the Italian Army, 1915–1918

John Gooch

On 9 May 1915, some two weeks before Italy formally declared war on Austria-Hungary, the former prime minister, Giovanni Giolitti, voiced grave doubts about the fighting capacity of the nation in the war which was shortly to begin. The peasantry, he believed, would no longer respond instinctively to war, unlike more backward counterparts in Russia; nor did they yet possess the concept of citizenship which was apparent in Germany, France and Great Britain. If the raw material of the rank and file left a lot to be desired, so did the generals: having joined up in the days when families sent into the army only their most stupid sons, with whom they did not know what to do, they were worth little. Only the junior officers were of any quality.[1]

The views of a statesman whose political cynicism matched – if it did not exceed – that of Cavour and who was, moreover, a convinced opponent of Italian intervention cannot be taken as an objective evaluation of the cohesiveness and moral worth of Italy's soldiery at the moment when the trumpet summoned them to war, but they reflect fundamental anxieties about the nation-in-arms which were both deeply-rooted and widespread. After 1871, Italy had forged a conscript army in imitation of Germany and France, but one with particular characteristics which raised doubts about its power and likely performance.[2] For economic and social reasons, a smaller proportion of the adult male population served in the main contingent than was the case in Germany, France or even Austria–Hungary: in 1913, only 24.7 per cent of adult males did full military service.[3] Two-year service, introduced in 1910, raised professional doubts as to whether the necessary *spirito di corpo* – with all its undertones of obedience, discipline and loyalty – could be generated in such an abbreviated period. The army had reached neither very widely nor very deeply into Italian society before

1915, so that mass mobilization for war meant that new demands would have to be made of Giolitti's peasants.

Whether the peasants, and the much smaller urban proletariat, would be biddable when called was a matter of even greater doubt. The rise of socialism and anti-militarism in the 1890s introduced new divisions into a state whose solidarity was far from self-evident. As well as bearing the obligation of defending the state against its external enemies, the army now was called upon to form a bulwark against the fissiparous domestic forces of socialism and syndicalism. Acting to maintain public order – a task which it heartily disliked – made it unpopular in many quarters. More importantly for the war-time relationship between the high command and the troops, although there was much talk about the need for a liberal education for the modern soldier, who was more politically aware and less malleable than his *ottocento* predecessors, nothing was done to reform this dimension of soldiering until 1917. Wishing both to alter and to solidify society, the army fell back on its traditional preference for discipline as the basis of military education.[4]

National morale – the bedrock upon which the morale of the war-time armies had to be built – was not reinforced by the manner in which Italy entered the war. There were no external threats to national autonomy and integrity in 1914 and 1915. Nor was there a collectively recognisable national interest which could be achieved or maintained only by war. Instead, Italy entered upon hostilities as the result of political calculations effected by the king and his leading ministers and backed by a minority of interventionists. The 'voluntary' war, as it has been termed, was therefore easily and frequently regarded as serving someone else's interests. Extreme conservatives saw it as a war of revolutionaries; social democrats attacked it as an imperialists' and plutocrats' war; to the populace at large it was the war of the *signori*.[5] For all this, Giolitti turned out to be at least partly wrong: despite their disinterestedness (to put it no higher) in the stated goals of national policy, Italy's mass armies fought stubbornly for twenty-eight months before being overtaken by disaster at Caporetto.

When she entered the Great War, Italy was not militarily well-prepared in terms of morale and social cohesion. Nor was her state of material preparation much better. On becoming chief of the general staff in August 1914, general Luigi Cadorna listed an array of deficiencies: reserves were insufficiently trained, there were shortages of equipment and munitions (stocks of small arms ammunition were said to amount to only 700 rounds per rifle) and serious deficiencies in respect of medium and heavy artillery, and there were too few machine-gun sections.[6] Although the government spent two billion lire between August 1914 and June 1915, and a good deal more thereafter, shortages of artillery and ammunition both hampered operations and shaped strategy, with palpable consequences for military morale, throughout the first two and a half years of war.

In July, 1915, Italy mobilised a force comprising 31,000 officers and 1,058,000 non-commissioned officers and men. The proportion of absentees among those due to present themselves to conscription boards, which had been running at an annual rate of 10 per cent between 1910 and 1914, immediately mounted to 12.1 per cent, the highest figure since Italian unification. In all, 5,200,000 men did military service between 1915 and 1918 and 470,000 potential candidates failed to appear before the authorities.[7] The bulk of the absentees (370,000) were emigrants who had left Italy in the 1890s and 1900s, but a 'net' rate of absenteeism of almost 2 per cent suggests a not inconsiderable degree of disaffection. The continuation in wartime of a phenomenon which had greatly exercised the military authorities ever since 1863 probably reinforced the decision to take a harsh line over discipline from the outset.

Assumptions about morale and decisions about discipline, like much else about the manner in which the Italian army fought the war, were shaped by the commander-in-chief from 1915 to 1917, Luigi Cadorna. Highly conservative by temperament, authoritarian by nature and possessed of a well-developed persecution complex, Cadorna saw the army in abstract terms as a machine which had to perform certain tasks which he set it. Preoccupied from the outset with *matériel*, he lacked an appreciation of *la parte spirituale* of the force under his command. His views, which were wholly unchallengeable for as long as he retained his exalted status and unquestioned authority, were reinforced as a consequence of his isolation within his own circle. From the start, he determined to rule his armies with an iron hand: punishing a company of bersaglieri who had been taken by surprise in August 1915, he explained 'It is the usual discipline of persuasion which Italy needs.'[8]

In August 1914, the Italian army had no plan for an offensive war against Austria-Hungary. By December, Cadorna had decided to launch the attack across the eastern frontier towards Vienna; two battles in forty-eight days would bring his armies to the Lubliana plain, whereupon the prize would be in his grasp. Considered in the abstract, this plan appears highly ambitious; in reality even its first stage proved quite unattainable. In July 1915, when such a strategy still seemed viable, Cadorna issued a circular stating that 'every soldier . . . must be convinced that his superior has the sacred duty to shoot all cowards and recalcitrants immediately.'[9] A contemporaneous proclamation announcing prison sentences for anyone spreading war news which differed from that handed down by the government or the high command revealed his anxiety that indiscipline on the home front might weaken the fighting powers of his armies.[10]

By December 1915, Cadorna had privately recognised that even an initial breakthrough on the Carso would simply confront more obstacles and that the war had become one of attrition in which the loser would be the side which first ran out of men and weapons – 'and Austria is much nearer to that than we are.'[11] The tasks he set his armies, to bludgeon their way across the uplands of the Carso in the east while defending the northern mountain front on the Trentino and the Cadore, necessitated fighting a well-entrenched opponent in the most taxing of physical conditions. High temperatures and poor sanitation led to outbreaks of cholera and typhus on the Isonzo in the summer of 1915, while fighting on the stone-covered slopes of the Carso was made yet more lethal by the way in which nature aided the enemy: the increase in fragmentation caused by exploding shells produced 70 per cent more casualties there than on other fronts. Climatic conditions made combat yet more arduous: rain, snow and avalanches created enormous difficulties and fighting efficiency at altitudes which exceeded 2,000 metres was lowered by the effects of climbing, reduced atmospheric pressure and lower night-time temperatures, which fell to −32 C in the Trentino. Transporting food and ammunition up to the front line and bringing back the wounded in areas with few or no roads taxed even Italian ingenuity.[12]

The Italian armies could make little or no headway against the combination of the enemy's strength, shortages of ammunition and heavy artillery and the obstacles of nature, and in the eleven battles fought on the Isonzo between May 1915 and September 1917 they suffered a series of bloody rebuffs. To maintain the necessary offensive spirit in these circumstances, Cadorna acted on the brutally simple assumption that only the most severe disciplinary measures could keep morale from crumbling. In the words of a contemporary observer posted to his headquarters staff, refusing to confront the need to change his operational methods, he sacked generals and shot soldiers.[13]

The war-time expansion of the army required a parallel expansion of the officer corps, and 160,191 new commissions were awarded between 1915 and 1918. The result of this policy was that a number of company and battalion commanders were unequal to their tasks, as were many staff officers, especially those with liaison functions.[14] Inadequate performance at more elevated levels was punished by dismissal: in little more than two years, Cadorna sacked 217 generals, 255 colonels and 337 lieutenant-colonels.[15] The general effect of this policy was to make front line commanders feel that they stood between two fires, and that the one at their rear was the more dangerous. Army commanders imitated Cadorna, sacking or threatening corps commanders, and their staff officers followed suit. General Capello, commanding II Army, terrorised General Vanzo (XXVII corps) by telephone, and Capello's chief of staff did likewise to Vanzo's chief of staff. Vanzo reportedly often left the phone weeping and in turn began to threaten to shoot his brigadiers.[16] In these circumstances it is perhaps remarkable that so many divisional and brigade commanders were able to display serenity and affection when they visited their troops.[17]

In his engaging memoirs of the First World War, Paolo Monelli recorded just such an incident:

> Bonan, D'Incà's batman, is strolling along the road from Primolano to Feltre, with a little wine in his legs and a great longing for the family he is going to see again after so many months of war. What is that down there at the end of the road? A glittering motor, waiting. The mere notion of getting a ride in it would be mad. That is what generals ride in, majors, brass hats, those who send the yellow envelopes, after which come the alarms and orders to stand by. But close to it there is an old soldier, with a long white moustache like Pupo's, who is a driver. But Pupo has a little beard and short moustache, while this old soldier has only two long snow-white moustaches. He is standing still and looking at the motor. A patronising gaiety darts across the thoughts of the Alpino, who staggers a little as he comes along. So old as he is, they have taken him too to be a soldier! We'll ask him if he'll take a drop of wine with me, the old boy.
> Bonan has come up to the old soldier, and claps him on the shoulder. 'So they've got thee too, old 'un, in the army?'
> But his eye travels down to the old man's sleeve, and click! the terrified Alpino stiffens hastily to attention, with his fingers rigid at his hat and two eyes full of fear: a general, b— it; and now amid the fumes of wine and fear he recognises him, for he was his colonel in the 7th, when he was a recruit, many years ago. General Etna.
> 'Now he'll tick me off.'
> And the general smiles, and gives him a cigar: and then, since the puncture is mended and they can go on again, Bonan is made to get in, and there he sits puffing out his chest, triumphant, bursting with pride, coming back to the town beside the driver, his half-yard of cigar slanting from his mouth.[18]

The maintenance of discipline among the troops was a central and enduring concern for Cadorna. In consequence, and like its officers, the rank and file of the army had to endure a régime of unremitting harshness. Of the 5,200,000 men mobilised for military service between 1915 and 1918, 870,000 faced charges for military crimes. Of this total, absentees who had emigrated accounted for 370,000 cases and a further 61,927 were civilians, mostly charged with crimes committed in war zones. The 'net' figure of 330,000 charged with military crimes therefore represents 6·4 per cent of the mobilised army. Approximately one soldier in seventeen faced disciplinary charge, of whom some 61 per cent were found guilty.[19]

Cadorna's main instruments for exercising disciplinary control were the decree of 28 July 1915, which made punishable even the most general expressions against the war, and which made local magistrates the absolute arbiters in interpreting the meaning of the terms 'denigration' and 'public order', and the military penal code. The code in force in May 1915 was that of 28 November 1869, which in effect reproduced the substance of the Sardinian military penal code of 28 June 1840. Compiled to regulate an army entirely different in size, composition and function from that to which it was now applied, it contained a catch-all clause for desertion which prescribed the death penalty for actions 'in the presence' as well as 'in the face' of the enemy. Another article made the abandonment of one's post 'in the presence of the enemy' punishable by death or imprisonment. All these terms, but particularly the latter, were open to varying interpretation.[20]

Statistically, the most common crime committed in the war-time army was desertion: 189,425 soldiers were tried for the offence and 101,665 were found guilty (62.6%). Penalties differed according to whether the accused went over to the enemy, deserted 'in the face of the enemy' or deserted behind the front. The vast majority of cases – approximately 92,500 – involved 'internal desertion'; those found guilty were sentenced to terms of between three and fifteen years. Although they fell within the legal definition of the term, it is by no means certain that these were all cases of intentional desertion. Even when the front was stable, difficulties with transportation when returning from leave could – and did – result in 'inadvertent desertion'. Authority recognised this, but only to a limited and differential degree: officers were given fifteen days to report to any military authority, while their men had five days' grace. The distribution of guilty findings across the three and a half years of war clearly reveals the crisis in 1917–18 as a consequence of Caporetto:

TABLE 1: DESERTION

Year 1 (June 1915–May 1916)	10,000 guilty findings
Year 2 (June 1916–May 1917)	28,000 guilty findings
Year 3 (June 1917–May 1918)	55,000 guilty findings
Year 4 (June–October 1918)	8,500 guilty findings

[Taken from Forcella and Monticone, *Plotoni d'esecuzione*]

The next most frequent crime was indiscipline, for which 31,000 men were tried and 24,500 found guilty. This was followed by self-mutilation, for which 15,000 were tried and 10,000 found guilty. Judges could, if they chose, interpret self-mutilation as an act contrary to the duty to offer resistance to the enemy; if done in the trenches and therefore in the face of the enemy this was cowardice, for which the penalty under article 92 of the military penal code was death. Fourth in the list came surrender, for which 8,500 were tried and 5,300 convicted. The fact that over 4,000 of those convictions came in the first two years of the war gives some indication of the relative state of troop morale before and after the defeat at Caporetto. In all, 4,028 men were condemned to death by the courts, approximately

2 per cent of the total number of those accused who were adjudged guilty, of whom approximately 750 were shot.[21]

Military executions put the troops who were called on to carry them out under intense moral and psychological pressure. They also generated a combination of disdain and contempt for the higher ranks who ordered them as Monelli's account of one such event demonstrates:

> The firing party – pain and horror on all faces – breaks its ranks and comes back slowly. All day long there is a lot of talking in low voices in the huts and great dismay all through the battalion . . .
>
> Only the man who has come alive out of the crushing-mill of battle, only the man who has crawled forward to the attack and gone white with horror under the bombardment, and prayed for death in the night of battle, oppressed by cold and hunger – only he would be a competent judge; and perhaps he too would pronounce sentence of death, with the knowledge of what it means. But not those men down there, whited sepulchres with temporary rank, nicely shaved, with clean sheets and their war a memory of school manuals and an edition of the penal code annotated far from the agony of the front line.[22]

Even a draconian legal code such as this did not offer Cadorna enough certainty that cases of indiscipline were being swiftly and condignly punished and during 1916 he tightened the disciplinary ratchet. On 22 March, during the fifth battle of the Isonzo, he sent out a circular censuring the military tribunals for the mildness of their sentences. When the Austrian army launched the *Strafexpedition* in the Trentino on 15 May 1916, the initial reaction of some Italian units was surprise and panic. Cadorna wrote to the front commander, General Lequio, complaining that important positions had been ceded to the enemy with little or no resistance. 'Y[our] E[xcellency] should take the most energetic and severe measures,' he suggested; 'if necessary, shoot at once and without trial those guilty of such enormous scandals, no matter what their rank.'[23] The first of five known cases of killing by lottery (two of which were specifically decimation) followed almost immediately: a lieutenant, three sergeants and eight men were selected by lot from a company which had broken under unexpected attack and shot. Summary executions were to be a feature of the aftermath of Caporetto, but the practice was already well-established by October 1917.

Continued stalemate on the Isonzo strengthened Cadorna's innate conviction that the roots of weak military morale went deep into Italian society itself. In a circular issued on 4 January 1917 he claimed, on the basis of the appearance of common ideas and phrases in censored letters and of the number of soldiers' letters to parliamentary deputies written in different hands from their signatures, that a widespread covert conspiracy existed within the army, supposedly fuelled by left-wing and anti-militarist propaganda.[24] As he remarked to the newspaper editor Olindo Malagodi, 'the nation was indisciplined and therefore so too was the army.'[25]

Italian domestic politics became markedly more febrile during 1917 and pronouncements against the war by Claudio Treves, a prominent socialist deputy, in July and by Pope Benedict XV in August, and strikes in Turin during the latter month, nourished Cadorna's prejudices. However, in attributing the evident symptoms of tiredness and discouragement in the army to defeatist internal propaganda, he was looking to the wrong source. The soldiers were becoming increasingly disillusioned with the official doctrine that the artillery would conquer ground and leave the infantry merely to mop up, which – as they knew all too well – simply did not correspond to reality.[26] Disregarding such considerations, Cadorna promulgated new disciplinary norms, but desertion rates increased none the less: the commission of enquiry into Caporetto reported that 2,137 men had deserted in April 1917 and 5,471 had deserted in August.[27]

Acting on Cadorna's suspicions, the *Carabinieri* conducted enquiries which resulted in 43 accused being brought to trial but revealed no evidence of the kind of conspiracy which was flowering in the mind of the commander-in-chief.[28] Putting the blame firmly where it did not belong, Cadorna wrote four letters of complaint to the prime minister between 6 June and 18 August 1917, castigating the government for allowing strikes, demonstrations and open references to peace negotiations to sap the morale of the army. France, at least, seemed to have found the solution to the problem. General Garrucio, the head of Cadorna's intelligence service, believed the French army to be much sounder after April 1917 as a result of mass executions carried out by the Senegalese.[29]

Serious mutinies broke out in Ravenna brigade in March 1917 and the Catanzaro brigade in July 1917 as spontaneous reactions to the strategy of attrition and the harshness of military discipline. Reports began to reach headquarters that soldiers were advancing into the attack weeping.[30] Then, on 17 August, Cadorna began the eleventh and last battle of the Isonzo. Although the army responded once more to the call, the losses it suffered now mounted to what in retrospect can be seen to have been a critical level: Italian casualties sustained in the main engagement, the battle of Bainsizza, were 25 per cent heavier than those suffered by the French in Nivelle's offensive on the Aisne in April. The army was fast approaching the end of its tether and when, on 24 October, it was struck by combined German and Austro-Hungarian forces in a hurricane offensive, it temporarily collapsed.

The attack at Caporetto was by no means unexpected: by late September, II Army intelligence indicated that it would be of considerable dimensions. Front line units were alerted to the likely use of gas and warned on the afternoon of 23rd October that the enemy bombardment would start at 2.00 a.m. the following morning.[31] Foreseeing neither its full extent nor its nature, Cadorna laid his plans for partial counter-offensives, and on the day of the attack he awaited the enemy with a confidence which was boosted by bad weather and a falling barometer.[32] In the sudden and widespread collapse and retreat which followed, and which finally came to a halt on the river Piave on 9 November, the army lost 40,000 killed or wounded, 280,000 taken prisoner and 350,000 deserters or stragglers.

The sudden defeat and temporary rout of the Italian armies generated a plethora of explanations and kindled a debate which is far from over.[33] Cadorna's immediate reaction was to believe that the army was failing because of the blows it had suffered from its domestic enemies.[34] Next, on 28 October, he issued a communiqué blaming elements of Capello's II Army for cowardice in retreating without fighting or ignominiously surrendering without fighting. By 3 November he had come to conceive of the defeat as 'a kind of military strike' caused by a combination of anti-militarism, social indiscipline and defeatism in the country at large and manifested in betrayal at the front – a view from which he never departed.[35]

In the hurly-burly of retreat after Caporetto, order and discipline not unnaturally broke down. Curzio Malaparte claimed to have witnessed troops triumphantly carrying naked prostitutes from the military brothels and the occasional corpulent officer as in a bacchanalia.[36] Less spectacularly, many eyewitnesses reported a sense of enormous liberation among those fleeing from the front. During the retreat there was resort to the brutal and obtuse notions of discipline which Cadorna had long been propounding. General Andrea Graziani, an infamous disciplinarian who went on inspection tours attended by a truck containing a personal execution detail, had thirty-four men shot during November 1917.[37] Summary executions seem, however, to have been few in number: official sources give a total of 141 such executions during the course of the war.

In trying to halt the collapse, the authorities made considerable use of the penal code, interpreting it harshly. Examples of their ferocity are legion. During the retreat an officer cadet from the Alpini remarked 'I am pleased that they have broken the lines. With luck, they might have got to Milan and then it would be finished for everyone.' He was reported and shot.[38] Nor, initially, were the authorities prepared to make any allowances for the extraordinary confusion and disruption which marked the army's retreat to the Piave. On 2 November an order was issued requiring soldiers who had become separated from their units to report to military authority within five days or be shot in the back as deserters. On this occasion sanity prevailed, and the date was first deferred to 18 November and then until 29 December. At the same time, though, strong penalties were introduced for anyone having assisted a deserter.

On 10 November 1917, an outnumbered force of 33 Italian divisions and 3,800 guns faced the first of a series of attacks by Austro-German forces amounting to 50 divisions and 4,500 guns. By the time that Allied forces entered the line in December, a stubborn Italian resistance had both held off the attacks and demonstrated that morale in the army was actually much stronger than Cadorna had feared. Fighting now to defend Italy from national defeat, and often lacking even fire support as a result of the loss of artillery and shortages of ammunition, the infantry was sometimes reduced to using bayonets, rocks and even their bare hands. The successful 'Three Mountains' offensive of 27–31 January 1918, although limited in extent, showed quite clearly that, despite Caporetto, morale had not broken and that the Italian army had not lost its ability to take the offensive.[39]

Early in November 1917, the king replaced Cadorna, appointing General Armando Diaz as the new commander-in-chief.[40] Diaz was assigned two deputies: General Gaetano Giardino took responsibility for strategy and liaison with the government, and General Pietro Badoglio set about rebuilding army morale. Rapid steps were taken to ease both the lot and the mind of the common soldier. In November 1917 a new ministry for soldiers and war pensioners was created, and in the following month the government introduced non-contributory insurance policies, payable on death, for NCOs and Privates. Rations were improved and a second annual period of 10 days' leave was added to the 15 days already allowed. Rest periods no longer entailed new forms of duress but now included small shows, lectures and talks by veteran combatants – who were doubtless carefully selected. All combatants were given the right to vote. Greater attention was also paid to propaganda and the war was now portrayed as being fought for the liberty of peoples and for a better future. Finally, more care was given to the award of medals and decorations.[41]

Steps were also taken to improve the collective morale of the army by altering organisational practices. Diaz believed that Caporetto had been the consequence of a general demoralization which was in turn caused by frequent changes in the composition of corps so that they lacked cohesion.[42] Accordingly, corps and divisions were given fixed components. Cadorna's practice of dismissing senior officers with unsettling frequency was discontinued, although in the twelve months between his departure and the end of the war a further 176 officers were sacked. Greater consideration was also given to maintaining the morale of new troops. Instead of being incorporated willy-nilly into existing units as drafts, incoming recruits of the class of 1899 were formed into separate regiments to avoid intermingling them with tried and tired troops, with beneficial results.[43]

The plan devised by Diaz and Badoglio for reviving the army gave priority to strengthening the mass of the infantry by improving their weapons, training and conditions. In these circumstances it became necessary to reconsider the organisation and role of what were perhaps the best known and certainly the most publicised Italian units – the *Arditi*.[44] Modelled on the Austro-Hungarian *Sturmtruppen*, and on the lessons drawn from the battle of the Somme by the Germans as to the need for special training for assault troops, the *Arditi* officially came into being on 29 July 1917. Armed with special weapons which included not merely the celebrated dagger and Thevenot grenade but also machine-guns, machine pistols and 65mm guns, the *Arditi* enjoyed better food and quarters than the rest of the army, a special uniform, extra pay, less formal discipline and more leave. Contrary to later legends which they themselves liked to foster, their high morale, to which these privileges contributed, was not due to their being a wholly volunteer force (which they were not) nor to the fact that they welcomed convicted criminals into their ranks: men convicted of civil crimes were excluded, although those guilty of military crimes whose punishments had been deferred for the duration of the war could join, and were encouraged to do so.

The *Arditi* were perceived not simply as a functionally specialised élite but as models for a new breed of soldier. By forcing men to adapt to suffering and develop the capacity to sustain a form of war requiring passive obedience, trench warfare, it was believed, had reduced soldiers to supine subservience.[45] The assault detachments, imbued with the desire to test themselves against ever greater dangers and marching off to battle with 'explosions of barbaric joy', displayed an individualism and an enthusiasm which were far removed from the resignation with which the peasant soldier went about his duties. In the aftermath of Caporetto, the high command initially decided that it could make the best use of such troops by spreading them broadly *pour encourager les autres*: accordingly, in April 1918 *Arditi* detachments were allotted to each individual army corps. Then, as a consequence of the last Austrian attack in June, they were gathered together to form two assault divisions.

Although much-publicised by the High Command – and themselves – the *Arditi* did not achieve the same kind of infiltration as the German *Stosstruppen* and failed to modify the somewhat clumsy and mechanical nature of Italian attacks in the last months of the war. They may also have presented the wrong kind of model through which to raise the general morale: their special treatment and their cruelty to prisoners made them unpopular in the army at large.[46] One of the assault divisions played a limited part in the battle of Vittorio Veneto, but in general the *Arditi* made no great impact in the latter stages of the war, though far-sighted men felt some anxieties about the role they might play in a post-war Italy – with considerable justification.

During spring 1918 army morale gradually improved.[47] The consequent recovery in military efficiency, which was demonstrated in June when the Austrian offensive was swiftly brought to a halt, was the result of a combination of factors, many of which indirectly but powerfully reinforced the measure the new commander-in-chief had taken to improve the soldier's lot. In addition to relaxing the iron grip of disciplinary norms on the army,

Diaz modernised its tactical doctrine in the light of experience in recent battles.[48] On the home front, the government mobilised genuine enthusiasm for the war with promises of land for peasants, jobs for the workers and education for veterans when it was won. And after a massive feat of reorganisation, Italian industry was at last able to supply the army with sufficient quantities of heavy artillery and ammunition, as well as producing large numbers of aeroplanes and automobiles.[49] Finally, Diaz cautiously husbanded his military strength, rejecting Allied pleas for action to relieve pressure on the Western front in June and July 1918. In late October, regarding the enemy as sufficiently weakened, Diaz launched an improvised attack on Monte Grappa and then a general assault against a quavering Austro-Hungarian line which quickly crumbled. A much celebrated victory, Vittorio Veneto was an Austrian Caporetto but one from which the dual monarchy would not recover.

In 1915, national unity became a central priority for Italy, as it did for every major combatant. Without it, the war simply could not be won. Yet Italy, though legally united for over half a century, was in almost every other respect still a divided society. Ever since Unification these divisions had caused great anxiety in generals and politicians alike. When he became commander-in-chief, Cadorna faced the task of tempering that society to withstand the stresses of a lengthy war of attrition. He brought to his task the prejudices of generations of Italian generals who never really trusted a national army, who had often not trusted one another, and who were well aware that Italy's politicians – remembering the defeats of 1849, 1866 and 1896 – did not put much faith in them or in their men. The outcome was a disciplinary system of considerable severity which was designed to maintain morale by force but which could not prevent a dissolution of the front following military defeat in October 1917. Italy's recovery from that defeat suggests the existence of reserves of national morale of which Cadorna was never aware.

Notes

1   Olindo Malagodi [ed. Brunello Vigezzi], *Conversazioni della Guerra* (Milan-Naples: Ricciardi, 1960), Vol. 1, p.56 (9 May 1915).
2   For general studies of the Italian army before 1915, see: John Whittam, *The Politics of the Italian Army* (London: Croom Helm, 1977); John Gooch, *Army, State and Society in Italy, 1870–1915* (London, Macmillan, 1989).
3   Piero Del Negro, *Esercito, stato, società* (Bologna: Capelli, 1979), p.227.
4   Nichola Labanca, 'I programmi dell'educazione morale del soldato. Per uno studio sulla pedogogia militare nell'Italia liberale' in *Esercito e città dall'Unita agli anni trenta* (Convegno nazionale di studio: Bologna, 1989) pp.521–536.
5   Gioacchino Volpe, 'Esercito e popolo, autorità e paese', in Mario Isnenghi, ed., *La prima guerra mondiale* (Bologna: Zanichelli, 1977), pp.126–128.
6   Amadeo Tosti, *Storia dell'esercito italiano* (1861–1936) (Milan: Istituto per gli studi di politica internazionale, 1942), pp.168–71. In July 1914, Italy had 300 Vickers machine-guns; by May 1915 she possessed only 618.

7   Del Negro, op.cit., pp.230–1.

8   Luigi Cadorna to Ninetta Cadorna, 19 August 1915. Quo. Luigi Cadorna, ed., *Lettere famigliari* (Verona: Mondadori, 1967), p.123. See also Gianni Rocca, *Cardorna* (Milan: Le Scie, 1985).

9   Mario Isnenghi, *I vinti di Caporetto nella letteratura di guerra* (Vicenza: Marsilio, 1967), p.30.

10 Giorgio Rochat. 'Gli storici italiani e la grande guerra: ora i miti crollano', in Isnenghi, *La prima guerra mondiale* op.cit., p.107.

11 Cadorna to Carla Cadorna, 17 December 1915. Quo. *Lettere famigliari* op.cit., p.135.

12 J.E. Edmonds and H.R. Davies, *Military Operations: Italy 1915–1919* (London: H.M.S.O., 1949), pp. 11, 30–1; Ministero della Guerra, *L'Esercito italiano nella grande guerra (1915–1918)* Vol. III Tomo 1 (Rome: 1931), pp.289–90, 325–6.

13 Angelo Gatti [ed. Alberto Monticone], *Caporetto. Dal diario di guerra inedito (maggio-dicembre 1917)* (Bologna: Il Mulino, 1964), p.146 (27 June 1917).

14 Filippo Stefani, *La Storia della dottrina e degli ordinamenti dell'esercito italiano* Vol. I (Rome: Ufficio storico dello Stato maggiore dell'esercito, 1984), pp.679–80.

15 C. De Biase, *Aquila d'oro-Storia dello Stato Maggiore Italiano (1861–1945)* (Milan: Edizioni del Borghese, 1969), p.311.

16 Gatti, *op.cit.*, pp.212–3 (2 September 1917). For an account of Cadorna's 'telephone torpedoes' and their effects, see Tito A. Spagnol, *Memoriette marziali e veneree* (Vicenza: Mario Spagnol, 1970), p.41.

17 For examples, see *Lucangelo Bracci, Testasecca nel ricordo degli amici e nel suo diario di guerra* (Rome: Edizione Colombo, 1957), pp.133–4, 135, 153 (12 & 16 August, 15 September 1917).

18 Paolo Monelli, *Toes Up: A chronicle of gay and doleful adventures, of Alpini and mules and wine* (London: Duckworth 1930), pp.35–6. See also *ibid*, pp.102–3.

19 Enzo Forcella and Alberto Monticone, *Plotone d'esecuzione: I processi della prima guerra mondiale* (Bari: Laterza, 1968), pp. 433–436. A further 100,000 absentees had not gone abroad.

20 *ibid*, pp.417 et seq.

21 *ibid.*, pp.441–2.

22 Monelli, op.cit. pp. 150–151.

23 Cadorna to Lequio, 26 May 1916. Quo. *ibid.*, p.448 fn. 45. A useful, if somewhat dated, narrative account of the *Straffexpedition* can be found in Pompilio Schiarini, *L'offensiva austriaca nel Trentino* (Rome: Libreria del littorio, 1929).

24 Isnenghi, *I vinti di Caporetto, op.cit.*, pp. 37, 108.

25 Malagodi, *op.cit.*, Vol. I, p.106 (23 January 1917).

26 Piero Pieri and Giorgio Rohat, *Badoglio* (Turin: U.T.E.T., 1974), p.207–8.

27 Isnenghi, *I vinti di Caporetto, op.cit.*, p.40.

28 The belief that, by 1917, pacifist propaganda was everywhere and was affecting the discipline of the rank and file persisted in the official mind nevertheless: see Ministero della guerra, *L'esercito italiano nella grande guerra*, op.cit., Vol. IV, Tomo 2, p.5.

29 Gatti, *op.cit.*, p.161 (7 August 1917).

30   *ibid*, p.61 (2 June 1917).

31   Carlo Emilio Gadda, *Taccuini di Caporetto: Diario di guerra e di prigonia (Ottobre 1917-Aprile 1918)* (Milan: Garzanti, 1991), pp.70, 73.

32   Cadorna to Carla Cadorna, 24 October 1917. *Lettere famigliari, op.cit.*, p.227. Cadorna expected 10–15 Austrian and German divisions to attack, taking advantage of surprise and gas.

33   See especially Giorgio Rochat, *L'Italia nella prima guerra mondiale* (Milan: Feltrinelli, 1976), *passim*; Isnenghi, *I Vinti di Caporetto, op.cit.*

34   Telegram, Cadorna to Boselli, 17 October 1917. Quo. Pieri and Rochat, *op.cit.*, pp. 403–4.

35   For a revealing summary of Cadorna's views shortly after the battle, see Malagodi, *op.cit.*, pp. 207–225 (23 November 1917). The legend of betrayals, understandings with the enemy and of a deliberate wish to end the war regardless of who won is demolished in Piero Pieri, 'La leggenda di Caporetto', *Il Ponte* Vol. VIII (1951), pp.1443–56, 1581–92.

36   Isnenghi, *I vinti di Caporetto, op.cit.*, p.68.

37   Forcella and Monticone, *op.cit.*, p.445, fn. 31.

38   *ibid.*, p.ix.

39   See Brian R. Sullivan, 'Caporetto: Recovery and Consequences, October 1917-October 1922', in George J. Andreopoulos and Harold E. Selesky, *The Aftermath of Defeat: Societies, Armed Forces and the Challenge of Recovery* (New Haven & London: Yale University Press, forthcoming). For a contemporary British view of what Italian troops might be capable of, see Edmonds and Davies, *op.cit.*, p.137.

40   The only study of Diaz available in English is dated and unsatisfactory: Alberto Baldini, *Diaz*, (London: Humphrey Toulmin, 1935).

41   Piero Pieri, *L'Italia nella prima guerra mondiale*, (Turin: Einaudi, 1965), pp.176–80.

42   Malagodi, *op.cit.*, Vol. II p.448 (16 November 1918).

43   Lucio Ceva, *Le forze armate* (Tutin: U.T.E.T., 1981), p.145.

44   For what follows I have drawn on Giorgio Rochat, *Gli arditi della grande guerra: origini, battaglie e miti* (Milan: Fletrinelli, 1981).

45   These were the views of Agnostino Gemelli, a mass psychologist serving at Cadorna's headquarters: ibid., pp.31, 40.

46   Ceva, *op.cit.*, p.145.

47   Wilson Papers. Delmé-Radcliffe to Wilson, 26 May 1918. Imperial War Museum, Wilson 73/1/11/7.

48   Stefani, *op.cit.*, p.162.

49   See Rosario Romeo, *Breve storia della grande industria* (Bologna: Capelli, 1967); Massimo Mazzetti, *L'industria italiana nella grande guerra* (Rome: Ufficio Storico dello Stato Maggiore dell'Esercito, 1979).

Part VII

Medicine and Experience

Chapter 33

Health Systems in Khaki: The British and American Medical Experience

Nick Bosanquet

For health services, the First World War was a forced transition in attitudes, systems and personnel. It was a short, intensive experience which completely changed both the way health services worked and perceptions of their effectiveness. It gave the medical profession in Europe its first taste of success and power. The sheer scale of treatment and the frequency of contact between mass armies and doctors led to a rise in the reputation of medicine in general and the army medical service in particular. In the phrase of a widely sold review published in 1919 it was 'The Triumph of the Doctor'.[1]

The new systems included the use of managed medical research, the extension of surgery through teamwork, wider employment of technology in X-Rays and anaesthetics, along with the use of psychiatry and the rise of dental, optical and rehabilitation services. These innovations were sought compulsively to meet overwhelming and urgent problems. Not much new technology was invented in the war, but the conflict provided a great clinical trial and laboratory in which to refine concepts and practices from the civilian world.

The crises of disease and treatment varied with the progress of the war and the changes in the battle environment, but from day-to-day a key medical task remained, that of sanitation and infection control. For all its wealth and advanced equipment, the American Expeditionary Force had equally to give its attention to the basic reality of prevention and sanitation. Ironically the 'Triumph of the Doctor' was achieved by taking on roles which had always been considered auxiliary or undignified.

Past research on the impact of the First World War on health services has had its main focus on hospital services. Abel-Smith in his general history presented a critical picture: 'The price of these unco-ordinated policies was paid by the civilians who lost half their supply of doctors and roughly a third of their already inadequate stock of hospital beds. Nevertheless no one had suffered as much as the soldiers at the front – many of them volunteers'.[2] More recently Rosemary Stevens has charted the impact of the war on the power of the teaching hospitals in the US: 'Superintendents and clinicians of the base hospitals returned as heroes, bringing their experienced staff, their new knowledge, and their War stories back home with them to rejuvenate teaching hospitals across the country – and to dominate the post-war hospital scene.'[3]

The British medical services entered the war soon after a period of reorganisation with lessons drawn from the British medical disaster in South Africa and the Japanese medical triumph in the Russo-Japanese War. The 'bible' of command in Field Service Regulations set out the doctrine: 'Every Officer is responsible that all orders affecting the health of an army are rigidly carried out by the troops under his command. Neglect of sanitary precautions inevitably results in great loss of life and efficiency'.[4] The Regulations went on to set out key tasks for the medical services:

> The personnel of the medical services of the forces in the field has four distinct functions; the preservation of the health of the troops: the professional treatment and care of the sick and the wounded: the replenishing of medical and surgical equipment: and the collection and evacuation of sick and wounded from the theatre of operations. All these functions are of equal importance because no one of them can be performed efficiently without the others.[5]

These signposts may have helped in pointing towards a diversified effort covering all areas of medical activity, but the tasks had to be discharged through a series of crises most of which were unexpected. However useful as long term guides to action, these doctrines did not lead to effective services on the ground at the start. As the official history was later to admit 'The organisation of the British army medical services was faulty at the beginning of the Great War'.[6] Despite this the leadership of the RAMC under Sir Alfred Keogh, Sir Arthur Sloggett and Sir W.G. Macpherson showed great drive and flair in meeting problems, especially in meeting the 'invisible enemy' of microbes. In the first few weeks, numbers in the RAMC expanded rapidly with a key contribution from the territorial forces rejected by Kitchener for other services.

The first few months of the war were dominated by the crises of mobilisation and of movement after the retreat from Mons. The arrival of troops from Canada in the UK in 1914 was one source of new problems with a virulent outbreak of cerebro-spinal meningitis as young men from isolated farm backgrounds met new sources of infection. There were new challenges in setting standards of mass recruitment. There was also the threat of typhoid which was dealt with through inoculation. The Army Council had considered and rejected compulsory inoculation in 1912 so that the

BEF arrived in France with inadequate levels of immunisation. Contact with the French army, which suffered 60,000 cases of typhoid in the first six months of the war, led to urgent efforts to increase inoculation so that by early 1915, 90–92 per cent of the BEF had been immunised.

The retreat from Mons meant there was little chance of using the inadequate ambulance services and many wounded had to be left behind. Many were left without medical attention for hours or even days. There was some improvement in the later stages of the retreat, when it became possible to evacuate some of the wounded to Paris using American and French volunteers. The shift of clearing hospitals to the Loire and shortage of motorised ambulances made for persisting problems in evacuation during and after the retreat. Many patients were treated in a converted sugar shed on the quay at Boulogne. One nursing sister wrote: 'What an indescribable scene! In the first huge shed there were hundreds of wounded walking cases: as long as a man could crawl he *had* to be a walking case. All were caked with mud, in torn clothes, hardly any caps, and with bloodstained bandages on hands, arms and legs. Many were lying asleep in the straw that had been left in the hastily cleared sheds, looking weary to death; others were sitting on empty boxes or barrels, eating the contents of a tin of "maconochie" with the help of a clasp knife.'[7] Stretcher cases were put behind temporary partitions: 'The beds as soon as they arrived were occupied by badly wounded men who had to be put into them as they were, clothes and all, until time could be found to cut off the clothing, wash the patient and dress his wounds.'

The coming of trench warfare led to new threats. The heavily manured ground led to great danger of tetanus and of gas gangrene infection. Tetanus was eliminated by giving an immediate anti-tetanic injection to wounded men: the problem of gas gangrene was harder to resolve. By 1915 an international research programme led by the French-American surgeon Alexis Carrel and the British chemist, Dakin, had developed an effective answer through continuous irrigation of wounds with a mild antiseptic fluid, 'Dakin's solution', made up of chloride of lime (chlorine) together with boric acid. By April 1915 the new approaches to battle-field wound healing were already generating a sense of achievement among an international group of doctors and scientists. George Crile, the specialist in treating surgical shock from the Cleveland Institute, recorded in his memoirs:

At eight I gave a dinner for eighteen at the Ritz. It was an extraordinary gathering of talent. Among the guests were Dr Helm, a facile and graceful French writer – in French medical literature what Osler is in English; Professor Weinberg, the head of the bacteriology laboratories of the Pasteur Institute; Professor Dakin, the biochemist of the Rockefeller Institute who has scarcely a rival; Alexis Carrel who along surgical and biological lines had no living superior; Professor Tuffier of brilliant intellect, Bourbon ancestry, and wealth, the foremost French surgeon; Berkeley Moynihan easily the first surgeon of the British Empire; and Sir Almroth Wright who stands alone in preventive medicine. It was Wright's genius more than that of any other that was sustaining the health of the twelve to fifteen million troops on the battlefields of Europe.[8]

Once the immediate crisis of 1914 was over, the RAMC began to develop a distinctive approach to the problems of siege warfare in the trenches. Its duties were to provide treatment for wounded soldiers, to prevent the spread of disease, and to restore as many wounded men as possible to health. The medical managers were willing to seek new solutions to the new problems thrown up by trench warfare and by treatment of wounds in fit youth. They found little in pre-war medicine to help them. 'At the beginning of the war European medicine was static. It was felt that old methods had been largely worked out. The study of disease in its advanced stages – which was the only stage of disease seen in great hospitals, and so the only stage of disease upon which detailed and careful study was possible – had yielded only meagre results'.[9]

Keogh had played an important role in recruiting to the international research effort through contacts with leading hospital consultants who served as experts on the Western Front. But most of the work of the RAMC was concerned with sanitation and the maintenance of health and day to day morale. During the first period of trench warfare, the regimental medical officer (RMO) began his daily service in sick parade, and routines were established for purifying water with chlorine, fumigating clothes and ensuring regular bathing during rotation out of the line. It was the RMO who had to solve the threatening problem of trench foot, a kind of massive chilblain arising from restriction of circulation in cold and damp. Regular change of socks, washing of feet and improvement of boots meant that by the second winter of the war trench feet were rare. Laundry and bathing were assisted by the development of special bathing centres using old brewery vats and labour from French civilians. One later verdict was that 'The good health of armies in the western theatre of conflict was a very remarkable feature of the first nine months of war. This was the more surprising because the number of dead bodies befouling the fields of France and Flanders was enormous. In the inundated area of the Yser alone some 120,000 corpses lay submerged.'[10] RAMC and local improvisation also devised respirators for gas attacks so that during the whole of the war only some 6000 deaths on the Western Front resulted from gas, a commendable result, even if one also achieved by other armies. The introduction of the steel helmet from the French army in 1915 was also a success. There was less success however, either for the RAMC or the international research team, in dealing with the novel problem of shell shock. Crile recorded an important discussion on shell shock and war neurasthenia, which had become an overwhelming problem: 'During quiet periods at the front, three-to-one of the cases that were admitted were neurasthenia. During periods of battle the ratio was increased to eight-to-one . . . Only rest, change of scene, rationalisation and in some cases operation, I was convinced would cure it.'[11] In the first stages of the war the term 'shell shock' was applied to physical casualties such as men who were found dead even though apparently unharmed. Later the term came to apply to the longer term effects on mental stability of prolonged exposure to shell fire.

By mid 1915 the American medical contribution on the Western Front was reduced as some of the principals returned to the USA. However the team led by Wright remained with mobile laboratories and a watching brief on any first signs of outbreaks of infectious disease: 'The Military Hospital became, therefore, much more than a mere clearing house for the injured. It became a kind of detective bureau for the discovery of the first indications of epidemic disease'.[12] Before the battle of Loos, the offensives of 1915 were relatively small and short and many casualties were evacuated to the UK. Expansion of armies in 1916 and the prolonged offensive on the Somme were to bring new challenges.

In 1916 the focus of effort shifted to the development of a hospital system in France and battlefield evacuation which could treat many thousands of wounded men a week: in the first 24 hours of the Somme battle 797 officers and 13,603 other ranks were brought to casualty clearing stations from the Fourth Army area alone.[13] This was well in excess of the 9,500 places available. The system faced fairly severe stresses and was only saved by using additional ambulance trains, barges and road convoys so that 14,930 wounded were evacuated from the Fourth Army Area on 2 July.

The RAMC system was based on treatment of the wounded at a Regimental Aid Post with the Regimental Medical Officer and orderlies close to the front line. They were carried by stretcher bearers to Advanced Dressing Stations 500–2000 yards behind the front line: there would then be road transport to the Casualty Clearing Stations, followed by rail transport to the Stationary Base Hospitals and evacuation to the U.K. One variable across the war was in the role of the casualty clearing station. This had originally been called a 'casualty clearing hospital' in the pre-war scheme, but the name was changed to casualty clearing station in early 1915 so as not to leave any doubt about its limited function. Pressure from below changed the function once again in the course of 1916, even though the new name remained:

In order to provide for the additional work at the casualty clearing stations, an enormous amount of equipment was added not only for medical and surgical purposes, but also in order to provide well equipped beds and hospital comforts for the more seriously wounded, and better shelter and accommodation. Officers commanding casualty clearing stations indented very extensively on ordnance stores for additional equipment.[14]

Staff faced a massive challenge in the size and acute nature of the wounds caused by shellfire, which were usually far larger and more complex than those caused by rifle fire.

The next year, 1917, saw further development of the casualty clearing stations with the introduction of 100 fully equipped hospital beds at each of the thirteen stations in Flanders prepared for the 1917 offensive. Four of these units had been stationed near Poperinghe at Remy siding since 1915. Each station was allocated three extra surgical teams and special experts such as the American neuro-surgeon, Harvey Cushing, who recorded how they were now getting used to 6–8 major operations a day compared with the normal ratio of one in peace time.[15] The medical complex around Ypres benefited from a growing contribution from nursing sisters in key roles in providing and organising care as well as providing new services as nurse anaesthetists and in other technical roles. Between 31 July and 16 November 61,400 surgical operations were carried out in these casualty clearing stations involving intensive use of anaesthetics and X-Ray and the first attempts at blood transfusion. 1917 also saw a fundamental change in policy, facilitated by the development of new hospitals in the Boulogne area, and treating the great majority of wounded men in France. This was made possible by an investment in 70,000 beds and 10,000 places in rehabilitation centres.

The Flanders campaigns of 1917 represented the high point of medical concentration with the network of casualty clearing stations close to the front lines linked by effective transport systems to the base areas. Long distance shell fire meant that the siting of some of the stations had to be changed several times. Even so there was still conflict between doctors and General Sir Hubert Gough, Army Commander in the Fifth Army area:

> Colonel Soltau, the consulting physician of the Northern Armies, it may be noted, had also made an emphatic protest to the DMS against retaining serious chest injuries in the forward position. The surgeons on duty at Brandhoek had also reported that the noise of artillery fire in the vicinity had a bad effect on the wounded, and that the locality was not suitable for retaining them under treatment, and the determination of the Army Commander and his DMS to retain casualty clearing stations there must be regarded as strategically unsound from a medical point of view.[16]

The concentration also led to serious problems with bombing and shelling, and the only time of the war in which there were serious questions about breaches of the Geneva Convention. There was a contrast however between the increasing sophistication in treatment and technology and the basic problems of the stretcher bearers in the Flanders mud. The intensity of shellfire changed the battle environment for all soldiers, but it was the stretcher bearers who had to move most in the mud. Their efforts supplied some of the best known images of the war as eight-man parties were required to carry wounded men long distances out of the deep mud.

There was less change in the day to day routines of battalion medical services than in the treatment of casualties behind the line. After problems with dysentery in the Somme brought about by poor sanitation when divisions were rotating rapidly in and out of the line, a new system of permanent sanitary detachments was introduced. While the specialist services played a crucial part during the great offensives, the RMO had a key role in facing the developing problems of long-term siege. The primary care of the RMO was the crucial factor for maintaining manpower during the routines of trench warfare.

The battalion 'performance indicator' was the proportion of a unit's strength reporting sick:

'An empirical figure of 0.3 per cent had been accepted as the permissible limit of inefficiency due to sickness in an army in the field . . . It was remarkable how sensitive was the reaction of this means of indicating the sanitary conditions of units in the field. Divisions on first arriving from home showed a daily admission-rate for sickness much higher than 0.3 per cent of strength, sometimes as high as 1.0 per cent. But when they were taken in hand by administrative medical and sanitary officers and became better acquainted with the necessity of enforcing sanitary measures, the percentage of inefficiency dropped to well below the limit of 0.3 so much so that it was rare to find divisions with a higher rate than 0.3 per cent.'[17]

Captain J.C. Dunn, as an RMO, clearly used this performance indicator with the daily sick parade as a barometer of morale and a test of the RMO's prestige.[18]

By mid 1917 the numbers of RMOs were depleted as a result of enormous courage and consequent heavy casualties during actions. At the time the vastly expanded army had a need for a much larger medical service – so much so that the first appeal of the Foreign Secretary Arthur Balfour on his special mission to the US in April 1917 was for medical manpower. The appeal was answered so that by mid 1918, 1200 American medical officers were serving with the BEF.

The official history records that 'during the critical years of 1917 and 1918 the total number of officers lent to the British forces remained at a high figure and thus contributed in a large measure to the maintenance of the Royal Army Medical Corps services which were so severely tried during these years.'[19]

Captain Dunn reports how in September 1918 'During this hectic time our American M.O. was fully occupied. He showed that day that he had the infantry outlook and had made himself one of the Battalion. He set up his Aid Post well forward'.[20] Chapin's post-war chronicle of American medical officers, *The Lost Legion*, recorded their problems in detecting malingering and their success in generating patient satisfaction: 'The enlisted men always seemed to prefer an American doctor, perhaps because of the novelty, but avowedly because of the latter's ability to cope with the situation at any time and of always standing out for a sick man against the routine and red tape of the Army.'[21]

Like their surviving British colleagues the new medical officers faced problems of lengthening sick parades and new threats from infectious disease. The problems of stress and exhaustion generated shell shock: they also led to soldier's heart, trench nephritis and trench mouth. All these problems were in part due to overstrain and exhaustion. For some the problem was of identifying 'martial misfits': for others such as the RMO Captain Charles McMoran Wilson (later Lord Moran and Churchill's doctor) courage came to be seen as a store: even very brave men could only stand so much.[22]

Trench fever was a new problem of infection under siege conditions. Long research, including a trial involving elderly volunteers who submitted to having four hundred lice crawling over them and biting them, was required to prove that the real cause lay in the scratching-in of louse excreta. Once again the RMO had the main responsibility of improving cleanliness in the trenches.

In the last months of the war a new and major infection problem of influenza was to emerge. Although this caused far fewer deaths among soldiers with their relatively good level of nutrition than among civilians, it could reduce availability of manpower for front line duties. The Armistice did not end the war against the invisible enemy as the army medical services struggled to treat influenza and then stop the spread of infectious disease among civilians in liberated areas of France and Belgium. After the war came new challenges in rehabilitation for the 2.4m individuals left with some continuing disability. For many whose conditions were not stabilised, their entitlement to war pensions remained in doubt well into the 1920s.

At home the RAMC had a major task in selecting recruits through medical examinations. When war was declared the system in existence was geared to receive 50,000 recruits annually. In September 1914 as many as 500,000 men came up for enlistment. Recruiting doctors, many of whom had no experience of the physical requirements for the army, were faced with a situation in which their decisions would be tested relatively soon and stringently in the trenches. Thus we find at the beginning of the war, men being discharged with less than three months service or reservists sent back from the expeditionary force as unfit; the chief disabilities suffered being hernia, defective vision, varicose veins, deficient teeth, middle-ear disease, debility and old age.

To encourage more uniformity in the standards of selection the army medical services gradually developed a standard classification system:[23]

A. – Fit for service at home or abroad.

B. – Temporarily unfit for service abroad.

C. – Fit for service at home only.

D. – Unfit for service at home or abroad.

The RAMC role in medical recruitment led it to expand certain kinds of service which were useful in raising numbers in the A category. The dental service was found to be particularly effective and the issue of spectacles increased. By the end of the war, recruits were being classified as type A when they had a quarter normal sight in one eye, so long as their sight in the other could be brought up to half normal standard by the use of spectacles.

At the end of the war the RAMC and its supporters hastened to record success. The official history of the medical services was well under way by 1924, recording success in sanitation and treatment. Even earlier, in 1919, the triumph of the doctor had been well chronicled:

> Our armies in Flanders and Northern France in the winter of 1917–18, out in open trenches in some of the vilest and 'sickliest' weather troops ever had to face, had less sickness and fewer deaths from pneumonia and all other diseases than soldiers used to have in barracks in time of peace, and far less than the general civil population at home.
>
> Inoculation protected them against typhoid; splendid feeding, with plenty of meat and fat, against pneumonia and consumption; fly campaigns, against dysentery and diarrhoea; shower baths and clean underwear against spotted typhus; and quarantine, against measles, summer diarrhoea, diphtheria and influenza.[24]

In the past the ratio of deaths from disease to deaths in battle had been variable, but could reach five deaths to diseases for every one in battle. The World War saw one death from disease for every fifteen in battle.

The RAMC also developed success indicators in treating battle casualties. The greatest success was in survival of battle casualties admitted to medical units, where 92 per cent recovered. For the Western Front 29 per cent of the two million casualties returned to duty there: many had to be evacuated to the UK. The official history calculated that 82 per cent of the wounded were 'ultimately returned to some form of duty.'[25] However the services did better in ensuring survival than in preventing long-term disability.

THE AMERICAN RESPONSE

The initial American contribution was in surgery, research and advanced technology. The success of the American hospital in Neuilly, Paris, in 1914 was followed by a continuing contribution and the arrival in 1917 of six University hospitals each associated with a leading American teaching centre. Their innovations included the use of blood transfusions, more effective treatment of trauma and shock and the use of nitrous oxide as an anaesthetic. Harvey Cushing was given the task of developing neuro-surgery for the BEF as a whole. In 1917 American surgeons were particularly active in expanding orthopaedics and helping to bring about an expansion from 250 orthopaedic beds in 1914 to 25,000 by the end of the war. These new units were particularly effective in reducing numbers of amputations.

The influence of American surgery remained an important theme. The long-term impact of the war may well have been to raise the influence and confidence of the teaching hospitals: but the main concerns during the actual war period were rather different, concentrating upon sanitation, control of infection and transport. The predominant role of the university hospitals was greater in the period before America fully entered the war. The problems of maintaining health in a mass army proved menacing so that non-battle casualties caused as much stress for the American Expeditionary Force as did battle casualties.

The AEF started the war with a doctrine of the offensive: 'The mobile army is primarily organised for offensive operations against an enemy, and on this account requires the maximum degree of mobility.'[26] The manual for the medical department went on to stress that 'The mobility of an army may be the factor which determines its success or its failure. It is therefore highly important that the army should be relieved as quickly as possible of the encumbrance of its sick and wounded.'[27] This doctrine of mobility combined with the promise of ample resources to produce a massive programme of hospital building in base areas using special ambulance trains to carry the wounded. The early stage of treatment involved carriage from a battalion aid post to a field hospital some five miles behind the front line, which acted as a triage centre. This sorted out those severely wounded for transport by motor ambulance to evacuation hospitals twenty miles behind the front line: 'The field hospitals of the World War were places where only emergency surgery was done, wounds re-dressed and splints re-applied, pain relieved, nourishment given, shock treated and the patient prepared for further progress towards the rear.' The evacuation hospitals were 'much better equipped and larger institutions with women nurses'[28] However, wartime conditions led to some change, especially with the presence of psychiatrists in field hospitals to assess cases of battle neurosis and shell shock.

In practice, shortages of wood and of supply shipments from the US meant that only 70,000 places in base hospitals were finished in time for the Armistice – far short of the target of 200,000 beds. The RAMC official history commented:

> The administrative officers of the American Medical Department had a hard struggle to obtain an organisation capable of handling the ramifications of their medical services and to get information which they considered absolutely essential if their army and their country were to benefit by having a medical personnel in Europe varying from 8.6 per cent to 10 per cent of the total strength with provision for the hospitalisation of their cases on a 15 per cent basis.[29]

In the event, shipping and recruitment difficulties meant that medical department personnel never exceeded 7.65 per cent of the total.

The first crises emerged soon after mobilisation. The War Department, often against medical advice, had selected sites for training camps in the American South and East for year round training. The sheer size of the camps, with as many as 50,000 troops brought together from all areas of the US, led to massive infection problems: their siting in low lying areas brought the threat of malaria and typhoid. Only the use of inoculation and an urgent programme to disinfect and clear swamps prevented a repetition on a larger scale of the disasters of the Spanish American War. The size of the camps may have contributed however to the spread of the first influenza epidemic which began in recruitment camps in New Jersey and New England, since the control of infection and isolation of infected individuals was particularly difficult in such large camps. The passage to Europe produced new problems with infection. The carriage of two million men in fifteen months packed 5,000 to a ship inevitably meant that some men with infection developed it on the voyage and passed it on to others. The influenza epidemics then presented new challenges beginning in the spring and recurring with an even more virulent strain in the autumn. Few troops had the more fatal complication of pneumonia but even hospital care of troops with influenza put severe strain on the availability of beds. On arrival in France the units faced problems in their training areas. For typhoid:

> every training area occupied by the Americans was infected and practically all water supplies contaminated. Rural sanitation was almost unknown. Billets were usually overcrowded, were often in stables and outhouses and were generally in the midst of very unsanitary surroundings. Prostitution was more in evidence than at home and sexual temptations frequent. In the Zone of the Armies conditions were even

worse. Muddy trenches and crowded dug outs, lice, itch and lack of bathing facilities reproduced conditions reminiscent of bad mediaeval times.[30]

The six major US hospital centres were behind the British lines in Northern France. For the first few months they worked mainly with British casualty clearing stations to make up for British shortages of medical manpower, and most of the casualties treated were British. These hospitals were not well placed to deal with the casualties in the actions fought by American troops who were suddenly engaged to meet the crisis in the French sector on the Second Marne near Chateau Thierry. Pershing in his memoirs recorded that 'we had to rely largely on the assistance of the French to care for our wounded.'[31] The care was inadequate and a major scandal was only narrowly averted. Once the US Army had its own front from mid 1918 onwards the base hospitals were moved round behind it.

The system faced further problems during the great offensives in the Argonne at the end of the war. The terrain of the American front was thickly wooded with poor roads. Mobility in the last stages of the war presented problems for the system even though the mobility of field hospitals was increased. Movement of casualties, however, remained a problem. There was a shortage of ambulances. In the peak of the shortage during the Argonne offensive, sight-seeing buses had to be borrowed from the French government as the ambulance allowance was based on a 12–20 miles haul between field and evacuation base hospital; in fact 'during the Argonne offensive the average one way haul . . . amounted to nearly twenty-eight miles for 24,000 trips.'[32] Shortage of places in evacuation hospitals made it necessary to borrow forty-five trains from the French: 'Trains of box cars without special fittings were also used for the movement of sitting patients, carrying as many as 1000 or 1500 at a trip.'[33]

A longer war would have led to change in the system: it would also have increased the problems of sanitation and after care of veterans. As it was the US medical services had to deal with new and unexpected crises, which meant that the commitment to a high level of preparedness and hospital investment could not be followed through on the ground, although those concerned with American medical services showed considerable drive and initiatives in meeting new problems.

THE LEGACY OF THE WORLD WAR

The Times History of the War concluded that 'medicine and surgery were reborn on the fields of France and Flanders.' Certainly there was a massive increase in resources and activity in hospital beds, surgery and medical specialisation. The war was an absorbing and conditioning experience for most doctors. Their participation rate was higher than that of any group other than the professional military: within the UK half of the 22,000

doctors were mobilised. The war also saw an unprecedented rise in international cooperation and the first emergence of America on the world stage
as the leader of medical research. At the end the official histories can be
allowed their share of self congratulation. This was certainly the first
European war in which the medical services made a real difference in terms
of a reduced death toll, and in which their effect in conserving manpower
may well have had some impact on the outcome. There could be congratulation too on the respect for the Geneva Convention and the
standards of treatment of enemy wounded on both sides.

The long term legacy of the war and its impact on the health system
remained uncertain. In lectures published in *The Lancet* followed by an
official report, Major General Dawson stressed the role of health promotion and of an expanded duty for the general practitioner.[34] However this
vision set out in the Dawson Report of a chain of health centres operating
within an integrated health service concerned with prevention and sanitation as well as with treatment, was not to be. In the short-term the war
gave powerful impetus to the development of hospitals and of medical
research based in hospitals. Even the development of psychiatry within the
health services was mainly on a hospital base: but there were enough longer
term effects for there to be reality in the judgment of *The Times*. Among
the key developments were, first, the development of medical research:
before 1914 medical research had been far more advanced in tropical medicine. Now the techniques of trials and clinical specialism, which had been
pursued by Sir Henry Wellcome and Walter Reed on yellow fever and
malaria, had been more widely adapted to problems in the northern hemi-
sphere. At the same time new sources of supply and pharmaceutical
enterprise had emerged to replace the predominant German role before
1914. German medicine was never to regain its pre-1914 status: the
search for the magic bullet had shifted to the Anglo-American world.

Second, there was the wider use of surgery as a system and a process
capable of carrying out a wide range of operations. With the extension of
surgery went technology in anaesthetics, X-rays and the use of prosthetic
material. The teams came to involve a much enhanced role for operating
department assistants and for theatre nurses. Large operations became
much more common helped along by the further development of blood
transfusion. Many young doctors were exposed to new standards of practice and took them home. The specialties of orthopaedics and plastic
surgery, which had only existed in the US before the war, now came to be
established in the UK.

A third development occurred in medical specialisation, involving the
subdivision of the old main categories of surgery and medicine and the rise
of new specialisms such as orthopaedics and plastic surgery. This was also
evident in the expansion of pathology and radiology.

Fourth there was the increased role of the nursing profession within the

463

hospital service. The pre-war qualified nurse was as likely to work in a home setting as in the hospital. The war gave a great impetus to the role of the matron and the sister.

Fifth there was the development of psychiatry in the UK concerned particularly with mental stress affecting ordinary individuals, rather than with the special problems of 'lunacy'.

The war led to a greater confidence in medical endeavour, symbolised by the foundation of the Ministry of Health in 1918. For some it began a period of improvement in health standards. By 1939 Neville Chamberlain was to point to a transition for the younger generation from a C3 to an A1 nation, with only 2.7 per cent of recruits being rejected as unfit.[35] War created a system and confidence in shared endeavour in health services which set patterns and acted as an enduring legacy. Above all, the war shifted views about the potential for innovation. Instead of change wrought by the occasional lone genius, a Lister or a Pasteur, there came to be an expectation of permanent change in the process of care and improvement in results. Ironically, the long term effect of the war was to generate optimism about health services and a belief in medical progress.

Notes

I am most grateful for help and discussion to Hugh McNeal, Jim Sherval, Professor Robert Joy and Stuart Ingham, and particular thanks to Peter Liddle. Frances Daniels gave indispensable help. My thanks also to William Bosanquet, for an extensive (and continuing) loan of *The Times History of the War*.

1   Woods Hutchinson, *The Doctor in War*, London, Cassell, 1919. pp. 1–13.
2   B. Abel Smith,. *The Hospitals 1800–1948*. London, Heinemann, 1964, pp. 282–3.
3   R. Stevens, *In Sickness and in Wealth. American hospitals in the twentieth century*, New York, Basic Books. 1989.
4   General Staff War Office. *Field Service Regulations*. Part I. HMSO, London. 1914, p. 73.
5   *Field Service Regulations*. Part II. p. 111.
6   T.J. Mitchell, and G.M. Smith, *History of the Great War. Medical Services: Casualties and medical statistics of the Great War*. London, HMSO, 1931. p. 35.
7   I. Hay, *One Hundred Years of Army Nursing*. London, Cassell, 1953. pp. 89–90.
8   G. Crile, *An Autobiography*. Philadelphia, Lippincott, 1947. p. 258.
9   *The Times History of the War*. 1914: The army medical services and the new medicine. Vol. XIV, Chap. CCXVIII. p. 334. London 1918.
10 *The Times History of the War*: Medical Work in the field and at home. Vol. IV Chap. LXVI. p. 66.
11 G. Crile, op. cit. p.259.
12 *The Times History of the War*. Vol. XIV. pp. 327–8.
13 W.G. Macpherson, *Medical Services General History*. Vol. III. HMSO, London. 1924. p. 46.

14 W.G. Macpherson, *Medical Services General History*. Vol. III. p. 34.

15 H. Cushing, *From a Surgeon's Journal* 1915–18. London, Constable, 1936. p. 187.

16 W.G. Macpherson, *Medical Services General History*. Vol. III. p. 156.

17 W.G. Macpherson, W.H. Horrocks W.W.O. Beveridge, *Medical Services, Hygiene of the War*. Vol. I. p.ix. HMSO, London, 1923.

18 Captain J.C. Dunn, *The War the Infantry Knew 1914–19: a chronicle of service in France and Belgium*, London, Jane's, 1987.

19 W.G. Macpherson, Vol. I. pp. 149–50.

20 J.C. Dunn, op cit. p. 532.

21 W.A.R. Chapin, *The Lost Legion*, Springfield, Mass. 1926. p. 95.

22 Lord Moran, *The Anatomy of Courage*. London, Constable, 1945.

23 W.G. Macpherson, Vol. I. pp. 119–120.

24 Woods Hutchinson, op cit. p. 3.

25 Mitchell and Smith. op cit. p. 19.

26 Field Service Regulations. Part 1. Organisation, in M.W. Ireland, *The Medical Department of the United States Army in the World War*. Vol. VIII, p. 1021. Washington. Government Printing Office 1925.

27 Manual of the Medical Department. Article XII. in M.W. Ireland, op cit. p. 1026.

28 P.M. Ashburn, *A History of the Medical Department of the United States Army* Houghton Mifflin, Boston. 1929. p. 341.

29 Mitchell and Smith. op cit. p. 35.

30 P.M. Ashburn, op cit. p. 334.

31 J.J. Pershing. *My Experiences in the World War*. Vol. 2. Stokes, New York. 1931, p. 127.

32 P.M. Ashburn, op cit. p. 342.

33 P.M. Ashburn, op cit. p. 343.

34 Sir B. Dawson, The future of the medical profession. *The Lancet*, July 20, 1918, pp. 83–87.

35 I. Macleod, *Neville Chamberlain*. Muller, London. 1962. p. 275.

Chapter 34

Not a Doctor's Work? The Role of the British Regimental Medical Officer in the Field

Ian Whitehead

During the First World War, one of the commonest criticisms of the RAMC was that its employment of medical men as Regimental Medical Officers (RMOs) was wasteful. The work was said to be undemanding of medical skill, and to involve too great a risk to the lives of the officers concerned, especially given the growing scarcity of doctors.[1] It was not just armchair critics in the UK who made these complaints. Numerous letters appeared in the medical press from RMOs complaining that they had little work to do. Typical of these was J.C. Ashton who, having served for six months, was convinced that the work of an RMO 'could easily be done in three or four hours'.[2] These sentiments were echoed in the private letters and diaries of medical men. Captain E.C. Deane felt that an RMO was a skilled life wasted, and believed that his trained stretcher bearers could have carried out his work just as effectively.[3]

The duties of RMOs certainly exposed them to a good deal of danger, and unlike combatants it was often difficult for them to know how much risk to run.[4] In theory, the duty of the RMO was to establish an Aid Post, in whatever shelter he could find, and as near to the firing line as was deemed safe. He was to remain there, awaiting the arrival of the sick and wounded. The job of retrieving the wounded fell to the regimental stretcher bearers, of whom there were usually sixteen, under the RMO's command (although this number could be doubled in times of heavy fighting). In practice, however, many RMOs were leaving the comparative safety of their Aid Posts and going forward with their bearers. There can be no doubt that it was sometimes essential for them to tend men in advanced positions, since there were cases which could not be moved until they had received medical attention. But, many RMOs were going forward as a matter of course. One such was Captain Hugh Llewelyn Glyn-Hughes, RMO to the First Battalion Wiltshire Regiment, who was remembered by an officer of the Regiment as always being in the thick of the fighting, 'going over the top with the men, attending to them as they got wounded'.[5] In one attack, he even assumed command of two companies, the other officers having been killed or wounded.[6] But for the vast majority of RMOs, their experience of front-line service did not take them beyond the confines of their medical work.

However, many shared Glyn-Hughes's approach to his duties, choosing to go into the trenches rather than remain at their Aid Posts. From some quarters this definition of an RMO's duties received encouragement. An article appeared in *The Great War*, in 1915, heaping praise on doctors who advanced under fire. It declared that there were 'few more splendid records than those of the eager young medicos who put regulations on one side and went where danger was greatest'.[7] But, whilst the bravery and devotion of RMOs won them deserved praise, there was concern that they were taking unnecessary risks.

Many medical officers were uncomfortable with their non-combatant status. They tended to look upon work as an RMO as a chance to prove themselves as equally willing to risk their lives for their country, as were their combatant brethren. G.D. Fairley expressed a common view, with his observation that it was the duty of all young medical men to serve in the front-line.[8] Much more challenging medical work (professionally speaking) was available at the Base, but there was a sense amongst many doctors that their war service, however commendable it might seem to others, was incomplete unless they experienced close physical contact with the fighting. Once at the front, many took great risks in pursuit of their medical duties. However, front-line experience led some to become even more frustrated with their non-combatant role. With friends dying around them, it was difficult for doctors to resist the urge to hit back. In his diary, Lieutenant-Colonel F.C. Fenwick describes an occasion when an MO gave way to this desire to retaliate; shooting a sniper at 400 yards. According to Fenwick, the MO in question was not reprimanded.[9] Such an action contravened the Geneva Convention and does not appear to have been a regular occurrence. However, the emotions which this action expressed were widely shared.

Others felt that, as non-combatants, they should steer clear of the fighting, and should have nothing to do with weapons. A.A. Martin saw the possession of arms as completely at odds with the role of a Medical Officer. He refused to obtain a revolver, and found doctors who did so highly ridiculous.[10] The justification for issuing arms to Medical Officers was that they might need them to defend the wounded. However, such a situation was unlikely to arise, and the military authorities were keen to prevent them from fighting. Colonel Arthur Lee, who made a series of reports to Kitchener on the medical arrangements in France, concluded that 'Medical Officers are inclined to expose themselves too recklessly and that in consequence of gallant but fatal attempts to succour one wounded man a whole unit may be deprived of medical assistance for the remainder of a day's fighting'. He felt that this situation needed to be remedied by the issuing of clear orders restraining Medical Officers from what he called 'acts of mistaken gallantry'.[11]

In September 1916, the Deputy Assistant Director of Medical Services (DADMS), Sixth Division, recorded an order 'forbidding MOs to hop over the parapet at once'.[12] Such orders received the wholehearted support of the B.M.J., which expressed the confident belief that Medical Officers' sense of duty would prevent them from taking unnecessary risks.[13] But, by 1917, with a growing shortage of doctors, there was serious concern that despite being 'severely warned'[14] against dangerous exploits, many were still failing to exercise sufficient caution.

Mounting concern about the shortage of doctors, combined with a belief that the Army's employment of doctors was wasteful, led to the appointment, in 1917, of a *Commission On Medical Establishments In France*. Its conclusions, in 1918, stressed the importance of battalion commanders impressing upon the RMOs that the proper place for them was either at their Aid Post, or with their C.Os., and that they should resist the temptation to go over the top. It also felt that the RMOs should be given better instruction with regard to this matter.[15] Indeed, the Commission was critical of the lack of systematic training for Medical Officers. At the outbreak of the War it was assumed that civilian doctors being recruited into the RAMC would require little training, and that their professional qualification would be sufficient. But, it soon became clear that this was not the case. Doctors were arriving at the front knowing little of their role, or the extent of their duties. On joining the Seventeenth (Service) Battalion Northumberland Fusiliers, J.M. McLachlan wrote: 'I'm sort of feeling my way, and am in a slightly fogged condition as to how much I'm supposed actually to do'.[16] The Commission recommended that provision for front-line training be improved, to remedy the deficiencies in Medical Officers' knowledge. Following the Commission's Report, there were moves to extend the provision of RAMC training in the front-line; for instance, the RAMC School of Instruction formed in France by the First Army. These developments were in tune with the Commission's recommendations, but were cut short by the German offensive in 1918; in a war of rapid movement front-line training centres were impossible to operate.[17]

It is clear that there were times when there was advantage in the RMO leaving his Aid Post. Occasional visits to the firing trench were beneficial, from the point of view of troop morale, as they reminded the men that the 'Doc' was with them in the line. Also, with serious cases, such as severe fractures, when it was difficult to move patients, RMOs could go forward to administer aid and oversee the arrangements – as long as this did not take them too near to the thick of the fighting.[18]

Given the nature of their duties, RMOs were always going to be exposed to danger. As the war progressed, every effort was made to ensure that they were fully aware of the limits of their role, and of the most effective ways of minimising the risks to their lives. However, it remains to be seen whether the quantity of work undertaken by RMOs, and the demands that it made on their medical skills, were sufficient to justify any risk at all.

Throughout the War, there were those who, concerned at the disruption being caused to the civilian medical service, claimed that the Army's demands for Medical Officers were excessive, and that it should exercise greater economy in its employment of medical personnel. The high casualty rate amongst RMOs (altogether 1,000 were killed during the War) reinforced the conviction that their skills could have been better employed elsewhere:[19] a conviction fuelled by the claims by some RMOs that they generally had only a few hours work a day, amounting to little more than basic first aid.[20] In 1917, however, the Medical Establishment Commission concluded that good RMOs should always be able to find work to do, and that their elimination would cause great harm to battalions.[21] Charles McKerrow, RMO, agreed with this conclusion, and believed that no man without some years of general practice would be the least use in maintaining the health of the men.[22] He found the work interesting, and noted signs that his endeavours were bearing fruit, as regarded the general health of the men. According to McKerrow, there was no reason why RMOs should be idle, but it was up to the individual how much he felt duty bound to do.[23] Sir Wilmot Herringham, who served as a Consultant with the RAMC, was less diplomatic. In his view, any RMO who claimed to have only half an hour's work a day had not been doing his duty.[24]

How can these opinions be squared with those who felt their talents wasted? The Medical Establishment Committee pointed the way to the answer, observing that there was no systematic training of RMOs.[25] The problem lay in the failure of RMOs to realise that there was more to their work than treating wounded. Their principal function was maintaining the health and fitness of the men, which was a full time job. However, in civilian life most doctors had a limited acquaintance with preventative work. For instance, much of an RMO's time would be taken up with sanitary matters, yet only Medical Officers of Health had much relevant experience. Thus, it was a lack of training which meant that some RMOs failed to appreciate that, in the lulls between battles, there was a good deal of work to be done. Pamphlets and instructions were issued to them as guidance, however, and from the papers of RMOs consulted, it would appear that the majority appreciated the broad range of their duties.

Moreover, the efforts to introduce more systematic training into the RAMC, mentioned above, met with some success.

The most obvious duty of the RMO was that of receiving and treating the wounded, and then evacuating them to the Field Ambulances.[26] This included training the stretcher bearers in first aid, with particular attention to the question of arresting haemorrhage, so that some immediate treatment could be given to the wounded, prior to their arrival at the Aid Post.[27] Once the wounded man arrived at the Aid Post, the RMO would check that the wound was clean, carry out any emergency amputations that were required, oversee the splinting of fractures and ensure that everything possible was done to prevent the onset of shock. More extensive operative treatment was discouraged; the prime concern being to evacuate the wounded to hospitals in safer locations, where the settled environment would contribute to their chances of survival.[28] It was the job of the regimental medical personnel to fit the wounded for their journey down the line. Thus, the quality of the treatment received at the Aid Post was vital to the patients' subsequent recovery, and it was essential that a qualified medical practitioner be there to supervise it.

The RMO's primary duty was to maintain the fighting strength of the unit. He kept a close eye on the health of the men at daily sick parades. In judging the health of a man, the RMO's main concern had to be the efficiency of the Army; he could not afford to indulge the individual. Early in the War inexperienced Medical Officers were often too lenient with the men, sending trivial cases down the line unnecessarily. The need for greater strictness was impressed upon RMOs by the RAMC authorities.[29] J. Hartsilver, a private in the RAMC, recalled a Medical Officer with a garrison battalion, who had clearly heeded this advice: '[he] was a most brutal sort of fellow and made things as uncomfortable as he possibly could for everyone going sick, unless they were nearly dying'.[30] For Charles Huxtable, this need to be hard-hearted was the worst part of the job. He recalled having to insist upon a man with sore legs participating in an attack. Although this made him feel rotten, he knew the consequence of doing otherwise: 'if you relax and give favours to one man you may get a flood of others'.[31]

RMOs had to be on the look-out for malingering, as there undoubtedly were professional malingerers.[32] On the whole, however, a consensus appears to emerge from Medical Officers' papers to the effect that serious cases of malingering were rare, and usually easily detected. According to Charles McKerrow some men would 'try it on' out of the line, but men very rarely went sick in the trenches.[33] The prevailing mood in the line, where men about to go on a stunt would not report sick, for fear of missing the action, was recorded by W. Brown.[34]

A high incidence of malingering in a unit reflected badly on the RMO. A Medical Officer who judged the men fairly and firmly would win their respect. One who showed weakness would produce a large sickness rate; consequently undermining the strength and morale of the unit. At the same time, however, it was essential that the RMO's need to be firm did not cause him to be unnecessarily harsh. Some Medical Officers tended to treat every man attending a sick parade as a malingerer,[35] and failed to appreciate the point at which firmness became harshness. Max Plowman describes the 'callous brutality' which a Medical Officer in France displayed towards a Gallipoli veteran, who had suffered from fever.[36] Such an approach did nothing for the reputation of the RAMC, and the activities of a minority of poor RMOs have helped to perpetuate an image of doctors in the trenches as lazy and callous. But, a more worrying consequence of a harsh doctor was the detrimental effect upon the morale of his unit.

A good RMO would maintain the strength of his unit by adopting a firm yet fair attitude towards men going sick; an attitude which had a good moral effect, and so further strengthened the unit. Indeed, the Medical Officer had an important role to play in sustaining a regiment's morale. Frequent inspection of the trenches by the RMO boosted the spirits of a unit, as it was important for the men to see that skilled medical assistance was at hand. These inspections, along with the sick parades, allowed the RMO to get to know all the officers and men in his battalion, enabling him to detect the earliest signs of fatigue, mental breakdown or the recurrence of previous illnesses. Charles McKerrow's diligent fulfilment of these duties won him the respect of his entire battalion. On McKerrow's death, his battalion commander wrote that 'no man in the Battalion was more loved, admired and respected. I believe he had the Medical History of every man in the Battalion, who had passed through his hands, written down in his private diary'.[37] Thus, by taking a keen interest in the health of his men, and making himself well-known and approachable, the RMO could avert the loss of valuable fighting material. F.J. Blackley noted that the men 'sometimes come to see me chilly, nervy and eyes dropping out for want of sleep so although not ill I generally pack them into my dugout for wounded and let them have hot drinks and three hours' sleep before sending them back'.[38]

The RMO helped to sustain the health of the unit through the enforcement of strict measures for the avoidance of preventable diseases, which had obvious benefits for the maintenance of morale. Thus, the sanitary work of RMOs, so often underestimated by wartime critics of the RAMC, was of great value. Frequent inspections of the trenches were essential to maintain adequate standards of hygiene. Out of the line, too, it was important that the RMO retain his sanitary vigilance.[39] This role, as guardian of the unit's health, required constant attention and involved a variety of tasks, including: checking the safety of water and food supplies; supervising the siting of camps and the erection of latrines; and ensuring that the men maintained good standards of bodily hygiene.[40] The RMO also had to be on the alert for outbreaks of contagious diseases, such as typhoid and malaria, and had a crucial part to play in schemes for their prevention. This often included attendance upon the local civilian population with whom the troops were likely to come into contact.[41]

Despite the vigilance of even the most conscientious Medical Officer, some disease was always going to break out. This was especially the case during heavy fighting, when the difficulties of maintaining adequate sanitary standards were immense. In these conditions, the best defence against the spread of diseases, such as typhoid, was inoculation. However, inoculation was not compulsory in the British Army, and RMOs consequently had an important role to play in persuading their men to agree.[42] The B.M.J. believed that an 'RMO's personal influence' was the principal factor in the success of such measures to keep men fit.[43]

The RMO acted as health education officer to the unit, instructing officers and men in first aid, and teaching the elements of hygiene and sanitation. It was proposed that particular attention be paid to platoon officers and section NCOs, who could then be enlisted in the campaign to educate the men.[44] Thus, officers and NCOs were lectured on such subjects as the care of feet; hygiene; and the avoidance of gas poisoning. It was also the RMO's duty to provide expert medical advice to the Commanding Officer, on all questions bearing upon the health of the men; and to ensure that this advice was acted upon.

Nevertheless, although it was essential that qualified medical men were in the front-line, professionally speaking the work was not stimulating. After a while, RMOs began to feel cut off from professional developments, and longed for more challenging work. Consideration needed to be given to the well being of the RMOs themselves. Front-line work placed them under a heavy physical and emotional strain. Having become so close to the officers and men with whom they served, it was difficult for RMOs to maintain a calm, dispassionate approach when dealing with sometimes horrific wounds. Unsurprisingly, the incidence of nervous collapse amongst RMOs was high.[45] The combination of physical and emotional strain, when added to the mundane, routine nature of the work, meant that, in the majority of cases, it was wise to limit a Medical Officer's length of service with a battalion.[46] In the French Army, doctors were supposed to spend no more than six months in the front-line.[47] The Committee on Medical Establishments in France concluded that a similar restriction should apply in the British Army, with doctors doing RMO work for no longer than twelve months.[48]

To conclude, there seem to be no grounds for saying that the RMO was a medical man wasted. On the contrary, he played a critical part, both in the rapid treatment of the sick and wounded, and in the prevention of disease. It is evident that those who complained about their employment being wasteful simply had too narrow a perception of the work involved; and that, especially in the early years of the war, RAMC training could have done more to broaden their understanding. Nevertheless, most recognised that their work, though often necessarily dull, needed the skills and knowledge of a qualified medical practitioner.

Notes

1   Throughout the War, there was a body of medical opinion which argued that military demands upon the medical profession were excessive, and that insufficient consideration was being given to the needs of the civilian population. See chapter two, 'The Recruitment Of Medical Officers', in I.R. Whitehead, *Medical Officers And The British Army During The First World War*, Leeds University Ph.D., 1993, pp. 35–109.
2   *The Need Of Doctors For The Army*, letter from J.C. Ashton, *British Medical Journal (B.M.J.)*, 1915 (II), p. 943.
3   Captain E.C. Deane, Liddle Collection, Brotherton Library, University of Leeds (LC), Diary: 28 November 1914, pp. 8–10; 29 November 1914, p. 10.
4   Second Lieutenant Charles Symonds, LC, extract from letter dated 26 April 1917.
5   Captain Hugh Llewelyn Glyn-Hughes, Wellcome Institute for the History of Medicine (WI), RAMC 1218, Papers: transcript of *This Is Your Life* television programme, 9 March 1959, p. 10.
6   ibid.
7   H.W. Wilson & J.A. Hammerton, *The Great War*, Volume 4, The Amalgamated Press, 1915, p. 124.
8   G.D. Fairley, LC, tape-recorded interview.
9   *F.C. Fenwick*, LC, Diary: 5 May 1915, p. 8.
10   A.A. Martin, *Surgeon In Khaki*, Arnold, 1915, pp. 9–10.
11   Sir C. Burtchaell, WI, RAMC 446/7: Papers: letters of Lee to Kitchener, letter 12 October 1914.
12   Sir Neil Cantlie, WI RAMC 465, Papers: War Diary when DADMS Sixth Division, 24 September 1916.
13   *The Medical Service On the Somme, B.M.J.*, 1916 (II), pp. 397–398.
14   N.J.C. Rutherford, *Memories Of An Army Surgeon*, Stanley Paul, 1939, p. 29.
15   Report Of The Commission On Medical Establishments, WI, RAMC 1165, p. 65.
16   J.M. McLachlan, LC, Letters: letter 321, 3 April 1915.
17   For a fuller discussion of some of the problems involved in the training of Medical Officers see chapter six, 'Doctors And Military Medicine: The Training Of Medical Officers' in I.R. Whitehead, *Medical Officers And The British Army During The First World War*, Leeds University Ph.D., 1993, pp. 174–226.
18   *The Royal Army Medical Corps And Its Work, B.M.J*, 1917 (II), p. 218.
19   J. Ellis, *Eye-Deep In Hell*, Fontana, 1977, p. 110.
20   *The War Emergency – An Opinion From France, B.M.J.*, 1915 (II), p. 539.
21   *Commission On Medical Establishments*, WI, RAMC 1165, pp. 63 & 66.
22   C. McKerrow, LC, Letters: letter 19 December 1915, pp. 75–76.
23   C. McKerrow, LC, Letters: letter 19 January 1916.

24 Sir W. Herringham, *A Physician In France*, Edward Arnold, 1919, p.97.

25 *Commission On Medical Establishments*, WI, RAMC, 1165, p. 63.

26 The role of Medical Officers at Field Ambulances was itself controversial. See I.R. Whitehead, *Medical Officers And The British Army During The First World War*, Leeds University Ph.D., 1993, pp.335-345.

27 Sometimes, as when a Division held a narrow front, RMOs might combine to form a Joint Aid Post. See Sir Neil Cantlie, WI, RAMC 465, Papers: War Diary when DADMS Sixth Division, 24 September 1916. Also, A.L.P. Gould, LC, Diary: 25 March 1918, p. 60.

28 *Manual of Injuries And Diseases of War*, HMSO, 1918, p. 2.

29 WO 95/52, PRO, Medical Inspector of Drafts, Diary April 1915-March 1916: 14 October 1915; 17 November 1915; 20 November 1915.

30 J Hartsilver, LC, memoirs, pp. 298-299.

31 C. Huxtable, LC, tape-recorded interview.

32 For more details on the problems which RMOs had with malingering, see I.R. Whitehead, *Medical Officers And The British Army During The First World War*, Leeds University Ph.D., 1993, pp. 323-324.

33 C. McKerrow, LC, Letters: letter 25 October 1915.

34 W. Brown, LC, Diary: 20 February 1917.

35 M. Brown, *Tommy Goes To War*, J.M. Dent, 1978, p. 218.

36 Max Plowman [Mark VII], *A Subaltern On The Somme*, J.M. Dent, 1927, pp. 55-56.

37 C. McKerrow, LC, Letters: letter from Robert Manners, Lieutenant-Colonel commanding Tenth Battalion Northumberland Fusiliers, to McKerrow's mother, 27 December 1916, p. 291.

38 F.J. Blackley, LC, Diary: 29 September 1915.

39 *The Medical Needs Of The Army*, B.M.J., 1915 (I), p. 511.

40 ibid.

41 I.R. Whitehead, *Medical Officers And The British Army During The First World War*, Leeds University Ph.D., 1993, pp. 329-331.

42 L. Gameson, Imperial War Museum (IWM), memoirs, p. 202. C. McKerrow, LC, Letters: letter 21 April 1916. N. King-Wilson, LC, memoirs, p. 9.

43 *The Medical Needs Of The Army*, B.M.J., 1915 (I), p. 511.

44 Lieutenant-Colonel W. Beveridge, WI, RAMC 543, War Diary, Volume XXIX, Appendix 2, 5 December 1916.

45 C. McKerrow, LC, Letters: letter, 29 July 1916.

46 *The Army Medical Service By Medical Officer In Charge Of An Infantry Battalion*, B.M.J., 1916 (II), p. 528.

47 *The French Army Medical Service: Recruitment, Organisation And Work*, B.M.J., 1917 (I), p. 628.

48 *Commission On Medical Establishments*, WI, RAMC, 1165, p. 64.

Chapter 25

The Fight Against Disease in the Mesopotamia Campaign

Mark Harrison

The First World War is often remembered as one of the first wars in which wounds inflicted in battle were responsible for more fatalities than disease – excepting the terrible influenza pandemic of 1918–19. In virtually all major conflicts that took place prior to 1914 – with the exception of the Russo-Japanese War of 1904–5 – the reverse had been true.[2] During the South African War of 1899–1902, for example, no less than two-thirds of the 22,000 deaths among British soldiers were attributed to disease.[3] The First World War, then, marked an important break with the past, yet sickness – rather than battlefield casualties – continued to be the main cause of admissions to hospital and seriously hampered the conduct of campaigns. This was especially true of operations outside Western Europe: in Salonika French and British troops were ravaged by malaria; in Eastern Europe typhus claimed the lives of countless German, Austrian, Russian and Serbian soldiers; in Gallipoli, East Africa and Mesopotamia, a host of diseases – among them, malaria, dysentery and typhoid – drastically reduced the fighting strength of all sides.[1]

This chapter is concerned with one of the least documented aspects of disease and medicine during the First World War but one which was – from both medical and military points of view – amongst the most important.[4] So-called 'deficiency diseases', such as anaemia, beri-beri and scurvy, were a major cause of sickness in several theatres, but most notably in Mesopotamia, where over 11,000 Indian troops succumbed to scurvy in the last six months of 1916. During this period, scurvy was the most important factor in the ill health of the Mesopotamian Expeditionary Force (MEF) and a major drain on fighting efficiency and morale. Scurvy and other 'deficiency diseases' also served as powerful metaphors for the failure of logistical planning during the campaign, as well as highlighting grievances and discontent within the armies involved. By the summer of 1916 it became evident that a 'danger line' had been crossed in both medical and disciplinary senses.

I

In 1914 the very concept of a 'deficiency disease' was unfamiliar to many doctors, for whom disease was very much a matter of 'germs' and 'infection'. From the 1880s the identification of numerous microbes causing disease had obscured important empirical and experimental work into the link between disease and nutrition. Thus, although the association of scurvy with the absence of certain foodstuffs was generally acknowledged, the causation of other diseases now associated with malnutrition, such as beri-beri, was hotly disputed into the present century; as was the possibility that these diseases were due to the absence of some *specific* substance other than the generally acknowledged constituents of food: protein, fats and carbohydrates.

The existence of 'vitamines' (the terminal 'e' was later dropped) was postulated just a few years before the war, and the term itself was coined only in 1912 by Dr Casimir Funk, who suggested that beri-beri, scurvy, rickets and pellagra were all due to the absence of *specific* substances found in different kinds of food. Detailed quantitative evidence supporting this hypothesis came in the same year from the Cambridge physiologist Sir Frederick Gowland Hopkins, who in 1929 was to be awarded the Nobel Prize for medicine for these experiments.[5] Although this work marked a major shift in thinking about disease and nutrition, the concept of 'vitamins' and their relation to certain diseases had made relatively little impression on medical practice by the time war was declared. Indeed, there were many doctors who contested the vitamin theory, and who continued to think in terms of a bacterial cause for diseases such as beri-beri. Mesopotamia was to be the proving ground on which the theory of vitamins was tested.

II

From a military point of view, the most important of the deficiency diseases to appear in Mesopotamia was scurvy, which we now know to be caused by an inadequate intake of the substance known as 'vitamin C' (being so named in 1920). In its mildest form, scurvy causes blistering of the gums, minor palatal haemorrhages and slight anaemia and debility. It may therefore go un-noticed or undetected for some time. Serious cases show more marked changes of the gums, anaemia and debility, together with definite haemorrhages of the muscles and loss of teeth. The most severe forms of scurvy are typified by substantial haemorrhages of the muscles and joints, pronounced anaemia and very often by dilation of the heart. Recovery from severe scurvy is a slow process and unless properly treated the disease may end in death.[6] The effects of such a disease on both manpower and morale are not hard to imagine.

The existence of scurvy among the MEF was first noticed early in March 1915, when Colonel Hehir, the Assistant Director of Medical Services (ADMS) in Mesopotamia, notified his superior, the Director of Medical Services (DMS) in India, Surgeon-General William Babtie, that some Indian troops had contracted the disease owing to inadequate supplies of green vegetables.[7] It seemed that supplies had been disrupted owing to chronic shortages in transport which were adversely affecting all aspects of military operations in Mesopotamia at that stage.[8] However, perhaps owing to the fact that the number of cases soon began to fall, the military medical authorities in Delhi took no further action. But Hehir suspected that the problem ran deeper than any temporary interruption of supplies. In his report to Babtie on 8 April, he drew attention to the fact that 'the present field service diet of Indian troops and followers has certain intrinsic defects and it is suggested that the whole question should be reconsidered'. The basic ration, according to Hehir, was defective in both fresh vegetables and meat[9] – an opinion which was to be endorsed by subsequent inquiries into the incidence of the disease.

Little more was heard of scurvy until April 1916, just after the fall of Kut-el-Amara to the Turks. The combined effects of transport shortages and extended lines of supply (the position south of Kut was nearly 400 miles from the Base at Basra) together with the onset of the hot weather, meant that few units received regular supplies of fresh vegetables. The official figures state that 1,290 cases diagnosed as scurvy were admitted to hospital from the beginning of April 1916 to the end of June, and a further 11,445 in the last six months of the year.[10] During this period, scurvy was the single greatest cause of admissions to hospital among Indian members of the Mesopotamian force.

By the beginning of May it became evident that the incidence of scurvy was high. On the 7th, Major T.J.B. Williams of the Indian Medical Service (IMS) reported that as many as twenty-six of the fifty-five cases his hospital had received from the Tigris Front had been suffering from scurvy or 'prescurvy anaemia'. As far as Williams was concerned, the underlying problem was that Indian rations were insufficient: 'The Indian Army as a whole is a badly fed army ... defective dietary conditions exist in a marked degree in Mesopotamia and are responsible for a large amount of the casualties from disease in this Army.[11] There were essentially two problems with the Indian ration. First, the overall quantity of most dietary items was too small for active service, since sepoys traditionally received an additional allowance with which to purchase food of their choice. Second, the ration was high in cereals and low in fresh meat and vegetables – the foodstuffs generally acknowledged to prevent scurvy. At this stage of the campaign, the Indian daily ration for troops on active service was as follows:

Atta (chick pea flower)	1½ lb
Fresh meat	4 ozs
Dhal (lentils)	4 ozs
Ghee (clarified butter)	2 ozs
Gur (sugar cake)	1 oz
Garlic	1/6 oz
Potatoes	2 ozs (or 4 ozs of green vegetables)
Tea	1/3 oz
Ginger	1/3 oz
Chillies	1/6 oz
Turmeric	1/6 oz
Suet	½ oz
Fuel	1½ lb

There was a marked disparity between this ration and that allocated to British troops in Mesopotamia. As Major Williams noted, 'The British fighting man needs 1 lb of fresh meat daily to keep him fit – the Indian sepoy is supposed to be fighting fit on 4 oz'. The British soldier similarly received 1 lb of potatoes, or its 'equivalent' in green vegetables, while sepoys had to make do with less than a quarter of that amount.[12] This inequality, he explained, accounted for the fact that only a handful of British troops suffered from scurvy, while Indians were particularly prone to the disease. This was especially true of sepoys who did not eat meat for religious reasons and whose scruples were maintained even under the most trying of conditions, such as during the 147 day siege of Kut.[13] But though meat was thought to have some antiscorbutic value, it is doubtful, in view of current medical knowledge, that it was of much significance in the prevention of scurvy. A more likely reason lay in the lack of green vegetables in the sepoy's diet prior to his arriving in Mesopotamia. Colonel William Willcox – the newly appointed Chief Consultant Physician in Mesopotamia – noted that:

Indian troops on their arrival in Mesopotamia had little or no capital in their Anti-Scorbutic Vitamine Bank. A few weeks of dieting on rations very greatly deficient in Anti-Scorbutic Vitamines was sufficient to cause the development of scurvy. The British soldier had much more capital in his bank, and could withstand the deficiency of Anti-Scorbutic Vitamines for a much longer period without developing scurvy.[14]

Willcox's colleague, Major Williams, blamed this state of affairs on the Government of India, which was then coming under attack from several quarters for its handling of the campaign:

478

In India, only after much trouble, and when scurvy had broken out in some regiments, could the Government be induced to give an active service ration, and then only for those troops out on the actual [North-West] frontier. The remainder . . . are still going on in the same easy-going style feeding themselves *how they like* and *when they like* [original emphasis]. Consequently, regiments are being sent out to Mesopotamia which are below par and in the 'Scurvy danger line' to start with.[15]

The IMS had never enjoyed an harmonious relationship with the Government of India, and was often critical of its 'parsimony' and bureaucratic ways.[16] Indeed, similar criticisms were made of the Government by the Mesopotamia Commission, which published its report on the handling of the campaign in late 1917 and, later, in the official medical history of the war. If anything can be said in the Government of India's defence it is that it was its general policy to keep intervention in the everyday life of the sepoy at a minimum, in case regulations gave offence to caste or religion.

Whatever their views on the causes of the scurvy outbreak, medical officers were unanimous in their estimation of the seriousness of the problem. In June 1916, Colonel Willcox joined Williams in urging in the strongest terms 'the necessity of taking immediate measures to improve the ration of the troops at the front on the lines indicated. The defects in the dietary of the troops are at present *GREAT* and demand *urgent attention*' [original emphasis].[17] In the coming months the disease showed no signs of abating – indeed, the prevalence of scurvy at the front seemed to increase, being highest in the 3rd Division which was furthest from the base. At this point, Willcox estimated that scurvy was responsible for between one-third and one-fifth of all sickness in the force, the other chief problems being heat-stroke, dysentery and typhoid.[18]

Scurvy thus constituted a major drain on manpower and morale. As is well known, the fighting spirit of the Indian Expeditionary Force in Mesopotamia was at a low ebb by 1916. The initial reluctance of many Moslem sepoys to fight their Turkish co-religionists had been compounded by the trying climatic conditions of the campaign, failure at Ctesiphon and defeat at Kut, and the low standard of equipment and medical provisions. On top of this, the paucity of the active service ration and the depressing effects of anaemia, scurvy and other 'deficiency diseases' rendered some units more or less ineffective.[19] Although there were only two 'mutinies' by Indian units against British officers in Mesopotamia, desertions from the ranks were common and the incidence of so-called 'malingering' was high.[20] As the civil servant A.N. Bingley put in a report to the Government of India at the end of March 1916: 'The attitude of our Musalmans is not satisfactory. There is much malingering. They are not fighting with much keenness. The troops are rather homesick and would like to see the end of this long war.'[21] It would be going too far to suggest that dietary deficiency was the sole, or even the most important, cause of these incidents, but it was undoubtedly a contributory factor. It is worth noting that dissatisfaction with diet had figured prominently in numerous cases of insubordination in the Indian Army prior to 1914. During the First Burma War of 1824–6, for example, the absence of ghee angered Bengali sepoys, who were also dissatisfied with local varieties of rice.[22]

Ironically, however, scurvy provided sepoys with a way of escaping the fighting in Mesopotamia. For the first two years of the campaign, most scurvy cases were evacuated to Basra, or to India, and some took as long as six months to recover, for even fairly mild cases would apparently 'break down' if subjected to prolonged mental and physical strain.[23] Some scurvy may even have been feigned or deliberately induced – the military authorities certainly thought so. According to a memorandum on scurvy issued in 1918, its symptoms were sometimes faked by sepoys who tied ligatures around their legs and used corrosives on their gums.[24] However, the Medical Advisory Committee for Mesopotamia – appointed in 1916 – felt that the number of bogus cases had been exaggerated:

> Disciplinary measures have had to be taken in some instances when scurvy has been self-induced by abstention from food, or simulated by malingering . . . We are convinced, however, that self-induced scurvy or malingering has been only a minor factor in the epidemic, and feel much sympathy with the protests which we frequently received against the idea that the Indian troops generally were adopting this means of evading their duty.[25]

It might also be added in defence of the reputation of Indian troops, that what was seen by some British officers as a deliberate attempt to induce scurvy through abstinence from certain foods, may have been no more than religious scruples which forbade the eating of meat.

The first major attempt to tackle the problem of scurvy came in July 1916, when Indian rations were improved – on Willcox's recommendation – by the addition of 2 oz of fresh fruit and 4 oz of fresh vegetables. However, the new ration was still deficient in anti-scorbutics unless an extra 4 oz of vegetables and 2 oz of meat was consumed daily. Rations were further amended on 31 October 1916, when the quantity of fresh meat and vegetables was increased to 6 oz per day respectively, and the fresh fruit ration by 2 oz. Willcox believed that this new scale was 'entirely satisfactory', and the General Officers Commanding the Army in Mesopotamia – Sir Percy Lake and later Major-General F.S. Maude – apparently did all they could to see that these rations reached the troops. Willcox also expressed his gratitude for the co-operation of those officers in charge of transport and supplies, such as Major-General Sir George MacMunn, the Inspector-General of the Lines of Communication.[26]

Yet there were continuing problems owing to the shortage of river barges throughout 1916, and supplies of fresh fruit and vegetables continued to perish under the scorching summer sun.[27] In August Willcox told the DMS Mesopotamia – Surgeon-General Treherne – that 'Such articles as sour limes, potatoes, fruit or other vegetables often arrive in a condition unsuitable for consumption owing to the great heat to which they have been subjected in transit and to the delay necessitated by the long and difficult journey up the Tigris'.[28] Fresh meat was also subject to the unwelcome attentions of Mesopotamia's vast insect population: 'There were literally millions of insects, mosquitoes, ants and even large hornets', recalled Dr E.H. Cameron, a medical officer at 32nd General Hospital at Amara, 'It was impossible to keep food from insect infection as a couple of seconds of exposure was sufficient time to allow numbers of flies to alight on the piece of food to which one was helping himself.'[29] However, continuing transport difficulties and Mesopotamia's harsh environment were not the only factors hindering supplies of food to troops at the front. According to the Medical Advisory Committee's report on the lines of communication, the failure of supply *was* sometimes due to the shortage of transport, but

> in other cases it appeared that vegetables or perhaps meat up to the sanctioned scale could have been obtained if the drawing up of the supplies had been sufficiently seen to. The Officers Commanding Supply and Transport depots informed us that in the case of some units it is exceptional for any officer (including quartermaster and medical officer) to make inquiries of them regarding food supplies, or for any officer to go to the depot to check the drawing of the rations of his unit. There seems to be some room for improvement in the amount of attention given in some Indian units both to the nature of the rations drawn and the way in which they are utilised.[30]

A similar point was made by some regimental medical officers. The MO for 15th Indian Division believed that dietary deficiencies were hard to avoid on active service in a country like Mesopotamia, but reported that:

> A supplementary cause is no doubt to be found in the defective interior economy of the units themselves. Officers commanding and junior officers do not often realise the importance of dietetics and its relation to scurvy.[31]

There was little that medical officers could do by themselves to remedy these defects, but regimental MOs did attempt to educate their men in the rudiments of nutrition,[32] and senior MOs such as Willcox did their best to ensure supplies of anti-scorbutic items to the front.[33] At his suggestion, in August 1916, fresh lime juice was prepared in India with the addition of small quantities of alcohol and salicylic acid as preservatives. By 1917 some 250 gallons of lime juice were reaching the front every day. This new juice appeared to give better results in the treatment of scurvy, though Willcox was later to conclude that its value as a prophylactic was uncertain.[34] By the end of 1916 river transport on the Tigris had also improved, and refrigeration barges with cold storage chambers for fresh meat were coming into use – an accomplishment which Willcox rated as one of the most important factors in bringing scurvy under control in Mesopotamia.[35] But no less important was the capture of Baghdad in March 1917, which gave troops access to abundant fresh fruit and vegetables grown locally. The Director of Local Resources, General Dickson, ensured that adequate quantities of fresh produce were purchased and distributed to the troops.[36]

However, there were reservations in some quarters about the cost of these provisions. Willcox was aware of the great expense entailed in furnishing large numbers of troops with generous quantities of fresh food but he emphasised that 'this expense has been a great economy since the saving of sickness has been enormous as a result, and there has been a great improvement in the general physique and vigour of the troops in consequence of this'.[37] Indeed, in 1917 the number of admissions to hospital from scurvy was drastically reduced to 2,199, compared with over 11,000 in July-December 1916. A slight increase was noted in the spring of 1918 among some Indian units fighting along the Euphrates,[38] but most cases were mild in nature, and responded readily to improved diet and rest. In 1918 only 825 cases were recorded, of which five were fatal.[39] For Captain A.N. Stevenson, RAMC, such low figures represented a mark of the 'efficiency of the great attention now paid to the proper rationing amongst the Indian troops'.[40] In 1917 significant strides were also made in the treatment of scurvy cases. Previously, most cases had been evacuated to Basra or Bombay, but the establishment of special 'scurvy sections' in stationary hospitals from September 1917 meant that more cases could be treated nearer the front. Treatments for scurvy were also improved, and patients underwent a combination of dietary measures, physical exercise, and 'local treatment' such as antiseptic mouthwashes. A suitable diet for convalescents was now possible because many hospitals had taken to growing their own vegetables. By August 1918, as many as forty percent of cases were being returned to the front within five months of admission to hospital.[41]

The language of 'efficiency' is evident in most of the reports written by medical officers on deficiency diseases during the Great War. Willcox and others who had assimilated new developments in the field of nutrition were anxious to show that medical science could be of service to the state and thereby claim legitimacy for their enterprise. It should be remembered that the vitamin theory of deficiency disease was still in its infancy and the subject of some controversy in scientific circles. Willcox was later to claim that the Mesopotamian campaign had provided just the kind of practical demonstration that the theory required in order to gain acceptance outside of a small elite of medical scientists. 'It is very doubtful', he wrote in a report to the DMS, India, in 1919, 'if any campaign has ever furnished such very important and interesting data on the very close bearing which rations have on the health of the soldier, and the great danger of Vitamin Deficiency in a ration has been demonstrated on a very large scale.'[42]

One important consequence of the reports made by Willcox and his fellow medical officers was that the British and Indian armies gradually refined their formulations of nutritional status. Willcox told a meeting of the Royal Society of Medicine in 1920 that:

> The experiences of the War, especially in distant countries such as Mesopotamia, called for special attention to the scientific rationing of troops. The old idea of sufficiency of calories, or of proteins, fat and carbohydrates, is quite inadequate to meet the needs.[43]

In the case of the Indian Army, the experience of the Mesopotamia campaign also culminated in an unprecedented degree of control over the rationing of sepoys, whose individual allowance for food was progressively reduced in favour of an enhanced ration for active service. Whilst it is true that some moves had been made in the direction of 'messing' sepoys in the years before the war, these had not progressed very far, and the war ushered in a more interventionist phase in the management of the Indian Army.[44] Yet the Indian soldier was still given some latitude in deciding his diet, and in 1919 Willcox was still protesting against the ten anna per month allowance given to sepoys serving in India. He thought that all Indian troops, even those based at home, should receive a ration sufficient for all their needs; that is, the post–1917 active service ration devised for Mesopotamia.[45]

III

Compared to their Indian comrades, British soldiers in Mesopotamia fared rather better in terms of diet, the only clearly identifiable deficiency disease being beri-beri, of which there were 104 recorded cases in 1916, eighty-four in 1917, and fifty-one in 1918.[46] However, one must regard these figures with some caution, since mild cases of the disease may have been hard to spot. The early symptoms of beri-beri are shortness of breath, tiredness, and weight loss – all of which might be expected in a force fighting in trying conditions and with inadequate rations. The more serious symptoms of beri-beri – such as parasthesia and loss of sensation in the limbs – usually (but not always) occurred at a later stage.[47] However, some senior officers claimed that doctors were too quick to diagnose beri-beri. Surgeon-General Treherne – the DMS for Mesopotamia – wrote to Willcox in November 1916 that 'There is one gentleman at the front whose diagnostic powers are perhaps not great, and he has beri-beri on his brain'.[48]

But the low official figures for beri-beri should not obscure the fact that

British troops in Mesopotamia suffered from the more general effects of malnutrition. In June 1916 Willcox reported that 'A large number of the British patients are suffering from general weakness and "debility" which is in my opinion due to malnutrition coupled with the strain involved by the climatic conditions'. British troops had little fresh meat and were forced to rely on their old staples – 'biscuit and bully'.[49] Nor is this surprising, for supplies to British units were hampered by the same transport and climatic difficulties which stemmed the flow of fresh produce to Indian troops.

Willcox acknowledged that these problems were due, in part, to the chronic shortage of river transport, but he discerned a more fundamental inadequacy in the rations of British troops. The basic problem was a deficiency of the 'anti-beri-beri vitamin' – later identified as vitamin 'B1' – in the rations supplied to British soldiers. Willcox and some other officers had already suggested that this might be the case, following an outbreak of beri-beri among British and Commonwealth troops in the Dardanelles. It seemed that even a slight variation from standard rations could be enough to induce beri-beri. 'Curiously enough, beri-beri has turned up here . . . ', wrote Major C.J. Makin, after inspecting the hospitals on Mudros,

> The ordinary ration evidently runs very near the margin, and officers are more likely to fall than men, because if the bread is sour and the fresh milk beastly they substitute sardines and rice biscuits . . . and various luxuries.[50]

Based on the evidence of the fifty clinical cases that he treated in the Dardanelles, Willcox concluded that the foodstuff yielding the highest quantity of the 'anti-beri-beri vitamin' was yeast. The disease seemed to respond well to diets rich in this substance,[51] and the yeast extract 'Marmite' was issued as a prophylactic against beri-beri to British troops in Mesopotamia from October 1916 with encouraging results.[52]

Willcox's research seemed to confirm the emerging consensus that beri-beri was a 'deficiency disease' (rather than one caused by some infective agent, as some doctors had previously believed), and an outbreak of beri-beri among Chinese labourers in Mesopotamia further confirmed research done in India and the Far East prior to the war, linking the disease with the consumption of milled rice (The husk of the rice grain had also been identified as rich in anti-beri-beri vitamins). As in the case of scurvy, the experience of campaigning in Mesopotamia produced much persuasive evidence in favour of the vitamin theorists, and the army's decision to revise ration scales in the light of these findings gave their views the stamp of official approval.

As far as the military effects of malnutrition among British troops are concerned, there can be little doubt that it had a serious effect on morale. As Colonel Willcox observed,

The problem of supplying an adequate ration to the troops does not appear to have been arranged for or thought out . . . The British troops got no potatoes or fresh vegetables with the possible exception of an occasional issue of onions. The British troops suffered as a result from debility and anaemia, and general lack of vigour and morale.[53]

The combined effects of climate, exhaustion and poor diet served to render many British troops ineffective. As Walter Ogilvie – a medical officer with the 7th Indian Division – put it in a letter to Willcox in August 1917:

Quite a number of officers and senior NCOs are about at the end of their tether . . . There is no distinct disease to put one's finger on, but from my experience of the tropics in general, and of this show in particular, I am sure that these men are no longer fit to carry on as officers or NCOs on active service . . . [54]

There were other similar reports. The medical officer Mathew Fell, for example, wrote to his wife in July 1916 telling her that many men no longer had the stamina needed for campaigning in such trying conditions.[55] However, there is little evidence that depressed morale led, as in the case of some Indian troops, to insubordination and active dissent. In the case of sepoys, diet was one among a whole range of grievances which threatened to loosen their bonds of loyalty to the Raj. Malnutrition was also a factor in the mass desertions that occurred in the Turkish Army in Mesopotamia, where food supplies were scarce owing to the British naval blockade and over-burdened lines of communication.[56] In the case of the Indian Army, the fact the British troops seemed to be largely free from scurvy may have also led some sepoys to believe they were being treated unfairly. However, what may have appeared to some sepoys – and even some medical officers – as systematic neglect, was in fact a reflection of the time-honoured policy of limited intervention in the private lives of Indian troops.

The problem of diet thus epitomised the Indian Army's great dilemma in the management of its troops: of achieving a balance between measures necessary to ensure the fighting efficiency of sepoys, and of allowing them to exercise preference according to custom, caste and religion. This dilemma was never fully resolved during the First World War, although the new ration scales introduced in Mesopotamia did represent a marked shift towards a more interventionist style of management. The wisdom of this move seemed to have been borne out by the general improvement reported in the morale and fighting efficiency of Indian troops from 1917. Such achievements – although due in part to improvements in transport and supplies – did much to enhance the standing of medical officers within the British and Indian armies. In particular, the experience of war in

Mesopotamia helped to establish the reputation of medical specialists, such as Willcox, as well as the authority of the vitamin theory they expounded.

Notes

1   The author acknowledges with gratitude the support of the Wellcome Trust. This chapter has also benefitted from the assistance of Peter Liddle and Dr Michael Worboys.

2   See Roger Cooter, 'War and modern medicine', in W.F. Bynum and R. Porter (eds.), *Companion Encyclopedia of the History of Medicine* (London & New York, Routledge, 1993, pp.1536–73; Richard A. Gabriel & Karen S. Metz, *A History of Military Medicine, Vol II: From the Renaissance Through Modern Times* (New York & London: Greenwood Press, 1992), p.243.

3   Gabriel & Metz, *Military Medicine*, p.217.

4   The story of deficiency disease in Mesopotamia is very much a neglected aspect of a 'neglected war'. A.J. Barker's excellent narrative of the Mesopotamia campaign – *The Neglected War: Mesopotamia 1914–1918* (London: Faber & Faber, 1967) – while considering medical arrangements, makes no mention of deficiency disease. Barker's silence is understandable in view of the fact that major collections of papers (such as those of Colonel Willcox, Consulting Physician in Mesopotamia) have only recently been made available to the public. However, problems of diet and disease do receive attention in the official medical histories, and in some recent surveys of soldiers' experiences during the Great War. See W.G. MacPherson (ed.), *Medical Services. Diseases of the War, Vol.II* (London: HMSO, 1923), pp.409–410 and Peter Liddle, *The Soldier's War 1914–1918* (London: Blandford, 1988), pp.178–191.

5   See Leslie J. Harris, 'The discovery of vitamins', in Joseph Needham (ed.), *The Chemistry of Life: Eight Lectures on the History of Biochemistry* (Cambridge: Cambridge University Press, 1970), pp.156–170; Christine Sinding, 'The history of resistant rickets: a model for understanding the growth of biomedical knowledge', *Journal of the History of Biology*, 22, 3 (1989), pp.461–495.

6   As described and classified by Captain A. Stevenson, 'Report on scurvy. Cases treated in a special scurvy section of 61st Indian Stationary Hospital', W[illcox] P[apers], L[iddle] C[ollection], University of Leeds.

7   Statement of Capt. Shaw to Vincent-Bingley Commission; Col. Hehir (ADMS Mesopotamia) to Surgeon-General W. Babtie (DMS India), 8 April 1915, CAB 19/21, P[ublic] R[ecord] O[ffice].

8   Barker, *Neglected War*, see esp. pp.134–5.

9   *Mesopotamia Commission: Report and Minority Report by Commander J. Wedgewood, D.S.O., M.P.*(London: HMSO, 1917), p.71.

10 W.H. Willcox, 'Further report on scurvy, 12 August 1916', p.1, LC; W.H. Willcox, 'Discussion on the treatment and management of diseases due to dietetic deficiencies', *Proceedings of the Royal Society of Medicine*, 13, 3 (1920), p.16.

11 Major T.J.B. Williams, 'Scurvy and unfitness in the Indian Army in Mesopotamia', 7 May 1916, W[illcox] P[apers], Library of the I[nternational] I[nstitute] of H[uman] N[utrition].

12 *ibid.*

13 Maj. S. van B. Laing, 76th Punjabis, letter 25, 11 January 1917, LC.

14 Willcox, 'Report on scurvy', 12 January 1919, WP, IIHN.

15 T.J.B. Williams, 'Report on scurvy', 16 May 1916, WP, IIHN.

16 On the IMS see Mark Harrison, *Public Health in British India: Anglo-Indian Preventive Medicine, 1860–1914* (Cambridge and Delhi: CUP, 1994.)

17 Willcox, 'Report on rations for British and Indian troops' made to DMS, MEF, 13 June 1916, WP, IIHN.

18 Willcox, 'Report on scurvy', 8 August 1916, WP, IIHN.

19 Statement to Mesopotamia Commission by Lieutenant-General Aylmer, CAB 19/22, PRO.

20 David Omissi, *The Sepoy and the Raj: The Indian Army, 1860–1940* (London: MacMillan, 1994), chapter 4.

21 Report on medical arrangements by A.N. Bingley, 26 March 1916, L/MIL/5/767, I[ndia] O[ffice] R[ecords].

22 Douglas M. Peers, 'Contours of the garrison state: the army and the historiography of early nineteenth century India', in Nancy Cassel (ed.), *Orientalism, Evangelism and the Military Cantonment in Early Nineteenth-Century India* (Lewiston, NY: Edwin Mellen Press, 1991), p.114.

23 Willcox, 'Report on scurvy', 8 August 1916, WP, LC.

24 'Memorandum on scurvy', MEF 1918, R[oyal] A[rmy] M[edical] C[orps] 2052/25, C[ontemporary] M[edical] A[rchives] C[entre], Wellcome Institute for the History of Medicine.

25 Medical Advisory Committee, 'Report on health conditions in the Advanced Area (Corps), October 1916', WO 32/5114, PRO.

26 Willcox, 'Notes on rations for the Mesopotamian Expeditionary Force', p.3, 1 January 1919, LC; *idem, Mesopotamia (1916–1919)* (London: Morton & Burt, 1919), pp.9, 19.

27 Willcox, 'Notes on rations', p.4, LC.

28 Willcox, 'Report on the prevention of scurvy', 26 August, 1916, LC.

29 Papers of E.H. Cameron, typescript of recollections, p.3, LC.

30 Medical Advisory Committee, *Report on Lines of Communications, Sheikh Saad to Basrah, November 1916* (Delhi: Government Press, 1917), p.11.

31 General report on the medical history of 15th Indian Division, 2 May 1918 – 31 December 1918, CMAC, RAMC 1186/2.

32 Memoranda on nutrition were drawn up in such a way that they could be understood by combatant units. See Willcox, 'Discussion on the treatment and management of diseases', p.22.

33 Willcox, 'Further report on scurvy', 12 August 1916, p.3, LC.

34 Willcox 'Discussion on the treatment and management of diseases', p.14. Recent research had also confirmed lemon juice to be a better prophylactic than lime juice; *idem,* 'Report on the prevention of scurvy', 26 August 1916, LC.

35 Willcox, 'Discussion on the treatment and management of diseases', pp. 12–13, LC, P.H.A. Willcox, *The Detective-Physician: The Life and Work of Sir William Willcox 1870–1941* (London: Heinemann, 1970), pp.15–16.

36 Willcox, 'Notes on rations for Mesopotamian Expeditionary Force', p.4, 1 January 1919, LC.

37 *ibid.,* p.2.

38 War diary of Colonel E.W.W. Cochrane, IMS (advance along the Euphrates), entries of 11 & 21 November 1917, CMAC, RAMC 1186/1' General report on medical history of 15th Indian Division, 16 Sept. 1917–30 April 1917, CMAC, RAMC 1186/2.

39 Willcox, 'Discussion on the treatment and management of diseases', p.16.

40 Captain A.N. Stevenson, 'Report on scurvy', 31 August 1918, p.1, LC.

41 ibid., p.1; idem, 'Report on scurvy cases treated in special scurvy section of 61 Indian Stationary Hospital', August 1917, LC; G. Grey Turner, Medical and Surgical Notes from Mesopotamia (London: British Medical Association, 1917), p.4.

42 Willcox, 'Report re rations for Indian soldiers serving in India', 17 February 1919, WP, IIHN.

43 Willcox, 'Discussion on the treatment and management of diseases', Proceedings of the Royal Society of Medicine, 1920, 13, 3, p.21.

44 The generally accepted view is that there was relatively little intervention to secure the health of sepoys when compared with medical arrangements for the British Army in India, prior to the Great War at least. See Peter Burroughs, 'The human cost of imperial defence in the early Victorian age', Victorian Studies, XXIV (1980), pp.31–32; Peers, 'Contours of the garrison state', pp.111–113; Omissi, The Sepoy and the Raj, pp.61–63; Mark Harrison, 'Health, medicine and the crisis of command in the Indian Army, 1914–1918', unpublished manuscript. David Arnold also stresses the army's laissez faire approach regarding the health of sepoys, but points to exceptions such as vaccination and the practice of 'messing': David Arnold, Colonizing the Body: State Medicine and Epidemic Disease in Nineteenth-century India (Berkeley & London: University of California Press, 1993), pp.91–96.

45 Willcox, 'Report re rations for Indian soldiers serving in India', 17 February 1919, WP, IIHN.

46 Willcox, 'Discussion on the treatment and management of disease', p.16.

47 The 'test' used by most medical officers in the diagnosis of beri-beri was the 'squatting test' in which the patient was asked to bend on his knees and assume a squatting position with buttocks a few inches from the ground. A man with beri-beri was supposed to be unable to raise himself from this position. W.H. Willcox, 'Beri-beri with special reference to prophylaxis and treatment', Lancet, 11 March 1916, p.554; Diary of Lieutenant-Colonel T. Osmond, entry of 17 October 1915, LC.

48 Treherne to Willcox, 18 November 1916, LC.

49 Willcox, 'Report on rations', 13 June 1916, p.2, LC.

50 C.J. Makin, letter of 15 November 1915, cited in 'Memo on prevention of beri-beri', by Maj. E.H. Standing, OC Hygiene Dept., Royal Army Medical College, 21 February 1916, WP, IIHN.

51 Willcox, 'Beri-beri with special reference to prophylaxis and treatment', Lancet, 11 March 1916, pp.553–7.

52 Willcox, 'Discussion on the treatment and management of diseases due to dietetic deficiencies', p.15; idem, 'Notes re rations for MEF', 1 January 1919, LC.

53 Willcox, 'Notes re rations for MEF', LC.

54 Ogilvie to Willcox, 31 August 1917, LC.

55 Papers of Mathew Fell, letter of 10 July 1916, CAMC, RAMC 1153/5.
56 See Erik Zürcher, 'Little Mehmet in the desert: the Ottoman soldier's experience in the Great War', in this volume. I am grateful to the author and to Peter Liddle for making this chapter available prior to publication.

Chapter 36

Facial Surgery: The Patient's Experience

Andrew Bamji

The art of plastic surgery is an old one; ancient texts from India indicate that reconstruction of the nose was practised widely many hundreds of years ago and the techniques of facial reconstruction became of interest to European surgeons in the early part of the 19th century.[1] Advances were slow; in the absence of anaesthetics, most surgery had to be conducted at great speed with little regard for accuracy or tidiness and the problems of infection awaited the work of Lister and Semmelweiss whose experiments showed the importance of aseptic technique. Thus it was only in the latter part of the 19th century that surgical advances began.

The Great War was to change all that. Although it is widely believed that plastic surgery of the face developed in the Second World War under the guidance of such famous names as Archibald McIndoe, the foundations were laid by others twenty years earlier. While modern plastic surgery may have had East Grinstead as its nursery, its birthplace and cradle were at Sidcup, a South-East London suburb.

The Great War was accompanied by many new medical problems. Not the least of these was the problem of facial injury as a direct consequence of trench warfare. Never before had armies been subjected to such heavy continuous shelling in fixed positions, and any soldier exposing his head above the parapet of a trench ran the risk of being shot. Soft caps were replaced by steel helmets; these gave some protection against shell fragments and shrapnel that would have penetrated the brain, but the face remained exposed. By 1915 surgeons in the field were being confronted with increasing numbers of facial casualties.

The close range and relatively low muzzle velocity of the rifles meant that when a bullet struck it produced a big entry wound, but that its energy was rapidly dissipated. Shot side on, a soldier would lose his nose and face, and perhaps be blinded, as was Gilbert Nobbs of the London Rifle Brigade.

My head at the moment was inclined to the right, for I was shouting at the men. Like a flash I remembered that about fifty yards to the left of me there was a 'German strong point' still occupied by the Germans. A bullet had entered my left temple; it must have come from a sniper in that strong point, for I found some days later that it had emerged through the centre of my right eye.

I remember distinctly clutching my head and sinking to the ground, and all the time I was thinking, 'So this is the end – the finish of it all; shot through the head, mine is a fatal wound.'[2]

Behind the front line it was little safer. The supply roads, tightly packed with wagons or trucks bringing food and ammunition, or with troops moving up to the front or back into reserve, were a prime target for shells and bombs. Casualties here augmented those coming down the line:

Thousands of . . . lightly wounded men swarmed about a long ambulance train standing in a field . . . They crowded the carriages, leaned out of the windows with their bandaged heads and arms, shouting at friends they saw in the other crowds . . .

There were other wounded men from whom no laughter came, nor any sound. They were carried on to the train on stretchers, laid down awhile on the wooden platforms, covered with blankets up to their chins . . . I saw one young Londoner so smashed about the face that only his eyes were uncovered between layers of bandages, and they were glazed with the first film of death. Another had his jaw clean blown away, so the doctor told me . . . Outside a square brick building . . . the 'bad' cases were unloaded: men with chunks of steel in their lungs and bowels were vomiting great gobs of blood, men with arms and legs torn from their trunks, men without noses, and their brains throbbing through opened scalps, men without faces . . . [3]

The soldier's war could be over almost before it began. Lieutenant William Carr of the Royal Field Artillery described the destruction of a German machine-gun post in a hut by the River Ancre, effected by stealthy observation from an exposed point in a barley field:

On return from this expedition, I went straight to the mess to clean up. There I found Suthey with an officer newly arrived from cadet school. After introductions Suthey, knowing I would be going to congratulate the gunners, suggested that I took the young man along to have a look around. As we went out towards the gun positions Jerry decided to retaliate. As the shell came over I dropped flat to the ground. The shell landed some thirty yards behind us. I got to my feet and noting that the new officer had remained standing told him that whenever he heard a shell coming he should get down quickly – it was our usual practice. He was a very tall young man, he looked down at me in disbelief as clearly

491

he thought that things were coming to a pretty pass with the war being fought by these windy old fellows. Patiently I made another attempt, explaining the dangers of splinters and flying debris, adding that this was one of the survival drills not taught at cadet school. The words were scarcely out of my mouth when another shell came towards us – down I flopped. After the dust cleared I got up to find the young man still on his feet but clutching his head moaning in agony. A splinter had gone in through one cheek and out at the other. It was a blighty one and we never saw him again.[4]

The majority of casualties who passed through the Regimental Aid Posts, Advanced Dressing Stations and Casualty Clearing Stations reached the base hospitals by ambulance train. Then the sufferer from a Blighty wound was transported to England by ship and, after another train ride, might be admitted to a military hospital or, if less seriously injured, to one of the Voluntary Aid Detachment hospitals dotted about the nation and mostly converted from private houses or church halls.

Soldiers died anywhere along this line from shock due to blood loss, from asphyxiation (it was rapidly realised that the facial casualty had to be nursed sitting forward, to avoid choking), or from the almost inevitable sepsis. The fertile fields of the Flanders plain, heavily manured in peacetime, harboured many highly infectious organisms such as *Clostridium Tetani*, the cause of gas gangrene. This condition had never before been encountered on such a scale. Insanitary conditions in the trenches were universal. Tissue loss, infection and scarring combined to produce dreadful deformity in those who survived. There were of course no antibiotics; the best that could be done was to operate early, and by July 1917 surgeons were being moved out of the base hospitals towards the front line and even the nurses resorted to steel helmets.

John Bagot Glubb joined the 7th Field Company, Royal Engineers, in November 1915 at the age of 18. He was wounded to the south-east of Arras, on 21 August 1917. His account epitomises the initial inexperience of the facial casualty:

The road beyond St Martin was in view of the enemy, and it was not yet quite dark. I dismounted and sat on a stone for a short time, and then rode back through St Martin 'village', which consisted of untidy mounds of broken bricks, covered with grass.

Some long range shells whined over, and burst about 120 yards beyond the road. It seemed to me to be a 4-inch gun at extreme range. I began to trot at first, but finding shells bursting well over I pulled back to a walk, determined not to run away. Just as I left St Martin, the shelling ceased. Here I met Driver Gowans coming up with a G.S. wagon, and stopped to tell him he would have to do two trips, as the infantry wagons had failed to come. No shells had fallen in the last five minutes, since those which had passed over my head a few hundred yards back.

As I spoke to Gowans, I think I heard for a second a distant shell whine, then felt a tremendous explosion almost on top of me. For an instant I appeared to rise slowly into the air and then slowly to fall again . . .

Scarcely had I begun to run towards Hénin, when the floodgates in my neck seemed to burst, and the blood poured out in torrents . . . I was in a kind of dazed panic . . . I could not speak, but I paused in the middle of the road, and gave one or two sobbing groans, whereupon the traffic man appeared, from where he had been crouching in a shellhole to avoid the shells. He called to a gunner driver to watch the post, and led me a little further down the road to a dressing station in an old cellar under a mound of bricks. I could feel something lying loosely in my left cheek, as though I had a chicken bone in my mouth. It was in reality half my jaw, which had been broken off, teeth and all, and was floating about in my mouth.

I sat on the table in the cellar, while they dressed my wound. The R.A.M.C. orderly put some plug into my neck which stopped the bleeding. They also put a rubber tube in my wound, sticking out of the bandage. They told me there was no ambulance in Hénin and I should have to walk to Boiry-Becquerelle. We accordingly set out, I leaning on the medical orderly's arm. I was not looking forward to the long walk at all, but luckily the orderly remembered that there was some regimental medical officer, who lived in a dugout at the south end of the village . . . I heard him tell the orderly that it was a good thing they dressed me at once, or I should have been done for.

Glubb was taken to the main Casualty Clearing Station at Ficheux, a mile or so to the west. There he was operated on and remained for several days.

I had apparently nearly swallowed my tongue during the operation and, to prevent this, they had pierced my tongue and threaded a wire through it with a wooden rod on the end of it. This was extremely uncomfortable. A good deal of discharge came from my mouth, and I was very miserable, with my pillow always covered with blood and slime. I was later told that I looked very bad, with my mouth dragged down, discharging and filthy . . .

After six days in the C.C.S. we were driven away one morning in a motor ambulance to Boisleux-au-Mont and loaded onto a hospital train . . . The British hospital trains were wonderfully fitted up, regardless of expense, and painted spotlessly white.

Glubb's train carried him on to Rouen and he was driven to one of the British Red Cross hospitals where

... I noticed a very evil decaying smell, which I attributed to some foul drains which must be near by, but when my wound was dressed the stench suddenly became so overpowering that I realised that it came from myself ... Next day I was told I was for England and was taken in the ambulance to the station. From Rouen to Le Havre, we travelled in what we were told was the French method – stretchers laid side-by-side in a covered cattle truck. In the afternoon we reached Le Havre and were carried straight on to a ship. I was in a deck cabin, but all the cots were already full and I was just put down on the floor ... I did not know what would happen if I were seasick with my mouth in such a state ... I was quite a spectacular sight. There were not enough doctors or nurses on board to change anyone's dressings, so whenever mine worked loose, the sister hastily tied another bandage over it ...

They laid out our stretchers on the public platform at Southampton station for a while, and then put us on an ambulance coach hooked on to the back of an ordinary passenger train. The train was a slow one and as I was lying at a big window, a crowd collected on the platform of every station to stare at me. An old sister was in charge of us. I asked her for a drink, which she gave me in a feeding cup, bearing the inscription *South Africa 1900*. Some of the dust of the veldt must have lain in the spout those seventeen years, for I got a mouthful of it with my first gulp.[5]

An ear, nose and throat surgeon, Harold Gillies, attached to the Red Cross, was seconded in 1915 to assist a French-American dentist called Valadier at the 'Dublin' hospital, Wimereux. Valadier was not medically qualified, and so was treated with some suspicion by the army medical establishment, being forced as a condition of his continuing employment to suffer the indignity of a medical 'minder'. Gillies was fascinated by the injuries he saw. On his return to the Cambridge Military Hospital at Aldershot he did his best to convince the army medical establishment that special facilities for facial casualties were urgently needed. He was successful, gaining wards at the Cambridge and beginning the development of a team of dedicated facial surgeons, dentists and anaesthetists, together with support services in the form of radiologists and medical illustrators, perhaps the most famous of these being Henry Tonks, Professor of Fine Art at the Slade School, and the Australian Daryl Lindsay.

The Cambridge Military Hospital was not big enough. On 1 July 1916 the Somme offensive turned the flood of facial casualties into a tidal wave. Gillies was allocated an extra two hundred beds at Aldershot by the Commandant, Sir Arbuthnot Lane, but two thousand patients arrived. Working flat out all hours of the day, inventing techniques as he went along, pushing patients into convalescent beds as fast as he could, Gillies and his little team could not cope. He wrote:

Men without half their faces; men burned and maimed to the condition of animals. Day after day, the tragic, grotesque procession disembarked from the hospital ships and made its way towards us.[6]

More facilities were needed, and in a planning exercise which can only be envied by those who work in today's NHS, a new hospital, specifically for facial injuries (to be run along the lines of the Roehampton hospital for amputees) was designed, built, and opened, within a year. The enthusiasm of Charles Kenderdine, who had been influential in establishing Roehampton, contributed greatly to the speed with which money was raised. Sidcup was chosen as the site because it was relatively near to London, on the rail route from the Channel ports, and because Frognal House, the mansion in whose grounds it was built, was for sale.

The facilities were extensive. By early 1918 over a thousand beds were available at Sidcup and a series of convalescent hospitals around. Contemporary postcards illustrated the grounds, the operating theatres, wards and workshops, while the public was exhorted to raise money to support the hospital by numerous articles in the national and local press.

The hospital was organised on national lines, with separate contingents of medical staff from Great Britain, Canada, New Zealand and Australia. Some five thousand servicemen were treated at Sidcup and its associated hospitals between 1917 and 1925, with over 11,000 operations being performed.

Publicised records of work at Sidcup were confined to Gillies' textbooks, the first published in 1920; the casenotes on which they were based disappeared, having been removed when the respective sections left the hospital. A museum established at the hospital, containing a large collection of facial casts and many of Tonks' pastels, also vanished, although the pastels survived in the hands of the Royal College of Surgeons, London. Quite by chance I came across the New Zealand records; nearly 300 folders of notes, 77 watercolours and a life-size wax model demonstrating many of the surgical techniques, which had all been rescued from destruction in Dunedin by the former Dean of Dental Surgery, Professor A.D. Macalister. Rather than see them go on a skip he kept them in his garage, and later kindly donated them to us at Sidcup.

As the result of a journal article about the New Zealand casenotes, which was read by the medical photographers at Queen Mary's Hospital, Roehampton, I learned that the British Section records had made their way to Roehampton and were languishing in two filing cabinets in the photography department, where no-one quite knew what to do with them. In this collection were, it transpired, some 2500 sets of casenotes, including many seminal cases with original techniques illustrated by thousands of photographs, diagrams and other illustrations. These records too were recovered.

Only by looking through these records can the full horror of wartime facial injury be appreciated. The images are both disturbing and fascinating; suddenly one is transported from the calm realms of death to the indignity of disfigurement. Many contemporary reports, such as that of Ward Muir (an orderly corporal at the 3rd London General Hospital, Wandsworth) dwell on this aspect:

There is one perturbing experience . . . that is inevitable. It is this. He (the hospital worker) finds that he must fraternise with his fellow-men at whom he cannot look without the grievous risk of betraying, by his expression, how awful is their appearance. Myself, I confess that this discovery came as a surprise. I had not known before how usual and necessary a thing it is . . . to gaze straight at anybody to whom one is speaking, and to gaze with no embarassment . . .

Hideous is the only word for these smashed faces: the socket with some twisted, moist slit, with a lash or two adhering feebly, which is all that is traceable of the forfeited eye; the skewed mouth which sometimes – in spite of brilliant dentistry contrivances – results from the loss of a segment of jaw; and worse, far the worst, the incredibly brutalising effects which are the consequence of wounds in the nose, and which reach a climax of mournful grotesquerie when the nose is missing altogether.

To talk to a lad who, six months ago, was probably a wholesome and pleasing specimen of English youth, and is now a gargoyle, and a broken gargoyle at that . . . is something of an ordeal. You know very well that he has examined himself in a mirror. That one eye of his has contemplated the mangled mess which is his face – all the more hopeless because 'healed'. He has seen himself without a nose. Skilled skin-grafting has reconstructed a something which owns two small orifices that are his nostrils; but the something is emphatically not a nose. He is aware of just what he looks like: therefore you feel intensely that he is aware you are aware, and that some unguarded glance of yours may cause him hurt. This, then, is the patient at whom you are afraid to gaze unflinchingly: not afraid for yourself but afraid for *him* . . .

Without surgery's aid his face might have been unspeakably worse than it is. He has every reason to bless surgery. And yet –! Surgery has at last washed its hands of him; and in his mirror he is greeted by a gargoyle.

Suppose he is married, or engaged to be married . . . Could any woman come near that gargoyle without repugnance? His children . . . Why, a child would run screaming from such a sight. To be fled from by children! That must be a heavy cross for some souls to bear.[7]

Ward Muir also wrote of the construction of masks, known as 'Tin Faces', to cover large facial defects. It is said that at Aldershot there was a riot of 'Tin Face' patients; I have not been able to confirm this but clearly the development of plastic surgery, with reconstruction rather than concealment, mitigated the psychological effects of injury.

John Glubb, wounded three days after the Queen's Hospital officially opened, ended up in the 3rd London General.

At Rouen, I had been marked with a label, *Cambridge Hospital, Aldershot,* which was the chief place for face wounds. But on the boat they said there was no room there, so I was sent up to London. When we got to Waterloo, a man came in and gave us all tickets for hospitals. Mine was the 3rd London General.

I lay for three months in my bed at Wandsworth, during which my wound remained septic, and received no medical attention . . . At last, in November 1917, three months after I had been hit, I was transferred to a new hospital for face injuries at Frognal, Sidcup, in Kent.

Here things were very different. My broken and septic teeth were extracted and my wound cleaned. The problem then was how to reunite the broken fragments of my lower jaw bone, which were still hanging loosely in my mouth. The solution adopted was to set the broken bones of the lower jaw and then cement it to the upper jaw, which thereby acted as a splint . . . As most of my lower jaw had gone, I was shown an album of photographs of handsome young men and asked to choose the chin I would like to have![8]

Nevertheless Nurse Catherine Black, who worked for Gillies at Aldershot, wrote:

Hardest of all was the task of trying to rekindle the desire to live in men condemned to lie week after week smothered in bandages, unable to talk, unable to taste, unable even to sleep, and all the while knowing themselves to be appallingly disfigured . . .

I shall never forget the case of a young corporal who had been, judging from the photograph his mother showed me, very handsome. He was brought in with the mud of the trenches still on him. It was not long before I heard of Molly. She wrote to him by nearly every post, letters full of plans for the day when she would be able to come and see him. He kept putting her off . . .

'I don't want her to come until I get some of these beastly bandages off, Sister,' he used to say. 'It would scare her to death to see me lying here looking like a mummy.'

Mirrors were prohibited in that ward, but to my dismay I found the corporal in possession of one the evening that his bandages were taken off. I pretended not to see it when he called me over and asked me to put the screens round his bed. The next morning he asked for pen and paper and wrote a letter to Molly. 'You're well enough to see her now,' I said. 'Why not let her come down?'

'She will never come now,' he said quietly, and there was the finality of despair in his voice . . . [9]

The *Daily Mail* carried a piece in the late spring of 1918 which described a visit. We possess Bates' casenotes; he was in the Rifle Brigade, and was wounded on 18th October 1916.

'You want to see Sergeant Bates.'

'Yes if you please ma'am.'

The little woman looked almost as if she expected the Matron to produce him by sleight-of-hand there and then.

'He told you of his wound.'

'He said he was hit by shrapnel, ma'am but not bad.'

Matron motioned her to sit down, and then, with an infinite pity in her face, this terror of all V.A.D's, this alleged martinet, told the little woman before her in a few words what Sergeant Bates in his agony of mind could not write.

'So you see, Mrs Bates,' she ended gently 'you must be brave when you see him, because – he dreads this meeting – for your sake.'

'I'm not complaining, mum, if he don't,' she said; 'and now, if you don't mind, I'll see him.'

Sister came into the small ward rather hurriedly and, drawing the screen round the Sergeant's bed, told him very gently that his wife was waiting to see him.

'Sister,' the man turned abruptly, as he groped for the kindly hand she held out 'I'm a bloomin' coward, that's what I am,'

'Sergeant, she knows it all!' She paused, feeling more than a 'bloomin' coward' herself. 'Come now, you're my prize patient, you know!'

'Right you are, sister,' said the soldier.

The door opened and shut – steps came towards the screens, and Bates still gripped the sister's hand as first matron appeared and then his wife.

'Well, Bates——' began Matron, but the little woman was past her. She took one searching glance as involuntarily he turned his 'good' side to her and then, deliberately choosing the other, she went right up to the bed, and with a hand on each shoulder, kissed him – ever so lightly – on the worst scar of all.[10]

The public were shielded from the worst of the disfigurements. Although soldiers were encouraged to 'take the air' some of the benches along the road from the Queen's Hospital to Sidcup, were painted blue for wounded soldiers only, so that local residents would know that the occupant of such a bench was likely to have some hideous facial injury. The stigma of disfigurement was often very difficult to cope with. Corporal Davidson of the RAMC married a local girl, but if people came to dinner he would dine alone in the kitchen, embarassed by his inability to eat quietly.

One of Gillies's maxims was 'never do today what can honourably be put off till tomorrow' – which meant that operations were not hurried and were often done in many stages. Our notes record frequent re-admission. The Sidcup experience required much patience. Some men, like Private

Reid who arrived in 1918 ten months after injury, could not cope. Photographs taken four years later showed there was still room for improvement but Reid had had enough; he refused further surgery. The surgeons tried for two months to persuade him but the last entry in the notes reads 'refusal not considered reasonable.'

Nevertheless the end results did much to mitigate the terrible injuries and their effects on others. Sometimes full reconstruction was not possible and 'Tin Faces' were made at Sidcup.

It is too late now to adduce directly the psychological effect of facial injury. The men's own accounts, against all the odds, are remarkably cheerful – witness the essays written in a Queen's Hospital English class, now deposited in the Liddle Collection at Leeds. They did not talk of their fears, their depression or their despair. But circumstantial evidence indicates that there were major problems and this is clear from the accounts of their attendants, like Ward Muir, the nurses or the surgeons. Some men, like Davidson, worked on at the hospital and hid from the world. Some developed hysterical symptoms; some put on a front. Pte Anderson celebrated his 50th operation by getting utterly drunk and smashing all the ward windows. One can presume that it took courage to face the world and perhaps that is why the hospital football team had a fearsome reputation. Enormous efforts were made to enable the wounded men to get back to a normal life; the occupational therapy facilities at the hospital provided teaching of a wide range of skills from coach-building to chicken-farming, and the Sidcup toys were famous throughout London for their quality.

Many of the results were excellent. Bell was referred to Gillies by Valadier in Wimereux for a second opinion. The primary repair had resulted in gross deformity, and the suture lines were re-cut, allowing tissues to spring back into normal positions so the surgeon could see how extensive was the loss and decide how to move other tissues to fill the gaps.

Such excellent results are all the more amazing because almost every facial injury was infected, and there were no antibiotics. Gunner Ashworth was depicted by Tonks severely disfigured and receiving the usual antiseptic treatment – the flushing through the wounds of sterile water, which is caught in the bowl below. Yet the final photographs show a marked improvement in the facial appearance.

Reconstructions were often aided by pre-operative photographs, and recording techniques were remarkably sophisticated – colour, of course, was confined to watercolour and pastel, but some stereo photographs survive.

The publicity of the Second World War 'Guinea Pigs' – airmen operated on by Archibald McIndoe at East Grinstead – has overshadowed the origins of burns surgery at Sidcup some twenty-five years earlier. Indeed it was Gillies who gave his junior cousin his first break in plastic surgery. The

Sidcup records illustrate many examples of severe burns. A plastic surgery first was Vicarage, a seaman who served on HMS *Malaya* in the starboard 6 inch gun battery, and suffered severe burns when the battery cordite store was ignited by a direct hit at the Battle of Jutland. He arrived at Sidcup a year after the injury, severely scarred and unable to close his mouth. It was while a huge flap was being raised from the chest that its tendency to roll up was noted and Gillies sutured the two sides into tubes, finding that they stayed clean, and that the blood supply along them was enhanced. This was the first 'tube pedicle'.

Lieutenant Wallace, a Canadian artillery observer, may be used to represent the airmen of the First War and the injuries they suffered if their aircraft caught fire and they survived a crash landing. His notes are thick with photographs, diagrams and a series of watercolours illustrating the failure of a large cheek flap. Other burns victims came from the Tank Corps, and one from a local explosives factory.

While one cannot speculate closely on the effects of these injuries on the psyche, it is necessary to remember that sometimes the psychological disturbance caused the injury. Shellshock was a well recognised entity, but sometimes soldiers who could no longer face the front line inflicted injuries on themselves. The Sidcup archives show at least two cases of self-inflicted facial injury.

The patient experience at Sidcup is dimmed by the passage of time. The horror of facial disfigurement is universal and enduring; yet, thanks to those at Sidcup, those disfigured by war could look forward to a better life than would otherwise have been their lot.

The Queen's Hospital records are a remarkable testament to the skills of the surgeons, anaesthetists, technicians and illustrators of almost 80 years ago. There is no doubt that the casualties of the Western Front were the vital experimental subjects which enabled the modern specialty of plastic surgery to develop. The team approach to facial surgery, involving plastic surgeons, dentists, anaesthetists and the technical support staff in close attendance, is perhaps Sidcup's greatest legacy to that specialty.

Notes

1   M. Maltz, *Evolution of Plastic Surgery*. New York, Froben Press, 1946.
2   G. Nobbs, *Englishman Kamerad! Right of the British Line*. London, Heinemann, 1918.
3   Anon., *Diary of a Nursing Sister on the Western Front 1914–1915*. Edinburgh and London, Blackwood and Sons, 1915.
4   W. Carr, *A Time to Leave the Ploughshares. A Gunner Remembers 1917–18*. London, Robert Hale, 1985.
5   J. Glubb, *Into Battle; A Soldier's Diary of the Great War*. London, Cassell, 1978.
6   Sir H. Gillies, D.R. Millard, *The Principles and Art of Plastic Surgery*. London, Butterworth; New York, Little, Brown and Co, 1957.

7   W. Muir, *The Happy Hospital*. London, Simpkin, Marshall, Hamilton, Kent & Co., 1918.
8   See note 5 above.
9   See note 6 above.
10 Sunday Chronicle, May/June 1918 (reprinting earlier *Daily Mail* article).

Chapter 37

Dr James Dunn and Shell-shock

Keith Simpson

This paper seeks to examine the experiences of one temporary doctor in the Royal Army Medical Corps (RAMC) during the First World War and to consider his reflections on his own role as a Regimental Medical Officer, his awareness of his own reactions to stress and fear in battle and his attitude towards war neuroses. James Churchill Dunn was a temporary officer in the RAMC who served as Regimental Medical Officer (RMO) to the Second Battalion The Royal Welsh Fusiliers (2/RWF) between November 1915 and May 1918. During that thirty months of continuous service with a regular infantry battalion Dunn was to be awarded the MC and Bar and the DSO. His experiences during the war, based upon a diary and the letters he sent home, as well as over fifty contributions from all ranks of 2/RWF, were to help form the basis of *The War The Infantry Knew 1914–1919,* anonymously edited by Dunn and which was published in a limited edition in 1938. It was a unique history of a regular infantry battalion through four and a half years of continuous service on the Western Front.[1]

James Dunn was born on 24 February 1871, and studied medicine at Edinburgh University, qualifying MD in 1897. Dunn then moved to London, serving as a House Physician and later as Resident Medical Officer at the St. Pancras North Dispensary. It was whilst he was in London that he volunteered for military service during the South African War. Dunn volunteered during 'Black Week' of December 1899 and instead of serving as an army doctor enlisted as a trooper in the Montgomeryshire Yeomanry. Dunn served for over a year in South Africa and was awarded the Distinguished Conduct medal (DCM) for bravery. After serving as a civil surgeon with the South African Field Force he returned to Britain and in 1903 was a physician in a Lambeth Hospital. Before 1914 his address was Portland Square, London, probably where he was taking in private patients. After the outbreak of war in August 1914, Dunn took several months to put his affairs in order before volunteering, at the age of forty-three, for military service. On 18 January 1915 he was commissioned as a temporary Lieutenant in the RAMC, and on 23 July 1915 he was posted to the 19th Field Ambulance, 19th Brigade in France. On 7 November 1915 he succeeded Captain Harbison as RMO of 2/RWF, a position he was to hold until he was temporarily incapacitated by gas on 22 May 1918. Following his recovery in June 1918 Dunn asked to be transferred to another battalion as he could not work with the new acting CO of 2/RWF. Until the end of the war, Dunn served, somewhat unhappily, with a Service battalion of the East Yorkshire Regiment.

After the Armistice, Dunn was demobilised, and in 1919 he worked as a doctor in Rye where he received the thanks of the local council for his outstanding work during the Spanish influenza epidemic. He then moved to Glasgow to live with his aunts, serving as a member of a Pensions Appeal Tribunal, for those claiming War Disabilities, and in 1922 he gave evidence as a witness to the War Office Committee Enquiry into 'Shell Shock'. Dunn continued to live in Glasgow following his retirement, considered something of a local celebrity, not least because of his association with the RWF. He died on the 30 March 1955 aged eighty-four.

Taken together, *The War The Infantry Knew,* his post-war correspondence with Siegfried Sassoon, Robert Graves and Edmund Blunden, and the detailed evidence he submitted to the 'Shell Shock' Committee in 1922, help us to understand Dunn's role as an RMO, his own reaction to stress in battle, and his attitude towards war neuroses. When Dunn received his temporary commission in the RAMC he was joining a medical corps that had only received its Royal Warrant in 1898. During the nineteenth century the old Army Medical Department had suffered as a depressed branch of the Victorian medical profession unable to recruit the best medical students. Within the army, doctors had been regarded with disdain by combatant officers because medicine itself lacked professional status. Regular Army doctors were predominantly from a lower social status and in military eyes were not quite 'officers and gentlemen'. By 1914 many of these anomalies had disappeared and the new conditions of service in the RAMC meant that the army doctor had become more accepted as a military man.[2] During the First World War Dunn was to display a very critical attitude towards the bureaucracy of the RAMC and what he saw as its unwillingness actively to support the combat units of the Army. Ironically, when Dunn was posted as RMO to 2/RWF in November 1915, he was to join a pre-war regular infantry battalion which still maintained the rigid peacetime social and professional conventions against outsiders. As a civilian doctor, a Scotsman of humble social origins, and someone who had served in the ranks and with the ranker's DCM, he could have expected a degree of ostracism comparable, although for different reasons, to that endured by Robert Graves. But there is no indication by Dunn that this occurred and his outstanding abilities combined with his natural reserve must have quickly overcome any prejudices within 2/RWF.

Dunn's opinions and prejudices were influenced by his experience in civil medical practice before the war; his experience of soldiering and active service during the South African War; and his thirty months continuous service with an infantry battalion on the Western Front. In war as in peace much of an RMO's job consisted of medical inspections of new drafts, sick parades, dealing with hygiene, and distinguishing between those who were considered to be really ill and those who were thought to be malingerers. In their marvellous military and social lexicon of the British soldier's experience of the First World War, John Brophy and Eric Partridge wrote in 1931 that medical officers

> varied considerably in quality; some were brutes, some were weak underlings of the C.O., but most were quite human. In the line all worked like niggers, and many of them heroically. (Work has always been a cloak to cover the doctor's sins).

In their revised 1965 edition this was amended, deleting the racist language, and with this additional sentence on medical officers: 'they were good to wounded men unless they suspected S.I. [Self-Inflicted Wound].' Interestingly, in both editions the authors were convinced that malingerers could get away with it and genuinely ill men were ordered back to duty.[3] As Brophy and Partridge have observed,

> when a soldier was, in his opinion, so ill that he was unable to perform his duties, he went sick by giving his name to the orderly Corporal, and reported the next morning very early for sick parade. The Regimental Medical Officer saw him in his turn, asked him a question or two, invariably gave him a standardised purgative pill, known as Number 9, and marked him down as M.D., i.e., medicine and duty, Light Duty or Excused Duty. Malingerers were reported for punishment if the M.O. was sufficiently sure of his diagnosis; those who were unable to hold themselves upright were – in time – removed to an ambulance.[4]

Dunn believed that

> The work, the outlook, of a battalion medical officer is not purely medical and surgical, certainly not in war-time. As much knowledge of one's fellow-man as of medicine is needed.[5]

Dunn claimed that in November 1915 as a new and inexperienced RMO with 2/RWF, his medical orderly, Corporal Roberts, had taught me that the first duty of a battalion officer in War is to discourage the evasion of duty. That has to be done not seldom against one's better feeling, sometimes to the temporary hurt of an individual, but justice to all other men as well as discipline demands it.[6]

Dunn underlines this in his evidence to the 'Shell Shock' Committee in 1922, writing:

My practice as RMO was determined by the conviction that the first duty of an RMO is to maintain the discipline and morale of his unit. To effect that the health of individuals may have to be sacrificed temporarily, even permanently.[7]

Dunn's conviction was endorsed by two other temporary RMOs. Charles McMoran Wilson served as RMO to 1/Royal Fusiliers for thirty months between 1914–1917. Later as Lord Moran, and Churchill's doctor, he was to write, 'My job as medical officer was to value the assets of the battalion – to take stock – to guard against depreciation.'[8] Harold Dearden served in 1917 as RMO with 3/Grenadier Guards, and wrote,

When a soldier presented himself for treatment, especially in or near the trenches, his physician – by much training – was led to adopt towards him an attitude of mind guaranteed to ruin the same physician in the shortest possible time in any other place on earth. That is to say, he endeavoured to prove, exclusively to his own satisfaction, that there was nothing whatever the matter with his patient; and the fact that the latter rarely accepted his diagnosis did not in the least degree affect the nature of his treatment. Having arrived at this conclusion (and to the sufferer it must have seemed that nothing short of an audible death rattle could prevent him from doing so), he was accustomed to administer a brisk aperient and mark his card 'Medicine and Duty'.[9]

When an infantry battalion went into the line, the RMO and the Regimental Aid Post (RAP) were positioned in support, but Dunn like many RMOs did not remain in a static RAP but went forward to the front line trenches to see for himself and personally deal with wounded and injured men. When a battalion was taking part in offensive operations the RAP would be moved forward to a dug-out, a cellar, or the ruins of a cottage, and eventually to a trench or even a shell hole. The RAP would consist of the RMO, his medical orderlies and the battalion stretcher bearers, normally sixteen bandsmen and pioneers, but the number could be doubled. These men were regarded by the battalion as more reliable than RAMC bearers because they were part of the battalion and knew the men. Only in emergencies or for large-scale attacks would field ambulance bearers be detailed to help them. The job of the battalion stretcher bearers was to follow the attack and provide first aid to the wounded before bringing them back to the RAP where the RMO would provide further medical attention, perhaps giving a morphia injection and even carrying out emergency surgery before the wounded could be removed to a Casualty Clearing Station. Dunn, like many RMOs, refused to be tied to the RAP, and would move forward with his medical orderlies to search out the wounded. His decorations for bravery were associated with this work. Frank Richards noted that during a battalion attack on the 27 May 1917 Dunn,

> had been wandering about no-man's land attending to the wounded and doing what he could for them. How he didn't get riddled was a mystery. Some of the men who did not know him so well as the rest of us were saying that he was fed up with life and was doing his level best to get killed.[10]

Dunn's active role as RMO reflected his physical courage, his admitted dislike of remaining in any enclosed space under shell fire, and one suspects at times his frustration over not being a combatant soldier. In 1934 in a letter to Edmund Blunden, Dunn expressed his disapproval of 'a prevalent non-combatant attitude in the RAMC, and its not-to-be-exposed-to-risk-corollary'.[11] Whilst Dunn could document occasions when he had felt frustrated with the administrative bureaucracy of the RAMC, he was being unfair and inaccurate when applying his censure to the traditions of the RAMC and the behaviour of his fellow RMOs during the First World War. Physical courage was an attribute valued by the RAMC, and during the nineteenth century army doctors had received numerous decorations for bravery, sometimes for actions incompatible with their non-combatant status. Certainly in the First World War Dunn was not unique as an RMO either in his physical courage or his behaviour, and there were many other RMOs who were as well decorated. Lieutenant-Colonel Martin-Leake had won the Victoria Cross during the South African War and was awarded a bar to it at Ypres in 1914, and Captain Chavasse was to win both the VC and Bar during the First World War. The physical risks involved can be seen in the casualties for RAMC officers during the War. In July 1914 there were 970 RAMC officers and by April 1918 at maximum strength there were 12,432.[12] 743 RAMC officers lost their lives, the majority of them RMOs who were killed in action or died of wounds.[13] In fact Dunn was remarkably lucky to escape unharmed apart from receiving a temporary incapacity from gas in May 1918.

Dunn had no illusion about the nature of war in the battle zone between antagonists of equal tenacity and resources – in his words it was 'prolonged drudgery'. As Siegfried Sassoon described it in his contribution to *The War The Infantry Knew*,

The truth is that infantry soldiering in the battle-zone was an overwhelming physical experience. Such human elements as food, warmth and sleep were the living realities, and it may not have occurred to many a writer of military histories that the weather was a more effective General than Foch, Haig or Ludendorff. A bad blister on a man's heel might be the only thing he could clearly remember after a week of intense experience which added a battle honour to the colours of his regiment.[14]

Given the great physical strains imposed on the infantry who did not have the same amount of transport or lifting aids as other arms and corps, Dunn concluded that 'no man should be posted to the infantry to begin with who is not capable of carrying the great weight to which infantry equipment now amounts'.[15] Dunn had observed that the infantry was worn down by the sheer physical labour involved in soldiering on the Western Front. Even out of the line when 'resting', many men were allocated to fatigues, including moving stores, digging roads, trenches and dug-outs, and this was only partially addressed by the formation of the Labour Corps. Exposure to the elements, particularly extreme cold or long periods of wet weather was very debilitating, as Dunn noted on 18 December 1916,

> Two weeks of continuously bad weather extended over this time. There was snow and rain, frost and thaw by turn – the conditions which cause trench foot. A four days tour cost us 30 to hospital with broken chilblains and a few trench foot cases. This was quite a new experience for the Battalion, but the number was said to be the smallest in the Division; one battalion was debited – by report – with 200 cases.[16]

Dunn was convinced that as the war progressed increasing numbers of men were reporting sick because the quality of drafts sent to the battalion deteriorated and the drafts failed to look after themselves. In January 1917 he observed:

> The daily sick parade had become a serious affair by this date in the War. A year ago it was very exceptional to see a dozen 'sick'; now nothing was too trivial to be a pretext for 'going sick', and 60 was the daily average. Cleanly habits kept the old Army men remarkably free from minor ailments. Neglect of cleanliness caused most of the foot sores, and the vast amount of itch, lousiness and consequent debilitating maladies that ravaged the Territorial and 'duration' troops and taxed the capacity of the hospitals.[17]

Although Dunn did recognise the link between bad weather, the amount of fatigues and the intensity of the fighting with the size of the sick parade, the real conclusion he drew was that it was due to a decline in the physical and mental quality of drafts sent to the battalion. Until July 1916, 2/RWF escaped heavy casualties and retained a remarkably large number of regulars and reservists in all ranks. After the casualties suffered during the attack on High Wood in July 1916 the battalion received 540 drafts of all ranks. Dunn was horrified: 'The quality of the drafts made those of us who were used to a different personnel fearful of the immediate future, so every working hour was given to trying to get them into some sort of shape.'[18] Furthermore, Dunn noted that the majority of the drafts had received only limited basic training, and many did not know how to load and unload a rifle. The increasingly poor physique of drafts received throughout the war and their lack of basic training was compounded, in Dunn's eyes, by those who were drafted in from non-combatant or auxiliary service to 2/RWF and who objected to their transfer to a combatant unit. As Dunn told the "Shell Shock" Committee:

> That mental attitude is not compatible with the morale that is essential to achieve objects at a minimum cost. Rarely, if ever, have I known a man join in the Pioneer Battalion or Garrison Battalion frame of mind and rise out of it. It creates skulking; skulking is terribly infectious; it leads to the sacrifice of the good men in the unit and prevents responsible officers relying on an attack being pressed or a defence maintained with sufficient numbers.[19]

Dunn makes no mention of venereal diseases in *The War The Infantry Knew* and only a passing reference in his submission to the 'Shell Shock' Enquiry. We know from official sources that venereal disease was an increasingly significant problem in the British Army on the Western Front. Between 1914 and 1918 there were 153,531 admissions to hospital for venereal disease, with in 1918 a ratio of 32 to every 1,000 on the ration strength.[20] The contraction of venereal disease was regarded as a disciplinary offence in the sense that it could be regarded as malingering or self-inflicted wound. Dunn's omission means that venereal disease was either not a significant problem in 2/RWF or not something that Dunn wished to draw attention to out of regimental loyalty.

In *The War The Infantry Knew* Dunn recounts examples of what he describes as 'skulking', being 'gun-shy' or 'trench-shy', to support his views on the importance of training and discipline. On 27 June 1917 2/RWF participated in a major raid with a battalion of the Cameronians. Dunn noted how the attack collapsed and

> the dribble became a surge, on they came but none sought to go beyond the trench. Cameronians too were back. The collapse was stupefying in its suddenness, the manner of it was sickening. Some men said they 'were stopped by wire', others that they 'had orders to retire'. There were, however, no officers and very few NCOs among them . . . Sergeants Ibbotson and Onions had most to say about the collapse. Onions summed it up as 'panic among men without enough training and

discipline'; but he nodded assent when Ibbotson said that the capture of Tunnel Trench 'only wanted running forward instead of running away' ... It was fairly plain that there had been no lack of leadership, but the irresolute mass had not been trained out of the habit of the turnstile, or into the use of the rifle ... Our Battalion casualties in this calamitous affair of minutes were 10 officers and 155 other ranks, almost half of whom were dead.[21]

And yet Dunn was an unfair perfectionist, who looked back to the professionalism of the pre-war regular battalion, and failed to appreciate or accept that by 1917 for all intents and purposes there was little to distinguish 2/RWF in the quality of its drafts from Territorial or Service battalions. Although Dunn maintained that the quality and effectiveness of 2/RWF declined after 1916, it was a largely conscript battalion in a conscript British Army that helped beat the German Army in the summer and autumn of 1918.

The characteristics of infantry soldiering – exposure to the elements, hard physical labour, and the bloody business of battle, placed great stress on all ranks of 2/RWF. The duration and intensity of service for the infantry on the Western Front created physical and mental stress on a scale not hitherto seen either in civil life or in previous wars. What was initially and erroneously named 'Shell Shock', or later more accurately 'war neurosis', proved a major challenge both to the medical profession and the army. Before the war British medicine recognised functional nervous diseases in two forms – hysteria and neurasthenia.[22] Both the medical profession and the public regarded hysteria and neurasthenia with distaste, and tended to believe that the origins lay in an hereditary disposition or the individual's 'lack of moral fibre'. In 1914 British medical psychology had no carefully articulated theory, no consistent and agreed upon means of diagnosis, and no specific therapy for such disorders. Although the British Army had experienced cases of functional mental and nervous disorders in previous campaigns they were not prepared for the numbers involved in the First World War.

In war the crucial issue for all armies is to persuade or coerce soldiers against their natural inclinations to remain on the battlefield. Both the military authorities and army doctors regarded any soldier reporting sick without a demonstrable physical ailment or wound as somebody attempting to avoid his duty and therefore liable for punishment. In the British Army, medical psychology, military medicine and military discipline were combined in the person of the Regimental Medical Officer. Whether a pre-war regular or a uniformed civilian, army doctors were trained to regard nervous collapse as mainly a question of 'moral fibre' and were inclined to tell a soldier to, 'get a grip' before returning him to duty.

Cases of functional nervous disorder began to appear in the BEF in the first few weeks of the war, and by 1915 had reached – at least as far as the military authorities were concerned – alarming numbers.[23] The majority of these cases were not conducive to traditional military medical treatment, and were evacuated to Britain. What was particularly alarming to the military authorities was the number of officers in this category.[24] In February 1915 Dr Charles Myers, in an article in *The Lancet*, referred to cases he had dealt with as suffering from 'shell-shock', and almost immediately this became the accepted description of war neurosis. The sheer scale of artillery fire and the impact of high explosives had been recognised from the early weeks of the war both by the military and medical authorities. The belief that shell fire was mainly the cause in the increase of those suffering from war neuroses had an appeal to both the military and medical authorities as it had understandable and definable characteristics. Unfortunately, as far as the military authorities were concerned, only direct trauma from shell fire could render a man at the front free from the charge of cowardice or desertion, whilst many doctors ignored or misdiagnosed many cases of war neurosis as they were looking for the symptoms of 'shell-shock'. There appears to have been a refusal to consider that many of those suffering from 'shell-shock' were traumatised by fears associated with 'survivability'.[25] For the Regimental Medical Officer, 'shell-shock' posed disciplinary, medical and personal dilemmas which increased his own stress at fulfilling an ambivalent and dangerous role.

Dunn himself endured considerable shock and strain in the thirty months he was RMO with 2/RWF. In *The War The Infantry Knew* there are glimpses of Dunn's self-awareness of what he called 'a certain loss of nerve'. Shell fire was a fear he fought continuously, and it was the fear of being under shell fire in an enclosed space that held a particular horror for him. At Passchendaele on 27 September 1917, when 2/RWF was badly knocked about in the attack at Polygon Wood, Dunn found himself sheltering in a shell hole near a pillbox which was being used as battalion HQ when it came under shell fire:

> Beginning near 6 o'clock there was an hour's sustained shelling of HQ, so accurate, so concentrated, that my confidence in a new shell-hole as the safest shelter was shaken. I came to date a failure of nerve from impressions taken then.[26]

This was confirmed four months later during a two and a half hour bombardment around another pill-box used as HQ. Confined inside, Dunn realised with dismay 'that my nerve was failing.'[27] By May 1918 Dunn found that he had lost his sense of placing and timing shells and it had become a horrible worry to him. After he was affected by gas he claimed that he had requested a transfer from 2/RWF because he didn't want to serve under the new acting CO. But there may have been a subconscious recognition that his nerve was failing and he would have been worried about showing fear in front of the battalion. Two months enforced absence from the shelled area, but not from a sometimes bombed area, restored his self-confidence and Dunn was to serve for the last six months of the war as an RMO, but with a different battalion. But it wasn't just the physical strain of war – fear of shelling, fear of being mutilated, the discomforts of weather, fatigue and recurring bouts of influenza – which wore down the resistance of Dunn and other RMOs. It was the emotional strain over a period of thirty months of surviving fresh intakes of all ranks who were killed, wounded or transferred from the battalion. By the end of his thirty months with 2/RWF the only surviving officers still serving were Yates the Quartermaster and Radford a Company Commander, and perhaps three dozen other ranks. This emotional strain was movingly summarised by Lord Moran, who as RMO to 1/RF had a similar experience to Dunn:

> But the revolt that grew in my heart against this killing business – the constant fret of casualties – was another story. The battalion kept changing, seven Colonels came and went and I could never school myself to grow indifferent to these gaps. They left wounds which even now are hardly healed [in 1945] and my own decline in morale in the first months of the winter of 1916–1917 – obvious enough to me though not, I think to others – was probably the outcome of those wounds.[28]

After 1918 there was considerable public debate concerning the treatment of those suffering from war neuroses and a suspicion that some of the 346 British soldiers shot during the war for desertion, cowardice or refusing to obey orders, had in fact been suffering from war neuroses. In September 1920 a War Office Committee of Enquiry into 'Shell Shock' met under the chairmanship of Lord Southborough, and published its report in 1922. Out of the fifteen members, eleven were medically qualified. They examined 59 witnesses, most of whom had experience either of active service or of the treatment of servicemen suffering from hysteria and traumatic neurosis; among those who appeared were staff officers, regimental and battalion commanders, medical officers, neurologists and psychologists, Ministry of Pensions officials and at least six men who had suffered or were still suffering from war neurosis. Each witness was provided in advance with a questionnaire of thirty-eight questions concerning problems of military recruiting and training and the nature of shell shock. The final report of the Committee contains both excerpts from, and a summary of, witnesses' testimony. Dunn appeared as a witness because of his experience of service in the ranks during the South African War; his three years service as an RMO; and his service after the war as a member of a Pensions Appeal Tribunal. Dunn's completed questionnaire, held in the Royal Welch Fusiliers Archive, appears to be the only surviving questionnaire from those submitted by witnesses.[29]

In his evidence to the 'Shell Shock' Enquiry and later in *The War The*

Infantry Knew, Dunn displayed an ambivalent attitude about war neuroses. His approach to the subject was medically and militarily conservative, and yet he showed some sensitivity to what stress in battle and front line soldiering could mean to individuals. In his questionnaire Dunn gave his definition of shell shock and war strain:

> By shell shock and war strain I understand the acute and chronic states of a condition of being: fundamentally mental and subjective but generally, if not always, accompanied by physical sign: induced by the experience of injury or by the anticipation of danger to life or person arising out of a state of war: occurring when a man fails to gain or loses control of his thought (and action) in a situation of actual or imagined risk: multiform in expression and transient or recurring or of varying duration: caused by fear.[30]

In fact Dunn made clear distinctions between those who were suffering from shock and strain and those whom he described as shirkers and malingerers. The latter group he believed would adopt the symptoms of shock, strain or illness to evade their duty. To Dunn, 'the most potent cause of shock and strain in my experience are an intense bombardment or repeated bombardments and exposure to machine gun or concentrated rifle fire', and he argued that: 'strain of battle, prolonged responsibilities, long service alone as causes for war strain cannot, in my experience, be separated from exposure to bombing or shelling and rifle fire'.[31] Dunn noted in *The War The Infantry Knew* that under shell fire 'the idea of cover acts strongly on the mind. Men will sit calmly under no more than a corrugated-iron sheet or even a groundsheet, when shells are dropping about, whose eyes would be starting were there nothing over them'.[32] Dunn's emphasis on the effect of shell fire and its direct relation to shock and strain may also reflect his own admitted fears. He had noted on 9 January 1918 concerning himself, that 'any confined space under shell-fire had always been hateful.'[33]

Dunn believed that it was impossible to establish any one type of individual who by physique, temperament or degree of intelligence could be recognised as predisposed to shock or strain, nor were there any general characteristics. He used four examples from 2/RWF – Fletcher, Sassoon, Greaves and Coster – who were all of artistic temperament and who thus might be considered more than ordinarily susceptible to shock and strain, and yet who were 'remarkably stout men and showed no signs of war nerves'. Dunn referred to Sassoon's nervous collapse in 1917 by writing that he

> was declared officially to be shocked and treated accordingly, but that was a disciplinary measure – he said in public at home what 'everyone' in the infantry said in France. He said 'Amen' to the charge of a pacifist

publicist that men were being thrown away in wanton and futile attacks.[34]

Dunn believed that Sassoon's treatment for 'shell shock' had been 'an astute official means of denying our cold-blooded, cold-footed, superior persons the martyr they are too precious to find from their own unruly ranks'.[35] Dunn would appear then to have been ignorant of or naive about Sassoon's emotional problems and gives no indication of what value he placed on the work of Dr Rivers and others at the Craiglockhart War Hospital and their therapy for removing a patient's repressed emotions and experiences in peace and war.[36]

Dunn had found that the incidence of shock and strain was highest amongst young men aged 18 and 19 and to troops quite new to the line when they first experienced shell fire. Dunn described the symptoms of actual shell shock thus:

> a man acutely shocked by a bombardment may sit down violently tremulous, weeping or silent, staring or with tight-shut eyes, incapable of walking unaided the 100 yards that would take him out of the shelled area: or, he may lie or fall down clutching at the ground as for an aperture through which to escape.[37]

Over a period of time men could lose their nerves without being able to point to any particular causal experience. As Dunn wrote,

> some may, in retrospect, indicate when they became aware of the change in themselves. The officer or man may be less of a good fellow than he was; he ducks as he did not do; he is less enterprising than formerly: he is apt to prefer the safe detour to the more direct route; he who could carry on any routine occupation under a shelling is now distracted; there is a momentary look of apprehension, perhaps a little erection of the body, as each shell approaches, followed by an assumed look of unconcern when it has burst some distance off. Some take a little more alcohol than was their custom.[38]

Dunn distinguished between those who were affected by shock and strain and those who were shirkers and malingerers:

> The shirker never can be efficient. He's a serious service problem. My experience of him, for the purpose of this enquiry, is that he does not suffer from shock (except by accident) nor from strain. He employs self-protective devices to meet all situations. The shirker is not discoverable till he has been tried. He may have roughed it in new countries; he may have been in the Army for years – a terror on the square; he may have been a good and plucky boxer.[39]

Dunn claimed that 'the men were very reliable appraisers of cold feet, shirking and neurosis'. Dunn's ethnocentric prejudices were displayed when he wrote that his remarks applied only to the British races: 'In South Africa and in the recent War my experience of the Jew is that he's not worth his uniform'.[40]

How did Dunn think the Army could prevent and cope with shock, strain and malingering? He was convinced that much greater care had to be taken over the types of men selected to serve in the infantry. Second, that more emphasis should be placed on training before a recruit reached his unit, and that this should include what a later generation referred to as 'battle inoculation' – exposure to shell and rifle fire. Dunn believed that experienced soldiers soon became uneasy if they were joined by drafts who had no training and were unable even to fire their weapons. In *The War The Infantry Knew* Dunn had described how on 21 August 1916, during a very bad period in the line under intense shell-fire, this factor affected morale:

> All the companies are rattled. The Old Lot show it too, although there are some splendid stoics. This morning three of B, all good men, came and begged to be sent to the Transport for a rest: they said that they could not stand being in with the drafts any longer. One fell on his knees and wept when told that they must stick it and show a good example, but they were taken for a few hours rest to a trench where I had slept . . . [41]

Third, it was imperative to inculcate high morale amongst all ranks. This depended upon the careful selection of officers, particularly the commanding officer. It is difficult for someone without military experience to realise just how important the personality, character, physical courage, professionalism and sheer leadership of a commanding officer is for an infantry battalion in war. Dunn was thoroughly convinced of this, noting on 31 January 1916, 'To a detached onlooker at close quarters the supreme importance of the character of a commanding officer to the efficiency of a battalion was strikingly shown. Time was to show the grave misfortune of a slackness in any command'. Apart from acting temporary appointments, 2/RWF had seven commanding officers from 1914 to 1918. Dunn recalled:

> Except for one unpointed remark I made no reference to what every thoughtful officer and NCO said, each in his own way: that the undoubted serious deterioration of the battalion from March 1917 to July/August 1918 was due in a very large measure to the incompetence and indifference of the C.O.[42]

Furthermore, he suggested that those officers regarded as 'inefficient and gun shy to be superseded regardless of seniority and reverted – not sent back or home to safety, probably a cushy job and promotion'.[43] Morale also depended upon the individual soldier's conscience, grit and a strong sense of duty. Dunn was convinced that good morale lessened shock and strain, writing: 'it was in the second half of the war when morale was very low that I became familiar with cases of acute shock'.[44] Regimental pride Dunn believed was invaluable in maintaining ésprit de corps.

Finally, Dunn supported rigorously enforced discipline, 'distinguishing between a lapse that matters and one that does not and *always* punishing the former', and suggested that, 'the main reason for the demoralisation of the Army was the virtual suspension early in 1917 of the death penalty for desertion and flagrant shirking'.[45] In expressing this opinion Dunn came close to meeting Judge Anthony Babington's strictures about army doctors in the First World War:

> If soldiers accused of cowardice or desertion in the face of the enemy had looked to the medical officers for assistance or compassion then they were likely to have looked in vain. The army doctors as a whole seem to have set themselves up as an extra branch of the provost corps, intent on securing the extreme penalty for such offenders wherever possible.[46]

But Dunn saw the death penalty as a deterrent to those soldiers who wanted to run away during a battle. As he had noted in anger on 15 October 1917:

> Plainly no action whatever is to be taken against our habitual deserter, clear as is the evidence of wilfulness if it were offered. And yet, what use? To gratify a mawkish humanitarianism two or three score mean fellows are encouraged to slip away every time there is a risk to their skins, so more and more average men learn to shirk with impunity; attacks fail, and losses run into untold thousands, because the most dutiful men are not backed up.[47]

Dunn's robust attitude towards 'shirking', 'malingering' and the deterrent value of the death penalty was supported by other RMOs. Harold Dearden (3/GG) recalled attending a Court Martial of a Guardsman accused of desertion who he described as 'a pitiful degenerate, has drunk a lot in his time, and is obviously of no use to anyone'. To Dearden's amazement the accused asked him to appear as a character witness. 'I went to the trial determined to give him no help of any sort, for I detest this type, and seeing so many good fellows go out during the night's shelling made me all the more bitter against him for trying to back down. I really hoped he would be shot, as indeed was anticipated by all of us'.

In the event Dearden described the accused as being of a highly nervous temperament with no self-control and mentally below standard. Dearden's evidence may have helped him escape the death penalty, but the doctor believed he would 'bolt again the first chance he gets. They tell me he'll probably get shot by his own mates the next time we go over the top.'[48] M.S. Esler, another temporary officer in the RAMC, who was RMO to 2/Middlesex Regiment in France in 1917–1918, attended the execution of a deserter from his battalion and was later asked whether at the time he had considered the penalty to be a reasonable one. He replied,

> I think it was absolutely essential. It was setting a bad example to the men. They would have begun to feel that you only had to walk off during a battle and then come back afterwards and you escaped death or mutilation . . . I think it was a necessary punishment.[49]

Dunn believed that many new drafts were frightened by the strangeness and noise of the front lines, and he suggested sending them to the battalion transport for a couple of weeks to get accustomed to the noise and fears of the front line by going up nightly with the rations. He was convinced that frequent removal from the front line lessened the liability to strain if not shock by providing respite from the irritant and giving opportunity for adequate sleep and food. By 1917 it was recognised that the veteran in all ranks was too good to lose from shock or strain, 'so he was left out frequently, sent on courses, given temporary staff jobs and otherwise given respites'.[50] Finally, Dunn argued that 'the less talk about shock the better, it is calculated to suggest shock',[51] and gave examples where new troops sought medical attention in the belief that they were suffering from shock as a result of being near shell fire or hearing a rumour about gas.

Absent from Dunn's consideration of morale and discipline is any mention of religious or spiritual beliefs to sustain a soldier in war. In *The War The Infantry Knew* chaplains and church services receive a passing mention, and usually in a casual or even derogatory way. Dunn did note in 1918 'the Battalion has never received Chaplains gladly', and in July 1917 the chaplain had told him that 'he had got a real voluntary congregation of 30; the number reached 70 to 80 later still – Caernarvonshire was largely represented in these numbers. We had a much respected Chaplain at this time'.[52] Although ostensibly a Welsh Regiment, before 1914 2/RWF was nicknamed the 'Birmingham Fusiliers' on account of the very high proportion of recruits from that city. Dunn calculated that in 1914 only ten per cent of the Second Battalion were Welsh although by the summer of 1917 it had become eighty-five per cent Welsh, recruited from the nonconformist areas of North Wales.

Perhaps through modesty or because he genuinely didn't consider it to be significant, Dunn failed to mention the importance of the character, personality and professionalism of the RMO in maintaining the morale and discipline of an infantry battalion. Despite Dunn's reservations, 2/RWF throughout the war was regarded as a very effective infantry battalion by brigade and divisional commanders. It is reasonable to conclude that some at least of 2/RWF's military effectiveness between November 1915 and May 1918 was due to Dunn's role as RMO. This appears to have been substantiated by the direct evidence of Robert Graves, Siegfried Sassoon and Frank Richards, and indirectly through the recollections of other contributors to *The War The Infantry Knew*.

Dunn's evidence to the 'Shell Shock' Enquiry reflected the general tone of evidence submitted by other witnesses. The recommendations of the War Office Committee in 1922 were predictable and conservative – no soldier should be allowed to think that loss of 'nervous or mental control' provided an escape from the battlefield; if possible, slight cases of mental collapse should be prevented from leaving the front; the 'simplest form of psycho-therapy' was adequate for the majority of cases; proper medical screening of recruits was of the utmost importance; the term 'shell shock' should be abolished; concussion victims should be listed as battle casualties, while other types of mental illness should not; shell-shock cases should be treated separately from those with physical wounds; officers should study the psychology of the soldier; unit morale and discipline were of critical importance in preventing war neurosis; short tours of duty, frequent rotation and home leave were recommended; good sanitation, physical comfort and opportunities for rest of those under strain were encouraged. Although the report rejected the 'mental' origins of war neuroses, and attempted to concentrate on the moral and physical attributes, nevertheless, it was forced to confront a problem which neither the pre-war medical profession nor the military authorities had been able to diagnose, prevent or cure.

Dunn saw courage very much in terms later described by Lord Moran:

> Courage is will-power, whereof no man has an unlimited stock; and when in war it is used up, he is finished. A man's courage is his capital and he is always spending. The call on the bank may be only the daily drain of the front line or it may be a sudden draft which threatens to close the account. His will is perhaps almost destroyed by intensive shelling, by heavy bombing or by a bloody battle, or it is gradually used up by monotony, by exposure, by the loss of the support of stauncher spirits on whom he has come to depend, by physical exhaustion, by a wrong attitude to danger, to casualties, to war, to death itself.[53]

Given Dunn's definition of the role of an RMO, he approached battle stress in a traditional way, believing in rough and ready treatment, common sense and experience to distinguish between those who were really affected and those who acquired the symptoms to malinger. Like Moran, Dunn displayed an ambivalence regarding the origins of war neuroses, but had sympathy for its genuine victims.

Notes

1. For further background on Dunn see my introduction to Captain J.C. Dunn, *The War The Infantry Knew 1914–1919*, London, Jane's, 1987, hereafter referred to as *TWTIK*.

2. For background to the Army Medical Department in the nineteenth century and the development of the RAMC after 1898 see Nelson Lankford, 'Status, Professionalism, and Bureaucracy: The Surgeon in the British Army, 1860–1940', Ph.D. thesis, Indiana University, USA, 1976.

3. John Brophy and Eric Partridge, (eds), *Songs and Slang of the British Soldier: 1914–1918*, London, The Scholartis Press, 1931, p.140 and John Brophy and Eric Partridge, *The Long Trail*, London, Andre Deutsch, 1965, p.149. Both Brophy (1899–1965) and Partridge (1894–1979) were veterans having served in the ranks as volunteers – Brophy in the King's Liverpool Regiment and Partridge in the Australian Army.

4. Brophy and Partridge, *Songs and Slang*, p.161.

5. *TWTIK* p.323.

6. ibid.

7. Dunn's answer to the questionnaire sent by the 'Shell Shock' Committee L/2653/25 p1, Archives of The Royal Welch Fusiliers, Caernarvon, hereafter referred to as Dunn 'Shell Shock' Questionnaire. Quoted by kind permission of the Colonel of the Royal Welch Fusiliers.

8. Lord Moran, *The Anatomy of Courage*, London, Sphere Books, 1968, p.22. (Originally published 1945). Moran had a very paternalistic attitude towards other ranks to whom he soon acquired a reputation for being very strict at medical parades. It was noticed that when he went on leave the sick list doubled. See Richard Lovell, *Churchill's Doctor. A Biography of Lord Moran*, London, Royal Society of Medicine Services Ltd, 1992, p.41.

9. Harold Dearden, *Medicine and Duty: A War Diary*, London, William Heinemann, 1928, p.viii.

10. Frank Richards, *Old Soldiers Never Die*, London, Faber & Faber, 1953, p.218.

11. James Dunn to Edmund Blunden, 27 July 1934, quoted by kind permission of the Harry Ransom Humanities Research Center, The University of Texas at Austin and Mrs Edmund Blunden

12. *General Annual Reports on the British Army for the Period from 1 October 1913 to 30 September 1919*, London, HMSO, 1921, Part II, Strength and Distribution Tables 1A–1E, pp.17–21.

13. Peter Lovegrove, *Not Least in the Crusade: A Short History of the Royal Army Medical Corps*, Aldershot, Gale & Polden, 1951, p.47.

14. *TWTIK* p.314.

15. Dunn, 'Shell-Shock' Questionnaire, p.5.

16. *TWTIK* p.285.

17. ibid p.289. Battle to non-battle casualties as a percentage of average strength France and Flanders was 49.3 to 64.5, including of course venereal disease, T.J. Mitchell and G.M. Smith *History of the Great War Medical Services: Casualties and Medical Statistics of the Great War*, Vol 7, London, HMSO, 1931, Table 14, p.38.

18. *TWTIK* p.245.

19. Dunn, 'Shell Shock' Questionnaire p.4.

20 Mitchell and Smith, *Casualties and Medical Statistics*, Table 13, p.73.

21 *TWTIK* p.352.

22 For a more detailed background to the medical and military understanding of nervous disorders and war neuroses see P.J. Lynch 'The Exploitation of Courage: Psychiatric Care in the British Army, 1914–1918', M.Phil thesis, University College, London 1977; Martin Stone, 'Shell-shock and the psychologists' in W.F. Bynum, Roy Porter and Michael Shepherd (eds), *The Anatomy of Madness*, Vol II, London, 1985, pp.242–271 and Ted Bogacz, 'War Neurosis and Cultural Change in England 1914–1922: The Work of the War Office Committee of Enquiry into "Shell-Shock",' *Journal of Contemporary History*, 1989, Vol 24, pp.227–256.

23 According to incomplete official figures some 80,000 'shell-shock' cases passed through army hospitals during the war. Mitchell and Smith, *History of the Great War Medical Services: Diseases of the War*, London, HMSO, 1923, p.7.

24 In fact officers were more than twice as likely as other ranks to suffer mental breakdown. ibid p.17.

25 For the British Army, and particularly the infantry, the deadliest theatre of operations was the Western Front, where for every nine men sent out five were killed, wounded or missing (*Statistics of the Military Effort of the British Empire 1914–1920*, London, HMSO, 1922, p.248). An officer stood approximately a one in six chance of being killed and a one in three chance of being wounded, and was nearly twice as likely to be killed as an other rank (see J.M. Winter, *The Great War and the British People*, London, Macmillan, 1985, pp.83–92). What these general statistics fail to bring out is that the percentage of casualties over the establishment of the average infantry battalion was frequently higher – and soldiers could soon calculate their own 'survivability'.

26 *TWTIK* p.403.

27 *TWTIK* p.432.

28 Moran, *The Anatomy of Courage*, p.68.

29 See Bogacz, 'War Neurosis and Cultural Change in England' footnote 73, p.255.

30 Dunn, 'Shell Shock' Questionnaire p.8.

31 ibid, p.14. Dunn's impressions were confirmed by the postwar official history which showed that 58.51 per cent of casualties were caused by artillery and trench mortar fire as against 38.98 per cent by rifle and machine gun fire, Mitchell and Smith, *Casualties and Medical Statistics*, p.40.

32 *TWTIK* p.377.

33 ibid p.432.

34 Dunn, 'Shell Shock' Questionnaire p.9.

35 *TWTIK* p.372.

36 For a recent interpretation of the origins of the emotional stress suffered by Rupert Brooke, Siegfried Sassoon, Wilfred Owen and Robert Graves see Adrian Caesar, *Taking it like a Man: Suffering, Sexuality and the War Poets*, Manchester University Press, 1993

37 Dunn, 'Shell Shock' Questionnaire p.12.

38 ibid p.14.

39 ibid p.6.

40 ibid.

41 *TWTIK* p.253.

42 Dunn to Blunden, 19 March 1930.

43 Dunn, 'Shell Shock' Questionnaire p.19

44 ibid.

45 ibid p.26. Dunn was correct in the sense that there was a decline in the number of soldiers executed in 1918. British military executions on the Western Front 1914–1918 were as follows – 1914 – 4; 1915 – 22; 1916 – 105; 1917 – 100; 1918 – 52. Compiled from Appendix 1 in Julian Putkowski and Julian Sykes, *Shot at Dawn, Executions in World War One by Authority of the British Army Act*, Barnsley, Wharncliffe Publishing, 1989.

46 Anthony Babington, *For the Sake of Example: Capital Courts Martial 1914–1920*, London, Leo Cooper, 1983, p.x. This image of army doctors had been established by the portrayal by Leo McKern of an RMO in Joseph Losey's film, *King and Country*, 1964, which showed the fictional court martial and execution of a soldier for desertion. On the current debate over the issue of pardons for those executed see the review article by Professor Peter Rowe, Faculty of Law, University of Liverpool, of the 1993 revised edition of *For the Sake of Example* in *The RUSI Journal*, Vol 139, No.4, August 1994, pp.61–62.

47 *TWTIK* p.410.

48 Dearden, *Medicine and Duty*, pp.154–155.

49 Quoted in Babington, *For the Sake of Example*, p.249.

50 Dunn, 'Shell Shock' Questionnaire p.24.

51 ibid p.20.

52 *TWTIK* p.442 and p.430.

53 Moran, *The Anatomy of Courage*, p.13.

Part VIII

Peoples at War

Chapter 38

British Loyalties: The Evidence of an Archive

Peter Liddle

Historians today are increasingly aware of the inconsistency between the history of Britain during the First World War and the way in which succeeding generations have perceived that history. It is incontestable that Britain played a huge part in securing Allied victory and that she had the right to a distinctive place on the Allied triumphal podium. Russia had been lost to revolution, France's military reputation had been stained by soldier mutinies, Italy's by near terminal defeat and the United States, entering the war in that same penultimate year, had no track record of long-term endurance: the British people however, if we were to exclude the special case of Irish nationalism, had withstood their four and a half years without serious fracture and her servicemen had played an unfaltering, perhaps even a dominant role in securing victory.

Such facts have not proved easy to fit into the thinking of changed times. While attention has been directed consistently towards demonstrating the incompetence of military high command, to featuring the enlightenment and persecution of the conscientious objector, the work of that superior engine for the distortion of the truth, British propaganda, and then to showing how the jingoistic lemmings of 1914 became the universally disillusioned of the subsequent years, far less interest has been shown in the sustained positive response of British people to the prolonged challenge of the war. After more than thirty years of accumulating and studying an archival collection furnishing exhaustive evidence of the contemporary reaction to the war by Britons on active service and at home, this writer never ceases to be surprised at the longevity of myths and imbalanced perceptions of the British experience of the Great War. The soldier in his war service and women in their response to the war years have certainly been the subject of such thinking. This paper is designed to reflect what soldiers and women actually wrote of their experience at the time and, in a few cases, what they recorded in retrospect. The evidence will reveal a picture at variance with the image uncritically accepted by many.

Was the British soldier held to his duty by the ruthless brutality of army discipline? Did he soon jettison the ideals which called him as a volunteer in 1914? When the concept of God, King and Country was less in the forefront of a man's motivation or provided an ennobling cloak for what was largely an escape from labouring class deprivation and hardship into a world of change, adventure and the attractions of regular food, clothing, comradeship and freedom from domestic responsibility, did a sense of betrayal or alienation follow swiftly from experiencing the reality of twentieth century warfare? With the extended periods of boredom, the discomfort, the moments of stark fear, is there no evidence of a kind of relish in facing the challenge? Were all the ideals shattered? After more than three years of war we find one man writing 'I am glad of this experience if one pulls through,'[1] another, after a demanding period in the line, 'I wouldn't have missed it for anything but I am quite glad that it is over'[2] and a third describing a day in the Ypres Salient in the winter of 1917 as 'the best day of my life.'[3] In 1918 a sergeant reflected that 'it is all an interesting, exciting and wearisome game but I am not tired of things out here, there is so much to see and hear that will never happen again',[4] and also in the final year of the war there is the expression of a sentiment which one might have expected of the first weeks of the war: 'By Jove I am proud of our British Empire'.[5]

Earlier in the war but already experienced in action, a man in the ranks had written before an attack: 'It is almost certain that a lot of us will go under and in case it should fall to my lot to be one of them. I for one am well content if by my death our righteous cause is aided by the merest fraction'.[6] Another soldier in the ranks, writing to a friend serving in a different unit, reflected: 'What a game war is. There are more thrills in one second than at a dozen footer matches but we still keep jogging on, very happy and jolly for the most part. Truly life's pathway is strange yet intensely interesting even in its uncertainty, or perhaps I should say because of it.'[7] Even a less philosophical Non Commissioned Officer, also writing in 1915 and finding life in France 'a rotten existence', stated 'of course we all make the best of it and are all surprisingly cheerful'.[8] In the following year, a soldier in the ranks, wrote of the Kaiser 'Old Bill keeps trying to break through all along the line but he forgets he as (sic) the British Bulldog to beat and that will never be for we will not be beaten and he knows it.'[9] Stoicism is nearly always there in abundance, even when all naive enthusiasm has been scraped away. Indeed, in late 1917, there were still men for whom the squalid conditions of the line had not effaced beyond recognition the nobility of spirit with which so many had commenced their service. In the final months of the fighting a private in the Royal Scots wrote of his service that it was 'a great, a glorious, a romantic and adventurous life and we are fighting for civilisation'.[10] The sense of mission, interdependence and reliability of men received an attractive tribute from another officer: 'Life out here is a very wonderful thing. People are seen at their best.'[11]

Let there be no doubt about it, the cosy, politically correct picture of the British soldier identifying in sympathy with his field grey counterpart across no-man's land as a man equally imprisoned by the war into a circumstance not of his making, is an image which is not supported by contemporary evidence, however much it plays a part in post-war novels or films.

There is certainly a sort of wonderment at the German capacity to 'seem to be able to fight the world,'[12] 'a nation of the most wonderful organisation and discipline as has ever existed or will exist,'[13] but of communality of feeling there was little. It is unknown whether K.A. Townsend in August 1916 would have found many to echo his sentiment that 'after Germany's unspeakable vileness', he 'would destroy the whole race with pleasure'[14] but we may note an officer writing home asking if the photos in the papers were to have shown the enemy 'squashed to jelly under the tanks. How I hate the Huns'.[15] At the end of the war another officer did not want to go into occupied Germany 'I have seen all I want to see of the Hun and his ways',[16] and in Cologne such views were embellished with prophesy when an officer wrote that where the khaki soldiers marched, 'the streets are full of boys who I suppose will grow up to try to conquer the world again'.[17]

In the same way that delusions of soldiering fraternity with the enemy are held, we are often encouraged to believe in an unanimity of yearning for the slight wound to take a man back to Blighty and away from the danger, dirt, stench, and squalor of life at the Front. In fact there is plenty of evidence to the contrary. There was a magnetic attraction in the spirit of indivisible togetherness in the line and we should not wonder at an officer recovering from a wound, dismissing its seriousness, refusing the safety offered in home service and avowing 'It's France for me as soon as I can'.[18]

Now there is indeed evidence of sheer physical weariness, lack of sleep, of low morale, but an examination of great numbers of soldier letter and diary collections shows in a majority of cases men responding resiliently and with a measure of cheerfulness rather than otherwise to even prolonged strain.

In looking at those areas where primary evidence is at variance with the simplistic overview, it might be noted that the soldier's attitude towards those on the Home Front is also more complex than is often presented. We are rightly familiar with the lack of any real comprehension on the part of those at home with what was actually entailed in the front line service of their loved ones or acquaintances. We can appreciate too that a soldier on leave might experience a range of reactions to this. However, many soldiers were aware that home front morale was a vital weapon in the national armoury and no good purpose was served if it were drained by over-stimulated anxiety for loved ones on active service abroad. On the part of the soldier overseas picturing home, there could well be an ambivalence in his emotional response. When love had been expressed for nearest and dearest, wistfulness indicated over what had been left behind, there was room for scornful mention of those subjectively deemed to be too comfortably ensconced at home, perhaps in profit as well as under protection. Those who were seen as not pulling their weight, refusing to play their part, exercising influence to evade responsibility, inspired anger, and soldier letters frequently reflect such views.

Evidence of love for parents is so consistently present in letters that it needs no illustration here except when it is attractively widened by a man writing that we 'wouldn't have anything to fight with or fight for if it were not that we had those at home.'[19] Similarly for another in his diary: 'When I am on guard for 2 hours I always think about England and all the good times I have had there.'[20] The cross currents flow when concern for safety of parents under air raids is mixed with the thought that air raids ought to be a useful reminder to those 'who seem unaware of what is going on out here'.[21]

Grumblers in England would 'realise how well off they were' if they were sharing 2nd Lt Hopthrow's final week of March 1918 experience on the Western Front, as this officer confided to his diary.[22] I.H. Macdonell focused his resentment more sharply still: 'The striker strikes, and the shirker shirks (and) Uncle John and his pals at the Reform Club and in the House are worth an Army Corps to the Hun'.[23] Striking munitions workers were 'slack criminals' hindering the soldiers' best endeavours according to T.C. Clayton Nunn.[24] There is much along the same lines, T. Tarlton, in the final year of the war, writing in his diary of the 'outrage of the troops' that there should be industrial disputes.[25]

Unsurprisingly, Conscientious Objectors are a frequent target. A year before the passing of the first Military Service Act in January 1916, A.W.L. Turner felt no doubt about the need for the total commitment of young men to the nation's cause: 'non recruits shouldn't be allowed to marry and breed.'[26] Two years later, such was his frustration, E.G. Bates recommended that 'Every one of them should be shot instead of sending them to Wormwood Scrubs'.[27] Even the most mild of reproofs was couched in terms which fairly express the overall soldier verdict in 1916–18. Andrew Sagar, observing a physical struggle by several men to get an unwilling Conscientious Objector into uniform, affirmed that he 'would not be like that for anything'[28] and H.V. Hart writing to his sister who was married to a C.O. acknowledged that it was 'not his business' but as far as he (Hart) was concerned, it was a 'privilege' to serve.[29]

The fear of the censor may well have something to do with the fact that soldier letters have little to say about the High Command but we should note that criticism of the High Command by men in the ranks and by their officers was for various reasons less within their thinking than is commonly assumed. The same may be said of comments on politicians. There is a diary entry of Pte R. Chambers: 'Rumours of our going over the top again. Some frizzy whiskered old bugger wants shooting if we do',[30] but we have to note that it is the same soldier who, two months later, condemns the Prime Minister: 'Old Lloyd George ought to suffer what some of these poor devils (the soldiers) had'.[31] F.D. Day considered all politicians 'gas bags and traitors',[32] and on 11 November 1917, T.C. Clayton Nunn scornfully recorded in his diary that he 'hated' all staff officers, they were fat headed . . . white faced . . . corpulent . . . facetious . . . boot licking', and 'made him sick bobbing about like a lot of girls – swelling with pride.'[33] Generalisations of the sort enunciated by Day and Clayton Nunn do find their echo in personal documentation but certainly not in such numbers as to suggest that it was a preoccupying mental sore.

There is a parallel with the soldiers' view of the Press. The way the war was presented interested many, amused some and infuriated others. Among the latter was C.E. Raven who despised the way the Press was full of 'cowardly rumblings and dirty intrigues'.[34] More bitterly after the heavy losses suffered by his battalion, Lt Colonel Cordeaux wrote 'how wild the papers at home make me with their casualties "very slight". My God the British Public are fools.'[35] A letter which expresses scathing contempt for the press was in fact sent by a Company Commander to the Editor of the Daily Express acknowledging receipt of some 'tin victory trumpets' for his men, the trumpets currently doing duty as candle holders: 'If you think that men, after a hard tour in the line, appreciate such useless trumpery things . . . then your estimate of the average Tommy must indeed be a low one'.[36]

So uniformly well attested is the comradeship of the men in the line, a comradeship which in a distinctive sense included the junior officers, that this response of the British soldier at war needs no further endorsement here. The same, by extension, can be said for the overall excellence of the officer/men relationship and for the way in which regimental pride was consistently upheld. There are other matters however which inspired a range of differing response. An example of this would be the soldier's reaction to the French and Belgian peasants or townsfolk upon whom he was billeted. Men certainly wrote of what they considered to be the cupidity of Belgians and insanitary practices of the French. It cannot be expected that they would expand upon circumstances where their own behaviour will have seemed unreasonable to their involuntary hosts.

Sympathy for refugees and admiration for those who continued to till the land amidst danger and destruction – such sentiments frequently appear in both letters and diaries. Bernard Eyre Walker wrote of France and the French being 'tremendously human if squalid' and then cryptically of 'really kind Flamands for once.'[37] Meirion Thomas's opinion was that the French peasants 'wallow in filth.'[38] P.H. Rawson several times mentioned their hard working women,[39] and W.A. Miller wrote of the French being 'a wonderful nation' as in the late evening he watched a heavily laden hay-cart wending its way in the war zone past a tank.[40]

We come upon differing reactions too as men record the impact of active service upon their spiritual convictions. It has to be accepted that it is not easy to set up agreed parameters for a serious investigation of this issue. There would be little agreement over the degree to which pre-war church or chapel attendance truly represented a faith which determined a man's conduct outside his Sunday observance. Anyone generalising upon the impact of war on something as difficult to define as faith faces problems. There is however some general understanding that the war eroded the religious beliefs of a great number, challenged and overcame them for a fair number, for some reaffirmed their faith and for others, far fewer in number, brought them for the first time into a positive spiritual conviction.

J.B. MacLean thought 'Most Chaplains out here are only a nuisance.'[41] Harry Old heard the Chaplain read the Sixth Commandment in a firm voice and not a man winced and judged that 'Truly Christianity is double-faced,'[42] and yet R.H. Bradley, whose correspondence attests his abiding faith, wanted 'to go right through the experience that war has to offer to gain from it what God will let one.'[43] There were religiously inclined men who would not have agreed with Bradley's position. J.R. Bellerby was one. In his memoirs written soon after the war he considered that God could surely not have been identified in any way with the Western Front so he had seen no point in praying.[44] The numbers of men like G.M.C. Bowman who have 'put myself entirely in His keeping',[45] and J.J. Fisher who put his 'trust in God to see me through',[46] are large enough to encourage thought of a wide affirmation of faith in times of special danger or in the anticipation of battle. However, one wonders if this were lasting and, as some would argue that faith is at constant war with logic, for how long would N.M. McLeod's immediate post Armistice reflection stand dialectical testing: 'No one who has seen the thousands and thousands of little graves [can have] any doubt about the Resurrection'?[47]

In another book the author has accepted that institutionalised religion was one of the casualties of war but it seems appropriate to conclude this brief airing of a subject which will always present food for thought, with a statement strongly at odds with that verdict.[48] Hubert Worthington wrote of the progression of his spiritual thinking 'towards absolute conviction of faith in the Church of England . . . England and the world are going to turn the war into the greatest instrument for the Kingdom of Heaven yet known or we are going to become mere beasts and worse than before . . . I suppose people will argue with me but of course argument in religion is sheer bilge. It comes to me through sheer experience and not through priests and books.'[49] Parenthetically, and perhaps mischievously, because the author does not know the answer in Worthington's case, is this letter writer not offering us here yet another piece of evidence that disillusionment may follow the war but is not automatically to be seen as a concurrent element within its timespan? And so to women.

If the horizons of men as a result of the war expand far beyond their local community, the opportunities for women in all terms, including that of claiming by right a less subordinate place throughout society, were there as never before. Their response to the crisis of war is demonstrated over and over again as one of readiness, even eagerness, to serve and conviction as to the righteousness of the cause. In both respects the response was sustained. Family reasons as well as the national need demanded that a woman played her part. The poster which invited women to take up this work or that was valuable in a directional sense; it was far less necessary as an appeal to conscience. Much has been written about women in general terms having little idea of the real nature of the fighting at the front. Even those in uniformed service overseas, it was said, were very seldom in any danger. However, this patronising disqualification of women and their response to the reality of war understates one point and more significantly misses another altogether. First, some women did face danger: Mary Marshall, for example, in France with the First Aid Nursing Yeomanry, was awarded the Military Medal for 'gallantry and coolness' during a bombing raid by hostile aircraft on 23 September 1918. After the first bomb she 'rallied the medical orderlies who had become temporarily disorganised, and throughout the raid, in exceedingly trying and dangerous circumstances she displayed the utmost disregard for danger'.[50] Second, and really far more to the point, the war could not have been waged, never mind won, without the war effort of women in munitions, heavy industry, on the land, in substitute labour, in expanded medical services and through economy and imagination in the kitchen. Furthermore, a woman's universal burden in wartime is that of anxiety for her menfolk on active service, an anxiety which in 1914 –18 so frequently became the reality of bereavement. To this burden might be added a woman's personal vulnerability against the very essence of war – her compassion and pain at the suffering of humanity. No one should underestimate what was required of women in wartime: for all, a sense of anxiety, for so many, a sense of loss, while at the same time a home had to be run, children brought up, economies made, new jobs undertaken. There were new opportunities and freedoms but for women to continue to fulfil a war-winning role, the national cause had to hold sustainable attraction – and it did.

Recalling her war work many years later, Mrs P. Burton, whose father and brothers worked at Hylton Colliery in Sunderland, drew together the simple reasons which conditioned her response to the war: 'There was a war on, we wanted to do our little bit, also we thought of the money . . . my two brothers had enlisted and my mother could manage without help . . . I could send money home and I could send parcels to my brothers and my friend and I had two holidays in Blackpool and in those days you were lucky to have a holiday.'[51] Such recollections have the ring of truth but they miss what was for many women in all classes of society the sense of an exciting departure from the normal humdrum way of life – a sense of leaving that which was to be expected and embarking upon something of an adventure. Munitions work was often physically heavy, demanded still more discipline than was in any event required in an industrial workplace and it could be dangerous. Mrs Burton herself narrowly escaped injury in the explosion at the White Lund factory, Morecambe. However, in her recollections, she had failed to record the fact that she had left home for the first time, travelled by train across the country from the East to the West coast, lived in a hutted dormitory with girls from far afield, was free from the overseeing eye of her parents and was enjoying an independence which in the ordinary run of things she would not have achieved. It was a hard-working freedom but there can be no doubt that her horizon was extended. It is unfortunate that we do not know whether she were to have recorded this at the time. It is not likely that she would have written long, descriptive letters or kept a personal diary and if she were to have done so, nothing has survived.

The same is regrettably true of Mrs E.N. Smith but she did record subsequently that when she arrived at the new munitions factory at Gretna after a journey from Sunderland 'there were girls from everywhere, from Scotland, Ireland, Wales and England and some lovely girls from Inverness but the main girls who came to begin the work were from Fraserburgh in the North of Scotland – they were very nice but very broad Scot. It took a long time to understand them.'[52]

After training at Shoreditch, a London-based girl was sent to work at a tool makers in Coventry. She worked night shift for two years and in retrospect remembered concerts, dances, and friendships maintained over fifty years. When potential areas of dissatisfaction were put to her, the cold of the work premises, poor conditions in digs or a hostel, she would have none of it. Perhaps distance had lent enchantment but clearly there was a good deal of fun and fellowship: 'I taught a few Birmingham girls to dance' in the lunch breaks.[53]

Mrs Emily Hubble, a munitions girl at Gretna who received commendation and promotion for prompt action when a nitro-glycerine emergency occurred, did remember it being desperately cold in the dormitory cubicles but 'we were very happy. We had no responsibilities. We were being fed and looked after. It was kind of a Lady's life in a way'.[54]

The dearth of contemporary personal documentation of women in the labouring classes is general but not without exception. All too frequently the exception relates to bereavement. Here there is what one might expect, moving testimony that these women bore their tragic ordeal with courageous composure. Alice Leek for example wrote to a Padre Evers on receipt of his letter of condolence following the death in action of her stretcher-bearer husband: 'Truly it is glorious to have died for ones country, but it is hard for those who are left behind.' She asked that 'the little family left to mourn his loss may be remembered in your prayers.'[55]

Munitions, shipbuilding and other heavy industries, clothing factories making uniforms, agriculture, forestry, the three military services, each was offering an opportunity for women to respond to national needs and in so doing it seems quite reasonable to conclude that many would find fulfilment of unspoken even unguessed areas for personal development. For the better educated even more doors were opening. More precisely it should be stated that some doors were already open but were now opening wider. The medical profession and clerical/secretarial work fall nicely within this latter bracket.

Of the generally positive response to a war crisis now extending beyond three years, Alice Sims wrote to her sister: 'You see girls in every capacity from milk girls to Carter Patterson girls, coal girls and sweeps. I think you must agree with me that the women have come forward splendidly'.[56]

It is instructive to examine the diary of a teenage girl from a privileged background. Patricia Hanbury's record illustrates the way in which the war took over her young life just as it refocussed the daily concerns of people from every class. Patricia lived at Hitcham House, near Windsor, its stables turned into a convalescent home for Canadian soldiers who had been in the very stately hospital at Clivedon. Her father commanded a battalion in France and her eldest brother also served there. One sister nursed in a war hospital in Boulogne, another nursed children during the war. An indoor household staff of seven, with three gardeners, a groom and a chauffeur, left Hitcham at intervals for various war service or war related jobs. The war, even amidst leisure, never seems to leave Patricia's thoughts. In a September 1916 week's holiday visiting Clovelly she wrote: 'It almost made one forget war to look at these peaceful little cottages with happy children playing on the doorsteps. And yet some of those homes may have been anxious with some loved one absent.' In the evening on a beach "one of the rocks was just like a crouching British lion. It was looking out over the sea and one felt as though it was guarding England with the great billows dashing all around it.'

A Zeppelin raid over London is recorded next and a visit to the cinema to see 'very wonderful war pictures of Salonica, Kut, French Army and Navy and the Russian Army then we saw some pictures of the Somme Battle. They were very thrilling as they had been taken so lately.' A close family friend died of wounds: 'It was an awful blow and one could not take it in at first.' On 28 September 'Our ten convalescents all returned to hospital as Betty was just off for a holiday after massaging for five months without a rest. The men gave three large cheers for Hitcham House as they left.'

Grandmother and Patricia on 30 September took three of the convalescents for a drive but Miss Hanbury learned that her father was so physically drained that he was to be sent home and there was further disquieting news, financial irregularities at Clivedon Hospital, arrests and a scandal. Patricia's father was met at Victoria Station looking 'tired and thin but otherwise alright.' More convalescents arrived and Betty resumed her massage work. On 26 October 'We priced and arranged "rummage" all morning for a rummage sale in the evening . . . our sale in the evening was a great success and we got £23.00. Patients from the hospital were entertained for the day and the Christmas parcels were packed for the men at the front from this village. There were about 43–50.' A newly bereaved woman visited them looking 'so sad and ill' but a few days later that same lady and her daughter 'went to a place near to Verdun to work at a canteen for men straight out of the trenches'.

When her brother Reg came home from France on leave, he also looked 'tired and thin'. His arrival coincided with the family's support of 'National Mission Week'. Two Zeppelins were recorded as having been brought down and before the end of November there was an unexpected arrival of an aeroplane landing in a nearby field; the pilot was a family friend. As it was too misty for 'Mark to go on to Farnborough that night more friends were rustled up and we danced and sang until quite late.'

There were of course Christmas dinners for the soldiers, a service of Intercession and some family celebrations but she recorded for 31 December that war was still raging and that there was not much hope of peace. The year 1916 'had not been a very happy one.' Indeed it had not been a happy year at home or abroad but the Hanbury family and its circle had unfalteringly identified with the national cause.[57]

In trying to gauge in general terms the way women reacted to the changed circumstances in which many found themselves, a recurring image emerges, one which has a parallel even in the trenches during quiet periods. Routine and a new normality reign in settings which scarcely could have been forecast. A phrase in a letter from Gwynneth Milburn captures the essence of this. Having experienced at close hand in Hull a 1915 Zeppelin raid, from London during the daylight raids of 1917 she wrote: 'Thank goodness if they are coming often, they are coming earlier, one does get a good night afterwards'.[58] A female worker with the Scottish Churches Hut in No 5 Convalescent Camp in France, Netta Hamilton, wrote letters which are overlaid by such a presumption that the war continues and does not need mention that she might well be describing the daily life at some seaside resort except that everyone is wearing similar clothes and all a drab lightish brown. On 26 August 1916 she had some free time before the counter of her hut opened and she wrote home: 'Our little party on Saturday came off alright and I enjoyed it immensely. We had a lovely dinner in a little tea-room at Cayeau and had the most gorgeous cakes which were ripping, then we went to see the revue which is pronounced as great a success as previously. The "girls" were simply splendid and except for their voices one could hardly have told that they were men . . . Tell Elsie that a man came to the counter the other day and laid off a great screed to me in the middle of a tea rush the gist of which was that a Sgt Major Evans was asking for her and said he is with the Canadians and misses the Scottish Church Hut ladies very much.'[59]

The same extraordinary normalcy of wartime life appears in the papers of polio victim Mrs Emily MacLeod. She had two sons on active service and twin girls who combined teacher training college life with a range of voluntary war work. She lived in comfortable middle class circumstances in Cambridge. Her physical disability was countered by the determination with which she rode a tricycle. She kept open house for family and friends, doing all the food shopping for meals carefully planned to keep within the food restrictions. These restrictions made their impact upon the parcels regularly sent to her boys. She undertook a significant commitment to the 1st Eastern General Hospital, adopting soldiers in particular from the Highland regiments. She visited them, taking comforts and supported their visitors some of whom had travelled from the North of Scotland. She acted as Paymaster to the soldiers of the hospital, allocating a weekly allowance for their needs.

Not the least of Mrs MacLeod's daily tasks was that of regular correspondence with her four children. The letters reveal her as engaged upon a quite remarkable degree of service to others. Occasionally, with an economy of words, the letters are very moving: 'The MacKenzie boy is worse – 'serious' – his parents are staying till Monday. Mrs McTaggart and I went to the memorial service in King's today. Boyce McKenzie's name was read out and also of course Donald Innes – at the end, 4 buglers standing on altar steps sounded the Last Post and then Mrs Innes broke down – I could not watch her.'[60]

It is not the purpose of this paper to diminish or to divert attention from the grief of Mrs Innes and of those who suffered similarly. The author does not seek to underestimate the strain which stretched the fibres of a woman's heart as she awaited telegrams of death or wounds for her menfolk. It is rather to put beside such images others which also deserve their place – the strong sense of national and local identity which animates so many personal documents. It is an identity which has called for a positive response to the challenge facing all. This response may well have been through voluntary unpaid or paid work, something which in itself brought satisfaction at several levels. It will have called for concern and care for others and it required that one did one's best to keep cheerful because times for all were harsh.

The fact that there were women who devoted their energies to the support of Conscientious Objectors or who took part in strikes at their work place does not seriously influence the overall conclusion which can be drawn from any survey of women's contemporary documentation of the war. Furthermore, so many diaries or letters pay private tribute to receiving small kindnesses or being warmed by someone's cheery considerate demeanour that the painting of women's war in uniformly bleak colours will not do. It is a denial of individual responses which collectively accounted for the national resolve.

A factory girl might not have recorded at the time her reaction to a work place accident as Mary Marshall in the First Aid Nursing Yeomanry did: ('In trying to disinfect my hands I put them into pure disinfectant thinking it was solution. Of course I have burnt myself . . . I expect they will skin. Fortunately it doesn't stop my work'[61] but the social divide between the two women was bridged by a common attitude: with the country at war, who could allow her work to be impeded?

As a Sister with three years active service experience in Hospital Ships, and then in France in Queen Alexandra's Imperial Military Nursing Service, Priscilla Simpson prepared herself as did so many more in France for the anticipated German offensive in March 1918. She wrote in her diary 'one cannot help dreading it a little now all the troops are released from Russia and they will be able to bring overwhelming numbers against us – but our faith is strong in the cause of right and justice and what are numbers with God on our side. When one thinks of the early days of the war and how our little contemptible army held back all those hordes of Germans it gives me confidence for the future.'[62] She knew what was going on: she looked back and drew comfort. It is not insignificant to my theme of the positive response of women as well as men to war that this Sister, less than a week after the Armistice and while rejoicing that there would be no more wounded coming in, added that 'there will be many things to regret when we come to disband for there have been some very happy times in spite of all the dreadful experiences of war.'[63]

As with soldiers, for women too there are common misperceptions like their supposed gullibility to propaganda images of German beastliness. A woman had her new factory workmates to get along with or her Voluntary Aid Detachment nursing colleagues. She had her brother's, her boyfriend's or husband's safety to preoccupy her when she was not busy filling shells or changing wound dressings. In her exciting new independence, whatever the personal strains, there was little time to contemplate the iniquities of the Kaiser, just possibly time to smile at the cartoon of him, a figure of derision, even of fun. Bitter thought or even angry words were usually reserved for those not playing their part.

Quite deliberately there has been no focus of attention here on those women whose war service was so exceptional as to mark them as just that, exceptional. Edith Cavell's sad fate ensures that her record lives on but scarcely known Sister White who nursed with her may be mentioned. She hid two wounded men in her accommodation at Miss Cavell's request and in her recollection of this denied any awareness of danger inhibiting compliance: 'It was impossible to send a wounded man away like that. He had to be looked after and [in a place] to be looked after . . . it was expected of a nurse.'[64]

Loyalty to one's country, to the Entente, to Belgium or Serbia and humanitarian instinct animated other women who like Cavell were to become celebrated. Florence Farmborough and Violet Thurstan in Russia, Mrs Elsie Knocker and Mhairi Chisholm in Belgium spring to mind. Dr Elsie Inglis, Dr May Dickinson Berry and Mrs St Clair Stobart did outstanding work in the Balkans and, of course, Flora Sandes was engaged in active military service as a soldier with the Serbs.

There were other women whose fame in a sense disqualifies them from more than fleeting appearance in this paper, Lena Ashwell with her concert parties, and Katherine Furse in the organisation of women's uniformed voluntary services. A case which has not yet got the recognition it deserves is that of Soeur Marguerite, the English Nun caught in the German occupation of areas of North Eastern France. She nursed wounded under conditions of German control, and was for some time captive in Germany but by independent-minded, determined agitation secured permission to return to France and then worked in a military hospital behind the French lines.[65]

Leaving aside all such special cases, an examination of the response of British women to the challenge of the Great War mirrors that of the response of the British soldier in France – a perception of the nation's need and a sense of duty interwoven with opportunity. The protracted length and the nature of the war would have a major impact upon the soldier. As duty became statutory with compulsory military service and opportunity became far less attractive in the reality of conditions on the Western Front, enthusiasm waned but war was forging something more enduring in its place, stoic resilience. For women too the years of war and the fact or anxiety over bereavement gave sombre colours to the record of their service. Nevertheless the evidence is there of a sustained unity of purpose. Is this phenomenon to be viewed patronisingly as the product of pre-war educational systems, values self-interestedly inculcated by political parties, the social system, institutionalised religion and the Press all fruiting in ground well fertilised by wartime propaganda? Do we explain national endeavour through the years of war as if it were an unnatural phenomenon of mass delusion? It is possible that we might be better employed in considering whether nations were to have accumulated over centuries or decades characteristics of behaviour in times of war. Ernest Haden, an RFA Signaller, wrote to his brother of the March 1918 crisis, 'we began to wonder how things would turn out after so big a defeat. Still we manage somehow to do our best when we have to face the worst. I suppose it is one of the characteristics of the British people to do their utmost when necessity requires no less.'[66] The question as to whether Haden were indeed representative needs addressing. However difficult it may be, we need to consider from all the evidence available, the collective response of countless individuals each in his or her own wartime crisis. An attempt so to do has led this author to the conclusion that there was not only a considerable degree of unity of purpose throughout British society during the First World War but that British historians have no need to begin their explanation of this in an exculpatory fashion.

Notes :

All personal experience documentation quoted is from the Liddle Collection, the Library, the University of Leeds.

1   G. Verity, 2nd Lt 5th Bn Lancashire Fusiliers, Diary 5.5.17
2   C.E. Raven, Padre, Letter 24.11.17
3   T.H.E. Helby, Lt RGA, Diary 29.12.17
4   A.D. Wills, Sgt 100th Bn Canadian Expeditionary Force, Letter 22.1.18
5   A. Hooper, 2nd Lt Queen's Own Royal West Kent Regt, Letter 7.7.18
6   Charlie Bosher, Rank and Unit unknown, Letter 21.9.15 [See Battle of Loos: Item 12]
7   Thomas Dyson, Cpl 4th Bn Duke of Wellington's Regt, Letter 12.7.15 [See H.W. Harwood Papers]
8   C. Turner, L Cpl 1st/1st West Riding Field Ambulance RAMC, Letter 13.6.15 [See H Oldham Papers]
9   T. Jackson, Pte 8th Bn East Lancashire Regt, Letter 2.3.16
10   J.D. Urquhart Pte 15th Bn Royal Scots, Letter 26.10.17
11   'Burmah' signatory of a letter dated 7.5.17 to A.S.G. Butler
12   R.J.W. Ledingham. Lt RFA, Diary for end of May 1918
13   L.F.S. Sotheby, 2nd Lt Argyll and Sutherland Highlanders, Letter 24.5.15
14   K.A. Townsend, Lt RHA, Letter 24.8.16
15   E.G. Bates, 3rd Bn attached 9th Northumberland Fusiliers, Letter 2.16.17
16   E.A. Smith, Gnr RGA, Letter 5.12.18
17   P.N. Ellis, Lt RHA, Letter 13.2.19
18   N. F. Humphreys, Capt HBMGC, Letter 17.5.17
19   A. D. Wills, Sgt 100th Bn Canadian Expeditionary Force, Letter 4
20   T.R. Bennett, Pte 9th Bn Middlesex Regt, Diary 4.3.18
21   H.W. Sims, Rifleman 1st Bn Queen's Westminster Rifles, Letter 72
22   H.E. Hopthrow, 2nd Lt Royal Engineers, Diary 27.3.18

23 I.H. Macdonell, Major 2nd Bn Inniskilling Fusiliers, Letter 28.1.1917
24 T.C. Clayton Nunn, Major 1st Bn Royal West Kent Regt, Diary 9.5.15
25 T. Tarlton, Clerk to APM Military Police, 26.7.18
26 A.W.L. Turner, Pte Ceylon Planters Rifles, Letter 1.1.15
27 E.G. Bates, Lt 3rd Bn attached 9th Bn Northumberland Fusiliers, Letter 28.3.17
28 A. Sagar, Pte 5th Bn Lancashire Fusiliers, Letter 18.5.17
29 H.V. Hart, Lt 6th Bn London Regt, Letter 6.8.16
30 R. Chambers, Cpl 1st Bn Hertfordshire Regt, 27.7.18
31 R. Chambers, Cpl 1st Bn Hertfordshire Regt, 27.9.18
32 F.D. Day, Sgt Royal Engineers, Letter 170
33 T.C. Clayton Nunn, Major 1st Bn Royal West Kent Regt, Diary 11.11.17
34 C.E. Raven, Padre, Letter, 19.2.18.
35 Lt Col E.K. Cordeaux, 10th Bn Lincolnshire Regt, Letter 7.7.16
36 J.E. Smart, Capt 5th Bn Manchester Regt, Letter 4.1.18
37 Bernard Eyre Walker, Pte RAMC 81st Field Ambulance, Diary 18.11.17, 1.2.15
38 Meirion Thomas, 2nd Lt 13th Bn South Wales Borderers, Letter 14.9.15
39 P.H. Rawson, Capt RAMC attached to 8th South Staffordshire Regt, Letters 95, 99, 165
40 W.A. Miller, Capt 2nd King Edward's Horse attached 11th Bn Tank Corps, Letter 18.9.18
41 J.B. MacLean, Lt 1st Bn Cameronians, Letter 33, 12.12.17
42 Harry Old, Pte 15th Bn London Regt, Letter 4.4.15
43 R.H. Bradley, Capt 22nd Bn London Regt, Letter 19.9.15
44 J.R. Bellerby, 2nd Lt 8th Bn West Yorkshire Regt, Memoir
45 G.M.C. Bowman, Pte 1st Bn HAC, Letter 16.12.16
46 J.J. Fisher, L Cpl 1/7th Bn Cheshire Regt, Letter 1915
47 N.M. McLeod, Major RFA, Letter 16.11.18
48 Peter Liddle, *The Soldier's War 1914–18* (London, Blandford Press 1988) p.218
49 Hubert Worthington, 2nd Lt 6th Bn Manchester Regt, Letter 7.2.17
50 Mary D. Marshall Papers, Military Medal Citation
51 Mrs P. Burton, 1969 Recollections letter
52 Mrs E.N. Smith, Taperecording No. 167 April 1971
53 Mrs Ainsley, Taperecording No. 200 December 1973
54 Mrs Emily Hubble, Taperecording No. 303 September 1975
55 From the papers of Rev M.S. Evers, Capt Chaplain to the Forces 74th Bde 4th Army
56 From the papers of H.W. Sims : See end note 21
57 Patricia Hanbury, Diary Sept-Dec 1916
58 Gwynneth Milburn, Letter 26.9.17
59 Netta Hamilton, Letter 26.8.16
60 Mrs E.M. MacLeod, Letter 1.11.18
61 Mary Marshall, Letter 17.5.16
62 Priscilla Simpson, Sister QAIMNS, Diary 8.3.18
63 ibid, Diary 16.11.18
64 Sister White (Mrs Battrum) Taperecording No. 36 1969
65 There is documentation in the Liddle Collection on Florence Farmborough,

Violet Thurstan, Elsie Knocker, Mhairi Chisholm, Soeur Marguerite, Lena Ashwell, Katherine Furse and numbers of women who served with The Scottish Women's Hospital Units. For Soeur Marguerite, see *The Poppy and the Owl, the Journal of the Friends of the Liddle Collection*, Number 15, February 1995, article by Tony Sutton.

66 Ernest W. Haden, Signaller RFA, Letter 3.2.19

Chapter 39

A Nation at War: The Russian Experience

THE NATIONAL EXPERIENCE OF WAR, 1914–1917
Vladimir Buldakov

The social experience of World War I is still not studied in Russia, despite the fact that the country's human losses were so great in that war. 1,660,000 Russian citizens were killed, died in hospitals and disappeared without trace. Only now is the conviction that World War 1 was the real turning point of modern Russian history beginning to penetrate public opinion. As an historian of revolution, I think that only through a realistic picture of her people at war can one fully explain the history of modern Russia and her greatest social conflicts.

There have been various reasons why the importance of World War I has been discounted by Soviet society. The first is that, after the war against foreign enemies, the great internal civil war of 1918 – 1920 began. The victims of this civil war were so terribly numerous as to make the losses in World War I seem less tragic. Second, there was the view of the the official communist historiography that the so-called Great October Socialist Revolution was the only event of supreme importance in the whole history of modern mankind. Of course, Soviet historians reckoned World War I to be an 'accelerator' of the 'socialist' revolution, but their main interest was 'objective' – i.e. in the economic, not the social, preconditions of socialism.

Third, World War I was labelled by communists as 'the imperialist war', not as a patriotic war of national defence. There is some truth in this, and not a single monument devoted to the victims of World War I was built in the U.S.S.R.

Finally, there has been a concrete obstacle to research on the experience of the war. The greater part of documents with information about the conditions of the Imperial Russian Army was secret and the Soviet Empire tried to perpetuate all the mysteries of the Tsarist Empire. Just recently all the documents in the Russian war-history archives have become accessible to scholars, but in these state archives there were no documents about how human beings lived through the war.

The soldiers of this greatest of empires were never seen by its ruling class as persons, but only as talking animals in grey uniform. Its authorities, in spite of an officially paternal attitude, paid no attention to its loyal citizens. It was only when soldiers became an anti-governmental force, that the authorities began to pay heed to them. The archives contained all too many documents about the crimes of soldiers and mutinies in the army, but little information about the ordinary life of rank-and-file fighters. The soldiers' everyday lives and the state of their minds and spirit were ignored also in the patriotic literature of the period.

It has only been through military censorship that soldiers' letters have been brought together in a collection,[1] but censors usually did not have any detailed instructions about their duties and these assemblages of letters, published only as extracts,[2] could not give full information about the mood of rank-and-file participants of the war and their relatives. Moreover, the letters that we do have furnish little information about day-to-day life in the trenches.

Personal reminiscences of soldiers are very rare.[3] Nobody collected them. About eighty per cent of the Russian wartime army consisted of former peasants and while the artillery and staff included representatives of the pre-war working and the middle class, the infantry was drawn from this rural workforce which was in large part illiterate.

A proper study of the everyday life of Russian soldiers is therefore almost impossible. This reflects a general tendency of Russian historiography: using the documents of state archives one can write a story of the state and the educated classes, but not a full story of the people. Private collections of documents disappeared in the Soviet period. Scholars may of course try to reconstruct a picture by combining different kinds of documents, but with possibly inaccurate results. The soldiers, especially former peasants, have usually appeared as a bizarre assemblage of heroes and traitors, not in their role as trained troops.

But first, before further consideration of the question, a few words about the main reasons why the imperial army and Russia were defeated. It is incorrect to think, as did many of the Tsarist and Soviet officials, that Russia was absolutely unprepared for the Great War. From the 1870s, the Russian General Staff pointed out Germany as likely to be the main enemy in a future war. They stated also their principal aims: to annex the Black Sea Straits, Galicia, German and Austrian Poland; and they also spoke of the inevitable annexation of Eastern Prussia.[4] By 1914 a detailed plan of mobilization had been elaborated. This mobilization was very successful at every stage. There was, of course, an initial shortage of artillery shells and machine-guns, but by the end of 1916 the situation had improved and the Russian army was getting enough guns, shells and manpower for its planned grand-scale offensive, which would finally accelerate the destruction of Germany and Austria-Hungary.

Russia had enough raw materials and foodstuffs to sustain a total war. Despite the shortage of hands and horses in agriculture,[5] after she ceased to export grain, Russia's bread supply problems seemed to be over. Not only government bodies, but economists as well, were confident that their agriculture, albeit primitive, gave a great advantage in supplying provisions under war conditions.[6] The projected day ration allowance of a soldier included 2.5 pounds of bread and 1.5 pounds of meat.[7] Later the meat ration was reduced to one pound. Admittedly, food was temporarily in short supply, but the Russian soldier was never so hungry as the German.

The reasons for the Russian army's defeat were not therefore just to do with quantities of guns, men, resources and foodstuffs. The fact was that the old regime was incapable of waging a modern total war. Russia was the only great power which began to disintegrate during wartime – and this was not an economic disintegration. The hunger riots in Petrograd of February 1917, which ended by the overthrowing of the Tsarist government, were provoked by the incapacity of the railroads to supply foodstuffs to the capital. There was enough grain in the country, but the urban population were not getting enough bread. In this situation the soldiers in February 1917 refused to shoot demonstrators. The fate of the autocracy in Russia was resolved by peasants with rifles. In October 1917 the end of Russia's external war came when the soldiers of the Petrograd garrison demanded peace. Again, one should remember that eighty per cent of the Russian army consisted of former peasants.

Thus the revolution in Russia was not the archetypical social conflict between proletariat and bourgeoisie in the manner predicted. It was also, importantly, a peasant rebellion against the militarized empire. The roots of this conflict were in the army. The main reason for such a conflict lay in the soldiers' attitudes.

Now I shall try to illustrate some aspects of the behaviour of this army of mainly peasant foot-soldiers. First there was the peasant soldier's attitude towards Russia's aims in the war. The idea of annexation of the territories mentioned was absolutely alien to the understanding of the Russian soldier. But the generals and official propagandists were not in the habit of recalling to them the idea of defending their Fatherland, which would have made sense, and preferred to speak about 'the Slav's hegemony in the postwar world'. So in the peasant-soldier's mind the war came to be seen not as something they could comprehend, but as a kind of penalty from God [8] – not for their own sin, but for those of the ruling class.

The behaviour of peasants during mobilization was very characteristic. There were many riots involving bloody conflicts with the police.[9] The government prohibited the sale of vodka during the mobilization. The recruits usually looted wine-shops. Although, thenceforth, the sale of grape wines and beer was also banned, the soldiers always tried to obtain alcohol and substitutes. Sometimes their readiness to attack in battle was inspired by the hope of capturing alcohol from the enemy.[10] The war and later the revolution were accompanied by heavy drinking.

The so-called fraternisation with the enemy across the lines was also connected with drinking. Usually the Russian soldier tried to exchange bread for German schnaps or Austrian rum drinks.[11] So the idea of peace increasingly became connected in the soldiers' minds with drinking

Though these peasant soldiers did have elements of a primitive chauvinism, patriotism in the modern sense was unknown to them and a friendly attitude to most prisoners-of-war, especially of Slavonic origin, was characteristic.[12] Very often the Russian soldier preferred to surrender. In 1915, while retreating from Galicia, about a million Russian soldiers became prisoners-of-war, three-quarters of them freely.[13] The tendency of Russian soldiers to desert is also well known. This was not cowardice. They seldom deserted while in the trenches, but in most cases when out of the line.[14] Strikingly, these included men decorated for bravery.

Peasant soldiers found the psychology of professional soldiers unfathomable. They themselves regarded their new duty as temporary and pointless. They were not fond of training and were disinclined to dig trenches properly and make themselves comfortable.[15] Their only thoughts were for the war to end, regardless of conditions, and of staying alive.

It is most important to understand the nature of the relationship between these soldiers and their officers. For the peasant conscripts the officers were not only their commanders – they also represented the hated landlord class, as well as in some cases an unfamiliar non-traditional culture. It was for this reason that in 1917 soldiers demanded that officers with 'German' names [16] should be weeded out of the army. Some of the soldiers dreamed of the land of these 'German colonists' being confiscated by the government and put at their own disposal after the war – a primitive agrarian variety of 'nationalism'.[17]

Of course the hatred felt by the soldiers for the officers was also connected with a brutal discipline and the practice of using fists and birches. The soldiers never forgave officers for cowardliness, drinking, or for having quarters which were comfortable and safe.[18] Moreover, many Russian officers and generals were known to be corrupt. Members of a truly privileged ruling caste, their ethics tended to exclude friendly relationships with the soldiers.[19] At the time of the February revolution and later, dozens of officers were killed by the soldiers, though it was usual to divide all the officers into 'good' and 'bad' categories, with only the latter being executed.

The worst elements among the officers had a corrupting effect on their men. Peasant conscripts, accustomed to plunder, were also influenced by the anti-semitic mood of the highest commanders, the officers and especially the Cossacks.[20,21] All the evils of the war influenced these peasant representatives of traditional Russian culture and many became habituated to robbery to rape. Not all soldiers, of course, became revolutionaries of the looting and massacring type of 1917–1918; but as the chroniclers pointed out, it was the defeats of 1915 which began chiefly to demoralise these former peasants,[22] who were affected by the shortages of ammunition and foodstuffs. At the time, the censors drew attention to the fact that the soldiers had begun to wish for peace without conditions by the beginning of 1916. In the summer of 1917 the collapse of morale became inevitable.

Notes

1   See military censorship memoirs in the State Archive of the Russian Federation (GARF), Collection 5881, description 1, folder 201, folios 6–8, 10–11; description 2, folder 377, folios 276–277.

2   Soldatskie pisma v gody mirovoi voiny (1915–1917) – Krasnyi arkhiv, 1934, n° 4–5; Soldatskie pisma 1917 goda, Moscow-Leningrad, 1927.

3   S.F. Ershov, Stranitsy proshlogo: Zapiski starogo soldata, Leningrad, 1962; D. Oskin, Zapiski soldata, Moscow, 1929; A.M. Pireiko, V tylu i na fronte imperialisticheskoi voiny: Vospominaniya ryadovogo, Leningrad, 1926.

4   GARF, Collection 5881, description 2, folder 530, folio 16.

5   A.M. Anfimov, Rossiiskaya derevnya v gody pervoi mirovoi voiny (1914 – fevral 1917). Moscow, 1962, p. 130.

6   See: I.S. Bliokh, Budushchaya voina v tekhnicheskom i politicheskom otnosheniyakh, vol. II, St. Petersburg, 1898, pp. 624–626.

7   GARF, Collection 5881, description 2, folder 110, folios 25, 74.

8   Voina i kostromskaya derevnya (Po dannym ankety statisticheskogo otdeleniya). Kostroma, 1915, pp. 66–71.

9   A.B. Berkevich, Krestyanstvo i vseobshchaya mobilizatsiya v iyule 1914 g.-Istoricheskie zapiski 1947, vol. 23, pp. 3–43; Krasnaya revolyutsionnaya borba krestyan v Rossii v gody imperialisticheskoi voiny (1914–1916 gg.), Moscow, 1932, p. 48–49; Yu. I.Kiryanov, Krestyanstvo Ekaterinoslavskoi gubernii v gody pervoi mirovoi voiny, Moscow, 1960, p. 26; D.Oskin, op. cit., p. 68.

10   D. Oskin, op. cit., pp. 115, 207–210, 274.

11   M.I. Akhun, V.A. Petrov, Tsarskaya armiya v gody imperialisticheskoi voiny, Moscow, 1929.

12   F. Stepun, Iz pisem praporshchika-artillerista, Odessa, 1919, p. 59; A. Ksyunin, Narod na voine: iz zapisok voennogo korrespondenta. St.Petersburg, 1919, pp. 5–11.

13   GARF, Collection 5881, description 2, folder 532, folio 54.

14   A.M. Pireiko, op. cit., pp. 29, 37, 40.

15   F. Stepun, op.cit., p. 53.

16   M.I. Akhun, V.A.Petrov, op. cit., pp. 47–48.

17   RGVIA, Collection 2003, description 1, folder 1486, folio 98.

18   D. Oskin, op. cit., pp. 35, 45–46, 71, 94–95, 119, 127–129, 138, 143–144, 148–149, 164–166, 167–168, 229; A.M. Pireiko, op. cit., pp. 40, 55

19 D. Oskin, op. cit., pp. 170–173, 225–226, 249, 316; S.F. Ershov, op.cit., pp. 162, 169–170.
20 GARF, Collection 523, description 2, folder 14, folios 22–41; description 3, folder 37, folios 2–8, 17, 23; F. Stepun, op. cit., pp.21–22, 75–76; A.M. Pireiko, op. cit., pp. 25, 46; D.Oskin, op.cit., pp. 180, 269.
21 D. Oskin, op. cit., p. 269; F. Stepun, op. cit., p. 16.
22 D. Oskin, op. cit., pp. 259, 264, 267; A.M. Pireiko, op. cit., p. 22.
23 RGVIA, Collection 2067, description 1, folder 2933, folio 470; Soldatskie pisma 1917 goda, p. 8.

The Russian Worker at War
Sergei Kudryashov

The general impact of the First World War on mankind is undeniable. Even nowadays, in many national or political conflicts, one is always noticing issues which date from that time, eighty years ago. At the same time it is true to say that Russia has its own, rather specific, perception of the war. For many Russians, the war went on until the Revolution in October 1917, after which the only fighting was between the Reds and Whites.

Certainly that was the picture deliberately drawn by Soviet propaganda which sought to create a good image of Soviet power and put the war efforts of Tsarist Russia in the shade. As a result there is a huge historiography of the 1914–1918 period but it is politically and ideologically angled and narrow-minded. Thousands of books and articles deal specifically with three subjects:

1 The activity of the Bolsheviks and the revolutionary movement in Russia.
2 The non-stop struggle of workers and peasants against the bourgeoisie and the Tsarist regime.
3 The appalling conditions of the everyday proletarian life in Russia and the crisis of the regime.

Many other problems are still untouched or insufficiently studied. Amongst them are the different aspects of personal experience and perception of the war. What was the war like according to a worker, a peasant or a soldier? The official historiography paid little attention to these questions and in this respect the First World War is still 'an unknown war' for Russians.

The huge historiography of the 'revolutionary workers' movement' gives the impression that there is a mass of well-classified source material, but this is hardly the case. In fact, scholars have relied on a very narrow documentary base, mainly of governmental origin: materials from different ministries concerning workers' problems, and police and factory inspection reports. Little evidence comes from the workers themselves. There are few memoirs and a tiny collection of workers' letters in the State Russian Archive. I failed to find any original diaries written by a worker during the war.[1]

Why did things turn out as they did in Russia? This question is still endlessly discussed among historians. In all European countries the economic situation came under strain during the war and inevitably workers suffered. Everywhere there were workers' strikes but it was only in Russia that the most disastrous social explosion took place, which caused the total collapse of the existing regime. It is obvious that war accelerated the crisis and workers took an active part in it, but I think we are still far from a clear picture.

The number of Russian industrial workers during the First World War was constantly increasing, despite the army mobilisation, as the figures show: 1913 – 2,598,600; 1914 – 2,667,000; 1915 – 2,641,500; 1916 – 2,926,000; 1917 – 3,240,300. Some historians tend to believe in a larger growth in worker numbers and would add one more million to the last figure (4,253,000); but however computed, there could not be more than 4.5 million workers in Russia in 1917. Of the total labour population of Russia during the war period, workers constituted four to six per cent (twenty-three per cent of them were employed in industry) and thirty per cent of all industrial workers were concentrated in two big cities, Moscow and Petrograd.[2]

The news of the outbreak of war was received by many of these workers without any markedly cheerful support. The general reaction was very passive. According to a governmental statistic of that time there were 1,410 registered workers' strikes and demonstrations in the period 1914–1917 and only fifteen of these were accompanied by patriotic slogans supporting the war. Although it is obvious that the total number of strikes was deliberately underestimated by the Tsarist officials, the number of patriotic demonstrations is amazingly small.[3]

On the other hand, although nobody wanted to fight, one should not exaggerate the degree of anti-war feelings. Even the Soviet historiography, which did its best to register each 'proletarian protest' against the regime, states that in 1914 in Russia there were only thirty-seven political strikes, in which 29,597 workers took part. The number of strikes gives us a general picture of the worker militancy during the war. The table shown here is based on the police and factory inspection reports. It differs from the official government figures since it included information from all rural and far regions in Russia.

These reliable figures gathered from the whole country show us that the total number of strikers was nearly equal to the number of all Russian workers. The overwhelming majority of economic strikes over the political ones is also clear. At the same time the notion of a 'political strike' needs be explained. In fact it is not very precise. Under the category of political strikes come all protests against the policy of the Tsarist government, which slightly distorts the real picture. In one instance there was a demonstration under the slogan 'We do not want this war' and in another, quite different case, workers went into streets with red banners and the slogan 'Down with the Tsar'. In the first case the protest against the regime was not obvious at all but the Soviet historiography never said so and lumped both cases together in one anti-government political trend. Today, as every scholar must realise, it requires special and rather difficult

STRIKES IN RUSSIA, 1914–1917

Year	Total number and number of participants	Economical aims	Political aims
1914	183	146	37
	109,219 participants	72,629	29,597
1915	1,946	1,381	565
	897,088 participants	643,771	253,317
1916	2,306	1,959	347
	1,784,731 participants	1,364,619	420,112
1917	751	339	412
two month	579,000	268,431	372,142
All years of war – 5,186 strikes		3,825 Economical	1,362 Political
1914 – Feb. 1917 – 3,424, 617 participants.		2,349,449	1,075,168

(Source: see footnote 4)

research to be able to divide political strikes, for example, into 'passive' or 'active' categories.

In our case we assume this terminology to prove the following: according to the same sources there were 599 political strikes in Moscow and about 650 in Petrograd. The total number of strikes in the two cities was 1,249. Comparing these figures it is easy to calculate that in the rest of Russia, with a population of some 140 million people, there can only have been 113 political strikes.[5]

Some Soviet historians trying to prove a higher record of political activity among Russian workers have estimated the number of political strikers in Petrograd as 1,091,993 and in Moscow as 429,322, making a total of 1,521,315. This is more than in the police and factory inspection reports (1,075,168). But anyway, even assuming this very 'favourable' approach, one reaches a picture of workers in the country at large being politically very passive and the fate of Russia being decided in the two biggest cities – Petrograd and Moscow.[6]

The still popular view that the poor brought down the regime is wrong. The workers of Petrograd and Moscow were the most educated, skilful and well-paid workers of Russia. The Petrograd workers were in an even better position. They were exempt from army recruitment and their average working day was ten hours as opposed to eleven or twelve hours in the rest of the country.[7]

Various reasons influenced the activity of the workers of Petrograd and Moscow. I would like to stress that nobody in the Government really cared about the workers. Only left-wing parties – of which the Bolsheviks were the most successful – paid attention to workers' needs. They constantly appealed to the social and human dignity of the Russian worker. This point, which I regard as crucial, is very rarely mentioned. At the same time the Government response towards workers' movement was mainly repressive. By sending the most radical workers to the front, the Tsar and his government were digging their own grave; and the food shortage was the last element which made the social explosion inevitable.

Notes

1   See: Military censorship. The State Russian Archive (GARF). Collection 5881, description 1–2. Soldatskie pisma 1917 goda, Moscow-Leningrad, 1927; A.M. Pireiko, V tylu i na fronte imperialisticheskoi voiny, Leningrad, 1926.
2   Istoriya SSSR. Vol.VI. Moscow, 1968, pp.581–591; A.L. Sidorov, Ekonomicheskoe polozhenie v Rossii v gody pervoi mirovoi voiny, Moscow, 1973, p.413.
3   Istoriya SSSR. op. cit., p.592.
4   Stachki v Rossii v 1914 -fevral 1917: Khronika, Moscow, 1989, p.4;14.
5   Istoriya rabochikh Leningrada. Vol.1. 1703-fevr.1917, Leningrad, 1972., p.492; G.G. Kasarov, Moskovskie rabochie v gody pervoi mirovoi voiny. (Thesis), Moscow, 1974, p.21.
6   ibid.
7   Rabochie Leningrada, op. cit, pp.472, 474; E.D. Rumyantsev, Rabochii klass Povolzhiya v gody pervoi mirovoi voiny i fevralskoi revolyutsii, Kazan, 1989, pp.159–173; Yu.I. Kiryanov, Rabochie Yuga Rossii. 1914-fevr.1917, Moscow, 1971, pp.59–64; Reformy ili revolyutsiya? Rossiya 1861–1917, St. Petersburg, 1992, pp.88,97–99,138,143,302.

THE FIRST WORLD WAR AND SOCIAL DEVIANCE* IN RUSSIA

Genadii Bordiugov

It is a matter for regret that Russian historians have never tried to tackle the issue of how the First World War affected 'anomalous behaviour' – that is to say deviant social conduct, such as alcoholism, prostitution, destitution, or the abandonment of children. After the 1917 revolution and right through to the period of perestroika, this theme was not considered to be a serious one, and consequently deemed unworthy of the historian's attention. Indeed, a feeling of shame made historians keep quiet about the very existence of such phenomena, although, as I believe, it is these 'social anomalies' which are the clearest indicators of the state of morality – or lack of it – in a human society. In this respect, the years of the First World War were tragic for Russia. Here I shall try to show why, though there are difficulties in doing so, for two reasons.

First, all statistics on criminal issues connected with public morals for the year 1914 were destroyed during the February revolution of 1917. Statistics for 1915 and 1916 are incomplete and often inaccurate. The occupation of part of the Russian Empire by German forces brought the collection of this information to a stop. From 1917, the acquisition of statistical material became completely fortuitous. The only way to study this problem, therefore, is to collect the very incomplete and fragmentary evidence from various sources and to try to detect general tendencies, during the war period, towards change in the scale and character of 'social deviance'. It would be very complicated to speak about all manifestations of such deviance, and I shall here deal only with alcoholism, prostitution and especially with abandoned children.

The second reason for our difficulties with the evidence is that in the period 1914–17 the amount of 'deviant behaviour' declined in Russia, as it did in England, France, Germany and the other combatant states. This is shown from their national statistical collections on such issues. In England, for instance, the numbers arrested for drunkenness decreased almost by one and a half times, from 58,000 in 1909–13 to 41,000 in 1914–18; prostitution was almost halved, from 11,000 to 6,000 prosecutions in the same years; the destitute decreased almost by five times, from 29,000 to 6,000.[1] Approximately the same picture can be observed in Russia, despite the big gaps in the Russian statistics. The basic cause of this paradox was identified as the 'morale factor': political enthusiasm and the creation of a co-operative spirit.

However in my research into the causes of this decrease in 'social

---

*The phrase is, literally, 'social anomalies' in the Russian.

anomalies' I was faced with the obvious question – surely the cause of this decrease lay in the very fact that a significant part of the Russian population was being called up into the army? During the course of the war, approximately fifteen million men were mobilized. Having said this, the available statistics show that there was also a corresponding decrease in 'social deviance' among those sections of the population which were not subject to conscription. Nevertheless, it is difficult to accept that the 'morale factor' really did play such a significant role in this decrease as was believed. The right way to reach a correct answer, it seems, must lie in subjecting each of these 'social anomalies' to separate scrutiny; and above all else, then to look for the causes of the apparent decrease in such tendencies in Russian society which took place during the war.

It is hardly convincing to attribute the decline in the consumption of alcohol in Russia at this time to 'an improvement in morals', but two causes of this change can be clearly identified. The first was that the conscription of young males inevitably restricted their opportunities of drinking hard liquor. The second was the prohibition of the sale of spirits in 1914, as also in France, Finland and, later, America. This measure had a positive, if temporary influence, as for instance in Kazan (the capital of Tataria): in 1916 the provincial zemstvo, or local organ of government, published a study under the following title, 'A year of sobriety in the province of Kazan'. It was based on material collected from questionnaires distributed among the urban workers and craftsmen, peasants, officials and others. It appeared that the prohibition of the sale of alcohol led to serious changes in the whole pattern of consumption. The consumption of tea, sugar and confectionery had sharply increased: deposits in national savings banks and private banks by the population had increased.[2] After the prohibition of vodka, the number of criminal cases in Petrograd fell by almost eighty per cent. It is curious that the number of the poverty-stricken also decreased, among men by seventy-five per cent, and among women by sixty-eight per cent,[3] showing how much the lure of vodka often tempted them into destitution so that they could collect charitable aid to buy it. Thus the introduction of regulation led to positive results.

So where was the tragedy? First, the effect of the ban was temporary. By the end of the war, secret drunkenness was developing strongly: people began to drink 'denatured alcohol', varnish, eau-de-cologne, and, on a huge scale, 'samogon' or home brew. Secondly, it is clear that female and adolescent drunkenness increased.

These were two sections of the population where it is hard to believe that 'love of country' exercised a limiting influence on alcoholism or other manifestations of 'anomalous behaviour'. Youths aged up to sixteen were hardly so interested in the political and social life of Russia that a growing feeling of patriotism would have held them back from committing crimes if they were so inclined. Women were also too remote from participation in public life, and too tied to family duties to be suddenly seized by an interest in political life and by high moral imperatives only to descend to their former level after the end of the war.

In Russia, the number of cases of 'social anomalies' among women grew rather than diminished – for example, from 17 per cent in 1912 to 24.1 per cent in 1915.[4] Admittedly the judicial and police organs speak of a decrease in prostitution. This is not surprising, because it was subjected to greater regulation: the brothels worked under police control, while street prostitution was harshly persecuted. One has to take into account, too, the fact that as a result of the war the normal clientele of the brothels was drastically reduced. However the war itself quickly changed the character of prostitution and the kind of person drawn into it. In short, while it is reasonable to talk about a decline in professional prostitution, this was more than made up for by non-professional prostitution – the part-timers. The war forced many women, against their will, temporarily and secretly, to join the ranks of 'social deviants' to earn something extra for their families. A woman might have a job but, as a result of shortage of money, would from time to time go on the streets to sell her body. Often it was very difficult for the police to be sure of the intentions of a nicely-dressed, modest-seeming woman sitting in a cafe or club or cinema, or walking about in the livelier parts of town.

What was far worse was that very young girls, below the age of seventeen, were being dragged into prostitution. From the Moscow and Petrograd court lists of 1915, for example, one sees that ten out of every hundred homeless girls who were detained were engaged in this trade.[5] All of this was known and seen by the administration, by the judges, by the local government organs and by society at large – and all remained silent. However the relationship of adults to these fallen girls was not passive. What was saddest for their relatives and close friends was the phenomenon of the 'girls with big purses'.[6] Adults could pester these girls for their earnings, use all their arts of persuasion or simply seize them. On the other hand it is clear that such people as lackeys and coachmen respected these girls on account of their money. Moreover, a 'large purse' fortified the legal position of these girl-prostitutes. They did not need internal passports, the police helped them to keep out of the way of the judges, and they were not subjected to compulsory registration. Mothers often quietly obeyed their 'fallen' daughters. They were materially dependent on them. From this example alone one can see the terrible damage to family relationships that was inflicted by the war.

All the legislation of the First World War epoch proclaimed that the family was the 'foundation of all society', 'the main foundation of the state'. Millions of fathers, however, went off to fight leaving their families defenceless, without material means of support. The departure of the fathers for the war meant that those members of the family left behind, including the children, were thrown into the arena of struggle for existence. Whilst their fathers were dying under their enemies' bullets, their children were subjected to the blows of harsh reality and turned into moral cripples and invalids.

When the children were prematurely pushed into adult life, this was a form of 'mobilization' where there were no privileges, and which could not be postponed. No account was taken of their age or health. The longer the war raged, the greater became the scale of this 'mobilization of the children'. Who were these children? In Russia, this destitute social group included youngsters without homes, in poverty and in prostitution. They were popularly known as: 'no one's children'. The majority of these *bezprizornye* or destitute and homeless children were those whose fathers were on active service in the army (the phenomenon of 'fatherlessness'), or who were children of refugees (by the beginning of 1916 the general figure of refugees in Russia reached 4 million, including approximately 40,000 children on their own).[7] We can add to this the orphans and the children of the destitute, the vagrants and the drunkards. They were to be encountered everywhere: on the streets and in the markets, in front of the churches and in the cemeteries, in robbers' hideouts and dosshouses. It was natural that this milieu of homeless children should produce criminals. As opposed to 20, 000 in 1913,[8] in 1914 child criminality rose to 4.2 per cent of the total; by 1915 it had reached 6.5 per cent and by 1916 to 8.6 per cent.[9] The consequences of this early and accelerated adulthood cast a long shadow over their subsequent development. Whereas for adults in Russia, peace and demobilization came first in 1917 and then, (after the Civil War) in 1920–1922, for the children, 'demobilization' took place only towards the end of the 1920's. By then they had succeeded all too well in getting to know the social depths of life.

By way of conclusion, I draw attention to two points: first, while the war did not increase the scale of deviant behaviour, and while there *was* a decline in its incidence, we know how quickly after the war the former state of affairs was restored. Moreover there were varieties of 'social deviance' during the war that would never have occurred during peacetime. We are talking about what happened to women who were wives, and had families and, of course, to children. It is one of the darkest pages in the history of the World War.

Second, in prewar Russia, 'social deviance' could be equated with crime. After the war and the revolution, this had already ceased to be formally treated as criminal. At this stage society came at last to understand that it was necessary to struggle not against prostitution, destitution, homelessness and homeless children as such, but rather against the conditions which gave birth to them, including war.[10]

Notes

1   M.N. Gernet, Prestupnost i samoubiistva vo vremya voiny i posle nee, Moscow, 1927, pp. 48–49.
2   God trezvosti v Kazanskoi gubernii, Kazan, 1916.
3   Osobye sudy dlya maloletnikh, Petrograd, 1914, no 1 (November), p.10.
4   M.N. Gernet, Moralnaya statistika, Moscow, 1922, p.222.
5   V.I. Kufaev, Yunye pravonarushiteli, Moscow, 1924, pp.191–193.
6   A. Yablonskii, Bezdomnye devochki. – Kievskaya mysl, Kiev, 1916, no 32. p. 173; V. Levitskii, Deti-prostitutki v dni voiny. – Vestnik vospitaniia, Petrograd, 1917, no 2.
7   Prizrenie i blagotvoritelnost v Rossii, Petrograd, 1916, no 1–2, p. 82.
8   ibid. p.64; V.Levitskii, Voina i detskii sud, Moscow, 1916.
9   V.I. Kufaev, Deti i voina, Kiev, 1916, p.87.
10   See: G. Bordyugov, Sotsialnye anomalii ili sotsialnyi parazitizm? – Istoriya SSSR. Moscow,1989, no 6.

Chapter 40

Germany, The Home Front (1): The Physical and Psychological Consequences of Home Front Hardship

Peter Loewenberg

World War One was the original, the primary, catastrophe of the twentieth century. It was the first total war in history, involving the lives and the full energies of its peoples as no previous war had. Europe lost her dominance in the world. Central European society was highly stratified in 1914. The war meant an end to the empires of Germany, Austria, and Russia and a breakdown of the established social value systems of these traditional polities. Communism was triumphant in Russia in 1917. Fascism rose in Italy in 1922. The most drastic hyper-inflation in history, which wiped out the middle class and made its virtues of thrift and calculation irrelevant, occurred in Germany in 1923 as a consequence of the war and the peace treaties. Adolf Hitler came to power in Germany in 1933, establishing the Third Reich.

Blockade is a traditional weapon of modern warfare intended to crush and demoralize the civilian population and weaken the productivity of an economy. Cardinal Richelieu brought the Huguenots of La Rochelle to starvation and surrender in 1628 using a land and sea blockade. The British fleet isolated Napoleonic Europe from international trade, while Bonaparte in the Berlin Decrees of 1806 proclaimed an ineffective 'paper blockade' of Great Britain which he called 'the Continental System'. During the American Civil War, naval blockade was a Union instrument constricting exports and imports to enervate the Confederacy. In 1948–1949 the Soviets imposed a land blockade on West Berlin which was circumvented by an airlift. The blockade was utilized by the United Nations as a weapon of coercive diplomacy toward Serbia and Iraq.

In the half century prior to the First World War Germany underwent a rapid transformation from an agriculturally self-sufficient land of forty million people to a food and raw material importing industrial economy of sixty-seven million. Germany was dependent on the import of food, fats, oils, and strategic metals and chemicals. The first Allied war measure in 1914, as in 1939, was the imposition of a naval blockade and mine barrage across the North Sea from Scotland to Norway. Bread rationing cards were introduced in Germany on 25 January, 1915. On February 20, the physician Alfred Grotjahn, a SPD member of the Reichstag, noted in his diary: 'Slowly but surely we are slipping into a, now still well organized, famine.' On 5 July he wrote: 'Now the real starvation begins. Today a former patient who has lost 66 *Pfund* [72.6 English lbs.] visited me. In the ministry we are experimenting with turnip bread.'[1] *Kriegsbrot* [war bread] consisted of flour mixed with turnips and potatoes. Two meatless days were imposed and rationing was extended to other items. Meat and farm produce went to the black market.[2]

All strategic raw materials were sequestered and allocated by the German government in what became the world's first controlled economy. Under the direction of Walther Rathenau (1867–1922), the chairman of the *AEG,* the German General Electric Corporation, a *Kriegs-Rohstoff-Abteilung [KRA]* was created in the war ministry which: 1.) Organized the uses and disposal of raw materials in the country. Rathenau instituted a policy of sequestering strategic raw materials and administering their use for the war effort by mixed private and government companies. 2.) Imported war material via neutral neighbours, often through phoney companies, and requisitioned anything needed from occupied territories. 3.) Researched and developed new technologies to create methods of synthetic manufacture of alternative [*ersatz*] materials. Rathenau's friend, the chemist Fritz Haber (1868–1934) developed a synthetic process for extracting ammonia from atmospheric nitrogen. The Haber-Bosch nitrogen fixation process freed Germany from dependence on imported Chilean nitrates essential for the manufacture of explosives. [Haber also developed and supervised at Ypres in April 1915 the first use of poison gas in warfare].[3] 4.) Substituted lighter, sometimes inferior, alternative products to replace standard but now unavailable materials.[4] This German initiative in government economic planning had a lasting world wide impact in the twentieth century, including the Third Reich. Other states followed this model during and after both wars.

Under the National Auxiliary Service Law [*Vaterländischer Hilfsdienst Gesetz*] of December 5, 1916, every male between the ages of seventeen and sixty was placed at the disposal of the war ministry for employment in industrial production. Trade unions gained new importance, bargaining power, and recognition by a government interested in avoiding strikes and work stoppages.[5] Thousands of Belgian, French and Polish labourers were drafted and deported to the Reich to work as slave labour in war industry.

The German civilian population first felt severe shortages in 1916. The harvests of both the years 1916 and 1917 were exceptionally poor. Grain production fell from 21.8 million tons to 14.9 million tons in those two years.[6] The winter of 1916–1917 was known as the 'turnip winter' due to the exclusive, unnourishing and monotonous diet. Official food rations in 1917 were 1000 calories per day, while the health ministry considered 2,280 calories a subsistence minimum. Three quarters of a million people died of starvation in Germany between 1914 and 1918.[7] The number of live births declined from 1,353,714 in 1915 to 926,813 in 1918. The birth rate per 1,000 population went from 28.25 in 1913 to 14.73 in 1918. Deaths among the civilian population over one year old rose from 729,000 in 1914 to 1,084,000 in 1918. Specific causes of death that increased during the war years were influenza, lung infections and pneumonia, tuberculosis, diseases of the circulatory system, diphtheria, typhus, dysentery, and diseases of the urinary and reproductive organs.[8] In the war's third year the weight of neonates was 50 to 100 grammes less at birth than before the war. Among neonates and infants there was a decline in weight and size at birth, a decline in the ability of mothers to nurse, and an increase of rickets and tuberculosis.[9] By the third year of war three year old children were 2.2 pounds lighter than normal body weight for their age. A study comparing 300 Berlin children in 1908–09 with children of the same age in 1919 showed that boys were retarded in growth by 1.5 years and the girls were 1.25 years behind normal.[10] Young children were also particularly afflicted with rickets, tuberculosis, and parasites. These diseases are specific to a population whose biological ability to maintain health and counter infection was undermined in the malnutrition and deprivation of the war.

Family life was dislocated by the war, not only because the husbands, fathers, sons, and brothers were in the military, but because wives and mothers were engaged in war work. In Germany 1.2 million women joined the labour force of medium and large industrial plants during the war. The women workers in the armaments industry rose by 500 per cent, from 113,750 in 1913 to 702,100 in 1917. In Prussia the number of women engaged in industrial labour increased by 76 per cent, from 788,100 in 1913 to 1,393,000 in 1917. Women railway workers in Prussia increased from 10,000 in 1914 to 100,000 in 1918.[11]

Central European folklore found the food shortages and the exigencies of the ration card economy the stuff of sarcastic parody, as this 'middle-class recipe' demonstrates:

Take a meat card, turn it in an egg card and fry it until nice and brown in a butter card. Cook the potato card and the vegetable card and add the flour card. To cook it quickly and under high heat, lay the coal card and the liquor card underneath and light them. For dessert brew the coffee card and add the milk card to it. Gourmets dissolve the sugar card in it. After the meal one washes oneself with the soap card and dries oneself with the ration coupon.[12]

After the armistice of 11 November, 1918 the blockade was continued and extended to the Baltic Sea to coerce Germany to surrender her merchant fleet to the Allies.[13] The winter 1918–1919 was a time of famine in Central Europe. The blockade of Germany was terminated on 12 July 1919. Two American historians concluded: 'the suffering of the German children, women, and men, . . . was greater under the continued blockade than prior to the armistice.'[14] A tripartite commission from the medical faculties of the Netherlands, Sweden and Norway that examined health conditions in Germany after the armistice reported in the spring of 1919:

> Tuberculosis, especially in children, is increasing in an appalling way, and generally speaking, is malignant. In the same way rickets is more serious and widely prevalent . . . Tuberculosis is assuming almost unprecedented aspects, such as have hitherto only been known in exceptional cases. The whole body is attacked simultaneously, and the illness in this form is practically incurable . . . Tuberculosis is nearly always fatal now among adults . . . It appears in the most terrible forms, such as glandular tuberculosis, which turns into purulent dissolution.[15]

The economist John Maynard Keynes posed the prescient question: 'Who can say how much is endurable, or in what direction men will seek at last to escape from their misfortunes?'[16] The emotional constellations of infancy and childhood are the foundations of a human being's sense of core self, of emergent subjective feelings and subjectivity, of physical social relatedness, and the capacity for intersubjectivity, and of verbal relatedness.[17] John Bowlby terms separation from the mothering figure the 'primal anxiety' in the child's life.[18] As Daniel Stern puts it: 'Once a baby starts to become a reader of the human heart and mind, the central social action is now and forever the human drama made up of motives and feelings and desires and goals, the invisible subjective contents of mind.'[19]

When a child is struggling with his aggressive and destructive impulses in a society at war, the hatred and violence around them in the outer world meet the as yet untamed aggression of his inner world. At the time when socialization and education are attempting to cope and direct the hostile inner impulses, these same fantasies receive validation from a polity at war.[20] It is not possible to repress destructive and murderous wishes when fighting, maiming, and killing are the preoccupations of the people among whom the child lives. The horrors and atrocities of war arouse primitive excitement in both children and adults.[21] The official ideology and mass media of a nation at war re-enforce the self-image of virtue of 'our cause' and the justification of murder of the wicked enemy.

In Germany nationalistic hate was stimulated by slogans such as: *Jeder*

(v) *'Wien stirbt! Rettet seine Kinder!'* – 'Vienna is Starving! Save Her Children!'
(Robert Gore Rifkind Collection, Beverly Hills, California)

A poster (1920) by the famous German artist Käthe Kollwitz (1867–1945), whose son was killed in the war. She devoted much of her life's work to depicting the sufferings of humanity, particularly of women. Austria, like Germany, took long to recover from the extended Allied blockade of the Central Powers (See for example, Anne Eisenmenger, *Blockade: The Diary of an Austrian Middle-Class Woman, 1914–1924,* London, 1932).

Schuss ein Russ ['Every shot a Russian']; *Jeder Stoss ein Franzos* ['Every punch a Frenchman']; *Jeder Tritt ein Britt* ['Every kick a Brit']; *Jeder Klaps ein Japs* ['Every slap a Jap']. Ernst Lissauer composed a 'Hymn of Hate' against England:

> Hate by water and hate by land;
> Hate of heart and hate of the hand;
> We love as one and hate as one;
> We have but one foe alone – England.[22]

In the middle of the war Sigmund Freud commented evocatively and sadly on the emotional 'splitting' of the world into such good and bad parts:

> Science herself has lost her passionless impartiality; her deeply embittered servants seek for weapons from her with which to contribute towards the struggle with the enemy. Anthropologists feel driven to declare him inferior and degenerate, psychiatrists issue a diagnosis of his disease of mind or spirit . . . A belligerent state permits itself every . . . misdeed, every . . . act of violence, as would disgrace the individual. It makes use against the enemy not only of the accepted *ruses de guerre,* but of deliberate lying and deception as well – and to a degree which seems to exceed the usage of former wars.[23]

The role of career opportunity in the Nazi movement was symbolized by the former corporal who ruled Europe and humbled the generals, aristocrats, and bankers.[24] He also appeared to embody a will to action, a positive dynamism, and a restored national pride that defied and reversed the 'humiliation of Versailles'. The administrators of the National Socialist Party have been termed 'plebeians on the make' who used Nazism as a path to upward social mobility.[25] Young people of plebeian, working class, or petit-bourgeois background used Nazism as a vehicle to achieve positions of prestige and deference in German and Austrian society. Another pattern existed among the Nazi intellectuals, propagandists, and ideologists born and raised within the middle income 'skill groups' of Imperial Germany who were alienated from 'the prevailing structure of symbols and sanctions in the societies that nurture them'.[26] In both cases the psycho-ideological dynamic was a generational revolt against the traditional social norms and deference values of the 'old order' of the Bismarckian-Wilhelmine and Habsburg empires.

Among the political consequences of the traumas for the children of Germany and Austria, who came to adulthood in the two decades after the war, were: 1.) A low tolerance of frustration, dealing in an impulsive manner with problems (for example, a hyper-inflation or an economic depression) that require patience and rationality; seeking simplistic immediate solutions. 2.) Projection of all negative, asocial, morally ambivalent qualities (such as greed, sexuality, cowardice) onto racial and ethnic minorities and foreign peoples; 3.) Responding to internal stress and tension with externalized aggression and violence. In a defeated, atomized, inorganic, alienated, industrialized, and apparently hopeless world, Nazism appealed to a caricature of virility, the male bonding of closed ranks, heroism and exclusive community.

The relationship between the moral, physical, and psychic trauma of the First World War on the civilian populations, particularly the children, of Central Europe and the Nazi appeal to them during the crisis of the Great Depression after 1929, was causal.[27] The experience of civilian deprivation and trauma during the war conditioned a generation of central European youth to make Adolf Hitler a charismatic figure and his programme politically attractive to them in the early 1930s. These traumas were: 1.) Extreme hunger and physical privation; 2.) National defeat accompanied by the discredit, collapse, and humiliation of political and social authority. 3.) Prolonged absence and unavailability of the parents. The absence of fathers in the army and mothers in war work was equally significant for male and female children.

The factors of long term starvation and the return of the father in defeat were unique to central Europe. French and British civilian populations, particularly children, were also traumatized by the war and its losses. The critical difference was that in the West the suffering was legitimized as being in the service of ideals of democratic freedom and future security while in Germany and Austria the entire political-social world was overturned. The German Kaiser and his court had fled. The Austrian Kaiser abdicated. They were replaced with socialist republics which had to deal with defeat, demobilization and unemployment, peace-making and reparations, inflation and depression. For central Europe the defeat in World War One meant that much more than a war was lost – an entire organization of the state and society was destroyed. It had to be reconstituted under conditions of desperation and at ominous physical and emotional cost.

Notes

1 D. and R. Glatzer, *Berliner Leben 1914–1918: Eine historische Reportage aus Erinnerungen und Berichten,* vol. II (Berlin, 1983), p. 335 f., as quoted in Sigrid and Wolfgang Jacobeit, *Illustrierte Alltags-und-Sozialgeschichte Deutschlands 1900–1945* (Münster, 1995), p 242.

2 Koppel S. Pinson, *Modern Germany: its History and Civilization* (New York, second ed., 1966), p.322

3 Fritz Stern, 'Fritz Haber: The Scientist in Power and in Exile,' in *Dreams and Delusions: The Drama of German History* (New York, 1987), pp. 51–76.

4 Walther Rathenau, *'Deutschlands Rohstoffversorgung.'* (December, 1915) in *Gesammelte Schriften* (Berlin, 1918), Vol. 5, pp. 31–32.

5 Gerald D. Feldman, *Army, Industry and Labor in Germany, 1914–1918* (Princeton, 1966)

6   Volker R. Berghahn, *Modern Germany: Society, Economy and Politics in the Twentieth Century* (Cambridge, second ed., 1987), p. 50.

7   Karl Dietrich Erdmann, 'Die Zahl der Weltkriege,' in Bruno Gebhardt, ed., *Handbuch der Deutschen Geschichte* (Stuttgart, 1963), 4: 49, 77.

8   Dr. Roesle, 'Die Geburts und Sterblichkeitsverhältnisse in Franz Bumm, ed., *Deutschlands gesundheitsverhältnisse unter dem Einfluss des Weltkrieges* (Stuttgart, 1928), 1: 15, 17, 25, 58

9   L. Langstein and F. Rott, 'Der Gesundheitsstand unter den Sauglingen und Kleinkindern,' in *ibid.*, 90.

10 *ibid.*, 93, 95.

11 Marie-Elisabeth Lüders, *Das Unbekannte Heer: Frauen Kämpfen für Deutschland, 1914–1918* (Berlin, 1937), pp. 84–86, 151, 151 n. 1; 153 n. 2.

12 *Hochlarmarker Lesebuch: Kohle war nicht alles – 100 Jahre Ruhrgebietsgeschichte* (Oberhausen 1981), p. 61, as quoted in S. and W. Jacobeit, *Alltags-und-Sozialgeschichte*, p. 250.

13 James A. Huston, 'The Allied Blockade of Germany 1918–1919,' *Journal of Central European Affairs*, 10 (1950), 161; Erdmann, 'Weltkriege,' 88.

14 Suda Lorena Bane and Ralph Haswell Lutz, eds., *The blockade of Germany after the Armistice 1918–1919: Selected Documents of the Supreme Economic Council, Superior Blockade Council, American Relief Administration and Other Wartime Organizations* (Stanford, 1942), v.

15 Swedish press of April 1919, as reported in John Maynard Keynes, *The Economic Consequences of the Peace* (New York, 1920), p. 250 n.

16 Keynes, *Economic Consequences*, p.251.

17 Daniel N. Stern, *The Interpersonal World of the Infant: A View from Psychoanalysis and Developmental Psychology* (New York, 1985). I am indebted to Gordon M. Berger for sharing with me his pre-publication paper, 'Psycho-Historical Considerations of the Causes of War' which organizes the Sternian categories of the development of a subjective self for the analysis of modern Japanese history.

18 John Bowlby, 'Separation Anxiety,' *International Journal of Psychoanalysis*, 41 (1960), 105.

19 Daniel N. Stern, *Diary of a Baby* (New York, 1990), p. 84.

20 Anna Freud and Dorothy T. Burlingham, *War and Children* (New York, 1943).

21 D.W. Winnicott, 'Residential Management as Treatment for Difficult Children' (1947), *The Child and the Outside World: Studies in Developing Relationships* (New York, 1957)

22 Pinson, *Modern Germany*, p. 315.

23 Sigmund Freud, 'Thoughts for the Times on War and Death' (1915), in James Strachey, Anna Freud, Alix Strachey and Alan Tyson (eds and trans.), *Standard Edition of the Complete Psychological Works* (London, 1957), XIV, 275, 279.

24 David Schoenbaum, *Hitler's Social Revolution: Class and Status in Nazi Germany* (New York, 1966).

25 Harold D. Lasswell and Daniel Lerner, eds., *World Revolutionary Elites: Studies in Coercive Ideological Movements* (Cambridge, MA 1965), p. 284.

26 Lasswell and Lerner, *Elites* p.203.

27 For a detailed elaboration of this argument, see Peter Loewenberg, 'The Psychohistorical Origins of the Nazi Youth Cohort', in *Decoding the Past: The Psychohistorical Approach* (New York, 1983; Berkeley, 1985; New Brunswick, N.J., 1966), pp. 240–283.

Chapter 41

Germany, The Home Front (2): Blockade, Government and Revolution

Alyson Jackson

In the trenches when they had spoken of the scarcity at home, many had said: 'They shouldn't make such a fuss about it. We go hungry for twenty-four hours when we're under fire. They exaggerate.'

But Otto saw at once that everything was much worse, a hundred times worse than they in the trenches had believed. It wasn't only hunger – seeing these hopeless faces one realised how dreadful was the complete joylessness, the lack of everything which really made life worth living, which was hope.[1]

Hans Fallada's novel, *Iron Gustav*, bitterly recalled in 1938 the wartime hardships, which, as the previous chapter relates, were to have such fearful effects on the psyche of the German nation. The world war had expanded the use of the economic weapon far beyond any previous scope. By the end of the war there was a world-wide Allied network, naval and diplomatic, working against the commerce of the Central Powers. Did the results justify the efforts – not to mention the inhumanity – involved ?

This chapter concentrates on the ways in which the blockade undermined relations between the German population and the Kaiser's government and on the contribution of domestic hardship to the growth of revolutionary feeling at the war's end. Aside from the inclusion of documentation newly available from the Liddle Collection, this paper draws together some of the work of scholars currently involved in this field, such as Belinda Davis, Richard Bessel, Nicholas Howard, Jürgen Kocka and Avner Offer, furnishing further background for Dr Loewenberg's study.[2]

The effect of the blockade on German health and morale was gradual, although food shortages began to occur as soon as late autumn 1914, with bread particularly scarce.[3] Contemporary accounts furnish indications of how members of the community were affected. Edith Doerry (later Mrs E.

Roseveare) was a child in Berlin during the war years. She was the daughter of a well-known German athlete and was from a comfortable middle class home, unused to privation. In her personal account of those years, now in the Liddle Collection, she has described the early impact of rationing:

by and by a change could be felt: rationing had steadily reduced our standard of living, though we never actually went without in the early days. There is nothing dramatic about slow starvation. Its effect is upon you before you know, and it can become almost a way of life, something monotonous, something one gets used to, like traffic noise. Soon the quantity and quality of the food at our disposal declined so much that we were always hungry. After all, we were four lively, growing children and had by no means forgotten the meals we once enjoyed: large slices of good bread, crisp rolls with plenty of fresh butter and our favourite type of sausages on them. Cakes, whipped cream, chops, chicken, ham and lovely puddings became a tantalising memory. The bread was now almost uneatable, like putty, made with the addition of potatoes and swedes. It took years before I could look upon a swede again as a desirable vegetable, because swedes, carrots and now and then kale was all that could be found in the shops. The bread caused much discomfort and embarrassment to people. It swelled up inside them, very likely reducing that gnawing feeling of emptiness. Yet, as I said, there was still always something to eat.[4]

Edith Doerry's life as a child in war-torn Berlin was more privileged than most. She was sent to a private school 'For the daughters of Gentlemen' when her progress at the state school was deemed unsatisfactory. At both schools the children were required to take sandwiches:

There are no lunches served in German schools, because lessons start early. We left home at about 7.30a.m. after a breakfast of Ersatz coffee, soggy bread with jam made mainly of carrots and unidentifiable fruit. For our elevenses we carried a packet of a few slices of bread, generally smeared with jam or sometimes filled with a scraping of soft cheese. Often we swapped these with other children. Some had mashed apple in their sandwiches, others a mysterious paste. It was all the same to us.[5]

Another girl, also a child in Germany at this time, who later married a German war hero, Colonel Lubinski, left another account, also held at Leeds, of her life in the war. In it she described the rationing and her own frugal allowance of food :

Not only sugar, meat and coffee, we were short of everything. When I went to school I remember that I had one loaf of bread per week. I put that in my wardrobe, locked the wardrobe and took the key with me to school. I measured the loaf in so many centimetres and had a piece per

(vi)   A propaganda image far from sustainable in reality: Kriegsküche, from the front
cover of Lustige Blätter, 1916. [per H.P. Cecil]

day of perhaps 2 or 3 centimetres. My grandparents were great patriots and wouldn't buy anything on the black market so we really were short of any food at all.[6]

Although a *Burgfried* and the general confidence in the national leadership at the start of the conflict ensured, for a while, a broadly loyal and submissive response to the demands of war, within a year the government was faced with deteriorating public morale as economic hardship grew and the expected victory had not transpired. Even before the war, the German people had already become distrustful of the state, particularly over the provision of adequate, good quality food. The urban populace had become suspicious of government motives and distrustful of rural producers. In 1902, to secure wealthy landowners' support for an intensified naval programme, officials had imposed agricultural tariffs protecting the East Elbian Junkers from cheap food imports. The result was to increase food prices, sparking off riots and contributing to the Social Democratic Party victories of 1912. Shopkeepers and middlemen were suspected of overcharging and even of food adulteration by a burgeoning immigrant population from rural communities used to either growing their own food or dealing directly with producers. All this laid the foundations of the antagonism between industrial and rural communities in the war years.[7]

There had been significant changes in eating habits throughout Europe during the later nineteenth century, and in perceptions of what constituted a 'proper German diet'. Potatoes, bread baked from expensive imported wheat (largely replacing native rye), pork, lard, white granular sugar, chocolate and coffee had all come to be regarded as essential. Germany was dependent upon imports for one-third of its food supply. Many of these imported foods would be the first casualties of the blockade. The influential Eltzbacher Report of 1914, however, estimated that pre-war production and imports of food exceeded physiological needs by 50 per cent, and even with the loss of imports, it concluded, about 90 per cent of pre-war calories would be available, and about 87 per cent of protein, through appropriate measures of economy and substitution. Though the soundness of this report has been questioned, its views reinforced the policies of the government which believed a loss of imports would have no serious physiological effects.[8]

Even more serious, perhaps, was the effect the blockade had on the supply of certain other commodities: first, coal and oil essential for power generation and the transport system. The railways' shortage of coal[9] affected food distribution in its turn. Secondly, German farmers had relied heavily on artificial fertilisers, importing much of the phosphoric and nitrogenous varieties – chemicals also required for explosives. Although potash remained widely available during the war years, phosphoric fertiliser fell by some 50% while pure nitrogen declined by over 60%. As we have seen, however, a significant development in the early 1900's was the preparation of synthetic nitrogen sources.[10] Third, animal feed was affected both by the loss of imports – six million tons a year before the war – and the loss of domestic feed products diverted for human use. Rye replaced the lost imported wheat for bread-making. Potatoes and turnips were taken to feed people rather than the pigs. Fertiliser shortage seriously affected the production of sugar beet. By 1915–16 the available fodder had fallen by one-third.[11]

Such reductions in animal fodder, fertiliser and fuel were sure to have a serious impact on food production and distribution – even without the additional load imposed on food production by a nation supporting a huge war effort involving the withdrawal of labour into the army and the requisitioning of animals for military use.[12]

How did the state respond? In any prolonged conflict, the needs of the people sustaining the war effort at home must be considered alongside those of the military,[13] but Germany had relied on the rapid success of her armies and had not planned a long-term war. Consequently those on the Home Front were doomed to suffer. In the early years, satisfied that even with a loss of imports, sufficient food would be available, the German state responded to the reduction in the food supply primarily by controlling prices and rationing, but also by attempting to control arable and livestock resources.[14]

Established by the beginning of 1915, the Imperial Grain Bureau fixed prices, rationed bread and even authorised adulteration with up to 10% potato flour. Meat prices were not controlled. The German people had become accustomed to a diet involving large quantities of animal products but, as Offer reminds us, animals use grain inefficiently – the amount of grain used in meat production can have up to eight times the calories and protein of the meat produced. The Eltzbacher Commission had recommended a reduction in livestock and up to mid-April 1915 nine million pigs, one-third of the total herd, were slaughtered. Reduced meat supplies and the lack of price controls caused a swift rise in meat and fat prices with the result that farmers diverted grain and potatoes intended for human consumption to their livestock in order to secure higher returns. Traders also exploited the system: as price controls were locally imposed they simply shifted supplies to areas without controls. Thus price controls, imposed extensively in the first two years of the war to protect the consumer, worked to alienate farmers accustomed to pre-war protectionist tariffs and provoked them to divert their efforts into uncontrolled products.[15]

Could domestic production have been better geared to satisfy nutritional requirements, as was the case in Britain? The case of bread supply is a microcosm of the problems faced. Imported wheat had replaced in large part traditional domestic rye. When wheat was lost two options were clearly available – to grow more rye or to switch rye from animal feed to bread-making. Growing more rye required advance planning and, as Davis has pointed out, this was not in place. Switching rye from animal feed had the extra benefit of increasing the level of nutrition, given the inefficient conversion of grain to meat, and so the government's response of whole-sale slaughter of animals would, superficially, seem to help to solve the problem. However, the measures did not take into account the existence of the black market for meat which, coupled with price-controlled grain, caused farmers to continue meat production illicitly.[16]

The authorities' efforts at controlling demand through propaganda were so aggressive as to be largely self-defeating, or turned one section of the community against another with talk of those who ate too much being 'traitors to the fatherland.'[17] Whereas British and French propaganda efforts increasingly held out bribes of a better world after the war, the government dominated by General Ludendorff offered the German public no 'land fit for heroes' to fight for, but only the honour of sacrifice for Emperor and country.

By the beginning of 1915, shifts in government propaganda led to poorer consumers accusing shopkeepers, distributors and rural producers of holding back produce for increased profit. The police, now deployed to control rebellious food queues, found themselves increasingly sympa-thethic with the unhappy housewives :

> ... since this [difficulty in procuring food] concerns predominantly the population of little means and the lower civil servants, bitterness against the big, rich rural producers and business people grows daily. In general one considers the latter as the most evil enemies, who haven't the faintest glimmer of love of country, nor love for their fellow humanity.[18]

By the end of 1915 all the foods regarded as most important, including bread, potatoes and pork, were in very short supply or so overpriced as to be unobtainable by a large percentage of the population; ration cards were introduced for fat, sugar, bread and soap. Spontaneous food riots became a daily occurrence. Such evidence of a breakdown in morale and discipline and the resulting disunity unsettled the men at the front and reassured the enemy that the blockade was working.[19]

On 22 May 1916 the government established the War Food Office (Kriegsernährungsamt) empowered to control food at a national level, with the virtue, in theory, of removing the exploitation of uneven price controls. On 28 August 1916, Paul von Hindenburg was appointed Chief of the General Staff and Erich Ludendorff First Quartermaster General; in effect the German government had handed over responsibility to the military. Bessel points out that the German people were initially enthusiastic, hoping for a quick end to their privations, but the implementation of a radical plan for 'total mobilisation' of the German economy was to bring even greater hardship. The civilian population was compelled, through the Auxiliary Service Law of 5 December 1916 to rise to the demands of the Hindenburg plan for a massive increase in armaments production. Such demands were made at a time when human and economic resources were stretched to the limit and both the Hindenburg plan and the Auxiliary Service Law were failures, serving only to increase discontent – the civilian population became increasingly of the opinion that the war should end soon whether Germany were victorious or not.[20]

The poor harvest of 1916, coupled with the lack of transport, led to a winter of real deprivation, the notorious 'turnip winter'. Germany was not well-equipped with storage facilities and required an efficient transport system to deliver fresh food to the urban areas. Thus, as transport problems increased, towns suffered disproportionately from the food shortages.[21]

Food production was further hampered by the loss of labour. Almost 60% of male agricultural labour – the strongest and most efficient of the work force – about 3.3 million, was called up during the course of the war. Government remedies included the deployment of 430,000 migrant workers and 900,000 prisoners of war; soldiers were given harvest leave and many farm managers were not drafted, sometimes being asked to manage more than one farm. Although schoolchildren and volunteers helped, labour remained in short supply. Economic mobilisation during the second half of the war consisted largely of the mobilisation of women for both agricultural and industrial work. It was the women, too, who needed to be persuaded to purchase war bonds – something they increasingly declined to do; in the final stages of the war, soldiers on leave were actively advising against signing up for the Ninth War Loan because of the poor military situation . According to Bessel, attempts in February 1917 to persuade women from the cities to take up agricultural work were completely unsuccessful and the campaign was discontinued in November – Germany's women apparently preferred to use the black market or to steal food, activities which increased hugely in the latter years of the war.[22]

Much food was distributed illegally to the black market, making available statistics somewhat unreliable, but with shortages of draft animals, fodder and fertilisers contributing to huge reductions in food production (35% in the case of rye and 45% for potatoes are cited by Offer) the consequences for the nation must have been serious, even if the pre-war estimates of over-production were correct. After the failure of the Hindenburg plan, the black market had flourished. By the time of the Armistice, shortages were severe and widespread and black market pricing largely responsible for the uneven food distribution. A quarter to a third of milk, butter and cheese, one-third to a half of meat, eggs and fruit and one-eighth to one-seventh of flour, meal and vegetables went for black market prices up to ten times pre-war price levels.[23]

The typical German diet, therefore, increasingly became one of potatoes and swedes, though the wonderful foods of the past were not forgotten. The town of Niederlahnstein even expressed its yearning for good food on its local emergency currency : above a picture of a ham, a line from Schiller, 'Zarte sehnsucht, susses hoffen' ('tender longing, sweet hopes') while above a picture of swedes, a line from an old German song, 'So leben wir, so leben wir' ('thus we live, thus we live'). The German government evidently disapproved and ordered this note to be recalled.[24]

In the last two years of the war food supply and distribution were in crisis, with many 'ersatz' goods replacing normal food, being cosmetically similar but with little or no nutritional value, for example, the use of ash instead of pepper . Thus the worst fears of pre-war Germans were realised – the dramatic reduction in both quality and quantity of food was finally a reality.[25]

The rationing of soap – to as little as one small bar per month – and also of coal, meant a dirtier, colder population.[26] Cotton and woollen goods were no longer manufactured and warm clothing had to be handed over to a government seriously short of fabrics later in the war. A 'make do and mend' philosophy prevailed in the Doerry household: 'I went about in the boots my elder brother discarded till they began to pinch my toes', wrote Edith, 'They were soled with thin slats of wood and noisy to walk on.'[27]

How disastrous was the blockade to life and vigour? The German people, not unnaturally, lost weight but Offer suggests that it was not so much the reduction in energy as the change in diet which was felt by the German people. It was a psychological rather than a physical deprivation, and he concludes that the siege economy did not give rise to actual famine, although hunger, cold and insanitary conditions led to an increase in deaths due to infectious diseases such as pneumonia and tuberculosis and the influenza epidemic of 1918.[28] Here, however, there are differences of view: according to Howard, imminent famine *was* a distinct possibility in 1918. In January of that year a Swedish newspaper published reports from German life insurance companies that the death rate of the civilian population was approaching the death rate in battle. In 1913 the average monthly number of civilian deaths was 78,820; in November 1918 this had reached 184,896 – of these more than half were due to hunger and malnutrition.

Howard again cites statistics from J. Flemming, this time to compare average daily meat consumption throughout the war by various groups. Whereas consumption by army personnel, with a controlled supply, dropped by only a half and meat suppliers with access at source *increased* their own by a third, the hapless consumer, increasingly reliant on the over-priced black market, was reduced to eating between a fifth and a sixth of the pre-war amount.[29]

The average diet might have been sufficient in calorie intake to sustain moderate work loads, but those involved in heavy manual work required much more nutrition than the wartime diet provided and evidently German miners, who as Offer has observed, 'dug more coal in 1918 than in 1914 and only 15% less iron ore' did get enough to sustain these efforts. This contrasts with British government reports cited by Howard of 'considerable malnutrition in mining districts' and evidence of 'greater losses among heavy manual and industrial workers than in other occupation groups and social classes'.[30]

Estimates of civilian deaths in the war years vary. According to Offer:

> Just after the war the imperial statistical office calculated the excess of civilian deaths over the pre-war level at a grand total of 762,000, more than a third of battlefield deaths, excluding the victims of the great influenza epidemic of 1918. A more sober estimate a decade later arrived at a number of 424,000 excess civilian deaths (over the age of one), plus 209,000 deaths in the influenza pandemic of 1918, making a total of 633,000 (excluding Alsace-Lorraine).'[31]

However all these statistics are computed, the precise figures, whether more or less, can hardly have mattered to the very large number who did die, or to their families. It was the contemporary *perception* of the scale of disaster, in combination with a very widespread loss of life and health which was really significant to morale and subsequent reactions. Moreover, after the Armistice, Howard estimates, 'the continued food blockade brought about a quarter of a million additional deaths among the civilian population of Germany, within its post–1919 boundaries' – and here particularly, the long-term effects, as the previous chapter shows, were tragic.[32]

In all this, women suffered disproportionately. The additional five million women involved in war work had also to cope with increasingly arduous domestic responsibilities. The reduction in the diet together with the increased physical and psychological stress often proved fatal. The growing 'war weariness' was expressed by an observer: 'Why should we work, starve, send our men out to fight? What is it all going to bring us? More work, more poverty, our men cripples, our homes ruined. What is it all for? . . . The state which called upon us to fight cannot even give us decent food'. Offer quotes statistics on the female death rate during and after the war years: in 1918, at its maximum, it was 50% above the pre-war level. The highest mortality, however, was among children and young adults between the ages of 5 and 25. Adolescents, in particular, requiring large amounts of vitamins and protein, often received less than the full adult ration.[33]

Those living close to the centre of food production suffered less than those living in large towns and cities who relied increasingly on the black market. Resort to it involved a humiliating erosion of traditional middle class values. As Offer points out, the effects of the black market were far-reaching and encompassed a moral conflict well-illustrated by two excerpts from contemporary letters he quotes: 'this beastly usury with the bare necessities of life sickens me, and one meets it at every turn, and nobody seems to mind taking part in it, or feels any sort of responsibility in doing it,' and 'Where everything is forbidden, you simply have to break the laws if you want to go on living'.[34]

Although rural communities suffered less than town dwellers at times of food shortage, they, nevertheless, had their own grievances. Many agricultural workers had been enticed to the city by better paid industrial work which left a shortage of labour, exacerbated by the above-average rate of conscription in rural areas, and consequent over-working of those who were not self-supporting. With the removal of the additional rations of barley given to harvesters and general food shortages, labour relations became tense. Increasing state controls were bitterly resented – frequently seen as being applied unjustly to small and medium sized farmsteads. There were also complaints that controlled prices paid to producers were too low in contrast with the prices of industrial products which remained uncontrolled. In the face of growing discontent among the lower classes, the major industrialists and Junkers began to draw closer together. Jürgen Kocka identifies three reasons for this alliance; first, the economic boom and protectionist effect of the blockade negated some central points of conflict, in particular the question of tariffs; second, the threat of organised labour; and finally the common cause of resistance to state intervention.[35]

Meanwhile the antagonism between town and country dwellers – those with ration cards and those who were self-supporting – intensified and provoked a unification, within each community, of the lower and middle strata of society. Townspeople regarded farmers as selfishly causing shortages through food-hoarding, while farmers, who had a hard life, and were often poor, were envious of the higher-earning industrial worker and saw towns in general as a symbol of the hated state controls. In an effort to obtain food, town dwellers would swallow their pride and travel into the countryside to beg from the farmers who regarded this activity with a malicious pleasure. Often such encounters led to conflict.[36]

Offer quotes Kocka's *Total War*: 'the more deeply and intensively the State authorities intervened in most peoples' lives, the more they became identified with the increasing hardships and difficulties.'[37] By the winter of 1916–17, malnutrition was common and there was general disbelief in the promises of the state to provide a victorious peace in return for the extreme privations and increased war effort of the civilian population.[38]

What of the post-war consequences? That German morale was crumbling towards the end of the war was obvious to the Allies from army intelligence reports and the German press. At the front this was manifested by desertion and by the formation of Soldiers' Councils which began to operate independently of the military. 10,000 of these sprang up when the old German command structure collapsed in 1918; by early August 1918 desertion from the army had begun in earnest and was linked, by the German High Command, to plundering of army food stocks and other stores. Much of the food was distributed among the civilian population. The French Secret Service reported on 13 January 1919 that ' soldiers were to be seen in all the large towns of Germany as well as Berlin, selling cocoa, tea, flour, potatoes which are punctually delivered.' The report also claimed that hoarded food was beginning to appear because the law against such activity was not being enforced.[39]

Edith Doerry remembered events in Berlin around the time of the armistice:

> It was the 8th November 1918, a cold but sunny day as far as I remember ... We noticed armed men on the roof of the palace watching the milling crowd below. It seemed that the Kaiser was still in residence. A lot of rough-looking people were standing about and silently staring. There was something threatening in the air, and I was frightened. A couple of scowling men pushed past me, and one shoved his elbow in my back. I urged my brother to come away. In spite of my poor coat I looked probably more prosperous than many of the people there. Soon we heard gun-fire, and at last we began to run ... On the 9th November the revolution was a fact, and on the 10th the Kaiser had fled to Doorn.[40]

Although it was feared that Bolshevism would spread more rapidly in a country on the verge of starvation, the blockade was continued after the armistice for political reasons. As the British War Office put it on 16 February 1919: 'while Germany is still an enemy country, it would be inadvisable to remove the menace of starvation by a too sudden and abundant supply of foodstuffs. This menace is a powerful lever for negotiation at an important moment.' Since the Soldiers and Workers Councils (S.W.C.s) were seen as the source of the spread of Bolshevism, the Allies imposed conditions in the Armistice Agreement which sought to deny them funds. Armistice terms were intended to favour those areas which resisted Bolshevism; the continued control of the food supply was essential in this aim. Following the setting up of the new Weimar Republic, Fritz Ebert's fledgling government was already in conflict with the Soldiers and Workers' Councils in trying to regain control of the domestic food stocks in the months after the signing of the armistice, resorting to military violence as well as legal and political means. As a direct consequence of the continuing blockade, civil war erupted between government and S.W.C.s in 1919 and many lives were lost.[41]

During these months, Berlin itself was torn by the same strife and the Doerrys suffered further:

Officers returning from the front were stood against the wall and shot out of hand. Young men with haggard faces came late at night in fear of their lives to shelter with us. We had neither gas nor light, and I can still see my mother trying to cook a pot of split peas over a fire of a few sticks picked in the garden. Food was scarcer than ever because most of the shops were shut. Soon, however, soup-kitchens were opened and we were able to get a hot meal. I cried all the time I sat there, looking into my plate, feeling degraded and miserable.[42]

The Councils were effectively suppressed in time for the signing of the Versailles Peace Treaty on 28 June 1919, and the blockade was officially lifted two weeks later.

To sum up, although the blockade contributed to the reduction in food supplies it is difficult to quantify its precise effect, but it was part of the chain of events – in which the black market played a significant role – which led to general mistrust of the authorities and those traditionally in control. The mistrust had existed to a degree before the war, but the tangible loss of the basic requirement of adequate food served to crystallise feelings against the existing order. Davis has concluded recently that 'The state . . . lost the psychological war, by its own mistakes, and, in turn, it lost the right to rule'. Bessel also concludes that the attempt to achieve total mobilisation undermined the political order, widening the distance between rulers and ruled.[43]

The second direct effect of the loss of imports was on morale. Whatever the necessary nutritional requirement was, the perceived erosion of the German diet was a severe psychological blow. Loss of faith in the government to keep its promises, and survival on a subsistence diet were conditions which could, perhaps, be endured in a victorious situation, but with little to support the government's assurances towards the end of the war that victory could still be achieved, declining morale at home spread to the men at the front. Both the massive desertions and formation of the Soldiers' Councils, which preceded the end of the war, were linked to the plundering of army food supplies, in the case of the S.W.C.s specifically for redistribution to the German civilian population. In this sense the blockade may well have made an additional, minor, contribution to the timing of the end of the war. The failing military situation, however, was crucial. After its last desperate and momentarily effective efforts on the Western Front, from March to July 1918, Germany's army could not hope to outmatch her enemies and her defeat was certain.[44]

Finally there is the question of how far the blockade caused internal de-stabilisation leading to revolution. On the whole the Soldiers Councils adopted, as they believed, the right tactic in systematically redistributing army food rations to the near-starving German people. Within three months of the signing of the Armistice, Soldiers Councils had handed out an estimated one million tons of food, including stocks removed from the barns of wealthier farmers. The S.W.C.s were the nucleus of Bolshevism at the time, formed as a reaction to the collapse of the command structure. The food situation provided them with an immediate purpose, and saved their members, as Howard says, from recriminations as deserters. No doubt their ability to bring food to the people was contrasted favourably with the state's past failures. It was chiefly, however, the combination of the collapse of traditional authority in the military, through the failure of the army on the Western Front, with the disillusion with all forms of authority at home, which served to stimulate the formation of the S.W.C.s. The blockade thus had only a minor role in the rise of Bolshevik activity.[45]

It is arguable however that the blockade played a more significant role in crushing German Bolshevism – the lever being used as much by the new German government as by the Allies. The terms of the Armistice and the particular requirements denying relief to areas sympathetic to the Bolsheviks would seem to have been realisable only while the blockade remained in place, allowing continued control of the food supply.

Notes

1   Hans Fallada, *Iron Gustav*, Putnam, London, 1940, first published 1938.
2   Belinda Davis, 'State versus Society: Provisioning Berlin' delivered at 'Mobilising for Total War: Society and State in Europe, 1914–1918', Trinity College, Dublin, 23–24 June 1993; Richard Bessel, 'Mobilisation and Demobilisation in Germany, 1916–1919', in John Horne ed., *State, Society and Mobilisation in Europe during the First World War*, to be published by the Cambridge University Press; N.P.Howard, 'The Social and Political Consequences of the Allied Food Blockade of Germany, 1918–19', *German History, Journal of the German History Society*, London and Edinburgh, June 1993, Vol. 11 No. 2 pp 161–188; Jürgen Kocka, *Facing Total War, German Society 1914–18*, Oxford, Berg, 1973; Avner Offer, *The First World War: an Agrarian Interpretation*, Oxford, the Clarendon Press, 1989.
3   Davis, op. cit., p.8.
4   Mrs. E. Roseveare (Edith Doerry), Personal account, Liddle Collection, University of Leeds, pp. 1–4.
5   LC, ibid.
6   LC, ibid, Mrs.K. Lubinski.
7   Davis, op. cit., pp.3–6
8   ibid., and Offer, op.cit., p.25.
9   Offer, op.cit., p.63.
10 ibid., and Kirk-Othmer, *Encyclopaedia of Chemical Technology* Fourth Edition, Vol. 2., Ammonia.
11 Offer, op.cit., p.63.
12 Davis, p.6.
13 See Bessel, op. cit.
14 Davis, op. cit, pp.1, 6.
15 ibid., p.3; Offer, op.cit. pp.25–6, 64.
16 Davis, op.cit. p.6.
17 ibid., p.7.

18 ibid., p.9.
19 ibid., pp.8,10; Offer, op.cit., p.27.
20 Offer, op.cit., p.28; Bessel, pp.3–4; Davis, op.cit., p.14.
21 Offer, op.cit., pp.64–69.
22 ibid., p.62; Bessel, op.cit., pp.7,9.
23 Offer, op.cit., pp.62–3.; Howard, op.cit., p.164.
24 Benjamin White, *The Currency of the Great War,* Waterlow and Sons Ltd., London, 1921, p.27.
25 Davis,op.cit., p.5.
26 Offer, op.cit., p.30
27 LC, Roseveare, op.cit.,p.2.
28 Offer, op.cit., pp.38, 46, 50, 51–52.
29 Howard, op.cit., pp.164–165.
30 ibid, p.167; Offer, op.cit., p.51.
31 Offer, op.cit., p.34.
32 Howard, op.cit., p.162; Peter Loewenberg, 'The Psychohistorical Origins of the Nazi Youth Cohort' in *Decoding the Past: the Psychohistorical Approach,* Los Angeles, University of California Press, 1985 (new edition New Brunswick, N.J. 1996), p.254.
33 For this para., See: Howard, op.cit., p.168; Davis, op.cit., p.12; Offer, op.cit., pp.35–7; Loewenberg, op.cit., pp.257–8.
34 Offer, op.cit., pp.58–9.
35 Kocka, op.cit., pp.116–120.
36 ibid., p.121.
37 Offer, op.cit., p.59.
38 Davis, op.cit., p.12.
39 ibid., p.71; Howard op.cit., pp.171,176.
40 LC, Roseveare, loc.cit., p.4.
41 Howard, op.cit., pp162, 178,180–5.
42 LC, Roseveare, loc.cit. p.5.
43 Davis, op.cit., p.15; Bessel, op.cit., p.12.
44 See, Martin Middlebrook *The Kaiser's Battle*, Allen Lane, 1978.
45 Howard, op.cit., p.171.

Chapter 42

The Home Front in Italy

Luigi Tomassini

NEUTRALITY

Italy only entered the war on 24 May, 1915, nine months after the European contest began. In August 1914 the government and almost all of the political groupings, except a few small bodies of nationalists, had agreed that Italy's intervention in the war was premature. There had been the widespread conviction that the country was unprepared for conflict, and that its motives were insufficient and clearly not comparable with those of the other great powers struggling for a world supremacy far beyond the aspirations of the Italian State. Moreover, only a few weeks before the outbreak of the war, the 'Red Week' (a popular uprising which had spread across large areas of northern Italy and caused dozens of deaths), had roused extreme apprehensions among the ruling classes regarding the state of mind of the masses.

In fact, the process of national integration in Italy had advanced more slowly than in other countries. Not only had Italy been divided into a series of independent, or at any rate separate, states until 1861, but even after unification, completed only in 1870 with the seizure of Rome, the real unification of the Italian masses had proceeded at a rather more leisurely pace. 'Making the Italian people', according to a famous saying, turned out to be an even longer and more complex process than 'making Italy'.[1]

The way in which Italy delayed over her entry into the war was indicative of the nation's limitations and difficulties.[2] It was very significant that Italy only declared war on Austria. Not until the summer of 1916, following strong pressure from the Allies, did the government decide to extend the war to Germany. Even then there remained the impression of a separate Italian war, for its own limited and particular aims, not at all in step with the wider vision of the war waged by Russia, France and Great Britain. This limited nature of the commitment to war of the country was clear even to contemporaries and was summed up in the phrase used by the Prime Minister Salandra in his famous speech in which he maintained that a 'holy egoism' had inspired Italian intervention. This was not a prospect likely to inflame hearts and mobilise the home front.[3]

The Italian Socialist Party, alone among the 'official' large socialist parties of the major Allied and enemy nations, declared itself against the war.[4] The parliamentary majority, led by Giolitti, was against intervention, and voted for war credits only after the King had committed himself by signing the Treaty of London. Even public opinion – although a considerable part of the middle class sympathised for various reasons with France and England – had not been united behind intervention.[5]

All this meant that Italy was entering the war with her home front less cohesive and united than that of the other major allied and enemy nations. It therefore required a strong commitment to mobilising the energies of the nation in order to create a home front capable of supporting the military effort.

MOBILISATION OF THE HOME FRONT.

For all these reasons, the forms of mobilisation of Italian society during the war were profound and extensive, to a degree beyond that of other countries – such as Germany – in which the political system was less liberal, but in which there had developed a *'burgfrieden'* lacking in Italy.[6]

The outstanding characteristic of the forms of mobilisation of the home front in Italy was the important role of the Army and of civilian society, in the absence of a strong state structure. The liberal state in Italy was characterised by a particularly fragile structure, with limited means of intervention, especially in areas concerning the economy and civilian society. Above all, Italy had a tradition, profoundly rooted in the political culture of the ruling classes, of liberalism and laissez-faire, which had not been significantly overturned by the change to protection in 1887.

Despite the large increase in ministries (from 12 to 22 in the course of the war), and of Committees and public bodies of various kinds responsible for managing all aspects of the life of the nation in war-time, and despite the marked growth in the size and competence of the central administrative apparatus, the effort of mobilising the nation at war was not initially based on direct state intervention. There was indirect intervention, in which some previously existing institutions (notably the Army) carried great weight. In addition, other specially constituted bodies, comprised of a typically singular mixture of public and private, exercised a role. There remained however, a notable reluctance on the part of the ruling-classes to abandon the old mental patterns of laissez-faire, even in the context of a world-wide upheaval, which everywhere required an unprecented development of state authority.

In the three areas in which the mobilisation of the home front was most obvious (mobilisation of production equipment, the coordination and regulation of supplies, and organisation of consensus and war propaganda), this dual-natured State intervention emerged very clearly in various forms.[7]

INDUSTRIAL MOBILISATION: THE 'OTHER ARMY'.
In the case of Italian industrial mobilisation,[8] the leading role was entrusted to the Army, first because for almost the entire duration of the war the Under-Secretary and then the Minister for Arms and Munitions was (unlike elsewhere) a soldier, General Alfredo Dallolio. Second, and more particularly, because all the organisation of the Mobilitazione Industriale (MI) hinged on the military structure: the presidents of the mobilisation committees and all their bureaucracies were made up of soldiers. Workers in the mobilised companies were militarised. According to age and military rank, they wore a uniform and were subject to the usual military obligations (including sleeping in barracks). Others were obliged to wear a special badge, but were allowed to stay with their families. In all cases they were subject to the military code, the application of which was managed by detachments of soldiers, commanded by officers or carabinieri, located near the factories. The severe military discipline was applied formally even to women, children, and older workers, with occasionally counterproductive effects, which forced some revision of the initial legislation.

In the course of the war, the MI involved over 900,000 workers in about 2,000 firms – that is the majority of the industrial apparatus. For these workers the innovations caused by militarisation brought drastic changes. Primarily, the composition of the workforce itself changed. Now, as the industrial machine grew massively to meet war requirements, the factories drew workers previously occupied in minor production or craft sectors. Particularly crucial were new workers from the agricultural sector, especially women, whose employment was strongly supported by the government, as they naturally replaced the male workforce which had been drastically reduced by military mobilisation. At the end of the war, there were about 200,000 women employed in the mobilised factories – a lower percentage than in other countries, but none the less considerable.

These developments caused exceptional changes in the internal structure of industrial organisation, in the relationships between skilled and unskilled workers, and between workers and their families. For example, much resistance had to be overcome from families to female employment, even by means of protective measures and facilities such as dormitories, rest and washing areas, and canteens. The periodic reports between the peripheral bodies of the MI concentrated, in some cases almost obsessively, on how to avoid the numerous absences of workers still too tied to an agricultural working-day or to popular tradition. For example, night-work, for women workers, was viewed with particular hostility.

As a manufacturer warned in 1916, the women workers recruited in wartime were :

> peasant women, who all carry with them the burden of their ignorance and their prejudices, not least among which is the refusal of their husband's permission to do night work, which makes it impossible for us to organize rotas . . . Other difficulties are caused for us by agricultural work . . . at the approach of spring, a large part of our female workforce . . . take their leave, and it is by now clear that a male or female worker who is kept back by force when they wish to leave, works so badly and so unwillingly, and produces so little, as to force us in our turn to request them to leave.[9]

Even Sunday working, introduced half-way through the war, led to widespread forms of protest and serious concern. In many cases the protests of the people and the workers were supported even by the clergy.[10] However the most obvious way in which factory life was altered concerned the organization of discipline. Workers could now be punished not only with fines and sackings (which meant, under the circumstances, being returned to the Front) but also with prison and other penalties allowed for in the military code. This situation also had strange consequences which had certainly not been foreseen by the legislator.

For example, women and children, who, despite formal equivalence of rights, in practice were rather less subject to the punitive effects of the military code, assumed a fairly active role in the union struggles in the factories. They were certainly in agreement with, and sometimes inspired by, the male workforce, who were more subject to repressive control; but in any case the result was to reverse the pre-war roles.[11]

The presence of the Army officers or the carabinieri responsible for discipline in the factories notably altered the workers' experience of this 'other army'. Frequent cases of conflict between soldiers and industrialists arose, since the latter tended to use the disciplinary forces to keep wage levels low, while obviously the army's task was to maintain order and discipline. The industrialists made this duty more difficult if they followed particularly restrictive practices regarding wages.

The very presence of an authority distinct from that of the owner-manager in the factory, even under the guise of the military, gave the workers a new awareness that there existed a different and higher authority than that of the owner. This new awareness kept pace with the importance of their own role in the life of the nation. The elevation of the role of industrial work to patriotic ends, which took the form of large patriotic messages posted up in the workshops, of meetings inside the factories, or in the widespread distribution of pamphlets and propaganda materials, was all meant to exploit the role of labour and production as essential for the fate of the nation and for victory. It contributed to the creation of a self-image of the industrial worker very different from that of the pre-war period. According to the language used by, for example, some of the major political exponents of Italian political culture of the time such as – on opposite fronts – Antonio Gramsci and Benito Mussolini, the worker was now taking on the characteristics of a 'producer'. No longer a seller of labour on the open market, regulated only by the laws of economic interest, he was now an essential cog in the production machine, of vital importance for the functioning and very existence of the nation.[12]

This new position was also confirmed by legislation. There was formal compensation for the workers' loss of their normal freedoms and rights, and for the objective worsening of their conditions due to increased work shifts and the drop in real wages as a result of rapid inflation. A series of rules was adopted to protect living and working conditions. These ranged from health regulations to controls over wages in relation to the cost of living (index-linked wages); and from forms of wage supplement in case of involuntary unemployment (which foreshadowed today's redundancy fund), to the general adoption of social security measures which were extended after the war.[13]

SUPPLIES AND GOODS: THE 'HEROES OF POVERTY '

The State had a similar role, in more obvious ways, in the organisation of supplies and goods for the country at war.[14] In this case too it was decided initially to entrust this function to the Army. General Tettoni was made responsible for managing the first centralised body responsible for co-ordinating supplies.[15] Above all, it was decided to approach the first phase of the war along mainly laissez-faire lines, which did not allow for any direct state intervention, only coordination and verification.

At first, therefore, the experience of the general population did not change significantly. Soon, however, the price of goods began to rise to previously unknown levels. Consumers, who had been used for decades to considerable monetary stability, found themselves faced with unexpected price rises unknown in living memory. Such inflation had not even been seen during the troubled events of the national Risorgimento.

Furthermore, prices were not rising in a uniform manner; the increases affected different goods in different ways. This caused noticeable changes in the eating habits of the population, not just in the poorest classes, but also in the lower-middle classses. Finally, food shortages as well as price rises caused unrest. The long queues outside the shops after the first price-control and quota-restriction measures were a new experience for Italian city-dwellers, and there were repercussions for productivity. As an official of the Ministry for Arms and Munitions warned:

> There is serious discontent among the working class who are absenting themselves from work . . . in a manner exceedingly dangerous for the

industrial economy and the battle on the Home Front. Too often workers are ... excusing themselves with having had to spend long hours at the shops in order to provide basic necessities.'[16]

Balancing the family budget became a difficult task for the workers, whose wages had previously been near to purely subsistence levels. Ironically, but not inappropriately, the leading socialist newspaper, in talking about industrial workers, whom the patriots were referring to as 'the other army', called them 'the heroes of poverty.'[17]

On the other hand, hardship was only one facet of life in the cities behind the lines. In reality, the great development of the economy and monetary inflation itself had an effect which could not go unnoticed: to the soldiers returning on leave, the cities appeared festive, illuminated and gay, demonstrating an altogether new luxuriousness and lack of concern which were out of keeping with the tragic reality of the front.

This caused the local and government authorities to pass a series of measures to limit the consumption of luxury goods. This was less because of actual supply requirements, than the declared aim of 'avoiding the irritation felt by the soldiers returning from the front at the sight of the thoughtless gaiety which the numerous crowded stores of the cities offered.'[18]

In this situation, popular discontent was channelled against certain stereotypical figures in Italian society who could be firmly identified and blamed, such as speculators and war profiteers. These were now given such names as: 'sharks', 'bloodsuckers' and 'vampires'. As is well documented, the spread of these notions was even promoted by the principal bourgeois and interventionist newspapers because such cases of disreputable behaviour provided an excellent and obvious way of diverting popular discontent from the general management of the war. In contrast, the publications of the socialist opposition clearly refused to descend to this level, in some cases openly defending the most controversial groups, such as the small traders, and putting the blame on the government and its direction of the war effort.[19]

The transformation of the war experience did not just involve the consumers. Besides traders, who were in the ambivalent position of being able to draw economic advantage, but were exposed to popular discontent, producers, too, experienced previously unknown forms of state interference. Those in agriculture were affected by price controls, requisitions and quota restrictions, especially concerning basic goods, such as meat and grain. These measures impressed themselves in an entirely new and unforeseen way on habits and certainties reinforced in the public mind. So much was this the case, that the promoters of these policies themselves had considerable fears about enacting them.

Sidney Sonnino, recognised leader of the conservatives in Parliament, and someone who knew in depth the situation in the Italian countryside, had pointed out the particular danger which the grain requisitions presented:

> You do not know the countryside of Italy and the psychology of the peasants. They have given their sons and even their livestock to their country, but they will not give up their wheat; you are worried that there may be riots in the cities because of bread shortages; there will be even more serious ones in the countryside.[20]

Subsequently, in fact, the measures adopted did not have such serious repercussions. All in all, the prices of agricultural products put the producers in a favourable position.

However, one of the innovations which of all the profound changes brought by the war, had perhaps the greatest influence on the public mind and awareness, was the introduction of identity cards.

In fact, after the various beneficent and charitable institutions already operating widely in the main Italian cities had made their greatest effort to distribute free food and meals to those worst off, it became necessary to operate a more systematic structure so as to control the distribution problem in a centralised and organised way. Ration cards, introduced in the main Italian centres from 1917 onwards, and subsequently kept on for reasons of morale rather than economic regulation, bore clear witness to the fact that the public considered the provision of basic food requirements, at prices compatible with wage levels, to be an inalienable right. As Salandra observed, to his prime ministerial successor in 1917, the peasants and the city workers, especially in the south, lived 'on bread and flour, and nothing else . . . but as much bread as necessary is considered a natural right, on which no authority in the world can impose limits. If the opinion were to form that bread is in short supply because of the war, the war would be hated and condemned.'[21]

However, the introduction of identity cards showed clearly the new fact that this task was now taken on by the State administration, without any delegation to private bodies or charitable organisations; further, that the common interest was not limited to ensuring a minimum of food for the poor people, but also implied a reduction in privilege and an equalising tendency for all classes confronted with the national sacrifice.

PUBLIC OPINION AND PROPAGANDA: THE MOBILISATION OF THE INTELLECTUALS.

The third major area in which the war gave rise to forms of mobilisation aimed at consolidating the home front, was the organisation and management of consensus. Indeed, this is the area which can most aptly be described as the 'home front', since the dense network of associations and structures created was in fact held to be the heart of the country's resistance.[22] In this case especially, involving the mingling of public and private, the role of civilian society standing in for the state was particularly evident. The search for consensus by involvement of the masses and by direct propaganda was initially absent from the Italian government's mental horizon, according to an idea analogous to that of the military command in the last phase of the war.[23]

If, in this initial phase of the war, the Government did not act directly to bring propaganda to the masses, it did, on the other hand support and encourage an intense mobilisation effort among the middle classes and the interventionist forces, which in some way compensated for, and replaced, this lack of intervention. In fact, from the beginning of the conflict there sprang up a myriad of little civil committees, for mobilisation or welfare, who gave themselves the task of carrying out a 'patriotic' action to support the effort of the nation at war.[24] These committees combined the 'morale-boosting' activities of propaganda for war aims with concrete tasks of welfare and charity performed through the most disparate means: through the setting up and expansion of public kitchens, through the distribution of food to the poorest classes, or indirectly through the distribution of work at home, especially in the area of army supplies, to the wives of the recalled servicemen or in general to working-class women. In many cases, private donations were integrated with the corresponding government subsidies for the families of recalled servicemen.[25]

Economically the importance of these measures was considerable, but even more so politically and adminstratively. The private welfare associations, the mobilisation committees for either welfare or civil preparations, united, very interestingly, characteristics of both Italy's past and future political system . On the one hand, in the past, committees of this kind had taken the form of very flexible, functional and also important associations – for special and urgent requirements – of the local ruling classes. These handled relations with the central power, at a historic moment in which political representation was not yet managed by organised and centralised parties of the modern kind.[26] On the other hand, they functioned as an extension of a very limited state apparatus, which expressed itself through them for occasional particular requirements. The war brought on to this scene some substantial changes. First, by increasing the size of this phenomenon; second, by giving it a noticeable continuity, because the war went on so long; and finally by introducing a strong element of centralisation and co-ordination both nationally and locally. The picture which resulted, although it appeared to involve only the intensification of pre-existing features, was such that it profoundly changed the experience and awareness of all concerned.

Recent studies have shown how the working people, who were the intended recipients of this welfare and assistance work, nursed ambivalent feelings towards these bodies and the people who represented them. They saw in them both those who provided concrete help in difficult situations and those who by personifying interventionist ideals, had caused the war, which in the final analysis was the source of the present hardship. There were private individuals who used their own time and energy and sometimes even their own money, but at the same time such people were also often themselves handling the state's contribution and organising the distribution of subsidies or work on behalf of the state administration.

The capacity of those holding power, the middle class, to organise and coordinate themselves at local and national levels found expression in a series of local 'fasci' [branches] for welfare organisation and civilian and patriotic mobilisation. It was not a question of specifically political bodies; nor should the name 'fasci', which they often adopted, be taken as anticipating Fascism, since the word was already used in Italian political tradition with a very different significance. However, in these 'fasci' there also formed associations which had a clear political meaning, foreshadowing the 'national blocs' which in the postwar period brought the Fascist movement to power. Furthermore, it confirmed a kind of experience which definitely suggested the possibility of active bourgeois minorities 'shifting for themselves' in helping and integrating with state activities, when these were held to be ineffective or restricted by existing obstructive laws.

HARDSHIP

Despite all the forms of mobilisation and consensus put into action during the war, the Italian home front gave on many occasions clear and worrying symptoms of collapse. The hardship caused by the war hit – in different ways, but none the less seriously – not only the soldiers at the front, but also the civilian population. The number of deaths among the civilian population during the war was 600,000 in excess of the previous (prewar) estimated average, or roughly the same number as those killed at the front. This fact bears witness to the fact that the war led to a worsening in living conditions, inseparable from which were individual illnesses and actual epidemics (such as influenza, which claimed hundreds of thousands of victims in the last year of the war), responsible for damage far greater than they would have done under normal conditions.[27]

Hardship was a general fact, but it originated from various sources and operated along very unequal lines within Italian society. Undoubtedly among the worst affected were families (mainly those of the urban working classes) who, because of their limited nuclear structure, were deprived by the call to arms of their main source of maintenance. They relied on the meagre state subsidy, or on charity or work subsidised by it – often at home – from the civilian mobilisation and welfare committees. In general those of the humbler urban proletariat who were not in factory work were amongst the least successful in adapting themselves to war. The actual industrial working classes – although badly affected financially by the special measures adopted in the militarisation of the factories – were much more successful in coping, despite the steadily increasing inflation. To a large extent they retained, thanks to exemption from military service, the possibility of drawing an income and staying with their families.

The peasants were without any possibility of exemption from the military draft. However, in many parts of Italy the extended structure of the peasant family and the possibility of remaining connected to land which produced basic necessities, the prices of which were rising rapidly, helped considerably in alleviating hardship. In the areas near to the city where the peasant family could have direct access to the market, there were even cases of profits being made. Where these conditions did not exist, as for example in the case of the farm-labouring classes and in large areas of southern Italy, hardship seriously affected even the peasant classes.

Senator Camporeale, after a visit to the south and to Sicily, wrote to Giolitti in November 1916 that the state of poverty was worrying given that 'more than half of the land is uncultivated and with us poverty and rebellion and revolt are synonymous . . . [The countryside] is swarming with thousands – 20 to 30 thousand – deserters.'

On the eve of Caporetto, in September 1917, the Italian Supreme Command calculated that there were about 100,000 deserters in the country, with a higher concentration in some regions.[28] The deserters hid especially in the countryside, both because many of these men themselves were of peasant origin, and because it was easier to remain hidden and helped by the country people, who in some cases valued the work they could do in the fields. In many cases the deserters organised themselves into gangs, carrying out thefts and robberies and frequently coming under fire from the police.[29]

This last extreme instance shows how directly the difficulties of the military front could have repercussions on the home front. More generally, however, the war and hardship brought about a profound change in collective behaviour; from the transformation of habits and behaviour in everyday life and the private moral sphere, to widespread cases of social conflict.

MORALITY AND WAR

In Italy about 5,900,000 men wore military uniform out of a total of about 7,000,000 able-bodied men of military age. For those who stayed in the country, and especially for young people and women, war meant a necessary change of habits and a greater independence, which gave rise to different collective behaviour than in the past. The slackening of family ties caused effects at first sight unperceived, but the signs could appear in new forms. In an enquiry promoted by the Humanitarian Society of Milan one reads: 'The war having broken out we are witnessing a sad and painful spectacle: women and boys are not only taking on the jobs of men called to arms but also the deleterious habit of drinking. It appears that in the province of Milan during the war about 23% of women and 27% of boys took to drinking . . . and we must record another pernicious effect of the war, the shocking encouragement it has given to nicotinism in young people'[30]

Family ties had been in some ways eroded by the war, especially for young people and adolescents, who were left more and more to themselves because of their fathers' call-up and their mothers' work. This meant that the problem of a deterioration of links in the moral order, basic to civil co-existence, posed itself to the ruling classes in increasingly worrying ways.

The problem affected women, as we have already seen, because of new working practices for them, but also in a more general way. For example, in some cases the local authorities even went so far as to wonder if the subsidy should be maintained or lessened to the wives of drafted men in cases where it was certain that the women had been unfaithful to their husbands. This suggestion was not followed up, but it shows a concern among the ruling classes because of what in many instances was seen as a worrying moral decline on the home front.[31]

The fact which chiefly alarmed the ruling classes was the rapid increase and spread of petty crime among juveniles. During the war juvenile criminality increased markedly; but it was particularly shocking because the increase involved especially the lowest age groups, those from 9–13, as well as those from 14–17. There was a decrease for young people from 18–20 (who were mostly of course under military discipline). Offences were mainly small thefts, but the problem took many forms: aggressive begging, assault and conflict with the forces of law and the military, night-time rowdiness, vandalism and violent attacks, often with groups organised into gangs of youths. In the cities criminality resembled in some ways that of the gangs of deserters in the countryside.

Such crimes varied a great deal in their seriousness and were very often treated by the police with remarkable tolerance. This may have provoked indignant comments from the patriotic associations and the press, but severe repression appeared at times to be counterproductive. In July 1917, justifying police reluctance about intervening to stop coal thefts, the prefect of Naples wrote,

It is regular practice among countless groups of urchins less than ten years old, who come out of the alleyways opening on to the port, to clamber over the railings at various points and throw down the coal from the wagons, so that adults can carry it off. Any attempts to stamp out this practice among such a large number of women and boys would undoubtedly have caused popular unrest.[32]

This attitude, however, appeared very risky to the middle classes who considered that there was a dangerous link between such deviance of a criminal type and political opposition. In 1918, on the subject of widespread attitudes among Florentine boys during the war, the Florence civil welfare committee expressed itself thus:

> These boys of our city, the cheeky street urchins who sneer at work or thought, with their crude taunts, coarse laughs, insults and vulgar songs, are in the vanguard of the defeatists. The Florentine urchin is an ill-brought up brat risen from the slums to the surface and dangerous if you confront him.

The link between individual deviance (petty crime) and social danger (in the form of opposition to the war), was an almost obsessive *leitmotiv* of the press and the political journalism in urban bourgeois circles. In fact, deprivation and worsening of living conditions beyond a certain limit, tended to look in the popular perception like deprivation of a natural right, and this triggered off forms of protest which, in these circumstances, naturally tended to become anti-war protest.

PROTEST

Anti-war protest in Italy dated from the period of Italy's neutrality. The socialists organised various pro-neutrality demonstrations, including a national one on 21 February 1915, which was remarkably successful. There were less organised and more spontaneous forms of protest in various places when drafted soldiers departed for troop assembly points; but at the moment of intervention there were no open and generalised forms of protest, since the hardship of the population had not yet reached the levels which months of war would produce. In fact, given the high unemployment and the crisis in the labour market caused by the high number of returning temporary emigrants, the war came at the right moment and could have appeared to some as a solution to some of the most pressing social problems. However, from the second year of the war onwards, hardship became generalised and an increasingly widespread source of conflict.[33]

The places in which popular discontent was chiefly concentrated were in the countryside – especially the urban suburbs and the countryside near to the city, where there were large groups of workers between the agricultural and industrial sectors. As a prefect related in 1917:

> in the countryside, particularly in areas near to provincial industrial centres, one notes lack of public spirit, dissatisfaction and war-weariness ... [and] among the rural masses, especially women, there has taken root the idea that the war was wished on them by their overlords, who desire it to continue, because they want to see most of the proletariat destroyed

. . . another conviction which has taken root in women's minds is that the war will end if there are hostile public demonstrations.[34]

Typical places for popular protest to arise were the queues for the distribution of subsidies provided for the families of those who had relatives at the front, and who were in difficult circumstances. These occasions in fact brought together the social groups *most* affected by hardship because of the war. Often their demands for better economic conditions were accompanied, and even taken over, by demands for an end to the war, so that their husbands and sons might be able to return from the front.

This endemic form of protest became increasingly apparent and reached its peak in 1917, when a wave of popular demonstrations in both countryside and city, led especially by women, involved large areas of central northern Italy. This was the crucial area for the nation at war, causing considerable concern to the police forces, to the ruling classes and parliament.[35]

Amidst this unrest there also came together the protest of large groups of those male and female industrial workers, who in common with a large proportion of the new war workforce, originated from, or had maintained links with, the agricultural sector. The processions they formed tended mostly to be made up of women, but with male workers often joining them as they passed through the city streets singing protest songs and calling for immediate peace. At the beginning of May 1917, demonstrations of this kind began to converge on the outskirts of Milan (the largest Italian industrial centre), where they were joined by many factory workers. The demonstrators were 'masters of the city for 24 hours',[36] but there were no serious consequences, partly because the workers' and socialists' organisations did not join the protest.

SOCIAL CONFLICT AND POLITICAL CONFLICT

The most important protest movement against the war happened in Turin in August 1917 and had a more obvious political content. It was sparked off by bread shortages, which caused a popular uprising in which the extremists (anarchists and socialists) actively intervened. Although supplies of bread were quickly guaranteed, the uproar did not stop but continued as an anti-war protest. To halt it, the Army had to step in, leaving fifty of the civilian population dead and two hundred injured.[37]

The fact that the revolt had happened in Turin seriously worried the ruling classes, as this was one of the major industrial centres of the country; furthermore, in the other heavily industrial areas, such as Liguria, Lombardy, Tuscany, there were threats of massive worker protests against inadequate wages. These, according to the industrialists, also had the political motive of opposition to the war. No less worrying was the fact that the socialist press had meanwhile been following events in Russia with great interest. Soviet correspondents from Petrograd and Moscow, on a propaganda tour (which actually urged continuing the war) were welcomed by large popular demonstrations which sang Lenin's praises.

The harsh repression of the Turin disturbances affected even the major leaders of the Italian Socialist Party, that is Lazzari and Serrati, respectively party secretary and editor of its daily newspaper, *Avanti!*. This fitted into a wide-sweeping context of repression. Large areas of Piedmont and Liguria were declared 'war zones', coming under direct military control. A further series of restrictions was imposed and on 4 October a decree was pronounced (the 'Sacchi decree', from the name of the Chancellor of that period) which severely punished all forms of dissent, even simple verbal opposition to the war. Increasingly, however, anti-war tendencies were developing within the Socialist Party.[38]

Also in 1917, the social conflict in the factories was becoming more radical. Intense unrest continued in Liguria and Lombardy. According to the industrialists' reports, unrest in these leading industrial areas was increasingly a reflection of anti-war protest rather than of economic claims.

After Caporetto, the Government, while continuing with strict repression,[39] tried also to regain a kind of consensus, both in the Army and in the country. Besides, food supplies were noticeably improving and there were no further alarming shortages of basic necessities in the big cities. Finally, the fact that the war now appeared like a war of national defence caused a new wave of patriotism in the middle classes, and to a certain extent also influenced some sections of the working classes. Some outstanding representatives of reformist socialism, like Turati and Treves, on their own initiative and with open opposition from the party leaders, made declarations which greatly limited their opposition to the war at such a dramatic moment.

Taken overall, this mixture of repression and search for consensus had some effect, and the last year of the war was less characterised by open social conflict. Nonetheless by now a deep rift had been revealed in the body of the country. It was to reappear forcefully in the postwar period.

CONCLUSIONS

The home front in Italy was characterised by the strong presence of state structures (i.e. the army) and by forces of civilian society (committees for such matters as internal resistance, civilian mobilisation and welfare), which ensured extensive and efficient forms of mobilisation.

There were also however great hardships, which led to widespread forms of protest and dissent. These protests covered a broad spectrum of demonstrations: (i) traditional political protest, embodied by the Italian Socialist Party, (ii) union conflict, (iii) spontaneous protest by women and the people of the cities and, (iv) forms of rebellion and even draft dodging in the countryside, especially in the south. In many cases, as we have seen, protest even took a moral form, being moved not only by hardship itself, but by the conviction that basic and undeniable rights, rooted in a long tradition, were being damaged. After the war all these elements combined, leading to bitter political and social dispute.

The first occasion on which these forces coalesced was the so-called 'cost of living riots' of July 1919.[40] Elements from the food riots and trades unions joined forces with the infectious violence of the young urban gangs. To this was added the resentment of the soldiers returned from the front, uprooted from the context they had left behind. The 'outbreak of peace', as it was defined at the time, brought about the sudden and rapid dissolution of all the emergency war measures, in a situation where the old modes of behaviour were no longer appropriate. The experience of war had profoundly changed the expectations, the behaviour, and the ideas of the masses.

To reach a new equilibrium a long and troubled journey was required.

Notes

1   After the end of the Risorgimento, the Italian ruling classes had made conspicuous efforts to move towards raising the national consciousness of the masses, precisely around the myth of a national Risorgimento, of the Third Italy (after the Rome of the Caesars and that of the Popes) which was to be an Italy founded on the values of science, of reason, of liberalism. In reality, these values had reached only the middle and lower-middle classes. The peasant masses, whose living standards were still extremely poor, particularly in the south of Italy, had been affected very little in any national sense by these processes of integration. On the contrary,they had been affected by a phenomenon of a very different kind, that is, large-scale emigration: it has been calculated that in the first decade of the century alone about 1,600,000 emigrants moved permanently abroad, while another considerable number emigrated temporarily to other European countries. For a general picture see: E. Sori, *L'emigrazione italiana dall'unita all seconda guerra mondiale*, Bologna, Il Mulino, 1979.

2   The Treaty of London (April 1915), which defined the conditions of Italy's entry into the war beside the powers of the Entente, reveals an uncertainty, as between, on the one hand, irredentist and anti-Austrian concepts of the conflict – being reshaped in the tradition of the Risorgimento as objectives – and between imperialist aims, on the other, though these were fairly narrow and limited in the context of a conflict which was deciding the military and political hegemony on a world scale. The return of Trentino and Trieste was requested, on grounds of nationality, and also a series of territories in Dalmatia and on the Adriatic, contrary to this principle, and in tendential conflict with the Slav peoples. Meanwhile, in the Adriatic, there were indications of a Mediterranean expansion, with some hint, however vague, of remuneration in a colonial form.

3   See B.Vigezzi, *L'Italia di fronte alla prima guerra mondiale*, I, *L'Italia neutrale*, Naples, Ricciardi, 1966; B. Vigezzi: *I problemi della neutralita e della guerra nel carteggio Salandra-Sonnino 1914–1917*, MI-RO-NA, Dante Alighieri,1962. From this point of view, the months of neutrality had certainly

not made matters easy. The wave of enthusiasm of August 1914, which had swept away and probably hidden in the surprise and excitement of the moment the possibility of expression of popular dissent in other European countries could not be repeated in Italy. Even in Italy there was in May 1915 a wave of pro-intervention demonstrations, but these were demonstrations which reached their peak only after the signing of the Treaty of London, that is in favour of things already decided. They were violent and bitter, but in essence they were expressive of a minority opinion and had been preceded by strong neutralist demonstrations.

4   L.Valiani, *Il Partito Socialista Italiano nel periodo della neutralita (1914–1915)*, Milan, Feltrinelli, 1977.

5   Some major newspapers had remained fairly equivocal until the eve of the conflict. In the intellectual-scientific circles themselves the debate had been fully developed, showing up opposing positions, and there had not been in Italian high culture that emotional and almost unanimous involvement in favour of war that following the manifesto of the German intellectuals and scientists of 4th October 1914, which characterised the intellectual environments of the Great Powers at war. The greatest Italian thinker of the era, Benedetto Croce,preserved throughout the war an equidistant attitude to both sides,and in scientific circles there was very strong resistance to aligning on an uncritically patriotic and interventionist front. On this point cf L. Tomassini, 'Guerra e scienzia. Lo Stato e l'organizazzione della ricerca in Italia, 1915–1919', in *Ricerche Storiche*, a XXI, no3,Sept-Dec,1991, pp.747–802.

6   For a comparative examination of the different social realities of the various countries at war cf the special edition of the review *Ricerche Storiche*, XXI, n.3, Sept-Dec. 1991, entitled *Studi recenti sulla prima guerra mondiale*, edited by Giovanna Procacci and Luigi Tomassini, with writings by Jean-Louis Robert, Jay M. Winter, John Horne,Martin H. Geyer, Berthold Unfried, Giannarita Mele, Bruna Bianchi.

7   This confirmed a pattern similar to earlier moments of comparable difficulty.On the occasion of the Messina earthquake (1908),the Italian State had not intervened directly, not even allocating funds for the affected people: the intervention had been managed, under the supervision of the Crown, by the Army, by charitable committees and by institutions spanning public and private spheres, like the Red Cross.

8   Italian industrial mobilisation, legally set up on 22 August 1915, forecast the establishing of an undersecretariat, later ministry, of Arms and Munitions, which was to regulate all materials, and to see to the ordering of materials for the Army.The organisational structure was decentralised, taking into account the profound differences in Italian industrial apparatus,to 7 and later 11 regional committees. These, in contrast to what had happened in France, which had served as a model for this part of the Italian organisation, were not part of the Chambers of Commerce and of the industrial circles, but were bureaucratic bodies under the War Ministry, had military staff from the territorial divisions, and were chaired by soldiers (generals or admirals).In this environment, a series of companies, initially limited to the arms sector, then gradually extended to all areas of production,from foodstuffs to textiles, from energy production to ceramics and aeronautics, was declared mobilised.In these companies the workforce was militarised.In this way, the workers lost

both the right to strike,and any possibility of moving to other jobs.At the same time,wage levels were frozen at the level in force at the outbreak of hostilities. In exchange, the workers avoided being sent to the front.On the other hand,the Italian Government, unlike the English for example,or in other ways the German or the French, did not foresee any kind of restriction for manufacturers and in fact agreed to rather high price levels. In this way, even the less organised or modern – and more improvised – businesses, such as those of craftsmen, were able to remain on the market, raising the overall level of industrial production, in spite of their low levels of individual productivity, while the better organised companies were to realise enormous profits, which they would be better able to reinvest in the improvement of plant and so in further improvement in their productivity. On this point, see L.Tomassini, 'Industrial mobilisation and the labour market in Italy during the First World War, *Social History*, vol. 16, no.1 (Jan 1991), pp.59–87 (original in English).

9 Letter of 6.12.1916 from the Mechanical Workshops of Lissone (province of Milan), in the Archivio Centrale dello Stato (ACS), Ministero delle Armi e Munizioni (MAM), Comitato Centrale di Mobilizione Industriale (CCMI), b.30.

10 On this point see A.Camarda-S.Peli, ' "Mai la Domenica". La sospensione del riposo festivo durante la grande guerra', in *Studi Bresciani* 15 (1984).

11 G. Procacci, 'Repressione e dissenso nella prima guerra mondiale', in *Studi Storici*, 22, n. 1 (1981),pp.119–150.

12 On these points see L. Tomassini, 'Intervenciòn del Estado y relaciones industriales en Italia durante la primera guerra mundial (1915–1918)', in *Sociologia del Trabajo*, 21,(spring 1994), pp. 159–187.

13 L. Tomassini, 'Industrial mobilization and State Intervention in Italy in the First World War: Effects on Labour Unrest', (original in English) in L.Haimson & G.Sapelli eds, *Strikes, Social Conflict and the First World War. An International Perspective*, Annali della Fondazione Feltrinelli, XXVII, Milan, 1992, pp.179–211.

14 See M.C. Dentoni, '"Questione alimentare" e "questione sociale" durante la prima guerra mondiale in Italia' in *Societa e storia*, no.37, 1987, pp.607–636, c.f. also M.C, Dentoni, ' "L'Arte di viver bene mangiando poco" ', in *Annali dell' Instituto Alcide Cervi*, 13 (1991), pp.133–147; and M.C. Dentoni, *Annona e consenso in Italia 1914–1919*, Milan, Angeli, 1995. On the eve of war, the trade balance in Italy for exchange of agricultural products was roughly equalised,but while Italian exports were chiefly goods such as wine, fruit, citrus fruits, tomatoes, etc, over 80% of imports were goods essential in the diet, chiefly grain (57% of food imports in 1913).

15 In January 1916, a commission was set up chaired by General Tettoni. He was one of the military leaders in whom the Prime Minister Antonio Salandra placed his trust, (c.f. the highly commendatory appraisals in A. Salandra, *La Neutralità italiana. Ricordi e pensieri*, Milano, Mondadori, 1928, pp. 270, 271, 291), and was in charge of the central committee for supplies, for the purchasing and distribution of cereals,set up in January 1916 at the War Ministry, up to May 1916.

16 Report from the Ufficio Vigilanza Igienico-Sanitaria (Health Supervisory Office) on 'Food supplies to auxiliary workers', in, ACS, MAM, CCMI, b . 24.

17 *Avanti!*, 25th September,1915, 'Agitazione nello stabilimento Ansaldo':

Fundamentally, the industrial workers were not among the worst-off sectors of the population, who included above all the families whose able-bodied men were at the front,and who had to rely for a living on the meagre State subsidy.

18 V.Giuffrida-G. Pietra, *Provital. Approvvigionamenti alimentari d'Italia durante la grande guerra 1914–1918*, Padua, Cedam, 1936, p.165, cit, in M.C.Dentoni, ' "Questione alimentare" . . . ' .cit., p.624.

19 L. Tomassini, 'The State and civil provisioning in Italy during the First World War', paper (original in English) at the conference, 'Mobilising for Total War: Society and State in Europe 1914–18', Trinity College, Dublin, 23–25 June 1993, now being published in the review *Guerres mondiales et conflits contemporains*.

20 Sonnino's words are reported in V. Giuffrida- G.Pietra, *Provital*, op. cit., p.142.

21 Salandra's words are reported by G. Procacci, 'Dalla rassegnazione alla rivolta: osservazioni sul comportamento popolare in Italia negli anni della prima guerra mondiale', in *Ricerche Storiche*, XIX, 1, (gennaio-aprile 1989), p.66.

22 See A. Fava, 'Assistenza e propaganda nei regime di guerra (1915–18)', in M. Isnenghi,(ed), *Operai e contadini nella grande guerra*, Bologna, Nuova Cappelli, 1982.

23 See P. Melograni, *Storia politica della grande guerra 1915–1918*, Bari, Laterza, 1972.

24 These were bodies whose creation had been called for by the government (Salandra had wished for every town council to have a committee), but which remained entirely entrusted to the initiative and management of private people. Only after some time did the government realise the necessity for its presence in this area, nominating the republican Comandini responsible for the civil welfare committee set up in August 1916. In July 1917 there was added to the responsibility of the committee that of 'internal propaganda'. Shortly after, Comandini was also nominated president of the central Committee for the 'Federated Welfare and National Propaganda enterprises,' that is, the most important federation of private welfare and civil mobilisation organisations, which was really set up between July and August 1917, soon including 4,500 commissariats and 60 provincial secretariats.With only Comandini at the head of this state and private organisation, the intersection of public and private bodies discussed above could be clearly seen. See A. Fava, 'Assistenza e propaganda', op.cit.

25 B. Pisa, 'Una azienda di stato a domicilio: la confezione di indumenti militari durante la Grande Guerra' in *Storia Contemporanea* 1989, no.6; A.Staderini, 'Le forniture militari a Roma (1915–1918)',in *Storia Contemporanea*, 1990, 1.

26 See A. Fava's presentation paper to the conference: ' La società in guerra. Giornate di studio sul fronte interno nella prima guerra mondiale', Camerino, 23–24 May, 1995.

27 P. Giovannini, 'L' influenza espagnola: controllo instituzionale e reazioni popolari (1918–19)', in *Sanità e sociteà. Emilia-Romagna,Toscana, Marche, Umbria e Lazio secoli XVI-XX*, edited by A. Pastore and P. Sorcinelli, Udine, Casamassima, 1987.

28 See B. Bianchi, *Crescere in tempo di guerra. Il lavoro e la protesta dei ragazzi in Italia 1915–1918*, Venezia, Libreria Editrice Foscarina, 1995, p.133.

29 ibid., p.135.

30 A. Pugliese, *Brevi cenni sulle condizioni igieniche della provinzia di Milano con speciale riguardo all alcoholismo e nicotinismo negli adolescenti, Milan,1920*, cit., in B. Bianchi, op.cit., p.111.

31 ACS,PCM,1917,f. 1,2,1004,('Donne che durante l'assenza del marito perché richiamato alle armi, abbiano tradito la fede coniugale. Revoca dell'esonero giornalero.').More generally about women during the war, see A. Bravo, (ed), *Donne e uomini nelle guerre mondiali,* Bari, Laterza, 1991.

32 PDG.,b.234, f. Naples, Prefect's Report, July 1917, quoted in B. Bianchi, op.cit., p.161; for further testimonies to reactions to the excessive police indulgence towards little delinquents, see p.130 ff.

33 See G. Procacci, 'Popular protest and labour conflict in Italy, 1915–1918,' in *Social History,* vol.14,no.1. (Jan,1989), and G. Proccaci: 'State coercion and worker solidarity in Italy, (1915–18) :the moral and political content of social unrest', in: L. Haimson & G. Sapelli eds., *Strikes, Social Conflict and the First World War, An International Perspective,* Annali della Fondazione Feltrinelli, XXVII, Milan, 1992, pp.145–177.

34 ACS, A5G,81, 162,1, cit., in G. Procacci, 'Dalla rassegnazione alla rivolta' op.cit., p.89.

35 G. Procacci, 'La protesta delle donne delle campagne in tempo di guerra', in *Annali dell'Instituto Alcide Cervi,* 13 (1991), pp. 57–86.

36 Martini, *Diario,* cited in Procacci, op.cit., p.90.

37 P. Spriano, *Storia di Torino operaia e socialista da De Amicis a Gramsci,* Turin, Einaudi, 1972.

38 Already in 1915 the PSI delegation, the only 'official ' party of the great powers not to support the war, had had an important role in the preparation for the Zimmerwald conference, the first occasion on which it had been attempted to start up an international socialist organisation based on opposition to war; in 1917 the splinter group 'intransigente revoluzionaria' formed, with a meeting where among others Amedeo Bordiga and Antonio Gramsci were present. More radically against the war than the PSI policies: see E. Ragionieri, 'Il socialismo italiano e il movimento di Zimmerwald', in *Belfagor,* XXVIII, (1973), pp.129–160; also ibid., E. Ragioneri: 'La terza Internazionale e il partito comunista italiano', pp.79–118; also see P.Spriano, *Storia del partito comunista italiano, vol 1, Da Bordiga a Gramsci,* Turin, Einaudi, 1967.

39 See G. Procacci, 'State coercion', pp.174 ff.

40 On the cost of living riots, and more generally on the postwar crisis in Italy, see R. Vivarelli, *Storia delle origini del fascismo, I, L'Italia dalla grande guerra alla marcia su Roma,* Bologna, Il Mulino, 1991, p.448.

Chapter 43

Peoples of the Underdeveloped World

Bernard Waites

The 1914–1918 war was the first to be fought at the industrialised core of the world economy in which extra-European resources of food, *matériel*, and manpower were indispensable for victory, and resource denial was a central part of wartime strategy. Britain was crucially dependent on the agrarian producers of the frontier democracies for foodstuffs, and thanks to ethnic and imperial solidarity they volunteered highly motivated recruits in significant numbers.[1] But, additionally, both Britain and France could command resources in the 'underdeveloped world' of their African and Asian colonial empires, and British sea power and financial strength made the Allies monopoly purchasers from the export-oriented economies of South America.[2]

Colonial status determined that India and Africa were involuntary belligerents, but 'colonialism' can be a misleading starting point for analysing the war's consequences for these regions. Most colonies in 1914 were not economic dependencies of a single power in the old mercantilist sense, but rather open markets in a world of multilateral trade.[3] The disruption of international commerce and the knock-on effects on local exchange economies was the key mechanism in diffusing the impact of war through India and West Africa. Its longer-term global significance lay in the exposure and testing of the links between industrialised and peasant societies, between urban consumers and 'native' producers. True, a 'local' colonial war led to widespread suffering in central East Africa, but the social intensity of the experience resulted from the region's fragile demography and the impossibility of mobilising labour without coercion in communities where waged work was virtually unknown. For most of Africa, the real colonial era began with *the end of war* and the completion of pacification.

Admittedly, 'underdevelopment' is a relatively recent concept whose present-day correlates are explosive demographic growth and delayed industrialisation, resulting in a chronic disparity between population and material resources. In the 1900s, 'underdevelopment' was more usually associated with slow or negative population growth. Between 1881 and 1921, India's population increased by less than a quarter. During the same period, the population of Black Africa declined as the opening up of the continent exposed Africans to epidemic diseases from which they had been relatively isolated in the past.[4] Mortality from the natural calamities that coincidentally afflicted Asia and Africa greatly exceeded combatant deaths in 1914–18. The influenza pandemic which struck western India at the end of June 1918 killed at least six million people in the sub-continent by the end of the year. The final death toll for 1918–19 was later reckoned at twelve to thirteen million or more than four per cent of the population.[5] The Indian government's official account of these years implies that war-time circumstances exacerbated the tragedy: sanitary and medical services were severely depleted with the absence of British personnel on war service, and the prices of nourishing food, blankets and warm clothing were abnormally high because of the economic dislocation caused by the war.[6] But, since the ravages of the epidemic were as great in 1919 as they were in 1918, the arguments for an exceptional mortality because of the war are not compelling. In proportion to Africa's population, influenza probably had a lesser impact, but certainly overshadowed all other determinants of human experience in 1918–19, with a mortality tentatively estimated at 1.5–2 million.[7] The war was incidentally important to its onset because the disease was introduced by soldiers returning from the European theatre, and in central East Africa spread along military lines of communication linking the region to South Africa.[8] But with respect to both India and Africa we are confronted by coincidence not conjuncture. The predominant determinant of human experience was a mutant virus, not the global military conflict.

The most far-reaching repercussion of July 1914 was a financial and commercial crisis affecting developed and underdeveloped countries alike. With the maritime transport revolution after c.1870, Indian trade and finance had become increasingly geared to primary exports, and were immediately disrupted by the news of the war's outbreak. There was a run on savings bank deposits and a panic cashing of Indian currency notes for silver coin. The expatriate community of administrators and businessmen rushed to remit money to London and the international exchange value of the rupee came under such attack that it had to be supported by the Indian Imperial Government.[9] In colonial West Africa, the shipping shortage at the beginning of the war reduced the flow of exports to a trickle, and because of the region's 'open' trade economy, a re-orientation of exports was a prerequisite for their recovery. The treaties establishing colonial rule had forbidden discriminatory tariffs and the operations of European trading firms were not limited by imperial frontiers. Germany's soap and margarine industries were based on the crushing of palm-kernels, a West African staple. Three quarters of Nigerian palm kernels and forty-four per cent of total exports went to Germany in 1913 which furnished 14 per cent of total commercial imports. Since these consisted largely of cheap gin, their cessation had a crippling effect on government revenue. Duties on trade spirits accounted for £14 million in 1913 (or 30 per cent of the total revenue); by 1917 they had shrunk to £89,000.[10]

In reconstructing the experience of war and its longer term consequences for the peoples of India, the best point of departure is to evaluate the military and economic resources the sub-continent afforded the Allies, and then consider how the exploitation of those resources strained the colonial relationship and exacted its price of political concessions on the part of the imperial power. With a population of over three hundred million in 1914, a standing army of over 300,000, and a large mercantile sector dealing in raw cotton, jute, food-grains, oil-seeds, hides and nonferrous ores, the Indian sub-continent was a considerable military and economic asset. The BEF's first reinforcements were from India and in the winter of 1914–15 about a quarter of the British army in France was either native or British Indian Army units. Between August 1914 and the end of 1918, 877,068 combatants and 563,369 non-combatants were recruited in India; during the same period, 1,096,013 Indian and 285,037 British soldiers were despatched overseas from the sub-continent.[11] In 1917–18, the Indian Imperial government made an outright grant to the British Exchequer of £100 million – a sum equal to more than a year's British Indian annual revenue – towards the cost of the war. A further financial contribution took the form of deferred payments from the British government for the use of Indian troops outside India.[12] Remittance was impossible because of wartime bullion shortages, and, while India's credit banked up in London, local taxation was required to meet British obligations. A British Government agency, the Royal Commission on Wheat Supplies, purchased nearly five million tons of Indian foodstuffs totalling £40 million in value, although the economic benefit of these purchases was greater because Indian food prices were much lower than those in the rest of the world by early 1917.[13] Included in this total were nearly three million tons of Indian wheat shipped to the Allies – equivalent to about six months worth of British war-time wheat imports. Raw hides were acquired in India and accounted for at least three fifths of the upper leather used in the United Kingdom to make British and Allied army boots.[14] India had a narrow modern industrial sector which allowed it to furnish certain manufactures for the war effort: the British-owned Calcutta jute industry was the largest in the world and supplied the Allied armies with sand-bags and the merchant marine with gunny-bags. The Bombay cotton mills turned out army cotton supplies. All campaigns required railway lines for military transport, and in Mesopotamia, East Africa and Palestine the chief source was the Tata Iron and Steel works. In the course of the war, Tata supplied the Indian government with nearly 300,000 tons of steel.

This bare recital of India's contribution in manpower and *matériel* to the war disguises security liabilities which Britain incurred because of its presence in India, and deficiencies in military and economic organisation. Both have to be placed on the debit side of the imperial account. British vulnerability was heightened because the war at first denuded India of British troops but did little to allay chronic security concerns on the North West frontier.[15] More portentous were British anxieties about Muslim loyalty following Turkey's entry into the war. The Ottoman Sultan was spiritual leader of India's Sunni Muslims and the religious conservatives amongst them – who were traditional allies of the British – were deeply uneasy about a war on the Caliph and the possible defilement of the Holy Places by unbelievers during the Arab revolt and the Palestine campaign.

India's economic contribution to the war was stringently limited by industrial backwardness and virtually complete dependence on imported capital goods. Nationalists had long charged that British colonialism had retarded the Indian economy by inserting it into an international division of labour based upon the exchange of raw materials for imported manufactures. This accusation gained authority from an unexpected quarter when the Indian Government appointed an Industrial Commission in 1916. Its principal witness was the Indian Munitions Board, a central authority created to control the purchase and manufacture of military stores in India because of the difficulty of obtaining supplies from Britain. The state's attempt to organise production revealed gross strategic deficiencies: apart from the railway workshops (which were mainly concerned with maintenance and repair) there was no mechanical engineering industry to speak of, not even a single machine to make nails or screws. Primary materials – ranging from oil seeds to hides and nonferrous ores to mica – had to be exported in a raw state for want of industrial processing capacity. The Commission's proposals for removing these strategic weaknesses constituted major concessions to Indian economic nationalism: they included a new government purchasing policy to favour Indian industrialists and the provision of entrepreneurial capital through state-aided and state-supervised banks.[16] Most vital of all to the nationalists was protection of the home market, and in this respect the exigencies of war finance reinforced the proposed industrial policy. Until 1914 the Lancashire cotton lobby had always managed to persuade the British government that, to ensure a level playing field in international trade, any revenue tariff on cotton imports had to be matched by a countervailing excise on Indian manufactured exports. Lancashire's ability to dictate Indian tariffs ended when government finances deteriorated with massive increases in military expenditure, and the re-introduction of revenue tariffs became inevitable. In 1917 the Government raised the duty on cotton imports from 3 and a half to 7 and a half per cent, without any corresponding increase in the countervailing excise, and publicly declared industrialisation to be the paramount objective of fiscal policy.[17]

India's military contribution to the war was seriously compromised by a standard of equipment suitable only for frontier wars and combating civil disorder. Since the Mutiny, British policy had kept the Indian Army one generation behind in weaponry, and it entered the war grossly under-equipped in artillery, and with neither motor transport nor wireless. Recruitment was confined to the martial castes – which effectively eliminated most Indians from the manpower pool – and heavily concentrated in the western Muslim Punjab, the North West Frontier Province and Nepal. Indian army regiments were either composed entirely of the same ethnic or caste group or their three constituent companies were ethnically pure. Discounting the Gurkhas, only thirty per cent of the 1914 Indian army were Hindus. With less than one thirteenth of the population of the Indian Empire, the Punjab furnished sixty per cent of recruits.[18] Some of the highest military participation ratios in the world were to be found in a triangle of territory around Rawalpindi where 40 per cent of the males of military age flocked to the colours during the war, with the most heavily-recruited villages and tribes sending virtually all their eligible men.[19] Recruiting according to caste and communal criteria deprived the Indian army of a common disciplinary framework – since Indians holding the Viceroy's Commission could not exercise command over ranks from another caste – and was a hopelessly inefficient way of replenishing under-manned units. Replacements could not be assigned where needed but had to go to those units restricted to their caste.

The Indian soldier was usually an illiterate peasant, unfamiliar with the infrastructure of the industrial world, and sought honour and security within the extended family in the widest sense. He was scarcely touched by modern secular ideologies, and only in 1918 did an occasional letter from an Indian soldier exhibit a nationalist political vision.[20] Morale in Indian Army units was very dependent on the paternalism, language skills and ethnic sensitivities of a small elite of British officers – the only ones to hold the King's Commission. Exposure to industrialised warfare on the Western Front tested the morale of Indian forces to the breaking point. A very high incidence of self-inflicted wounds amongst Indian troops, and the complete rout of some units during German offensives of 1915, persuaded the General Staff that Indians were unsuited to the Western Front.[21] On the dubious assumption that cold and rain were the chief cause of their failure in Europe, they were despatched to the warmer climes (and lethal disease environments) of East Africa, Gallipoli, Mesopotamia and Palestine.

For the vast majority of Indians the experience of war was mediated through prices not military participation, and came as a check to rising expectations. Though many economic transactions in village India were not yet monetised, money was essential to pay the land tax and buy indispensable commodities, such as cotton goods, at local markets. Peasants had no confidence in paper money and were notoriously prone to hoard coinage for its bullion value. With the revival of Indian exports after 1915, coupled with the restrictions on the imports of manufactures as a result of shipping shortages, demand for silver became virtually insatiable. Between August 1914 and 31 March 1918, over 270 million ounces of silver (or more than two fifths of the entire world production) was added to the monetary 'stock' in India. Silver flowed out to the regional and local markets to purchase peasant primary produce, but the return flow to the ports and commercial centres was restricted. With shortages of international and inland transport, the reciprocal basis of commerce broke down, and hoarding removed vast quantities of bullion from circulation. By April 1918, after raw cotton prices peaked, the Government of India's silver reserves had dwindled so low that special arrangements had to be made to buy US silver on generous terms.[22]

Paradoxically, the peasantry's growing money wealth was accompanied by falling real prosperity measured in terms of the consumption of such basic items as cotton piece goods, kerosene and salt. By 1918, cotton cloth imports were two thirds below their pre-war level and, though Indian mill output had overtaken imports, there were simply insufficient powered looms to compensate for the shortfall. Indians consumed, on average, less cotton cloth in 1918–19 than they did in 1900.[23] India produced insufficient salt to meet domestic consumption, and dwindling imports, together with an increased salt tax, drove its price unprecedentedly high. As a result of inland transport shortages, hitherto coordinated price levels in the Indian economy began to diverge. The cost of essential commodity imports rose much faster than agricultural producers' prices which were kept low by a succession of good harvests until the last season of the war. After the 1917 harvest, the grain merchants, who mostly profited from price differences between inland markets, were unwilling to buy in their usual quantities because of freight restrictions. The harvest was good and the absence of transport kept the prices of all foodstuffs low. But ordinary commodity prices – including spices, oil, cloth, kerosene and salt – were raised abnormally high by shortages and profiteering. Discontent and uneasiness soon turned to sporadic looting in Bombay, Bengal, Bihar and Assam. In reaction the government took steps to increase salt production, control its sale and impose maximum prices where necessary. It also tried to stop cotton speculation.

The other price relationship disturbed by shortages of inland transport was that between rural and urban food prices, and this generated industrial unrest on a scale hitherto unknown in India. The cost of living of the

Bombay working classes rose very rapidly in 1917, causing widespread strikes amongst mill-hands and service workers. The police establishment of Bombay and other cities fell dangerously low because a constable's pay ceased to be a living wage and many volunteered for the army, then offering a special bonus to new recruits. This was of particular concern because all provincial governments, except the Punjab and North West Frontier Province, were reporting substantial increases in crime against property. With the monsoon failure of 1918, mass discontent and a new sensitivity to nationalist opinion placed the Government under an urgent political compulsion to relieve distress, even though this would interfere with India's economic contribution to the war. In the summer of 1918 the Secretary of State was informed that the Government could no longer purchase and export wheat and other foodstuffs, except for Mesopotamia, and the export of food grains was subsequently prohibited.

The incident demonstrates in miniature the balance the Government of India had to maintain between meeting imperial commitments and minimising the burdens these imposed on its impoverished subjects.[24] The war upset this balance: military expenditure, and the recurring charges on the capital grant, demanded additional excise duties and purchase taxes, and income tax was enhanced and graduated. While the last touched only a tiny minority of townspeople, many more were exposed to the indiscriminate taxation effected by inflation. Restoring the balance required political concessions of a kind the Viceroy had dismissed as 'ridiculous and absurd . . . ' in 1912. In an attempt to win back 'moderate' allegiance to the Raj, the Secretary of State announced, in August 1917, 'a policy of increasing association of Indians in every branch of the administration, with a view to the progressive realisation of responsible government in India as an integral part of the British Empire.' This circumlocution implied evolution towards dominion status, and the first steps were the constitutional reforms of 1919 enlarging the legislative councils and devolving considerable power to Indians who could command the support of those councils.[25] These concessions were made to a colonial nationalism whose presence and political style had changed radically under the impetus of war. As the official record of India's 'moral and material progress in 1917–18' records: 'The time has gone by when the topic of constitutional reform . . . could be dismissed summarily with the remark that those who demand it form but a small fraction of the population.'[26]

India was subjected to a single paramount power and we can relate her experience of the war to the loosening of that subjection and the emergence of modern nationhood. We cannot impose anything like that thematic coherence on the African experience. The diversity of African states and societies, and of the forms of colonial rule to which they had been so recently subjected, make synthesis difficult. Though all the colonial empires were involved in the conflict and territorially re-adjusted by its outcome, the modes and degree of involvement varied. In French West Africa, the war achieved its greatest impact through military conscription, while in British West Africa economic processes were dominant. The African empire where, it would seem, the most decisive changes were occurring during the years 1914–18 was the Portuguese: it was the time when tribal resistance to Portugal's rule was decisively overcome, although only in northern Mozambique was this a direct consequence of the war.[27] In late 1917 retreating German forces crossed the border and the territory experienced all the socially disruptive pressures of the East African campaign.

This campaign and French conscription must necessarily claim our attention: the first brought the novel experience of war between European colonial states on African soil, the second led to the induction of hundreds of thousands of Africans into the French colonial army and their experience of modern war in theatres outside Africa, including the Western Front, Salonika and Gallipoli. The raising of French colonial forces for fighting in distant theatres of war was not new in itself: Senegalese *tirailleurs* had fought in the Franco-Prussian war, for example. But like Indians, these were professionals recruited from 'warrior races', or at least what French thinking stereotyped as warrior races. The scale of military conscription after 1914 was clearly new, but so too was the fact that it made no distinction between 'warrior' and 'non-warrior races', nor – in the vast French Sudan where *de facto* slavery still prevailed – between slaves and the sons of slave masters. Partly at the prompting of Charles Mangin, conscription had been extended to the French colonies in 1912 (though kept as a reserve measure in sub-Saharan Africa until the outbreak of war). Approximately 600,000 colonial soldiers were recruited during the war, about 300,000 from North Africa, just over 160,000 from the West African Federation. Between 66,000 and 71,000 colonial soldiers died for France. The most decorated unit in the French army was a Moroccan regiment. The French Empire also provided about 200,000 labour conscripts, of whom 140,000 were North Africans.[28]

The colonial empires rested on the active consent of at least large minorities amongst the peoples they governed, and we cannot pass over the way both *évolué* groups and representatives of 'traditional' society rallied to France. Much of the Muslim manpower of Algeria, for example, was contributed willingly. The last time France had been at war, in 1870–1, an Algerian rebellion had ensued, and after its ferocious repression native lands had been confiscated on a wide scale. In August 1914, by contrast, the French administration and *colon* opinion were gratified by a remarkable display of Muslim loyalty. Algerian society enjoyed its own, rather briefer version of metropolitan France's *Union sacrée*. Muslim clerics endorsed the French cause and encouraged Muslims to volunteer. There are even accounts of native peasants spontaneously offering to care for the families and properties of European *colons* who were called up. A governor's decree of December 1914 exempted all Muslim volunteers, and their fathers, from the *indigénat* (or native penal code). Included in this exemption were all Muslims spending more than a year in metropolitan France as civilian workers.[29] Since the goal of virtually all Muslim Algerians who had formed modern political aspirations was full assimilation to French citizenship without loss of Muslim personal status, the war was an exceptional opportunity to overcome the deep divide in Algerian colonial society between its minority of European *citoyens* and the majority of *sujets*. That this opportunity was missed was due to *colon* intransigence.

The civil status of Africans from the French empire was crucial in determining their military experience, both in Africa and Europe. A small minority of enfranchised Black Africans from the Four Communes of Senegal, known as *originaires*, demanded the imposition of conscription on black electors in order to protect their voting rights. In 1916, their spokesman, Blaise Diagne, the first black African deputy to the National Assembly, secured a law confirming their citizenship and their obligation for military service, though in the metropolitan army, not as *tirailleurs*.[30] However, the great majority of Africans were conscripted to the colonial army as *sujets*, men whose legal status was defined by the *indigénat*. They received one half of the pay of the citizen in uniform, were not given beds, had no prospect of promotion to the officer grades, were debarred from holding authority over French troops, and on discharge received under a third of the pension granted to those with citizen status. When serving behind the lines in France, they were isolated in special camps (with the privilege of 'wintering' in the Midi to protect their health), fed a familiar diet, instructed by marabouts if they were Muslims, and discouraged from mixing with the local population. Few spent any time in a large city. This was not because of racism on the part of the French command, who refused an American request to institute segregation towards the end of the war, and we should recall that to Black Americans and educated Africans from the British colonies French conduct to 'men of colour' was a model of democratic solidarity.[31] Rather, there was a paternalistic concern for the welfare of men wrenched from a world almost incomprehensibly different from modern France.

Some inkling of that difference can be gathered from the recollections of a volunteer from Futa Jalon, recorded in the early 1970s.[32] The son of a Muslim chief, with eighty siblings and half-siblings, his father had wanted to shield his free-born sons from conscription because a universal obligation to serve struck at the distinction between the servile and well-born. At first, 'the chiefs sent only their slaves, and the members of the community with little status . . .' According to rumour, the French promised to make every slave who went to war a chief on his return, and this threat, together with an immense pride in the warrior tradition, persuaded the young man to volunteer. He was a devout Muslim, but his faith was a syncretic Islam that had absorbed elements of local animism. Long after the war, he could convey the intensity of the experience only by likening it to the key Islamic religious rite of circumcision.

There is probably insufficient evidence for a systematic analysis of the cultural terms in which Africans handled their experiences but a series of private letters by Dahomeans to Governor Noufflard suggests that literate *évolués* assimilated the purest patriotism of the French.[33] We cannot altogether exclude the possibility that these men wrote what the recipient wanted to read, but there can be no grounds for doubting the Senegalese veteran who told Marc Michel in 1972: 'Everywhere we used to meet strangers from Dahomey, Mali, the Ivory Coast . . . We all had the same ambition, which was to beat the enemy. France's victory meant our victory.'

We must bear in mind, however, that identification with the French cause on the part of Africans inducted into the army was a process quite discrete from the imposition of conscription on French West Africa in the first instance. It is all too evident that the latter met with bitter resentment and caused widespread social dislocation. A thinly-spread French administration could not follow bureaucratic procedures and arbitrary impressment, using the leaders of traditional society, was the norm. Some joined up more or less willingly in the expectation of a post on the bottom rung of the administration. But because communal leaders sought to screen their healthiest young men, a high proportion of those presented to the call up were enfeebled by disease and malnutrition. When the demands of the military authorities became more pressing in 1916, a large number – variously estimated between 60,000 and 150,000 – fled to Liberia and neighbouring British territories. New conscripts deserted in droves from columns on the march and military camps. Three spontaneous armed insurrections broke out in animist regions where French rule had not yet found collaborative allies equivalent to the Muslim clergy or the *évolués*.

Besides these inchoate popular protests, the French faced 'aristocratic' rebellions in recently pacified areas where collaborative relations with local chiefs came under stress.[34] Conscription undermined the servile basis of chiefly authority because recruits were promised relief from labour service. Furthermore, chiefly assent to colonial rule was strained by the withdrawal of French troops in 1914, rumours of France's military disasters in Europe, and shortages of the imported luxuries that had helped secure the collaboration of the local aristocracies.

Resistance of one form or another to conscription was so widespread that, in September 1917, the Governor-General warned that a 'general revolt' in West Africa would result from further recruitment. Despite this, when French manpower needs became desperate, Blaise Diagne accepted a special commission from Clemenceau, with the rank of governor-general, to raise recruits throughout the Federation. This was on the understanding that veterans would be exempted from the *prestation* or obligatory labour service on public works, given preference in appointing to government jobs, whilst distinguished service would be rewarded by French citizenship when requested, and that African education in agriculture and medicine would be instituted and public health facilities expanded. Diagne's success in mobilising many more recruits than had been expected of him belied the Governor-General's prediction of a 'general revolt' and demonstrated that an African could rally other Africans to France more successfully than the French. But Diagne appears to have acted in belief that the post-war settlement would see a collective improvement in the status of France's African *sujets*. Instead, the demobilisation of Africans saw the emergence of a new social cluster of the petty privileged, exempt from obligatory public labour, often appointed to posts in the bottom rungs of the colonial administration such as *agent de cercle* – men who tended to be allies of the French in any conflict with traditional leaders. The status of the *sujet* itself remained a keystone of the colonial legal structure.[35]

In focusing on these military aspects of war, we are liable to overlook the fact that in the most populous region of Black Africa, between Sierra Leone and Eastern Nigeria, the years between 1916 and 1920 saw unparalleled prosperity for producers of primary exports. The war broke out in the aftermath of prolonged drought and famine affecting most of West Africa, and recovery was retarded by the sharp fall in exports of cash crops. Exports of Nigerian groundnuts, for example, fell by half between 1914 and 1915. Government recruitment for carrier service provided some relief for continuing distress: about 40,000 men were raised for military carrier service alone in Nigeria and Sierra Leone, while others were recruited for road and railway construction.[36] General recovery came with the reopening of the shipping lanes and booming Allied demand for groundnuts and palm products – both raw materials for soap and margarine – and other cash crops. Nigerian groundnut exports in 1916 were three times the volume of 1914, and in 1918 reached a level not surpassed until the mid-1920s.[37] Export prices rose much faster than the local costs of subsistence, reaching an all time high in 1920. The terms of trade had never been more favourable for African producers. Slavery had been the basis of the Northern Nigerian economy when the territory was conquered at the turn of the century, and boom conditions accelerated the substitution of paid for slave labour because, with the increased opportunities to earn cash incomes, slaves were able to raise their redemption fees. In the Gold Coast colony, where small-scale African capitalism was most developed, the war was an opportunity for Africans to acquire new skills. With the withdrawal of white artisans and blue collar workers for war service, a range of jobs and promotion opportunities was opened to them. They became engine drivers on the railways, fitters and mechanics in the mines, and were less closely supervised in a wide range of jobs. Eleven hundred men were raised in the Gold Coast for Military Motor Transport, and this experience was put to use after the war in the road transport businesses set up by Africans.[38]

The war had its most intense impact on Africans in the mass where the most protracted and determined of all the satellite campaigns was waged, in central East Africa. Had the provisions of the Berlin Act for the continent's neutrality in the event of war elsewhere been observed, Africa would have been spared its use as a battleground for European colonialists, but the Defence Force commander in German East Africa, Paul von Lettow-Vorbeck, seized the opportunity to divert enemy forces from more important theatres by harassing the Uganda railway. Distance, terrain and poor communications favoured guerrilla warfare. The German colony's frontiers were half as long again as all the battle-fronts of Europe, but the campaign ranged even wider, spilling over into Mozambique and Northern Rhodesia in its final phase. The numbers of soldiers engaged were tiny compared to the millions massed on the European fronts, and the weaponry necessarily light because of the formidable difficulties of transporting any heavy load in a continent so inhospitable to draught animals and so recently introduced to any form of wheeled vehicle. Von Lettow's forces at the beginning of his campaign numbered 260 Germans and 2,472 askaris, and they were always short of modern rifles and smokeless powder. At his maximum strength in March 1916, he had 12,100 askaris. Over the course of the war, the British Empire alone used over 114,000 troops against von Lettow, and at one point had 55,000 men in the field, yet never defeated him. When he surrendered in Mozambique in November 1918, his force consisted of 155 Europeans, 1,168 askaris and 1,522 porters. Many of the women amongst his followers had borne children on the march.[39]

Such tiny numbers rightly indicate von Lettow's remarkable military skills and tenacity but may give the entirely wrong impression that the East African campaign was a trifling matter to the local societies. In fact, the impact of war penetrated deep into communities hundreds of miles from the fighting, and persisted long after hostilities ended. To understand why, we must recall certain immemorial features of Africa's landscape, demography and disease ecology. Quinine prophylaxis had made it a less lethal environment for human incomers, but livestock diseases were still uncontrolled. With tsetse fly – the vector for sleeping sickness trypanosomes – so prevalent, pack and draught animals were useless throughout much of the bush and wheeled transport was unknown in the pre-colonial era. Before 1914, the German authorities reckoned that about a third of Tanganyika was infested with tsetse. Attempts to deploy cavalry during the campaign merely confirmed that tropical Africa could not be conquered on horseback. Sleeping sickness decimated the mounts. With few motorable roads and only two railway lines into the Tanganyika interior, any movement of goods, weaponry or equipment required the massive mobilisation of auxiliary labour. For the populations of central East Africa, the labour demands placed on them by the combatants – British, Belgian, Portuguese and German – were especially crushing because the region had undergone a Malthusian crisis of epidemics, famine and pestilence in the decades before 1914. That the war saw the culmination of these natural disasters was, to some extent coincidental, but conditions were created where epidemics spread more rapidly and there were fewer checks on pestilences. Tsetse flourish in uncontrolled bush, and the loss of men's labour to clear the bush was a factor in the extension of the infested area, which covered about two thirds of Tanganyika by the early 1920s.[40]

The British at first assumed that the military issue could be settled by using Indian troops, supplemented, if need be, by South African and settler forces. The civil authorities in East Africa were reluctant to see large numbers of Africans familiarised with modern weaponry. But the failures of the Indian expeditionary force, its weakening by disease, and the demands of the Mesopotamian theatre, led to the Africanisation of the war. The British eventually raised about 50,000 African troops; two thirds were enlisted locally, and the rest shipped from Nigeria and the Gold Coast. Volunteers were easily found amongst the young tribesmen of Nyasaland and the East African Protectorate, partly because the warrior role was embedded in their culture, but also because askaris were paid more than three times the most generous prevailing local wage rates.

To support their troops, the British employed during the course of the war over one million African 'followers', about half compulsorily conscripted under ordinances issued in Nyasaland in late 1914 and in the East African Protectorate in August 1915.[41] Since their allies and the Germans also recruited heavily, the total number who at one time or another performed carrier service must have been much higher. The only precedent for the mobilisation of labour on this scale in Africa was recruitment for the South African mines. Parts of East Africa experienced something close to the universal labour conscription of able-bodied men. A recent estimate is that over 83 per cent of the manpower available in Nyasaland served at one time or another. In the four provinces of the East African Protectorate, where recruitment was concentrated, the only able-bodied men not conscripted were those who fled to the bush.[42] Labour was needed on this scale to maintain lines of communication over vast distances where weapons, ammunition, food and other supplies had to be head-carried. Every military detachment had its tail of gun carriers, stretcher bearers and front-line porters, but the majority of labour conscripts worked far from the fighting zones as human transport chains, road and rail labourers, and canoemen.

Caravan porterage was by far the commonest form of hired labour in central East Africa before 1914, but the work was seasonal and a particularly despised and arduous task of the kind which a pre-capitalist society often relegates to casual wage-labourers who are regarded as socially inferior even to slaves.[43] Reluctance to serve can only have been compounded by the wage-cut for porters announced under the pressure of European settlers because the rates offered by the East Africa Transport Corps were higher than those on white farms.[44] Men were impressed into service in Kenya and Nyasaland by tactics resembling, at their most brutal, the slave raiding only recently suppressed by colonial rule. Tax defaulters were rounded up and forced to act as carriers or to work on the roads, and subsequently given only a tax receipt as payment for their efforts. The wives of defaulters were taken hostage until men gave themselves up; chiefs and headmen were threatened with removal from office unless they produced enough recruits to meet military labour requirements.

Only a minority of carriers witnessed combat. But those common experiences of war – separation from home, subjection to novel forms of discipline, forced marching and monotonous labour on inadequate rations, exposure to severe weather and new disease environments, depression and nostalgia – were as generalised in the East African populations as they were in Europe. Debilitated men routinely succumbed to dysentery and intestinal diseases. In the second half of 1917, the death rate in the British carrier corps was officially reckoned at 2 per cent per month, while the 'rate of wastage' from illness, disablement and desertion was reckoned at 15 per cent per month. One tentative estimate is that throughout the war 10 per cent of British conscripted followers, or over 100,000 men, must have died. Followers recruited by other combatants probably fared much worse: almost a quarter of the porters used by the Belgians in Rwanda-Burundi died in 1917–18.[45]

The campaign was the last act of the 'pacification' phase of European colonialism in central East Africa. With so much labour expended improving roads and railways, the greater use of motor transport, and the closer control of chiefs to ensure they yielded up able-bodied men, European administration was given the means to penetrate more deeply into society. For the first time, too, authority was exercised over peoples whose remoteness or turbulence had left them beyond the reach of European rule. Before 1914, no British official had ever been seen in Lugbaraland, a stateless tribal confederation on the Congo-Nilotic watershed where eastern Uganda now borders on western Zaire. Contact with the wider world economy was through the petty Indian traders whose enterprise had opened central East Africa to monetised exchange. By 1918, British officials had imposed hut taxes and recruited several hundred young

Lugbara men for carrier corps service.[46] In 1914, northern Mozambique was a fiefdom of the Niassa concessionary company that had been delegated administrative and police functions by the Portuguese, but never effectively occupied its territory. When German forces crossed into northern Mozambique in November 1917, the Portuguese were already preoccupied by a rebellion in Zambesia, far to the south. Many of the Makua chiefs in the North transferred their allegiance to the Germans. When the region was re-occupied by Allied forces at the end of 1918, the Portuguese seized the occasion to pacify the region for good, and eliminated the chiefs who had collaborated with the Germans.[47]

The African experience of the war has been linked to the emergence of a modern sense of national identity and pan-African solidarity, but to this non-specialist the traces seem faint and dubious. The brutal fact which circumscribed any collective consequences for Africans of their war-time experience was their political passivity in European eyes.[48] The post-war repartition of Africa amongst the victorious colonial powers (including the Union of South Africa) took place without any reference to ethnic identities and differences, let alone the political will of local populations. The 1919 Peace Conference largely confirmed the division of German East Africa along the lines of the existing military occupation by Belgian, Portuguese and British forces. The main beneficiaries of British rule in Tanganyika were Asian merchants, who purchased the smaller sisal and coffee plantations at low prices, and immigrant clerks and artisans from India. The political consciousness most raised by the war in Tanganyika was Indian, partly because by then the idea had been floated of the conquered territory becoming an Indian settler colony for migrants excluded by the racism of Kenya and the white Dominions.[49]

Is it possible, by way of conclusion, to stand back and assess the consequences of the war for the 'underdeveloped world'? Perhaps the first point to make is a negative one: the temporary uncoupling of the periphery of the capitalist world economy from its core did little to promote autonomous development. Even the favourably placed South American economies were handicapped when they could not import machinery, skilled labour, iron and steel, and coal between 1914–18.[50] Existing Indian industrial enterprises benefited hugely by de facto protection from British competition in war-time: total profits of the Bombay cotton mills quadrupled between 1913 and 1920.[51] But import substitution occurred only in textiles, iron and steel, and coal, sectors with a strong basis in 1914. Industrialisation was not extended to other sectors, and its limits were underlined by Japanese and American import penetration during the war. The second point worth making is that, in the post-war world, the European economic stake in those areas of the underdeveloped world under European political control was greater, often substantially so, than before 1914. This was most obvious in the case of France, and the reasons are not hard to seek. Only nine per cent of pre-war foreign investment had been in the French empire before 1914 and imperial commerce accounted for only twelve per cent of foreign trade. Between two-thirds and three-quarters of French foreign investments were lost with the collapse of Tsarist Russia. In the difficult economic circumstances of the inter-war years, the French economy fell back on the empire, whose protected markets became the *chasse gardée* of French exporters, and where French overseas investors found a favoured field.[52] The final point worth making is that though relations between core and periphery were not fundamentally disturbed, the ideological frameworks in which they were perceived were radically altered. No piece of war-time writing had a greater influence on the twentieth century than Lenin's *Imperialism*.[53] It defined monopoly capitalism as a universal system of colonial oppression and financial strangulation by a handful of advanced countries of the great majority of humanity. The fiction of 'underdevelopment' as an economic retardation imposed on peripheral societies derives largely from Lenin, and he gave these societies a compelling rationale for skipping the highest stage of capitalism and embarking on alternative form of modernisation. Another, liberal framework actually shared Lenin's thesis that the war revolved about the exploitation of weak territories, but proposed an internationalist regime which would obviate the need for private enterprise in the advanced economies to rely on the support of the national state when venturing into backward regions. The idea of the mandate vested in a trustee power, and the League of Nations' Permanent Mandates Commission, derived from this impulse to internationalise the colonial problem.[54] The same impulse strengthened the conviction that the trustee powers had an obligation to develop the backward regions in their care economically and socially, in the interests both of the native inhabitants and humanity at large.[55] Though no single element of these conflicting frameworks was new, the polarities of 'underdevelopment' and guided 'development' crystallised during the world crisis sparked off by the war.

Notes

1 For further, detailed exploration of these themes see Avner Offer, *The First World War: An Agrarian Interpretation*, Clarendon Press, Oxford, 1989.

2 Space precludes discussion of the South American export economies here; I must refer readers to Bill Albert, *South America and the First World War*, CUP, 1988.

3 For a particularly influential analysis of an 'open economy' in the underdeveloped world, see A.G. Hopkins, *An Economic History of West Africa*, 2nd edition, Longmans, 1988.

4 On Indian population, see Leela Visaria and Pravin Visaria, 'Population (1757–1947)', *Cambridge Economic History of India*, vol.2, edited by Dharma Kumar, CUP, 1983, Table 5.7, p.488; a good introduction to African historical demography can be found in Catherine Coquery-Vidrovitch, *Africa*:

Endurance and Change South of the Sahara, University of Calif. Press, 1988, especially pp.32–45.

5 See *Statement exhibiting the Moral and Material Progress and Condition of India during 1917–18,* PP1919, p.75, (hereafter cited as *Indian Moral and Material Progress); East India (Census 1921) Tables giving the main statistics of the census of the Indian Empire of 1921,* PP1923, vol.23.

6 *Indian Moral and Material Progress,* pp.182–183.

7 K. David Patterson, 'The demographic impact of the 1918–19 influenza pandemic in sub-Saharan Africa: a tentative estimate', in Christopher Fyfe and David McMaster, eds., *African Historical Demography,* II, Edinburgh, 1981.

8 Catherine Coquery-Vidrovitch, *Africa: Endurance and Change South of the Sahara,* p.42; Melvin E. Page, 'Malawians in the Great War and After – 1914–25', University of Michigan State, PhD, 1977, pp.217–218.

9 *Indian Moral and Material Progress,* p.74

10 Sir Alan Burns, *History of Nigeria,* 4th edition, 1948, Allen and Unwin, p.206, p.215.

11 On India's military contribution to the war, see Jeffrey Greenhut, 'The Imperial reserve: the Indian Corps on the Western front, 1914–15', *The Journal of Imperial and Commonwealth History,* 12, Oct.1983, 1, pp.54–73; S.D. Pradhan, 'Indian Army and the First World War', in Dewitt C. Ellinwood and S.D. Pradhan, editors, *India and World War 1,* Manohar, 1978.

12 *Indian Moral and Material Progress,* p.72, p.76.

13 See Krishan G. Sainie, 'The Economic Aspects of India's Participation in the First World War', in Ellinwood and Pradhan, eds., pp.141–176; B.R. Tomlinson, 'India and the British Empire, 1880–1935', *Indian Economic and Social History Review,* 12, 1975, 4, pp.337–380.

14 *Indian Moral and Material Progress,* p104.

15 In the Spring of 1918 rumours were rife of an approaching invasion by large German and Turkish armies; *Indian Moral and Material Progress,* pp.4–5.

16 *Report of the Indian Industrial Commission, 1916–18, passim.*

17 See Clive Dewey, 'The Government of India's "New Industrial Policy", 1900–1925: Formation and Failure', in K.N. Chaudhuri and Clive J. Dewey, *Economy and Society: Essays in Indian Economic and Social History,* OUP, Delhi, 1979, pp.215–257.

18 I have drawn heavily on Dewitt C. Ellinwood, 'The Indian Soldier, the Indian Army, and Change, 1914–18', in Ellinwood and Pradhan, eds., pp.177–211.

19 See Clive Dewey, 'Some Consequences of Military Expenditure in British India: The Case of the Upper Sind Sagar Doab, 1849–1947', in Clive Dewey, editor, *Arrested Development in India,* Manohar, 1988, pp.93–169.

20 Ellinwood, *loc.cit.* (n.18), p.201

21 Greenhut, *loc.cit.,* (n.11).

22 *Indian Moral and Material Progress,* pp.78–81.

23 *Government Annual Report for India, 1930–31,* cited in Joan Beauchamp, *British Imperialism in India,* Martin Lawrence, 1935, p.62. Annual per capita consumption of cotton piece goods rose from 7.79 yards in 1900 to 13.29 in 1913–14. In 1918–19, consumption was down to 7.62 yards. My account of economic and social conditions in India is based on *Indian Moral and Material Progress.*

24 See, in particular, Tomlinson, 'India and the British Empire, 1880–1935', (n.13).

25 See Judith M. Brown, 'War and the Colonial Relationship: Britain, India and the War of 1914–18', in Ellinwood and Pradhan, eds., pp.19–47.

26 *Indian Moral and Material Progress,* p.67.

27 See Malyn Newitt, *Portugal in Africa,* Hurst, 1981, p.70.

28 Round figures for the French empire's military contribution are given in Charles-Robert Ageron, *La décolonisation française,* Colin, pp.31–32. A more detailed breakdown of the military contribution of the French empire can be found in Marc Michel, *L'Appel à l'Afrique: Contributions et Réactions à l'effort de Guerre en AOF (1914–19),* Publications de la Sorbonne, 1982, p.404. See also, C.M. Andrew and A.S. Kanya-Forstner, 'France, Africa and the First World War: *Journal of African History,* 19, 1, 1978, pp.11–23.

29 See Charles-Robert Ageron, *Les Algériens musulmans et la France (1871–1919),* vol.2, PUF, 1968, pp.1140–1147.

30 See Michael Crowder, 'Blaise Diagne and the Recruitment of African Troops for the 1914–18 war', in Crowder, *Colonial West Africa: Collected Essays,* Frank Cass, 1978, pp.104–121

31 The definitive study of wartime French West Africa is Marc Michel, *L'Appel à l'Afrique: Contributions et Réactions à l'effort de Guerre en AOF (1914–19),* Publications de la Sorbonne, 1982, 'Conclusions'.

32 The following is drawn from Joe Harris Lunn, 'Kande Kamara Speaks: An Oral History of the West African Experience in France, 1914–18', in Melvin E. Page, ed., *Africa and the First World War,* 1987, Macmillan.

33 These are given in Michel, op.cit., pp.357–367.

34 The recently pacified Oulimiden Tuareg rebelled as early as the autumn of 1914, under their chief Firhoum, on rumours of French military disasters. Though the French quickly restored control, they pardoned the rebellious chief with untypical leniency and in February 1916 he again rebelled, defying the colonial authorities until defeated in May. In 1917, the Sultan of Agades raised his standard; British forces in Nigeria had to be mobilised to support the French against him.

35 Apart from Crowder, 'Blaise Diagne' (n.30) and Michel, *L'Appel à l'Afrique,* reference should also be made to Anne Summers and R.W. Johnson, 'World War I Conscription and Social Change in Guinea', *Journal of African History,* 19, 1, 1978, pp.25–38.

36 PRO CO 879/121/1089, *Report on the Combatant Manpower of the Native Races of British West Africa,* cited in David Killingray, 'Repercussions of World War I in the Gold Coast', *Journal of African History,* 19, 1, 1978, p46, n.36. See also Michael Crowder, 'The 1914–1918 European War and West Africa', in J.F.A. Ajayi and Crowder, *History of West Africa,* vol.2. Longmans, 1974.

37 See Paul E. Lovejoy and Jan S. Hogendorn, *Slow death for slavery,* Table 7.3, p.199, CUP, 1993.

38 David Killingray, 'Repercussions of World War I in the Gold Coast', (n.36).

39 These figures are given in H. Moyse-Bartlett, *The King's African Rifles,* Gale and Polden, Aldershot, 1956, which provides the clearest account of the military aspects of East African campaign in English. See also P. von

Lettow-Vorbeck, *My Reminiscences of East Africa*, London, Hurst, (n.d.) and John Iliffe, *A Modern History of Tanganyika*, CUP, 1979, Ch.8.

40 Iliffe, op.cit., pp.270–271.

41 The estimate arrived at in G.W.T. Hodges, 'African Manpower Statistics for the British Forces in East Africa, 1914–1918', *Journal of African History*, 19, 1, 1978, pp.101–115; see also, *idem.*, *The Carrier Corps: Military Labor in the East African Campaign, 1914–1918*, Greenwood Press, 1986.

42 Hodges, loc.cit., p.113.

43 John Iliffe, *The Emergence of African Capitalism*, Macmillan, 1983, p.7.

44 *The Leader of British East Africa* welcomed the Native Followers' Recruitment Ordinance as an expression of the Europeans' 'natural right to compel loyal service from the African', adding that 'our idle, irresponsible natives will at last be compelled to do their duty towards the Empire . . .'; 21 August 1915, cited in Donald C. Savage and J. Forbes Munro, 'Carrier Corps Recruitment in the British East Africa Protectorate 1914–1918', *Journal of African History*, 7,2, 1966, pp.313–432, p.320.

45 Hodges, loc.cit., (n.41), p.115, p.106, n.28.

46 John Middleton, 'Some effects of colonial rule among the Lugbara', in Victor Turner, editor, *Colonialism in Africa*: vol.3, *Profiles of Change: African Society and Colonial Rule*, CUP, 1971.

47 Newitt, op.cit., (n.27), p.63, p.84. The scandalous state of the Portuguese Niassa caused such embarrassment to the British government in 1919 that Balfour, the Foreign Secretary, suggested extending the Mandate system to the Portuguese African empire.

48 If it seems naive to imagine anything else, let us recall that Lloyd George had, in January 1918, declared the 'general principle of national self-determination' to be as 'applicable' to Germany's African colonies as to European peoples. David Lloyd George, *War Memoirs*, Odhams, (n.d.) vol.2, p.1515.

49 Iliffe, *A Modern History of Tanganyika*, pp.263–264.

50 See Albert, *South America and the First World War*.

51 Beauchamp, op.cit., (n.23) p.37.

52 For an overview, see Jean Bouvier, René Girault and Jacques Thobie, *L'Impérialisme à la française*, Editions de la découverte, 1986.

53 Originally published in 1916 as *Imperialism: the Latest Stage of Capitalism*. In subsequent editions this was amended to '*Highest Stage*'.

54 For a dated but still useful discussion of the Mandate idea see Parker T. Moon, *Imperialism and World Politics*, Macmillan, 1926, Ch.18.

55 For two influential expressions of the 'dual mandate' idea, see Frederick Lugard, *The Dual Mandate in British Tropical Africa*, London, 1922; Albert Sarraut, *La Mise en valeur des colonies françaises*, Paris, 1923.

Part IX

Resisters, Rebels and Dissenters

Chapter 44

The Flames of Louvain: The War Experience of an Academic Community

Mark Derez

In 1914 Leuven (Louvain) was a quiet provincial town with a population of slightly more than 40,000 and a rather large university of 2,500 students. The combination had resulted in a typical European university town. In the First World War Leuven became a symbol, a jab at the conscience of the world, a martyred town in an occupied country.[1]

It was late summer of 1914. At ten o'clock on the evening of Tuesday, 25 August, a German transport unit set out from University Hall. Earlier that day, this historic main building of Leuven University had been requisitioned to serve as the unit's stables. The university's doorkeeper then did a final check of the entrance of the University Library, housed in an adjacent wing fronting the Old Market. Here all was quiet.

At that very moment, however, about a kilometre away, most of the houses facing the railway station were already a mass of flames. Within an hour, the Old Market too was ablaze, and about half an hour before midnight, eye witnesses saw German soldiers starting fires in the cellar of the University Library. Thus began the three-day long ravaging of Leuven, during which an 'incendiary column' of German soldiers criss-crossed the city, forcibly entered houses and public buildings and, using phosphorus, set fire to them one by one.[2]

When the smoke cleared there were some 1,100 burnt out buildings in the city, and a thousand more in neighbouring communities. Even more houses were plundered. Only the borough of Heverlee at the outskirts was somewhat spared, since it contained much property owned by the Duke of Arenberg, a German subject. In Leuven itself, one ninth of all buildings were burnt, but the ravaged districts actually covered a far greater portion of the city's total area. The devastation extended beyond the historic centre to the more recently laid-out avenues and streets inhabited by professors, members of the professions, and the more affluent bourgeoisie.

The destruction of elegant private dwellings was in itself an appalling aspect of what was soon to be known as 'The Sack of Louvain', yet the deepest impressions were those produced by the ruined historic structures and university buildings. The fourteenth-century Cloth Hall which housed the University Hall, the eighteenth-century University Library, Driutius College (an immensely imposing Louis XVI-style building), the law court complex connecting the St. Ives's College with the old seat of the Arts Faculty (the *Vicus Artium*), all were gutted. The roof of the fifteenth century St. Peter's Church had collapsed. At least Dirk Bouts's famous painted triptych, 'The Last Supper' had been spared, as was the gothic Town Hall where the German army's Local Commander was installed.

It is very difficult now to picture the extent of the damage; there are still traces to be seen, but reconstruction has caused the worst scars to disappear. The damage was not limited to buildings, however. With the loss of the city's commercial centre, food supplies were limited and public life was paralysed. The inhabitants were victims of such terrorisation that contemporaries at first believed the tales emerging from Leuven were simply blood-curdling propaganda. There was intimidation by mock-executions, and there was even a sham bombing with forcible evacuation of all 42,000 inhabitants on 27 August, thereby leaving the city wide open to plundering. Even after an interim local government had been formed and an end to the plundering had been promised, houses were still put to the torch as late as 2 September. 650 civilians were transported to Germany like cattle and imprisoned there for months. Others were forced to walk before the German troops as hostages or were tied together and were marched about the countryside for days on end. 209 civilians were killed: allegedly some were strangled or burnt; most were shot, either singly as they crawled out of their cellars, like the Luxembourg professor Vincent Lenertz crying for mercy in German, or in groups, such as the fifty whose bodies were discovered in 1915 near the railway station.

What had unleashed this German fury, this *'Furor teutonicus'*? The Germans themselves glossed it over as *'Strafgericht über Löwen'* (the punishment of Leuven). But what had so enraged the Germans on that evening of 25 August? Belgian troops had made a sortie from the Antwerp Fortress and had come to within 10 km. of Leuven. The first shots were fired about 8 p.m. It appears that in the dusk, German soldiers mistook a retreating German spearhead for a Belgian unit, and fired in panic on their own men. After the officers had re-established order, a scapegoat was speedily found. The shots were said to have been fired by civilian snipers from Leuven, the so-called *franc-tireurs* who, expecting Leuven to be soon liberated, started shooting at the occupying troops. This story was later proved to be a myth. From the first day of the occupation, 19 August, there had been intimidations, hostages were taken, and there were threats of executions and of destruction by fire. Further, there were German artillery regiments stationed on the surrounding hills with their weapons trained on the city.

It is hardly likely that an intimidated populace which had had most of its able-bodied men mobilised would take action against enemy troops, especially when, as on that infamous 25 August, they were 10,000 strong. It is just as unlikely that the world's mightiest military power would need four days to quell an uprising in a small provincial city. The Germans, however, in a White Book issued by their Ministry of Foreign Affairs in May 1915, maintained that fire had been opened by snipers from Leuven: *'Man hat geschossen'*. There is no doubt that this is what the German soldiers did believe. What was more to the point was the existence of a collective 'sniper psychosis' among the Germans. It was deeply rooted in the prevailing militaristic doctrine, in publications of a war-mongering nature and in a journalistic campaign initiated at the beginning of the war.[3]

To understand how the notion of snipers or *franc-tireurs* was given such credibility, one must be aware of certain circumstances. First of all, when the Germans invaded Belgium, they expected no armed opposition, and at the most a verbal protest. Belgium's rejection of the German ultimatum had not been made known in Germany. Further, not only were the invaders surprised to meet with opposition, but they were irritated that the Belgian army avoided encounters out in the open. The Belgians preferred to operate with small groups such as units of cyclists who caught German scouts unawares, thereby hampering communications. Such guerrilla tactics could only strengthen the belief in the existence of Belgian irregulars, thereby turning suspicion on the local populace. The German occupiers were infected, at all ranks and levels, with the *franc-tireur* psychosis. As a consequence, Belgian military actions were laid at the door of the civilian populace, which were seen as violating the Hague Convention. German terrorisation of civilian could then be explained as reprisals.

The term *franc-tireur* originated in the War of 1870–71 between France and Prussia. It was applied to French civilians who took up arms after the defeat at Sedan. The Prussian Junkers saw this type of informal military action as a negation of the noble art of conducting well-regulated warfare. The concept of *franc-tireur* was kept very much alive in the Prussian army. It also enlivened pre-war literature. One novel, published in 130,000 copies in 1907, even prefigured a war with an attack on Belgium, where fanatical priests roused the Belgian population, and where there was a revolt of Socialistic terrorists. These became clichés frequently appearing in the German press in August 1914. Other standard ingredients were women who poured boiling oil from windows and who castrated wounded German soldiers. The 'Popish' University of Leuven was also the victim of this Protestant-inspired Prussian anti-clericalism. It was even reported that there was a student revolt in Leuven, whereas most of the students had left after the last examinations in July, and the presence of Russian students was noted, though not one Russian had matriculated in the previous academic year. We might also mention that in Poland, in that very same August 1914, Germans were fired upon by Jews, or so they claimed. As a result, the city of Kalisch had to endure the same fate as Leuven.

In the 'legend of the *franc-tireurs*', identical elements kept on re-surfacing. Furthermore, the Germans maintained that they encountered snipers not only in Belgium, but also in Russia and in Serbia. The suspicion arises that these rumours were the result of systematic orchestration, particularly since the press was subject to very strict censorship. What is certain is that many letters purporting to come from German soldiers and recounting their experiences with snipers were actually written at Military Headquarters in Coblenz. That this manipulation of German public opinion even continued after hostilities were ended, can be seen in the German White Book (where, however, not one sniper is cited by name), and in the continuing, vivid presence of these legendary snipers in the minds of the veterans. The *franc-tireurs*, therefore, constitute the subjective element behind the terrorisation mechanism.

The objective element is to be found in German military logic, in the '*Kriegsnotwendigkeit*' which was an inherent aspect of the '*Blitzkrieg*' the Germans intended to carry out. The aim was to make a rapid advance, straight across Belgium, to surround the French army as quickly as possible, and to transfer the troops which would then be available to the Eastern Front to fight the Russians. German strategists following upon von Clausewitz's dicta were very clear as to how this advance should be hastened. The way to subdue an occupied people and to control a whole country with a small occupying force was simply this: the application of stark terror. As Chancellor von Bethman Hollweg told the Reichstag on 4 August 1914, *Not kennt kein Gebot*. Thus from the start of the invasion on 4 August to the foundering of the Western Offensive, 18,000 houses were destroyed in four Belgian provinces and 5,000 civilians were killed. This was the cost of deterrence by terror.

In 1958, the German historian Peter Schöller and a mixed commission of Belgian and German historians arrived at the conclusion that the German White Book had no claim to credibility, since its approach to sources did not meet the standards of historical enquiry. Schöller did not believe, however, that the burning of Leuven was an act of conscious German provocation.[4] Not until twenty years later did a German scholar, Lothar Wieland, state albeit with some trepidation, that Leuven was intentionally destroyed ('*Leuven sei vorsàtzlich zerstört worden*'). Yet, Barbara Tuchman, the American historian, was already convinced in 1962 that Leuven was *not* ravaged as a reprisal for *franc-tireur* attacks, but purely as an act of intimidation and a warning. Her conviction was reinforced by the unequivocal statement which a German officer had made to the First Secretary of the American Embassy, Hugh Gibson. Leuven, he indicated, was to be made an example, a terrifying warning for generations to come, so that all would learn *'Deutschland zu respectieren'*. Although the threat of not leaving one stone upon another was proceeded with, the example of Leuven backfired.[5]

Instead of instilling respect, the Germans were the target of universal indignation. From Copenhagen to Rome, protests rained down upon the German embassies. The flames of Leuven had by no means demoralised the Allies, but gave them fresh determination. Politicians were more resolved than ever to destroy the German war machine. After Leuven, the war once more took on a moral dimension. It became a just war. Sir Arthur Conan Doyle took up his pen to denounce German military methods. He was later joined by Arnold Toynbee, who published *The German Terror in Belgium* in 1917. In French, works such as *Le Supplice de Louvain* and *Louvain – Ville martyre* appeared in 1915 and 1916 respectively. As a French writer, Auguste Mélot put it, *Le martyre de Louvain, c'est comme la synthèse des attentats que les Allemands ont commis en Belgique.*

The example of Leuven was not lost on the neutral countries. When the Belgian government-in-exile sent a distinguished delegation to Washington, the German Kaiser tried to forestall any effect it might have. He sent a telegram lamenting Leuven's fate, and giving excuses based on the atrocities committed by women and the Catholic clergy. The Belgian delegation was received in the White House on 16 September, and though President Wilson may still have sat on the fence, American public opinion clearly recognised a 'good' and a 'bad' cause. The phrase 'Poor little Belgium' acquired a moral force which was fanned by 'the Flames of Louvain'.

Leuven's fate was by no means unique. In other Belgian towns too, hundreds of civilians were shot in late August of 1914. Leuven, however, was larger, and it was a city which enjoyed high prestige abroad. It was above all a university town with a long history, 'the Oxford of Belgium', as *The Times* styled it on 29 August. It was a major European cultural centre, and 'the Huns' had attacked it.

Rudyard Kipling wrote a polemical poem on these Huns. The image of the Huns also occurred to Romain Rolland who was in neutral Switzerland, and who wrote an open letter on 29 August to Gerhard Hauptmann. Hauptmann was Germany's leading literary figure, and he supported the war-making. Rolland urged his German colleague to protest against German despoiling of cultural values, and to choose to be among the spiritual heirs of Goethe, not Attila the Hun. Hauptmann replied that Germans would rather be seen as sons of Attila, and this uncompromising answer produced a decoration for him on the Kaiser's birthday.

Rolland, who was awarded the Nobel Prize for Literature in 1915, had been France's most outspokenly pro-German intellectual. Hauptmann, before the war, was known to be critical of Prussian nationalism. After '*le sac de Louvain*', intellectuals could no longer stay out of the fight. They *had* to take sides. As Wolfgang Schievelbusch phrased it, 'Löwen wurde zum Sarajewo der europäischen Intelligenz'.[6] Indeed, the intellectuals now began to enter the fray. Manifestos rained down. Under the title *Louvain*, English universities and institutes of higher learning voiced their disgust. On 11 October German intellectuals published their reply in all the fatherland's newspapers. Their infamous manifesto, '*Anruf an die Kulturwelt*', was signed by 93 leading figures in the arts and sciences, including Karl Lamprecht, Max Planck, Wilhem Röntgen and Wilhelm Wundt. They endorsed the *franc-tireur* hypothesis and the right to reprisal, and claimed that if it had not been for German soldiers, German culture would long have been swept away.

The University Library of Leuven, with its 230,000 books, its 800 incunabulae and its 950 manuscripts which were now nothing but ashes, became the symbol of the threat to European civilisation. The double photo, before and after, of the library's showpiece – its handsome main reading room, was a propagandist's dream. It raised the age-old spectre of library-burning. The analogy with the destruction of the Alexandria library by the 'Saracens' was obvious. A young Jesuit in Leuven, Robert Dupierreux, is said to have been shot by a firing-squad on the 27 August because he had written this comparison in his notebook.[7]

After the Germans shelled Rheims cathedral on 20 September, Leuven and Rheims together formed a line of demarcation between civilisation and German 'Kultur'. Western democracy was seen as 'moral', and Prussian militarism, which was a part of the German way of life, was 'amoral'. *Kultur* became a sarcastic slogan in Allied propaganda. According to the Rector in a quite academic analysis, it was all the fault of the eighteenth century German philosopher Immanuel Kant who with his system of autonomous morality had made the Germans proud and arrogant. They lacked '*l'objectivité scholastique de la philosophie chrétienne*' a kind of objectivity which was obviously not applied to his fellow catholics from over the Rhine who the rector called, less academically, '*les catholiques bâtards de la Rhénanie*'.

The burning of Leuven and the shooting of its citizens provided the Allies with a moral argument. Neutral nations began to revise their attitudes. The university's charred library had driven a symbolic wedge between the spheres of civilisation and of *Kultur*.

Even before the end of the war, the outrage against the attack on the library and its irreplaceable treasures led to world-wide gestures of solidarity. Committees to collect money and books were formed in twenty-five countries. The impetus for the rebuilding of the library came from the

Institut de France in Paris. America stole the show by offering to build an entirely new library. The site chosen was the highest, most imposing in central Leuven. The building's architect, the American Whitney Warren, served as liaison to combine French cultural prestige and American fund-raising. He had been trained at the *Ecole des Beaux-Arts* in Paris, and was himself a member of the *Institut de France*. Warren had made his name by building railway stations and luxury hotels in New York. He had also written many pamphlets urging America to enter the war. For the new library, he sought his inspiration in the native tradition, the brick and grey stone Northern Renaissance style. In the outside walls of the building, the names of generous donors are immortalised on hundreds of commemorative stones: almost all of them are American educational institutions.

From the beginning, the library was conceived as an elaborate monument with an extensive iconographical programme. The helmeted virgin on the top gable and the whole menagerie of heraldic animals associated with the Allies make it into a war memorial, a souvenir of the German terror and the Allied co-operation in reconstruction. Begun in 1921, the edifice was completed in 1928, and at the time of its inauguration only one thing was still lacking: a much disputed Latin inscription which had divided the university, caused a passionate controversy to rage in Belgian newspapers for years and finally would not be added to the building's exterior. It read, *'Furore teutonico diruta, dono americano restituta'*, freely translated: *'Demolished by German fury and reconstructed by American gifts.'*[8]

To understand the bitterness of this dispute, it will be helpful to return to the war-experience of the academic community.[9] At the end of August 1914, the university was like an orphan sitting among the charred ruins. It was a small community in disarray, badly shaken by the events. Most of the professors had fled, and only the prefects of the residential colleges remained at their posts.

The Rector and Vice-Rector were treated like hostages and were mishandled by the occupiers. After he was freed on 27 August, the Rector's first thought was to escape to England or the Netherlands, but he resisted the urge. In point of fact, during the first weeks he resided in Brussels where he could make contact with members of the university's General Council. These were all wealthy and influential figures within the Catholic sector of the Belgian Establishment. He even managed to pry an interest-free loan from the principal bank of Belgium, the *Société Générale*. By this means, and throughout the war, he was able to pay the salaries of the professors still in Leuven.

Every week the Rector travelled to Leuven and to Mechelen. The twenty-mile journey to Leuven was sometimes made on foot, in order to keep an eye on things. He went to Mechelen, the Archbishop's seat, to confer with Cardinal Mercier. The Cardinal was not only a former professor at the university's Higher Institute of Philosophy, but as Archbishop of Mechelen he was *ex officio* the High Chancellor of the university. As a result of the pastoral letter he issued at Christmas of 1914, Cardinal Mercier became an international symbol of the Belgian Church's opposition to the German occupation.

In mid-September it was announced, via the American Embassy in Brussels, that Oxford would offer hospitality to professors from Leuven and their families. At about the same time, Cambridge University proposed that the University of Leuven should move temporarily to Cambridge. That same month a similar invitation had come from Paris, where the *Institut Catholique* offered its facilities to Leuven professors and their Belgian students. Also, Dutch Catholics invited the Leuven Faculties of Theology, Law and Philosophy to move north of the border. These were all welcome signs of sympathy, but in fact there was no way in which the university could be moved abroad. The occupation authorities would never permit the students to leave the country, and it would be quite as difficult to gather all the scattered professors together.

Relocation in England could never be. It would infuriate the Germans, who would then confiscate every university building that had escaped destruction. The Rector wished to avoid this at any cost. Moreover, the four Belgian universities had mutually agreed that there would be no lectures given for the duration of the war. This was both passive resistance and a way to prevent the enemy's censorship from infringing on academic liberty. In addition, the academic authorities did not wish to disadvantage the students who were at the front, and to sharpen the opposition between combatants and non-combatants. A lot of them had gone as volunteers. Thus, the university remained closed.

The German occupiers tried separately to have this decision reversed; to no avail. They used both threats and blandishments in the hope of getting the Rector, Monsignor Ladeuze, to vacillate. They also played on the impatience of certain families to see their children's education completed. As the war dragged on, the pressure increased. The academic leaders could not foresee, of course, that the war would last for four long years. Each year, in his New Year's greetings, the Rector expressed the hope that the university would reopen that year.

In July 1916 certain Germans who called themselves 'friends', let it be known that the Rector was to be 'punished' like the two professors from Ghent, Frédéricq and Pirenne, who had been deported. It was also said that the German government, which had a strong Catholic *Zentrum* element, was prepared to give preferment to Leuven at the expense of the Universities of Liège and of Brussels, all in the cause of 'protecting Christian values'. In 1918 industrialists from the Walloon region of Hainault asked that courses be partially resumed because of the shortage of qualified engineers. None of this had any effect. Monsignor Ladeuze held his ground to the end. The only activities, in Leuven as in other universities, were limited to entrance-exams for commercial and engineering studies, certain non-credit courses in general culture, and a few seminars for post-graduates.

As for the city of Leuven, September saw a certain calm restored, replacing the fury that had been unleashed in August. The Mayor and the entire City Council had fled, as had the city fathers before them in 1541. At that time, Emperor Charles the Fifth had commented, 'My good burghers of Leuven are no soldiers'. Now, a committee composed of leading citizens was formed to fill the void and to see to the burial of the victims, the clearing of the streets, food supplies and health care. Of these fifteen prominent citizens, six were professors and the others were all alumni. The chairman, acting as mayor, was Nerincx, a professor of law. Thus the university had, in a sense, taken upon itself the governing of the city. It was the final triumph of the university in the eternal struggle of town and gown.

The 165 professors and lecturers were scattered. Ten of them had gone to the front as volunteers, mainly as chaplains or army doctors. A hundred or so professors eventually returned to the city, where they found not only their wine-cellars plundered, but their collections of books and professional equipment destroyed by fire. The city's chief printing presses had also been put to the torch. As a consequence huge stocks of academic publications were lost, as were the manuscripts of books then in press. Some professors never recovered from this blow; they were too old to start on a new academic project or to begin assembling fresh material for their studies. They abandoned academic inquiry. Others used their enforced leisure to take up or complete time-consuming projects. One such was the noted Professor of English literature De Vocht, who used the war years to make an inventory of the university's archives from pre-French Revolution times. His form of passive resistance was to copy excerpts into notebooks, using, black, yellow and red inks – the Belgian national colours. Others, looking ahead to the post-war years, devised major curriculum reforms.

A good many professors left their ivory towers for the ruins and rubble. They rolled up their sleeves and helped to restore order and to arrange the provisioning of food and health services. Professor Nerincx who was first acting mayor and later auxiliary mayor, was the go-between between the city government and the German military authorities. This suited the academic administrators nicely, since Nerincx was naturally in contact with them almost daily. In this way the university kept an eye on city affairs all through the war, something which was not possible in normal times when the anti-clerical Liberal Party held the municipal reins.

At the very outbreak of the war, the Higher Institute of Philosophy, the world famous School of St. Tomas, transformed its lecture halls and laboratories into the so-called 'Saint Thomas Field Hospital'. There, severely wounded French and Belgian soldiers were cared for, and later on, civilian war victims were nursed there. One professor, Lemaire, took up the fight against tuberculosis, which was on the increase. Two residential colleges fed weakened children in their refectories. These same colleges also housed citizens whose houses had been burnt down. Everywhere, professors stepped into the breach. A professor of agriculture organised the food supplies. The food he and his committee distributed came from the American Commission for Relief in Belgium. This commission was housed in the American College, where clergy from the United States were trained. The College continued to fly the Stars and Stripes right until America entered the war.

Thirty-five professors were scattered abroad. One single professor went to Germany, but he had come from there in the first place. In Cambridge, nine 'Louvainists' set up the *Université Belge de Cambridge*. Cambridge was delighted that Leuven, like the ancient English universities, had kept its colleges: *'velut Angliae Universitates antiquissimae non modo Universitatem sed Collegia habere gloriamini'*. At that time the correspondence between Leuven and Cambridge was in Latin. The philosopher Leon Noël, who was in Oxford on his own, appointed himself Secretary of the *Comité universitaire anglo-belge d'Oxford*. The mathematician, de la Vallée Poussin, and the specialist in medieval philosophy, De Wulf, taught at Harvard.

There were others who travelled round the world, giving lectures on the University of Leuven and its tragic fate. At that time, they were not permitted to take collections for the university, for the Rector wanted to avoid making a greedy impression. Yet they scouted the terrain, searched out willing donors, and created a climate which would be favourable to a huge post-war campaign of solidarity.

And some there were who found contact with the outside world so stimulating that they never returned to the bosom of the Alma Mater. One such was the promising librarian, Father Paul Delannoy. He was giving lectures at the *Collège de France* on the history of the university when he suddenly disappeared from the academic scene and the annals of the university. He had met a woman in Paris, and discarded his clerical garb!

The war brought people closer together, yet under the patriotic surface, old feuds continued to smoulder. The university, with its new-found power in city affairs, hoped that it would at last acquire full ownership of University Hall. The Rector felt that this was the least the city could do to thank the university for its many services performed in the first six months of the war. This, evidently, was asking just too much. University Hall has remained city property to this day.

Certain conflicts of interest were muffled by the war, yet they continued to dictate university policy. Take, for example, the old Belgian antagonism between Catholics and free-thinkers, between clericalists and anticlericalists. The Universities of Leuven and of Brussels represented the two camps. They were of course united now by an *entente cordiale*, and were together firmly resolved not to resume academic activities. Yet this firmness, as far as Catholic Leuven was concerned, was also rooted in the fear that a reopening would benefit Brussels. Leuven had a scarcity of student lodgings and poor transportation to and from the countryside, and therefore it would attract fewer students.

Then too, there were the lectures given at the Socialists' House of the People in a framework somewhat like that of university extension. There were professors, and even priests, who willingly participated, and this displeased the Rector. It was certainly no task of Catholic professors to deliver people into the hands of the Socialists, even in wartime.

The Rector was even more shocked by one professor abroad, and a priest at that, who published one tirade after another against the Belgian state. Though Belgian nationalism had been strengthened by the war, the Germans nevertheless cleverly played upon Flemish frustrations in a state that was dominated by French-speakers. And behind the front lines, too, there was increasing frustration among Flemish soldiers who were under the command of French-speaking officers. The Rector could only note that these Flemish professors had little inclination to disavow their enraged anti-Belgian colleague. The professor in question lost his chair after the war, but in the meantime the auditoria were bursting with students as radical as he, demanding Home Rule and an exclusively Flemish university.

Among the professors themselves, some who felt that they were cut off at home, resented their colleagues who were able to shine in America or Paris, and who were none too eager to return. Such misunderstandings were not helped by poor communications, which were only possible via the Apostolic Nuncio's diplomatic pouch, or via neutral Dutchmen.

Not even the relations between Leuven and Rome were free from misunderstanding and suspicion. In 1915, the Rector could not understand why Rome was dragging its feet and did not pronounce an official condemnation of the university's tragic lot. The truth was that the new pope, Benedict the Fifteenth, favoured neutralism and pacifism. He was not enthused by Cardinal Mercier's independent methods, for the Cardinal not only took 'poor little Belgium' under his wing, but also set himself up as the Allies' spiritual leader. Later, in 1917, the Rector was designated Apostolic Protonotary, and there was no mistaking the gesture – it was a clear positive signal from the Holy See to Leuven. These, then, were some of the old tensions and new irritations which confronted the academic community at this time of stress.

On the other hand, the war brought to the university opportunities for new friendships and for new perceptions of its identity. Hitherto, the professors in the humanities had been confined within a Latin-based cultural sphere dominated by France, and the scientists had been oriented toward Central Europe. Now, those who had emigrated, got to know the Anglo-Saxon world in its many facets. The post-war result of this was to be a radical turn to the West. After the war, physicians no longer went to Berlin, Vienna or Leipzig to specialise. They went to the United States with a fellowship from the Belgian American Educational Foundation, dispensed by the Commission for Relief in Belgium

It was a paradox that the university emerged from the blackened rubble with increased international standing. In the flattering light of American appreciation of Europe's history, the university suddenly discovered its ancient roots. Whereas in 1909 it had celebrated the mere 75th anniversary of its post-Napoleonic re-founding, in 1927 – less than twenty years later – the University of Leuven duly commemorated its five hundredth anniversary!

Moreover, this flirtation with America forced the university to be more tolerant of dissenters. Back in Leuven, the Rector was still fulminating against Prussian Protestantism, but in America the New York Herald was painting another picture for its readers: '. . . This name is the Catholic University of Louvain, but it admits all creeds, and every variety of religious opinion is tolerated among the students'. Although, in fact, the university's Code of Order did contain thorough directives regarding the students' religious obligations, this was demurely passed over. The outside world was presented with a broader definition of the university's religious alignment than that which applied at home.

In the final analysis, the university entered the post-war period stronger than before, international in fame and orientation, more broad-minded and even much older – or at least more aware of its own ancient traditions. In 1914, before the occupation, the university saw itself as a militant Catholic institution in a Belgian context. After the war, the University of Leuven stood forth as an age-old seat of learning, and as an intellectual beacon of Western civilisation, radiating an 'open-minded Christianity' to Europe and beyond.

Notes

1 The research is mainly based on archival sources in the University Archives of the University of Leuven and on the *Analectes pour servir à l'histoire de l'Université Catholique* in the *Annuaire de l'Université Catholique de Louvain*, 1915 and 1920–1926.

2 Lode Wils, *Augustus 1914 – Leuven brandt*, in: *Onze Alma Mater*, 1990, nr.2, p. 147–155.

3 Lothar Wieland, *Belgien 1914. Die Frage des belgischen 'Franktireurkrieges' und die deutsche Öffentlichè Meinung von 1914 bis 1936*, New York 1984; Carlo Lejeune, *Die deutsch-belgischen Kulturbeziehungen 1925–1980*, Köln-Weimar-Wien 1992.

4 Peter Schöller, *Le cas de Louvain et le Livre Blanc allemand*, Louvain-Paris 1958.

5   Barbara Tuchman, *The Guns of August,* New York 1962.
6   Wolfgang Schivelbusch, *Die Bibliothek von Löwen. Eine Episode aus der Zeit der Weltkriege,* München-Wien 1988.
7   Arnold J. Toynbee, *The German Terror in Belgium,* London-New York-Toronto 1917, p. 137–138.
8   Pierre de Soete, *The Louvain Library controversy. The Misadventures of an American Artist or "Furore Teutonico Diruta: Dono Americano Restituta",* Concord, 1929.
9   To understand the intensity of the dispute, it would also be useful to return to the non-existent but ever-present *franc-tireurs*. Indeed, the phantom of the *franc-tireurs* continued to dominate the Weimar Republic's self justification throughout the 1920s. The stakes were high: they were no less than the Treaty of Versailles itself – whether it should be enforced or revised. It should be noted here that with respect to one part of the Treaty of Versailles, Article 247, Germany was carrying out the stipulated donation of books and manuscripts for the new library much more fully than the University had anticipated. The sections of the treaty having to do with atrocities committed by the Germans were more problematic. They could not be separated from the question of guilt. In the first instance, Germany was considered guilty of starting the war, of invading neutral Belgium. Even more, however, the German Empire was held to be guilty of barbaric practices in wartime, of war crimes in short. The poison-gas attacks and the submarine warfare were bad enough, but the reprisals against Belgian civilians were deemed even worse. In the 1920's, Belgium demanded not only reparation payments, but also moral redress.

The Weimar Republic, however, once again brought out the arguments used during the war, especially the *franc-tireurs*. A climax was reached in 1928 when two eminent opponents, Professor Christian Meurer – a German, and Professor Ferdinand Mayence of Leuven, crossed swords in the American journal *Current History*. The German Ministry of Foreign Affairs was also involved, and defended the *franc-tireur* hypothesis in every possible way. 1928 was also the year of the library's completion. The question to be decided at this point was whether or not an inscription that had been proposed in 1921 should be added.

629

Chapter 45

Life in an Occupied Zone: Lille, Roubaix, Tourcoing

Annette Becker

The territories of Northern France and Belgium which suffered particularly from the wars of the twentieth century – after having done so in those of the eighteenth and nineteenth centuries, and even earlier – can serve as involuntary laboratories for a study of the European peoples at war with one another. In the North of France, French people, Germans, Belgians, English, and even Poles and Czechs, some of whom were subjects of Austria, others of Prussia, were placed from August 1914 onwards in terrible conditions in which it became impossible, earlier than anywhere else, to tell the difference between civilians and soldiers. Once the front had stabilised, at the end of 1914, most of Belgium and of 10 French *Départements* remained under German military occupation until the end of the war. The population of these areas was, in fact, on their own 'front line', and discovered the miseries of total war in their region. They drew no advantage from the French victory at the Battle of the Marne, and remained on the other side of the front line, occupied by the German army, until October 1918. In addition to the 'ordinary' sufferings undergone by the families of all those involved in the war throughout Europe – the fear of being wounded or killed – they also had to undergo the impossibility of any news reaching them across a front which had become an impassable frontier, as well as the rigours of being occupied. It was not possible for them to receive either newspapers or letters from 'non-occupied' France. As an occupied population, they were also in the front line in a war in which no suffering was spared them 'in the course of the captivity of occupation'.[1]

The large towns of Lille, Roubaix and Tourcoing were at the centre of the occupation system. The Germans could billet a large number of soldiers, requisition men and material and impose enormous compulsory payments. Such are the laws of war, in which might is right, from which stem all forms of suffering and acts of injustice.[2]

It is difficult today to define what is meant by 'atrocity' during and after the Great War.[3] It is the word most frequently used by the inhabitants of the occupied regions in order to talk about what they have been through. In theory, an atrocity is an act which violates the Hague convention, the 'laws of war' ratified by a large number of countries in 1907. Compulsory labour, in particular for the enemy and against the war effort of one's own country, was contrary to these conventions. It is obvious that for these people in Belgium and the North of France, it was the very fact of being occupied which was an atrocity. Thus 'German atrocities' does not mean the same thing as 'atrocities committed by the Germans'.[4]

As French people cut off from France itself, and even more from France at war, the inhabitants of these northern territories made the daily discovery of the peculiar wretchedness of their fate. The harshness inseparable from war itself was mingled with physical and moral brutality. In the meaning given to the word by the inhabitants of this part of France, the word 'atrocities' meant all the suffering, unhappiness and death stemming from the fact that they were occupied. In order to describe them, I shall rely on an exceptional piece of evidence, the diary kept between 1914 and 1918 by David Hirsch at Roubaix.[5] David Hirsch was a shop-keeper who kept daily accounts. On August 1, 1914, he made the first mention of anything happening outside his immediate preoccupations, that is to say the war, when he wrote down in the margin of his accounts 'Midnight: mobilisation'. These short notes, with few details, soon occupied the whole margin, and eventually, as all commercial activity slowed down and came to a complete halt as a result of the war, the whole page. The physical appearance of the diary itself bears witness to the way the war took over everything. As the months and years go by, nothing could stand in its way.

Since it was impossible to communicate with 'unoccupied France', all news of military operations came through the *Gazette de Cologne*, the *Gazette des Ardennes,* and from the *Bulletin de Lille,* all newspapers published by the German occupying authorities. And, above all, there was 'what people say' and 'what people think', echoes of different rumours, and especially of troop movements. People heard the news in the version put out by the Germans, and especially the military communiqués which were then turned round and interpreted, deprived of the propaganda element given to them by the Germans, and presented in such a way as to make the position of the allies, always referred to as 'us', more comprehensible. News of disasters came first of all in the form of sound, especially that of the guns, which can be heard constantly, since the front line was so close. Bombs, shells and aeroplanes were constantly falling, killing civilians in the middle of the town. The bells rang out triumphantly to announce every German victory, leaving an impression, as Hirsch recorded: 'which nobody who has not had the experience can possibly appreciate. Since you know nothing of what is really happening, you always expect the worst'. (December 6, 1916). For a long time, at least until the summer of 1916, Hirsch continued to hope that the war would be a short one. Then the failure of the Somme offensive affected his morale, and he wrote: 'I think we shall have to accept that the war is going to last much longer than I had expected, perhaps for another year. But', he noted in October 1916, 'we shall doubtless soon see the end of the occupation'. However, on 21 May, 1917, he observed: 'I am beginning to fear that the war will not be over for another year, and that we shall still be occupied in winter'. On page after page he came back to the fact that nobody knew anything about what had happened to their loved ones who went off to the war. 'Still no news of our people. The situation is becoming almost impossible to bear. There could have been people killed, or wounded, or who have lost a limb, without our knowing anything of them (October 24, 1916).'

He tried to believe that, cut off from France though he was in Roubaix, he was still taking part in the war effort: 'We close on Sunday afternoon. It's mainly the Germans who do their shopping on Sundays. This enables us to make a slight contribution to the blockade'. (25 January, 1917). At the end of 1917, Hirsch wondered for the first time if the only solution would be to make peace:

> Is it in France's interest, even to obtain a brilliant victory, to lose so much blood? Would it not be more in her interest to make peace without getting back Alsace-Lorraine, with making the Germans pay an indemnity? In peace time, our neighbours increase their population much more rapidly than we do. What will happen when we have even fewer people producing children? (29 December, 1917).

The conditions under German occupation must indeed have been terrible for this French patriot originally from Alsace, whose family had chosen to come and live in France after 1871, to have allowed himself to make such a comment. The whole of his diary is a fairly good reflection, on which most modern historians would now agree, of how the morale of the French population of the French Home Front in general developed during the war:[6] there was the beginning of a weakening of morale at the end of 1916, which grew worse until the summer of 1917, before a return of a spirit of resolution and hope of victory:

> In spite of the 42 months of occupation, it is extraordinary to see what confidence and optimism can still be found. While you do find people who are becoming discouraged, there are relatively few of them. People quite calmly envisage the war going on for another year, for another 18 months (April 1918).

THE OCCUPATION: PRIVATIONS AND REQUISITIONS

The harshness of the occupation, of this war without conventional fighting, but which was nevertheless full of suffering and death, provided the main theme for Hirsch's entries. The days went by to the rhythm of the sound of the guns, the increase in the price of bread and the decline in its quality. People grew weaker and saw their neighbours die:

> Everybody is getting thinner . . . there are lots of deaths. Normally, Roubaix could get along with two grave diggers. Now, there are six . . . Food is more and more expensive. My trousers have had to be taken in from 54 to 46 centimetres. People grow weaker for lack of food. Since we no longer have sugar, milk, meat, pasta, eggs or wine, it's not surprising (11, 29 March; 7 June, 1916; 22 November, 1917).

Hirsch described the suffering imposed on the population of Lille, Roubaix and Tourcoing, men, women and children, throughout the war. Houses were gradually emptied as clothes, leather, copper, wood and wool for mattresses were requisitioned. The North was being emptied of everything and was suffering acutely from hunger and cold. All that David Hirsch could do as the last mattresses were taken from his house was to make a joke: 'It's no longer accurate to say that when you ruin somebody that you have reduced them to sleeping on straw' (30 March, 1918). He consoled himself, if that were the right word, in seeing in all these requisitions the proof of the shortages which must exist in Germany itself: 'There must be serious food shortages in Germany. German soldiers steal food to send it to their relatives' (29 May 1916). Civilian prisoners who had been re-patriated talked to him about demonstrations 'for peace and bread' in Germany (17 May 1917). Industrial requisitions did not deprive him of his normal sense of humour:

> It gives you an odd feeling to see a great nation like Germany take away all the pipes from a little factory like the one belonging to the Desbonnets. They must indeed be short of things in Germany, since they've taken away all the latches, the name plates for houses, the hangers for wardrobes, the coat stands, the door knockers, the coffee mills, etc. (9 February, 1916; 3 July, 1917).

In winter, the schools closed for lack of fuel. In the spring of 1918, the inhabitants started to cultivate small allotments which had to be guarded night and day against theft, and they did so with the permission of the German authorities: 'This morning, Marx[7] had a meeting at six o'clock with 18 tenants to decide everybody's share. Sign of the times: communism and war' (18 March, 1918).

In addition to the continuous worsening of their living conditions, the population had to endure collective atrocities stemming, for the most part, from the difficulty which the Germans had in obtaining the goods they tried to requisition. The taking of hostages began in Autumn 1914, especially of the leading citizens of the towns, the mayors, the town councillors, the industrialists and, at Lille, even the Bishop, Monseigneur Charost. David Hirsch, himself President of the Jewish community in Lille, praised the Bishop for his 'vehement and patriotic refusal to deconsecrate the bells so that the Germans can take them for their metal without committing sacrilege' (18 August, 1917). Hirsch was delighted to see the general reluctance on the part of industrialists and workers alike to co-operate with the Germans on an industrial and economic level, or even to work alongside them. After the war, the inscription on the monument put up in Roubaix to the honour of the leading industrialist and former Mayor, Eugène Motte, bore witness to his impeccably patriotic behaviour throughout the war:

> We cannot accept the role of people who work alongside the enemy. You can requisition our possessions, you cannot requisition our persons. Our conscience as French people will not allow it.

This state of mind is absolutely identical to the attitude revealed in David Hirsch's diary. Maxence van der Meersch may well have shown in his novel *Invasion 14* (1935) that not everyone was equally patriotic, but it would appear that the number of people who agreed to work with the Germans during the Great War was very small.[8] The Mayor of Roubaix himself, Jean-Baptiste Lebas, spent a great part of the war as a prisoner in a German fortress. Talking in particular about the taking of hostages in the Aisne in 1870, the historian Ernest Lavisse wrote: 'The hatred of Germans is a virtue which the Germans themselves made very easy, and our excessive sufferings have made it impossible for us to forget.[9] The treatment of civilians in Northern France between 1914 and 1918 gives far more reason than the events of 1870 to talk about these 'excessive sufferings'.

NORTHERN FRANCE'S EXCESSIVE SUFFERINGS
For example, the Germans started, by requiring French workers to dig trenches for them. Not only did they not respect the Hague convention, they also placed these inhabitants of the north in a morally unbearable position: every moment they worked placed them in a situation where they were helping to kill their fellow-citizens and, worse still, their fathers, sons and brothers: hence the disturbances in Lille, Roubaix and Tourcoing, when the Germans used the population of these occupied towns to make sandbags to protect their own trenches: 'We shall not spin winding sheets for our own children'.[10] This refusal of the workers to work for the Germans in 1915 led to the taking of new hostages and then the establishment of forced labour in 1916. These young men, like their aged companions, received the name of 'red armbands' ('brassards rouges')

because of the sign which they wore enabling them to be recognised. Hirsch speculated on their fate: 'Nine hundred men taken by railway to cut wood in the forest? To plant potatoes? Or to be taken into Germany? The Germans continue to take men away from here: one group, who have reached the age when they are liable to call up is taken to a concentration camp in Sedan' (7, 9 April, 1918).

Five classes due for call up, men who reached the age of 14 between 1914 and 1918, grew up to a life of forced labour, in conditions of undernourishment and high mortality which enable us to see that there is nothing anachronistic about the term 'concentration camp' used by David Hirsch.[11] At Easter 1916, the Germans used the excuse of the English blockade of Germany – and the refusal of the French population to hate their English allies – to justify the deportation of a part of the population of Lille, Roubaix and Tourcoing. A proclamation by the German authorities was issued at the time:

> The attitude of England makes it more and more difficult to feed the population. To reduce these food shortages, the Germans recently asked for volunteers to go and work in the fields. This request did not find an appropriate response. Consequently, inhabitants will be evacuated compulsorily and taken into the country . . . Since this is an irrevocable decision, it is in the population's own interest to remain calm and obedient.[12]

Some 2000 people were thus taken to other French *départements* occupied by the Germans, where in order to ensure that those who had been deported from Northern France were badly received, care had been taken to proclaim that they were voluntary workers. It was essentially the taking away of women and young girls which provoked the greatest terror and resentment. Witnesses have described the sufferings caused by the promiscuity, the way women were raped, their fear of never seeing their families again, their inability to understand why they were being deported since in the end most of them did not do any work and came back in small groups during the following months. All these women, including the very young girls, were made to undergo a very detailed gynaecological examination, which was all the more traumatising since they were thus openly given the status of prostitutes. Some were certainly sent to Germany to fulfil this role:

> A first patrol went from house to house, distributing tickets; 'Order: Within half an hour, the inhabitants of this house must assemble in a room on the ground floor to await the arrival of the next patrol. The people indicated must prepare their luggage, which must not weigh more than 30 kilograms. Any attempt to avoid carrying out this order will be severely punished'. Half an hour later, the officers responsible for deciding who should go came to each house. They made their choice in

a highly arbitrary fashion. As is always the case with the Germans, it was the working class men and women who suffered most. Sometimes, they took the sister and left the brother. . . The people evacuated were locked into cattle trucks, and sent to the *départements* of the Aisne and the Ardennes.[13]

The occupation was thus experienced by the people of the North as open warfare which was all the more atrocious since it was directed against women, children and pigeons, in an area where pigeon-keeping is a passion. The fury with which the occupying German authorities pursued these unfortunate birds, and the execution of at least 16 pigeon fanciers for not having obeyed the order to give them up, is a clear indication, if looked at from the point of view of Germans, of how afraid they were of the civilian population, a fear dating back to the activities of the partisans (*franc-tireurs*) of the 1870 war. What was prudence on their part – the ban on pigeons – became an atrocity as a result of the death sentences, even if it were really true that some of the pigeon fanciers used their birds to send messages to the allies, that is to say to take part in the resistance.

ESCAPE NETWORKS AND RESISTANCE MOVEMENTS

In 1914, within the German occupation zone, French, English and Belgian soldiers who had been taken prisoner managed to escape and hide. Some of them, who had been wounded, needed medical attention. They all tried to escape into Holland, which had remained neutral, either in order to spend the rest of the war there or to use it as a stepping stone from which to escape to England and rejoin their unit. Either through patriotism, or through compassion for these soldiers, a number of French people – in the main, women – began as early as 1914 to organise networks enabling these soldiers to escape. From the north of France, and from Belgium, this new kind of smuggler managed to observe the greatest secrecy in evacuating allied fighting men.

> Both the French and English armies needed to know about the enemy's movements. Some of the people in the occupied zones began to work for the Intelligence Service. For the Germans, these manifestations of patriotism and compassion were seen as resistance, spying and treason. In wartime, and under military occupation, such crimes are normally punished by death. French women, French men, Belgians and an English woman, Edith Cavell, paid for their resistance to the Germans with their lives.

How did one become a member of the resistance movement in 1914? In so far as one can reconstruct what happened to individuals who, for the most part, were taken prisoner and shot, it was often by ignorance and without any serious thought as to the consequences. Princess de Croy and Princess

CROIX-ROUGE FRANÇAISE

SOCIÉTÉ FRANÇAISE DE SECOURS AUX BLESSÉS MILITAIRES

DÉLÉGATION DE LA 1ᵉ RÉGION

Comité de Roubaix

Le Président du Comité de Roubaix

certifie que M⁰ Sœur Marguerite de l'ordre de
Saint Vincent de Paul née Corballis Emilie Marie

inscrit sur les contrôles de la Délégation sous le numéro 1800

a fait partie du Personnel de l'ambulance St Louis, comme chef de salle
du 20 Avril 1914 au 10 Juillet 1915, puis comme Directrice de l'ambulance
à partir de cette date, fonctions qu'elle a remplies à la satisfaction
de tous. A rendu en maintes circonstances les plus signalés
services aux personnes ayant à faire à l'autorité allemande
du 20 août 1914 actuellement encore de service.

Fait à Roubaix le 15 Mai 1916

LE PRÉSIDENT DE COMITÉ LOCAL,

Guy Mathon

VU:
LE DÉLÉGUÉ RÉGIONAL,

(vii)   The local French Red Cross Committee in Roubaix acknowledges the work done for wounded in Roubaix by a British Nun in a French Religious Order, the work having been done under 'l'autorité allemande'. Soeur Marguerite's account of her experience in the Lille Roubaix area has graphic description of German deportation of French civilians for work in Germany. [Soeur Marguerite: Liddle Collection]

Belleville gave shelter to wounded soldiers in their chateaux not far from the border between France and Belgium. An English nurse, Edith Cavell, had since 1907, been running the Berkedael Institute in Brussels. Her school for nurses became a Red Cross hospital, in which during the first few months of the war as many German soldiers became patients as Belgian ones. Then allied soldiers who were in danger of being taken prisoner tried to find an escape route into Holland. A Brussels architect, Philippe Baucq, provided money and helpers. A network was set up through which soldiers who had been saved by the two princesses and some of their trusted friends managed to get back to Brussels. In exactly the same way and at the same time another network was set up in Lille, consisting principally of four men, Eugène Jacquet, Ernest Deconinck, George Maertens and Sylvère Verhulst.

Those who, like Edith Cavell, set up these networks, cannot really be called spies. On the other hand, resistance workers of this kind had to keep track of the movements of enemy soldiers, and make sure of being able to receive help from the many people whom they would meet on the way. With Lille as her base, Louise de Bettignes set up a veritable network of information for the Intelligence Service. It was hard for these various activities to pass unnoticed and the Germans rapidly became suspicious of what was happening. In 1915, in Belgium and France, there were more and more arrests and summary trials and executions. The Germans put up notices to warn the population of the consequences of spying and enabling soldiers to escape. A note in David Hirsch's diary reads:

A man has just been shot at Liévin for having hidden pigeons. This morning, at Lille, four Frenchmen were shot for having enabled French soldiers who had gone into hiding to stay in France. According to the priest who was with them in their last moments, they died with the cry of "Long Live France, Long Live the Republic" on their lips . . . This morning, at the Citadelle of Lille, a poor little lad of sixteen and a half called Léon Trulin, a Belgian living in Lille, was shot on the accusation of having been involved in spying. . . It was said that he had photographed trenches and passed the photographs on to the English. How could he have done this? (6, and 22 September; 8 November, 1915).

The execution of women and of adolescents – though Trulin's youth had been exaggerated – increased the anti-German feelings of a population which was already physically in the front line and living in a particularly intense warlike atmosphere. Henry Cochin expressed this atmosphere well in 1917 in a speech given in Paris on *The invasion of Northern France*: 'There is something special about the patriotism of the Northern France. We are a frontier. But what kind of frontier? Nothing really marks it. It is drawn on the map. It is not a creation of nature. This makes it only the stronger and the more real. It is marked in our hearts'.

In the first weeks of the war, during the German advance, there had already been a number of atrocities: villages burned, women raped, hostages shot. The Germans, genuinely obsessed by the memory of the partisan fighters of the Franco-Prussian war, suspected the whole of the civilian population, and were not inclined to be merciful. How could the population, fleeing before the rapid advance of the German forces, have avoided telling stories which depicted the Germans in an increasingly monstrous light? It was obvious to them that the German troops were made up of criminals since they did not respect the Hague convention of 1907. The war secreted violence and hatred. Men advancing into enemy territory, as the Germans were, could not be anything but barbarians. The war that they were waging, unlike that of their adversaries, was not one for justice and right. Moreover, the way they destroyed churches and executed priests proved that the Germans were attacking God himself. There were more and more stories about French and Belgian people being crucified by a brutal and licentious soldiery. Some of God's innocent children were said to have had their hands cut off. There were many witnesses who swore that they had seen, as they fled from the Germans, children with their hands wrapped around with bandages.[14] It is against this nightmare background of genuine terror that we must imagine what it was like during the occupation. Inhabitants already overwhelmed by defeat were required to receive into their own homes, and feed at their own tables, invaders whom they had made up their minds to regard as nothing but barbarians. When the women were taken away, in 1916, there was rumour that 'they have been summoned to the Kommandatur to have their breasts cut off' (17 April, 1916). Hirsch talks about 'stupid rumours', and the clarity of his vision inevitably recalls Marc Bloch's statement that 'A piece of misinformation is inevitably the result of a collective state of mind preceding it. It is only apparently accidental . . . One can never over-emphasise the extent to which emotion and fatigue destroy the critical faculties'.[15]

Emotion and weariness had indeed reached a climax in France during the deportations of 1916, and the population of the occupied North of France was at the end of its tether: 'It is against all the laws of war and of humanity, especially as far as women are concerned', wrote Hirsch on 21 April, 1916. For him, the Germans were an inferior people because of their readiness to treat in this manner those whom they should most respect, namely women and children. He was also very harsh on French women who agreed to have relationships with German soldiers, even outside the framework of prostitution – perhaps even more so in such cases. 'It is', he wrote, 'a state of mind which it is painful to notice, but which has to be acknowledged for what it is. A young girl can perfectly well go to a shop to buy a wedding ring to marry a German . . . After all, she may say, he is no different from other men . . . And there are said to be a fair number of girls like that. You need to be totally lacking in any feeling for your country to accept or express this kind of argument, especially at a time like this' (18 April, 1918).

France was seen as a woman, who had been raped by the invaders. How then could one come to regard these invaders and rapists as men whom one could accept as husbands? But while Hirsch gave large numbers of examples of individual atrocities committed by German soldiers, he was honest enough to recognise that there were some who behaved with dignity. He did not theorise, and limited himself to noting what happened. His notes were, naturally, not intended to be published. The same questions recur: 'Are the Germans a great people? Is this, all in all, the way one expects a great people to behave?' The account of the visit of a German Jewish doctor to the Jewish community of Roubaix is, in this respect, highly significant: 'He wants to mix with the population. We keep him at arms length . . . In what he has to say, he expresses surprise that French Jews are treated in exactly the same way as other citizens. He even adds that they are better off in France than they are elsewhere'. (29 November, 1918). This German Jewish officer was not treated by his fellow Jews as a Jew, but as a German, and yet what he had to say was noted down, since it reinforced the certainty of the Jews of Roubaix that they were, as the German proverb puts it 'as happy as God in France'.

Thus the war and the occupation were experienced as a struggle between two civilisations from which all points of common contact had disappeared. The inhabitants of Northern France had discovered, at the same time as the Serbians, the Poles, the Russians, the Germans living in Eastern Prussia and, above all the Armenians, that war had ceased to be a matter of military encounters and even of the struggle between national cultures in a state of total mobilisation. In occupied territory, war is total war. Hitler, in 1939, could make fun of the weakness of the European memory on the subject of the massacre by the Turks of the Armenians. After all, he asked on 22 August, 1939, 'who now remembers the way the Armenians were wiped out?' Even Hitler in his cynicism had failed to recollect what had happened in the occupied territories during the First World War. Over and above the certainty of these murderers that they could always win the memory battle, one may also wonder whether the efforts of the pacifist may not have helped to produce the same forgetfulness. The conceptual screen erected during the twenties and thirties by militant pacifists determined to condemn war as an atrocity in itself, rather than individual atrocities committed during the war, is in no small degree responsible for this failure of memory.

Notes

1   Jean Saint-Quentin, speech inaugurating the monument to the memory of Henry Legrand, a Valenciennes schoolteacher shot for having tried to send a message by carrier pigeon in 1917, Valenciennes, 1927. (Municipal Archives

of Valenciennes; I should like to thank everyone working in these archives, and especially William Maufroy, for their constant helpfulness).

2   Peter Haggenmacher, 'L'occupation militaire en droit international: Genèse et profil d'une institution juridique'. *Relations Internationales*, no.79, autumn 1994, pp. 285–301.

3   See Les atrocités allemandes à Lille, trois témoignages de députés socialistes, Delory, Ragheboom, Inghels. Chambre des députés, séance du 22 octobre 1918.

4   See in particular the study of 'atrocities' by John Horne and Alan Kramer, and especially their forthcoming book.

5   I warmly thank Jean-Pierre Hirsch who has generously let me read and use the manuscript of his grandfather's diary.

6   Centre de recherche de l'Historial de la Grande Guerre, S. Audoin-Rouzeau, A. Becker, J.J. Becker, G. Krumeich, J. Winter, *La très Grande Guerre, 1914–1918*, Le Monde-Editions, 1994.

7   David Hirsch's son. Agrégé d'histoire, a teacher in Lille.

8   Annette Becker, 'Mémoire et commémoration, les "atrocités" allemandes de la Première Guerre mondiale dans le Nord de la France'. Revue du Nord, juin 1992, pp.339–354, and 'D'une guerre à l'autre: mémoire de l'occupation et de la résistance:1914–1940', *Revue du Nord* no. 306, juillet-septembre 1994, pp.453–465. Philippe Burin, La France à l'heure allemande, 1940–44, Le Seuil, 1995. Robert Frank, 'L'occupation allemande dans l'imaginaire français' *Relations internationales,* no. 80, hiver 1994, pp.491–500.

9   Ernest Lavisse. *L'invasion dans le département de l'Aisne*, Laon, 1872, p.96, p.10.

10 *Le Cordon de Saint François*, Roubaix, August 1915, no.3. Printed in an unoccupied zone.

11 See the Master's diploma submitted by Muriel Rigole, *Le travail forcé dans le Nord de la France, 1914–1918*, supervised by Annette Becker, 1995. Université Charles de Gaulle/Lille III. From the point of view of food the Germans were no better off: 'In certain groups of civilian workers, the soldiers guarding them were so badly fed that they begged the French to give them the remains of their food, or stole their bread from them. In other groups, they said that they would prefer to go to the front, where at least they would be able to eat'.

12 *Bulletin de Lille*, April 23, 1916.

13 A typed account by Max Hirsch, dating from 1919.

14 Annette Becker. *La Guerre et la foi, de la mort à la mémoire, 1914–1930*, Armand-Colin, 1994, chapter 1 to be published by C.U.P. under the title: 'The Religious Imagination at War', 1996; John Horne, '"les mains coupées", "atrocités allemandes" et opinion française en 1914' in *Guerre et Cultures, 1914–1918* (edited by S. Audoin-Rouzeau, A. Becker, J.J. Becker, G. Krumeich, J. Winter) Armand Colin, 1994.

15 Marc Bloch. 'Réflexions d'un historien sur les fausses nouvelles de la guerre', *Revue de synthèses historique*, Vol. XXXIII, pp. 13–15.

Chapter 46

The Arab Experience of the War

Rashid Khalidi

The First World War completely transformed the Arab world, as it did much of the rest of the globe. In many Arab countries, it brought with it the end of an era, introducing massive, permanent changes, some of whose effects are not yet clear. Most notably, the First World War ended over 400 years of Ottoman rule of most of the Arab world; it brought many important centres of Arab civilization like Damascus and Baghdad under lasting European control for the first time in their history; and it produced political divisions, frontiers and entities which by and large have lasted to this day.

In addition to these profound political upheavals for which the war was responsible, it devastated several Arab countries, particularly those parts of Palestine and Iraq which were the scenes of intense combat, causing untold material and human damage. Finally, through the widespread famine, disease and deprivation, death in battle, human dislocation and political repression which were all results of the First World War in the Arab world, it scarred an entire generation of men and women who fought and suffered through it.

The impact of the First World War was particularly devastating since it followed several generations of peace, rapid economic and population growth, and relative stability in most parts of the Arab world. Although the Ottoman Empire had been involved in a series of localized, regional conflicts – a brief war with Greece in 1897, the Libyan conflict of 1911–1912, and the two Balkan Wars of 1912–1913, it had not fought a major war which encompassed large expanses of its territory since 1878, nor had there been serious combat in the Arab parts of the Empire since well before that. And in spite of occasional unrest, European occupations (as in Egypt and Tunisia in 1881–82) and other conflicts (in the Sudan for example), throughout most of the rest of the region peace had long prevailed.

There were a number of achievements during the war, some military, some human, some political, and some material, but on balance the First World War was a deeply traumatic experience for many, perhaps most, of the people of the Arab world. The end of the Ottoman era, which had lasted for nearly twenty generations in the Arab world, was not easy to adjust to, and it was exacerbated by the intense Arab-Turkish mistrust and ill-feeling which accompanied and followed it. The war nevertheless gave a powerful stimulus to the ongoing process of the definition of a modern national identity among the Arab peoples, and began the long and difficult process of the establishment of the independence of Arab states.[1]

This growth of nationalist sentiment could be seen in Egypt, Palestine, Syria, Iraq and several other Arab countries as soon as the fighting stopped, and powerful national movements emerged. Most of these national movements faced repression by the military forces of the victorious Allied powers in the immediate post-war period, several of which hoped to find barely-disguised colonial compensations in the Middle East for their horrendous war losses. Before detailing aspects of the Arab human experience during the course of the First World War, it is necessary to discuss some of the war's general effects on the Arab world as a whole.

II

The Arab world – the area where the Arabic language is spoken – is a varied region, encompassing as it does enormous distances stretching from northwest Africa to the Indian Ocean, and from the Sahara Desert to the edges of the Iranian and Anatolian highlands. Its geographical diversity has been complemented by a wide variety of human adaptations to the harsh climate and great distances, the lack of water and the relatively limited amount of arable land. It is thus hard to summarize the impact on the Arab world of a world war fought in several separate parts of its vast expanses – the first such modern European war to involve the region to this extent, although much earlier the Napoleonic wars had affected it deeply, particularly as a result of the French occupation of Egypt.

Beyond these geographical variations and the distances involved, before the First World War the Arab world was already subject to a broad range of different sovereignties and political arrangements. These included contested attempts to impose Spanish rule in parts of western Morocco, French protectorates in Morocco and Tunisia, direct French colonial rule in Algeria, an Italian occupation of Libya which was still being fiercely resisted in 1914, and British dominion in varied forms over Egypt, the Sudan, Aden, and several small Gulf principalities stretching from Kuwait to Oman. The rest of the Arab world, including Syria, Palestine, Lebanon,

Iraq, the Hijaz, the Najd and Yemen, formally constituted part of the Ottoman Empire and was subject to greater or lesser degrees of Ottoman control.

The Ottoman Empire came into the First World War on the side of Germany and Austria-Hungary in late October 1914 with a surprise attack on Russian naval bases in the Black Sea by two German naval vessels, the battle-cruiser Goeben and the Breslau, which had been trapped in Ottoman waters by pursuing British vessels, 'sold' to the Ottoman Navy, and used with their German crews as the spearhead of this attack. The war very quickly encompassed the Caucasus, the Balkans, Gallipoli, and in the Arab world, Mesopotamia and the Egypt-Palestine front, as well as different parts of the Arabian Peninsula.

Arab soldiers, like all other Ottoman subjects, were drafted into the army or called up with the reserves (there were in addition many Arab soldiers and officers in the regular standing army, particularly from Iraq), but until 1916, conscripts and reservists tended to serve in units stationed in or around their home regions. Thus most of the units of the Ottoman Fourth Army under Cemal Pasa (Jamal Pasha), which launched attacks on the Suez Canal in 1915 and 1916, were composed of troops originally from Syria and Iraq.[2] Similarly, most of the Ottoman troops in Mesopotamia who fought the Anglo-Indian expeditionary force which occupied Basra in 1914, and thereafter advanced northwards, were originally from Iraq, and many other units serving in different parts of the Arab world were locally raised.

As time went on, however, military requirements imposed the necessity for transfers and troop movements which changed this situation. In the case of Syria, this change was accelerated by growing fears of possible disloyalty among Arab troops in the Ottoman high command, which decided to decrease the potential danger by transferring Arab units of the Fourth Army out of Syria.[3] From an Ottoman point of view, this measure was probably a wise one, as Arab-British plans for a rising involving these forces existed,[4] but in the end these plans could not be implemented due to the sudden troop transfers. And as a result, Arab soldiers fought and died not only on the Mesopotamian, Palestinian and Yemeni/Hijazi fronts, but in the Caucasus, at Gallipoli and in the Balkans.

As is clear from the above discussion, the main arenas of the First World War within the Arab world centered on the frontiers of the Ottoman domains. The Egypt-Palestine and Mesopotamian fronts were the Arab regions where the most fiercely contested battlefields were located, and combat continued there, sometimes sporadically and sometimes quite intensely, from 1914 until 1918. In addition, the Yemen-Aden frontier, the Holy Cities of Mecca and Medina in the Hijaz and the communications lines linking them to Syria[5], as well as the deserts of Libya and those of Najd in eastern Arabia, were also the scenes of occasional heavy fighting.

In all these areas where combat took place some damage was done, with the most severe fighting and the greatest damage in parts of Iraq and Palestine.

The war was experienced painfully and immediately in all these regions by the Arab civilian population, which in addition to losing many of its able-bodied men to conscription for the duration of the war, and losing large numbers of its draft animals to confiscation, often also lost its homes in the fighting, particularly in areas like Gaza in Palestine and Kut al-'Amara in Iraq, where heavy shelling took place in the context of entrenched positional warfare. In much of Lebanon and Palestine, the heavily wooded mountain and hill areas were completely deforested and many people lost their fruit and olive groves, as large numbers of trees were cut down to meet the needs for fuel of the Ottoman railway system in transporting troops.

Finally, and most cruelly, there was famine, which was particularly severe in Lebanon and Palestine. Several factors played a role in this. The first was the fact that of the Ottoman Empire's Arab domains, these two regions had by 1914 become the most integrated into the world economy, with Lebanon producing silk, and Palestine growing cotton and grain, and later citrus, for export since the eighteenth century. The blockade imposed on enemy regions by the Allied navies hit hard at these two areas, which had developed a reliance on imports to meet some of their food needs, and could no longer export their surplus production in the way of citrus, olives and other products. The absence of so many men at the front was another factor in restraining food production, and in hindering the shift backwards from production for the export market to subsistence agriculture and the production of locally-consumed food crops. On top of all this, the harvests of several years during the war were poor, and the winter of 1917–1918 was extremely bitter in the eastern Mediterranean, with heavy snows in areas which rarely saw freezing temperatures in winter-time.

In addition to these factors, which might be described as indirect causes of the famine, some of them natural, there were other, more sinister, direct man-made ones. Explaining them will require a short but important digression. As the war went on, and as the Ottoman authorities amassed evidence of what they claimed was the involvement of a number of Arab leaders and organizations in plotting for independence in collusion with the Allied powers, they began putting some of the individuals concerned on trial. They were materially aided in this endeavour by the failure of the French Consulate-General in Beirut to destroy its archives on the outbreak of the war.[6] This inexcusable lapse enabled the Ottoman military authorities to use a number of incriminating documents in these individuals' trials. They were later published in Turkish, French and Arabic.[7] Two trials, by court martial at 'Alay in Lebanon in 1915 and 1916, resulted in numerous convictions and in the executions, in the main squares of Beirut and

Damascus, of dozens of Lebanese, Syrian and Palestinian leaders, including several former members of the Ottoman Parliament, a number of newspaper editors, army officers, and other notable figures, and in the imprisonment and exile of hundreds more.[8] One source puts the total number of those exiled from Syria during the war as high as 50,000.[9] Many others were tried and executed after these two main trials.[10]

Those hanged in 1915 and 1916 have gone down in Arab history as *martyrs*, and both execution sites, in the centers of the Lebanese and Syrian capitals, have since been renamed Sāḥat al-Shuhadā', 'Martyrs' Square'. It is worth noting that while a few of these individuals had apparently conspired with foreign powers, and others had been involved with nationalist or proto-nationalist secret societies, some appear to have been innocent of the specific charges against them.[11] Nevertheless, having to their own satisfaction proven the treason of the individuals concerned, and the untrustworthiness of the Arabs in general, the Ottoman authorities under the direction of the vindictive Fourth Army commander, Cemal Pasa, proceeded to punish the general population with exactions including a tax of 50 per cent on personal property and 25 per cent on land. In the case of the Mount Lebanon region, these exactions extended to a blockade to prevent food from reaching the area.[12]

To what degree such Ottoman measures were responsible for, or contributed to, the famine which followed in 1917 and 1918 is probably impossible to discern at this remove in time. The famine has certainly gone down in popular memory as having been caused by 'Turkish' actions,[13] and there is evidence in Cemal's own autobiography that he held much of the population responsible for the 'treason' of some of their leaders.[14] That these sentiments were heartily reciprocated is indicated by the fact that Cemal is frequently described in Arab history books with the epithet 'the Butcher'.

Whatever the precise role played by the Ottoman authorities in causing the famine, there can be little question as to its impact. The demographer Justin McCarthy has established from a careful study of Ottoman and British Mandate statistics that after growing in the prewar period by slightly over one per cent annually, the total population of Palestine declined by more than six per cent during the war years, from over 720,000 to about 670,000, as a result of famine and disease, as well as war casualties.[15] These numbers indicate a total decrease in population due to war-related causes of over 80,000, assuming a natural peace-time population increase of one per cent.

It is very likely that the decline in population was considerably greater in Mount Lebanon, where the famine was unquestionably more severe, although demographic research similar to that of McCarthy for Palestine does not exist to quantify the suffering in Lebanon. War-time deaths due to famine and disease, according to estimates of varying reliability, ranged from 100,000 to 200,000 in Mount Lebanon.[16] The stories of the famine told by eye-witnesses are heart-rending, however: the writer Anbara Salam al-Khalidi recounts in her memoirs that she often saw starving refugees from the Lebanese mountains who had fled to Beirut, where some food was available, and who could be found there begging pitifully in the streets during the last years of the war.[17] She and other Beirut women set up relief facilities for those in need which served thousands daily.

III

Clearly, the material effect of events such as these was devastating. What was the *political* impact of the First World War, and how did it affect those who lived through it? The nationalist historiography (both Arab and Turkish) which has developed in the decades since 1918 has obscured the fact that at the outset of the war there was little doubt about the loyalty to the Empire and the Sultan of most Arabs within the Ottoman domains, and an assumption among most politically active Arabs and Turks that with the end of the Balkan Wars in 1913, the Empire had survived the worst, and could look forward to a period of renewed stability.[18]

It is true that previous to the war there had been a growth of national sentiment among both Arabs and Turks, in the wake of the spread of Balkan and Armenian nationalisms, and there was strong support for political decentralization, reform and local self-government in a number of Arab regions, including Syria and parts of Iraq.[19] Moreover, many Arabs were coming to see the Ottoman Empire as acting at the expense of Arab interests and as being increasingly dominated by Turks, through the Turkish-run Committee of Union and Progress (CUP)[20] which dominated the government for most of the 1908–1918 period. There was also a strong desire for cultural rights such as education in Arabic instead of Turkish, and for appointments of local officials in their own localities. But it is important to note that in the pre-war period this Arabist, or cultural nationalist, sentiment had not reached the point of outright support for Arab independence from the Empire on the part of even the most advanced Arabist thinkers.

Although the ill-advised Ottoman entry into the war, and other factors, had won a number of Arab leaders in Greater Syria (Syria, Lebanon, Palestine and Jordan), as well as Sharif Husayn of Mecca, over to the idea of Arab independence from the Turks by some time in 1915 or 1916, until this point most Arabs supported the Ottoman cause, albeit with misgivings in many cases. The fact that so many of their sons, father, husbands and brothers were serving at the front in the Ottoman army after 1914 contributed to this sentiment, as did four centuries of loyalty to the greatest Islamic state by the majority Muslim population, and well-founded fears among many that the Allied powers sought the dismemberment of the

Empire and its absorption within their colonial domains. Thus there was some satisfaction during the first two years of the war in the Arab provinces of the Empire at Ottoman successes in holding off the superior forces of the Allied powers along the Suez Canal, in the Caucasus, in Iraq and at Gallipoli.[21]

A combination of factors led to a change in this situation. One was British blandishments to the Hashemites in the Hijaz, where the Allied blockade had had a devastating effect, interrupting the pilgrimage to the Islamic holy places on which many depended for their income, and initially cutting off food supplies (although these were soon restored as a means of inducement to the Hashemites). Another was the repression of Cemal Pasa in Syria, as he drew a net tighter and tighter around Arabist leaders, even before the first court martial began. Perhaps in the end there was also the sense for many Arab leaders who before the war had formerly entertained the illusion that they shared power in the Empire, that they no longer had control over their own fate or that of their people. They had seen how a few CUP leaders could secretly decide to throw in the lot of the entire Empire with Germany, for reasons still hard for historians to divine to this day, in a situation where the overwhelming naval superiority of Britain in the Mediterranean and the Indian Ocean exposed much of the Arab world to danger.

In any case, for many of those who had not decided to revolt, Cemal Pasa made the decision for them. By hanging the best and brightest among an entire generation of Arab leaders in Syria, Lebanon and Palestine in 1915 and 1916, he gave the revolt both a number of martyrs and an impetus it would not otherwise have had. The story is told by George Antonius that upon hearing the news of the executions while visiting Damascus, Amir Faysal, third son of Sharif Husayn, threw his *kaffiyya* to the ground in bitter anger and exclaimed, 'Death has become sweet, oh Arabs!'.[22] Whether Faysal actually underwent so rapid a conversion is impossible to discern: Antonius was the first to have access to Hashemite documents and other sources provided him by Sharif Husayn and other members of the family, but he mentions none of his sources for specific statements. Nevertheless, his words seem to reflect a widespread attitude at the time.[23]

In spite of the existence of some memoirs, we are handicapped in trying to discern personal feelings in much of the Arab world at this time, because of the destruction of so much source material in areas where fighting took place during the war,[24] and because of strict Ottoman censorship of the press and other publications and British and French military censorship in Egypt and North Africa. The press, which for the pre-war period is an invaluable source,[25] was almost entirely muzzled during the war: the number of newspapers decreased precipitously in both the Ottoman domains and Egypt, as many were shut by the authorities, fell victim to

26. Officers of the 10th Battalion, Essex Regiment at Lamotte, Buleux, France, in
December 1916. In operations on the Somme that year the battalion had suffered
900 casualties including 100 killed but it was brought up to strength by successive
drafts. The 10th Essex served with the 18th Division throughout the war.
(Note the jackdaw on the arm of one of the seated officers).
(R.A. Chell: Liddle Collection).
See Chapter 24: The War Experience of a typical Kitchener Division - The 18th
Division.

27. The Band of the 6th Battalion Highland Light Infantry leading the battalion
through desert scrub near Gaza in May 1917. 'Scotland the Brave, our
Regimental March often made the last wee bit a lot easier. Our Pipers never failed
us'. (T.M. MacQuaker: Liddle Collection).
See Chapter 25: The Scottish Soldier at War.

28. A member of 186 Company RE, Special Brigade, at Hallines in France 22.5.16 with a gas cylinder and barrow for short distance transportation when ground conditions allowed. (G.I Higson: Liddle Collection). See Chapter 27: The Experience of the British Special Brigade in Gas Warfare.

29. Friendships in France. The original caption, 'The Smilers', witness to the comradeship within the Q.M.A.A.C. is paralleled by an inscription on another photograph of these girls. It recorded that they were 'warranted to stick together like glue until chucked out on the mat'. They came from Pontypridd, Bradford, Jarrow, Durham, Sunderland, Doncaster and from Scotland. Nora Steer is on the front left. (Nora Steer: Liddle Collection). See Chapter 28: The Forgotten Army of Women.

30. German underground bunker. Though posed, this pre-1917 picture conveys a close-knit community and good living standards - generous headroom, tables, bunks, wine, tin of veal. (Charles G.Adams (A.E.F.): Liddle Collection).
See Chapter 29: The Morale of the German Army in 1917-18.

31. Austro-Hungarian wounded on the Izonzo Front, 1916. (Österreichisches Kriegsarchiv, Vienna)
See Chapter 30: Morale in the Austro-Hungarian Army.

32. Russian prisoners under guard. (H. Meyer: Liddle Collection).
    See Chapter 32: The Russian Soldier's Morale.

33. Italian troops, Autumn 1917, not long before defeat at Caporetto. (L. Struthers:
    Liddle Collection).
    See Chapter 33: Morale and Discipline in the Italian Army 1915-18

34. Caporetto casualties. (L.
Struthers: Liddle Collection).
See Chapter 33. Morale and
Discipline in the Italian Army
1915-18.

35. A Medical Officer, Capt R.S.
Goodman, left, bends over a
stretcher case brought in to
his Field Dressing Station
(Ypres – Menin Road A.D.S)
by German P.O.W's acting as
stretcher bearers. (Dr.R.S.
Goodman: Liddle Collection)
See Chapter 35. Not a
Doctor's Work.

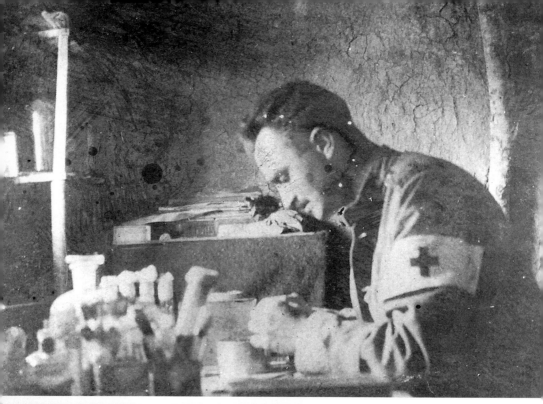

36. Corporal A.E. Clay RAMC at work in an improvised Advanced Field Laboratory, 27.4.18, Deli Abbas, Mesopotamia. (A.E. Clay: Liddle Collection).
See Chapter 36: The Fight against Disease in the Mesopotamia Campaign.

37. Sir Harold Gillies. (British Association of Plastic Surgeons).
See Chapter 37: Facial Surgery: The Patient's Experience.

38. Private Bell (A). After initial surgery in France, May 1918, B). With Gillies's annotations to show planned surgical procedure, operation performed 23.7.18, C). Final appearance 22.9.19 after six operations. (St.Mary's Hospital N.H. Trust Archives, Sidcup).
See Chapter 37: Facial Surgery: The Patient's Experience.

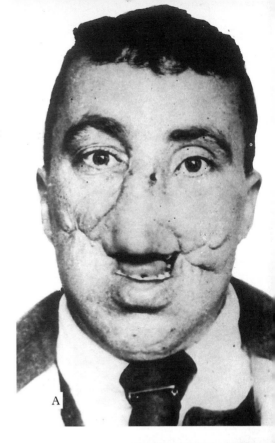

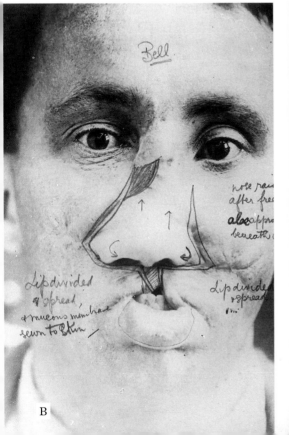

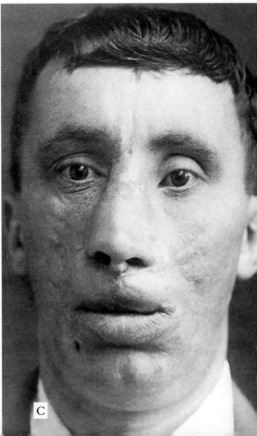

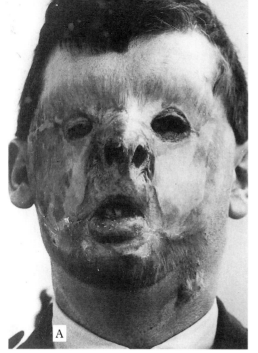 

39. Lieutenant Wallace (Canadian Field Artillery attached RFC) A) three days after his admission, 21.5.18 and B) his final appearance 9.11.21. (St. Mary's Hospital N.H. Trust Archives, Sidcup).
See Chapter 37: Facial Surgery: The Patient's Experience.

40. Officers of the 2nd Battalion Royal Welsh Fusiliers on the Somme, August 1916. Dr. James Dunn is in the centre. (The Royal Welch Fusiliers). See note page XIV.
See Chapter 38: Dr. James Dunn and Shell Shock.

severe newsprint shortages, or lost their editors to political repression (of the 31 most prominent Arab martyrs executed by the Ottoman authorities in 1915 and 1916, 16 were journalists).[26] In the words of an authority on this subject:

> World War I, spilling over into the Middle East, brought political upheaval and economic hardship unprecedented in the region's recent memory. For the press this meant near-complete paralysis: most of the existing papers collapsed, hardly any new ones were allowed to appear, and the few that survived faced tremendous difficulties.[27]

Even in Egypt, where the repression was far less brutal than in the Ottoman domains, the press suffered from war-time pressures. It is thus possible to follow the impact of the war on Egyptian society, but one of our main windows into its workings is nearly shut as a result. Nevertheless, a separate discussion of the impact of the First World War on Egypt is necessary because of its long-term political impact. Egypt was nominally under Ottoman suzerainty until October 1914, although it had been under British occupation, and effective British control, since 1882. Upon the entry of the Ottoman Empire into the war, Great Britain proclaimed a protectorate over Egypt, ousting the Khedive, Abbas Hilmi II, and installing another member of the ruling family, Husayn Kamil, with the new title of Sultan.

In the years preceding the war, Egypt had witnessed the development of powerful nationalist political currents, focused on opposition to the British occupation. With the proclamation of the protectorate, and the imposition of direct British control of political life, the veil had been removed from the reality of power in Egypt. On the political level, this meant little other than the arrest of a number of nationalists, the closure of many newspapers, the banning of some political parties and groups, and strict maintenance of public order. But Egypt was a scene of combat during the first three years of the war, as Cemal Pasa's Fourth Army made attacks upon the Canal Zone, and the staging area for the British forces under Generals Murray and Allenby which ultimately pushed north into Palestine. As a result, Egyptians felt the impact of the war directly as well as on other levels.

There had been much concern among British strategic planners in the pre-war years about the danger to British interests represented by a German-supported Ottoman attack on Egypt, co-ordinated with a rising by Egyptian nationalists.[28] In the event, these fears proved misplaced, as there was no rising in Egypt during the First World War, in spite of Ottoman and German efforts to foster one.[29] But despite the fact that overt Egyptian expressions of opposition to the British during the war were successfully repressed, there was deep dissatisfaction among many Egyptians. One of the primary causes was the conscription of large numbers of peasants into a Labour Corps which built roads and dug trenches for British troops in Egypt and later on in Palestine (and 23,000 of whom were serving in France by 1917). Initially, recruitment for this Corps, and for a Camel Transport Corps raised in Egypt, had been voluntary, and they had reached a strength of 100,000 by 1917.[30] Starting in that year, however, tens of thousands of Egyptians were forcibly enrolled in the Labour Corps, where they remained for the duration of the war, although Egypt was technically neither a belligerent nor an allied power. Draft animals were also confiscated and foodstuffs necessary for the army requisitioned from 1917. Combined with the impact of conscription, and with the paralysis caused by the war to the international trade upon which Egypt's economy had come to depend, the result was severe economic dislocation, and extreme hardship for many sectors of the population.[31]

Pent-up during war-time, these feelings of resentment exploded immediately after the war's end. Egyptians, like so many other colonized and subjugated peoples, were inspired by American President Wilson's promise of self-determination in his Fourteen Points, and by their adoption as Allied war aims. They were thereby encouraged to bear the deprivation which the war brought with it by the hope that in consequence of this pledge, and of the war-time sacrifices the country had made, Egypt would receive its independence as part of the peace settlement. There was outrage among Egyptians when their country was refused representation at the Paris Peace Conference, even though states many Egyptians regarded as less worthy of independence than themselves – such as the Hijaz – received seats at the conference table. When a delegation (*Wafd* in Arabic) of four Egyptian nationalist leaders nevertheless proclaimed its intention to set off for Paris in 1919, and its members were detained by the British in Malta, the response was a violent all-out national revolution under the banner of the *Wafd Party* in March and April of that year. These events shook British rule of the country to its foundations, and ultimately forced Great Britain to grant Egypt limited independence in 1922.[32]

IV

The Egyptian case highlights one of the most important effects of the First World War in the Arab world: the war heightened the expectations of millions of people, and led them to hope that they might gain greater control over their lives. The Fourteen Points were certainly part of this, as were British assurances to Sharif Husayn which constituted part of the correspondence between him and the British High Commissioner in Egypt, Sir Henry McMahon, in 1915 and 1916, whereby Britain agreed to support Arab independence within purposely ill-defined limits, in return for an Arab revolt against the Ottomans.[33] In his negotiations with the British, Sharif Husayn was representing a coalition of Arabist groups in greater Syria who had authorized him to speak on their behalf. The resulting understandings thus became widely known in many parts of the Arab world: even in areas under Ottoman control, Ambara Salam al-Khalidi testifies in her memoirs, leaflets propagating the Sharifís views were dropped by Allied planes.[34]

At the same time as British officials in Egypt were exchanging letters with Sharif Husayn in Mecca, others were engaged in defining post-war British interests in the Middle East with their French and Russian allies. The resulting agreements as they related to the Arab world, the Sykes-Picot accords of 1916, divided Syria and Mesopotamia between France and Great Britain into spheres of influence and zones of direct control which, while not directly contradicting the letter of the Husayn-McMahon correspondence, certainly did not conform with its spirit.

Although they were not published at the time, we have seen that Britain's assurances to Sharif Husayn soon became generally known. Towards the end of the war they were publicly restated and amplified in several documents, notably an Anglo-French joint declaration issued in November 1918 just before the armistice in which the two countries promised the peoples of the Arab world 'complete liberation and the establishment of popular governments which will draw their power from the free choice of the citizens' and encouraged 'the establishment of popular governments in Syria and Iraq, which the allies have already liberated . . . '[35]

It was to be many years before these countries and others 'liberated' from Ottoman rule by Britain and France were to enjoy such conditions, and indeed the gap between these promises and the harsh realities which ensued defined the contested political terrain of the inter-war years in Syria, Lebanon, Iraq, Jordan and Palestine. Palestine requires separate mention, however. For, with the Balfour Declaration of November 1917, Britain had made yet another war-time commitment with regard to Palestine in particular: this was to 'support the establishment in Palestine of a national home for the Jewish people'.

The impact of this pledge in Palestine and other parts of the Arab world can be imagined. Already before 1914 there had developed a strong awareness of and opposition to Zionism in Palestine and other parts of the Arab world.[36] Many pre-war Zionist spokesmen had denied that their movement had as its objective taking control of Palestine away from the Arab majority of its inhabitants (who formed about 92 per cent of the pre-war population of over 720,000).[37] The Balfour Declaration, with its ill-defined terminology (did 'a national home in Palestine' mean the transformation of the entire country into a national home? what precisely was meant by the term 'a national home'?), aroused renewed fears for their future among Palestinians, and started the process of disillusionment with the Allies among the Arabs generally. This process was accelerated in November 1917 when the new Bolshevik regime in Russia released the texts of the

Sykes-Picot accords and other secret war-time agreements between the Allies.[38] The Palestinian educator Khalil al-Sakakini wrote a few years later that the revelation of these accords, combined with the impact of the war itself, had a great impact on Palestine:

> A nation which has long been in the depths of sleep only awakes if it is rudely shaken by events, and only arises little by little . . . This was the situation of Palestine, which for many centuries had been in the deepest sleep, until it was shaken by the Great War, shocked by the Zionist movement, and violated by the illegal policy [of the British], and it awoke, little by little.[39]

There can be little question that the First World War shook Palestine, as it did other parts of the Arab world like Iraq which were also battlefields. But the effect of this shock was intensified by the commitment of Great Britain, the greatest power of its day, to Zionism, which was publicly announced only a few weeks before Allenby's troops entered Jerusalem in December 1917, at a time when it had become clear that the British would be the new rulers of the country. Indeed, it was partly to counter the negative effects in the Arab world of the Balfour Declaration and of the Bolsheviks' revelations regarding the Sykes-Picot accords, effects intensified by the problems which had arisen during a year of uneasy British military occupation of most of Palestine and Iraq, that the Anglo-French declaration of November 1918 was issued.

In the end, most of the high hopes and heady expectations aroused in the Arab world by promises such as those made during the First World War were disappointed. Whether they had fought on the side of the victors, as had the Hijazis and the many Arabs who joined their Arab Legion which helped Allenby's troops capture Damascus[40] (and as had many North Africans in the French forces who found themselves in trenches in Flanders and elsewhere, and many Egyptians in the Labour Corps), whether they had fought in the Ottoman ranks, or whether they had been unwillingly conscripted like the Egyptians, most had little to show for all the sacrifices imposed by the war.

The people of the Arab world, on all sides, had faced an ordeal which had been imposed upon them by others – it was the CUP, the Turks, the Germans, the Allies who had made the decisions which brought the region into the war, not its inhabitants – and at its end few could feel that they had won anything. And much of what appeared to have been gained, whether the right of self-determination promised in the Fourteen Points, or the independent Arab government which ruled Syria for two years until suppressed by the French, was extinguished soon after the war's end.

During the First World War, many parts of the Arab world endured suffering greater than anything in living memory, many people lost their lives, and an era of Islamic rule ended, to be replaced by another era of

European control, sometimes direct, and sometimes under the murky rules of the League of Nations mandate system. But in the end few people were better off than they had been at the outset of the war, and few faced a more certain future. Although the war affected people differently all over the Arab world, for most it was a traumatic experience, as it was for others elsewhere. And in most areas of this region, as in the rest of the world, it ended an era of relative stability and ushered in one of unprecedented turmoil and uncertainty.

Notes

1   For a brief overview of this process, see Albert Hourani, *A History of the Arab Peoples*, Cambridge: Harvard University Press, 1991, pp. 315–319.
2   This is clear from: Djemal Pasha [Cemal Pasa, Commander of the 4th Army], *Memories of a Turkish Statesman, 1913–1919*, London: Hutchinson, 1922, p. 213. Acc. to Eliezer Tauber, *The Arab Movements in World War I*, London: Cass, 1993, p. 59, five of the six divisions of the 4th Army were composed of Arab troops, and the sixth was partly Arab.
3   ibid., pp. 65–66.
4   For details, see ibid., pp. 19–21 and 59–66.
5   Although the Hijaz Railway, lifeline for Ottoman forces in the Hijaz and Yemen, was never cut by repeated raids on it by Arabs, Ottoman troops were forced to garrison its vulnerable length: *Military Operations, Egypt and Palestine*, 2 vols. London: HMSO, 1928; Col. A.P. Wavell, *The Palestine Campaigns: The Campaigns and their Lessons*, London: Constable, 1936. Much credit claimed by T.E. Lawrence for this in *Seven Pillars of Wisdom* and elsewhere, in fact belonged to others, Arabs and British – see Suleiman Mousa, *T.E. Lawrence: an Arab View*, London: OUP, 1966. The vast T.E. Lawrence industry focuses relatively little on what really happened in Western Arabia during the war.
6   These archives contained material incriminating such Lebanese leaders as Saíid 'Aql and Philippe al-Khazin, who had favoured French control of Lebanon, and other much more ambiguous documents, i.e. those re. the former parliamentary deputy for Damascus, Shafiq al-Muíayyad, which were nonetheless used as evidence of treasonous intentions. Ottoman Fourth Army, *'Idāhāt hawla al-ma'ala al-sūriyya* [Clarifications concerning the Syrian question], Istanbul: Tanin, 1916. The title of the French version is *La verité sur la question syrienne*.
7   ibid.
8   For how wide a net Cemal Pasa cast see: memoirs of Muhammad 'Izzat Darwaza, who for over a year during the War hid from the Ottoman authorities after coming under suspicion, *Khamsa wa-tis'īna yawman fī al-hayā: Mudhakirāt wa-tasjīlat* [95 years of life: memoirs and records], eds., Ali Jarbawi and Husam Shakhshir, vol. 1, Jerusalem: Arab Thought Forum, 1993, pp. 261 ff.
9   Tauber, op.cit., p. 54.
10   Bayan Nuwayhid al-Hut, *al-Qiyādāt wal-mu'assasāt al-siyāsiyya fī Filastīn, 1917–1948* [Political leaderships and institutions in Palestine, 1917–1948], Beirut: Institute for Palestine Studies, 1981, pp. 46–52, discusses the cases of

nine leading Palestinian personalities executed by the Ottoman authorities or who died in prison after trial on similar charges, most of them after 1916.

11 A 'revisionist' trend in Arab historiography rejects this nationalist version, treating these individuals as traitors working for foreign powers: see Wajih Kawtharani, *Bilād al-shām*, Beirut: Ma'had al-Inmā', 1981.

12 Tauber, op.cit., p. 37. Cit. article by Cemal's aide.

13 Ambara Salam al-Khalidi, *Jawla fil-dhikrayat bayna Lubnān wa Filastīn* [A journey through memories between Lebanon and Palestine], Beirut: al-Nahar, 1979, pp. 103–104.

14 *Memories of a Turkish Statesman*, pp. 197 ff.

15 Justin McCarthy, *The Population of Palestine: Population Statistics of the Late Ottoman Period and the Mandate*, New York: Columbia University Press, 1990, pp. 25–27, points out that by contrast, in spite of horrendous losses, only 1% of the French population was lost during the Great War, during which England and Germany 'suffered no loss of total population'.

16 Tauber, op.cit., p. 37. The same estimates for the Beirut and Damascus provinces range as high as 150,000 and 300,000 respectively.

17 al-Khalidi, *Jawla fil-dhikrayat*, pp. 106 ff.

18 R. Khalidi, *British Policy Towards Syria and Palestine, 1906–1914*, London: Ithaca Press, 1980, chs. 5 and 6 deal with this period.

19 See R. Khalidi, 'Ottomanism and Arabism in Syria before 1914: A Reassessment', in R. Khalidi, Lisa Anderson, Reeva Simon and Muhammad Muslih, eds., *The Origins of Arab Nationalism*, New York: Columbia University Press, 1991, pp. 50–69.

20 For more on the Turkish nationalism of the CUP at a very early stage, even before it came to power, see Sukru Hanioglu, 'The Young Turks and the Arabs before the Revolution of 1908,' in R. Khalidi et. al., eds., *The Origins of Arab Nationalism*, pp. 31–49; and his book, *The Young Turks in Opposition*, New York: OUP, 1995.

21 For propaganda along these lines, see Muhammad Kurd 'Ali, *al-Rahla al-Anwariyya'ilā al-isqā' al-Hijāziyaa wal-Shāmiyya* [Enver's visit to the lands of Hijaz and Syria], Beirut: al-Matbaa al-'Ilmiyya, 1334/1916, a fawning description of a visit by the 'first man of the Ottomans, hero of Islam and the Muslims, His Highness and His Excellency, Enver Pasa, Deputy Commander-in-Chief, Minister of War, to al-Medina, Syria and Palestine'. A similar work, *al-Ba'tha al-'ilmiyya' ila Dār al-Khilāfa al-islāmiyya* [A learned visit to the seat of the Islamic Caliphate], Beirut: al-Matba'a al-'Ilmiyya, 1334/1916, describes a visit to Istanbul and the Dardanelles front by a group of Syrian religious dignitaries with four Arab journalists: Muhammad al-Baqir, owner of al-Balāgh, Kurd 'Ali, owner of al-Muqtabas, Husayn al-Habbal, owner of Abābil, and 'Abd al-Basit an-Unsi, owner of Iqbal, all of whom also published glowing reports of Ottoman military accomplishments in their papers: for details, see Darwaza Memoirs in *Khamsa wa-tis'ūna yawman*, p. 265.

22 G. Antonius, *The Arab Awakening*, London: Hamish Hamilton, 1938, p. 191.

23 Darwaza, in *Khamsa wa-tis'ūna yawman*, p. 261, and al-Khalidi, *Jawla fil-dhikrayat*, pp. 94 ff., on the shock re the 1916 executions in particular.

24 An example is Gaza, scene of heavy fighting in 1917 which destroyed the city's ancient Islamic court records. These currently date from December 1917: see

Beshara Doumani, 'Palestinian Islamic Court Records: A Source for Socioeconomic History,' *MESA Bulletin*, 19, 1975, pp. 166–67.

25 See R. Khalidi, 'The Press as a Source for Modern Arab Political History,' *Arab Studies Quarterly*, 3, 1, Winter, 1981, pp. 22–42.

26 Ami Ayalon, *The Press in the Arab Middle East: A History*, Oxford: OUP, 1995, p. 71, citing Amin Saíid, *al-Thawra al-'arabiyya al-kubrā* [The great Arab revolt], Cairo: Dar al-íIlm lil-Malayin, 1934, vol. I, pp. 58–92.

27 Ayalon, *The Press in the Arab Middle East*, p. 69.

28 R. Khalidi, British Policy Towards Syria and Palestine, chs. 1 and 2, deals with the strategic aftermath of the 'Aqaba incident of 1906, which first alerted British planners to this possibility.

29 i.e. in May 1915 before one of the assaults on the Canal, the Ottoman authorities published a 10-pp. propaganda pamphlet, in Arabic 'Sahifa min tarikh ingiltera fi-Misr' [A page from this history of the English in Egypt], and in English 'Lest We Forget: A Page from the History of the English in Egypt'. It contains 6 pictures (suppressed earlier by the British) of the 1906 executions in Dinshwai, Egypt, of peasants blamed for the death of a British officer from heat-stroke after an altercation over the shooting of the villagers' pigeons. This had caused widespread unrest. Khalidi Library, Jerusalem.

30 Lord Lloyd, *Egypt after Cromer*, vol. I, London: Macmillan, 1933, pp. 237–238.

31 For the impact of these measures, see ibid., also Mahmoud Zayid, *Egypt's Struggle for Independence*, Beirut: Khayat, 1965, pp. 63–79, and Jacques Berque, *Egypt, Imperialism and Revolution*, London: Faber, 1972, pp. 269 ff.

32 ibid., as well as Lloyd, *Egypt after Cromer*, pp. 280–313.

33 The political/scholarly debate on this subject is vast: see, e.g., Antonius, *The Arab Awakening*; A.L. Tibawi, *Anglo-Arab Relations and the Question of Palestine, 1914–1921*, London: Luzac, 1977; and Elie Kedourie, *In the Anglo-Arab Labyrinth*, London: Weidenfeld & Nicolson, 1977.

34 al-Khalidi, *Jawla fil-dhikrayāt*, p. 118.

35 Text is in J.C. Hurewitz, ed. *The Middle East and North Africa in World Politics*, New Haven: Yale University Press, 1979, vol. 2, pp. 111–112. A copy of the communiqué distributed by the Muslim-Christian Association in Jerusalem, by order of the British Military Governor in Jerusalem, 7 November, 1918 can be found in the uncatalogued papers, Khalidi Library, Jerusalem, showing the widespread diffusion of this declaration.

36 See Neville Mandel, *Arab Reactions to Zionism 1882–1914*, Berkeley: University of California Press, 1986; and R. Khalidi, 'The Role of the Press in the Early Arab Reaction to Zionism,' *Peuples Mediterraneans/ Mediterranean Peoples*, 20 (July-Sept. 1982), pp. 105–124.

37 Population figures from McCarthy, *The Population of Palestine*, pp. 25–27.

38 See Hurewitz, ed., *The Middle East and North Africa*, pp. 108–110.

39 Khalil al-Sakakini, *Filāstin ba'd al-ḥarb al-kubrā* [Palestine after the great War], Jerusalem: Bayt al-Maqdis Press, 1925, p. 9. (a collection of articles originally published in the Cairo newspaper al-Siyasa, 1923).

40 Did the British or Arab forces enter Damascus first? Acc. recently, to Tauber, op.cit., pp. 231–238, Australian (perhaps an hour earlier) and Arab forces entered the city from different directions on the morning of 1 October 1918.

Chapter 47

The Experience of Yugoslav Agitation in Austria–Hungary, 1917–1918

Mark Cornwall

It was the wartime experience in the southern regions of the Habsburg Empire which made possible the creation of a new Yugoslav state in 1918. Until 1917 the principal centres agitating for unification of Serbs, Croats and Slovenes in an independent state were outside the Monarchy: namely the exiled Serbian government based on Corfu, which chiefly thought in terms of a Greater Serbia; and the Yugoslav Committee of exiled southern Slav politicians from Austria, who were based mainly in London and dreamt of a new unitary Yugoslav structure. From the second half of 1917 they were matched by a third centre of agitation within the Monarchy itself. Although this third centre was stimulated and interacted to some extent with those abroad,[1] it is generally agreed that the launch-pad for the new movement was the 'May Declaration', of 30 May 1917, by the 33 southern Slav politicians in the Austrian Parliament. Taking advantage of the new forum created when Emperor Karl at last reconvened the Reichsrat in April, and stimulated particularly by the example of their Czech comrades, the southern Slav leaders in this statement attacked the stale dualist structure of the Empire by demanding unity for Serbs, Croats and Slovenes in a special democratic entity under the Habsburg dynasty. This was the start of the 'declaration movement' which in the next eighteen months spread out of Slovene regions and into Dalmatia, Croatia and Bosnia-Hercegovina. There is, as a leading Slovene historian noted recently, no full history of this crucial movement.[2] Yet by 1918 it was specifically in the face of this agitation that all southern Slav clergy, politicians and civilians within Austria-Hungary had to take some stand – positive or negative – with regard to a future Yugoslav structure. The movement, moreover, had notable characteristics. First, it was inspired especially by Slovenes, notably the leader of the Yugoslav Club in the Reichsrat, Monsignor Anton Korošec, something which caused one

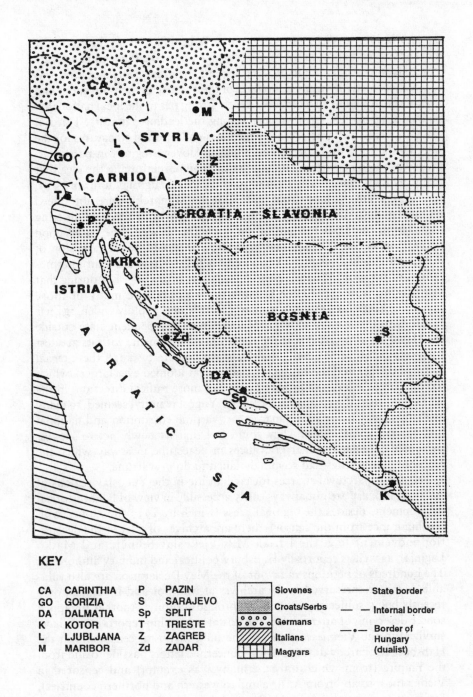

(viii)   The Southern Slav regions of Austria–Hungary.

657

military lawyer in Vienna to surmise that radical Slovenes ('the culturally most advanced nation of the South Slavs') would take the lead in a future Yugoslav state.[3] Second, in Slovene regions the grass-roots agitation was conducted chiefly by women, because of the absence of their husbands and sons at the front and also because of their strong ties to the local nationally-minded Catholic clergy who were among the leading agitators. Third, it was a movement characterized by the mass-collection of signatures for the May Declaration and later mass-rallies; in Slovene regions in particular, there was popular participation in the campaign, reinforcing the idea that many civilians consciously desired to enter some Yugoslav unit. In 1917, the various Slovene and Croat leaders of the Monarchy were not agreed on the regions to be included in this Yugoslav unit, and also held differing ideas about the basis for unification – whether it would be based upon natural rights (on the 'national principle') or would be an extension of 'Croat state rights' (as many Croats envisaged).[4] These different interpretations of the word 'Yugoslav' did not disappear in 1918. But during that year as the war experience became more oppressive many of those favouring Yugoslav unity – in whatever form – were rapidly widening their horizons to think more in terms of unity in an independent state outside the Habsburg Empire. It was the declaration movement, with its greatest successes in 'Slovenia', Istria and Dalmatia (where by 1918 the internal German danger and the external Italian threat loomed ever larger), which led the Yugoslavs of the Empire in an ever more radical direction. In the war's final year, the campaign for tighter Yugoslav unity, seemed, to many civilians experiencing it, a panacea for wartime corruption and national and economic insecurity. They could feel that its newly active spokespersons would satisfy their grievances in peacetime in a way which the Habsburg authorities had seemingly failed to do in wartime.

The diverse archival sources for civilian life in the Yugoslav regions of Austria-Hungary are not always easily accessible in view of later historical development. Besides the regional press (which by 1917 functioned with less hindrance from the censor), there are archives of part of the declaration movement (e.g. the Istrian MPs Vjekoslav Spinčić and Matko Laginja), as well as reports by Habsburg political and military authorities. The hundreds of petitions in favour of the May Declaration are also valuable; many are preserved in the archives at Maribor and Ljubljana, only recently being subjected to a more thorough scrutiny. Another untapped source deserving of attention are the postal censorship reports which have survived in the Viennese archives. The bulk of postal censorship in the Habsburg Monarchy during the war concerned letters passing to and from the Empire (from which only Germany was exempt) and censored in Vienna (post to and from Austria and to western and northern countries), Budapest (post to and from Hungary and in a Balkan direction), and at Feldkirch on the Swiss border for material passing to and from

Switzerland. Each of the three centres produced monthly reports, including usually a section on southern Slav correspondence. However, most internal post in the Empire was, as in Italy, immune from censorship. Exceptions were Bosnia-Herçegovina and Dalmatia, from 1915 under the control of Baron Stjepan Sarkotić, where an attempt was still made to control all correspondence. The post in Bosnia was censored at Sarajevo; for Dalmatia, at Split, Zadar, Kotor and Metković. This undoubtedly yielded useful Intelligence for the military authorities, but it also came up against the inevitable issue of suitable manpower: by August 1918 Sarkotić was complaining that women staff were unsatisfactory.[5] From May 1915 certain regions in the rear of the Italian front had been designated as part of the 'war zone', in which civilian correspondence was subject to censorship: they included the southern Slav regions of Istria, Gorizia, part of Carniola, the Modrus-Rijeka komitat of Croatia and the northern islands off the Croatian coast. Censor offices scattered around this region (e.g. Trieste, Pazin, Pula and Krk), sent monthly reports to the military intelligence centre at Udine, providing a valuable picture for 1918 of a civilian population in dire economic straits which was succumbing increasingly to radical Yugoslav agitation. The censors' reports as a whole clearly outline the grass-roots trend in the south of Austria-Hungary from 1917. While in June 1917 all the censors could portray the southern Slavs as 'thoroughly loyal', a year later the Vienna censor office painted a gloomy picture for the south: the Yugoslav issue was now the main talking-point, with most Slovene and Croat letters protesting at arbitrary government measures and hardly any containing a patriotic note.[6]

Economic misery was important in the success of the declaration movement because it stimulated radicalism. As the Entente's blockade began to bite, the Monarchy's grain production diminished (by over 40 per cent in the war years)[7] and became ever more unevenly divided up among the Monarchy's regions. While Austria's 'bread-basket' in Galicia was under Russian occupation until August 1917, leaving her dependent largely on Hungary for making good her grain deficiencies, Hungary (including Croatia-Slavonia) remained self-sufficient and always looked to her own needs first. There was no equality of rationing and no attempts were made to equalize prices until the middle of 1918. As the Empire increasingly ceased to act as an economic unit, it was only Croatia – of the southern Slav regions – which held its head above water. In May 1917, General Ottokar Landwehr, newly appointed to the thankless task of co-ordinating the Monarchy's food supplies, travelled by train to Zagreb: he passed only women and children working in the fields, but noted good bread available at the stations. He found however the Ban, Ivan Skerlecz, unwilling to tighten rationing within the kingdom, let alone supply food to Bosnia (as the Hungarian Prime Minister, Count Tisza, had recommended).[8] A year later when Landwehr returned to Zagreb he could still observe confidently that 'everything swims in fat and the black-market blossoms';[9] although it was now forbidden to sell bread in public places, much of Croatia was still suffering less than elsewhere, as evidenced by the migrant beggars from Istria or Bosnia who loitered around the railway stations.[10] By this time at least the new Ban of Croatia, Antun Mihalovich (picked by the Emperor out of the Croatian Parliament – the Sabor), was more receptive to the idea of sharp requisitioning; he promised, for example, to supply forty waggons of macaroni, potatoes and fat, with the express hope that it would be used to relieve suffering in Istria, Dalmatia and Bosnia. Mihalovich's concern for these neighbouring 'Croat lands' reflected his own 'southern Slav sympathies'; when appointed as Ban in June 1917 he had made a stirring speech to the Sabor that his government would be 'democratic and Croat', defending the interests of all Croat people.[11] By early summer 1918, Landwehr felt there was a fast-accelerating Yugoslav band-waggon in Croatia, on which Mihalovich himself (perceiving Yugoslav unity largely in pan-Croatian terms) had already climbed.[12]

In contrast to most of Croatia, the population in southern Austria and in Bosnia had been living from hand to mouth for years, their poverty exacerbated by wartime economic inefficiency. In June 1917, for example, maps produced by the Vienna censor office on the basis of censored correspondence, revealed cases of famine in most towns in southern Styria, Istria, Dalmatia, south-west Bosnia and the islands.[13] The maps also correctly predicted bad harvests in these regions for the summer of 1917. As Anton Korošec noted a few months later, the barley harvest yielded only 51,000 waggons compared to 85,000 in 1916, the oats harvest only 76,000 waggons compared to 138,000 the previous year: Austria, in his view, was faced with a food catastrophe.[14] The Yugoslav Club in the Reichsrat made regular loud protests about the chronic lack of food supplies to the south. On the one hand they attacked Hungary's attitude: according to the vociferous deputy Karel Verstovšek, 'our Slovene nation has always had only the feeblest impression of the Magyars. We wished from of old that all Slavs should be separated from those "hunnish" people ... Because of their economic exploitation the Magyars are the most hated people among all Austrians irrespective of nationality'.[15] On the other hand, as the deputies complained, the situation was compounded by inefficiency or corruption on the spot. Korošec, having visited Bosnia on a fact-finding mission in the summer of 1917, made regular attacks on the Sarkotić regime, including the Baron's ignorance of economics.[16] In reality Bosnia could not survive on its own resources even in peacetime (and now needed to be bailed out by Hungary); its economy suffered from a weak workforce, a series of bad harvests, and villagers who vehemently opposed requisitioning to aid cities like Sarajevo or Mostar.[17] This situation was very similar to that in Austria. There the southern Slav politicians regularly complained that through strict requisitioning, the countryside of Carinthia or Istria was constantly exploited, benefiting urban areas (such as Ljubljana or Trieste); meanwhile, in Istria and Dalmatia many rural supply centres or supply routes (served by steamers on the Adriatic for example) had ceased to function. On top of this was an inequality of prices which could only encourage smuggling and profiteering: stories were rife of intrepid Istrian women who visited Trieste to barter their local produce in return for bread, or tried to smuggle more attractive merchandise back across the border from Croatia.[18]

This situation slowly worsened during the last year of war. While in 1917 economic issues were certainly taking precedence in censored correspondence, by mid-1918 90 per cent of the letters handled at Vienna and Feldkirch concerned food problems.[19] The local experience, to give one example, is revealed in correspondence from Pazin [Mitterburg], high up in the centre of Istria. The joy of the inhabitants of Pazin at a visit from the Emperor in April 1918 was undoubtedly short-lived. In late May the Pazin censor told of 47 deaths from starvation and summed up: 'the plight is so great that people are forced to live on wild plants, water and some milk without bread and this, coupled with terribly high prices for even the most basic foodstuffs, steadily increases the exasperation of the population'.[20] A month later the censor reported that 'food provisioning' in central Istria had broken down completely, producing starvation and some suicides: the local inhabitants, while placing all hope on the forthcoming harvest, were cutting even half-ripe grain to make flour and 'preparing for their meals not only nettles but also all kinds of edible and inedible grasses'.[21] In the words of one correspondent, a chemist's wife in the coastal town of Rovinj, 'the land looks as if the enemy had destroyed everything, dried up and contaminated . . . People wander around like ghosts, dead from hunger . . . [but] one minister has said, "the people down there should get used to starving and dying"'.[22] Not surprisingly, the Istrian peninsula by this time was one of the most fertile areas where the declaration movement could take root; agitation flourished wherever civilians felt most threatened, either personally or nationally, by the war.

The movement[23] had only begun in early autumn 1917 because of the negative attitude of the Austrian government. The Yugoslav Club had at first been hopeful, especially after the Emperor's amnesty for political prisoners (including some of their own number), that their May Declaration would gain a fair hearing. But any goodwill from the court (to which Korošec later declared he had an 'open door') was offset by the consistent view of Ernst von Seidler's Germanophile government, that only some national autonomy for the Slovenes could be permitted but certainly no restructuring of Dualism.[24] By August 1917 the Club was in opposition in the Reichsrat. There were already signs of scattered support for the declaration around 'Slovenia' – the first hints of the declaration movement.[25] But, as the Feldkirch reported, public opinion as yet seemed rather unclear, waiting on events.[26] The real impetus to a mass-movement – what turned almost into a plebiscite among the Slovene civilian population – came only with the public statement of support from Bishop Anton Jeglič of Ljubljana. Jeglič's statement, signed by a number of clergy and politicians and published in the radical Slovene press on 15 September, expressed solidarity with the peace initiative of Pope Benedict XV as well as with the Yugoslav Club: and above all, it finally alerted broad swathes of the population to the May Declaration.[27] It is clear that Jeglič, and perhaps even Korošec and other members of the Club, continued for a long time to view the declaration as a demand for Yugoslav unity within the Habsburg Empire rather than in an independent state. Looking back in July 1920, Jeglič insisted that he had always been a loyal Austrian, disgusted at those working against Austria, but at the same time he had long hoped for some kind of Yugoslav unity. He therefore perceived the May Declaration as an opportunity which he had to seize, to protect the southern Slavs internally (especially against German dominance), but at the same time to strengthen Austria's position in the south against external threats (notably Italy):

> I felt that all would be lost and we would be powerless if at this propitious moment we did not rise up; I acted so that all parties would sign. My signature was authoritative and started the movement which made Yugoslavia possible. Thank God that He guided everything in such a way that my steps at the end of the war were completely legalized.[28]

Korošec too would later marvel at the push which Jeglič's statement gave towards southern Slav unity.[29] From October 1917 parish councils in Carniola – the only pure Slovene crownland – began to announce adherence to the May Declaration, and a machinery of mass signature-gathering began to grind into action. The high-point of this process was late 1917 and spring 1918, for from March the movement changed tactics and developed into a series of mass-rallies in support of the May Declaration.

Historians have tended to view the declaration itself as increasingly a legal cloak under which a more radical agitation was fermenting during 1918. In other words, the agitators paid lip-service to a declaration loyal to the Habsburgs while actually working towards an independent Yugoslav state outside the Empire. However, the latest research by a Slovene historian, Vlasta Stavbar, suggests a more complex series of motives inspiring those who signed or supported statements backing the declaration.[30] She implies, on the basis of hundreds of statements contained in the archives at Maribor, that many of the signatories continued to feel strong allegiance to the Habsburg dynasty as well as to the concept of Yugoslav unity. True, some may have signed with a more radical political design in mind, while some were simply jumping on a band-waggon of war-generated social distress, demanding peace or protesting at taxes on wine or grain requisitioning. But others may well have experienced Bishop Jeglič's crisis of conscience – torn between loyalty to Austria and to Yugoslav unity. Indeed, one is tempted to suggest that if the Slovene regions had been more carefully handled by Vienna as late as mid-1918, they could have been saved for some future Austrian state.

On the evidence of Stavbar's research, the main declaration movement started first in Carniola in the wake of Jeglič's statement. In one village the inhabitants added their personal feelings to the basic declaration as follows: 'we love the Habsburg Monarchy; and for that reason we demand for her peoples their own statehood and for us Yugoslavs our own independent state within her, for only thus can the Monarchy continue'.[31] On the whole, however, the statements sent into the Yugoslav Club from Carniola were made primarily by parish councils, over a period of six months or more. Over half the councils of this crownland finally adhered to the declaration.[32] Their number seems to have been weakened firstly because part of Carniola remained in the war zone, subject to military vigilance, and secondly because of the influence of the controversial MP Ivan Šušteršić who by late 1917 had left the Yugoslav Club, insistent that the pure May Declaration was the maximum demand for the Empire's South Slavs.

In southern Styria, Korošec's home-base, particularly because of the proximity of the German language border, the movement was livelier than in Carniola but at times more cautious. According to Stavbar, 70 per cent of parish councils adhered to the declaration while over 70,000 signatures were collected, chiefly of women and girls; the statements revealed more individual initiative than in Carniola, as many were handwritten rather than signed printed texts.[33] Many statements contained a special Habsburg clause (such as 'Long live Yugoslavia, long live our Emperor Karl!' or 'Long live the beloved Habsburg dynasty and happy Yugoslavia under its glorious sceptre!'). Mass-meetings from the spring of 1918 also seemed at first to be spontaneously loyal. At one in March, when Korošec spoke about the wonderful Yugoslav future, the mass cry went up, 'we want to be free in a great Habsburg Yugoslavia'; at another, as late as 21 April, the final resolution still mentioned the Habsburg clause of the May Declaration.[34] Although Slovene anxiety in Styria about German opposition or intimidation was often noticeable, one statement sent to Korošec in January by 558 women from near Maribor remained optimistic:

> With regard to the audacious plan of our religious and national opponents who wish with the help of the [German] *Schulverein* (*Südmark*) to seize by force our beautiful Slovene lands which have been owned by the Slovene people for centuries, we are inspired by the thought of unification of all the Yugoslav regions of Austria-Hungary [under the Habsburg

sceptre], with the cheerful hope that all the efforts of our national enemies will be in vain.[35]

The German threat, however, seemed especially dangerous to the Slovenes of Carinthia who from the war's start had been under a severe German administration. As Pleterski's excellent analysis shows, German persecution in Carinthia and Styria was a 'crucial mass political experience' making numerous Slovenes conscious of the peril to their national existence should Austria–Hungary win the war.[36] Even after May 1917 when the Emperor had restored constitutional rule to most of Austria, the *Statthalter* of Carinthia, Count Lodron, a German nationalist speaking no Slovene, was determined to suppress the declaration movement: the only Carinthian Slovene MP, Franc Grafenauer, remained in prison for 'treasonable statements' and the Slovene press remained strictly censored. Rallies were banned,[37] and only ten parishes actively declared their support. Yet 19,000 signatures were collected – perhaps over 20% of the Slovene population. Lodron dismissively asserted that most Slovenes had little idea about what they were signing. Certainly, there may have been abuses in the gathering of signatures, while some villagers simply signed on seeing their clergy's adherence.[38] Against this must be set Pleterski's analysis of those statements preserved in the Ljubljana archives, showing individual grievances, widespread among Slovene inhabitants of Carinthia,[39] against the war and German aggressiveness.

Indeed, on the whole it seems possible from the evidence to characterise the declaration movement as a broad church within which thousands of Slovene civilians by 1918 were expressing their frustrations at the wartime experience and sometimes their national aspirations as well. As the Feldkirch censor noted in April, ordinary people who 'normally ignored such things' had been indoctrinated with the main ideas of the declaration; this was clear from the correspondence of the lower classes and even working women, who were 'not tired of asserting that everyone fights for "Yugoslavia", admonishing their relatives and friends in neutral foreign countries to remain true to the Slovene cause in mind and heart'.[40] The gendarmerie commander at Celje concurred in the same month that the agitation was unstoppable: 'it includes all people without distinction of party bias . . . the agitationary work has been skilfully organized and skilfully executed. People who lived in peace up to now have been shaken to the core'.[41] In the face of the movement, the Habsburg authorities in most areas remained relatively powerless. Already in February 1918 the *Statthalter* of Carniola, Count Attems, warned the Ministry of Interior about a phenomenon which seemed to be spreading into all Yugoslav regions and all layers of the population. However, not only were Korošec and his comrades protected by parliamentary immunity, but a legal ruling in February announced that the agitation – because of the Habsburg clause – was still within the law. Count Lodron's arbitrary behaviour was therefore rather exceptional, preempting the Minister of Interior who only on 12 May forbade further meetings or agitation in support of the May Declaration.[42]

This ban was prompted by events in Ljubljana where the agitation, as well as feeding off basic social grievances, was beginning to infect the armed forces. On 22–24 April spontaneous food demonstrations had occurred in the city. Many of the demonstrators displayed their Yugoslav sympathies, directing their frustration against Ivan Šušteršić, the Reichsrat deputy who still advocated loyalty to the Habsburg state, as well as against German property. According to Attems, whose office was invaded by 200 Slovene women,

> Through systematic agitation in the press and in meetings dealing in essence with the Yugoslav question, a great mass of inflammable material has been brought together; it has now blazed up, on the one hand against the head of the provincial diet [Šušteršić] and on the other against Germans.

Even more important was the fact that Slovene troops of the 2nd Gebirgsschützenregiment had refused to move against the rioters, clear evidence for the military authorities that 'Yugoslav propaganda' was beginning to enter the armed forces.[43] A military investigation revealed that, a few evenings before the disturbances, two officers of the regiment had been heard shouting Yugoslav and treasonable slogans in the streets of Ljubljana. The local military commanders were quite clear that the blame lay with the Korošec party because:

> 'many men – even the companies who left in April – wore national (tricolour) ribbons and cockades on the march to the railway station; furthermore, because of cases of seditious utterances in recent times, and finally because sundry supporting battalions have not behaved with sufficient energy on 24 April . . . Everybody was agreed on one point: that the agitation originates with a section of the Slovene clergy, incited and supported by the Bishop [Jeglič]; the rural population is only roused with difficulty and reluctantly, whereas the urban population – first and foremost, part of the educated classes and the younger generation – follows more willingly.[44]

Reports such as this led the Austrian Defence Minister, Feldmarshall Czapp (who had always wanted the movement suppressed), to warn the Austrian cabinet on 1 May of 'the unbridled agitation of the Korošec party, which is beginning to react in a demoralizing way upon Slovene troops also'.[45] The politicians quickly bowed to military pressure. The declaration movement was officially banned on 12 May, and both Emperor Karl and Ernst von Seidler at this time publicly refuted the idea that Slovene regions would be allowed to join any Yugoslav union or even be permitted to form a Slovene unit within Austria. These official decisions, however, were no longer enforceable. Indeed, the speeches by the Emperor and the Prime Minister (who was himself veering ever more upon a 'German course') simply confirmed for the Slovene leaders that, in their quest for national security through southern Slav unity, they could expect no help from Vienna: they were therefore pushed in a more radical direction, to seek unity outside the Habsburg Empire.[46]

Nor could their increasingly radical agitation be prevented. The security forces were not strong enough to enforce the ban, with the result that in the early summer dozens of mass-meetings continued to be held.

On 2 July, for example, at a large, officially-prohibited gathering in Vrhnika, Korošec was able to address large crowds from a hotel balcony while local gendarmes were prevented from acting. Later at the railway station, Korošec attributed the rally's tremendous success largely to the government's wisdom in banning it, for that had simply increased enthusiasm as well as confirming the need for a constitutional Yugoslav state.[47] Although the authorities were suitably alarmed, Korošec himself was quite free, inspiring Slovene women to wear his portrait in a locket upon their breast; at the same time, the pulpits of southern Styria and Carniola were now entirely devoted to spreading 'anti-state propaganda'.[48] A further alarming sign was that the security forces themselves were not immune from the 'Korošec agitation'. When six military revolts occurred in the hinterland in late May, the basic causes were war-weariness, inadequate food and leave, and the influence of troops who had recently returned from Russian captivity. But the three rebellions involving Slovene soldiers – at Judenburg, Murau and Radkersburg (all in Styria) – all contained some nationalist ingredient through direct or indirect contact with domestic agitation; while the mayor of Radkersburg attributed everything to Korošec's treasonable activity, in Judenburg 130 men in one battalion were found to be subscribing to Slovene nationalist newspapers.[49] The real danger was that domestic agitation was also reaching troops at the front, who might also respond to it by deserting or rebelling. As yet, the incidence of open Slovene or Croat insubordination in the front-line seems to have been small (especially in comparison to the Czechs or Poles). But several notorious cases of intrigue and desertion to Italy – particularly those of one Slovene officer, Ljudevit Pivko, in September 1917 and several Croat officers of the 42nd Honvéd infantry division in May 1918[50] – amply confirmed military fears that the 'agitation by men of the stamp of a Korošec or Verstovšek' was slowly spreading poison into the war zone as well.[51]

The agitation in 'Slovenia' was to climax in mid-August in the famous 'Slav days' in Ljubljana. There, in defiance of the authorities, a National Council of Austria's South Slavs was proclaimed, part of a future, wider national council which would work towards Yugoslav unity.[52] Korošec read out a letter from Bishop Jeglič urging those assembled to continue to fight for the May Declaration. But as one police report noted, 'the birthday of the Emperor was not mentioned. It appears that Dr Korošec intentionally chose 17 August for the Slav gathering.[53]

The Slovene lands witnessed the most overt and extensive Yugoslav agitation during 1918. For the Slovene civilians' experience of war was not simply characterised by a food crisis and the absence of loved ones: it also meant, for the more educated, recognizing that Italy had clear designs upon Slovene territory and, in particular, that the Germans of Austria (from their Easter programme of 1916) were determined to shore-up their position at Slovene and Czech expense. Combined, these personal and national anxieties gave great force to the declaration movement in 'Slovenia'.

For the same reasons, agitation by Slovene-Croat clergy and teachers under the guidance of Reichsrat deputies was particularly successful in the more southerly Austrian crownlands. In Istria, for example, on 7 April a national gathering summoned by the Reichsrat deputy Vjekoslav Spinčić voted for Yugoslav unity.[54] Spinčić and his fellow Croat Matko Laginja – both members of the Starčević party with its main base in Croatia – had been very active in the Istrian peninsula, supported in their agitation by the local press and the dire food conditions. The provincial gendarmerie commander suggested in late May that although these deputies had managed to convince the inhabitants of Volosca by their propaganda, in general the Istrian population was showing little interest.[55] But that this was a fallacy is now evident from Stavbar's research, which shows that at least 15,000 signatures were collected in the peninsula in early 1918.[56] It is also clear from the censored correspondence. This was revealing reasonable support (over 2,000 signatures) for the movement in the northern islands, where strong backing came from the influential Croat Bishop of Krk [Veglia], Antun Mahnić.[57] But also among the starving people of Pazin, the censor noted in June that

> there is a very lively interest in the South Slav Declaration. In the correspondence of intelligent people there are more detailed statements about it, while in that of the less educated one reads only short allusions like the greeting 'Long live Yugoslavia'.[58]

Three months later, the censor observed ever stronger support for the declaration in central Istria, and joy at news of the National Council founded in Ljubljana:

> The people are convinced that [the declaration] will be realized and therefore expect a better future. They have full confidence in the Reichsrat deputies and are pleased that they have finally chosen the radical path . . . The national struggle between Croats, Slovenes and

Italians has ceased – all hatred is directed against the Germans and Magyars.[59]

The story was the same further south in Dalmatia, where the movement was perhaps even more strongly stimulated by the leaders of the Yugoslav Club. According to the *Statthalter* in Zadar, already in March 1918 the Slovene leadership enjoyed a great reputation in Dalmatia with the result that educated people had certainly decided for Yugoslav unity – but still within the Habsburg Empire.[60] We know that over 16,000 signatures were collected in this crownland with statements of support from such unlikely sources as the Croat reading-room in the Serb bastion of Knin.[61] In early April Anton Korošec himself visited Split, having received a petition and invitation from 7,000 of its inhabitants. A few days later the amnestied Dalmation MP Ante Tresić-Pavičić finally arrived and was given a tumultuous welcome: about 2,000 people assembled with cries of 'Long live Croatia in a united Yugoslav state'; while students unfurled the Yugoslav tricolour.[62] The armed forces too were not immune from this atmosphere. A few months earlier, the serious naval mutiny at Kotor [Cattaro] had in fact had few nationalist overtones: both General Sarkotić and the naval authorities had wrongly assumed close links to Ljubljana.[63] But in April 1918 the military authorities noted that some men on leave had taken part in the rallies to welcome Tresić-Pavičić, while in one reserve battalion in Dalmatia the men had worn Yugoslav rather than Habsburg colours on the Empress's birthday (7 May).[64] Although still able to check these individual cases of military insubordination, it was the case as elsewhere that the authorities no longer had the resources or the powers to control more widespread subversion. Despite repeated requests from Sarkotić there was no state police in Dalmatia, nor registration offices for inhabitants in Split or the other coastal towns; as a result hundreds of deserters could hide undetected amongst the civilian population. The fact also that the *Statthalter* of Dalmatia allowed freedom of assembly and a rather lax censorship law impeded military efforts to curtail Yugoslav agitation.[65] On 2 July, Croat and Serb delegates from all parts of Dalmatia were able to assemble at Split, announce their goal of an independent Yugoslav state and form a committee to agitate in this direction.[66]

Turning to Croatia and Bosnia, in both, as abroad,[67] there were echoes of the declaration movement – or the 'Korošec movement' as many termed it. But in both, the political environment and the geographical location prevented the type of widespread agitation witnessed in Austria. In Croatia, compared to 'Slovenia', the political parties were less united and – more importantly – lacked the grass-roots organization so characteristic of Slovene Catholic politics. The ruling Serb-Croat Coalition, although its origins lay in the explicit rejection of the dualist system, declined to embrace the May Declaration and preferred to wait on opportunity until October 1918. Instead it was the small Starčević party, forming only a seventh of deputies in the Croatian Sabor but with vociferous representatives also in Austria (Spinčić and Laginja), which picked up the Yugoslav torch; on 5 June 1917 its leader, Ante Pavelić, had welcomed the declaration and proceeded to announce that a campaign would be waged inside and outside the Sabor for its fulfilment.[68] In the following months it was the Starčević party which became the 'axis for rallying and co-ordinating' the new policy, both within Croatia, where it was joined by some prominent Serb defectors from the Coalition, and outside, in strengthening ties to the Yugoslav Club.[69] However, the initiative for mobilizing the masses still lay chiefly with the Yugoslav Club because of the Coalition's continued reserve. That the Coalition was a major obstacle was clearly revealed when members of the Club and the Starčević party met in Zagreb on 2–3 March 1918: although the idea of 'national councils' developed from this meeting, the Slovene leaders saw little purpose at this time in making a new joint declaration with Croatian representatives because of the lack of consensus in Croatia itself. To some extent the same reasoning underlay Korosec's moves in the early summer. By then, more Coalition supporters were defecting (notably at a public assembly of intellectuals on 12 May) and the volatile Peasant party leader, Stjepan Radić, had 'crossed the Rubicon of his political career' by announcing his adherence to the May Declaration.[70] But Korošec still decided to forge ahead with a National Council in Ljubljana, rather than waiting for some joint initiative in Zagreb; as one radical newspaper reported, the Slovenes 'who have the longest and most threatened national border, cannot wait for conditions in the Banovina [Croatia-Slavonia] to clear up completely'.[71]

In Croatia, therefore, there was lacking that clear political lead and focus which was provided in Austria by the Slovene People's party under the banner of the May Declaration and stimulated by apparent threats to Slovene existence. In Croatia, Yugoslav propaganda, along the lines of the declaration, was certainly in circulation, but its chief propagators appear to have been the radical press: notably *Jug* in Osijek, *Glas Slovenaca Hrvata i Srba* in Zagreb, and even *Novine*, the organ of Archbishop Bauer of Zagreb, which commented in January 1918 that the Yugoslav problem was a 'Gordian knot' which awaited its own Alexander (a clear allusion to Regent Alexander of Serbia).[72] In addition, the evidence suggests that Yugoslav agitation stemmed chiefly from diverse groups among the educated elite – the students and clergy of Zagreb for example – or that it was fomented by the declaration movement seeping across the dualist border. Indeed, Ban Mihalovich tried to assure the Austro-Hungarian leaders that Austria was the real source of the Yugoslav movement.[73] There was perhaps some substance to this claim as far as grass-roots agitation was concerned; thus, in the western-most Modrus-Rijeka komitat, military Intelligence in May 1918 could observe how 'today there are only Yugoslavs left . . . In the whole region signatures are collected to be used if necessary as a plebiscite'.[74] Yet in most of Croatia this type of mass-mobilization was not taking place (and perhaps only 7,500 signatures were to be collected for the May Declaration).[75] The fact was that the 'educated classes' remained the bearers of the Yugoslav message in Croatia, but they failed to achieve the type of national concentration so evident in 'Slovenia' or Dalmatia; the Croatian clergy, for example were themselves divided between those who backed the declaration and those who envisaged the future in terms of some 'Great Croatian' solution.[76] More importantly, for many Croatian civilians Yugoslav agitation was not part of their wartime experience, either because it did not exist in their locality or because they associated it wholly with the political elite. The reality of the situation was correctly summarized by a supporter of the Serb-Croat Coalition, Živko Bertić, when he addressed the Sabor in July 1918. Although he was sure from his own experience at the front that many Croat soldiers were indeed inclining towards the idea of southern Slav unity, he warned his colleagues that the movement remained 'young and green' in Croatia: 'broad layers of our people still act more according to their dark instincts than under the influence of this great idea which is still in the course of development'.[77] These 'dark instincts' – reacting to basic wartime privations – were to come to the fore at the end of the war: while the political elite were engaged in discussions to bring about Yugoslav unity, many of the peasantry in league with thousands of deserters (the so-called 'green cadres') vented their anger from the war years upon the symbols of authority, pillaging towns and estates.[78] Croatia therefore was taken into the Yugoslav state by its intelligentsia, but they had failed to carry the masses with them.

In Bosnia-Herçegovina, Yugoslav agitation was even less widely part of civilians' wartime experience. Just as it was partly true that for Croatia the declaration movement acted as a stimulant across the dualist border, so in Bosnia General Sarkotić also portrayed Yugoslav agitation as largely external, something from which his territory needed to be immunized. On arrival in the province in early 1915 he had been only too aware of 'sitting on a volcano', but hoped 'with God's help to prevent any outbreak of lava'.[79] His maxim throughout remained, 'no politics in Bosnia-Hercegovina is the best politics': he refused to recall the Bosnian Sabor (perhaps wisely in view of the Reichsrat example) and acted particularly severely against signs of Serb organization, culminating in the famous Banjaluka trials of 156 Serbs in early 1916,[80] though the resulting publicity may well have reactivated political tensions. He was probably correct in viewing the real stimulus as external, having long felt that a clear and concerted policy by all Habsburg authorities towards the southern Slav question was crucial; the unequal treatment had dangerous implications for Bosnia since, as he noted, borders were no obstacles to ideas.[81] This was clear in the wake of the May Declaration. Sarajevo's Serb and Croat politicians were now increasingly in contact with Reichsrat deputies, and in September 1917 Korošec made a well-publicized visit to the Bosnian capital to drum up support for the declaration. From Vienna Count Burián, the Joint Finance Minister (with special responsibility for Bosnia), observed that Korošec could indeed do great damage, that the authorities were trying to confine his movement to Austria – but that his journey to Sarajevo was legal and could not be prevented. With Korošec able to meet almost all the leading Bosnian politicians, his visit seems to have moved most parties in a Yugoslav direction, and encouraged them to take some stand over southern Slav unity.[82] True, the Moslem leaders chiefly remained hostile to the declaration until the end of the war, fearing engulfment in any Yugoslav organism; but Korošec found some sympathetic Moslems, and by 1918 an alarming number of Moslem women were backing the pro-Yugoslav Social Democratic Party. Many Croats, as in Croatia, were divided between those like Archbishop Stadler of Sarajevo who opted for a 'Greater Croatia', and those like Jozo Sunarić and the Franciscan clergy who openly favoured the declaration; that the Franciscans made such a stand, on Christmas Eve of 1917, was all the more important in view of their local influence. As for the Bosnian Serbs their 'Yugoslav' credentials were taken as read by Sarkotić, but their leaders like Vojislav Šola or Danilo Dimović with links to Vienna and Zagreb were, nevertheless, more cautious and opportunistic than the Croats in their public pronouncements during the final year of war.

In the early summer of 1918 Sarkotić read the report of a lawyer, Milan Katičić, who had travelled through the southern Slav regions and painted a dismal picture. Everywhere the Austro-Hungarian state idea was allegedly losing ground; even in Bosnia most politicians were in the enemy camp and the climate ripe for revolution. Sarkotić did not fully agree. He continued to view Dalmatia, Carniola and Croatia as the principal sources of Yugoslav agitation.[83] The lack of security in Dalmatia was all the more alarming since it seemed to be affecting military discipline. The dangers from Carniola and Croatia had also been vividly brought home to him, personified in Bishops Jeglič and Bauer who in June visited Sarajevo to attend celebrations to mark the 50th anniversary of Stadler's consecration. This encounter with clergy who seemed to be 'swimming in the South Slav Declaration' certainly increased Sarkotić's anxiety.[84] The relative calm in Bosnia – in terms of nationalist agitation – could well be a surface phenomenon, kept in place by the military régime. As Sarkotić warned Burián:

foreign and domestic propaganda is working in a Yugoslav – in other words in a Serbian sense – and the danger exists that this propaganda will overwhelm not only the [Bosnian] Serbs but also the Moslems. For it is clear that those who have a positive goal – like the Yugoslavs, who steer unswervingly towards that goal and spare neither toil or effort, also have a real chance of success. To view this propaganda with folded arms, in other words not to pursue our own goals with the same determination, can really only bring us disappointments.[85]

The reality, however, was that the Habsburg authorities could never all agree on the goal which they were pursuing in the south, nor provide any attractive alternative to the dualist system. In this environment 'Yugoslav agitation' – in whatever form – could flourish. From summer 1917 it increasingly became part of the experience of war in the south of Austria-Hungary as many civilians were caught up in a movement which they expected to solve their personal as well as national grievances. Its main domestic source in 1917–18 was, as we have seen, the Yugoslav Club of the Reichsrat and particularly the Slovene Catholic leaders who were increasingly anxious about German and Italian encroachment on their territory. Their May Declaration, with its demand for Yugoslav unity within the Empire, found a receptive audience when it was propagated in the southern crownlands: for most people it symbolized a more secure future as well as a defiant stance against economic misery and government incompetence or German-Magyar intransigence. It therefore served as a focal point in mobilizing the masses in southern Austria, while in Croatia and Bosnia, even if broad swathes of the population remained ignorant or indifferent, it certainly acted as a stimulant upon the educated elite. Thus a movement shaped notably by wartime insecurities, accelerated the development of a Yugoslav consciousness among many individuals. When the Habsburg authorities provided no solutions, the movement slowly took a more radical direction and finally created, in the form of national councils, one of the main bases for a new Yugoslav state. Many, including perhaps even Anton Korošec, would undoubtedly have preferred autonomy and security within the Empire, but by October 1918 this option was still not clearly available. The alternative – of unity outside the Empire – was therefore chosen. Korošec proceeded to announce in one of his last speeches to the Reichsrat that, 'in all southern Slav regions there is only one cry, deep and powerful and unchanging: complete freedom or death!' As for the prospect of remaining in an Austrian framework, he dismissed it with a final prophetic flourish: 'no frame is so covered in gold, no picture so enticing that it could separate the brothers of our three-titled nation'.[86]

Notes

1   See for example, Bogdan Krizman, 'Povjerljive veze izmedju Jugoslavenskog odbora i domaćih političara za I svetskog rata, *Historijski Zbornik*, 1962, vol.XV.

2   Janko Pleterski, 'Zapis ob razpravi o izjavah za majniško deklaracijo', *Zgodovinski Časopis*, 1993, vol.47/4, p.569. The subject receives no mention in two excellent works published in the west: Dimitrije Djordjević (ed.), *The Creation of Yugoslavia 1914–1918*, Santa Barbara-Oxford, Clio Books, 1980;

and Ivo Banac, *The National Question in Yugoslavia. Origins, History, Politics,* Ithaca-London, 1984.

3 K.k. Militäranwalt des Milkmdo in Wien to Evidenzbüro [hereafter EvB], A 12633/17, 31 January 1918, EvB 1918, Faszikel [Fasz.] 5743, Nr 3442, Kriegsarchiv, Vienna [hereafter KA]

4 For a good summary of South Slav attitudes before and after the May Declaration see, Dragovan Šepić, *Italija, Saveznici i jugslavensko pitanje 1914–1918,* Zagreb, 1970, pp. 197–205.

5 Sarkotić to EvB, Na No 3163 res, 15 August 1918, EvB 1918, Fasz. 5758, Nr 25251, KA.

6 'Referat über die Stimmung der Bevölkerung der Monarchie im In-und Auslande' (on basis of censor reports from Vienna, Budapest and Feldkirch), June 1917, EvB 1917, Fasz.5697, Nr 9336, KA; Zensurstelle Wien, monthly report (Beilage 27,28), 30 June 1918, EvB 1918, Fasz.5754, Nr 19867, KA.

7 Gustav Gratz and Richard Schüller, *Der Wirtschaftliche Zusammenbruch Österreich-Ungarns. Die Tragödie der Erschöpfung,* Vienna, 1930, p.46.

8 Ottokar Landwehr, *Hunger. Die Erschöpfungsjahre der Mittelmächte 1917/18,* Zurich-Leipzig-Vienna, 1931, p.56.

9 Landwehr to Militärkanzlei Seiner Majestät [MKSM], E.Nr 5111/Sekt I Res, 5 May 1918, MKSM 1918, 93–2/35, KA.

10 Josip Horvat, *Politička Povijest Hrvatske,* Zagreb, 1990, vol.2, pp.22, 42.

11 Bogdan Krizman, *Hrvatska u prvom svjetskom ratu. Hrvatsko-srpski politički odnosi,* Zagreb, 1989, p.113.

12 Landwehr, *op. cit.,* pp.182, 235, 239.

13 Zensurstelle Wien to EvB, K. Nr 2000, 7 July 1917, EvB 1917, Fasz.5698, Nr 11609, KA: Vranja, near Opatija in Istria, was singled out as a town for emergency attention.

14 *Stenographische Protokolle über die Sitzungen des Hauses der Abgeordneten des Österreichischen Reichsrates,* XXII Session, vol.III, Vienna, 1918 [hereafter *Reichsrat*], pp.2184ff: 41. Sitzung, 21 November 1917, speech by Anton Korošec.

15 *Reichsrat,* pp.2558–2560: 48.Sitzung, 4 Dec 1917, speech by K. Verstovšek.

16 For example, see *Reichsrat,* p.2186: 'heuer gab es dort durch sieben Monate keinen Tropfen Regen..und das Land Bosnien und die Hercegovina stehen schon jetzt in der Hungersnot'.

17 Hamdija Kapidžić, *Bosna i Hercegovina pod Austro-Ugarskom upravom,* Sarajevo, 1962, pp.214, 216; Landwehr, *op.cit.,* pp.58–9, for a survey of the situation in mid-1917.

18 See for example the speeches in *Reichsrat,* pp.2186 (Korošec), 2809 (Korošec), 2410–11 (Spadaro), 2857 (Jarc), 3010ff (Laginja).

19 EvB 1918, Fasz.5756, Nrs 23324, 23412, KA.

20 Na[chrichten] Stelle Udine to EvB, Na Nr 2298, 15 June 1918, EvB 1918, Fasz.5752, Nr 17812, KA; NaStelle Udine to EvB, Na Nr 1807, 21 May 1918, EvB 1918, Fasz.5751, Nr 15118, KA.

21 NaStelle Udine to EvB, Na Nr 2719, 16 July 1918, EvB 1918, Fasz.5755, Nr 21616, KA.

22 Zensurstelle Udine to HGK Feldmarschall von Boroević, Res.Nr 263, 5 September 1918, EvB 1918, Fasz.5759, Nr 28731, KA.

23 The best general surveys remain (all from the Slovene perspective): Janko

Pleterski, *Prvo opredeljenje Slovenaca za Jugoslaviju,* Belgrade, 1976 [Serbo-Croat translation]; and the work of Lojze Ude: 'Declaracijsko gibanje na Slovenskem', in *Naučni skup u povodu 50-godišnjice raspada Austro-Ugarske Monarhije i stvaranja Jugoslavenske države* (eds. V. Čubrilović, F. Čulinović and M. Kostrenčić), Zagreb, 1969; and 'Declaracijsko gibanje pri Slovencih', *Zgodovinski Časopis,* 1970, vol.24.

24 Dragovan Šepić, 'Oktobarska revolucija i jugoslavensko pitanje u Austro-Ugarskoj 1917/18', *Historijski Zbornik,* 1958–9, vols.XI-XII, pp.9–12.

25 See Pleterski, *Prvo opredeljenje,* pp.192–6 for this period.

26 Zensurstelle Feldkirch zu Res.Nr 1700: 'Südslavische Bewegung' (Beilage 6 of monthly report for August 1917), EvB 1917, Fasz.5697, Nr 9336/III, KA.

27 Fran Erjavec, *Zgodovina katoliškega gibanja na Slovenskem,* Ljubljana, 1928, p.227.

28 Pleterski, 'Zapis ob razpravi o izjavah', p.572. For a good general survey of Jeglič's position, see Pleterski, *Prvo opredeljenje,* pp.197ff.

29 Šepić, 'Oktobarska revolucija', p.17 note (26).

30 Vlasta Stavbar, 'Izjave v podporo Majniško Deklaracije', *Zgodovinski Časopis,* 1992–3, vols.46/3, pp.357–381, 46/4, pp.497–507, 47/1, pp.99–106.

31 Stavbar, *op.cit.,* p.498.

32 Stavbar sets the figure at 198 parish councils, while Lojze Ude suggested 189 ('Declaracijsko gibanje na Slovenskem', p.149). Stavbar also calculates that about 30,000 signatures were collected, apart from the famous occasion on 24 March 1918 when a petition with the signatures of 200,000 women was presented to Korošec in Ljubljana (Stavbar *op.cit.,* pp.502, 507).

33 ibid., pp.358–9, 497. 70,000 signatures would represent about 17% of the Slovene population of Styria according to the census of 1910.

34 ibid., pp.359, 363, 372: this is the latest recorded inclusion of the Habsburg clause at a mass meeting for the May Declaration.

35 ibid., pp.371.

36 Janko Pleterski, 'Koroški Slovenci med prvo svetovno vojno', in *Koroški plebiscit. Razprave in članki* (eds. Janko Pleterski, Lojze Ude and Tone Zorn), Ljubljana, 1970, p. 85.

37 An exception was a rally at Klagenfurt on 24 January 1918 (the first such Slovene gathering during the whole war) when a thousand people proclaimed the May Declaration; thereafter, Lodron effectively banned Slovene but not German rallies.

38 See the report by Austrian military Intelligence which downplays the actual success of the declaration movement: Armeeoberkommando [AOK] NaAbt, 'Studie über die südslavische Frage und ihre Rückwirkung auf die Armee', 4 July 1918, EvB 1918, Fasz.5754, Nr 19617, KA.

39 Pleterski, 'Koroški Slovenci', pp. 104ff.

40 Zensurstelle Feldkirch, Monatsbericht für April 1918, Beilage 29 (Südslavische Bewegung), 29 April, Fasz.5952, KA.

41 Pleterski, *Prvo opredeljenje,* p. 260.

42 ibid., pp.246, 248, 255.

43 Pleterski, *Prvo opredeljenje,* pp.321–3.

44 Generalmajor Otto Herzmansky [investigating officer] to k.k. Ministry of Defence, 5 May 1918: in Franjo Barac (ed.), *Croats and Slovenes – Friends of the Entente in the World War,* Paris, 1919, p.69.

45 Czapp to AOK, Op. Nr 13155, 2 May 1918: Barac, *op.cit.*, p.68. The Gebirgsschützenregiment was moved to Enns and replaced by Magyar troops.

46 See the public declaration against Seidler and his 'undemocratic behaviour', made on 7 May by the Yugoslav and Czech Clubs: Horvat, *op.cit.*, pp.43–4.

47 Ude, 'Declaracijsko gibanje pri Slovencih', pp. 201–2; pp. 198ff., give a full review of the mass-rallies.

48 Feindespropaganda-Abwehrstelle [FAst] to AOK Op.Abt, Res Nr 185, 19 June 1918, FAst 1918, Fasz.5994, KA.

49 See the detailed account in Richard Plaschka, Horst Haselsteiner and Arnold Suppan, *Innere Front. Militärassistenz, Widerstand und Umsturz in der Donaumonarchie 1918,* Vienna, 1974, vol.1, pp.324ff: no concrete proof ever came to light to link the mutinies directly with Slovene politicians.

50 Pivko's entertaining memoirs have recently been republished: Ljudevit Pivko, *Proti Avstriji 1914–1918,* Maribor, 1991. For the 42nd HID desertions, see especially the documents in Op.Nr 112745, Fasz.377, AOK Op.Abt 1918, KA: investigation showed that many young Croat officers sympathized with 'Yugoslav propaganda' even if they did not necessarily view it as incompatible with their allegiance to the Emperor.

51 Max Ronge, *Kriegs- und Industriespionage. Zwölf Jahre Kundschaftsdienst,* Zurich-Leipzig-Vienna, 1930, p.311.

52 Representatives from Dalmatia did not officially join this council because of the distance from Ljubljana; on 2 July they had already set up a special committee at Split and awaited the creation of a larger council in Zagreb.

53 Ude, 'Declaracijsko gibanje na Slovenskem', p.156.

54 Šepić. *Italija, Saveznici,* p.310.

55 Pleterski, *Prvo opredeljenje,* p. 262.

56 Stavbar, *op.cit.*, pp.102–4: over 6000 of these were indeed from the Volosca political district. 15,000 signatures represented 7% of the Slovene-Croat population of Istria (acc. to 1910 census).

57 Zensurstelle Udine to HGK Boreović (Abw.Stelle), Res. Nr 31, 18 April 1918, EvB 1918, Fasz.5749, Nr 11932, KA. On Mahnić (the third major Croat bishop after Strossmajer and Stadler), see Ivan Vitezić, 'Die Römisch-Katolische Kirche bei den Kroaten', in *Die Habsburgermonarchie 1848–1918,* IV, *Die Konfessionen* (eds. A Wandruszka and P. Urbanitsch), Vienna, 1985, pp.367ff.

58 NaStelle Udine to EvB, Na Nr 2298, 15 June 1918, EvB 1918, Fasz.5752, Nr 17812, KA. Already in January over 800 women and girls had signed a statement backing the declaration (Stavbar, *op.cit.*, p.103).

59 Zensurstelle Udine to HGK FM von Boreović (N-St.), Res.Nr 263, 5 September 1918, EvB 1918, Fasz.5759, Nr 28731, KA.

60 Pleterski, *Prvo opredeljenje,* p.257.

61 Stavbar, *op.cit.*, p.105. But N.B.: 16,000 represented only 3% of 1910 Serbo-Croat population of Dalmatia.

62 Sarkotić to AOK NaAbt, Op.Nr 2669, 18 May 1918, EvB 1918, Fasz.5751, Nr 15181/18, KA; *Bosnische Post,* 5 April 1918 (p.4); Stavbar, *op.cit.*, p.105.

63 See the standard account of the Cattaro mutiny: Richard Plaschka, *Cattaro-Prag. Revolte und Revolution,* Graz-Cologne, 1963; and the shorter version in Plaschka, Haselsteiner, Suppan, *op.cit.*, pp.107ff: the number of Serbs,

Croats and Slovenes who took part in the mutiny was roughly proportional to their (high) percentage in the navy (p.146 note (178)).

64 AOK to HGK Joseph, Op.Nr 109942, 5 August 1918, AOK Op.Abt 1918, Fasz.377, Nr 11257, KA.

65 See for example, Sarkotić to AOK Op.Abt, Na Nr 2635/1 res, 26 July 1918, AOK Op.Abt 1918, Fasz.371, Nr 110077, KA.

66 Gradja o stvaranju jugoslovenske države [hereafter Gradja], eds.Dragoslav Janković & Bogdan Krizman, Belgrade 1964, vol.1, pp.221–2.

67 See Janko Pleterski, 'Zunaji odmevi declaracijskega gibanja', Zgodovinski Časopis, 1989, vol.43/1, pp.59–64.

68 Krizman, Hrvatska, pp.109, 114.

69 Horvat, op.cit., p.32.

70 Gradja, vol.1, p.185; Horvat, op.cit., p.38.

71 Glas Slovenca Hrvata i Srba, quoted in Pleterski, Prvo opredeljenje, p.337.

72 Horvat, op.cit., p.34.

73 Sarkotić diary, entry for 30 May 1918, Sarkotić MSS, Arhiv Hrvatske Zagreb [AHZ: Croatian State Archives].

74 NaStelle Udine (Major von Walzel) to EvB, Na Nr 210 Geheim, 5 May 1918, EvB 1918, Fasz.5750, Nr 13508, KA.

75 Stavbar, op.cit., p.104: only 46 declarations exist in the Maribor archives.

76 Zensurstelle Feldkirch to EvB, Res Nr 3200, 5 March 1918 (Beilage 35: 'Südslavische Bewegung'), EvB 1918, Fasz.5745, Nr 6552, KA.

77 Horvat, op.cit., pp.56–8.

78 See Ivo Blanc, '"Emperor Karl has become a Comitadji": the Croatian disturbances of autumn 1918', The Slavonic and East European Review, April 1992, vol.70/2.

79 Signe Klein, Freiherr Sarkotić von Lovćen. Die Zeit seiner Verwaltung in Bosnien-Herzegovina von 1914 bis 1918, PhD, Vienna, 1969, p.38.

80 Kapidžić, op.cit., pp.211–3.

81 ibid., pp.207–8.

82 ibid., pp.221ff.

83 Klein, Freiherr Sarkotić von Lovćen, pp.190–1.

84 Sarkotić diary, entry for 10 June 1918, AHZ.

85 Sarkotić to Burián, 16 June 1918, Sarkotić MSS, AHZ.

86 Reichsrat, vol.IV, Vienna, 1918, p.4326 (2 October 1918).

Chapter 48

Opposition to the War in France: The Case of Clovis Andrieu

Jean-Jacques Becker

Throughout the war, the vast majority of the French remained faithful to the attitude of Sacred Union which they had adopted from the very beginning. Opposition to the war was a marginal phenomenon. It is not very difficult to draw up an account of it.

Even if, as far as the press was concerned, some newspapers such as Gustave Téry's *L'Oeuvre*, which was published as a daily from September 1915 onwards, or the *Canard Enchaîné*, which was really born in July 1916, refused to repeat the mindless propaganda put out by the government, they did not question the need for the country to defend itself. *L'Humanité*, for the socialist party, and the *Bataille syndicaliste* for the *Confédération du Travail*, had also firmly taken up a position of support for national defence. There was really only one newspaper which, having been vigorously patriotic at the beginning of the war, was often vigorously attacked later on as the mouthpiece of pacifism, and indeed of defeatism: the *Bonnet Rouge*,[1] and it refuted the accusation. In fact, it was first and foremost a corrupt newspaper, all the more so since, its director, Miguel Almereyda, needed a great deal of money. Before the war, he had been in the habit of receiving large sums from Joseph Caillaux, president of the radical party, and during the war, from 1914 to March 1916, he was subsidised by the Minister of the Interior, Louis Malvy, and by various more or less like-minded industrialists. In April 1916, its new administrator, Emile-Joseph Duval, received German subsidies paid to him via Switzerland. In point of fact, the pacifism of the *Bonnet Rouge* was not particularly aggressive, and had little ability to influence French opinion. Almereyda was arrested on 7 August, 1917, and is said to have committed suicide a few days later, in prison. As far as the administrator of the newspaper is concerned, he was sentenced to death and shot on 17 July, 1918.

The *Bonnet Rouge* took up a position half way between opposition to the war and treason. It is naturally the case that censorship would have prevented newspapers from expressing excessively pacifist views. A few small opposition newspapers nevertheless did enjoy a certain success, such as *La Vague,* launched by the socialist député of the Allier, Pierre Brizon, in January 1919.

Outside the press, opposition to the war showed itself mainly on the margins of the working-class movement. There was some opposition in the socialist party, where a minority around Jean Longuet, a grandson of Karl Marx, thought that greater efforts should be made to find a peaceful solution to the conflict, but did not call into question the right of France to defend herself. This minority became in fact a majority during 1918. The opposition was strongest among certain trade-unionists. A group, inspired by Leon Trotsky, who had been a refugee in France since 1914, set itself up around a trade-union newspaper, *La Vie ouvrière*, whose director, Pierre Monatta, had resigned from the 'Bureau confédéral' of the *Confédération Générale du Travail*, in order to protest against its participation in the Sacred Union for the defence of France. This fairly heterogeneous opposition, which had as one of its leaders Alphonse Merrheim, one of the main organisers of the CGT, secretary of the *Confédération des Métaux* (Metal workers Union), set up the Committee for the Resumption of International Relations, while a short time afterwards a minority of trade unionists formed a group on the Committee for the Defence of Trade-Unionism. It was two trade-unionists, Alphonse Merrheim and Albert Boredon, who went to the Zimmerwald Conference in September 1915, accompanied by three socialist *députés* at the Kienthal Conference in April 1916. All in all, the importance of these different forms of more or less radical opposition to the war derive their importance more from the fact of having been much studied than for any real influence they exercised.[2]

In contrast, the action of one man throughout the war has remained widely unrecognised for a long time. A few years ago, interest began to grow about the personality of Clovis Andrieu and the movement which he inspired in the Département de la Loire in 1918. As Gérard Raffaelli and Michelle Zancarini have written, 'he found himself in particularly important circumstances, at the centre of a pacifist and revolutionary movement which is unique in France'.[3] It is the only example, throughout the war, of which one can meaningfully speak of an attempt at revolutionary activity.

In 1914, Clovis Andrieu was 38. He was born in Picardy at Pont-Rémy, a small industrial town, near Abbeville, on 27 June, 1876. He was therefore called up, but the following year, like a large number of other workers, while still in the army, was sent back in order to work in war production. He was sent to Firminy, in the Loire, first of all in the *Verdié* metal works. It must be emphasised that even if an enquiry had been carried out, something which does not seem very probable, the military authorities were not afraid to send experienced trade-union leaders, who were known for their militant attitude, to work in war factories. The fact that there was no political selection is proof of a general feeling of virtually unanimous patriotism. Clovis Andrieu was not in fact unknown to the police.

By trade, he was a skilled metal worker, and while still very young had come to work in the Paris area. As a revolutionary syndicalist, he belonged to the anarchist tendency which, before the war, dominated the trade-union movement in France, and he was a leading militant in the CGT. In his capacity as the secretary of the metal workers union of the Seine area, he took part in the Congrès d'Amiens in October 1906. It was at this conference that the majority to which Andrieu belonged adopted anti-militarism and anti-patriotism as the doctrine of the trade-union movement.[4] He also took part in subsequent conferences organised by the *Confédération Générale du Travail*, but remained essentially one of those whose central preoccupation was anti-militarism, and who showed this by taking part in the *Sou du Soldat*[5] (The soldier's farthing). This organisation was run by a secretary of the CGT, Georges Yvetot, the son of a fiercely anti-militaristic policeman, and in theory its aim was to help young trade-unionists, when they were called to the colours, by sending them small sums of money. In practice, the *Sûreté générale* – the section of the police responsible for keeping an eye on political organisations, especially if they had revolutionary tendencies – considered that the main activity of the *Sou du Soldat* was to carry out revolutionary propaganda in the army.[6]

After the demonstrations in the barracks, in the spring of 1913, against the extension of the period of compulsory military service, a number of leaders of the CGT had been arrested on 1 July, 1913 for their involvement with the *Sou du Soldat*, and charged with 'incitement to disobedience of members of the armed services'. Clovis Andrieu was one of them, and they were freed shortly afterwards, the trial taking place later, on 26 March, 1914. In addition to Georges Yvetot, who was sentenced to a year in prison and the payment of a fine of 100 francs, twelve others were severely punished, with prison sentences of eight months and fines of 100 francs. And, once again, Clovis Andrieu was one of them. But the trial took place in their absence, with the verdict being confirmed in their presence only in May 1914. Those sentenced lodged an appeal, and war broke out before it could be heard. The names of all these revolutionaries obviously figured in the *Carnet B*, the document giving the names of those suspected of seeking to sabotage any possible mobilisation, and who were to be arrested when the order to mobilise was published. Because of the overwhelming upsurge of patriotism which marked the outbreak of war in 1914, there was no attempt to arrest anyone whose name was in the *Carnet B*[7], so that those awaiting sentence for membership of the *Sou du Soldat* who were of military age, like Clovis Andrieu, joined their regiment.

It was thus a revolutionary militant with a number of charges recorded against him who arrived at Firminy in 1915.

We know that all the countries involved in the first world war were taken aback by the unbelievable consumption of arms and munitions caused by the outbreak of the first industrial war in the history of mankind. Enormous programmes of war production had to be implemented in order to satisfy the needs of the armies. In France, the industrial area around St Étienne became a vast centre for war production. The population of the Département de la Loire doubled as a result of the arrival of war workers.[8] This work force contained a large number of workers who had earlier been in the army.

What caused the outbreak of protests in the Saint-Étienne area was the arrival on Tuesday, 27 November, 1917, of the order from the local labour control office of the order to Clovis Andrieu, who was working at the time in the Holtzer metal factories at Unieux, a small town near Firminy, to rejoin his regiment, the 86th infantry, stationed at Le Puy (Haute Loire) that very evening.

Up to then, the Saint-Étienne region had scarcely been touched by any social unrest.

Over the whole of France, the trade-union movement had virtually disappeared at the outbreak of the war, and was not to reappear until 1916. The unions themselves did very little: there were few strikes, involving only a very small number of workers. In contrast, 1917 had been marked by two major conflicts, particularly affecting the Paris area in January and in May-June of the same year. Although, in both cases, the movements had been launched by women working in the clothing sector, the 'midinettes', they had also spread to involve workers involved in the war factory, especially in July.

These strikes were characterised by the major role played by women – even in the war factories, the men, who were often still officially under military discipline, played a subordinate role – and were generally short-lived. There was little co-ordination between the movements, which aimed at obtaining advantages for particular groups of workers. Prices had risen very rapidly in the early part of 1917. It was this sudden increase in the cost of living which explained the demand for higher wages.

In wartime, however, demands of this kind can never be seen entirely out of context. The fact that the war was lasting so long was leading to a certain weariness, which was increased by the failure of the offensive on the Chemin-des-Dames on 16 April, 1917, itself the starting point for a series of mutinies which shook the French army. A survey organised by the *Préfets* in June 1916 revealed widespread feelings of depression in France. Moreover, on 1 May, 1917, to the surprise of the authorities as well as of that of the organisers themselves, meetings and demonstrations enjoyed a much greater success than in 1915 and 1916. They were vigorous in their

41. A cheerful comradeship. On the extreme right Private Victor McConnell, twice
    wounded. (V. McConnell: Liddle Collection).
    See Chapter 39: British Loyalties: The Evidence of an Archive.

42. Munition girls and other staff at the Gretna Green factory. Emily Hubble, née
    Davidson, front row, 2nd from left in dark mob cap. (Mrs.E. Hubble: Liddle
    Collection). See Chapter 39: British Loyalties: The Evidence of an Archive.

43. Demonstration in Tverskaya
    Street, Moscow, February 1917.
    (Museum of the Revolution,
    Moscow).
    See Chapter 40: A Nation at War:
    The Russian Experience.

44. Political Meeting on the Russian
    South West Front during the
    February 1917 Revolution.
    (Museum of the Revolution,
    Moscow).
    See Chapter 40: A Nation at War:
    The Russian Experience.

45. German children of the occupation, 1919. A British officer, E.P. Neville, wrote these thoughts of the future in a letter home, 'The streets are full of boys who I suppose will grow up to try and conquer the world again.' (J.C.H. Willett: Liddle Collection). See Chapter 41: Germany, the Home Front (1).

46. Anxious Italian women and children of a frontier town greet Allied military aid (British) which began to arrive from November 1917. Italy's privations continued beyond the war's end. (French War Office official photograph).
See Chapter 43: The Home Front in Italy.

47. German troops and their officers pose for a photograph in front of Louvain's celebrated Gothic Town Hall, a building preserved (amidst so much that was destroyed) because Platzkommandant von Manteuffel had swiftly installed his headquarters there. (Archives of the Catholic University of Louvain).
See Chapter 45: The Flames of Louvain.

48. Louvain: a cyclist skirts the
    ruins. (Archives of the Catholic
    University of Louvain).
    See Chapter 45. The Flames of
    Louvain.

49. Requisitioning bedding in the
    Rue Ratisbonne, Lille. (From
    Michelin Battlefield Guide, Lille,
    1921).
    See Chapter 46: Life in an
    Occupied Zone.

50. Need and opportunity meet: Arabs bargaining with British officers over forage rates, (C.P.Carlson: Liddle Collection). See Chapter 47: The Arab Experience of the War.

51. Richard Blaker, author of *Medal Without Bar* as a Second Lieutenant, Royal Field Artillery. (Mrs.E.Ingleby). See Chapter 57: British War Novelists.

52. On the left, Louis Ferdinand Céline, as a French cavalryman. (Frank Field).
    See Chapter 59: The French War Novel.

53. Inspirational surroundings for an artist. Glencorse Wood, Ypres Salient. (E.T.S.
    Bonnett: Liddle Collection).
    See Chapter 61: Painting Armageddon.

54. Sir Ian Hamilton at the unveiling of a War Memorial. (Liddell Hart Centre for
Military Archives, King's College, London).
See Chapter 62: Sir Ian Hamilton after the War.

opposition to the government, and even, in Paris in particular, expressed markedly pacifist views. There were shouts of 'Peace Now', and 'Down with the War'.[9] But in spite of this, the demands of the strikers in the spring of 1917 were for higher wages rather than for political changes.

From the summer of 1917 onwards, tension gradually grew in the Saint-Étienne area, but mainly in favour of compelling a rather reluctant set of factory owners to increase wages, with the owners themselves preferring to keep their workers well under control. It was from autumn onwards that the movement became a revolutionary one with pacifist overtones.

There were three main phases, the first being from 27 November, 1917 to 6 December, and taking the form of a massive strike by metal workers in the Saint-Étienne area. Thousands of workers attended meetings. Violent incidents took place at Firminy and at Saint-Étienne, and it was only because the authorities followed the advice of Pams, Clemenceau's Interior Minister, to deal with the situation with the greatest caution, that more serious outbreaks were avoided.

The second phase took place in the first months of 1918, when preparations were made in the Loire area for an almost openly revolutionary movement. There was constant agitation, very frequent meetings, and intense activity by trade-union leaders with revolutionary sympathies. It was no longer a question of asking for higher wages. The demonstrations were accompanied by the singing of the *Internationale,* and were clearly political with the aim of compelling the government to make peace. On several occasions, the departmental authorities were seriously concerned about what might happen, speaking of how the Russian revolution had 'raised the hopes' of the revolutionaries, with the success of the Bolsheviks arousing 'great admiration'. At Firminy, men spoke of establishing Soviets.

The third and shortest phase took place between 18 and 28 May. From its starting point in Chambon and Firminy, the strike spread to the whole of the metal industry, thus affecting the war factories around Saint-Étienne, and even reaching Roanne, where textile workers also became involved. At the meetings setting out the aims of the movement, there was enthusiasm for strikes which, it was said, would last until the government made peace.

Some speakers showed no hesitation in using the language of revolution, and in calling for open rebellion, so much so that on 23 May, this almost took place. A police officer was stabbed twice and revolver shots fired at the police sent to restore order. But in spite of this, only a minority of the strikers was involved in the violence, and the movement gradually grew weaker. This led the authorities, who had earlier been seriously worried, to react with some vigour. In the night of 25–26 May, trade-union leaders in the Saint-Étienne area were arrested, among them Clovis Andrieu. Protest movements against this arrest were weak, the strikers having been taken by surprise. On 28 May at 23.15 hours, Théophile Barnier, 'sous-chef de cabinet' in Clemenceau's government, who had been sent to co-ordinate the maintenance of order, was able to cable victoriously that he considered that industrial activity was now back to normal throughout the Département. Two cavalry brigades which had been summoned from the Front were able to go back there. A few days later, the same happened for 15 squadrons sent from elsewhere in France itself, as well as for units of the gendarmerie sent as reinforcements.

What role had Clovis Andrieu played in these events? We know little of his activity before 1917, when he became secretary, first on a provisional and then on a permanent basis (25 May, 1917) of the metal workers union in Firminy. There is little doubt about his feelings since shortly beforehand he had declared to a 'secret' meeting of the union, attended by 200 people, that: 'The war was brought about by people like Holstzer, Verdié and Krupp, by all the capitalists and factory owners of the whole world'.[10]

But during the spring and summer of 1917, it soon became apparent that his ambitions extended beyond the immediate Saint-Étienne area, that he wanted to make Firminy into a centre for all the trade-union activity of the Département, an activity with strong political overtones.

The authorities made no mistake about what was happening. In a letter to the Minister for Munitions (Louis Loucheur) on 22 November, 1917,[11] General Dantant, commander of the 15th region, reminded him that he had already, on 11 June, asked for Andrieu to be called back to his regiment. According to him he was 'a trouble-maker', and this punishment would be an example to others. In the General's view, Andrieu's speeches at trade-union movements expressed pacifist, revolutionary and even defeatist ideas, calling as he did on his listeners to set out for a 'real' war, this time against 'the owners'. 'The people must not', the General reported Andrieu as saying, 'exhaust itself working so that its brothers can become cannon fodder, food for machine-guns sacrificed for the scum of the earth (de la chair à mitraille pour le profit de la canaille)'.

The General indeed felt that he was confronted by an adversary who was dangerous because of the influence he had obtained over the workers. This was why he wished to avoid an open arrest, which would be followed by a trial that could give rise to movements of support and protest. General Dantant was not mistaken, except for the fact that sending Andrieu back to his regiment was going to have the same result.

As soon as the news broke, the workers assembled. When Andrieu pretended to go to the station to obey the order to rejoin his unit, the workers brought him triumphantly back to the 'Bourse du Travail'. The Holtzer factories where Andrieu was working, and which employed 4000 workers, immediately went on strike. This rapidly spread to the factories in the neighbourhood, and then to the whole of the Saint-Étienne area. The owners asked for the workers to be compelled to go back to work, but the government, aware of how few forces it had at its disposal, did not accept this view. On 2 November, the Minister of the Interior sent a cable saying that it was 'essential to act with the greatest care and moderation'. In order to disguise its weakness, it concluded by saying that 'at the present time, every effort should be made to preserve national unity'.

In fact, negotiations took place between the authorities and the trade-unionists of the Loire area, and Andrieu finally rejoined his regiment at Le Puy. He was, moreover, rapidly awarded a period of leave, which he used to go to Paris, where he claimed to have met Clemenceau. A compromise was gradually reached, and a set of fairly theoretical conditions agreed whereby Andrieu was allowed to go back to Firminy and reinstated as a member of the work force of the factory in which he was supposed to be working. By 8 December, after a strike lasting 10 days, work had been resumed everywhere.

The movement had been an impressive one: more than 100,000 workers had gone on strike, most of them in war industries. There had nevertheless been some ambiguity about it. Demands for higher wages had rapidly come to take precedence over the demand for Andrieu to be brought back into the factory, and for many of the strikers, it was not enough to have won on this particular point. But although the pacifist movement was still in the background, the fact remains that a large number of the metal workers in the Loire area had come together to prevent one of their number from being punished for his opposition to the war. It was probably the first time that the pacifist movement had won a victory, and this at the very moment when the Clemenceau government, whose programme was a ruthless pursuit of the war, had just come to power.

By the beginning of 1918, there had been a considerable change in the atmosphere in the *Département de la Loire*. The trade-union leaders were aware that they had won a victory, and were no longer prepared to show the same moderation in their slogans that they had used up to then. What was coming into being was a genuine movement of protest against the war itself. Two bodies took charge of this, the *Commission exécutive de l'Union des syndicats de la Loire*, wholly dominated by the supposed minority of pacifists in the CGT, and whose secretary was Charles-Eugène Flageollet, a thirty-five year-old paper worker of marked anarchist tendencies, and the *Comité intercorporatif de la Loire*, which had some 20,000 members, either in the metal or the building industry. But the real driving force was in the 'Bourse du Travail' at Firminy, and the leader of the movement was Clovis Andrieu. He urged the different groups in the Loire to consider means of bringing about an immediate end to the war.

Andrieu was nevertheless fully aware of the fact that however important the armament factories were in the Loire area, he had no chance of succeeding if he remained isolated. The movement had, he realised, to become nation-wide. Since it was recognised that all that the Loire workers could do was set the movement in motion, contacts were made with the pacifist wing of the CGT, grouped together in the *Comité de défense syndicaliste*, which was seen as the co-ordinating force for the workers in the whole of France. Delegates from the metal workers of the Loire were sent to Paris to make contact with the CDS, as well as with the Federations of workers in the metal and building industries.[12]

On the ground, there were more and more protest meetings, and several demonstrations took place against the sending of soldiers up to the front. On 28 January, a number were prevented from leaving, and there were shouts of 'Down with the War, Long Live Peace'. When, finally, the soldiers were allowed to leave, they shouted seditious slogans, sang the *Internationale*, and made themselves conspicuous by their 'rowdiness' and 'scandalous behaviour'.[13] Pacifist meetings were held every day, with speakers competing in revolutionary fervour in the presence of thousands of workers. Thus, on 3 February, the joint committee claimed to have brought together 7000 workers at Saint-Étienne, with the Préfecture estimating the numbers at between 3000 and 3500. The meeting ended with the formation of a procession which went to demonstrate in front of the Préfecture, demanding peace and singing the *Internationale*. Clovis Andrieu seemed to be everywhere at the same time, all the more so since he and his comrades spread out into the neighbouring *Départements*. On 8 February, Andrieu was speaking in Bourges, while others were at Alais, in the *Département du Gard*, or at Lyons.

The government was amazed that one man such as Andrieu could do so much. After all, like a number of his most active comrades, he was technically in the army and under military orders. How could these people, it was asked, be at one and the same time workers in armaments factories and political agitators? On 22 February, a note arrived from the Prime Minister's office for the *Préfet de la Loire*, asking how many times Andrieu had been absent from work, for what reason, and on whose authority? The authorities at Saint-Étienne were unable to give a satisfactory answer, replying that 'as far as they knew, the soldier Andrieu had, since 1 February, worked for only one day'.[14]

In point of fact, the local authorities felt overwhelmed by the situation, and were constantly warning the central government of the dangers, with the *Préfet de la Loire* sending a long, eleven-page report to the Minister of the Interior. In his list of speakers, he signalled out 'the famous Andrieu' as one of the most violent. He and his comrades, the report stated, were 'now operating quite openly'. He reported what was being said, particularly the remarks of 'this man Andrieu' who on 1 February had concluded his 'rabble-rousing speech' to 1500 metal workers at Firminy with the words:

'Last week, your female comrades came out to demonstrate against the war. They prevented the class of 1913 from setting out for the front (the soldiers in question were members of this class who had been finally called to the colours). If, tomorrow, the authorities try to call up the class of 1912, you should oppose this. In Austria-Hungary, the people had arisen to demand peace. In Germany, the workers have followed this example. In turn, comrades, the hour has come for you to follow the example of your German and Austrian comrades.'

The authorities also noted a motion for one meeting in which

'those present commit themselves to fight with all means at their disposal to bring an end to the war, this terrible cataclysm which has caused more than 15 million deaths and 20 million casualties'.

In the *Préfet's* view, this was more than just pacifism. It was defeatism. He thought that there was going to be an attempted uprising, even if he found reassurance in the fact that most of the workers did not come to the meetings, even though they were not opposed to their revolutionary overtones either. More significantly, he noted that the miners had so far refused to be involved, something which, he added, Andrieu had publicly regretted. This fact, added the *Préfet*, offered some reassurance to the authorities, and might reassure a rather nervous public opinion.In conclusion, the *Préfet* wondered whether an uprising could still be avoided, and stressed that the forces at his disposal were inadequate to prevent it.

The next day, 5 February, the *Préfet* sent a new report, stating that Andrieu himself could not now control the situation, that 'rioters' had realised how weak the forces of law and order were, that they were terrorising or influencing the moderate trade-unions, and in which he underlined the need to send 2000 extra mounted policemen so that at least he would be able to defend public buildings.

On 4 February, the special commissioner at Saint-Étienne claimed that the coming revolutionary movement would involve a million workers, principally from the metal, textile and glass industries, that it had ramifications in a whole series of *Départements*, notably the Loire, obviously, but also in the Haute-Loire, the Rhône, Montluçon, Bourges, Dijon and Paris, and that even if no date had yet been decided, 'the slightest incident could set off the explosion'.[15] This was also the view of the General commanding the Region. On the basis of 'very serious information', he believed an insurrectionary movement to be imminent.[16]

It is possible that the local authorities, the *Préfets*, and Special Commissioners – that is to say, those with the special responsibility for keeping a watch on subversive organisations, particularly those involving members of the working class -were exaggerating the danger, in order to cover themselves if there were serious disturbances. However, the man who, from 1914, had symbolised opposition to the war, Alphonse Merrheim, secretary of the metal workers federation, who took part in the

Zimmerwald conference of 1915, and who came to the Loire region at the time, noted the same 'state of excitement' among the militants in that area. 'You have brought them to fever pitch'[17] he told the local leaders on 22 February; and he did not intend this as a compliment. For some time, Merrheim had been distancing himself from his friends in the *Comité de Défense syndicaliste*.

Suddenly, however, when the uprising was felt to be imminent, tension fell in the whole *Département*. Andrieu was partly responsible for this. He was aware that if people were perhaps ready in the Loire, this was not the case elsewhere. Unlike the less well-educated trade-union leaders, he felt the need for an overall strategy. This did, in fact, cause him some difficulties. He was not understood when he tried to avoid premature action, and at Firminy, on 31 January, he was accused of being in the pay of the government, and of being a traitor and a coward. He needed all his energy to make sure that an uprising did not take place the next day.[18]

There were also other causes for this sudden relaxation of tension: the arrival in the Saint-Étienne area of a large number of fresh troops, rumours of the arrest of trade-union leaders, a spy scandal in which trade-unionists were said to be involved.

This last incident, which was soon shown to be without foundation, was nevertheless important on the psychological level, and explains some of the hesitations which then afflicted the movement. For pacifist and revolutionary leaders, accusations of this kind are unbearable, since they are well aware of how much more unbearable they are to their 'troops', and this not only for political reasons. Thus, the more they describe themselves as pacifist, the less are they prepared to be called defeatists. Thus Andrieu, at the meeting of the administrative commission of the Union of Metal Workers, vigorously rejected any idea, according to a police spy, that he was 'in the pay of the Boches'. He was for peace, he insisted, but 'did not mean by that the Germans should be allowed to keep Belgium, the North of France, Serbia, Montenegro and Rumania'.[19]. And this was the whole problem: how could one bring about a peaceful settlement to the conflict while still arguing that the Germans should not be allowed to hold on to their conquests, for which they were so favourably placed by the actual position of the armies?

When one looks at the matter more closely, it becomes clear that, on a much smaller scale, the revolutionaries of the Loire were faced with the same difficulties as the Bolsheviks. In the same way that the accusations that Lenin was in the pay of the Germans were almost fatal to him, so the trade-unionists in the Loire had to make the greatest efforts to avoid the same accusations. Even pacifist workers were patriots. For the workers around Saint-Étienne, what was happening in Russia was at one and the same time a source of pride and of great concern. In this same month of March, 1918, the news of the signature of the Peace Treaty of Brest-Litovsk was given a very cool reception, precisely because it was the proof that the Bolsheviks had accepted 'a German peace', while Merrheim, a few days earlier, had declared that they would sign only 'a people's peace'.[20]

Under these conditions, at a time when the actions of the workers of the Loire area had been taking place without any particular concern as to what was happening elsewhere, events such as the victorious German offensive of 21 March, and the shelling of Paris, began to affect their revolutionary enthusiasm. The military situation transformed what was happening on the political front.

After the decline of the revolutionary movement from late February, there were two distinct tendencies among the revolutionaries of the Loire. One of these was inspired by Charles Flageollet, and consisted of the ambition to recover lost ground and go forward, with the idea that the mobilisation of the local workers would soon bring with it that of the rest of France. The second was represented by Clovis Andrieu, and consisted of withdrawing on the local front, and adopting a national strategy, one which was more or less closely combined with that of Raymond Péricat, a 55-year-old building worker, the secretary of the Committee for the defence of trade-unions (*Comité de défense syndicaliste*). The aim was to compel the CGT to assume the leadership of the movement, or, if it would not do so, to have the CDS take its place. Andrieu devoted the whole of March and April to this more or less public activity, but even between Andrieu, who spent most of the time in the Loire, and Péricat, who was based mainly in Paris, there were differences of emphasis. Péricat was much more cautious than Andrieu, and more aware of the need to take account of what was happening elsewhere because of its impact on the readiness of the workers to mobilise to support the peace movement. Andrieu put it quite nicely when he said that in the CGT, but also in the CDS, people were worried about 'moving frontiers'; but what was actually happening was the result of the German offensives.

In April, the activism of Flageollet and Andrieu, who seemed to be more or less in agreement, was a cause of concern for the *Préfet*, who once again did not seem to have sufficient forces at his disposal, and who asked for them from the Interior Ministry. But although it was not possible to allow him to keep military forces who might be needed elsewhere, the authorities in Paris gave their approval. Matters were clearly being taken seriously.

What mattered in fact was the lack of agreement among the different trade-union leaders. Georges Dumoulin, one of the main CGT leaders before the war, and who had been called up in the Loire as a miner in Roche-la-Molière, looked at the situation and commented on it in a letter, writing that there were divisions in the metal industries, and wondering whose side to take. 'I can understand Merrheim and his colleagues in the "Bureau de la Fédération des métaux"', he wrote, 'but I can also understand Andrieu and the others. Here, little account is taken of the German offensive. In Paris, it dominates the situation. At the top, people are aware of the need to be careful; down below, what matters is the need to do something'.[21]

Discussions crystallised around the date of 1 May, which Andrieu wanted to make the starting point for action, something which turned out to be impossible. As was often the case, what turned out to be a trial of strength was brought about by an accidental event, the dismissal of eleven workers, of whom five had been sent back to their unit by the management of the 'Aciéries et Forges de Firminy' because they had not turned up for work on 1 May, an absence which had caused the loss of several days production and the closing down of three furnaces.

After several days discussion, Andrieu gave the authorities, at eight in the evening of 8 May, a week's notice either to take the workers back or face a general strike. And a week later, in the night of 17–18 May, notices calling for a strike appeared on the walls at Chambon. At Firminy, where the notices had not been posted in time, work began normally on the morning of 18 May, but during the day, Andrieu gave the order – which was obeyed – to cease work. His aim was probably to exert pressure at the same time on the 'Congrès national du Comité de défense syndicaliste', which was meeting on 19 and 20 May at Saint-Étienne, to issue the order for a general strike.

In fact, without being complete, as it was at Firmin, the strike extended to the whole area. At meetings, speakers stated clearly that the strike was to last *until the signature of a peace treaty*. On 21 May, the workers at Chambon-Feugerolles voted a motion to that effect, saying that they were 'more than ever determined not to go back to work until the government had signed an armistice'.[22]

As we now know, the strike which was to last until the end of the war was over after only a few days. Andrieu was forced to recognise his failure, since in spite of his rhetoric and the decisions taken by the Congress at Saint-Étienne, the Loire remained completely isolated. Strikes began in the Paris region on 13 May, but were virtually over by the 18th. At the same time as the strikes were taking place in the Loire, there were other strikes elsewhere, in l'Isère and the Gard, but they were unco-ordinated and relatively small. When he was arrested, Andrieu could say cheekily to the policeman who arrested him, Commissioner Oudaille, and who had been sent from Paris to take charge of events, 'You are a day too late. We were going back to work on Monday anyway'.

Andrieu was no Lenin. But although he was certainly no great thinker, he had great gifts of leadership. He was an expert at the grass roots level, and the man who brought about the only major movement of opposition to the war which took place in France. It is in fact very curious, from a historiographical point of view, that events which had no immediate effect on the progress of the war, such as the Zimmerwald conference, should figure so widely in the history books, while strike movements in the major area of armament production in France should be virtually ignored. For the Loire was the centre of France's war industry, and a prolonged stoppage could have brought about a virtual end to France's war effort. To some extent, it is a result of the war censorship that these events should have remained unknown long after the censorship itself has ended.

There are other reasons for this. The movement inspired by Andrieu was the exception which proves the rule. This, throughout, was that the vast majority of French people accepted the war, or at least remained convinced that France should not be beaten, even though war was, in itself, something abominable. Whatever they may have said, some of the trade-union leaders in the Loire were probably defeatists, in particular Andrieu, even though what they said varied from day to day, was contradictory, or could have been understood in a number of different ways. But they knew, or a least they felt, that the workers who followed them were in their vast majority deeply opposed to any defeatist attitude, and that there was a threshold which could not be passed if you still wanted to be followed, the invisible but impassable threshold of national feeling. It should also be added that it was very much a minority movement, that apart from the metal workers, the other working-class organisations were not involved, and that even among the metal workers of the Loire any revolutionary enthusiasm, which certainly existed in January 1918, had lost its impetus a few weeks later, if only because of the concern caused by the German offensives.

It is the fact that the only movement of opposition to the war to have existed in France was so much of an exception which explains why it should have been forgotten. It is significant that its leaders, in the Paris area as well in the Loire, did not make a career in the working-class movement after the war. Andrieu himself, outstanding though he may have been as a leader of men, and by no means devoid of the ability to think in tactical and strategic terms, was able to employ all his talents only at one particular moment, and was not sufficiently clear-sighted to envisage a specific goal which took account of all the realities of the situation.

Clovis Andrieu was released from prison on 15 February, 1919, and settled in the Loire area. He involved himself in organising the unions which he, like the other pre-war trade-union leaders, saw as the basis for the working class movement. Although he was very favourable to the Bolshevik movement, he was soon marginalised, being neither in favour of the CGT, which was at the time very hostile to communism, nor on the side of the communists, for whom political organisation was at the heart of everything. He died in 1936, almost blind, just sixty, and forgotten, as forgotten as the movement of opposition to the war which he had inspired.

Notes

1 See Pierre Albert, *Histoire de la Press française* (Claude Bellanger, Jacques Godechot, Pierre Guiral, Fernand Terrou) volume III (1871–1940), Press Universitaires de France, 1972, p. 439 *passim*.

2 See, in particular, Annie Kriegel, *Aux Origines du parti communiste français*, two volumes Mouton, 1964, part I, Section I. Also Jean-Jacques Becker, *La France en guerre*, 1914–1918, Editions complexe, 1988.

3 See 'Clovis Andrieu' in *Dictionnaire biographique du mouvement ouvrier en France*, published under the direction of Jean Maitron, Part IV, 1914 – 1939, volume 1, p. 158 *passim*, Les éditions ouvrières.

4 See Henri Dubief. *Le Syndicalisme révolutionnaire*, Paris, Armand Colin, Collection U, 1969.

5 See Jean-Jacques Becker. *Le Carnet B. Les pouvoirs publics et l'antimilitarisme avant la guerre de 1914*. Préface de Pierre Renouvin, Editions Klincksieck, 1973, chapter 1.

6 For example, in 1912, the police prepared two long summaries on the question: on January 3, 1912, 'La propagande révolutionnaire dans l'armée, *Le Sou du Soldat* (Archives Nationales, F7 12911); and on September 1, 'Une oeuvre de la CGT, *Le Sou du Soldat*, A.N. F7 13333)

7 Jean-Jacques Becker. *1914. Comment les Français sont entrés dans la guerre. (Contribution à l'étude de l'opinion publique, printemps-été, 1914)* Presses de la Fondation nationale des Sciences politiques, 1977, p. 379 *passim*.

8 Gérard Raffael, 'Les movements pacifistes dans les usines d'armements de la région de Saint-Étienne' in *Actes du 98e congrès national des Sociétés savantes*, Saint Étienne, 1973.

9 Archives Nationales F 7 13272.

10 *Dictionnaire biographique du mouvement ouvrier français*.

11 Archives Nationales F 14607.

12 A.N. F7 12994, documents 83 and 84.

13 A.N. F7 12994. Documents 107, 108 and 109.

14 ibid.,, document 124.

15 A.N. F 12994. Document 124.

16 ibid.,. Document 160.

17 ibid.,, Document 188.

18 ibid.,. Document 125.

19 A.N. F 12994. Report of a police spy on the meeting of the administrative committee of the Metal Workers Union for February 26,1918. Document 200.

20 ibid., Document 161.

21 Letter from Georges Dumoulin to Pierre Monatte on April 22nd, 1918, in *Syndicalisme révolutionnaire et communisme, les archives de Pierre Monatte*, presented by Jean Maitron and Colette Chambelland. François Maspéro, 1968, p. 257.

22 A.N. 12994, Document 514.

690

Chapter 49

The British Experience of Conscientious Objection

Keith Robbins

In a book which concentrates upon 'the war experience' there is, perhaps, something paradoxical in a contribution on the subject of conscientious objection. Conscientious objectors, by definition, set themselves against 'experiencing' war. Many, perhaps most, did not need actually to 'experience' war to be convinced that it was unjustifiable and they would have no part in it. In most cases, that conviction had been formed by reading and reflection rather than by direct encounter with warfare – though there were, of course, some individuals, for whom direct contact with the war changed their minds[1]. From 1914 onwards, however, as the war unfolded, nothing which could be read about its progress would cause pre-war objectors to change their minds about its intrinsic unacceptability. It was not for them the scale of the war or its duration which triggered 'objection' – though it may have strengthened it – but simply the fact that war was war. No doubt some wars were worse than others, and the war of 1914 showed every sign of becoming a particularly awful example of the species, but the resort to force and the attendant killing were intrinsically 'objectionable' whether hundreds, thousands or millions were involved. A priori, war was 'wrong'. It was not necessary specifically to 'experience' war to know that was the case.

Although it is undoubtedly possible in pre–1914 Britain to locate voices who believed that the tensions of Europe could only be resolved by resort to war or were positively anxious for such a conflict, I have argued elsewhere, however, that there was no dominant desire in pre–1914 Britain for war[2]. The Edwardian Liberal Party still professed an ideological commitment to 'peace' – though that did not mean that it was 'pacifist', a word full of ambiguity. The vacillations and uncertainties of the Liberal Cabinet in the summer of 1914 need no further rehearsal here. In other words, in articulating the conviction that war was 'unacceptable', those who did so in the pre–1914 decade had not already set themselves clearly 'against the tide'. Notwithstanding 'militaristic' aspects, British society was not, as a whole, 'militarist'. Of course, Britain did go to war in 1914 but, despite the agitation for 'National Service' which had surfaced a few years earlier, it did so without conscription.

The outbreak of hostilities, and the British government's decision to join in, necessarily provoked a crisis in that broad swathe of radical Liberal/Labour opinion whose opposition to war, up to this point, was general rather than specific. Before 1914, opposition to war had found expression in rallies and demonstrations, though often there had remained a pervasive feeling amongst those taking part that, somehow or other, in the last analysis, war would be avoided. In August 1914, however, individuals and organizations – churches and political parties – had to make up their minds whether to support or oppose the war.[3] This decision was frequently agonizingly difficult. Within what we may loosely label 'the peace movement' it provoked a crisis. Some erstwhile 'pacifists' came to the conclusion that this particular war was the exception which proved the rule. On the part of those who continued to oppose intervention, however, such changes of front were deemed a 'betrayal'[4].

Was such objection to British intervention 'conscientious'? It is here that we begin to move into a thicket of conceptual difficulties. Some objections to participation in the war seemed in the eyes of contemporaries to be prudential, pragmatic or, as it were, methodological. Prudential arguments could rest on cost-benefit analysis – war did not 'pay' and was therefore not worth anyone engaging in. Norman Angell and his followers believed that war was 'The Great Illusion'. Was that conscience? Pragmatically, objections could rest on calculations that British interests would be better served if France and Germany fought themselves to a standstill. Was that conscience? Methodologically, they could rest on the proposition that 'the people' had not been consulted and that war had only occurred because of a 'secret diplomacy' only concerned with the 'Balance of Power'. These views could be held separately or clustered together to make what seemed to those who held them to be a comprehensively convincing case. It was not clear, however, that objections of this kind were 'conscientious'.

In the short term, in the British context, no attempt at definition was necessary. Those who were uncertain or unwilling did not respond to 'duty's call' but stood back as the volunteers came forward, stimulated, in some cases by the songs of Phyllis Dare or the eloquence of Horatio Bottomley. The climate of enthusiastic patriotism thus engendered does not need elaboration here. At a time of heightened emotion, however, the 'instincts of the herd' asserted themselves. Through the Parliamentary Recruiting Committee, and other means, the emphasis from government was placed upon duty: 'Don't Lag! Follow your flag!'. The householders' return, signed by the party leaders, asked all eligible men from nineteen to thirty-eight to indicate their willingness to enlist. It is well-known, however, that the pace of recruitment slackened. It was in this context that social pressure began to manifest itself.

Within families, clubs, churches, chapels or other social groups, young men found themselves required to explain why they were not volunteering. The famous or infamous 'White Feathers' made their appearance with the clear implication that young men who were not preparing to fight were 'cowards'. It became necessary for them, in their own minds and in a social context, to clarify the nature of their objections. The act of 'not fighting' certainly ran counter to the propaganda of the state and, so far as we can judge, to the initial mood of the country at large. However, while it might bring social unpopularity or ostracism, it was legal not to fight.

The prospect of conscription would narrow down the issues. There is no call here to examine the pressures within the government which led to the agitated consideration of compulsory military service. The prospect that it would be introduced, however, gave rise to as varied a set of objections as the war itself had provoked. For some, of course, the opposition to conscription was not necessarily 'anti-war'. Such voices argued either that conscription was not in fact an efficient way of deploying national resources or that to introduce it would only imperil national unity at a crucial juncture. These views were advanced by prominent Liberals within and without the government. As is well-known, Sir John Simon, the Home Secretary, resigned rather than be party to compelling a man to be a soldier[5]. He was probably disappointed that no other cabinet minister followed him onto the back benches. And, in the debate on the Military Service Bill in January 1916, in which he spoke, the government majority was 403 to 105 (of whom 60 were Irish Nationalists). The British opposition was reduced to eleven Labour members and thirty-four Liberals. The anticipated opposition outside Parliament, especially from trade unions, largely failed to materialize. The outcome, naturally, was a disappointment for the groups which had sprung up to campaign against conscription. The passage of the legislation, however, inevitably entailed that the meaning of 'conscientious objection' was about to be put to the test.

In introducing the Military Service Bill, Asquith had announced, amongst other grounds for exemption, 'conscientious objection to undertaking combatant service'[6]. In part he no doubt wished to mollify Liberal opinion, but it is not entirely fair to regard the decision as 'political' rather than 'ideological' or 'ethical'. With the exception of the United States (subsequently), the British government was the only major belligerent to seek to make provision for 'conscientious objection'. It seems that Asquith's statement was greeted with groans, catcalls and laughter. The Prime Minister cited the fact that Pitt had exempted Quakers from the provisions of the Militia Acts during the war against France at the end of

693

the eighteenth century. However, although some Tory back-benchers tried to limit the exemption so that it applied only to religious bodies with a long-established tradition of 'pacifism', Bonar Law made it clear in the debate that an 'objection' could also be founded on a non-religious basis. It seems fairly certain, indeed, that the government believed that the provisions it was making would cater adequately for such categories of 'conscientious objection' as it was able to identify. It was, however, also anxious to protect itself against the accusation that it was providing a 'shirker's charter'. Local tribunals of responsible citizens were to have the task of testing consciences. In the event, the composition of the tribunals and their conflicting interpretations of their task ensured disparity of treatment. In addition, there was confusion about the exemptions to be offered – 'absolute', from combatant service only, 'work of national importance' – to those who refused to fight. It was naively assumed in some official quarters that the formation of a Non-Combatant Corps, whose members would undertake supply but not combat duties, would satisfy most conscientious objectors. Although some three thousand joined, it did not in fact do so.

Difficulty in framing and implementing legislation of this character was only to be expected in all the circumstances. The philosophical difficulties surrounding the concept of 'conscience' must be mentioned but cannot be elaborated. Do its promptings require rational elaboration and justification or are they overarching? How is the coherence of conscience to be judged? In addition, there were issues relating to the nature of political obligation and the State which could not be avoided. Sir Henry Jones, moral philosopher and 'the greatest living Welshman' (after Lloyd George!) argued that 'the state had a right to compel, provided it stood for its own welfare . . . It owned us, we belonged to it. We derived the very substance of our soul from the organized community in which we lived and which we called the State'[7]. How could a 'conscientious objector' contract out of such a community? In short, the issues involved in a claim to 'conscientious objection' would have taxed even the diligent students of moral philosophy at the University of Glasgow where Sir Henry taught. It is not surprising that such exchanges as survive between local tribunal and applicant take on a rather cruder form. In any case, it was the task of the tribunal to make an assessment of 'character' and 'genuineness' rather than award an alpha for cogency of argument. Their task was not made any easier by the fact that they also had to consider the validity of claims for exemption on grounds other than conscience – family and employment circumstances, for example. Tribunals themselves clearly felt the moral force of 'equality of sacrifice' as a guiding principle. There was a reluctance to grant 'total exemption' – though the legislation was clarified to make it plain that this was possible – insofar as it seemed to suggest that someone who would not fight had no obligations of any kind to the community.

Legend has it that the tribunals were invariably harsh, obscurantist and insensitive. Certainly the Military Representative had the right to appear as a party to every application and in many cases his presence set the tone. Nevertheless, such a generalization about the work of the Tribunals, while no doubt true in many instances, ignores the difficulty which 'conscientious objection' posed for those tribunal members who were trying, conscientiously, to accommodate and understand its basis. Thus, the 'experience of conscientious objection' in wartime has two sides, though it is perhaps inevitable that our image of the role of tribunals is largely formed from the comments of conscientious objectors themselves.

Having established the context in which 'conscientious objection' emerged, therefore, it is time to see things from the perspective of conscientious objectors themselves. How should we understand that 'experience'? Is it even possible to talk about *the* experience of the conscientious objector, given the diversity of standpoints involved?

Although the definition of a conscientious objector cannot be absolutely rigid, it is helpful at the outset to state the generally agreed figure of roughly 16,500 – 0.33 per cent of the total number of men recruited voluntarily and compulsorily during the war. Most were satisfied with the kind of exemption which was allowed. In the eyes of certain sections of the press it was these men, by their willingness to accept what the law provided and, in many cases, to accept irksome restrictions on their freedom so long as they were not complled to fight, who demonstrated that conscientious objection was a valid position which had to be respected even in a society at war. However, there was a large minority of around 6,000 men who either declined to appear before the tribunals or would not accept their verdict. They were subjected to military or civil detention. The 'hard core' – involving around 1300 men - were totally intransigent in their attitude and received repeated sentences each time the initial sentence was completed. This figure indicates, therefore, that we are dealing with a small body of men, but it is very often this rump and their experiences which are held to be 'normative' in discussion of First World War 'conscientious objection'.

However, within this core, we can discern a wide variety of beliefs, motives and actions. The label 'conscientious objector' is therefore only a loose description and masks internal disagreement, even conflict. It also makes generalization about treatment difficult. It is true that in society at large 'conscientious objection' could appear a single category – to be treated appropriately. Nevertheless, in more informed circles, there was some awareness of the different reasons which led men to claim to be conscientious objectors. Some of these reasons received more public sympathy and understanding than others.

The diversity should occasion no surprise. In a sense, 'individuality' lay at the heart of the conscientious objector's argument. Whatever the precise nature of the case being articulated, it was intensely individual. It sprang from reflection that was personal in its very essence. A conscientious objector, as things stood, was *contra mundum*. His role was prophetic [8]. He could do no other. Cultivation of the individual conscience could bring together a political Liberalism and a religious Dissent in potent fusion. The 'Nonconformist Conscience' did not hold the State in awe – 'passive resistance' was in the blood [9]. This pedigree is very apparent in the background of many conscientious objectors, but emphasis upon *The Majesty of Conscience*, to quote the title of a book published by a leading Baptist, F.B. Meyer, in 1917, could not ignore the fact that conscience clearly prompted different men in different directions [10]. We therefore discover a tension at the heart of 'conscientious objection', by no means only latent, between the 'right of private judgment' and the belief that certain private judgments were right.

It was not clear, therefore, precisely what 'conscientious objection' implied and the grounds on which it could be claimed. This was a problem as much for conscientious objectors between themselves as it was in dealings between conscientious objectors and various branches of government. Unanimity of conviction was perhaps not even to be looked for since, on principle, a right of dissent ruled amongst themselves when conscientious objectors sought to reach a common position. In addition, almost by definition, conscientious objectors were articulate and eager to discuss and debate. This reflected, in many cases, their previous involvement in Nonconformist chapel life or in ILP politics. Their social background was mixed but skilled workers or lower middle-class clerical or professional workers probably predominated. Their viewpoint, defended tenaciously against the wider society, could be defended equally tenaciously against their fellows. 'Leadership' and 'Organization' posed particular problems. Thus, although many conscientious objectors went through the same formal experiences – appearance before tribunal, detention and imprisonment – there was no unanimity in interpreting the significance of these experiences.

The dissidence of Dissent, however, had awkwardly to coexist with the collectivism of Socialism and, very often, to coexist within the same individual. The fact that 'conscientious objection' could be allowed under the Act without any religious foundation opened the way to endless complications. The division in Labour's ranks in August 1914 and thereafter cannot be elaborated in detail here [11]. However, anti-war sentiments continued to be strongly expressed in certain I.L.P. branches where the view was taken that the war was only being waged for the sake of armament rings. The workers of Europe, it was argued, continued to have no quarrel with each other [12]. A campaign against conscription would be one facet of a continuing opposition to the war.

The youthful editor of the *Labour Leader*, Fenner Brockway, played a leading part, together with Clifford Allen and C.H. Norman – all three Socialists – in establishing the No-Conscription Fellowship at the end of 1914 [13]. In its statement in the spring of 1915, the N.C.F. based its opposition to conscription on the principle that human life was sacred. In addition, governments had no right to compel anyone to bear arms. Into the Fellowship came many, probably a majority, who described themselves as Socialist war-resisters – and their objections went further. They were asking themselves whether it might be right to kill in order to overthrow capitalism. By the end of 1915, the N.C.F. claimed to have nearly two hundred branches, but despite intensive lobbying in the early months of 1916, success was to elude it. Conscientious objectors had therefore to decide on their next move. There was still some talk of leading a campaign in the country, but that seemed a difficult if not hopeless cause.

Generalization about 'public opinion and the conscientious objector' is inevitably difficult. Although not all historians are agreed, the picture rather seems to be one of increasing public exasperation with 'conchies' and 'pastyfaces'[14], certainly in 1916. Allen subsequently conceded that 'a certain spiritual pride' had crept into the ranks which stiffened opposition to the cause and, in his own words, 'engendered really bitter hatred'. Even so, experiences of individuals could vary very considerably, depending on their social milieu. They were unpopular and subject to some degree of social ostracism before 1916 but rarely physically assaulted. A distinction can perhaps usefully be drawn between attitudes towards individual conscientious objectors and attitudes towards any gathering which they organized.

One such public assembly was a N.C.F. national convention held in London at Devonshire House, then the Quaker headquarters, on 8–9 April 1916, to take stock. The *Daily Express* saw fit to alert its readers to the event and there were fears of violence. It is interesting to note that Allen contacted the Metropolitan Police Commissioner who provided police protection – some sections of the N.C.F. had been establishing an elaborate 'shadow' organization on the grounds that the police constituted the enemy. A hostile crowd did gather outside and, in order not to be provocative, the fifteen hundred or so people inside were asked not to cheer the speakers. The assembly declared, almost unanimously, that it would only recognize the legitimacy of absolute exemption. In effect, every effort would be made to make the Military Service Acts unworkable and to spurn the efforts that the government had made to cater for men who would not fight. Beatrice Webb, who was an unsympathetic witness, concluded that those present were 'not so much conscientious objectors as a militant minority of elects, intent on thwarting the will of the majority of ordinary citizens in a national policy'[15]. Bertrand Russell, however, who had been recently drawn into the work of the N.C.F. was in high spirits. He believed that the young men would defeat the government and wreck conscription. In a letter to Lady Ottoline Morrell, he described the spirit of the young men as 'magnificent'. They were not *seeking* martyrdom, he claimed, but accepting it with great willingness [16]. Some press reaction to this gathering was extremely hostile. The *Evening Standard* spoke of the 'hordes of cowards' who merited severe treatment, while the *Glasgow Herald* thought they should be interned for the duration of the war and deported thereafter. It was a common assumption that, whatever their ostensible 'reasons', conscientious objectors were in fact cowards hiding behind high moral sentiments.

In the months immediately following the Devonshire House Convention, it became clear that the government had no intention of wilting. It could be argued that the 'sanctity of life' had ceased to be the issue. The government was not going to stop the war but, making use of the Defence of the Realm Act, it was going to stop or at least drastically curtail the N.C.F.'s proselytizing activities. The entire national committee, with the exception of Allen, was successfully prosecuted for publishing a leaflet *Repeal the Act*. Partly under this pressure, which ran with the tide of press opinion, the ardent unanimity of the Devonshire House meeting began to dissolve, although the fragmentation of opinion did not follow straightforward lines.

It would be too simple, for example, to distinguish between 'religious' and 'non-religious' objectors, though it was inevitable that there should be a certain difference of perspective between religious and non-religious men. It was evident that in some sense 'religion' was central to the 'objections' of conscientious objectors. Yet in many cases there was a resolute refusal to distinguish between 'religion' and 'politics'. Socialists became Quakers and Quakers became Socialists. There was, thus, a unitary vision in which religious language and political programme fused. In other cases, 'official' Christianity had been rejected and a radical religion espoused which had little connection with organized churches. In yet other cases, all religion had been rejected absolutely. These different combinations and emphases necessarily meant that the experience of being a conscientious objector did not have a common framework. For some, suffering was something which strengthened their convictions; for others, it was simply intolerable.

There were certainly figures in the outside world, however, who continued very firmly to distinguish between the two categories in their own minds. Lord William Cecil, for example, the Bishop of Exeter, expressed himself firmly in a letter to *The Times* in October 1917. After visiting the centre for objectors at Princetown on Dartmoor, he had become convinced that sacks of letters came and went 'conveying instructions for those plans of bloodshed which may at some future time bring, according to their view, liberty, and to our view, ruin, to England'. He suggested that all genuine religious objectors should be released as good citizens 'with fanatic views' whereas political objectors should be transported, without money or rations, to 'that portion of England which is frequently visited by the enemy aeroplane'.[17] The experiences of conscientious objectors, therefore, inevitably varied to the extent that such views were shared by those with whom they came into contact.

As was only to be expected, this was predominantly a movement of youthful and enthusiastic but politically inexperienced young men – Allen, for example, was born in 1889 and Brockway a year earlier – drawn from the age group involved. It was dispiriting for some of these young men to observe other contemporaries, perhaps initially sympathetic, who decided not to go through with the absolutist stand which entailed refusal of any kind of alternative if total exemption were not granted. Was the 'alternativist' to be regarded as a 'weak brother' and cast out, or should the N.C.F. hold a watching brief for all? The controversy on this issue in the summer and autumn of 1916 threatened to split the N.C.F. completely. Another source of bitter controversy revolved around the amount of contact, direct or indirect, to be had with the military authorities. Men who had been turned down by tribunals but who persisted, in the army, in regarding themselves as conscientious objectors constituted a major problem. It is well-known that one group came close to losing their lives in France. Inevitably, however, in some eyes, for supporters of conscientious objectors to seek to work effectively with the military in order to reach some kind of accommodation on this and other matters was to 'collaborate'. Not surprisingly, men who were perceived as being utterly and completely hostile to 'the military machine' did not invariably receive the same treatment at the hands of that machine as those whose behaviour, from a military or prison standpoint, seemed 'reasonable'. The death in September 1916 of Walter Roberts, a conscientious objector held at the Dyce camp in Aberdeenshire, was presented as a martyrdom by fellow-objectors and their supporters. He had fallen victim to influenza – a direct consequence, it was argued, of damp conditions. Hostile commentators noted that even damper conditions were to be encountered in France.

The details of these disagreements cannot be followed through here. On issue after issue, however, conscientious objectors, despite warm affirmations of their continuing unity in the struggle against militarism and their desire for peace, differed on the extent to which their principles would be compromised if they accepted the schemes that were on offer. In 1917, for example, in connexion with the Home Office scheme which had established camps – not prisons – at Wakefield, Princetown and elsewhere, there were disturbances and protests which divided the Conscientious Objectors themselves. Should they honour the conditions on which they had been sent to such centres or should they sabotage everything? Opinions and actions differed.

The harshness of the conditions experienced by the hard core of 'absolutists' who refused any kind of alternative came as a shock, at least to those among their number who had talked a little glibly of 'going off to prison'. Herbert Samuel, as Home Secretary, had determined that conscientious objectors should not be subjected to a regimen any more favourable (or unfavourable) than that experienced by 'ordinary' prisoners. It is impossible, in this contribution, to review all the experiences systematically, but a number of prominent individuals will now be looked at in more detail. Of course, 'experience' can have short- or long-term consequences and be primarily physical, intellectual or spiritual. It is characteristic of those we shall be considering that all these elements were involved and that their years as conscientious objectors became central in the shape and purpose of their lives.

The experience of prison proved shattering, in some cases literally so, for members of the 'hard core'. The extent of their physical breakdown naturally varied since they did not begin the experience of detention in the same physical condition. Clifford Allen, chairman of the NCF, emerged from detention gravely weakened in body.[18] Indeed, he was subsequently rarely anything more than a semi-invalid and died before he was fifty. That was not a fate which his Conservative Anglican parents had in mind when they sent him to an English public school. Bristol and Cambridge universities followed, where he was converted to socialism and pacifism - holding the two to be virtually synonymous. Allen himself, who served some sixteen months hard labour in a variety of locations since he absolutely refused all compromise with the authorities, took the view that the experience of detention was worse than the experience of war. It may be, of course, that prison life came especially hard to someone of his background. In his, and other cases, what made their fate worse was the fact that, unlike 'ordinary' prisoners with finite sentences, theirs was in effect without limit. Once a particular sentence was concluded, after due process another one began.

Beyond the loss of health, what had the experience meant? Allen never stopped worrying over its significance for the rest of his life. On the one hand, that his health had suffered was a clear vindication of his integrity. It could not be said that he was a coward, concerned only for his own survival. He was as wounded as any soldier. Yet he had not carried his objection to the lengths he had done merely to demonstrate his personal integrity. It had been part of a programme designed to stop the war. As such, while stirrings could be detected in 1917, it had undoubtedly failed. So, in the post-war decade, he moved somewhat erratically on a political course which was to take him to the House of Lords with a peerage on the formation of the National Government in 1931. His experience led him, and certain others, as Martin Ceadel puts it, to define pacifism as a personal faith but one which could not in any realistic time-scale be expected to be a political creed. He died in 1939 before seeing the failure of his 'constructive pacifism' to avert another war.

Morgan Jones, MP for Caerphilly from 1921, was the first ex-conscientious objector to be elected to the House of Commons – he was to be followed by a trickle of others including Fenner Brockway and Walter Ayles. Jones represented the constituency until he too died young in 1939. A school teacher and local I.L.P. councillor in South Wales, he was dismissed from his post because of his objection to the war and joined the N.C.F. He wrote to Allen in May 1916 from the police cells in Bargoed that he had 'no regrets, no remorse and no misgiving' for the stand that was being taken, adding 'Our fellowship is dealing smashing blows to militarism in this country and it is my confident belief that it will never recover'. He was, however, anxious that Allen should conserve his energy and strength so that he could grapple with future problems:

> you have no right, by a reckless waste of your physical strength, to put the future to that extent in jeopardy. Be advised, dear comrade, in time. Take more leisure. I beg of you to take more exercise in the open air . . . you are sacrificing yourself too much.

Six months later, Jones was confessing that the effect of prison on his own mind had been 'to entirely deprive me of the power of mentally concentrating upon any subject for any length of time'. He had felt himself to be under intense pressure in the experience through which he had been passing. In the solitude of his cell he was 'almost borne down with the burden I bear'. Things were very shaky at home and he had come to doubt the wisdom of the Absolutist stand. He wrote to Allen:

> 'We are all watching your magnificent fight with unwearied interest. We note each piece of news about you and those who take your view and though at the moment we differ – I am astonished to think how far I have travelled from my old standpoint – we are entirely at one in the desire that each and all of us may be enabled to fight the battle of conscience to the uttermost degree that we may think it necessary'.

There were other ways, too, in which he was changing. As he put it, gaol was a wonderful place for self introspection. 'More and more' he wrote 'I am compelled to recognise and appreciate the value of individual character and the formulative influence of religion thereon.'[19]

The experience and outlook of another South Walian teacher (and subsequent MP) Emrys Hughes was somewhat different. He wrote as follows in his own ironically entitled 'Journal of a Coward':

> 'I never thought of going to prison as something vaguely negative, as an act of passive refusal, as a futile personal protest. Going to prison to me

meant focussing public attention on certain principles, the constructive International Socialist principles as an alternative to the war policy of the Government. We would be the advance guard of the attack of the young democracy on the old imperialism'.

He drew a parallel between the persecution of Plato, Jesus, Savonarola, Hus 'and thousands more in the eternal struggle between Tyranny and Freedom, between the Law and the fanatic'. Hughes was himself the son of a Nonconformist minister.

But where was the boundary to be drawn, if anywhere, in this 'eternal struggle'? Somewhat later, in response to criticism of the treatment which absolutists received in prison, the Government set up a detention centre for them in Wakefield prison under less harsh conditions. However, the experiment failed because of the opposition, led by Walter Ayles, chairman of the prisoners involved, who was able to carry a collective policy of refusing any special concessions other than unconditional release. Fenner Brockway, on his own account, took every opportunity, during his incarceration not only to proclaim his own anti-war stand but also to challenge authority. When he was at Devizes, a military camp where he was first sent, Hughes refused to dress himself in army uniform or to obey orders but he was prepared to polish rusty farm implements. However under Army Order X, Hughes was subsequently transferred to the civil prison at Shepton Mallet in Somerset where he would be out of sight of khaki. A hostile crowd outside booed him into the prison. 'The thought flashed through my mind', he wrote, 'as the door closed behind us, how bad things must be when anyone could give a sigh of relief when leaving human beings behind and going into prison.' He went through a series of courts martial and transfers from prison to prison in the years ahead. He refused the Home Office scheme of civil work under civil control. His reading matter in his varied locations ranged from *Pilgrim's Progress* to Carlyle's *French Revolution*. His father, brother and sister could come to visit him once a month when he was in Cardiff gaol. Nevertheless, he recalls that his health began to suffer. He slept very badly and felt that he would eventually go mad. By the summer of 1917, however, when he was in the small prison at Caernarfon, he found himself 'enjoying the rest' and he could think about life 'without anxiety and terror'.[20]

Although his health suffered in the short term, on his own account he left the peace of his cell eventually in April 1919 almost reluctantly. 'I was leaving its seclusion', he wrote, 'for the life of the world, the life of struggle, of noise, of striving, of humiliation, and of defeat. It had been so easy to be good alone. One saw so little of humanity'. Unlike others, a long and rebellious political career lay ahead of him and he was seventy-five when he died.

Although, there was some alleviation of their circumstances by the end of the war, there was equally a hardening of their own resistance, and some work and hunger strikes. The condition of the absolutists in prison did evoke outside concern. *I Appeal unto Caesar*, published in mid-1917 and largely written, it seems, by Bertrand Russell, arose out of Mrs Henry Hobhouse's concern for her son Stephen, and had some effect on the general climate of opinion, at least in Russell's own estimation, but did not result in a general change of government policy. However, the announcement that seriously ill objectors might be released did allow both Hobhouse and Allen to leave prison.

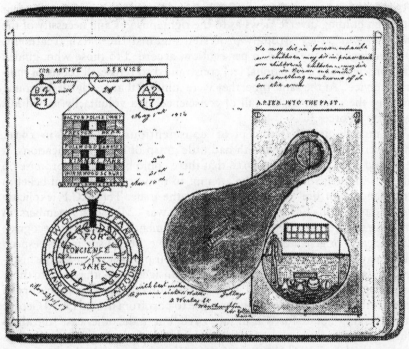

(ix)   In an autograph album, Conscientious Objector Walter Jolley, imprisoned in Kinmel Camp, North Wales, designs a medal award for his service for Conscience. Note the medal bar showing cells and floors he occupied. [J.N. Carter: Liddle Collection]

The experiences which have been sketched cannot easily be summarized and the issues which they raise still remain to some extent contentious, even at this juncture. The concept of 'conscientious objection' was inescapably problematic. The juxtaposition of the two words caused offence and irritation for the bulk of the population which was left with the imputation that a combatant had no conscience. It was offensive for conscientious objectors, on the other hand, to be described, both in private and public, as 'cranks' or 'misfits'. It is not surprising, at a time of heightened emotion, suffering and loss, that strong opinions were expressed. For some, conscientious objectors had been treated with excessive concern, in parliament and elsewhere, at a time when the fate of the nation was at stake. For others, they had been unnecessarily and inappropriately pilloried for their convictions. No liberal state at war has found that balance easy to attain. Individuals and institutions had to strike it as best they could. Trinity College, Cambridge, as is well known, deprived Bertrand Russell of a lectureship in July 1916 after he had been convicted of prejudicing the recruitment and discipline of the armed forces. The members of The Downs Congregational Church, Bowdon, Cheshire whose minister, Leyton Richards, was a prominent pacifist, had resolved a few months earlier that 'though holding diverse views as to the righteousness and necessity of the present war', they strongly protested 'against the harsh treatment, amounting in many cases to persecution, accorded to those who, guided by conscientious convictions, feel constrained to refuse all forms of military service'. At the same time, they were mindful that nearly all the young men of the church 'at the call of conscience' had voluntarily joined His Majesty's Forces.[21]

In introducing the concept of 'conscientious objection' in 1916, however, it seems that Asquith had little grasp of its full implications. It emerged after the spring of 1916 that there could be little compromise on the government's part once the attempt to respect an individual belief in 'the sanctity of life' was seen not to be the issue. The N.C.F. explicitly wished to smash conscription and 'stop the war'. Most of its members, in varying degrees, saw no merit in the government's attempts to recognize 'conscience' or give it credit for its comparative 'liberalism' in this respect. This may have been a sensible attitude on their part – it is not for the historian to say – but intransigence fostered intransigence. 'With regard to those who object to shedding blood it is the traditional policy of this country to respect that view, and we do not propose to part from it' said Lloyd George as Secretary of State for War in July 1916 'but in the other case [the absolutists] I shall only consider the best means of making the path of that class a very hard one'.[22] The experience of objectors was indeed a 'very hard one' in many instances.[23] A later age may think it too hard.

Notes

1   Max Plowman, *Bridge into the Future: Letters*, London, Andrew Dakers, 1944, pp.112–17.
2   Keith Robbins, 'L'Ambiguité du mot "Paix" au Royaume-Uni avant 1914' in *1914: Les Psychoses de Guerre*, Rouen, Publications de l'Université, 1984, pp.59–73.
3   Keith Robbins, 'Britain in the Summer of 1914' in Keith Robbins, *Politicians, Diplomacy and War in Modern British History*, London, Hambledon, 1994, pp.175–88; Michael Brock, 'Britain Enters the War' in R.J.W.Evans and Hartmut Pogge von Strandmann (eds.), *The Coming of the First World War*, Oxford, Oxford University Press, 1988, pp.145–78.

4   Keith Robbins, *The Abolition of War: The 'Peace Movement' in Britain, 1914–1919*, Cardiff, University of Wales Press, 1976, pp.27–47.

5   David Dutton, *Simon: A Political Biography*, London, Aurum, 1992, pp.37–41.

6   See the discussion in J.M. Rae, *Conscience & Politics: The British Government and the Conscientious Objector to Military Service 1916–1919*, Oxford, Oxford University Press, 1970, pp.22–67; John W. Dalton, *Conscription and Conscience: A History 1916–1919*, London, Allen & Unwin, 1922, is a committed early study still worth reading; Julian Bell, ed., *We Did Not Fight: 1914–1918 Experiences of War Resisters*, London, Cobden-Sanderson, 1935; M. Ceadel, *Pacifism in Britain 1914–1945: The Defining of a Faith*, Oxford, Oxford University Press, 1980.

7   David Boucher and Andrew Vincent, *A Radical Hegelian: The Political and Social Philosophy of Henry Jones* Cardiff, University of Wales Press, 1993 p.163; Henry Jones, 'The War and Morality' in J.Estlin Carpenter (ed.), *Ethical and Religious Problems of the War*, London, Lindsey, 1916, pp.21–45.

8   Keith Robbins, 'On Prophecy and Politics: Some Pragmatic Reflexions' in Keith Robbins, *History, Religion and Identity in Modern Britain*, London, Hambledon, 1993, pp.105–18.

9   David Bebbington, *The Nonconformist Conscience: Chapel and Politics 1870–1914*, London, Allen & Unwin, 1982.

10 F.B. Meyer, *The Majesty of Conscience*, London, National Labour Press, 1917: For Meyer see I. Randall, 'Mere Denominationalism: F.B. Meyer and Baptist Life', *The Baptist Quarterly* XXXV (January 1993) pp.19–34.

11 Douglas J. Newton, *British Labour, European Socialism and the Struggle for Peace 1889–1914*, Oxford, Oxford University Press, 1985.

12 F.L. Carsten, *War against War: British and German Radical Movements in the First World War*, London, Batsford, 1982, pp.54–5.

13 Thomas C. Kennedy, *The Hound of Conscience: A History of the No-Conscription Fellowship, 1914–1919*, Fayetteville, University of Kentucky Press, 1981, is the best account and what follows is substantially indebted to his work which corrects my own comments in *The Abolition of War* in a number of places. The wealth of his references to relevant literature makes repetition unnecessary here.

14 Thomas C. Kennedy, 'Public Opinion and the Conscientious Objector, 1915–1919', *Journal of British Studies*, 12 (May 1973) pp.105–19.

15 Robbins, *Abolition of War*, pp.81–2.

16 Jo Vellacott, *Bertrand Russell and the Pacifists in the First World War*, Brighton, Harvester, 1980, p.43. and p.47.

17 Kennedy, *Hound of Conscience*, p.175.

18 For Allen see Arthur Marwick, *Clifford Allen*, Edinburgh, Edinburgh University Press, 1964; M.Gilbert (ed.) *Plough My Own Furrow* (London, 1965).

19 Keith Robbins, 'Morgan Jones in 1916', *Llafur*, 1, 4 (1975), pp.38–43; for a general survey of the Welsh scene see K.O.Morgan, 'Peace Movements in Wales, 1899–1945', *Welsh History Review* 10 (1980–81) pp.398–430.

20 Anthony More-O'Brien, '"Conchie": Emrys Hughes and the First World War', *Welsh History Review*, 13 (1986–87) pp.343–51.

21 Clyde Binfield, *So Down to Prayers: Studies in English Nonconformity*

1780–1920, London, J.M.Dent, 1977, p.244; Alan Wilkinson, *Dissent or Conform: War, Peace and the English Churches, 1900–1945*, London, S.C.M., 1986; Paul R. Dekar, 'Twentieth-Century British Baptist Conscientious Objectors' *Baptist Quarterly* XXXV (January, 1994) 1 pp.35–44; Jill Wallis, *Valiant for Peace: A History of the Fellowship of Reconciliation 1914–1989*, London, Fellowship of Reconciliation, 1991.

22 Cited in Rae, *Conscription & Conscience*, p.206.

23 For a comparative perspective on this British-centred paper see Edward R. Cain, 'Conscientious Objection in France, Britain and the United States', *Comparative Politics* 2 (1970) pp.274–307.

Part X

The War Experience Projected: Propagandists and Their Audiences

Chapter 50

German Teachers at War

Eberhard Demm

After the battle of Sadowa (Königgrätz) which decided the Austro-Prussian War of 1866 in favour of the Prussians, the French said: 'It was not General von Moltke who won this battle, it was the Prussian schoolmaster.' The idea was of course that the Prussian soldiers defeated the Austrians because of their superior standard of instruction which they owed to the excellence of the Prussian primary school system. In 1914 the German schoolmaster was back again, but this time it was not simply a metaphor, now he really fought on the front. I do not mean the military front – there of course the schoolmaster did his duty in the same way as all the other people: 54,000 German schoolmasters, that is about one third of them, enrolled, and around 15 per cent were killed in battle[1] – but I mean the home front. His task in this area was threefold:

First he worked, in practice, as a propaganda agent of the state. He brainwashed the children at school, and he was supposed to influence – directly or indirectly – the adults as well. Second, he organized the collection of all sorts of items, from scrap metal to stinging nettles for the embattled German economy. Third, he was engaged in many supplementary administrative tasks: from the distribution of the rationing cards over the so-called 'Lebensmittelerfassung' – that is the control of hoarding and hamstering, to the filling out of numerous useless questionnaires for the administration.

I now invite the reader to accompany a German schoolteacher in a small town of the Grand Duchy of Baden to his work on a day in October 1917.[2] He gets up at seven, washes himself at a sink without soap because there isn't any, eats a modest breakfast consisting of the famous K-Brot, bread baked of ersatz (potato) flour, with turnip jam and ersatz sausage, and he drinks ersatz tea made of fruit kernels or heather. After breakfast he hurries, not to his school, but to an ersatz school of course, that is a large room lent to him by the Church. His school has already in August 1914 been requisitioned by the army which has transformed it into a military barrack.[3] The room is badly lit and not heated because there is not enough coal. In his class there are eighty pupils, because two classes have been merged. Why? fifty-six per cent of his colleagues are serving at the front – this is the highest percentage of all German states. In Prussia only 34.8 per cent of the teachers serve, the German average is around one third,[4] and some women and inexperienced auxiliary teachers or seminarists cannot make up for this loss. There is a deficit of 2276 teachers in the Grand Duchy of Baden alone.[5] For this reason the number of hours for the pupils has been reduced to sixteen a week, and our teacher teaches only on Mondays, Tuesdays and Fridays. The other days, however, he is not free, but has to go to a neighbouring village and teach there.[6] Fortunately not all his pupils are there, as quite a few cut his lessons. Others have been sent away to work on farms in the countryside. To-day five of them have returned from a farm; they complain bitterly of the bad conditions there: not enough to eat, dirty plates, sleeping on straw mattresses, all suffer from dysentery because the water was polluted.[7] The teacher lets them go and promises that he will inform his superiors so that in the future no pupils will be sent to this farmer any more. The cutting of lessons is not always a result of negligence, but of higher necessities: the children have to queue for food, make 'Hamsterfahrten' into the countryside (that is to beg for or steal food) or they pilfer food or coal at railway stations; others look after little brothers and sisters because the mother works; others have no shoes any more or are simply too tired because they are severely undernourished.[8]

To-day the first lesson is German. The pupils were supposed to read at home as a preparation for this lesson a story called 'Ich hatt' einen Kameraden' (I had a comrade). The teacher, who probably does not trust the quality of the preparation, gives an 'einleitende Vorerzählung', that is a sort of resumé of the story: Two little boys always play together, then go to school, they are called the good comrades. Then comes the war, they become soldiers and learn how to shoot. When they see a village destroyed by the enemy they say: 'We want to fight courageously so that the French cannot come into our homeland and destroy our village'.[9] On the front they built trenches, and are always on their guard because the French want to attack them. They make a dangerous incursion into enemy territory with success and get the Iron Cross. Then starts the battle: 'The French want to chase us away and take our mountain', says the captain. 'They must not do this. We fight with God for Kaiser and Reich. The Kaiser Hurrah!'[10] In the battle the French lose and run away, but one of the two comrades dies. After this resumé the teacher starts the 'Vertiefung', a sort of guided discussion. The teachers asks when the two friends have gone to war; he shows the children an announcement of mobilization and reads some of it to them. Then he asks: 'Why is this posted at the town hall?' 'Which man also has a uniform? Describe a uniform?' Then the teacher shows pictures of uniforms. He asks: 'Why are they now grey?' One intelligent pupil says that the grey colour will protect the soldier against being seen by the enemy. He nevertheless gets a bad mark and has to pay five pfennigs into a sheet metal box, because in his answer he used a foreign word, and this has been forbidden since the beginning of the war.[11] Then the teacher goes on: 'What do you remember when our soldiers went to war?' The children answer that some people cried. 'Who cried and why?', insists the teacher. Then he organizes a role play in the church yard: the boys go to war, the girls sing and wave. He shows a picture of soldiers leaving for the front. In the end the children write down some basic phrases to remember into their copy-book: 'Germany is superior to all other nations in the world. I love Germany, because it is my fatherland. Our soldiers are courageous.'[12] Our teacher is an excellent pedagogue, and his lesson is well delivered and very effective. Above all he does not talk all the time himself, but poses questions which oblige the children to find the truth by thinking for themselves. There is a great variety of approaches: questions and answers, role play, interpretation of pictures, and practical exercises, such as drawing a rifle, performing exercises with a toy rifle, packing a parcel for a soldier, or planting a 'hero oak' in the yard. He is not very severe: in some cases he even allows some pupils to put their heads on their arms and sleep. He knows that because of malnutrition they are starving and simply fall asleep because they have become too weak.[13]

After a pause of ten minutes the religious lesson starts. The teacher tells the famous story of the New Testament when Jesus fed some people with two fishes and five loaves of bread – a very well chosen subject. The children, undernourished and most of them always hungry, pay little heed. The teacher, although hungry himself, tries to bring home the following reasoning: as in the time of Jesus, there is now in Germany enough to eat for everybody even if it seems little; but we have to save food and consume it moderately. The teacher dwells a long time on the eating of barley bread by Jesus and his followers and asks: 'If Jesus were content with barley-bread, why should we need bread made of wheat? We should not say that we don't like the K-bread, that would be ungrateful to God and also show that we do not love our fatherland. God blessed the bread so that a very small quantity of it was enough for many people. The same has happened in Germany. After two years of war and a bad harvest, everybody still gets his daily bread'. The teacher resumes: 'We shall ask God to bless our food, so that we shall not be starved by the English'. Great attention is drawn to the fact that after the feeding of the five thousand the followers of Jesus collected all the bread crumbs. The teacher exhorts his pupils to do the same and concludes: whoever throws away food commits two sins – against God, and against the fatherland: 'If you do not want to save food, you are an enemy like the English'. Then the pupils write down a phrase to memorise: 'I shall keep the bread holy and shall not waste any food'. At the end of the lesson the teacher speaks of the children's duties: they must help to win the victory, but how? They must learn to renounce, not always eat when they are hungry, but work painstakingly, and give savings to the Red Cross instead of spending them on toys. Thus the war, concludes the teacher, is our great educator and inculcates important virtues like frugality, thriftiness, helpfulness. In the end the teacher collects gifts for packets which will be sent to the front: tobacco, books, cigarettes, chocolate, soap, newspapers.[16] The subject for the homework for the next religion lesson is either: 'One can put up with everything except too many good days' or: 'Which are the duties imposed on you by the War?'

The next lesson is mathematics. The teacher calculates with the children such things as British ship losses, the costs of war, the war loans, and pensions of war invalids.[17] Some examples would be : 'A German prisoner in England receives 200 marks from his family in Germany, how much will he be paid in English pounds?' 'A family consisting of mother and three children has eaten three loafs of K-bread and one loaf of 1 kg in a week. How much bread can they still buy on her bread card?' The following example makes a strong impression: 'In the battle of Neuve Chapelle the British have advanced and conquered a small strip of land three kilometers long and 950 meters deep. This "success" has cost them 25,000 dead. How many soldiers do they have to sacrifice in order to liberate the entire French territory under German occupation (22,300 square kilometers)?' The children calculate and arrive at the number of 195,600,000. 'This is impossible', says one of them. 'Yes', confirms the teacher, 'that's why they can't win the war – don't forget to tell this to your parents.'[19] Then he poses a rather simple question: 'How many marks has a golden piece of twenty marks?' The children are surprised and one of them finally says: 'Well, twenty marks of course.' 'But if you bring it to the Central Bank?', insists the teacher and explains to the children that in this case the bank can issue sixty paper marks. He speaks about the importance of collecting gold for the German central bank, exhorts his pupils to collect this at home and promises one day off school if they succeed in gathering a mark's worth of gold.[20]

In the following history lesson the teacher reads the daily report of the Military High command,[21] and shows on the map the enormous advance of the German-Austrian army after the brilliant victory of Caporetto (Karfreit) against the Italians. He announces a great school festivity and a day off because of this victory. He tries to inculcate new hope for a final victory of Germany and urges his children to discuss this brilliant success with their parents. At the end of the lesson one of the pupils offers him an English helmet which his father has brought from the front. Very happy about this sign of interest the teacher takes it and puts it into the small war museum he has established in a huge cupboard in a corner. There the following items are assembled: A Scottish cap, parts of French red trousers, a rifle sling, a buckle, parts of shells, helmets, cooking utensils, a war poem ('The Hymn of Hate' by Ernst Lissauer), letters of soldiers, the order of mobilisation, the plan of the battle of Tannenberg, a photograph of the pupils collecting metal, a military rucksack, an album with postcards from the front.[22]

The last lesson is music. The teacher proposes selecting three songs for the coming school festival celebrating the victory of Caporetto. The pupils discuss and decide who sings which song and which songs are sung by all. When one pupil suggests inventing a war story in order to combine the different songs this suggestion is accepted.[23] In the end the teacher distributes pamphlets with patriotic appeals by the Kaiser.[24] Then some of the children go home to have lunch. Others, the children of the poorer families, stay and get lunch at the church.[25]

The teacher walks to another building where a school conference takes place. There the school principal tells the colleagues that the teacher of needlework has been arrested because she has been 'a danger for the security of the Reich.' She has tried to stir up the people at an assembly of the independent Socialist party of which she was a member. She had suggested, for instance, that women should go on strike in order to compel the government to make peace. Fortunately a policeman in civilian clothes has been present and has noted all her remarks. The director underlines that he has not been aware of her political activities and that she has directed her lessons to the full satisfaction of all and refrained from any political remarks. Under her direction the girls of the school have knitted a lot of caps and socks for the soldiers at the front. Then he informs his colleagues about a new circular of the Ministry of Education: the teachers have the high patriotic duty to counteract utterances of discontent and pusillanimity and the influence of the propaganda of the enemy countries and to encourage the spirit of sacrifice and the hope of victory. They are exhorted not only to influence the children at school and out of school, but also the population, especially the women, workers, and house employees, less by public lectures, but by such means as in personal discussions at pubs, in the street, or on the trains and excursions. The following arguments are to be used: the favourable war situation, the recent successes of the army, the brilliant financial situation, (war loans), the number of foreign territories in German hands and the sparing of German territory from the war, the public welfare for families of soldiers, the role of prisoners as workers, and the difficult situation of the enemy, who nevertheless persists in fervent patriotism and refuses a humiliating peace, which should serve as a model for Germans. The teachers are especially encouraged to direct the discontent about the bad food supply away from the German rationing organization and on to the British and their blockade. Then he formally announces a day off because of the victory at Caporetto and calls everyone to come to the patriotic assembly which will take place this evening at 6 pm at the town hall. The aim is clear: Complete mobilisation of the people for the war. As Karl Liebknecht has put it in the Prussian chamber on March 16, 1916: 'War, war and war again is the slogan of the school, the schools have become "*Dressurnstalten*" (training institutions) for the war.'[28]

The teacher now goes back to the classroom where the pupils have returned in order to be examined by a school doctor. The doctor finds that eleven per cent of the pupils have abnormal hearts, 33 per cent defects of vision, and 88.8 per cent have a goitre. He says that the comparative figures for 1914 were 5 per cent, 5.5 per cent and 0 per cent and concludes that this is due to the malnutrition during the war.[29] On the whole the nutritional status of the children is unsatisfactory and has declined considerably since 1916: half of the children suffer from anaemia, where before 1916 it had been just one third.[30] Because of the lack of soap quite a few have lice and boils. After the examination the teacher takes his children to a small forest where they collect large stinging nettles which will be made into nettle cotton and for such uses as making pullovers. The pupils put the nettles in a large cart and draw this cart to a building near their old school which looks like a warehouse of junk: scrap metal, cherry kernels, old copper tubes, and, most touching, tin soldiers the children have given from their own toys for the sake of German victory; then, rubber, acorns, scrap paper, bones, coffee-grounds. In 1916 the school had collected 55 kg. of scrap metal and 258 kg. of cherry kernels, and thirty-nine old copper tubes.[32] The teacher makes some remarks on the subject: 'That's how we succeed in beating the British and their pernicious blockade.' In the same room where this stuff is stocked awaiting transport to a larger town, takes place a cooking course organized by a female colleague. Thirty housewives learn how to prepare tasty dishes without any fat, meat, and sugar and how to cook with ersatz.[33]

It is now 5 pm and the teacher rushes to his classroom where six soldiers' wives are already waiting for him, because from 5 to 6 he helps them to write letters for their husbands at the front, which he does according to Ministry of Education instructions, avoiding any subject matter which might discourage the soldiers. At 6 p.m. he goes to the patriotic assembly in the town hall where he meets the Catholic priest, the mayor and some colleagues. The children's choir is already there. The meeting starts with the song 'The honour of the German arms'. The participation of the school choir is very important because their patriotic songs are supposed to improve the low morale of the war-tired population. Singing in a group is supposed to lead to the 'integration of the individual in the nation', and to bring about discipline, the sense of sacrifice, and hate against the enemy.[35] Then the Mayor speaks on the subject of the great victory at Karfreit (Caporetto). Then comes another song and then our teacher speaks on the subject: 'What are we still fighting for?' He elaborates the great scheme of a German dominated *Mitteleuropa* where all peoples would live in peace and freedom instead of slaving along for the British and the Russians. Then a female colleague recites a poem 'The fight of the 17er before Luneville.[36] Then the priest makes a special appeal to the rural population not to hoard food but to sell everything to the state agents. He stresses that it is not only a crime against the state but also a sin against God to feed cattle with cereals while a lot of people have not enough bread to eat.[37] Then are sung the songs '*Immer fest druff*' and '*Wir müssen siegen*'. The teacher again mounts the platform and speaks of the necessity to buy war loans. Even poorer people could participate because of the possibility of collective subscription.[38] Unfortunately a soldier on leave tries to interrupt the teacher by complaining about the conditions at the front, and finally concluding: 'Whoever signs war loans will only prolong the war.' But patriotic people are in the majority and the soldier has to shut up. Then a theatre troupe of the theatre of Karlsruhe is playing a so-called war picture 'On the field of honour'. In the end a lottery is organized for the benefit of the soldiers at the front and the patriotic assembly is closed with the National anthem and the 'Trumpets of Jericho'.[40]

At 8 p.m. the teacher goes to see a farmer at the outskirts of the town. He has to walk because the rubber tires of his bike have been requisitioned for war purposes[41] – and practises the so-called '*Lebensmittelerfassung*' – that is, he checks his stocks and tries to find out if he has not hoarded provisions for the Black Market.[42] On his way back he drops into a bar where he refutes the anti-war arguments of angry soldiers on leave and tries to console a war widow.[43]

Back at home he has dinner: potatoes with ersatz sausage and ersatz lemonade. Then he writes a report about his activity to the '*Kreisschulamt*', emphasizing that he has no problems inculcating his ideas to the pupils, but has encountered heavy resistance on the part of adults: 'The population here is tired of the war and has prejudiced opinions which are difficult to correct.'[44] After this he prepares his rationing cards for the distribution, because the next day, instead of teaching, he will hand out these cards to the population.[45] Fortunately somebody has sold him some kerosene for his lamp on the black market because otherwise he could not have worked so late.

There are surveys about the health of the pupils but I have so far found very little about the health of the teachers. At all events some of them had a complete nervous breakdown because of the permanent strain on them.[46]

Modris Eksteins in his book *Rites of Spring* asks the question, 'What kept the soldiers in the trenches?'[47] 'One could ask the same question about the teachers: what kept these completely overworked and stressed people in school and in all their other activities? Not all teachers, of course, were like the especially zealous example given here. There were teachers arrested for pacifist propaganda; others showed in their reports to the *'Kreisschulämter'* that they did not work very hard for the victory,[48] but most of the cases I have examined on the basis of the documents of the Badenian Ministry of Education were eager to demonstrate their un-relenting activities, and some of them even received an important war medal for this, the *'Kriegsverdienstkreuz'*.[49] The reason for this, I believe, was the same as the one Eksteins gave to his own question – it was the sense of duty, the subjugation of the individual interests to the necessities and aims of society. 'You are nothing, your people is everything,' the Nazis were to say later on, and this was not by chance. Hitler himself and most of his followers belonged to the war generation, and the 'war experience' for them was their main source of inspiration.[50] The totalitarian state they built was nothing less than the pursuit of the total mobilization of the society which had begun in World War I. The teachers started to practise the same kind of brain-washing which later was more thoroughly elabo-rated in the totalitarian state of the Third Reich.

Notes

1   'Die Militärverhältnisse der Lehrer im Krieg', in F.Führen, Lehrer im *Krieg.Ein Ehrenbuch deutscher Volsschullehrer*, vol. 2, Leipzig, 1936, p. 187.

2   I have tried to construct an 'ideal type', a model of an especially zealous teacher. All documentary evidence has been drawn from the files of the 'Großherzogl Ministerium für Unterricht und Kultur' (Ministry of Education of Baden, abbreviated as GMU) preserved in the 'Generallandesarchiv Karlsruhe', subsequently abbreviated as GLA; especially useful were the reports of the teachers of Schopfheim contained in file 235/16173, Großherzogl. Bad. Kreisschulamt Schopfheim, Generalakten, Volks-aufklärung, Beilage, Bericht der Lehrer (auf Aufforderung) gelegentlich der amtl. Konferenz, Sept. Okt. 1916. Some supplementary material has been found in the Polish archives of Szczeczin and Wrowlaw. Especially useful also were the various teacher's manuals preserved in the 'Bibliothèque de docu-mentation internationale contemporaine', Nanterre, and the documentation by K.Saul: *Jugend im Schatten des Krieges*, Militärgeschichtliche Mitteilungen 1983, vol.2, pp.91–184.

3   GLA 235/16172, GMU, Mitteilungen des Unterrichtsministeriums über die Einwirkungen des Krieges in seinem Geschäftsbereich (Höhere Schule und Volksschule), 20 Dec. 1915, Anlage 21.

4   Führen, op.cit., p.187.

5   GLA 235/16172, GMU, Unterricht an Schulen und Gesundheit der Schüler, Mitteilungen des Ministeriums über die Einwirkungen des Krieges in seinem Geschäftsbereich vom 20 Dec. 1915, Anlage 21. In Prussia the situation was the same. In the Budget committee on 6 February 1916 the Prussian Minister of Education gave the following figures for Prussia: 51,118 masters were mobi-lized, 6,000 had fallen, 20 per cent of the seminarists had fallen as well, cited after V.H.Friedel, *The German school as a War Nursery*, London 1918, p.43.

6   GLA 235/16172, (as note 5) Anlage 21; H. Lemmermann, Kriegserziehung im

Kaiserreich. *Studien zur politischen Funktion von Schule und Schulmusik 1890–1918*, Bremen 1984, p.840.

7 Archives of the district of Sczczeczin, Akten des Provinzialschulkollegiums, vol.11, Bericht Preußners vom 25 July 1917.

8 Saul,op.cit., p.114, p.170 note 135.

9 K.König, *Kriegsstoffe für die Unter- und Mittelstufe*, 3rd edition Strasbourg 1916, p.16f.

10 Ibid. p.25

11 Führen, op.cit. p.27; J.Mihaly, . . . *da gibt's ein Wiedersehen! Kriegstagebuch eines Mädchens*, Freiburg Heidelberg 1982. 3 August 1914, p.16f.

12 König, op.cit., p.24.

13 Mihaly, op.cit., p.246.

14 König,. op.cit., p.10.

15 K.Wendling, *Kriegslektionen*,umgearbeitete Aufl. Straßburg 1916. *Hilfsbücher für Kriegsstunden* ed.by Konig und Wendling, p.24, see also A.Knable (Rektor in Guben): Der Religionsunterricht im Weltkriege 1914/15, (Friedrich Mann's *Pädagogisches Magazin* 615, 1915).

16 Führen, op.cit., p.63.

17 *Rechenunterricht und Krieg. Eine zeitgemäße Aufgabensammlung.*

18 ibid., p.96f.

19 ibid.

20 R.Braun (ed.), *Deutschlands Jugend in großer Zeit. Ein Buch vom Weltkriege für jung und alt*, Potsdam 1916, p.93ff.

21 GLA 235/16173 (like note 2), reports of the following teachers: Maria Liesl, Unterlehrerin in Gerrichwind, 8 Oct. 1916; Franz Gräser, Hilfslehrer in Hogschür, 22 Sept. 1916; Graf, Oberlehrer in Murg, Amt Säckingen, 28 Sept. 1916; L.Matt, Hauptlehrer, 1 Oct. 1916; Gruner (?), Rippolingen, 18 Oct 1916.

22 K.Lotz, *Kriegstagebücher von Schülern, Schoenichen, Kriegsmuseum einer Dorfschule*, in: *Krieg und Schule*, Berlin 1916, p.59–63, p.204–206.

23 F.Jode: *Eine Wiederholung.Skizze aus dem Gesangunterricht, Monatsschrift fur den Schulgesang, 1913/14*, vol.8, pp.207–210, cited after Lemmermann, Document 139, S.902–904).

24 Saul, op.cit., p.116.

25 Führen, op.cit., p.42.

26 V.Ullrich, *Kriegsalltag.Hamburg im ersten Weltkrieg*, Köln 1982, 15.5. 1917, p.109f.

27 GLA 235/16167, GMU, Gerneralia, Militär-und Kriegssachen, secret circular letter to the secondary schools and headmasters of Volksschulen, 28 Nov. 1916.

28 K.Liebknecht, *Gesammelte Werke und Schriften*, vol.8, Berlin, 1966, 16.3.1916, p.531ff.

29 GLA 235/16172, Kreisschulamt Schopfheim, Die Einwirkungen des Krieges auf den Gesundheitszustand der Kinder, 3 March 1917 and 30 April 1918. 37472, GMU, Generalia, Medizinalwesen. Die Jahresberichte der Schulärzte der Volksschulen.

30 R.Wall, 'English and German Families and the First World War, 1914–1918', in Idem/J.Winter (eds.), *The Upheaval of War, Family, Work, and Welfare in Europe 1914–1918*, Cambridge 1988, p.53.

31 Saul, op.cit., p.114.
32 GLA 235/29244a, GMU, Sammlungen der Schüler 1917.
33 GLA 235/16670, GMU, Maßnahmen zur Sicherung der Volksernährung während des Krieges; 16081/16082, Kreisschulamt Schopfheim, Generalakten, Volksernährung.
34 GLA 235/16167, GMU, Generalia, Aufklärung der Schuljugend über Kriegsmaßnahmen und die Abhaltung von Vorträgen durch Lehrer zur Hebung der Volksstimmung während des Krieges. Letter of the GMU to all headmasters of primary and secondary schools and 'Kreissschulämter', 10 June 1916.
35 Lemmermann, op.cit.
36 Archive of the district of Wroclaw, Acta Maista Wroclaw, III/23474 fol.21.
37 GLA 235/16173, Kreisschulamt Schopfheim, Generalakten, Volksaufklärung. Bericht der Lehrer (auf Aufforderung) gelegentlich der amtl Konferenz, Sept./Okt. 1916, report of Theber, Hauptlehrer, Herrischried. 1.10.1916.Cf. W.Pressel, *Die Kriegspredigt 1914–1918 in der evangelischen Kirche Deutschlands*, Göttingen 1967; H.Missalla, '*Gott mit uns*'. *Die deutsche katholische Kriegspredigt 1914–1918*, Munich 1970.
38 ibid., see also the report of Wehr, 6 Oct. 1916,.Matt, Hauptlehrer, 2 Oct. 1916, and Schultes, Hauptlehrer, Todtnauberg, 4 Oct. 1916.
39 Frey, Hauptlehrer, Obersäckingen, ibid.
40 Lemmermann,op.cit.p.155.
41 ibid., p.286, Führen, op.cit., p.37.
42 GLA 235/19394, GMU, Generalia, Miltär-und Kriegssachen, letter of Kreisschulamt Freiburg to GMU 18 April 1917, letter of GMU to Kreisschulamt Bruchsal, 6.2. 1918.
43 GLA 235/16173 (as note 35), report of Kübler, Fahrnau.
44 ibid., reports of Anna Ringler, Bergalingen, 28 Sept.1916, and Franz Gärser, Hogschür.
45 GLA 235/19394, GMU Beiziehung von Lehren zur Hilfeleistung bei der Lebensmittel-und Brennstoffversorgung sowie bei sonstigen wirtschaftlichen Maßnahmen während des Krieges.
46 Führen,op.cit.,p.102, no statistics cited.
47 M.Eksteins, *Rites of Spring. The Great War and the Birth of the Modern Age*, Toronto 1990, p.171ff.
48 One teacher wrote a report of only two sentences: 'In my school lessons and also especially in talking to the adults I have made use of every opportunity to inform the population. There were no new viewpoints.' GLA 235/16173 (as note 35), report of Thinnig, Hauptlehrer, Wieslet, 21 Oct. 1916.
49 ibid., report of Wenck, headmaster of the school of Nollingen-Bad Rheinfelden.
50 Eksteins, op.cit., p.308.

Chapter 51

War Correspondents and Conducting Officers on the Western Front from 1915

Keith Grieves

One of the most sensitive intersections of civil-military relations in the British war effort in the years 1915–18 existed at the press camp in close proximity to General Headquarters (GHQ) on the Western Front, as part of the burgeoning 'tail' of rearward services of the British armies in France. In the words of Philip Gibbs, arguably the most well-known British war correspondent of the Great War, the journalists and their allocated conducting officers lived in close proximity to each other as 'a kind of jailer and spy, eating, sleeping, walking and driving together'.[1] This duality of journalists as gatherers and processors of news, and conducting officers as censors and managers of information, was less obvious than the close personal relationships which facilitated the vital function of reporting a vast impersonal war of increasing scale and complexity.

The war correspondents officially authorised by the War Office were originally five in number in 1915 and wore an officer's uniform with a green arm band without badges of rank, but they received the honorary rank of captain. They were part of the British military structure in France but not soldiers and their expenses were paid by the Newspaper Proprietors Association. The strain of collecting news under a highly regulated procedure was intense, and was exacerbated by the rigid schedule of each working day. William Beach Thomas noted that,

> Day after day we spent hours in a car going at high speed over roads full of military transport, saw and heard terrible and glorious dramas, and without any gap for reflection, poured out the experience in thousands of words, triplicated by military orders, from a typewriter.[2]

The nervously watchful Intelligence Department at GHQ monitored the daily reports of the war correspondents through late afternoon 'censorship while you wait' procedures which ensured the 'blue lining' of praise or blame in matters of command and forbade mention of specific names of units which would reveal the composition of British divisions and the order of battle. Most of all, reports were monitored to ensure that they synchronised with the publication of the official daily communique from GHQ. The Press camp maintained separate mess and accommodation arrangements, but the value of journalistic work was increasingly measured by Intelligence officers according to its contribution to the plans of defence and attack on the Western Front. As Chief of Intelligence after January 1916 Brigadier-General Charteris expressed the assumption that the 'steadying' effect of journalistic output should be of foremost importance. He summarised this approach after Haig was interviewed in February 1917 by noting 'all that we allowed to appear was the customary "Union Jack over the door, cow grazing in a meadow, strong, silent man, blue eyes, white moustache, raised maps" and such-like drivel'.[3]

During 1916 the age-old 'eyewitness' system of providing war news, which might be defined as 'official "word painting" by some Regular officer with a tincture of letters,'[4] was replaced by the reports of war correspondents because they could behave like 'officers and gentlemen', with all the unspoken assumptions which these words embraced. Furthermore, they rarely challenged the overriding constraint of the secrecy and security of operations on the front line. From the position of pariahs in 1914 the war correspondents were to emerge from the war as potential knights of the realm for their contribution to victory. This transformation reflected the all-engulfing character of mass attritional war, in which few agencies and individuals resisted the state's demands in pursuit of an efficient, resilient and national response to Prussian militarism.

The incorporation of war correspondents as an organisational responsibility of the Intelligence Department at GHQ required an accompanying establishment of serving officers, often of older men. They knew front line conditions from personal experience early in the war and paid diplomatic attendance on journalists as their conductor and censor, and as the personification of British high command. As journalists gradually assumed the *appearance* of pseudo-army officers attached to GHQ, these officers were required to undertake the quasi-civilian task of managing the control of news flow from the British armies in France to the War Office and hence to national daily newspapers. Alongside the well-known journalists, military participants in this process had equal cause to reflect on the presentation of large-scale war. Their wartime careers became immersed in an unforeseen unsoldierly sphere of activity where the drama of battle was replaced by the stress of everyday antagonistic social relationships, which was caused by the quest for more independence of thought and action on the correspondent's part and the unyielding implementation of censorship codes by conducting officers. Major A. N. Lee became a conducting officer in July 1916 and fulfilled this function for one year. In his diary he soon noted that he hated this new job, particularly when compared with the more coveted and desirable post in the traditional chain of command of a brigade-major in an infantry brigade. His diaries record a litany of rows which originated in the gap of comprehension between traditional soldiering and the war correspondent's yearning for freelance conditions.

At the end of 1916 Lee used such terms as 'stress', 'toil', 'disappointment' and 'difficulty' to describe his new role with 'nervy and disgruntled' press-men, many of whom were 'riff-raff'.[5] Of this 'jumpy profession' he reflected,

> all of them had been brought up to carry on their jobs in perfect freedom until this one came along – even in our earlier small wars they were more or less freelances and could do what they liked, go where they liked and write what they liked – and they felt the effects of the necessary restraint put upon them during this War.[6]

Lee's diaries juxtaposed the 'pettiness associated with Press people' which, in actuality were practical expressions of serious demarcation disputes which increased in intensity as definitions of military and civilian activity became blurred, with the brief intensely comradely meetings of friends from his battalion and other regimental officers on their way up to the front line, many of whom were killed in action shortly afterwards.

Although Lee resented references to staff officers as leading 'gilded' lives, his reluctant detachment from the operational imperatives of the front line was presented in his diaries as a temporary and ignoble role of censoring texts, photographs and paintings. It was a measure of the all-pervasive consequences of war that the most dramatic news in Lee's diary originated in England, not in France, early in 1918,

> I had a letter from my wife from Eastbourne, a most desperate affair, which showed she must be nearly at breaking point. The children had been unwell and trying, the food at home was inadequate for the needs of young children and my wife had 'gone without' for their benefit. Then also she had been cooking for some hundreds of sick soldiers at the local hospital and generally overdoing it.[7]

In effect, although Major Lee was much closer than his wife to the decisive front, the most dominant feature of their respective wartime experiences was a shared one – exhaustion caused by long hours of toil, exacerbated in his wife's case by lack of sufficient food. In the occasional pause for reflection Lee noted the privileged insight he gained into the British war effort in France and, even if he preferred to be closer to the guns, his testimony provides evidence of unforeseen working conditions where the impact of the 'war experienced' could start to be considered in relation to a panoramic understanding of the scale of effort – individual and collective – on the Western Front.

To consider in more detail the contrasting roles of war correspondent and conducting officer, and the impact of personal experience of these functions, the wartime careers and post-war writings of two personalities will be considered. A comparison of their reflections on war after 1918 will suggest the possibility of emergent diverse consequences of war. H. M. Tomlinson and C. E. Montague were leader-writers at the *Daily News* and *Manchester Guardian* respectively before 1914. At the outbreak of war these liberal-minded journalists were 41 and 47 years of age respectively and both were anxious to experience the war at close hand but in different ways. Tomlinson crossed to France to observe the Battle of the Marne and the autumn campaign of 1914 in his professional capacity. Montague enlisted in December 1914 despite 'my few years over the limit of age' and grey hair with the 'romantic' intention of serving the national cause in a direct way as an infantryman in a battalion of hoary ancients without reference to his professional expertise. In due course he became the best war correspondent the Western Front never had. Tomlinson admired Montague's writings in the post-war era and they both reflected on their experience of war in memoirs and thinly disguised fictional accounts as a war correspondent in the quest for truth, and as a conducting officer, for whom the notion of reliable information was more problematic.[8] Their interest in the political and social dimensions of war enabled them to place press activity within a wider context. Furthermore, their writings on the presentation of war were published by 1930, and much of it earlier, so that most of their reflections contributed to the early historiography of the war. The intermingling of their ideological *loci* with the process of gathering or sifting news heightened the effect of their early responses to the outbreak of war. Montague quickly adopted a new vantage point based on a belief in comradeship, efficiency and patriotism which was derived from membership of a Kitchener battalion.

In his post-war writings, H. M. Tomlinson constantly reiterated the point that he was not a soldier and did not pretend to be one, but suffered the moral quandary of *appearing* to be an army officer to others. In his invaluable volume, *Waiting for Daylight,* his self-conscious awareness of a gulf between the rearward security of his billet and the constantly endangered enlisted men, was conveyed in his reaction to passing through Ypres under shellfire. Tomlinson noted, 'it is not dignified to hurry when one looks like an officer. One ought to fill a pipe. I did so.'[9] He was an observer of the Contemptibles, Kitchener men, Derby men and conscripts in and out of the line and he relished his conversations with the uniformed working class, particularly with enlisted men from Limehouse and Wapping. Philip Gibbs described the constituent elements of Tomlinson's philosophy as

'Christian in tradition, Cockney in colloquial expression, and Greek in its sense of truth and human folly and the agony of man, and the mystery of the Unknown God'.[10] He had a mystical faith in the defeat of Germany and a compassionate regard for soldiers in the main theatre of war. He himself felt uneasy and self-critical, a representative of an 'outer world' lacking, by contrast, in integrity as was symbolised by the daily journey to the front by motor car. In the guise of a visitor Tomlinson recorded the questions of front-line troops,

> 'I'd love to see G.H.Q. Really, what is it like? Is it true you have parlour-maids?' 'And is it true,' added another fellow, 'you don't reckon we are men, but only insufficient numbers?' They always rubbed it in like this. It was a privilege of theirs.[11]

From this passage it was a short step to the conclusion that the press had let the troops down because newspaper reports on unfolding offensives were cheerful rather than circumspect and provided unlimited opportunities for armchair publicists who were 'patriots in full stampede'.[12] Tomlinson made the important point that at least the correspondents in France were less subject to these pernicious influences and avoided the role of martial leader-writers, but he also acknowledged that a dominant feature of all press activity was the ready espousal of sacrificial values.

This theme was emphasised in his essay 'Holiday Reading' in which a convalescent young man was handed a newspaper by an elderly man who said 'Splendid news this morning'. Tomlinson continued, 'The soldier indifferently handed back the glorious news, without inspecting it, with words which youth should never address to age'.[13] Tomlinson acknowledged the complicity of war correspondents in their 'genuine rapture'[14] about the war, rather than their deceitful reporting. As a liberal-minded journalist, he was one of the first Western Front correspondents to reflect on their collusion with the war policy of the State.[15] His stance has had a profound and dominant effect on the historiography of the press in wartime. Consequently the personal experience of war correspondents fuelled their individual commitment to the war effort. Their acceptance of constraints on the production of news for home and neutral opinion reflected the tendency to self-censorship 'from below'. In particular, Tomlinson drew attention to the problem of reporting in conditions of total war and his 'confessions' strongly influenced the way historians viewed Press involvement in the Great War.

In fact on the subject of reporting the fog of war a variety of stances quickly emerged. Tomlinson was doubtful that the Great War had 'just origins', and he exhibited few crusading tendencies. He reported the view of a subaltern in the London Rifles who 'wanted the blood of all war correspondents – seemed to want to paddle in it. He hated them – he said they were decoy ducks'.[16] With different emphasis, which neatly encapsulated the difference between public perception and private persuasion, Philip Gibbs told C. E. Montague in 1922, 'I hate to be classed among the Liars, as I shall be for all time, not by you but by the judgment of History itself, as one of the war correspondents – though God knows, I humbly and indeed, desperately endeavoured to let the truth shine through'.[17] In the following year he emphasised that he 'wrote always with heavy stress on the suffering and tragedy of warfare'.[18] Over twenty years later the more conservative-inclined Sir William Beach Thomas reflected on his experience during the First World War and phlegmatically recorded,

> For myself, I had lived through those grim years without any paralysing depression, thanks chiefly to a definite, conscious, perhaps cowardly, determination not to think at all, but to live so far as might be in the day's events, to bear what was bad in them and to enjoy what was good.[19]

The diverse opinions which war correspondents voiced in the post-war years reflected *particular* admixtures of personal experience in war and ideological commitments shaped before 1914. In Tomlinson's case his left-ward path in the post-war years from the *Daily News* to the more radical *Nation*, stemmed chiefly from the role of a detached onlooker in war whose proximity to the unchanging traditional hierarchy of military decision-making heightened his repellent feelings about the cost of war. For example, Beach Thomas observed of Tomlinson, 'It was a liberal education to hear him tell a high Tory General that he, the General, was a cog in a marvellously socialistic State, paid by the State, fed by the State, given a particular job with other men all fed, paid and compelled by the State to do particular work in a national cause'.[20]

As a staunch unreconstructed liberal, Montague could never have shared Tomlinson's exuberant comments on the un-availing 'marvellously socialistic State' in wartime. However, they both had an abiding interest in war-related books and thoughts after 1918. Tomlinson commented favourably on Montague's writings and recognised his war credentials. He also noted Montague's interest in 'niceties of honour and duty',[21] which separated their subsequent remarks on press activity in the military war effort. Montague displayed no wholesale regret for the untruthful elements of news reporting in the war years and exuded a 'oneness' with the troops, if not with all his designated administrative roles. In September 1914 Montague asked A. N. Monkhouse, fellow journalist at the *Manchester Guardian*, 'Do you find the war an absolute disabler to any coherent effort of your mind? I can't get the idea of anything with any fulness'.[22] His mental disablement was resolved by acceptance of his claim as an Alpinist and thus eligible for the second Sportsman's battalion, 24th Royal Fusiliers at the Cecil Hotel, London. In his correspondence he relished training ('a good healthy life'), trench digging ('fine, satisfying work'), technical manuals, active service leave and, briefly in March 1916, front line service.[23]

Montague's profound admiration of the 'Tommy' stemmed directly from his brief experience of being one. His idealisation of battalion life, to which he yearned to return as late as June 1918, was reflected in his novel *Rough Justice,* where as the conducting officer Auberon Garth, 'he watched from afar the dwindling of his friends'.[24] In the novel Garth insistently returns to the site of his fallen friends, accompanied by a visiting Romanian general, to commune with the front line action of the 'Comfies' or Kings Own Middlesex Fusiliers. He 'reflected silently and sagaciously'.[25] Due to C. P. Scott's intervention as the *Manchester Guardian*'s powerful owner-editor, the 'crocked' Montague, who was injured at bomb practice, became an intelligence officer in France in July 1916 to undertake censoring work, semi-official writings and additionally, in 1917, conducting work. Tomlinson observed Montague at the press camp at Chateau de Rollencourt and depicted him as Houghton in *All Our Yesterdays.* Tomlinson wrote that the patient, unemotional, ascetic Houghton was 'A poet and a scholar, he had served as a sergeant in the line and continued to mortify himself with the punctilious saluting of brigadiers who would never reach his exact knowledge of English drama and the use and abuse of hand grenades'.[26] In this penetrating and barely-fictionalised account of press work, Tomlinson again referred to the commonly-held view that the job of war correspondents was to maintain 'courage and cheerfulness'.[27] He also noted that Montague (as Houghton), although slightly aloof in a 'chill and distant corner of the room', was directly and purposefully employed in the military war effort, if also warily and watchfully.[28]

Unlike Tomlinson, Montague wanted to learn in detail about the technicalities of the artillery war as an unfit, older and thoroughly engaged junior officer who believed strongly in the 'necessity of getting on with the war' so that ideals could be resumed when peace was restored.[29] His own sacrifice was to become a painfully modest, deferential, subordinate under military discipline, as a personal commitment to British military victory.[30] This commitment involved full participation in the censoring process, the authorship of semi-official articles, and constant reference to military imperatives in his relations with war correspondents. Montague's involvement in these tasks enabled him to explore and reflect on the relationship of press work and propaganda in a nation mobilised for war. He quickly 'sickened' of the process of writing leaflets to be dropped over German trenches and billets and was soon relieved of this duty.[31] During the Somme offensive in 1916 he wrote official war articles as an 'eyewitness' observer which emphasised topographical interest, superior firepower, relentless advance, Anglo-French co-operation and diminishing German manpower in accounts which were steadying, sometimes subdued, but always indefatigable.[32] The problems inherent in explaining the condition of stalemate were evident in 1916 and encountered in each subsequent literary endeavour sanctioned by GHQ.

For official purposes, Montague became 'a distinguished soldier-writer whose impressions are vivid and comprehensive', as noted in the prospectus for Muirhead Bone's drawings published as *The Western Front*.[33] Montague wrote the letterpress for this publication and also for the volumes of *British Artists at the Front* in 1918. In both projects Montague encountered stringent constraints, but his writings or 'drivelettes' were not without some elements of individuality.[34] In each case his own brief experience of front-line service was an important point of reference. *The Western Front* volumes placed emphasis on avoiding the feeling of horror by depicting damaged property – not the suffering of men – and the empty battlefield.[35] Consequently, Montague wrote of destruction and discomfort rather that of death and disaster. The war was rendered familiar in many ways, for example, by comparing the Somme summit ridge to the Hog's Back in Surrey, by highlighting everyday activity, such as policemen in khaki who directed the traffic, and by using Shakespearian imagery.[36] As head of Wellington House, C. F. G. Masterman intended to allow Montague to write 'exactly what he thinks appropriate'.[37] Although this was not possible in practice, Montague maintained an approach to the letterpress for *British Artists at the Front* which was firmly grounded on this view.

Consequently, his introduction on 'Trench Housekeeping' in the volume devoted to Eric Kennington's war art, was criticised 'because it focused on details of life that I had seen in the trenches when I lived there, and not a general descant on the British soldier, such as a war correspondent might do'.[38] Montague felt sufficiently well placed to insist that he would continue the work his way. In his essay 'Strange, but True' for the paintings of Paul Nash (in volume three) he suggested that at his best the artist had distilled the essence of the front line and with personal insight insisted that the pictures 'express well what a sentry may see'.[39] More broadly, Montague recognised that the paintings would be understood by those who had experienced trench warfare and scandalise those who had not. In his writings in support of propagandist activity Montague aired opinions on artistic modernism which were by no means acceptable to all, and he explored the value of this activity in his correspondence. He thought that the propaganda value of *British Artists at the Front* would be considerable but, in a semi-independent way, he felt that John Buchan's descriptions of generals to accompany the portraits drawn by Francis Dodd were unduly generous.[40]

All the while Montague undertook the task of censoring the reports of war correspondents alongside his own 'scraps of bleat' of direct or indirect 'use to the cause'. Consequently, he participated fully in the process of generating different types of persuasive writing on a spectrum which ran from newspaper reports, through officially inspired prints of paintings with 'slanted' captions, to the manufacture of leaflets for enemy consumption. It was a measure of Montague's commitment to his official duties that Lee found him to be an 'old marvel and grand chap in every way'.[41] Lee also described him as 'terribly "genuine"' and suggested that Montague sought every opportunity to be under fire, which perhaps helped him in his writing.[42] In an irritated, sometimes irascible way, Montague's vantage point was a military rather than a journalistic one, even if, like Lee, he regretted his subsidiary status as a *visitor* to the forward zone.

In the light of his war experience and professional expertise, Montague's comments on the relationship of the press to war policy were quickly available in the early post war years. He wrote speculative essays on the extent to which the press should be mobilised in wartime and suggested that 'Most of the fibs that we used in the war were mere nothings, and clumsy at that'.[43] In that sentence the particular impact of war experience on Montague's liberal mind shone through strongly. This pivotal figure at the *Manchester Guardian* suggested that one of the lessons of the war for a future large conflict should be the value of seriously making 'ourselves an enigma', like a 'painted canvas'. In his article 'To Lie or not to lie' in May 1921, he opposed 'halfness' and proposed, rhetorically, the need for a clear choice between 'cooked news' or 'clean chivalry'. Montague accepted the necessity for lies during wartime because a crusading cause created its own moral condition until the restoration of peace.[44] Consequently, his main complaint in 1921 was not the munitions of mendacity in war but the willingness of journalists to continue their dependence on governmental sources of information and thereby sustain untruthfulness into peace.

Like Tomlinson, Montague acknowledged that a delicate balance existed between the utility of falsified news in wartime and the morale of the front-line troops who lived in an atmosphere of lies, but, unlike many war correspondents, he recognised circumstances which might necessitate 'poison gas projected in print'. A further measure of Montague's understanding of the war as a literal test of national survival was his explanatory point 'Every war, even the most honourable, most just and most necessary, such as the Great War was for ourselves, must bring to the combatant rank and file much disillusion'.[45] For Montague the emergence of propaganda had relativised truth as surely as the arrival of poison gas and flame-throwers had diminished chivalry, but the more important post-war task was to stop ex-servicemen saying 'You can't believe a word you read'. He noted 'An inky war-after-the-war has been waged, and still wages, among the many politicians and others whom the original conflict left rubbing painful wounds'.[46] For example, the novel entitled *The First Hundred Thousand* by Ian Hay (John Hay Beith) was an acceptable 'stiffening' novel of New Army training in 1915, but his article on the enrolment of 'The New Hundred Thousand' during the coal miners' dispute in April 1921 was a piece of anti-labour propaganda commissioned by the Board of

Trade which should not be presented by newspapers as if it were an ordinary article.[47]

For Montague this continuation of war morality was of greater concern than the admission in 1925 by Brigadier-General Charteris that there was no substance in the 'Corpse Factory Story'. Montague concluded that Intelligence officers should not be criticised for specific instances of departure from truth in conditions of general falsehood and distraction. From his personal experience of official duties he reminded his readers of the new scale of concerted delusiveness which occurred in the Great War:

> the daily communique is hardly ever truthful; almost every despatch from a war correspondent must to get through the censor's hands, contain at least lies of omission; to bring off any surprise attack on a large scale your Intelligence Corps must put down a perfect smoke barrage of lies – forged letters, false newspaper articles, every description of ingenious falsehood.[48]

In contrast to his noble intentions of joining the army in 1914 to campaign in the Low Countries, Montague was forced to recognise the indivisibility of news and opinion in wartime and the intimate connection between press activity and the plans of High Command.

His position closely resembled the viewpoint of Major the Hon Neville Lytton who was head of the Allied Press Camp. Montague reviewed Lytton's *Press and the General Staff* very favourably in the *Manchester Guardian* in 1921 and described him as a 'marvel' who through the development of press facilities for French journalists at GHQ during 1917 had contributed to the maintenance of the Entente in that desperate year.[49] As a painter, musician, amateur tennis champion and diplomatic presence in charge of foreign correspondents, Lytton belonged to a different age. However, his regimental service as a company commander and respect for 'military method', if not for all aspects of the Regular Army, prepared him for the task of managing news in pursuit of operational aims, while maintaining a common-sensical reasonableness regarding the limits of censorship.

Lytton was much impressed by the independent-mindedness of his first battalion commander who was angry at the cheerful view which the press took of the Somme offensive. In a letter home Lytton noted, 'When you think of chaps lying out with a leg blown off, you can hardly wonder that everybody in the army wishes to murder those correspondents who bring in "the bank holiday touch"'.[50] During 1917 Lytton maintained two aims as a premier conducting officer which focused on the necessity of some realist reporting while promoting good relations with Britain's foremost ally. Lytton was disconcerted by the lingering effect of football and picnic imagery associated with 'going over the top'. He highlighted the aim of producing reports which contained 'facts of good and bad fortune' so that tragic events were sometimes seen for what they were. To that end he noted, 'I used to try and drive some of this sense of tragedy into the temper of General Charteris, but I was not altogether successful'.[51]

His regard for the security of the front line and for the realist outlook of its inhabitants was derived from personal insights into the suffering of men in the war. For that reason he was concerned to sustain a sensitivity of outlook at the press camp. Late in 1917 he noted in some exasperation, 'Whole coveys of Colonels turned up, peers amongst them, none of whom had seen any regimental service during the war'.[52] Ultimately, Lytton's attention to the development of social niceties and friendships at this vital juncture of civil-military relations ensured that his *raison d'être* was fulfilled, namely, 'I was able to prove to the French nation how magnificent our men were under fire and how splendidly they met death'.[53] Alongside the cultural shift from tolerating journalistic activity as a nuisance to accepting its legitimacy as a weapon, both Lytton and Montague, as conducting officers, recognised the onset of a more total war than they had foreseen in 1914.

In the privileged setting of the press camp, war correspondents and conducting officers drew the conclusion that the resilience of the 'common man' was more important than the leadership qualities of British High Command. Tomlinson expressed appreciation of the 'mere Nobodies',[54] and Montague drew attention to the 'indestructible soundness of the common sort of man' in *Rough Justice*.[55] As an old Etonian, Lytton concluded that the Great War was not won on the playing fields of Eton;[56] 'this war has brought out the uncommon virtues of the common man, it is owing to his heroism that we are able to hold up our heads today'.[57] Consequently their war demonology was not dissimilar. Tomlinson took exception to Colonel Repington's diary and the memoirs of Field Marshal Lord French.[58] Montague criticised the professional soldier who disliked 'New Army bounders' and who took refuge from the war by obtaining a series of 'special employments' in France, as depicted in the competition for medals and decorations between Colin March and Claude Barbason in his short story 'Honours Easy'.[59]

Montague sympathised with Lytton when he was awarded the OBE for liaison work in 1918 and their writings shared a general antipathy towards the career soldier in 1917–18, excepting their profound respect for Plumer, Harington and the Second Army at the Battle of Messines where so much effort was taken to brief the war correspondents. Otherwise Lytton's remarks on Charteris were typical; 'I found him extremely good-humoured and affable, and the warmth of his greeting was so human that I could hardly believe him to be a regular soldier'.[60] Lytton left the Press camp as it wound down in December 1918 and briefly returned to a purely military mess of 'narrow outlook and lack of versatility'.[61] Both Lytton's and Montague's personal commitment to the censoring and management of news on behalf of GHQ and in support of offensive plans for the Western Front should not be mistaken for an abiding respect for traditional military structures.

Most war correspondents and conducting officers drew attention in their post-war writings to the 'wear and tear' of a strange life in comfortable *châteaux* near GHQ but not of its nature, which took the form of daily news gathering expeditions to viewing points as far forward as a car could go, supplemented by discussions at Corps headquarters. Philip Gibbs drew a conclusion which has become of almost universal application in the history of war in the twentieth century for it acknowledged the plight of the war correspondent who could no longer freely wander around the margins of the battlefield;

> we were between two worlds, and belonged to neither, and though I think our job was worth doing (and the spirit of the people would have broken if we had not done it) we felt at times (or I did) that the only honest job was to join the fighting men and die like the best of British manhood did.[62]

Gibbs recognised his own inevitable commitment to the war effort as a whole and noted the worthwhile tasks he undertook, but was obliged to remain a civilian onlooker without the freedom of thought and deed which William Russell obtained in his reporting on the Crimean War. Between the two worlds of front line and GHQ/Home Front, there existed staff officers, including the conducting variety, who manned a bureaucratised procedure to ensure that news reporting took place within the wider context of strategic planning as well as the operational conduct of the war. In his discussion of 'the much abused staff' Lee noted that they were spared 'much of the filth and dirt of War and also the periods of "Chances of Death", but they had no rest period and were at it from 8 a.m. to midnight and 2 and 3 for seven days in every week'.[63] There is little doubt that these conditions gave cause for much reflection after 1918, as contributions emerged on the widened definition of war work in an absolute conflict.

For conducting officers the paramountcy of soldiering was a still evident feature of their outlook and they tended to dismiss too easily the significance of their work because they were unable to assess its contributory effect on the course of the war. Montague came to appreciate that a war effort of such attritional length and scale might include, rather than ignore, procedures and routines which facilitated the transmission of 'appropriate' reports to newspaper offices in London. Fatiguing hours spent poring over texts and photographs late at night in Nissen huts for signs of information helpful to the enemy were gradually accepted as vital tasks in support of operational activity. As a soldier-writer, Montague accomplished an accommodation of mind and role in a cause for which he had no doubt. Like Lytton he developed a vantage point which war correspondents, such as Tomlinson, could not share. Their different roles determined their experience of war which was constantly evident in their contrasting post-war writings. Tomlinson's dismay was generalised and impressionistic and Montague's adherence to the notion of a 'just war' was a specific organising theme.

In his novels and essays, Tomlinson provided impressions of war in conversational format which lacked the technical vocabulary of military service and insights on the nature of warfare but conveyed the sense of momentous events in a vivid form. Montague and Lytton wrote of the particularities of war in literary responses which stressed authenticated episodes but maintained a critical distance from the assumptions which emphasised British military success in the Great War. The wide ranging intrusiveness of the machinery of war on 'personal home rule' altered the perspective of many reflective writers, not least in the acceptance and justifications which were attached to the increasing malleability of truth in the Great War. Gibbs recognised this development and it troubled him, acting almost as the mainspring of his urgent and repetitive volumes on the war. Beach Thomas noted the need for a balance between a democracy's right to know and the prevailing instinct of self-censorship, and then got on with becoming a countryman. He remembered a most pleasing letter from an employer – 'without your dispatch we could never have persuaded the men to work through the bank holiday'.[64] His pragmatic conservatism remained intact. Tomlinson was radicalised by his experience of war. Montague remained liberal-minded in a literary sense but eventually placed his political faith in the consensual rhetoric of Baldwinism.

The interplay of war, experience and personality had its varying effects according to the expectations and exigencies of human interrelationships and endeavour. At the heart of these experiences in war was a curious informal 'jailer and spy' relationship of war correspondent and conducting officer. These well-defined roles were mediated by personal relationships in such a way that human truths sometimes emerged alongside the respect accorded to the secrecy of battle, even if reputations of command were too easily shielded from public scrutiny. Press censorship was undoubtedly a contributory factor in disillusionment but Montague surmised that the essential question remained the level of falsehood which could be withstood in pursuit of successful surprise attacks. His threshold was higher than might at first be thought.

In the early historiography of the Great War the divergent opinions on the presentation of the war indicated how variable the impact of the conflict would be in the minds of its participants, well before it became a literary cliché of anti-heroism. The writers who shared an interest in the presentation of the war, and were therefore connected in their wartime roles, noted the contradiction of a meaningful but uncontrollable war which would gradually take the form of an abyss in modern history.[65] In 1924 Tomlinson wrote of remaining awake at nights thinking about the war.[66] In one respect at least he spoke for many when he wrote 'The shadow of what once was in France is an abiding presence for us. We know nothing can happen again which will release us from it'.[67]

Notes

I am grateful to Dr Hugh Cecil and participants at the University of Leeds International Conference on the 'War Experienced', September 1994, for their comments on an earlier draft of this paper.

1 P. Gibbs, *Adventures in Journalism,* London, Heinemann, 1923, p.234.

2 W. Beach Thomas, *The Way of a Countryman,* Michael Joseph, London, 1944, p. 113. He wrote for the *Daily Mail* and in 1918 he went to the United States on a lecture tour in support of the Allied war effort. As one of the original five designated war correspondents he received the KBE in 1920.

3 Brig. Gen. J. Charteris, *At G.H.Q.,* Cassell, London, 1931, p. 194.

4 C. E. Montague review, 'The Press and the General Staff' *Manchester Guardian,* 28 April 1921, Montague mss. II(A)23, John Rylands University Library of Manchester.

5 The First World War Diaries of Lt. Col. A. N. Lee, pp.95, 100, 107, 128 (microfilm), Imperial War Museum (IWM). All extracts from the Lee diaries in this paper are quoted by permission of Mr P. M. Lee and the Imperial War Museum. For a critical view of Lee see W. Orpen, *An Onlooker in France 1917–1919,* William and Norgate, London, 1921, pp. 67, 69, 72.

6 Lee diaries, 14 July 1917, p. 137. IWM.

7 Lee diaries, 4 January 1918, p. 164, IWM.

8 For an illuminating discussion of autobiography as thinly disguised fictional accounts see Rosa Maria Bracco, *Merchants of Hope. British Middlebrow Writers and the First World War 1919–1939,* Berg, Oxford, 1993, p. 13.

9 H. M. Tomlinson, *Waiting for Daylight,* Cassell, London, 1922, p. 3. See also J. Onions, *English Fiction and Drama of the Great War,* Macmillan, London, 1990, p. 112. Tomlinson started his working life in a shipping office and joined the radical *Morning Leader* in 1904 which amalgamated with the *Daily News* in 1912.

10 P. Gibbs, *The Pageant of the Years. An Autobiography,* Heinemann, London, 1946, p. 138.

11 H. M. Tomlinson, *All Our Yesterdays,* Heinemann, London, 1930, p. 414.

12 H. M. Tomlinson, *Waiting for Daylight, op.cit.,* p. 13.

13 *ibid.* pp. 65–6.

14 H. M. Tomlinson, *All Our Yesterdays, op.cit.,* p. 522.

15 P. Knightly, *The First Casualty. The War Correspondent as Hero, Propagandist and Myth Maker,* Quartet, London, rev. ed. 1982, p. 65.

16 H. M. Tomlinson, *All Our Yesterdays, op. cit.,* p. 391.

17 P. Gibbs to C. E. Montague, 25 July 1922, Montague mss. III. 2. After brief periods at the *Daily Mail, Daily Express, Daily Chronicle* and *Tribune,* Gibbs rejoined the *Daily Chronicle* in 1908 and his war despatches were published in that paper and the *Daily Telegraph.*

18 P. Gibbs, *Adventures in Journalism, op. cit.,* p. 246.

19 W. Beach Thomas, *The Way of a Countryman, op. cit.,* p. 131.

20 W. Beach Thomas, *A Traveller in News,* Chapman and Hall, London, 1925, p. 133.

21 H. M. Tomlinson, *Christian Science Monitor,* 2 August 1922, Montague mss. II(B)6.

22 C. E. Montague to A. N. Monkhouse, 17 September 1914, Monkhouse general literary letters, Box 5, John Rylands University Library of Manchester.

23 C. E. Montague to A. N. Monkhouse, 28 July 1915, Monkhouse mss. and C.E. Montague to F. Dodd, 2 May 1915 and 18 September 1915, Dodd mss. Add. Ms.45910, British Library, London. See also O. Elton, *C. E. Montague. A Memoir,* Chatto and Windus, London, 1929, pp. 101–115.

24 C. E. Montague, *Rough Justice. A Novel,* Chatto and Windus, London, 1927, p. 307. See also C. E. Montague to F. Dodd, 16 June 1918, Dodd mss. Add. Ms.45910.

25 C. E. Montague, *Rough Justice op. cit.,* p.306.

26 H. M. Tomlinson, *All Our Yesterdays, op. cit.,* p.441.

27 *ibid.* p. 345.

28 *ibid.* p. 451; C. E. Montague, *Rough Justice. op. cit.,* p. 337.

29 P. Gibbs, *The Pageant of the Years, op. cit.,* p. 166.

30 For further contemporary comments on Montague as a conducting officer see H. W. Nevinson, *Last Changes, Last Chances,* Nisbet, London, 1928, p. 140; G. Bernard Shaw, *What I Really Wrote About the War,* Constable, London, 1917, p. 251; H. G. Wells, *Experiment in Autobiography,* Faber and Faber, London, 1934 (1984 ed.) Vol. 2, p. 682; P. Gibbs, *Adventures in Journalism op. cit.,* pp. 240–1.

31 Undated manuscript fragment on propaganda leaflets, Montague mss. I.9.

32 Cuttings of official war articles by C. E. Montague, August-December 1916, Montague mss.II.7.

33 The Muirhead Bone Prospectus, *The Western Front* [1916] and M. Bone to C. F. G. Masterman, 12 November 1916, correspondence file, M. Bone 427/9, Dept. of Art, IWM.

34 M. and S. Harries, *The War Artists. British Official War Art of the Twentieth Century,* Michael Joseph, London, 1983, p. 13.

35 C. F. G. Masterman to M. Bone, 7 November 1916, 427/9, IWM.

36 M. Bone, *The Western Front,* with text by C. E. Montague, Country Life, London, 1917, Vol. 1. See in particular part 2 (January 1917) and part 3 (March 1917).

37 L. Masterman, *C. F. G. Masterman. A Biography,* Nicholson and Watson, London, 1939, p. 287.

38 C. E. Montague to F. Dodd, 16 June 1918, Add. Ms. 45910 and A. Yockney to C. E. Montague, correspondence file 'British Artists at the Front' 458/10, Dept. of Art, IWM; *British Artists at the Front,* Vol. 4, Eric Kennington, Country Life, London, 1918, Introduction 'Trench Housekeeping' by C. E. Montague.

39 *British Artists at the Front,* Vol. 3, Paul Nash, Country Life, London, 1918, Introduction; M. and S. Harries, *The War Artists, op. cit.,* p. 59.

40 C. E. Montague to F. Dodd, 12 October 1917, Dodd mss. Add. Ms. 45910; C. E. Montague to A. Yockney, 7 March 1918, 458/10, IWM; F. Dodd, *Generals of the British Army,* Country Life, London, 1917–18, 2 parts.

41 Lee diaries, 30 October 1916, p. 102, IWM.

42 Lee diaries, 19 January 1917, p. 110, IWM.

43 C. E. Montague, 'To lie or not to lie', *The Nineteenth Century and After*, May 1921, No. 531, p. 831. For a recent discussion of state-supported manipulation of public opinion see G. S. Messinger, *British Propaganda and the State in the First World War*, Manchester University Press, 1992, pp. 9–23.

44 Philip Gibbs noted that Montague had 'declared a kind of moratorium on Christian ethics during the war' in his *The Pageant of the Years op. cit.*, p. 166.

45 C. E. Montague, 'Would Truth or Lies Cost More?', *The Nineteenth Century and After*, July 1921, No. 533, p. 32. See also his leading articles in the *Manchester Guardian* 'The "Propaganda" Morass', 15 January 1920 and 'News and Opinions', 3 May 1921. Montague mss. II(A)22.

46 C. E. Montague, Manuscript preface to the American edition of *Fiery Particles*, signed and dated May 1923, Montague I.6. See also R. Graves and A. Hodge, *The Long Weekend*, Hutchinson, London, 1940 (1985 ed.), p. 26.

47 C. E. Montague, 'Propaganda Again', *Manchester Guardian*, 20 April 1921, Montague mss. II(A)23.

48 C. E. Montague, 'Corpse Factory Story', *Manchester Guardian*, 26 October 1925, Montague mss. II(A)25.

49 C. E. Montague review 'The Press and the General Staff', *Manchester Guardian*, 28 April 1921, Montague mss. II(A)23. For a contrary view see the *Times Literary Supplement*, 28 April 1921.

50 N. Lytton, *The Press and the General Staff*, Collins, London, 1920, N. Lytton to Lady Wentworth, 13 April 1917, p. 94. By 1917 the press was required to present victories in cautious terms so that a prolonged war remained uppermost in the public mind. D. Hopkin, 'Domestic censorship in the First World War', *Journal of Contemporary History*, Vol. 5, No. 4, 1970, p. 155.

51 *ibid.* p. 126. For comments on the perceptions of battle held by Charteris see T. Wilson, *The Myriad Faces of War*, Polity, Cambridge, 1988, pp. 477, 479, 547.

52 N. Lytton, *The Press and the General Staff, op. cit.*, p. 141.

53 *ibid.* N. Lytton to Lady Wentworth, 11 November 1918, p. 211.

54 H. M. Tomlinson, *Waiting for Daylight, op. cit.*, p. 94.

55 C. E. Montague, *Rough Justice, op. cit.*, p. 360.

56 N. Lytton, *The English Country Gentleman*, Hurst and Blackett, London, [1925], p. 183.

57 N. Lytton, *The Press and the General Staff, op. cit.*, p. 210.

58 Col. C à C. Repington, *The First World War*, Constable, London, 1920, 2 Vols.; Field Marshal Lord French, *1914*, Constable, London, 1919.

59 C. E. Montague, *Fiery Particles*, Chatto and Windus, London, 1923, pp. 25 and 49.

60 N. Lytton, *The Press and the General Staff, op. cit.*, p. 56.

61 *ibid.* p. 221.

62 P. Gibbs, *Adventures in Journalism, op. cit.*, p. 244.

63 Lee diaries, 24 October 1918, p. 156, IWM.

64 W. Beach Thomas, *The Way of a Countryman, op. cit.*, p. 112.

65 On 'uncontrollable' war as a source of schism in modern history see D. Pick, *War Machine: The Rationalisation of Slaughter in the Modern Age*, Yale University Press, 1993, p. 170.
66 H. M. Tomlinson to C. E. Montague, 20 February 1922, Montague mss. III.2.
67 H. M. Tomlinson, *Waiting for Daylight, op. cit.*, p. 194.

Chapter 52

Tommy's Sisters: The Representation of Working Women's Experience

Sharon Ouditt

It has become conventional to represent women's role in the First World War as dedicated, splendid, and although tinged with grief and tragedy, quietly triumphant. It was as a result of the war (according to this line of thought) that women gained the vote: they proved themselves worthy of citizenship by hard work, unstinting service and the ability to fuel, not only the home, but the industrial fires while the men offered the ultimate sacrifice on the battlefronts. The war also had its heroines – the martyred Nurse Edith Cavell, the two women of Pervyse, Mrs St Clair Stobart, Dr Elsie Inglis, Violetta Thurstan. Hagiographies were published during the war with titles such as *Women who Dared: Heroines of the Great War, Women of the War* and *The Roll-call of Serving Women*[1] and were augmented in the 1960s with David Mitchell's *Women on the Warpath*. Women were seen to have found themselves. They threw off the shackles of decorous femininity (chaperones, corsets, flowing hair) and offered their services in a true manifestation of the British spirit.

Not surprisingly this notion was grist to the mill of a particular brand of modern feminism. To Sandra Gilbert and Susan Gubar:

> women seemed to become [. . .] ever more powerful. As nurses, as mistresses, as munitions workers, bus drivers, or soldiers in the 'land army', even as wives and mothers, these formerly subservient creatures began to loom malevolently larger.[2]

These women, liberated into the war-workforce, apparently 'swooped over the waste lands of the war with the energetic love of Valkyries'[3] in confident anticipation of upsetting the laws of patrilineal succession. Now, such celebration of lost heroines is vital to the general project of rescuing women from a history of meek subordination. The problem with it,

736

The Gretna Girls.

THE Gretna girls are here, lads—Gretna women, too,
   From sweet sixteen to sixty, seeing "Tommy"
     through :
Girls from Scottish hillsides, strong in health and vigour,
Girls from desk and counter, neat in style and figure ;
" Hinnies " from the Tyneside, Geordie's bonnie bairns—
At Whitley Bay they'll show them what the Gretna lassie
     earns ;
Jolly girls from Yorkshire—tha' knows th' sort Ah mean—
"Gradely" girls from Lancashire with eyes devoid of green.
Sure ! there's winsome Irish colleens, with lashes black
     as sloes,
They've "stuck it" all the winter through Border frost
     and snows.
Hear them in the morning, singing through the streets,
With their little nose-bags full of grub——and sweets.
"There's a long, long trail a-winding" to the stations
     every day,
To " keep the home fires burning" for laddies far away.
"When Irish eyes are smiling," Scotch and English are
     not sad,
They all sing " Tipperary " as though they had gone mad.
Pouring from the hostels, happy, gay, and bright—
Week-day, Sunday, holiday, morning, noon, and night.
Pink cheeks from the country, pale cheeks from the town,
A month or two at Gretna turns them ruddy brown.
Rosy cheeks or white cheeks, each is doing her best
To help our gallant warriors fighting East and West.
Write and tell your soldier pal, it's sure to cheer his heart
To know the girl he left behind so nobly plays her part,
If he hears about her " clicking," tell him not to worry,
When he returns the " home reserves" will " dismiss "
     in a hurry.
So three cheers for the Gretna lasses ! give another three,
They're doing their bit right heartily to keep old Britain
     free.
" Tom " and " Jack " when they come back will show
     appreciation
By " joining up " with girls who are a credit to the nation.

Copyright, 1917, by A. BURNS, *Carlisle.*

(x)   Munitions girls at a large new factory at Gretna, as depicted by a local patriotic poet. {Liddle Collection} however, is that it gives priority to a certain kind of experience: that of particular members of the educated middle and upper classes who had the time, the financial and domestic resources and the ideological inclination to dedicate themselves to the service of 'the greatest Democracy in the world'.[4] There is little scope in this rendition for the ambivalences and uncertainties that one finds after reading the published and unpublished accounts of V.A.D. nurses, for example. And the experiences of the unglamorous go unrecorded.[5]

Furthermore, it is clear that women had an uphill struggle to gain any sort of status in the war *at all*. Initially they were not welcome in medical, military or industrial structures as the testimonies of Katharine Furse, Elsie Inglis, and May Wedderburn Cannan suggest.[6] As female participation became indispensable to the management of the war, however, it became necessary to defend the potentially alarming social change that their inclusion represented. A reassuring picture of mobilised womanhood was composed of higher-class women in positions of national importance, a strategy aided by their association with ideals of constancy: 'In these extraordinarily unpleasant times,' wrote W.L. George, 'women seem the only permanent things. [They] stand in a society of flux, like living reefs of coral in stormy seas, which will go down and leave them undisturbed by and by.'[7] At a time of social turmoil it was important that women's recruitment to industry should not signal radical political change. This concern for traditional values in the context of instability was reflected in the representation of those working women who might have had a great deal to gain from wage increases and the promise of a permanent place in industry.

This paper examines the representation of working-class female experience in propaganda written to encourage women's participation in the war effort. It seems that the combination, in the written propaganda, of the nobility of Britain's war aims[8] with the need for women's service, sanctioned the provision of greater opportunities for better-off women. In the promotion of *their* cause, however, the representation of working-class women becomes correspondingly derogatory. This is not to suggest that the slackers, shirkers and self-indulgers of the middle and upper class escaped censure, or that there was anything approaching uniformity to actual working-class experience. My point here concerns the means of representation in a particular kind of writing and the social implications that are carried with it. For, underpinning the celebration of the war-time benefactresses was a trope, or rhetorical strategy, that performed the function of dividing the elevated from the vulgar, the pure of spirit from the debased and material. The effectiveness of any rhetorical formula tends to rely on its applying to larger spheres of meaning than the purely literal or referential, and on the implied connections between the various levels of meaning. Such is the case here where the form of speech to which I am referring was reflected not only in abstract or moral propositions where to be 'high-minded' is preferable to having base thoughts, but in the social hierarchy, where the upper classes reign over the lower, and in physical topography, where the wisdom of the 'head' is preferred over the licentious 'seat' of the passions. This rhetorical formula by no means emerged as a result of the First World War, but its use became exaggerated in some of the written propaganda, with the result that while educated women were seen to occupy the high moral ground, working women became increasingly associated with immorality and fecklessness. The broader social and moral resonances of what is essentially a figure of speech deserve some examination.

Of course much propaganda was concerned to naturalise women's involvement in war work and to play down its radical implications. On the one hand it was made to appear inevitably an extension of normal female behaviour ('It is surprising how speedily the women have wooed and won this new kind of male monster', said the author Hall Caine, where the monster in question is a piece of munitions machinery[9]) but on the other, as something inspiring. One way of registering the latter was to present women's new power as classless. L. K. Yates wrote that:

Even in the early days of the advent of women in the munitions shops, I have seen working together, side by side, the daughter of an Earl, a shop keeper's widow, a graduate from Girton, a domestic servant, and a young woman from a lonely farm in Rhodesia, whose husband had joined the colours. Social status, so stiff a barrier in this country in pre-war days, was forgotten in the factory, as in the trenches, and they were all working together as happily as the members of a united family.[10]

The metaphor is telling, recalling the traditional mythology of the family as microcosm of the state. Neither family nor state, of course, is a unit in which all elements are equal: the father would be the head; the sons would take precedence over the daughters (as Vera Brittain discovered) and below stairs the family structure would be replicated. The reference to Rhodesia is also interesting as it expands the metaphor to suggest the British Empire as a universal family. This Kiplingesque mythology, while supportive of women's contribution to the war effort, was clearly flawed. Social barriers were not forgotten in the trenches, but largely reestablished along lines of rank. The responsibilities of protection, leadership and setting a good example accrued to those of higher rank in family, army and factory alike. Those lower down the scale were still expected to be respectful, and prepared to deal with the grubbiness of life.

A further example came from Thekla Bowser (Honorary Serving Sister of the Order of St John of Jerusalem) in her laudatory account of V.A.D. work:

739

... they did not know that they were giving birth to an organization that was to do more for the bringing together of all classes of society – a real and splendid socialism that has no connexion with the men or women who belong to socialistic societies – than any other movement has ever achieved. [11]

Again there is the insistence on classless community, but here it is used to undermine politically-organised socialism. Bowser clearly has little time for socialism, but her point is that war has revealed its disquieting aims as *unnatural* by restoring a sense of community which *is* 'natural', 'real and splendid', in keeping with the British spirit and tradition that relies so heavily on voluntary contributions and a deeply-structured sense of place and position.

Women's war experience, on the whole, did little to fracture this tradition. V.A.D. nurses were picked from the middle and upper classes, which led to some friction with the less well-to-do trained nursing Sisters; farmers expressed a preference for educated women as land workers; in the munitions factories the 'ladies' were given the supervisory jobs and work in the welfare departments. On the home front, as in the trenches, social divisions were merely reconstituted. Of course there were exceptions, but they were rare.

Sylvia Pankhurst wrote that 'For women of means, undreamed of activities, opportunities, positions, opened on the horizon. The War brought a vast unlocking of their energies.'[12] Ideals of service and individualism are important here. May Sinclair speaks of the 'ecstasy' of service, Vera Brittain of its 'sacred glamour', Ruth Whitaker of the 'sublimation and fulfilment' she found as a V.A.D. nurse.[13] Brittain also insists on describing herself as an 'individualist', as do Katharine Furse and May Wedderburn Cannan.[14] But if Marwick is right and approximately 80 per cent of the population were working class, at least 18 per cent middle-class and the remainder upper-class,[15] then there was presumably little room for individualism among the so-called lower orders. The term 'individualism' also suggests a movement away from community towards personal gain and fulfilment, perhaps in the service of the greater good, but inevitably at the expense of one's contemporaries. Lying behind it is the idea of being a chosen one or a romantic spokesperson. There is nothing reprehensible in this, but, as a trope, it tends to situate the rest of the ordinary working women as 'other', as alien, incomprehensible, outside a perceived set of values. And the broader rhetorical framework suggests the separation of high ideals from material mundanities; refined or abstract preoccupations from vulgar or specific details.

Virginia Woolf articulated it thus: the middle-classes have 'wit and detachment, learning and poetry, and all those good gifts which those who have never answered bells or minded machines enjoy by right.'[16] This comes from a woman who felt deep political sympathy with working-class women, but she calls this sympathy 'fictional' rather than 'real' because it is not based on shared, unconscious emotion. The abstractions that are the province of the educated classes are compared with 'the demand for an extra shilling, for another year at school, for eight hours instead of nine behind a counter or in a mill'. Her point is by no means to derogate those mundanities, but to say that they are not part of her (elevated, erudite) world and that, therefore, she cannot experience 'real' sympathy for them.

This seems usefully to articulate the chasm of understanding between the language of literary propaganda and working-class experience. I have already suggested that higher-class women were used as models of conservative values, that there was a drive to conceal the differences of interest represented by different class experiences, and that ideals of service and individualism tended to marginalize working-class women. Literary propaganda, like Virginia Woolf, does not 'understand' working-class experience. There is a difference in register and in practical concerns that renders the representation of working-class lives at best awkward, at worst patronising and disempowering. Most of those who signed Masterman's 'Authors' Manifesto',[17] for example, would have had little in common with factory workers. This does not rule out the possibility of political sympathy and, of course, the image of working-class women heaving sacks of coal and operating industrial machinery was crucial to the picture of the English nation pulling together. The specific preoccupations of these women, however, which often concerned rates of pay, sanitation arrangements, ventilation, protection from dangerous chemicals and so on, were hardly going to be used to convince the allies and America of the righteousness of the cause and the glamour of those fighting for it. The segregation of the elevated from the mundane is thus maintained as much through the discourse of the representation of the nation-at-war as it is through political and economic practices.

In the high diction of some of the war propaganda, an attempt is made to see the re-organisation of the munitions industry as one of the wonders of the world. Hall Caine, in his book, *Our Girls: Their Work for the War* described the operation of Woolwich Arsenal in the following terms:

> To think of the building of the Pyramids of Egypt is to fill the mind's eye with visions of innumerable armies of labourers, like trains of human ants, conveying gigantic masses of stone across the desert from the quarries of the Mokattam Hills to the plains of Mena. But Woolwich is a yet greater and more awesome vision than that. . . . [18]

This is the view from the erudite metropolitan centre, and as in the Bowser piece, reference to the splendour of organised labour simultaneously denigrates the force of socialism by representing the workforce as anonymous and alien specks of insect life. Zooming into close focus, however, Caine describes a person he names as Tommy's sister: 'Here she comes sailing into the superintendent's office, Tommy's sister, one of the many varieties, wearing a hat as big as a fish-basket, and with her pretty face painted red as the sun with rouge.' The description attempts to induce a warm affection for this girl with a 'saucy mouth' and lunatic head-gear; to make her unthreatening, familiar – not one of the unionised workers, but the loyal, cheeky sibling of the lad in the trenches. She remains anonymous. She is her brother's sister. One of the many varieties. Later she is Alice or Annie or Rose; later still, 'Lily Something, commonly called Lil', who is engaged to 'William Somebody, commonly called Will'. A rhyming couplet. Stereotyping the jolly working classes from this bemused, bourgeois perspective renders them interchangeable; disempowers them while claiming to celebrate their power.

It is the question of power, and specifically of leadership, which lies at the heart of middle-class rhetoric about working women. Mrs Alec-Tweedie FRGS, philanthropist and author of travel books, published a book in 1918 that set out to praise women's roles in the war. She commented on the ubiquity of women in all kinds of occupations, their farsightedness, their superior practical and organisational skills: 'Women are wonderful. They always have been', she says.[19] But it is only women of the 'right sort' who have made the advances of which she was boasting:

> The best sort of forewomen [. . .] are better-class ladies. The aristocrat who is accustomed to rule a household has learnt to rule in a sympathetic way. Her girls respect her, love her, follow her. Like Tommy, they prefer not to follow their own class.

In fact, many working-class women moved away from domestic labour precisely because of their poor relations with the 'better-class ladies' who were their employers (Rosa Freedman, Miss O. M. Taylor, Rosina Whyatt),[20] and Lady Peggy Hamilton's comment on the welfare department at her factory was that 'It was staffed by people largely unaccustomed to the work'.[21]

A more democratic example of natural leadership came from the popular novelist Berta Ruck, whose novel *The Land-Girl's Love Story* she described as her 'tiny bit of useful propaganda':[22]

> In every community of girls is one who will always take the lead by virtue of her vitality and initiative. Here it was Victoria Jelks, the ex-coster girl from Kentish Town, who stood out as one of the handsomest, 'goeyest', and most efficient women I have met.[23]

Even here war work – and specifically land work, with its connotations of natural healthiness – is seen to have eradicated in Vic the less savoury features seen to be proper to her class:

[S]he belonged to the class that we have seen blackening Hampstead Heath on Bank Holidays, grimy and anaemic, made ugly by the life and toil of town.

Connotations of blight, of dirt, disease, of unpleasant and anonymous infestation are surely unavoidable.

And the general denigration did not stop there. Working-class women were often credited en masse with ungovernable sexual appetites, and the fear of sexually-transmitted diseases underpins many of the comments made about them. Actions were taken to control or supervise them, including the introduction of women police officers. The imagery of blight and slovenliness seems consciously or unconsciously to be related to genuine fears of the British army being severely debilitated by the spread of syphilis, and even fears of the British race being undermined by the same cause.[24]

The account of Miss O. M. Taylor, however, a working-class woman whose war-work included service in the W.A.A.C.s, states that:

We privates had a terrible shock to learn that there were to be women police. What kind of woman could volunteer for such a position we could not envisage. Naturally, we were prepared to hate them. Their main task was to try and catch us talking to a soldier, or out after hours.[25]

The experience from the other side of the social division, then, is that governing-class women, rather than being 'extraordinarily efficacious', were disliked as interfering busybodies, determined to persecute anyone taking the most innocent advantage of their rather restricted freedoms.

Evidence from some of the letters and articles in the home-orientated popular women's magazines suggests that factory life in itself was seen as a potential site of moral danger.[26] This uneasiness with female freedom is reinforced by a 'Report on Industrial Welfare Conditions in Coventry', which looks to hostels to provide accommodation for imported labour, but comments that their general homeliness needs to be improved: 'There are no small rooms in which girls could gather round a stove or fire and have facilities for quiet writing, reading or sewing.' The irrelevance of this Jane Austen-like idyll to the normal lives of working women is astonishing enough. The reason for this assiduous concern is arguably more insulting: 'Responsible medical evidence was forthcoming of a serious increase already of venereal disease and of loose and immoral conduct in recreation grounds and dark streets.' Women's police and good recreation facilities are strongly recommended. Control, it seems, is the order of the day: control of the threat represented by the (temporarily) liberated female masses.[27]

The development of the women's police force and of the welfare system in factories is particularly interesting in this context. It suggests that the

743

influx of women into industrial areas not only brought liberation from the constraints of domestic service and offered a decent wage, it also led to a perceived need for surveillance and social discipline. The twin assumptions that a) working women were sexually dangerous, and b) that the natural good sense and moral standards of higher-class women made them appropriate authority figures, led to the replication on the streets and in the factories of the politics of the upper-class household or the girls' school.

It is, of course, absurd to imagine that working-class experience was anything but highly stratified, diverse and inhospitable to the caricatures drawn of it by the self-designated upholders of social discipline. We only have to look at some working women's accounts of their own sexuality, to see that far from expressing carnal familiarity, they repeatedly return to their own innocence and ignorance. 'About a month before the baby was born' one woman said, 'I remember asking my aunt where the baby would come from. She was astounded and did not make me much wiser.'[28] 'My mother, a dear, pious soul', noted another, 'thought ignorance was innocence, and the only thing I remember her saying on the subject of childbirth was: "God never sends a babe without bread to feed it." Dame Experience long ago knocked the bottom out of that argument for me.' Miss O.M. Taylor, in her vivid, unpublished account said that she was 'completely innocent of sex' at the age seventeen, about which time she started walking out with her first young man: 'Walking out was the right expression to use as that is all young couples did at that time.' She moved from farm work to a munitions factory. 'It was in this factory that to my disgust I was told how babies were made. I refused to believe it and told those women in no uncertain terms what I thought of them, remarking, "My mum & dad would never do that!" How those women laughed!' She said that in those days countrywomen had no idea what would happen to them when they married. Working as a WAAC she had to be a little more wary: 'we could never trust a Coldstream Guard. They would even threaten to throw us into the Brookwood canal if they couldn't have their way with us & they seemed to have only one thought in mind. What did it matter to them if a girl lost her character and ended up in the workhouse with a baby?'[29]

It is hardly surprising that most working women relied on their own judgement and resources rather than depending on the protective moral guidance of their social superiors. Miss Taylor considered herself physically equal to any man, having carried weights of up to sixteen stones in her farm labouring days. And furthermore, the working classes did have their defenders. Someone who signed himself 'A Brother in "Social Service"', writing in the *Millgate Monthly* about Lancashire Mill Girls, said: 'These toiling girls are splendidly straight and good. . . . The factory lass has well learned the art of taking care of herself. She is as ready with

744

her hand as with her tongue. If unwelcome attentions are persisted in, the objectionable male is very apt to find himself woman handled.'[30]

Sylvia Pankhurst was a tireless supporter of the poor women amongst whom she lived in the East End. She channelled her energies – and money – into practical schemes (cost-price restaurants, a maternity centre, a toy factory) and against the insulting moral surveillance that took the form of police supervision of soldiers' wives, a practice whereby their separation allowance could be stopped if they were found guilty of unchastity, drunkenness, or neglect of children. The question of double standards was inevitable. One soldier's wife wrote:

> The Government ought not to issue such an order unless the wives of all Government paid men are to come under the same rules. Why should it not be applied to the wives of postmen, why not the wives of the police themselves?[31]

An enquiry into 'Alleged Drinking Among Women' states that 'Taken as a whole the evidence led irresistibly to the conclusion that the majority of women were doing well by their children, their homes, and their absent husbands.' Many did suffer from loneliness and anxiety, but where there was evidence of intemperance, it was not restricted to one class.[32] As if to confirm that sexual impropriety was not simply a matter of social class, in the context of the divorce rate amongst the gentry, Lady Angela Forbes describes a visitor as saying: 'I hear there are only two things to do in Leicestershire – and I don't hunt!'[33]

Perhaps the only way to counteract the general defamation of the working classes was to turn the whole rhetorical kit upside down. Sylvia Pankhurst tried it by saying that war was being fought 'not for the benefit of democracy or to avenge the rights of poor Belgium, but is geared to the interests of bankers, financiers and big business men who make massive profits while unemployment soars, food prices rise, [and] babies starve.'[34] But even in her 460-page account of the experiences of East End women, *The Home Front*, the women themselves remain anonymous. 'A woman', 'A soldier's wife', 'A widow' – the people themselves become statistics, symbols, representatives. Their human details, the complex textures of their lives are no better scrutinised, let alone celebrated, than in a narrative by Mrs Alec-Tweedie. The heroine of this book is Pankhurst herself: the working women on whose behalf she campaigns so relentlessly merely occupy her symbolic landscape as the victims of an unjust system.

Some middle ground where we might better understand the experiences of working women would be their own narratives. But these are sparse. The Imperial War Museum and the The Liddle Collection have a handful in written form and a few more on audio tape. Literary production has historically been the preserve of the leisured classes: many working women may have been illiterate or unused to literary expression.[35] It is clear, however, that working-class women did have their achievements during the war, whether in mainstream politics, like Ellen Wilkinson, who became an MP and a novelist; on the level of suffragist activism, like Selina Cooper and Hannah Mitchell or simply in terms of an increased self-perception and understanding as recounted by contributors to volumes such as Margaret Llewelyn Davies's *Maternity: Letters from Working Women* or John Burnett's *Useful Toil*. For many the war provided an 'escape route from domestic slavery', a finding upheld by the unpublished accounts of Miss O. M. Taylor and Rosa Freedman.[36]

Let us return to the rhetorical formula that separates the elevated from the mundane. Several working-class narratives share the notion that the mundanities of life are given form and meaning through social idealism. Rather than derogating – or even eliding – the number of pennies earned per hour or the precise length of the working day, these accounts absorb such details into a narrative that is driven forwards by the notion of the pursuit of an ideal. The style in which they were written is often naive, and descriptive, lacking the rhetorical flourishes and pithy certainties of the professional opinion formers, but their ideals arise from the preoccupations of their own communities, rather than those of Sir Hall Caine or Mrs Alec-Tweedie.

Life as We Have Known It was a collection of letters by women of the Women's Co-Operative Guild, handed over to Woolf (in her own account of events) so that the working women, for whom she could muster only a 'fictitious' sympathy, should cease to be symbols and begin instead to be individuals.[37] They are narratives of transformation. The effect of the Guild, often combined with war experiences, empowers them as individuals with social vision. Mrs Layton, who began to earn her living at 10, went into domestic service at 13 and later became a midwife. 'My neighbours tried very hard to induce me to go [to the pub]' she said, 'and possibly, if I had not been connected with the Guild, when my baby died, I might have fallen a victim to the drink habit.'[38] Not only was she 'rescued' from disaster, but she became active and vocal in deputations to the government to increase maternity care for women during the war. Mrs Wrigley, a plate-layer's wife, lost her eldest son and her husband during the war. 'Had it not been that I took an interest in public work, I could not have stood it', she said. '[H]aving had such a hard and difficult life myself, I thought I would do all I could to relieve the sufferings of others.'[39] Mrs Scott, a hat worker, said that 'There are thousands of Guildswomen who have given of their best ungrudgingly with no hope of material gain, but only the thoughts of making the path a little easier for those who follow.'[40]

These are crude, experiential accounts, whose interest lies as much in the fact that they were written at all, in the struggle to untie the tongue, as in the information they impart. They have in common a narrative drive to explain how the details of their lives are seen to have relevance in the context of broader social movements. Furthermore they see beyond questions of personal gain and look to ideals of social progress. And there are other accounts which represent, not the Guild, but socialism, for example, or trades unionism as an agent which revitalises and reorientates their lives. Winifred Griffiths was in domestic service in May 1914 when she 'discovered' socialism by reading an article in a magazine:

> It changed my thinking about life so completely that I no longer felt the urge of personal ambition. Henceforth I had a guiding light which gave life a new meaning. I imagined a society in which men and women worked together gladly to provide all that was needed to banish poverty and distress, and equally gladly went without luxuries and services they had been used to, in order to further the common good.[41]

This is a strikingly idealistic comment which, again, seems to demonstrate the displacement of individual gain by impersonal ideals. At the outbreak of war Griffiths took a post at the Co-Operative Stores in Basingstoke in order to train as a grocery assistant to replace men who were joining up. She was paid (we are told) a pound a week and spent 12/6 on board and lodging. The skills of her new trade are described in detail – weighing, measuring, packing, carrying, and later patting butter, cutting cheeses, butchering bacon. She formed new friendships: 'I was quite thrilled to meet a real live socialist, for I had known, in a sense, that I was one ever since I read the economist's article . . . ' and went on: 'Up till now I had been a loyal supporter of the war effort, only wishing I could play a more useful part in helping the country. But now under the influence of this young Welshman, I was to revise my ideas [. . .] and gradually I came round to thinking he was right.'[42]

Her war experience, then, is one of finding not only a form of satisfaction in her work (she too had been in domestic service beforehand) but also, and more importantly, ideological direction. The narrative enacts a vacillation between ideals and practicalities, in which – not unlike the propagandist pieces – the latter are given structure by the former. The difference is that Griffiths envisages a permanent change in the social formation rather than a temporary redistribution of roles. She described, for example, taking a less well-paid job in an inferior store, but so that she might be closer to her fiancé, and the socialist centre to which he belongs. The ideology she espouses, then, is resistant to mainstream values of patriotism and national duty, but it is interesting that she, like some of the V.A.D. nurses, used the idiom of religious conversion – 'a guiding light that gave life a new meaning' – in the service of 'the common good'. Furthermore, the journey towards 'the common good' paradoxically takes her away from the values of the ordinary people who had previously formed her social circle. Like Mrs Layton, she resists the working-class culture that surrounds her in favour of the pursuit of an ideal to be found in another manifestation of working-class culture: that of radical politics. The place of the war in this narrative is not as a means to an end, but a turning point, at which stray aspects of her life assemble and re-emerge in a new form.

Rosina Whyatt's transforming experience is based on an idealism less abstract than that of Griffiths. It is more of a personal transformation in which her dedication to her work leads to her own advancement within the structures of trades unionism. The attention to detail then, is not balanced by the visionary language of service, but the more earthly considerations of performing a job well and doing what is practically possible to ameliorate conditions for the vast numbers of women newly imported into munitions work. She, in the autobiographical role of 'Jenny', nevertheless finds a sense of purpose and identity in discovering trades unionism which had previously been missing from her life:

> Jenny learnt a lot that night about the principles for which trade unionism stood: protection of workers in industry, dealing with problems of wages, hours of work and conditions, factory acts (concerning ventilation, lighting and heating). She came to the conclusion very soon that here was something interesting and exciting.[43]

It may not appeal to Virginia Woolf, but it offers her a new way forward. She finds branch discussions 'an outlet for her pent-up impressions and emotions' and successfully channels her newly-discovered talents as an organiser and administrator into liaising between workforce and management to produce more harmonious working conditions. The account catalogues the dangers of working with munitions (in particular the effects of TNT poisoning) and Whyatt's own small successes. It is not an heroic narrative, but one of steady progress, suggesting equable relations with her employers, particularly when she is appointed union representative at her factory:

> This gave her an opportunity of coming into contact with the management, and she was able to discuss with them improvements of conditions, particularly in personal welfare and lavatory accommodation for the girls. She never obtained all she wanted, but she was always well received and she gained quite a lot of small but important concessions . . . .[44]

The narrative closes with her accepting a job as a full-time officer of the W.U. in April 1918. Again, she moves away from her immediate community of workers to join those working for structural social change.

These narratives, then, combine social idealism with mundane material details, so that the latter are seen to make sense and have meaning within an ideological or political framework, rather than being the unspoken

748

detritus of a world made according to middle-class values. The middle-class writers used the high/low trope as an agent of control; the working-classes used it as an agent of release. The rhetoric of Caine and Tweedie is overtly patronising, but implicitly fearful; that of the working-class narratives naive, dull, perhaps, in terms of self-consciousness and literary complexity, but infused with enthusiasm for social change. One particularly intriguing paradox that emerges from these writings, though, is that those who are writing from a liberal/conservative position (Caine, Tweedie) engaged with the language later associated with totalitarian regimes – armies of labourers, armies of women, the anonymity and magnificence of organised labour – while those writing from a position associated with left-wing social change used the rhetoric of individualism – each used her political discovery as a means of releasing herself from the culture of constraint imposed by her immediate industrial or social context.

Notes

1   Kent Carr, *Women Who Dared: Heroines of the Great War*, London, S.W. Partridge, 1920; Barbara McLaren, *Women of the War*, London, Hodder & Stoughton, 1917; Mary Frances Billington, *The Roll-call of Serving Women: A Record of Women's Work for Combatants and Sufferers in the Great War*, London, The Religious Tract Society, 1915. David Mitchell, *Women on the Warpath: The Story of the Women of the First World War*, London, Jonathan Cape, 1966.

2   S. Gilbert and S. Gubar, *Sexchanges*, vol. II of *No Man's Land: The Place of the Woman Writer in the Twentieth Century*, New Haven, CT and London, Yale University Press, 1989, p. 263.

3   ibid., p.291

4   Mrs Alec-Tweedie, *Women and Soldiers*, London, John Lane, The Bodley Head, 1918, p. 33.

5   For a detailed critique of Sandra Gilbert's argument see Claire M. Tylee, '"Maleness Run Riot" – The Great War and Women's Resistance to Militarism' *Women's Studies International Forum* 2(3)1988: 199–210. See also my *Fighting Forces, Writing Women* London, Routledge, 1994: p7ff, for an analysis of V.A.D.s' narratives.

6   K. Furse, *Hearts and Pomegranates*, London, Peter Davies, 1940; M. Lawrence, *Shadow of Swords: A Biography of Elsie Inglis*, London, Michael Joseph, 1971; M.W. Cannan 'Recollections of a British Red Cross Voluntary Aid Detachment, No. 12, Oxford University, March 26th 1911 – April 24th 1919, Dept of Documents, Imperial War Museum, 1971.

7   W.L. George, *The Intelligence of Women*, London, Herbert Jenkins Ltd, 1917, p.x.

8   Much has been written on the elevated language of and the involvement of literary figures in war propaganda, particularly in relation to C.F.G. Masterman's bureau at Wellington House. See Irene Cooper Willis *England's Holy War*, New York, 1928; M. Sanders and P. Taylor *British Propaganda During the First World War*, London, Macmillan, 1982; P. Buitenhuis *The*

Great War of Words, London, B.T. Batsford, 1989, G. Messinger *British Propaganda and the State in the First World War*, Manchester, MUP, 1992.

9   Hall Caine, *Our Girls: Their Work for the War*, London, Hutchinson, 1916, p.23. See my *Fighting Forces, Writing Women* op. cit. pp.77–80 for a fuller analysis of this construction, also Claire Culleton 'Gender-charged Munitions: the Language of World War One Munitions Reports', *Women's Studies International Forum* 11 (2) 1988: 109–16.

10 L.K. Yates, *The Woman's Part: A Record of Munitions Work*, London, Hodder & Stoughton, 1918, p.9.

11 Thekla Bowser, *The Story of British V.A.D. Work in the Great War*, London, Andrew Melrose, 1917, p.13.

12 Sylvia Pankhurst, *The Home Front*, London, Hutchinson, 1932, p.38.

13 May Sinclair, A *Journal of Impressions in Belgium*, London, Hutchinson, 1915, p.14; Vera Brittain, *Testament of Youth* (1933), rpt. London, Fontana Paperbacks, 1979, p.210; R. Whitaker, 'The First World War Memoirs of Miss R. Whitaker, c. 1970, Dept of Documents, IWM p.106.

14 Vera Brittain *War Diary 1913–17: Chronicle of Youth* ed. Alan Bishop with Terry Smart, London, Victor Gollancz, pp.118–123; see also *Testament of Youth* where she speaks of herself and Roland as 'strong individualists' (op. cit.. p.175). K. Furse in *Hearts and Pomegranates* speaks of always having been an individualist, never a member of a team (op. cit., p.291); Cannan uses a similar metaphor in her novel *The Lonely Generation* London, Hutchinson, 1934.

15 A. Marwick, *The Deluge*, Harmondsworth, Penguin, 1965, p.21.

16 M.L. Davies, ed. *Life as We Have Known It*, (1931) rpt. London, Virago, 1977, p.p. xxx, xx–xxi.

17 A statement of their support of the war by fifty-four major British authors, including Kipling, Bennett, Conan Doyle. The statement was published in *The Times* and the *New York Times* in September 1914. Most of the signatories were established literary figures who were above the age-limit for recruitment. For a full account of this, see Peter Buitenhuis *The Great War of Words*, London, B.T. Batsford, 1989.

18 Hall Caine, op. cit., p.11; also p. 69.

19 Mrs Alec-Tweedie, op. cit., p.7, also p. 18.

20 See IWM accounts and John Burnett ed. *Useful Toil*, London, Routledge, 1974 and 1994.

21 Peggy Hamilton, *Three Years or the Duration: The Memoirs of a Munitions Worker*, London, Peter Owen, 1978, p.78.

22 Berta Ruck, *A Story-Teller Tells the Truth*, London, Hutchinson & Co. 1935, p. 107.

23 Berta Ruck, *The Land-Girl's Love Story*, London, Hodder & Stoughton, 1919, pp. 86–87.

24 See, e.g. Havelock Ellis 'The Conquest of Venereal Disease' in *Essays in War-Time*, London, Constable and Co, Ltd., 1916.

25 Miss Olive M. Taylor 'Recollections of the Great War 1914–18' np, nd, MS, Dept of Documents, Imperial War Museum.

26 The women's magazines offered their share of moral guidance. One of *Woman's World's* 'Straight Talks to Wives and Mothers of the British Empire' speaks against 'having a good time', and exhorts readers to 'Be ashamed of the

cheap flirtations of an idle hour' (Aug 29, 1914, no. 476). One young woman who writes in, in a state of moral confusion, having fallen in love with a man at her factory while her soldier sweetheart is in France, is told to 'Send him about his business at once'. He is condemned as a slacker and a coward and she should do her duty by the lad out there who loves her (Nov 20, 1915, no 531).

27 Emp 45/7: Advisory Committee on Women's Employment (Industrial). Report on Industrial Welfare Conditions in Coventry by Miss Anderson and Miss Markham. November 1916. Women's Work Collection, IWM.

28 M.L. Davies ed., *Maternity: Letters From Working Women* (1915), rpt. New York and London, W. W. Norton, 1978, pp. 30, 44.

29 op. cit., np.

30 J. T. Taylor 'The Mill Girl' in *Millgate Monthly*, October 1914, 14–15. Gertrude Tuckwell, TUC.

31 S. Pankhurst, op. cit., p.100.

32 The results of this enquiry were published in the Birmingham publication *Women Workers* (June 1916, vol xxvi, No 1).

33 Lady Angela Forbes *Memories and Base Details*, London, Hutchinson,1921.

34 Pankhurst, op. cit., p. 129

35 See Angela Woolacott's 'Sisters and Brothers in Arms: Family, Class and Gendering in World War 1 Britain', in Miriam Cooke and Angela Woolacott eds., *Gendering War Talk*, Princeton, Princeton University Press, 1993 for further discussion of textual and experiential differences between middle- and working-class women's accounts of the war.

36 Miss Margery Williamson, unpublished memoir, The Liddle Collection, Domestic Front. Taylor, op. cit.; Freedman 'Memories of a Land Girl in the First World War', Dept of Documents, IWM.

37 op. cit., p.xxxi.

38 ibid, p.48.

39 ibid., p.65

40 ibid., pp.99–100.

41 Burnett, op. cit., pp.107–110.

42 ibid., p.110.

43 ibid., p.118

44 ibid., p.120.

Chapter 53

The Experience of War in American Patriotic Literature

Patrick Quinn

In its passionate appeals to national chivalry and manhood, America's wartime patriotic literature resembled its counterparts in Britain (and France) and for this reason sold widely in Britain as well as the U.S.A. There was, however, an essential difference. Whereas Britain's propagandist novels and plays, by writers such as John Oxenham, Ian Hay, Joseph Hocking or William J. Locke [1] were assertions of time-honoured loyalties to 'England, Home and Duty', reinforced by more recent imperial and school rhetoric, the American works, for historic reasons, were centred on their intense and complex feelings about individual rights and democracy.

It is when her fundamental beliefs in these god-ordained values have been felt to be under threat that the rhetoric of America's propaganda machine has been repeatedly wheeled into action. The American Civil War, though it forced communal action on both sides, was fought for individual rights: the right of the individual southern states to chose whether to drop slavery or not; and, in the other camp, the right of all men, black or white, to be free, which was believed by the bulk of the northern soldiers to be the reason they were at war.

Although Americans had long valued European culture as a source of enlightened thought and individual development, early twentieth century America suffered from a progressive tradition which allowed little time for reflection on its European folk heritage, the background of old pagan myths and harvest festivals which inculcate a particular sense of belonging to a cultural tradition. In Europe, writers can draw on this heritage, this tradition of communal sharing, and such myths often provide nourishment for good writers because they enrich the writers' subconscious and connect them with natural forces. American writers, lacking this communal foundation, must construct this mythos within themselves, and the affinity thus gained acts as a tie with the natural elements – by knowing the deeper self, one can perceive the fullness and richness of life that is almost instinctively part of the European writer's heritage. This very act of establishing the nature of existence from inner speculation as opposed to having organic access to an ensconced cultural heritage is what makes the American artist so consumed with the rights of the individual and the importance of individual action as a measure of self-worth.

The dilemma for Americans has been: 'should the sacred rights of individuals always come before the demands of a national military system, or are there times when a higher duty sometimes requires their surrender? This was explored in two American novels written after the Civil War [2]: Herman Melville's *Billy Budd*, set aboard HMS *Indomitable* during the French Revolutionary war, in which a sailor of saintly innocence strikes his evil tormentor in an act of involuntary mutiny and is hanged, blessing his captain at the moment of his death; and Stephen Crane's *The Red Badge of Courage*, about the Civil War, in which another, but less peerless, innocent, a young farmer's son, goes to war with dreams of glory and, finding the reality terrifying, flees, is accidentally wounded by one of his own side, is forced back into battle, and because of his bloodied head is mistaken for a hero. In the case of *Billy Budd*, the message is that notwithstanding the seeming injustice of Budd's execution, there is a higher justice, accepted by Budd, which requires that duty and discipline be served in time of war. In the other novel, the wound, 'the red badge of courage' symbolises for the chief character his acceptance that he is but a cog in the machine, that this, not individual heroics, however admirable, is the reality of war, and therein lies duty. In both books there is an indication of a loftier purpose at work to which individuals must bow.[3]

Both novels are instructive for an understanding of the wartime American literary response to the Great War, for they explore the same imperatives as did novelists and poets trying to make sense of the American entry into the European conflict: first that in order for Americans to relinquish their god-given individual rights of self-determination and liberty, the cause must be righteous and devoid of baser intentions. Spreading democracy and guaranteeing justice would be such inducements. Second that with the character-building opportunities for heroism that war affords, the individual hero must measure himself against an evil foe, and if he does not achieve victory, must die bravely with his Christian virtues intact. [4]

So well did the Allies understand the American psyche that, as early as 1914, they targeted certain classes of Americans who would accept most uncritically what today would be judged as manipulative propaganda. It was calculated that young college-educated males would respond most heartily to the call for adventure and to an opportunity to visit and to protect the countries where most of their Eurocentric studies were based. Why would the American college graduate want to stay at home when an

(xi)   The cover of a romantic, patriotic, American novel (1919) in which the central figure dies heroically for his country. [per H.G. Cecil]

exciting European War was deciding the future of civilisation?[5] The Allies also targeted the working-class man who would realise the war offered an opportunity to escape the drudgery of the sweat-shop and the assembly lines. In exchange, there would be the opportunity for the labourer to exert his individual freedom and reveal his heroic nature. More insidiously, the Allied propaganda machine recognised early on that if the unempowered female population could be convinced of the righteousness of their cause, they would shame their reluctant husbands, boy friends, and brothers into taking up arms to protect innocent women and children in Belgium and France.[6] It is not surprising that representatives of these classes bought and read most of the American literature written during the conflict and shortly after it was over.

Thus, though it was largely through economic pressures and such episodes as the sinking of the *Lusitania* in May 1915 that America's neutral stance was gradually eroded, one should not underestimate Allied propaganda, encouraging, among other things the wholesale acceptance by the Americans of the Christian rightness of the Allied cause, and of the battlefield as a proving-ground for manhood.[7] Despite Wilson's re-election as American President on a non-interventionist platform, a significant proportion of the American population was now waiting for a German miscalculation to open the way for active American involvement in the European war. By mid-March 1917, the exposure of a proposed German pact with Mexico drove the American public into an anti-German delirium. When war was finally declared on 2 April 1917, patriotism was as fervid in America as in Berlin, London, and Paris nearly three years earlier.

The bellicose pro-Allied literature of the period was finally unleashed, and within weeks of the war being declared, patriotic novels and poetry were being published by American presses at breakneck speed. The remaining section of this paper examines the war poetry of Alan Seeger and a selection of war novels which appeared in print between 1917–1918. Not surprisingly, these works reflected the dominant Allied propaganda. They ensured that the strong inherent American belief in individual freedom and heroic self-realisation was in no way threatened by contrary views, already expressed by writers such as Barbusse, Latzko or Rosenberg, that this war offered only dehumanisation.[8]

The case of the American poet Alan Seeger is interesting for a number of reasons. First, Seeger had been dead for almost a year when the Americans declared war on the Central Powers in April of 1917 and perhaps largely because of this became a 'Rupert Brooke figure' for the American public. *Poems and Letters and Diaries of Alan Seeger*[9] were published just as the U.S.A. entered the war, their completely sincere sentiments reflecting the expected patriotic responses to any horrors that might await the American soldier.

After graduating from Harvard in 1912, Seeger had gone to France to learn the craft of poetry. He enlisted in the French Foreign Legion in August 1914 to fight for France's liberation. His diary indicates that he saw the war as the supreme experience of life from which he could not shrink without disloyalty to his ideal. Further, as his letter to *The New Republic* in May 1915 indicates, he fought for Paris:

Paris – mystic, maternal, personified, to whom they owed the happiest moments of their lives – Paris was in peril. Were they not under a moral obligation, no less binding than [that by which] their comrades were bound legally, to put their breasts between her and destruction?[10]

Later, writing to his mother and explaining why his Harvard friend Thwing was enlisting, but clearly projecting his own motivations, Seeger stated:

He [Thwing] refused to be content . . . with lesser emotions while there are hours to be lived such as are being lived by young men in Flanders and Champagne . . .There should really be no neutrals in a conflict like this, where there is not a people whose interests are not involved. To neutrals who have stomached what America has consented to stomach from Germany – whose ideals are so opposite of hers – who in the event of a German victory would be so inevitably embroiled, the question he put to himself and so resolutely answered will become more and more pertinent.[11]

While convalescing from bronchitis in Paris in spring of 1916, Seeger wrote to his mother: 'I shall go back on the first of May without regrets. These visits to the rear confirm me in my conviction that the work up there on the front is so far the most interesting work that a man can be doing at this moment, that nothing counts in comparison.'[12] His poetry at the time reflected his sentiments:

Under the little crosses where they rise
The soldier rests. Now round him undismayed,
The cannon thunders, and at night he lies
At peace beneath the eternal fusillade

That other generations might possess –
From shame and menace free in years to come –
A richer heritage of happiness,
He marched to that heroic martyrdom.[13]

On 23 July 1916 (although William Archer, in his introduction to the *Poems*, moved the date to a more convenient Fourth of July) Seeger, aged 28, charged German trenches at Belloy-en-Santerre. His squad of French Foreign Legionnaires was caught in the flurry of machine-gun fire. He fell, cheering on his comrades, and died of his wounds.

No war poet, English or American, died more contentedly. Seeger's attitudes to the war and his poetry powerfully reflect the best of idealistic nineteenth century American high culture. He met a noble death fighting for French civilisation. From his letters, Seeger appears as the perfect role-model for the glorious campaign against the Hun who was draining the life-blood from America's great ally.[14]

But if the dead Seeger was the ideal abstract model for America's engagement in the war, Arthur Guy Empey was to be her living expression of heroism. His 1917 autobiographical novel, *From the Fire Step: The Experiences of an American Soldier in the British Army*[15] – in America published as *Over the Top* – was such a runaway best-seller that Empey was invited to speak at Liberty Bond rallies and wrote a follow-up book the next year.[16]

In the foreword to *From the Fire Step*, Empey wrote about his experiences with the British Expeditionary Forces. He stated:

> Through this elbow rubbing, and not from reading, I have become convinced of the nobility, truth, and justice of the Allies' cause, and know their fight to be our fight, because it espouses the principles of the United States of America – democracy, justice, and liberty.[17]

The last three words were to appear over and over again in the American war novel, and not until 1923 would they be used regularly in a satirical manner.

In Empey's novel, on an evening following the news of the *Lusitania* sinking, the protagonist sees the word REPAY emblazoned on a skyscraper.[18] Taking this as a sign, he travels to England where he enlists and becomes a recruitment officer whose task it is to stop stalwart-looking Englishmen on the street and shame them into joining up; but to be really effective, such work requires an English, not an American, accent, so he joyfully trains as a soldier instead.

His introduction to trench life is masterfully described. Surprisingly, the most human character we meet is a captured German prisoner, Carl Schmidt. Schmidt has lived in New York before the war, and the two enemies chat about the war, with the protagonist subtly pumping the seemingly good-natured Schmidt for information about the German snipers' uncanny effectiveness. Schmidt confides that there are financial inducements for killing English soldiers:

> For killing or wounding an English private, the sniper gets one mark. For killing or wounding an English officer he gets five marks, but if he kills a Red Cap or English General, the sniper gets 21 days tied to the wheel of a limber as punishment for his carelessness . . . You see, if all English Generals were killed, there would be no one left to make costly mistakes.[19]

With such lighter touches, the story moves briskly along, and – as with the English Ian Hay's *The First Hundred Thousand* – at times one forgets that this war is being fought in deadly earnest. Occasionally, however,

Empey adds a dark detail to remind the reader what happens, for example, to those who fail to follow orders. His ' Firing Squad' chapter recounts the unsavory details of an incident in which the 'Empey' character is involved. During the night, twelve soldiers are roused from their beds, brought to the woods and given rifles, one of which contains a blank cartridge. At some distance from them is a dark figure, bearing a white mark, vaguely discernible in the moonlight, at which the soldiers are told to aim. Empey, disobeying orders, aims for another white spot on the wall, and independently proclaims 'No blood of Tommy is on my hands.'[20]

As a corrective to this grim tale, Empey then relates the apocryphal story of Private Lloyd, a coward of Company D who had been ordered to be executed. About an hour before his sentence is to be carried out, the Germans attack and blow open the prison. Instead of escaping, Lloyd helps repulse a German offensive and dies a hero's death at the moment when his execution was to have taken place. The suggestion is that war can turn the base metal of cowardice into the gold of heroism, and while the rules of combat are difficult and dangerous, they offer a challenge and adventure in which all American boys would wish to participate.

War, claims Empey, 'is not a pink tea but in a worthwhile cause like ours, mud, rats, cooties [lice], shells, wounds, or death itself, are far outweighed by the deep sense of satisfaction felt by the man who does his bit.'[21] Private Empey, indeed, does his bit and is eventually wounded and is sent to 'Blighty' where at Paignton hospital he awakens to a team of nurses draping an American flag over his bed. It is then that he realises his duty: to make America aware of the British sacrifice in the war. There followed his return to America and his first book.

Just after America's entry in the war, Empey began work on a second work, First Call, which was published in January, 1918. The book might be called an 'Insider's Guide to the First World War', because women writers subsequently known for their descriptions of the Great War, such as Edith Wharton and Willa Cather, who were never near a trench, evidently drew on it for their depictions of life at the front in A Son at the Front and One of Ours.[22] First Call was largely intended for an uninformed and patriotic American public (mothers, fathers, and drafted sons) needing re-assurance of the righteousness of the Allied cause. Before launching into an appeal to Americans' sense of justice, Empey began by whipping up his readers' paranoia:

> The Germans in the trenches can be handled by our boys at the front, but what about the Germans at home here in the United States? The one who stabs us in the back! Are we going to let these snakes hinder or undermine our armies at the front or are we going to safeguard our boys and exterminate the pests? [23]

The second chapter was written expressly to mothers and commended them for having 'given' their son in 'God's war' to the cause of 'Justice, Democracy, and Liberty'. 'America has fought and shall fight only on the side of Right'. Empey even endeavoured to comfort soldiers' mothers with the soothing, if surprising, assertion that if their sons were to be wounded severely, the suffering would not be great: ' in fact, there is very little pain..' He explained the advantages of warfare to the mothers; their sons would mix with the best manhood of America: 'they are men among men. They are fast learning the meaning of true democracy, good fellowship, self-reliance ... They are profiting mentally and physically, and also spiritually, because they are fighting in the cause of right.' [24]

The next chapters took the recruit step by step through his training lessons and on to the battlefields themselves. There was discussion of the rest billets, the types of training – all of which were aimed at gearing the recruit for the excitement of arriving at the front line where, 'After being under fire for a few minutes, a warm glow of confidence steals over you, and you look proudly around at your mates; you have come into your own'.[25]

Astoundingly unsophisticated to a modern day reader, Empey's fabricated vision was in line with the romantic rendering of war which was being projected and accepted throughout the United States – 'the great adventure' as ex-President Roosevelt called it – presented on posters as a struggle between handsome, noble doughboys and grisly Huns, with a blood-spattered woman representing France, Belgium, liberty, or freedom in thrall.

Such simplistic pictures had earlier prepared the way for the over-whelmingly positive response to Wilson's declaration of war to Congress. Couched in a well-rehearsed rhetorical style, Wilson's address had portrayed the United States as an innocent virgin in the dark and murky world of international politics, who was being bullied into war by the ruthless Germans and their immoral friends.

It was ironical that a country which had recently tangled with Spain over Cuba, haggled with Britain over the annexation of Hawaii, sent troops into Nicaragua, and was fighting a border war with Mexico, should have come to perceive itself as an international innocent – but it did, and this myth of American innocence had also been readily used by British war propagandists, who were happy to hold up a mirror, showing manly, outraged decency, to the American people. [26]

The initial literary response upon the declaration of war included an urgent call, in the prestigious *Atlantic Monthly*, for universal military service. Subsequently, a large number of major American literary figures formed a group with the express purpose of propagandising the war effort: 'The Vigilantes', as they called themselves, included Edward Arlington Robinson, George Ade, Gertrude Atherton, and Mary Roberts Rinehart. The form and approach of their creative propaganda varied, but the message was almost always the same, and their format became standard for nearly all war literature produced in the USA up to five years after the American entry into the war. The reality of the conflict was concealed under a veil of ennobling rhetoric: while admitting war to be a dirty, bloody affair, they repeatedly stressed the honour of fighting for a godly cause alongside Britain and France, and the purification and strengthening of the soldiers through hardship.[27]

The authors of these war narratives were assured of a large readership, as the American literary historian Charles Genthe has observed:

> it is significant that the general reading public . . . reflected the narrators' simplistic views of war, morality, good versus bad, religion, and other scientific and cultural factors by providing a lucrative market for over four hundred narratives published in America during the war years. [28]

A very striking example of the formulaic romanticism of the kind pioneered by Empey, which appeared in most of these four hundred works published during the War, is Temple Bailey's *The Tin Soldier*, which appeared in 1918. The hero is a well-off idler, Derry Drake, who has enlisted in the American Expeditionary Force largely because his father is a retired general. During the novel he is converted from a superficial young scamp to a committed military man.

First, the author has to establish religious sanction for the war, so, just after hesitantly enlisting, Derry and his fiancée Jean are listening to a minister's sermon and are enraptured by his noble exhortation:

> I am too old to go myself, . . . but I have sent my sons. In the face of the world's need, no man has a right to hold another back. Personal consideration which might once have seemed sufficient must now be set aside. Things are at stake which involve not only the honour of a nation but the honour of the individual. To call a man a coward in the old days was to challenge his physical courage. To know him as a slacker in these modern times is to doubt the quality of his mind and spirit. 'I pray thee have me excused' is the word of one lost to the high meanings of justice of love and loyalty and liberty. [29]

Familiar words! But the minister's sacrifice of his sons in a virtuous cause is not the only sacrifice that must be made in time of crisis. While waiting for his fiancée in the US Capitol building, Derry studies a mural depicting frontier American history. When Jean arrives, he is lost in thought, and she follows his gaze; and her thoughts are expressed by the sympathetic narrator:

> She saw a girl with hope in her eyes, a young mother with a babe at her left breast; homely middle-aged women redeemed from the common-

760

place by that long gaze ahead of them; old women straining towards that sunset glow. She saw, indeed, the Vision of Brave Women. 'If it could only be like that for one, Derry. Do you see, they go with their husbands, those women, and I must stay behind.'[30]

Derry's reply, 'You will go with me, beloved, in spirit'.[31] affords Jean the realisation that she must dig deeply within her self and uncomplainingly accept the sacrifice of her husband for the sake of the American ethos; she must welcome the opportunity to take her place beside the brave women depicted in the mural.

Whilst at training camp, Derry sends his newly-married wife a letter lamenting the carping kind of woman who is sabotaging the war effort by moaning to her soldier-husband about his serving his country. He tells Jean:

> But, thank God, most of the women are the real thing: true as steel and brave. And it is those women that the men worship. It is a masculine trait to want to be a sort of a hero in the eyes of the woman you love. When she doesn't look at it that way, your plumes droop! [32]

Despite the perhaps unintended symbolic sexual inference, the real woman's role in this war is to encourage her man to heroic military action no matter what the cost. She becomes his spiritual conscience in case his courage should falter at the moment of battle.

But Derry, the American hero, will not falter. For him, the American soldier's duty is clear. Inspired by the Canadian Colonel John McCrae's famous patriotic poem 'In Flanders Fields', Derry vows to keep faith with those loyal Americans who have died in France before him, to take the torch and 'to do some deed to match that of the other fellow who slept in Flanders Fields'.[33]

In the novel, the realities of war are depicted as purifying agents, which act to improve the characters' perspectives. The three main characters encounter each other at a field hospital, and the reader discovers that as a result of their diverse experiences of war the socially flighty Drusilla has become a caring and saintly nurse, the cynical doctor Bruce McKenzie, who was unsure of what to do with himself in peace time, has found revelation by practising medicine on the battlefield; and the hero, Derry, the elegant idler, has become a gallant defender of liberty and freedom. The war has given meaning to each of their lives.

Edith Wharton's *The Marne* is a striking example of a more urbane and talented novelist handling the same formula, but her message is just as jingoistic and cliché-ridden as Temple Bailey's. Her hero Troy Belknap (the Homeric reference cannot be lost on the reader here) is on a crusade to save the European world from evil. In the process, the nobility of his ceaseless quest, much like the Grail Quest in Arthurian romance, will purify and make him worthy for the supreme sacrifice in what Wharton calls the 'dim land of the final'. This moral obligation in the novel to save Europe is, as Jeffrey Walsh perceives, often seen in conjunction with the recurring metaphor of the blood transfusion where the American Republic 'poured forth from the reservoirs of the new world' her willing and courageous troops in order 'to replenish the wasted veins of the old'.[34]

One need only to look at the portrait of the sensitive farmer, Claude Wheeler, painted by Willa Cather in her Pulitzer Prize-winning novel *One of Ours*, to see this romantic format at work again. As in *The Red Badge of Courage*, the mid-western farm boy sees the conflict as an opportunity to escape the drudgery of work on the homestead. Armed with a chivalric view of the battlefield and an idealistic view of life, Claude subscribes to the patriotic sentiments written by dead soldier poets Alan Seeger and Joyce Kilmer. When America finally declares war, Claude enlists immediately and discovers that the atrocities of war are mitigated by the companionship of his fellow American soldiers and the holiness of the American cause. He dies a death worthy of a hero, and his ideals, much like Alan Seeger's, are left largely intact.

A further and final example of this formula is to be found in Coningsby Dawson's highly successful *The Glory of the Trenches*.[35] Dawson, an Englishman living in New York, saw the war novel as an opportunity to issue propaganda about his own bugbear: the need for America to purge itself of its perfervid materialism and return to the principled and basic values of the Republic. Redolent of the musings of Rupert Brooke and the stories of Cincinnatus, Dawson's novel emphasises the benefits of war. The narrator echoes the thoughts of Dawson's hero in a speech which must contain as many clichés as it does impoverished metaphors:

> Nevertheless, there's many a man who has no love of war, who previous to the war had cramped his soul with littleness and was chased by his bayonet of duty into the bloodstained largeness of the trenches, who has learned to say, 'Thank God for this war.' He thanks God not because of the carnage, but because when the winepress of new ideals was being trodden, he was born in an age when he could do his share.[36]

All of the examples cited above and in endnotes 4 and 6 below are typical of the American literary response to the Great War, yet the positive and even naive elements that this literature projects must be seen in their proper perspective. For the American combat soldier, the Great War was an exceedingly brief affair: The United States joined the war in April, 1917; by 26 June 1917, the bulk of the US regular army had landed in France, and on 4 July 1917 the corps of the First and Second Army marched through Paris. However, the majority of the AEF was in combat only from July to November 1918, and that particular summer and autumn were largely free of mud and damp. Also, compared with his Allied counterparts earlier, the American soldier spent very little time in the trenches without progress, for most Americans arrived when there was a continuous movement on the battlefield, and only those well behind the lines had time for morose questions about the meaning of the war.[37] In fact, one of the most ironic refrains in American war literature in the years immediately following the war was that its conclusion had come too suddenly. The soldiers found themselves thrust back into the tedium of commonplace jobs after having been trained to do God's ennobling work and to make glorious sacrifices for one's country in the heat of combat.

The cessation of hostilities thus denied many enthusiastic volunteers (though some of those who registered for the draft had second thoughts once 'over there') their opportunity to prove their self-worth and individual prowess. Coningsby Dawson's hero in *The Glory of the Trenches* is thunderstruck when, at training camp in England, he sees a headline announcing PEACE RUMOURED. Before he realises what has happened, he is crying: 'I was furious with disappointment. If the war should end before I got there!' [38]

The sense of inconclusiveness aroused by the end of the war, which necessitated the return of many idealistically-motivated young men to drab farms and dingy factories in the United States, by 1922 generated a seething dissatisfaction with both the conduct of the war and the repressive society with which it was believed to be intimately connected. Out of this dissatisfaction was created the myth of the lost generation on which the literature of John Dos Passos, Ernest Hemingway, William Faulkner, and F. Scott Fitzgerald would write so powerfully. Their works manifested this dissatisfaction through

a brooding hostility towards the vacuity and artificiality of industrial civilisation. The older generation suggested combat offered adventure-filled liberation from the iron trend of peacetime society toward mechanisation, routine, and the suppression of the individual. The younger authors protested that war was, in fact, the supreme embodiment of those hated tendencies. Death-dealing technology, ennui, arbitrary authority, and loss of identity became the leading motifs of their war writing[39]

After the war, amidst President Harding's reign of 'normalcy' and the onset of isolationism, came the resurgence of the American ego. The individual's voice could be heard raging against the hysterical suppression of inalienable rights guaranteed by the Constitution; raging against the implementations of repressive moral imperatives; raging against what Ezra Pound in 'Hugh Selwyn Mauberley' called 'an old bitch gone in the teeth ... a botched civilization;' raging against the bureaucratic depreciation of the individual capital 'I' to a lower case 'i' in a progressively dehumanised society; and raging about the self-serving machinations of petty bureaucrats in governments which allowed the Treaty of Versailles to be signed only at the cost of unrealistic demands on the defeated nations.

This strident voice of post-war America offered a direct antithesis to the passive spirit of acceptance symbolised by the body of the unknown American soldier which graces the sarcophagus in Arlington National Cemetery in Virginia. For that soldier, the shell which had his number on it was his ticket to eternal veneration and glory. For Thomas Boyd, William March, Charles Yale Harrison, James Stevens, Ernest Hemingway, Scott Fitzgerald, William Faulkner, and John Dos Passos, the unified (though not identical) voices of the 'lost generation', the unknown soldier's sacrifice was more personal and more tragic than ever conceived in the patriotic writing of a few years earlier, for they saw it in terms of deceit, dehumanisation and callous waste:

> The blood ran into the ground . . . The blood ran into the the ground,
> the brains oozed out of the cracked skull and were licked up by the
> trench rats, the belly swelled and raised
> a generation of bluebottle flies,
> and the incorruptible skeleton
> and the scraps of dried viscera and skin bundled in khaki
> they took to Chalons-sur-Marne
> and laid it out neat in a pine coffin
> and took it home to God's Country on a battleship . . .
> and draped the Old Glory over it
> and the bugler played taps
> and Mr. Harding prayed to God and the diplomats and the generals
> and the admirals and the brass hats and the politicians and the
> handsomely dressed ladies out of the society column of the
> *Washington Post* stood up solemn.
> All the Washingtonians brought flowers. Woodrow Wilson
> brought a bouquet of poppies.[40]

A new response towards war and a tougher type of war novel had taken root in the American literary world. Although many ex-soldiers continued to speak up in their memoirs for wartime values[41], no amount of government propaganda or patriotic reminiscence would stem the disillusion with war and its disheartening aftermath that found expression in the writings of the lost generation.

Notes

1   John Oxenham, 1914 , London, Methuen, 1916; Ian Hay, (John Hay Beith), *The First Hundred Thousand, Being the Unofficial Chronicle of a Unit of 'K(1)'* London Wm. Blackwood, 1915 ; Joseph Hocking, *The Curtain of Fire*, London, Hodder & Stoughton, 1916; William J. Locke, *The Rough Road*, London, John Lane: the Bodley Head, 1918.

2   See Peter Aichinger's study of the American attitudes toward warfare, *The*

American Soldier in Fiction 1880–1963: A History of Attitudes Toward Warfare and the Military Establishment, Ames, Iowa State Press,1975.

3   See Malcolm Bradbury: *The Modern American Novel*, Oxford: Oxford U.P., 1984, p.12.

4   See for example, Warren Lee Goss, *Jed's Boy: a Story of Adventures in the Great World War*, New York, Thomas Y. Crowell Company, 1919, p.234: 'He was a hero without a stain of selfishness. He was willing to sacrifice all he held dear, to go down to death branded as a traitor by the friends he loved best, that he might serve his country.'

5   See, for example Amos N. Wilder, *Armageddon Revisited: a World War 1 Journal*, New Haven, Yale University Press, 1994.

6   See for example, the well-known American recruiting poster, reading: 'Gee I wish I were A Man. I'd join the Navy'. The same theme is taken up in the novel by Credo Harris, *Where the Souls of Men Are Calling*, New York, Britton Pub. Co. 1918, in which a young man is shamed into uniform and heroism by the indomitable woman he loves.

7   See Stanley Cooperman, *World War I and the American Novel*, Baltimore, Johns Hopkins U.P., 1967; see also Ernest R. May, *The World War and American Isolation*, Cambridge Mass., Harvard U.P., 1959., and Doreen Collins, *Aspects of British Politics 1904 –19*, Oxford Pergamon Press 1965.

8   Siegfried Sassoon ed., Isaac Rosenberg, *Collected Poems*; Andreas Latzko, *Men in Battle*, London, Cassell, 1918; Henri Barbusse, *Le Feu*, (The Fire) English Tr.W.Fitzwalter Wray, London, Dent, 1917.

9   Alan Seeger, *Letters and Diary of Alan Seeger*, New York, Charles Scribner's Sons, 1917; *Poems*, London: Constable, 1917.

10   *The New Republic* , 22 May 1915, quoted in introduction to Alan Seeger, *Poems*, p.xxvi.

11   Seeger, *Letters* , 25 October 1915, p. 173.

12   Seeger, *Letters*, 13 April, 1916, pp.190–1.

13   Seeger, *Poems*, 'Champagne (1914–15)', pp.134–5.

14   David Kennedy, *Over Here The First World War and American Society*, Oxford: Oxford U.P., 1980, p. 182.

15   Arthur Guy Empey, *From the Fire Step: The Experiences of an American Soldier in the British Army* London: Putnam, 1917.

16   Empey, *First Call, Guide Posts to Berlin*, New York & London: The Knickerbocker Press, G.P. Putnam, 1918.

17   Empey, *From the Fire Step* p.7

18   ibid. p.12.

19   ibid. pp.137–8.

20   ibid. p.172.

21   ibid., p.180

22   Edith Wharton, *The Marne*, New York, D. Appleton, 1918; Willa Cather, *One of Ours*, New York: Knopf, 1922.

23   Empey, *First Call*, p.3

24   ibid., p.6–7

25   ibid., p.16

26   See for example, the character of the American 'Mr Direck' in H.G. Wells, *Mr Britling Sees it Through* London, Cassell, 1916

27 See David Lundberg, 'The American Literature of War', *American Quarterly*, Vol 36 (3), 373–88.

28 Charles Genthe, *American War Narratives 1917–1918*, New York, D. Lewis, 1969, p.3.

29 Temple Bailey, *The Tin Soldier*, 1918, London, Skeffington, 1918, p.178.

30 ibid.p.180.

31 ibid., p.181.

32 ibid . p.260

33 ibid. p.260

34 Jeffrey Walsh, *American War Literature 1914 to Vietnam*, London, Macmillan, 1982, p.17

35 Coningsby Dawson, *The Glory of the Trenches*, London, John Lane, 1918.

36 ibid., p.50.

37 Morale was not universally high in the American Army. See Amos Wilder, op. cit., p.137: October 1918: 'The drafted soldiers here in camp as replacements – who have only a dull experience on top of their first homesickness . . . really hope not to go to the front.'

38 ibid, p.80.

39 Kennedy, op. cit., p 228 .

40 John. Dos Passos, *USA: Nineteen Nineteen*, London: Constable, 1938, pp472–73; see also Stanley Cooperman, 'John Dos Passos *Three Soldiers*: Aesthetics and the Doom of Individualism', in Holger Klein ed., *The First World War in Literature* London, Macmillan, 1976.

41 See for example, Capt.Wendell Westover, *Suicide Batttalions*, New York, G.P.Putnam's,The Knickerbocker Press, 1929.

Chapter 54

French Children as Target for Propaganda

Stephane Audoin-Rouzeau

Children were fully integrated into the war. In all the combatant nations – and this paper is concerned particularly with the French – childhood was the target for intense propaganda designed to bring the youngest citizens whole-heartedly into the war. They too had to be *mobilised*.

Many means of instruction were employed to promote this mobilisation, but their themes and objectives converged to form a cultural universe specifically for the consumption of young people, including the very youngest. Books,[1] illustrated magazines, toys and games were all heavily influenced by war themes from the very beginning and played a decisive role in adults' interpretation of the world conflict for children.

The Catholic church also occupied a central role in their mobilisation: in 1915, for example, on the initiative of pupils in a private school in Bordeaux, it launched the 'Children's crusade'; this was organised systematically on a national and even international scale, with the object of creating a veritable children's 'army of prayer', established on the basis of school year-groups. The mission of these 'soldiers' was to gain the aid of the Almighty in achieving victory for the French and her allies but also, more prosaically, to 'adopt' different sectors of the front so as to offer support for the soldiers there and to express solidarity through prayers at the moment of combat.[2]

The republic's primary schools also played a significant part: teachers' journals, inspectors' reports, manuals, teaching material and the topics set for pupils show that, particularly at the beginning, the nation's schools made the war their focus of interest[3]. All teaching and all apprenticeships were undertaken from the starting-point of an educational presentation of the war. Teaching of French, history, geography, ethics and even mathematics, was wholly transformed: the war was henceforward the point of departure for everything; and everything came back to it.

767

This all-embracing management of childhood had a prominently stated objective. As the Dean of Poitiers Academy noted in 1916, at the prize-giving for the town's *lycée*,

> there is no place for ordinary children at an extraordinary time like this
> ... If you have feelings you cannot see others getting killed on your behalf
> without wanting to be worthy of this sacrifice.[4]

Children were required to feel continuously mobilised, continuously 'at war'.

This 'mobilisation of childhood' indicates the full scale of French society's stake in the war. Since it was seen as a war for civilisation, and even as a war committed to a certain concept of humanity, logic demanded that no age-group could be exempt; what would be the point of children's lives, for example, if the greater civilisation which France felt she embodied, lost the war? In France the old Jacobin culture of war as emancipator and civiliser created a predisposition towards a particularly strong mobilisation of the youngest citizens.

Study of propaganda aimed at children reveals the interesting aspect of making it possible to reach the heart of the 'war culture' of societies engaged in the war. But my object here is not to evoke propaganda for its own sake: it is to attempt to define the degree to which children assimilated the war culture created for their consumption.

Unfortunately the children of the war period have left very few direct accounts of their state of mind at the time. Further, the impact of propaganda on all areas of childhood is extremely difficult to measure: cultural history is more at home in analysing *methods* of propaganda management and manipulation than their *effectiveness*. In the present case, apart from scattered elements, information is depressingly scarce. Our aim is therefore limited to suggesting some paths of research and to attempting an initial approach.[5]

The simplest way is undoubtedly to begin with the certainties of the adult world. From this point of view the younger generation was as admirable then as it would be in the future. The war, essentially a learning experience, was creating an élite generation. The adult message concerning children assumed that these results were gained through promotion of children's innate patriotism. No doubt appears on this point: the children of the war were perfect children. As Madame Hollebecque wrote at the end of her book on French youth and the war:

> The rising generation ... has earned the sacrifice of its elders who have
> given their lives on the battlefield for their nation's well-being and for
> the freedom of those who are to come.[6]

This adult conviction of 'perfect childhood', wholly centred on the single concept of the defence of the nation, clearly deserves examination. It would indeed be too simple to see the description of certain children's attitudes during the war as pure propaganda. Going by the evidence of certain round-robin letters[7], when the Minister of Public Education demanded in May 1915 that school children should abandon their plans to give the cost of their prize books to charity, he was probably opposing a movement that was at least partly spontaneous among school-children.[8] When, particularly at the beginning of the war, the heads and inspectors noted a genuine enthusiasm among pupils in the school workrooms undertaking tasks for the soldiers, they were probably not entirely mistaken.[9] When the girls who read *Fillette* asked their magazine to act as an intermediary to put them in touch with one or more 'war godsons',[10] when pupils adopted soldiers collectively, there was undoubtedly real devotion. Whatever the role (through permission or encouragement) played by the adult world, organisations like the *Ligue fraternelle des enfants de France* (set up in 1915 to establish teams of war 'godfathers' and 'godmothers' for refugee children), or like the *Union fraternelle des enfants de la France*, created in the same year (so that children of prosperous families could help the child of a soldier killed in battle), certainly released juvenile devotion that was wholly sincere. Equally sincere was the maintenance of soldiers' graves by children behind the front lines, or their visits, which are known to have taken place, to wounded men in hospitals.

The young Simone de Beauvoir, whose patriotic enthusiasm, according to her memoirs, surpassed that of her parents (despite their links with *Action française*) was a good example of a type of child from the urban bourgeoisie particularly strongly 'integrated' into the war. This also applied to Françoise Marette, aged 6 at the end of 1914,[11] or the young Anaïs Nin (aged 11 in 1914), who left Europe for the United States at the end of July 1914 but whose pulse continued, throughout the war, to beat for France. She scattered her 'diary of childhood' with hopes of victory, patriotic and anti-German poems, regrets at not being a man and at not being able to take part. 'The war is very good,' she wrote on 14 September 1914. 'France is winning, is always winning, I have no sympathy for the Germans, they are too cruel.'[12] On 25 January 1915, before she was 12, she was calling for a new Joan of Arc to arise, none other than herself:

> I dreamed that I was saving France, that Jeanne d'Arc was with me and that she was singing: Come on Anaïs, rescue France because that is your wish, and I threw myself forward, and fifteen minutes later all the cities were shouting, Victory! Vive la France! Vive Jeanne d'Arc who has given strength to Anaïs! Oh, I would be so happy if it could come true![13]

Her patriotic urge was fundamentally no different from that of the young Yves Congar when, at the age of 10½, he witnessed the German entry into Sedan. He drew a black line across the page of his diary, then wrote beneath the line that divided two eras: 'This is the beginning of a tragedy, a sad and sombre story written by a child who has always loved and respected his nation and has great and justified hatred for a cruel and unjust nation.' [14]

In making use of these remarkable note-books written by remarkable children, the historian may lose his way at the precise moment when he thinks he is reaching his goal; yet a certain level of children's involvement in the war cannot be denied. Observers of childhood were surely not wrong, for example, when they noted that the children sometimes believed that *they were capable of doing something* to preserve one soldier or another from danger. For example, one little girl in a Paris school wrote, 'Dear soldier, I am sending you this parcel so that you can kill the accursed Boches. You will not die; therefore, do not be afraid.' [15]

These same observers were also probably correct when they noted the extent to which the war had penetrated into children's games, with all the appropriate military vocabulary. Some were delighted; others saw more clearly what this annexation concealed: Since the beginning of the war we have seen games change . . . All children have *played* at war and turned themselves and their objects into elements of the action . . . Most of these games are violent, rough and, we must admit, often cruel. [16]

Play could thus register – and thus no doubt exorcise – the most dreadful circumstances of the war: for example, little girls seen in a school play-ground enacting the announcement to a woman of her husband's death and who acted out 'with astonishing realism the gesture of terror, the fainting, the recovery and instinctive turn to fictitious children and soon, the renewed faint'. [17]

Children's drawings and their letters to soldiers, school-children's essays published in educational publications or journals, usually revealed a perfect match between the language of childhood and that of propaganda. In the first school year of the war, Jacques Cardinaud, born in 1903, wrote about the Battle of the Marne:

> Paris was saved! I was full of overflowing delight, I admired the magnif-
> icent heroism that symbolised the ordinary French men who saved Paris
> and our beloved Montmartre from the German grasp. Everyone's face
> radiated happiness – Oh, yes, this victory was the salvation of France,
> vengeance for Senlis, Termonde, Rheims, Louvain, and so many others!
> German 'Kultur' was wiped out! Hail to Joffre! . . . [18]

There are still fewer false notes in this description of a cache of weapons, taken from an exhibition on 'school and war' and presented by the *Revue pédagogique* at the end of 1917:

> These soldiers must have sublime thoughts. They saw themselves at the
> heart of enemy machine-gun fire, bayonets on their rifles, their hands red

with blood, returning from an attack . . . Brave little Frenchmen, I am proud to be your brother and, if I can, I will avenge you: I swear it.[19]

These children's essays also gave an uncompromising image of the enemy, a perfect reproduction of the official presentation: a pupil wrote in 1916:

We cannot look at them without a feeling of very natural hatred . . . This hatred will always exist between the French nation and the German nation, for what they have done is unforgivable and unforgettable.[20]

This was imitation in the spirit of the original. Drawings too were in the same spirit: those collected from schools by the *Société libre pour l'étude psychologique de l'enfant*,[21] and published in 1917 in a fascinating study under the title *Nos enfants et la guerre*, show identical conformity: the most junior classes show lines of soldiers and hand-to-hand fighting, with a marked fascination with the German helmet; in the middle age-groups, the dead, the trenches, the various different troops and, in addition, among the girls, the figure of the nurse, overwhelmingly; by the time they reached the senior classes, the accent was on technical details while the boy/girl dichotomy grew stronger (pictures of battle from the former, drawings of hospitals, men on leave, the dead, and shelled houses from the latter). In fact the authors of the survey did not hide their relative disappointment at these creations which appeared to have been carried out to order, when they had hoped for a 'spontaneous' response. The patriotic allegories appear to have been based on the same persuasive images in posters and the press. Caricatures, strongly anti-German, were copied from the work of Poulbot or Abel Faivre: surely this response from the children corresponded perfectly to the schools' *demands*? Whatever the truth of the matter, the first glance reveals exemplary pupils and equally exemplary essays, letters and drawings.[22] Undoubtedly such work was carefully selected, but exercise books and copies of school-leaving certificates that have been preserved also show the conformity of most school-children to the demands of the war culture. 'Always hate the Germans' said a pupil's exercise book preserved by the national museum of education.[23]

And yet the 'mobilisation of childhood' in war-time clashed with a major contradiction, both social and cultural, which was impossible to resolve. To be successful, the all-encompassing management of childhood required the net that in normal times surrounded the world of childhood to be drawn even tighter.[24] The multifarious demands of the war (school premises requisitioned, departure of teachers, the need to keep children at home more often to work on the land, the attraction of urban employment in a context of labour shortages, family members coming home on leave), all interfered with the national scholastic effort which since the 1880s had concentrated specifically on achieving regular school attendance. From the beginning of the war, and even more at its end with the deterioration in material conditions, school inspectors raised the alarm.[25] The situation was particularly serious in the directly exposed areas behind the front line, with the *département* of the Somme providing a good example of the problem. Confusion in daily existence caused by battles and incoming troops was great, although the picture of the school year 1914–1915 is less alarming than might have been expected. But matters deteriorated during the following school years with the growing poverty of the local labour force. The reasons for absence cited at the beginning of 1916 were generally connected with the need to keep children away from school for agricultural work, often from the age of 9–10 years. From 1916–1917 other factors were added: the shelling of Amiens, the use of children to help collect the family food and fuel supplies or for minor trade with passing troops and to look after young brothers and sisters, and if a family were in mourning or a soldier returning to them on leave; but work in the fields remained the principal cause of absenteeism.

Teachers' determination to teach no doubt did much to prevent the collapse of the school system; for those schools in the Somme for which information survives, school attendance for the year 1916–1917 was assessed at nil, poor or mediocre for 75, fairly good for 51, good or very good for 103. The year 1917–1918, the period of the final enemy offensives, was to be much worse, to the extent of eliminating all statistics.[26] Absenteeism in *Seine et Oise*, which in 1913–1914 had stood at 13 per cent, exceeded 25 per cent during the war and even 50 per cent in certain schools.[27]

Disorganisation of life, particularly significant near to the front lines, also applied elsewhere, although to a lesser extent. On 1 October 1917, a ministerial memorandum noted that 'the regular attendance of our pupils had never before been so severely hindered'.[28] It recommended repression of 'vagabondage among children of school age' and advised that they should be brought back to school by the police.[29]

Yet the problem was too great for the schools themselves and had wider causes than simply the material difficulties of life. The prolonged absence of mobilised men – fathers, older brothers, uncles – undermined the whole family structure as a unit where masculine presence, particularly paternal authority, so strongly reasserted at the evening meal among the popular classes, played a role all the more significant[30] because, since the turn of the century, a type of nuclear family model had become the norm, with the child as its pivotal element. It was children who were hit most severely by the war, in households where there was now no paternal presence. No doubt the impact of this paternal absence should not be exaggerated: in the case of Vienna, Reinhard Sieder has shown that most working-class families were able to replace paternal authority with that of the oldest son, or another adult in the family (uncle, brother-in-law, etc.) and this pattern, noted elsewhere, no doubt applied to most of the other combatant nations.[31] And yet it is probably true that this 'patriarchal pattern', the key-stone shaping the whole of family life, was missing for too long. This was the conclusion of deeply grieved observers of childhood,[32] whether laymen or clerics, and most particularly in working-class circles when the women joined the labour market or increased their hours of work to the detriment of their presence at home. It was moreover in these same circles that the war culture created for juvenile consumption took hold with the greatest difficulty. Without even returning to schools, the cultural means of instruction aimed at young people (books, albums, magazines, toys, etc.) reached middle-class children more substantially than those of the urban working classes, who were in turn more accessible than rural children.

While 'the relative abandonment of children',[33] feared by psychologists during the war, was only to a limited extent a reality, the concern was revealing: the youngest children, whom the war propaganda made such efforts to mobilise from 1914 onwards, undoubtedly *had* increased their independence because of the war. It was a paradox: the war required the mobilisation of children just at the time when it moved them largely out of reach.

Further, the inevitable erosion of the effect of propaganda aimed at children, must be admitted, once the first months of the war had passed. The development of a substantial number of magazines for young people between 1914 and 1918 provides a prime indication of this decline. Although from the beginning of the war until its end the war culture for children changed much less obviously than that aimed at adults, a certain 're-learning' of the war propaganda nevertheless took place once the very powerful initial efforts at mobilisation had passed. From 1916 onwards, most of the illustrated periodicals devoted diminishing amounts of space to the war. The initial indoctrination eventually lost its effectiveness in a prolonged war.

War propaganda in education also lost much of its force.[34] Close examination of the *Revue de l'enseignement primaire* shows, for example, that if the 'presence' of the war always remained strong in the topics studied, its tone altered noticeably from the beginning of the school year in September 1916; in particular this included the appearance of a theme which had hitherto received little attention: the absence of fathers. From the school year 1916–1917, the bond between education and the war weakened, and the teachers' obsession with the war died away noticeably as the school year drew to its end. Among the 'subjects' set by the journal that year there were only nine (out of a total of 34) which related to the continuing conflict: the war was becoming a side-issue. The journal turned to preoccupations simultaneously broader and more traditional, and during the course of the year 1917–1918 this evolution reached its limit:

the 'focus of interest' at the beginning of the school year was 'being a pupil',[35] and the war, without being altogether ignored, found itself reduced to a minor element.

The dominant discourse was quickly challenged *from within*. From 1916, no doubt the turning point for the topic under consideration, a school inspector corrected certain initial options for teachers in the Basses-Alpes:

> The school must continue to provide suitable space for current events. However, I think I should alert you to certain dangers: it is important not to neglect essential teaching in the programme, not to ignore the purpose for which the teaching periods were intended under the pretext of discussing with children the events of the war.

They must no longer think in terms of using the war as the basis for all lessons nor of systematically integrating current events into them, except in the case of very significant events. It was even necessary:

> to be on guard against distorting certain parts of teaching, history for example, by denigrating certain hostile nations systematically.

The teachers must also

> take care not to upset the feelings of pupils through descriptions of terrible events, too often repeated.[36]

This development turned its back on the original recommendations: in 1918, teaching had thus distanced itself largely from that of 1914–1915. From 1917, moreover, the report on 'the school at war' prepared by the survey *Nos enfants et la guerre* was not optimistic; by basing itself on questionnaires returned by teachers in 22 schools, the publication concluded that 'a lowering in the level of children's instruction' had taken place, a drop linked to material difficulties but also to 'problems with behaviour'.[37]

Once the exceptional tensions of the outbreak of war had passed, schools had in fact largely failed in their mobilisation of childhood. A revealing setback was that of the 'school allotments' launched officially in 1917 by the ministry for public information in an attempt to counteract the national crisis in agriculture. The initial target of 1500 hectares was never achieved. The *Revue pédagogique*, in its first report in June 1917 and the second in March 1918, confirmed that apart from unforeseen material obstacles, the abandonment by pupils and the irritation among parents suspicious of a scheme that appeared to interfere with their children's education, the jeers from farmworkers and the refusal of more than half the communes to provide any support, all led to the collapse of the only genuine attempt –

apart from school workrooms – to make use of juvenile labour on a grand scale.

Further, pupils' submission to their schools' patriotic demands proved nothing. André Bellessort was well aware of this in the introduction to his none the less unfailingly patriotic educational manual:

> The drawback of these subjects is that they encourage insincerity. You encourage it each time that you put the child in the position of telling you officially about his intimate feelings (and school exercise books are official by nature). Except in a very few rare cases, he will have no intention of expressing his genuine thoughts or feelings; but he will try to guess what, according to you, he is supposed to feel and think.[38]

In fact André Bellessort was already expressing a rule well-known to modern teachers, on children's conformism in school and their natural submission to what they perceive to be the adult world's expectations of them. This was underlined in the survey carried out by the '*Société libre pour l'étude psychologique de l'enfant*'. It was based on a twofold survey questionnaire in the primary schools in the Rhône department in 1916, one aimed at children to assess the extent of their knowledge of what was happening in the war and the other designed to learn from teachers and head-teachers what impact the war was having on the pupils. The results, received by academic inspectors in July 1916, dealt with only 316, or 20 per cent, of the answers. They showed great awareness on the part of the children, which brought the teachers the congratulations of the survey's authors on their 'excellent labours'.[39] On other points, however, the survey tended towards pessimism, bemoaning in particular the 'schoolroom style' of the answers and the fact that the war was 'seen and felt through the school'.[40] The survey had in fact encountered nothing but complete submission among the pupils, who had responded to the best of their ability to what they thought was expected of them. 'It would no doubt be illusory to suppose that we could reach these young minds in their entirety through a survey in school', they added, perceiving that not all aspects of childhood were open to their explorations.[41]

This was perceptive. Even in the most formal school exercises, selected to demonstrate the full excellence of childhood at war, the children effectively gave themselves away, mostly in part and sometimes completely. And what they then expressed was their profound sadness at the war, their despair in the face of the absence or death of their fathers, brothers, cousins – their anguish over death, their weariness in this unending trial. Under the essay heading 'New Year's Day at Home' for his *Certificat d'études*, one pupil wrote as follows: 'The new year is beginning in sadness for everyone because of this terrible war which is creating so many victims. We were particularly unhappy in our family because on New Year's Eve itself we had heard bad news: one of our cousins had been killed in battle on the

Yser, doing his duty as a good Frenchman. When we greeted each other on January 1st we felt more like weeping than wishing each other a Happy New Year . . . that evening we sat round the fire, hardly speaking, thinking about our dear cousin, who we wouldn't see again, and also about all our brave soldiers and their heroic struggle to defend our nation. I shall never forget New Year's Day 1915 for as long as I live . . . and I shall never stop hating those damned Germans.'[42] This is unmistakable – this essay is not a reflection of generalised family pacifism: the cousin's death was blamed not on the war but on the Germans, and the passages on the enduring hatred for them, the 'duty as a good Frenchman' and the 'heroic struggle to defend our nation,' provide ample proof. But the text betrays profound disgust.

A certain degree of autonomy was therefore possible in childhood. Further, the writings of some children showed irrefutable pacifism, as seen in these essays written by pupils after the German withdrawal in February 1917. In answer to the blunt question, 'What is your opinion of the war?',

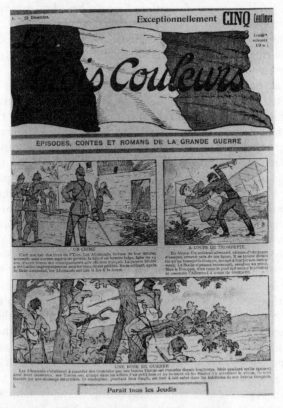

(xii)   'The Three Colours' a children's weekly first produced in December 1914. [l'Historial de la Grande Guerre, Péronne]

776

an 11-year-old girl, Rose, responded: 'In the last three years since war was declared, we have had time to learn what wretchedness is . . . It would be good if this awful killing could end soon and everyone get back to their families and to happiness again, not like before the war because nearly everyone is in mourning'.[43] The presence of death was also emphasised in illustrations of daily life drawn at the beginning of the war in a Montmartre school;[44] it was present too in some children's letters, in a style devoid of all expression: 'Dear Aunt and Uncle, I am writing to tell you that my dear Papa is dead, who I loved so much . . . '[45]

Substantial surveys undertaken during the war and dealing with fairly broad pupil samples show the extent to which children, far from being miniature adults as generally assumed, retained an independent view of the war, which they saw through different eyes from adults. The blend of heroic conformity and independence seems to us to express well what it meant, in general, to be a child in wartime. Propaganda themes were in effect interiorised but at the same time worked over, in unpredictable ways, by the children themselves.

Countering widespread optimism in the world of education, some teachers complained of a noticeable deterioration in behaviour in school, in pupils' speech and games. One such teacher was Jeanne Galzy, who in 1919 published *La femme chez les garçons*. In this book she described her work as an *agregée de lettres* from 1915 to 1917 in a boys' *lycée* where she replaced a teacher killed at the Front, for the teaching of French and history. With total detachment from her pupils, she noted their overwhelming indifference to the war and the dramas going on around them, such as the teaching assistant whose son was at Verdun and of whom no news had been heard for weeks, or the boy whose father had just been killed and who was envied by the others because he would get out of doing the Maths test. She also saw clearly that the pupils knew very well how to avoid any personal comment or any truly sincere opinion when they offered her 'unlikely war stories' in the guise of an essay.[46] Though tough, her judgement was probably justified, at least in part, when she wrote: 'I have learned only one fact for certain: the burden of war does not weigh them down. In vain, naive romanticism thinks of them suffocating under the horrors and anxieties that surround them. They have all got used to it because nothing affects them materially. It should not be said of them that "They will have lost their childhood". We must see things as they are, without frills. Irreplaceable, unconcerned and unconscious childhood – they will have had that. For them the war is only a theme around which their imagination evolves. For them it operates much more as a pastime than as a source of emotion.'[47]

These children's successful maintenance of their autonomy varied from a denial of the war to an enthusiasm, which if sincere, was almost certainly momentary and selective. Such a frame of mind derived from a combination of their forced submission and their actual indifference. This result corresponded ill with what education experts wished to see in children in wartime or with what most adults wanted and created for them; and it lies at the heart of the problem of why there was a failure to instil a war culture for juvenile consumption. Because it was impossible to sustain the initial tension over four and a half years or to resist the reduction of the war to an everyday matter, those in charge were unable to give a concrete reality to their ambitions. It seems, therefore, as if war failed to conquer completely those childhood territories which it had hoped to claim for itself.

Notes

1   See the catalogue of the exhibition: *Livre, mon ami. Lectures enfantines.* *1914–1954*, Paris, 1991.
2   A. Bessières, *La croisade des enfants. Ligue eucharistique des enfants pour la victoire de la France, le salut des mourants, la pacification et la restauration chrétienne des patries*. Paris, Beauchesnes, 1917.
3   There is no overall study of this aspect. For secondary education, however, see Paul Gerbod, 'L'enseignement secondaire public en France de 1914 à 1920', *L'Information historique*, no.1, January–February 1971, pp 18–28.
4   *Revue pédagogique*, August 1916, no.8, p.167.
5   For a more extensive approach see: S. Audoin-Rouzeau, *La guerre des enfants, 1914–1918. Essai d'histoire culturelle*, Paris, Armand Colin, 1993.
6   Madame Hollebecque, *La jeunesse de France et la guerre*, Paris, Didier, 1916, p.101.
7   A. Faria de Vasconcellos, *Les enfants et la guerre*, Geneva, Atar, 1915, pp.23–4.
8   Circular relating to prize-givings, 15 May 1915, *Bulletin administratif du Ministère de l'Instruction Publique*, no. 2172, p.507.
9   Charles Adam, Rector of the Academy of Nancy, *Revue Pédagogique*, 15 October–15 November 1915, no.10–11, p.113.
10   *Fillette*, 20 August 1916, no.441, p.12.
11   Her letters written during the war have recently been published: Françoise Dolto, *Correspondance, 1913–1938*, Paris, Hatier, 1991.
12   Anaïs Nin, *Journal d'enfance*, 1914–1919, Paris, Stock, 1979, p.42.
13   ibid., p.91.
14   Père Yves Congar, 'Enfances sedanaises, 1904–1919', *Pays sedanais*, 1978, 5, p.28.
15   Madame Hollebecque, op.cit., pp.22–23.
16   ibid., pp.86–7.
17   Madame Hollebecque, op.cit., pp.87–8.
18   'La France de demain, la vie à Montmartre pendant la guerre racontée et dess-inée par les écoliers montmartrois de l'école Sainte Isaure, no.18. School year 1914–1915', *Bulletin de guerre du Vieux Montmartre*, no. 88.
19   *Revue pédagogique*, October 1917, no.10. p.355.
20   *Revue pédagogique*, July 1916, no.7, p.42.
21   *Nos enfants et la guerre. Enquête de la société libre pour l'étude psychologique*

de l'enfant, Paris, F. Alcan, 1917. The society was formed in 1908 by F. Buisson and A. Binet.

22 This model effect can be seen in a selection of drawings by the children of Nantes in 1914–1918 and published in: Didier Guyvarc'h, *Moi, Marie Rocher, écolière en guerre. Dessins d'enfants 1914–1918*, Rennes, Apogée, 1993.

23 *P comme Patrie (en France entre 1850 et 1950)* INRP, Musée National de l'Education, p.69.

24 For the problems of the child in society and in the family at the beginning of the twentieth century, see Maurice Crubellier, *L'enfance et la jeunesse dans la société française, 1800–1950*, Paris, A. Colin, 1979.

25 *Revue pédagogique*, February 1918, no.2, p.141.

26 Valérie Dehay, *L'enfance et l'école dans la Somme en 1914–1918*, maîtrise dissertation, University of Picardy 1992, p.231ff.

27 Serge Lesmanne, 'L'école et la guerre (1914–1918)', *Mémoires de la Société d'histoire et d'archéologie de Pontoise*, 1985–1986, vol. 73, p.274.

28 *Bulletin administratif du Ministère de l'Instruction Publique*, 13 October 1917, no. 2295, p.723.

29 Circular relating to school attendance, *Bulletin administratif du Ministère de l'Instruction Publique*, 13 October 1917, op.cit..

30 For comparison, see Reinhard Sieder, 'Behind the lines; working-class family life in wartime Vienna' in *The Upheaval of War, Family*, op.cit., pp.109–38.

31 For example in rural French life: Françoise Thébaud, *La femme au temps de la guerre de 1914*, Paris, Stock, 1986, p.152.

32 Mme Hollebecque, *La jeunesse de France et la guerre*, Paris, Didier, 1916. See also, *Nos enfants et la guerre*, survey by the Société libre pour l'étude psychologique de l'enfant, Paris, F. Alcan, 1917.

33 *Nos enfants et la guerre*, op.cit., p.76.

34 Paul Gerbod, 'L'enseignement secondaire public en France de 1914 à 1920', *L'Information historique*, no.1, January-February 1971, pp.18–28.

35 *Revue de l'enseignement primaire*, 30 September 1917, no.1. The same development can be seen in the *Revue pédagogique* from 1916 onwards, but particularly in 1917–1918.

36 Memorandum to teachers in the Basses-Alpes by the Academy Inspector, *Revue pédagogique*, January-June 1916, no.1, p.88.

37 *Nos enfants et la guerre*, op.cit., p.75.

38 André Bellessort, *Petit recueil de compositions françaises. Episodes de la guerre, 1914–1915*, Paris, Belin, 1916, p.7.

39 *Nos enfants et la guerre*, op.cit., p.13.

40 ibid., p.14.

41 ibid., p.14.

42 Jean Guirbal, *La Grande Guerre en compositions françaises*, Paris, Nathan, 1915, pp.72–3.

43 *Revue pédagogique*, July 1917, no.7, pp.86–7.

44 La France de demain, op.cit.

45 *Les Trois Couleurs*, 25 March 1915, no.16.

46 Jeanne Galzy, *La femme chez les garçons*, Paris, Payot, 1919, p.205. 'Jeanne Galzy' was the pseudonym of Jeanne Baraduc, from Sèvres.

47 ibid., p.36.

Chapter 55

Through the Eye of the Camera: Contemporary Cinema Audiences and their 'Experience' of War in the film, *Battle of the Somme*

Nicholas Reeves

Geoffrey Malins, the most famous of that small group of official British film-makers who worked on the Western Front in the months after November 1915, wrote at the conclusion of his own, very distinctive account of his wartime service:

> In all the pictures that it has been my good fortune to take during the two and a half years that I have been kept at work on the great European battlefield, I have always tried to remember that it was through the eye of the camera, directed by my own sense of observation, that the millions of people at home would gain their only first-hand knowledge of what was happening at the front.[1]

It was a very large claim to make and, given the nature of Malins' book, many readers must have concluded that this was simply the most overblown of a series of exaggerated claims that he had made about his wartime career as an official British cameraman. And yet, for all his talent for hyperbole, is his claim quite as exaggerated as it appears at first sight? Did 'the millions of people at home' see his films, and, if so, did those films give them a 'first-hand knowledge of what was happening at the front'? The answers to these questions will enable us to understand a little more about the nature of the domestic experience of the war. For while that experience was shaped in large measure by the myriad changes in social, economic and personal circumstances brought about by the war, another important element was that 'knowledge' of the war which was constructed for the mass of the people by that small minority whose access to the traditional media of communication had now been supplemented by access to the new media of mass communication. Nor were they slow to take advantage of the special opportunities which war presented. A plethora of words and images confronted the people at every turn as journalists and painters, advertisers and politicians, churchmen and poets, constructed and communicated their own particular images of the war. And of course within that mass of information were those moving images of the war which had been constructed by Malins and a handful of other official cameramen who had filmed the war on the Western Front.

While cinema was a comparatively recent phenomenon in British society,[2] it had quickly established itself as the major force in British popular culture. With a pricing policy which undercut the theatres and the music hall,[3] it was already at the outbreak of the war the dominant form of popular entertainment, with more money being spent on cinema tickets each week than the combined receipts of all other forms of commercial entertainment put together – indeed, by the summer of 1916 twenty million tickets were being sold each week.[4] So, the millions to whom Malins referred were going to the cinema. But it was not official, factual, war films that they were going to see. The heart of the cinema programme consisted of a variety of fiction films, in which drama and comedy, romance and adventure, reinforced by an ever more important star system, persuaded ordinary people to spend some of their hard-earned cash on the two hours or so of entertainment which a typical programme provided.

Official film propaganda, on the other hand, was firmly wedded to the factual, non-fiction, film. Both the cinema trade and the government's own propagandists had been convinced that this was the only appropriate form for official wartime film propaganda to take, and it was this very approach which delayed the launch of the official films until the end of 1915. For of course factual war films, films of the army or navy, required the agreement of the service departments – and securing that agreement proved to be a long and difficult process. Not only did those advocating official film propaganda have to overcome the usual military and naval concerns with secrecy and security, they had to win the consent of people who were almost entirely ignorant of the new mass medium, who regarded it as a distasteful form of commercial, working-class entertainment, a medium which therefore, by definition, could play no proper part in the deadly serious business of prosecuting the war.[5] Thus, it took over a year to overcome this opposition, and it was not until the very end of 1915 that the first official film reached British cinema screens.[6] Malins himself, as one of the first two official cameramen to be sent to the Western Front, did not arrive in France until November 1915 and the first British footage from France was not publicly exhibited until the following January.

Six series of short films drawing on this Western Front footage were released to British cinemas in the first six months of 1916, and while their novelty did attract some attention and certainly ensured a wider distribution than comparable factual films would normally have achieved, nothing in these early months of official film propaganda substantiates Malins' grandiose claims.[7] All that changed, however, and changed dramatically with the release of *Battle of the Somme* in August 1916. For here at last was a film which really caught the popular imagination, and its release inaugurated a brief period of immense success for the official films. *Battle of the Somme* was followed in October 1916 by *The King Visits His Armies in the Great Advance*, and a trio of popular films was completed with *Battle of the Ancre and the Advance of the Tanks,* released in January 1917. That said, the release of *Battle of the Ancre* already revealed the first signs of some wavering in public interest in the films,[8] and by the time the third 'Battle' film was released in June 1917,[9] official film propaganda had passed its peak. Indeed, from the early summer of 1917 until the end of the war, the official propagandists were engaged in an (ultimately fruitless) attempt to try to win back the audiences they had lost.[10] Thus, at best Malins' claim can only apply to a very short period of the war: it was not until the late summer of 1916 that the vast majority of British cinema-goers saw the official films, and by the following spring they had lost interest in them.

That said, the mere fact that the films did not sustain their popularity over a long period of time does not in itself deny them any value; what matters is how many people saw them, and what sense they made of what they saw. In exploring these issues, this analysis will concentrate entirely on the first of these popular official films, *Battle of the Somme*. The middle film, *The King Visits His Armies in the Great Advance*, is only indirectly concerned with the experience of war on the Western Front,[11] and with the exception of the footage of the tanks, *Battle of the Ancre* covers much the same ground as *Battle of the Somme*. Most important of all, however, *Battle of the Somme* attracted far and away the most contemporary discussion – indeed, few if any films in the history of British cinema have been discussed so widely. Thus the trade press lavished fulsome attention on the film, but at a time when cinema was still largely ignored by considerable sections of the press, this film was also discussed in every major national daily paper and large numbers of regional and local papers as well. Moreover, a wide cross-section of other publications discussed the film, ranging from the Anglican *Guardian* and the free church *British Journal,* to service journals like the *Regiment* and the *Army and Navy Gazette* to less specialised journals like the *Illustrated London News,* the *Sphere* and the *Spectator.*

Battle of the Somme draws on footage shot by two official cameramen, Geoffrey Malins, and J. B. McDowell. Malins started filming on 25 June 1916; on 29 June he was joined by McDowell, and they continued to film the preliminaries, including the massive artillery bombardment.[12] Then on

1 July they were in position at two different locations with Rawlinson's Fourth Army to film the opening day of the battle of the Somme. They continued to film on the Somme until, on 10 July, they left the front; two days later, the first rushes of their footage were seen in London by the Trade Committee which supervised their work. The Committee was so impressed with what it saw that, whereas up until then it had released short films (the longest ran just under 12 minutes), the decision was taken to release the Somme footage in one consolidated film. Just under a month later, on 7 August 1916, the completed film (which ran for an hour and a quarter) had its first trade show, and three days later it was screened to an invited audience. At that screening an enthusiastic message of support for the film from Lloyd George (the recently appointed Secretary of State for War) was read to the audience, and the film was extensively reported in the national press the following day. Three weeks later it received the most prestigious endorsement of all for, following a private screening at Windsor, the King urged people to see it, and this too was widely reported. This initial publicity was complemented by extensive advertising in the trade press and a number of additional trade shows. All this vigorous promotion clearly paid off, for when *Battle of the Somme* went on public exhibition in London on 21 August, it opened at no less than thirty-four cinemas simultaneously; a week later it went on national release, a hundred prints being distributed nationwide.

The film did extraordinarily good business wherever it was shown. The opening week in London proved enormously popular, with numerous cinemas reporting that they were simply unable to cope with the scale of demand, [13] and the London experience of screening the film simultaneously at a number of different cinemas (a most unusual practice at the time) was repeated in most of the major centres of population. Thus the film was screened at twenty cinemas in Birmingham, most adopting the equally unusual strategy of showing the film all week (where normally programmes changed mid week); [14] in Dublin's Theatre Royal, no less than 10,000 people saw the film in the first half of the week in which it was shown. [15] In Leeds the film was screened simultaneously at the Picture House, the Assembly Rooms and the Harehills Picture House, [16] and the distributor reported that 'never has a war picture been so much in demand'. [17] In Glasgow and Edinburgh, the film opened simultaneously in at least a dozen cinemas, playing to full houses throughout the week, from eleven in the morning until ten thirty in the evening. [18] In Cardiff six cinemas ran the film simultaneously, while at Swansea huge crowds were reported and special morning performances had to be arranged to meet the demand. [19] In west London, the two Ealing cinemas shared the film between them, each launching it with a special performance attended by local dignitaries – both cinemas were sold out for the whole week, with police being required to control the crowds outside the Kinema in West Ealing, [20] while outside the Walpole in Ealing Broadway there were queues five deep all along the road between four and nine every evening.[21]

Queuing was a common experience for people wanting to see the film, and the fact that the trade press saw it as newsworthy is evidence in itself of how unusual it was.[22] In all, cinemas simply could not keep up with the scale of popular demand and there are frequent references to people being turned away from cinemas which were full.[23] Nor was it just a question of numbers. The film succeeded in attracting middle-class customers, many of whom may never have been to a cinema before. Thus one correspondent commented that the audience which he saw in the Southport Palladium included 'several of the leading citizens in the district who are more usually to be found a performances of legitimate drama of the "intellectual" type'.[24] In all, *Battle of the Somme* proved immensely popular wherever it was shown. Cinema after cinema played the film to full houses, often having to turn would-be patrons away. And although no national box-office statistics for the film were collected, Nicholas Hiley has calculated that the film probably achieved twenty million attendances in its first six weeks. Moreover, it continued to be shown in British cinemas for many months thereafter, and it is thus very likely that a majority of the domestic population saw the film.[25] It was indeed an extraordinary phenomenon, quite without precedent in the history of the British cinema. And it means of course that Malins' claim about the size of the audience, at least in respect of *Battle of the Somme*, was not exaggerated; the 'millions of people at home' did see this film.

But what of the second question: millions of people may have seen the film, but what did it mean to them? In exploring that second question, the most obvious point to make is that the film received universally favourable reviews, in marked contrast to reviews of the earlier, Western Front films which had been distinctly mixed,[26] with the trade press often openly hostile.[27] This time the trade press was unanimously enthusiastic in its view – *Kine Weekly* for example wrote:

> Speaking for ourselves, we never remember in all our long experience, to have seen any picture which, for power of appeal and intense gripping interest comes within measurable distance of this wonderful kinematograph record . . . The film record of 'the Battle of the Somme' is the greatest five-reel drama that will ever be shown in this or any land . . . [28]

Bioscope claimed that no other medium, literary or visual, could 'hope to convey to the man at home the reality of modern warfare, with the force and conviction shown in the marvellous pictures taken by the British Topical Committee for War films', [29] while for the *Cinema* it was quite simply 'the greatest war picture ever shown'.[30] This fulsome praise was echoed right across the national press,[31] with the *Daily Express* arguing

ℂ ALL THIS WEEK

OFFICIAL WAR FILM

The Battle of
The Somme

FIVE REELS

" If the exhibition of this Picture
all over the world does not end
War, God help civilisation ! "—

Mr. Lloyd George

"THE BATTLE OF THE SOMME" is the greatest moving
picture in the world—the greatest that has ever been produced.
A great war picture, it is the finest peace picture the world
has ever seen; it is worth a thousand Hague conferences. Where-
ever it is shown it should make an end in the minds of men to
the pretensions of pompous princes who have too long claimed the
right as the "All Highest" to doom their fellow-creatures to suffering
and destruction for the gratification of their mad ambitions. It is
impossible to believe that the world will ever forget this picture;
its impression will never fade from the memory of this generation.
Men who see it will never lightly talk of war again. In this picture
the world will obtain some idea of what it costs in human suffering
to put down the devil's domination."—*London Evening News.*

BRIGGATE, LEEDS.

(xiii) The *Yorkshire Evening Post* of 28.8.16 and an advertisement for the Battle of
the Somme film in Leeds. [Yorkshire Post Newspapers Plc]

that 'for sheer realism, there has perhaps never been anything to excel this wonderful film',[32] while for the *Daily Mirror* it was 'a glorious tribute to British valour . . . [which] should be shown in every British and neutral picture theatre the world over'.[33] The *Daily Telegraph* argued that 'nothing like the new series of war films has hitherto been seen, nothing so vivid, so detailed and so consecutive',[34] and *The Times* claimed that when in the future historians would 'wish to know the conditions under which the great offensive was launched, they will only have to send for these films'.[35] The local and provincial press was equally enthusiastic: for the *Leeds Mercury* the film was a 'great war picture [that] depicts in a most realistic fashion the grim and glorious incidents connected with this episode of the war',[36] while the *Yorkshire Evening Press* commented that 'never before has such a production been screened . . . it is all so real'.[37] The *Birmingham Gazette* asserted that it was 'very thrilling, very intimate, and very touching', [38] while for the *Glasgow Citizen* it was 'a great picture and one that cannot fail to grip and hold the attention'.[39]

There is a certain irony in this emphasis on the 'realism' of the film, for while it consisted largely of footage filmed at the time and place claimed for it in the film, it does include a number of sequences where the presence of the camera clearly influenced the events that were being filmed. This does not in itself distinguish it from most other factual film-making, but what is different here is that these sequences are shot and edited in such a way that the intervention of the cameraman is rather more apparent.[40] On the other hand, there is a crucial sequence in the film, which apparently shows men climbing out of a trench, going 'over the top', into battle, and here the charge against the film-makers is much more serious. This twenty-one second sequence, which attracted so much attention at the time was, in all probability, faked.[41] The evidence is not absolutely conclusive, but even if we assume for the moment that it was, it is quite clear that, in the main, the contemporary audience was quite unaware of this possibility. For the vast majority, this was, as the *Manchester Guardian* put it, 'the real thing at last';[42] overwhelmingly the contemporary audience accepted at face value the authenticity of the Somme footage presented to them.[43]

Particular characteristics were singled out in the public discussion of the film. The 'over the top' sequence won especial praise, described variously as 'perhaps the most striking part of the picture',[44] 'an amazing scene'[45] and 'a thrilling and inspiring sight'.[46] Moreover, it was the fact that it apparently showed men being killed that gave it its power – as the *Spectator* put it:

It would indeed be a cold heart that could resist the thrill of the battle that rushes upon one from the shivering screen. In the right-hand corner of the picture, one of the brown clad, helmeted men, just as he tops the parapet, instead of going over, slides back flattened out with arms extended against the wall of the trench – the first life sacrificed in the assault. It is a wonderful example of how reality – remember this is no arranged piece of play acting but a record taken in the agony of battle – transcends fiction.[47]

The *Bath and Wiltshire Chronicle* made a similar point in contrasting the film's 'vivid pictures' with 'how little cold print conveys',[48] and the *Daily Express* argued that: 'For sheer realism, there has perhaps never been anything to excel this wonderful film. You are in the battle and of it'.[49] Thus it was the film's ability to construct realistic images of the war which was emphasised again and again. The *Daily Mirror* saw the film as 'a visualisation of the hell that is war. It is a true picture, and is therefore stark and realistic';[50] the *Morning Post* described the film as 'extraordinarily realistic' showing 'all the grim horrors of war',[51] and the *Daily Sketch* wrote simply: 'It is war, grim, red war; the real thing'.[52] The *Manchester Guardian* made the point even more clearly: 'The film casts no glamour over war. It leaves out many terrors that we know to exist; but on the whole, it reveals war in its true aspect – as a grimly destructive and infernal thing'.[53] And that sentiment was echoed by *Bioscope*'s Leeds correspondent who argued that 'whereas the battle pictures of the past have incited to war and tried to show the "glory" of war, these Somme pictures teach what war really means'.[54] A journalist who had visited both the British and French fronts claimed that 'it was not until I saw these pictures the other night that I seemed to grasp this great thing'[55].

Moreover, these claims about the film's realism can also be found in journals written for a service audience. An emotional piece by the editor of the *Regiment*, reiterates a common view in journals of this kind that civilians were woefully ignorant of the reality of war, but argues that this film might perhaps shake them out of their complacency, claiming it would teach 'millions . . . the true meaning of war'.[56] It was reported that men watched a rest area screening of the film in France 'rapt and attentive'.[57] That said, some soldiers emphasised the limits of its realism – one, asked whether the film was 'like the real thing' replied, 'Yes . . . about as like as a silhouette is like a real person, or as a dream is like a waking experience. There is so much left out – the stupefying din, the stinks, the excitement, the fighting at close quarters'.[58] But such comments (which derive of course from serving soldiers, not civilians) are extremely rare, and the overwhelming picture presented by the surviving evidence suggests that Malins was right in believing that the film offered the audience at home a degree of access to the war that was quite outside their experience.

Perhaps the most striking evidence of audience response to the film is revealed in the intense debate which its screening provoked. For while people shared a common view that the film was realistic and powerful, this very realism led them to disagree passionately about whether or not it should be shown. Even before its public release, J.A. Farrar had written to the editor of the *Manchester Guardian* protesting that the film included scenes:

> . . . so gruesome in their realism as to be hardly bearable; nor will a public view make them more so. Is it tolerable that our brave soldiers cannot go through the ordeal of their self-sacrifice without the details of their manifold sufferings being turned into a spectacle for the pleasure of those who like to gloat, in perfect safety themselves, over the agonies of others?[59]

And four days later, James Douglas in the *Star* reported that:

> There is no doubt that the Somme pictures have stirred London more passionately than anything has stirred it since the war. Everybody is talking about them. Everybody is discussing them. Everybody is discussing the question whether they are too painful for public exhibition. It is evident that they have brought the war closer to us than it has ever been brought by the written word or by the photograph.[60]

The shape of the debate was given a sharper focus at the beginning of September with the publication of another letter in the *Manchester Guardian* arguing that the film 'merely satisfied the morbid or idle curiosity of the people',[61] and two further letters in *The Times*, the first of which, from Hensley Henson (the Dean of Durham), protested that:

> . . . crowds of Londoners feel no scruple at feasting their eyes on pictures which present the passion and death of British soldiers in the Battle of the Somme . . . a 'film' of war's hideous tragedy is welcomed. I beg leave respectfully to enter a protest against an entertainment which wounds the heart and violates the very sanctities of bereavement.[62]

Two days later, his protest was supported by Professor Ray Lankester, the eminent zoologist, who was 'surprised and disappointed' that so many people could 'find pleasure in experiencing the thrills of horror . . . which such exhibitions provide'; after all, people had long since stopped 'witnessing the hangings at Newgate and the floggings of the mad-men at Bedlam'.[63] These two letters provoked a vigorous response in *The Times*' letter columns over the next six days, all of which rejected Henson's and Lankester's claims – indeed, such was the size of the correspondence that it prompted an editorial giving the film an enthusiastic endorsement.[64]

Nor was the debate about the morality of screening footage of this kind limited to *The Times*. Even before the publication of Henson's letter, the evangelical journal, the *English Churchman*, had argued that 'many have been deeply distressed' by the film,[65] and the following week a second editorial quoted Henson's letter with approval, arguing the case even more powerfully:

> The matter is one of proper feeling, and the feelings of the bereaved should not be harrowed by the knowledge that the loved forms of their sons and brothers who fell in that awful battle are now on show to gratify the jaded and degraded taste of sight-seers.[66]

This provoked the Anglican *Guardian* to respond that it was 'highly desirable . . . that the realities of war should be made clear to those who stay at home',[67] and further responses to Henson's criticism can be found right across the national, provincial and local press – a *Daily Sketch* columnist, for example, berated 'Durham's doleful Dean' on the grounds that such an eminent person 'ought to know better'.[68] Even the service press joined in, with the *Army and Navy Gazette*[69] attacking Henson's views, citing (like many others) the King's approval of the film in its defence.[70] On the other hand, another service journal reported that a screening of the film attended by a group of serving soldiers (some of whom had been wounded in action) had provoked vigorous debate. Some argued that 'civilians want waking up! They should know what the horrors of war are and nine-tenths of the horrors are not seen at all in these pictures'. But others took a wholly opposed position, claiming that the film was:

> . . . too poignantly tragic for the eyes of women and children. Almost every woman has someone out there; or, worse still, has lost son, husband, or sweetheart. These pictures would stab them to the heart. These pictures of the huddled dead, too, would create an indelible impression of horror in the minds of children, of whom there were many in the theatre.[71]

Thus, once again, it was the film's unprecedented realism that was so striking to so many in the domestic audience, and this led many to argue that the film gave them an entirely new understanding of the nature of the war. Thus one of *The Times'* correspondents wrote: 'I have already lost two near relatives, yet I never understood their sacrifice until I had seen this film';[72] another explained:

> I have lost a son in battle, and I have seen the Somme films twice. I am going to see them again. I want to know what was the life, and the life-in-death, that our dear ones endured, and to be with them again in their great adventure . . . If the Dean had lost what I have lost, he would know that his objections are squeamish and sentimental.[73]

Perhaps even more remarkable, after a private viewing of the film, Frances

Stevenson (Lloyd George's Secretary and mistress) wrote in her diary in very much the same terms about the film's ability to enable her to understand her brother's death: 'I have often tried to imagine myself what he went through, but now I *know*, and I shall never forget'.[74]

Many of these correspondents also argue that the audiences with whom they saw the film had responded in much the same way. Thus James Cooper asserted that:

> It is, in my opinion, as untrue as it is uncharitable to say that crowds of Londoners feast their eyes on pictures representing the passion and death of British soldiers. The tears in many people's eyes and the silence which prevailed when I saw the films showed that every heart was full of love and sympathy for our soldiers . . . [75]

Another wrote: 'I have been twice to see these films and was profoundly struck by the emotion, and almost reverence with which they were followed'.[76] The women's correspondent in the free church *British Weekly* reported that the audience with whom she saw the film was 'as quiet as worshippers in a cathedral',[77] a view echoed by the *Star*'s columnist who wrote of 'a depth of reverence as profound and pure as any ever evoked in the Cathedral aisle'.[78] *Kine Weekly*'s Manchester correspondent writes of 'the "tenseness" of the atmosphere while the film was running',[79] while a Birmingham trade paper described the intensely emotional response of the audience – 'Strong men found unexpected lumps in their throats, and were thankful for the "dim religious light" of the theatre. Women audibly sighed'.[80] The *Spectator* argued that 'there was nothing but the deepest sense of respect for a brave soldier shown by the audience when the present writer saw the film',[81] and the *Army and Navy Gazette* commented both on the silence in which the films were viewed and the 'sympathy for our soldiers which they evoke'.[82] For the *Birmingham Daily Mail* 'the tense silence with which scenes of the dead were received were significant of the emotions which stirred the audiences',[83] while the *Nation*'s London diarist noted that 'women wept when the wounded came in'.[84]

These comments provide a rare insight into the way in which contemporary audiences responded to *Battle of the Somme*, and this evidence is all the more striking because at that time audiences did not watch films in respectful silence; rather they responded actively to what they saw on the screeen in a vocal and often rowdy manner.[85] And at least some of the evidence suggests that not every audience responded in the deferential, almost religious tone suggested thus far. One account draws attention to the fact that what the writer called 'the marching and lighter scenes', were met with vigorous cheers;[86] at the original London trade show, the famous sequence of a soldier carrying a wounded comrade over his shoulders, evoked 'a thunderous cheer'.[87] And some footage provoked even more distinctive responses. Thus one cinemagoer's response to the whole film was apparently summed up in the words: 'Praise God, from whom all blessing flow, A few more Germans gone below'.[88] German prisoners, who played an important part in the film,[89] were described variously as 'nerve-wracked and cowed',[90] 'staggering along "like drunken men"',[91] 'demented'[92] and most commonly, following the film's own inter-titles, 'nerve-shattered';[93] indeed, one Leeds audience laughed at the images of German prisoners.[94] But even that audience was moved by that part of the film

> . . . which shows the dead . . . Here is the meaning of war. It is Death.
> At last the hardened picturegoer is moved. It is war in all the stark nakedness of the 'thriller' to which he is accustomed. Dead bodies with upturned faces, and the grave ready. They are German dead, but here the dullest imagination is stirred into activity . . . This is why, in the end, we all leave the building chastened and silent.[95]

We are back with the clear, central conclusion which emerges from this wealth of evidence. The film made an immense emotional impact on audiences who were stunned by the apparent realism of what they saw. Very many would surely have endorsed Malins' claim that this was indeed 'their only first-hand knowledge of what was happening at the front'.

There remains one last, critical issue. Millions of people saw *Battle of the Somme* and they were clearly powerfully moved by what they saw – but what conclusions did they draw from viewing the film? What did it tell them about the nature of war? Most important of all, did it lead any to question their commitment to the continued prosecution of the war? In the politics of the situation these were crucial questions, and the evidence makes it clear that there was no single, unambiguous response. In endorsing the film in the first place, Lloyd George had argued that it would reinforce popular commitment to the war, and in particular encourage munition workers to work even harder,[96] and clearly part of the audience responded to the film in just these terms. Thus the *Army and Navy Gazette* suggested that in enabling civilians better to understand the nature of the war, it would make them even more determined 'that the nation must be utterly crushed that has brought so dreadful a war upon mankind',[97] and this notion of shaking complacent civilians into a proper recognition of the sacrifices that were being made on their behalf is echoed in a number of other reviews.[98] James Douglas in the *Star* went so far as to assert that the film was 'the only substitute for invasion', demonstrating 'the power of the moving picture to carry the war to British soil'.[99] Probably the most direct expression of a straightforward, patriotic response to the film came from those whose viewing of the film prompted them to write to the press. A correspondent in the *Manchester Guardian* argued that:

Anything that takes us from our smug security and gives us an insight into the horrors and discomforts our troops are suffering must awaken in us a sense of admiration for their bravery and inspire us with a desire to do all we can for them whilst on the field of battle, and on their return home.[100]

Another wrote:

I came away feeling humiliated and ashamed, for at last I was able to realise what Britain's soldiers were doing for her. If my turn comes, I hope that the memory of that film will stay with me to keep me as brave and smiling as they are.[101]

While yet another, who had three sons serving in the army, argued that the film 'if possible, increased my admiration and sympathy for them and their fellows and their cause'.[102]

On the other hand, this was not the only conclusion which audiences drew from the film. In reporting on Leeds audiences' response to the film, *Bioscope*'s correspondent argued that they formed a rather different conclusion:

. . . these Somme pictures teach what war really means. They will do more to preserve the peace of the world than a hundred peace societies and thousands of sermons.[103]

In writing in the film's defence in *The Times*, James Cooper argued that 'no better means could be found of making English men and women determined to stop the repetition of such a war as the present one',[104] and the *Manchester Guardian* editorial concluded:

As for the horror of them [the Somme pictures], no good can come of gilding war into a romance. The more of its trappings that are stripped from it, the more will men see its waste, its madness and its cruelty, as well as its glory, and the more earnestly will they cleave to peace.[105]

None of this discussion goes the further step of arguing that, on the basis of the evidence of the film, war is so terrible that a way should be found of bringing it to an immediate end, but the more cautious conclusion that the film demonstrated, the need to avoid any repetition of the war, could perhaps be seen as a step in that direction. British public opinion in the summer and autumn of 1916 (when most people saw *Battle of the Somme*) was still broadly committed to the war effort, though there was a shift from this conformity, demonstrated by industrial unrest that winter. It is possible that exhibition of the film may have played a part in this shift. It is at the very least intriguing that, after the exhibition of the *Battle of the*

Ancre at the start of 1917, no subsequent official British film included graphic and detailed images of the dead and wounded.[106] Certainly the surviving evidence makes it clear that some audiences *outside* Britain drew much more radical conclusions from the exhibition of the film,[107] and it may be that the propagandists did have evidence to suggest that some in the domestic audience responded in the same way.

But set against speculation of that kind, there is overwhelming evidence testifying to the way in which, for all its emotional impact, *Battle of the Somme* was incorporated into the audience's own existing ideology. Images which at another time or in another place might have served to convince audiences of the inhumanity and barbarity of war, served in Britain in the summer and autumn of 1916 to reconfirm existing convictions that Britain's cause was just. Nowhere is this demonstrated more clearly than in James Douglas' lengthy and strongly felt review, for while he shared with so many others an acute sense of the pain and horror of the war as recorded in the film, it is abundantly clear that he integrated that response into his own clear conviction of the essential justice of Britain's cause. And it seems fair therefore to leave the last word with him. He concluded his review with these words:

The bravery of our boys is past our imagining. 'Every one of them', said a wounded officer to me who fought on the First of July, 'every one of them is a hero.' His eyes filled with tears as he spoke. I thought of his words as I saw our soldiers bringing in a dying comrade under shell-fire. He died half-an-hour after he passed on the back of a soldier. I shall not soon forget his good English face. Nor shall I soon forget the face of the dead German soldier who is lying there waiting to be buried by the British soldiers who are digging the graves on the battlefield. These are dreadful sights, but their dreadfulness is as wholesome as Tolstoy's 'War and Peace'. It shakes the kaleidoscope of war into human reality. Now I know why soldiers are nobler than civilians in their tenderness and their chivalry and their charity. They have seen war, and they hate it as we can never hate it.

Therefore I say that these pictures are good for us. The dead on the battlefield, the drivers of the gun-teams steering the wheels clear of the corpse, the demented German prisoners, the kindly British soldiers showering cigarettes upon their captives, the mangled heap of anguish on the stretcher, the half-naked wounded men in the dressing-station – let our men and women see it all and vow that earth shall be delivered from it all. Dying men, dead horses, the dead dog lying beside his dead master – these vilenesses are war. War is the enemy, and Germany is its patentee, its idolater, its worshipper. It is our task to beat the German sword into a ploughshare so that the nations may learn war no more.[108]

Notes

1 Geoffrey H. Malins (edited by Low Warren), *How I Filmed the War*, London, 1920, pp. 303–304. In 1993, Malins' memoir was republished by the Imperial War Museum with an introduction by Nicholas Hiley.

2 The first public demonstration of the new technology had taken place early in 1896.

3 Prices ranged from 1d. to 1s. with a majority of seats being sold for 4d. or less.

4 For a fuller discussion of the nature of the contemporary cinema audience see Nicholas Hiley, 'A Proletarian Public Sphere. The British Cinema Auditorium in the First World War', a paper presented to the International IAMHIST Conference *Film and the First World War*, Amsterdam, July 1993, pp. 1–3.

5 For a fuller discussion of the problems encountered in winning the approval of the Service Departments and the way in which they were overcome, see Nicholas Reeves, *Official British Film Propaganda*, London, 1986, pp. 45–56.

6 *Britain Prepared*, premièred on 29 December 1915 – for further discussion see Reeves (1986), pp. 222–3.

7 For a fuller discussion of these early films and their reception see Reeves (1986) pp. 145–157 and 238.

8 The Scottish Section of the trade journal *Bioscope* reported that while the film did good business for the first two days, thereafter attendances fell off so badly that some cinemas took the film off for the last two days of the week – *Bioscope*, 15 February 1917, p. 737.

9 The film was *The German Retreat and the Battle of Arras*.

10 For a fuller discussion of the limited success of official film propaganda see Nicholas Reeves, 'The Power of Film Propaganda – myth or reality?', *Historical Journal of Film Radio and Television*, Vol. 13, No. 2, 1993, pp. 181–201.

11 For further discussion of this film see Reeves (1986) pp. 194–197.

12 For a more detailed discussion of the circumstances in which the cameramen worked and the production of the film see Reeves (1986), pp. 94–113; S.D. Badsey, 'Battle of the Somme: British war-propaganda', *Historical Journal of Film, Radio and Television*, Vol. 3, No. c 2, 1983, pp. 99–115; Nicholas Hiley's introduction to Malins' *How I Filmed the War*, London, 1993, pp. xxiii-xxvi. The remainder of this paragraph is drawn from these three sources.

13 'War Film Crowds' in the London *Evening News*, 22 August 1916, p. 3.

14 'Birmingham Notes', *The Cinema News and Property Gazette*, (hereafter *Cinema*), 14 September 1916, p. 78.

15 'Irish Times' in *Cinema*, 21 September 1916, p. 69.

16 'Provincial Film Centres. Leeds', *Bioscope*, 31 August 1916, p. 852.

17 'Provincial Film Centres. Leeds', *Bioscope*, 14 September 1916, p. 1053.

18 'Scottish Section', *Bioscope*, 7 September 1916, p. 943.

19 *ibid.*, p. 68.

20 *Ealing Gazette*, 26 August 1916, p. 3 and p. 6; 2 September 1916, p. 2 and p. 3.

21 'Our Visit to the London Shows', *The Kinematograph and Lantern Weekly*, (hereafter *Kine Weekly*), 21 September 1916, p. 109.

22 See for example, 'Northern Notes' by 'Gossip' in *Kine Weekly*, 7 September 1916, p. 118.

23 For example, a friend of the *Bioscope*'s Manchester columnist reported that

after trying repeatedly to gain admission to one of the many cinemas that was showing the film, he eventually gave up in disgust – *Bioscope*, 14 September 1916, p. 1051.

24 See for example 'With the Exhibitors, Southport', *Bioscope*, 28 September 1916, Supplement p. v.

25 Hiley argued this estimate in a paper titled 'The Battle of the Somme and the British News Media' which he presented at a conference held at the *Centre de Recherche de l'Historial de la Grande Guerre*, in Péronne on 21 July 1992.

26 See for example contrasting reviews in *The Times* and the *Star* – Reeves (1986) p. 238.

27 See for example 'Done Again!', 17 January 1916, p. 2.

28 'Film That Will Make History', *Kine Weekly*, 10 August 1916, p. 7.

29 'Battle of the Somme. The Reality of War', *Bioscope*, 10 August 1916, p. 476.

30 Editorial, 'The Cinema and "The Big Push"', 10 August 1916, p. 2.

31 Few papers had yet developed the practice of reviewing films as a matter of course, and thus those outside the trade press who wrote about the film were not regular film reviewers and their responses may therefore have been more typical of the audience as a whole.

32 'Somme Battle on the Film. Thrilling Pictures of the "Big Push"', *Daily Express*, 11 August 1916.

33 'This Morning's Gossip by "The Rambler"', *Daily Mirror*, 11 August 1916, p. 10.

34 'Somme Battle Films', *Daily Telegraph*, 11 August 1916, p. 9.

35 'War History on the Cinema. The British Offensive', *The Times*, 11 August 1916, p. 3.

36 'Amusements. "War Pictures in Leeds"', *Leeds Mercury*, 29 August 1916, p. 4.

37 'Amusements in York. The Picture House'. *Yorkshire Evening Press*, 29 August 1916, p. 3.

38 'The Somme Battle. Great Film Pictures in Birmingham', *Birmingham Gazette*, 5 September 1916, p. 3.

39 'City and Round About', *Glasgow Citizen*, 29 August 1916, p. 2.

40 Thus, for example, in a sequence in Part IV of the film where we see post from home being distributed to soldiers at the front, it is clear that the participants wait for a signal (presumably from the cameramen) before they start to give out the parcels and letters – *Battle of the Somme*, Part IV, 690' to 734'.

41 The extent of faking in the film has been explored with immense rigour and intelligence by Roger Smither in '"A Wonderful Idea of the Fighting": the question of fakes in "The Battle of the Somme"', *Historical Journal of Film, Radio and Television*, Vol. 13, No. 2, 1993, pp. 149–168.

42 'Film Pictures from the Somme', *Manchester Guardian*, 11 August 1916.

43 There is just one public comment at the time which refers to the issue, although only to argue that the footage is in fact genuine ('The Somme Films and the Men Who Have Taken Them', *Sphere*, 23 September 1916, p. 263). Furthermore, some of the publicity for *Battle of the Ancre* asserts explicitly that 'nothing in the nature of a "fake" has been allowed to be shown' (Smither, *op. cit.*, p. 151). There is just one reference to the issue in the surviving papers of the propagandists themselves; in February 1917 Beaverbrook claimed a statement had been 'systematically circulated with intent to do damage, that

portions of the last Official films are of a faked description', although of course at the time of writing, 'the last Official films' would have been *Battle of the Ancre* (House of Lords Record Office, Beaverbrook Papers, Series E. Vol. 14, File 'Cinema General January, February, March 1917 3–2', Beaverbrook to Secretary War Office, 16 February 1917).

44 'Amusements. War Pictures in Leeds', *Leeds Mercury*, 29 August 1916, p. 4.
45 Third leader, 'The Battle of the Somme', *Evening Times*, Glasgow, 29 August 1916, p. 2.
46 'Somme Battle on the Film. Thrilling Pictures of the "Big Push"', *Daily Express*, 11 August 1916, p. 00
47 'News of the Week', *Spectator*, 26 August 1916, p. 227.
48 'The Battle of the Somme. What Our Soldier Boys Are Enduring. Vivid Pictures in Bath this week', *Bath and Wilts. Chronicle*, 11 September 1916, p. 3.
49 'Somme battle on the Film. Thrilling Pictures of the "Big Push"', *Daily Express*, 11 August 1916, p. 00
50 'The Morning's Gossip by "The Rambler"', *Daily Mirror*, 11 August 1916, p. 10.
51 'Somme Battle Pictures. Mr Lloyd George's Appeal', *Morning Post*, 11 August 1916, p. 00
52 'Somme Battle on the Films. Pictures Taken in the Fighting Line, Which Show War As It Really Is, *Daily Sketch*, 11 August 1916, p. 12.
53 'Kinema Pictures of the Somme Battles', *Manchester Guardian*, 16 August 1916, p. 4.
54 'Leeds', *Bioscope*, 7 September 1916, p. 957.
55 'Ought we to see the Pictures', by 'Alpha of the Plough', *Star*, 6 September 1916, p. 2.
56 'Quite Between Ourselves', *Regiment*, 2 September 1916, p. 219.
57 Lyn Macdonald, *Somme*, Harmondsworth, 1993, p. 256.
58 'A correspondent', *Manchester Guardian*, 1 September 1916, p. 3.
59 J.A. Farrar to the Editor, *Manchester Guardian*, 15 August 1916, p. 10.
60 James Douglas, 'The Somme Pictures. Are They Too Painful for Public Exhibition?', *Star*, 25 August 1916, p. 2.
61 Frank E. Marshall to the Editor, *Manchester Guardian*, 1 September 1916, p. 3.
62 H. Hensley Henson to the Editor, *The Times*, 1 September 1916, p. 7.
63 E. Ray Lankester to the Editor, *The Times*, 4 September 1916, p. 11.
64 'The Somme Films' in *The Times*, 5 September 1916, p. 9.
65 Editorial in *The English Churchman and St James's Chronicle*, 31 August 1916, p. 447.
66 Editorial, *The English Churchman and St James's Chronicle*, 7 September 1916, p. 459.
67 'The Week', *Guardian. The Church Newspaper*, 7 September 1916, p. 749.
68 'Echoes of the Town', *Daily Sketch*, 5 September 1916, p. 5.
69 The journal of the reserve and territorial forces.
70 'Army Notes. The Somme Films', *Army and Navy Gazette*, 9 September 1916, p. 582.
71 'Heard in the Army. News and Views by "Khaki"' in *Regiment*, 9 September 1916, p. 249.

72 'Forty-Six' to the Editor, *The Times*, 2 September 1916, p. 3.
73 'Orbatus' to the Editor, *The Times*, 2 September 1916, p. 3.
74 A.J.P. Taylor (ed.), *Lloyd George: a Diary by Frances Stevenson*, London, 1971, p. 112.
75 James Cooper to the Editor, *The Times*, 2 September 1916, p. 3.
76 '70' to the Editor, *The Times*, 5 September 1916, p. 6.
77 'The Woman's World' by 'Lorna' in *British Weekly. A Journal of Social and Christian Progress*, 7 September 1916.
78 'Ought we to see the Pictures', by Alpha of the Plough, *Star*, 6 September 1916, p. 2.
79 'Northern Notes by "The Gossip"', *Kine Weekly*, 7 September 1916, p. 118.
80 'History in a Nation's Eyes. "The Battle of the Somme"', *Films. The Cinema Trade Journal*, 24 August 1916, p. 12.
81 'News of the Week', *Spectator*, 26 August 1916, p. 227.
82 'Army Notes. The Somme Films', *Army and Navy Gazette*, 9 September 1916, p. 582.
83 'Battle of the Somme. Official Pictures Shown in Birmingham', *The Birmingham Daily Mail*, 4 September 1916, p. 5.
84 'A London Diary by "A Wayfarer"', *Nation*, 26 August 1916, p. 654.
85 For a fuller discussion of this see Nicholas Hiley, 'A Proletarian Public Sphere. The British Cinema Auditorium in the First World War', a paper presented to the International IAMHIST Conference *Film and the First World War*, Amsterdam, July 1993, pp. 1–3.
86 Lucy Clifford to the Editor, *The Times*, 6 September 1916, p. 11.
87 'The Greatest Picture in the World' by W.G. Faulkner, *Evening News*, 11 August 1916, p. 2.
88 'In Cinemaland', *Yorkshire Evening News*, 19 August 1916, p. 2.
89 It occupied just over ten per cent of the whole film.
90 'Somme Battle Pictures. Mr Lloyd George's Appeal', *Morning Post*, Friday 11 August 1916, p. oo
91 J.A. Farrar to the Editor, *Manchester Guardian*, 15 August 1916, p. 10.
92 James Douglas *op. cit.*
93 See for example 'The Somme Battle. Great Film Pictures in Birmingham', *Birmingham Gazette*, 5 September 1916, p. 3.
94 'The Battle Film As Seen By one of the Crowd. Thoughts in a Yorkshire Picture Theatre', *Yorkshire Evening Post*, 29 August 1916, p. 5.
95 *ibid.*
96 'War History on the Cinema. The British Offensive', *The Times*, 11 August 1916, p. 3.
97 'Army Notes. The Somme Films', *Army and Navy Gazette*, 9 September 1916, p. 582.
98 See for example 'The Woman's World by "Lorna". Impression of the War Films', *op. cit.*
99 James Douglas, *op. cit.*
100 Robert Heatley to the Editor, *Manchester Guardian*, 2 September 1916, p. 4.
101 'Forty-Six' to the Editor, *The Times*, 2 September 1916, p. 3.
102 Jas Walmsley to the Editor, *The Times*, 4 September 1916, p. 11.
103 *Bioscope*, 7 September 1916, p. 957.

104 James A. Cooper to the Editor, *The Times*, 2 September 1916.
105 'The Pictures on the Somme', *Manchester Guardian*, 21 August 1916, p. 00
106 For further discussion of this decision see Reeves, (1986), pp. 167–168.
107 *ibid.*, pp. 245–6.
108 James Douglas, *op. cit.*

Part XI

Interpreting War Experience: The Arts and Post War Reflection

Chapter 56

British War Novelists

Hugh Cecil

After the war, particularly in the late 1920s, thousands of veterans from the front, including women, turned their hand to war novels.They were hopeful, naturally, of literary fame, but what they chiefly wanted was to express the inexpressible, to create something which would somehow convey the overwhelming horror and the importance of what they had experienced. At a rough estimate something like 400 works of British war fiction (including plays and boys' thriller stories) were published in the period 1918–1939 and one may safely assume that the majority of war novel manuscripts that were offered were turned down, as are most manuscripts which arrive on publishers' desks. Nearly all of these rejects have presumably been destroyed.

War novel writing started early, much of it during the conflict, the object being partly propaganda – such as novels by William J. Locke, H.G. Wells and John Galsworthy.[1] All three had attended the historic meeting at the start of the war in the government's secret propaganda headquarters at Wellington House; there, they and other best-selling writers were asked to place their expertise at the disposal of the Allied cause, writing as if the books came from their own inspiration. Results varied. Locke's novels, *The Red Planet* and *The Rough Road*,[2] were second-rate romantic works by a fashionable middlebrow writer and their only interest now is the context of their appearance. For all their superficially sophisticated air, their patriotic message was crude: 'I'm an English girl and I can't marry a coward.' exclaims the beautiful Phyllis Gedge as she spurns the unfortunate Randall Holmes – who later redeems himself heroically.

H.G. Wells, as to be expected, produced a far better war book, one of his most interesting works, *Mr. Britling Sees It Through* (1916), evoking the atmosphere in Britain in the first months of war and describing vividly the sense of a great divide between a pre-war world and the new reality which the sheltered English now confronted. In addition to the book's useful function of persuading America – the powerful neutral whose goodwill Britain and France needed so badly – that the English were humane, self-critical and unbelligerent, it is largely drawn from the life and is witty and moving.[3] Doubtless the many popular war melodramas by authors such as Dorota Flatau and Joseph Hocking[4] represented in their fiercely patriotic sentiments a genuine strain of British feeling; but no later reader would go to them, as they would to Wells' book, to find out what it was like to live in those times.

In a different category were those wartime novels whose authors such as Ian Hay and 'Sapper' (Cyril McNeile), had actually served at the front. Their function was to foster a sense of national purpose and to inform the public through partly cheerful and partly harrowing detail, what the soldiers were going through, so as to lessen the gulf of understanding between combatant and non-combatant. The short stories of 'Sapper', which appeared regularly in *Blackwood's Magazine*, were tough-minded and anti-sentimental, with knockabout comedy relief provided by drunken heroes like Sergeant Michael Cassidy, whose ferocious devotion to England's cause was supposed to demonstrate the healthy relationship between England and Ireland at the time.[5] Ian Hay (John Hay Beith), served early in the war and his most famous work, *The First Hundred Thousand, 'K(1)'*, reconstructs the life of a volunteer battalion early in the war, not inaccurately as regards the exuberant spirit and sense of companionship as well as the first acquaintance with tragedy. If its jocularity and boyishness seem to us curiously remote, they were certainly a strong element in the spirit of the volunteer army of 1914–15.[6] What his books could not do was burrow much below the surface of soldiers' feelings which combined with the courage and selfless devotion of what C.E. Montague called 'the second boyhood' other, darker forebodings: 'soldiers have to pretend they're not afraid' confided one officer to his fiancée in the summer of 1915, before going out to the front.[7]

There were in fact few British novels written in wartime that carried any contrary message, in the manner of Henri Barbusse's powerful story set in the trenches, *Le Feu* (1916), which combined stark horror and misery with a socialist critique of the war machine. In England during the years 1914–18 such works were not likely to be tolerated and the spirit of 'pack up your troubles in your old kit-bag' discouraged profounder speculation. Unsurprisingly the authorities banned a pacifist British novel about homosexual men and women resisting the war, Rose Allatini's *Despised and Rejected* (1918).[8] Despite clearly anti-war sentiments, however, Mary Agnes Hamilton's *Dead Yesterday* (1916) was treated with respect; it was less artless than Allatini's courageous and more than slightly absurd book, and it escaped condemnation because the character most held up for contempt in it was a young man of ultra-patriotic views who did not have the courage to join the army.[9] Readers readily shared the author's feelings about this hypocritical figure. The book, a *roman à clef*, is revealing about the wartime life of the upper-middle class intelligensia. Arnold Bennett's pictures of society and the world of politics in war, *The Pretty Lady* and *Lord Raingo* are also interesting documents of their time.[10]

The line separating early post-war fiction from wartime fiction was a very fine one. Gilbert Frankau's *Peter Jackson, Cigar Merchant* was begun in 1917, when the author who had served in 107th Brigade, Royal Field Artillery, was making a slow recovery from shell-shock. In many ways the book was indistinguishable from the superficial variety of wartime romance; it contained two elaborate and unconvincing sub-plots – one about spying, the other about love. It threw in, for good measure, a countryside idyll of the then fashionable variety; and it was fervently patriotic. Yet it broke new ground, dealing with the delicate topics of shell-shock, army corruption and military incompetence. In some ways, therefore, this artilleryman's book, which was well-received by other soldiers, was ahead of its time in Britain.[11] Most of the novels more or less contemporary with it (it was serialised and then appeared in book form in 1920) were less critical of the British Army. These included Wilfrid Ewart's *Way of Revelation* (1921), Robert Keable's *Simon Called Peter* (1921) and Ernest Raymond's *Tell England* (1922), all of which were best-sellers.[12] It is often forgotten that this early wave of patriotic war books enjoyed far more acclaim than any of the later 'disenchanted' British war novels, such as Richard Aldington's *Death of a Hero* (1929).[13] Only the translation of the German *All Quiet On the Western Front* (1929), far and away the most successful First World War novel, drew a larger readership in Britain. Its success and that of R.C. Sherriff's play *Journey's End* distorts the picture. Book for book, the British public, over a thirty-year period (*Tell England* and A.S.M. Hutchinson's *If Winter Comes* were still selling in the 1950s), seem to have preferred the patriotic to the disenchanted type of war book.[14] This not to say that these early war novels were artistically superior to the books of Aldington or Sassoon, or even remotely approached those authors in quality, though as literature they were not greatly inferior to *All Quiet on the Western Front*.[15]

In the mid-twenties the output of war novels slackened, with the occasional *succés d'estime* such as Ford Madox Ford's *Tietjens Tetralogy* – a brilliant attack on the failure of the majority of the British aristocracy to live up to their honourable past, and on the generals and politicians managing the war;[16] and Patrick Miller's disturbing *The Natural Man*[17] – which depicted war as a road to personal development. More successful commercially than either of these was R.H. Mottram's sober and detached *Spanish Farm Trilogy*, which won the Hawthornden Prize and was another indictment of military mismanagement and the destructive effects of war on English and French culture and civilisation.[18]

By 1929, and largely inspired by the success of *All Quiet*, there was a new rush of war books, often disenchanted in message, but not necessarily so; indeed it is striking how many ex-servicemen, such as Ronald Gurner, in *Pass Guard At Ypres*, (1930), William Barnet Logan, in *Dress of the Day* (1930), and Edward Thompson in *Lament for Adonis* (1932), hit back at those who pronounced the war futile. [19]

There were a few more – and notable – successes as the thirties continued; Siegfried Sassoon's *Sherston Trilogy* was completed by 1936 and Robert Briffault's *Europa* and *Europa in Limbo* came out in 1936 and 1937. Both were rebellious, questioning works by men who had displayed exceptional courage on numerous occasions during the war and had earned the right, if anyone had, to speak critically. Sassoon's has rarely, if ever, been out of print; while Briffault's satirical apologia (at times almost pornographic) for communist revolution, had very large sales despite some unfriendly reviews.[20] By 1939, however, public interest in the First World War had faded. In the words of Louis Golding (whose own portrait of wartime Manchester had been well-received earlier), 'it's a bloody truth, but the last war is now considerably deader than mutton'.[21] If we were to leave out the continued popularity of Ernest Raymond's and A.S.M. Hutchinson's works (more by then as romances than as pictures of war and its effects) and the surprise success of the Penguin edition of Pamela Hinkson's *The Ladies' Road* in 1946,[22] the truth of Golding's remark is borne out by the general eclipse of First World War literature, of any kind, by a vast body of work on the Second World War. Writers had found the language to convey the 'truth about the war' more convincingly, and works such as David Piper's *Trial By Battle* matched the best from the previous conflict.

Nonetheless a few First War veterans continued to try their hand at getting their experiences out of their system in the form of fiction. James Lansdale Hodson, author of an interesting pre-war book about a Kitchener Army volunteer, *Grey Dawn, Red Night* (1929) came back to the subject in 1955, with *Return to the Wood*.[23] Stuart Cloete's *How Young They Died* (1968) was probably the last war novel by a veteran; although full of racy and presumably authentic information about fornicating officers, it seems now in its way as dated as anything written in 1920s.[24] A curiosity is Carl Fallas's poignant *St. Mary's Village, Through the Eyes of an Unknown Soldier Who Lived On*, a prose elegy on the English soldier – the beauty of young life, the closeness of companionship, the tragedy of loss. It owes much to influences such as those of Edmund Blunden, H.M. Tomlinson and even David Jones (another late writer on the war), but, not surprisingly, given the lapse of time, the war appears in Fallas's work as something more dreamlike and remote than in the works of any of those writers.[25] By contrast, Henry Williamson's multi-volume *Chronicle of Ancient Sunlight*, for all its stress on times gone beyond recall, has a remarkable immediacy in its descriptions of battle and life behind the lines, considering that the war sections of this fifteen-volume *roman fleuve* were written during the 1950s.[26]

Clearly such novels have an historical value, in the sense that they throw light on wartime and postwar literary tastes and attitudes to war. How valuable are they, however, for gaining a deeper understanding of the nature of war experience? In a number of chapters in this volume – by Audoin-Rouzeau and Richter, for example – they are treated with some suspicion and certainly as less useful than contemporary correspondence, diaries and trench journals. One can see that they are not so close to their subject matter as such sources and that they may indeed offer conclusions which are very different from those felt by soldiers at the time. With some justification, too, it may be held that they express unrepresentative views, simply because people who write novels or poetry are not typical of the mass of humanity.

Do they have any value as evidence? First let a former First World War soldier speak! It was Gerald Brenan M.C., author of *The Spanish Labyrinth*, who told the historian Sir Raymond Carr when he was a young man: 'You can't get at the truth by history; you can only get it through novels'. Carr never forgot this; his *Spain*, like Brenan's great work, is, Brenan's biographer observes, one of the few works of history to give an important place in the bibliography to novels as evidence.[27] Fiction is indeed probably the most effective medium for evoking atmosphere. It has been the means whereby some of the most vivid writers have been able to describe in minute detail the life at the front. Without a trench scribe on hand, the flow of conversation, for example, could only be recaptured as a fictional reconstruction. Frederic Manning, in the most moving and subtlest of all Great War novels, *The Middle Parts of Fortune* (1929), describes the roll-call after a company returns from a battle. The pathos of the scene is none less piercing for the crudity of the language (which was only restored to the original text in a 1977 edition):

It was a long business . They had gauged the extent of the losses suffered by the company as soon as they went on parade. Name after name was called, and in many cases no particulars were available. Then, for a moment the general sense of loss would become focused on one individual name, while some meagre details would be given by witnesses of the man's fate; and after that, he too, faded into the past. Behind Bourne was a big stevedore from Liverpool, though he was of Cockney origin; a man called Pike, a rough, hard-bitten character, with a good heart.

'Redmain' was the name called out; and as at first there was no reply, it was repeated. 'Has anyone seen anything of Redmain?'

'Yes, sir,' cried Pike, with sullen anger in his voice. 'The poor bastard's dead, sir.'

'Are you sure of that, Pike?' Captain Malet asked him quietly, ignoring everything but the question of fact. 'I mean are you sure the man you saw was Redmain?'

'I saw 'im, sir; 'e were just blown to buggery,' said Pike, with a feeling that was almost brutal in its directness. ' 'e were a chum o' mine, sir, an' I seen 'im blown into fuckin' bits. 'e got it just before we got to their first line, sir.'[28]

Another area where the novelist appeared to advantage, was in the description of battle. Some memoirs written close to the time, it is true, such as Edward Liveing's *Attack* (Heinemann 1918) describing July 1 1916, at Gommecourt and Herbert Read's *In Retreat* (1919), on the March 1918 retreat, do contain particularly good accounts; [29] but what is striking is that among the finest depictions of battle are passages from two *novels*, *Death of a Hero*, by Richard Aldington and *How Dear is Life*, by Henry Williamson, the first of which appeared in 1929 and the latter as late as 1954. Aldington's is pure destruction and awesome sound:

> The whole thing was indescribable – a terrific spectacle, a stupendous symphony of sound. The devil-artist who had staged it was a master, in comparison with whom all other artists of the sublime and terrible were babies. The roar of the guns was beyond clamour – it was an immense rhythmic harmony, a superjazz of tremendous drums, a ride of the Walkyrie played by three thousand cannon. The intense rattle of the machine-guns played a minor motif of terror. It was too dark to see the attacking troops, but Winterbourne thought with agony how every one of those dreadful vibrations of sound meant death or mutilation. He thought of the ragged lines of British troops stumbling forward in smoke and flame and a chaos of sound, crumbling away before the German protective barrage and the Reserve line machine-guns. He thought of the German front lines, already obliterated under that ruthless tempest of explosions and flying metal. Nothing could live within the area of that storm except by a miraculous hazard. Already in this first half-hour of bombardment hundreds upon hundreds of men would have been violently slain, smashed, torn, gouged, crushed, mutilated. The colossal harmony seemed to roar louder as the drum-fire lifted from the Front line to the Reserve. The battle was begun.[30]

Williamson's battle is similarly awe-inspiring but explores also the feelings of fear and loss of fear in action:

> Mr Ogilby was moving his sword from his head towards the right. They were too far to the left. Right incline! shouted Baldwin's voice only just audible in the noise. Right incline! How thin his own voice felt. He could now hear machine-guns firing. Each bullet passed with a sharp hissing. He broke into a sweat. Why was Baldwin kneeling down? He seemed to be sick. Then he saw that he was vomiting blood from his mouth. He fell

sideways, hands clutching face, fingers streaming bright red jerking blood.

Movement thereafter for Phillip became automatic. He was stumbling over brown furrows of a ploughed field, near a tall hedge red with hawthorn haws. There were stacks at the far end of the field, and a windmill. Near the windmill was a farm house, with a red roof. He was a walking mass of perspiration. A jumble of memories rose before him, his head was filled with a high singing note, a steel wire seemed to make him go on after each automatic bending down, arms shielding face, from great black metallic-rending crumps in the field. He thought wildly of himself as a bony skeleton rushing down Westerham Hill on his unsteerable rigid Swift, white dust rushing up behind, the pace too fast on the hill, too steep to put on brakes after he had turned the corner and seen with awful suddenness what lay below him, the straight steepness of the white dusty road, on which he would skid and crash if he put on the brakes. It was the same sort of feeling now, a thin steel wire from below his stomach to above his eyes. With a broken-glass-like glance to the left, he saw the brown mass of Wytschaete as a flat and painful upright surface. In front he could see the straggling first line of attack beginning to bunch, like iron-filings under the hidden magnet of the field. Black blots of shrapnel were thick in the sky, floating above the huge upspouting steel-fragments of Jack Johnsons. [31]

Besides the great freedom they had in expressing themselves in such descriptive passages, novelists had one clear advantage over the memoirist in another sense – they could speak frankly about contemporaries while concealing their identities and that of their unit, passing the whole thing off as fiction to avoid a writ for libel. Pseudonyms such as the 'Loyal Southshires', the 'Chalkshires' or 'The Loamshires' were conventionally used for regiments. Richard Blaker in *Medal Without Bar* (1930) introduced a host of characters easily identifiable by members of his battery, D.58, but concealed from the rest of the world, such as the lively young subaltern Reynolds (2nd Lieut Hugh Hope M.C.) and the odious 'Taffy' Dolby (Capt. 'Gaddy' Monks M.C.). [32]

Gilbert Frankau had been appalled on joining the 9th East Surreys by the adjutant, who had encouraged fellow-officers to purchase promotion from him at a time when it was crucial that the very best men should be moved up fastest. In *Peter Jackson, Cigar Merchant*, his portrait of 'Lieut. Locksley-Jones' was uncomplimentary: 'a pair of puffy eyes under a thatch of sandy hair, two ears rather full in the lobe, a goodish nose, and a set of bad teeth between thin lips'. In fact Frankau hardly attempted disguise, for he wanted, after the war to expose this officer. 'With one solitary exception, all the soldier characters in that book are composites and purely fictitious,' he wrote later, 'The solitary exception, over whom I took particular care, did not fail to recognise his own portrait. He died, as he had lived, peaceably in his unsoiled uniform, before he could bring his threatened libel case . . . At the time I regretted his death keenly.'[33]

In general, then, novels freed writers to speak their minds, for which we must be grateful. However the arguments *against* treating fiction as a serious form of evidence are of course very strong. There is no doubt that many of the war novels now seem very contrived. An example of this is Wilfrid Ewart's *Way of Revelation* (1921) – a sincere, though sentimental and now dated, work by a former Scots Guards officer. Its story is melodramatic and unconvincing and the battle episodes do not have the vigour of Ewart's journalism or letters describing, much more forcibly, the same scenes. Ewart stressed the tragedy rather than the horror. Frankau, on the other hand, did not shrink from lurid details, but again the over-theatrical language of some of his battle scenes in *Peter Jackson, Cigar Merchant* marred – to the point of absurdity – what was in some respects a valuable description of wartime life in the artillery.

> Each still saw the same bestial vision; smashed pit, half-buried gun, mangled men writhing and groaning, mangled men lying deadly still, Charlie Straker's face white and drawn in the light of the hurricane lamp – and the Head that watched him, the Head that still grinned under its shrapnel-helmet, the Head which had been Pettigrew . . .[34]

Moreover the ability of novelists to convey convincing soldier talk, as claimed above, has been questioned. Even writers of talent equal to Manning's did not always have his sensitive ear for dialogue; Ford Madox Ford in *A Man Could Stand Up*, for example, used conversation as a means of expressing his own subtle ideas rather than as a faithful reproduction of what soldiers said, and the effect was far from realistic; there is the key passage, for example, where a sergeant is talking with Ford's protagonist, Tietjens. Ford singled out, as symbolic of war's tyranny, the fact that for years on end trench warfare had forced men in the front line to crouch down like apes, epitomising the humiliating and unnatural life required of all soldiers:

> The Sergeant beside him said:
>
> 'Then a man could stand hup on an ill . . . You really mean to say sir, that you think a man will be able to stand up on a bleedin'ill . . . '
> Presumably Tietjens had been putting heart into the acting temporary Sergeant-Major. He could not remember what he had been saying to the N.C.O. because his mind had been so occupied with the image of Perowne . . . He said:
> 'You're a Lincolnshire man, aren't you? You come from a Fen country. What do you want to stand up on a hill for?'
> The man said:

'Ah but you *do*, sir!'
He added:
'You want to stand up! Take a look round . . .' He struggled for
expression: 'Like as if you wanted to breathe deep after bein in a stoopin
posture for a long time!'[35]

The unreality of the language, however, should not detract from the
value of Ford's observations. Other writers' authenticity in recording
soldiers' talk has also been questioned, though not necessarily for the same
reasons. One is V.M.Yeates, author of *Winged Victory*, a powerful novel
on the wearing-down effects of air combat during 1918, who included
numerous conversations between pilots about politics and the possible
future of the world. [36]

Two of those advising Yeates on the manuscript of his book,
T.E. Lawrence and Henry Williamson, cautioned him that many of the
ideas he put into officers' mouths which were critical of English society had
not been expressed in 1918, though the germ of them may have existed
then. 'I fear this dialogue is not of war vintage.' wrote Williamson apolo-
getically of one passage, 'It's 1928–30.' Yeates disagreed, and kept it in the
book. At least one reviewer supported his view that such topics were
standard fare in officers' conversations in 1918 on the Western Front.[37]

What has exercised war historians above all is that some well-known
novels have spread the misleading impression that soldiers at the front were
constantly denouncing the generals and railing against the deception that
had pitched them into the war. For example there is Liam o' Flaherty's *The
Return of the Brute* describing a demoralised and brutish platoon of the
Irish Guards being gradually killed off during the Battle of Arras. One is
killed while defaecating, another goes mad and is gunned to death running
in a frenzy across no-man's land after murdering one of his comrades. The
book is a deliberate satire: it represents what the shell-shocked o'Flaherty
felt, but it cannot be taken as a literal portrait of life at the front. It was
accepted by a publisher at the height of the anti-war novel period, 1930.
o'Flaherty apparently regarded it as his worst book.[38]

Much more famous and influential was Erich Maria Remarque's *All
Quiet on the Western Front*, which in translation was probably read by
more British people than any other single book on the First World War.
Doubts have been cast on its authenticity not only by German nationalists,
but by English ex-officers, such as Henry Williamson and Edmund
Blunden, who examined the text carefully. As Professor Modris Eksteins
has demonstrated convincingly in *Rites of Spring*, Remarque's book is
more valuable as a guide to how the German war generation viewed the
impact of the war after it was over, than to his actual military experience.
In *All Quiet*, the soldiers' talk reflects their preoccupation with the loss of
their future; this is the heart of the book:

We are not youth any longer. We don't want to take the world by storm. We are fleeing. We fly from ourselves. From our life. We were eighteen and had begun to love life and the world; and we had to shoot it to pieces. The first bomb, the first explosion, burst in our hearts. We are cut off from activity, from striving, from progress. We believe in such things no longer, we believe in the war. [39]

There is no denying the power of Remarque's message; yet it would be wrong to accept even these allegedly authentic conversations as being the way that most soldiers thought, most of the time, while at the front. The melodramatic quality of the quoted statement should put readers on their guard. Edmund Blunden took Remarque to task for a host of unlikely details, including guns giving off smoke – like the weaponry of Napoleonic days – soldiers kneading boots as hard as iron for *twenty* hours (with intervals) 'until they became soft as butter,' or scrubbing the Corporal's Mess 'with a tooth-brush'; and men running on the stumps of their feet after they had been blown off. [40]

With such conspicuous examples of unreal treatment of war subjects, it is small wonder that many have looked sceptically on novels as evidence. The important thing, however, is to determine in each case something of these novelists' credentials. In *Peter Jackson*, Gilbert Frankau's fine account of the battle of Loos can be checked against battalion records, some of which bear his signature. A hall-mark of Frankau's undistinguished but professionally crafted (and very successful) novels was their close attention to accuracy. One of his aims in *Peter Jackson* was to expose the army life 'in all its naked, beastly disorganisation' [41] and he spared the reader no detail to show how this contrasted with the patriotic spirit of volunteers and professionals whose sincere aim was to tackle 'the Beast in grey' and save their country.

Likewise accounts by Richard Blaker, Richard Aldington, Siegfried Sassoon, V.M. Yeates and many others can be checked against their papers and against battalion diaries. The results are instructive. A surprising number of novels follow the record closely. It is exciting to find in the 9th Royal Sussex battalion diaries in the summer of 1918, confirmation of Richard Aldington's account of the raw quality of the new drafts. The number of deaths from gas, from accidents and from at least one case of a self-inflicted wound are eloquent of the bewildered inexperience which he describes with such force:

He found most of the recruits were hopelessly slow in getting on their gas-masks, and appeared to be in such a state of hebetude that they did not realise that gas was dangerous. They did preposterous things. They would, for instance, entirely abandon a Lewis-gun post to get their dinners. It was ten days before Winterbourne discovered this. The subalterns had seen it, of course, but had not known that they ought to report it. Winterbourne 'ran' the responsible N.C.O. as an example. He 'ran' a boy for sleeping on sentry duty, and then washed out the charge when he reflected that the poor wretch might be shot for so serious a military crime.[42]

Novelists may have been concerned, on the whole, with giving a precise record of what they experienced in battle, but editors and friends advising them were often more concerned with what would sell well, would make a better literary product and would not give offence. Reading the correspondence of some writers is revealing about the kind of pressure they were under to distort the record in order to please the reader. A good example was the case of Richard Blaker, author of *Medal Without Bar*; Blaker's book is patriotic but it is chiefly about the damage that war does to the emotional life – separating those who fought from those who stayed at home – and coming between husbands and wives even in a good marriage. If he failed to convey faithfully all he had seen, it was because of inhibition rather than any lack of sincerity. In *Medal without Bar*, he dwelt on the faults as well as the virtues of his fellow officers. His publisher, Ralph Hodder-Williams, (himself a war veteran) admired the book greatly, but the publisher's reader (a former major), had pointed out that Blaker seemed to show personal ill-feeling towards everyone who was not in the firing line and who was above the rank of major. Although an exaggeration, this indicated how sensitive the army had become to criticism by war writers, since the appearance of All Quiet on the Western Front and the play *Journey's End*. Hodder-Williams objected to a dismissive remark about the war stories of Sapper (Cyril McNeile), who was a personal friend of his. It would be taken as a sneer and McNeile, he told Blaker, was about the most sensitive man he knew– which may surprise anyone who has sampled his works.

He also disliked Blaker introducing a drunken officer into the narrative, one Capt. 'Voo Voo' Parley, clearly drawn from the life, who was, as one of the characters says 'just as wet and fatuous when he's dead sober – if a man could ever be dead sober after a dozen years of sizzling in his blasted "Kel-cutta."' Hodder-Williams, upset, asked if Blaker could not stress how extraordinarily rare such drunken swine really were, considering the number of people involved and the strain they were under. *Journey's End* (in which the heroic leading character is drunk most of the time) had given terrible offence, he told Blaker, and what was still more important, terrible pain.

Hodder-Williams, in the manner of other publishers of his day, censored Blaker's stronger language, such as the ejaculation 'Christ!' and the word 'arse'. He was very concerned about the female readership, and for this reason wanted technical detail trimmed as well. It would have sold better had it been more of a 'woman's book', he told Blaker later (it sold a respectable 10,000), the passion for detail, he thought, being too much for most of them. The very quality which still makes it a valuable source on life in the Royal Artillery was its shortcoming as a popular work.[43]

Another novelist whose approach to his subject was queried before it was completed was V.M. Yeates, author of *Winged Victory*, which was recognised by pilots at the beginning of the Second World War to contain the most realistic passages, up to that time, on air combat. Its drawback as a work of art is that though much of it is beautifully written it lacks form. Yeates was insistent that he should not be forced into any literary strait-jacket. 'Art is selection, not alteration,' he wrote to his friend, the writer Henry Williamson, who had a strong proprietory interest in the Yeates book. They had been at school together in Lewisham. Yeates, who had a wife and four children and was suffering from T.B. as a direct result of war strain, had been in and out of sanatoria for many years and had turned to writing to supplement his intermittent income as an insurance broker. Williamson had urged him to concentrate entirely on a novel about the war. Yeates used his flying log book and his wartime letters to his wife as his documentary sources and wrote whenever he could in and out of hospital during the years 1932–3.

Reading through drafts, Williamson had no serious doubt about Yeates, whom he believed to be a genius like himself; but he urged him to make large cuts and also to insert a strong story line about a friendship between two pilots, which ends when one of them was killed. It was only reluctantly that Yeates accepted the idea, since this had not been his personal experience; and he felt that to trim his narrative too drastically might make it a better book, but less authentic. Williamson was almost certainly right. Yeates' *Winged Victory* is not as deftly shaped as it should have been. In all, Yeates cut eight or nine thousand words, but Williamson pressed him to make further alterations, and even added a few hundred highly effective words of his own, towards the end. Overall, the literary shortcomings of this brilliant, unconventional book are balanced by its undoubted veracity. The impression of unremitting strain is admirably conveyed. [44]

The publishers were, as they say, only doing a job, when they asked their authors to consider a wider readership: 'You cannot write your book just for the soldiers,' Richard Blaker was told.[45] Yet that was exactly what he did; and for the student of war, as opposed to the discerning literary critic, or the ordinary reader, this, in the last analysis, is the kind of work that is by far the most valuable. It is instructive to see what soldiers and airmen, who had served, had to say about Yeates and Blaker's books. Their approval is surely a clear indicator of these novels' worth to the historian. Among the many enthusiastic letters to Blaker after *Medal Without Bar* appeared in 1930, there were these words from a former 3rd Canadian Division private: 'Its beauty lies in its truth, its strength in the cleanness with which it was built, and its character in the utter lack of hypocrisy as much as in the absence of non-essentials.' Another twice-wounded soldier,

G.V. Baxter, told Blaker that all those who had been out on the Western Front 'look back on the war as brotherhood. It is therefore *the* war book – brotherhood runs all through it.' To a Major Fred Fish of the Royal Field Artillery it was 'the finest war book.' One of Blaker's friends wrote to tell him of how his 'bungalow-mate' out in Singapore, an ex-soldier, had reacted to *Medal Without Bar*: 'The funny old boy wept at the dinner table one evening as the vividness of the chapter he'd been reading recalled incidents that had happened in his company.'[46]

V.M. Yeates received a flood of correspondence from admiring ex-fliers, and many of his reviewers had also served as airmen. J.E.L. Skelton, writing to Williamson in 1935, said 'Although my flying experience and skill were insignificant compared with his, I can see the incidents and hear the conversations he describes in "Winged Victory", as clearly as if I had witnessed them or taken part in them yesterday.' [47]

Of the book's picture of the wearing-down effects of war, a former wartime pilot observed in the *Army and Navy Gazette* : 'It was not until the murderous fighting of mid-1915 and of the Somme had reft away the cream of our youth, that the real spontaneity of the fighting man's spirit became dulled. As this book goes on, the reader may appreciate the processes by which the psychical voltage became lowered. For this reason, the work is one for future leaders of airmen to read.' [48] One ex-pilot, Claydon Knight, found the book evoked memories almost too powerful: 'I am recommending it to any who wish to know what it was all about, but I wonder how many will truly appreciate it who were not knocking around the air over France during the war. Especially such parts as when he describes "My guts turned to jelly." I was exhausted for days while I read it.' [49] Ben Ray Redman, an American airman who had been on the Western Front with 79 Squadron Royal Flying Corps wrote an appreciative piece in the *Saturday Review of Literature* : 'If any historian, in any future generation, wishes to know what it meant to be a fighting pilot on active service with the Royal Flying Corps during 1918, he need only read "Winged Victory." . . . in the literature of war flying it stands superb and alone.'[50]

Winged Victory was an outstanding book, which has not dated in language nor tone. Blaker's *Medal Without Bar* is less effective today. Yet for the historian, his testimony deserves equal attention, and both, in this sense, are entitled to equal consideration with Richard Aldington's *Death of a Hero*, still grudgingly accepted as a masterpiece in England, where the author is otherwise under-appreciated. Aldington's book was praised by a fellow-infantryman, Edmund Blunden, as a book which captured the feeling of the front in a way that *All Quiet on the Western Front*, in his view, failed to do. Aldington himself gave the fighting man's tribute to Henry Williamson's war volumes of the novel sequence, *A Chronicle of Ancient Sunlight:* 'absolutely accurate in every particular.'[51]

Although it is true that war novels were usually written long after the event, when subsequent judgements had altered the focus and the value judgements about the purpose of the war, this does not mean that all the evidence in them was therefore worthless. In fact those readiest to reject the evidence of much of this fiction are not necessarily historians of war experience, so much as critics who, knowing the period but patchily, are disturbed to find that the majority of neglected First World War novelists (who include Yeates, Frankau, Blaker and for these purposes, Williamson) do not fit precisely with the myths about the Great War which prevail today. For this reason such critics reject their evidence, hiding behind the excuse that their literary quality is so inferior as to render their views worthless. *All Quiet on the Western Front* (*pace* Edmund Blunden's dismissal of that work as 'piddling, lying rubbish' [52]), continues to reign supreme, whilst the subtle undertones of Sassoon, so ambiguous in his message, as Brian Bond points out in the next chapter, are also misunderstood. The novels of experience from the Great War were uneven in quality; often the spirit of the stiff upper lip, so useful in battle, prevented the easy flow of feeling from the heart to the pen; but these writers' evidence is invaluable, especially if the facts behind them can be checked from other sources. These are the words of men who wondered why they were still alive to tell the tale. Collectively they add up to a testimony which must not be ignored, not least because in their variety they provide yet further proof of a more complex picture than the stereotypical image still believed by many to be the message of First World War creative writers.

Notes

1   William J. Locke (see note 2 below), H.G. Wells (see note 3 below), John Galsworthy, *The Burning Spear*, London, Chatto & Windus, 1919.

2   William J. Locke, *The Red Planet, The Rough Road*, London, John Lane, the Bodley Head, 1916, 1918.

3   H.G.Wells, *Mr. Britling Sees it Through*, London, Cassell, 1916.

4   Dorota Flatau, *Yellow English*, Hutchinson,1918; Joseph P. Hocking, *The Curtain of Fire*, London, Hodder & Stoughton,1916

5   'Sapper', *Sergeant Michael Cassidy R.E.*, Hodder & Stoughton1916.

6   Ian Hay, *The First Hundred Thousand 'K.(1.)'* , London, Wm. Blackwood, 1915.

7   R.H. Mottram papers, Norfolk County Record Office, Mottram to Madge Allen, 29 June,1915.

8   Rose Allatini, (pseud A.T. Fitzroy) *Despised and Rejected*, 1st ed., London, C.W.Daniel, 1918.

9   Mary Agnes Hamilton, *Dead Yesterday*, London, Duckworth 1916.

10 Arnold Bennett, *The Pretty Lady*, London, Cassell, 1918; *Lord Raingo*, London, Cassell, 1926.

11 Gilbert Frankau, *Peter Jackson, Cigar Merchant*, London, Hutchinson, 1920.

12 Wilfrid Ewart, *Way of Revelation*, London, G.P. Putnam's,1921; Robert

Keable, *Simon Called Peter*, London, Constable,1921; Ernest Raymond, *Tell England*, London, Cassell, 1922.

13 Richard Aldington, *Death of a Hero*, London, 1929.

14 A.S.M. Hutchinson, *If Winter Comes*, London, McLelland & Stuart, 1922.

15 Erich Maria Remarque, *All Quiet on the Western Front*, tr. A.W. Wheen, London, G.P.Putnam's,1929.

16 Ford Madox Ford: *Some Do Not;No More Parades; A Man Could Stand Up*; *Last Post*, London, Duckworth, 1924,1925,1926, 1928.

17 Patrick Miller, *The Natural Man*, London, Grant Richards, 1924.

18 R.H. Mottram, *The Spanish Farm Trilogy*, London 1927.

19 Ronald Gurner, *Pass Guard at Ypres*, London, Dent, 1930; William Barnet Logan, *Dress of the Day*, London, Marriott,1930; Edward Thompson, *Lament for Adonis*, London, Ernest Benn,1932.

20 Siegfried Sassoon, *Memoirs of a Fox-Hunting Man; Memoirs of an Infantry Officer; Sherston's Progress*, London, Faber & Faber, 1928, 1930, 1936; Robert Briffault, *Europa, Europa in Limbo*, London, Robert Hale, 1936, 1937.

21 Bodleian Library, Richard Blaker Papers, ms Eng. Lett. c.318, f.194, 8 Sept. 1939, Louis Golding to Richard Blaker.

22 Pamela Hinkson, *The Ladies' Road*, First edition was London, Victor Gollancz, 1932.

23 James Lansdale Hodson, *Grey Dawn, Red Night*, London, Victor Gollancz 1929; *Return to the Wood*, London, Victor Gollancz 1955

24 Stuart Cloete, *How Young They Died*, London, Collins, 1969.

25 Carl Fallas, *St.Mary's Village, Through the Eyes of an Unknown Soldier Who Lived On*, London, Hodder & Stoughton, 1954.

26 Henry Williamson, *How Dear Is Life, A Fox Under My Cloak, The Golden Virgin, Love and the Loveless, A Test to Destruction*, London, Macdonald, 1954, 1955, 1957, 1958, 1960.

27 Jonathan Gathorne Hardy, *The Interior Castle, a Life of Gerald Brenan*, London, Sinclair Stevenson, 1992, p.356.

28 Frederic Manning, *The Middle Parts of Fortune*, London, Peter Davies, 1929.

29 Edward Liveing, *Attack*, London, Heinemann, 1918; Herbert Read, *In Retreat*, London, Faber & Faber, 1930 (1st pub. 1919)

30 Aldington, *op.cit.*, pp.373.

31 Henry Williamson, *How Dear Is Life*, pp.257-8.

32 see Blaker Papers, ms Eng. Lett. c.319, f.86; and Richard Blaker, *Medal Without Bar*, London, Hodder & Stoughton, 1930, pp.436-7.

33 *Gilbert Frankau's Self-Portait, a Novel of His Own Life*, 2nd edn. London, Macdonald, 1944.

34 Gilbert Frankau, *Peter Jackson, Cigar Merchant*, part XXVIII, section 2.

35 Ford Madox Ford, *A Man could Stand Up*, London, Bodley Head edn.,1980, p.343.

36 V.M.Yeates, *Winged Victory*, London, Cape, 1934.

37 Harry Ransom Humanities Research Center (HRHRC), the University of Texas at Austin, V.M.Yeates Papers, ms of *Winged Victory*, notes by Williamson.

38 Liam o'Flaherty, *The Return of the Brute*, London, Mandrake Press, 1930.

39 Remarque *op.cit*; see also Modris Eksteins, 'All Quiet on the Western Front

and the Face of a War,' *Journal of Contemporary History*, vol. 15, no.2, April 1980; and Modris Eksteins, *Rites of Spring: the Great War and the Birth of the Modern Age*, London, Bantam Press, 1989.

40 HRHRC, Sassoon Papers, Blunden to Sassoon, 15 July, 1929.

41 HRHRC, Gilbert Frankau Papers, Frankau's 'Scenario of "Peter Jackson, Cigar Merchant"'.

42 Aldington, *op.cit.*, p.426.

43 Blaker papers, ms Eng.Lett. c.319, f.134 et seq., letters of Ralph Hodder-Williams, 14, 18 Nov. 1929.

44 HRHRC, see note 37 above.

45 See note 43 above.

46 Blaker papers, ms Eng.Lett c.317, Roy Bower – Blaker, 9 May 1930; c.317, W.E. Baker to Blaker, 7 Jan. 1932; G.V. Baxter, 2 May 1930.

47 From papers of V.M.Yeates in the possession of his family.

48 ibid. (*Army & Navy Gazette* press cutting, 1934).

49 *ibid*.

50 *ibid*. (*Saturday Review of Literature* press cutting,1934).

51 Diana Mosley, 'A Tribute to Henry Williamson in Brocard Sewell ed., *Henry Williamson, the Man, the Writings*, Padstow, Tabb House, 1980, p. 36.

52 HRHRC, mss Sassoon, Edmund Blunden to Siegfried Sassoon, 15 July 1929. The Blunden passages are quoted from Hugh Cecil, 'Edmund Blunden and First World War Writing, 1919–36' in *Focus on Robert Graves and His Contemporaries* vol. 2. no. 1. University of Maryland Press, Spring 1993; I am indebted to the HRHRC and Mrs Edmund Blunden for permission to quote in the article. I am also indebted to the Bodleian Library and Lilian Wynn (Louis Golding) for permission to quote from the Blaker Papers. I have been unable to trace the literary heirs of Blaker's other correspondents.

Chapter 57

British 'Anti-War' Writers and Their Critics

Brian Bond

This paper is concerned to challenge both the cohesion and representativeness of the 'anti-war' writers who are so much discussed by literary and cultural critics such as Paul Fussell and Samuel Hynes, but there are problems of identification and terminology. One has only to mention the best-known 'anti-war' memoirs, poetry and plays to see that they contain many inconsistencies, ambiguities and paradoxes, while it would be grossly unjust to label their critics 'pro-war', and even 'patriotic' seems inadequate. Ultimately, perhaps, the distinction to be drawn is between those writers whose view of the First World War is negative (with 'futility' as their watchword), and those who stress its positive features and legacy, despite full awareness of the destruction, suffering and heavy casualties.

The paradox has long been recognised that some of the best anti-war satirists were not pacifists or conscientious objectors but brave, efficient and even zealous subalterns, such as Siegfried Sassoon, Robert Graves and – to a lesser extent – Wilfred Owen, who voluntarily returned to the front after recovering from wounds or illness despite the fact that they had become disillusioned about the justice of the war. Recently, in his study *Taking it like a man: suffering, sexuality and the war poets*, Adrian Caesar has argued that these three writers (and Rupert Brooke) were not really anti-war at all in the usual interpretation of that term because a great deal of their mental turmoil and the resulting frustration and anger were due to sexual problems deriving from their education and repressive home environment. To a degree their war experience was only incidental to their personal 'hang ups'. More positively they needed the war to obtain personal freedom and to seek love and consolation through suffering:

> The poet must emulate the soldiers' suffering in order to be worthy of their love . . . Any potential critique of the politics of the war is subordinated to the personal, emotional and erotic implications of suffering.

Caesar suggests that Sassoon's poetry in particular covertly supports war by providing positive consolations based on the idea that suffering is good.[1]

These famous 'anti-war' writers also believed that protest against the war depended upon participation in it. Owen, especially, hated 'washy pacifists' as much as 'whiskered prussianists'. His readers are asked to pity the suffering soldiers, but also told that they cannot understand or pity unless they too go and fight. Contrary to the myth, then, these anti-war poems become in subtle ways war poems – war is celebrated as well as detested. Ample evidence is quoted by Caesar to prove that Owen enjoyed his second spell of active service in France but wished this to be concealed from friends and readers who thought he was having a bad time. Caesar's conclusion is that the four poets studied have come to 'represent' the First World War through partial readings which have highlighted a compassionate denunciation of war, whereas he believes their complex and equivocal attitude to war and suffering has exerted a dangerous influence:

> This liberal-humanist reception of the texts works finally to accommodate the grotesque and enables societies to wage further wars in the name of England, Christ and freedom. The sentimental attitude prevails.[2]

Sassoon did, of course, make a famous public protest under the guidance of pacifist friends, including the Morrells and Bertrand Russell. His anti-war declaration, published in *The Times* on 31 July 1917 read in part:

> I believe that this War, upon which I entered as a war of defence and liberation, has now become a war of aggression and conquest. I believe that the purposes for which I and my fellow soldiers entered upon this War should have been so clearly stated as to have made it impossible to change them and that, had this been done, the objects which actuated us would now be attainable by negotiation.[3]

He expressly stated that he was not protesting against the conduct of the war, but only the deception practised by the politicians. One might comment that the conduct of the war *was* open to criticism, but Britain's political objectives could certainly not have been achieved by negotiation in 1917. Robert Graves, who saved his friend from a court martial, believed that Sassoon's action met with approval at the regiment's Liverpool depot, but his colleagues at the front deplored it, telling him that they had to stick it out until Germany was beaten, and lamenting his association with pacifist 'croakers' at home. Sassoon did return to active service and later admitted that his protest had been a mistake.

The political naivety of Sassoon's protest highlights the perennial difficult – or near-impossibility – of the front-line combatant understanding what the war is 'about' and how it is progressing from the government's viewpoint. But it also illustrates the specific problem of presenting Britain's political and strategic objectives in the First World War. Most historians would probably now agree that there were compelling reasons for entry into the war in 1914, and very little chance thereafter of a negotiated peace without victory on acceptable terms. Unfortunately, from the viewpoint of justifying to the people a long, attritional conflict, Britain's war aims were essentially negative and defensive; namely to prevent German domination of central and western Europe. However, even allowing for the excesses of anti-Hun propaganda and the exaggeration of enemy atrocities, the vast majority of the troops and the civil population seem to have believed that the cause was just and that the struggle must continue until a clear victory was achieved. A victorious conclusion to the war was far from certain at the time of Sassoon's protest, and even in mid-1918 still seemed far-distant, so that the maintenance of resolute military morale and the almost complete absence of mutinies presents a very different picture from that outlined by Sassoon and others who would like to have 'stopped the war'. Where Sassoon and other soldier-critics, such as C. E. Montague, were on firmer ground was in their understanding that home-front propaganda for grandiose, abstract war aims, such as 'crushing German militarism', did not impress front-line combatants, who were more concerned with the practicalities of unit pride, comradeship and survival against a tough and generally respected enemy.[4] In short there was more empty rhetoric and militaristic sentiments on the home front than in the trenches. Much of what has commonly been accepted as 'anti-war' writing really refers to this antagonism and mutual lack of empathy between the home and military fronts.

Sassoon's failure to address the complex issues of military strategy, foreign policy and diplomacy in 1917 is understandable; far less so is the almost complete avoidance of these matters by the post-war writers who shaped the anti-war 'myth' which had become deeply rooted by 1930. Samuel Hynes, though primarily interested in 'the myth' as a cultural phenomenon, does at least appreciate why military historians and generals are intensely irritated by it; namely that it renders the whole war effort meaningless:

> If the myth-making authors . . . were right, then the war had no history,
> in the sense of a story expressing the meaning of events, but was anti-
> historical, apocalyptic, an incoherence, a gap in time.[5]

There is no need here to develop in detail the historian's response to this enormous defect in the anti-war literature, which has already been casti-gated with typical verve and pugnacity by Correlli Barnett.[6] The anti-war writers, he points out, failed to tackle the hard questions such as the German occupation of Belgium and northern France which largely deter-mined allied strategy. Instead they poured out their emotional revulsion at the dreadful conditions and heavy casualties with impressive power and cumulative effect. It remains puzzling, nonetheless, as to why the middle-class reading public responded so approvingly to this superficial emotional revulsion as 'the truth' about the war. Some explanations will be advanced at the end of this paper, but a full analysis would require a long account of the class system, reading habits and the pre-war liberal cast of mind regarding peace and war. What really causes historians intense annoyance is that influential literary experts, such as Paul Fussell, not only continue to purvey the anti-war myth as 'the truth' about the war, but also provide an inadequate, erroneous and contradictory historical context.[7]

One of the main contentions in this paper is that much of what passes for anti-war literature written after 1918 was really provoked by the shattering of war-time idealism and disappointment with the results of victory in the early post-war years. This viewpoint was forcefully expressed by Charles Carrington (under the pseudonym Charles Edmonds) in *A Subaltern's War*, published in July 1929 avowedly to counter the prevailing literary fashion of disillusionment with the war. He described 1919 as 'the maddest year of all' in which the spell which had bound the soldiers for such a long time was broken:

> Disillusion came in with peace, not with war; peace at first was the futile state. In war a man at least did know what he was at . . . but peace seemed to lead nowhere: it was anti-climax.[8]

If the events between 1914 and 1919 were to be characterized as sheer futility, why had he and his comrades been such fools as to take part in them? The answer was self-evident: there had been absolutely no other course open to plain, honest men.

An early post-war publication which set a fashion for war memoirs and by its title provided a key word for much that followed was C. E. Montague's *Disenchantment* (1922). One suspects that the apposite title is invoked by many commentators who have not read the book. Montague was untypical of the 'anti-war' writers in terms of his age and background. Educated at the City of London School and Balliol College, Oxford, by 1914 he was a distinguished leader-writer for the *Manchester Guardian* and 47 years old. Montague's idealism was so intense that he dyed his grey hair and lied about his age to gain entrance to the army. His polemic is beautifully written but clearly reveals why he was more thoroughly disenchanted than much younger and more robust volunteers such as Carrington, Guy Chapman or Graham Greenwell, who entertained fewer illusions about the nature of military service and combat. Montague's sympathy throughout is with his fellow volunteers whose early idealism was rapidly eroded by the Regulars, by bloodthirsty chaplains, mendacious politicians, civilian war-mongers, profiteers and shirkers. He is also scathing, however, about the lack of 'brain power' and the amateur incompetence of the staff and higher command. But his book seems to have been inspired mainly by outrage at the harsh terms imposed on Germany in the Treaty of Versailles which, he said, was an insult to the dead. In rhetoric reminiscent of Thomas Carlyle at his most dyspeptic, Montague contended that Prussia:

> Beaten out of the field, had won in the souls of her conquerors' rulers; they had become her pupils; they took her word for it that she, and not the older England, knew how to use victory.

England, in short, had won the fight and lost the prize by becoming militaristic and vindictive.[9]

Sergeant (later Professor) R. H. Tawney shared Montague's idealistic approach to war service but believed that the soldiers' idealism had endured, while that on the home front diminished, because only if those ideals were valid could their sacrifices be justified. This explains the sense of alienation experienced by many returning troops, their reluctance to discuss the war, and the frequently expressed regret that the 'home' they had found in their regiment and in the trenches was not replicated when they returned to Britain.[10]

Another famous book title routinely but dubiously cited as an anti-war classic is Robert Graves' *Goodbye to All That* (1929). Graves avowedly exploited the current publishing fashion to write a pot-boiler when he was desperately short of money, embellishing and embroidering his war experiences so as to make the maximum impact. Significantly the compiler of the excellent regimental history of the Royal Welch Fusiliers, (J. C. Dunn (ed) *The War the Infantry Knew*), rejected Graves' proffered contributions on the grounds that they were heavily infiltrated by fiction.[11]

In any case Graves' title was accurate: he was saying goodbye to *all* that; including the stuffy conventions of pre-war society; war-time hysteria and immorality on the home front; and personal problems at the time of writing, including a marital crisis and being grilled by the police on suspicion of attempted murder. Finally, despite his criticisms of the regular officers' snobbery, Graves was extremely proud of his war service with the Royal Welch Fusiliers and remained so throughout his long life. In 1930 he expressed surprise that his memoirs were being included in the category of anti-war literature.[12]

By this date (1930) the anti-war myth was firmly established, in the sense that books, plays and poetry which were critical of the war experience in various ways were deemed to represent 'the truth' while other works, including a patriotic, and even 'gung-ho' film series, about the Somme and other campaigns produced by British Instructional Films (BIF) in the late 1920s, were severely handled by the critics.[13]

There is no need here to list in full the spate of publications which established the anti-war conventions between 1928 and 1931. The evidence for their popularity is undeniable. For example, R. C. Sherriff's play *Journey's*

End was reprinted thirteen times in 1929, and in that year alone sold 45,000 copies. Edmund Blunden's *Undertones of War* was reprinted three times in one month, and Frederic Manning's *Her Privates We* four times in a month. Wilfred Owen's poems by contrast had not yet had a wide impact: only 730 copies of the 1920 edition were printed and a second edition of a similar number sold poorly. Rupert Brooke, by contrast, remained enormously popular: by 1930 his *Collected Poems* had sold 300,000 copies.[14]

For all their differences in style and emphasis, a common viewpoint emerged from the 'trench memoirs': of idealism turning into sour disenchantment; of the terrors of battle and the obscenity of death and mutilation, and all for no comprehensible reason; the suffering and sacrifice had been futile.

Samuel Hynes conveys a clear idea of how this interpretation developed and summarises the myth as follows:

> the idealism betrayed; the early high-mindedness that turned in mid-war to bitterness and cynicism; the growing feeling among soldiers of alienation from the people at home for whom they were fighting; the rising resentment of politicians and profiteers and ignorant, patriotic women; the growing sympathy for the men on the other side, betrayed in the same ways and suffering the same hardships; the emerging sense of the war as a machine and of all soldiers as its victims; the bitter conviction that the men in the trenches fought for no cause, in a war that could not be stopped.[15]

The single work which presented the most poignant expression of the myth, and probably exercised the widest influence, was Erich Maria Remarque's book (and subsequent film) *All Quiet on the Western Front* (1929). The novel was launched with calculated publicity in Germany and was received there and in other countries, including Britain and the United States, with enormous enthusiasm. It rapidly became one of the best-sellers of all time. It was repeatedly referred to as 'the greatest of war novels', and in semi-religious terms as 'the Bible of the common soldier'. Above all, it told 'the truth about the war', which was that it had been an irrational, nihilistic slaughter; that its protagonists and victims had no sense of purpose; and that it had been fought in vain. This message seemed congenial to the liberal left and socialists in Europe and the Anglo-Saxon world, but was denounced by fascists for whom war was an essential part of their outlook. The Nazis banned it as pacifist Marxist propaganda and burnt all the copies they could lay their hands on.

As Modris Eksteins astutely observed, the novel was more a reflection of the post-war than the wartime mind, telling 'the truth' not so much about the war as about Erich Maria Remarque in 1929. The author exploited the prevailing view of the war to make a fortune, but his admirers and critics were no more objective. His first person narrative epitomized the widely-held assumption that only on the level of individual suffering could the war have meaning. The war was a matter of individual experience rather than collective endeavour. Art had become more important than history. Historians up to that date (and, some would argue, to the present), had allegedly failed to meet the challenge of explaining and describing the horrendous realities of the war.[16]

In the British case it is difficult to claim that the anti-war myth was countered by 'pro-war' writers. True, Henry Williamson became a fascist, but his First World War novels, notably *The Patriot's Progress* (1930) are anything but pro-war. The hero of that work, John Bullock, is portrayed as an archetypal victim. Britain, it seems, produced no equivalent of Ernst Jünger with his mystical and nationalistic reverence for war. Jünger, for example, likened the human race to a primeval forest

> From whose dark and misty depths emerged the cry of victims ripped out of their nests by . . . beasts of prey. To live meant to kill . . . Man would never overcome war because it was greater than he was, and woe to him if he tried to escape from its grasp, for it was in war that men fulfilled themselves most completely . . . War was a creative force. It made men and their times what they were . . . Territories and war aims were mere symbols necessary to get men to die. War was an eternal rite in which young celebrants strove after moral perfection. In the performance of this rite death was unimportant.[17]

At least it should be noted that Jünger practised what he preached, being outstandingly brave as a platoon and company commander and suffering fourteen wounds. Despite his celebration of the supreme experience of death in battle he is still alive and approaching his hundred and first year as this is written.

Indeed, it is hard to think of any British author who approaches war in Jünger's ecstatic manner. Nevertheless, as Robert Wohl acutely observes, some intellectuals who later recalled the First World War mainly in terms of horror, fear and brutalization also experienced it as an opportunity, a privilege and a revelation:

> Ambivalence towards the war is the main characteristic of the best and most honest of the war literature.[18]

There is more than a hint of the Romantic reaction in the young Graham Greenwell, whose incredibly frank letters to his mother were first published in 1935 under the title *An Infant in Arms*. Greenwell aroused some reviewers' distaste by the admission in his preface that 'I look back on the years 1914–1918 as among the happiest I have ever spent', sentiments he had expressed in a letter home in December 1918.[19] This was clearly a politically incorrect line to make public in the mid-1930s, but by no means unique. The late Field Marshal Earl Alexander told the present writer with, one suspects, only slight exaggeration that he had 'enjoyed every minute of the war. It was great fun'. But then he was a *beau sabreur*, not an intellectual or a writer.

The most overt, combative and polemical riposte to the outpouring of anti-war literature was Douglas Jerrold's pamphlet *The Lie About the War* which appeared in February 1930. Jerrold had served with the Royal Naval Division in the war and had written its history, also that of the 36th (Ulster) Division and other books about the war. In reviewing sixteen war books Jerrold's main aim was to show that the war was not futile or meaningless but rather a great tragedy because it was a great historical event. It had accomplished many good things politically while even for individuals its effects were by no means all negative. His most palpable hits on his literary targets were, first, that the authors were unusually sensitive and imaginative individuals whose obsession with the ghastly nature of combat was unrepresentative of the vast majority of ordinary soldiers. Second, and as a corollary, these writers travestied the variety of war experience by portraying it as four years of ceaseless, sanguinary attrition, thereby creating in the minds of the public 'a love of peace foolishly based on a barren fear of useless suffering'.[20] Third, and most important, Jerrold pointed out that the authors under review ignored the wider purposes and meaning of the war by focusing on individual experience. These wider purposes are seldom apparent to the private soldier in a trench, but war is *par excellence* a competition between large disciplined groups. Jerrold's critique received support from his fellow official historian Cyril Falls, whose more comprehensive review, *War Books* (1930) also argued that the war made sense politically, and that most accounts had grossly caricatured the common experience by, for example, omitting any reference to periods of rest and games.

Charles Carrington had written a plain, objective account of his battle experiences as a young officer just after the war, but did not publish it until July 1929 (as *A Subaltern's War*), in an effort to counteract the over-emotional and pessimistic tone of the anti-war books then receiving so much attention. Then, and for the rest of his life, he remained a sharp critic of the 'disenchantment' school, contending that he and his fellow volunteers had known from the outset that they faced a terrible ordeal but were determined to see it through. His epilogue, provocatively entitled 'An essay on militarism' was really an eloquent riposte to the caricature of front-line experience as one of unrelieved suffering, fear and deprivation. Such accounts deny both the soldier's capacity for an inner life and also his capacity for intense happiness despite, or even because of, appalling physical conditions:

Further, it is not honest to deny the existence of happiness which was actually derived from the war. First, the horrors and the discomforts, indescribable as they are, were not continuous. The unluckiest soldiers, whose leave was always stopped, who never had a 'blighty' wound, still spent only a comparatively few days in the face of the enemy, and of these only a few were of the most horrible kind. Their intensity, when they came, sharpened the senses and made the intervals correspondingly delightful.[21]

Second, young men like adventures, even those where their life is put at risk. This is an imaginative challenge to all historians over forty. Third, there was comradeship, 'richer, stronger in war than we have ever known since'. Carrington's rather harsh remarks about 'comfortable folk who hate war because it shakes them out of their routine and whose motto is "Safety First",' became more strident in his later book *Soldier from the Wars Returning* (1964), but he still maintained a robust defence of the motives, values and positive experience of the 1914–1918 generation of soldiers.

By contrast, Frederic Manning was by temperament an aesthete, a classical scholar and poet, whose chronic ill-health also unfitted him for a soldier's life. He served in the ranks in the battle of the Somme and eventually obtained a commission; but he proved to be an incompetent officer, was frequently inebriated, and was fortunate to avoid a court martial by being allowed to retire.[22] It seems pointless to try to place Manning in a pro- or anti-war category, but his war fiction *The Middle Parts of Fortune* (originally published in a bowdlerised edition as *Her Privates We* in 1930), is unsurpassed as an account of real soldiering, about being (in Michael Howard's words)

the scrounging, drilling, yarning, gossiping, gambling, drinking and womanizing which has always constituted the great bulk of military experience.

If this novel did nothing else, it provided graphic evidence that 1st July 1916 was not a typical day on the Western Front.

Although Manning clearly imparts some of his own qualities to his enigmatic hero, Bourne, he achieved artistic detachment by describing the experience of *a group of soldiers*. Despite his personal inadequacies, Manning also conveys the idea of combat as a supreme test of character in which those who come through achieve a lasting sense of liberation and self-knowledge. As he wrote to William Rothenstein:

I found that I felt most free in precisely those conditions when freedom seems to the normal mind least possible – an extraordinary feeling of self-reliance and self-assertion.[23]

Guy Chapman records a similar sense of liberation, exaltation, and almost divine energy in recalling an escape from extreme danger in which many of his comrades had been killed in 1917. He reflected (in the 1970s) on

> how much less alive I am than I was then . . . What is missing is the sense, fleeting, beyond price, of living in every nerve and cell of one's body and with every ghostly impulse of one's mind. I am grateful to have had it.[24]

Numerous other memoirists of the First World War combatted or countered the 'disenchanted' school. Their books, many reprinted in recent years, are treasured by military historians but not so well known by the general public, especially to younger generations brought up on the assumption that the 'war poets' and Graves are authoritative sources for the meaning of the war. In addition to Graham Greenwell, mentioned earlier, Sidney Rogerson's *Twelve Days*, about the 2nd West Yorkshire Regiment during a quiet period in the Somme campaign, was originally published in the unpropitious year 1933. Rogerson praised the courage, resolution and, not least, the cheerfulness of ordinary soldiers against those who had recently portrayed the war as one long nightmare:

> The bemused survivor is slightly irritated to find his experience exploited by the marrow-freezing agents of peace for all time . . . But this post-war propaganda, piling corpse on corpse, heaping terror on futility, seems bound to fail from every point of view. In its distortion, the soldier looks in vain for the scenes he knew.[25]

There has surely been no more honest or moving evocation of the fascination of war than that reluctantly admitted by Guy Chapman:

> Once you have lain in her arms you can admit no other mistress. You may loathe, you may execrate, but you cannot deny her. No lover can offer you defter caresses, more exquisite tortures, such breaking delights. No wine gives fiercer intoxication, no drug more vivid exaltation. Every writer of imagination who has set down in honesty his experience has confessed it. Even those who hate her most are prisoners to her spell. They rise from her embraces, pillaged, soiled, it may be ashamed; but they are still hers.[26]

Chapman, a humane scholar and certainly no militarist, also wrote of the life-long spell which the war had exerted over him. Apart from meeting his wife (the novelist Storm Jameson), Chapman reflected in his autobiography that his battalion was the only wholly good thing in his life:

> To the years between 1914 and 1918 I owe everything of lasting value in my make-up. For any cost I paid in physical and mental vigour they gave me back a supreme fulfilment I should never otherwise have had.[27]

Among the many other writers who have expressed similar positive views about the war's enhancing effects on the rest of their lives may be mentioned R. H. Tawney, Vivian de Sola Pinto, Lord Reith, Sir Maurice Bowra, Harold Macmillan and P. J. Campbell – but the list could be greatly extended. True, with the important exception of Tawney, these authors were all officers, but the more recently published memoirs or letters of Norman Gladden, George Coppard, Frank Dunham and others provide evidence that the other ranks were far from inarticulate, and could also recall their war service with pride.

Why, then, have these positive and often moving testaments in defence of the British war effort, and its meaning for thoughtful writers, failed to overshadow the anti-war literature and images in the public consciousness? First, no amount of honesty and eloquence can counter 750,000 deaths, their names recorded in every village church. Second, the desolate battlescapes depicted by Paul Nash, C. R. W. Nevinson and others have created an indelible image of what the Western Front was 'really like'; no one wants to be told, for example, of the dry and dusty spell during the Passchendaele campaign. On the Western Front it was always raining, when it was not snowing, and men and horses were always knee-deep in mud. Third, the war poets, Remarque and the popular memoirists, such as Vera Brittain (*Testament of Youth*) appeal strongly to the emotions with their accounts of wasted lives, a lost generation and the soldiers as victims or martyrs in a pointless war. On the last aspect, Adrian Caesar does well to remind us that Owen's and Sassoon's soldiers were also killers; indeed Sassoon himself was unusual for an officer in the enthusiasm he displayed in despatching Germans.[28]

Fourth, the beneficial results of Britain's unprecedented war effort were hard to discern either at home or in international relations by the early 1930s. Moreover, for those like C. E. Montague who had cherished illusions of a better world, the bitter post-war reaction was exacerbated by excessive promises of the 'war to end wars' and of a 'land fit for heroes'. Here perhaps is the sharpest divide in post-war attitudes between the majority who had simply fought doggedly to defeat Germany and thus preserve their homes and way of life, and the minority like Montague for whom the conflict only made sense if regarded as a crusade to secure a better world.

Finally, influential sections of the educated middle classes (i.e., readers of the 'quality' newspapers and of the literature discussed here) seem to have reacted very strongly in the 1920s against war in general and against the British Army and its leaders in particular. There was a long 'open season' for journalistic attacks on incompetent generals (if there were competent ones the critics were not interested) and 'Colonel Blimps', as exemplified by Major-General J. F. C. Fuller's savage satires; while his fellow military critic Captain B. H. Liddell Hart, advanced the seductive theories that Britain could and should have avoided a total commitment to mass, Continental warfare, and that Germany had been defeated by the blockade rather than the wasteful attrition on the Western Front.[29]

The anti-war myth spawned in the late 1920s and early 1930s is still very influential, notably in setting the agenda and tone for anniversaries and other commemorations of the First World War (for example in the annual television programmes on the Somme and the Armistice).

In addition many facets of the myth were resuscitated and given a new lease of life during the 1960s at the time of the 50th anniversaries.[30] Books such as Alan Clark's *The Donkeys* (1961) and Leon Wolff's *In Flanders Fields* (1958), and Joan Littlewood's play *Oh! What a Lovely War* (1963) gave a tremendous boost to the myth of the bloody, muddy conflict, incompetently conducted and ultimately futile – in that it set the scene for an even more titanic struggle against Germany. On the other hand, the same decade witnessed a new phase of serious historical interest in the war led by John Terraine and later developed by academic scholars including Tim Travers, Dominick Graham, David French, Trevor Wilson and Robin Prior. But the tendency to present the whole complex conflict in terms of 'butchers and bunglers' remains strong.

It does not require any great intellectual or moral effort to be 'anti-war', and the First World War is an easy target from almost any standpoint. Nevertheless the literary-cultural anti-war myth as outlined in this paper must be challenged on at least three counts which need only be briefly recapitulated here.

First, despite the fact that the war was a terrible tragedy if evaluated in Clausewitzian terms as an instrument of policy, it was nevertheless fought about great national and international issues. Furthermore, albeit unpredictably and at great cost, it did bring about enormous political changes affecting individual states and empires and the relationship between them. In the light of available information and assumptions, the British government had little option but to enter the war in August 1914, and it is very hard to see how a 'peace without victory' could have been honourably negotiated at any point in the next four years.[31]

Second, this paper supports the line taken by Charles Carrington, Correlli Barnett and others that the anti-war writers were not at all representative of the vast majority of civilians in uniform who experienced active service. Indeed, it is salutary to remember that the generation which grew up in the 1920s and 1930s was not deterred by the pervasive, 'disenchanted' legacy of the First World War from fighting the second.[32]

Finally, the phrase 'anti-war' and the collection of ideas and assumptions which constitute the 'myth' as discussed earlier, are far too sweeping and imprecise to encourage serious study and understanding of the First World War. On the contrary, they inhibit fresh thinking by their complacent assumption of the moral high ground. To take just one aspect:

much of the most bitter criticism during the war and through the 1920s was (justifiably we may feel), directed at the failings on the home front rather than at the reasons for fighting or the conduct of operations. Paradoxically, as Adrian Caesar has reminded us, the 'anti-war' label has become attached to soldier poets, writers and artists whose attitudes to the war were ambivalent if not actually supportive, whereas the true civilian anti-war campaigners receive little public attention.

It is difficult to undermine the popular basis of the anti-war myth; indeed the endeavour is about as rewarding as disputing the merits of apple pie or motherhood. Nevertheless, even in the prevailing climate of opinion in Britain in the 1990s, it ought to be possible to gain a sympathetic hearing for the historian's view of the war and the positive – though not militaristic – interpretations to be found in the writings of Douglas Jerrold, Charles Carrington, Frederic Manning and Guy Chapman, who spoke for a vast number of ordinary soldiers. Perhaps in the course of the twenty-first century those who shape British public opinion will come to accept the First World War as history (like the earlier Great War against Napoleonic France), rather than in predominantly literary terms as a black hole or national trauma – a gap in history – redeemed and rendered meaningful for them only by disenchanted memoirs and the poetry of pity.

Notes

1 Adrian Caesar, *Taking It Like a Man: Suffering, Sexuality and the War Poets* (1990) pp. 97–8.
2 *ibid*, pp. 104, 158, 162, 233.
3 Robert Wohl, *The Generation of 1914* (1980) pp. 262. Samuel Hynes, *A War Imagined: the First World War and English Culture* (1990) pp. 175–80.
4 Modris Eksteins, *Rites of Spring. The Great War and the Birth of the Modern Age* (1989) pp. 175–6. See also Michael Howard's introduction to Frederic Manning, *The Middle Parts of Fortune* (1977 edition).
5 Hynes, pp. 455, 166–7, 215.
6 Correlli Barnett, *The Collapse of British Power* (1972) pp. 433–4.
7 See Robin Prior and Trevor Wilson 'Paul Fussell at War' in *War in History* Vol. I, No I, 1994 pp. 63–80.
8 Charles Edmonds, *A Subaltern's War* (1929) pp. 206–8.
9 C. E. Montague, *Disenchantment* (1929 Phoenix library edition) pp. 188–9. Hynes pp. 307–310.
10 Hynes, pp. 118–9.
11 Keith Simpson (ed) *The War the Infantry Knew* (1987) p. xxxi.
12 Robert Graves, *Goodbye to All That* (1957 edition) Prologue. Hynes, pp. 427–30.
13 Hynes, pp. 446–7. Also my own comments on the Somme film in 'The Somme in British History', (unpublished paper, 1992).
14 Barnett, *op. cit.*, pp. 428–9. Hynes, p. 302.
15 Hynes, p. 439.
16 Eksteins pp. 285–99.
17 Wohl, pp. 58–9.

18 *ibid*. p. 219.

19 John Terraine's introduction to Graham H. Greenwell, *An Infant in Arms* (1972 edition), pp. ix–xix

20 Douglas Jerrold, *The Lie about the War* (1929), p. 46. Hynes, pp. 451–4.

21 Charles Edmonds (Carrington), *A Subaltern's War* (1929), pp. 194–5.

22 Jonathan Marwil, *Frederic Manning: an Unfinished Life* (1988).

23 *ibid*., p. 179.

24 Guy Chapman, *A Kind of Survivor* (1975), pp. 158–9.

25 John Terraine quoting Rogerson in his introduction to Greenwell, op. cit., p. xiii.

26 Guy Chapman, *A Passionate Prodigality* (1933). The quotation is from the second edition (1965), p. 226.

27 Guy Chapman, *A Kind of Survivor*, p. 280.

28 Caesar *op. cit.*, p. 144. 'On one occasion he ignored a written order . . . in order to occupy and hold a German trench – alone. Sassoon had badly wanted to kill a German at close quarters', Wohl, p. 97.

29 See for example, J. F. C. Fuller, *Generalship: Its Diseases and their Cure* (1933), *The Army in my Time* (1935), and *Memoirs of an Unconventional Soldier* (1936); B. H. Liddell Hart, *The British Way in Warfare* (1932).

30 See the editor's introduction and Alex Danchev's '"Bunking" and Debunking: the controversies of the 1960s' in Brian Bond, (editor) *The First World War and British Military History* (1991) p.1-12, 263-288.

31 See, for example, the robust conclusions of Trevor Wilson in *The Myriad Faces of War* (1986) pp. 848–853. For a recent statement of the case that Britain could and should have remained neutral in 1914 see Niall Ferguson 'Were we right to fight the Great War?' *Sunday Telegraph* 31 July 1994.

32 Wilson, p. 852.

Chapter 58

The French War Novel: The Case of Louis-Ferdinand Céline

Frank Field

It is not difficult to see why the French today make less fuss about the memory of the Great War than do the British. Far more psychologically prepared for battle with Germany in 1914 (although not for the scale of that conflict) the French do not have quite the same preoccupation with the loss of innocence as the British. Defeated and occupied during the Second World War, France since 1945 has been far more conspicuously and successfully concerned with dealing with the challenges of the modern world and the creation of a new Europe than with looking back to the past.

But this is not to deny that for over a generation the memory of the terrible wounds of the First World War dominated the minds of the French. Not only was the war in the West fought in the main on French soil, but French fatalities were higher in percentage terms than those of the Germans, twice those of the British, and against this background it is not surprising that for many years the war provided a major theme in French literature.

Unfortunately much of this literature is now largely forgotten. In part this is due to the extent to which the divisions and humiliations of the Second World War have overlaid the sufferings of the First. But it has also been the result of the preoccupation of French critics with the avant garde. In the last decade or so, however, the situation has begun to change. Now that Modernism has waned, for example, there are the beginnings of a reassessment of French war poetry. Leaving overtly patriotic verse on one side, it was previously held that the influence of Symbolism and later of Surrealism, with their common obsession with the alchemy of language, meant that French poets, unlike their English counterparts, were not primarily interested in responding to the experience of the First World War in direct terms. Although this view is not entirely wrong, we can now see from studies such as Elizabeth Marsland's *The Nation's Cause: French, English and German poetry of the First World War* (1991) that this is an inadequate judgement. Although Aragon in his Surrealist phase prided himself on never referring to the war in his poetry (despite the fact that he had had first-hand experience of it) we can now appreciate that there were other responses to the conflict, and that for a number of writers – from Cocteau to Blaise Cendrars – the Great War inspired a body of poetry that possesses an immediacy that can be compared with that produced in Britain and Germany.

In the history of the war novel, too, there are signs of movement. As the French become acclimatised to the world of post-Modernism, and as they become less and less preoccupied with ideological issues, it is likely that Jean Giono's depiction of the suffering of man and the natural world in time of war in *Le grand troupeau* will receive greater attention, and when the scandal over Henry de Montherlant's lately revealed pederasty is over it may be possible to achieve a more balanced view of this complicated and elusive writer and to do justice to his understanding of the male fraternity of the soldiers in *Le Songe*. Meanwhile the rediscovery of the richness and variety of the response to the war by French novelists continues apace. Bernard-Henri Lévy[1] has drawn attention to the neglect of *Ceux de Verdun* by Maurice Genevoix, while the merits of the liberal humanism of Georges Duhamel's *La vie des martyrs* and of his correspondence are now being increasingly valued by historians.

Perhaps inevitably up to now, however, it has tended to be those writers who responded to the war with a particular extremism and intensity whose work has been remembered. The names of Barbusse, Drieu la Rochelle and Bernanos immediately spring to mind, and to these must surely be added that of Céline, nom de plume of Louis-Ferdinand Destouches, whose novel *Voyage au bout de la nuit* created a sensation when it appeared in 1932. For in this novel a new note is struck within French war literature. To other responses to the war – Barbusse's Communism, Drieu's Fascism and the militant Catholicism of Bernanos – there must now be added another vision, that of the Absurd.

The literature of the Absurd did not achieve definition and make its real mark in France until many years later, and it is understandable that critics in the early 1930s should have regarded Céline's novel as a variation within the Naturalist tradition. But even at the time Céline caused a scandal. This was due not merely to his use of slang and obscenity (an onslaught on the petrified conventions of literary French which he carried much further in later novels) but was also due to his unremitting pessimism.

It was this which distinguished his response from that of other writers of the war. In *Le Feu* Barbusse had produced a harrowing indictment of the suffering of the soldiers at the front, the first novel to expose the reality of the conflict, but the horror was alleviated to a certain extent by the experience of fraternity in the midst of suffering. It was this that inspired him to make his later commitment to Communism. The comradeship of those who had truly been 'dans le bain' was also a source of inspiration to Bernanos. The latter never wrote a 'war novel' in the conventional sense, but all his work reflects the conflict. Terrified that the war had demonstrated the degree to which the world was moving into a post-Christian era, the brotherhood that he had witnessed in the trenches convinced him that the doctrine of the communion of saints still possessed its validity and that this could be a source of hope to a world given over to despair. Drieu la Rochelle, too, was continually beset by the temptation of despair. Obsessed by a sense of the decadence of himself and France in the modern world, he plunged into hedonism and dissipation in the 1920s. But he could never remain indifferent to the freemasonry that had existed between those who had been through the war experience. Nor, despite his horror of modern warfare, could he forget the sense of mystical exaltation that he had experienced in a bayonet charge at the very beginning of the war, an experience that he recorded in *La Comédie de Charleroi* which appeared in 1934. It was in the hope of rediscovering this sense of heroism and self-transcendence that he turned to an idealised form of Fascism.

In *Voyage au bout de la nuit* by contrast, there is no heroism, no transcendence, no true fraternity. Everything that happens is random and absurd. Bardamu, the central character of the novel becomes involved in the war through accident. He is sitting in a café denouncing nationalism when war is announced. He joins a column of soldiers marching to the front. There he finds himself in a world of total chaos, a world in which the Germans are largely invisible, and where one suffers as much from friendly fire as from that of the enemy. He tries to explain to his colonel that the war must be stopped, but the latter is killed before his eyes:

> The colonel's stomach was slit open and he was making an ugly face about that. It must have been painful when that happened. So much the worse for him. If he'd gone away when the firing began, he wouldn't have had it.[2]

Bardamu is then employed as a runner, but he can never make contact with the main body of the troops. He decides to desert but is wounded and given a medal before he can escape. Sent to various hospitals he then encounters the world of the Derrière where 'the women were in heat and the old men had greed written all over them':

> Back at home they'd been pretty quick to pick up honour and glory from the boys at the front, and had learnt how to resign themselves to it all bravely and without flinching. The mothers, all nurses or martyrs, were never without their sombre livery and the little diplomas so promptly presented to them by the War Office.[3]

In the hospitals he encounters Sergeant Branledore, a splendid comic creation, who plays on his wounds and his patriotic utterances to charm the nurses and to avoid further involvement in the war. Bardamu also meets up with Lola, an American nurse, who regards France as a sort of chivalrous entity, not clearly defined within space or time, but grievously wounded and, for that reason, extremely exciting. Bardamu is interested in her body, while she is obsessed with France. They break up when Bardamu tries to disabuse her of her ideas about the glory of war. He subsequently pursues an actress with whom he is determined not to make the same mistake. He gives her a highly coloured version of his bravery in the war. She then uses this information to enable a poet friend of hers to create a patriotic sensation at the Comédie Française. At this performance Branledore and the poet, 'a melodious invert', steal all the glory. Eventually Bardamu is invalided out of the army.

The war itself only takes up about a quarter of *Voyage au bout de la nuit*. The rest is concerned with Bardamu's life after the army. He goes as a clerk to the colony of Bambola Bragamance in Africa, a tropical hell, where the whites brutally oppress the acquiescent blacks while everybody is periodically the victim of appalling diseases. Struck down by fever Bardamu believes that the blacks have sold him into slavery and that he is rowing his way to America in the galley of a slave ship. Once in America he experiences the American version of Hell, working on a totally de-humanised assembly line in Detroit. Back in France he qualifies as a doctor and runs a poverty-stricken practice where his patients rarely pay him, where death lies in wait for everyone, and where he regularly deals with the victims of boredom and depression – alcoholics, wife-beaters and seekers after abortion. Madness is another form of escape from the human condition. He becomes head of a lunatic asylum operating a new kind of therapy, a system of Cinematic Cures for Cretins. At the very end of the novel the mysterious Robinson, an alter ego or spiritual brother of Bardamu, who has appeared at certain crucial points in Bardamu's life from the time of his period at the front, is killed by his girlfriend after he himself has murdered an old woman. Bardamu is left contemplating the boats on the Seine canal, aware that Robinson has advanced further than him into the journey to the end of the night. Although biographical infor-mation is meagre on the years before his fame, it is clear that Céline drew upon many of his own experiences in writing *Voyage au bout de la nuit*. He was a rebellious youth who after his discharge from the army in 1915 worked as a clerk first in the French passport office in London and then in the Cameroons. After the war he qualified as a doctor, worked for a time for the League of Nations and visited the United States before going into private practice.

All these episodes of his life are reflected, refracted, distorted and magni-fied in his writings. But undoubtedly it was the war that was the crucial event in Céline's career, and on this subject what he wrote about Bardamu in his novel was a travesty of the true situation. The fact is that Céline had already been in the army as a conscript in the cavalry for nearly two years when the war broke out and although at first he did not relish the discipline and the boredom of military life in peacetime, and even contemplated desertion at one point, he eventually became a good soldier. He delighted in the beauty and precision of the great parades at Longchamps on Bastille Day (he was always passionately devoted to the ballet) and did not seem to object when he was called upon to put down striking workers in the Rue des Pyramides. His friends noticed his capacity for mockery and his sly subversive humour, but it looked at this stage that he had decided to conform. He was made an N.C.O., and, when the war came, he greeted it with enthusiasm.

On 25 October 1914 his regiment was in action at Poelcapelle near Ypres. The fire was intense. When the regular runners were reluctant to deliver a message Céline volunteered to go. He accomplished his mission but was severely wounded. In recognition of his action he was awarded the médaille militaire and received a citation signed by Joffre, the French commander-in-chief. His courage was also celebrated some months later in the pages of *L'Illustré National*. With his craving for drama and excitement (and his secret fascination with violence) Céline embellished his own copy of this report to make it appear even more striking, thus creating problems for his early biographers. Having taken all his hyperbole into account, however, the fact remains that, far from being a consistent opponent of the war, Céline, unlike Bardamu, was a genuine patriot in 1914 and, however brief his period of service in time of war, a genuine war hero.

He was also seriously wounded, and, after going through a series of hospitals, where at one point he received electrical therapy, he was discharged from the army in 1915 as being unfit for military service. With typical exaggeration he claimed in later life that in addition to a severe injury to his arm he was also wounded so badly in the head that he needed trepanation. There is no truth in this, but he seems to have suffered from a trapped nerve in his ear caused by blast, and his second wife, Lucette, has testified to his suffering in later years from blinding headaches in which he felt that his skull was splitting in two. Significantly enough when the pacifist Céline attempted to enlist again in 1939 he was turned down and awarded a 70 per cent disability war pension. It is more than likely that the hysteria he manifested as another war approached in the 1930s, and the venom that he was to direct against the Jews, were exacerbated by the lasting pain he experienced as a result of his war experience.

He was enormously proud of his military service, however, and throughout his work there is a pronounced nostalgia for the France of the Belle Époque and the bravery of 1914. But, as the true dimensions of the war became clear, his enthusiasm turned into disgust at the absurdity of the blood-letting, and, when *Voyage au bout de la nuit* appeared, it was widely assumed that Céline, like Barbusse, was a man of the Left.

This was mistaken. Céline was certainly a pacifist and an anarchist. He admired Barbusse and when he was invited to give an address at the annual reunion of the Zola society in 1933 he used the occasion to denounce the forces of nationalism that were leading Europe into further carnage and war. But he distanced himself from Zola's Naturalism and in the course of this remarkable address, an address that deserves to be read by every serious student of the 1930s, he described the world since 1914 in Pascalian terms as tragic and grotesque. The harrowing but ordered world of the Naturalists is no longer sufficient. Life now can only be depicted in terms of nightmare. Men were turning towards totalitarianism out of spiritual despair, but in truth none of the existing political systems, whether liberal, Marxist or Fascist, could last for two months if mankind really faced up to the inescapable misery of its situation.[4]

To Céline, then, the ultimate optimism of men like Zola and Barbusse was offensive, and his alienation from the Left was confirmed by the trip that he made to the Soviet Union in August 1936 to spend his royalties that were accumulating there. *Voyage au bout de la nuit* had been translated into Russian in a bowdlerised version by Aragon and Elsa Triolet, and Communists hoped that he would return, if not a Marxist, certainly as a fellow-traveller. In this they were deceived. In the pamphlet *Mea Culpa* he wrote on his return he talked instead about the atmosphere of terror, and mocked the charges that were being made by the régime at the show trials of the old Bolsheviks that were just beginning. Only three things worked in the Soviet nightmare – the army, the police and propaganda. Worse even than the terror were the lies and hypocrisy. The Russian system has the effrontery to dress up a turd and then pass it off as caramel. [5]

If Communism was a gigantic fraud, where, then, did salvation lie? Faithful to his anarchism and pacifism Céline could not accept the authoritarianism, the élitism, and the worship of the heroic myth, that lay at the heart of Fascism. Nor could he find any solution in religious belief. Meanwhile France was moving towards another major war. It was against this background that he turned to antisemitism. In 1937 there appeared *Bagatelles pour un massacre*, a work that can hardly be described as a pamphlet at all, a diatribe of several hundred pages against the Jews, a publication from which Céline's reputation was never to recover.

Faced with the seeming collapse of capitalism, the challenge of Communism and the growing danger of war there was a constant search for scapegoats in the France of the 1930s. Already in 1931, for example, Bernanos (an admirer of *Voyage au bout de la nuit* and a man whom Céline in turn regarded as belonging to the same family of visionaries as himself) published *La grande peur des bien-pensants*, a biography of Drumont, the father of French antisemitism, in which Bernanos calls upon the youth of France to fight against the power of money symbolised by the Jews, a force which is overwhelming French society and rendering meaningless the sacrifices of the Great War. This, however, only represented a phase in Bernanos' evolution. After the intense spiritual despair that had haunted him in the early 1930s, and after he had witnessed the Falangist purges in Majorca during the Spanish Civil War, he turned away from the Fascist temptation to attack all the tyrannies of the modern world. In Brazil during the Second World War he denounced the persecution of the Jews and the silence of the Pope over the Final Solution.

In his review of *Voyage au bout de la nuit* Bernanos had been quick to detect the undertone of spiritual anguish in Céline and had expressed the hope that the latter would discover God's pity at the end of his journey.[6] But Céline could not take this path. Confronted with the growing threat of war his nerve failed and he sought refuge in dementia. Once again it should be pointed out that antisemitism was widespread in a France faced with the Popular Front and terrified by the prospect of another war. Even by the standard of publications like *Gringoire* and *Je suis partout*, however, the tone that Céline adopted in *Bagatelles pour un massacre* and another pamphlet, *l'École des cadavres* which came out in 1938, was one of extraordinary hysteria. Pages and pages of invective against the 'Yids', including extracts from publications like that notorious forgery, the 'Protocols of the Elders of Zion',[7] swirl round with ballet scenarios and elements of black farce as Céline attacks Hollywood, Léon Blum, Karl Marx and the English, while mercilessly satirising the French. In so far as any 'argument' can be discerned in these pamphlets, it is that the Jews are the secret power behind capitalism and communism and are the mortal enemies of France. In their hatred of Adolf Hitler they are intent on forcing France into a conflict with Nazi Germany in which the decadent French, drained of their vitality by the Great War, hopelessly addicted to the comfort of apéritifs, paid holidays and a declining birth-rate, will be annihilated. Bereft of the Russian alliance of 1914 the French are bagatelles for a coming massacre and will be destroyed in 15 days. No help can be expected from England. The French people will be maggots before the first Oxford queers disembark in Flanders.[8] Anyone who does not take a pacifist line towards the coming war is automatically Jewish. Thus Maurras, the antisemitic leader of the Action Française is Jewish. The Pope is Jewish. George VI is half-Jewish, while Queen Elizabeth and Mrs Simpson are fully Jewish. But then, so is the entire English nation . . .

So demented is the tone that it was claimed (by Gide amongst others) that Céline was not being serious and that he was working himself up into a passion to create a work of art. This explanation, like the theory that Céline was consciously going further into the Absurd or was engaged in a Baudelairian exploration of evil, provides touching evidence of the innocence of literary critics, but it is too subtle. The sophisticated nature of Céline's intelligence can never be in doubt, but less elevated factors were at work here. Céline's antisemitism had its origins in his petit-bourgeois background. It was reactivated by his terror at the prospect of war, but it then toppled over into delirium, a delirium that, in however wayward a fashion, did not hesitate to use the language of racialism. At the beginning of *Voyage au bout de la nuit* Bardamu had denounced the idea of a French 'race', and in his Zola address Céline had described Hitler's nationalism as 'epileptic'. Now Dr Destouches begins to talk about biology and urges an alliance with Hitler to foil the Jewish threat to Aryan civilisation. [9]

In 1940 France collapsed with almost the speed that Céline had predicted, and in his final 'pamphlet', *Les beaux draps* (1941), there is a vivid description of the refugees trying in vain to catch up with the French army in retreat.[10] But once France fell it was the turn of the collaborators and the Germans to be the objects of his mockery. In the winter of 1940 he told Lucien Rebatet that the Fritz had lost the war because they had not brought a social revolution to France.[11] In December 1941 he informed an appalled Ernst Jünger that he was stupefied that the Germans were not exterminating the Jews. Had the Bolsheviks occupied Paris they would have shown the Germans how to be ruthless.[12] This, perhaps, should not be interpreted too literally. Céline did not love the Germans. His behaviour was capricious and his definition of Jews remained elastic. In 1943 at a dinner given by Otto Abetz in Paris which was attended by Drieu and other collaborators, he suddenly exclaimed that the Germans were losing the war because the real Hitler was dead and a Jew substituted in his place. One of Céline's friends, who had lost a leg in the First World War, then began to imitate a speech by the 'real' Hitler, while Céline provided a satirical commentary. After the general consternation provoked by their behaviour had died down, it was agreed by those present that they were, after all, invalids of the Great War and not quite right in the head.[13] When one considers that the deportations of French Jews to the extermination camps had started in July 1942 it may be felt that this is by far the most charitable view it is possible to take on Céline's war-time record.

At the Liberation he escaped to Germany where, after many adventures, including a period acting as a doctor to the forces of the bizarre government in exile of the French collaborators at Sigmaringen, he eventually managed to reach Denmark where he was imprisoned for a year. He returned to France under an amnesty in 1951 and devoted himself to writing a trilogy – *D'un château l'autre* (sic), *Nord* and *Rigodon* – which presents a hallucinatory picture of the chaos and collapse of Nazi Germany. He died in 1961.

After his return to France Céline did not suffer from any undue remorse for his antisemitic activities, taking the line that both the Jews and himself had suffered so much that the whole thing should be forgotten. But

Western civilization was still doomed. While the French drugged themselves with television, the theatrical hamming of de Gaulle and the novels of Françoise Sagan, their fate was being decided elsewhere. If France was not overrun by the Russians, it would be the Chinese who would give the coup de grâce.

He was heartened by the growing signs that his literary stature was being recognised, however, and this process has gathered pace since his death. It is clear that his influence has been extensive, not only on the early Sartre, Genet and Henry Miller, but also on the whole literature of war. Joseph Heller has acknowledged his debt, while Pynchon's 'Gravity's Rainbow' reminds one irresistibly of Céline. If the experience of war represents the Absurd in its most concentrated form, then Céline in his writings on both World Wars is one of its greatest chroniclers.

But, like so many human inventions, the literature of the Absurd has its limitations. 'This century deceives us'.[14] Bernanos made this remark in 1915 when his early illusions about the Great War had been shattered, and in saying this he was articulating one of the great truths that came out of that war – that reality has an infinite capacity to match and then to overtake any horror of human imagining. Nowhere can this be seen more clearly than in the career of Céline. For if Barbusse ended up as a canting apologist for Stalin, and Drieu a suicide evading the vengeance of the Resistance, the destiny of Céline was even more terrifying. Unable to bear the realities of the 1930s he escaped into a world of sadistic fantasy. Unable to face the consequences of his nihilism he betrayed the integrity of his own powerful vision. His hatred of war was passionate. His pain was real. As an extreme example of, and as a penetrating commentary on, the physical and psychological damage done to France by the Great War, the case of Céline has a continuing fascination. But at the end it was not he, but those he had attacked and vilified, who made the real and unimaginable journey to the end of the night.

Notes

1   B-H Lévy, *Les aventures de la liberté*, Paris, 1991, pp. 51–6.
2   L-F Céline, *Journey to the end of the night*, translated by J. H. P. Marks, London 1966, p. 16.
3   *ibid.*, p. 42
4   L-F Céline, Hommage à Zola, *Oeuvres de Louis-Ferdinand Céline*, Vol. II, Paris 1967, pp. 503–7.
5   L-F Céline, *Mea Culpa*, Paris 1936, pp. 33–4.
6   G. Bernanos, *Le crépuscule des vieux*, Paris, 1956, p. 346.
7   L-F Céline, *Bagatelles pour un massacre*, Paris, 1937, p. 279.
8   *ibid.*, p. 89. Quoted by P. McCarthy, *Céline*, London, 1975, p. 149. Despite all this, Céline's widow assures us that he loved England and momentarily thought of escaping there at the time of the French defeat in 1940. See F. Vitoux, *La vie de Céline*, Paris, 1988, p. 341.
9   L-F Céline, *L'École des cadavres*, Paris, 1938, p. 140.

10 L-F Céline, *Les beaux draps*, Paris, 1941, pp. 110–112.
11 Les Cahiers de l'Herne: *Louis-Ferdinand Céline*, Paris, 1963, p. 46.
12 Vitoux, *La vie de Céline*, p. 378.
13 *ibid.*, p. 387.
14 A. Béguin (ed.), *Georges Bernanos. Essais et témoignages*, Paris, 1949, p. 31.

BIBLIOGRAPHICAL INFORMATION
(not already contained in the References)
1   *General*:
    L. Riegel   *Guerre et littérature: le bouleversement des consciences dans la littérature romanesque inspirée par la Grande Guerre*, Paris, 1978. A comprehensive general survey.
    F. Field   *Three French Writers and the Great War*, Cambridge, 1975. For a detailed examination of Barbusse, Drieu la Rochelle and Bernanos.
2   *On Céline*:
    P. Alméras   *Céline*, Paris, 1994. The most recent biography.
    N. Hewitt   *The Golden Age of Louis-Ferdinand Céline*, Leamington Spa, 1987. A stimulating analysis of Céline's literary achievement in terms of his fidelity to the doomed values of the petite bourgeoisie before 1914.
3   *On Céline's works*
    Not mentioned in the references
    a) *Death on the Instalment Plan*, translated by J. H. P. Marks, London, 1968. A translation of *Mort à crédit*, Paris, 1936, Céline's second major novel of the 1930s, which deals with the world before 1914.
    b) *Guignol's Band*, translated by B. Frechtman and J. T. Niles, New York, 1954. A translation of *Guignol's Band*, Paris, 1944, which deals with aspects of Céline's experiences in both World Wars.
    c) *Castle to Castle*, translated by R. Manheim, New York, 1968. A translation of *D'un château l'autre* (sic), Paris, 1957. The most accessible of Céline's trilogy on the fall of Nazi Germany.

Chapter 59

The Experience of British Artists in the Great War

Paul Gough

Much of the debate about the British art of the Great War centres around two themes: the innovatory official war art schemes devised and funded by the Ministry of Information and the problems faced by radical modernist artists working under the repressive nature of these schemes.[1] So far, little attention has been paid to the vast body of work produced outside the circle of the modernist avant garde, nor to the practical conditions that inspired and frustrated attempts to depict the face of modern war. This article attempts to redress that balance by focusing on the key experience of soldier-artists [2] on the Western Front.

By way of setting the scene, it might be worth examining the experience of one artist who made the transformation from a front-line soldier to official war artist. When he went overseas with the 13th London Regiment in late 1914 Eric Kennington was no ordinary soldier. At 26 he was a painter of extraordinary skills, widely recognised for his technical virtuosity and exceptional draughtsmanship. Trained at Lambeth School of Art and at the City and Guilds School, Kennington found little room for artistic pursuit in his two months service with the Kensingtons on the Western Front. In poor trenches on the Lys valley, Kennington experienced the hardships of infantry duty, a period brought ignominiously to a close after a shooting accident in which he was wounded in the foot. But his time at the front yielded quite unexpected results. While convalescing in England he composed and completed perhaps the first great painting of the war – *The Kensingtons at Laventie*.[3] A complex multi-figure composition of a platoon at rest, it is painted in reverse on a sheet of glass some 5 by 4 feet, a technique that lends the picture a surprising luminosity and intensity. Shown first at the Goupil Gallery in 1916 it was an unparalleled success; *The Times* admiring its force of expression while recognising its peculiar beauty.[4] Others agreed and after some heavy lobbying Kennington was eventually employed, in August 1917, as an official war artist. Yet, ironically, he did not thrive. His terms of commission were strict, he had no official car, no expenses, no salary; his materials failed to arrive in France and he was constantly troubled by petty officials. Furthermore, his subject matter – the 'fighting man' upon which his reputation had been built – proved elusive and he was reduced to drawing 'tents and shacks and camp rubbish'.[5] His subsequent one-man show in London was spoilt by a prolonged wrangle over the censoring of many of the titles and a graceless dispute with the war museum over the pricing of his work. Despite the critical acclaim which heralded the show – Robert Graves applauded his ability to capture 'the trench point of view' – Kennington felt artistically and financially impoverished by his experience as a war artist.

If we have dealt at length with this artist's story it is because he is a paradigm of the dilemma faced by many war artists – inspired by witnessing conflict: undermined by the expectations of market and propaganda. Kennington epitomises many of the challenges and problems faced by artists in the Great War and many aspects of his story will be heard again as we continue to examine the experience of artists on the Western Front.

I

Like any other profession, painters and sculptors – professional and amateur, famous and obscure – flocked to enlist in the first months of the war. *The Studio* magazine ran long lists of artists who had enlisted;[6] many joined the Artists Rifles, an officer training unit which attracted painters, poets, architects, surveyors, and others with artistic pretensions – if not the talent. In most military units though, artists soon found themselves in steady demand.

Bombardier William Roberts' first 'artistic' task was to paint his battery crest on two German field guns captured by the 51st Brigade in early 1918.[7] The eminent salon painter William Orpen turned his hand to sculpture, helping to model and cast a number of plaster heads for target practice. The sculptor Derwent Wood worked in the 'tin noses' room at the 3rd London General Hospital, fashioning face masks out of flesh coloured electroplate.[qv Chapter Six] Stanley Spencer's painterly duties were a little less edifying. He had to paint the letters designating the men's and the sergeant's toilets, though, as ever, Spencer brought a delicate touch to this mundane task by decorating the S for Sergeant's with a halo of painted dog-roses.[8] In addition, professional artists, along with pre-war surveyors, architects, draughtsmen and civil engineers found themselves sought-after men, transferred into the newly formed Camouflage Corps or detailed for drawing work with various branches of the Royal Engineers. These postings were not always free from danger. While his fellow camouflage artists worked safely in depots and paint sheds miles behind the lines, the young painter Leon Underwood was sent on regular hazardous missions out in to No Man's Land. With his back to the enemy he had to make detailed drawings of trees on the British line. His drawings were then used to construct an exact replica of a particular tree which, hollowed out and lined with metal, was installed at night as an observation post.[9]

Working with paint, plaster and scrim in the Camouflage Corps may have satisfied the artistic urges in many soldiers, but it appears that the creative sense was fairly widespread – exacerbated, perhaps, by the mundane ugliness of much of the front-line world. The need to nurture some sort of creative life in the trench world was recalled by the machine-gunner George Coppard who wrote of the 'boyish satisfaction' gained

> out of making replicas of Regimental cap badges (by) melting the lead content of several bullets (and pouring) the boiling liquid into a mould made by pressing a badge on the clay bottom of the trench.

'The new brightness of the moulded badges', wrote Coppard, 'was something created, however trifling.'[10] Furthermore, in the despoilt world of the trenches artistically inclined soldiers were often awarded special respect: Frank Richards recalled the talents of 'Bob' an old signaller, whom he considered a 'very humorous sketcher' and cartoonist. Bob had sent a sketch to the editor of Punch and received an autographed reply complimenting him on his skill – a letter he 'prized more highly than anything he possessed'.[11]

As the war settled down to a protracted siege, soldier-artists contributed to the design of Christmas cards, programmes for boxing tournaments, menu cards, regimental crests, anything that might enliven the dullness of typeface and army-issue stationery.

Having established the range of artistic activity let us now examine the core experiences of the soldier-artist at war. We can use five key headings:

Motivation	– what made any soldier want to put pencil to paper?
Hardship	– how did artists overcome the physical difficulties of trench life?
Practicalities	– How did they physically manage to produce art?
Control	– how did they overcome the rigorous censorship laws?
Market	– What became of their work once it was done?

First, the concept of motivation. The stereotypical idea of the Western Front is of a blasted, featureless wasteland beyond any creative re-invention. Artist and cavalry officer Keith Henderson would not have

(xiv)   From the 1915 diary of a Corporal in the R.A.M.C. Bernard Eyre Walker, 26
March 1915: Ypres before the German bombardment in April. [B. Eyre Walker:
Liddle Collection]

agreed. 'I tell you', he wrote to his wife, Helen, in October 1916, 'the
"subjects" are endless, and in particular I long to do great big stretches of
this bleak brown land.'[12] The young Paul Nash, a subaltern in the
Hampshires, marvelled at the rejuvenating power of nature. In 1917, he
wrote of his astonishment at the transformation of a wood 'a most desolate and ruinous place two months back' into a riot of vivid green leafage
and nightingale song. For Nash this 'Ridiculous mad incongruity' would
be the key to his war art.[13]

   Many other soldier-artists expressed their excitement and amazement at
the spectacle of war on the Western Front, but there were perhaps five
reasons why they should want to record their sensations in pictures. First,
they may have wanted to record these sensations in a single summative
image. Many soldier-artists made just a single powerful statement about
their war, others made multiple records of the same image. Artillery soldier
E. J. Mears, for example, made at least four identical versions of a watercolour of a battered avenue. Mears was obsessed by this viewpoint which
he described as 'a picture of shattered trees crying aloud . . . against the
horror of it all, of dark, sinister pools of mud; of a troubled sky and of
insignificant little crouching figures running across a shell swept road'.[14]
Soldier-artist David Baxter painted the ruined stump of the Cloth Hall at
Ypres no fewer than 23 times – an obsession with the devastation that
borders on being psychotic.[15]

844

The second motivation may well have been commercial. By the second year of the war, the illustrated newspapers in London were desperate for fresh pictures from the front. Official pictures released by the army censor were dull and uneventful, the line drawings produced by the established illustrators smacked of inauthenticity. Unlike previous wars, the 'specials' were forbidden to enter the war zones. Illustrators such as Frederic Villiers and Sidney Begg had to concoct their images from second hand accounts, adding visual spice to their illustrations in their London studios. Villiers' drawing of a 'portable trench', and his semi-aerial panoramas of Hill 60 are typical of the fictions being created by studio-based military artists, often under the ruse that the material was 'supplied by one who was present'.[16]

By mid 1916 newspaper editors were regularly running requests, with financial inducements, for original drawings made at the front. Despite the official line on secrecy and censorship a trickle of eye-witness images began to appear in print. In early 1916, for example, The Graphic illustrated paper ran a page of drawings by an officer who signed himself JRCB. The drawings depicted a cratered no man's land, the entrance to a mine gallery, and night scenes lit by star shells. Despite their slight awkwardness and naivety, they have the authority of eye-witness incident. The slight tilt in the heads of two figures, in one drawing, tentatively peeping over the trench parapet is wonderfully observed, an important expression of the parapet as a distinct edge between safety and danger – a point that might have been lost on a studio-based illustrator working from hearsay accounts.[17]

Joseph Gray was one of the few whose art made the transition from the trenches to the printed page. Trained as a marine painter in South Shields, Gray served at the front with the 4th Black Watch and regularly sent sketches of the front to a number of the illustrated papers. Invalided out of the army he was employed during the latter part of the war as a staff artist with The Graphic. He drew and wrote with some authority even though most of his published work drew too heavily on his limited front-line experience around Neuve Chapelle (steel helmets, for example, seldom appear). But his front-line credentials were a selling point for the newspaper.[18]

If money was one motivation, our third category was its pole opposite – the illustrated letter or diary. Although it was against military rules to keep a diary, many soldiers did so. Artistically inclined soldiers may have found the idea of keeping a visual diary – a sketchbook – a safer occupation. A sketchbook gave away fewer military secrets than a diary, though to the observant eye it told just as much, perhaps more. For most artists sketchbooks offer a particular satisfaction that derives from their sequential style. They are a logbook of unfolding ideas, places and events. Turning over page after page we can follow the pictorial invention of an artist as an idea forms, modifies and mutates. Similarly a travelling artist records the changing landscape around him. A particularly fine example of this in wartime are the 156 sketchbook pages made by Geoffrey Rose, a major in the Ox. and Bucks. L.I.[19] The drawings tell the continuous story of his movements from the Messines Road sector in mid-1915 to Bourlon Wood in late 1918. Rose used his pencil drawings to chart the gradual, but inexorable, disintegration of the battlefield landscape. Possibly without realising it, Rose was invariably drawn to the same motif – avenues and lines of trees that might have suggested the pre-war patterns and sub-structure of the French woods and forests. As the war continues and the devastation spreads, so these neat avenue lines become lost in a mass of broken boughs and fallen branches. The sketches come to an end in the smashed chaos of Bourlon Wood.[20]

Besides its use as a visual *aide-memoire* the illustrated letter was the perfect fusion of content and form. Nowhere has this format been bettered than in the remarkable number of letters written and illustrated by the youngest official war artist Adrian Hill. His service in a Sniping and Scouting section of the Honourable Artillery Company prepared him remarkably well for his eventual role as an official war artist. He wrote later of his drawing patrols in No Man's Land:

> I advanced in short rushes, mostly on my hands and knees with my sketching kit dangling around my neck. As I slowly approached, the wood gradually took a more definite shape, and as I crept nearer I saw that what was hidden from our own line, now revealed itself as a cunningly contrived observation post in one of the battered trees.[21]

Other soldiers use the illustrated letter or journal as a means of lending a visual narrative to unfolding events. The war diary of Hiram Sturdy incorporates image and text in a quite remarkable fashion. Sturdy, a Scottish gunner in the Royal Artillery wrote by hand a 150 page book that tells his brutal, often cynical, story. But it is illustrated with some of the most delicate and thoughtfully designed watercolours to come out of the war.[22] One of the most interesting structural devices used in his book is the page of text and image that tells the sad story of 'George Chalk' who dies from the bullet of a German sniper. The British soldier, who is in the act of rebuilding a trench parapet, is depicted in four tiny vignettes running vertically down the page between lines of text. On the right there are four corresponding images that show 'Fritz' alerted first to movement on the other side of the page. In the second vignette he takes aim, in the third he fires across the page of No Man's Land and in the fourth 'Fritz' receives the congratulations of his fellow soldiers. In the corresponding watercolours on the left hand side George is shown flattening down a high sandbag, revealing too much of himself to the enemy sniper and finally collapsing back into the sergeant's arms. Dead. This is a clever and masterful understanding of the relationship between words and pictures. Sturdy has used the layout of the images to underpin the intensity of the narrative – he has also conveyed an interesting truth about the form of the war on the Western Front, using the width of the paper to speak for the critical distance of no man's land between the lines.

The fourth aspect in this theme of artistic motivation is the functional role of art. This might take a number of forms. Artillery officer Richard Talbot Kelly, for example, was able to send drawings back to England where his father, a professional artist, would turn them into finished oil paintings. Captain Edward Handley Read turned his skills as a landscape painter to good use as an instructor in the Machine Gun Corps. Having served at the front for six months he was commissioned to set up a studio and staff at the home of the MGC in Grantham, where he produced instructional leaflets, coloured diagrams, landscape models and other training material.

But probably the greatest functional use of art and artists was in recon-naissance and panoramic work. Ever since the establishment of the Royal Military Academy at Woolwich in 1741 drawing had been an important part of the syllabus. Artillery and Engineer cadets were trained to 'break ground' – the art of analysing and recording the tactical features of a battle-field. Although the teaching of landscape drawing had become an adjunct to map-making by the early 1900s, it was still a mandatory part of officer training at both Woolwich and Sandhurst.[23] Because of its utilitarian func-tion very few panoramas were considered worth saving and only a few remain. What do survive are the dozens of army issue and commercial sketching manuals. Typical of the official treatises is the 1912 *Manual of Map Reading and Sketching* which stressed the value of Panorama Drawing in illustrating a report while warning that:

> . . . it is better almost that the artistic sense should be absent, and that instead of idealising a landscape, it should be looked at with a cold, matter-of-fact military eye. Thus the sketcher would note rather the capabilities of the country for military purposes than its beauties of colouring or the artistic effect of light and shade.[24]

Not all soldiers turned artists wanted to reach this level of cool, diagram-matic perfection. Paul Maze worked as a liaison officer for the 5th Army and was given the freedom to roam the front making rapid sketches of the state of the battlefield. The few drawings that survive are a remarkable example of the urgency of front line life under fire. Maze seems to have known no fear, he was wounded three times and won four decorations. His drawings reflect these battle honours – they are frenetic, rather scrib-bled affairs made under extreme circumstances: indeed, one of his drawings had to remain incomplete, scribbled in hurried writing in the bottom corner is the inscription 'Could not go on through heavy shelling'.[25]

Finally on this issue of motivation: the fifth, perhaps the most important, reason why so much artistic work came out of the war in Flanders was because so many artists wanted to be there, to witness this vast event whose outcome could change the shape of the modern world. To the young, modernist avant garde the war was a rallying cry for all that they stood for. 'You must not miss a war, if one is going. You cannot afford to miss that experience' argued the leader of the Vorticists, Wyndham Lewis: warfare would wipe the slate clean, would empty the museums and smash revered reputations, it would usher in a new machine age of sleek lines and technological dynamism. Although many of these ambitions would turn sour on the young zealots in the English and Italian avant garde, there were others who sensed that war in Europe offered opportunities that no artist could miss. Painters bombarded the war office for permits and official accreditation. A visit to the bomb-shattered city of Ypres, wrote one painter, would compensate for his failure to see, and draw, the ruins of the 1910 earthquake in Messina.

Few artists won the commissions they so urgently sought. The plight of amateur painter Rowland Hill is typical. He wrote repeatedly to the government, to the Ministry of Information, and to the war museum asking to be sent to France to paint the war. His own war had been rather quiet: as a lance-corporal in the Royal Defence Corps he was considered too old to serve overseas. By April 1919 his requests had turned to pleas. He wrote asking for permission to travel to the war zones 'to make some record of our true battlegrounds, and of the immensely picturesque material before it is all "mended" and tidied up'.[26] Eventually he obtained a passport, though not a Drawing Permit, and somehow managed to make a painting of the ruins of Ypres. While the work itself may have lacked artistic worth, Hill's quest had proved worthwhile. His obituary in *The Whitby Gazette*, in 1952, rated his visit to the battlefields in 1919 as the 'one definite step . . . in his career'.[27]

These then comprise the various factors that may have motivated and inspired soldier-artists to make a pictorial record of the war. But there were also plenty of obstacles to this motivation – indeed so many that one might wonder how any art was produced at all.

II

The greatest disincentive to the creative urge was the widespread fear of spying. In Britain, the artist Sir John Lavery, working for the Department of Information, was not allowed anywhere close to his subject – the Fleet off Rosyth. His Special Joint Permit in fact disqualified him from drawing docks, harbours, munitions factories, captured ships or planes and 'any other place or thing guarded by His Majesty's Forces'. The permit did little to protect him from the police or from vigilant members of the public: 'No sooner had I got to work than I was stopped by the local police', he wrote 'and marched off to Headquarters. They thought the permit too good to be true.'[28] Fellow painter Alfred Munnings concluded after several abortive sketching trips in England that 'there came a time when an artist dare not be seen sketching out of doors in the country'.[29]

In the war zones these annoyances became major tribulations – the Fleet Street special artist Frederic Villiers had to disguise himself as a Belgian peasant to avoid the attentions of the military police. His most memorable scoop of the war – drawings of the siege battles on the Aisne – were smuggled out of the war zone stuffed into his boots.[30] On active service these problems were inevitably compounded by the rigorous censorship. The painter John Nash, an NCO in the Artists Rifles, remembered that 'drawing wouldn't have been encouraged by a commanding officer in the Line; I might have been taken for a spy.'[31] On the other hand, another member of the Artists Rifles, Private James Parkes, thrilled at escaping detection:

> I had become a keen and fairly competent sketcher in the army. It had started with military sketching as a scout, but it soon went on to filling sketch books with records of the towns and villages of Flanders, and of the trenches. As it was strictly illegal, the necessary care not to be detected added to the pleasure.[32]

and his drawings are strewn with references to his illicit activity. A drawing of Cassel is inscribed 'spotted by Military Police, got today's permit from APM', another of a farm gateway at the monastery at Mont des Cats was made, according to the inscription, from the 'security of [an] ASC limber'.[33]

Even with official clearance artists were a constant irritant to officialdom. In France all visitors – press, politicians, dignitaries and artists – came under the jurisdiction of Military Press Control, a branch of Military Intelligence, MI7. From mid 1917 to the spring of 1919 the officer entrusted with controlling the flow of official war artists to the front was Major (later Colonel) A. N. Lee, who acted as logistics, organiser and censor – a remarkably powerful post. He tended to agree with his superior, the intelligence chief General Sir John Charteris, that artists were an unruly and difficult lot, who had to be handled firmly and without special favours. According to Charteris, however, the main problem with artists was their tendency to 'want to sit down and look at a place for a long time'.[34] Tales of artists' rows and differences of opinion with Major Lee are well documented. His infamous dispute with the young modernist painter Christopher Nevinson is often cited as proof of the philistinism of military authorities. The truth is, of course, much more complex.

Having worked at the front as an ambulance orderly and as an official war artist, Nevinson was ready to exhibit the results in early 1918. He had first, though, to pass the censor. On details of fact he had to give way –

849

Nevinson had to correct the traffic flow from the left side to the right on his painting of the road from Bapaume to Arras. But on principles of interpretation he and Lee clashed immediately. Lee wanted to hold back from display Nevinson's canvas of *A Group of Soldiers* arguing that 'the type of man represented is not worthy of the British Army'. Nevinson's written reply is worth quoting in full:

> I will not paint 'castrated lancelots' though I know this is how Tommies are usually represented in illustrated papers etc. – high souled eunuchs looking mild-eyed, unable to melt butter on their tongues and mentally and physically incapable of killing a German. I refuse to insult the British army with such sentimental bilge.[35]

In his defence Lee did not cite aesthetic reasons. He argued that 'if [the picture] ever gets into German hands I will lay a shade of odds that the Germans use it against us'.[36] In this instance, however, he would lose to Nevinson. Not so with his painting, the ironically titled *Paths of Glory*. Lee's views prevailed and the picture was held back from the London show. The painter, though, as always, had the last word. Ever the showman, Nevinson displayed the canvas with a large banner of brown paper marked 'Censored' plastered across the offending images of dead infantry.

All artists were warned off drawing or painting subjects that might have some obvious strategic value, or from depicting new technological innovations or operational procedures. But painters could easily stray into controversial areas – the etcher Martin Hardie, for example, had a number of his pictures censored because they seemed to show Britain's allies in a dim light – his painting *The Bathing Corner at Boulogne* was considered to be in poor taste because it showed French troops frolicking about in an unbecoming manner, similarly his image of black troops landing at the same port was criticised by native authorities who felt it 'accentuated the Kaffir features unduly'. The picture was withheld from public show.[37]

As one might expect, there was some concern over the depiction of dead bodies. After the battle of Passchendaele there was a complete ban on the rendition of corpses, of either side. In most official war art the convention was soon understood. Gilbert Rogers, who was specially employed by the Royal Army Medical Corps, could paint dead or dying stretcher bearers if they were whole in limb, but there was no such consideration extended to the German dead. In his famous oil painting *Stretcher Bearers after the Battle of Messines*[38] the British wounded are depicted with minor injuries, they are whole in body and limb and are being looked after. By contrast, the German corpses are seen as fragments scattered to the edges of the canvas.

This takes us conveniently from the issue of censorship and official control of images onto the issue of practicalities – what were the practical problems that had to be overcome?

The most pressing requirement was how to keep paper and sketchbooks dry. Arthur Bradbury, a subaltern in the 2nd Royal Iniskillings remembered the ubiquitous mud on the Somme battlefield in 1916:

> some of the trenches were *waist* deep in liquid mud . . . I always carried a sketchbook in my pack but conditions often made sketching impossible.[39]

Cold weather brought different hazards – Paul Maze wrote in his war memoir, *A Frenchman in Khaki*, of a period in the appalling winter of 1916–1917 when it was impossible to make any art because his watercolour brush kept freezing to the paper.[40] The physical trials of handling sheets of paper or watercolour boxes in the trenches, while demanding, could be overcome by the versatile artist. As we have seen, the young Adrian Hill regularly ventured into No Man's Land with his sketching gear dangling around his neck. He also recalled making drawings with the rain pouring off his paper and gratefully using shell hole water to dilute his Indian ink washes.[41] But others though found the demands too trying. The eminent painter Philip Wilson Steer who was commissioned by the British government to paint naval subjects, laid down quite extraordinary conditions before he picked up his paintbrush. Amongst these were: 1)Shelter from the wind; 2)proximity to a lavatory; 3)shade from the sun; 4) protection from children; and 5) a suitable subject.[42]

At the front the sketchbook was the preferred format for most amateur artists – it was compact, light and easy to conceal. Lt Colonel Frank Palmer Cook, a trainee architect, carried his sketchbook 'tucked inside his tunic like a breastplate'.[43] Studying front line sketchbooks offers us a quite unique insight into the lives of trench soldiers; they combine the extraordinary intimacy of the hand-written letter with a pictorial veracity of documentary art; they also offer an idea of an individual's changing priorities. A sketchbook by Henry Russell of the London Rifle Brigade, for instance, starts with competent topographical drawings of Rouen and French Flanders, but ends with a diagrammatic drawing of an X-ray of his arm broken on the Somme in late 1916 and, on another page, a curious drawing and written explanation of his attempt to take his own life while sheltering in a shell-hole after the failed attack on Gommecourt.[44] Some artists faced with quite particular tasks had no choice but to use larger drawing paper. Paul Maze, a liaison officer working directly for General Hubert Gough south of the Somme, drew from exposed front line positions on quite large sheets of good quality French paper which were then glued together to form extended panoramas. One can only marvel at his manual dexterity in handling these huge sheets of unrolled paper in trench conditions. There was also a lighter side to his work: once while trying to reach an observation position near Mouquet Farm, Maze was carrying his paper rolled and tied with a red ribbon. As Maze struggled to get through the trenches he heard an infantryman remark 'for God's sake let him pass, it's a bloke with the Peace Treaty'.[45]

Using Eric Kennington as an opening case study this paper has weighed up the factors that motivated solder-artists on the Western Front – whether they be commercial, artistic, professional, or opportunistic. Counterbalancing these motivations we have identified various disincentives – censorship, lethargy, poor material, physical hardships, and spy-fever that could so easily have prevented any soldier-artist from working at all. Even professional painters and draughtsmen working for one of the official war art schemes faced such hardships. Like their non-commissioned colleagues they wanted, despite the difficulties, to capture the key aesthetic themes of the war on the Western Front: an obsession with the vastness of the desolation; the 'dread fascination' with the enemy-held landscape; the 'pleasure of ruins'; the spectacle and colour of night barrages; the picturesque character of the soldier-turned-cave dweller, the abstract qualities of the machinery of war. It is a complex, contradictory aesthetic superbly summarised by Wyndham Lewis:

> Those grinning skeletons in field-gray, the skull still protected by the metal helmet: those festoons of mud-caked wire, those miniature mountain-ranges of saffron earth, and trees like gibbets – these were the properties only of those titanic casts of dying and shell-shocked actors, who charged this stage with a romantic electricity.[46]

Notes

1 See M. and S. Harries, *The War Artists*, London, Michael Joseph, 1983, for a full administrative history.
2 The term 'soldier-artist' is used to define artists with some front-line experience.
3 Imperial War Museum (IWM) Department of Art no.15661.
4 *The Times*, 20 May 1916.
5 William Rothenstein, *Men and Memories*, London, Faber, 1932, Vol. II, pp. 328.
6 *The Studio*, December 1914 and August 1915.
7 William Roberts, *4.5 Howitzer Gunner RFA: The War to End All Wars*, London, Canada Press, 1974, pp. 27–28.
8 Richard Carline, *Stanley Spencer at War*, London, Faber, 1978, pp. 81.
9 Imperial War Museum (IWM) Department of Art no.2283.
10 George Coppard, *With a Machine Gun to Cambrai*, London, HMSO, pp. 28.
11 Frank Richards, *Old Soldiers Never Die*, London, Faber, 1933, pp. 220.
12 Keith Henderson, *Letters to Helen*, (October 26 1916) privately published, 1917, pp. 66.
13 Paul Nash, *Outline: An Autobiography and Other Writings*, Faber, 1949, pp. 187.
14 *The Daily News*, 7 May 1920. IWM Art Dept. nos.6023, 5855.
15 See *A Concise Catalogue of Paintings, Prints and Sculpture of the First World War*, London, IWM, 1963, pp. 11–14, 321–323.

16 *Illustrated London News*, 24 April 1915 and 4 September 1915.

17 *The Graphic*, 8 January 1916.

18 See for example 'In Action – How an Attack is Delivered', *The Graphic*, 10 June 1916; 'Between the Lines at Night', February 1917.

19 IWM Art Dept. nos.4775–4930.

20 IWM Art Dept. nos.4727, 4928.

21 *The Graphic*, 15 November 1930.

22 IWM Dept. of Documents.

23 Paul Gough, 'Military Landscape Sketching', *The Artist*, June 1993, pp. 13–15. See also 'Drawing Fire: Servicemen's Art, 1741–1994' documentary by HTV Bristol, 1995.

24 Manual of Map-Reading and Sketching, London, HMSO, 1912, pp. 75.

25 For a full account see Paul Maze, *A Frenchman in Khaki*, London, Heinemann, 1934.

26 Rowland Hill correspondence, IWM Art Dept. 156/5 part ii.

27 *Whitby Gazette*, 12 September 1952.

28 John Lavery, *Life of a Painter*, London, Cassell, 1940, pp. 145–146.

29 Alfred Munnings, *An Artist's Life*, London, Museum Press, 1950, pp. 296.

30 Frederic Villiers, *Five Decades of Adventure*, London, 1921, Vol. 2, pp. 316–318.

31 IWM, Department of Sound Records.

32 James Parkes, *Voyage of Discoveries*, London, Gollancz, 1969, pp. 52. See also Parkes' sketchbook 'The Red Book Volume 1 – April-May 1917' Liddle Collection, Leeds.

33 *ibid.*, pp. 52.

34 Charteris to Masterman, 12 March 1917, IWM Art Dept.

35 Nevinson to Masterman, 25 November 1917, IWM Art Dept.

36 Lee to Yockney, 13 December 1917, IWM Art Dept.

37 IWM Art Dept. No.939.

38 IWM Art Dept. No.2757.

39 Bradbury to Blaikley, Keeper of Art IWM, 14 January 1933, IWM Art Dept.file 150/4 part i.

40 Paul Maze, *op. cit.*, pp. 205–206.

41 *The Graphic*, 15 November 1930.

42 D. S. McColl, *Life, Work and Setting of Philip Wilson Steer*, London, Faber, 1945, pp. 118.

43 Quoted in Caroline Dakers, *The Countryside at War, 1914–1918*, London, Constable, 1987, pp. 168.

44 IWM Art Dept. Nos. 6272–6277.

45 Paul Maze, *op. cit.*, pp. 183.

46 Wyndham Lewis, *Blasting and Bombardiering*, London, Eyre and Spottiswoode, 1937, pp. 131.

Chapter 60

Painting Armageddon
Some aspects of the Apocalyptic imagination in art:
from anticipation to allegory

Jay Winter

Eschatology, the science of last things, flourished during and after the Great War. Among its most powerful and lasting forms were painting and sculpture produced by both soldiers and civilians. Through an examination of the work of a number of artists, we can appreciate the richness and diversity of the search for older forms and images by means of which enduring visions of the Great War were fashioned.

Most of these works revived facets of the nineteenth-century romantic tradition. Within the literature of art history, this finding breaks no new ground. Apocalyptic motifs have preoccupied artists of many different schools and periods.[1] But by placing these twentieth-century renderings of a set of ancient themes within the wider cultural history of the war, it may be possible to show how a number of artists drew upon and amplified other currents of cultural expression in the period following the outbreak of war in 1914.

To develop this point may prove useful in another way. It may help obliterate the outmoded distinction between elite and masses, between avant-garde and rear guard, between high-brow and middle-brow, which still bifurcates scholarship in cultural history. The art discussed in this chapter was little known at the time of its creation; its dissemination in later years was limited. But the work of Beckmann, Dix, Rouault, and Stanley Spencer was neither marginal nor esoteric; they were closer to the centre of their culture than may appear at first sight, and shared much with the peoples among whom they lived and worked. What they had in common above all was a sense that, at a time of universal mourning, their task was not to reject the sacred as a language of expression, but to recast its message. To this end, they created art which took older artistic forms about the Apocalypse and other Biblical themes and turned them to new uses.

1. Before the Apocalypse: 'Theology beyond reason'

In the two decades before the 1914–18 war, artists working in distant parts of Europe shared a surge of interest in apocalyptic themes.[2] A number of commentators have explored the question as to the prophetic character of these images.[3] It is true that in the decade or so before the outbreak of war in 1914, there was much discussion of violent upheavals to come. Apocalypticians rarely agreed among themselves, but the spectrum of calamities they used before the Great War did not extend to the one that actually occurred. However feverish their language, the Somme and Verdun were beyond their wildest dreams. What these artists left us, there-fore, was not prophecy but a visual language from which later imaginings of war were formed.

That pre-war upsurge in apocalyptic reference revived older romantic, religious and spiritualist motifs.[4] Many were drawn from unconventional sources, and in particular from theosophy. Here was a body of thought which shared some (but not all) of the premises of spiritualism. Both were havens for Victorian dissenters. On both sides of the Atlantic, throughout Europe, and in India, men and women uncomfortable with sedate Victorian religious teachings and with scientific materialism were drawn to the Theosophical Society, founded in 1875 in New York. Its leading light was Madame Helena Petrova Blavatsky, author of *Isis Unveiled* (1877) and a host of other meditations on the one eternal truth, obscured by warring churches and contemporary materialism.[5] She pointed to a clairvoyant future, the foundations for which were being laid by many enquiring minds, including some of the finest scientists of the day. One prominent exponent of this faith was Annie Besant, English freethinker and pioneer in the fight for contraception, and president of the Theosophical Society from 1907.[6] The German branch of the movement broke away in 1913 to form the Anthroposophical Society. Its guiding light was Rudolf Steiner, a prominent Goethe scholar.[7] Many theosophists were humanists; others blended elements of it with racialist ideas. Theosophy was a house of many mansions.[8]

This mixture of the occult, Eastern exoticism, and nineteenth-century romantic speculation on the sublime, drawing in particular on Schiller and Goethe, proved attractive to many artists in the prewar period. Piet Mondrian joined the Theosophical Society in 1909, after a decade of spec-ulation on theosophical themes. The composers Scriabin, Stravinsky, and Arnold Schönberg were familiar with the work of Blavatsky and Steiner. Many other artists and writers dabbled in this ecumenical movement.[9] Paul Klee emphatically denied that he was a theosophist, though much of his work shows both a familiarity with and an affinity for spiritualist ideas. 'My hand', he wrote,

> is wholly the instrument of some remote power. It is not my intellect that runs the show, but something different, something higher, and more distant – somewhere else. I must have great friends there, bright ones, but sombre ones, too.[10]

One scholar has suggested that the source of Klee's interest in theosophy in his period in Munich before the First World War was his association with Wassily Kandinsky.[11] Indeed the pre–1914 blending of Russian and German idealism and theosophy may be seen most strikingly in Kandinsky's work and reflections. Born in Moscow in 1866, and resident in Munich from 1896, he repeatedly meditated on theosophical themes, and in particular on the universal catastrophe he believed was on the way. In 1912, he wrote of the coming collapse as a cosmic vibration, a resonance (*Klang*), which would both destroy all, but would be 'a detached praise of life, like a hymn of rebirth'.[12]

Kandinsky's Russian Orthodox beliefs, to which he adhered throughout his life,[13] predisposed him to explore the mystical realm. And 'nowhere else in Europe', James Billington tells us, 'was the volume and intensity of apocalyptic literature comparable to that found in Russia' in the last decades of the Romanov dynasty.[14] Echoing strains in popular religion, this apocalypticism took on many forms before 1914. The master of modern ballet Serge Diaghilev spoke in 1905 of a coming day of judgment, a 'summing-up' prepared by artists but which would sweep them all away. 'The only wish that I, an incorrigible sensualist, can express', he added 'is that the forthcoming struggle should be as beautiful and as illuminating as the resurrection'. [15] Aleksander Blok's poetry spoke of the 'last day' and damned the city as 'a curse of the beast'. Vladimir Maiakovskii liked to wear the mantle of 'the thirteenth Apostle', the man who alone would 'come through the buildings on fire' to see the 'second tidal flood'. To him Apocalyptic images were a form of 'theology beyond reason'.[16]

Two publications show the variety of Kandinsky's artistic interests and his ongoing preoccupations with the occult world of theosophy. The first is the *Blaue Reiter Almanac*, which first appeared in 1912.[17] The second is Kandinsky's essay *Concerning the Spiritual in Art*, of 1909. His prewar work fully reflects his philosophical preoccupations, steeped in theosophy and stoked by his admiration for the simplicity and clarity of Bavarian religious folk art.[18]

A second expression of the apocalyptic temperament in art before 1914 focused on a very terrestrial environment. This time the upheaval was envisioned in an urban landscape, that of imperial Berlin. Ludwig Meidner was born in Bernstadt in Silesia in 1884. After training in the *Königliche Kunstschule* (Royal School of Art) in Breslau, and a period of study in

Paris, where he befriended the Italian artist Modigliani, he returned to Germany and to an impoverished artist's life in Berlin.[19]

Meidner was one of millions who migrated to a city which was both a provincial capital and the seat of government of a world power. Berlin was also a massively growing industrial metropolis, with big chemical and electrical enterprises. The giant Siemens firm created its own industrial city of 100,000 people in *Siemensstadt* in the suburb of Spandau. In two generations the urban landscape had been transformed.[20]

It was this landscape which, in his dreams and nightmares, Ludwig Meidner tore apart. Meidner was a polemicist who delighted in insulting other artists or distancing his work from what he called their 'shabby goods'.[21] But behind the polemics, histrionics and idiosyncrasies, Meidner's work expressed a second form of the prewar art of catastrophe. His apocalypticism drew on the international tension surrounding chronic Balkan conflicts, to be sure, but primarily it presented the coming upheaval as an urban event.

The history of landscape painting in the eighteenth century is replete with doom-ridden anti-urban figuration,[22] as is much nineteenth-century fiction, poetry and critical writing. For Meidner's generation there was another source of urban apocalypticism. He was not alone in drawing deeply from Nietzsche's writings,[23] and in particular, his Jeremiads in *Thus Spake Zarathustra* on the coming destruction of cities, where 'everything infirm, infamous, lustful, dusky, overmusty, pussy and plotting putrefies together . . . ' Zarathustra prophesies:

> Woe unto this great city! And I wish I already saw the pillar of fire in which it will be burned. For such pillars of fire must precede the great noon. But this has its own time and its own destiny.[24]

The 'pillar of fire' – in Hebrew 'Shoah' – reverts back to the original Biblical meaning of Holocaust, as a ritual purification or sacrifice.[25]

Meidner's attitude to city life was ambivalent. Though he lived in extreme poverty, his vision of urban life was not at all wholly negative. Berlin was a city he both loved and hated.[26] In one sense, his subject was the dynamism of the metropolis, 'our real homeland', its shapes, its sounds, its dangers. He celebrated the muscular newness of metropolitan life, while probing the explosive potential of such vast concentrations of people. In 1914 he wrote:

> Let's paint what is close to us, our city world! The wild streets, the elegance of iron suspension bridges, gas tanks which hang in white-clad mountains, the roaring colours of buses and express locomotives, the rushing telephone wires (aren't they like music?), the harlequinade of advertising pillars, and then night . . . big city night . . . [27]

857

This was the positive side of his outlook. Not far below the surface was a darker vision: Here he spoke of his strolls around Berlin during the heat wave of 1912:

> Sometimes when I feel a nocturnal need I venture forth into the city . . . and hustle headlong along the pavements . . . The screams of clouds echo around me, burning bushes, a distant beating of wings, and people shadowy and spitting. The moon burns against my hot temples . . . The city nears. My body crackles. The giggles of the city ignite against my skin. I hear eruptions at the base of my skull. The houses near. Their catastrophes explode from their windows, stairways silently collapse. People laugh beneath the ruins.[28]

The 'ruins' are what he painted, in strokes of feverish anticipation of chaos and the triumph of evil. Cities shelled; women raped; people trapped in a world gone mad; mutilated soldiers: these are his urban citizens. In 1920 he recalled the stiflingly hot summer eight years before, when he began painting this cycle of apocalyptic visions. 'My brain bled dreadful visions. I could see nothing but a thousand skeletons jigging in a row. Many graves and burnt cities writhed across the plains'.[29]

> I unloaded my obsessions onto canvas day and night – Judgment days, world's ends, and gibbets of skulls, for in those days the great universal storm was already baring its teeth and casting its glaring yellow shadow across my whimpering brush-hand.[30]

This sense of art as anticipation is more flattering to the artist than it need be. An examination of Meidner's apocalyptic painting leads to an alternative reading. In these works he was responding to urban upheaval and violence invading the cities, both well-worn nineteenth-century themes expressing middle-class fears of crime, revolution, 'degeneration' and rapid urban development.[31] Prewar painting captured this older mood, deeply imprinted in nineteenth-century cultural life. Meidner was aware of visions of international tensions. But his war did not anticipate the Great War; he materialises fears of urban chaos which were the commonplace of late-Victorian pessimism.[32] For decades the Cassandras had spoken of the explosive social mixture in these new urban worlds. Berlin was teeming with tenements, or human barracks – *Mietkasernen* in German.[33] Meidner lived among them, in the belly of the whale. Here is a neglected source of his apocalyptic visions, one remote from the battlefields soon to engulf the European continent.[34]

Instead of perpetuating the romantic myth of the artist as 'Seer', so dear to Kandinsky and so many of his contemporaries,[35] and proclaiming his work and that of Meidner as intimations of the Great War, historians would be better advised to recognize that the environment of domestic political conflict, and in particular class conflict, was sufficiently over-heated to supply these artists with more than enough ominous material for their eschatological explorations. That material was there on the streets of Berlin, for anyone with eyes to see it.[36]

Equally it would be a mistake to reduce Meidner's art (or Kandinsky's) to a mere reflection of political tensions. Much more was involved than that. I have shown two forms of prewar apocalyptic art. On the one hand, there were the cosmic speculations of Kandinsky and his excursions into theosophy. On the other hand, Ludwig Meidner drew visions from the daily realities of urban dynamism and political tensions. Both created a visual grammar for those who, after the outbreak of war in 1914, brooded on the future and put their minds to the task of imagining the Apocalypse.

2. Apocalyptic images: from anticipation to allegory

It is not my intention to provide a broad or representative survey of wartime art or of postwar visual meditations on trench warfare.[37] Nor is it possible to offer more than a glimpse of the vast range of religious refer-ence in the art of all combatant countries.[38] My purpose is more modest: it is simply to demonstrate the gap which separates the prewar apocalyptic tradition in painting from a number of later explorations of the genre.

The outbreak of war abruptly ended one phase of apocalyptic art, the art of anticipation. Instead, apocalyptic motifs became the core of a series of visual allegories about war. The use of allegory, a device of indirection, of the interposition of a narrative form between artists and audience,[39] was important for many artists after 1914. Allegory was there for those unwilling or unable to resort to abstract or realistic descriptive techniques in their approach to imagining the war. For sources of such allegorical art, many painters turned back to the old masters, and in particular the art of the sixteenth century. The shadows of Holbein and Grünewald, among others, fell over this work, and provide another link between old and new in the complex attempts made after 1914 to imagine the catastrophe of war.

A. Otto Dix, the trenches and the Flood

When it came, the Apocalypse was neither urban nor cosmic. The war experienced by soldiers and imagined by those in and out of uniform after 1914 was located in a different kind of landscape from that envisioned by Kandinsky or Meidner. The scene of war was essentially rural, but with such marks of carnage and devastation as to resemble a desert covered in mud, twisted metal and putrefaction. Above all, it was an infernal land-scape. The German artist Otto Dix put it this way: 'Lice, rats, barbed wire, fleas, shells, bombs, underground caves, corpses, blood, liquor, mice, cats, artillery, filth, bullets, mortars, fire, steel: that is what war is. It is the work of the devil'.[40]

No one could capture directly what the war was really like; those who tried usually trivialised the subject. 'What we soldiers have experienced out here in the past few months', wrote Franz Marc in early 1915, 'is beyond belief'.[41] War, he told his mother, 'is more frightful than I could ever have dreamed'.[42] He was dead ten months later, killed on horseback near Verdun. Instead of resorting to the visual clichés of propaganda, so remote from the soldier's war, or adopting the naive approach of *imagerie d'Epinal*, a number of artists both during and after the conflict chose the language of allegory to express their amazement and their horror about the war.

Dix is the first of the apocalypticians in uniform to be discussed in this chapter. In 1914 he was a 24-year-old art student in Dresden.[43] His early work on 'Night in the city' and 'Sunrise 1913' show both his formal affinities with the strong lines of Van Gogh, whose work was exhibited in Dresden in 1912, and with Meidner's (and the Futurists') fascination with urban landscapes.[44] We see here too evidence of Dix's engagement with the writings of Nietzsche, whose head he sculpted in plaster in 1912, and whose shadow was cast over so much of the art of the first decades of the twentieth century.[45]

A number of Dix's drawings and paintings at this time express a set of interests which would preoccupy him in later years. He explored religious symbols in 'The Nun' (1914), mythical themes in 'Dying Warrior' (1913), and outcast sexuality in 'The Prostitute' (1913). Although never a conventionally religious man, he was thoroughly conversant with the Bible, and was drawn to deviants as those who were, in a way, closer to God than were conventional people.[46]

Dix volunteered in 1914. He shared the naive view of many young soldiers that the war would bring them into contact with a range of 'tremendous' experiences inaccessible in civilian life.[47] It is said that he carried in his soldier's pack both the Bible and Nietzsche,[48] and his self-portrait in 1914, as a bald warrior, attests to his embrace of the excitement of the war in its early phase.[49]

In another 1914 painting, 'Self-portrait as Mars', Dix's taste for allegory can be seen. Here the collage of shapes, colours and animal forms recalls prewar apocalyptic images. Only this time, the Apocalypse suggests older motifs; after 1914, in a sense, classical mythology, mediated by Nietzsche, had come alive. In his later drawings from the Front, Dix followed this mythical perspective, so powerfully captured by another Nietzschean in uniform, Ernst Jünger.[50]

Many of his wartime drawings sketch the uncanny, surreal landscape of the trenches. Many were drawn on the back of postcards sent back to a friend in Dresden, Helene Jakob. Partly to counteract boredom, Dix tried to fix in his mind some of the images of the four years he spent in uniform, as an artilleryman and machine-gunner in Champagne, on the Somme, and in Russia. But underlying this descriptive approach was the beginning of a revulsion about the war which became more pronounced after the Armistice. Like Jeremiah, he wrote in his diary at the Somme front, 'Cursed be the day on which I was born; the day on which my mother gave birth must have been unblessed'.[51] Later it was this darker side of apocalyptic art which Dix would make his own, but during the war he still retained some elements of prewar apocalypticism. Witness his painting 'Awakening' (1918), which mixes forms, colours and horses in a manner reminiscent of Kandinsky and Marc's prewar work.[52]

How different in style and content were his postwar meditations on trench warfare. From the early 1920s, Dix dropped any element of celebration of the warrior or neutrality about the nobility of his calling. Back in Dresden in 1920, he painted grotesque images of prostitutes and German soldiers, for instance in his 'Memories of the mirrored rooms in Brussels' and mutilated veterans on 'Prager Strasse' and in 'Skat players'. In Düsseldorf in 1923, he painted 'The Trench', the first of a series of epic works which borrowed heavily from Grünewald and German Renaissance art.[53]

In the following year, Dix created a cycle of 50 etchings, simply entitled 'Der Krieg'. They are among the most searing works on war in any artistic tradition. To depict the dehumanization of soldiers in war, Dix went back to photographs of the devastation of the trenches. We know of his interest in Goya in this period,[54] but there is also much here to indicate his growing exploration of the hideous images of Grünewald and Cranach.

These etchings were completed in the same year that a pacifist activist, Ernst Friedrich, published a two-volume set of photographs of mutilated bodies, hanging prisoners-of-war, and disfigured veterans. *War against War!* is almost unbearable to look at, and that may have limited the impact of the photographs displayed in his 'Anti-Kriegsmuseum' in Berlin.[55]

It was Dix who showed how to capture the infernal character of the Great War, for in this task, allegory was far more powerful than photographic realism. Allegory was a form Dix explored in many other paintings,[56] but for our purposes there are two which firmly establish the character of his postwar apocalypticism.

The first is the triptych with predella he painted in 1932 entitled 'War'; the second is entitled 'Flanders' (after Henri Barbusse's *Under Fire*), painted four years later in 1936. The triptych's left panel shows a column of marching soldiers.

Initially accompanied by a dog in an early sketch, these men pass a wheel in the final version. The central panel is dominated by an impaled figure, suspended on a tree above the battle, a dead man whose hand points to the carnage below. The echoes of Grünewald's Isenheim altarpiece in Dix's early drawings are unmistakable, especially in the pock-marked legs of one soldier buried upside down in the mud. In the right-hand panel, one soldier (with Dix's own features)[57] is dragging a wounded comrade from the trench; another is crawling away alone. As if to parallel the left-hand panel, these human, dignified responses of ordinary soldiers in an inhuman, undignified landscape, bracket the Crucifixion in the centre. A similar counterpoint is in the predella, where soldiers hang their food from the ceiling to keep the rats from devouring it. Their living quarters are surrounded by skulls and bones, buried in the walls of the trench system itself. In form, the predella recalls the bleak horizontal lines of Holbein's 'Christ in the Tomb' of 1521.

The religious iconography is clear: from the road to Calvary, to Crucifixion, to Descent from the Cross, to entombment. But the presence of images of decency does not imply the presence of God or salvation. Indeed, the reference to Holbein's extraordinary painting of 'Christ in the Tomb' is (from a Christian point of view) unnerving. In Holbein's master-piece, an entirely realistic Christ is laid out in the tomb in such a way as to suggest that though the Crucifixion has happened, that is the end of the story. There is no sign whatsoever of the Resurrection. The sheer horizontality of Holbein's composition challenges conventional Christian faith. As in the comparable case of post-1918 war memorials, it is clear that pure horizontality is too austere for most artists, wishing to provide a message of hope. It was not for them to dwell on the religious doubts that Holbein's painting created in the mind of Dostoyevsky's Prince Mishkin.[58] Dix's painting goes further. Human decency is affirmed, but faith in God is absent.

The retention of a humanist faith, and its expression in allegory, is even more directly evident in Dix's painting of 1936, entitled 'Flanders'. The subject is a celebrated scene in Henri Barbusse's novel *Under Fire*. Barbusse ended his novel allegorically, through the depiction of a modern version of the legend of the Flood. This scene describes the moment when soldiers from both sides awake from a night of infernal rain. Mud-encrusted soldiers become part of the landscape, growing out of trees and branches as if inhabiting one of Dante's *bolgias*. The sign of the crown of thorns is visible in the centre of the painting. But resurrection is near. Soldiers awaken from the infernal night, and in Barbusse's book, they rise to cry out against war as an abomination which must never happen again.[59] Thus the hopeful 'dawn' of Barbusse's *Under Fire*, published in 1916 and available in German in 1918, is present in Dix's painting, through a golden, though cloud-covered sunrise on the left and a blue sky, with the setting moon clearly visible on the right of the painting.

Barbusse had written an introduction to a book promoting Dix's 1924 cycle of etchings on the war.[60] The prominence of Barbusse in left-wing veterans' politics meant that anything to do with his work would be anathema to the Nazis. Dix's painting of 1936 is an act of defiance.

For our purposes, what is most important is that the allegory he has chosen is Noah and the Flood, a Biblical landscape in which those like Dix and Barbusse, who had been through the worst of war as enemies, cry out together against its repetition. Here the Apocalypse is reconfigured as an allegory of hope, just as Barbusse had intended 20 years before. Seven years later, in the midst of the Second World War, Dix painted his first 'Resurrection', once more returning to the German Renaissance, and to Grunewald's final, luminous vision of eternal glory.[61]

B. Beckmann's Resurrection

After the outbreak of the Great War, there are striking similarities between the apocalyptic art of Dix and that of his German contemporary Max Beckmann. Beckmann was 30 in 1914, six years older than Dix, and already an established artist in Berlin. He was a recognized member of the Berlin Secession, with powerful works to his credit, like 'The destruction of Messina' (1909) and 'The sinking of the Titanic' (1912).[62]

Like Dix, Beckmann initially supported the German war effort, though his reactions captured the turbulence of the period and the complexity of emotions stirred by these disturbing days. Witness the drypoint print entitled 'Declaration of War 1914'. It shows a group of people in Berlin trying to get a glimpse of a newspaper with the latest war news. Their faces show a range of reactions, from shock to concern to apparent detachment.[63]

Beckmann also volunteered, though exempted from military service in 1903 on medical grounds. Beckmann (like Dix) carried Nietzsche in his military gear. Like Dix, he saw the human wreckage of battle, this time in East Prussia in 1914 and near Ypres in Belgium in 1915, when gas warfare began. Unlike Dix, Beckmann saw no combat, but served as a hospital orderly, regularly attending to men with gruesome wounds and caring for them after they were operated on.[64]

Beckmann too saw on the Western front a landscape which gave the word 'fantastic' a new and heightened meaning. He passed 'strangely unreal cities like lunar mountains', cities of the dead, both the newly-massacred and the long-since buried, hurled into the air time and again like a mockery of the Resurrection.[65] He described one scene to his first wife Minna:

> Yesterday we came through a cemetery which was completely ruined by grenade fire. The tombs were ripped open, and the coffins lay around in uncomfortable positions. The indiscreet grenades had exposed the ladies and gentlemen to the light – bones, hair, clothing peeked out from the coffins.[66]

And it was the Resurrection among other religious motifs which he painted in 1916–18, after a breakdown occasioned by the strain of work as a medical orderly led to his being invalided out of the army.

In his wartime work, Beckmann developed a style both romantic and ironic, disclosed by his jibe to a friend that instead of serving in Belgium, he wished he could read Jean Paul on Mars.[67] Here Beckmann is referring to the author of dream visions, including 'Speech of the Dead Christ'.[68] Irony and bitterness had replaced the artist's curiosity in his approach to the war. Now the 'inexpressible absurdity of life', its character as a 'paradoxical joke' bore heavily on him.[69] By mid-1915, he likened torn-up streets to the scene of the Day of Judgment; he repeatedly dreamed of the 'destruction of the world'. 'Everything is foundering', he told his wife, 'and I keep thinking only of how I will paint the head of the resurrected one against the red stars in the sky of the Final Judgment'.[70] In 1916 he wrote a friend, 'if you cannot find a way out of this mess you are the biggest fool in the world'.[71] There were millions of such fools, whose madness at war Beckmann approached through the apocalyptic vision 'Resurrection'.

Beckmann's 'Resurrection' bears little resemblance to the work of the *Blaue Reiter* school.[72] Before the war, Beckmann had distanced himself from Marc and Kandinsky's apocalypticism, describing it acidly as empty mysticism.[73] And Beckmann quickly turned his back on those who felt gratitude for the war as a purifying force. On 26 September 1914 (as it happened, the day his fellow painter August Macke was killed), Franz Marc asked Kandinsky the rhetorical question: 'is there a single man who wishes the war had never occurred?'[74] There were many such men; after an initial period of reflection, Beckmann was one of them.

By the end of the war, Beckmann was even more emphatic in what kind of spiritual art he rejected and what kind he intended to create.

> Through four long years now we have gazed into the grimace of horror. Perhaps some of us have, thereby, gained a deeper understanding. We have got rid of much which was taken for granted. From a thoughtless imitation of the visible, from a weak archaism of empty decoration and from a falsely sentimental mysticism we may now proceed to a transcendental objective . . .

Among the guides he sought out to help him in this new enterprise, this attempt to build 'a new church' in which men could 'cry out their fury and despair, all their poor optimism, joy and wild longings' were Grünewald, Breughel, Cézanne and Van Gogh.[75]

Dominating the unfinished 'Resurrection' of 1916 are an exploding sun and a dark moon on the horizon. Houses are ripped open. In one of them, Beckmann, his wife, his son and friends are standing passively, gazing at a corpse hovering nearby. Above them is a recently revived figure, facing away from the viewer, head bowed and apparently still rubbing his eyes. Complex groups of people stand awaiting judgment to the left and right of this central section.[76]

Beckmann had addressed this theme in his oil painting 'Resurrection' of 1909, but in an entirely orderly and conventional manner. His wartime study is in another realm entirely. What sets apart the later painting was its enrichment by his experience of the chaos of war and by the studies he made of the wounded soldiers he cared for and of those beyond help. His resurrected men are his wartime companions, emerging from the long night of war into an uncertain day, lit by a dying sun.

Beckmann's wartime 'Resurrection' is emphatically non-triumphal. Its theme suggests hope, but in both the unfinished painting and in a drypoint sketch of 1918, that hope is literally disembodied. This detached point of view may point towards Beckmann's struggle with the problem of theodicy. As the writer Sarah O'Brien-Twohig has observed:

> Unable to reconcile the idea of a loving, benign God with the appalling suffering he witnessed as a voluntary medical orderly, he was 'filled with rage at God for having made us so we cannot love each other'. To find an explanation for such evil he turned to the mystical doctrines of Gnosticism, Buddhism and the Cabbala, and to the pessimistic philosophy of Schopenhauer.[77]

The Gnostic idea that 'the world was created by an evil demiurge as a prison for souls which must struggle to return to their original state in the realm of Good or Light beyond material creation'[78] has always been heretical within the Christian tradition. Beckmann's reference to the Resurrection in this painting is therefore a questioning of conventional beliefs through the exploration of the conventional setting of the Apocalypse. This gnostic pessimism, this sense of despair over the ugliness of the war and the suffering it entailed, marked this phase of Beckmann's art, created in the wake of his breakdown in Flanders in 1915. It is this brooding melancholy, this *soleil noir* (in Julia Kristeva's phrase),[79] which dominates Beckmann's 'Resurrection' of 1916–18.

Beckmann claimed that he was totally uninterested in politics.[80] And though he created lasting monuments to the violence accompanying the German revolution of 1919 in his masterpiece 'The Night' and in other works,[81] it is in the non-political realm that we should locate his apocalyptic painting.

After the war some saw links between Beckmann's visions of war and the anti-war writings of Henri Barbusse. I have already noted the same parallel with reference to Otto Dix's war painting.[82] The critic Eduard Bendemann wrote in the *Frankfurter Zeitung* on 7 June 1919 that Beckmann's graphic works were 'perhaps the only images with which the pictorial arts might compete with Henri Barbusse's representation of the war: they even seem like illustrations to Barbusse's book'.[83] A more critical line was taken by Paul Westheim, editor of the radical journal *Das Kunstblatt*. In 1923 he accused Beckmann of a lingering romanticism, in which radical political change mattered less than the exploration of mythical themes.[84] Both Bendemann and Westheim were right. Beckmann's apocalyptic works share the revulsion of Barbusse as to the waste, the suffering, the pointlessness of the war. But the cold, exploding sun of Beckmann's 'Resurrection' is not that of the Biblical dawn and the new covenant Barbusse and other political activists announced. Beckmann's is a harsher, more pessimistic, vision, brooding on the disaster rather than on the better days to come.

C. *English Apocalypse: Stanley Spencer of Cookham*

It would be a mistake to believe that the apocalyptic temperament was (or is) exclusively German. While it is true that many German artists meditated on the end of days in this period, other artists in Britain and France, with very different points of view, joined them in this search for a visual language appropriate to a catastrophe on the scale of the Great War. One such artist was Stanley Spencer. Born and raised in the Berkshire village of Cookham, Spencer studied at the Slade School of Art, exhibited in Roger Fry's second post-impressionist exhibition in 1912, and in 1915, at the age of 24, joined the Royal Army Medical Corps.

He was part of the British Army that never got into war literature: the men who also served, as orderlies, porters, cleaners, launderers, and the like. No glory here. Spencer, like thousands of other forgotten men, inhabited the vast underbelly of the British Army, and did so in very unheroic settings. The first was Beaufort War Hospital in Bristol, where the sick and wounded were cared for alongside civilian lunatics. The second was Macedonia, where he was attached to the 7th Royal Berkshire Regiment, a unit that had turned him down as physically unfit (too small) when he had tried to enlist in 1914.

After demobilization, Spencer returned to Cookham, and to religious art, but of a very unconventional kind. His was a spiritualism with marked similarities to that of Blake, albeit on a less powerful and certainly less beautiful plane. Nevertheless, Spencer followed Blake into the figurative world of the everydayness and the normality of the spiritual life. The war did not create this interest; it gave him the material and memories to extend it in striking ways.

Spencer spent the early postwar years on many different projects, but among the most important was a series of paintings on the passion of Christ, begun in 1920 and continued intermittently throughout his life. These paintings show how Spencer's prewar fascination with both the pre-Raphaelites and with Gauguin's rounded portraits developed after the war. The painting of Christ carrying the Cross (now in the Tate Gallery) was executed in 1921 while Spencer was living at Sir Henry Slessor's home in Bourne End, near Cookham. In this work, the obscurity of the Christ figure, masked and hidden by the local people of Cookham, echoes Breughel's compositions, and shares a positively Flemish taste for the particularism of local settings.[85] Between 1924 and 1926, Spencer worked on a 'Resurrection', located in Cookham churchyard. In the centre, at the entrance to the church, is a seated figure, carrying a book, whose form anticipates the Christ of his 'Resurrection of Soldiers', designed in the early 1920s and executed at Burghclere between 1928 and 1932.

This cycle of frescoes realized in a specially constructed chapel in Burghclere, near Newbury in Berkshire, is more original than any of these previous works. Spencer's benefactors, Mr and Mrs J. L. Behrend, gave him the chance to realize his vision, and then dedicated the chapel to the memory of Mrs Behrend's brother, who had died of illness contracted while on military service in Macedonia during the Great War.[86]

Again, the traditional character of the project is clear. The form of the enterprise recalls Giotto's frescoes in the Arena Chapel in Padua, or more likely, John Ruskin's description of them. But both in its evocation of the entirely ordinary and unheroic world of military life, at home and abroad, and in its treatment of the Resurrection, Spencer's work is unique in war art. A series of side panels takes us through scenes of Spencer's war, from the drab and dreary corridors of Beaufort Military Hospital, to the brown and dusty hillsides of Macedonia. In these paintings, nobody fights, no one kills, no one dies. There are some wounded men portrayed, one being painted with iodine, and one whose apparently frostbitten legs we see protected from contact with his sheets. But there is no pain in them. Nor is there any joy in the faces of the soldiers carrying on their mundane lives. It is as if they are all in a trance, stuck in a dreamworld of onerous tasks, avoided where possible, or simply endured. There is only one officer, sitting astride a blanket which only after careful scrutiny we discover is actually covering a horse. He is either trying to teach his men map-reading or simply telling them where they are. In either case, none of his men appears to take the slightest interest. In its unromantic, unmilitary, unofficered normality, Spencer's war memorial is like no other in Britain or (to the best of my knowledge) on the Continent.[87]

The most remarkable feature of Spencer's chapel is the central panel portraying the Resurrection. Just as in his painting of Christ carrying the Cross, here the Saviour is hard to find. He is near the top of the wall above the altar, seated, receiving from a group of risen soldiers the crosses which presumably marked their graves. This Christ resembles, though in complex ways, the seated figure in the earlier 'Resurrection at Cookham'. The centre of the Burghclere work is dominated by two horses, fallen down, craning their necks around to see why the cart they had carried had collapsed. Above them and below the Christ is a young soldier, staring at the wooden crucifix on his cross, seemingly oblivious of the risen Christ by his side.

All this takes place on a Macedonian hillside, where animals graze, soldiers sleep, rise from their graves in fur jackets, polish epaulets, unwind their puttees, cut the wire fallen on another soldier's head and body, and generally go about their business. As Spencer later recalled, the painting is

Resurrection as Armistice, when soldiers rise and hand in their crosses as they would hand in their guns when the need for them ended.[88] There are soldierly handshakes in one corner of the painting, but absolutely no joy.[89]

Most of the men in Spencer's frescoes share the same dark features, rounded heads and stubby figures. Either in menial tasks or in military routine, their bearing and manner have none of the marks of the cubist features of Nevinson's war art or of the individual portraiture of Muirhead Bone. Spencer evidently chose his own way, remote from both the avant-garde and the rearguard of British art, in the exploration of spiritual realities.

The image of the rising of the dead of the Great War which graces the Burghclere war memorial fresco was in no sense simply a reflection of Spencer's eccentric religiosity. He spoke a spiritual language many contemporaries used and adapted to their particular circumstances. Protestant iconography in England was more restrained than the reservoir of German Renaissance painting from which Dix and Beckmann drew their inspiration, but both Blake and the pre-Raphaelites provided ample artistic material for Spencer. When he came to paint his frescoes at Burghclere between 1928 and 1932, he testified both to the robustness of the English mystical tradition and to the capacity of the apocalyptic temperament to see transcendence even in the carnage of war. None of this needed the war to establish it; it was all there for those like Stanley Spencer who believed in the incontrovertible imminence of the spiritual life,[90] and who maintained that belief in the decades following 1914–18.

D.   Rouault and resistance to the apocalyptic temptation

Allegorical imagery has played a central role in Catholic devotion, and in the work of the French painter Georges Rouault there are many examples of the art of allegory as a means of placing the disaster of the Great War in a transcendental and religious framework. But here the use of allegory departs from that of Dix, Beckmann and many other painters. For Rouault allegory serves the purpose of affirming, rather than questioning, denying or transforming, the central tenets of Christian faith.

We can understand much about the temptation to succumb to nihilism, to give in to despair about human nature in the shadow of the Great War, to renounce religious beliefs, conventional or otherwise, by introducing the work of a man who refused to do so. The apocalyptic imagination speaks in a language halfway between hope and despair. And while despair was never far from the work of Georges Rouault, it is the hope, indeed the certainty, of mercy and salvation, which places his painting outside the Apocalyptic tradition.

In this sense, Rouault's art was conservative. He placed his trust in the Resurrection and not in the Apocalypse, in the risen Christ, and not directly in the transformation of this world. Among writers, socialists like Henri

Barbusse nurtured a different kind of apocalyptic hope, one far removed from the way of the Cross imagined by Rouault. Both saw meaning in the suffering of the war, but understood it in very different ways.[91]

The struggle to express Catholic hope in art is evident in much of Rouault's painting, and in particular in his war cycle, 'Miserere', painted from 1916 to 1928, and exhibited and published only after the Second World War.[92] Completed just before Spencer and Dix began their work on the Burghclere Chapel and the War Triptych, this set of meditations on war and suffering takes as its text the first verse of the 51st Psalm: 'Have mercy upon me, O God, according to thy loving-kindness'.

The aim of this work is, therefore, acceptance of the will of God. It provides a form of aesthetic redemption which fulfils the function of 'religious discourse' described by Julia Kristeva in *Black Sun*. She holds that, alongside 'aesthetic and particularly literary creation',

> religious discourse in its imaginary fictional essence, set[s] forth a device whose prosodic economy, interaction of characters, and implicit symbolism constitute a very faithful semiological representation of the subject's battle with symbolic collapse.

These symbols themselves are resurrected through art, and retain a power for healing, the effectiveness of which, in her view, lies in their being 'closer to catharsis than to elaboration'.[93] It was Rouault's aim in 'Miserere' to resurrect through art the symbolic universe of Catholicism, and thereby help heal the wounds of the Great War.

Born in war-torn Paris, on 27 May 1871, the day before the last resistance of the Paris Commune was snuffed out among the tombstones of the cemetery of Père Lachaise, Rouault was too infirm for military service in 1914. Already a celebrated painter, a pupil of Gustave Moreau alongside Matisse, and a fellow 'Fauve',[94] Rouault was a fervent Catholic, who came to his mature beliefs after the turn of the century. He had attended Protestant schools as a child, but after an early apprenticeship in a stained-glass workshop, Rouault developed a life-long affinity for the anonymous popular art of the medieval cathedrals. After the death of his teacher Moreau, he went through a personal crisis, from which he emerged a profoundly religious man, no longer weighed down by a conflict between his art and his religion.[95]

In part his convictions were formed through his association with the novelist Léon Bloy, who celebrated medieval piety and castigated the vulgar art of the modern secular world.[96] As one of his characters affirms in his novel *La femme pauvre*, 'If art does not go on its knees . . . it must necessarily go on its back or its belly'.[97] Rouault's search for Christ in his work was unmistakable, but the earthiness of his paintings of prostitutes and criminals went too far for Bloy. In 1907, he wrote to Rouault, that he was 'a lost friend . . . if you were a man of prayer, a eucharist, an obedient soul, you could not paint these horrible canvasses'.[98] Their association survived this rift, and the social vision and compassion of Bloy's Catholicism remained important for Rouault.[99]

Bloy died in 1917. By then Rouault had embarked on a project in religious art unparalleled in his generation. When war broke out, Rouault's heart went out to the people of France, to their 'resignation', their faith.[100] Through the sponsorship of the art-dealer and publisher Ambroise Vollard, he was able to embark three years later on an Herculean task: the creation of 100 etchings to illustrate a book, in either one or two volumes, on the sufferings of the war. The project took ten years to complete. In the end it constituted 'only' 58 etchings, published in 1948 after years of litigation between Rouault and Vollard's family.[101]

The working title of the book initially was 'Guerre et Miserere', and then reduced by Rouault to 'Miserere', both out of preference for the Latin and out of a belief that the single word suited the design of the first print.[102] As a whole, it is a war memorial of a kind not produced before or since. As one Catholic writer, Abbé Morel, put it:

> This was precisely the time when every town in France was commissioning stone, marble, or bronze monuments to the memory of the victims of the recent slaughter. Many such monuments were erected on the roads of France and the rest of Europe. But I know none other that attains, not the immensity, but the grandeur, the inwardness, and thus the effectiveness and spiritual power achieved by Rouault in this work.

Following Goya, Rouault had found a way

> to participate in the battle by rebuilding what the battle had destroyed in man. And there were a lot of things to fight against, as the war left great ruins in its aftermath – illusions, spiritual blindness, and despair.[103]

This was a war memorial that no one saw, until after two decades of wrangling over property rights. Essentially, it constituted a materialized prayer, a 'sort of last communion', in Abbé Morel's words, first drawn, then photographed onto copper, then painstakingly etched, then produced in the simplicity of black and white prints.[104]

'Miserere' has no clear-cut sequence or division into narrative sections. The first print looks like the frontispiece of a book. Christ's bowed head is below an angel. The same profile of Christ's submission appears in the second and third prints, but thereafter, Rouault presents the wretched of the earth: the vagabond (4), the outcast (5, 11), the prostitute (14, 15), the condemned (18). The 27th print introduces a non-Christian element, that of Orpheus searching hell for Eurydice. Thereafter, at approximately the mid-point of the cycle, the presence of death and the hope of Resurrection become more prevalent. The 28th print is of skulls in a charnel house, awaiting Resurrection, prefigured in the 29th print, entitled 'Sing Matins, a new day is born'. The 31st print (with the legend 'That ye love one another') is of Christ on the Cross. It is followed (32) by an image of Emmaus, of the proof of Christ's victory over death, registered as well in the face on Veronica's veil (33).

It is at this point that Rouault turned explicitly to the theme of war. The same bookish frame of the first print 'Miserere' appears in the 34th, entitled 'Guerre'. Here the bowed head of the dead soldier replaces the Christ of the first print, now suspended above the fallen man. The soldier's way of the cross begins with a son in uniform embracing his father, with the hollow words of reassurance, 'this will be the last time', as death awaits his departure. 'Homo homini lupus' (37), death with a soldier's cap, is followed by images of civilian culpability: a Chinaman as inventor of gunpowder (38); smiling civilians, captioned 'Nous sommes fous' (39); war factories (44). Anxious women (41–3) await the worst. In print 46, angels lift a fallen soldier. The caption reads: 'The just, like sandalwood, perfume the axe that strikes them'. He awaits burial in the next two prints (47–8).

Here the obvious development is towards Resurrection, but instead Rouault breaks the sequence, and turns to stylized images of the war: a stiff-necked Kaiser Wilhelm (49), a stoical France (50), the Archbishop of Reims (51), the long-suffering 'poilu' (52), and 'The Virgin of seven swords' (53), possibly the mourning mothers of France.

The 54th print is of a wartime legend, 'Debout les morts'. It shows death calling forth fallen soldiers to carry on the battle, a theme popularized by many Catholic writers in wartime, including Léon Bloy.[105] Rouault's print is entirely unsympathetic to Bloy's celebration of a trench miracle. Indeed, this sentiment of bellicose Catholicism, celebrated by Barrès and a host of lesser writers, is described as a travesty of the Resurrection, a misuse of Catholic faith for patriotic purposes.

The series ends with Christ on the Cross, 'obedient until death' (57), and with the injunction (58) taken from Isaiah 53.5 that it is 'through his stripes that we are healed'. Healing is the last word of the cycle, and the one word which captures its aim and direction.

One observer likened these prints, in their message about 'Miserere' and 'Guerre', to 'the arched doorway of a Cathedral', a 'dual entrance' to the House of God.[106] To another, the original engravings produced a book 'whose weight is over twenty-one kilogrammes' and which 'resembles a tombstone'.[107] Both have captured Rouault's intent. He sought and found a visual language of mourning, in part after the death of his own father in 1912,[108] in part in the aftermath of the death of his spiritual mentor Léon Bloy in 1917, and in part after the death of over one million Frenchmen in the First World War.

Rouault's art encapsulates a visual language of mourning, one which stops short of the mystical or the apocalyptic. There are no inscriptions taken from the Book of Revelation, from Daniel or Ezekiel, the traditional sources of apocalyptic art. His was not a theology of impatience, but of resignation. His art was intended to heal, but only through the one true hope: submission to the will of the Lord and an abiding faith in the truth of the Resurrection. 'You talk of [my] fervour', he replied to one observer of his work. 'Yes, it is my only possession, like the women at the sepulchre, I wait with continuing love the Resurrection'.[109]

E.   Visions of war, the sacred, and the language of healing
Apocalypticians can't wait. They see the end of time rushing towards them. Before the war, some of their visions, and the beliefs embedded in them, were hopeful. Following the crash would come rebirth and renewal. After 1914, the art of anticipation turned to allegory, the allegory of catastrophic disaster.

In the wake of the Great War, apocalyptic art took on new forms, appropriate to an age of mass bereavement. The artists who explored this terrain sought inspiration from a variety of spiritual sources, from the Bible, theosophy and the occult, and from the work of Blake, Goya, Grünewald and Holbein, in the effort to imagine the war and its human costs.

Rouault, it is true, was one who stopped short of the apocalyptic tradition. At times he came close to it, but ultimately stayed within the borders of the Church. He clung to faith in the Resurrection, and not in the Apocalypse.[110] His case is a useful one to describe the boundary conditions of what is as much a temperamental as a theological position.

And yet even across the yawning gap of doctrinal orthodoxy, these artists spoke a common language. After 1914, most sought in the Biblical tradition a range of signs and symbols through which to imagine the war and the loss of life entailed in it. The art they produced was intended to help heal, perhaps in precisely the way Kristeva has suggested, through 'catharsis', not 'elaboration'. Here is one essential point where the sacred returned in the period of the Great War: as a vocabulary of mourning, and as a code through which artists expressed in enduring ways the enormity of the war and the suffering left in its wake.

Notes
1   For a classic survey, see Montague Rhodes James's Schweich lectures of the British Academy for 1927, *The Apocalypse in Art* (London, Oxford University Press, 1931). See the catalogue of an exhibition on apocalyptic art held in the Wilhelm-Hack Museum in Ludwigshafen am Rhein in 1985, R. W. Gassen and B. Holeczek (eds.), *Apokalypse: Ein Princip Hoffnung* (Ludwigshafen, Wilhelm-Hack Museum, 1985).

2   For full references, see J. M. Winter, *Sites of Memory. Sites of Mourning: the Great War in European Cultural History* (Cambridge, Cambridge University Press, 1995), ch. 6.

3   F. Haskell, 'Art & the Apocalypse', *New York Review of Books*, 15 July 1993, pp. 25–29.

872

4   Y. F. Heibel, ' "They danced on volcanoes': Kandinsky's breakthrough to abstraction, the German avant-garde and the eve of the First World War', *Art History*, xii (1989), p. 357, on the way Kandinsky's painting points 'away from modernity'.

5   C. J. Ryan, *H. P. Blavatsky and the Theosophical Movement* (Pasadena, California, Theosophical University Press, 1975); J. Symonds, *Madame Blavatsky* (London, Odhams, 1959); J. O. Fuller, *Blavatsky and her Teachers* (London, Theosophical Publishing House, 1988); J. A. Santucci, *Theosophy and the Theosophical Society* (London, Theosophical History Centre, 1985).

6   A. Besant, *An Autobiography* (London, Allen & Unwin, 1908); J. A. and Olive Banks, *Feminism and Family Planning in Victorian England* (Liverpool, University of Liverpool Press, 1964), pp. 88–94.

7   R. Steiner, *Theosophy* (London, Kegan Paul Trench, 1908); see the original *Theosophie: einführung in ubersinnliche Welterkenntnis und Menschenbestimmung* (Leipzig, Altmann, 1920); *Goethes Weltanschaaung* (Weimar, E. Felber, 1897).

8   G. L. Mosse, *Towards the Final Solution: a history of European Racism* (Madison, Wisconsin, University of Wisconsin Press, 1985), pp. 95–8.

9   Sixten Ringbom, *The Sounding Cosmos. A Study of the Spiritualism of Kandinsky and the Genesis of Abstract Painting. Acta academiae Aboensis*, Ser. A., Humaniora, vol. 38, no. 2 (Abo, Abo Akademi, 1970), pp. 58–9.

10   S. Ringbom, 'Art in the "epoch of the Great Spiritual". Occult Elements in the Early Theory of Abstract Painting', *Journal of the Warburg and Courtault Institutes*, xxix (1966), p. 412. The citation is taken from W. Grohmann, *Paul Klee: Drawings* (London, Thames & Hudson, 1960), p. 17.

11   Ringbom, 'Art in the epoch of the "Great Spiritual"' , pp. 412–13.

12   Ringbom, *Sounding Cosmos*, p. 166.

13   Ringbom, *Sounding Cosmos*, p. 176.

14   James Billington, *The Icon and the Axe. An Interpretative History of Russian Culture* (London, Weidenfeld & Nicolson, 1966), p. 514.

15   as cited in Billington, *Icon*, p. 504.

16   V. Ehrlich, 'The Dead Hand of the Future: the Predicament of Vladimir Mayakovsky', *American Slavic and East European Review* (1962), pp. 433–40.

17   All references to the text are from W. Kandinsky and F. Marc (eds.), *The Blaue Reiter Almanac*, trans. H. Falkenstein (New York, the Viking Press, 1974). A German edition was published in 1965 by R. Piper, the original publisher.

18   Ringbom, *Sounding Cosmos*, pp. 162–3.

19   Carol S. Eliel, *The Apocalyptic Landscapes of Ludwig Meidner* (Munich, Prestel, 1991), pp. 11–13.

20   J. L. Robert, 'Paris, London and Berlin in 1914', in J. M. Winter and J. L. Robert, *Paris, London, Berlin: Capital Cities at War, 1914–1919* (Cambridge, Cambridge University Press, 1996).

21   L. Meidner, 'Anleitung zum Malen von Grossstadtnildern', *Kunst und Kunstler*, xii (1914), pp. 312–14, as cited in V. H. Miesel (ed.), *Voices of German Expressionism* (Englewood Cliffs, New Jersey, Prentice-Hall, 1970), p. 114. The reference is to Futurist art. For Meidner's rude remarks about Kandinsky, see Yule F. Heibel, ' "They danced on volcanoes": Kandinsky's

breakthrough to abstraction, the German avant-garde and the eve of the First World War', *Art History*, xii (1989), pp. 342–61.

22 See Simon Schama, *Landscape and Memory* (London, HarperCollins, 1995).

23 T. Grochowiak, *Ludwig Meidner* (Recklinghausen, Aurel Bongers, 1966), p. 25.

24 F. Nietzsche, *Thus spake Zarathustra*, trans, W. Kaufmann (Harmondsworth, Penguin, 1978), pp. 176–8.

25 See the discussion in chapter 4, pp. xx-xxi.

26 C. Brockhaus, 'Die ambivalente Faszination der Grossstadterfahrung in der deutschen Kunst des Expressionismus', in H. Meixner and S. Vietta (eds.), *Expressionismus: sozialer wandel und kunstlerische Erfahrung* (Munich, Wilhelm Fink, 1982).

27 L. Meidner, 'Anleitung zum Malen von Grossstadtnildern', as cited in Miesel (ed.), *Voices of German Expressionism*, pp. 111–15.

28 Eliel, *Meidner*, p. 45. The original citation is from Meidner, *Im Nacken das Sternemeer* (Leipzig, Kurt Wolff, n.d. [1918]), pp. 26–7.

29 Meidner, 'Vision des apokalyptischen Sommers', *Septemberschrei: Hymnen, Gebete, Lasternungen* (Berlin, Paul Cassirer, 1920), p. 8, as cited in E. Roters, 'The painter's nights', in Eliel, *Meidner*, p. 65.

30 Meidner, 'Mein Leben', im L. Brieger, *Ludwig Meidner* Junge Kunst, vol. 4 (Leipzig, Klinkhardt and Biermann, 1919), p. 12, as cited in Roters, 'The painter's nights', p. 65.

31 See for instance, Louis Chevalier, *Labouring Classes and Dangerous Classes in Paris During the First Half of the Nineteenth Century*, trans. F. Jellinek (London, Routledge, 1973); D. Pick, *Faces of Degeneration. A European Disorder, c.1848-c.1918* (Cambridge, Cambridge University Press, 1989).

32 S. Friedlander, 'Themes of Decline and End in Nineteenth-Century Imagination', in S. Friedlander (ed.), *Visions of Apocalypse* (London, Holmes & Meier, 1985), pp. 61–83.

33 S. Magri, 'Housing', in Winter and Robert, *Paris, London, Berlin*, ch. 13.

34 For some stimulating remarks on this subject, see R. Marz, 'L'expressionisme dans la métropole de 1910 à 1914', in *Figures du moderne*, p. 327, and J. Lloyd, 'The painted city as nature and artifice', in Irit Rogoff (ed.), *The Divided Heritage. Themes and Problems in German Modernism* (Cambridge, Cambridge University Press, 1992).

35 A. Weidmann, *Romantic Roots in Modern Art. Romanticism and Expressionism: a Study in Comparative Aesthetics* (London, Gresham Books, 1980), pp. 106–116; for Apollinaire's version of this romantic pose, see Julia Fagan-King, 'United on the threshold of the twentieth-century mystical ideal: Marie Laurencin's integral involvement with Guillaume Apollinaire and the inmates of the Bateau Lavoir', *Art History*, xi (1988), pp. 88–114.

36 E. Roters, 'Big-city expressionism: Berlin and German Expressionism', in *Expressionism: A German Intuition,1905–1920* (New York, Guggenheim Museum, 1980).

37 For an introduction to the subject, see: K. Silver, *Esprit de Corps: the Art of the Parisian Avant-garde and the First World War 1914–1925* (London, Thames & Hudson, 1989); S. Hynes, *A War Imagined*; M. Tippett, *Art at the service of war. Canada, Art and the Great War* (Toronto, University of Toronto Press, 1984); M. Eberle, *World War I and Weimar artists* (New

Haven, Yale University Press, 1988); E. L. Kahn, 'Art and the front, death imagined and the neglected majority', *Art History* (June 1985); Kahn, *The Neglected Majority, 'Les camoufleurs', Art History and World War I* (New York, Greenwood Press, 1980); M. and S. Harries, *The War Artists, British Official War Art of the Twentieth Century* (London, Imperial War Museum, 1980); R. H. Axsom, *'Parade: Cubism as Theater* (New York, Garland Press, 1979).

38 Winter op.cit., about war memorials. For more general and particular issues, see Annette Becker, *La guerre et la foi. De la mort à la mémoire* (Paris, Armand Colin, 1994); on symbolism and war art, see Gustave Adolf Mossa, *L'oeuvre symboliste 1903–1918* (Nice, n.p., 1992); for the use of triptych in war art, see *Polyptyques. Le tableau multiple du moyen âge au vingtième siècle* (Paris, Musée du Louvre, 1990). On the German side, see W. Schmied (ed.), *Zeichen des Glaubens. Geist der Avantgarde: Religiose Tendenzen in der Kunst des 20. Jahrhunderts* (Stuttgart, Electa/Klett-Cotta, 1980). For religious themes in poster art, there is much of interest in the Hoover Institution poster collection, Stanford University, in the BDIC in the Hôtel des Invalides, in the Imperial War Museum in London, and in the Bibliothek für Zeitgeschichte, Stuttgart.

39 Angus Fletcher, *Allegory* (Ithaca, New York, Cornell University Press, 1963).

40 as cited in E. Karcher, *Otto Dix, 1891–1964. Leben und werk* (Köln, Benedikt Taschen, 1988), p. 38.

41 F. Marc, 'In war's purifying fire', in Miesel (ed.), *Voices*, p. 160.

42 Levine, *The Apocalyptic Vision*, p. 161.

43 The fullest treatment of Dix is to be found in F. Loffler, *Otto Dix*, (Leipzig, 1977).

44 *Otto Dix 1891–1961* (London, Tate Gallery, 1992), pp. 70–1. (Hereafter cited as *Dix*).

45 We await the study of Sarah O'Brien-Twohig on Nietzsche and painting for the first full account of this subject.

46 I am grateful to Ursus Dix for advice on this point.

47 The word 'tremendous' is from an interview cited in D. Schmidt, *Otto Dix im Selbstbildnis* (Berlin, Henschelverlag, 1978), p. 237. The full citation is: 'The war was a horrible thing, but there was something tremendous about it, too'.

48 *Dix*, p. 73, has him carrying *Zarathustra* in his pack; M. Eberle, *World War I and the Weimar Artists: Dix, Grosz, Beckmann, Schlemmer*, trans. J. Gabriel (New Haven, Yale University Press, 1985), p. 22, has him carrying *The Joyous Science*.

49 Dietrich Schubert, *Otto Dix in Selbstzeugnissen und Bilddokumenten* (Reinbeck bei Hamburg, Rowolt-Taschenbuch Verlag, 1980), p. 24, disputes whether the painting is of Dix himself. This is unconvincing, since it is the mood of the early phase of the war which Dix has captured.

50 Winter, op.cit., p. 199.

51 as cited in O. Conzelmann, 'Nietzsches Nachklang in den Landschaften', in *Der anderen Dix – Sein Bild vom menschen und vom Kriege* (Stuttgart, Klett-Cotta, 1983), p.133.

52 *Dix*, p. 83.

53 *Dix*, p. 116.

54 Eberle, *Weimar artists*, p. 39.

55 E. Friedrich, *War against war!* (Seattle, the Real Comet Press, 1987), with an introduction by D. Kellner to a facsimile edition of the original.

56 *Dix*, p. 116.

57 *Dix*, p. 193. The image may have recalled classical motifs of 'Menelaus carrying the body of the dead Patroclus from the battlefield of Troy'.

58 Winter, op.cit., p. 93.

59 ibid, p. 186.

60 *Dix*, p. 201.

61 Eberle, *Weimar Artists*, pp. 52–3.

62 On his prewar work, see M. Beckmann, *Leben in Berlin. Tagebuch 1908/09* (ed. H. Kinkel) (Munich, Piper, 1966), and E. G. Guse, *Das Fruhwerk Max Beckmanns – zur Thematik seiner Bilder aus den Jahren 1904–1914* (Frankfurt, M. P. Lang, 1977); on the Berlin Secession, see P. Paret, *The Berlin Secession and its Enemies in Imperial Berlin* (Cambridge, Mass., Harvard University Press, 1980).

63 On the background to this drawing, and other facets of Beckmann's response to the 1914–18 war, see C. Schulz-Hoffmann and J. C. Weiss (eds.), *Max Beckmann Retrospective* (Munich and New York, Prestel, 1985), p. 388 and C. W. Haxthausen, 'Beckmann and the First World War' in the same volume, pp. 69–80. See also B. C. Buenger, 'Max Beckmann in the First World War', in R. Rumold and O. K. Werckmeister (eds.), *The Ideological Crisis of Expressionism. The Literary and Artistic German War Colony in Belgium 1914–1918*, Studies in German Literature, Linguistics and Culture, vol. 51 (Columbia, S.C., 1990), pp. 237–75.

64 B. C. Buenger, 'Max Beckmann's *Ideologues*: some forgotten faces', *Art Bulletin*, lxxi, 3 (1989), pp. 464–8.

65 Buenger, 'Max Beckmann', p. 257.

66 Lackner, *Beckmann*, p. 50.

67 Buenger, 'Max Beckmann', p. 257.

68 Dube, 'On the "Resurrection"', in *Max Beckmann Retrospective*, p. 88.

69 These phrases are taken from letters of Beckmann to his wife of 24 Sept. 1914 and 21 May 1915, as cited in W.-D. Dube, 'On the "Resurrection"', in *Max Beckmann Retrospective*, p. 82.

70 Max Beckmann, letters to his wife, 3 April 1915, 24 April 1915, 11 May 1915, as cited in Dube, 'On the "Resurrection"', in Max Beckmann, p. 82.

71 Buenger, 'Max Beckmann', p. 265.

72 S. O'Brien-Twohig, 'Max Beckmann', in C. M. Joachimides *et al* (eds.), *German Art in the 20th Century. Painting and Sculpture 1905–1985* (London, Prestel-Verlag, 1985), p. 440.

73 Buenger, 'Max Beckmann, p. 245.

74 as cited in W.-D. Dube, *Expressionists and Expressionism*, trans. J. Emmons (Geneva, Skira, 1983), pp. 86–7.

75 S. Lackner, *Beckmann* (London, Thames & Hudson, 1991), pp. 15–16.

76 The best decoding of the painting is in Dube, 'On the "Resurrection"', in *Max Beckmann Retrospective*, pp. 84ff; see also S. von Wiese, *Max Beckmanns zeichnerisches Werk 1903–1925* (Düsseldorf, Droste Verlag, 1978), pp. 100–108.

77 S. O'Brien-Twohig, 'Max Beckmann', p. 440. The phrase 'filled with rage at God' is from a conversation between Beckmann and Reinhard Piper in 1917.

78   S. O'Brien-Twohig, 'Max Beckmann', p. 440.

79   J. Kristeva, *Black Sun. Depression and Melancholy*, trans. L. S. Roudiez (New York, Columbia University Press, 1989), p. 3.

80   Max Beckmann, 'On my painting', in Max Beckmann, *A Small loan retrospective of painting, centring around his visit to London in 1938* (London, Marlborough Gallery, 1987); the remark was made in a lecture in London in 1938; see also S. Lacker, Max Beckmann's mystical pageant of the world', in *Max Beckmann Retrospective*, pp. 39–53.

81   Eberle, *Weimar artists*, ch. 4.

82   See above, pp.861–2.

83   Bendemann, 'Max Beckmann', *Frankfurter Zeitung*, 7 June 1919, as cited in B. C. Buenger, 'Max Beckmann in the First World War', in R. Rumold and O. K. Werckmeister (eds.), *The Ideological Crisis of Expressionism. The Literary and Artistic German War Colony in Belgium 1914–1918* (Columbia, S.C., Camden House, 1990), p. 267.

84   Westheim, *Für und Wider* (Potsdam, G. Klepenheuer, 1923), p. 102, as cited in Buenger, 'Max Beckmann', p. 268.

85   *Stanley Spencer. The Passion.* (Edinburgh, Scottish National Gallery of Modern Art, 1986).

86   G. Behrend, *Stanley Spencer at Burghclere* (London, Macdonald, 1965), p. 62.

87   Winter, op.cit.

88   R. Carline, *Stanley Spencer at War* (London, Faber, 1978), p. 184.

89   Samuel Hynes calls the scene 'joyous', an emotion remote from the faces and postures of every single figure in the cycle. See S. Hynes, *A War Imagined*, p. 463.

90   G. Behrend, *Stanley Spencer at Burghclere* (London, 1965); Arts Council, *Stanley Spencer, 1851–1959* (London, 1976); R. Carline, *Stanley Spencer at War*.

91   I am grateful to Diana Goodrich for discussions on this point.

92   G. Rouault, *Miserere*, (Paris, Editions le léopard d'or, 1990).

93   J. Kristeva, 'Psychoanalysis: a counter-depressant', in *Black Sun*, p. 25

94   S. Whitfield, ' "An outrageous lyricism"', in F. Hergott and S. Whitfield, *Georges Rouault. The early years 1903–1920* (London, Royal Academy of Arts, 1993), pp. 11–14.

95   Whitfield, 'An outrageous lyricism', p.16.

96   F. Hergott, 'The early Rouault', in *Georges Rouault. The early years*, p.23.

97   L. Bloy, *La femme pauvre* (Paris, Mercure de France, 1937), p. 171.

98   As cited in L. Venturi, *Georges Rouault* (New York, Wylie, 1940), p. 16.

99   J. T. Soby, *Georges Rouault* (New York, Arno Press, 1972), pp. 10–11.

100 Letter of Rouault to André Saurès, 8 Aug. 1914, in *Georges Rouault – André Saurès Correspondance* (Paris, Gallimard, 1960), pp. 106–7.

101 Soby, *Rouault*, pp. 28, 28n.

102 Rouault to Saurès, 2 May 1922, in *Correspondance*, pp. 172–3.

103 'Abbé Morel's presentation', in *Miserere*, p. 40.

104 Soby, *Rouault*, pp. 22.

105 *Miserere* includes a number of illustrative citations, added by Rouault's daughter to the edition. (See 'Note', p. 35 Opposite print 54, is a direct citation of Léon Bloy's 'Au seuil de l'Apocalypse', 18 April 1915, celebrating this incident.'

106 F. Chapon, 'This hymn of dolours . . . ', *Miserere*, p. 55.

107 C. -R. Marx, 'Rouault's legacy', *Miserere*, p. 53.

108 *Miserere*, p. 59.

109 *Miserere*, p. 62.

110 I am grateful to Antoine Prost for our discussions on this point.

Chapter 61

Sir Ian Hamilton After the War:
A Liberal General Reflects

John Lee

'Material victories are often spiritual defeats'.[1] This aphorism, which Sir Ian Hamilton used in an article to the Central Press Agency on the unveiling of the Cenotaph on 11 November 1920, is a coded message signifying his increasing disillusion with the post-war settlement unfolding at Versailles.

Even while the war was still in progress he was beginning to spell out his hopes for the future. At the opening of a YMCA hostel in Walthamstow, London, on 12 October 1918, he reminded his audience that they were gathered to honour soldiers who fought, not for conquest, but to defend their homes and end 'this frenzied orgy of hate'.[2] He closed his address with an appeal that the spirit of the YMCA would win a victory over those who saw in the coming peace 'merely an opening for Capital, for combines, for boycotts and for concessions'. In April 1920 he told a gathering held to unveil a memorial to the fallen from Dr Barnardo homes: 'We still await the mutual agreement between victors and vanquished which alone is worthy of the name of peace'. In October of that year he declared that 'one beautiful gesture might have lifted this civilisation onto a higher plane and given it a fresh lease of life – the gesture familiar to every public schoolboy in England of the victor holding out his hand.'

Unveiling a war memorial at Spalding on 8 June 1922 he repeated what was by now his well-worn theme that all the strife in the world did not mean that the men of 1914–18 had died in vain: 'Peace or war are the results of a frame of mind. Don't be too hard on your enemies. Don't grind them down now that they are beaten. Then I believe you will be acting up to the ideals for which the brave men we commemorate laid down their lives.'[3] Later in the wearying round of unveilings, which he later said had contributed to his determination to see an end to war forever, he said, 'It is from the contempt and harshness of the victor that the spirit of revenge is bred in the defeated as surely as dirt breeds disease. Never mind the League of Nations but try to do something practical yourselves ... try the clean slate; try magnanimity; it's not too late yet ... These boys of yours did not die for reparations; nor for Mesopotamia; not even for Jerusalem. They hoped, God bless them, to kill war.'⁴

We are clearly in the company of a very unusual general as we listen to these desperate pleas to forgive and forget, so very soon after the end of the Great War. His pleas were not always received very favourably but no one ever accused Sir Ian Hamilton of lacking courage, physical or moral. Hamilton was the ultimate professional soldier – he had been commissioned in 1872 and, after a lifetime of battles in India, Africa and Turkey and staff posts in the highest echelons of the British Army, was the senior Lieutenant-General on the Army List. In 1914 the German High Command had regarded him as the most experienced soldier alive in the world. He often frankly confessed that he loved fighting and he wrote movingly about the nobility of the army as a profession, in ways that defy anyone to label him 'militarist'. But a love of soldiering is not the same as a love of war, and we do have a remarkably clear precedent for his immediate response to the ending of the First World War.

In 1902 Hamilton was Chief of Staff to Lord Kitchener in the closing stages of the Boer War, and he kept up a lively correspondence with that rising star in the Liberal Party, Winston Spencer Churchill. He repeatedly stressed, even in the midst of the last fighting, that the Boers were a fine race of people, who should be incorporated into the British Empire at the earliest opportunity. The soldiers tended to admire them, and often viewed them favourably compared with the politicians like Alfred Milner and his coterie of Johannesburg capitalists who looked for a vengeful peace.

This is how he used the experience in his unofficial campaign against the Versailles settlement: 'How is it that the Boer War put an end to the feuds, race hatreds, bankruptcies, disorders and bloodshed which had paralysed South African progress for a generation, whilst the Great War has on the contrary inflicted race hatred, bankruptcy and murder over the best part of the old world from Ireland in the West to the Near East; including the whole of Central Europe which has been turned into a seething cauldron of hate? I'll tell you why it is; it is because our Politicians entirely ignored the ideals of those to whom we have raised this memorial by making a vindictive instead of a generous peace ... Lord Kitchener forced them to make a good peace in South Africa. For six months Lord Kitchener fought the politicians who wanted to make a vindictive peace, an 'unconditional surrender' peace as they called it; a peace which would above all things humiliate and wound the feelings of the conquered ... He beat them and made his own peace; a generous, soldierly peace. He lent the Boers money;

he rebuilt their farms; he rebuilt their dams; he re-stocked their farms . . . within one year South Africa was smiling and so were we.'⁵

It was this bid to treat the defeated enemy in an open-handed and generous way which informed all Hamilton's work in this immediate post-war period. With our hindsight we can only admire his astonishing good sense; what a good deal of misery the world might have been saved if more people had taken his message to heart.

Here is one final reference to this 'campaign', which pulls together several important threads of the argument. It dates from August 1920: 'What we have to understand now is, to put an end to war by knocking out the bully, the aggressor, is to win half the battle only; to scotch the snake and make it change its skin onto someone else. True, to end war the first step is to overthrow the militarist nation: that's the first half of the business; after you have finished with them you have to turn against your own old self; your own war propaganda; knock it out and forget it. I don't say that the survivors are to shake hands with those who have done to them and to the world so cruel a wrong: that would be asking too much. But I say it is up to us to try and do what Kitchener did to the Boers – set our enemies going again in a generous, large-handed way . . . Perhaps you disagree but anyway . . . '⁶ Hamilton has clearly been interrupted here, but he is driving home his point in his usual combative way. He had a partic-ular loathing for the hatred whipped up by war propaganda; not just because he was a literate, sensitive, deeply civilised man, but because he knew such hatreds took a disproportionately long time to die down and he felt Europe had more pressing concerns to occupy it. For he ended the speech thus '. . . for Asia is coming on and Asiatic socialism and there's no other way out of it for Europe west of the Vistula but reconciliation or ruin.' (There is a double warning here. 'Asiatic socialism' is, of course, the new Bolshevist regime in All the Russias, and Hamilton always suspected, from his deep knowledge of the country and its culture, that Japan would before too long be a major threat to the West).

His concern for social peace in Europe and the wider world was central to his activities in the United Kingdom on behalf of the demobilised service men and women. In October 1918, Hamilton had been appointed by the Army Council to be chairman of a consultative committee on the disposal of the huge profits (amounting to several millions of pounds) made by the expeditionary forces canteen funds. His committee represented all the fighting services, including the Dominions. Now he was anxious to use the committee as a means of drawing together the already burgeoning – and splintering – ex-servicemen's organisations. His committee proposed the creation of an 'Empire Services League', backed by all three service ministries, and funded by the Army Council. The proposal was flatly refused by the War Office in February 1919, ostensibly because it wanted the money disposed of quickly and directly by the servicemen themselves.

There is, however, a strong suspicion that the government of the day did not want a single organisation with a potential membership of many millions embracing all the ex-servicemen's organisations, which could have wielded extraordinary political power.

Instead a new committee headed by Sir Julian Byng proceeded to spend the 'United Services Fund' like water, meeting requests for money to build ex-servicemen's clubs and the like. Hamilton was greatly disappointed that his old friend, Winston Churchill, now the Secretary of State for War, had failed to take the opportunity to 'wipe out these small Primrose, Radical, Socialist and Bolshevist federations and to bring them into one big league', of a non-political nature, which could have acted as a stabilising factor in a country going through a rather turbulent period in its domestic politics. Indeed this antagonism between the small groups did lead to disorderly clashes, culminating in the burning down of Leicester Town Hall. The government belatedly realised things were getting out of hand and recalled Lord Haig from South Africa, to begin a two year tour of the country arguing for a unified ex-servicemen's organisation. The founding of the British Legion in June 1921, is just one more testament to the visionary foresight of Sir Ian Hamilton, though he gave all the credit to Haig, whose authority was vital to the success of the venture.

Underlying all this concern for the ex-servicemen was a very real fear amongst the British ruling class, greatly exaggerated though it may have been, of the spread of Bolshevism. In his usual combative but educated way, Hamilton sought to engage the Social Democratic Federation (soon to become a founding component of the Communist Party of Great Britain) in debate through the pages of its journal 'Justice'. Having complained that, by employing ex-servicemen on his newly-acquired farm at Lullenden in Sussex, Hamilton, far from exploiting their labour for profit, was losing money rather heavily, the SDF explained in a charming and good-natured riposte that Sir Ian was not a capitalist at all but a decent philanthropist, incapable of solving the problems of society by his altruism!

In the midst of his work unveiling war memorials and addressing Old Comrades' Associations, Hamilton worked hard to build the British Legion and to win over non-Legion organisations to it, repeatedly telling the story of how his recommendations were ignored and two years wasted. His theme was the promotion of social peace and, again, he spoke a great deal of good sense in the process. At a dinner of the Glasgow and Lanarkshire London Association in November 1919, he told his audience, 'We seem less inclined to rejoice together over the victory than to come to blows over the division of the spoils! When war was declared we all stood shoulder to shoulder. There was no sort of enquiry whether a man was a reckless anarchist or a stiff-necked Tory. I don't suggest a peace between Capital and Labour – I like fighting – but, in the name of common sense, let's scrape together something worth fighting over before we strike one another dead.' He called for a one year armistice in industrial relations, 'till we get our trade back from America. When we took our coats off to fight we pawned them to the USA!' He wanted Capital and Labour to unite and wage war on the bureaucracy of central government.

We have to understand that Hamilton, from his earliest childhood, had developed a tremendous empathy with working people. In his military writings he would draw examples of good inner discipline from the working solidarity of miners and deep-sea fishermen. His comments on the denial of opportunity for education and self-expression to working-class children, even if written in the context of damaging the military potential of the nation and the empire, are emotionally moving for all that. His schemes for alleviating distress during the post-war slump were eminently sensible and have a resonance with the Beveridge Plan of later years. (The work of another great Liberal, of course.) He took up the idea, abroad in 1922, for the digging of a Forth-Clyde Canal. How better to use 50,000 men so newly trained in the digging of great trenches? The spending of £24,000,000 of public money would take 50,000 off the 'dole', create 80,000 ancillary jobs and transform the great central industrial belt of Scotland, giving a chance to plan and build lovely, healthy garden cities along the canal. In the 1990s Hamilton seems to be talking to us with great relevance on this, as on so many other subjects.

In 1923 he published a series of lectures addressed to the British Legion in the form of the book, 'The Friends of England'. It expanded the ideas of his 1918 pamphlet, 'The Millenium', about the economic stupidity of reparations and the need for a generous peace. He called on ex-servicemen everywhere to unite in the search for peace. He was not impressed with the way France seemed to dominate the new League of Nations with the sole intent of enforcing in the harshest way the Versailles settlement. He confessed that he couldn't see the logic of sacking coal miners in Wales because we were making German miners give their coal away (as reparations) to fulfil the terms of Versailles! He gave full vent to his detestation of the hate propaganda used by the press and politicians in wartime, and contrasting it with the easy-going attitude of the British troops sent to occupy Germany after the war. The British Legion should set the example for unselfish gesture towards Germany.

He personally grasped the nettle and began a series of visits and inter-changes with Germany, which invariably drew a great deal of publicity, leading to a fairly notorious incident in 1938. Hamilton had extensive connections with the old German Army before the war and spoke the language fluently.

In April 1922, Hamilton's old Gallipoli comrade, Alex Godley, was the new GOC British Forces in Germany and he invited his old chief out for a visit. Hamilton took the opportunity to interview Erich von Ludendorff, and was able to report back to his colleagues (like Sir Henry Rawlinson,

C in C India) important information on the failures of German strategy in March 1918, and the impact on Ludendorff of the collapse of Bulgaria in late September. It wasn't long before Ludendorff and his young aides were ranting about the Bolshevik threat to Europe and how it would take the German Army to subdue Russia and make it part of a European bulwark against America. Hamilton had a certain sympathy with these ideas, as he most certainly did with the German complaint that France was threatening to use black troops to enforce the Versailles Treaty in the Saar region.

He returned to England to tell the British Legion that 'the outstanding feature of German post-war life' was the German Legion, a gathering of hundreds of regimental associations, a coming together of veterans, which, unlike in Britain, had been encouraged by the state, which was additional to the two and a half million members of the Veterans Associations. 'What a bulwark against Bolshevism they are', he remarked.[7]

He publicly called for the British Legion to shake hands with the war veterans of Germany, and he was unanimously re-elected as President of the Metropolitan Area of the Legion by all its 224 delegates at the time. But he did seem to get a little too far ahead of the members in this respect for, when he was canvassed about the setting up of an Anglo-German Society in February 1929, he replied that he would have to take British Legion advice before agreeing. 'A little caution is desirable', he said, as he recalled that once in 1924 his area committee had asked for his resignation over his too-friendly attitude to Germany.

It is interesting, given the recent debate on whether Germans should be included in the fiftieth anniversary commemorations of the ending of the Second World War, that Hamilton treated sympathetically the idea that ceremonies at the Cenotaph in London should honour the dead of all sides. In a letter of 12 November 1928, replying to Commander Sir Graham Bower, RN, who had suggested the idea, he wrote, 'Any little turn of the political board which brought us momentarily greater friendliness with the Germans would make a difference.'

The publication in Germany in January 1929, of Erich Maria Remarque's *All Quiet on the Western Front* (soon translated into English in March of that year) led to an interesting exchange of letters between Hamilton and the author, via Remarque's publisher, Putnams, and Desmond MacCarthy's journal *Life and Letters*. Putnams, very shrewdly, sent an advance copy of the book to Sir Ian (which, in itself, tells us something of how he was regarded in the literary world in his day). Hamilton said he was glad someone had found a good translator 'clever enough to pick up Remarque's bomb and fling it across the Channel. We here just needed this bit of shaking up.' He saw it as a tale of a generation effectively lost to human progress through its suffering in the war. Having once been disposed to combat such inferences and conclusions he wrote, 'Now, sorrowfully, I must admit, there is a great deal of truth in them.' The terrible demands of attritional warfare had produced a 'lost' generation. How else could the flower of British youth now form such a high proportion of the country's down and outs? Hamilton the soldier still rebels at the full rigour of Remarque's message: 'This German goes too far . . . Even in the last and most accursed of all wars – the war "on the Western Front" . . . was there not the superb leading of forlorn hopes; the vague triumphs, vague but real, of dying for a cause?' Above all Hamilton praises those who came through the war with the courage to fight to make the world 'a better place for themselves and everyone else, including their ex-enemies'. McCarthy and other critics praised Sir Ian's letter because it alone brought the author out of his self-imposed purdah.

In an effusive, six page letter Remarque expressed his deep gratitude to 'Sir Hamilton' (sic) for his 'beautiful and understanding letter' and of his 'admiration that my work had been so clearly, accurately and absolutely understood. You can well imagine that I was very uncertain what the effect of my book would be outside Germany and whether I have succeeded in making myself understood.' Hamilton had clearly related to the book as a tale of youth suffering in common from their confrontation with death in what they saw, each in their own way, as their duty. Both writers could appreciate the quiet heroism of the ordinary soldier. Hamilton perceived that Remarque was not preaching resignation but was sending out 'a clarion call to face up to the difficulties caused by the war and begin to build for the future.'[8]

In his reply to this letter Hamilton once again wrote with enormous compassion for the unemployed in Britain: 'When they went to war they were the flowers, not the dregs, of our people.' During those vital years between the ages of eighteen and twenty-two, when they should have been mastering their trade, they were manning the trenches, which made them especially vulnerable when recession struck in the post-war era. For him, Remarque's book showed exactly how his young heroes were not only robbed of their education but of the energy and regenerative power to see them through their early struggles as citizens. He explained that his work in the British Legion was to get the veterans to band together to influence their own government, to help one another and to strive for some high ideal, the highest being peace. He finished by urging Remarque to write another book exposing the enormity of modern war. This old soldier knew only too well how seductive an appeal the military life could have: 'For great and terrible is the counter-power of the romance and beauty of war, to which you wisely make no reference in your book'. He reminds the author of the thrill of watching an entire German Army Corps move past at the parade march, flags flying and drums crashing: 'These are the legends and illusions you have got to transfix very quickly with your pen.'

This exchange of letters, published in November 1929, was very widely reported and commented upon in the press. For Arnold Bennett, writing in the *Evening Standard*, 'The contribution of both Erich Remarque and Sir Ian Hamilton have nobility.' This coincided with some of Hamilton's most strenuous denunciations of Versailles, during which he took issue with Professor H. A. L. Fisher, a fellow Vice President of the newly created Anglo-German Society. In a letter to the *Manchester Guardian* criticising Fisher's defence of the Versailles Treaty, Hamilton reminded the readers of the English maxims, 'Please don't kick a man when he's down' and 'Fair play's a jewel'. After particularly denouncing the creation of the utterly artificial state of Czechoslovakia and the 'monuments to revenge' called peace treaties, he concluded 'by stating my own firm belief that the peace treaties made after 9,000,000 soldiers had died to give a clear hand to the politicians were the worst settlement of world affairs after a great war recorded in modern or ancient history.'

Hamilton's next visit to Germany was an official one to the old Field Marshal von Hindenburg, to receive back the drums of the Gordon Highlanders which had been lost in 1914. The private conversations apparently avoided all references to the Great War, but Hamilton did, of course, begin to meet the officials of the new Nazi regime, including Rudolf Hess.

Again we must try and dispense with the wisdom of hindsight as we hear that, in July 1935, whilst addressing the Yorkshire West Riding British Legion, Hamilton makes a glowing reference to a speech by Hess of a few days before. In it Hess is reported as issuing an appeal 'to the front line soldiers in other states – they are more fitted to rebuild the bridge of understanding'. Hamilton remarked, 'At this meeting of front line soldiers it would be a shame not to respond to the challenge.' He described his meeting with Hess and assured his audience that 'Hess is a fine young fellow and that he is far more than the mere mouthpiece of Herr Hitler. As to his appeal to the front line ex-servicemen – he is right.' He went on to reinforce his pan-European, anti-Bolshevik message by concluding, 'If we want to support the cause of peace we must separate our opinions of the actions of a Government fighting for its existence from our feelings for the Germans as a whole. There are people in London and I daresay in Leeds who are only too pleased if they see misfortune closing in upon our ex-enemies. Alas that it should be so for, in my humble opinion, the collapse of Germany would be the most deadly misfortune to Europe. The one thing that can save Civilisation is sympathy between ex-enemies.'[9] (We should, perhaps, note that when Hess made his dash by 'plane to Britain in 1941, there was some confusion as to whether he had come to see the Duke of Hamilton or Sir Ian of that ilk!)

Hamilton's increasingly extreme anti-war stance reached its apogee in August 1938, when he was an extraordinarily spry 85 years old, in a somewhat bizarre and unfortunate turn of events which had an innocent enough beginning. The Metropolitan Area Council of the British Legion had organised a visit to Germany by some forty of its members, to lay some wreaths at German war memorials as a token of peace. The party was led by Sir Ian Hamilton.

His speeches, delivered in impeccable German, took on an increasingly sentimental tone. At the Barbarossa Memorial he declared, 'If the world could be run by old soldiers instead of Autocrats and Bureaucrats there would be no more wars.' A day or so later, during the Berlin phase of the trip, he was suddenly whisked off by air to Munich to lunch with 'that fine young fellow', Rudolf Hess. Within a few hours he was taking tea with Adolf Hitler at Berchtesgaden. Hitler soon realised that interpreters were unnecessary; he was said to be awestruck at being in the presence of a man who had learned his German amongst the heroes of 1871! The two men had private talks for some ninety minutes during which Hitler seems to have conducted a 'charm offensive' on the old general. Hamilton did recognise it for what it was, and has left us very full accounts of the meeting. But he did take Germany's side very strongly against Czech 'provocations', and came away convinced that Hitler was a democratic leader who was desperate to maintain peace in Europe and who was, if anything, restraining the 'war party' in Germany.

In an interview with the *Sunday Graphic* given on his return, Hamilton repeated his assertion that the old fighters of Europe alone were capable of making and keeping the peace: 'The bogey of the fire-eating Hitler is the greatest danger to peace today. It is dangerous in its effect on us; it is dangerous in its effect on Germany. But the ex-servicemen of the two nations are helping to lay it.'

This interview closed with a summary of what Hamilton had come to believe in these inter-war years:

'Yes, certainly, I have been a soldier all my life and have loved my profession. But for years after the war I unveiled a war memorial almost every week, and the people who were given the best seats were the widows and orphans, the mutilated, the blind and the parents who had lost their sons. It was this that brought about my change of heart and enlisted me in this new and greater campaign.'[10]

Notes

1   Ian Hamilton Archives. 39/12/19.
2   Ian Hamilton Archives. 39/12/1.
3   Ian Hamilton Archives. 39/12/41.
4   Ian Hamilton Archives. 39/12/48. Speech at Ashton-under-Lyne, Sept. 1922.
5   Ian Hamilton Archives. 39/12/45.
6   Ian Hamilton Archives. 39/12/17. Speech at the unveiling of a war memorial at Winchcombe, Gloucestershire, 4 August 1920.
7   Ian Hamilton Archives. 39/12/40. Speech to British Legion at Dudley, Worcestershire.
8   Ian Hamilton Archives. 41/4/1. Remarque to Hamilton, 1 June 1929.
9   Ian Hamilton Archives. 30/13.
10 Ian Hamilton Archives. 30/13.

Bibliography and Index

Facing Armageddon:
A Select Bibliography

Ian Beckett

Reflection on the historiography of the Great War since the 70th Anniversary Conference, also associated with the Liddle Archive but held on that occasion at the then Sunderland Polytechnic, suggests superficially that little progress has been made in our understanding of the impact of the first 'total' conflict of the Twentieth Century. This is most apparent in British popular publishing, which remains largely obsessed with its discovery in the 1970s of the apparent significance of 1 July 1916 and seemingly endless recapitulations of the old 'lions and donkeys' theme of the 1960s, itself merely reflecting the historiographical battles of the 1920s and 1930s. It has also been the case that interest in the Great War has been much slower to develop in Europe than in Britain where the spectacular growth of the Western Front Association, founded in 1980, has arguably stimulated academic publishing at the same time that it has fed the demand for popular treatments of less value.

In view of these academic developments, the reality, therefore, has been on balance, that knowledge of the experience of war has advanced materially in many areas since 1984. The benchmark against which publications which have appeared over this ten year period – at least in terms of the British experience – can be judged is taken to be the proceedings of the Sunderland conference as edited by Peter Liddle, *Home Fires and Foreign Fields* (London, Brasseys, 1985). Subsequent developments in the understanding of British experiences can be traced in Trevor Wilson, *The Myriad Faces of War* (Cambridge, Polity Press, 1986), David Turner (ed.), *Britain and the First World War* (London: Unwin Hyman, 1988), and John Bourne, *Britain and the Great War* (London, Edward Arnold, 1989). As indicated earlier, continental historians have been slower to produce similar overviews but one encouraging development has been the establishment of the Historial de la Grande Guerre at Péronne and its promotion of continental scholarship through conferences. The publication of the proceedings of a conference at the Université de Paris X-Nanterre in 1990 edited by Jean-Jacques Becker and Stéphane Audoin-Rouzeau, *Les sociétés européennes et la guerre de 1914–1918* (Paris, Centre d'Histoire de la France contemporaine, 1990), predated the opening of the research centre but Becker, Jay Winter, Gerd Krumeich and Audoin-Rouzeau have since edited the proceedings of the Historial's opening event, *Guerre et Cultures 1914–1918* (Paris, Armand Colin, 1994). Becker, of course, has also contributed a number of works on French war experiences, notably *La France en guerre 1914–18: La Grande Mutation* (Paris, Complexe, 1988) and *The Great War and the French People* (Leamington Spa, Berg, 1985). Winter has also edited with R. M. Wall, *The Upheaval of War: Family, Work and Welfare in Europe, 1914–18* (Cambridge University Press, 1988). Similar compilations to those of the Historial include, by mostly German historians, Gerhard Hirschfeld, Gerd Krumeich and Irina Den (eds.), *Keiner fühlt sich mehr als Mensch: Erebnis und Wirkung des Ersten Weltkriegs* (Essen, Klartext Verlag, 1993), Wolfram Wette (ed.), *Der Krieg des Kleinenmannes: Eine Militärgeschichte von Unten*(Munich, Piper, 1992) and Wolfgang Michalka (ed.), *Der Erste Weltkrieg: Wirkung, Wahrenehmung, Analyse* (Munich, 1994). Manfried Rauchensteiner provides the first reassessment of Austria-Hungary at war for many decades in *Der Tod des Doppeladlers: Österreich-Ungarn und der Erste Weltkrieg* (Vienna and Graz, Verlag Styria, 1994) and Antonio Gibelli fuses together anthropology, psychology and literature in his account of Italian experience, *L'Officina Della Guerra: La Grande Guerra e le Trasformazione Dei Mondo Mentale* (Turin, Ballati Boringhieri, 1991). For the Slovene lands, it is still necessary to consult Janko Pleterski, *Proa odlocitev Slovencev za Jugoslavijo 1914–18* (Ljubljana, 1971), subsequently translated into Serbo-Croat as *Provo opredel jenje Slovenaca za Jugoslaviju 1914–18* (Belgrade, 1976).

In terms of work on individual armies, the new parameters for scholarship already established ten years ago are apparent in Ian Beckett and Keith Simpson (eds.), *A Nation in Arms: A Social Study of the British Army in the First World War* (Manchester University Press, 1985). Surprisingly little more has been done in Britain on recruitment and enlistment patterns with the exception of studies of Ireland but there is the benefit of Jay Winter's essays on military participation and other demographic matters collected in one volume in *The Great War and the British People* (London, Macmillan, 1986), studies on manpower policy such as Keith Grieves, *The Politics of Manpower, 1914–18* (Manchester University Press, 1988) and, arguably the greatest single contribution to the knowledge of the social organisation of the British Army, Peter Simkins, *Kitchener's Army* (Manchester University Press, 1986). Of comparable value are possibly

Desmond Morton, *When Your Number's Up: The Canadian Soldier in the First World War* (Toronto, Random House, 1993) and, for the Polish Legion in the Austro-Hungarian Army, Wanda Wyganowska, *Sztuka Legionow Polskia, 1914–18.* The study of British conscripts other than conscientious objectors has been neglected, but for New Zealand there is Paul Baker, *King and Country Call: New Zealanders, Conscription and the Great War* (Auckland University Press, 1988).

In the case of the British Army, a fuller knowledge of the role of conscripts is important if a proper understanding of morale and discipline is to be achieved beyond the popular obsession with the relatively minor matter of 312 wartime executions and mutinous disorders, which principally occurred only during demobilisation. A brief article by David Englander, 'Mutiny and Myopia', *Bulletin of the Society for the Study of Labour History*, vol 52, 1987, pp. 5–7 is particularly apposite in reviewing contributions such as G. Dallas and D. Gill, *The Unknown Army* (London, Verso, 1985). Disciplinary matters are especially well treated in Christopher Pugsley, *On the Fringe of Hell: New Zealanders and Military Discipline in the First World War* (Auckland, Hodder & Stoughton, 1991) while Leonard Smith has re-examined the French Army mutinies in *Between Mutiny and Obedience: The Case of the French Fifth Infantry Division during World War One* (Princeton University Press, 1994). Wider issues of morale are dealt with by David Englander, 'The French Soldier, 1914–18', *French History* vol 1, 1. 1987, pp. 49–57; by Stéphane Audoin-Rouzeau, *Men at War 1914–18: National Sentiment and Trench Journalism in France during the First World War* (Oxford, Berg, 1992); and, using similar British trench journalism, by John Fuller, *Troop Morale and Popular Culture in the British and Dominion Armies* (Oxford, Clarendon Press, 1990). Another contribution to the evolving debate on the maintenance of morale is S. P. Mackenzie, *Politics and Military Morale: Current Affairs and Citizenship Education in the British Army, 1914–50* (Oxford, Clarendon Press, 1992) while the memoir of the late nonagenarian American classical scholar, Amos Wilder, *Armageddon Revisited: A World War One Journal* (Yale University Press, 1994) is revealing on American morale. It might be compared with the interesting use of oral testimony by historians of the Dominion forces such as Maurice Shadbolt, *Voices of Gallipoli* (Auckland, 1988) and Alistair Thomson, *Anzac Memories, Living with the Legend* (Oxford University Press, 1995), the latter in particular exposing 'hidden texts' in such evidence from dwindling numbers of veterans. This raises a lively area of debate involving English works on battle experience such as Jonathan Nicholls' *Cheerful Sacrifice: The Battle of Arras 1917* (London, Leo Cooper, 1990) which draws significantly on later recollections, oral and otherwise, and Peter Liddle's *The 1916 Battle of the Somme. A Reappraisal* (London, Leo Cooper, 1992), which however is based very largely upon contemporary sources in its description and analysis.

Turning to operational matters, the wider context of British strategy has continued to be well served through, for example, David French's trilogy, *British Economic and Strategic Planning, 1905–15* (London, Allen & Unwin, 1982), *British Strategy and War Aims, 1914–16* (London, Allen & Unwin, 1986) and *The Strategy of the Lloyd George Coalition, 1916–18* (Oxford, Clarendon Press, 1995) while the Great War volume of Allan Millett and Williamson Murray (eds.), *Military Effectiveness* (London and Boston, Allen & Unwin, 1988) provides an overview for all the major belligerents. However, neither British nor continental historians have contributed much as yet to a revival of interest in the actual conduct of combat, and the pioneering work has been undertaken by North American or Australian scholars. In two important works, *The Killing Ground* (London, Allen & Unwin, 1987) and *How the War Was Won* (London, Routledge, 1992), Tim Travers has advanced an explanation for the difficulties of the British Army in coming to terms with the new conditions of warfare in what might be characterised as largely managerial terms. By contrast, Robin Prior and Trevor Wilson have chosen to focus more on the technical problems of achieving breakthrough in *Command on the Western Front* (Oxford, Blackwell, 1992). The learning curve of all armies facing positional warfare is also well illustrated in Bill Rawling, *Surviving Trench Warfare: Technology and the Canadian Corps, 1914–18* (University of Toronto Press, 1992), Eric Andrews, *The Anzac Illusion: Anglo-Australian Relations during World War One* (Cambridge University Press, 1993), David Woodward, *Trial by Friendship: Anglo-American Relations, 1917–18* (Kentucky University Press, 1993) and David Trask, *The AEF and Coalition Warmaking, 1917–18* (University Press of Kansas, 1993). John Ferris, *The British Army and Signals Intelligence during the First World War* (Stroud, Alan Sutton for Army Records Society, 1992) represents another North American contribution to the understanding of operational matters and is useful as a supplement to the idiosyncratic study of British military intelligence by Michael Occleshaw, *Armour Against Fate* (London, Columbus Books, 1989). Equally idiosyncratic is one of the few British contributions to date, Paddy Griffith, *British Tactics of the Western Front* (New Haven, Yale University Press, 1994).

The revisionism implicit in the new operational studies raises the question of the reality of the image and collective memory of war and, in this regard, attention should be drawn to the devastating critique of Paul Fussell's still influential but seriously flawed *The Great War and Modern Memory* (Oxford, Clarendon Press, 1975) by Robin Prior and Trevor Wilson, 'Paul Fussell at War', *War in History* vol 1, 1, 1994, pp. 63–80. The failure of many cultural historians to comprehend military matters should always be borne in mind but there is increasing work being done on the war's varied cultural impact in volumes such as Modris Eksteins, *Rites of Spring: The Great War and the Birth of the Modern Age* (London, Bantam Press, 1989), Samuel Hynes, *A War Imagined: The First World War and English Culture* (London: Bodley Head, 1990), the superbly illustrated Richard Cork, *A Bitter Truth: Avant Garde Art and the Great War* (New Haven, Yale University Press, 1994), Annette Becker, *La Guerre et la foi: de la mort à la mémoire* (Paris, Armand Colin, 1994) and the slightly older Roland Stromberg, *Redemption by War: The Intellectuals and 1914* (Regents Press of Kansas, 1982). The literary impact is traced in Hugh Cecil, *The Flower of Battle: How Britain Wrote The Great War* (1996) and in *Intimate Enemies: English and German Literary Reactions to the Great War 1914–18*, edited by Franz Karl Stanzel and Martin Losnig (C. Winter Verlag, Heidelberg, 1992). Feminist, children's and gender perspectives are variously explored in Margaret Higgonet et al (eds.), *Behind the Lines: Gender and the Two World Wars* (New Haven, Yale University Press, 1987), Claire Tylee, *The Great War and Women's Consciousness: Images of Militarism and Womanhood in Women's Writings, 1914–64* (London, Macmillan, 1990), Christine Bard, *Les filles de Marianne: Histoire des femininismes, 1914–18* (Paris, Fayard, 1995), Miriam Cooke and Angela Woolacott, *Gendering War Talk* (Princeton University Press, 1993), Stéphane Audoin-Rouzeau, *La Guerre des enfants 1914–18: essai d'histoire culturelle* (Paris, A. Colin, 1993) and Klaus Thewelweit, *Male Fantasies* (Minneapolis, University of Minnesota Press, 1987), which deals primarily with writings by veterans who became members of the Freikorps. One of the first fruits of the increasing postgraduate investigation of the process of war commemoration is a study of armistice day in Britain, Adrian Gregory, *The Silence of Memory* (Oxford, Berg, 1994). For France, see Annette Becker, *Les monuments aux morts, mémoire de la Grande Guerre* (Paris, Errance, 1988) and, for Germany, Robert Weldon Whalen, *Bitter Wounds: German Victims of the Great War* (Ithaca and London, 1984) while a general overview is provided by George Mosse, *Fallen Soldiers: Shaping the Memory of the World Wars* (New York: Oxford University Press, 1990).

It has not been possible in the space available to mention more than a handful of books and even this has necessitated the omission of reference to most journal articles, conference papers, unpublished dissertations and theses and work in press. Naval and aerial aspects have also been omitted. For a more comprehensive coverage of recent publications on British military aspects of the Great War, reference may be had to Ian Beckett, 'Revisiting the Old Front Line', *Stand To* no. 43, 1995, pp. 10–14 and, for the evolution of British historiography of the war generally, the essays in Brian Bond (ed.), *The First World War and British Military History* (Oxford, Clarendon Press, 1991).

Notes on Contributors

Professor Stephane Audoin-Rouzeau, University of Picardie, Amiens and Co-Director of the Centre for Research at l'Historial de la Grande Guerre (Péronne-Somme).
French Children: as Target for Propaganda and *The French Soldier in the Trenches.* Professor Audoin-Rouzeau is the author of *La Guerre des Enfants (1914–18)* and *Men at War 1914–18* on French national sentiment and trench journalism and of *L'enfant de l'ennemi: (1914–18)*

Andrew Bamji, Consultant Rheumatologist, Queen Mary's Hospital, Sidcup.
Facial Surgery: The Patient's Experience. Andrew Bamji is Honorary Consultant Archivist at Queen Mary's and has lectured widely on the First World War facial surgery records at the hospital.

Professor Annette Becker, Charles de Gaulle University, Lille.
Life in an Occupied Zone: Lille, Roubaix, Tourcoing 1914–18. Co-director of the Centre for research at l'Historial de la Grande Guerre (Péronne-Somme). Her publications include *La Guerre et la foi, de la mort à la mémoire* (1994, English edition 1995).

Professor Jean-Jacques Becker, Nanterre University, Paris.
Opposition to the War in France: the Case of Clovis Andrieu. Dr Becker's many publications on France and the Great War include *The Great War and the French People* (1985).

Dr Ian Beckett, The Royal Military Academy, Sandhurst.
Facing Armageddon: a Select Bibliography. Dr Beckett, author of *The Amateur Military Tradition* (1991), has written extensively on the British Army and co-edited *A Nation in Arms*, a social study of the British Army in the First World War.

Professor Brian Bond, King's College, London.
British 'Anti-war' writers and their critics. Brian Bond is President of the British Commission for Military History. His numerous publications include (as editor) *The First World War and British Military History* and he is currently completing a book on *The Pursuit of Victory: Napoleon to Saddam Hussein.*

Dr Genadii Bordiugov, Moscow State University.
A Nation at War: The Russian Experience. Dr Bordiugov is General Editor of a new series of monographs on Russian History.

Professor Nick Bosanquet, Imperial College, The University of London.
Health Systems in Khaki: The British and American Experience. Professor Bosanquet's interest in military medicine has grown out of his research into the management of health services.

Dr John Bourne, The University of Birmingham.
The British Working Man in Arms. John Bourne is the author of *Great Britain and the First World War* and is working on a computer-based study of British divisional commanders.

Jack Bruce, former Visiting Professor at the Smithsonian Institute, Washington D.C.
The War in the Air: the Men and their Machines. Jack Bruce, through his aeroplane monographs and his book, *The Aeroplanes of the Royal Flying Corps (Military Wing)* is a recognised world expert on the British aeroplanes of the First World War.

Professor Vladimir Buldakov, Institute of Russian History, Russian Academy of Sciences, Moscow and General Secretary of the International Commission on the History of the October Revolution.
A Nation at War: The Russian Experience.

Professor George Cassar, Eastern Michigan University, Ypsilanti, Michigan.
Kitchener at the War Office. Professor Cassar's many published works include *Kitchener, Architect of Victory* and *Asquith as War Leader* [1994].

Dr Hugh Cecil, The University of Leeds.
British War Novelists. Dr Cecil is co-editor of *Facing Armageddon.* His most recent book is *The Flower of Battle: How Britain wrote the First World War* [U.S. edn. 1996].

Professor James Cooke, The University of Mississippi, U.S.A.
The American soldier in France 1917–19. Dr Cooke's publications include *The Rainbow Division in the Great War 1917–19* [1994]. He is currently writing on Pershing and his Generals.

Dr Mark Cornwall, The University of Dundee.
The Experience of Yugoslav Agitation in Austria–Hungary, 1917–18. Dr Cornwall, editor of a book of essays on *The Last Years of Austria–Hungary* [1990], is currently working upon military propaganda in this field.

Dr Irina Davidian, The Institute of National Problems in Education, Moscow.
The Russian Soldier's Morale by the Evidence of Tsarist Military Censorship.

Professor Eberhard Demm, Jean Moulin University, Lyon.
German Teachers at War. Professor Demm has published widely on German Ostpolitik and war ideology, including *Der erste Weltkrieg in der internationalen Karikatur*.

Mark Derez, The University Archives of the Catholic University of Louvain, Belgium.
The Flames of Louvain: The War Experience of an Academic Community. Marc Derez has published on the history of universities and higher education.

Dr Frank Field, The University of Keele.
The French War Novel: the Case of Louis-Ferdinand Céline. Dr Field is the author of *British and French Writers of the First World War* [1991] and of *Three French Writers of the Great War* [1975].

Professor Imanuel Geiss, The University of Bremen, Germany.
The Civilian Dimension of the War. Dr Geiss first achieved eminence through research into Germany and the origins of the First World War *July 1914* [1967 English translation]. More recently he has published a multi-volume world history.

Sir Martin Gilbert, Winston Churchill's Official Biographer.
Winston Churchill and the Strain of Office, 1914–1915. Dr Gilbert's many works on 20th-century history include *The First World War* [1994].

Professor John Gooch, The University of Leeds.
Morale and Discipline in the Italian Army 1915–18. Professor Gooch is the Director of the Leeds University Institute of International Studies. His publications on the military history of the period include, *The Plans of War: The General Staff and British Military Strategy 1900–1916.*

Dr Paul Gough, The University of the West of England, Bristol.
The Experience of British Artists in the Great War. Paul Gough's doctoral thesis was on British Art of the First World War. He has exhibited widely as a painter and is represented in the permanent collection of the Imperial War Museum. His recent publications cover the artist's response to the battle landscape of the Western Front.

Dr Keith Grieves, Kingston University, Kingston upon Thames.
War Correspondents and Conducting Officers on the Western Front from 1915. Dr Grieves is the author of *The Politics of Manpower 1914–18* and biographer of Sir Eric Geddes, who organised the British Expeditionary Force railways on the Western Front. Dr Grieves is currently working on the early historiography of the Great War.

Dr Mark Harrison, Sheffield Hallam University.
The Fight against Disease in the Mesopotamian Campaign. Dr Harrison is the author of articles on the medical aspects of war and imperialism and of *Public Health in British India: Anglo–Indian Preventive Medicine, 1859–1914.* He is currently completing a book entitled *Medicine and British Warfare, 1898–1918.*

Professor Richard Holmes, Co-director, Security Studies Institute, [Royal Military College of Science] Cranfield University.
The Last Hurrah: Cavalry on the Western Front, August–September 1914. Dr Holmes is Consultant Historian at the Army Staff College, Camberley. His publications include *The Little Field Marshal: Sir John French* and most recently, *Charger* which relates to the British retirement from Mons in August 1914.

Dr Alyson Jackson, The University of Leeds.
Germany, the Home Front: Blockade, Government and Revolution. Dr Jackson is a scientist with a scholarly interest in the First World War.

Professor Rashid Khalidi, Director of the Center for International Studies, University of Chicago.
The Arab Experience of the War. Dr Khalidi is the author of *British Policy Towards Syria and Palestine 1906–1914.* His forthcoming book is on the genesis of Palestinian national identity (Columbia University Press, 1996).

Peter Kilduff, Central Connecticut State University, New Britain, Connecticut.
A German Airman and his War: Oscar Bechtle. Peter Kilduff's publications on aviation history include *Germany's First Air Force 1914–1918* and most recently *Richthofen – Beyond the Legend of the Red Baron* [1993]. His work has earned him the Order of Merit of the Federal Republic of Germany.

Professor Martin Kitchen, Simon Fraser University, Burnaby, British Columbia.
Ludendorff and Germany's Defeat. Dr Kitchen has many books on German history to his credit, among them *The German Officer Corps 1890–1914* and *The Silent Dictatorship: The Politics of the German High Command 1916–18* and more recently, *Germany in the Age of Total War* [1981].

Dr Sergei Kudryashev, Moscow.
A Nation at War: The Russian Experience. Dr Koudryashev is an expert in Russian warfare of the 20th Century and has been responsible for publishing many documents from Stalin's personal archives.

Tony Lane, The University of Liverpool.
The Merchant Seaman at War. Tony Lane is an ex-seafarer and is the author of a book on the Second World War, *The Merchant Seamen's War.*

John Lee, London.
Sir Ian Hamilton after the War: A Liberal General Reflects. John Lee, Honorary Treasurer of the British Commission for Military History, is currently working on a biography of Sir Ian Hamilton. His other main interest is in the operational military history of the First World War.

Jane Leonard, The Institute of Irish Studies, The Queen's University, Belfast.
The Reactions of Irish Officers in the British Army to the Easter Rising of 1916. Jane Leonard has contributed actively to academic seminars in the UK and the Republic of Ireland. Her PhD thesis is on ex-servicemen and political change in Ireland.

Peter Liddle, The Liddle Collection, The University Of Leeds.
British Loyalties: the Evidence of an Archive. Peter Liddle is co-editor of *Facing Armageddon* and Founder and Keeper of the First World War Collection in Leeds. His publications include, *The Battle of the Somme* and *The Worst Ordeal: Britons at Home and Abroad 1914–18* [1994] and he is engaged in T.V. and multi-media consultancy on the War.

Professor Peter Loewenberg, The University of California, Los Angeles. *Germany, The Home Front. The Physical and Psychological Consequence of Home Front Hardship.* Dr Loewenberg is Professor of History and Political Psychology, teaching European cultural and intellectual history, and author of *Decoding the Past* and *Fantasy and Reality in History* [1995].

Dr Bullitt Lowry, The University of North Texas, Denton, Texas. *War Experience and Armistice Conditions: Generals and Politicians.* Dr Lowry has written extensively on the First World War. His most recent book is entitled *Armistice, 1918* [1995].

Professor Thomas Nevin, John Carroll University, Cleveland, Ohio. *Ernst Jünger: German Stormtrooper Chronicler.* Dr Nevin's book on Ernst Jünger is to be published in Britain and the U.S.A.

Dr Sharon Ouditt, Nottingham Trent University. *Tommy's Sisters: The Representation of Working Women's Experience.* Dr Ouditt, author of *Fighting Forces, Writing Women* [1994], is working on a bibliography of women's writings of the First World War.

Captain Chris Page R.N., Head of Defence Studies, Royal Navy, Royal Naval College, Greenwich. *The British Experience of Enforcing Blockade: the Armed Merchant Cruisers in 1915.* Captain Page is currently researching a biography of Arthur Asquith.

Dr Robin Prior, Australian Defence Force Academy, Canberra. *British Decision-making 1917: Lloyd George, the Generals and Passchendaele.* Dr Prior has collaborated with Trevor Wilson in the production of *Command on the Western Front: the Military Career of Sir Henry Rawlinson* and on *Passchendaele: the Untold Story* [1995].

Professor Patrick Quinn, Nene College, Northampton. *The Experience of War in American Patriotic Literature.* Dr Quinn, an American, is Professor of English Literature and editor of *Focus*, the literary journal on Robert Graves and his contemporaries.

Dr Werner Rahn, Kapitän zur See, Militärgeschichtliches Forschungsamt, Potsdam. *The German Naval War 1914–18: Strategy and Experience.* Dr Rahn is Director of the Military History Research Office in Potsdam. He is the author of several articles and a book (*Reichsmarine und Landesverteidigung 1919–1928*) on the German navy in the twentieth century.

Dr Nicholas Reeves, Thames Valley University, London.
Through the Eye of the Camera: Contemporary Cinema Audiences and their Experience of War in the Film, "Battle of the Somme". Dr Reeves has published *Official British Film Propaganda during the First World War* [1986].

Professor Donald Richter, Ohio University, Athens, Ohio.
The Experience of the British Special Brigade in Gas Warfare. Dr Richter is the author of *Chemical Soldiers*, the British use of gas in the First World War. He is preparing for publication the letters of Lionel Sotheby, a British infantry officer killed in France in 1915.

Professor Keith Robbins, Principal, University of Wales, Lampeter.
The British Experience of Conscientious Objection. President of the Historical Association 1988–91 and Editor of *History* 1977–86, Professor Robbins' numerous publications include *The Abolition of War: The British Peace Movement 1914–19* and *The First World War.*

Diana Shaw.
The Forgotten Army of Women: Queen Mary's Army Auxiliary Corps. Diana Shaw is a civil servant working with a government agency under the Cabinet Office.

Dr Gary Sheffield, Royal Military Academy, Sandhurst.
Officer–Man Relations, Discipline and Morale in the British Army of the Great War. Gary Sheffield has edited the letters of Christopher Stone, an officer in the 22nd Royal Fusiliers: *From Vimy Ridge to the Rhine.* His work on the Military Police appeared in 1995.

Vice Admiral Renato Sicurezza, Former Head of Ufficio Storico della Marina Militare, Rome.
Italy and the War in the Adriatic. Admiral Sicurezza has recently retired from his post as the Chief Historian in the Italian Navy. In this position and as President of the Italian Commission for Military History he organised conferences, published many articles and edited books on related themes.

Peter Simkins, Imperial War Museum, London.
The War Experience of a Typical Kitchener Division – the 18th Division. Senior Historian for the Imperial War Museum since 1976, Peter Simkins is the author of *Kitchener's Army*, the definitive work on British voluntary recruitment in the First World War and he is currently engaged on research for a book entitled *Haig's Army.*

Keith Simpson, Co-director, Security Studies Institute, [Royal Military College of Science] Cranfield University.
Dr James Dunn and Shell-shock. Keith Simpson, who has published *The Old Contemptibles*, [1981], was co-editor of *A Nation in Arms* [1985] and editor of the reissued *The War the Infantry Knew* by Captain J.C. Dunn.

Dr Leonard Smith, Oberlin College, Oberlin, Ohio.
The French High Command and the Mutinies of Spring 1917. Dr Smith has written *Between Mutiny and Obedience: the Case of the French Fifth Infantry Division during World War I* [1994].

Professor Edward Spiers, The University of Leeds.
The Scottish Soldier at War. Professor Spiers is the author of *Haldane: An Army Reformer; Chemical Warfare; The Army and Society 1815–1914* and *The Late Victorian Army.*

Professor Hew Strachan, The University of Glasgow.
The Morale of the German Army, 1917–18. Professor Strachan is a leading historian of Europe's armies in the modern age. He is currently working on the *Oxford History of the First World War* and is joint editor of a new journal *War in History.*

John Terraine
The Substance of the War. John Terraine has written some of the most widely discussed and influential works of the past 30 years on the British General Staff and the myths surrounding the First World War. They include *Douglas Haig, the Educated Soldier* and *White Heat: the New Warfare 1914–18* and his celebrated television series on the history of the Great War.

Professor Geoffrey Till, Royal Naval College, Greenwich.
Brothers in Arms: The British Army and Navy at the Dardanelles. Professor Till holds the Chair of History and International Affairs at Greenwich. His many works include *Modern Sea Power* and *The Sea in Soviet Strategy.*

Professor Luigi Tomassini, The University of Florence.
The Home Front in Italy. Dr Tomassini, who has published articles on industrial mobilisation and state intervention in Italy during the First World War, is currently working on 'scientific mobilisation' in this period.

Dr Frank Vandiver, Texas A & M University, College Station, Texas.
Haig and Pershing. Dr Vandiver, President Emeritus of his University, is

the author of numerous books on the American Civil War and the biographer of General Pershing, *Black Jack*.

Dr Bernard Waites, The Open University, Milton Keynes.
Peoples of the Underdeveloped World. Bernard Waites is the author of *A Class Society at War 1914–18*. He is currently working on the political and economic relationship of the Third World and the developed countries.

Dr Geoffrey Wawro, Oakland University, Rochester, Michigan.
Morale in the Austro–Hungarian Army. Dr Wawro's book, *The Austro–Prussian War: Austria's War with Prussia and Italy in 1866* will be published by Cambridge University Press in 1996.

Dr Ian Whitehead, The University of Derby.
Not a Doctor's Work? The Role of the British Regimental Medical Officer in the Field. Ian Whitehead is extending his doctoral research in the work of the British Medical Officer at the front.

Professor Trevor Wilson, The University of Adelaide, South Australia.
British Decision-making, 1917: Lloyd George, the Generals and Passchendaele. Professor Wilson is the author of the most comprehensive history of Britain's part in the First World War, *The Myriad Faces of War*. With Robin Prior he has written on Sir Henry Rawlinson and most recently *Passchendaele: the Untold Story* (1995).

Dr Jay Winter, Pembroke College, Cambridge.
Painting Armageddon. Dr Winter is the author of *The Great War and the British People* [1986] and is the General Editor of a series on the legacy of the First World War, sponsored by l'Historial de la Grande Guerre, Péronne.

Professor Erik Zürcher, The University of Amsterdam and The Catholic University of Nijmegen.
Little Mehmet in the Desert: The Ottoman Soldier's Experience. Professor of Ottoman and Turkish History and Senior Lecturer in Middle East History, Professor Zürcher has published on the political and social history of the late Ottoman Empire and the Turkish Republic.

Index

Alexander, FM H. 1st Earl of Tunis (1891–1969), 824
Alexander, Regent of Serbia, 670
Algeo, Capt., 420
Algeria, support for war, 603–4
Allatini, Rose, 802
Allen, Clifford, 697, 698, 699, 700
Allenby, FM Sir Edmund H.H., Visct. Megiddo (1861–1936), in Egypt, 649; and Palestine, 279, 652; style of command, 279
alliances, 12–13, 127, 231, 755
Almeida, P. Camena d', on German deserters, 387
Almereyda, Miguel, 677
Alsace, 56, 61, 104, 105, 106, 111, 632
Alsatian, 141
Altrichter, Friedrich, 388, 395–6
Amalfi, 182, 183, 192
America see United States
American Expeditionary Force see also United States army; Allied expectations of, 110; attitudes to the French, 249; attitudes to the Germans, 249; French attitudes to, 249; impressions of Europe, 247–8; learning period, 110–11; training; logistics failure, 251; medical services see medical services; morale, 245, 247; numbers, 242–3; occupation forces, 251; and prostitution, 248–9, 461; reactions to casualties, 250–1; resentment over order of return to US, 251–2; returning troops, reception of, 252–4; soldiers' experiences, 242–54; status of, 111; training, 245–7, 249–50
Amiens, 303
amphibious operations, 160, 161
Amphion, 5
Ancre, 302
Andrieu, Clovis, 678–90; background, 679; and St.Étienne strikes, 680–8
Angell, Sir Norman, 692
Anglo-German Society, 884, 886
Angus, Piper Archie, retrieved pipes from No Man's Land, 322
anti-submarine warfare, 5–6
Aonzo, Midshpmn. Giuseppe, commander of MAS21, 188–9
Arab world, Br. and Fr. spheres of influence, 651; Br. occupation of Palestine and Iraq, 652; effect of blockade, 645; impact of war on

civilians, 645; and independence from Turks, 647; loyalties, 647; main war theatres, 644–5; newspapers, 648–9; poor harvests, 645; pre-1914 European occupation, 643; and Pres. Wilson's 14 Points, 650–1, 652; Sykes-Picot accords, 651, 652; trial and execution of Arab nationalists, 645–6, 648; troops see Turkish army, Arab troops; and WWI, pl.50, 642–53
Aragon, Louis, 832, 836
Aragon, 155–8
Arcadian, 165, 170
Archer, William, and Alan Seeger, 756
Ardant du Picq, Charles, on infantry tactics, 281
Argonne, 269, 462
armed merchant cruisers, British, 134–43
Armenian, massacres, 19, 238, 640; migration from Turkey, 238
Armistice see also Versailles Treaty; reactions to terms, 103–16
armoured cars, 193, 194
armoured trains, 184–5
Arras, 275, 279, 302, 360, 893; Loretto Heights, 269; Mars offensive, 54
Art, and allegory, 853, 859, 861, 862, 863, 868, 872; Apocalyptic, 854–72; British Artists at the Front, 726; and censorship, 850; children's drawings, 771; motivation, 843–8; official artists, 558, 726, 841, 842; reconnaissance landscapes, 847; sketchbooks, 845–6, 851; soldier artists, 136, 841–52, 844; and spying, 848–50; *The Western* Front, 726; and Theosophy, 855; vorticists, 848
Arthur, George, 39
ASDIC, 6
Ashley, Charles, and gas, 361
Ashmead-Bartlett, Ellis, and the Dardanelles, 172
Ashton, J.C. RMO, 466
Ashwell, Lena, concert parties, 535
Ashworth, Gunner, 499
Asquith, H.H., 1st Earl of Oxford (1852–1928), and Churchill, 27–8, 30, 31, 32, 33, 34, 41; and conscientious objection, 693, 704; drinking, 27; and Kitchener, 42, 47; on munitions supplies, 42; ousted by Lloyd George, 85; strain,

163; support for Dardanelles expedition, 41, 44
Asquith, Margot, Countess of Oxford, 31
Atkinson, Capt. MN, 155
Atkinson, H., MN, 155–8
Atlantic Monthly, 759
atrocities *see also* executions; allegations and their effect on Scot. troops, 326; destruction of Kalisch, 18, 620; East African campaign, pl.2; gas warfare, 360; Habsburg army on Serbian civilians, 402, 406; in Kosovo and Albania, 17; Louvain, 18, 617–28; massacre of Armenians, 19, 238, 640; and occupation, 631, 633–4, 636, 638–40; Ruthenian peasants hanged by Austrian troops, 20
Attems, Count, 665
Aubers Ridge, 42, 321
Audacious, 6
Audoin-Rouzeau, Stéphane, rationale for war, 391
'Augusterlebnis', 17
Australian Imperial Force, attitude to Germans, 279, 325; oral history, 893; at Pozières, 279; respect for Turks, 279; at Villers-Bretonneux, 303; 3rd Light Horse Brigade, 279
Austria, Italy's age old enemy, 180
Austria-Hungary, army *see* Austro-Hungarian army; and censorship, 660–1, 667, 670; espionage network in Italy, 186; ethnic tensions, 399–400, 407, 409–10; food, demonstrations, 665; supply problems, 660–2
hunger in, 20, 21, 408–9, 661–2; Magyars hated, 661; May Declaration, 656, 658, 662–6, 668–72; navy *see* Austro-Hungarian navy; Reichsrat, and S. Slavs, 658; Social Democratic Party, 671; Starcevič party, 668; war with Italy, 180–92, 402; Yugoslav agitation, 657–73
Austro-Hungarian army, atrocities, 402, 406; Bosnian Serbs, 401; chronic failure, 400–1; collapse of, 404, 408; composition of, 400; Croats, 401; Czechs, 399, 401; defeat in Galicia, 401; desertions, 402, 404, 407–9; and ethnic divisions, 399–400, 401, 407, 409–10;

Germanisation and effects of, 399–400; hostility to Habsburgs, 400–1; indiscipline, 405–6; invasion of Serbia, 401, 404–6; loyalty problems, 404, 666, 667; Magyars, 401, 402; mass surrenders, 402, 404, 408, 409; morale, 401–10; mutiny, 405, 408; as opponents, 278; Piave offensive, 407–9; propped up by Reich Germans, 401, 402; reliability of national units, 401; restructuring, 399; routed in Serbia, 401–2; and Schlieffen Plan, 401; shirkers, 406; 'shock' troops, 403; Slovenes, 666, 667; Trentino *Straffexpedition*, 440; Tyrol offensive shattered, 402; Ukraine, failed defence of, 402; unable to defend itself, 403
Austro-Hungarian army,
South Army, 401, 404
2nd Army, 404–5
5th Army, 405
VIII Corps, 406
36th Croatian Division, 405
21st Landwehr Division, 405
1st Hungarian Honvéd Regiment, 407
31st Rumanian Regiment, 409
44th Regiment, 405
53rd Croatian Regiment, 405
64th Regiment, 407
65th Hungarian Regiment, 409
96th Croatian Regiment, 405, 408
Austro-Hungarian navy, bombards Italian coastal towns, 184–5; composition of fleet, 181; mutiny, 187–8, 407; sabotage mission against Brindisi, 186; submarines, 150, 182
Austro-Prussian War, 1866, 709
aviation, development of, 195–6; early military use, 7–8
Ayles, Walter, 701, 702

Babington, Judge Anthony, on army doctors, 515
Baboeuf, 303, 308
Babtie, Surg.-Gen. W., 477
Bacon, Adm. Sir R.H.S. (1863–1947), 87
Badoglio, Gen. Pietro, 443
Bahr, Sgt.Mjr. Erich, 207, 209–10
Bailey, Temple, *The Tin Soldier*, 760–1
Bainsizza, 403, 441

British army *(continued)*
  51st (Highland) Division, 316, 317, 324
  Royal Artillery, 9–10, 283–4
  Royal Field Artillery, 283, 284, 289
  Royal Horse Artillery, 283, 290
  53rd Trench Mortar Battery, 303
  Royal Engineers,
    Air Battalion, 194
    field survey companies, 10
    Signal Service, 284
    Special [gas] Brigade, pl.28, 354–62
  Camouflage Corps, 843
  Royal Flying Corps *see* British air force
  Royal Army Medical Corps, pl.35, 452,
    454, 455, 458–9, 466–73, 502, 503,
    506
  Women's Army Auxiliary Corps, 365–76
British cavalry,
  Cavalry Corps, 285, 290
  5th Cavalry Brigade, 290
  regiments,
    4th Dragoon Guards, 286, 291
    14th Hussars, 288
    15th Hussars, 282
    12th Lancers, 280, 290
    Royal Scots Greys, 290
British Expeditionary Force (BEF) *see
  also* British army; British cavalry;
  British infantry; weapons; acute
  shortages in, 1914, 298; adoption
  of steel helmet, 454, 490;
  artillery, 8, 10; allied superiority in,
    1918, 384; at Mons, 286; training,
    298–9
  attitudes, to enemy, 325–7, 525; to High
    Command, 527; to homefront
    'shirkers', 525–7; to politicians,
    527; to the press, 527
  bantam battalions, 315; cavalry,
    279–80, 285–92; comradeship,
    pl.41, 318–19, 527; and
    conscription, 308; convoying of,
    33–4; discipline, 307, 321–2,
    324–5, 344–5; divisions,
    reorganisation, 384–5; drafts,
    quality of, 507–8; evolution of
    1915 to, 1918, 298;
  GHQ, and artists, 849; intelligence
    section, 286, 719, 720; irrelevance
    of in, 1918, 297; press camp, 720,
    728, 729
  high command incompetence, myth
    of, 523; 'Hundred Days', 303–4,
    309; inadequate supplies, 12;
    landing and advance missed by

Germans, 8; leadership in 18th
  Div., 304–5; medical services *see*
  medical services; morale, aspects of,
  322, 323, 413–21; mutiny at
  Étaples, 421;
New Army Divisions, 297–309, 338;
  shortage of experienced regulars,
  298–9, 338
officer-man relations, 305–7, 319–20,
  338, 413–21, 527; officers *see*
  British army, officers;
  overwhelmingly working class,
  336; pals battalions, 315;
  reorganisation in, 1918, 298; and
  the RFC, 196; shyness in attack,
  508–9; Soldiers and Workers
  Council, 421; success on the
  battlefield, factors, 308–9;
tactics, all-arms small unit, 303;
  decentralisation of, 297
values, Regular Army v. civilian,
  339–41; views of French and
  Belgian civilians, 527–8; weapons,
  341; welfare facilities, 349; wounds
  and Blighty ones, 525
British infantry *see also* British Expeditionary
  Force (BEF)
  53rd Brigade, 298, 302, 307
  54th Brigade, 302, 303, 304
  55th Brigade, 304, 306, 307
  regiments,
    Argyll and Suth. Highlndrs, 318, 320,
    321, 325, 327
    Artists Rifles, 842
    Bedfords, 304, 305
    Black Watch, 315, 316, 320, 321, 322,
    323, 324, 327
    Border Regt., 323
    Buffs (East Kent), 302, 306, 307, 308
    Cameron Highlanders, 316, 317, 320,
    321, 324
    Connaught Rangers, 259, 260
    Dublin University OTC, 257–8
    East Surrey, 282, 298, 302, 306, 307
    East Yorkshire, 503, 511
    Essex, pl.26, 303, 305–6, 308
    Glasgow Highlanders, 317
    Gordon Highlanders, 317, 319–20,
    321, 322, 323, 324
    Highland Light Infantry, pl.27,
    314–15, 316, 317, 321, 323
    Inniskilling Fusiliers, 263
    Kings Own Scottish Borderers, 318,
    322

Ciano, Constanzo, commander of MAS craft, 185–6

cinema *see also* literature; British, 780–93, 821; documentary, 781–93; German, 392; post-war, 525

Clan Davidson, 149

Clan Macrae, pl.11

Clark, Alan, 828

Clarke, Pte. 'Nobby', and a lost horse, 289

Clausewitz, Karl von (1780–1831), and challenge to military authority, 84, 89; 'friction' in the military machine, 84; *On War*, 79

Claxton, B. Brooke, soldiering a form of work, 345

Clayton, Lt. Lancashire Fus., 170

Clemenceau, George (1841–1929), animosity against Foch, 110; armistice terms, 104, 107, 110, 111, 112; and Clovis Andrieu, 683; and Pershing, 75

climate, effect on troops, 359–60, 485, 507; effect on war, 278

Cloete, Stuart, 804

Co-operative Movement, 346

coastal bombardment, 122, 123, 184–5

Cocteau, Jean, 832

codes, diplomatic, 127; German navy, 6–7

Comité de défence syndicaliste, 684, 686, 687, 688

Comité intercorporatif de la Loire, 683

command, style, 279, 285

Committee for the Resumption of International Relations, 678

communications, 7, 284–5; radio telephony, in aircraft, 195–6; semaphore, 283; telephone, land lines, 7, 283, 284; wireless telegraphy, 6–7, 9

comradeship, 318–19, 345–6

concentration camps, 635

concert parties, 349

Confédération des Métaux, 678, 686

Confédération Générale du Travail, 677, 678, 679, 684, 687, 689

Congo, Belgian, rise of Joseph Kimbangu, 22

Congrès d'Amiens, 679

Connolly, James (1870–1916), 257, 260, 262

Conrad, Gen. Franz von Hötzendorf,

and Falkenhayn, 402; and the Piave, 403, 407–8

conscientious objection, 523, 526–7, 534, 691–704; pacifism; and Defence of the Realm Act, 698; definition, 692; and Military Service Act, 693, 697; No-Conscription Fellowship, 697–700, 704; and Non-Combatant Corps, 694; numbers, 695; and public opinion, 697; reasons for, 695–6; and religion, 693–4, 696, 698; and Socialism, 696–701; tribunals, 694–5; and 'White Feathers', 693; and William Pitt, 693

convoys, 128, 149, 153–4

Cook, Lt-Col. Frank P., 851

Cooksey, Pte. C., 305–6

Coolidge, 2nd Lt. Hamilton (U.S.Army), 247–8

Cooper, Selina, 746

Coppard, George, 827, 843

Coquet, 150

Corbett, Sir Julian S., 161, 165, 167, 168

Cordeaux, Lt-Col., 527

Cornford, L.Cope, on merchant seamen, 147, 148

Cornwall, Col. Marshall, 72

Coronel, 125

Cortelazzo, 187, 192

Crabbe, Maj. John R.S.Greys, 325

Craiglockhart War Hospital, 513

Cranach, Lucas, 861

Crane, Stephen, *The Red Badge of Courage*, 753, 762

Crapouillot, Le, trench newspaper, 224, 227, 228, 229n

Creighton, Basil, translation of *Storm of Steel*, 270

Crile, George, shell-shock specialist, 453, 454–5

Croatia, 399, 552, 657, 659, 660, 661, 667, 668, 669–72

Croy, Princess de, 636

Cude, Robert (battalion runner), 306, 307–8

Cunningham, Adm. Sir Andrew B. (1883–1963) 1st Visct. Hyndhope, 171

Cunningham, Lt. James C., 325

Cunnington, Sgt. Humphrey, 306

Curzon, Lord George (1859–1925), 100, 173

Cushing, Harvey, neuro-surgeon, 456, 460

cyclists, and cavalry tasks, 286
Czapp, FM, Austrian Defence Minister,
    666

Dahomey, Fr. patriotism among évolués,
    605
Dakin, H.D., wound treatment, 453–4
Dallolio, Gen. Alfredo, 579
Dalmatia, 657, 659, 660, 661, 668, 669,
    670, 672
Dalrymple, James, and the 15th HLI,
    315
Danant, Gen., and Clovis Andrieu, 682
Dardanelles Commission, 160
Dardanelles Committee, 43, 44, 45, 47
Dardanelles expedition, 29, 32–3, 35–6,
    41, 44; Gallipoli; artillery
    deficiencies, 172–3; and beri-beri,
    484; cooperation of army and
    navy, 160–77, 174–77; departure
    of battleships, 42, 163, 164, 175;
    evacuation, 163, 164, 167, 173;
    gunfire, naval, support for
    landings, 169–71, 172; naval cutter
    crews under fire, 156, 169, 176;
    sickness and strain of commanders,
    164–5; strategic decision making,
    84; successes, 168
Dare, Phyllis, 692
Davidson, Cpl. RAMC, 498, 499
Davies, Leslie, MN, 153
Dawes, Capt.G.W.P. RFC, 194
Dawson, Maj-Gen. Sir B., 463
Dawson, Coningsby, 762, 763
Day, Sgt. F.D., 527
Day, Fl.Lt. M.J. RFC, 201
De Havilland, Sir Geoffrey, aircraft
    designer, 196, 198, 200–1
De Robeck, Adm. Sir John M.
    (1862–1928), 163, 164, 165, 167
De Valera, Eamon (1882–1975), 263
Deane, Capt. E.C. RMO, 466
Dearden, Harold RMO, 505, 515
Deist, Wilhelm, 385, 391
Delmira, 148
Dent, Capt., 170
Derby, Sir Edward G.V.S.
    K.G.(1865–1948) 17th Earl, 101,
    367
desertion, aid Societies, 393; Austro-
    Hungarian army, 402, 404, 407–9;
    and death penalty, 515–16; Fr,
    African conscripts, 605; German
    army, 385, 387–8, 391, 393–4,
    395, 573, 574; Indian troops, 479;

Italian army, 439, 441, 442, 586;
    merchant seamen, 151–2; New
    Army Divisions, 307; Poles in
    German army, 388; Russian army,
    430, 542; and shell-shock, 511;
    Turkish army, 234, 235, 485
Diagne, Blaise, Senegalese Deputy, 604,
    605–6
Diaz, Gen. A., concern for morale,
    443–5; Piave offensive, 409;
    replaces Cadorna, 443
Dickens, Arthur, 264
Dickson, Capt. Bertram, 197
Dickson, Gen. DLR MEF, 482
Dimovic, Danilo, 671
direction-finding, wireless, 7
discipline, 141–3, 191–2, 307, 321–2,
    324–5, 338, 344–5, 416, 436–42,
    515, 516; mutinies
diseases *see* medical services
Dix, Otto, 854, 859–63
Dodd, John, 726
Doerry, Edith, and homefront Germany,
    563–4, 573–4
Dogger Bank, 123, 135
Dos Passos, John, 763, 764
Douglas, MRAF William Sholto
    (1893–1969), 198–9
Douglas-Hamilton, Lt-Col. A.F. VC, 320
Doyle, Sir A.C., and Louvain, 621
Drieu La Rochelle, 832, 833–4, 838, 839
drink, intrepid when fortified, 273;
    merchant seamen, 152–3; and
    Russia, 549, 550; Russian soldiers,
    541–2; and Scot. troops, 320–1
Druid, 135
Dublin, 1916 Easter Rising, pl.22, 257–8
Dubost, Antonin (President of French
    Senate), 81
Duchêne, Gen. Denis, 81, 85
Duff, Charles, 261–2
Duhamel, Georges, 832
Dumoulin, Georges, 687–8
Dunalley, Lord, 259–60
Duncan, Lt-Col. F.J., 320
Duncan, *Rev*.G.S., chaplain to Haig, 73
Dundas, Capt. R.H., 327
Dunham, Frank, 827
Dunn, Capt. James C. RAMC, as an
    RMO, pl.40, 457, 503–11, 515–17;
    background, 502–3; and death
    penalty, 515; gassed, 510; and loss
    of nerve, 510–11; and malingerers,
    504–5, 512, 513–14; and Pensions
    Appeal Tribunal, 6511; and

performance indicators, 457; and shell shock, 502–17; *The War the Infantry Knew*, 502, 506–17passim, 821; and training, 508–9, 514
Dunning, Sqd.Cdr. E.H. RNAS, 203
Dupierreux, Robert, and Louvain, 622
Duval, Emile-Joseph, 677

East African Protectorate, and E. African campaign, 608
Ebert, Friedrich, 573
Ecole (Supérieure) de Guerre, 8, 105
economic planning, 555
Edgar, 141
Edmonds, Charles, 820
Edmonds, Sir James, on Allenby, 279
education, and Scot. troops, 321; teachers as propagandists, 709–16, 767–8
Edwards, Lt-Col. (Ind.Army), 288
Edwards, Pte. F.J. VC, 301
Egerton, Maj-Gen. G.G., 315
Egypt, Br. censorship, 648; Br. protectorate, 649; Camel Corps, 650; conscription into Labour Corps, 649–50; impact of WWI, 649–50; limited independence, 650; nationalist sentiment, 643, 649; and Paris Peace Conference, 650; and Pres. Wilson's 'Fourteen Points', 650; the press, 649; Wafd, and revolution, 650
Eichler, Lt. Gustav, 207
Eksteins, Modris, 715, 809, 822–3
Ellis, I.P., MN, 154
Elouges, 283
Emden, 122, 124
Empey, Arthur Guy, 757–9, 760; *First Call*, 758–9; *From the Fire Step*, 757–8; *Over the Top*, 757
Engels, Friedrich, 17
English-Murphy, Brig. William, 261
Enver Pasha, 232, 233
Esher, Lord R.B.B.(1852–1930), on conscription, 4
Esler, M.S. RMO, 516
espionage *see also* intelligence; Austrian network in Italy, 186; Italian coup in Zurich, 186
Ettinger, Pfc. Albert, 248
Euryalus, 165, 170, 171, 174
Ewart, Wilfrid, 803, 808
executions, 307, 321, 395, 437, 438–40, 441, 442, 511, 515; atrocities

Fairley, G.D. RMO, 467
Falkenhayn, Gen. Erich von (1861–1922), reinforces Austrians, 402; and tactics, 384
Falklands, 125
Fallada, Hans, *Iron Gustav*, 563
Fallas, Carl, *St.Mary's Village*, 804
Falls, Cyril, 824
Farie, Capt. RNR, 142
Faulkner, William, 763, 764
Fayolle, Gen. M.E., 82
Faysal, Amir, 648
Fell, Matthew, on diet and morale, 485
Fenwick, Lt-Col. F.C., 467
Ferguson, Lionel, recruiting for the Liverpool Scottish, 316
Ferry, Sub-Lt. Abel, 225
Fielder, Sgt. Eustace (U.S.Army), 252
film *see* cinema
Findlay, Col. J.M., 325
Fisher, L/Cpl. J.J., 528
Fisher, Adm. Sir John A. 1st Baron Kilverstone (1841–1920), 28, 32, 35; and Dardanelles, 162, 163–4; strain, 163
Fisher, H.A.L., 886
Fitzgerald, F. Scott, 763, 764
Fitzgerald, Lt-Col. O.A.G., 39
Fiume, 185
Flageollet, Charles-Eugène, 683, 687
Flatau, Dorota, 802
Fleet, Pte.G.A., 303, 307
flies, 317
flooding, defence of Venice, 187
flying instruction, 204
Foch, Marshal Ferdinand (1851–1929), and armistice, 104–5, 111, 112, 113, 114; character, 105; and Clemenceau, 110; estimate of, 115; Guillaumat's opinion of him, 82; and Haig, 70–1; and Pershing, 75
Fokker, Anthony [Anton H.G.] Dutch aeroplane builder, 12, 198
Ford, Ford Madox, 803, 808–9
Forrest, Harry MN, 152
Fossetti, *mignatta* attacks, 190
Foster, Cecil MN, 151
Foster, Lt-Col. C.E., 177
Foulkes, Maj. Charles H., i/c Special (gas) Brigade, 355, 357, 361, 362
Fowler, Flt.Cdr. B.F. RNAS, pl.17, 203
Fowler, Pte. J.P., 323
Fowler, Pte. N.J., 316
Fowler, Pte. Ted 15th Hussars, 282

Fox, Gas Cpl. Sidney, 359
France, and Africa, 22; and African
    conscription, 603–6; air force, 8,
    pl.15; army see French army;
    aviation, 7; and black people, 22,
    604; casualties, 14, 221, 223;
    censorship in N. Africa, 648;
    children, 767–78; education,
    767–9, 771–6;
    enlistment/mobilisation, 4, 221;
    forced labour, 555, 631, 634; and
    Greek offer of help to Serbia, 45;
    homefront, 21; attitude to troops
    sufferings, 225–6; morale, 632
    navy see French navy; occupied
    Départements see occupied
    territory; pacifism, 677–90;
    population, 4; post-war investment,
    610–11; the press, 677–8; refugees
    in, 19; strategic problem, 13;
    strikes, 680–3; trades unions,
    678–89; and trench warfare,
    221–8; 'Union Sacrée', 17, 603,
    677, 678
Francesco Caracciolo, 183
Franchet d'Esperey, Marshal Louis, 81,
    83, 85, 87
Franco-Prussian War (1870–71), 16,
    280, 281, 603, 639
Frankau, Gilbert, Peter Jackson Cigar
    Merchant, 803, 807, 808, 810, 814
Frankfurt trench, 323
Franz Joseph, Emperor of Austria-
    Hungary (1830–1916), 399, 401
Franz Joseph, Prince, on the Emden, 122
Fraser, Antonia, The Warrior Queens,
    370
Fraser, Hon William, 324
Freedman, Rosa, 746
Frégicourt, 304
French, FM John D.P. 1st Earl of Ypres
    (1852–1925), and Aubers Ridge,
    42; and cavalry tactics, 287; and
    Haig, 69; his desire to retreat, 40;
    memoirs, 729; tribute to RFC, 193
French army, and African troops, 603;
    artillery, 8–9; allied superiority in,
    1918, 384; reorganisation, 385
    attitude to death, 222–3;
    cavalry, and horses, pl.25, pl.52, 290;
    tactics, 288
    cavalry tactics, 288; civilians in
    uniform, 226; composition of,
    221–2; concept of duty, 227–8;

confidence in ultimate victory, 227;
    hatred for the Boche, 226–7;
    internal collapse, 385; mutinies
    (1917), pl.7, 79–89, 225, 228; non-
    combative contact with enemy,
    226; and trench warfare, pl.19,
    221–8; and typhoid, 453
French army,
    Army Group East, 85
    Army Group North, 83, 85
    II Army, 75
    IV Army, 75
    X Army, 81
    5th Infantry Division, 83
    41st Infantry Division, 83
    152nd Regiment, 81
Freud, Sigmund, 559
Fried, Hans, on Stormtroopers, 274
Friedrich, Ernst, 861
Friendly Societies, 346
Fuller, Maj-Gen. J.F.C., 6, 827
Funk, Dr. Casimir, 476
Furious, 203
Furse, Dame Katherine WRNS, 535,
    738, 740
Fussell, Paul, 817, 820

Galicia, 403
Gallagher, Lt. Edward, 263
Gallipoli see also Dardanelles expedition,
    pl.1, pl.12, pl.20, 42, 43, 48, 160,
    233, 279, 325, 416, 648; account
    of landings, 156; Anzac Cove, 173;
    books about, 893; Chunuk Bair,
    169, 172; effect of climate, 278;
    Suvla, 166, 167, 168, 169, 174,
    257
Galsworthy, John, 801
Galtier-Boissière, Jean, 227, 229n
Gameson, Capt. L. RAMC, 328
Garibaldi, 182
Garrod, Pte., 289
Garros, Roland, developments in aircraft
    armament, pl.15, 197
Garrucio, Gen., head of Cadorna's
    intelligence service, 441
gas, 353; after effects, 263, 353–4; anti-
    gas defence, 354; Brit. gas
    retaliation, 354–62; Brit. use at
    Loos, 326, 355, 357, 362; chlorine
    (Red Star), 353, 354, 355, 358;
    French use, 358, 362; gas mask
    (anti-gas respirators), 354, 454;
    Geneva Protocol, 1925, 361;

making, 83–4; and destitution, 549;
and drunkenness, 549; homefront,
loyalties, 523, 529–36; and India,
596; lack of military capability, 41;
Liberal Party, 691–2; Military
Service Bill (ACT), 693, 697;
Ministry of Health, 464; Ministry
of Information, 841; myths about
strategy, 83–4; navy *see* British
navy; normality of wartime life,
532–3; pacifism, 691–704;
population, 4; and prostitution,
549; reasons for war, 819, 828;
War Cabinet, 88–9, 100–1, 102;
War Council, 41, 42, 43, 45; War
Office Shell Shock Committee,
1922, 503, 505, 508, 511, 517;
War Policy Committee, 87–8; and
Zionism, 651–2
Greece, and Serbia, 45
Greeks, migration from Turkey, 238
Green, Pte. Alfred, 282
Greenwell, Graham, 820, 823–4, 826
Grey, C.G., editor of *The Aeroplane*,
199–200
Grey, Sir Edward (1862–1933), 17
Grierson, Lt.Gen. Sir James
(1859–1914), 7, 8, 12
Griffith, Paddy, *Forward into Battle*,
281; on Gen. Maxse, 300; and later
BEF fighting methods, 297
Griffith, Wyn RWF, 415–16
Griffiths, Pte. Joe, 419
Griffiths, Winifred, discovers socialism,
747
Groener, Gen. Wilhelm (1867–1939),
58, 388
Groom, Pte. W.H., 349
Grotjahn, Alfred, SPD member of
Reichstag, 555
Grundy, Charis WAAC, 368–9
Grünewald, Mathis, 859, 861, 864, 872
Gudmundsson, Bruce, suggests poor
leadership in small units, 304
Guillaumat, Gen. M.L.A. (1863–1940),
81, 82, 84–5, 86
guns *see also* weapons; creeping barrage,
301; defence of Venice, 183
Gurner, Ronald, 803
Gurney, Ivor (poet), response to
authority, 344
Gwynn, Capt. Stephen, 260, 264, 266
Gwynne-Vaughan, Dame Helen
(1879–1967) WAAC, 366, 372–3,
376

Haber, Fritz, 555
Haber-Bosch nitrogen fixation process,
555
Haden, Signaller Ernest W. RFA, 536
Haeften, OHL envoy, 61
Hague Convention, 631
Haig, FM Douglas 1st Earl (1861–1928),
pl.5, pl.8, 278; and armistice, 106,
107, 110, 111; and aviation, 7;
background, 68; becomes C-in-C
BEF, 69; and BEF tactics, 297;
breaks Hindenburg Line, 76; and
the British Legion, 882; and
Cambrai, 75; and casualties, 72,
101; on cavalry tactics, 287;
character, 68, 106–7; criticisms, 67,
72–3; estimate of, 115; and Foch,
70–1, 75, 106; and the French, 14,
69–70; and gas, use of, 357, 362;
and German Spring 1918 offensive,
53; and manpower, 383; at Mons,
69, 284; and Passchendaele, 87;
and soldier education, 340; and
strategy, 13, 69, 72–3; stress on,
69, 71, 72, 73, 76; and WAAC,
365, 367
Haldane, Maj-Gen. Sir Aylmer, on
Allenby, 279; encounters a poor
officer, 319; non-combat deaths in
trenches, 317; and Scots gallantry
at Loos, 321; and Scots history and
traditions, 324; and trench
discipline, 322
Hall, Bert, Am. pilot, on first Spad, 198
Hamilton, Gen. Sir Ian (1853–1947),
and Anglo-German Society, 884,
886; anti-Bolshevik stance, 881,
882, 886; anti-war stance, 884–5,
886, 887; and the British Legion,
pl.54, 882, 883, 884, 885, 886–7;
and Churchill, 880, 882; and
Czechoslovakia, 886, 887; and
Gallipoli, pl.12, 42, 43, 164, 165,
166, 172; and German leaders,
883–4, 886–7; on Kitchener, 162,
880–1; opposition to Versailles
treaty, 880, 884, 886–7; plans for
industrial renewal, 883; and post-
war Germany, 879–80, 883–7; and
Remarque, 884–6; and social
peace, 881, 882; and unemployed,
883, 885
Hamilton, Mary A., 802
Hamilton, Netta, 533
Hampshire, 37

Hanbury, Patricia, 531–2
Hankey, Donald, gentleman in ranks, 420
Hankey, Col. Sir Maurice (1877–1963), Sec. to War Cabinet, 13, 162, 167
Hanna Larsen, 148
Harbison, Capt. RMO, 503
Harbord, Gen. James, 75
Hardie, Martin, 850
Harding, Pres. Warren G. (1865–1923), 763
Hardinge, B.A. MN, 149
Hare, Walter, 354
Harington, Gen. Sir Charles (1872–1940), 729
Harper, Maj-Gen. G.M., 321
Hart, Basil Liddell, on Gen. Maxse, 300, 827–8
Hart, Lt. H.V., 526–7
Hart, 1st Lt. Percival G. (U.S.Army), 252
Hartsilver, Pte. J. RAMC, 470
Hašek, Jaroslav, *Adventures of the Good Soldier Švejk*, 406
Hauptmann, Gerhard, and Louvain, 621–2
Hay, Ian *see* Beith, John Hay
Hehir, Col. ADMS MEF, 477
Heller, Joseph, 839
Hemingway, Ernest, 763, 764
Hemming, Harold RFA, 300
Hemphill, Lt. Patrick, 262
Henderson, Keith, 843–4
Henderson, Sir David, and the RFC, 193
Herbert, Pfc. Craig S., 248
Herringham, Sir Wilmot RAMC, 469
Hertling, Georg, Count von (1843–1919), German chancellor, 57, 59, 60
Hess, Rudolph (1894–1987), 886, 887
Heuston, Sean, executed rebel leader, 266
Heye, Col. aide to Ludendorff, 57, 58, 59
Higginson, Brig.Gen. H.W., 303
Hijaz, Britain woos Hashemites, 648
Hill, Adrian, 846, 851
Hill, Rowland, 848
Hill, Pfc. Walter, 246, 250, 254
Hindenburg, FM Paul von (1847–1934), and Armistice, 59–60, 61; Chief of General Staff, 568; embraces technology, 383; and Ludendorff, pl.23, 57; offers resignation, 62; and Sir Ian Hamilton, 886; and

submarine warfare, 127; and tactics, 384
Hindenburg Line, 11, 76, 210, 302, 303, 304; Siegfried Line
Hindenburg Programme [weapons production], 51, 384, 394, 569
Hinkson, Pamela, 804
Hintze, Adm. von, German Foreign Secretary, 56, 57, 59–60, 61
Hipper, Adm. von (1863–1932), 130
Hirsch, David, occupation diary, 631–4, 638, 639
Hirschauer, Fr.Gen., 86–7
Hiscock, H., MN, in hospital ship *Goorkha*, 155
Hitler, Adolf (1889–1945), and Armenian massacres, 19, 640; and Céline, 837, 838; and Ludendorff, 63; and Sir Ian Hamilton, 887; and Third Reich, 554, 559–60, 716
Hobhouse, Stephen, 703
Hochheimer, Dr., and Ludendorff, 57–8
Hocking, J.P., 752, 802
Hodder-Williams, Ralph, 811
Hodgson, 2nd Lt. Clarrie RFA, 284
Hodson, J.L., 804
Holbein, Hans, 859, 862, 872
Holland, Col. A.E., 320
Hollebecque, Mme., Fr. youth and the war, 768
Hollins, Pte., 499
Holme, Marjorie WAAC, 372
Hopkins, Sir F. Gowland (1861–1947), 476
Hopthrow, 2nd Lt. H.E. RE, 526
Hopwood, Sir Francis, 35
Horthy, Adm. Miklós (1868–1957), 187, 190
Hoskins, R.D., MN, 153
Hubble, Mrs Emily, munitions work, pl.42, 530–1
Hughes, Emrys, 701–2
Hulluch, 263
Hulse, Capt. Sir Edward, 327
Humbert, Gen. Georges, 84
'Hundred Days', 303–4
Hungary, 399
hunger, Arab world, 645–7; Austria, 408–9, 560; German army, 391; Germany, 20–1, 391–2, 555, 556–7, 560, 570–1; Russia, 432, 540
Hunter-Weston, Gen. Sir Aylmer G. (1864–1940), 164, 165
Husayn Kamil, Sultan of Egypt, 649

Hutchinson, A.S.M., 803, 804
Huxtable, Charles RAMC, 470
Hynes, Samuel, 817, 819, 822

Implacable, 171
India, constitutional reforms, 602;
    contribution of manpower and
    matériel, 598–9; cotton tariffs,
    599–600; and dominion status,
    602; economy and prices, 598–9,
    601–2; impact of war on, 596, 597,
    598–602; industry, 599, 610; and
    influenza, 597; military
    contribution, 600; Muslim
    loyalties, 599; nationalists, 602;
    need to raise tax and duties, 602;
    NW frontier concerns, 599; strikes,
    602; trade and finance, 597
Indian army, composition, 600
Indian seamen, merchant navy crews,
    147
Indian troops, and diet, 477–9, 480,
    483, 485; and disease, 475,
    477–83; and E. African campaign,
    608; morale, 479, 485, 600
industrial revolution, 3–4
industrialism, and war, 3–4, 12, 555
industry, Entente access to American I.,
    384; heavy, growth of in Britain,
    341; opportunities for women, 531
infantry, changes in Br. army, 341–2;
    combat, 282; hand-to-hand, 282, 301
    tactics, 281
Ingenohl, Adm. Friedrich von
    (1857–1933), 123
innovations, 191
Insall, A.J. RFC, 197
Insall, Gilbert VC RFC, 197
intelligence *see also* espionage; French,
    387, 406, 638
Inverness Copse, 302, 304
Iraq, nationalist sentiment, 643;
    Ottoman successes, 648; and Sykes-
    Picot accords, 651; troops, 644
Ireland, Anglo-Irish Treaty (1921), 258,
    261; and conscription, 107, 257,
    258; Dail Eireann established, 258;
Easter Rising, 22, 257–8, 326; arrests
    and executions, pl.22, 258;
    composition of firing squads, 260;
    effects on nationalist officers,
    263–6; reactions of Ir. officers in
    Br. Army, 258–66; shift in public
    opinion, 258
Gaelic League, 261; Germans urge Irish

troops to desert, 263; Home Rule
    Act (1914), 256; Home Rule party
    and by-elections, 258;
IRA, 265; intimidation of ex-servicemen,
    265, 268n; military campaign, 258
Irish Citizen Army, 257; Irish Divisions
    in the Br. army, 256, 257, 263,
    265; Irish involvement in WWI,
    256–7; Irish National Volunteers
    (INV), 257, 265; Irish Volunteers,
    256, 257, 261; Sinn Fein, 258, 264,
    265; Ulster Volunteer Force, 256
Irwin, A.P.B. 8th East Surreys, 298, 299,
    304
Isonzo, pl.31, 400, 402, 403, 437, 440,
    441
Istria, 659, 661, 662, 668
Italian army, pl.33; *arditi* assault troops,
    444; casualties, 442; censorship,
    440–1; conscripts, 434; defeat at
    Caporetto, pl.34, 186, 440, 441–2;
    defence of Venice, 183, 186–7,
    192; deficiencies, 435; desertion,
    439, 441, 586; discipline, 436–42;
    and domestic politics, 441;
    expansion and its effects, 437–8;
    fails to achieve breakthrough, 181,
    436–7; high command, relations
    with troops, 435; improved
    conditions, 443; internal collapse,
    385; maintaining public order, 435;
    mobilisation, 436; morale, 435–45;
    mutinies, 441; response to
    Straffexpedition, 440; retreat from
    Caporetto, 442; role in industry,
    579; shortages of artillery and
    ammunition, 435; stubborn
    fighting, 435; tactics modernised,
    445; withstands Austro-German
    forces, 442–3
Italian army,
    artillery, Amalfi battery, 183–4, 192
    artillery, Naval Artillery Group, 187
    IInd Army, 186, 437, 442
    IIIrd Army, 183, 186–7, 192
    XXIII Army Corps, 187
    Naval Brigade, 187
    Naval Infantry Regiment, 187
Italian navy, composition of fleet, 181;
    discipline, 191–2; espionage coup,
    186; expansion of, 191; 'fleet in
    being', 182; MAS craft, pl.13,
    184–6, 187, 188–90, 192; *mignatta*
    manned torpedoes, 185, 190;
    Monfalcone company, 187; morale,

921

Italian navy *(continued)*
192; Naval Brigade, 187; Naval
Infantry Regiment, 187; permanent
patrols in the Adriatic, 182; use of
armoured trains, 184–5
Italy, anti-war protests, 588–9; civil
committees (fasci), 584–5;
coastline, vulnerability, 183–4; cost
of living riots, 1919, 591; crime,
587–8; defence of Venice, 183–4,
186–7, 192; food supply, 581–3;
homefront, diet, 581; family life eroded,
586–7; hardships, pl.46, 582,
585–6, 590; lack of cohesion, 578;
moral decline, 587–8; preparations,
578–9
illiteracy of population, 191; industrial
reorganisation, 445; industry,
579–81; influenza, 585; loss of
merchant tonnage to submarines,
182; militarisation of workers, 579;
national integration, 577;
propaganda, 583–5; public
opinion, 578, 583–5; rationing,
583; reasons for war, 435; 'Red
Week', 577; rise of Fascism, 554,
585; shortages, food, 581–3; social
unrest, 589–91; and socialism, 435;
socialists, 578, 582, 589–90;
supplies, organisation of, 581;
Treaty of London, 1915, 578; war
with Austria-Hungary, 180–92,
402, 435–45, 577; war with
Germany, 577; war pensions
ministry, 443;
women, anti-war protests, 589; workers,
579–80, 587
worker protection rules, 581

Jack, Brig.Gen. James, 320, 339
Jackson, Brig.Gen. T.D., 306
Jäger, Lt. Albrecht, 207
James, Lt., 8
Japan, enters war against Germany, 125;
offer of alliance with Germany,
127; Russo-Japanese War, 1904,
67, 475
Jeglic, Bp. Anton, 663–4, 667, 672
Jellicoe, Adm. Sir John (1859–1935), 6,
108
Jenkins, Roy 1st Baron Hillhead (1920-),
83
Jerrold, Douglas, 824, 829
Jersey City, 149

Jews, 19, 21, 63, 542–3, 651–2, 835,
836, 837–8
Joffre, Marshal Joseph J.C.
(1852–1931), 7, 13, 14, 280, 285,
835
Johnston, 2nd Lt. R.W. Royal Scots, 310
Jolley, Walter, 703
Jones, David RWF, 416–17, 804
Jones, Sir Henry, moral philosopher, 694
Jones, Morgan, 701
Joyce, Lt. Walter, 265
Jünger, Lt. Ernst (1895-), pl.24, 270–3,
823, 838, 860
Jutland, 123, 135

Kaiser Wilhelm II *see* Wilhelm, II
Kalisch, 18, 620
Kandinsky, W., 856, 864
Kane, Paddy MN, 152
Kant, Immanuel, and German arrogance,
622
Karl I, Emperor of Austria-Hungary
(1887–1922), 403, 560, 657, 666
Karlsruhe, 125
Karr, Able Seaman, *nil desperandum,*
139
Kars offensive, 233
Katicič, Milan, 671
Kavanagh, Lt-Gen., 285
Keable, Robert, and WAACs, 374–5;
war novels, 803
Keegan, John, on Fr. army mutinies, 89
Kelly, Richard T., 847
Kemal, Mustapha Kemel Atatürk, *see*
Cemal, 169–70
Kenderdine, Charles, and Queen's Hosp.
Sidcup, 495
Kennington, Eric, 726, 841–2, 852
Kent, William, 263
Kenya *see also* East African Protectorate;
and E. African campaign, 609;
Indian settlers excluded, 610
Keogh, Sir A. RAMC, 452, 454
Kershaw, 2nd Lt. Kenneth, 315
Kettle, Capt. Tom, 256, 260, 264
Keyes, Adm. Sir Roger (1872–1945), and
Gallipoli, 163, 164, 166, 167, 174;
report to Dardanelles Commission,
160
Keynes, John Maynard 1st Baron
(1883–1946), 557
Kieffer, Obermaschinist Karl, 124
Kienthal Conference, 1916, 678
Kilmer, Sgt. Joyce, war poet, 246, 762
Kimbangu, Joseph, 22

Kipling, Rudyard, 621
Kitchener, Horatio H. Visct. of
    Khartoum (1850–1916), pl.4, 280;
    and Balkans, 44–6; and the Boers,
    880–1; and Broome Park, 39–40;
    character, 37, 39; and Churchill,
    33; and conscription, 44; and
    Dardanelles, 35, 41, 42, 43–4,
    47–8, 157, 161, 162; drowned, 37;
    and Fisher, 163–4; and Fr.
    demands for more troops, 40; and
    France, 14; lack of verbal facility,
    41; and Lloyd George, 43; and
    Loos, 44; need to expand army, 38;
    and politicians, 47; and
    recruitment, 4; schedule, 38–9;
    shrewdness, 38; and [Sir] William
    Robertson, 48; strain, 163;
    strategy, 41; at the War Office,
    37–48
Kitchener divisions see Great Britain,
    army, New Army divisions
Klee, Paul, 855–6
Kluck, FM Heinrich R.A. von
    (1846–1934), 286
König, and sailors revolt, 131
Königsberg, 125
Korošec, Mgr. Anton, 657, 661–73
Kosovo, Serb atrocities, 17
Kraft zu Hohenlohe-Ingelfingen, Prince,
    287
Kristeva, Julia, 865, 869
Kuhl, Gen. von, chief of staff 2 Army, 53
Kurds, and the Armenian massacres, 19;
    in the Turkish army, 232
Kut-al-Amara, 233, 477, 645

Ladeuze, Mgr., Rector of Louvain,
    623–5
Laginja, Matko, 659, 667, 669
Laidlaw, Piper VC, 322
Lake, Gen. Sir Percy, 480
Landwehr, Gen. Ottokar, 660, 661
Lane, Sir Arbuthnot, 494
Langemarck, first use of gas, 353
Langille, Leslie (U.S.Army), 252
Larkhill, military aeroplane competition,
    193–4
Latvia, conquest of, 20
Lausanne treaty, and exchange of Greek
    and Muslim pops., 238
Lavery, Sir John, 848–9
Law, Andrew Bonar (1858–1923), 45,
    694
Law, Frank, 262

Lawrence, D.H., 348
Lawrence, T.E., 809
Lawrey, E.T.N., MN, 149–50, 152, 153
Le Cateau, 283–5
Leach, Florence Burleigh, Chief
    Controller WAAC, 372
leadership, 304–5; nature of, 176
League of Nations, 253, 880, 883;
    mandates, 611, 653
Lebanon, famine, 645–7; population
    decline, 646–7
Lee, Maj. A.N., 720–2, 726–7, 730,
    849–50
Lee, Col. Arthur, 468
Lee, Maj-Gen. Richard RE, i/c 18th Div.,
    302, 304
Leek, Alice, and bereavement, 531
Leigh-Fermor, Patrick, and uniforms,
    280
Leigh-Wood, Col., and WAAC, 366
Lenin, V.I. (1870–1924), 611, 686
Leon Gambetta, 182
Leonardo da Vinci, 186
Lequio, Gen., letter from Cadorna, 440
Lettow-Vorbeck, Gen. Paul von, 607
Leuven see Louvain
Lévy, B-H., 832
Lewis, Lt., 8
Lewis, Wyndham, 848, 852
Liddell, Capt. John A., 320–1
Lille, pl.49, 630, 633; occupied by
    RNAS, 193
Liman von Sanders, on Arab troops, 232
Lindsay, Daryl, medical illustrator, 494
Lissa, named for the battle of, 180
Lissauer, Ernst, 'Hymn of Hate', 559
literature see also cinema; newspapers; of
    the Absurd, 832, 837, 839;
    American, 752–64, 893, 895; anti-
    war, 803, 809–10, 811, 817–29;
    Australian, 894; British, 368–9,
    417, 801–14, 817–29, 891, 892,
    893–4, 895; Canadian, 893, 894;
    children's essays, 770–1; on
    combat, 894; commemoration,
    895; Czech, 406; feminist
    perspective, 895; French, 392,
    831–9, 892, 895; German, 270–2,
    563, 619, 892, 895; Italian, 438,
    892; middle class views, 336;
    military intelligence, 894; and
    myth, 752, 763, 817–29; New
    Zealand, 893; novels as evidence,
    805–14; oral history, 893–4;

literature *(continued)*
    Polish, 893; post-war, 525; on
    strategy, 894; Yugoslav, 892
Lithuania, 19, 20
Littlewood, Joan, 828
Liveing, Edward, 806
Ljubljana, 662, 665, 667
Lloyd George, David (1863–1945),
    argues for 'some other front', 84;
    and armistice, 108–10; and
    Asquith, 85; and the Balkans, 41,
    46; and Churchill, 29, 31, 33; and
    conscientious objectors, 704; on
    Germany's defeat, 11; and guns for
    Italy, 88, 99; and Haig, pl.8, 71;
    inclination towards a campaign in
    Italy, 86, 97, 98; and Kitchener, 43,
    45; misjudges alliance situation, 13;
    and Nivelle, 86, 99; and Palestine,
    88, 99–100; and Passchendaele,
    85–7, 102; secures Premiership, 85,
    96; and Serbia, 45; and the *Somme*
    film, 783, 791
Locke, William J., 752, 801
Lockyer, Capt. RN, 171
Lodron, Count, 665
Logan, W.B., 803–4
logistics, seaborne supplies, Dardanelles,
    171–2
Longmore, Sqd.Cdr. Arthur RNAS, 202
Longuet, Jean, 678
Loos, 12, 14, 44, 320, 321, 322, 326,
    355, 357, 362
Lorimer, Capt. James B., 324
Lorraine, 56, 61, 104, 105, 106, 111,
    632
Lossberg, Gen. von, 56
Louvain, pl.47; burning of, 18, pl.48,
    617–28; effect on allies, 621;
    German justification for burning,
    618–20; intellectuals' response,
    622; library rebuilding, 622–3;
    professors scattered abroad, 626;
    terrorisation of civilians, 618
Love, H.M., on women's new horizons,
    374
Loveday, Dorothy WAAC, 368, 370,
    372
Low, Capt. Claud, 321
Lubinski, Mrs K., on German rationing,
    564–6
Ludendorff, FM Erich von (1865–1938),
    pl.23; and armistice, 60, 61, 62,
    103; *Attack in Trench Warfare*, 52;
    and Baltic states, 20; embraces

technology, 383; estimate of, 63;
    First Quartermaster General, 568;
    and Hitler, 63; homefront
    propaganda, 568; Hotel
    Britannique meeting, 59–60;
    isolation of, 58; and Marne, 55, 56;
    medical help sought, 57–8; and
    'Michael' offensive, 53–5, 63; and
    morale, 385–7; and patriotic
    instruction, 386, 387, 393;
    pressures of office, 51; Prince Max
    supports, 62; psychological
    problems, 55, 56, 57, 61, 63;
    resignation, 62; response to tanks,
    385; and Sir Ian Hamilton, 883–4;
    and Somme, 54; and
    Stormtroopers, 274–5; and
    submarine campaign, 127; and
    tactics, 384
Lupfer, Timothy, on German tactics, 384
Lusitania, 126, 755
Lussin, 181
Lutyens, Lt. Lionel, at Le Cateau, 284
Lytton, Maj. Hon. Neville, 728–9, 731;
    and censorship, 729–30; *Press and
    the General Staff*, 728

Macalister, Prof. A.D. (Dunedin), 495
MacArthur, Gen. Douglas, 251–2
MacCarthy, Desmond, 884, 885
McCarthy, Justin, Palestine demography,
    646
McCrae, Col. John, *In Flanders Fields*,
    761
McCudden, James VC RFC, pl.16, 200
Macdonell, Maj. I.H., 526
MacDonough, Thomas, executed rebel
    leader, 264
McDowell, J.B., official film-maker, 782
Macedonian uprising (1903), 20
Macfarlane Grieve, Lt. A.A., 321
McGilchrist, A.M., on the kilt and
    mustard gas, 317
McIndoe, Sir Archibald, plastic surgeon,
    490, 499
MacKay, Lt. R.L., 323, 327
Macke, August, 864
Mackensen, FM A.L.F.August von
    (1849–1945), defeat of Serbia, 402;
    halts Rumanians, 402
Mackenzie, Sir [E.M.] Compton, 165,
    175
Mackenzie, Pte. Jack, 317, 318, 320
McKerrow, Charles RMO, 469, 470,
    471

McLachlan, J.M. RMO, 468
MacLean, Lt. J.B., 528
MacLean, Lt. Joseph, 320
MacLeod, Mrs Emily, 533
MacLeod, Lt. J.D., 321, 324
McLeod, N.M., 528
Macmillan, Harold 1st Earl Stockton (1894–1986), 827
Macmillan, Norman, *Into the Blue*, 199
MacMunn, Maj-Gen. Sir George, 480
McNeile, H. Cyril (Sapper), 802, 811
Macpherson, Sir W.G. RAMC, 452
Macready, Sir Neville Adjutant General, and WAAC, 370–1
Mahan, Adm. Alfred T. (1840–1914), 121
Mahnič, Bp. Antun, 668
Mahoney, Capt. George, 260
mail *see also* censorship; efficient flow of, 339; letters and morale, 427–33
Maistre, Gen. Joseph, on leaders of mutinies, 85–6
Majestic, 173
Makin, Maj. C.J., 484
Malagodi, Olindo, It. newspaper editor, 441
Malaparte, Curzio, and retreat from Caporetto, 442
Malawi *see* Nyasaland
Malaya, 500
malingering *see* medical services, malingering
Malins, Geoffrey, official film-maker, 780, 781, 782
Malvy, Louis, 677
Mangin, Gen. Charles (1866–1925), 82, 88, 603
Manning, Frederic, 805–6, 822, 825–6, 829
Marc, Franz, 860, 864
March, Gen. Peyton, Amer. Chief of Staff, 74
Marguerite, Soeur, 535, 637
Marmora, 134, 136, 139, 140, 141, 142, 143
Marne, 8, 55, 325, 462639
Marsh, Eddy, Churchill's Priv.Sec., 27
Marshall, Gen. George C. (1880–1959), and Pershing, 75, 76
Marshall, Mary D., First Aid Nursing Yeo, 529, 534
Marsland, Elizabeth, 831–2
Martin, A.A. RMO, 467
Martin-Leake, Lt-Col. VC RAMC, 506

Marwitz, Gen. Georg von der (1856–1929), at Mons, 286
massacres *see* atrocities
Masterman, C.F.G., 726, 741
Mather, C. MN, 150, 154–5
Maude, Gen. Sir F.S. (1864–1917), 480
Max, Prince von Baden (1867–1929), 60, 61, 62
Maxse, Maj-Gen. Ivor, i/c XVIII Corps, 302, 303; i/c 18th Division, 299, 306, 309; character and background, 299–300; methods, 300; and the Somme, 301; and training, 300
Maxwell, Lt-Col. Frank VC, and discipline, 307; relations with troops, 305; at Trones Wood, 304
Maxwell, Gen. Sir John G. (1859–1929), 261
Mayne, Lt.Cdr., First Lieutenant of *Marmora*, 142
Maze, Paul, 291, 847, 851–2
Mazel, Gen., i/c Fr. 5th Army, 82
Mears, E.J., 844
medical services, 451–64; Advanced Dressing Stations, pl.35, 455; ambulances, 453, 460, 462, 470, 491; American, 451, 455, 460–2; American MOs with BEF, 457–8, 462; anaemia, 475; anaesthetics, 451, 456, 460, 463; anti-gas respirators, 454; antibiotics, lack of, 492, 499; arms issued to RMOs, 467–8; bathing centres, 454; battalion performance indicators, 457; battlefield evacuation, 455; beri-beri, 475, 476, 483, 484; blood transfusions, 456, 460, 463; and Canadian troops, 452; Casualty Clearing Stations, 455–6, 462, 506; Dardanelles, 172, 174; dead bodies, 454; deaths from disease, 459; deficiency diseases, 475–84; dental, 451, 459; disruption to civilian services, 469; dysentery, 169, 457, 475; enemy, treatment of, 463; examinations at enlistment, 458–9; expansion of RAMC, 452; facial injury, pl.38, 490–500; Field Service Regulations, 452; gas gangrene, 453, 492; German medicine, 463; and health education, 472, 481;

medical services *(continued)*
    hospitals, 451–2, 453, 455, 460–1,
    462, 463, 482, 495–900; hygiene,
    472; in India, 479; infection, 451,
    458, 460, 461, 481, 492; influenza,
    458, 461, 475; inoculation, 452–3,
    461, 472; international
    cooperation, 462; legacy of the
    war, 462–4; and local civilians,
    472; malaria, 461, 463, 472, 475;
    malingering, 470–1, 479, 504–5,
    512, 513–14; malnutrition, 476,
    484, 485; meningitis, cerebro-
    spinal, 452; morale maintenance,
    454, 471, 479, 484, 505, 514–15,
    516; non-battle casualties, 460;
    nursing, 456, 463; optical, 451,
    459; orthopaedics, 463; plastic
    surgery, pl.38, pl.39, 463, 490,
    497–500; pneumonia, 461;
    psychiatry, 451, 460, 463, 464;
    Regimental Aid Post, 455, 466,
    468, 470, 505; Regimental Medical
    Officer, pl.35, 455, 457, 458,
    466–73, 502; rehabilitation, 451,
    458; reorganisation, 452; research,
    pl.36, 451, 460, 462, 463; retreat
    from Mons, 452, 453; sanitation,
    451, 454, 457, 459, 460, 461, 469,
    471–2, 492; scurvy, 475–83; shell-
    shock, 250, 305, 454–5, 458, 460,
    500, 502–17; shortage of doctors,
    452, 466, 468; sick parades, 454,
    457, 458, 470, 471, 507; sickness
    at Gallipoli, 164–5, 169; stress and
    exhaustion, 458, 460, 507, 509,
    525; stretcher bearers, 456–7, 466,
    470, 505–6; surgery, 451, 456,
    460, 463; technology, 451, 456,
    460, 463; and tetanus, 453; 'Tin
    Faces', 496, 499, 842; training for
    MOs, 468, 469–70; and trench
    warfare, 453–4, 455, 457–8, 461,
    467–72, 505–6; typhoid, 452–3,
    461, 472, 475; typhus, 475;
    venereal disease, 508; vitamins,
    476, 478, 482–3, 484, 486; war
    neurosis, 509, 510; water, 454,
    461, 471; wounded treatment of,
    453–4, 455–5, 459, 470; yellow
    fever, 463
Mediterranean, dominated by Entente
    Powers, 180
Meidner, Ludwig, 856–9
Mélot, Auguste, and Louvain, 621

Melville, Herman, *Billy Budd*, 753
merchant navy, Great Britain, pl.11,
    146–58
    Chinese crews, 147, 148; cosmopolitan
    crews, 146–7; Dardanelles, 155–8;
    deserters, 151–2; encounters with
    enemy ships, 154–5; hospital ships,
    155; Kru, 147; lascars, 147; losses,
    146, 149; and prostitutes, 152;
    public views of, 147–8; survivors
    attacked by Beduin, 150;
    troopships, 155–8; and U-boats,
    146, 148–51
Merrheim, Alphonse, 678, 686, 687, 688
Mesopotamia campaign, and disease,
    475–86; Ottoman troops, 644;
    push to Baghdad, 47, 327, 482;
    shortage of river barges, 480–1,
    482, 484
Mesopotamian Expeditionary Force
    (MEF), and disease, pl.36, 475–86;
    morale, 479, 484
Messines, 12, 71, 264, 729
Meuse-Argonne offensive, 250, 251, 252
Mexico, offer of alliance with Germany,
    127, 755
Meyer, F.B., *The Majesty of Conscience*,
    696
Miall-Smith, 2nd Lt. Eric, 8th Norfolks,
    307
'Michael' offensive, 51–5, 63, 271;
    German Spring offensive (1918)
Michel, Capt. 12th Lancers, killed at
    Cerizy, 291
Micheler, Gen. Joseph, correspondence
    with Dubost, 81
Michell, Midshipman in *Edgar*, 141
Middlebrook, Martin, *The First Day on
    the Somme*, 230
midget submarines (maiali), 185
migrant workers *see* Germany, slave
    labour
Mihalovich, Ban Antun, 661, 670
Milan, anti-war protest, 589
Milburn, Gwynneth, 532–3
Milewczyk, Torpedo-
    Oberbootsmannsmaat, 123–4
Miller, Henry, 839
Miller, Patrick, 803
Miller, Capt. W.A., 528
Milner, Sir Alfred (1854–1925), 110,
    880
Miquel, Pierre, mutiny in German army,
    387
Mitchell, Hannah, 746

926

Rathenau, Walther (1867–1922), and control of raw materials, 555; suggestion of levée en masse, 61
Ratinaud, Jean, on Fr. army mutinies, 88
Raven, 2nd Lt. G.E., 527
Rawlinson, FM Sir Henry (1864–1925), 12, 97, 279–80, 783
Rawson, Capt. P.H., 528
Raymond, Ernest, 803, 804
Read, Capt. E.H., 847
Read, Herbert, 806
rebellion and civil disorder *see* under separate countries
reconnaissance, aerial, 7, 8, 9–10, 12, 194, 207–8, 286; cavalry patrols, 286
Red Cross, founded, 1864, 16
Redmond, John Edward (1856–1918), 257
Redmond, William, 264
Reed, Walter, medical research, 463
refugees, 18–19, 327; Balkan Muslims, 237–8; Lebanese, 647
Reichle, Lt. Alfons, 207, 208, 209
Reid, Pte., 499
Reith, John C.W. 1st Baron (1889–1971), 315, 827
religion, chaplains, 73, 263–4, 325, 374, 516, 528; and conscientious objection, 693–4, 696, 698; Easter fraternisations, 431; and Louvain, 619, 626–7, 628; and Scot. troops, 320, 325; Theosophy, 855–6; war and spiritual convictions, 528–9; and Welsh troops, 516
Remarque, Erich Maria, 803, 809–10, 811, 822–3, 827, 884–6
reparations, and Foch, 105–6
Repington, Col. C.à.C., 42, 729
Revel, Adm. Paolo Th. de, naval support to IIIrd Army, 186–7; response to Adm. Horthy, 188; revamps It. navy plans, 181–2
revenge, drive for, leads to WWII, 23
Rheims, cathedral shelled, 622
Rhineland, and armistice terms, 104, 105, 111
Rhodesia, Northern, and E. African Campaign, 607
Richards, Frank, 506, 517, 843
Richards, Leyton, 704
riots *see* mutinies and riots
Ritter, Gerhard, and failure of the April [Spring] offensive, 391

River Clyde, landing craft at Suvla Bay, 169
Rivers, Dr., and Craiglockhart War Hospital, 513
Rizzo, Luigi, commander of MAS craft, 186, 187, 188–90
Roberts, Cpl., 504–5
Roberts, Walter, 699
Roberts, Bdr. William, 842
Robertson, Gen. [Sir] William (1860–1933), 12, 13, 47, 48, 99
Robinson, Capt. David, 261
Roe, A.V., aviation pioneer, 194
'Rogers', 356, 361
Rogers, Gilbert, 850
Rogerson, Sidney, 826
Rohr, Capt. Willy M.E., 269, 273, 275
Rolland, Romain, and Louvain, 621, 622
Ronssoy, 304
Roosevelt, Pres.Theodore (1858–1919), and Pershing, 68
Rose, Maj. Geoffrey, 846
Roseveare, Mrs E. *see* Doerry, Edith
Rossetti, Maj., designs *mignatta* manned torpedo, 185
Rouault, Georges, 854, 868–72
Roubaix, 630, 631–4
Roupell, Lt. George, at Mons, 282
Rousseau, and conscription, 392–3
Royal Aero Club, 194
Royal Aircraft Factory, 194, 198, 199, 200
Royal Flying Corps *see* Great Britain, air forces
Royal Navy *see* Great Britain, navy
Ruck, Berta, and working women, 742–3
Rumania, war with Central Powers, 402
Rupprecht, Crown Prince, on Ludendorff, 63; and the 'Michael' offensive, 53, 54
Russell, Bertrand 3rd Earl (1872–1970), 697–8, 703, 704, 818
Russell, Henry, 851
Russell, Lt. J.W.B., 415
Russell, Sir William (1820–1907), 730
Russia, Bolshevik revolution, 20, pl.43, pl.44, 340, 426, 433, 541; children, 552; defeat by Central Powers, 403; deportation of Jews, 19; destitution, 549–52; deviant social conduct, 549–52; drink, role of, 541–2; drunkenness, 549, 550; family relationships, 551–2;

Gendarme Dept. and military censors, 426; hunger riots, 541; illiterate peasantry, 540; incapable of waging modern war, 541; industrial workers, 546; initial sufficiency in raw-materials, 541; mobilisation, 540, 541–2; national experience of WWI, 539–43; not unprepared, 540; and prostitution, 549, 551, 552; Soviet propaganda view of WWI, 539, 545; State documents, 539–40, 545; strikes, 546–8; workers needs, concern for, 548

Russian army, anti-semitism, 542–3; artillery, 8, 428, 540; attitude to war aims, 541; behaviour of troops in Prussia, 18; casualties, 429; desertions, 430, 542; and domestic politics, pl.44, 432–3; effect of 1915 defeats, 543; fraternisations, 393, 430–1, 542; hatred for war, 430; influence of news from rear, 432; internal collapse, 385; Kerensky offensive, 403; mass surrenders, pl.32, 430, 542; military censors, 425–7, 540; morale, 427–33; munitions shortages, 428, 429, 540, 543; officer-man relations, 429, 542–3; punishments, 429; retreat from Galicia, 431; shortages, 428, 543; soldiers letters, 428–33, 540; surrendering tendencies, 542

Russo-Japanese War, 1904, 67, 475
Rutland, Sqd.Cdr. F.J. RNAS, 203
Ryder, Pte. R. VC, at Thiepval, 301

Sagan, Françoise, 839
Sagar, Andrew, and conscientious objectors, 526
St.Étienne, 680–2, 684–8
Saint George, 184
St.Mihiel, 75, 242, 251
St.Omer, RFC base, 195
St.Quentin, 52
Salam-al-Khalidi, Anbara, 647, 651
Salandra, PM of Italy, 578, 583
Salonika campaign, 45, 47, 94, 324, 325, 475
Samson, Cdr. C.R. RNAS, military career, pl.14, 194; occupies Lille, 193
Samuel, Sir Herbert 1st Visct., Home Secretary, 700

San Gregorio, 153
Sandeman, Dr. Laura, equal pay battle, 367
Sarajevo, 660, 661, 671, 672
Sarkotič, Baron Stjepan, 660, 668, 669, 671, 672
Sartre, J-P., 839
Sassoon, Siegfried, 503, 506–7, 512–13, 517, 804, 810, 814, 817, 818–19, 827
Saulnier, Robert, developments in aircraft armament, 197
Savoia, Lt.Gen. E.F.di, commander It. IIIrd Army, 192
Scapa Flow, 6, 112
Scharnhorst, 125
Schauwecker, Franz, on stormtroopers, 271
Scheer, Adm. Reinhard (1813–1928), 123, 129
Scheidemann, Philip (1865–1939), Social Democrat, 21, 393
Scheubner-Richter, and Armenian massacres, 19
Schjerning, Dr., informs Heye about Ludendorff, 59
Schlieffen Plan, 8, 13–14, 51, 401
Schöller, Peter, and Louvain, 620
Schulenburg, von der, chief of staff to C. P. Rupprecht, 53, 58
Scorpion, 171
Scott, C.P., 725
Scott, Pfc Everett, 247
Scott, 2nd Lt. John G., 322
Scottish troops, 314–28; and bagpipes, pl.27, 322–3; comradeship in the frontline, 318–19; diaspora units, 314, 317; discipline and lack of, 321–2, 324–5; drunkenness, 320–1; and education, 321; enlistment and recruiting, 314–16; esprit de corps, 316, 323, 324; fighting spirit, 321–8; hostility to Germans, 325–7; and the kilt, 317–18; leadership quality of officers, 319–20; looting, 321; a ludicrous night attack, 328; in Mesopotamia and Palestine, 327; nonchalance under fire, 327–8; and regimental rivalry, 323–4; and religion, 320, 325; in the trenches, 316–18
sea power, vital importance of, 191
Sebenico, 181
Seeadler, 125

931

Seed, Pte. Bertie, Indian musketry prize, 288
Seeger, Alan, war poet, 755–7, 762
Seely, Col.J.E.B. (1868–1947), 7
Seidler, Ernst von, 662, 666
Semmler, Lt. Willy, 207
Senegal, and Fr. conscription, 604
Senegalese *tirailleurs*, 603
Serb-Croat Coalition, 669
Serbia, army saved by naval forces, 190; and Austria, 399; and Greater Serbia, 657; invasion of, 44, 386, 401
Seydlitz, 124
Shaikh Sa'ad, 327
Sharif Husayn, 650–1
Shaw, Capt. Alexander KOSB, 319
Shaw, Surgeon James RNVR, 134, 135–6, 138–9, 140, 143
Sheehan, Capt. Daniel D., 265
Sheehy, Capt. Eugene, 260, 266
sheep dip, not recommended for lice, 317
Shepherd, Ernest, NCO 1/Dorsets, 420
Sherriff, R.C., *Journey's End*, 803, 821–2
Sherwood, Elmer (U.S.Army), 247
Shoubridge, Brig.Gen. T.H., 304
Siegfried Line, 55, 208; Hindenburg Line
Sierra Leone, and export prosperity, 606; recruitment for war work, 606
Simon, Sir John 1st Visct., 693
Simpson, Sister Priscilla QAIMNS, 534
Sims, Alice, and women at work, 531
Sinclair, May, on war service, 740
Skeffington, Francis Sheehy, murder of, 261
Skerlecz, Ban Ivan, 660
slave labour *see* Germany, slave labour
Sloggett, Sir Arthur RAMC, 452
Slovenes, 399, 657, 659, 664, 665, 666, 667, 669–70, 672
Slovenia, 659, 667, 669
Smiles, Lt. Walter, 263
Smith, 2nd Lt. G. Buchanan, 319–20
Smith, James M., Churchill's Admiralty Sec., 27
Smith, Mrs E.N., munitions work, 530
Smith, Pte. David, 315, 322
Smith-Barry, Robert, School of Special Flying, 203–4
Smith-Dorrien, Gen. Sir Horace, and Haig, 69; at Le Cateau, 284
Smuts, Gen. J.C. (1870–1950), 100

Snelling, Cpl. Percy, on French cavalry, 280
snipers, and the Louvain burning, 620
Šola, Vojislav, 671
Soltau, Col. physician, 456
Somerville, Alexander, on writing and Scots regiments, 314
Somme, 12, 94, 214–15, 387, 402, 415, 455, 457, 632, 851, 893; 18th Infantry Division, 300–1, 305; Irish Divisions, 259, 263; press view, 728;
Thiepval, 304, 305–6; Schwaben Redoubt, 301, 306
SONAR, 6
songs, American, 243, 247, 253, 254; BEF, 339, 361; British, 692; chanties, 159n; German, 559; Turkish army, 235–7
Sonnino, Sidney, and It. grain requisitions, 582–3
Sotheby, Lt. Lionel, 324, 327
Souchon, Adm., negotiates with sailor's council, 131
souvenirs, 248
Sparrow, Lt. Alan Hanbury-, use of sword, 280
Spee, Adm. Maximilian *Count* von (1861–1914), 125, 135
Spencer, Stanley, 842, 854, 866–8
Spiegel, Lt.Cdr. Freiherr von, 126
Spiers, Edward, on cavalry tactics, 287
Spincič, Vyekoslav, 659, 667, 669
Split, 668, 669
Stadler, Abp. of Sarajevo, 671
Stamfordham, Lord, on Churchill, 35
Stanley, Venetia, 27, 34
Stavbar, Vlasta, and Yugoslavia, 663, 664, 667–8
steam power, 3
steel, 3
Steer, Philip Wilson, 851
Steiner, Rudolf, 855
Steinmetz, Fr.Col., 88
Stenson, Lt.Cdr.F.J.RNR, pl.10, 134, 136, 139–43passim
Stern, Daniel, 557
Stevens, Rosemary, and American teaching hospitals, 452
Stevenson, Capt. A.N. RAMC, 482
Stewart, Lt-Col. John, 326
Stone, Maj. Christopher, 415
Stone, Norman, on the Austrian army, 402–3

Women's Army Auxiliary Corps
(*continued*)
chaperoning, 372; class
distinctions, 367; Commission of
Enquiry, 372–3; decorations for
bravery, 369; disbandment, 373–4;
disciplinary problems, 371–3; equal
pay success, 367; and French
prostitutes, 371; hygiene, 369;
numbers, 365, 366; Old Comrades
Association, 375; organisation,
366; return to civilian life, 375;
work and living conditions, 368
Women's Co-Operative Guild, 746–7
Women's Legion, ovens sabotaged, 367
Wood, Derwent, 842
Wood, Brig.Gen. E.A., 304, 306
Woodhead, Pte. Sam, 415
Woolf, Virginia, 740–1, 746, 748
Woollcott, Sgt. Alexander (U.S.Army),
249
working classes, and Br. army, 336–50;
communal solidarity, 346–8; Fr.,
opposition to war, 678; good army
material, 349–50; homes, 346–7;
and inequality of power, 342–3;
and military discipline, 344–5;
Russian industrial workers, 546;
social differentiations, 348; and
trades unions, 342–4, 346
workplace conditions, in Britain, 345
World War II, 23
Worthington, 2nd Lt. H., 528–9

Wright, Sir Almroth, and health of
troops, 454, 455
Wright, Wilbur and Orville, 243
Wynne, G.C., on German tactics, 384

Yarmouth, 203
Yates, QM 2/RWF, 511
Yeates, V.M., 809, 810, 812–13, 814
Yemen, 236–7
YMCA canteens, 349
Young, Lt-Col. James Field Ambulance
52nd Div., 320
youth organisations, Boy Scouts, 340;
Boys Brigade, 315, 340; Lads Drill
Association, 340
yperite *see* gas, mustard gas
Ypres, pl.35, 206, 207, 844; 2nd battle,
11; 3rd battle, 302–3, 388
Ypres *see also* Passchendaele; and gas,
353, 555
Yugoslav Club, 657, 661, 662, 663, 669,
672
Yugoslav Committee, 657
Yugoslavia *see* Austria-Hungary
Yvetot, Georges, and *Sou de Soldat*, 679
YWCA huts, for WAACs, 368
Zambia *see* Rhodesia, Northern
Zancarini, Michelle, on Clovis Andrieu,
678
Zimmerwald Conference, 1915, 678,
689
Zionism, 651–2